Twentieth-Century Literary Criticism

Guide to Gale Literary Criticism Series

When you need to review criticism of literary works, these are the Gale series to use:

If the author's death date is: **You should turn to:**

After Dec. 31, 1959
(or author is still living)

CONTEMPORARY LITERARY CRITICISM

for example: Jorge Luis Borges, Anthony Burgess,
William Faulkner, Mary Gordon,
Ernest Hemingway, Iris Murdoch

1900 through 1959

TWENTIETH-CENTURY LITERARY CRITICISM

for example: Willa Cather, F. Scott Fitzgerald,
Henry James, Mark Twain, Virginia Woolf

1800 through 1899

NINETEENTH-CENTURY LITERATURE CRITICISM

for example: Fedor Dostoevski, Nathaniel Hawthorne,
George Sand, William Wordsworth

1400 through 1799

LITERATURE CRITICISM FROM 1400 TO 1800
(excluding Shakespeare)

for example: Anne Bradstreet, Daniel Defoe,
Alexander Pope, François Rabelais,
Jonathan Swift, Phillis Wheatley

SHAKESPEAREAN CRITICISM

Shakespeare's plays and poetry

Antiquity through 1399

CLASSICAL AND MEDIEVAL LITERATURE CRITICISM

for example: Dante, Homer, Plato, Sophocles, Vergil,
the Beowulf poet

(Volume 1 forthcoming)

Gale also publishes related criticism series:

CHILDREN'S LITERATURE REVIEW

This ongoing series covers authors of all eras.
Presents criticism on authors and author/illustrators
who write for the preschool to junior-high audience.

CONTEMPORARY ISSUES CRITICISM

This two volume set presents criticism on
contemporary authors writing on current issues.
Topics covered include the social sciences,
philosophy, economics, natural science, law, and
related areas.

ISSN 0276-8178

R

Volume 25

Twentieth-Century Literary Criticism

**Excerpts from Criticism of the
Works of Novelists, Poets, Playwrights,
Short Story Writers, and Other Creative Writers
Who Died between 1900 and 1960,
from the First Published Critical Appraisals
to Current Evaluations**

Dennis Poupard
Editor

Marie Lazzari
Thomas Ligotti
Associate Editors

Gale Research Company
Book Tower
Detroit, Michigan 48226

Dennis Poupard, *Editor*

Paula Kepos, Marie Lazzari, Thomas Ligotti, *Associate Editors*

Serita Lanette Lockard, Joann Prosyniuk, Keith E. Schooley,
Laurie A. Sherman, *Senior Assistant Editors*

Faye Kuzma, Sandra Liddell, *Assistant Editors*

Derek T. Bell, Denise Michlewicz Broderick, Melissa Reiff Hug,
Jay P. Pederson, Debra A. Wells, Robyn V. Young, *Contributing Assistant Editors*

Sharon R. Gunton, Phyllis Carmel Mendelson, *Contributing Editors*

Jeanne A. Gough, *Permissions & Production Manager*
Lizbeth A. Purdy, *Production Supervisor*
Kathleen M. Cook, *Assistant Production Coordinator*
Suzanne Powers, Jani Prescott, Lee Ann Welsh, *Editorial Assistants*
Linda M. Pugliese, *Manuscript Coordinator*
Donna Craft, *Assistant Manuscript Coordinator*
Jennifer E. Gale, Maureen A. Puhl, Rosetta Irene Simms, *Manuscript Assistants*

Victoria B. Cariappa, *Research Supervisor*
Maureen R. Richards, *Research Coordinator*
Mary D. Wise, *Senior Research Assistant*
Joyce E. Doyle, Eric Priehs, Filomena Sgambati, Laura B. Standley, *Research Assistants*

Janice M. Mach, *Text Permissions Supervisor, LCS*
Susan D. Battista, Kathy Grell, *Assistant Permissions Coordinators*
Mabel E. Gurney, Josephine M. Keene, *Senior Permissions Assistants*
H. Diane Cooper, *Permissions Assistant*
Eileen Baehr, Martha A. Mulder, Kimberly Smilay,
Anita Lorraine Ransom, Lisa Wimmer, *Permissions Clerks*

Patricia A. Seefelt, *Picture Permissions Supervisor*
Margaret A. Chamberlain, *Assistant Permissions Coordinator*
Lillian Tyus, *Permissions Clerk*

Special thanks to Sharon K. Hall, Carolyn Bancroft, Donna Craft, Joyce A. Davis, Lizbeth A. Purdy,
and Derek T. Bell for their assistance on the Title Index.

Frederick G. Ruffner, *Chairman*
Thomas A. Paul, *President*
Dedria Bryfonski, *Publisher*
Ellen T. Crowley, *Associate Editorial Director*
Laurie Lanzen Harris, *Director, Literary Criticism Division*
Dennis Poupard, *Senior Editor, Literary Criticism Series*

Library of Congress Catalog Card Number 76-46132
ISBN 0-8103-2407-5
ISSN 0276-8178

Computerized photocomposition by
Typographics, Incorporated
Kansas City, Missouri

Printed in the United States

Contents

Preface   7

Authors to Be Featured in *TCLC*, Volumes 27 and 28   11

Additional Authors to Appear in Future Volumes   13

Appendix   461

Literary Criticism Series Cumulative Author Index   473

TCLC Cumulative Nationality Index   531

TCLC Cumulative Title Index   535

Preface

It is impossible to overvalue the importance of literature in the intellectual, emotional, and spiritual evolution of humanity. Literature is that which both lifts us out of everyday life and helps us to better understand it. Through the fictive lives of such characters as Anna Karenina, Jay Gatsby, or Leopold Bloom, our perceptions of the human condition are enlarged, and we are enriched.

Literary criticism can also give us insight into the human condition, as well as into the specific moral and intellectual atmosphere of an era, for the criteria by which a work of art is judged reflect contemporary philosophical and social attitudes. Literary criticism takes many forms: the traditional essay, the book or play review, even the parodic poem. Criticism can also be of several types: normative, descriptive, interpretive, textual, appreciative, generic. Collectively, the range of critical response helps us to understand a work of art, an author, an era.

Scope of the Series

Twentieth-Century Literary Criticism (TCLC) is designed to serve as an introduction for the student of twentieth-century literature to the authors of the period 1900 to 1960 and to the most significant commentators on these authors. The great poets, novelists, short story writers, playwrights, and philosophers of this period are by far the most popular writers for study in high school and college literature courses. Since a vast amount of relevant critical material confronts the student, *TCLC* presents significant passages from the most important published criticism to aid students in the location and selection of commentaries on authors who died between 1900 and 1960.

The need for *TCLC* was suggested by the usefulness of the Gale series *Contemporary Literary Criticism (CLC),* which excerpts criticism on current writing. Because of the difference in time span under consideration *(CLC* considers authors who were still living after 1959), there is no duplication of material between *CLC* and *TCLC.* For further information about *CLC* and Gale's other criticism series, users should consult the Guide to Gale Literary Criticism Series preceding the title page in this volume.

Each volume of *TCLC* is carefully compiled to include authors who represent a variety of genres and nationalities and who are currently regarded as the most important writers of this era. In addition to major authors, *TCLC* also presents criticism on lesser-known writers whose significant contributions to literary history are important to the study of twentieth-century literature.

Each author entry in *TCLC* is intended to provide an overview of major criticism on an author. Therefore, the editors include fifteen to twenty authors in each 600-page volume (compared with approximately fifty authors in a *CLC* volume of similar size) so that more attention may be given to an author. Each author entry represents a historical survey of the critical response to that author's work: some early criticism is presented to indicate initial reactions, later criticism is selected to represent any rise or decline in the author's reputation, and current retrospective analyses provide students with a modern view. The length of an author entry is intended to reflect the amount of critical attention the author has received from critics writing in English, and from foreign criticism in translation. Critical articles and books that have not been translated into English are excluded. Every attempt has been made to identify and include excerpts from the seminal essays on each author's work.

An author may appear more than once in the series because of the great quantity of critical material available, or because of a resurgence of criticism generated by events such as an author's centennial or anniversary celebration, the republication or posthumous publication of an author's works, or the publication of a newly translated work. Generally, a few author entries in each volume of *TCLC* feature criticism on single works by major authors who have appeared previously in the series. Only those individual works that have been the subjects of vast amounts of criticism and are widely studied in literature classes are selected for this in-depth treatment. Joseph Conrad's *Nostromo* is an example of such an entry in *TCLC,* Volume 25.

Organization of the Book

An author entry consists of the following elements: author heading, biographical and critical introduction, list of principal works, excerpts of criticism (each preceded by explanatory notes and followed by a bibliographical citation), and an additional bibliography for further reading.

- The *author heading* consists of the author's full name, followed by birth and death dates. The unbracketed portion of the name denotes the form under which the author most commonly wrote. If an author wrote consistently under a pseudonym, the pseudonym will be listed in the author heading and the real name given in parentheses on the first line of the biographical and critical introduction. Also located at the beginning of the introduction to the author entry are any name variations under which an author wrote, including transliterated forms for authors whose languages use nonroman alphabets. Uncertainty as to a birth or death date is indicated by a question mark.

- The *biographical and critical introduction* contains background information designed to introduce the reader to an author and to the critical debate surrounding his or her work. Parenthetical material following many of the introductions provides references to biographical and critical reference series published by Gale, including *Children's Literature Review, Contemporary Authors, Dictionary of Literary Biography, Something about the Author,* and past volumes of *TCLC.*

- Most *TCLC* entries include *portraits* of the author. Many entries also contain illustrations of materials pertinent to an author's career, including manuscript pages, title pages, dust jackets, letters, or representations of important people, places, and events in an author's life.

- The *list of principal works* is chronological by date of first book publication and identifies the genre of each work. In the case of foreign authors where there are both foreign language publications and English translations, the title and date of the first English-language edition are given in brackets. Unless otherwise indicated, dramas are dated by first performance, not first publication.

- *Criticism* is arranged chronologically in each author entry to provide a perspective on changes in critical evaluation over the years. All titles by the author featured in the critical entry are printed in boldface type to enable the user to ascertain without difficulty the works being discussed. Also for purposes of easier identification, the critic's name and the publication date of the essay are given at the beginning of each piece of criticism. Unsigned criticism is preceded by the title of the journal in which it appeared. When an anonymous essay is later attributed to a critic, the critic's name appears in brackets at the beginning of the excerpt and in the bibliographical citation. Many critical entries in *TCLC* also contain translated material to aid users. Unless otherwise noted, translations within brackets are by the editors; translations within parentheses or continuous with the text are by the author of the excerpt.

- Critical essays are prefaced by *explanatory notes* as an additional aid to students using *TCLC.* The explanatory notes provide several types of useful information, including the reputation of a critic, the importance of a work of criticism, the specific type of criticism (biographical, psychoanalytic, structuralist, etc.), a synopsis of the criticism, and the growth of critical controversy or changes in critical trends regarding an author's work. In some cases, these notes cross-reference the work of critics who agree or disagree with each other. Dates in parentheses within the explanatory notes refer to a book publication date when they follow a book title and to an essay date when they follow a critic's name.

- A complete *bibliographical citation* designed to facilitate location of the original essay or book by the interested reader follows each piece of criticism.

- The *additional bibliography* appearing at the end of each author entry suggests further reading on the author. In some cases it includes essays for which the editors could not obtain reprint rights.

An appendix lists the sources from which material in each volume has been reprinted. It does not, however, list every book or periodical consulted in the preparation of the volume.

Cumulative Indexes

Each volume of *TCLC* includes a cumulative index listing all the authors who have appeared in *Contemporary Literary Criticism, Twentieth-Century Literary Criticism, Nineteenth-Century Literature Criticism,* and *Literature Criticism from 1400 to 1800,* along with cross-references to the Gale series *Children's Literature Review, Authors in the News, Contemporary Authors, Contemporary Authors Autobiography Series, Dictionary of Literary Biography, Concise Dictionary of American Literary Biography, Something about the Author, Something about the Author Autobiography Series,* and *Yesterday's Authors of Books for Children.* Readers will welcome this cumulated author index as a useful tool for locating an author within the various series. The index, which lists birth and death dates when available, will be particularly valuable for those authors who are identified with a certain period but whose death date causes them to be placed in another, or for those authors whose careers span two periods. For example, F. Scott Fitzgerald is found in *TCLC,* yet a writer often associated with him, Ernest Hemingway, is found in *CLC.*

Each volume of *TCLC* also includes a cumulative nationality index. Author names are arranged alphabetically under their respective nationalities and followed by the volume numbers in which they appear.

New Index

An important feature that appeared for the first time in *TCLC,* Volume 24, is a cumulative index to titles, an alphabetical listing of the literary works discussed in the series since its inception. Each title listing includes the corresponding volume and page numbers where criticism may be located. Foreign language titles that have been translated are followed by the titles of the translations—for example, *Voina i mir (War and Peace).* Page numbers following these translated titles refer to all pages on which any form of the titles, either foreign language or translated, appear. Titles of novels, dramas, nonfiction books, and poetry, short story, or essay collections are printed in italics, while all individual poems, short stories, and essays are printed in roman type within quotation marks. In cases where the same title is used by different authors, the author's surname is given in parentheses after the title, e.g., *Collected Poems* (Housman) and *Collected Poems* (Yeats).

Acknowledgments

No work of this scope can be accomplished without the cooperation of many people. The editors especially wish to thank the copyright holders of the excerpted criticism included in this volume, the permissions managers of many book and magazine publishing companies for assisting us in securing reprint rights, and Anthony Bogucki for assistance with copyright research. We are also grateful to the staffs of the Detroit Public Library, the Library of Congress, the University of Detroit Library, the University of Michigan Library, and the Wayne State University Library for making their resources available to us. The editors also wish to acknowledge The Bettmann Archive, Inc. for the endpaper illustration of Thomas Wolfe and The Granger Collection, New York, for the endpaper illustrations of Joseph Conrad, Thomas Hardy, Franz Kafka, Gertrude Stein, Leo Tolstoy, Mark Twain, and Virginia Woolf.

Suggestions Are Welcome

In response to various suggestions, several features have been added to *TCLC* since the series began, including explanatory notes to excerpted criticism that provide important information regarding critics and their work, a cumulative author index listing authors in all Gale literary criticism series, entries devoted to criticism on a single work by a major author, more extensive illustrations, and a title index listing all literary works discussed in the series since its inception.

Readers who wish to suggest authors to appear in future volumes, or who have other suggestions, are cordially invited to write the editors.

Authors to Be Featured in *TCLC*, Volumes 27 and 28

Twentieth-Century Literary Criticism, Volume 26, will be an Archives volume devoted to criticism of various topics in twentieth-century literature, including the Surrealist and Harlem Renaissance movements, the literature of the Spanish Civil War and Russian Thaw, and the centennial of the first appearance of Sherlock Holmes.

E. F. Benson (English novelist and short story writer)—An enormously popular author of the late nineteenth and early twentieth centuries, Benson is best remembered for his creation of the characters Dodo and Lucia, each of whom was featured in a series of novels that are considered masterpieces of Edwardian comedy.

Henri Bergson (French philosopher)—One of the most influential philosophers of the twentieth century, Bergson is renowned for his opposition to the dominant materialist thought of his time and for his creation of theories that emphasize the supremacy and independence of supra-rational consciousness.

R. D. Blackmore (English novelist)—A minor historical novelist of the Victorian era, Blackmore is remembered as the author of *Lorna Doone.* This classic of historical fiction is often praised for its vivid evocation of the past and its entertaining melodrama.

Edgar Rice Burroughs (American novelist)—Burroughs was a science fiction writer who is best known as the creator of Tarzan. His *Tarzan of the Apes* and its numerous sequels have sold over thirty-five million copies in fifty-six languages, making Burroughs one of the most popular authors in the world.

Joyce Cary (Anglo-Irish novelist)—Regarded as an important contributor to the trilogy as a literary form, Cary wrote trilogies noted for their humor, vitality, sympathetic characterizations, and technical virtuosity.

Stephen Crane (American novelist and short story writer)—Crane was one of the foremost realistic writers in American literature. *TCLC* will devote an entry to his masterpiece, *The Red Badge of Courage,* in which he depicted the psychological complexities of fear and courage in battle.

Charles Doughty (English travel writer and poet)—Doughty is best remembered as the author of *Travels in Arabia Deserta,* one of the classics in the literature of travel and a celebrated model of epic prose.

F. Scott Fitzgerald (American novelist)—Fitzgerald is considered the principal chronicler of the ideals and disillusionments of the Jazz Age, and his *Tender is the Night* is one of his most celebrated novels. In an entry devoted solely to this work, *TCLC* will present major critical essays examining its meaning and importance.

Fyodor Gladkov (Russian novelist)—A proletarian realist writer, Gladkov is best known for his novel *Cement,* which portrays the post-revolutionary collectivization of a cement factory.

Edmund Gosse (English novelist and critic)—A prolific man of letters in late nineteenth-century England, Gosse is of primary importance for his autobiographical novel *Father and Son,* which is considered a seminal work for gaining insight into the major issues of the Victorian age, especially the conflict between science and religion inspired by Darwin's *The Origin of Species.* Gosse is also important for his introduction of Henrik Ibsen's "new drama" to English audiences and for his numerous critical studies of English and foreign authors.

Muhammad Iqbal (Indian poet and philosopher)—Considered one of the leading Muslim intellectual figures of the twentieth century, Iqbal was a political activist and the author of poetry calling for social and religious reform.

Franz Kafka (Austrian novelist and short story writer)—Kafka's novel *The Trial* is often considered the definitive expression of his alienated vision as well as one of the seminal works of modern literature. *TCLC* will devote an entire entry to critical discussion of this novel, which has been described by Alvin J. Seltzer as "one of the most unrelenting works of chaos created in the first half of this century."

Henry Lawson (Australian short story writer and poet)—Lawson's stories in such collections as *While the Billy Boils* and *Joe Wilson and His Mates* chronicle the hard lives of working people in the backcountry of Australia and are considered characteristic of Australian writing of the late nineteenth and early twentieth centuries.

Dmitri Merezhkovsky (Russian novelist, philosopher, poet, and critic)—Although his poetry and criticism are credited with initiating the Symbolist movement in Russian literature, Merezhkovsky is best known as a religious philosopher who sought in numerous essays and historical novels to reconcile the values of pagan religions with the teachings of Christ.

John Muir (American naturalist, essayist, and autobiographer)—In such works as *A Thousand Mile Walk to the Gulf* and *The Mountains of California,* Muir celebrated the North American wilderness. He was also a prominent conservationist who was instrumental in establishing the system of national parks in the United States.

Eugene O'Neill (American dramatist)—Generally considered America's foremost dramatist, O'Neill is the author of works examining the implacability of an indifferent universe, the materialistic greed of humanity, and the problems of individual identity. *TCLC* will devote an entry to O'Neill's *Long Day's Journey into Night,* a portrait of a tormented, self-destructive family that has been called one of the most powerful dramas in American theater.

George Orwell (English novelist and essayist)—Designated the "conscience of his generation" by V. S. Pritchett, Orwell is the author of influential novels and essays embodying his commitment to personal freedom and social justice. *TCLC* will devote an entry to Orwell's first major popular and critical success, *Animal Farm,* a satirical fable in which Orwell attacked the consequences of the Russian Revolution while suggesting reasons for the failure of most revolutionary ideals.

Wilfred Owen (English poet)—Inspired by his experiences in World War I, Owen's poetry exposed the grim realities of war and its effect on the human spirit.

Benito Perez Galdos (Spanish novelist and dramatist)—Considered the greatest Spanish novelist since Cervantes, Galdos is known for two vast cycles of novels: the *Episodios nacionales,* a forty-six volume portrayal of nineteenth-century Spanish history; and the *Novelas espanolas contemporaneas,* explorations of social and ethical problems in twentieth-century Spain which have been favorably compared to the works of Charles Dickens and Honore de Balzac.

Fernando Pessoa (Portuguese poet)—Pessoa is considered the greatest Portuguese poet since the sixteenth century, as well as a writer whose work epitomizes the experimental tendencies and alienated temper of the modern era. His most prominent theme—that an individual's identity is multifarious and indeterminate—is conspiciuously reflected in the fact that much of his work was written under the names of various fictitious personas, for each of whom he created a distinct personality and literary style.

Luigi Pirandello (Italian dramatist)—Considered one of the most important innovators of twentieth-century drama, Pirandello developed experimental techniques including improvisation, the play-within-the-play, and the play-outside-the-play in order to explore such themes as the fluidity of reality, the relativity of truth, and the tenuous line between sanity and madness.

Alexei Remizov (Russian prose writer)—Best known for his ornate prose style, which influenced a generation of Soviet writers, Remizov was the author of an enormously diverse body of work, including realistic depictions of the Russian underclass, adaptations of Russian legends, mystery plays, religious parables, historical chronicles, memoirs, and recorded dreams.

Gertrude Stein (American novelist and critic)—Stein is recognized as one of the principal figures of literary Modernism, both as a brilliant experimentalist in such works as *The Autobiography of Alice B. Toklas* and *Tender Buttons* and as an influence upon a generation of authors that included Ernest Hemingway and F. Scott Fitzgerald.

Italo Svevo (Italian novelist)—Svevo's ironic portrayals of the moral life of the bourgeoisie, which characteristically demonstrate the influence of the psychoanalytic theories of Sigmund Freud, earned him a reputation as the father of the modern Italian novel.

Leo Tolstoy (Russian novelist)—Along with *Anna Karenina, War and Peace* is considered Tolstoy's most important work and one of the greatest works in world literature. *TCLC* will devote an entire entry to the critical history of this epic novel.

Thorstein Veblen (American economist and social critic)—Veblen's seminal analyses of the nature, development, and consequences of business and industry—as well as his attack on bourgeois materialism in *The Theory of the Leisure Class*—distinguished him as one of the foremost American economists and social scientists of the twentieth century.

Edith Wharton (American novelist and short story writer)—Wharton is best known as a novelist of manners whose fiction exposed the cruel excesses of aristocratic society at the turn of the century. Her subject matter, tone, and style have often been compared with those of her friend and mentor Henry James.

Thomas Wolfe (American novelist)—Wolfe is considered one of the foremost American novelists of the twentieth century. His most important works present intense and lyrical portraits of life in both rural and urban America while portraying the struggle of the lonely, sensitive, and artistic individual to find spiritual fulfillment.

Additional Authors to Appear
in Future Volumes

Abbey, Henry 1842-1911
Abercrombie, Lascelles 1881-1938
Adamic, Louis 1898-1951
Ade, George 1866-1944
Agustini, Delmira 1886-1914
Akers, Elizabeth Chase 1832-1911
Akiko, Yosano 1878-1942
Alas, Leopoldo 1852-1901
Aldrich, Thomas Bailey 1836-1907
Aliyu, Dan Sidi 1902-1920
Allen, Hervey 1889-1949
Archer, William 1856-1924
Arlen, Michael 1895-1956
Arlt, Roberto 1900-1942
Austin, Alfred 1835-1913
Bahr, Hermann 1863-1934
Bailey, Philip James 1816-1902
Barbour, Ralph Henry 1870-1944
Benét, William Rose 1886-1950
Benjamin, Walter 1892-1940
Bennett, James Gordon, Jr. 1841-1918
Berdyaev, Nikolai Aleksandrovich
    1874-1948
Beresford, J(ohn) D(avys) 1873-1947
Binyon, Laurence 1869-1943
Bishop, John Peale 1892-1944
Blake, Lillie Devereux 1835-1913
Blest Gana, Alberto 1830-1920
Blum, Leon 1872-1950
Bodenheim, Maxwell 1892-1954
Bowen, Marjorie 1886-1952
Byrne, Donn 1889-1928
Caine, Hall 1853-1931
Cannan, Gilbert 1884-1955
Carducci, Giosue 1835-1907
Carswell, Catherine 1879-1946
Churchill, Winston 1871-1947
Corelli, Marie 1855-1924
Cotter, Joseph Seamon 1861-1949
Croce, Benedetto 1866-1952
Crofts, Freeman Wills 1879-1957
Cruze, James (Jens Cruz Bosen) 1884-
    1942
Curros, Enriquez Manuel 1851-1908
Dall, Caroline Wells (Healy) 1822-1912
Daudet, Leon 1867-1942
Delafield, E.M. (Edme Elizabeth Monica
    de la Pasture) 1890-1943
Deneson, Jacob 1836-1919
DeVoto, Bernard 1897-1955
Diego, Jose de 1866-1918
Douglas, (George) Norman 1868-1952
Douglas, Lloyd C(assel) 1877-1951
Dovzhenko, Alexander 1894-1956
Drinkwater, John 1882-1937

Dunne, Finley Peter 1867-1936
Durkheim, Emile 1858-1917
Duun, Olav 1876-1939
Eaton, Walter Prichard 1878-1957
Eggleston, Edward 1837-1902
Erskine, John 1879-1951
Fadeyev, Alexander 1901-1956
Ferland, Albert 1872-1943
Field, Rachel 1894-1924
Flecker, James Elroy 1884-1915
Fletcher, John Gould 1886-1950
Fogazzaro, Antonio 1842-1911
Francos, Karl Emil 1848-1904
Frank, Bruno 1886-1945
Frazer, (Sir) George 1854-1941
Freud, Sigmund 1853-1939
Froding, Gustaf 1860-1911
Fuller, Henry Blake 1857-1929
Futabatei, Shimei 1864-1909
Glaspell, Susan 1876-1948
Glyn, Elinor 1864-1943
Golding, Louis 1895-1958
Gould, Gerald 1885-1936
Guest, Edgar 1881-1959
Gumilyov, Nikolay 1886-1921
Gyulai, Pal 1826-1909
Hale, Edward Everett 1822-1909
Hansen, Martin 1909-1955
Hayashi, Fumiko 1904-1951
Hernandez, Miguel 1910-1942
Hewlett, Maurice 1861-1923
Heyward, DuBose 1885-1940
Hope, Anthony 1863-1933
Hudson, W(illiam) H(enry) 1841-1922
Huidobro, Vincente 1893-1948
Ilyas, Abu Shabaka 1903-1947
Imbs, Bravig 1904-1946
Iqbal, Mahammad 1877-1938
Ivanov, Vyacheslav Ivanovich 1866-
    1949
James, Will 1892-1942
Jammes, Francis 1868-1938
Johnson, Fenton 1888-1958
Johnston, Mary 1870-1936
Jorgensen, Johannes 1866-1956
King, Grace 1851-1932
Kirby, William 1817-1906
Kline, Otis Albert 1891-1946
Kohut, Adolph 1848-1916
Kreve, Bincas 1882-1954
Kuzmin, Mikhail Alexseyevich 1875-
    1936
Lamm, Martin 1880-1950
Leipoldt, C. Louis 1880-1947
Lima, Jorge De 1895-1953

Locke, Alain 1886-1954
Long, Frank Belknap 1903-1959
Lopez Portillo y Rojas, Jose 1850-1903
Louys, Pierre 1870-1925
Lucas, E(dward) V(errall) 1868-1938
Lyall, Edna 1857-1903
Maghar, Josef Suatopluk 1864-1945
Mander, Jane 1877-1949
Maragall, Joan 1860-1911
Marais, Eugene 1871-1936
Masaryk, Tomas 1850-1939
Mayor, Flora Macdonald 1872-1932
McClellan, George Marion 1860-1934
McCoy, Horace 1897-1955
Mirbeau, Octave 1850-1917
Mistral, Frederic 1830-1914
Monro, Harold 1879-1932
Moore, Thomas Sturge 1870-1944
Moricz, Zsigmond 1879-1942
Morley, Christopher 1890-1957
Morley, S. Griswold 1883-1948
Murray, (George) Gilbert 1866-1957
Nansen, Peter 1861-1918
Nobre, Antonio 1867-1900
O'Dowd, Bernard 1866-1959
Ophuls, Max 1902-1957
Orczy, Baroness 1865-1947
Owen, Seaman 1861-1936
Page, Thomas Nelson 1853-1922
Palma, Ricardo 1833-1919
Papadiamantis, Alexandros 1851-1911
Parrington, Vernon L. 1871-1929
Peck, George W. 1840-1916
Phillips, Ulrich B. 1877-1934
Pinero, Arthur Wing 1855-1934
Pontoppidan, Henrik 1857-1943
Powys, T. F. 1875-1953
Prevost, Marcel 1862-1941
Quiller-Couch, Arthur 1863-1944
Radiguet, Raymond 1903-1923
Randall, James G. 1881-1953
Rappoport, Solomon 1863-1944
Read, Opie 1852-1939
Rebreanu, Liviu 1885-1944
Reisen (Reizen), Abraham 1875-1953
Remington, Frederic 1861-1909
Riley, James Whitcomb 1849-1916
Rinehart, Mary Roberts 1876-1958
Ring, Max 1817-1901
Rivera, Jose Eustasio 1889-1928
Rohmer, Sax 1883-1959
Rozanov, Vasily Vasilyevich 1856-1919
Saar, Ferdinand von 1833-1906
Sabatini, Rafael 1875-1950
Saintsbury, George 1845-1933

Sakutaro, Hagiwara 1886-1942
Sanborn, Franklin Benjamin 1831-1917
Santayana, George 1863-1952
Sardou, Victorien 1831-1908
Schickele, René 1885-1940
Seabrook, William 1886-1945
Seton, Ernest Thompson 1860-1946
Shestov, Lev 1866-1938
Shiels, George 1886-1949
Sodergran, Edith Irene 1892-1923
Solovyov, Vladimir 1853-1900
Sorel, Georges 1847-1922
Spector, Mordechai 1859-1922
Squire, J(ohn) C(ollings) 1884-1958
Stavenhagen, Fritz 1876-1906

Stockton, Frank R. 1834-1902
Subrahmanya Bharati, C. 1882-1921
Sully-Prudhomme, René 1839-1907
Sylva, Carmen 1843-1916
Thoma, Ludwig 1867-1927
Tomlinson, Henry Major 1873-1958
Totovents, Vahan 1889-1937
Tuchmann, Jules 1830-1901
Turner, W(alter) J(ames) R(edfern)
    1889-1946
Upward, Allen 1863-1926
Vachell, Horace Annesley 1861-1955
Van Dyke, Henry 1852-1933
Veblen, Thorstein 1857-1929
Villaespesa, Francisco 1877-1936

Wallace, Edgar 1874-1932
Wallace, Lewis 1827-1905
Walsh, Ernest 1895-1926
Webster, Jean 1876-1916
Wen I-to 1899-1946
Whitlock, Brand 1869-1927
Wilson, Harry Leon 1867-1939
Wolf, Emma 1865-1932
Wood, Clement 1888-1950
Wren, P(ercival) C(hristopher) 1885-
    1941
Yonge, Charlotte Mary 1823-1901
Zecca, Ferdinand 1864-1947
Zeromski, Stefan 1864-1925

Readers are cordially invited to suggest additional authors to the editors.

Mary (Hunter) Austin

1868-1934

(Also wrote under pseudonym of Gordon Stairs) American essayist, novelist, short story writer, poet, autobiographer, and dramatist.

Austin is best known for her regional sketches and tales which portray the landscape, life, and lore of the American Southwest. Inspired by the desert, she was one of the first American writers to celebrate an environment commonly perceived as barren and hostile. *The Land of Little Rain,* a collection of sketches depicting the southern California desert, is her most acclaimed work of this kind and has been characteristically praised by Lawrence Clark Powell for giving ''voice in singing prose to the soul of a hitherto unsung land.'' Throughout her work, Austin is concerned with the relationship of people to their natural and social environments, particularly with respect to the conditioning influence of environments on individuals and cultures.

Austin was born in Carlinville, Illinois, to an attorney and his wife. Due to her father's lingering poor health, caused by the malaria he contracted while serving in the Civil War, the financial situation of Austin's family was precarious. Austin deeply admired her father, with whom she shared a love of books and of the outdoors, and his death when Austin was ten years old was a devastating loss. In contrast to her close relationship with her father, Austin was estranged from her mother and was acutely aware that her mother favored Austin's elder brother. When in conflict with her mother, Austin would withdraw into an inner self, a persona which she called ''I-Mary.'' As Austin explained in her autobiography, *Earth Horizon,* ''I-Mary'' became a refuge and the center of her creativity. Perhaps the most significant experience of Austin's childhood occurred at the age of six when, as she stood beneath a walnut tree near her house, she experienced an intense awareness of her oneness with nature and identified God as the source of this feeling. Nature and mysticism, as well as her small-town upbringing, were to become major influences in her life and writing.

Austin displayed an early talent for storytelling and was writing poetry by the age of ten. Later, while pursuing a science major at Blackburn College, she became the editor of her college journal and was elected Class Poet. Following her graduation in 1888, Austin and her family moved to southern California, where they became homesteaders. Although the homesteading venture failed, two short stories set in the region—''One Hundred Miles on Horseback'' and ''Mother of Felipe''—were the first of her works accepted for publication. More importantly, her attraction to the desert began at this time. For a number of years she studied the desert—including the plants, animals, and people who lived there—gradually accumulating the material and developing the ideas and attitudes which later became the basis for her most distinguished works. During her early years in California she also taught school in the San Joaquin Valley, and there met Stafford Austin, whom she married in 1891. At the time of their meeting, Stafford Austin was working on an irrigation project which ultimately failed, leaving Mary to support both of them until her husband finally found employment as a teacher. Austin's marriage lasted until 1905,

when the couple permanently separated prior to their divorce. During the marriage, Austin contributed her earnings from teaching and writing, greatly supplementing her husband's income. In her later works the problems of marriage and women's struggles to succeed outside of traditional roles were among the social issues she examined.

In 1903 Austin published her first major work, *The Land of Little Rain,* and in 1905 she settled in a colony of writers and artists in Carmel. At first rejected by the male members of the group because she was considered unattractive, she eventually became a vital part of the colony and associated with such West Coast literary figures as Jack London and George Sterling. During this time she published her first novel, *Isidro;* she also wrote a study of the California sheep industry, *The Flock,* which is considered one of her best works. In 1907 Austin left Carmel for Europe where, among other cultural studies, she pursued her interest in the historical and theological foundation of Christianity, which led to the writing of such works as *Christ in Italy, The Man Jesus,* and *Can Prayer Be Answered?* During her nearly three years in Italy, France, and England, she met such prominent writers as Joseph Conrad, H. G. Wells, William Butler Yeats, and Bernard Shaw, was hosted for a time by the Herbert Hoovers, and published *Outland,* a fantasy novel based in part on her experiences in Carmel. In addition, Austin's feminist ideas were strengthened by her association with European women who promoted such progressivist causes as women's suffrage and greater professional opportunities for women.

Austin returned from Europe in 1910 for the New York production of her play *The Arrow Maker,* which portrays the tribal role of a Paiute medicine woman. From 1912 through 1924 Austin divided her time primarily between New York City and Carmel, though she also developed a strong attraction for the desert of New Mexico. During these years she published books and essays, promoted feminist causes, and lectured widely. Among her works of this period are *Love and the Soul Maker,* which reflects her ideals for marriage and demonstrates her attempt to break away from the conventions of her day; *A Woman of Genius,* a somewhat autobiographical novel depicting a woman's unhappy marriage, promising artistic career, and the conditioning influence of midwestern American culture on women; and *The Man Jesus,* a study of Jesus in which Austin interprets the formative influences of the desert, small-town life, and social pressures on his development. Although these were productive years during which Austin received some recognition from the eastern literary establishment, she became dissatisfied with what she perceived as the rootless, success-driven New York society.

In 1924, having been attracted for some time to the Indian and Spanish cultures of New Mexico as well as to the desert itself, Austin settled permanently in Santa Fe. Her adobe house, called "Casa Querida," became a meeting place for literary people and a center for cultural activities. That same year she published *The Land of Journeys' Ending,* a collection of prose sketches based on her travels through New Mexico and Arizona, and *The American Rhythm.* In the latter work Austin translated a selection of Indian poetry and presented her theory that environment profoundly affects artistic expression in general and poetry writing in particular. She also discussed the artistic contributions of the American Indian, asserting the significance of Indian poetry as an example of what genuine American poetry could be like, as contrasted with American poetry based on European traditions. Although critics find this theory an original and interesting idea which contains elements of truth, and which was important for drawing attention to the often neglected art of the American Indian, it is nevertheless considered an untenable argument as a whole. Throughout her years in Santa Fe, Austin devoted much of her attention to affairs of regional interest, particularly the recognition and restoration of the Indian culture. Among the more notable studies of Indian life that she published during this period is *One-Smoke Stories,* which illustrates, according to T. M. Pearce, Austin's "greatest gift," that of "interpreting the land in outline and meaning," and "her second superlative gift," that of "portraying the inhabitants of a landscape, whether vegetable, animal, or human." Her autobiography, *Earth Horizon,* in which she identifies literature, nature, and mysticism as three major forces in her life, appeared near the end of this period. She died in 1934, and her ashes were sealed in the crevice of a mountain east of Casa Querida.

Critics often discuss Austin's work in an autobiographical context that accentuates the correspondence between her life and her writings. In particular, critics emphasize her personal development, the unhappy circumstances of her life, her views on various social issues, and her spiritual precepts. As Carl Van Doren has noted: "What she has written has been essentially the record of her growth, the growth of a deep and

powerful spirit." As a child Austin had felt unwanted by her mother, and as an adult she often lacked a sense of belonging—finding herself at odds with her family or society and describing herself as "Woman Alone." She perceived mainstream American society to be restrictive, narrow-minded, rootless, and over-industrialized, and felt more at home with rural inhabitants of the Southwest. Her attitudes toward mainstream America are present in her work; according to Dudley Wynn: "Criticism of American rootlessness is implied in almost everything Mary Austin wrote." Regarding Austin's spiritual orientation, it is evident from her writings that, while maintaining a special predilection for Christianity and the nature worship of American Indians, she nonetheless recognized all world religions as effective and authentic methods for realizing a supernatural reality that was, in her view, essentially animistic. As Pearce explains, Austin "believed that there were influences and powers working toward everyone through nature."

Critics agree that Austin's talents are best displayed in her regional portraits, most notably *The Land of Little Rain, The Flock, Lost Borders,* and *The Land of Journeys' Ending.* That she was a naturalist, mystic, and folklorist with a scientific education is evidenced throughout her works, which present the desert as neither beneficent nor malevolent, but as a suitable environment for all forms of life that adapt to its harsh demands. Austin believed that the native American cultures of the Southwest represented the proper relationship between humanity and nature, one based on a profound identification of a people with their natural environment. As a naturalist, Austin not only reported the observable data of the region but also, according to H. C. Tracy, conveyed "the spirit of the land, the spirit of the plant, and the spirit of man." Critics note the prophetic state of mind expressed in these works, both in the sense of envisioning the future and, more dependably, in the sense of speaking with knowledge and deep understanding of nature, human culture, and their interrelationship. Of all her regional works, *The Land of Little Rain* has received the most critical admiration. This first major work of Austin's prolific career has been especially praised for its faithful description of the region, for the eloquence, lyricism, and exactitude of its prose style, and for its philosophical perspective. Powell describes the work as being "a perfect conjunction of life, landscape, and literature. In this book Mary Austin found the words which perfectly expressed what she saw and felt and wanted to say."

Austin's nature writing is often compared with that of Henry David Thoreau and John Muir. The three writers had in common an ability to enjoy solitude and to appreciate nature for its own sake; from nature they derived personal satisfaction and inspiration. Yet critics such as Vernon Young and Henry Smith emphasize that unlike Thoreau and Muir, Austin's ultimate purpose in experiencing and studying nature was not to escape from civilization but to discover a sense of direction for society and to derive moral lessons from desert life that could provide models for human behavior. Thus, her purpose was ultimately social and ethical. During her lifetime Austin gained recognition for her achievements as a naturalist and social commentator, and although her reputation has considerably diminished, critics have nonetheless confirmed her distinctive contribution to American literature.

(See also *Contemporary Authors,* Vol. 109 and *Dictionary of Literary Biography,* Vol. 9: *American Novelists: 1910-1945.*)

PRINCIPAL WORKS

The Land of Little Rain   (sketches)   1903
The Basket Woman   (short stories)   1904

Isidro (novel) 1905
The Flock (sketches) 1906
Santa Lucia (novel) 1908
Lost Borders (sketches) 1909
Outland [as Gordon Stairs] (novel) 1909
The Arrow Maker (drama) 1911
Christ in Italy (essays) 1912
A Woman of Genius (novel) 1912
The Lovely Lady (novel) 1913
California: The Land of the Sun (sketches) 1914; also
    published as *The Lands of the Sun*, 1927
Love and the Soul Maker (novel) 1914
The Man Jesus (nonfiction) 1915; also published as *A
    Small Town Man*, 1925
The Ford (novel) 1917
No. 26 Jayne Street (novel) 1920
The American Rhythm (criticism and translations) 1923;
    also published as *The American Rhythm: Studies and
    Reexpressions of Amerindian Songs* [revised and
    enlarged edition], 1930
The Land of Journeys' Ending (sketches) 1924
The Children Sing in the Far West (poetry) 1928
Taos Pueblo [with photographs by Ansel Adams] (prose)
    1930
Experiences Facing Death (essays) 1931
Starry Adventure (novel) 1931
Earth Horizon (autobiography) 1932
Can Prayer Be Answered? (essays) 1934
One-Smoke Stories (short stories) 1934
Mother of Felipe, and Other Early Stories (short stories)
    1950

THE DIAL (essay date 1903)

[*In the following excerpt, the critic reviews* The Land of Little
Rain.]

"Between the high Sierras south from Yosemite—east and
south over a very great assemblage of broken ranges beyond
Death Valley, and on illimitably into the Mojave Desert,"—
there Mrs. Mary Austin tells us lies **The Land of Little Rain.**
The Indians call it the Country of Lost Borders; and she prefers
that name to "Desert" for a place that, to the patient observer,
is far from being void of life. There are hills there, "blunt,
burned, squeezed up out of chaos, chrome and vermilion
painted"; and between the hills are steep and narrow cañons,
oftener than not dry at the bottom, and high sun-baked mesas
where the dust-devils dance to the wind's piping. By day, the
land is very still, spell-bound in the glare of the sun; but in
the late afternoon the birds appear, and the little furry folk
creep out from cover and take to their tiny ribbon-like water
trails. Then the hawk and the eagle skim over the sage, the
coyote lurks by the rabbit-form, the "billy-owl," the bob-cat,
and the red fox gather at the water-holes, all watching their
chance to prey on smaller creatures. Wherever there are cattle
there are scavengers,—buzzards and ravens; and in the dry
years vultures, in terrible black clouds. There are men, too, in
the desert: cattlemen, miners bitten with tales of lost treasure,
and Paiute Indians; there is Jimville, a Bret Harte town, and
Las Uvas, a Mexican pueblo. There is indeed tragedy in the
desert; but Mrs. Austin wonders if convention has not over-
emphasized that note. The lonely land takes heavy toll of the

visitor, but it pays high returns; and once its charm is on you,
you may curse it and leave it, but you will surely come back.
Mrs. Austin did not go to the desert to write it up. She has
lived on its borders for years, and because she knows and loves
it she can reproduce its atmosphere of romance, of silence,
and of strangeness. (pp. 421-22)

> "Holiday Publications," *in* The Dial, *Vol. 35, No.*
> *419, December 1, 1903, pp. 421-34.*

THE NATION (essay date 1906)

[*In the following excerpt, the critic compares Austin with several
other authors, and favorably reviews* The Flock.]

In the Georgics, Virgil blended husbandry, beauty, and observation from a poetic angle, with knowledge of his own craft.
To make a long skip, Richard Jefferies recorded both what he
saw and the connection between things seen and things remembered—tradition, history, and an undercurrent of well-
subordinated science. In "The Life of the Bee," and in his
wonderful sketch of the dog, Maeterlinck adds to all of these
qualities his own poetic philosophy of life. With the same
sentiment for nature, Thomas Hardy uses his knowledge as a
setting for his groups of rustic human beings. While showing
points of likeness to all of these, Mary Austin, in **The Flock,**
at once establishes herself as their worthy kinswoman, never
their imitator. That strain runs in her blood which makes her
see and feel as they do. It is not the abstract and detached
observation of Thoreau, it is at once more purposeful and more
romantic, in fact, more warm-blooded.

Whether this be a question of personality, or of her inspiring
surroundings, the product stands quite apart. Baldly stated, it
is no more than a study of the sheep industry in California,
with a slender thread of historic narrative, a picture of sheep
herding, a word for irrigation. This summary of **The Flock,**
however, bears about as much relation to the actual achievement as a statement that the first book of the Georgics is a
treatise on agriculture, or that the *Pêcheurs d'Islande* has to
do with salt fish. In the opening chapter you learn how domestic
sheep first came to Monterey. You have no sense of being
instructed, you merely feel that the author is talking agreeably
and discursively on a subject of deep interest to herself, and
in a manner that makes you a willing listener.

Mary Austin's method is to give you the picture, sky, flowers,
animals, and men. You see it all as if you had just come from
your Pullman car to a shearing. Gradually she explains a little,
the breed of sheep, of dogs, of shepherds; how they have come
over long and weary trails, following feed and water; how
forest preservation has brought about struggles between herders
and rangers; how a beneficent law may, in its first working,
make for injustice, as when, at the end of a long journey, the
expected pasture is a preserve, and the ranger does his duty
while sheep starve and die, in order that the region may be
saved from perpetual drought. All this she tells, with anecdotes
of the ways of sheep, with bits of legend and of tradition, tales
of finessing on the part of herders and of sagacious dogs. She
likewise stops for queer speculations on the development of
the animal mind; and pauses to let you infer what analogy you
please between the "flock-mind" (of which she says "I cannot
very well say what it is, except that it is less than the sum of
all their intelligences") and the crowd-mind of humanity. With
the closest observation and sympathy where animals are concerned, she does not sentimentalize about them: she makes the
limits of instinct quite as clear as its scope. Of some five

hundred sheep charging over a precipice to escape a bear, she says: "The brute instinct had warned them asleep, but could not save them awake." Her chapter on the dog is particularly delightful, his business with the flock is described as "a trick man has played on the dog to constitute him the guardian of his natural prey"; and the whole analysis of what the collie means to the herd, and what the herd means to the collie, is entirely free from false observation or obstructive theorizing.

And so the book rambles on through a shepherd's year, leaving you with a sense of refreshment, with a desire to join the hairy little Basques and Frenchmen on their long journeys, to eat savory messes out of their black camp pots, to lie under the sky with dogs and flocks, lulled to sleep by the "blether" of ewes and the bark of distant coyotes. The charm of the whole lies in three qualities: the novelty and interest of the subject, the picturesque texture of the author's mind, and in a style which is both cultivated and racy, and adapted to conveying her unusual sense of beauty.

A review of "The Flock," in The Nation, New York, Vol. LXXXIII, No. 2162, December 6, 1906, p. 489.

CLAYTON HAMILTON   (essay date 1911)

[In the following excerpt, Hamilton summarizes the plot of The Arrow Maker, criticizing the work both as a dramatic production and as a literary composition.]

As a play, Mrs. Mary Austin's effort [The Arrow Maker] is ponderous and slow-moving; and as a literary composition, it is laboured and rhetorical. The action passes in the foot-hills of the California Sierras at some undetermined time prior to the appearance of white people; and all the actors in the story are members of the Sagharawites, a small tribe of the Paiute Indians. The Medicine Woman of the tribe is set apart from ordinary human intercourse and consecrated to communion with the gods. Nevertheless she loves the Arrow Maker, who visits her in secret. On the eve of battle with a neighbouring tribe, the warriors of the Sagharawites take counsel of the Medicine Woman concerning the selection of a leader; and persuaded by her love, she contrives that her incantations shall secure the election of the Arrow Maker. Subsequently, actuated by ambition, he marries the daughter of the chief. The Medicine Woman comes unbidden to his wedding; and in an outburst of passionate jealousy, she discloses his former relations with herself, curses his bride, and retracts from the service of the tribe the assistance of her supernatural powers. As a result, the tribe is subsequently defeated in battle and reduced to famine; whereupon the Arrow Maker is deposed from his leadership, and the Medicine Woman, finally appeased, brings her magic once again to save the tribe from ruin. There is nothing in this quite ordinary story of a woman's jealousy that is necessarily indigenous to the prehistoric setting that the author has chosen for it. If a mediaeval nun were substituted for the Medicine Woman and the tribesmen of the Sagharawites were supplanted by mail-clad knights, the essential story would remain unaltered. It would therefore be an error to regard Mrs. Austin's play as a special study of the peculiar emotions of the primitive red-man. The piece is Indian only in its setting. The story, as Mrs. Austin has developed it, would serve better as the libretto for an opera than as a play. In the theatre the action moves so slowly that the audience is wearied. The dialogue is written in a rhetorical prose that is monotonously magniloquent. Mrs. Austin is supposed to know all about the Indians; she has lived among them. Can it be possible that they are unable to conduct

a simple conversation about ordinary matters without couching their remarks in sentences that are lengthy and elaborately literary? Don't the Indians ever say, "I'm tired"?—must they always say, "My body is overborne with weariness, my muscles flaccid with fatigue"?—I admit that I have invented, and not quoted, the foregoing illustration; but it will serve. I don't know anything about the Indians; but I should imagine that primitive people moved by strong emotions would think quickly and talk directly. Mrs. Austin's Indians seem to have spent the leisure hours of their childhood reading out loud the "Eleonora" of Edgar Allan Poe and the Rasselas of Dr. Johnson. (pp. 140-41)

Clayton Hamilton, "The Personality of the Playwright," in The Bookman, New York, Vol. XXXIII, No. 2, April, 1911, pp. 130-41.

JACK LONDON   (letter date 1915)

[One of the most popular Naturalist writers of the early twentieth century, London combined adventure, socialism, mysticism, Darwinian determinism, and Nietzschean theories of race in such classic novels as Call of the Wild (1903) and The Sea-Wolf (1904). His high regard for the writings of Charles Darwin and Friedrich Nietzsche is demonstrated by the doctrines of rugged individualism and of the amoral übermensch ("superman") that dominate his early adventure novels and which in his later fiction took the more malignant form of advocating white supremacy. Nevertheless, London also wrote socialist novels and essays in support of labor reform and a united effort by the working class to bring about a better future. London was among the writers and artists of Carmel with whom Austin associated. In the following excerpt, London comments favorably on Austin's The Man Jesus, while criticizing the public reception of this work and of his own works. As explained by T. M. Pearce in his introduction to the letter from London to Austin from which the following excerpt was taken, "My Christ story" refers to an episode in London's The Star Rover.]

Your letter strikes me that you are serious. Now, why be serious with this bone-head world? Long ere this, I know that you have learned that the majority of the people who inhabit the planet Earth are bone-heads. Wherever the bone of their heads interferes there is no getting through.

I have read and enjoyed every bit of your "Jesus Christ" book as published serially in the North American Review. What if it does not get across? (pp. 73-4)

Heavens, have you read my "Christ" story? I doubt that anybody has read this "Christ" story of mine, though it has been published in book form on both sides of the Atlantic. Said book has been praised for its red-bloodedness and no mention has been made of my handling of the Christ situation in Jerusalem at all.

I tell you this, not because I am squealing, which I am not; but to show you that you are not alone in this miss-firing. Just be content with being called the "greatest American stylist."

Those who sit alone must sit alone. They must continue to sit alone. As I remember it, the prophets and seers of all times have been compelled to sit alone except at such times when they were stoned or burned at the stake. The world is mostly bone-head and nearly all boob, and you have no complaint if the world calls you the "great stylist" and fails to recognize that your style is merely the very heart and soul of your brain. The world has an idea that style is something apart from heart and brain. Neither you nor I can un-convince the world of that idea.

I do not know what more I can say, except, that, had I you here with me for half an hour I could make my point more strongly, namely that you are very lucky, and that you should be content to receive what the world gives you. The world will never give you due recognition for your "Christ" book. I, who never read serials, read your serial of the Christ and turned always to it first when my *North American Review* came in. I am not the world, you are not the world. The world feeds you, the world feeds me, but the world knows damn little of either of us. (pp. 74-5)

> *Jack London, in a letter to Mary Austin on November 5, 1915, in* Literary America: The Mary Austin Letters, 1903-1934, *edited by T. M. Pearce, Greenwood Press, 1979, pp. 73-5.*

LEWIS MUMFORD   (essay date 1923)

[*Mumford is an American sociologist, historian, philosopher, and author whose primary interest is the relationship between the modern individual and his or her environment. Influenced by the works of Patrick Geddes, a Scottish sociologist and pioneer in the field of city planning, Mumford has worked extensively in the area of city and regional planning and has written several important studies of cities, including* The Culture of Cities *(1938),* City Development *(1945), and* The City in History *(1961). All of these works examine the interrelationship between cities and civilization over the centuries. Also indicative of much of his work is Mumford's concern with firm moral values to assure the growth of civilization. Writing in the* Saturday Evening Post, *Mumford noted that "the test of maturity, for nations as well as for individuals is not the increase of power, but the increase of self-understanding, self-control, self-direction, and self-transcendence. For in a mature society, man himself, not his machines or his organizations, is the chief work of art." In the following excerpt, Mumford analyzes the thesis of* The American Rhythm, *noting the strengths and weaknesses of Austin's argument.*]

Many people, I believe, vaguely associate Mrs. Mary Austin with the notion of connecting art and literature in America with the culture of the Amerindian; and they have an a priori objection to the belief that a sophisticated culture can tie up with a primitive one, or that it can find common roots with a primitive culture when it is planted in the same geographic environment. This settled indifference to our squandered birthright makes it likely that Mrs. Austin's latest work will not get the attention that it deserves; all the more, perhaps, because Mrs. Austin has an original mind in which authentic intuitions, drawn from the wells of experience, have the misfortune to be poured into cracked and ugly academic bottles; and her art often sounds like that "braying of maimed voices, hybrids of art and sociology" of which she herself complains in one of her poems. Even Mrs. Austin's errors, however, have a certain fertility and vigor that a great many truths lack; and if every particular point in her thesis should turn out to be wrong, her work would still be an interesting contribution to criticism.

The essay on *The American Rhythm* is, superficially, an attempt to show that American poetry, if it arises out of genuine experience, will have a rhythm that is native to the landscape and the primitive occupations of the American scene—the free loping stride of the pioneer, the swing of the axe, and the empathy towards "free flung mountain ridges, untrimmed forests, evidence of structure and growth." Mrs. Austin observes that "in so far as verse forms are shaped by topography and

Austin around 1900.

the rhythm of food supply, the aboriginal American was singing in precisely the forms that were later to become native to the region of Spoon River, the Land of Little Rain, and the country of the Cornhuskers."

As long ago as 1904-05 Mrs. Austin predicted that "American poetry must inevitably take, at some period of its history, the mold of Amerind verse," and so, in a sense, she may well claim that she anticipated the arrival of Masters, Sandburg and Vachel Lindsay. As a demonstration of American verse-forms Mrs. Austin devotes the second half of *The American Rhythm* to her very poignant and beautiful "re-expressions" of Amerindian poems, and these verses are sufficiently different in content and achievement to assure one that there is more of the Indian than of Mrs. Austin in them.

Beneath the thesis that American poetry must be shaped by American experience is the much more important notion that all poetry is shaped and measured by primitive, organic experiences. "Rhythm," says Mrs. Austin, "in so far as it affects our poetic mode, has nothing to do with our intellectual life." The fundamental rhythms are given in the very nature of the human organism itself, the rise and fall of the breath, the iambic lub-*dub* of the heart. (p. 23)

Mrs. Austin says: "Man learned to dance when he felt helpless or fragmentary, when he felt dislocated in his universe. As he learned to know such states of psychic completion for states of power, he danced for the sake of the meal or the mate. Who

19

can doubt that the Allness is moved by our singing, since it immediately begins to throb in us as the dance progresses? Will not the corn fill out in the ear, even as the soul fills?'' In other words, at their deepest, poetry and drama and dance give one that feeling of fulfillment and kinship which the sexual embrace gives: they energize the organism and deliver it from the sense of frustration which the blind hazards of experience might otherwise leave it with.

In her interest in the communal environment of poetry, in her appreciation of literature, music and the dance as essential to the well-being of men, in her feeling that poetry is as necessary as bread rather than as trivial as push-pins, Mrs. Austin's work is as important as it is vigorous and wise—and it is very vigorous and wise. With her aid we can, I think, see a little more clearly why the urbane Addisons and Popes of the eighteenth century left English poetry in an impasse of epigram from which Burns and Wordsworth rescued it in a romantic ''return to Nature'' by way of the peasant's ballads, and this is but one path of reflection among a dozen, Mrs. Austin points to. What, then, are Mrs. Austin's weaknesses?

The first weakness is that it is easier to accept Mrs. Austin's general thesis than it is to follow her particular illustrations. An opponent, for example, would single out the fact that on one page the iambic lub-dub is attributed to the heart, and on another to the heavy Nordic walk; and when Mrs. Austin finds the rhythm of the woodland stride and the swinging ax in Lincoln's Gettysburg speech it seems to me, frankly, that she is letting her imagination run away with her. These fallacies of illustration arise, however, out of a second weakness; namely, that Mrs. Austin is interested in an Americanization program, and she is anxious to make clear, not the influence of rustic occupations and experiences upon poetry, but the influence of *American* occupations upon *American* poetry. In order to make out a better case for Americanism Mrs. Austin is compelled to deny, or at least to belittle, the universal significance of poetry derived from other environments and other cultures. Instead of showing the influence of a rustic background upon cultivated poetry, as one might so easily do with the great bards of England, Mrs. Austin casts the greater part of English poetry aside as ''the instrument of a selected class, the rhythms of privilege,'' in much the same fashion that, apparently, the Proletkult despises the art and literature of the ''bourgeois'' world.

Let us grant that cultivated people have been late in doing justice to the natural environment and to the culture of the folk: is not Mrs. Austin a little hasty in abandoning the acknowledged treasures of a more sophisticated state? If the great body of art and literature inevitably springs out of the soil, it comes to flower in the city: had Giotto not gone to Florence and Shakespeare not gone to London would the Italian have painted more than a wayside shrine, or would the Warwickshire lad have done more than give a ballad to the alehouse? . . . While the organic imprint of the original environment is lacking in us, we have a cerebral sensitiveness, a receptivity, a capacity for responding to the whole heritage of culture, which are not to be despised; and to talk about the great word-hoard which the poets of the world, like Widsith, have unlocked for us as the product of a privileged class is to damn gold by saying that it has a yellow streak. Moreover, literature itself is as much a part of our experience as the raw environment of field and mountain: the rhythms that have been fixed in literature come to us as a natural heritage, proper to us as men who inherit our own creations as well as nature's. To cast aside culture is

as great a folly as to cast aside nature; for in man they become one.

Finally, the thesis which Mrs. Austin puts to the front, that there is a distinct American rhythm akin to that expressed by the Indian, seems to me both distracting and unimportant. For in the nature of things, it either exists in the American poet or it does not: if it does exist it will take hold of him, as Whitman's vers libre finally conquered all his Sunday School verse; and if it does not, then the ''American rhythm'' will be as artificial as an Italian sonnet. It is one thing to go back to the soil in Rhode Island, with old, cultivated farms and a steady round of life and a landscape that at times recalls Kent or Sussex; and it is another to go back to it in the midst of the corn-carpeted prairie. If Mrs. Austin's essential theory is worth anything, a quite different rhythm will arise in poetry and music out of these two different backgrounds; and to call both of these American, or to attempt to identify them with the art of the aborigine, is to relate them to a political unit and to a past which, from the standpoint of our present culture, can scarcely be said to exist. (pp. 23-4)

> *Lewis Mumford, ''The American Rhythm,'' in* The New Republic, *Vol. XXXV, No. 443, May 30, 1923, pp. 23-4.*

THE BOOKMAN, NEW YORK   (essay date 1923)

[*In the following excerpt, the critic examines Austin's character and ideals, reviews* The Man Jesus, *and provides a general appraisal of Austin's work and philosophy.*]

[Great] minds are singularly standardized. They have the same acquisitive impulse, by and large, and the same matter of factness and the same perceived and unperceived shortcomings and the same fundamental ruthlessness. Mary Austin is, by most standards, of the company of great minds. Her one essential lack is the comic sense. But there is no cruelty in her, and without cruelty humor offers but a meagre refuge; a refuge, moreover, to which she would never voluntarily go, for she takes life too seriously and with too consistent kindliness.

She is deeply concerned with both deity and the universe. She is little interested by anything of less consequence. Desert and sea and timber line furnish man with the three mirrors in which the will of the universe is most clearly discernible. Of the three, the desert seems the truest mirror of the mind of deity. Mary Austin found many things to her liking in the desert—small life amid desperate privation, vast amplifications of color, limitless space of clean air, and the feel of a country coordinated to the movement of gigantic rhythms. More than all this, however, she found in the desert a universe in which, by degrees, she became thoroughly at home, and a deity with whom she struck up the honest relationship of frank understanding and unabashed eagerness to serve. These two were the things she most needed. She read the desert's riddles and solved its domestic difficulties and set them down in her early books which are among literature's supreme interpretations of country. She took from the desert an emotional philosophy and a concept of God.

Her God is very evidently created to her requirements and the desert's by the union between the desert's spirit and her own. He seems a sort of combination between the Great Spirit of the Indian and the Smithsonian Institute. In his honor she founded an ethnological faith in which she is herself the perfect worshiper and which follows the observances of a special creed made up of physical geography and political liberalism and colored by a strong predilection for natural history museums. She did this in all seriousness, as her books attest. She deified her interpretation of the desert and she waits now for the prophet who shall come out of the southwest.

Her God taught her the mysticism of desert sage and blue distance and the appreciation of the problems of natural life which so engross her attention, and they, in their turn, invested her with their own pantheism. It is a specialized and a highly individualized doctrine—the idealism of a sublime detachment from all concrete human problems and most human thought. It disregards mankind and concerns itself alone and apart with those natural matters which are naturally irremediable. Beyond a doubt she was born to be a great and self-constituted defender. But the desert motivated her too spaciously. Though she is self-dedicated to the disinterested defense of human lost causes, the desert leaves her scant patience with humanity. It has, one suspects, fomented in her a recognizable discontent with having been born in human form and persuaded her that she would have been far better off as a goddess or a physical law. It seems likely even that, failing godhead, she would have chosen for herself a small furry shape and spent her lifetime scampering along desert water trails between stalks of sage and mesquite. She might have felt divinity the more surely and so come more perfectly into the natural scheme in which the southwest has enveloped all her intellectual and spiritual reactions.

Humanity is either too strong for Mary Austin's taste or not quite feeble enough. She can take such downtrodden creatures as the Pueblo Indians and Jesus of Nazareth and defend the one against Congress and the other against Christianity. This she can do because the plight of each is readily transformed into large emotional abstraction. For smaller injustice the wise, wide energy of the desert forever unfitted her. Her long assertion of the rights of womankind, the least successful of all her works, is the clearest proof of this. However arduously she may have pressed it, it is an enterprise impelled by conscience and by little else. She felt, it is quite evident, that she must do something for her sisters and she has done her utmost. But her comprehension of them is curiously at sea. Her philosophy holds no place for those who will not be abstracted. You cannot abstract women; you succeed merely in offending them if you try and set them on a tangent of vituperative contradiction. Mary Austin has offered them all the most grandiose pigeon holes of her scheme of things and they have rioted in every one. Her sense of justice drove her into the woman problem; her really convinced non-humanity betrayed her. Let her deny this hotly as she will, it is none the less true. Woman is not colossal nor is she small, furred and squeaking. Wherefore womankind does not abide in Mary Austin's alley and the sooner she has done with it the better.

You may call this spirit proud, but her humility is only the more genuine for its impressive stature. The lowliness with which she bows to the unalterable is without affectation and wholly unafraid. Her danger is that she too often credits with importance to herself matters which, in reality, neither interest nor involve her. From the first day of her transplantation she has been committed to the inevitable and to nothing else.

All of this that is here said of her is clear in her books, above all, in the most important of them—*The Man Jesus*. There her imagination and her philosophy came together with their one real embodiment. The two forces met and, emotionally and spiritually, fitted one into the other as light fits into form. She brought to Jesus what the desert had given her and that is a nobler thing than theology. *The Man Jesus* is, by that, a stauncher book than Renan's *Vie de Jésus*. The credulous platitudes of Papini's latest shrivel beside it.

Mary Austin achieves a very perfection of courageous understanding whenever Jesus speaks. The errors of her historical scholarship do not matter. Her Holy Land is none the less holy for being in her recreation of its atmosphere mostly western and American. She knows the man and his disciples and the countryside through which they wandered because they were desert folk, bred in small and primitive communities, who had, in their time, looked upon her salty desolations and her verdant settlements and condoned the same small lives and great. She knows them for the fact that she and Jesus are both desert taught and live both by a kindred humility and a kindred awe and by the same ignorance of the human formula.

What is so fine in the best of her writing, suffers whenever she follows conscience or the guidance of the momentary into more personable ways. What has the desert to do with theatric silliness? Her plays brought fine emotion and fine truth to the stage, but emotion and truth alike turn to empty gesticulation in the mouths of the puppet characters which she draws to be their spokesmen. Her novels will be read always for the serene elegance of her writing. The best of them is not their personnel but the feeling they have for the land, by some character or feature, her own land always, whatever exterior change she sets upon it. The everlasting best of her is that widespread simplicity and straightness, at once so kind and so impersonal, which she attained when she went away from her middle western college town into the "land of lost borders." Her tales are good tales, especially of westerners and the west, but her eyes in them again are far sharper for the land and its meaning than for the businesses of men and women. (pp. 48-51)

She is greatly American by the chance that took her into her southwest and she reads her desert rhythms and symbols into all American institutions. American institutions do not always fit very precisely into the rhythms with which she clothes them but this disconcerts her very little. A sculptor must throw away a good deal of marble to make a statue; a thinker of Mary Austin's cast does not hesitate with the rebellious institution. She can, you may be sure, usually twist or compress it to her demands. Let Mary Austin loose upon marital relations and she will "understand" them all around the town. She likes her friends to call her "Chisera," which is to say "Witch Woman," or words to that effect. And this is not ridiculous. You may, if you resent ruthlessness and really bitter consistency, resent Mary Austin, but you do not laugh at her.

For she has that extraordinary completeness and self-sufficiency which makes a mess of many little matters and, on occasion, can cope fearlessly and triumphally with the authentic crisis. She is like an actress marked apart to play great rôles. Her writing and her thinking alike are set aside for noble subjects. When she comes down from her own standard and the desert's, her workmanship persists in all its beauty and sincerity; her inspiration abandons her. That is the decree laid upon her by her experience in the lonely west. And that is proper, too. The great mind is no less great for having only one idea so long as the idea remains a part of godhead.

There are two kinds of thinking; the purely emotional to which everything is important and inviolate, and the purely intellectual to which nothing matters very much. Mary Austin thinks principally through her emotions; her faults and weaknesses

George Sterling, Austin, Jack London, and Jimmy Hopper on the beach at Carmel. Courtesy of The Bancroft Library.

are all intellectual. She has great feeling and little skepticism. (pp. 51-2)

"The Literary Spotlight: Mary Austin," in The Bookman, *New York, Vol. LVIII, No. 1, September, 1923, pp. 47-52.*

CARL VAN DOREN   (essay date 1923)

[Van Doren is considered one of the most perceptive critics of the first half of the twentieth century. He worked for many years as a professor of English at Columbia University and served as literary editor and critic of the Nation *and the* Century *during the 1920s. A founder of the Literary Guild and author or editor of several American literary histories, Van Doren was also a critically acclaimed historian and biographer. Howard Moss wrote of him: "His virtues, honesty, clarity, and tolerance are rare. His vices, occasional dullness and a somewhat monotonous rhetoric, are merely, in most places, the reverse coin of his excellence." In the following excerpt, Van Doren discusses the formative influence of the desert on Austin's thought, notes the themes of her work as well as the central importance of prophecy in her writing, and offers an appraisal of her literary achievement.]*

[Mary Austin] lived her maturing years in a kind of desert isolation in California. There she had her vision, there she found what she felt to be her place in the cosmic scheme. "For

all the toll the desert takes of a man," she wrote in her first book, "it gives compensations, deep breaths, deep sleep, and the communion of the stars. It comes upon one with new force in the pauses of the night that the Chaldeans were a desert-bred people. It is hard to escape the sense of mastery as the stars move in the wide clear heavens to risings and settings unobscured. They look large and near and palpitant; as if they moved on some stately service not needful to declare. Wheeling to their stations in the sky, they make the poor world-fret of no account. Of no account you who lie out there watching, nor the lean coyote that stands off in the scrub from you and howls and howls." During this period in the desert, too, Mrs. Austin arrived at her conceptions of those human matters which have interested her: religion, art, love, character, society. In that simple universe, where she came to seem a kind of prophet to the simple people who lived around her, she watched the procession of birth, love, hate, aspiration, death, and the marching seasons. The first philosophers she knew were silent men innocent of sophistication; the first poets she knew were Indians whose songs had in them nothing of the divided art of white America. She endured hardships, she tasted immense bitterness, she healed herself with thought. The mark of the desert has never quite left her. It appears in the profound calm of her temper, in the large dimensions of her ideas, in her neglect of all that does not go to the roots of some matter or other, in her oracular habit of communication. Interpreting the desert to a more complicated world, she interprets that world to itself. By the desert she takes her measure of existence. (p. 152)

[When Mrs. Austin] published *The Land of Little Rain,* an older mood of romance was warring with the new mood of naturalism. Yielding herself to neither, she in a sense laid hold on both. Rich as the magic was with which she invested that dry land, she looked at it with singularly level eyes, relying upon history and science in her account and celebrating the human nature of the desert with an eloquence which somehow managed to be analytical. But though she won a prompt success with her report of the locality which she had discovered for literature, she seems seldom to have been tempted to repeat herself. Each new book has been notably unlike its predecessor. For this reason, if for no other, she has lacked the particular kind of reputation which is won by a continued strumming upon one note. Even if she had wanted to, she could probably never have achieved a strategic monotony. What she has written has been essentially the record of her growth, the growth of a deep and powerful spirit which has lived by extending its inquiries and its experiences. (pp. 152-53)

Though the range of her concerns has been great, they fall under a few large heads. She has studied landscape and climate, with their human consequences, in *The Land of Little Rain, The Flock,* and *Lost Borders.* She has studied the plight of genius, of the individual by some gift made incapable of conformity to an environment, in *A Woman of Genius, The Arrow-Maker, The Man Jesus.* She has specifically studied the nature of love in *Love and the Soul-Maker,* the position of women in *The Young Woman Citizen,* the basis of national art in *The American Rhythm.* She has made herself an expert, for all practical literary purposes, in Amerindian lore, and has in countless papers and addresses turned her grave scrutiny upon religion, sex, ethics, communal life, handicrafts, history, anthropology. In none of her concerns, however, is she far removed from any other. Her conception of landscape and climate touches all she writes. *A Woman of Genius* and *The Arrow-Maker* are, though works of art, none the less documents upon the struggle of women to lead, like men, lives not wholly circumscribed by their biological functions. The Jesus of her interpretation is a genius, taught by the desert, who goes to his mission and his fate among the people of towns who destroy him because his reverence to them seems blasphemy, so far are they strangers to habits of direct vision such as his. All that Mrs. Austin writes is interwoven, for she has, it appears, no tight compartments in her mind. The whole stream of her experience and reflection has passed through her and, no matter what the theme at any moment, has taken the color of her spirit. (p. 153)

Mrs. Austin . . . starts with the primary assumptions of a God, or Allness, and of a life-stream, and she sees all existence under the light of these assumptions. Doubt them, or fail to feel them, and you may wonder that she should be so impressive as she is. It is at this point that she comes into conflict with the brasher intellectuals, who will not share her long views. To such of her critics she seems solemn if not pompous; to her they seem thin and ephemeral intelligences playing with fragmentary toys. Rarely enough have prophets spoken the language of the people they came to serve.

As a prophet, however, Mrs. Austin must be judged. She stands in this respect even the vulgar test of being asked which of her prophecies have come true. A decade before the newer forms of verse came into fashion, she had forecast them and practised them, deriving her methods from those of the primitive Americans near whom she lived. Her interpretations of various movements of opinion and sentiment about religion, the status of women, the forms of society, have been delivered in instance after instance so early as to have, apparently, an element of prophecy in them. And in the less vulgar aspects of her calling she has always had more than a little, and often much, of the seer's technic. Without it she could never have cut, as she has done, through the surface of appearances to the reality beneath. Thanks to the long views which she takes, and which are the best signs of a prophet, she has not fallen fatally into any mere habits of thought or feeling. (pp. 154-55)

Any discussion of Mrs. Austin's achievement tends irresistibly to turn rather to her prophecy than to her art, as it tends to turn rather to her whole intentions than to her specific triumphs. No one of her books more than partially represents her. Her verse, for example, sounds slight by comparison with her searching plea for a native poetry that shall not content itself with the deft adaptation of this or that imported, sophisticated mode, but shall go down within the nation till it reaches the basic rhythms, the stroke of the paddle or of the ax, the curves of the landscape, the sequence of the weather and the crops. This indeed she admits: "mine," she says, "is not a singing gift." Nor does she succeed entirely in more dramatic undertakings. *The Arrow-Maker* has a theme to which Mrs. Austin has given as much thought and passion as to any other among the many which have engaged her: the conflict in a woman between the special endowment which parts her from her kind and the universal instinct which draws her back to the customary life of love and child-bearing. The setting of the play, among the Indians of the Southwest, is one of which Mrs. Austin has a masterly knowledge, as she has also of the tribal customs which give color to the action. Yet as a drama *The Arrow-Maker* does less than justice to theme or setting. Except for a few splendid moments, it does not move with the true, cruel rush of tragedy; though the language is high and pure, it lacks something of the authentic breath of human speech. On the whole Mrs. Austin is at her best when she is nearer to exposition or criticism than to invention or creation. To be explicit, she nowhere else quite equals the success she reaches in those lovely, luminous documents on the Southwest, *The Land of Little Rain, The Flock, Lost Borders,* and the forthcoming volume in which she will return to that territory, *The Land of Journeys' Ending.* To put it very broadly, she is much less than herself unless both her knowledge and her passion are so enlisted that they can be in something like equipoise.

What talent is it that is withheld from a writer like Mrs. Austin and is given to a writer like, say, H. G. Wells, who hardly knows as much or feels as profoundly as she does, yet who has twice the capacity for pouring himself into effective forms of art? Perhaps it is the talent for strategic ignorance, which she lacks as well as strategic monotony. Men and Wellses have the advantage over angels and Mrs. Austins that they rush in unafraid, no matter what the peril. Art, after all, is action, not reflection. The artist must strike, must put himself behind the blow, without too much weighing of the consequences, whether to himself or to abstract truth. Let it not appear that Mrs. Austin is always accurate or ever timid. But she has a spacious mind, with many inlets. Within it she revolves and broods, turning over all the sciences, building up huge structures of doctrine, constantly shaping the universe in reasonable forms. Then when she comes to utter what has taken shape within her, she hesitates. Or if she does not consciously hesitate, she is nevertheless held back by the weight of her speculations. So much as she has assembled cannot crowd with impetuous haste through the outlet of her art. Perhaps, however, it is wiser not to give much credit to ignorance, strategic or otherwise. It may be that what Mrs. Austin lacks is the ability to focus her diffused powers and interests, however great, within a necessarily narrow field. The farsighted sometimes fumble when they try to do neat tasks near at hand. (pp. 155-56)

> Carl Van Doren, "Mary Austin: Discoverer and Prophet," in The Century, Vol. 107, No. 1, November, 1923, pp. 151-56.

HENRY CHESTER TRACY   (essay date 1930)

[*In the following excerpt, Tracy analyzes the qualities of Austin's nature writing, defining her approach to nature and contrasting it with the visions of nature held by romantic and realistic writers.*]

Elsewhere I have answered the question put to me by a woman, why there are not more competent women naturists. Now it is time to explain why there are some; and, in passing, why one who is also a brilliant essayist and an intellectual person can be a naturist at all.

I find the clue not in a book which has come to stand for Mary Austin, as a sort of synonym for her out-of-door writing, but in one of her least known volumes, *The Flock*. It is more than a clue. It is explicit, and worth quoting as a paragraph, intact:

> By two years of homesteading on the borders of Tejon, by fifteen beside the Long Trail where it spindles out through Inyo, by all the errands of necessity and desire that made me to know its moods and the calendar of its shrubs and skies, by the chances of Sierra holidays where there were always bells jangling behind us in the pines or flocks blethering before us in the meadows, by the riot of shearings, by the faint winy smell in the streets of certain of the towns of the San Joaquin that apprises of the yearly inturning of the wandering shepherds, I grew aware of all that you read here and of much beside.

"I grew aware," describes it. There is no other way. "Errands of necessity and desire . . . made me know its moods and the calendar of its shrubs and skies." Persistent study and enterprising research have made good naturalists but they never made a naturist on God's earth. Both logic and imagination enter into scientific procedures but this kind of interpreter of a nature-world must "know its moods."

The book from which I quote is written lyrically and joyously. It is pleasant and illuminated reading; but its rewards are for the initiated, to whom content does not greatly matter, and who kindle quickly to the magic of mood.

But this magic in no way denies or distorts reality. For proof of this, read, if you like, the second chapter of the book we just named: "The Sun in Aries"—of lambing and the ways of lambs and ewes. There is more pure authentic science of behavior in it than you will find in many pages of heavier reading. There is in this, as in every other chapter, true natural history of the sheep, good natural history of the herder, and a naturism of the human observer that lifts it out of the dull category of information. There is a realism that does not break our mood.

"Mood" again. Why stress it? Because it is a dominant causal contribution. It makes the meaning of things, in a sense that every naturist understands and every scientist, *qua scientist* does not. Without sentiment there is no meaning. Mood is the carrier and container of sentiment, in the true and original sense of the word. Thackeray said: "Without sentiment there would be no flavor in life at all"; but we must go farther and say that without sentiment there would be no meaning in it. For meaning is value, not coercive logic, and not a state of hypnosis induced by facts.

This temper of mind—that makes values, makes meanings—appears plainly in a sentence that I shall quote from the earlier pages of the same book:

> All of the book that is mine is the temper of mind which makes it impossible that there should be any play not worth the candle.
>
> (pp. 245-46)

Suppose we plunge at once into an important work, a product of her mature genius, *The Land of Journeys' Ending*. From an Author's Preface we learn that it is a book of prophecy. Of course. No writing done in his or her proper mood, by a true naturist, could be anything else. All other writing would be a digression, on that author's part. And no matter what its pretence, or its subject matter, other nature-writing is spurious. So much for the first line of the Preface. At its end this author admits that she is also a prophet of human nature "which lives so much more by effects produced than by facts described." Right, again. There is your naturist. And, for failing to perceive that, you will see some nature men, such as Burroughs, diminished, and a host of others eliminated. They have attended only to facts; and human nature, duped for a while by their accuracy, rejects them in the end; and rightly.

In the body of the book you get at once the drive of that strong feeling for the land itself, in whatever guise, that is the urge of a true nature-writer. Even when we are viewing (in the first chapter) the first thrust northward, under Alcaráz, of the Spanish intruder, and thereafter the greedy and futile march of Coronado, we feel the spirit of this rugged land as a thing greater and more lasting than the historical pageant. It is felt as personal, not geographical. It must be won, like a woman. (pp. 248-49)

True, a traveler in this vast place feels, even from the train, relief and escape from over-crowding. He cannot believe that it can ever become a hog-wallow for competitive industries. But he cannot follow the flight of his eye to those distant boundaries—he cannot walk those mottled hills and lose himself in their scent and silence. He has not the leisure. He needs these pages. Therefore he is glad when, with a rush of poetic imagery the book lifts him off his feet and sets him on the "Wind's Trail," in the New Mexican highlands.

He is now in the second chapter. He expects a heightened language, does not confuse it with "fine writing"; for it emanates from the spirit of place, like the Rain-song of the Sia. It comes in vigorous metaphors, the language of chiaroscuro; or in the slower stroke of the simile:

> On the miraculous floor of the air the Rain stands upright between the mountains.
>
> East of the Rio Grande the junipers are small and widely interspersed among the green ro-

settes of the one-leaved pinon pines, with which
the pale hills are spotted like an ocelot.

(pp. 249-50)

It is not the land alone that is felt, as a physiographic unit.
Not alone the winds, rain, clouds, mists, and air-rivers. You
feel through quickened senses the sap in the shrubs and trees,
the rhythm of the herbs, and its seeming suspension. Not "she
feels," but you feel. If only half an initiate, but responsive,
you are carried over into shared experience, are at one with
this strange vegetation. But if not even half awakened—if perforce an outsider—surely any one may weigh and know the
difference between this and an ephemeral writing that leads
nowhere, that dabbles in surfaces.

We have felt the land, and its native moods. We have become
intimates of an arid vegetation, felt its pulse, imagined its
manward yearnings. And now, as we go deeper in this prophetic book we find ourselves in a third mode; we are seeing
with man in his primitive form. We are sharing an Indian's
approach to nature. Properly done—as it is done here—this is
not a caprice, a fancy. It is not one among many possible
choices. With the land duly felt, and the plant rightly sensed,
it becomes the completion: the inevitable. Of this the book
itself will convince you. And by that fact alone the book lifts
itself above other contemporary writing, goes below current
and accustomed insights, carves out and grips a new segment
of the nature experience. It is a new wholeness. See how it
stands apart:

—not aesthetic man, merely, appraising a world from which
he has become detached and against which he stands opposed
as critic;

—not inductive mind, with scientific procedures, explaining
and exploring things that must presently be exploited;

—not emotional man, as poet, seeking in picture-patterns a
literate enjoyment.

Something of all these, perhaps, but with another will, another
center. It is the will for, or to, identification. Oneness. The
self is to be made one with a profounder world. The sick
conscious self is to be drawn both down and up into a valid
unconscious one. There is health there. Man is felt as man-
and-nature; no longer an ailing off-shoot, a detached product
of greed and intellection.

It is easily possible that a reader who has, hitherto, looked
with contempt upon all savage lore, regarding it as childish
myth and fable, may change his view while under the influence
of these pages. He will not be argued out of his old position.
He will be caught by a new contagion. It will be that or nothing.
A point gained by argument is seldom worth holding. The
appeal is to common roots, to deep life sources. Here you have
that appeal, made effective in sound writing.

But here is more than sound writing. Can a page be both
authentic and ecstatic? Apparently it can, with Mary Austin,
and as one reads deeper and deeper into these chapters—as in
the one titled "The Days of Our Ancients"—one finds everywhere the touch of that mood which Machen showed must be
present if literature is to be pure and abiding: ecstasy. Behind
it is sure knowledge of the ascertainable facts; they are always
at command, not let loose to dominate and cripple the imagination. It is not only that an archaeologist's facts are made
luminous to the eye of the mind. It is that and much more: the
whole scene and scheme of it is pervaded by a powerful and
sympathetic vision. The result is, not a book to stir us to a
futile sympathy and a sentimental concern for vanished tribes

or persons—as a romance is likely to do, with its dramatic
excitement and special pleading—but to create in us a living
picture, an experience of the past, a great slant-light upon our
own present. For *Now* is nothing without perspective. It demands a large perspective, a deep background. And here prehistory is more pertinent than history; for in the hectic scenes
which make up a political picture of civilized men there is no
hint of our third mode—of man at one with nature. He has
split off. He has forgotten. He has "improved." *That* is his
civilization, his story of wars and greed, of convenience and
luxury and disillusion. With all of earth's powers at his command he is drinking the dregs of sophistication. And so he
needs renewal, an experience of nature and of nature-and-man.
If any writing could give him such experience vicariously, it
would be a book like this. (pp. 251-54)

The primitive approach to nature can never—with excuse—be
misconstrued again, since Mary Austin. A cold intellectual
view of it becomes impossible, a romantic one unnecessary.
Through the soil, the plants, the skies, the seasonal changes,
through hardship, necessity, death and birth—how else?—we
rise to its reality, and find ourselves on no superior platform,
arrogating to ourselves a supreme insight. Our mature, our
only sound view, must have shared the best of the Amerind's
sense of his world, shared his rhythms; not descended from a
great height to his humble level. But to come up, by every
perceptive sense and with a quickened pulse through all its
rhythms—this is the true enlightenment. . . . (p. 259)

> *Henry Chester Tracy, "Mary Austin," in his Amer-
> ican Naturists, E. P. Dutton & Co., Inc., 1930, pp.
> 244-63.*

HENRY SMITH (essay date 1931)

[*In the following excerpt, Smith notes some social issues and
traditions which figure in Austin's fiction, discusses her vision of
nature and her mysticism, and defines her most characteristic
works as prophetic writings.*]

After her first books had established her as a writer of promise,
Mary Austin laid the foundations for her future work by a
series of novels clarifying her attitude toward the society of
contemporary America. Although here, as in the earlier *Land
of Little Rain* . . . and *The Flock* . . . , the deep positive trends
of her thinking were manifest and important, she was also
engaged in a critical study of her inherited traditions and the
various forces of the life about her. She had apparently come
out of her dozen years in the desert convinced of her vocation
and concerned to take stock of the country to which she felt
herself called to speak. In *A Woman of Genius* . . . , particularly, she worked out her emancipation from the small-town-
ness of the Middle West from which she came. And in *The
Ford* . . . and *No. 26 Jayne Street* . . . , she touched other aspects of the American scene,—turbulent New York and the
California of development companies and irrigation projects
and oil fields.

This should be kept in mind in any estimate of Mary Austin,
because it is important. Critics who tend to think of her as a
sort of recluse in the Western deserts should remember this
critical work, closely in contact with a wide variety of environments and widely diverse characters: members of the Missionary Society in a small Indiana town, promoters in the ruthless development of California, theatrical people and labor
agitators in New York. Years before Sinclair Lewis she seized

and conveyed the deadliness of all that is confining in the rural Middle West and in the well-ordered life of the wealthy middle class in the cities. The conflict in *A Woman of Genius* is between the imperious surge of genius within the actress-heroine, and the superficial patterns of a society determined not to admit to itself the truth about anything. The book, by the way, is a document for the well-known thesis that American respectability has either made every great American artist a pariah or clipped his wings somewhat to the measure of its own littleness. But I am concerned only to make it plain that Mrs. Austin knows Main Street and does not love it. (pp. 17-18)

[Mary Austin] has talent for writing fiction, but her genius tends in another direction. She is too much interested in ideas to be able to give herself up to the almost a-moral mirror-passion of the great dramatist or novelist—the instinctive love of the fleeting moment for itself alone, the delight in presenting a vision of life unqualified by the opinion and thought of the artist. In *Lost Borders* . . . , for instance, while there are at least two stories ("**The Pocket-Hunter's Story**" and "**The House of Offence**") of superlative merit as stories, the main impulse is always dual: characters plus environment, men and women plus the desert: and the study of the influence of the desert, as might be expected in a book by the author of *The Land of Little Rain,* is the dominant theme. *A Woman of Genius* is a powerful book of social criticism, but of all its characters only the heroine seems real: for in her mind are worked out the analyses of American society and the psychology of genius. *The Ford* . . . extends the analysis to California in the hands of the openly Scythian big business of the beginning of the century, but the characters suffer because of the author's interests in social forces.

No. 26 Jayne Street . . . , again, is a novel of genuine importance, with a plot moving strongly along authentic lines of human motivation and characters definitely conceived and clearly presented. The reading of the book is an emotional and intellectual impact. Its power lies, however, not in the story or the characters as such, but in the relation of the characters to ideas; and here also one often feels that the ideas are the more important to the author. Mrs. Austin continues in this novel to work on the most serious problems of the twentieth century: the matter of allegiance in time of war; the international drift toward communism which everyone must confront and relate to himself; theoretical democracy as a possible basis for a reconstruction of personal relations. It is as if the author had left this commentary upon her experiences in New York, as if she had demonstrated her understanding of what the passionate young radicals are fighting for, had served her apprenticeship at politics and economics, and had assimilated Karl Marx, as well as Jesus, into the body of her meditation: with some personal interpretation, it should be said, of both, and with little orthodoxy of either the communist or the ecclesiastical variety.

In short, although these books of fiction are anything but negligible, and for a less versatile writer might make a respectable reputation, one feels that Mrs. Austin has not come home until she returns to the manner of her earliest books (*The Land of Little Rain* and *The Flock*) and addresses herself to the composition of *The Land of Journeys' Ending.* In this field of writing (it has no accepted name, and the term "nature literature" proposed by Henry Chester Tracy, is open to all the ambiguities of the word "nature") she has done something of transcendent meaning, definitive if not yet definable. She has enlarged the tradition of the "American Naturists"; she has

increased the scale of nature-writing to the measure of the continent; she has taken the unisonal melody of a Muir and scored it for full orchestra. Thus:

> . . . the march of the tall trees is with the wind along the trend of the tall mountains striking diagonally across from the turn of the Río Grande to the Grand Cañon, with scattered patches wherever the cumbres are high enough to drag down the clouds as snow, and hold it as a mulch for the pines.

> A little to the west of the continental divide, from the Fort Apache Reservation to the country of the Hualapai along the Colorado, the land drops off in broken ranges, along the Rim of the Mogollon Mesa. North of the Rim it lifts in alternate patches of grassland and forest which exhibit the wide spacing and monotony characteristic of arid regions. Both the grass and the trees run with the wind in patterns that on a European map would measure states and empires, reduced by the whole scale of the country to intimacy. Once you have accepted the scale, it is as easy to be familiar with a grass-plot the size of Rhode Island or a plantation of yellow pines half as big as Belgium, as with the posy-plots of your garden. . . .

> (pp. 20-2)

I have mentioned Henry Chester Tracy's placing of Mary Austin in the tradition of Thoreau, Muir, Burroughs, as a "naturist." If such classification and comparison clarifies her meaning or bolsters her admirers in their estimate of her, I have no objection to it. But between Mary Austin and any of these there is this important difference, that her interest in the environment (must one call it this, or, worse, "nature"?) is, in the real sense, ethical, and thus political. She is seeking not a retreat from men, cities, and society, but a real avenue of approach to them. She dwells in no ivory tower, but at the meeting of all the highways of modern life. (p. 23)

Mrs. Austin is above all things realistic: which is to say, she is not thinking of "nature" as an escape. She is not trying to get away from any of the bewildering complexities of modern life. She is a little un-American, perhaps, in her humility, but she is American in her optimism. Whatever else her inknowing has taught her, it has made her certain that life—taken by and large—is good, and that man can have confidence in the universe. Here and there in her work one is aware of the basis of her thinking—a view of things, for the most part complete, fundamental, untroubled, even though aware of the ruinous slowness and imperfection of the ways life takes toward its realization. She has a religion deeper than organized churches, a politics beyond parties and governmental machinery, an ethics untrammeled by the letter of codes, and a confidence in America independent of the bitter froth or the childish self-sufficiency of the moment. (pp. 23-4)

Mrs. Austin is interested in the wholeness and the harmony of human life, now, hour by hour, not theoretically but practically and passionately, as the resource and the activity of the moment, the day, the year. She is interested in botany, geology, archaeology, the psychology of genius, history, anthropology, literary history, sociology, prose fiction, regional culture, religion, and verse for children: but all because, and to the extent that, she is impelled toward the integration of the human personality as it actually exists, everywhere in some specific environment, and particularly in America in the environment which has seemed to her, after long experience of many others, most fundamentally American: the West, ultimately the Southwest. It is this unity of Mrs. Austin's thought, rather than any unity in her artistic impulse, which grows upon the student of her writings; for to her, art is the handmaiden of life, ministering to the fullness thereof, and else of no account. The purpose of art, she has one of her characters say, is "its re-kneading of the bread of life until it nourishes us toward greater achievement" (*A Woman of Genius* . . .). It is impossible to call her lifelong quest scholarship, politics, science, or art: it is all these, by turns or simultaneously, but at bottom it is a quest for the fullness of life. Mary Austin brands herself as an Occidental: she is a mystic, to be sure, but her beatific vision embraces experience instead of fleeing from it; her criteria are pragmatic, not speculative.

Nowhere is this better illustrated than *The American Rhythm,* a book which stands on library shelves as literary criticism. The thesis—to the effect that American verse will be fruitful only to the extent that it captures American rhythms, preserved best at present in Amerindian poetry—seemed twenty years ago, perhaps seems even now, fantastic enough; I shall not labor it here. The interesting thing about the book is the fact that it shows Mrs. Austin's characteristic attitude toward art: not as an end in itself, but as a means and a mode of spiritual

existence. She is engaged, she says, to find "a basis for the poetic quest, and for the establishment of a traditional poetic mode, provocative of the maximum of well-being"; that is, of the fullness of life. These two—poetry and well-being—go hand in hand; for "The rhythms which give pleasure are those into which the organism has naturally fallen in the satisfaction of the social urge, the ego urge, the mating urge." . . . Rhythm, then, in so far as it affects our poetic mode, has nothing to do without intellectual life." . . . But if not with our intellectual life, certainly with our subconscious: rhythm has much to do with environment. There are two variables in the equation, the poet and the milieu; and they must be harmonized before poetry becomes a release for the race and a servant of life. (pp. 24-6)

[In *The American Rhythm*] as in her others, even her novels, Mary Austin is unmistakably a mystic. Just here, I think, lies the reason why in the academies and côteries she is underestimated. For it is certainly not the fashion now to believe very strongly in a spiritual continuum back of the universe, of which individual minds are but incompletely isolated parts. . . . (p. 26)

It seems to me certain . . . that the importance of such books as *The Land of Journeys' Ending* and *The Flock* lies not in minute descriptions of flora and fauna, or of topographical features; but in the capture and expression of what Mrs. Austin calls the *rhythm* of the region. Here is the crux. You cannot see, hear, taste, smell, or touch the rhythm of an environment.

Austin's home in Independence. Reproduced by permission of The Huntington Library, San Marino, CA.

Knowledge of it must be acquired otherwise than through the senses, or through any combination of sensory experiences.

Mrs. Austin so defines mystical knowledge. It is "knowledge which arrives at the threshold of consciousness by processes recognizably different from the familiar sense perceptions" (*Everyman's Genius* . . .). This knowledge may make use of the minutiae of geology and botany and zoölogy, but it uses them, not as facts but as symbols, as avenues of meditation. For the expression of knowledge so acquired, none of the usual forms of prose is satisfactory, and Mrs. Austin has never shown an inclination to use a Wordsworthian blank verse or ballad stanza because so much of what she has to say consists of detailed bits of information out of which the total effect is gradually built up; she does not strive for an immediate statement like that, say, of "Tintern Abbey." Hence the use of such a form as that of *The Land of Little Rain, The Flock,* and *The Land of Journeys' Ending.* These books are only incidentally "nature-writing"; rather are they books of prophesy.

Mrs. Austin lays claim to this title in the preface to *The Land of Journeys' Ending.* "The function of all prophesy," she continues, "is to discern truth and declare it, and the only restriction on the prophet is that his means shall be at all points capable of sustaining what he discovers." . . . Let us define the term more explicitly. By a prophet let us understand a person gifted with a certain amount of insight into the present situation of his tribe: not a philosopher, for he is not speculative; not a preacher, for he does not appeal to a revelation or promulgate moral codes; not an artist, for he speaks directly, with little of the impersonal and ununderstandable compulsion of the artist to display the appearances of things for their own sake; not any of these things: a prophet. The connotation of mysterious foreknowledge of future events which the word has received is due, of course, to the fact that insight into the present situation—into its complexities and beyond them by a vision which can only be described (without any implication of mere praise) as mystical—inevitably brings a certainty of where the deep trends will lead. Mrs. Austin claims for herself this specific function with relation to the development of the American poetry revival of fifteen years ago. But however such a performance may impress the multitude eager for a sign, it is not important. The important thing about a prophet is that he has insight into the state of his tribe, and out of that insight speaks thoughts needful to be heard by his fellows.

It is in this sense that Mrs. Austin's most characteristic works are prophetic writings. The immediate state of her tribe is somewhat as follows: Fragments of European races have undertaken to live together on a new continent. This implies the construction of a form of government and the carrying on of all the necessary functions of life: in other words, the formation of a civilization. . . . The integration of various racial elements into a new race is closely dependent upon the environment of its formation. . . . Thus the importance of the American environment for the formation of the American race, and for the course of American civilization, is enormous. (pp. 27-9)

[The] passionate eagerness with which Mrs. Austin has studied the land and the people of the West—those lands and peoples which least resemble the parts of Europe from which most settlers in America came—is full of meaning. It is a preparation for living in America. She performs a symbolic act, and in part she experiences for the race the acts of acquaintance necessary to the taking up of a permanent abode here. In the Europe which thought into our Occidental memory most of the higher reaches of our philosophy and art, this process of acquaintance

with the terrain had gone long before—had taken place slowly, by means of mythologies which had grown antiquated before printing. For the Greeks, and perhaps for the Norse, primitive religions which we now call mythologies established and preserved that contact with the environment which is the basis of a racial art. But in America there has not been time for the growth of such a mythology, and besides, the sophisticated cultures of the immigrants who settled here made them little inclined to see any value in myths. Yet the growth of a national art depends upon some accommodation to the soil. Mrs. Austin is trying to do for the American race what myths did for the Greeks and for other European peoples. Modern skepticism makes this task hard; she has explored the mythology and the folk-lore of the Indians and the early Spanish settlers, but she has been forced in the end to express her meaning in philosophical terms and through the traditional form of nature-writing. Of course she has not been able to create an American mythology—it takes generations to do that. But she has seen the problem, and made it clear. (pp. 29-30)

She, and the others who have spoken before her, and those who shall speak after, impose upon Americans the task of becoming a tribe, of building a civilization. There is no alternative: it is the cosmic cycle of life renewing itself through birth, which is not only painful in itself ("the child also suffers"), but also involves the assumption of functions continually beyond the strength and understanding of the new organism. So it is in America. (p. 32)

Often in the history of human thought the important thinkers have been those who have been able to see the problems. Once they are perceived and clearly stated, journeyman thinkers can cooperate to solve them. The distinction of Mrs. Austin's writings is that they shed problems from almost every page. She seems to live at that outer fringe of the spotlight of accepted knowledge where most trains of thought emerge quickly from the light and lead out into the penumbra. These are the lines of advance. She has spent many years marking these trails at the point where they enter the shadow, and some she has followed a greater or a smaller way herself.

These are some of the meanings which I get from Mrs. Austin's work. They are not the whole story; but perhaps they will suggest to Southwesterners the importance of this citizen of Santa Fé. . . . She is connected with almost every enterprise which shows any tendency to enrich and deepen the life of the West. But more than any writer of comparable achievement, she has gone almost unrewarded by and almost unknown to the people for whom her prophecy is important. (p. 33)

Henry Smith, "The Feel of the Purposeful Earth: Mary Austin's Prophecy," in New Mexico Quarterly, *Vol. 1, No. 1, February, 1931, pp. 17-33.*

CONSTANCE ROURKE   (essay date 1932)

[*Rourke was a pioneer in the field of American cultural history. Her reputation was established by her* American Humor: A Study of the National Character *(1931), which is still widely studied. The work advances Rourke's opposition to such critics as Van Wyck Brooks and T. S. Eliot, who asserted that America had no cultural traditions other than those it had imported from Europe. Rourke theorized that an American cultural tradition indeed exists, and that it is based on humor. The findings presented in* American Humor *and in Rourke's later* The Roots of American Culture *(1942) were a major factor in leading Brooks and other critics to reassess and revise their previously held opinions of America as a cultural wasteland. In the following excerpt, Rourke considers* Earth Horizon *an exceptional autobiography and a valuable interpretation of the society in which Austin lived.*]

In **Earth Horizon** Mary Austin has explored her own life, and the book has the impactive power of character free in a natural medium. She is a born autobiographer, with an uncompromising interest in herself that flows without false hindrance through experiences achieved or imposed, bringing forth personal references in many moods, the play of wit, the torment and clearing of emotion, the unfolding of a long creative absorption. Those concerned with sheer personality, those who wish to follow an extraordinary career, will find these here in abundance. But the title is the farther measure of the book. Without loss of ardor or of the personal focus it creates large perspectives.

A primal source for Mary Austin was that rich bottom land of southern Illinois to which her people had been drawn, a country where Indian mounds might be seen "mysteriously arising among mazy creeks," a land sown with bindweed and wild phlox, where sheets of blue violets lay about rotting tree trunks in the woodlots, where old tunes might be heard, old ways of speech, cryptic Negro chants full of connoted history and lore. This country could also produce a principal of schools named Xenophon Xerxes Crum. There the florid and the stiltedly cultural were coming into bloom, temperance societies were afloat, and Frances Willard was exercising her highly personal sway. Mary Austin tells of these phenomena without missing a touch of the shallow or stunted; she is aware that if Lincoln was formed by this country, "there too Pegasus might be impounded among the cockleburs." But her analysis of Frances Willard is both trenchant and highly tolerant: it is a humanly complex piece of portraiture. Mary Austin sees these people as gradually forming a folk, under enormous difficulties. She has wise things to say of revivals and the profession of religion as efforts to establish common forms of communication. She defends Longfellow as offering a gesture they missed to those who had kept their inheritance of eighteenth-century gentility, and she notes that the pretty names of quilts and woven coverlets otherwise sustained them. With a certain hardihood she insists that the whatnot contained "the hidden life, the unconfessed root of the art impulse from which I am indubitably sprung," and she elucidates the whatnot, "with its odd, and for the most part attractive, collection of socio-historical fetishes . . . the tropic shells . . . the glass paper weights with flowers inside . . . the mineral specimens from California . . . the polished buffalo horn . . . all those curious keys that unlocked for the ancestors esthetic emotion and intellectual curiosity."

With a gift for bringing quite disparate events into striking synchronization, Mary Austin has created a torrent of remembrance whose factual values are superlative; but it is the breadth of her interpretation and her feeling for social coherences that give this a living force: and she transmutes this once again by continual synthesis with the creative, the imaginative, life. (p. 166)

The strong bias of Mary Austin's feminism, drawn through the entire fabric of her self-portrayal, could have sustained this autobiography if other, deeper elements had been lacking. Among the more personal turns her penetrative talk of individuals—Sterling, Bierce, the chance characters at Inyo—would have given distinction to any book. She links William James, with whom she once talked, and the Medicine Man of the Paiutes, who taught her the Indian technique of prayer. Here one may branch off, if one likes, into speculation as to the sequences

that have led Mary Austin, a daughter of pioneers, "a born pragmatist," to those "affective values" in religion and poetry which she here describes, encircling again a portion of the thesis of **The American Rhythm**. Many such fertile digressions may be made, leading to others in the procession of her books. This autobiography is indeed inexhaustible. It is unique in its testimony as to those ancestries and perceptions and social coherences fundamental for the imaginative writer. It is unique in portraying a powerful and difficult struggle to explore and maintain them. (p. 167)

Constance Rourke, *"The Unfolding Earth," in* The New Republic, *Vol. LXXIII, No. 942, December 21, 1932, pp. 166-67.*

VERNON YOUNG (essay date 1950)

[*Young is an English-born American critic. In the following excerpt, he examines Austin's life and her achievement as a writer.*]

During the early 1930's, immediately preceding and immediately after her death, Mary Austin was being lauded in various responsible places, such as the American fiction surveys of Carl Van Doren and Arthur Hobson Quinn and Henry Chester Tracy's more specialized *American Naturists* [see excerpt dated 1930]. If the regional agitations of that period had survived the New Deal, Mary Austin might have been submitted to the really rigorous criticism she deserved and brought permanently into the channels of praise which she merited by the major aspects of her work. Instead, the impulse, in any major creative sense, ran into the sands and now, except for a Maryolatrous group in northern New Mexico who sustain an uncritical praise far the other side idolatry, she is unhonored, unsung, and not reprinted. (p. 153)

Admittedly, the serious contemporary reader who thinks, upon a reckless recommendation, to explore the literature of Mary Austin needs to be cautioned. She wrote over two dozen volumes and the most liberal criticism cannot concede distinction to more than eight of them. Three are collections of folk stories, mainly—though far from being mere recordings. One is a book on the man, Jesus. The rest you may set down as nature studies, regional portraits, bionomic essays; they resist precise classification but they are not less definitive for that. These redeem, if they cannot nullify, the mediocrity of many of the other volumes, while pointing up the inception of their buried values. The southwestern items among them recite the transfiguring processes of nature, its wild life, its plant movement, its effects on the plastic eye, in prose unsurpassed by any writer in this domain. (pp. 153-54)

She unquestionably felt a deep and intimate relationship with nature from early childhood; she was equipped with a positive, sensitive, and uncompromising ego and therefore recapitulated the plight of a host of women in her day and before, at odds with and often superior to their social environment, restricted by the mores from outfacing it with an independent occupation. The restraints, in her case, were doubly galling by reason of what seems, on all the evidence, to have been an obsessive repugnance toward the male animal. (p. 154)

She . . . married a man with whom, in any deeper sense than mutual interests in the country, she evidently had little sympathy. By him she had a child who, according to her account, inherited from the father the disease that rendered it mentally deficient. Before her twenties were over, Mary Austin was divorced from her husband, had taught school in the small towns of the region and, at the same time,

> all her interior energies were bent on sorting her really voluminous notes about strange growths and unfamiliar creatures, flocks, herders, vaqueros, . . . pelicans dancing on Buena Vista, Indians, phylloxera, and a vast dim valley between great swinging ranges. Along with these things, there were collections of colloquial phrases, Spanish folklore, intensively pondered adjectives for the color and form of natural things, the exact word for a mule's cry— 'maimed noises'—the difference between the sound of ripe figs dropping and the patter of olives shaken down by the wind; . . .

The tribulations to which she was subjected in these formative literary years scored a psyche already vulnerable, innocent, overdemanding, and—more than she liked to think—conditioned by an incurable Protestantism. In the products of her later career, especially in the novels from *A Woman of Genius* . . . to *26 Jayne Street* . . . , intense frustration, injured egotism, and a resolute will to forensic grievance, notably against the male world, rose in a crescendo of testiness and recrimination embarrassing to the reader and fatal to Mary Austin's literary forms. No good can come of insulting a talent that was driven to waste itself in the interest of self-justification. These volumes sulk on the shelves of all fairly complete libraries. Concerned often and very bravely with the large social issues of her day—water conservation, sexual equality, socialism, the artist's role in the capitalist economy—they may have historical value for the Americana-hunter or the M.A. thesis-writer but they have no literary or critical virtues to attract anyone who has read the fiction of those years by, let us say, Edith Wharton, Willa Cather—or even Upton Sinclair.

The genius of Mary Austin operated confidently in two areas, not separable. She could indelibly reproduce landscape in words and she could define and make communicable sense out of the experience of affinity with powers and presences not definable, in her early days, with the vocabulary of science and, for that matter, restricted still to the as yet unfashionable frontiers of parapsychology. This property was no doubt sharpened in Mary Austin by her years on the solitary fringes of the desert and encouraged by her discovery of its central importance in the Indian communities she encountered and admired. Often she became proprietorial about her cognition, as if some superior and quite original style of insight had been dispensed to her alone. Her use of it in prose was unarguably unique; its mere ownership was common enough, as Dr. Carl Jung could have told her. Her vanity constantly overcame her humility and its least attractive feature resided in her failure ever to acknowledge that other minds were working, through metaphysics, psychodynamics, and cultural anthropology, in the same direction; in later years she gave grudging credit to the Freudian and Jungian techniques.

When Mary Austin met the wilderness and the aboriginal inhabitant face to face, she simply stepped with no hesitation into a religious mode not usually amenable to recent European man but with many honorable antecedents elsewhere. This mode rests its value on what John Collier, in *The Indians of the Americas,* has explained as "the ancient, lost reverence and passion for the earth and its web of life," operating through the assumption "that intensity of consciousness . . . and of union with the sources of being was effectual in the magical

control of nature. . . ." Its agency is what Mary Austin later was to define broadly as prayer—"an explicit motion of the inner self which puts you in touch with the living principle which controls the existing emergency."

Far from the civilization which, in effect, she was already rejecting, without benefit of sociological or formal philosophical discipline, Mary Austin discovered this mode and we need not scruple to observe that she found it simpler to enunciate and practice when removed from the disconcerting complications of mainstream society. Yet, any criticism that attempts to discount her apparatus of intuition-knowledge while accepting the pertinence of her nature-observations is untenable. One must assume that the convictions she cherished and the peculiar sentience she professed had everything to do with her style. True, the quotation of her note-taking, above, implies a self-conscious and diligent attention to the exact naming of things; and in the opening lines of her first book, *The Land of Little Rain* . . . , she sounded the note of sanguine but specified evocation which testified to this detachment:

> East away from the Sierras, south from Panamint and Amargosa, east and south many an uncounted mile, is the Country of Lost Borders.
>
> (pp. 154-56)

> This is the nature of that country. There are hills, rounded, blunt, burned, squeezed up out of chaos, chrome and vermilion painted, aspiring to the snow line. Between the hills lie high level-looking plains full of intolerable sun glare, or narrow valleys drowned in a blue haze. The hill surface is streaked with ash drift and black, unweathered lava flows. After rains water accumulates in the hollows of small closed valleys, and, evaporating, leaves hard dry levels of pure desertness that get the local name of dry lakes. Where the mountains are steep and the rains heavy, the pool is never quite dry, but dark and bitter, rimmed about with the efflorescence of alkaline deposits. . . . The sculpture of the hills here is more wind than water work, though the quick storms do sometimes scar them past many a year's redeeming. In all the Western desert edges there are essays in miniature at the famed, terrible Grand Cañon, to which, if you keep on long enough in this country, you will come at last.

Elliptical and muscular, this is the prose of a strong personality habituated to seeing truly, selecting relentlessly and correcting any indulgence of euphuism with an exacting ear. It is sparse but well-ordered, its color emphatic for not being diffused, like the landscape it describes. It is prose ridden with a martingale to check the involuntary urge of runaway rhythms. But without the finer sense of identification which she laid claim to, she could never have written other passages of equal exactitude but subtler perception, such as the following:

> The suffusion of light over the Sierra highlands is singular. Broad bands of atmosphere infiltrating the minareted crests seem not to be penetrated by it, but the sage, the rounded backs of the sheep, the clicking needles of the pines give it back in luminous particles infinitely divided. Airy floods of it pour about the plats of white and purple heather and deepen vapo-

rously blue at the bases of the headlands. Long shafts of it at evening fall so obliquely as to strike far under the ragged bellies of the sheep. Wind approaches from the high places; even at the highest it drops down from unimagined steeps of air. When it moves in a cañon, before ever the near torches of the castilleia are stirred by it, far up you hear the crescendo tone of the fretted waters, first as it were the foam of sound blown toward you, and under it the pounding of the falls. Then it runs with a patter in the quaking aspen; now it takes a fir and wrestles with it; it wakes the brushwood with a whistle; in the soft dark of night it tugs at the corners of the bed.

You may, if you like, explicate this text as pictorial, rhythmic, clairaudient, mimetic, capricious in its change of subject; still there remains an enclosing dimension which flouts analysis, something other than studied syllable or fidelity to scene. It lies somewhere in that nebulous region where imagination takes its ascendancy from the instincts, and in our ignorance we call it style. The prose registry of attunement may be the nearer rendering.

Among the professional naturalists of the last century, with whom the categorical mind likes to connect Mary Austin, there is no page so bitingly of the essence as these I have selected, and in our own time only Donald Culross Peattie, in *An Almanac for Moderns,* has served, in a wetter world, such meticulous notation. Whatever verities of nature lore were uncovered by Audubon, Thoreau, Burroughs, and Muir, no cadence in their work was so well adapted to the requirements of its objects as those of Mrs. Austin. Thoreau, alone of these, is frequently commended as a stylist, yet compare any paragraph of his applauded documentation and you will agree that if he is more poetic—that is, subjective and graceful—than the sober Burroughs or the pious and abstract Muir, he is, by comparison with Mary Austin, static, painfully sequential. His descriptions are argued, measured, proven and, though not unattractive, laboriously *defined.* H. C. Tracy included both Thoreau and Mary Austin as American ''naturists''; but the difference in texture between the gnomic method of Thoreau and the motility of Mary Austin's registration underlines the distinction Tracy, himself, had cleverly invented. ''A naturist does not tell you *about* nature. He drives you to it, or he remains a naturalist and nothing more . . . in this field right perception is original perception. Nothing else counts.'' (pp. 156-57)

In sight of any spectacle of nature or a planned life-in-nature, [Mary Austin] never failed to socialize her emotions. She felt all the thrill of restored identity that Thoreau felt, all the sublimity that John Muir experienced (and despaired of expressing in mere words), but she knew, as an Indian knew, that the end of her researches was to be neither purely lyrical nor purely practical; it was to be social in the broadest sense—it was to enter ''the web of life.'' Without the insistent sermonizing of the nineteenth-century male-in-the-woods, with references uncorrupted by classical allusion and rustic facetiousness, she always noted, in the strange symbiosis of animal and plant life, in the behavior of individual and group man in the changeless desert, a lesson in moral experience, a direction for all men on earth, hints for the fuller realization of their destinies or for the avoidance of their terrible follies.

Thus, in *The Land of Little Rain,* the stoicism of Jimville, the chimeras of the gold-seekers, the adaptative fortitude of the Paiutes, as well as the habits of the badger, the coyote, and the mountain stream, exemplify fundamental patterns of behavior. ''Something within all life knows all the ways possible to life.'' The wide reference is more explicit in her third book, *The Flock* . . . , where all the occupational and environmental factors of sheep-raising combine into the potency of symbol. (pp. 158-59)

Preceding and following *The Flock* were two books which, although not so impressive, nonetheless deserve attention: *The Basket Woman* . . . and *Lost Borders.* . . . Each is a collection of tales, heard, embroidered upon, or invented outright—it is never easy to say—and they represent the limits of Mary Austin's excellence in fiction. Directed at the juvenile mind, *The Basket Woman* established her gift for the allegorical, and in such personifications as ''The Cheerful Glacier'' and ''The Stream that Ran Away'' announced the danger of whimsy while avoiding that danger. No one can afford to patronize the genuine play of imagination in these slight tales if he has ever had any respect for the *Just So Stories* of Kipling. Mary Austin, herself, admired Kipling as a short-story writer, and wished to emulate him. *Lost Borders* is a further reach of adaptation from legend. The title denotes the Death Valley-Sierra country and, by extension, signifies the borders of socially accepted morality and the overlapping boundaries between truth and fiction. Following a lamentable poem which is almost enough to discourage the reader from beginning the prose body of the book at all, the introductory chapter presents another of those magnificent dioramas of Mrs. Austin's which baffle one by their reminders that although a good poet rarely writes bad prose, an excellent prose artist may write execrable verse. The stories in this collection are of the supernatural as well as of the realistic order; with the *One-Smoke Stories* . . . , they comprise a matchless and enduring contribution to the folklore of western America.

In *Lands of the Sun* . . . , a wider survey of the California scene was taken. Here the intention was frankly nostalgic. (The book was written for English readers and while Mary Austin was in New York City.) The great structural divisions of the state were built up as on a contour map, with a sweep of poetic prose epic in its character beyond anything else she had written. Then, turning to a remembrance of old Spanish gardens and missions, the port of Monterey, the *tulares* of the Sacramento River, and the orchards of the San Joaquin and San Gabriel valleys, she wrote in a more muted prose, affection in every line. Much of the Old-World quality of the California she had known had either vanished or been exploited to the bone by the time her 1927 edition came out in America; in her new introduction she breathed a moral indignation, with which the reader cannot fail to sympathize, at the vulgar utilizations of Los Angeles County.

Her feeling for the close identity of man and his tellurian source also gave beauty and unaffected sympathy to her portrait, *The Man Jesus.* . . . Special criticism of her historical reconstruction may belong to scholars who have authority in this matter; her interpretation impresses me with its wonderfully fresh and intelligent empathy. Her unfailing awareness of the place-influence on man lends a graphic flavor to this interpretation; for the accuracy of her geographical focus in this book she has been highly praised by the archeologist, Edgar Hewett, and this accuracy is the more imposing since, to my knowledge, Mary Austin never in her life visited Palestine. (pp. 159-60)

The Land of Journeys' Ending . . . has an even more studied unity of subject than *The Land of Little Rain* or *The Flock.* In the valleys of the Rio Grande, on the plateaus of the Colorado basin country, in the cactus acres of the Mexican border in Arizona, a complex of Indian peoples reached the still center, if not the apex, of their development. The Spanish empire in the Americas found here the northern and most challenging limits of its trail of bloody hope and the Nordic American settlers gained the margins of exploitable habitation. (pp. 160-61)

There is much of the original power and sortilege of her early years in [*The Land of Journeys' Ending*] and also less care with scientific data, as well as a straining of the style at many points. Many pathetic fallacies vulgarize her metaphor, together with bitter and barely sublimated images of the failing male, barren women, and golden young girls. The prophetic bravado of these pages, which she considered their most fruitful feature, rushes across the most unstable ground. For, with a curiously obstinate refusal to acknowledge that New Mexico and Arizona were irretrievably two of the forty-eight United States, subject to all the monopolistic and technological "acculturation" implied by this status, she "confidently predicted the rise there, within appreciable time, of the *next* great and fructifying world culture." Deceived by local adulation of her own dominating person, by the germinal interest in Indian and Spanish handcrafts, ceremony, and folklore, and by the unharnessed, rarefied expanses of southwestern scenery, she committed the error which she, of all people, should have been wisest to avoid: she confused restoration with birth, intellectual synthesis with organic determinism.

The Southwest is, as natural resource, simply another field of extended energy for the engineer, the ecologist and, lately, the physicist. As a mingling-ground for three races—the aspect on the basis of which Mary Austin took her most hopeful stand—it is hopelessly disunited. . . . Culture cannot be *contrived,* as Mrs. Austin almost made the mistake of expostulating. And in Santa Fe, especially, where she had her conceptive vision, a generalized view will see no evidence of the sort of creative rebirth she had in mind. Museums of anthropology and Indian ceremonial do not constitute the tools of new culture; they memorialize a vanishing culture. Socially, whatever spirit from the land may inform the rare individual, Santa Fe is a dry Sargasso of human wreckage beached on the shores of three cultural defeats.

As a prophetess, Mary Austin was irrelevant, unless she was projecting what to this writer is an astronomically long glance. As an observer and a moral poet of origins she was apposite to the last.

Carl Van Doren, commenting in 1922 on "the certain signs of a power" in Mary Austin, wondered that this power had "as yet failed to express itself completely in forms of art" [see Additional Bibliography]. His expectation was misdirected. Intensity, not completion, was her strength; the failures in completeness of expression derived from her lack of knowledge and sympathy whereby to import, into imagined situations of a society she did not quicken to, the lambent wisdom she had learned from the Wild. An academically insulated habit of approach has emphasized the strictly American voice of Mary Austin. . . . Negatively, Mary Austin was indeed a nearly tragic specimen of the isolated American writer who undertakes, with an imperfectly developed tradition and an inborn hostility to precedent, to create, from the sometimes desolate immediacy of his surroundings, a significant literary expression.

With this limitation, however, went with Mary Austin a presence not of this society. It is only an accident that the Southwest

Austin's Carmel wick-i-up, a platform built high in the branches of a tree, where she wrote each morning. Reproduced by permission of The Huntington Library, San Marino, CA.

of her literature is in the United States. She would have written to no different purpose but perhaps with a less frequently failing vividness if she had traveled instead to Guatemala, Tahiti, or Spain. Noticeably, it was the *foreign* flavor of the early West that she most eagerly depicted in her social panorama. If it is to the point of historical criticism that she should be placed in a line of "influence" or "tendency," it is evident that her truest material is far from the preoccupations of the midwestern folk-historians or the New England naturalists. . . . The Southwest was to Mary Austin what it later became, along with Mexico and Italy, to D. H. Lawrence, what the Orient was to Joseph Conrad, Rudyard Kipling, and Lafcadio Hearn, what Arabia was to T. E. Lawrence: a coast opposite to the Western world, a proving-ground of old insights eternally new, a different way of *being,* with power to re-create (or to destroy) the dwindling European identity. Like these men, she was a refugee from history and she failed to exchange her inherited personality for one she might have preferred to inhabit. Her try was her glory. She was one of those who have left affirmation of worlds foreign to ours which, if we read them rightly, at least jar our complacencies. (pp. 161-63)

Vernon Young, "Mary Austin and the Earth Performance," in Southwest Review, *Vol. XXXV, No. 3, Summer, 1950, pp. 153-63.*

EDWARD WAGENKNECHT (essay date 1952)

[*Wagenknecht is an American biographer and critic whose works include critical surveys of the English and American novel and studies of Charles Dickens, Mark Twain, and Henry James, among many others. His studies of Dickens and Twain employ the biographical technique of "psychography," derived from American biographer Gamaliel Bradford, who writes of this method: "Out of the perpetual flux of actions and circumstances that constitutes a man's whole life, it seeks to extract what is essential, what is*

Carl Van Doren said of Mary Austin that her books ''were wells driven into America to bring up water for her countrymen, though they may not have recognized their thirst.'' She was the foremost sybil of our time. ''What other woman,'' asked H. G. Wells, ''could touch her?'' Yet her place in the history of the novel is a comparatively small one. In her own words, her work belonged ''to the quality of experience called Folk, and to the frame of behavior known as Mystical.'' Disdaining ''the male ritual of rationalization'' in favor of more direct, intuitional methods, she experimented with ''the utterly familiar and still mysterious and exciting stuff of ourselves.'' Her best work lies in that shadowy No Man's Land which overlaps the boundaries of science, art, and scholarship. (p. 230)

[When] the eccentricities of Mary Austin's personality are taken into account, nobody should be surprised to learn that she was as bitterly hated as she was passionately loved. She was a curious combination of arrogance and selfless humility: she gave herself up to be ''used'' by impersonal forces, but those upon whose toes she trampled called her ''God's mother-in-law.'' Worse still, her admirers did not often understand her much better than her detractors. Indeed, she did not always understand herself, and even when she did, she was not always able to explain herself to others. Mary Austin conducted her explorations upon the frontiers of consciousness, and we have as yet no vocabulary which is adequate to describe the experiences of such persons. The next stage in the development of human personality was perhaps embodied as clearly in her as in any human being of our time. But it may be generations before we shall surely know.

Mary Austin never wrote a bad novel, yet it is hardly an exaggeration to say that she never produced a novel that was entirely successful. What the land meant to her was best expressed in such sketches and stories as those contained in [*The Land of Little Rain, The Flock, The American Rhythm,* and *The Land of Journeys' Ending*]. For her mystical experiences and what she came to believe about them, we must go to such books as [*Christ in Italy, The Man Jesus,* later *A Small Town Man, Everyman's Genius, Experiences Facing Death,* and *Can Prayer Be Answered?*]. . . . (pp. 231-32).

Mary Austin's first novel, *Isidro* . . . , was an historical romance of Spanish California in the days preceding the secularizing of the missions. It has a young hero designed for the priesthood, who falls in love with a girl disguised as a boy; it has murder, journeying friars and Indians, and a lost child restored to her father. The story, in other words, is conventional; it is the land that comes alive.

Mrs. Austin could probably have turned out any number of tales of this character, but 1905 was late to begin a course as historical romancer and she had no desire to sink into a groove. In 1908, with *Santa Lucia,* she turned to modern life and the problem of adjustment in marriage. She gets the feeling of the small Western college community exceedingly well, but her story has a continually shifting center of interest.

There is a deeper probing of the wrongs of women in a much better novel, *A Woman of Genius* . . . , which takes the form of the autobiography of a great actress, Olivia Lattimore. Olivia comes out of the same Middle Western world of whatnots and sexual repressions that Mary Hunter knew, and she makes her entry into the theater through amateur productions, community theatricals, and small barnstorming troupes playing the Middle West in the days when Chicago was still a producing center. She is even given a touch of the author's own mysticism: the Pan-like ''Snockerty'' is closer to the children of Taylorville than the God of the Sunday School can ever be, and in her darkest hour Olivia learns an experimental kind of prayer. Though Mrs. Austin was always ready to defend the small town against the rootless sophistication of the cities, all that was valid in the ''revolt'' from the village that was to come upon us with Sinclair Lewis and *Main Street* is already implied in *A Woman of Genius.* So is everything that is important in woman's rebellion against man, for on its deepest level the book is a study of creative power, of its connection with sexual power, of how it is differentiated from sexual power, and of the conflict between art and love.

Mary Austin was less successful with the two other novels involving social considerations: *The Ford* . . . and *No. 26 Jayne Street.* . . . The former gives an elaborate picture of the struggle between capitalist and farmer for water rights in California. Both here and in *No. 26 Jayne Street,* it is clear that Mrs. Austin, though herself often a rebel, is unfavorably impressed by the ''sleazy'' quality in American radicalism, primarily, it seems, because the radical, in his preoccupation with ''causes'' and other abstractions generally shows a tendency to forget human realities. In *The Ford,* however, the situation never seems quite clear cut, nor is there a satisfying climax. *No. 26 Jayne Street* is actually two books: the first part is merely a picture of American radicalism at the time of America's ill-starred entry into World War I; the rest, which is very Jamesian and very well done, shows up the shallowness of one radical, Adam Frear, who is all for the new ways in political affairs while he continues to act the autocrat in his personal relationships. The predatory lover of the Dreiser school is precisely what will not go down with Neith Schuyler; she tells Adam to his face that what she objects to in him is his feeling that the ''things we do ourselves can't be helped.'' The point of the book, of course, is that ''we can't hope to have pure Democracy in politics until we get it in our fundamental relations.''

I have disturbed chronology in order that I might consider Mary Austin's three ''mystical'' novels together. *The Lovely Lady* . . . is an idyll, the story of a poor boy who became a rich man, dreamed of the Lovely Lady, was betrayed by her at last when he thought that she had appeared, and then found her in the very woman to whom he imagined he had condescended. . . . [*Outland*] deals with the adventures of two Californians who make contact with a half-primitive, half-fairy race, living, quite unknown to Americans, in the Western forest. It is the kind of book which must succeed gloriously or utterly fail. For me, *Outland* does not succeed.

Mary Austin's last novel, *Starry Adventure* . . .—she was at work upon a sequel when she died—is at once the most rewarding and the most disappointing of her fictions. The realization of New Mexico in the first half, of Gard's growing into life in full awareness of his country, and of his mystical sensitiveness—which is Mary Austin's adventure under the walnut tree transplanted to a new land—all this is first-rate, full-bodied, many-dimensioned fiction. Unhappily the second half, which is the study of Gard's relations with two women, is merely a bore. Though it seems cruel to say it, there are times when his sense of impending "starry adventure" suggests nothing better than the futile awareness of the feckless hero of "The Beast in the Jungle."

Mary Austin had no elaborate theory of fiction. . . . In her article on the technique of the novel ["**The American Form of the Novel**"], the principal point she makes is that "The democratic novelist must be inside his novel, rather than outside in the Victorian fashion of Thackeray or the reforming fashion of Mr. Wells." She also declares that "Characteristic art form is seldom perfected until the culture of which it is an expression comes to rest," but this may be merely a justification of her own limitations. When she began, her technique was rather advanced for its time. She has little formal exposition: she flings her reader into the situation to find his bearings as best he can. Sometimes her method makes for unnecessary obscurity. In later years, she was somewhat given to complaints that her readers did not get the point of her novels. If this be so, the fault was not altogether theirs. (pp. 232-35)

> Edward Wagenknecht, "Voices of the New Century," in his Cavalcade of the American Novel: From the Birth of the Nation to the Middle of the Twentieth Century, *Holt, Rinehart and Winston, 1952, pp. 230-51.*

T. M. PEARCE   (essay date 1965)

[*Pearce is an American literary critic, historian, and biographer who has written and edited numerous works about the Southwest. In the following excerpt from his biographical and critical study of Austin, Pearce discusses her poetry and offers an appraisal of her literary achievement.*]

As a poet Mary Hunter began at an early age to range freely within the zodiac of her own wit. She entered Blackburn College when she was just sixteen, and in her junior year *The Blackburnian*, the literary magazine, published four poems and one prose essay which she had written. The first of the poems is untitled, but the others are called "**Oak Leaves,**" "**Endymion,**" and "**Class Poem.**" The best of these is "**Oak Leaves,**" for it contains thoughts that are repeated many years later though in somewhat different terms and meter. Young Mary writes that she is lying beneath a sacred oak, listening to the melody sung by the stars and the wind. She dreams and then sings to the oak, asking to be changed into a tree so that she may rest on the breast of nature. She supplicates to:

> Leave for all time earth's ceaseless toil,
> Strike my roots deep in thy soil,
> With each returning spring to feel
> The life-sap through my branches steal,
> And as each twig new strength receives
> Laugh my joy in a thousand leaves.
> Part, undivided, of the earth
> And the Great Will that gave it birth.

How many of Mary Hunter's later books have passages dealing with trees? . . . The trail in *Outland*, leading to the country of free people, begins at the Broken Tree with the hawk's nest. In *The Basket Woman*, a number of trees are personified and give interesting accounts of themselves. The sugar pine is at first jealous of the flowers surrounding it; but, finally, as it towers above them, it grows proud and outlives all of the flaming, bright creatures once its neighbors. The white-barked pine longs to see the other side of the mountain and finally does when it is cut to mend a pack saddle and rides on a mule to the other side. Then it discovers that the slope was just like the one it had left. The straight sapling fir believes itself superior to its mother, for she is bent and worn. The son is critical of her shape until with time its own great branches begin to feel the weight of winter snows. "Droop your boughs" creaks the fir mother, "and bend so you will not break." Soon the young fir discovers that it is shaped like the mother, but it boasts, "You can see by the curve of my trunk what a weight I have borne." An aspen grove is the setting where Gard Sitwell in *Starry Adventure* first feels the spirit of the mountains. . . . [In] "**Going West,**" written thirty-six years after "**Oak Leaves,**" Mary Austin said:

> Lay me where some contented oak can prove
> How much of me is nurture for a tree. . . .
> Or if the wheel should run too fast
> Run up and rest
> As a sequoia for a thousand years.

The Children Sing in the Far West, the only collection of her poetry, was brought together in 1928. In the Preface, Mrs. Austin states that the songs began to be made nearly forty years earlier when the author was quite young and was teaching school. She tried them out on her pupils at Mountain View Dairy and at Lone Pine, California. . . . The language of these poems is artfully simple, and the repetition of a melodious line is timed to appeal to a song-line rhythm. "**The Sandhill Crane**" is an instance:

> Whenever the days are cool and clear
> The sandhill crane goes walking
> Across the field by the flashing weir
> Slowly, solemnly stalking.
> The little frogs in the tules hear
> And jump for their lives when he comes near,
> The minnows scuttle away in fear,
> When the sandhill crane goes walking.
> The fieldfolk know if he comes that way
> Slowly, solemnly stalking,
> There is danger and death in the least delay
> When the sandhill crane goes walking.
> The chipmunks stop in the midst of their play,
> The gophers hide in their holes away
> And hush, oh hush! the field mice say,
> When the sandhill crane goes walking.

H. C. Tracy, in his book *American Naturists*, calls *The Children Sing in the Far West* a book of nature verse. "Often they surprise and enchant one," he declares, and then quotes "**At Carmel**" for its touch-of-nature feeling:

> There are people go to Carmel
> To see the blue bay pass
> Through green wave to white foam
> Like snow on new grass.
> But I go to hear the auklets crying
> Like dark glass on glass.
> I go to hear the herons talk
> The way that herons have, half asleep,
> As they come in past Carmel bar
> With a slow wing sweep;
> To hear the wood teams jingling up from Sur,
> And the contented blether of the Mission sheep.

The poet's ever-recurring search for the right word is hauntingly expressed in "**Whisper of the Wind**":

> Whisper of the wind along the sage
> Only wait till I can get the word—
> Never was it printed in a page,
> Never was it spoken, never heard.

Once I thought I had it when the moon
Stood up young and white behind the grass,
Ah, but it was gone again so soon,
On the scented hill I heard it pass!
Whisper of the wind along the sage—
That was it where once the lupine stirred—
At the moth-hour once I heard it plain,
Once. But I forget the very word.

The early days the author spent in a "gull-gray city by the sea" are recalled in her poem **"San Francisco."** The reader swings up the hill on cable cars, gazes at the "gray wall-sided" warships and the gray fog drifting in. The green tide, the slow sound of the ferries, and the long Pacific swells slipping past the Golden Gate—all are perpetuated in the images of the poem. (pp. 102-05)

While Mary Austin was testing her lyrics upon the imagination of children, she was also writing occasional poems upon subjects as varied as **"The Burgher's Wife,"** protesting the Boer War in 1901; to **"Drouth,"** a blight typical of the Southwest in 1930 or any other year. A collection of her poems, classified as to subjects and types might make possible a final judgment upon her total poetic skills. (p. 106)

In several articles dealing with poetry, her own and that of others, she urged a re-examination of the impulses of expression in an effort to revitalize the art in both England and America. She compared the responses of children to those of peoples in primitive stages of culture. Impulse and response develop with individual and group motor incentives and result in rhythm. With children many objects or creatures can inspire action, sometimes in desire of possession, sometimes just in imitation. Children reach for color or brightness found in flowers and stones. They imitate sounds and movement heard and seen in animals. These are the first stages of poetic response. Onomatopoetic cries, tones, and evocative words appear in nonsense verse and nursery rhymes as well as in primitive fertility rites. Mrs. Austin cites the imitative words and measure in both a children's jingle and a Navajo gambling song. The first is the rhyme called "Blacksmith, Blacksmith":

> Here a nail
> And there a nail
> Tick . . . Tack . . . Toe.

The second accompanies throwing dice as it parallels the motion of fingers picking up counters, associating the imagery with a dove picking up seeds:

> Glossy locks picks them up.
> Red Moccasin picks them up,
> The lucky ones
> The winning ones
> My . . . little . . . dove.

After the earliest stage, that of recognition, comes the stage of identification with the object, in which the child or the primitive establishes a relationship between himself and what he sees or feels. This co-relatedness of the object to the poet and the poet to the object creates an interweaving of the out-reacher and what is reached for: "To express a peculiar and precious intimacy between the observer and the thing seen, that is the first social service of poets." In a general way, Mrs. Austin's reference to a statement about an object as a re-creation between the observer and the thing observed anticipates T. S. Eliot's formula called the "objective correlative" which he describes as external fact measured in sensory experience

creating an emotion measured by means of words. Mrs. Austin says that, when she first began to teach poetry to children, the only specimens she could find which measured their early experience were Wordsworth's "Daffodils," Bryant's "Waterfowl," and Longfellow's "New England Mayflower." She decided to write similar verses about bears, rabbits, mountain flowers, and birds which were familiar to Western, American young people. She searched for imagery, sound, and movement to reproduce this type of correlative.

The third stage of poetic response, arrived at in both primitive and juvenile creative effort, is generalization about group sentiment. She feels that this often ties in with mysticism about the land and with communal activities, but she is speaking of the most elementary types of verse. Her analysis does not proceed to the stage of introspection and subjectivism which penetrates poetry at all advanced levels. Her search is for the basic response to image and movement. Since the practice of poetry has ranged all the way from utterances as inspired as the Delphic Oracle to lines as mechanical as *Robert's Rules of Order,* a new examination might begin just where Mary Austin started, antedating the critical creeds and exploring the earliest psychology of sound, image, and meaning. (pp. 108-09)

In the life story of every writer a question may be raised: how far was his life as a person interwoven with the subject matter of his books? To what degree did he dramatize himself in his work? Are the ideas and feelings of the characters in his novels or plays those of the author in disguise? For Mary Austin the problem may be stated: how far was Mary-by-Herself represented by I-Mary? As a friend of the first Mary and as a student of the second, I think that the two identities, the author and the author in disguise, are very close. Perhaps, then, the strength and weakness of each may be summarized in the other.

Like Henry Thoreau and John Muir, Mary Austin enjoyed solitude. The gathering of clouds behind a high ridge, the spread of wild flowers across a mesa, or the rush of water in an arroyo brought to her mind some fundamental principle of natural law. She felt the joy in color and movement, but she also saw herself as a part of this flow of energy. As a pattern within a pattern, she felt both a response and a responsibility to live in accord with the freedom and discipline of nature's laws. Yet to her, withdrawal to a pond or to a forest or a desert was not the way for any man or woman to repay the natural forces which had produced him and of which he was a part. Mary Austin believed that an individual inherited the gifts of his ancestors and that within him was the capacity to return those gifts to the main stream. Her greatest gifts did not lie in the social novel, however much she desired them to. Such works as *The Ford* and *No. 26 Jayne Street* are failures as novels although the problems they fictionize are real. *The Ford* is the more successful of the two because it draws upon the battles between individuals and within communities for the water resources in the West, a contest which involved Mary Austin's views about nature's design and will for men and society.

The social treatises she wrote—such as *Christ in Italy, Love and the Soul Maker,* and *The Man Jesus*—are likely to be regarded as stepping stones rather than as terminal stages in sociological thought. Yet some of the loveliest passages in Mary Austin's imaginative prose may be found in *Christ in Italy,* especially in the small volume excerpted from this book and entitled *The Green Bough: A Tale of the Resurrection.* Certainly *The American Rhythm* did more than introduce a phrase to poetic theory drawn from the example of American

Indian verse. Mary Austin pioneered the inquiry into esthetic principles based upon indigenous motifs in American life, motifs based upon the European as well as the Indian experience here. If one probes the sources of each of her books, he discovers this partly anthropological and partly philosophic quest as the deepest motivation behind them all.

The books Mary Austin wrote in which she portrayed the oneness of man with nature are her finest literary achievement: *The Land of Little Rain, The Flock, Lost Borders, The Land of Journeys' Ending,* and *One-Smoke Stories.* In them her creed is shaped into literary form. The reader returns from these volumes feeling that he has walked in sunlight, gazed at far horizons, breathed clear air, and met unforgettable people. Midway in her writing career, Mary Austin made a brief statement of the conviction she held as a person and as a writer. In **"I Believe,"** the words proclaim the breadth of her outlook, the positive character of her attitude, and the living quality of her faith:

> I believe that the ills of this world are remediable while we are in the world by no other means than the spirit of truth and brotherliness working their lawful occasions among men. I believe in Here and Now.
>
> I believe in Man and the Friend of the Soul of Man, and I am unconvinced of Death.
>
> (pp. 134-35)

> *T. M. Pearce, in his* Mary Hunter Austin, *Twayne Publishers, Inc., 1965, 158 p.*

THOMAS W. FORD (essay date 1970)

[*Ford is an American literary critic, poet, and educator. In the following excerpt, he discusses the validity and importance of Austin's theories regarding the poetry of native Americans.*]

A notable effort to define a peculiarly American rhythm was made by Mary Austin in 1923 in her book *The American Rhythm*—notable because of its almost radical simplicity and notable because of its even more radical departure from the tradition that sees American poetry as a scion of English and European fathers. Mrs. Austin sees the rhythms of American poetry not as descending from the Old World, but rather as originating in the New World—specifically in the American West, and even more specifically in the primal energy contained in the land itself. What is perhaps even more astonishing, she sees a kinship between American Indian poetry and later American poetry, if not, indeed, almost a continuous development from one to the other.

Her claim should not be summarily dismissed as the distorted vision of a woman whose views became clouded because of devotion to the American Indian, although her great love for the Amerind is common knowledge and quite naturally would affect her judgment. Nor should it be tagged as simply another assertion of American intellectual independence from English and European models, in the tradition of Emerson's "The American Scholar" or Melville's "Hawthorne and His Mosses." To do so would deny revelation of significant, if partial, truths about the nature of rhythm, and more particularly about the nature of American Indian poetry and, just quite possibly, about American poetry.

Mrs. Austin argues that rhythm is an *experience,* and as such is distinct from our intellectual perception of that experience.

Motor impulses are started in the body in response to certain stimuli, and a succession of muscular tensions and releases follows. The stimuli come from the environment, from the land, and a sense of well-being occurs in the human organism when the rhythms are coordinated. Rhythm, she believes, is something that comes from the autonomic centers of experience. The Amerind, receiving stimulation from the land, responded with the rhythms of his poetry. This muscular and motor response of the human organism to environmental stimuli continued, she argued, in some of our present poets; consequently, we should expect similarities between Indian poetry and later American poetry since both derive from response to the American land.

Proceeding, then, on the basis that rhythm is not an intellectual perception but a product of the autonomic centers of experience, Mrs. Austin attempts to show how Indian poetry was the Indian's way of linking himself with the energy, with the "god-stuff" of creation:

> The Amerind makes poetry because he believes it to be good for him. He makes it because he believes it a contribution to the well-being of his group. He makes it to put himself in sympathy with the *wokonda,* the *orenda* or god-stuff which he conceives to be to some degree in every created thing.

Making use of mimesis, the Indian attempts to know the universe by "doing as it does." Poetry for the Amerind, she maintains, is a method of communion, not of communication. Mary Austin rejects any Freudian interpretation, instead seeing the Indian's primary need as the desire to relate himself to nature or to the Allness. The Indian, then, is in tune with his environment, and the land itself is a most important factor in furnishing stimuli for rhythmic expression. It was the influence of the land in forming rhythmic responses, in fact, that first indicated to Mrs. Austin that there must be a relationship between Indian and American poetry. Showing an unusual capacity to identify locations from rhythms, she states:

> It was when I discovered that I could listen to aboriginal verses on the phonograph in unidentified Amerindian languages, and securely refer them by their dominant rhythms to the plains, the deserts and woodlands that had produced them, that I awoke to the relationships that must necessarily exist between aboriginal and later American forms.

In the early 1900's she became convinced that at some period American poetry must necessarily take the shape of Amerind verse. Just as there existed Hellenic influences on Greek literature, there must exist Indian influences on American literature, because all great verse forms "are developed from the soil native to the culture that perfected them." American democracy, she believed, would strive toward a communality, which might be comparable to the Indian's desire to relate himself to the Allness. Coupled with this was the "shared stream of rhythmic stimuli proceeding from the environment." It should not be at all surprising, then, that there would emerge a trend toward a similar form of expression.

Mrs. Austin felt that we would have come into our heritage of natural rhythms earlier if it had not been for the pull of schools toward classic measures. The early American Puritan writers, and then Emerson, Lowell, Longfellow all slowed down the process of receiving rhythms from the American scene. Truly

American rhythm, she believed, first began to show itself in oratory, particularly in that of Abraham Lincoln. Then Whitman, while not really achieving the mode himself, was at least able to say "out of what stuff the new poetry was to be made." The national consciousness had to be restated through the new motor complexes and from the rhythm flowing from the land. While Whitman failed, Mrs. Austin was convinced that Carl Sandburg, Vachel Lindsay, and Sherwood Anderson were occasionally succeeding.

Are these observations of Mary Austin concerning the relationship between Indian and American poetry valid? Certain immediate similarities suggest themselves. Accent and rhyme have little place in Indian poetry, and the predominant meter, if any such thing really exists, is like a somewhat regularly spaced and unaccented pyrrhic. In other words, much Amerind poetry seems close to the free verse form found in much of Sandburg, Lindsay, and Anderson. Furthermore, the effort to establish contact with the Allness from the Indian point of view resembles that yearning toward communality often expressed by these American poets. But such generalities, as always, must remain somewhat superficial without the concrete. Unfortunately, Mrs. Austin does not name specifically the American poems which she believed to be similar to those of the Indian. (pp. 3-6)

Before rendering any meaningful opinion on the success or failure of Mrs. Austin's theories, one must face the prickly problem of translation. The difficulties of giving translations that are faithful in meaning and emotion are present in any language, and may be perhaps even greater in the Indian languages. The great number of languages increases the problem. The rituals, myths, and narratives involved in the poetry make it difficult for white readers to clearly understand. Do Mrs. Austin's translations cope with these difficulties? To be accurate, one should not use the word "translation" in her case. She explains:

> If forced to affix a title to my work I should prefer to call it not translation, but re-expression. My method has been, by preference, to saturate myself in the poem, in the life that produced it and the environment that cradled that life, so that when the point of crystallization is reached, I myself give forth a poem which bears, I hope, a genetic resemblance to the Amerind song that was my point of contact.

If one believes that a saturation in a culture may aid in translations then she should qualify, for her contact with the Indian was, in her words, "the only intellectual life I was to have for sixteen years."

It is to her credit that she is aware of the problems existing in translations and attempts to overcome them. She sees Indian poetry as three-fold, consisting of movement, or dance; melody; and words. Only the words, of course, are received in translation, and of necessity something is lost. She believes, however, that if the interpreter understands the life he is attempting to translate:

> Of the dance, only so much is necessary to be taken into the poetic record of aboriginal experience as serves to indicate the determining urge.

By her own admission, the melody is what suffers most in her own translations, for the reason that she was less interested in the lyrical aspect of poetry.

The Indian, in order to fill out the melodic pattern, would insert meaningless vocables, which appeared as something like "a he ya-a hu ai ya a he ya a hu" in translation. These, and the repetitions which are largely ritualistic in character, Mary Austin omits in her translations. She also aims to omit all the devices which would only be stage props in ceremony, and attempts to include only those necessary to an understanding of the thought. She admits that this is indeed a problem:

> It is a nice point to determine just when a feathered stick, a headdress, or a girdle is properly an item of poetic realization, and when it is to be relegated to the department of stage setting.

She believes that a common error in translations is the mistaken idea that because Indian culture is primitive, all the words must be one syllable. The Indian speech is what she terms "holophrastic"; that is, quite a number of important words contain many syllables which are actually words in themselves. For example, how would one translate "fear-living-in-that-place-shakes-continually"? The translator will more than likely have to use many words for the Indian's single expression.

The problem, then, as she sees it, is to absorb the culture, seek out the thought, and then re-express it in terms faithful to the Indian version, yet intelligible to the white reader. In the words of one critic [Helen MacKnight Doyle (see Additional Bibliography)], Mary Austin's poems were "an interpretation of the feeling that prompted the poem." Did she succeed in her translations? If one believes that sincere effort to understand the nature of an art by living in the environment which produced it will result in favorable translations, then she should have succeeded. At least one magazine, however, doubted the authenticity of her Indian poetry. *The Century* "agreed to print it if she would acknowledge that she had made it up herself." Mrs. Austin, of course, emphatically asserted her faithfulness to the original. (pp. 10-11)

In considering the final value of **The American Rhythm,** one must not overlook the possibility that Mary Austin's great interest in all forms of Indian art and her sympathy for the Indian may have prejudiced her view. It is possible that this attitude may have prevented her from taking an objective approach in her attempt to establish a relationship between Indian and American poetry. It is possible that she read something into the poetry that was not there. It is possible that her own emotions hindered the validity of her translations.

On the other hand, she did demonstrate similarities between Indian and American poetry; and who can categorically deny that the similarities spring from common response to the American land? Her translations, while lacking in lyrical quality, express clearly the feeling behind Amerind poetry. She was a pioneer in giving to the public an opportunity to consider the possible relationship between Indian and American poetry. Most significantly, in her insistent (although exaggerated) assertions that American rhythm derived primarily from response of the human organism to the energy and pulses inherent in the land itself, she indicated *one* significant truth about the nature of rhythm. By her emphasis on the non-logical and non-literary source of poetic rhythm, she offered a valuable warning to those who would over emphasize an intellectual continuity between English and American poetry. (p. 14)

Thomas W. Ford, "'The American Rhythm': Mary Austin's Poetic Principle," in Western American Literature, *Vol. V, No. 1, Spring, 1970, pp. 3-14.*

LAWRENCE CLARK POWELL   (essay date 1971)

[*Powell is an American essayist whose wide-ranging interests include the history of the Southwest. In the following excerpt, he commends* The Land of Little Rain *as an authentic representation of the desert country and comments favorably on several of Austin's other works.*]

Where is it, that land of Mary Austin? Southwest of the Rio Grande all the lands receive little rain. People, even critics who should know better, often think it is Arizona or New Mexico. Theirs is an understandable mistake, for Mary Austin did live there during the last two decades of her life, and those two states are indeed semi-arid.

Her land is California, the high desert country at the eastern base of the Sierra Nevada, merging with sagebrush Nevada. . . .

It is a more subtle land to which Mary Hunter Austin came before the turn of the century. There in the county of Inyo she put down roots and absorbed the lore of the Paiute and Shoshone Indians and of the shepherds, ranchers and miners. With her feet on earth and her head in the sky, she gave voice in singing prose to the soul of a hitherto unsung land. (p. 44)

The Land of Little Rain was published in 1903, the first of thirty-five books Mary Austin was to write before her death at Santa Fe in 1934. . . .

One might think that such an active writer would produce books of increasing quality and popularity. This was not the case. *The Land of Little Rain,* a young writer's first book, remains her best book. It is also the only one of her many books that has remained in print.

What makes it more than a California classic, truly an American classic, is its fidelity to the landscape and lore of its region. Although not a guidebook, *The Land of Little Rain* is true to the look and the feel of that desert country, to the lay of the land. She was one of the first writers to exalt the desert.

Its overtones are philosophical, and yet it is not theoretical, speculative, or impressionistic. Evidence of what might be called its mirror quality is the beautiful edition of 1950, introduced by Carl Van Doren, and with dramatic photographs by Ansel Adams which are captioned with passages from the book.

Here we see a perfect conjunction of life, landscape and literature. In this book Mary Austin found the words which precisely expressed what she saw and felt and wanted to say. The register of her language is fully as sharp as that of Adams's photographs. (p. 45)

In 1924 Mary Austin settled in Santa Fe and for the remaining decade of her life she was its eccentric high priestess, a safe distance removed from Mabel Dodge Luhan, her Taos counterpart. . . .

Two good books came from her New Mexican residence, and although they do not reach the level of her masterpiece, they rank high in Southwestern writing. *The Land of Journeys' Ending* is based on reading and on a six-weeks field trip in Arizona and New Mexico. Among the Mary Austin papers in the Huntington Library is a notebook which she kept on this field trip. Comparison of it with the finished book reveals her creative power. Bare notes are expanded by knowledge, illumined by imagination, and transformed into literature.

Its high point is the chapter on Inscription Rock called by the Spaniards El Morro, that great buff-colored sandstone battle-

Photograph of Austin by Ansel Adams, circa 1929. Courtesy of the Trustees of The Ansel Adams' Publishing Trust. All rights reserved.

ment on the road between Acoma and Zuñi on which centuries of passing travellers have carved their names. (p. 48)

In *Taos Pueblo* her prose and Ansel Adams's photographs are again wed. This essay is free of the crankiness, self-conscious admiration, and careless writing that flawed her later work. For example, her autobiography, *Earth Horizon,* begins with a richly detailed account of her earliest years, and then thins out in slovenly writing.

Just as her first book of nature essays remains her finest book, so Mary Austin's first novel, *Isidro,* is the best of several she wrote. Published in 1905 and inspired by the vaquero stories heard when she lived in Kern County, it is compact, lyrical, and faithful to the landscape and seasons of a country she knew and loved. *The Basket Woman* is a book of Paiute Indian tales retold for children. "All of these stories are so nearly true," she teasingly wrote, "that you need not be troubled in the least about believing them." Later, when her fiction became turgid with causes and prophecies, sounding like D. H. Lawrence at his worst, its fate was sealed. Mary Austin had the zeal and the stamina of Helen Hunt Jackson, and yet she never wrote a novel to match *Ramona.* Only when she forgot her own abnormal ego was she able to write beautiful, lasting prose, and this happened all too rarely. (pp. 48-9)

Lawrence Clark Powell, "Mary Austin: 'The Land of Little Rain'," in his California Classics: The Creative Literature of the Golden State, *1971. Reprint by Capra Press, 1982, pp. 44-52.*

VERA NORWOOD (essay date 1982)

[*Norwood is an American critic and educator who has taught various courses about the Southwest, including women's responses to the landscape and nature of the region. In the following excerpt, Norwood discusses Austin's vision of nature and how it related to conservationist, preservationist, and feminist concerns of her day. Norwood also appraises the importance as well as the limitations of Austin's views on nature and culture.*]

Austin's nature writing centered on the heroic expanses of the Southwest and Far West. She wrote at a time when wilderness in the classic sense was still to be found. Yet, her scientific education, physical and financial security and participation in the feminist movement freed her from the constricted vision of the land held by so many women of previous generations.... [In addition], Austin engaged in the national ambivalence about a preservationist or conservationist vision of America's future and attempted to come to her own resolution of that problem. She was one of the first women to participate in (rather than passively experience, as had so many women of the previous generation) national decisions about the future development of America's landscape. (p. 1)

Her first major piece to be published, *The Land of Little Rain* . . . , provided the focus for the attitude toward landscape which Austin pursued until her death in 1934. The book is a collection of essays describing the desert landscape of Southern California. The physical qualities of the land are the heart of the work. It seems that what drew her to the desert was the inability of humans to have an impact on the place: "Not the law, but the land sets the limit.... Desert is a loose term to indicate land that supports no man; whether the land can be bitted and broken to that purpose is not proven." For her, this place was (for the moment at least) safe from the development which was sweeping the country. Here was a place which had no immediate use but to succor the sick, bring back health to the world-weary:

> There is the divinest, cleanest air to be breathed anywhere in God's world. Some day the world will understand that, and the little oases in the winding tops of hills will harbor for the healing its ailing, house-weary broods. There is promise of great wealth in ores and earths, which is no wealth by reason of being so far removed from water and workable conditions, but men are bewitched by it and tempted to try the impossible. . . .

Statements such as this fit a classic tradition of American nature writing which by the mid-nineteenth century had begun to see the wilderness as a place for retreat from the pressures of civilization while maintaining an ambivalent stance toward the future potential for commercial development.

That Austin had some feeling for the potential for destruction of the land through greater use is clear both in statements from *The Land of Little Rain* and in battles she fought throughout her life. She had first-hand experience with the encroachment of the cities upon the water reserves in rural areas and was a strong champion for rural water rights. She fought for policies which protected the integrity of the landscape from over-development. Additionally, she understood the potential for destruction of an aesthetic landscape which settlement and development can bring. . . .

Unlike many of her contemporaries in the preservationist movement, Austin's recognition of man's potential destruction of nature did not lead her to the conclusion that bits of wilderness should be protected from the human species. Her writing includes sentiments common to both the preservationist and the conservationist movements, but finally her faith in the primacy of the land, and her need to present that faith in the strongest possible terms placed her outside both camps.

Often Austin expressed the belief that the land existed above and was indifferent to human needs. In a description of a small-time miner—a "pocket-hunter"—she noted that the man became one with the landscape "taking on the protective color of his surroundings" which were "lonely, inhospitable, . . . beautiful, terrible." But the man was safe in the land because "the land tolerated him as it might a gopher or a badger. Of all its inhabitants it has the least concern for men." . . . She expressed a classic vision of nature and implied the reason one must preserve wilderness: land untouched by men provides the nearest and most direct approximation to pure creative energy we shall experience and provides a check to egotistical belief in our own power. (p. 2)

Austin often looked at nature and saw a land which supported and nurtured life as long as living creatures adapted to its rhythms. Describing the desert, she sought to disabuse her readers of its deathly image: "Void of life it never is, however dry the air and villainous the soil." . . . The early chapters of *The Land of Little Rain* catalogue the myriad forms of plant and animal life which thrive in the desert, stressing always the adaptations made to the land's requirements.... Furthermore, while Austin clearly enjoyed these adaptations of life to the landscape simply for their own beauty and purity, much in the same way Tracy describes Thoreau's appreciation of animal life, her real objective was to provide her readers with examples of appropriate interactions with nature: "The desert flowers shame us with their cheerful adaptation to the seasonal limitations." . . . The point is to observe nature in order to come to more responsible living terms with it. . . .

Involved herself in that ambivalence which was at the core of America's response to the land, Austin also believed that the land existed to meet human needs. The "Water Borders" chapters of *The Land of Little Rain* provide fine examples of this philosophy, a philosophy much akin to that of conservationists who saw nature as man's resource. Describing the irrigation systems of the desert she believed that "it is the proper destiny of every considerable stream in the West to become an irrigation ditch. It would seem the streams are willing. They go as far as they can, or dare, toward the tillable lands in their own boulder fenced gullies—but how much further in the man-made waterways." . . . Austin found in the Southwest a landscape which still offered the twentieth century mind the opportunity to imagine a new Utopia.

Austin envisioned the desert landscape as a place of retreat from an over-industrialized world, but her retreat was a permanent one. While she engaged in her generation's dialogue about appropriate response to wilderness—not herself clear whether the land was subject to human manipulation or whether the land held primacy and required men's adaptation—she always presented the relationship between the two as of immediate, living concern. While many of her contemporaries desired to preserve wilderness in order to provide a continued source of "virility" to the industrial world, or to refresh a fading spirit in urban man, Austin's concern with the wilderness life was that of one living in it, not visiting. Thus, she was unsympathetic with both the builders of the national park systems and the builders of cities because neither represented the interests of those who live in the wilds.

One finds the clearest statement of this feeling in *The Flock,* her record of sheepherding in California. Published in 1906, this account of the lives of shepherds in California valleys was written at a time when John Muir was referring to sheep as "hoofed locusts." While Austin comprehended the need for Muir's national park system, her real sympathies were with the shepherd who esteemed "the segregation of the Park for the use of a few beauty-loving folk, as against its natural use as pasture, rather a silly performance." On the other hand, neither did she admire or support efforts to commercialize and industrialize the sheep business, decrying the coming of the Frenchmen "who fed where feed was, kept to their own kind, turned money quickly, and went back to France to spend it." . . . (p. 3)

There was a specific type of male life in the wilderness which attracted Austin. The shepherds she most admired, in Austin's terminology the "outliers," lived in the wilderness accepting that the natural process went on "independently of the convenience and the powers of men." . . . Acceptance of this basic core of indifference brought a separation from the normal social concerns of men, concerns tied to the need to effect a change, make an impact on the wilderness, and meant that a woman like Austin could be freed from the sex-typed expectations of women in more "civilized" social situations. At the conclusion of *The Flock,* Austin explained her sense of connection to these men as opposed to the traditional life of the society of women. She commented that many of her friends could not understand how she could be safe in the "Wilds." "Safety" to her implied a suffocation of personal freedom. She noted that basic indifference of the men to her comings and goings in contrast to the more restrictive notice that other women gave to her wanderings:

> Women-folk, being house inhabiting, might assume a groundless intimacy, premise a community of interests when necessarily barred from whole blocks of your experience, even annoy by a baseless conceit of advantage, but cowboys and shepherds, trappers and forest rangers, make no such mistakes. . . .

Finally, Austin was a "free" woman, aware of the feminist issues of her day, who had discovered a place where she could live in terms of that new freedom. The men she was most drawn to were those who offered the most potential for women's exercise of personal choice. For Austin to live the freedom she so passionately desired, the life of these men and the place in which they lived must offer a viable future and not be subject either to an artificial preservation or total destruction.

Furthermore, it was not sufficient that the West remain a free place; the basic American myth about the land must be changed to fit the primary needs of the "emancipated" woman. Austin revised the myth of the feminine landscape to fit her own feminist needs for a landscape to which women could respond directly. (pp. 3-4)

References to land as woman are found throughout Austin's work. One of the least complex statements comes from *The Land of Journeys' Ending,* her paean to the Southwest as the hope for a new American future. In a description of the desert areas of the Southwest, she noted the "lack of surface cover for the naked, fine-colored sands" and stated that:

> To many people grass is as indispensable an index of fertility in the earth as long hair is of femininity in a woman. Actually, all that grass and other annual cover offered to the casual observer, is evidence of the quick, continuous rhythms of vegetating life. But in arid regions where the period of growth is confined to the short season of maximum rainfall, the processes of foliation and floration are pushed almost to explosion; followed by a long quiescence in which life merely persists. . . .

While not rejecting the myth of land as woman, Austin argued with the tenets of the myth, redefining both femininity and nature in the process in a context not even Tracy anticipated. Furthermore, she began the statement with a description of nature as experienced in the American East to show that Eastern terms do not apply in the West.

If one remembers that Austin's primary love for the Southwest landscape stems from its resistance to any life except that which exists on the land's terms and her conviction that the best use to make of the land's bounty was that which interfered least with existing physical qualities, then it is not surprising that the feminine metaphor she came to was rather different than the classic masculine vision. Austin's female landscape was not passive in the face of a male hero's ravishment and impregnation. At the beginning of *Lost Borders,* a series of essays on the area around the Mojave desert, she made her strongest direct statement of her vision of land as woman:

> If the desert were a woman, I know well what she would be like: deep-breasted, broad in the hips, tawny, with tawny hair, great masses of it lying smooth along her perfect curves, full lipped like a sphinx, but not heavy-lidded like one, eyes sane and steady as the polished jewel of her skies, such a countenance as should make men serve without desiring her, such a largeness of her mind as should make their sins of no account, passionate, but not necessitous, patient—and you could not move her, not if you had all the earth to give, so much as one tawny hair's-breadth beyond her own desires. If you cut very deeply into the soul that has the mark of the land upon it, you find such qualities as these. . . .

The "forgiving" nature Austin assigned this female land had less to do with any stereotyped vision of women than it had to do with Austin's overly optimistic vision of the land's ability to turn men's bad works to good, and to exist above and outside their petty concerns for progress. In terms of a redefinition of the myth of land as woman, the more important concept is that of self-sufficiency and an unwillingness to be molded by the needs of men, rather than, to mold men to her needs. She totally rejects here any possibility of the land being subject to male manipulation or ownership. This is a fairly unique vision of the female land and led Austin to her equally unique description of the method by which women can live in the wilderness.

Austin herself seemed to realize that she had defined land in a new way and might be expecting too much to ask other, more traditional women of her generation to respond in the same way she did to the landscape. She understood that, until her time, the West for the most part held terrors for women while attracting men. Immediately preceding the above description of desert as woman she noted that "men . . . who go mostly into the desert, . . . love it past all reasonableness, slack their ambitions, cast off old usages, neglect their families because of the pulse and beat of a life laid bare to its thews and sinews. Their women hate with implicitness the life like the land. . . ." . . . Knowing and understanding the tradition did not mean, however, that she had to accept it. If she found it difficult to describe white women actually living well in the wilderness, she could let American Indian women provide an example.

One of her most famous pieces is the description in *The Land of Little Rain* of the "Basket Maker." This essay tells of the life of Seyavi, an American Indian woman who lost her husband and was forced to survive alone in the wilderness for a time. Seyavi was one of those whose "soul has the mark of the land upon it" and who had a feminine strength equal to that of the land. The essay begins with a quote from Seyavi to the effect that "[a] man must have a woman, but a woman who has a child will do very well." . . . The comment sprang from Seyavi's experience hiding with her child in the wilderness after the defeat of her tribe: "That was the time Seyavi learned the sufficiency of mother wit, and how much more easily one can do without a man than might at first be supposed." . . . Part of what attracted Austin to this life was obviously the pure "survival in the wilderness" tale, but additionally she saw a woman able to put together a whole life based on the principle of self-sufficiency. (pp. 4-5)

While Seyavi made baskets and sold them for money, she also burned them in honor of the dead. She made her baskets "for the satisfaction of desire" rather than for use. The desire to be satisfied was the direct connection the activity gave her to nature: "The weaver and the warp lived next to the earth and were saturated with the same elements. . . . Whenever Seyavi cut willows for baskets was always a golden time, and the soul of the weaver went into the wood." . . . Austin contrasted Seyavi's attitude toward her baskets with her own "covetous" collector's spirit. . . . Seyavi provided Austin with a human incarnation of the spirit of the feminine Southwest land and since for Austin, under the best circumstances, land culture and human culture were one, the best human method for living on that land. This vision has little to do with the European tradition of aggression against the land and its people, but depends heavily on the opposite vision of wilderness as home which is commonly posited as the American Indian relationship to the land. Thus, Austin in confronting the Western desert sloughs off not only her acquired sexual stereotypes but also racial stereotypes common to women of the generation just preceding hers. Along with Helen Hunt Jackson, Austin became a central female figure in the move to recognize wrongs done to the American Indian and make some attempt to right these wrongs. She went one step further, however, and saw in the Indian culture of the Southwest the best hope for America's future. Such hope was based partially on the models of self-sufficiency in the new landscape which American Indian women provided women of her generation.

While Austin made an important contribution to the discussion of women's place in the wilderness, her basic ambivalence to the way Americans should live in terms of the land flowed directly from her generation's own inability to answer the question. As did most of her predecessors, she suffered from conflicting emotions when faced with wilderness: she at once wanted to maintain its pristine qualities and yet allow humans the opportunity to use those qualities for our own benefit. For herself, she resolved this difficulty by placing her faith in a nostalgic vision of the American Indian's relationship to the land. She was not so much a teller of natural truths as an interpreter of what she saw. This was stated throughout her work but never so succinctly as in the introduction to Shoshone life in *The Land of Little Rain.* (pp. 5-6)

In her nature writings, as in her other creative efforts, Austin had a tendency to simplify and stereotype cultures to fit her concepts. It is finally this strongly felt need to envision an ideal way of life and to frame that life in terms of a perfect fit with nature that dates her work. Austin was incapable of foreseeing the potential destruction of both land and culture which would come with increasing use of the Southwest's resources. In fact, she foretold the reverse in the conclusion of *The Land of Journeys' Ending.* Here she invited Easterners to vacation in the West rather than in Europe. . . . Given her optimistic vision of the new female wilderness' ability to overcome the mistakes of men, Austin could not foresee the days when the neon representation of the thunderbird would light up the skies more dramatically than its natural occurrence. (p. 6)

Vera Norwood, "The Photographer and the Naturalist: Laura Gilpin and Mary Austin in the Southwest," in Journal of American Culture, *Vol. 5, No. 2, Summer, 1982, pp. 1-28.*

JAMES C. WORK   (essay date 1982)

[*In the following excerpt, Work illustrates the impressionistic nature of Austin's writing style in* The Land of Little Rain *and analyzes the philosophical concerns addressed by Austin in this work.*]

In the final assessment of Mary Austin's contribution to literature—if a final assessment is ever possible—*The Land of Little Rain* . . . will be recognized as one of the touchstone works of American nature writing. In subject matter it may be said to be similar to Krutch's *The Desert Year* or Eiseley's *The Night Country,* and in its use of the autobiographical approach it reminds one of Thoreau's *Walden* or Muir's *Yosemite.* But there are two respects in which *The Land of Little Rain* is incomparable. One is the set of abstract impressions left by the book in the reader's mind, and the other is the set of moral statements concerning the proper relationship of the human animal to the land in its natural state.

The best initial approach to *The Land of Little Rain* is the impressionistic one; the reader should simply let the book affect the sensibilities and then should analyse the resulting impressions to whatever extent seems natural. No other approach, for the first-time reader, fits the material so well.

To begin such an impressionistic approach, we could hardly do better than to let our impressions be guided by the words Austin wrote in appreciation of her neighbor's field:

> It is a still field, this of my neighbor's, though
> so busy, and admirably compounded for variety
> and pleasantness,—a little sand, a little loam,
> a grassy plot, a stony rise or two, a full brown
> stream, a little touch of humanness, a footpath
> trodden out by moccasins.

The Land of Little Rain, being composed of tranquility, does seem to be a "still" little book, but just as patient vigils prove that the apparently still and lifeless desert is in fact full of movement, so does close reading prove this to be a "busy" book indeed. We have a sense of watching the author walking through the country, or riding through it, in constant motion. She is always coming away, it seems, from an encounter with her plants, her terrain, her animals, her people, it is a book busy with life—no passive statistics of "Economy" or bean fields, no tiresome detailing of motionless specimens. Of the dead and inanimate she has as little to say as possible, as if they were to her nothing more than objects of merely momentary curiosity:

> Once below Pastaria Little Pete showed me bones sticking out of the sand where a flock of two hundred had been smothered in a by-gone wind. In many places the four-foot posts of a cattle fence had been buried by the wind-blown dunes. . . .

She takes far more interest in the "unshepherded, small flocks" of clouds moving in the sky than in the bony remnants of the earthly kind.

Being busy, the book also has the "variety" of the neighbor's field. From the dry desert in the title chapter to the marshy "Water Borders," from lonely "Scavengers" and "The Pocket Hunter" to the less lonely individuals gathered in "Jimville" and "The Little Town of the Grape Vines," from the "Streets of the Mountains" to the starker scenery of "The Mesa Trail" and thence to the "Neighbor's Field," Mary Austin seems the most self-indulgent of authors in responding not just to the richness of things in her arid world nor just to the surprising fullness of life there, but to the sheer unending variety of terrain, creature, plant, weather, sky, and mood as well.

Like the busy and various field, her book has a rich "pleasantness" to it. Here are no urgings of a philosophic system, no real pressure put upon the reader to perceive deeper meaning; rather, Austin seems to offer an invitation to us to look over her shoulder as she contemplates—very closely—the arid land. A reader gets the pleasant sense of listening to one of those "lyric improvisations" she insists have died out. . . . We are tempted to confront her with her own lyric passages in the book—the meal described at Las Uvas, the tribute to the arid land, the picture of the wildfowl in the tulares, the poetry of a stream's course, the smells of sage. "Pleasant" seems, indeed, an inadequate term for a work of such lyric quality.

About that "touch of humanness" I intend to say more later. But one does have a sense, with Austin, that contact with land in the arid regions—where any life that can exist is precious and a marvel—has brought something of one's "humanness" closer to the surface, has caused the memory to be more acute, has somehow given new significance to thinking, to the sense of irony, to sadness, to joy. It is not a tale of Austin struggling to drive life into a corner to know it, but of Austin in deep yet self-forgetting sympathy with the desert life-struggles.

"A footpath trodden by moccasins"—*The Land of Little Rain* is that, certainly. It is a light trail to follow, made as if by one walking in moccasins that are soft to allow the feet that necessary "sense of intimacy" with the land. . . . (pp. 297-99)

If the neighbor's field is planned, is the book? I am content to leave the question to the formalists. There is, perhaps, some pairing of chapters—the scavenger and the pocket hunter have at least as much in common with each other as do the streets of the mountains, the water borders, and the nurslings of the sky—some sense of movement from the dry desert and its hard

Jimville town to the well-showered mountains and the green softness of Las Uvas. On a philosopic level the reader is first told that "after having lived there one does not wonder so much about those who stay," . . . then is shown the deep satisfactions of it all from barren flats to verdant mountains, and finally is invited to "come away" to enjoy the "even-breathing days" in the end. . . . (pp. 299-300)

Beyond these few abstract impressions, *The Land of Little Rain* presents an almost organic regularity. I began examining it by separating Austin's more philosophic comments into categories, of which there appear to be three of major importance: these include observations about the land, observations about the animal and plant life native to the land, and observations about humans in the land. Later, reviewing the quotations and notes I had gathered under each category heading, I realized that Austin is addressing three questions: What are the essential qualities of the land? What is the relation of life forms to the land and to each other? And what is the proper role of the human animal in relation to the land and the life of it?

The replies Austin gives to these questions are of far more importance than any sort of order she may put them in, for they support what she was later to set down as a central premise of her own humanistic beliefs:

> Man is not himself only, not solely a variation of his racial type in the pattern of his immediate experience. He is all that he sees; all that flows to him from a thousand sources, half noted, or noted not at all except by some sense that lies too deep for naming. He is the land, the life of its mountain processions, the involution and variation of its vegetal patterns. If there is in the country of his abiding, no more than a single refluent color, such as the veiled green of sagebrush or the splendid wine of sunset spilled along the Sangre de Cristo, he takes it in and gives it forth again in directions and occasions least suspected by himself, as a manner, as music, as a prevailing tone of thought, as the line of his rooftree, the pattern of his personal adornment.

The "prevailing tone of thought"—what does Austin tell us is the essential character of the land that can so determine our own character? It is first of all a rewarding land, this desert, and a seductive one. . . . The land is, moreover, a place where one can retain some measure of individuality, where one can have the joy of knowing "special places" and private pleasures. "The earth," Austin writes, "is no wanton to give up all her best to every comer, but keeps a sweet, separate intimacy for each." . . . (pp. 300-01)

But despite the lotus charm and sweet intimacy of the land, relation with it must be entered into with great care. In every chapter, death is never overlooked as a necessary adjunct to life: "Go as far as you dare in the heart of a lonely land, you cannot go so far that life and death are not before you." . . . And, pleasant as it is to know that the experience of the land becomes a part of one's very person, it is necessary to remember what is stamped on the other side of that coin: "The manner of the country makes the usage of life there, and the land will not be lived in except in its own fashion." . . .

Here, then, is a view of a nature that can be sweet, but not beneficent, a nature which, while not taking extreme measures to deprive an inhabitant of life, makes no effort to keep one alive. Neither malicious nor benevolent, Austin's is a nature much like that of Stephen Crane—the leaden sky and apathetic sea in his story, "The Open Boat," have their counterparts in her characterization of Death Valley:

> Properly equipped it is possible to go safely across that ghastly sink, yet every year it takes its toll of death, and yet men find there sundried mummies, of whom no trace or recollection is preserved. To underestimate one's thirst, to pass a given landmark to the right or left, to find a dry spring where one looked for running water—there is no help for any of these things. . . .
>
> (p. 301)

Perhaps it is because of the indifferent surroundings that Mary Austin so keenly feels the fellowship, the close interrelationships of the living things. These she largely personifies, thus bringing them, in her moral system, into kinship with the human intruder. Writing as she did within two or three years of the turn of the century, when each coyote and wolf had a price on its head and when anything with wings was considered only a challenging target, she extends a humanitarian fairmindedness to even the most repulsive of them. (p. 302)

The Land of Little Rain . . . employs personification—and pathetic fallacy—to lesson us in what appear to Austin to be some human-like qualities of interaction in nature. Her roadrunner, for instance, who reminds us of Twain's bluejay, goes "peeking and prying" about the desert; preferring dustbaths himself, he "never had any patience with the water baths of the sparrows," so "after daunting them with shrill abuse and feint of battle," he would go away "in fine disdain, only to return in a day or two to make sure the foolish birds were still at it." . . . (p. 303)

Examples of Austin's empathy toward the living inhabitants of the land—and "empathy" is here the exact word we want—are plentiful in *The Land of Little Rain*. The best one, however, is in the chapter titled "The Streets of the Mountains." In those water-canyons she finds the same oversoul sense that she did in the desert, what she calls here the "sense of the hills."

> Whether the wild things understand it or not they adapt themselves to its processes with the greater ease. The business that goes on in the street of the mountain is tremendous, world-formative. Here go birds, squirrels, and red deer, children crying small wares and playing in the street, but they do not obstruct its affairs. Summer is their holiday; "Come now," says the lord of the street, "I have need of a great work and no more playing."
>
> But they are left borders and breathing-space out of pure kindness. They are not pushed out except by the exigencies of the nobler plan which they accept with a dignity the rest of us have not yet learned. . . .
>
> (pp. 303-04)

The third category in *The Land of Little Rain* is the human animal. On this topic, Mary Austin's theme is consistently based upon two watchwords: "awareness" and "simplicity." To promote the first of these two virtues, she often surprises the reader with observations on human habits, such as "Men have their season on the mesa as much as plants and four-footed things, and one is not like to meet them out of their time" . . . and then challenges one to break out of them. . . .

Seeing humans and animals as co-equals in the land, and dealing with animals in human terms, it is natural that Austin discusses human beings as a species. At Jimville, for instance, she finds she cannot get into "any proper relation" with the town—meaning to be aware of the people—unless she could "slough off and swallow acquired prejudices as a lizard does his skin." . . . Having done that, she finds herself free to agree with the basic simplicity and rightness of the town's social codes. . . . (p. 304)

It is true, of course, that Austin becomes fascinated with individual specimens, such as the Pocket Hunter and Seyavi the basket maker, but even in her examination of these obviously unusual samples she formulates several generalizations about the race as a whole. She makes the reader see them not just as individuals, but as abstractions as well. . . .

Austin can, of course, see the human weaknesses. And she does not let her high moral perspective keep her from pointing out the mean and obvious examples:

> Man is a great blunderer going about in the woods, and there is no other except the bear makes so much noise. Being so well warned beforehand, it is a very stupid animal, or a very bold one, that cannot keep safely hid. The cunningest hunter is hunted in turn, and what he leaves of his kill is meat for some other. That is the economy of nature, but with it all there is not sufficient account taken of the works of man. There is no scavenger that eats tin cans, and no wild thing leaves a like disfigurement on the forest floor.
>
> (p. 305)

But more in the humanitarian vein—especially the examination of the human capability and need for improvement as a moral being—is the lesson in nature that humans are not some sort of elect beings. To the land, the human is just barely the equal of the other creatures and the plants. Speaking of the Pocket Hunter, Austin paints him as a creature of simplicity but one lacking in awareness of ". . . a big, mysterious land, a lonely inhospitable land, beautiful, terrible. But he came to harm in it; the land tolerated him as it might a gopher or a badger. Of all its inhabitants it has the least concern for man." . . . (pp. 305-06)

Even though he developed an unconscious sense for self-preservation, an attunement to nature that saved him from the flood . . . , and although he had acquired that "weather shell" that made all seasons the same to him . . . , the Pocket Hunter still went about his searching as a man more or less oblivious to the Spirit of Place. He is as morally blind to that Spirit as Browning's Caliban, this prospector who ". . . had seen destruction by the violence of nature and the violence of men, and felt himself in the grip of an All-wisdom that killed men or spared them as seemed for their good." . . . When he does leave the desert country, "the land seemed not to miss him any more than it had minded him." . . .

The Pocket Hunter seems a sort of tragic example of a person with the impulse for the simple life and the ability to live it, but without the awareness of the larger Impulse behind the life of the land. And Austin does not hesitate to apply the lesson to her reader: "You of the house habit," she writes, "can hardly understand the sense of the hills. No doubt the labor of being comfortable gives you an exaggerated opinion of yourself, an exaggerated pain to be set aside.". . . (p. 306)

Besides setting aside that overblown self-esteem, we need to adopt some proper perspectives for observing the land and the life. . . . To really see the life beneath our feet, we need to ascend, up to the "tall hills" if necessary, to that height which is "also the level of the hawks."

Even with that height, however, comes more need for awareness. Achieve the level of the hawks and you need to add inquisitiveness and perhaps some cunning—traits of the fox and coyote—to your improved viewpoint. . . . Or, sometimes, we need to look not down at the ground but up at the heavens to re-acquaint ourselves with our proper place in the large scheme of things. . . . Our proper awareness of ourself may indeed come from such apparently simple things as rat-level inspection, offal-watching, and sky scanning. The last of these, done in the night only, may finally make Calibans of us all, simple half-human-half-animals who believe we are free of moral obligation just because we are of "no account" in the universe. But our sky-watching must also be done in the daytime if we are to keep a balanced perspective, for daytime observations will bring us back to knowing ourselves to be subject to—and thereby responsible to—a Spirit of Place.

> The first effect of cloud study is a sense of presence and intention in storm processes. Weather does not happen. It is the visible manifestation of the Spirit moving itself in the void. It gathers itself together under the heavens; rains, snows, yearns mightily in wind, smiles; and the Weather Bureau, situated advantageously for that very business, taps the record on his instruments and going out on the streets denies his God, not having gathered the sense of what he has seen. Hardly anybody takes account of the fact that John Muir, who knows more of mountain storms than any other, is a devout man. . . .

> (pp. 306-08)

The Spirit that moves itself in the void. The Sense of Place. The "God" discovered under the walnut tree by Mary Austin at age six—or was it three? Surely we can exist unaware of it, and even with a measure of content, as does the Pocket Hunter. But how much the better for us, and for all of nature, to live in appreciation of it. We are creatures not only of being but of imagination: we create for ourselves, if we will, a constant spirit of wonder and belief, a spirit which science can neither explain away nor prove. A complex soul, indeed, and therefore the more in need of simple wonderment. "I am persuaded," Austin writes, in the final pages of *The Land of Little Rain,* "only a complex soul can get any good of a plain religion. Your earthborn is a poet and a symbolist. We breed in an environment of asphalt pavements a body of people whose creeds are chiefly restrictions against other people's way of life, and have kitchens and latrines under the same roof that houses their God.". . . (p. 308)

Far from being a naturalist who is an advocate of the hermit existence, Mary Austin recognizes the need for a social environment. But people in impersonal crowds which inhabit asphalt pavements are almost as isolated from the essential good of group living—and as isolated from the earth—as if they *were* alone there. People are at their best, in terms of moral behavior, in intimate association both with the land and with other humans, living in such an environment as she describes in the final chapter of *The Land of Little Rain.* It is significant in understanding her stance with regard to desirable human behavior, I believe, to realize that she does not recommend or even particularly condone the hermit life of the Pocket Hunter, the basket weaver, or the borax muleskinner, and to further note that she uses the final words of her book to recommend not the empty land, but rather the little town of the grape vines, where "every house is a piece of earth." Would you be better than you are? Then to that town,

> Come away, you who are obsessed with your own importance in the scheme of things, and have got nothing you did not sweat for, come away by the brown valleys and full-bosomed hills to the even-breathing days, to the kindliness, earthiness, ease of El Pueblo de Las Uvas. . . .

> (pp. 308-09)

James C. Work, "The Moral in Austin's 'The Land of Little Rain'," in Women and Western American Literature, *edited by Helen Winter Stauffer and Susan J. Rosowski, The Whitston Publishing Company, 1982, pp. 297-310.*

ADDITIONAL BIBLIOGRAPHY

Brooks, Van Wyck. "The Southwest." In his *The Confident Years: 1885-1915,* pp. 353-70. New York: E. P. Dutton & Co., 1952.
  Discusses the Southwest—the land, legends, and people—as the source for *The Land of Little Rain, Lost Borders,* and *The Flock.* Brooks describes these works as "three singularly happy books, both deeply felt and picturesque, though perhaps a little too cunningly, or too consciously, wrought."

Doyle, Helen MacKnight. *Mary Austin: Woman of Genius.* New York: Gotham House, 1931, 302 p.
  Sympathetic, detailed biography written by a woman who was a doctor for Austin's daughter and who became Austin's friend.

DuBois, Arthur E. "Mary Hunter Austin: 1868-1934." *Southwest Review* XX, (Spring 1935): 231-64.
  Discusses Austin's personality, compares her with other authors, and considers her in light of the scientific and artistic community in general.

Field, Louise Maunsell. "Mary Austin, American." *The Bookman,* New York LXXV, No. 8 (December 1932): 819-21.
  Discusses some of Austin's works, noting their common traits such as her seeming interest in theme and setting above characterization, and her sensitivity to the charm of words as well as to the rhythm of prose. Field also considers Austin's personality, interests, and varied experiences, and commends her efforts to preserve Indian culture.

Fink, Augusta. *I-Mary: A Biography of Mary Austin.* University of Arizona Press, 1983, 310 p.

Study of Austin's life and career. Fink focuses on Austin's personal relationships and her psychological development.

Forman, Henry James. "On a Letter from Mary Austin." *New Mexico Quarterly* XXI, No. 4 (Winter 1961-62): 339-44.
Discusses Austin's deep preoccupation with her methods of writing and her mental processes while writing. Forman also offers a largely unfavorable review of *A Woman of Genius*.

Gelfant, Blanche H. "'Lives' of Women Writers: Cather, Austin, Porter/and Willa, Mary, Katherine Anne." *Novel: A Forum on Fiction* 18, No. 1 (Fall 1984): 64-80.
Comparative study of the lives and works of Cather, Austin, and Porter with reference to three biographies—*Willa: The Life of Willa Cather*, by Phyllis C. Robinson; *I-Mary: A Biography of Mary Austin*, by Augusta Fink; and *Katherine Anne Porter: A Life*, by Joan Givner. Gelfant compares the three writers with Ernest Hemingway, and discusses their development in light of their Victorian backgrounds as well as from the perspective of feminist theory.

Jones, Llewellyn. "Indian Rhythms." *The Bookman* LVII, No. 6 (August 1923): 647-48.
Review of *The American Rhythm*. Jones points out some confusing points of Austin's argument, but commends Austin for preserving some Indian poetry.

Keiser, Albert. "The Indian Drama." In his *The Indian in American Literature*, pp. 65-100. New York: Oxford University Press, 1933.
Favorable review of *The Arrow Maker*.

Lummis, Charles. Letter to Mary Austin. In *Literary America: The Mary Austin Letters, 1903-1934*, edited by T. M. Pearce, pp. 19-21. Westport: Greenwood Press, 1979.
Criticizes Austin for her incorrect use of the Spanish language in her work and advises her to provide a more careful, respectful representation of Spanish. Lummis, the editor of *Out West* magazine and author of a number of books pertaining to the Indian and Spanish history of California and the Southwest, published some of Austin's early works prior to *The Land of Little Rain*, and at his home she met local writers. The relationship between Austin and Lummis is described by Pearce, in his introduction to this letter, as one of "friendly adversaries." Pearce notes that Austin "resented his admonitory attitude, but relied upon him for advice about details of Southwestern history, flowers, Spanish gardens, and local customs."

Lyday, Jo W. *Mary Austin: The Southwest Works*. Southwest Writers Series, edited by James W. Lee. Austin: Steck-Baughn, 1968, 37 p.
Biographical and critical study which includes a discussion of Austin's ideas about fiction and her attitude toward her critics. Lyday states, "A keen sense of observation, a poetic soul, a philosophical turn of mind . . . lift Mary Austin's writing far above the level of mere geographical description" in *California: The Land of the Sun; The Land of Little Rain; The Flock; The Land of Journeys' Ending;* and *Taos Pueblo*. According to Lyday, it is on these works—with the exception of *Taos Pueblo* and the addition of *The Man Jesus*—that Austin's place in literature rests.

Overton, Grant. "Mary Austin." In his *The Women Who Make Our Novels*, pp. 8-20. New York: Dodd, Mead & Co., 1928.
Discusses Austin's life, personality, and work. Overton points out the works in which Austin "completely expresses herself, or the genius that is in her," among them *The Land of Little Rain* and *The Flock*.

Paterson, Isabel. "Mary Austin's Story, the Story of America." *New York Herald Tribune Books* IX, No. 9 (6 November 1932): 1-2.
Discusses *Earth Horizon*, praising the work for its "quality of greatness" and for being a "significant contribution to American values." Paterson comments favorably on Austin's prose style in general, considering her an accomplished writer who was "handicapped by her originality."

Pattee, Fred Lewis. "The Feminine Novel." In his *The New American Literature, 1890-1930*, pp. 245-70. New York: D. Appleton-Century Co., 1930.
Survey of female novelists of the late nineteenth through the early twentieth centuries, with brief mention of Austin. Of her *The Land of Little Rain* he states, "the Desert is the principal character, alive, sinister, lovable, death-dealing, irresistible, beautiful. No stronger book of its variety exists in our literature."

Powell, Lawrence Clark. "A Dedication to the Memory of Mary Hunter Austin: 1868-1934." *Arizona and the West: A Quarterly Journal of History* X, No. 1 (Spring 1968): 1-4.
Survey of Austin's career and major works, with highlights of her personal life.

———. "Mary Austin: *The Land of Journeys' Ending*." In his *Southwest Classics*, pp. 95-105. Los Angeles: Ward Ritchie Press, 1974.
Biographical and psychological study, with an examination of *The Land of Journeys' Ending*. Powell praises this as Austin's "richest, ripest book" and states that "the chapters of this timeless book are a processional of the past that is also present and future."

Ruppert, James. "Mary Austin's Landscape Line in Native American Literature." *Southwest Review* LXVIII, No. 4 (Autumn 1983): 376-90.
In-depth discussion of Austin's abiding concern with the influence of environment on people and culture, emphasizing her interest in the relationship of a writer to his or her environment. Ruppert examines Austin's theory of "landscape line" in which she considers the influence of environment on poetry and folk stories, and he cites many examples to illuminate her ideas. While acknowledging that Austin was not a trained academic and that "her ideas may not be practical tools for literary analysis," he defends her ideas as "rich theoretical treasures" which have value for contemporary writers.

———. "Discovering America: Mary Austin and Imagism." In *Studies in American Indian Literature: Critical Essays and Course Designs*, edited by Paula Gunn Allen, pp. 243-58. Modern Language Association of America, 1983.
Considers Austin "an interesting person on whom to focus after surveying the wider general interest [during the early twentieth century] in American Indian studies." Ruppert discusses Austin's views regarding the relationship of Indian literature and modern American literature, particularly her interpretation of the similarities between Indian and modern American poetry. Austin's understanding of the nature of storytelling is also a focus of this essay.

Sergeant, Elizabeth Shepley. "Mary Austin: A Portrait." *The Saturday Review of Literature* XI, No. 8 (8 September 1934): 96.
A reminiscence of Austin following her death. Sergeant comments on her personality and writings, concluding that Austin's "work continued to the very end [to be] the central, basic joy, interest, and high adventure of her essentially lonely life."

Stearns, Mary Adams. "Love's Highway." *The Little Review* I, No. 10 (January 1915): 44-6.
Largely favorable review of *Love and the Soul Maker*. Stearns discusses some of Austin's ideas regarding love, sex, and marriage as expressed in this work.

Van Doren, Carl. "New Styles: Emergent Types." In his *Contemporary American Novelists: 1900-1920*, pp. 132-46. New York: Macmillan, 1922.
Surveys the subjects of Austin's works, commenting on her writing style and on her development as a writer. Van Doren states: "She wears something like the sibyl's robes and speaks with something like the sibyl's strong accents, but the cool, hard discipline of the artist or of the exact scholar only occasionally serves her. Much of her significance lies in her promise."

Walker, Franklin. "The Desert Grows Friendly." In his *Chronicles of California: A Literary History of Southern California,* pp. 180-208. Berkeley and Los Angeles: University of California Press, 1950.

> Discusses Austin's works, her mysticism, and the transcendental tenets of her thought; appraises her writing; and explains her view of the desert.

Wynn, Dudley. "Mary Austin, Woman Alone." *The Virginia Quarterly Review* XIII, No. 2 (Spring 1937): 243-56.

> Discusses the relationship of Austin's life to her work, her ideas about folk culture, and her involvement in American and Indian affairs. In examining the development and complexity of her views, Wynn finds some inconsistencies as well as paradoxes, but concludes that Austin "is valuable not for giving us a system but for making us more aware, for extending the range of our consciousness of our environment and our social possibilities."

Chaim Nachman Bialik

1873-1934

(Also transliterated as Hayim and Hayyim; also Nahman and Nahhman; also Byàlik) Ukrainian poet, short story writer, essayist, autobiographer, and lecturer.

Regarded as the most important Hebrew poet of the twentieth century, Bialik contributed greatly to the twentieth-century renaissance of Hebrew literature and modernization of the Hebrew language. His verses reflect the personal sufferings of his childhood as well as the sufferings of the Diaspora—the Jewish people in exile from their ancient homeland. Through works such as "The City of Slaughter" and "The Scroll of Fire," he called upon Jews to assert their national independence and to take pride in the traditions of their culture, and these concerns have led to his adoption as "the national poet of Israel." According to critic Israel Efros, Bialik "stirred Jewish life to its utmost and gave modern Hebrew literature a new and vigorous impulse and a place in contemporary world literature."

Born in a village in the Volhynia district of the Ukraine, Bialik was five years old when his family moved to Zhitomir where his father, a pious Talmudic scholar, supported his family by working as an innkeeper. Two years later, Bialik's father died unexpectedly, and Bialik was sent to live with his grandparents in order to ease the financial strain on his widowed mother. He was given rigorous instruction in Jewish law and tradition in his grandfather's orthodox household and, at sixteen, was enrolled in a prestigious Talmudic academy in Belorussia. He excelled equally in religious and secular studies there and, while still a student, composed his popular poem "To the Bird." In 1891 he left the academy and traveled to Odessa, the center of Eastern European Jewish culture. In Odessa Bialik was befriended by several prominent scholars, including Ahad Ha'am, a leading Zionist philosopher whose writings he greatly admired, and J. H. Ravnitzky, who later became Bialik's patron and business partner. Ha'am influenced and encouraged Bialik and effectively launched his literary career by publishing several of his verses in *Ha-Shiloach*, an influential Hebrew-language journal. When Bialik received news that his grandfather was dying, he returned home. He married in 1893 and worked for his father-in-law in the timber trade for several years before returning to Odessa where his friends had secured a teaching position for him. At about this time, due in part to the patronage of Ha'am, Ravnitzky, and others, Bialik's poetry began to receive international renown. On a visit to Palestine in 1909, for example, he was greeted everywhere as a national spokesman and hero. In Odessa he worked as a co-editor of *Ha-Shiloach* and established a publishing firm which prospered until it was closed by the Bolsheviks. In 1921 he left the Ukraine to join other Hebrew writers in Germany and eventually settled in Palestine in 1924. He died in Vienna after undergoing a medical operation in 1934.

Rooted in his orthodox religious training, Bialik's early works were largely inspired by Biblical and Talmudic writings. His extensive knowledge of Judaic tradition and literature enabled him to create verses based on ancient forms and themes while thoroughly transforming the academic Hebrew language in which he wrote. Agreeing with many scholars of the era, William A.

Drake wrote in 1928 that Bialik had "conclusively proven the supreme flexibility of Biblical Hebrew beneath the hand of an artist." Closely linked to his use of the Hebrew language is his choice of Zionist subjects and themes. Writing for the Diaspora, Bialik exhorted his audience to recognize its duty to defend itself against antisemitism, to resist cultural assimilation, and to reclaim its ancient homeland. In "The City of Slaughter" and other poems written after the 1903 Kishinev pogroms, Bialik denounced the cowardice of acquiescent Jews who had failed to defend themselves or their property. The visionary, though sometimes chastening nature of his nationalist poetry has led some admirers to proclaim him a prophet, while most observers have noted that at the very least he should be credited with rousing and inspiring the Jews of the Diaspora. Many appreciative critics, including Drake, Efros, and Israel Goldstein, have praised Bialik's patriotic verses. According to Goldstein, Jews everywhere are indebted to Bialik "who has given [them] a tongue to speak with, a national song to cherish and a national hope by which to live."

Several observers have suggested that very personal preoccupations lie beneath the nationalistic sentiment of Bialik's verses, and they have linked the sorrow associated with his childhood to the subsequent topics and themes of his poetry. These critics see the premature loss of his father and separation from his mother as an important emotional source of Bialik's poetry. In many of his verses he examined the pain of separation or exile, and in a number of his later works he brooded on death. Bialik's childhood environment offered him an escape from unhappiness, and his love of nature inspired his mature verses as well. Efros has called his nature poetry "radiant songs of nature, . . . novel in their joyousness and abandon." Other works are drawn on well-known Hebrew legends, such as "The Scroll of Fire," Bialik's allegorical epic, which is set at the time of the destruction of the first temple of Jerusalem.

Bialik's examination of universal issues and their implications in the lives of individuals has gained him international praise, and he has been enthusiastically proclaimed as the counterpart in Hebrew literature of such authors as Shakespeare and Goethe. His continuing appeal for the Jewish people has been concisely explained by critic David Aberbach, who has suggested that Bialik, "in life-long mourning for his childhood, . . . spoke meaningfully to a people in perpetual mourning for its lost nationhood." Bialik's unique expression of Jewish culture has led to his stature as the greatest Hebrew poet of this century, a judgment forcefully expressed by Amos Elon, who states that "none before Bialik nor after has expressed the Jewish will to live in words and rhymes of such beauty and poetic force; he is rightly known today as the national poet of Israel."

*PRINCIPAL WORKS

Poems from the Hebrew   (poetry)   1924
Law and Legend or Halakah and Aggada   (essay)   1925
Selected Poems   (poetry)   1926
And It Came to Pass   (legends and short stories)   1938
Aftergrowth, and Other Stories   (autobiography and short stories)   1939
Far over the Sea   (poetry)   1939
Knight of Onions and Knight of Garlic   (legend)   1939
Complete Poetic Works   (poetry)   1948
The Hebrew Book   (essay)   1951
Bialik Speaks   (conversations)   1970

*This list includes only works translated into English.

B. IBRY (essay date 1907)

[*In the following excerpt, Ibry examines the nationalistic aspects of Bialik's poetry.*]

Like the Hebrew writers of the past generation, Byàlik derives his inspiration almost exclusively from Jewish sources. But the older writers were ever unable to separate the kernel from the shell. Conscious or unconscious assimilators, they took upon themselves—with exception of the purely Biblical Judaism respected by the Jewish and Christian world alike—to look upon the whole of post-Biblical Jewish history and tradition as one tragic mistake. Criticizing the old customs and observances with heedless raillery, they called on Jewish youth to rebel against the Ghetto existence, and to shake themselves free from the stifling pressure of the past. But the generation to which Byàlik belongs, notwithstanding their usual freedom of attitude with regard to religious matters, have an intense admiration for the traditions of Judaism enshrined in the Talmud and the Kabbalah. They acknowledge that, only behind the walls of a Ghetto could such measure of individualism as

is possible for a people surrounded by foes and deprived of their country, have been preserved through the centuries. They see, at the same time, that no racial antagonism, no anti-Semitism or Judaeophobia, no complicated ritual, no external barriers would have saved the Jewish race from extinction without their deep-rooted love for the Torah—their joy in life, and their strength in death. In Heine's *Prinzessin Sabbath,* it is only on Friday evenings that the enchanted Prince Israel recovers his human form for twenty-four hours. In Byàlik's eyes, the starved and cowering creature "mit hündischen Gedanken" is never anything but a king's son, whose soul no evil magic has power to transform until he let go of his talisman—the Torah. Byàlik loves not only the Biblical Judaism clung to by the semi-assimilated, but also the Talmudical Judaism which has enriched the world with many spiritual treasures: the limitless devotion to the Torah, the resolve to endure affliction because of hope in the Messianic ideal, the abandonment of the argument of physical force, purity of morals and perseverance in all things. This spirituality of the Jewish race, conceived and formulated by the prophets in the territorial period of Israel's history, has been preserved through 2,000 years of persecution and exile. To the group which includes the remarkable poems concerning the Beth Hammidrash and the Yeshibah of the Russian Ghetto, belongs also: **"If Thou Would'st Know the Source . . ."** . . . . (pp. 453-54)

Byàlik, however, taking Jewish history *en bloc,* is not blind to the shadows in the picture. The intense spirituality of the Ghetto turned the Jews away from nature, from the fresh air, from a healthy normal life and simple pleasures. Byàlik sees and deplores the suppression, by the intellectual part of their being, of its physical complement—a suppression dangerous to heart and mind alike. He acknowledges the saving necessity for them to show some energy in self-defence, he is alarmed at the absence of primitive wildness in the character of the race. Especially sad in his eyes is the premature development of the Jewish children. Their happy time ends almost with their babyhood. Heder-life usually begins for them when they are five to six years old, and it is a very hard and dreary one for that tender age. Therefore, and if we remember the poet's own unhappy boyhood, it is easy to understand why, in his contributions to Hebrew pedagogic literature, he continually reverts to the non-existence of childhood among the Jews. In one of his best poems: **"Take Me beneath Thy Wing"** . . . , he expresses his own longing after youth and love:—

> O come and take thou me
> Beneath thy wing, safe sheltered from all cares.
> Thy breast the refuge of my head shall be,
> The hiding-place of my rejected prayers.
>
> In twilight's hour of ruth,
> Bend down and hear the secret of my pain:
> They say that somewhere in the world is youth—
> Then where is mine? for I have sought in vain.
>
> Hear yet again, I pray.
> Consumèd is my soul with inward fire;
> And somewhere in the world is love, they say—
> What *is* this love, to which all hearts aspire?
>
> The stars my gaze deceived.
> I had a dream, and now my dream has fled.
> I come with empty hands, of all bereaved,
> The last joy vanished and the last hope dead.
>
> O come and take thou me
> Beneath thy wing, safe sheltered from all cares.
> Thy breast the refuge of my head shall be,
> The hiding-place of my rejected prayers.

There is a whole series of his poems dealing with Nature; the former Yeshibah student, the *Yeshive-Boher* of the Gass, is as sensitive as any other poet to her beauty and her melancholy, to the subtle influences of sunshine and cloud. . . . Poems on other subjects express . . . a gloom verging on despair. Byàlik is cut to the heart to see the Jewish middle class, careless of the high traditions of their race, given over to the pursuit of wealth, and bent on nothing better worth having than titles and decorations. What are these descendants of Jacob not ready to give for Esau's lentil pottage? For a smile from a non-Jew they will renounce their own and their children's part in the heritage of Israel. (pp. 454-57)

Questions of social economy have no attraction for Byàlik in themselves, although there are echoes of them in many of his verses. In contrast to most Jewish poets, such as M. Rosenfeld in Yiddish and "Yehallel" in Hebrew, Byàlik is less concerned with the plight of the Jews than with the plight of Judaism. The economic side of his people's life interests him only in so far as the soul of a nation depends on the bodies of its component units—. . . "Where there is no bread, there is no Torah," said the old Fathers. In the beautiful poem: **"The Hope of the Poor Destitute,"** we find a sick *melammed* lying among strangers and dreaming of his return home—and even here the spiritual element predominates.

The more complicated became the life of the Russian Jews, the more Byàlik's muse inclined to tragedy. Then came the Kishineff thunderclap—Byàlik hastened thither to collect information, and the result of what he heard and saw was the poem: **"On the Massacre"**. . . . This powerful, bitter, and horrible description of the pogròm puts every other attempt at the same thing into the shade. . . . The author gives a ghastly picture of the barbarity of the rioters, and flings terrible accusations at the Jews themselves; but the climax of horror is reached in a few lines in which the yells, threats and tumult of the mob give place to the silent, despairing apathy of the victims—the apathy of the man who lets his hands drop and is unable even to shriek aloud. It is certain aspects of this hopeless resignation, this pitiable acquiescence of the Jews in the inevitable for them and theirs, that move Byàlik to anger. Is this anger of his justified? Only to a certain extent. But he is no photographer or reporter, rather a prophet whose very love for his people causes him to burn with indignation at their weakness. And he was still in Kishineff when he shook off his gloom and wrote the joyous poem: **"To the Sun,"** with which he speeded the delegates on their way to the sixth Zionist Congress.

But soon there followed new misfortunes and disappointments: the crisis at the sixth congress, the death of Herzl, the substitution of Territorialism for the cherished historic ideal. Then came the Russo-Japanese war, the assassination of Plehve, and the rise of the Russian nation for freedom.

A new life opened for Russian Jewry—and the whole people went over to the revolution! (pp. 457-58)

And now that Byàlik sees the Jews infected with the general savagery of the "civilized" world, and taking to knives, revolvers, and bombs, he is sorry. He grieves because the new life is not distinctively Jewish. He is afraid that the national elements will be swept away in the torrent of the revolution. (p. 459)

Byàlik . . . is no fanatical Nationalist; nothing of the sort. He desires no wall of partition between the Jews and other races, only its disappearance is to be the result, not of assimilation, but of mutual respect and of possibility for the Jews to follow freely the bent of their national genius. And if he wishes for the downfall of the tents of Shem, it is only that he may see the former palace rise in their stead. (p. 460)

The **"Scroll of Fire"** is a long symbolic poem in eight parts. After a beautiful opening in the style of the Agadah, it tells how a number of captive Jewish youths and maidens are cast by the foe upon the opposite shores of a desert island. The youths start to wander across the glaring, waterless plain. Typical of the Jews of the Rabbinical period, they shut their eyes on a cruel world, and their soul shrinks back upon itself. But the sound of a mysterious march, like the quiet beating of a heart, inspires them to advance, and the one who forces himself to peer from under his heavy lids sees among them two tall youths, one dark and one fair, in whose hearts beat the hearts of all. But the two youths are equal in stature one to the other, and there is no telling which of them is the real leader of the throng. Of these two genii of the Jewish race, the dark one is sent to mock and to destroy, and, in his scorn and hatred of the old Western civilizations in which he had, and might have, no part, he threatens not only what is rotten and pestilential, but that also which is of enduring worth and beauty. His is the song of revenge:—

> From out the abyss of curses lift the song of strife,
> Black as your smould'ring hearts,
> And bear it to the God-rejected nations,
> And blast them with its flame!
> The song sows devastation o'er their plains
> And ruin to their fields of rustling corn.
> And when you wander, singing, through their gardens,
> And touch the lilies, they shall droop and die,
> And when you look upon their sculptured marbles,
> Behold, they fall and crumble into dust.
> And laughter, bitter laughter, cold and cruel,
> Your sword wherewith to slay . . .

The fair youth, whose mission is to console and to uplift, reminds the excited company of the song of love and peace, the song of the future, but no one listens to him. . . . All but he drink of the River [of] Peril and eat of the wild, bitter saltwort. Now the troop of maidens appear in their turn, heedless of danger, above the steep bank of the stream. With their tightly closed eyes, thorn-encircled brow and beatific smile, they are the Jewish women who, in blind faith and sacrificial patience, have borne their lot through the centuries. "Like a flight of white storks" they plunge into the abyss. The horrified youths throw themselves in to the rescue, and all perish together—all but the fair youth who remains the sole type of the past and present of his race. The vision of his beloved of early days—his passion for whom he has since been taught to regard as sin—rises from the water and would lure him back into the depth. But the pillars of heaven are shaken, God himself destroys his Temple, a single spark of the holy fire on the altar is saved by a pitiful angel, and lies, tended by the Dawn, on a rock in the same island. The youth approaches the rock. Now he is torn between the earthly and the heavenly, the height and the depth—and in his anguish of desire he grasps at both. Snatching the divine spark to his breast, he leaps into the abyss, but the depth cannot swallow the spark, and casts him out . . . and now he wanders tormented by a threefold fire: the flame from the Temple altar, the flame of Satan, and the flame of earthly love—and still, because of the divine spark within him, he looks and longs for the Dawn. (pp. 462-63)

Hebrew critics are loud in their praise of those poems in which Byàlik treats of Nature and of love. It should be borne in mind that the Hebrew love-songs preserved to us are comparatively rare. The Biblical Song of Songs was interpreted as an allegory, and in the Hebrew revival in mediaeval Spain and Italy love, though a very frequent subject of occasional verses, did not inspire a love-poetry. We must, however, except the youthful poems of Jehudah Halevy in the twelfth, and the satirical work of Immanuel of Rome in the sixteenth century. (p. 464)

The following fact goes far to explain the origin of Byàlik's works of the kind. "When Byàlik wrote his poems on love"—we inquired of the friend of his youth, to whom the poet had directed us, "Was he in love with any one himself?"—"No (was the reply), he married early, and remained faithful to his wife like all good Jews, but he began to write his love-poems when he first became acquainted with the poetry of Immanuel of Rome." Hence, in these poems, the absence of the sensual *tempérament* of the Latin races and of the longing for *das Ewig Weibliche* of the Germans. Their leading theme is a sigh for the loss incurred during the Exile of the power to enjoy oneself "like other people," a complaint that the poet himself never knew the sweet intoxication of a pure and youthful passion, with its power to enrich and beautify the whole of after-life. (p. 465)

The Hebrew critics and readers are not a whit less enthusiastic over Byàlik's descriptions of Nature, in which the theme is the same—a continual lament over the exclusion of Nature from the daily life of the Jewish masses. Here again the enthusiasm is partly due to the fact that Byàlik and his contemporaries have succeeded in proving: that Hebrew, with the help of the language of Rabbinical literature, is capable of expressing all the effects of light, sound, and colour.

But this, however important for readers of their verses in the original, cannot be expected to interest others to anything like the same extent. To the general reader, that part of Byàlik's work will seem the most original and significant which deals with national-historical and cultural subjects. His poems on life in the Beth Hammidrash and the Yeshibah and their poetic outlook on contemporary Jewish existence have been mentioned. But the poem which stands pre-eminent, even among his very best, is the **"Tale (or *Sage*) of the Pogròm,"** not owing to its depth of thought, but because of its unwonted passion of expression and of its overwhelming effect on the reader, who feels every line fall like a hammer on his brain. The subject of the **"Scroll of Fire"** is larger and deeper in scope, but the poem betrays that want of the feeling for proportion characteristic of Jewish artistic creations in contradistinction to those of the Greeks. Undesirable, too, are its occasional lapses from the Biblical style, not that Hebrew is to be denied the right to some development in the course of 2,000 years, but because the Biblical form is the one best suited to the subject-matter of the poem. However—*la critique est aisée, l'art est difficile.* . . . It is to be hoped that Byàlik's best poems will appear before long in English translations. English readers will then judge for themselves, whether or not there exists in Russian Jewry a poet such as the whole Jewish people may find it worth while to claim for their own. (pp. 465-66)

> *B. Ibry, "H. N. Byàlik and His Poems," translated by Helena Frank, in* The Jewish Quarterly Review, *Vol. XIX, No. 75, April, 1907, pp. 445-66.*

WILLIAM A. DRAKE   (essay date 1928)

[*Drake was an American author, editor, and journalist who served on the editorial staffs of* Vanity Fair, Art News, *and* New York Herald Tribune Books. *The author of many screenplays, Drake also adapted several European dramas for the American stage. In the following excerpt, he discusses Bialik's career in the context of Jewish culture in the early twentieth century.*]

It is at once Bialik's greatness and his limitation as a poet that his work cannot be considered separately from the social situation and aspirations of the Jewish people. His talent arose at the time of his people's greatest need, when the wave of anti-Semitism had reduced Jews to abjectness and the horrible succession of pogroms in Central Europe had left them cowed and hunted. Bialik's first poems were composed in the gloom of the Beth Hamedrash, and are filled with the desolation of sterile wisdom and the pang of an anxious and too eager spirit that has already surmised a surer means of serving God. Those bleak years, which have crushed many a stouter spirit than his—years which the Russian Jews call "Bezvremenye," because they are the obliteration of time—only made his apprehension of life the more eager and poignant. Thus, in **"The Talmudic Student," "Alone," "If You Would Know," "A Lone Star"** and similar early poems, his faltering spirit seeks the light; in such verses as **"On My Return,"** his growing pessimism spits out its bitterest spleen; in **"The Midnight Service,"** he remembers the traditions of his home; and in **"In the Cornfield,"** the beauty of the fields he had roamed in his boyhood. In **"Her Eyes"** composed when he was twenty, he has written as beautiful a love poem as any by Schnaiur; and later, in such verses as **"A Daughter of Israel," "Where Are You," "Summer Song"** and **"Tidings,"** he returns to the theme of love with an authentic, if limited, lyricism. Bialik's pseudo-folk songs, as a whole, and such poems as **"The Apple's Guilt,"** reveal in his work, as early as 1896, the influence of Heine. (pp. 281-82)

[Bialik's] true mission was to stir his people out of the lethargy of their despair and ignominy. The voice of the prophet gradually rises, through **"On Pisgah Height," "Surely the People Are Grass,"** the address to the delegates to the first Zionist Conference at Basel in 1897, and **"The Exile's Tear,"** to its first full utterance in **"The Dead of the Wilderness."** This remarkable poem is based upon the Talmudic legend that the rebellious Jews who left Egypt for Canaan did not perish in the desert, as the Bible states, but were cast into a deep slumber from which, from time to time, they awaken to struggle onward through eternity toward the goal which they are destined never to reach. Filled with the rebellious grandeur of Lucifer and the stubborn courage of the Maccabees, the example of these insurgent heroes, to Bialik, indicated by contrast the abyss of enslavement into which the Russian Jews had fallen.

"The Dead of the Wilderness" was written in 1902. In the next year occurred the massacre at Kishinev. Bialik emerged from the shock of that bestiality in his full stature as a prophet. In such flaming poems as **"On the Butchery"** and **"The City of Slaughter,"** he flays his people for their submission to such infamies, for their cowardice in not fighting back as their homes were pillaged and their daughters ravished, for their abjectness in praying through the carnage for forgiveness of the sins that had brought these misfortunes upon them, when their manhood required that they should die defending their honor. "How could such creatures sin?" he makes God exclaim, in scorn. The events of 1903 brought Bialik to his richest maturity and his greatest celebrity. The utterance of his poems, such as **"When I Am Dead," "And If the Angel Asks," "Logos," "God's Chastisement is This Curse," "The Curse of the Wilderness," "A Dirge," "At Sunrise,"** becomes thenceforth more sure and deep. He undertook prose, and his fantasies possess the same purity and beauty as his poems. Then he ceased writing, and in all the years since, there has been no new volume to swell the slight, though remarkably rich, corpus of Bialik's work. The patriotic task of organizing the movement to rehabilitate and repopulate the Holy Land as a homeland for the Jews of the world has claimed a poet who, as it would seem, might easily have become great in a world sense.

It is as yet too early to determine Bialik's place in literature. It is certain, at all events, that he is a poet of the stature of Jehudah Halevi and Ibn Gabirol; and he is still, as creative artists go, in his prime. His choice of the Hebrew language as a medium limits his audience severely, but he uses that language in its full purity and with a verbal virtuosity which constantly recalls the poignant eloquence of the Biblical psalmists. In his poems, Bialik has conclusively proven the supreme flexibility of Biblical Hebrew beneath the hand of an artist. A prophetic poet, nationalistic without bigotry, pious without austerity, and alert to every actual flavor of life, Chaim Nachman Bialik has missed unquestionable greatness only by his impetuosity in relinquishing his art before having achieved fullness, or even roundness, of his presumable utterance. Unless all the signs lie, he had only touched his true richness when he turned to another creative endeavor, to him more exigent and consequential. But there is still time, should he at length return to poetry. (pp. 282-84)

> *William A. Drake, "Chaim Nachman Bialik," in his* Contemporary European Writers, *The John Day Company, 1928, pp. 279-84.*

ISRAEL GOLDSTEIN   (lecture date 1938)

[*An educator, critic, and prominent American rabbi, Goldstein wrote several works chronicling the history of Judaism in America. In the following excerpt from an address delivered at the Bialik Memorial Meeting, New York City, 20 July 1938, Goldstein praises Bialik as a particularly Jewish genius and recognizes in his work a challenge for American Jews.*]

Chaim Nachman Bialik was truly the poet laureate of the Jewish people.

He has made it possible for us to say that Hebrew is not a dead language but a living tongue. He has taken the language of the Prophets and the Psalmists, of the sages and the scholars, and has so molded it and fashioned it and wrought it that it has become an instrument, both delicate and versatile, capable of expressing the finest shades of thought and feeling, the most delicate nuances of light, sound and color. He has taken the old forms of speech and breathed into them new life and meaning. (p. 197)

The Hebrew tongue is the "Lashon Kodesh," the holy tongue. Its content, its constituent elements, may change, but the vessel, the language as such has always been revered.

Bialik has poured new wine into the old vessels of the Hebrew speech, a new life-stream into the old arteries. He has taken the sacred heritage of an ancient tongue and made it live. It has become in our time the modern counterpart of Ezekiel's vision of the "dry bones." For that miracle of rejuvenation we lift the voice of gratitude to Chaim Nachman Bialik. He is the great master of the Hebrew tongue whose lips have been touched by the burning coals from the sacred altar.

Bialik has done more. He has made it possible for us to say not only that we have a living national speech, but that we have a contemporary national poetry which compares with the great poetry of our time. He has expressed the soul of his people as only one or two others have done in a thousand years of Jewish history.

We Jews have been all too long content to shine in reflected glory, to feel second-hand pride. When Heine sang the sweet lyrics of Germany, we boasted; when Antokolsky carved the marble masterpieces of Russian theme, we gloried; when Israels painted lovely Dutch pictures, we prided ourselves. Is it always to be the glory of the Jew that he should bring his talent and offering to the altars of all the nations except his own and pour the libations of his genius into every shrine except his own? Isaiah's rebuke is not obsolete, "In the children of strangers do they take abundant delight."

Bialik did not go to alien shrines. He made the offering of his genius at the altar of the Jewish people in whose lap he was reared, from whose breasts he was nourished. Therefore we hail Bialik as Israel's national poet.

Perhaps the greatest service that Bialik has rendered his people has been that he has stirred the Jew to a sense of self-respect as did no other poet of his time. With prophetic fury he lashed the weakling and the coward. With burning indignation he excoriated the "mah yofisnik," the sycophant who would sell his heritage for a smile from the non-Jew. With bitter rebuke he chided the anemic passivity of those who accepted the hooligan's kick as if they were dogs, and bore the yoke of oppression as if they were cattle. Bialik has taught the Jew to stand up and battle for his life and for his rights. Bialik has taught the Jew to understand that his greatest tragedy is not his sad plight but his supine attitude toward it.

> My father—bitter exile, my mother—want,
> 'Tis not my staff or the shameful scrip I dread!
> More cruel than these, more bitter sevenfold
> Is life without hope or brightness for the eyes;
> The life of a hungry dog, bound by its rope
> How art thou cursed, thou life without a hope!
> Illumine, star, my soul that has despaired
> Through pagan worship and 'neath exile's weight.

Bialik has lifted the vision of the Jew to a star, the star of Zion which points the way of hope. In **"El Hazipor," "To the Bird,"** he has given winged expression to his yearning for the hills of Judaea, the Valley of the Sharon, and the dews of Hermon. It is a paradox, of which only genius is capable, that he, the product of the Yeshivah, the "Mathmid," should have been able to feel the call of the soil and to give his people a foretaste of the song of the soil, with which Jewish life in Palestine was to hum a generation later. (pp. 198-99)

We are indebted to Chaim Nachman Bialik, who has given us a tongue to speak with, a national song to cherish and a national hope by which to live.

We who have been born in America, or, if not born here, at least reared upon the lap of this new continent, we who have not ourselves lived through the "shehitah" and the "harega," the ordeals of pogrom, tragic experiences which have moved Bialik to utter his immortal threnodies, we who cannot identify from first-hand experiences the rich picturization of the Mathmid, the student, and of the old "Beth Hamidrash," where he studied, we too, of this American generation, are profoundly indebted to Chaim Nachman Bialik.

Can we repay the debt? No more than we can repay the sun for shining, or the dew for bringing refreshment to the earth. For us it is to prove that we deserve to call him our own. We

A photograph of Bialik published in 1912.

must give a sign that the flame of his soul has touched us. We must let him see that we are not as the withered grass, of which he sings in plaintive tones, when he says: "Verily the people is grass, it has become as dry as wood."

Let us give proof that American Israel, which used to be regarded as the withered branch of the Jewish tree, is not without vitality. Let us show that this branch can give forth blossoms and bear fruit. Let us give the sign that the star of Zion to which he turned our gaze has captured our hearts, that Eretz Israel is our "Eretz Hemdah," the land in which we delight because it is the cradle of renascent Hebrew speech, renascent Hebrew genius and renascent self-respect.

In the same words with which Bialik hailed Ahad Haam, his teacher, do we hail his memory, our teacher and our poet.

> Accept our blessing, o teacher, our blessing sincere,
> The blessing which years without end our hearts did
>   contain;
> Now in pure untarnished love we bear thee thanks
> For every seed of nobleness thou didst implant
> Which in our barren hearts did blossom into fruit.
> And if it should in our generation come to pass
> That the sacred spark will glow in Israel's soul,
> It will be because among all the sons of Exile
> In thy noble soul it first did flash.

In Bialik's great masterpiece, **"The Dead of the Wilderness,"** he makes those ancient speak a mighty word. "We are to be the last generation under bondage and the first to be free."

Would that it might become our fate to be that generation which shall be the last to bear the yoke and the first to see the light of redemption, when the land of our past shall become the land of our present and of our future. Then it will be time for the poet of that day to write a sequel to Bialik's doleful **"Evening Song."** It will be the "Song of the Morning," the song of the new awakening. (pp. 200-01)

> *Israel Goldstein, "Bialik—The Hebrew Poet Laureate," in his* Toward a Solution, *G. P. Putnam's Sons, 1940, pp. 197-201.*

MENACHEM RIBALOW (essay date 1959)

[*An editor, lecturer, and critic, Ribalow was a central figure in the Hebrew cultural movement in the United States in the first half of the twentieth century. For over thirty years he was the editor of* Hadoar, *the only Hebrew-language weekly published outside of Israel, and he was a prominent supporter of the Histadruth Ivrith, an organization promoting Hebrew culture in America. His literary criticism was influential in the United States and Israel and demonstrated his abiding love for and mastery of the Hebrew language. According to Harold U. Ribalow: "Bialik was Ribalow's literary idol and Ribalow never ceased reading, studying, analyzing his poetry and prose." In the following excerpt, Ribalow offers a general appraisal of Bialik's poetry and examines the significance of Jewish legend in Bialik's life and works.*]

Hayyim Nahman Bialik is without question the greatest name in modern Hebrew poetry, one of the greatest in the entire history of Jewish literature. One must go back to the prophets for a parallel to Bialik in the use of the Hebrew idiom. Since the close of the Biblical canon, no writer has ever used the Hebrew language with such perfection. (p. 25)

Hayyim Nahman Bialik was one of those creative personalities who are unique and everlasting in the annals of literary history. When such personalities appear, they set their sign and seal upon the life and spiritual creativeness of their generation. A great poet is more than the product of his age or the child of his environment. Great poets stand above their times. They cannot be fitted into a Procrustean bed of neatly formulated concepts that tend to delimit and diminish their world. On the contrary, in their case there is a distinct and palpable influence by the individual upon the group. It is the poet that affects his environment. He imparts new energy and new values to old concepts and accepted norms. He opens new vistas in the life of his people. As the old Hebrew saying has it, he renews the work of Creation.

Bialik was such a force. Through his poetic creations he brought about the Hebrew literary renascence of his period and the rejuvenation of the Hebrew language. And with his cry of revolt and protest he quickened the pulse of his people and moved them to historic action.

In addition to his poetic genius, Bialik was endowed with the divine spark of prophecy. He was a man of inspiration. More than that, he was a child of the *Shekhinah*—the Divine Spirit. As he once wrote in a letter to Professor Joseph Klausner, "At times it seems to me that I am the only begotten son of the Holy One, blessed be His name, the favorite child of His divine spirit." Inspiration is the heritage of any poet who sings of himself and to himself. But the divine spirit, the *Shekhinah*, is the soul of a people, revealed only to chosen ones and to prophets of God.

The ordinary poet sings about his own life, nature, man's tribulations or the mystery of existence. But the prophetic poet not only sings; he preaches and chastises, he lashes out against the people and its God. The artist-poet, singing his individual song, reflects upon the world and upon man who inhabits it, and he sings his song with poetic imagery. But the prophet-poet, even when he is alone, never concentrates only upon himself. His is a threefold visual front: himself, his people and his God. This threefold conflict takes place within his inner soul: between himself and his people, between both and their God. (pp. 28-9)

The legend plays a special role in the drama of Bialik's life and work. From his earliest days he was drawn, as though by magic bonds, after the inner charm that lies hidden in the legend.

In one of his first poems, **"To the Legend,"** upon which the freshness of youth rests like the morning dew upon garden blossoms, the Yeshivah student confesses to the pages of his Talmud tome:

> In you, my worn, moth-eaten Talmud-leaves,
> Dwell ancient legends, captivating tales;
> In you, my soul finds soothing from its woes,
> To you I come whenever grief assails.

In the secret shelter of these pages of the Talmud that preserve in their columns those charming and bewitching legends "the sorrow-laden soul" of the young poet "finds its repose from the tyrant's wrath." When he walks in darkness in the vale of gloom there rise up to confront him these faded pages from which sparkle those legends like precious stones, opening wide "the gates of heaven" and

> . . . into his anguished soul
> A new supernal light streams ceaselessly.

Since Bialik was the kind of man who kept faith with all the sights and events, with all the precious images and early experiences of his distant childhood and since he was a poet with excellent memory and with his roots in the past, all his life he spun this web whose first strands he discovered in the spring-time of his being. He kept faith with the legend and fulfilled the promise he had made to it. During the very years of his torrential poetic creativity, he was working diligently on the great undertaking of *Safer Ha-agadah (The Book of the Legend)*, destined to become a most popular work, a glorious memorial to the poet and to his loyal co-worker, Ravnitzky.

Together with this collaborator, who could throw himself into uninterrupted research because of his devotion to the subject, the poet entered the inner sanctum of the legend and there in its secret gardens he plucked its choicest blossoms and became intoxicated with their fragrance, a fragrance with which he scented all of modern Hebrew literature and Hebrew education.

Thus the great poet of the Hebrew literary renaissance became the great exegete of the ancient legend. The relics of our distant forefathers' creative imagination, scattered over the expanse of the wide "sea of the Talmud" and concealed like pearls in its depths were gathered together and strung on one rope, arranged chronologically and presented in a most palatable Hebrew.

In this work of bringing to life again the ancient legend and finding a place for it within the framework of the Hebrew

literature of our times, Bialik found final fulfillment for his creative talent and, at the same time, a specific for the sick soul of his generation that searched for the new while yet yearning for the old. He was most eager to discover the happy blend of past and present. He grasped the artistic preciseness and the ethical meaning, the Jewish *apercu* and the human wisdom of the legend and with poetic grace presented his readers with a rediscovered treasure. To the flavor of the Biblical Hebrew which Jews savored from the days of childhood and the time of the literature of the Haskalah, a new flavor was added. (pp. 58-9)

Bialik was accepted as the people's poet with the speed of lightning, the kind of immediate acceptance won by few. However, in this blessing, to which so few attain, there lies also something perilous.

The peril lies in "the first impression." It is the strongest one and remains unchanging, preventing the readers, even the most faithful of them, from budging one whit from their first reaction to the poet so as to see him in a different light, in a new revelation. When the first edition of Bialik's collected poetry appeared in 1923 in honor of his fiftieth birthday (including also the rest of his works, short stories, essays and translations, all in four volumes), his stature had already been fixed in the imagination of the reader of Hebrew. But as a result, Bialik's own *terminus ad quem* was, as it were, also fixed. What he had created until that time was popularly known and accepted; while what he was to create henceforward would not be as widespread nor as greatly appreciated as it deserved. It was as though both reader and critic had agreed: What the poet has given us until now is more than enough—for what can be added to the unique and overwhelming gift he has given us? (p. 60)

However, now it is indeed known that more could have been added and, in truth, more was added, of basic and lasting value, to Bialik's poetry—even something new to his autobiographical poems (such as the poems of his "orphaned years"): **"Avi"** (**"My Father"**), **"Shivah"** (**"The Seven Days of Mourning"**), **"Almenut"** (**"Widowhood"**), **"Pridah"** (**"Separation"**), as well as other poems, and the writing of the legends collected in his book, *Vayehi Hayom (And It Came To Pass)*.

The new elements in this book of legends are the lucidity and the penetration, the breadth of knowledge and the very joy of telling a story, of describing a scene, the good humor and the keen observation and, most important of all, the author's emergence upon the broad square of popular imaginative writing while climbing the heights of universalism, especially in **"Aga-dat Sheloshah Ve'arba'ah"** (**"The Legend of the Three and the Four"**).

It would seem that in these legends Bialik freed himself from the spiritual tension that had gripped him all through his years, years heavy with creative toil and weighty with the great national burden. In the legends he entered a world translucent and pure, a world for which his soul had ever yearned. (p. 61)

Into this arena Bialik stepped armed with all the necessary weapons, a great literary style, a mastery of Biblical Hebrew and a spiritual and aesthetic maturity. When one reads his book, *And It Came To Pass* and, especially **"The Legend of the Three and the Four,"** **"The Stalled Ox and the Dish of Herbs"** and even the rhymed humorous story of **"Duke Onion and Duke Garlic,"** one marvels at the rare linguistic ability and the artistic and imaginative power of this contemporary poet who could so successfully penetrate to the very core of the Biblical idiom, to the manner of speech of ancient man and the way of thinking of the sage of the remote past.

Other authors who preceded him in the use of Biblical style, from Abraham Mapu to David Frischman, moved along a simple and straight path. Having grasped the general spirit of the Biblical story, they poured the hot metal of their own literary expression into the molds of phrases and sentences exactly as found in the Bible. The authors of the *Haskalah* period were enslaved to the complete literary structure of Biblical style. It was as though they were caught in self-imposed chains so that they could make no progress. (pp. 61-2)

But Bialik, original creator that he was, was concerned about the essence and substance of things. Therefore, he could not be satisfied with a literary imitation, even though it be an imitation of great beauty. Nor was it enough for him merely to tell a story charmingly, for the sole purpose of creating delightful reading.

In the legend he sought an additional means, a new medium, for giving expression to his creative talents that had reached their climax in his long-perfected poetry and now looked for a new outlet along other paths and in new directions. (pp. 62-3)

In this new form of literary creation Bialik forsook the Biblical formalism characteristic of his predecessors and chose to go his own way, the royal road of the poet. He absorbed the fragrance and the spirit of the style of the Bible but he did not become enslaved to its crystallized and congealed form of expression. There are in many of his legends and especially in **"The Legend of the Three and the Four"** expressions and descriptions reminiscent of his poems, particularly, **"The Scroll of Fire."** Here Bialik was not an imitator but an original creator. He poured the melody of his own style—and style is the soul—into the Biblical style. The manner of speech of the characters of his legends, the portrayal of their virtues and vices, the descriptions of nature, the methods of development of events are all given not skimpily but with largesse through all the blessed means granted to a twentieth-century poet-story-teller, even though he may treat of events and personalities of a much earlier era.

It was because of his great poetic ability and linguistic preeminence that he could completely free himself of Biblical formulas and break the fetters of the Biblical verses that had bound the hands of his predecessors. When one delves into his book, ***And It Came To Pass,*** he is aware of the gentle and peaceful atmosphere of the Bible, yet without being disturbed by the slightest trace of fragments of Biblical verses or expressions taken whole from the Biblical text and placed in the mouths of characters according to the whim and by the dictate of the author, standing behind them and compelling them so to speak.

The figures who live in these stories are living personalities, true to their times, their spirit and their proper character—no artificiality here. The poet-narrator, who walks along with them, recording their words, describing their deeds, tracing their movements and setting down their experiences in a book, is their comrade and cherished friend. He feels altogether like a habitué of that ancient but close world which is legendary and real at the same time.

Since the chief characters in these legends are kings and poets, renowned for both their wisdom and their poetry, the eminent poet of our era has an excellent opportunity to prompt the utterances of ancient sages and to cause the readers to savor something of the greatness of spirit and depth of understanding

of two folk-heroes who accompany every Jew along the path of life and upon the byways of his imagination.

King Solomon, the principal subject and chief character of **"The Legend of the Three and the Four,"** appears in his classical impressive figure—"Divine wisdom lights up his countenance; his mouth utters words of understanding." When he speaks, it is with profound wisdom "of the ways of God and His dominion over the earth and of all the wonders of His doings." When the spirit rests upon him, he delivers a prophetic utterance even about "the stars of the heavens and their constellations, all the hosts on high that make their appearance by the command of God."

Only a wise poet could have written about a wise king as Bialik writes about Solomon. He does not disclose the king's words of wisdom until he first reveals his deeds of wisdom. Bialik can control the story-teller's spirit within himself and postpone things that beg to be written down until the propitious time come. (pp. 64-5)

In the beginning comes the deed. At first there is the experience. Only afterwards come words of wisdom and understanding. That is a basic Hebrew concept and that is the way of the Hebrew king. And that too is the method of narration of this Hebrew poet and story-teller.

Bialik wrote two versions of **"The Legend of the Three and the Four,"** one version concise and simple, the other more elaborate and profound.

In the first version he limited himself to the telling of the familiar Hebrew legend of Solomon and his daughter based upon the words of *Agur ben Yakeh* in the Book of Proverbs (30:18-19).

> There are three things which are too wonderful for me,
> Yea, four which I know not:
> The way of an eagle in the air;
> The way of a serpent upon a rock;
> The way of a ship in the midst of the sea;
> And the way of a man with a young woman.

In brief, the story is this.

King Solomon has a beautiful daughter whom he loves more than self. But she worries him because of her strangeness and her desire to be alone. She is a dreamer; her eyes have a faraway stare. She wanders alone through the lanes of the vineyards. Princes come to woo her but she gives their words no heed. Her anxious father ascends to the palace roof to read the stars to see "who will be the prince destined by God for his daughter and when will he come. He examines the heavenly portents and behold, neither a king nor the son of a king has been fated by God for his daughter, but instead an indigent youth from among the poor of the people, such a one will come at the appointed time to wed her."

The king is sorely grieved at what he has seen in the stars "and he seeks a stratagem for the upsetting of heaven's plan." He decides to conceal the maiden until the heavenly decree will no longer be effective. He finds a solitary island in the midst of the sea upon which he builds a high tower, surrounded by a fortified wall. In this tower cut off from the world, he places his beloved daughter together with seventy eunuchs from among the Jewish elders to guard and serve her. He stores great amounts of provisions, all kinds of food and drink, every luxury—nothing is lacking. He then shuts up all the gates of the tower with iron bars and locks, making impossible any exit or entry, and says to himself, "Now I shall see what God can do, whether the prediction of the stars shall come true or not."

The stellar prophecy does come true.

> An impoverished youth, the son of good people and of a family of scribes sets out from his native city, Acre, for his soul longs for distant places.

Thus he goes to and fro in the land, wandering through cities and villages, until one day nightfall finds him in a foresaken and desolate place. Hungry and thirsty, he lies down to sleep inside an ox's skeleton in the field. While he sleeps, a great and mighty eagle swoops down upon the skeleton and snatches it up, together with its contents, the indigent and famished lad from Acre.

The eagle carries its burden to the roof of the tower where Solomon's daughter dwells and there leaves it. Thus meet the two whom God has meant for each other and they plight their eternal troth.

> And the lad arises and pricks his hand and with his blood writes down the words of their troth in a document, inscribed and sealed, and weds her according to law, saying, "The Lord be our witness and his angels, Michael and Gabriel."

When the time forecast by the stars has passed, Solomon comes to the tower and discovers the pair together. When he hears of the incredible but true occurrences, he understands that this indeed must be the poor youth revealed to him in the stars. Solomon admits, "Now I know that there is no wisdom, no intelligence, no design that can stand against the Lord."

This, in brief, is the legend in one version. But with this version the poet was not satisfied.

First of all, there is no development of all the four "ways," alluded to in the words of Proverbs. This version exploits only "the way of an eagle in the air" and "the way of a man with a young woman," but there is no reference to "the way of a serpent upon a rock" and "the way of a ship in the midst of the sea."

Secondly, even the "ways" that are found in this version, the way of the eagle and the way of the young man, are used in brief and simple fashion. The bounds of utter simplicity are never exceeded; no symbolism arises from the tale. It is a folk legend, based on two Biblical verses, told briefly and unaffectedly to prove a point and no more. If this be so, what does the poet succeed in accomplishing, coming, after a long period of about three thousand years and telling the same legend anew?

Bialik, therefore, could not rest content until he rewrote the legend, incorporating the emendations and improvements he sought, resulting in the second version of the tale. In his letter of April 2, 1933 to Doctor Jacob Nacht, he writes, "When I first wrote **"The Legend of the Three and the Four,"** I relied principally upon the abbreviated form of the legend as found in the introduction to Buber's edition of *Midrash Tanhuma* (Vilna, 1885, p. 136), and upon my supposition that this legend had been given birth to by the verses in Proverbs, 'There are three things which are too wonderful for me, etc.' This conjecture was fortified later when, by chance, I heard some additional details of the story from my wife. According to her version, which she as a child had heard from an old woman, a snake also played a part in that same legend. *Upon this basis*

I rewove the legend, giving it artistic completeness, so that it became an entire novella, full of action. I am not aware of any other sources for this legend."

The force of this second version and its innovation lie in the fact that the author here foresakes the narrow path of the folk legend, with its simplicity and naturalness, and sets forth upon the broad highway of epic creation, based upon the legend, but not enslaved to it, for it rises above it.

True, the story's rhythm and outward form are in the spirit of the Bible, without departing from its style, without doing the slightest violence to its simplicity, its clarity or its integrity—even the opening words of the story are the classical words, "And it came to pass." But into this framework, extended by Bialik, the poet poured a richness of imagination, a talent for description, a felicity of conception and a beauty of language whose compare is difficult to find.

The entire structure of the story is amazing both for its beauty and its completeness. Each chapter, and there are nineteen, has its own purpose, its own central idea, its own unity. Most of these chapters, if not all, can stand on their own feet; they are themselves stories or descriptions which, because of their content, form and abundance of charm shine forth with light of their own, glittering like emeralds.

The first line of each chapter foreshadows its entire contents. Each new chapter is joined to the previous one, developing the

An example of Bialik's handwriting from a manuscript.

plot farther, ascending the scale higher and higher until the climax is reached and the vision seen by the poet in his imagination is fulfilled.

From the first sentence of the first chapter, ''And it came to pass that the King, Solomon, made a great feast in his palace,'' until the two last chapters, wherein is described the second feast, the wedding feast of Natanyah and Ketsiah, there is unrolled the life's scroll of the young lovers in the lengthy and predestined fashion of two souls yearning for each other and despite many obstacles, finally reaching each other. The opening sentences of each chapter, that may be joined together to tell the story in brief, are the early notes of a symphony of wisdom and beauty directed by a wise poet singing the praises of a wise king. This story is a chef d'oeuvre of Hebrew creativity for in it are united the wisdom of past and present, while Judaism and humanity are fused together into one poetic harmony.

The greatest innovation in this second version of the legend is that the heroine, the instrumentality for the testing of man's fate and love's might, is no longer Solomon's daughter, but Ketsiah, the only daughter of the King of Aram. It was not without purpose that Bialik enlarged the *mise en scène* and made this aspect of the legend a subject for a universalistic story.

In the first version, built entirely upon the foundation of a folk legend, the Jewish king defies the stars and challenges fate, through his own daughter. Thus the theme remains a parochial one, a Jewish one. But just as Bialik was not content with the entire elementary structure of the first version, so too was he not satisfied with the setting placed between the national boundaries of the Kingdom of Judah. He, therefore, lifted the story's great challenge beyond these bounds, into the domain of the wide world itself.

For it was the poet's great aspiration to make of the legend's theme a broad humanitarian and universal one. It was not only the stars of fate that the Jewish king was testing but also the kings of the East and West in order to discern whether there yet lived in man's heart the great prophetic vision of the unity of mankind and the brotherhood of nations, the vision without which there could be neither order nor peace in the world.

It is for that reason that the prisoner in her symbolic tower is not a Jewish maiden but an Aramean. It is a Hebrew youth, Natanyah, son of Malkishua, whom the author brings to her in her tower of dreams and joins them together in a covenant of everlasting love. The fact of these two being united in love becomes all the more significant by the author's making of Malkishua and the King of Aram relatives by marriage in the end. For this very Malkishua, when he was young, strong and thirsty for adventure, had enlisted with the forces of Joab to wage war against Aram. In the hot and fierce battle that ensued, Malkishua shot an arrow straight to the heart of the brother of the King of Aram, the father of Ketsiah, and killed him. From that time on the King of Aram had carried in his heart a consuming hatred against Malkishua. Now fate appoints this same man to be his relative by marriage. And his only beloved daughter, who has borne her burden of loneliness and anxiety on the island tower, it is she whom fate gives as wife to Natanyah, the son of his enemy.

It is this novel though seemingly minor detail that contains the spark of dramatic action and that set Bialik's heart on fire. This he makes the paramount point at the feast and the chief burden of Solomon's lofty message on the brotherhood of na-

tions and the love of man for his fellow. For the seed of this universal love, according to both the king and the poet, is the love between man and woman, which is the builder of life upon earth. (pp. 66-70)

Love, in Bialik's poetry, was always something more than the love of man and woman, more than physical, sensual pleasure. In **''The Scroll of Fire''** and in all his love poetry, woman possesses a unique kind of beauty, distant and ethereal, spiritual and heavenly, for which the soul yearns more than the flesh. The figure of the beloved is that of the hind of the dawn. She is not alone the only one of his life, but she is also ''the divine dwelling-place of his desires.'' She is ''his heart's angel'' who appears to him upon the peaks of cliffs beneath the wings of the dawn and the morning-star. She is ''in appearance as the daughter of God.'' Most important of all, she is his redeemer. The poet prays to her with great tenderness,

> ''While yet there may be redemption for me,
> Come redeem me and rule over my destiny.''

In **''The Legend of the Three and the Four''** Natanyah, the lover, also appears as a redeemer and in the manner of the prayer in **''The Scroll of Fire,''** he asks, ''Am I not the redeemer, even I? Is it not I whom God has appointed to bring deliverance to the maiden?''

Under this great pressure of sanctity and of redemption, love becomes in **''The Legend of the Three and the Four''** a mighty force, not only in the life of the individual, but also of all creation, a force that brooks no resistance. It smashes its way across the expanses of roaring seas. It is victorious over waste places, distant isles and prison walls. ''For all of these together cannot stand before the might of love and the trumpet-blast of its power when, in its seemly but terrifying manner, full of God-given prowess, it storms its way to its gladsome goal and when, in spite of all obstacles, it carves out its mysterious path to its destination.''

And if the walls of the lofty tower could not withstand the Jewish lad in his undaunted climb to the Aramean maiden, Solomon asks the King of Aram still nursing his wrath against Malkishua, the Jew, ''How can you possibly think that the anger stemming from your picayunish heart will keep them apart? Is not the hind of Aram proper for the stag of Israel?''

Thus love fulfills a double mission. Not only does it unite two innocent spirits who yearn for each other, but it also spans the breach between two peoples, separated from each other through hate, the causeless hate dividing man from man, nation from nation. But ''when love's voice rings clear,'' say the two, the king and the poet, ''hate becomes utterly dumb.'' Love bears a healing salve for the wounded soul of the individual; it offers too a cure for the sick soul of the world. It ''joins together persons far apart by ways past understanding'' and ''unites the separated by means of a mysterious wisdom.'' All this is in order to ''blend together one blood with another, one fountain of life with another so as to make fruitful God's many fields and bring forth good produce upon the earth.'' This love comes from God for it quiets the hot blood of the man that longs for a woman's love and it redeems the blood spilled by fratricide. For it is not ''the redemption of the blood,'' tribal revenge, indulged in by oriental peoples and of which the King of Aram dreams, that is true redemption. For, the Jewish sage remarks, ''God will not place the means for redemption in the hands of Satan but in the good hands of his angels, in the hands of love. True, 'blood for blood and life for a life.' But not by the spilling of blood and by the cutting off of life does God redeem but by the creating of new life and by its multiplication upon earth, a newer and better life than the earlier.''

Thus does the King of Judah speak to the King of Aram and with these words comforting him by showing that the redemption of his slain brother's blood, of which he has long dreamed, has actually come to pass. For that spilled blood has now found a peaceful redemption through the covenant of love between his daughter, Ketsiah, and Natanyah, son of Malkishua. Through this means is his brother's soul redeemed from the hate that has poisoned it for many years and instead of shedding additional blood to that already shed in war, there will come forth new blood, the blood of a new and rejoicing life which love will give to two families in Judah and Aram. (pp. 71-3)

Thus the circle of humanity comes a full turn to the beginnings of Jewish history, to Abraham, Isaac and Jacob, who went back and forth between Canaan and Aram, and, too, to Sarah, Rebecca, Rachel and Leah, all the daughters of Aram. From this Canaanite-Aramean union came the Jewish people. Thus too was it with Israel and Moab, for from the union of Boaz, the Hebrew, and Ruth, the Moabitess, came the house of David.

And Solomon, the son of David, who, with his guests goes up to worship in the House of the Lord, offers seventy bullocks upon the altar according to the number of peoples upon the earth and on their behalf.

Such is the historic instruction, humanitarian and universal, that King Solomon offers to the guests at his banquet. To the reader it seems that not only are the Kings of the East and the West present at that banquet table but he is there as well. And the instructor is fitting for the instruction. For who can compare to King Solomon as a citizen of the world in the full meaning of that concept? Does not his very name, *Shlomo* (in the Hebrew) and the name of his beloved, *Shulamit,* point to the Jewish aspiration for the perfection (*shlemut* in the Hebrew) of humanity and the peace (*shalom* in the Hebrew) of the peoples of the world?

It was to give a new poetic expression to this ancient lofty idea that Bialik wrote **"The Legend of the Three and the Four."** And he chose Solomon, the king-poet, the great citizen of the world, to be the director of this wonderful orchestra that blends together stirring music and profound wisdom into one perfect harmony. (p. 74)

> *Menachem Ribalow, ''Hayyim Nahman Bialik, Poet Laureate of the Jewish People,'' and ''Bialik, Teller of Legends,'' in his* The Flowering of Modern Hebrew Literature: A Volume of Literary Evaluation, *edited and translated by Judah Nadich, Twayne Publishers, 1959, pp. 25-57, 58-87.*

ISRAEL EFROS (essay date 1965)

[*A Polish-born poet, lexicographer, and critic, Efros is best remembered for his numerous studies of Jewish theology and literature, including several works on Bialik. In the following excerpt, he examines the preoccupations of three distinct periods in Bialik's career.*]

Bialik penetrated into all the arcana of the Hebrew language. He made himself master of the grand style of the Bible with its antiphonal parallelisms and resonant echoes and re-echoes, as well as of the charm of the concrete, concise, but succulent language of the Mishna; of the dialectical style of the Talmud as well as of the music of the medieval Spanish-Hebrew poets.

He mastered all these styles, and he has majestically grand in his greater poems, prosaically charming in his short stories, dialectically clever in his essays, and entrancingly musical in his lighter verse. The Hebrew language seems to have been the congenital instrument of his genius. His tones sometimes cried, chastised and thundered, and sometimes they sounded plastically playful, whimsically Heinesque; but they were always endowed with warmth, luster and classicality. Bialik's language, like iron in a flame, always glowed in the fire of his genius.

During the first period in his poetic career, Bialik was almost entirely occupied with national themes. He bewailed the plight of his people in dark Czardom. He questioned the storm and searched the clouds: When will the darkness pass and the whirlwind die? When will the clouds scatter and light shine forth again? But there was no sight nor sound, only storm and night. He saw his people as if doomed from its very birth to wander, to have to buy air and steal light, to carry from door to door a beggar's pack, to crook its knees for bread; "I am weary with wandering; God my God, when will the road end?" But no end in sight, and no hope. "My father is bitter exile, my mother—black poverty. No! I fear not my staff, nor the heavy pack. Far more cruel and bitter than these is life without hope, without light—the life of a hungry, chain-tied dog. Oh, curse on you, hopeless life!'' And the inner pain, the burning shame of standing in the midst of a cornfield with the feeling that you have no right to enjoy it because it is not yours, because it is not your hands and your sweat that have brought forth this golden blessing!—And the worst of it all is the loss of confidence in the existence of some reason and purpose, which had turned all our former suffering into a sanctification of God's name and had enabled our ancestors to march to martyrdom with the hymn "It is upon us to praise" on their lips. Where is that reassuring sense of ultimate meaningfulness and purposefulness, that martyr's exultation, without which our cry is only animal pain?

Thus the poet sat on ruin and desolation and sang jeremiads to his people. The word most frequently used in that period is "tear." He addresses his tear tenderly, lovingly, and with a touch of self-pity which is perhaps characteristic of the ghetto-orphan. Childhood is so much behind all artistic expression. Out of its earliest complex of wonders and emotions, it distills some drops into the inner cup of the poet, and these are what the poet drinks during all his life. Bialik's orphaned childhood, which saw poverty, bitterness and suffering, gave him drops of tears which often mingled freely with the tears of his people. (pp. xx-xxii)

But even during that period, Bialik had his comforts. The pages of the Talmud with their dreamy legends lured him away from thoughts of the present. The reaction of that period to the centrifugal forces of Enlightenment that had looked askance at the old houses of learning as citadels of obscurantism, found its warmest and most eloquent articulation in Bialik's poetry. "Thou wilt not totter, tent of Shem. I shall yet cause thy rebuilding. From heaps of dust I'll revive thy walls. Thou wilt survive all the stately mansions, even as on the day of the great destruction, when towers fell.''

One long poem called **"The Talmud-Student,"** the outstanding poem of this period, glorifies those heroic lads who flocked to the house of learning, where for days and nights they swayed forward and backward over the tomes of the Talmud, singing *"Oi, oi, amar Raba, oi Tanu Rabbanan."* Springs and summers, forests and lakes, failed to lure them from their gray corners. "What art thou rock" Bialik exclaimed, "and what art thou flint, compared with a Hebrew lad studying the Torah?" He had great pity for these young ascetic lives, but he also sensed that those houses of learning have been the historic power-centers of his people.

Zion, too, dotted with just a few colonies of young students from Russia, awakened in Bialik a cheerful strain. To those early colonists he dedicated a poem **"The Blessing of a People,"** which became a rousing anthem. And in **"A Little Letter,"** he says to these struggling brothers in Zion: "Fields of corn, ancestral possession, broad spaces, freedom! Who is as blessed as you? And I here freeze in the cold, wander like a dog in a confused land. No hope here, my brother. No hope for a dove in the claws of a hawk. My eyes are lifted to the East. I know not as yet the meaning of my dreams, but my soul is like a bird scenting its freedom. It is the goal of my spirit, the hope of my hopes, my moon and my sun pouring light into me." Nevertheless when Herzl's clarion call was not sufficiently heeded, how like a prophet he thundered! "Surely the people are grass. They will not stir unless awakened by the whip. They will not rise unless raised by violence. A withering leaf of a tree, moss growing on stones, an emptied vine, a decayed plant—can the dead revive? Even when the clarion calls and the banner is hoisted, will the dead awake? Will the dead stir?"

The chastising tone of this poem is the first of the thunders that are to reverberate later with crushing fury.

It was at the turn of the century that Bialik, almost suddenly, threw off the glorious yoke of a national poet; and the other influence of his childhood, nature, entered joyously into his singing.

His poem **"Morning Spirits,"** written in 1900, may be said to open this new and short period, during which he wrote *inter alia* his four greatest poems. The few nature-poems that Bialik had written before were mainly nocturnes: dim sounds, whispering shadows, secrets upon secrets, and night-dwarfs coming down to dig gold in the valley. But now *light* enters as a motive in Bialik's poetry. Morning-spirits, little fluttering light-beings, beckon to him through the window: "Come out! Let us splash and spurt light everywhere, on cornfields, on flowing streams, on the smile of a sleeping child, on the heart of a merciful mother, on a drop of dew, on a child's tear, on a butterfly's wing, on a broken glass, on a soap bubble, on a brass button, and on verses of song." Thus they sing and call, their eyes glisten, their little faces beam, their luminous wings beat on the window-panes, and the poet exclaims: "God, I am flooded with light!"

In his poem **"Radiance,"** he continues the theme. He now joins the company of light-spirits, and together they scamper to the meadow, wallowing in its dewy grass, frightening a grazing calf and brood of hens, until the whole meadow flashes like suns and sapphires shaken in a sieve; then—to the field, weltering and floundering in the corn, with swallows jubilantly greeting them from above, with colorful butterflies fluttering as if someone were playfully throwing handfuls of living flowers, and with grasshoppers and crickets agitating the quiet air like cymbals and castanets; and then—to the lake, creating in it a riot of light, smashing its dreaming sun into splinters. Thus the poet gives himself to his newly-discovered light with a peculiar hunger, with an epicurean abandon, as if to compensate for two thousand years of ghetto darkness; and he flings a voluptuous cry heavenward: "God! even if Thou hadst hung up seven suns on high, Thou couldst not quench my spirit's

thirst for light!" The poem **"Radiance"** is a thematic continuation of his **"Morning Spirits,"** and out of the latter grew with a deeper motivation his greatly admired poem **"The Pool,"** about which—more anon.

Another motive in this period is the new call of the time, strength. We have already found it in his **"Talmud-Student"**— "what art thou, rock, what art thou, flint, compared with a Hebrew lad studying the Torah?"—but there it was moral strength; whereas now, as in the case of the theme of light, it is physical. To this he dedicates his beautiful **"Winter Songs."** He describes a white frosty day, "stronger than flint." The oak in the forest bursts with power, and so does the human heart. All faces are aflame, the muscles—drawn, the steps— firm. The lungs draw icy air. "O seize me, frost! Singe, burn, flame, and pierce. Freeze my breath upon my lips, and pour your iron into my blood!" "Drive on! Where? Do not ask! Wherever a bit of life is stirring, and a drop of blood is seething." The poet wants to snatch the cup of life and gulp it down to its last drop. He is ready to pour out all his strength and warmth in one grand revelry. When his heart is emptied, drained to the bottom, he will go to an old snow-covered forest of silvery silence, where, he knows, a hammer and an anvil are hidden; there he will draw out his heart, place it on the anvil, and strike and strike: Be strong! And the whole forest will respond with its echoes: Be strong!

There is another poem, called **"The Dead of the Wilderness,"** which is permeated with this apotheosis of power. It is based on an old legend that the sixty myriads of Israelites who left Egypt and were doomed to die in the wilderness belonged to a race of giants and never died but were only put to an everlasting sleep. With great vigor and bold strokes, Bialik paints here the glowing desert and the quietly sleeping Titans. Sometimes a great eagle flying above spies the bronze bodies, as they lie side by side below, and is about to swoop down upon them with its open beak and talons; sometimes a fiery serpent, crawling over the burning sand and drawing nigh, raises itself halfway like a hieroglyphic column with its pronged fluttering tongue; and sometimes a kingly lion comes and his roar reverberates through the desert; but overawed by the majesty of slumbering strength, they all retrace their paths, and the giants sleep on as calmly as before. But then a storm breaks out in the desert, hurling and whirling sand and stones and howling beasts in one flaming mass. It is then that the giants arise and sing:

> Come, we'll ascend.
> If God withdraw from us His hands,
> And His ark moves not from its place,
> Then we'll ascend alone!

The storm subsides, the sun appears, and passing caravans kneel in thanksgiving. A fleet horseman, hurling his javelin forward and catching it in its flight, suddenly sees the calmly sleeping giants and spurs his horse back to his comrades, to whom he relates in terror what his eyes have seen. Then the old sheik of the tribe lifts up his voice:

> Blessed be Allah! By the beard of the prophet,
> your eyes have seen the dead of the wilderness.
> Verily they were fierce and hard like the rocks
> of Araby. They provoked the spirit of their
> prophet and enraged their God, so that, shutting
> them up among the mountains, He cast upon
> them an eternal sleep and charged the wilder-
> ness to keep them for an everlasting memorial.

And may Allah keep the faithful from touching the hems of their coverings! Once an Arab took one thread of the fringes of their garments and at once his body withered until he returned the theft to its place.—And these are the fathers of the People of the Book.

Then the caravan moves on, and for a long time the white turbans gleam and the humps of the camels sway until they disappear in the bright distance, carrying away another tale, and the stillness returns to the desolate desert.

It is a great poem, perhaps the greatest, a paean of glory to strength and daring. But soon after, in 1903, the massacre of Kishineff occurs; and Bialik, forced to put the national yoke again on his neck, produces a harrowing account and a bitter outcry in the form of a long and moving poem called **"In the City of Slaughter."** He takes us to the scene. We see the courtyards and walls still plastered with black blood and sticky marrow. We see a heap upon which a Jew and a dog were beheaded, and pigs wallow in their mingled blood. We go up to a dark attic where we see stomachs ripped open and filled with the feathers of torn pillows, heads smashed with hammers, a child sucking the cold breast of its mother; and all around in the dark, we see eyes, eyes of pain and terror, asking why and wherefore. We climb down to a cellar where girls were defiled and murdered, and their fathers, brothers, and lovers found shelter behind the barrels. "See," the poet says bitterly, "where the sons of your people, the descendants of the Maccabees, were hiding!" Then the poet takes us to the graves of the victims:

See, see, the slaughtered calves, so smitten and so laid;
Is there a price for their death? How shall that price be
    paid?
Forgive, ye shamed of the earth, yours is a pauper-
    Lord!
Poor was He during your life, and poorer still of late.
When to my door you come to ask for your reward,
I'll open wide: See, I am fallen from my high estate.

Thus the national theme breaks into his human, universal period; no longer, however, as Jewish suffering but as a Jewish shame. "See where the descendants of the Maccabees were hiding!" This stinging condemnation of Jewish weakness had its effect on the youth, which soon organized itself for self-defense in various Russian towns. But the tragedy and the humiliation produced a crisis in the poet's heart, a burning sense of duality, a clash between his individual and national personalities, between the internal and the external claims; and the impress of this duality is found in the next two great poems: **"The Pool"** and **"The Scroll of Fire."**

In the first of these two poems, Bialik describes a vision of a twofold world in a forest-pool nestling in the shade of an enormous oak. Charming scenes follow one another. In the morning when the sun Delilah-like binds the oak with golden ropes, the pool silently hugs the feet of its protector, happy to be the mirror of this giant, and—who knows?—perhaps dreaming that it holds not the mere reflection but the actual being of the oak. In a moonlight-night when all is a silent and silvery mystery, and the whole forest seems to keep some dark, closely guarded secret, perhaps a princess on a bed of gold waiting for her prince-redeemer, the pool—who knows?—dreams perchance that the prince roams the world in vain, for the princess is here in its own sleeping heart. And in a storm when violent winds shake the trees, and skies flash with anger, the

pool like a frightened child clings closely to the tree, blinking its eyes with every lightning, and—who knows?—it may be anxious about the safety of the stately tree or "about the beauty of its hidden world, with its bright dreams and radiant visions, which a sudden passing wind made turbid." Is not this apprehension the poet's very own for his own "hidden world of bright dreams and radiant visions," which the sudden downpour of pain on the heads of his people has made turbid? Formerly he proudly said: "For me there is only one world, the world within my heart." He is not so sure now. On the brink of the pool he sits and gazes into this duality, into the world-world and the lake-world, and wonders which is prior.

This poem, the last and the climax of his nature-poems, is of particular interest as a synthesis in a struggle between the mystic and the artist in Bialik. The former, leading him in his childhood to the reading of esoteric literature, was intent upon the vague, shady, misty aspects of nature, upon the inner essence, the genius, or as he called it, "the prince of the night," upon the intangible, the internal, the metaphysical. He himself said later "from the body of the world for its light I pined," and he meant the inner light—a mystical concept. This mystic element dominated the artist in his first period. During the second he was still interested in the metaphysical, and saw the morning lights as morning *genii;* but the artist in Bialik, exuberant and unrestrained, showered upon them such an abundance of imagery that the metaphysical itself began to flutter with life and sensuous physicality. But in **"The Pool,"** the artist and the mystic create a greater beauty by their mutual reconciliation, and the poet sees the truth of the two worlds; the external and the internal, sense and dream; and the trees and clouds above live their life side by side with the lake-life, "the open eye of the forest-genius, great in mysteries and long in thoughts."

In the other poem, the **"Scroll of Fire,"** . . . the swan-song of his radiant intermezzo, he deals more directly with the tragic struggle of the heart to escape its national yoke. This great epic, the long lyrical part of which contains much that is autobiographical, unfolds a legend from the time of the Roman conquest of Jerusalem. The temple is reduced to ashes. The Lion of Fire, always crouching on the altar, is extinguished, except for one curl of its mane. A young angel flies down from the Hind of Dawn, seizes the curl and wings away. Far off on an island, along a pitch-black river, two hundred young captives were left by the Romans. One among them, with angry eyes, sings a song of hate. In the moonlight, they see young female captives on a cliff jutting out of the opposite shore, marching down to the brink with eyes closed and wreaths of thorns on their heads, and, like white birds, flying into the black waters. The lads jump into the river to save them, and perish. One remains, a bright-eyed youth, whose song was of love; and, seeing the River of Destruction covering all, he falls on his face and weeps. In the morning he rises and sees on the opposite cliff under the Hind of the Dawn a young angelic woman, and his heart is moved: "Art thou the one?" He has carried her image in his heart ever since his childhood on the mountains of Samaria. He was orphaned and adopted by an old hermit who taught him the way of self-immolation, to sacrifice his youth and his crown of curls on God's altar. But all the time he felt the sin of secret longings; he lustrated himself and continued longing. "Are thou the one?" He lifts his eyes, and lo, she is gone; only the River of Destruction beneath still carries her reflection. He cries out: Heaven or destruction? But the Hind of the Dawn winks to him and fills him with a blue calm. "God," he vows, "even the fire of my heart I consecrate to Thee!'' He rises to go. A white cloud leads him on along the river until he halts. He descries a light in the distance on a high crag. Sensing a holiness in that light, he rushes toward it. The nearer he draws, the larger it grows; until he discerns the flaming curl of the Lion of Fire. He leaps to the top of the cliff, seizes the curl, and stands erect triumphantly with salvation's torch in his hand. Suddenly he beholds again the enchanting image of the girl in the waters below; and pressing the hallowed flame to his heart, he calls: Heaven—destruction—thou! And he hurls himself from the top of the precipice into the outstretched arms in the River of Destruction.

Again we see a culminating synthesis of conflicting tendencies. At first, when he had just come out of the cloistered halls of Rabbinic learning, Bialik saw the sensuous, the demonic, in woman. "Almighty God, chase away the devil! Lilith caught me in her trap." Later he noticed in her an angelic spirit, and he bowed before her in adoration. "Too pure art thou to be my friend, too hallowed thou to sit with me." In the **"Scroll of Fire,"** the two extremes, the demon and the angel, dance together in one woman. But the story of the lad is essentially the agony of a soul whom destiny faces with the alternatives: self or unself, earth or heaven, freedom or the sacred fire. The lad chose one way, Bialik another. There is rue in either choice for one who has seen both.

Disillusionment, retreat, and a brooding on death, marked his third period.

It was foreshadowed just before the close of the radiant intermezzo in the poem **"The Last Word":**

> Throw away the burning coal from the altar, prophet, and leave it to the villains. Let them roast their roast on it, place their pot and warm the palm of their hands on it. Wipe off the spider-threads which were drawn like violin-chords upon thy heart and of which thou hast woven a revival-song and a salvation-vision, a prophecy of naught and falsehood. And whatever curse God's wrath puts in thy mouth, utter it without a quiver on thy lips. Let thy word be as bitter as death, let it be death itself— proclaim it and we shall know.

(pp. xxii-xxxiii)

Crushed by his people's weakness and overcome by a sense of futility—"I have searched your small coin and lost my gold-piece," "my axe struck decayed wood," "what he sought not, was given him; and the one thing he sought, he found not"— and feeling now estranged from his former comforters, whose language he no longer understands: the Talmud-tomes below and the golden stars above, he decides to retreat, to stick his tools into his girdle and leave. A long period of silence begins, while the poet is only at the beginning of his forties. Events are happening in the Jewish world and from all sides a plaint is heard: Bialik, where art thou? But the poet is in retreat. Only at long intervals a poem of his appears, limpid like a crystal stream and calm with resignation, concerning "those who weave their life in secret, modest of thought and deed, unknown dreamers, of few words but of much beauty," and particularly concerning his longing for a revisitation of the wonders of his childhood, for the mystical rapture of life when it bends back and closes at its source. "I know that man drinks only once from the golden cup, and a beatific vision comes not twice, that there is a blueness in the sky, a greenness in the grass, a hidden light in the whole world, and a luminous

face upon all God's creatures, which are revealed to a child's eye only once and never again; yet God has a sudden blessing in store, and to one who is true in His eyes He grants it.''

It was toward the end when this "sudden blessing" came, and Bialik began to relive his childhood in song. (pp. xxxiv-xxxv)

In Bialik's folk songs, the prophetic sternness gives way to a geniality and a broad sympathy which were inherent in Bialik's nature. In a light and humorous vein, the poet presents to us the ghetto-town with its poverty and economic rootlessness; the poor *ba'al 'agalah,* the "wagon-man," whose pocket is empty, whose throat is "dry," whose wife is a shrew, and who explains why he cannot join any other profession; the girl who charges a golden peacock to bring her a lover, or who propounds all kinds of questions to an acacia tree concerning her future suitor; and the impecunious father with three daughters, with the dowry-seeking fellows coming and going, and the same eternal oranges and nuts making their rounds in vain from the buffet to the table and back. To these the poet added, many years later, a Palestinian song concerning the girls of Shefeya "who have no father nor mother, whose sisters are birds and lizards, and whose brothers are heavenly stars." (pp. xxxv-xxxvi)

In prose, too, Bialik achieved a high degree of eminence. His short stories, like **"Aryeh the Gross"** and **"Behind the Fence,"** are realistic studies of raw earthly life. There are characters that do not seem to be written down but chiseled in rocks. His **"Aftergrowth"** is autobiographic; and here, too, as wherever Bialik touched on his childhood, there is a warmth, a throbbing longing, and a sheer singing.

His essays have a pathos and a ringing appeal. In **"Halakah and Aggadah"** he pleads that Jewishness should not be merely "legend" but also "law," not merely a poetic effusion, but also duties, demands, deeds, and a crystallization of life. "We bend our neck: where is the iron yoke? Why does not the strong hand and the outstretched arm come?"

In other essays, he develops his idea of *kinnus,* the need of *gathering* into one corpus the most vital and lasting products of the Hebraic genius of all ages, so as to make Jewish culture, in the Arnoldian conception of the term, a potent factor in the life and thought of the people as well as in the creative work of the writer, which would then acquire a continuity, a freshness, a rootedness.

It is with this aim in view that Bialik published together with Ravnitzky the *Book of Legends,* the first order of the Mishna with a running commentary, and a critical edition of the poems of the great medieval poets and thinkers, Solomon ibn Gabirol and Moses ibn Ezra. Yet it was not only the idea of *kinnus* that impelled Bialik to these vast and important labors, but also a love of learning and the feeling that inspired many of his poems, that the beginning of a national revival is the reaffirmation of the past, that the ship of a people must sink halfway in the waters of history in order to steer straight and sure in the free air of today. (pp. xxxvi-xxxvii)

But it is through his poetry that Bialik left his deepest impress. Through his free and powerful rhythms, through his radiant songs of nature, which were novel in their joyousness and abandon, and through those poems in which directly and indirectly the call of the time for national action found fiery expression, he stirred Jewish life to its utmost and gave modern Hebrew literature a new and vigorous impulse and a place in contemporary world-literature. (p. xxxvii)

Israel Efros, in an introduction to Selected Poems of Hayyim Nahman Bialik *by Hayyim Nahman Bialik, edited by Israel Efros, revised edition, Bloch Publishing Company, 1965, pp. xvii-xxxvii.*

LEON I. YUDKIN   (essay date 1974)

[*An English educator and critic, Yudkin is a frequent contributor of essays on modern Jewish literature to periodicals in the United States and abroad. His book-length studies include several works on Hebrew literary history and literary figures. In the following excerpt, Yudkin discusses the essential thematic and technical elements of Bialik's poetry and the influence of his work on other Hebrew writers.*]

Modern Hebrew Literature operates within a very different framework from the Hebrew literature of the Jewish tradition, and yet it speaks to the heirs of that tradition in the same language. Bialik, perhaps more accurately than anyone else, sensed this break, tried to bridge the chasm, and despaired of achieving this ambition. Thus, his poetry is an expression of that national crisis of identity which . . . [is] peculiar to Modern Hebrew Literature. But he also managed to incorporate this national experience into his own individuality, so that corporate and individual identity become one within his work. National disaster is a personal disaster for him, just as the lyrical expression of his own uniqueness is, in some sense, characteristic of the corporate whole. Bialik, it is true, has often been called the "national poet," the one who so successfully epitomized the yearnings of the people at the time of the emergence of a nation established anew on the soil of Palestine. But he was also the poet to insist on his own uniqueness, his separateness from other humanity, the exceptionality of his suffering and his state of mind, and the ultimate incommunicability of his work. Life for him was, as we shall see, necessarily a disaster. His poetry was an attempt to render this to the ultimate of its capacity, but even this was doomed at least to partial failure. Poetry can at best hint at the disaster perhaps by its very existence. In one of his own images, poetry, as opposed to prose, is like thin ice aware of the abyss beneath—necessary but precarious (see his essay on language **"Gilui we-chisui be-lashon" "Exposure and Cover in Language"**). Bialik, in reaching back to the past, also has a very strong contemporary sense of potential nothingness. This has been fundamentally sensed for a half-century or more, and continues to be so in Israeli terms. This is certainly modern literature.

Much confusion has reigned with regard to the twin voices of Bialik—the public and the private. His public voice was taken over by the Hebrew readership, and the poet was made the articulate spokesman of resurgent Israel. With this, various titles were appended to him—"national poet," "prophet," "Zionist poet," etc. On the other hand, we are aware of a great deal of tension within the poetry itself, which not only refuses its label, but asserts the very opposite tendency. Thus, we witness an exaggerated regard for his own private voice, unique in expression and alone in possession. What I have done, Bialik seems to assert, has proceeded from me alone, I owe it to no one—and I myself, again alone, will be involved in the consequences. Not only has the reader no part in the creation of the experience, but neither is he a participant in the product, because the poem goes from the poet and returns to his poet. That such a very private character (with regard to his poetry) should be awarded the title "national poet" and even "prophet" is a great irony.

Nevertheless, this is the case. In the earliest reactions to and discussions of Bialik's poetry there are opinions of this type. By the time David Frishman wrote his letter on Bialik in 1908 [*Mikhtabim 'al d'bar sifrut,* letter 13] these titles were already assumed. Frishman indeed complains bitterly of this title given to Bialik, and argues that it reduces his status as a poet, even influencing him in a "wrong" direction, making him write pseudo-prophecy. But we do see that, even at this early stage, Bialik had thus been firmly labelled. "First of all, Bialik is not the prophet that people call him, and you know to what degree they have given him this title." Frishman had a personal predilection for what he would have regarded as the pure aesthetic, and thought that Bialik was damaging his art by these "prophetic" tendencies. "Bialik is everything you want only not a prophet. On the contrary, Bialik is the very opposite of the prophet. He is an artist, perhaps the first artist of really excellent cast that Hebrew poetry has had." So he does not deny the validity of prophecy as a category, nor that a poet, even in contemporary society, can be a prophet, but thinks rather that its appearance mitigates against Bialik's true nature as a poet.

> It is nearer to the truth to say that he is the eternal type of tender, suffering soul, the modern soul with eternal longings in the heart and with a certain tendency to produce artistic forms . . . neither is he a national poet.

This same discussion was still being carried on decades later—Bialik poet or prophet, and if so, good or bad? Y. Fichman has an essay in his book on Bialik [*Shirath Bialik*] on the nature of poetry and prophecy, and continues to validate the distinction. He makes the assumption that different periods of history have different needs, and that a crisis situation calls for a crisis message—this being the nature of prophecy . . . :

> For such a generation, prophecy was not a creative necessity, but a necessity for existence . . . as long as the world had not been mightily stirred, the demand grew for poetry, for the cultivating element, the directive element, the straightening element, but on the outbreak of the storm, all hearts asked for a prophet.

In this sense, for Fichman, Bialik was responding to a national need, in spite of his own personal inclinations elsewhere. But "poetry is the expression of the individual's soul, whilst prophecy is the expression of the world's soul—poetry is release, whilst prophecy is compulsion." This sort of emotive, generalized description does not, of course, establish poetry and prophecy as separate, clear-cut categories, nor does it precisely define them, as Søren Kierkegaard had done, when establishing that there was a radical difference of function between the two. Prophecy, after all, is not characterized by individual genius, poetic aspiration or personal expression; it can even be most inartistic and untalented. What it must be is simply the channel of communication between an external agent, that is God, and other people. The prophet, or apostle in Kierkegaard's terminology, is merely an agent, a neutral pipeline, whereas the poet has an artistic purpose. The terms in Hebrew literary criticism were used emotionally and colourfully, rather than helpfully in terms of precise distinction. . . . Presumably what critics such as Frishman and Fichman had in mind in their deployment of this terminology is a certain elevation of tone, an address to the people, Biblical language, and other such external characteristics. Frishman disapproves of this tone in Bialik, and Fichman is prepared to accept it for national purposes, but both think that it can usefully be distinguished, and is important to a categorization of Bialik's poetry. What later critics have tended to do is to undermine this fundamental notion. Of course, we are still aware that Bialik does sometimes use a very elevated Biblical-type language, but the context within which he operates negates rather than supports any "prophetic" tendency within his writing. If we want to be able to understand Bialik's world and its effect on the reader, we should do it rather from within, and not with pre-established categories. Neither should we adopt the old method of seeking correspondences between his life (that is external events, historical and biographical) and his work. Literature does not work in this simple way, and even when there is an external correspondence, we are, rather, interested in the literature itself.

What, then, was Bialik's poetry? And if we deny him the title of prophet as one of inappropriate nature, do we then have to substitute another? The trouble quite frequently with the discussion of literature is that non-literary categories are imposed on it, and these non-literary categories are often then used by literary critics and historians themselves. This is perhaps an inevitable danger, as literature is not a world to itself—the word is very much part of the outer world, and must constantly refer to it. It can only be autonomous with the greatest difficulty, and paradoxically. It is not surprising then that the writer is shunted off into non-literary compartments, and made to speak for non-literary ideologies. But Kurzweil said: "One cannot speak of a Zionistic Bialik any more than one can speak of a religious Bialik or a Marxist Bialik." This is an attempt to counter rigid, ideological categorization; it does not, of course, mean that Bialik had no contact with these various ideological streams. As an active human being, it would have been most surprising if he had not, and as a poet, sensitive to trends of thought, movements, people, virtually impossible. He had such contacts, and he declared opinions, some of which might also come through in his poetry. However, in view of Bialik's understanding of poetry, and in view of the nature of poetry itself, Kurzweil's statement is not surprising. Poetry does not operate according to the simplistic categories of the world around—it is much more aware of the ultimate truth which goes beyond that of the prosaic world. The poem may touch the world of ideology and the world of political action, but it also transcends it. The poem may, and in this respect it might have something in common with prophecy, also transcend the prose consciousness of the poet himself. This is a way of saying that the poem could not be restated and still mean the same thing; it could not be paraphrased. The poet's personality retires into the background, and gives place to the poem, which then stands supreme and autonomous. (pp. 19-23)

It is true, however, that Bialik did write some poems of a specifically ideological nature. . . . Let us examine this type of poem. An ideological poem, by definition, would be paraphrasable, because what it is seeking to achieve, after all, is the transmission of an ideology which already exists in the outside world. Thus it is already a paraphrase. This sort of poem would be simple and unambivalent, because any ambivalence would militate against its ideological tendency and create confusion in the mind of the reader. It is not related uniquely to itself as proceeding from a unique mind, but rather to something else, about which the reader already had knowledge. Bialik, for example, could write a nationalistic hymn, since adopted by a Zionist youth movement, attempting to embody these qualities. The purpose of **"Birkath 'Am"** (**"People's Blessing"**) is limited and defined. It demands national preparedness:

> Let the hands be strong of our brethren who tend
> The dust of our land, wherever they may be;
> May your spirit not fall, be glad, exult.
> Come with one shoulder to the help of the people.

There is nothing here of the personality of the poet. The poem has the qualities of song. In Hebrew it is easy to remember, nicely expressed and has a direct appeal in that it embodies accepted national sentiments of the sort that are to be found in his first poem **"El Ha-zipor"** (**"To the Bird"**), and many other nationalistic-type poems of the earlier movement of Hibbat Zion (Love of Zion)—a late nineteenth-century Zionist movement in eastern Europe, whose poetry contained much aspiration towards a national home in the traditional sense of Zion. This poem has nothing of the complexity or the problematics peculiarly characteristic of Bialik, nor of the expression of his unique ego. He was only speaking here from the top layer of his mind. Prosaically, he thought of himself as a disciple of the famous Zionist teacher and essayist Ahad Haam, as a good Zionist, and as a loyal son to his people. In this poem he tried to express a good national sentiment. But it is the very nature of this generalized sentiment which makes it so suitable for adoption as a collective hymn that also precludes it from being poetry in the sense outlined above. This does not mean that Bialik was not a great poet when he treated of the national themes. We would in asserting this be denying him the title of great poet by implication—the national theme is so manifest in his work, explicitly or implicitly. But we must make a distinction between the national theme as explored by Bialik, official spokesman of the people, translator of Zionist longings and national aspirations into verse, and Bialik the real poet, who sees the national theme and his own individual soul as one and indivisible, who saw himself as unique in his sense of national identification and national in his sense of orphaned loneliness. Only when he sees the nation unambivalently through other people's eyes, does his poetry not reach heights. It is his own special, personal attitude to his environment and the outer world that catalyses his greatness. That is to say that it is not national subjects in their abstract form that produce the imprint of substantial quality, but those subjects in their concrete and individual expression, in the way that they elicit a personal response. It was precisely the conflict between the external world as he knew it and his own self, that constituted the quintessence of his poetry. His confrontation with tradition, his many-sided and personal view of the Jewish world, are central factors in his work, because it is in these respects that the poet could express his own personal psychological truth, in all its complexity and contradictions. Personal truth cannot be simple or one-sided, and Bialik's poetry does, after all, reflect the personality of the poet, if in a rather special way. Bialik could well be called the National Poet—the fact that he has been awarded that title does clearly indicate something about his effect on the Jewish population. If people see him as the national poet, that is what he is for them. But if we want to understand the ways in which he operates to achieve this effect, we have to be true to the nature of the poetry itself. And we see that Bialik is a national poet in that he is affected by national experiences common to many Jews of his time. But especially interesting for us is his personal, lyrical reaction, which, in spite of its individuality, still manages to speak to us. Our feelings expand towards the absorption of this phenomenon called Hayim Nachman Bialik. (pp. 24-6)

One of the most noticeable characteristics of Bialik's poetry is the description of the constant search. There is a restless dissatisfaction that occurs throughout his lines, when the poet grasps at hints and solutions, only to search for them without the sense of ultimate fulfilment. The springs of this dissatisfaction have not been adequately located. In reading the text, we want, after all, to understand the material which has proved so enigmatic. We are aware of the search, but as there is no prosaic expression of the sources of dissatisfaction, or of the object of identification, a further examination is called for. What is he looking for? In a poem, written in 1905, addressed to "my son" and about his soul, called **"We-'im yish'al ha-malach"** (**"And if the Angel Asks"**), he characterizes this restless, wandering soul as searching for love. The son says of himself (and his soul) that he has been lonely, "tender, alone and dreaming" (a frequent self-characterization), longing for a "delightful cloud." But it found itself instead on the pages of a Talmud, still longing for something beyond. And in the end:

It still flies wandering about the world,
Wandering, straying, and finding no comfort:
And on modest nights at the beginning of each month,
Whilst the world prays about the incompleteness of the
  moon,
It leans with its wing on the gate of love,
Leaning knocking and crying quietly,
Praying for love.

The climax of the poem is ultimate dissatisfaction, because the search has not succeeded, and the hunt goes on. The soul/lad/poet yearns for a love which he has never known, as he says in his well-known poem **"Hachnisini tahath kenafech"** (**"Take Me under Your Wing"**), also written in 1905, when confessing his "secret":

They say that there is love in the world—
What is love?

Here seems to be the object of the search—love, which has hitherto evaded him. But love in any language is a notoriously ambiguous concept. Without knowing more about the precise nature of this love, our knowledge, that the search is for love, is in itself limited. What sort of love is it that is required? In the poem **"Hachnisini,"** he asks not for a mistress, but for "a mother and sister," who surely represent non-sexual, even "ideal" love. We see in another poem of his, **"Ha-eynayim ha-re 'eboth"** (**"Hungry Eyes"**), also expressed in an intensely autobiographical way, that "he" (whether we can identify the "I" of the poet with the external, autobiographical author is really not to the point) was severely, and perhaps finally, disappointed by physical contact with a woman/the flesh. In that poem he vividly and erotically describes the intense appeal of the woman, whom he here also addresses directly, made to the innocent nature of the poet:

I was pure, the storm had not sullied my pure feelings
Until you came, beautiful one, and blew with your
  breath. Then I was sullied.

This is his own Paradise Lost, his own loss of innocence as imagined by erotic contact. As he says in the last lines:

In a short moment of pleasure, of happiness and joy,
  over me was destroyed
A whole world—how great is the price that I paid for
  your flesh.

He had longed for this flesh, but the sacrifice of his innocence and purity was simply not a worth-while price to pay. The object of desire in the poem **"Ha-eynayim ha-re 'eboth"** returns in various Bialik poems to wreak her havoc. Her touch, like the sight of Medusa's head, kills—her presence is associated with death, and we have here the well-known association of Eros and Thanatos. The poem **"Ziporeth"** (**"Butterfly"**), written in 1904, uses much of the same imagery. He addresses himself here as well to a woman, and is again engaged in ecstatic adventure, and the "cloud" again makes it appearance as an object of desire. He is invited by the environment, by her eyes, by her actual presence, which is ambiguous, seeming both modest and sensuous, to partake of the act of love, to bestow a kiss. And he ends:

Hurry, hurry, my sister, let us go to the forest,
Where under the canopy of the groves I will take out all
  my soul.
And with all my love which hangs on a hair
Let us put ourselves to death together with a kiss.

If the longed-for love is that which is identified here in these poems, its attainment is possible but fatal. Desire can certainly be satisfied, but that is the end of satisfaction. This is indeed death in the old ambiguous sense. (pp. 27-9)

Another facet of this search is seen in Bialik's attitude to the Jewish tradition. It is implied from our discussion of Bialik's identification of the personal and the national theme that he would also identify as one and the same the religious crisis of the nation and his own crisis. The great theme of the death of tradition is taken over by him and personalized so that the death of tradition induces a sense of personal loss, and leaves him isolated. He laments in the poem **"Levadi"** (**"By Myself"**), 1902, that everyone has been swept away by the wind and by the light, that very light, symbol of Enlightenment and Haskalah, that heralded a new era which others greeted rapturously—it was "the morning of their lives." But he is in a different state. While others welcome the dawn, the poet is left solitary, without solace, to mourn the death of the world, and to seek what inadequate crumb of comfort is available in the residue:

Alone, alone I remained, and the Shekhinah [Divine
  Presence]
Rested the palm of her trembling, broken right wing on
  my head.

The right (chief supporting) wing, which has traditionally offered protection and succour, is broken, so the power of the Divine Presence, the active agent of God in the universe, is now impaired. This is, of course, an image of the declining function of Jewish religious tradition in the contemporary world, but the poet's particular conribution to an otherwise objective assessment is the total self-involvement in the loss. The "death of God" for Bialik is expressed as though it were the death of a father or mother, or in fact both together. Here we have a new sort of tension within the poem—the tension that produces greatness. There are two forces at work as represented here—one, an old force no longer viable, and the other new, which is not accepted by the narrator of the poem. He is poised in the middle, moving in neither direction positively. He remains attached to something in which he no longer believes. (pp. 30-1)

One might challenge the action of the poet in returning to a source which has already failed him. He also seems to seek an answer from something whose power he doubts. In the poem **"Al ha-shehitah"** (**"On Slaughter"**), 1903, he has also displayed a scepticism in the source of the power to whom he appeals. In response to the pogrom at Kishinev, he wants to appeal to a court of justice for his people. So he turns to the heavens, where God is supposed to reside. But he has no certain knowledge of the presence of God there:

Heavens, seek mercy for me!
If there is a God amongst you, and if to God there is a
   path,
Which I have not found.

He is sceptical here about two things—firstly, about the presence of God, and secondly, about the possibility of establishing contact with him. In **"Al ha-shehitah,"** he is prepared to accept the possibility of the existence of God and of the path, although he asserts that if they do exist, he himself must be defective for not having found them. And in **"Lifne' aron ha-sefarim"** [**"Before the Bookcase"**], he is similarly prepared to accept the possibility that the fault lies in himself, that he has forgotten the language of the stars, and cannot now understand what they say.

But who is this "I" to whom the poet relates so sceptically? How does he strike the world and himself? At the end of **"Megillath ha-'esh"** [**"Scroll of Fire"**], after he has been spewed up by the waters to "a very distant land," we read a description of the person who has gone through the experiences here described. He has fallen into the abyss of extinction, and the lamps of God on high have already gone out for him. He then finds himself in "the land of exile," "where he was strange and a man of riddles to everyone." He was strange to everyone else, and everyone else was strange to him: "And he saw the Heavens and they were strange to him, and he looked upon a land, and behold it was foreign." This description is of one who has become alienated from his environment, who has lost the direct link with the world—it is a description which is well known to us in Bialik's poetry. We already know this "I" of his, the one lonely and removed, who cannot easily locate his place in the new world, though mourning, as one in "exile," the old which is no more. This "young man," then, in **"Megillath ha-'esh"** is the same figure who so often crops up in the poetry. And we become aware of a certain paradox; that in spite of his separation from the world, he continues to display a sympathy towards it and interest in it. He also shares its sorrows: "And he went out to his brother exiles and saw them in their lowliness and affliction. He felt the pain of them all, and he roared with them." Bialik the poet does echo the public grief and pour out his anger on paper. An outstanding example of this is **"Be'ir ha-haregah"** (**"In the City of Execution"**), 1904. But here again in **"Megillath ha-'esh"** there is a tension, this time between the demands of the world on the one hand, which he attempts to fulfil, and his separation from it (his estrangement). And another quality already noted also appears in the lad at the end of the poem—he continues to search and to yearn: "Yet his eyes thirsted for nothing but the dawn, and the radiance was the mark of his soul, and the half-light of dawn the poetry of his life." Here he is yearning for the "radiance" which we had before in the earlier description of the maiden from the abyss of extinction: "And she appeared in her full splendour with a radiance on her brow." This image of Eros clings to him then even after the fall. He yearns towards it constantly; this is the content of the "poetry of his life." (pp. 33-4)

We can perhaps number five central themes as expressed by Bialik's poetry: Tension, Search, Struggle, Death, the Sorrow of the Individual. These do not always appear in this order.

The tension is that between the external world and the "I," and the influence of the world on the "I." The search, without any hope of satisfaction, for what can be called, to use the poet's words "the fiftieth gate," runs like a golden thread throughout all his poetry. The struggle, as manifest particularly in such a poem as **"Megillath ha-'esh"** results from the tension of opposed forces, attracting and repelling. Death represents the point of despair in his poetry, where we have the recognition that it must necessarily intervene before the achievement of his solution, or, to put it differently, before he can obtain access into the fiftieth gate of the orchard. The sorrow of the individual is Bialik's characteristic note. In these words does he characterize the lad at the conclusion of **"Megillath ha-'esh":** "And he closed his eyes, and looked into the abyss of his soul, lingering on, and was silent with all the world in his great sorrow, the sorrow of the individual." Bialik's poetry is almost always sorrowful, but we can see why.

This ultimate sadness, the sense of nihilism and the sense of the absurd, all place Bialik well in the tradition of the modern. That these are allied to an identification with the Jewish people in eastern Europe and Palestine during the period of emergent Israel confirms his centrality in the Hebrew literature of the period. His language is traditional and flexible, rhetorical and rich-textured, rooted in the past, but also speaking of the present. For Bialik, the past is an untimely corrective to the unavoidable present. Even now, forty years after his death, Bialik's presence is still very much with us. (pp. 37-8)

Leon I. Yudkin, "The Quintessence of H. N. Bialik's Poetry and Its Seminal Influence," in his Escape into Siege: A Survey of Israeli Literature Today, *Routledge & Kegan Paul, 1974, pp. 19-38.*

DAVID ABERBACH   (essay date 1981)

[*In the following excerpt, Aberbach discusses the influence of Bialik's life on his poetry and compares Bialik's works with those of William Wordsworth and T. S. Eliot.*]

One of the great, unexplained ironies of modern Jewish history is that Chaim Nachman Bialik . . . , whom Weizmann called a giant of the Zionist movement, and who was hailed in his lifetime and until the present day as the poet laureate of the Jewish national renaissance, had painfully ambivalent feelings about this role to the point of rejecting it.

Instead, he saw himself in the humble role of an artist struggling with his personal agonies. Though he appeared in his poetry to be the virtual reincarnation of a Biblical prophet (Maxim Gorky, who read him in Jabotinsky's Russian translations, called him a "modern Jeremiah"), he was emphatic in dismissing his public role, echoing the prophet Amos: "I am no prophet, no poet, / But a chopper of wood." His cynicism about writing of Zion is put frankly: "When you see me weeping for some wondrous land . . . do not mourn or comfort me, my tears are false." He twice removed the poem containing these lines from his *Collected Poems*. . . .

At the turn of the century, the growth of Hebrew literature was unavoidably bound up with the rise of Jewish nationalism, so that a Hebrew writer was generally expected to write about national themes. Though in a remarkably short time there would be an eruption of Hebrew talent, in the 1890s (when Bialik began to publish verse) really original Hebrew poetry was scarce. . . . By becoming the first great artist in modern Hebrew, Bialik automatically became a cultural hero, with accompanying responsibilities. (p. 41)

Bialik had no ambitions to become a national institution, but this is exactly what happened in his lifetime. He shunned the idea of being celebrated by the people, and suffered acute self-reproach over his status as national poet, feeling it to be undeserved.... His view of his poetry as illegitimate offspring, "hybrid children of mixed seed ... fruit of harlotry," might, among other things, reflect his guilt at writing personal poetry mistakenly thought to be national.

To all appearances, however, Bialik played the role of national poet to the hilt. His best poetry, written mostly in Odessa in the years 1900-1911, was "national" both in its enormous impact upon the Jews and, to some degree, in its intent. His poetic genius and rare knowledge of Hebrew sources, gained through his Talmudic education, thrust him into the vanguard of Jewish writers who believed that if the nation was to be resurrected the language would have to be revived. He was adulated accordingly. The emotional climate which he helped to create was a windfall for political Zionism. (pp. 41-2)

After the murderous Kishinev pogrom in 1903, Bialik was driven to write **"The City of Slaughter,"** the poem which cemented his reputation as national poet. He was barely 30 years old. No other modern Hebrew poem has stirred up such a public outcry in the Jewish world. It is the only poem of Bialik's which, in the aftermath of the Holocaust, has the ring of prophecy. Yet for all its power to inspire national outrage, the poem is grotesquely dependent for its artistic success upon Bialik's uniquely personal stress. Moving like a funeral procession, the poem tells, at times with nauseating detail, of a journey into hell, revisiting the scenes of violence, the streets and yards stained with blood, the vandalised houses, the cellars where women were raped and their children murdered. The explosion of sarcasm and bitterness to which this leads at the end of the poem has for its target the cowardly, parasitical survivors who roused Bialik's ire for using this national tragedy to elicit sympathy and funds for themselves:

> Away, you beggars, to the charnel-house!
> The bones of your father disinter!
> Cram them into your knapsacks, bear
> Them on your shoulders, and go forth
> To do your business with these precious
>   wares
> At all the country fairs!
>
>   (tr. A. M. Klein)

Bialik's chastisement, while it makes for extraordinary poetry—and shook the Jewish people in a way that they needed at the time—does not do justice to the historical facts. Bialik had been sent to Kishinev by Jews in Odessa to find out exactly what had happened, and to write a report. He knew at first hand, therefore, that the pogrom was as severe as it was precisely because some Jews did take up arms and defend themselves; yet in the poem there is no mention of this. The opportunists who so infuriated Bialik were a minority, and their unheroic conduct did not warrant the emphasis which Bialik gives it.

An explanation of these distortions is that Bialik, perhaps unconsciously, identified himself with these *schnorrers* as he does elsewhere: his indignation with them for using national tragedy for personal aims might partly have been a displaced form of self-chastisement for doing the same thing. In one of his poems, God chooses him to be a *schnorrer*-prophet: "Go round from

door to door, knapsack on shoulder, go to the doors of generous men, bend down for a scrap of bread."

Even in poetry which appears to express fierce nationalism, the mark of a troubled personality is found. Bialik's central achievement, **"The Scroll of Fire,"** begins with a spectacular account of the ruin of the Temple in Jerusalem, but abandons national catastrophe to confess the ruin of one man, apparently the poet himself, by the fire of passion. (p. 42)

To modern Israelis, Bialik is still the national poet *par excellence,* a classic who is highly praised and seldom read carefully. Amos Elon, in his book on *The Israelis* [see Additional Bibliography], writes that "None before Bialik nor after has expressed the Jewish will to live in words and rhymes of such beauty and poetic force; he is rightly known today as the national poet of Israel." Clichés such as these are typical of the literature on Bialik. They reflect the popular response to him as the servant of a cause rather than to the content of his work. Jewish nationalists naturally saw in his poetry what was most meaningful to them. The most influential of Bialik's "national" poems, **"The City of Slaughter,"** is known to have inspired the formation of Jewish defence groups in East European towns; but the poem itself is pessimistic to the point of despair. Bialik's mature poetry has little of the "will to live" for which he is commemorated in the traditional stereotype. Quite the opposite is true. In one of his morbid poems, the poet considers ways in which he might die, including suicide:

> ... perhaps through my very hunger and thirst
> for life and its pleasantness, with disgust of
> soul, braving the fury of the Creator, I will kick
> at his gift, and cast my life at his feet, like a
> defiled shoe torn from the foot.
>
>   (p. 43)

Bialik's art, like that of T. S. Eliot, was taken up by a movement which preferred to ignore—or remained ignorant of—the private, psychological reasons for writing, necessarily giving it instead a predominantly socio-political interpretation. Eliot's profession of the need for art to be impersonal did not stop him from disavowing the social import of "The Waste Land" which critics had read into it: "To me it was only the relief of a personal and wholly insignificant grouse against life."

And yet, it is not always undesirable to be misread. Bialik was fascinated, as Eliot was, by the subtleties of revelation, concealment, and deception in language—knowing, as Eliot put it, that "there may be personal causes which make it impossible for a poet to express himself in any but an obscure way." In an essay dealing with **"Revelation and Concealment in Language,"** Bialik put forward the view that "language in all its forms does not reveal its inner meaning ... but serves as a partition, hiding it." The persona of national poet was a convenient stay against over-inquisitiveness into his buried life. He writes in a late poem:

> Therefore he reveals himself, to be invisible
> and to deceive you. In vain you search the re-
> cesses of his verses—these too but cover his
> hidden thoughts. ...
>
>   (pp. 43-4)

"My Poetry" purports to be a confession of the emotional sources of [Bialik's] poetry, particularly the period between his father's death and his removal to his grandfather's house. According to this poem his mother would labour in the market during the day and at home until midnight. At dawn she got up to bake bread: "And my heart knows that her tears fell into the dough. In the morning, when she cut the warm bread, salty with tears, and I swallowed it, her sighs entered my bones. . . ." Bialik never forgot the poverty of this period of his mother's degradation; he indicated that his endeavours for literary success were attempts to ensure that he would never know such poverty again. "**Orphanhood,**" Bialik's last poem, is the longest and most impassioned account of this troubled period. Comparing himself in his suffering to the fathers of the three main religions, he emphasises the universality of his tragedy: he is not only Isaac on the verge of being sacrificed, but also Ishmael abandoned by his mother, and Christ crucified.

One of the likely effects of his orphanhood was the heightening of his response to the natural world, finding in it some of the attributes of parental love and care, and the paradisal emblem of the lost time before his father's death. There are startling similarities between his poetry of childhood and that of William Wordsworth, who also suffered orphanhood and the complete disruption of his family at the age of seven (and also passed into the care of grandparents with whom he was miserably unhappy). In his semi-biographical prose-poem, "**After-growth,**" Bialik writes of the language of nature, comparing it to the love which silently radiates from a mother to her child, constituting his bond with external reality:

> There was no speech and no words—only a vision. Such utterance as there was came without words or even sounds. It was a mystic utterance, especially created, from which all sound had evaporated, yet which still remained. Nor did I hear it with my ears, but it entered my soul through another medium. In the same way a mother's tenderness and loving gaze penetrate the soul of her baby, asleep in the cradle, when she stands over him anxious and excited—and he knows nothing.
>
> (tr. David Patterson)

The same idea is found in Wordsworth's "The Prelude":

> . . . blest the Babe
> Nursed in his Mother's arms, who sinks to sleep
> Upon his mother's breast; who, with his soul
> Drinks in the feelings of his Mother's eye! . . .
> Along his infant veins are interfused
> The gravitation and the filial bond
> Of Nature that connect him with the world.

Separation from the mother or, in Wordsworth's case, her death, seems to have created in both poets the need for a mystic bond with the natural world, a bond so strong that even inanimate objects would appear to have the breath of life . . . (p. 45)

The bond with natural objects carried over from the bond with the mother appears to have been an integral factor in the development of the imagination. Bialik writes that as a child he was always imaginatively "entering" objects such as trees or stones. In one such anecdote in which he "enters" the stove mouth, his mother pulls him in. Wordsworth's similar tendencies to incorporate himself within natural objects and his self-confessed need to convince himself of their reality might also be attributed in part to the loss of his mother and the uncertainties aroused by this loss. . . .

In writing of early childhood, though in a somewhat idealised way, both poets were engaged in a form of self-analysis, as if

in creative response to the trauma of loss. The poetry of childhood might also have been an expression of a desire for children. After Wordsworth's first legitimate daughter was born, in 1803, he practically stopped writing about childhood; Bialik returned to this theme for the rest of his life. Most of the poetry which he wrote during his last quarter-century was for children, and he poured into this work the love which he wanted to give to children of his own: "I will arise and go to the children, playing innocently by the gate, I will mix in their company, learn their talk and chatter—and become pure from their breath, wash my lips in their cleanliness." But his poetry for children is no escape, for Bialik cannot suppress the themes of longing and deprivation which permeate his other poems. In some children's poems these themes are presented even more starkly:

> How shall I enter the gates
> Of the treasured land,
> If my key is broken,
> And the door is locked?

Or, in another poem:

> In a corner, widower and orphan—
> A pale lulav, an ethrog with cut stem.
> . . . My garden is ruined, its stalks crushed.
> Its ways untrodden.

The infertile landscape in Bialik's poetry, as in that of T. S. Eliot, might be the metaphoric landscape of his own infertility: the desert, the dry tree, the ruin, thunder without rain, melancholy in spring, the loss of hope and desire for death which accompany these images and others might reflect the emotional state of being childless. In one of Bialik's poems, the theme of "April is the cruellest month" is particularly striking:

> Spring will sprout once more, and I,
> Upon my bough I'll hang in grief—
> A sceptre bald, no flower his, nor blossom,
> No fruit, no leaf.

Elsewhere, too, the comparison with a dry tree is found: ". . . a root of dust, a withered flower . . . a single nest of thorns and thistles, an empty shell, at my loins the staff of an oppressor—is this the tree of life?" Bialik's prose and poetry are filled with imagery of this sort. The same imagery—the "dead tree," the tree "crookt and dry," the "withered tree," the "land of barren boughs," the "hollow tree"—is found frequently in the works of T. S. Eliot. . . .

Bialik's writings both illuminate and are illuminated by the works of Eliot. Bialik's constant use of the landscape of ruin and waste land found in Jewish legend and history—the destruction of the Temple ("**The Scroll of Fire**"); the wanderings of the Israelites in the wilderness ("**Aftergrowth**"); the impotent Israelite warriors stranded in the desert ("**The Dead of the Wilderness**"); the quest beginning and ending with a ruin to bring the Messiah ("**King David in his Tomb**")—may have symbolic significance in the same way as Eliot's use in "The Waste Land" of the story of the impotent Fisher King, the quest for the Holy Grail, and the desert journey to Emmaus with the resurrected Christ: these legends and stories might, on one level, point to the infertility of the poet, and his desire for and failure to achieve sexual rebirth. (p. 46)

An analysis of the themes of bereavement and infertility in Bialik's writings, while making clearer his significance as a deeply personal artist of universal interest, does nothing to diminish his stature as a national poet. In fact, his mesmeric national appeal can be attributed partly to this side of his work, which seems, on the surface, to have the least to do with Jewish nationalism. The great blows to Jewish nationhood have traditionally been expressed in imagery of bereavement and infertility, and in a tone of loss remarkably like that in Bialik's poetry. Bialik's longing for his childhood and for his mother (who while still alive was, nevertheless, out of reach) seems to have corresponded with the national longing for Zion, for the imaginary lost paradise of the nation's childhood, for a land which, like the mother, still existed, but seemed equally beyond reach. Partly for this reason, he spoke to his "orphaned generation" with particular conviction.

The personal equivalent of the loss of the national homeland is bereavement, for a bereaved person, especially an orphan deprived of a secure home, knows most intimately the resulting confusions, the instability, and the terrors. Already in the Book of *Ezekiel* the tragedy of the individual and of the nation are symbolic of each other: the death of the prophet's wife both represents and is represented by the destruction of the Temple and the fall of Judah. Not surprisingly, the greatest Hebrew poet of Zion before Bialik, Judah Halevi, also suffered bereavement in early childhood.

The imagery of infertility is also found in traditional depictions of national calamity. In the Bible, the fall of the kingdoms of Israel and Judah is described in images of barren fields and vineyards, rotten fruit, leaves, and roots. In the Book of *Ezekiel,* the fall of Judah is related both in imagery of infertility and bereavement. . . . (pp. 47-8)

One of the persistent themes in Jewish liturgy is the yearning to renew the days gone by, a motif prominent in Bialik's poetry of childhood. The hope for national renewal, for "a new heart and a new spirit," dates from the time of the exile of the Israelite nation by the Babylonians—when it became politically impotent and spiritually an orphan. Bialik occasionally, though not frequently, identified the nation's hopes as his own:

> My might is that of the nation, I too have power enough! In open spaces set free my imprisoned strength! From the smell of the field the impoverished nation will blossom, and bones that decayed shall flower like grass.

Elsewhere, the poet imagines himself cutting out his heart and hammering it, filling it with new strength. For the most part, a halo of sadness and pain hovers over Bialik's work. The hope for the renewal of the self—as of the nation—is defeated.

More clearly than most poets, Bialik bears out Lionel Trilling's contention that "the elements of art are not limited to the world of art . . . anything we may learn about the artist himself may be enriching and legitimate."

Bialik is the principal subject of his poetry, a Romantic tormented by what he had lost in life and could never regain. In life-long mourning for his childhood, he spoke meaningfully to a people in perpetual mourning for its lost nationhood. The elegiac tone of his poetry is that of the Jewish people in exile. Bialik's private agony mirrored national trauma in such an extraordinary way that the two became intertwined and inextricably linked in the poetry. (p. 48)

> *David Aberbach, "On Rereading Bialik: Paradoxes of a 'National Poet'," in* Encounter, *Vol. LVI, No. 6, June, 1981, pp. 41-8.*

ADDITIONAL BIBLIOGRAPHY

Aleichem, Sholem. "My Acquaintance with Chaim Nachman Bialik." *Yiddish* I, No. 2 (Fall 1973): 75-9.

>Personal reminiscence of Bialik's attendance at the 1907 Zionist Conference in The Hague and his subsequent visit to Aleichem in Geneva.

Alter, Robert. "The Kidnapping of Bialik and Tchernichovsky." In his *The Tradition: Modern Jewish Writing,* pp. 226-40. New York: E. P. Dutton & Co., 1969.

>Challenges the prevalent critical assessments of the two "national" poets of the Israeli renaissance, claiming that "Hebrew critics often fail to see what is actually said in a piece of literature because they are so anxious to make it a symbol, allegory, portent, or at least example of something else."

Bateson, Mary Catherine. "'A Riddle of Two Worlds': An Interpretation of the Poetry of H. N. Bialik." *Daedalus* 95, No. 3 (Summer 1966): 740-62.

>Analysis of Bialik's works according to Freudian theory.

Elon, Amos. *The Israelis: Founders and Sons.* New York: Holt, Rinehart and Winston, 1971, 359 p.

>Includes several appreciative references to Bialik's works. According to Elon: "None before Bialik nor after has expressed the Jewish will to live in words and rhymes of such beauty and poetic force; he is rightly known today as *the* national poet of Israel."

Halkin, Simon. *Modern Hebrew Literature: Trends and Values.* New York: Schocken Books, 1950, 76ff.

>Literary history. In his chapter "Religious Motifs in Modern Hebrew Poetry," Halkin briefly examines the nature of God as presented in Bialik's verses. According to Halkin: "Few among us realize Bialik's abiding clinging to the God of his fathers, in the most traditional sense of the phrase."

Lerner, Anne Lapidus. "Shabbat haMalkah." *Judaism* 33, No. 3 (Summer 1984): 301-08.

>A close analysis of Bialik's "Shabbat the Queen" which concludes that a "consistent pattern of overlooking the religious, while emphasizing the folk elements, is what distinguishes the poem. It is not . . . a religious poem; it is an areligious, national poem."

Lipsky, Louis. "Chaim Nachman Bialik." In his *A Gallery of Zionist Profiles,* pp. 106-12. New York: Farrar, Straus and Cudahy, 1956.

>An appreciative biographical and critical sketch. According to Lipsky: "[Bialik] was . . . at home with all Jews in the dust and dirt of everyday life. He brought light and warmth and hope into thousands of Jewish homes."

Ribalow, Menachem. "Bialik: Poet and Prophet." In *The Great Jewish Books: And Their Influence on History,* edited by Samuel Caplan and Harold U. Ribalow, pp. 317-39. New York: Horizon Press, 1952.

>Celebrates Bialik as a prophetic poet and spokesperson of Israel and discusses the importance of legend in Bialik's works.

Rübner, Tuvya. "Chaim Nachman Bialik (1873-1934)." In *The Modern Hebrew Poem Itself,* edited by Stanley Burnshaw, T. Carmi, and Ezra Spicehandler, pp. 18-34. San Francisco: Holt, Rinehart and Winston, 1965.

>Close analyses of several Bialik poems, including "On the Slaughter."

Spiegel, Shalom. "The Mouthpiece of the Folk." In his *Hebrew Reborn,* pp. 293-312. Cleveland and New York: Meridian Books, 1930.

>Surveys Bialik's principal works and summarizes his career. According to Spiegel: "However great and significant Bialik's achievements, the fame he enjoys extends far beyond his own deeds: it is nurtured by the forces produced by the whole epoch, but which the people, in an overflow of gratitude, has attached

to his name. It is as if the folk-memory did not care to cherish its minor gods, and heaped all their conquests upon the single chosen one.''

Waxman, Meyer. ''The Poetry of the Post Haskalah Period.'' In his *A History of Jewish Literature: Volume IV, from 1880 to 1935,* Part One, pp. 199-338. New York: Thomas Yoseloff, 1941.

Brief biography and survey of Bialik's career. According to Waxman: ''The title 'national poet' so frequently bestowed upon Bialik really belongs to him in the widest sense, for if there was ever a poet in modern times whose songs expressed the manifold of the Jewish national spirit, it was he. . . . [Bialik's poetry] marks the close of a period of poetic activity in Israel which began with the psalmists and ended with him.''

Joseph Conrad

1857-1924

(Born Tedor Josef Konrad Nalecz Korzenowski) Polish-born English novelist, short story writer, essayist, and autobiographer.

The following entry presents criticism of Conrad's novel *Nostromo*. For a complete discussion of Conrad's career, see *TCLC*, Volumes 1 and 6; for a comprehensive discussion of Conrad's novella *Heart of Darkness*, see Volume 13.

Nostromo is widely recognized as Conrad's most ambitious novel and is acclaimed by many critics as his greatest. An account of a revolution in the fictitious South American country of Costaguana, *Nostromo* examines the ideals, motivations, and failures of several participants in that conflict. Critics agree that *Nostromo* represents an important development in Conrad's career. His earlier works, including *Lord Jim* and *Heart of Darkness*, provide an intense analysis of a few characters, while in the political novels, beginning with *Nostromo* and including *The Secret Agent* and *Under Western Eyes*, Conrad widened his scope to examine an entire society. Conrad himself referred to *Nostromo* as his "largest canvas," and many critics consider the novel one of the greatest of the twentieth century.

In *Nostromo*, Conrad explored various aspects of modern life and society in a manner so artistically rich that critics have been able to examine the novel as folklore, epic, veristic narrative, and allegory, with much attention paid to the thematic and aesthetic complexities of the work. One of the most important themes of this and many other Conrad novels is the proposition that every ideal is fallible and contains within it the seeds of its own debasement. In *Nostromo*, Conrad emphasizes this theme by relating the events of the story in a chronologically disarranged order, a structure that often reveals the collapse of an endeavor before its idealistic beginning is portrayed. The effect of this presentation is to create in the reader a fatalistic sense that progress is impossible, underscoring another of the novel's major themes—that human endeavor, including political action, is ultimately ineffective. An important unifying device linking these themes is the symbolic role played by silver, described in the novel as the "incorruptible metal," which serves to corrupt even the most morally sound characters. Because of the nonchronological organization, critics have focused upon such unifying devices in their discussions of the structure of the novel, noting in particular that Conrad compensated for an intentional lack of straightforward narrative development by emphasizing the development of four major characters: Charles Gould, Dr. Monygham, Nostromo, and Martin Decoud.

Gould, an English aristocrat, reopens an abandoned silver mine in the Occidental Province of Costaguana, believing that the project will benefit Sulaco, the major city of the province. The enterprise in fact works to the detriment of the people of the city and precipitates a revolt against the dictatorial government of Costaguana. Because of his material interests, Gould supports the government and obsessively tries to save the mine from disaster. As a consequence of this obsession, he neglects his wife Emilia, one of the most sympathetic characters in the novel, who finally resigns herself to the effective dissolution

of her marriage. As Gould's love for Emilia wanes, another man, Dr. Monygham, falls in love with her. Monygham is a cynic who loathes himself for betraying several friends while under torture, but his cynicism is softened by the influence of Emilia's compassionate nature. When the Goulds and the silver mine are threatened by revolutionary forces, Monygham risks his life to save Emilia's by pretending to betray the Goulds while actually giving the revolutionaries false information.

"Nostromo" is the nickname of Giovanni Battista Fidanza, an Italian boatswain who abandons his ship on the coast of Costaguana and becomes a hero to the people of Sulaco. Although the word "nostromo" is an Italian nautical term meaning boatswain, many critics consider the name a contraction of the Italian "nostro uomo," meaning "our man," for Nostromo is the only character in the novel trusted by both the government authorities and the common people. When entrusted during the revolution with silver from the San Tomé mine, he buries it on an island, leaving Martin Decoud to guard it. Decoud, one of Conrad's most nihilistic characters, had become one of the leaders of the revolt due to his love for the revolutionary Antonia Avellanos, but while on the island he gradually loses the will to live and commits suicide by rowing out into the ocean, weighing himself down with four silver ingots from the hoard, and shooting himself. When Nostromo returns to the island, he discovers that the ingots are missing and thus cannot return the silver without being suspected as a thief. To avoid the appearance of theft, he claims that the barge sank and the silver was lost. He periodically steals from the hoard and is mistakenly shot by the island's lighthouse keeper while returning from a visit to the cache.

While early criticism of *Nostromo* often expressed dissatisfaction with the discontinuity of the novel's narrative structure, many critics nevertheless admired the fictional world Conrad had created. In an ambivalent review, Virginia Woolf wrote that "it is a world of bewildering fullness, fineness, and intricacy. . . . It would be difficult to find half a dozen thin, colourless, or perfunctory sentences in the length of the book. Each is consciously shaped and contributes its stroke to the building up of a structure to which we are sometimes tempted to apply terms more applicable to the painter's art than to the writer's." Conrad's portrayal of Costaguana was seen as especially remarkable since his only experience of South America was a two-day stop in Venezuela twenty-five years before he wrote *Nostromo*. One critic, Gustav Morf, has asserted that the origin of the novel lies not in Conrad's visit to Latin America but rather in his youth in Poland. Morf's contention is buttressed by the "Author's Note" to *Nostromo*, in which Conrad states that the character of Antonia Avellanos was based on his first love in Poland. Morf thus postulates that Decoud, Antonia's lover, is an autobiographical character. Many other critics have since identified Conrad with Decoud, based on what they perceive as the similarity between Conrad's philosophical outlook and that of Decoud.

An early critical disagreement concerning *Nostromo* focused on its complex rendering of moral issues. F. R. Leavis asserted that the greatness of *Nostromo* lay primarily in Conrad's realistic, amoral depiction of its characters and events, and not in its presentation of a consistent philosophy of life. Robert Penn Warren disagreed with Leavis's conclusion that Conrad had no philosophy, noting that even though an imperfect philosopher, "he is still, in the fullest sense of the term, a philosophical novelist." Warren's essay is an unusually optimistic reading of *Nostromo*, asserting that "there has been a civil war but the forces of 'progress'—i.e., the San Tomé mine and the capitalistic order—have won. And we must admit that the society at the end of the book is preferable to that at the beginning." Nevertheless, Warren views *Nostromo* as critical of exploitive, imperialistic forms of capitalism, and notes that conditions which would produce another civil war are developing as the novel concludes.

The standard interpretation of many of Conrad's works, including *Nostromo*, was established by Albert Guerard in his 1958 study *Conrad the Novelist*. Guerard characterized *Nostromo* as a "philosophical novel: a meditation on politics, on history, on motivation," but considered its philosophy to be far more pessimistic than did Warren. Guerard asserted that "*Nostromo* is a deeply skeptical novel," and demonstrated this thesis in a discussion of several elements of the novel, most importantly the characterization of Martin Decoud. While Leavis and Warren had accepted the authorial repudiation of Decoud as evidence of Conrad's rejection of skepticism, Guerard postulated that Conrad was in fact even more pessimistic than Decoud, but recognized and disparaged the paralysis and self-destruction which such an outlook may precipitate. Most later critics have implicitly accepted Guerard's view of Conrad's nihilism and identification with Decoud.

Later criticism of *Nostromo* reveals the diversity of approaches which may be brought to the novel. These approaches typically work toward a single end: to discover a thematic thread which will unify the seemingly disparate elements of the novel. Dorothy Van Ghent has pointed to elements of folklore in the narrative and sees the silver as a type of treasure which is associated with Emilia Gould, who in her innate goodness takes the role of a "fairy princess." The various male characters, in this scheme, become rivalling knights who endure various ordeals to win either the treasure or the princess. In another interpretation, E. M. W. Tillyard has perceived the novel as an epic, noting the depiction of the entire South American cultural milieu in Conrad's depiction of the small country of Costaguana. In an allegorical reading of the novel, Dougald McMillan writes: "The guilt and redemption which dominate the book are worked out specifically in terms of Christian myth and theology. To overlook this is to miss one of the most central sources of unity in the novel." Similarly, C. B. Cox views *Nostromo* as essentially a conflict of religious standards represented at one extreme by Decoud's nihilism and at the other by Emilia Gould's exemplary moral strength. By contrast, Stanley Tick demonstrates Conrad's ambiguous and distanced view of every religious perspective represented in the novel, including Decoud's skepticism.

The diverse interpretations of *Nostromo* demonstrate the depth and complexity of the work. Its structure, misunderstood when the novel was first published, is now recognized as an integral part of the work and a forerunner of modernist experimentation with nonchronological narrative. While the unity of *Nostromo* may be questioned, the novel is now more often praised for its realistic and complex characterization and honest exploration of human corruption. Conrad's most profound and intricate expression of his major themes, *Nostromo* is considered by many critics to be one of the greatest novels of the twentieth century.

(See also *Contemporary Authors*, Vol. 104; *Dictionary of Literary Biography*, Vol. 10: *Modern British Dramatists, 1900-1945;* Vol. 34: *British Novelists, 1890-1929: Traditionalists;* and *Something about the Author*, Vol. 27.)

THE SPECTATOR (essay date 1904)

[In the following excerpt from an early review of Nostromo, *the critic faults Conrad for a confusing multiplicity of plotlines.]*

Mr. Conrad's new book [*Nostromo*] shows in the highest relief the characteristic merits and defects of his work. He has a greater range of knowledge—subtle idiomatic knowledge—of the strange ways of the world than any contemporary writer. He has an imaginative force which at times can only be paralleled among the greatest; he has a profound sense of drama, and the logic of events which lesser people call fate; and he has a style which is often careless, involved, and harsh, but, like all true style, has moments of superb inspiration. On the other hand, he is burdened with the wealth of his equipment. A slender talent finds it easy to be lucid and orderly; but Mr. Conrad, seeing his people before him with such tremendous clearness, and entering into their loves and hates with such gusto, does not know where to begin or to end their tale. His characters crowd upon him, demanding that each have his story told with the same patient realism, till the great motive is so overlaid with minor dramas that it loses much of its appeal. His books, in consequence, tend to be a series of brilliant episodes connected by a trickle of narrative, rather than romance with the stream of story running strongly to the close. And the misfortune is that the drama which is pushed into the background is nearly always of exceptional power, capable, were the rest only duly subordinated to it, of raising the work to the highest level of art. In the book before us the story, which gives the title to the whole, is of one Nostromo, an Italian sailor, who becomes Capataz de Cargadores in the service of a steamboat company at a port in a South American Republic. He is the masterly egotist, the leader among his own class, trusted and used by his masters, happy in his second-rate greatness. But there come events which show, or seem to show, that he is a tool rather than a principal. His pride takes fire, he is all but in revolt, but his egotism comforts itself, and he does heroic work for his masters. And then somehow the story ebbs away. We see Nostromo an embryo revolutionary, spending himself in amours and a hurry to get rich, and killed at last by an accident. And the reason is that another and stronger drama comes athwart his. An Englishman and his wife have taken upon themselves the regeneration of the Republic of Costaguana by means of the silver industry which they control. The story of the regeneration, the revolution, and the creation of the Occidental Republic is the compelling interest of the book, and Nostromo comes in only as a handy *deus ex machinâ* in the greater story. The true story ends with the reminiscences of old Captain Mitchell, and the bitter reflection of Dr. Monygham that some day it would have to be done all over again,—the justification of the moral on the title-page: "So foul a sky clears not without a storm." The last two chapters belong to Nostromo's story alone, and are therefore irrelevant to the main drama, and a narrative which at times is profoundly moving and inspired with a kind of cosmic dignity ends bewilderingly with a mishap to a minor character. Either the politics of Sulaco should have been a mere background to Nostromo's tragedy, or his career should have been merely an episode in the story of the Republic. The separate interests are too potent to harmonise within one romance.

But though the construction of the book is topsy-turvy, beginning in the middle and finishing at the start, the story, considered even as narrative, is of surprising interest. Mr. Conrad has flung around his work the mystery of a cloud-covered sea and high remote mountains. All his characters, in spite of the close realism of his method, are invested with the glamour of romance. No one is perfunctorily treated; each is a living man or woman, adequately understood, drawn with firm, clean strokes. He has gone for many to the backways of life, but, strange as some are, the human blood of each is unmistakable. The most elaborate study is Nostromo, who misses being a masterpiece because of his habit of suddenly becoming a puppet in the development of another tale. But in the scene where he is adrift alone with Decoud and the treasure, in the fog, listening to the beat of the enemy's screws, there comes one of those intense moments of natural self-revelation which are the triumph of the psychologist. Mrs. Gould is an exquisite figure, the good angel of a troubled time; and if any one desires proofs of Mr. Conrad's genius, let him turn to those wonderful scenes during the Revolution when she sees for the first time the defects of her husband's regenerating policy, and shuts her lips to accept the second-best. But the greatest achievements are in the minor personages,—Decoud, the cynical and belated nationalist; Antonia; Hernandez, the brigand; the old Garibaldist Viola and his daughter; and the amazing crowd of schemers and swaggerers who play at politics in those Repub-

lics. We have said that every character is an adequate portrait. But Mr. Conrad's achievement is still greater, for he has managed to make clear the strife of ideals in a sordid warfare, and to show the core of seriousness in mock-heroics. It is not a book which the casual reader will appreciate. The sequence of events has to be sought painfully through the mazes of irrelevancy with which the author tries to mislead us. But it is a book which will well repay those who give it the close attention which it deserves. It shows signs of haste both in style and construction, and we trust that this may be the explanation of the main defects. It would be a thousand pities if an author who has few equals in talent should habitually spoil his work by an inability to do the pruning and selecting which his art demands. (pp. 800-01)

> *A review of "Nostromo," in* The Spectator, *Vol. 93, No. 3986, November 19, 1904, pp. 800-01.*

RICHARD CURLE (essay date 1914)

[*Curle was a Scottish novelist, nonfiction writer, and critic specializing in the works of Joseph Conrad. In the following excerpt, he pronounces* Nostromo *Conrad's greatest novel and discusses the main characters of the work.*]

[*Nostromo*] . . . is the history of a South American revolution. But on this leading theme there hang such a multitude of side-issues and of individual experiences that it is certainly the hardest of Conrad's novels to summarise. In this story of vast riches, of unbridled passions, of patriotism, of greed, of barbaric cruelty, of the most debased and of the most noble impulses, the whole history of South America seems to be epitomised. (p. 37)

[*Nostromo*] is a book containing so many threads of interest and so many individualities of the first order that to condense it with any realism is impossible. And how is one to recreate the romance of atmosphere? To read *Nostromo* is like drinking from a cold spring on the mountain side—it thrills you to the very marrow of your bones with a gulp of breathless and exhilarating life. *Nostromo* is Conrad's longest novel, and in my opinion, it is by far his greatest. It is a book singularly little known and one which many people find a difficulty in reading (probably owing to the confused way in which time is indicated), but it is one of the most astounding *tours de force* in all literature. For sheer creative genius it overtops all Conrad's work. Its manner of narration is, perhaps, involved, but its intricacy is highly artistic, and the continuity of the whole is convincing. In dramatic vigour, in psychological subtlety, and in the sustained feeling of a mood (an atmosphere at once physical and mental) *Nostromo* is a phenomenal masterpiece. It is Conrad's genius incarnate. (pp. 39-40)

[Not] only in its general atmosphere but in the very characters that pass through its pages, *Nostromo* is the most imaginative and original of all Conrad's books. There is, for instance, Charles Gould, the husband of Doña Emilia and the owner of the San Tomé concession. Outwardly taciturn, inwardly consumed by a passionate hatred of inefficiency, this silent man, so English amidst the excitable Costaguanos and yet so subtly a Costaguano himself, pursues his aim with the rigid inevitability of a fanatic. And, indeed, he *is* a fanatic, a man of one idea, a man intrepid, dangerous, incapable of turning back. His treatment of his wife is, of course, an integral part of his whole character—she is the slow victim of his consuming idea.

And then there is Nostromo (Gian' Battista, Captain Fidanza), a man with a genius for initiative and command, a man craving for the narrow romance of perpetual success and perpetual recognition, a man of strength and courage but of morbid sensibility, always brooding over imaginary slights, a man with a grievance which he could hardly have expressed in words but which leads him into deception and dishonour, a man of the people truly, but a man with an aristocratic aloofness of heart. I used to think that Nostromo was not a success but I now think quite otherwise. He is, perhaps, the one man of real genius in all Conrad's books. For he has the type of personality that amounts to genius. And, indeed, his grasp of a situation and his capacity for carrying out a scheme have genius in them. His whole actions during the revolution show an extraordinarily quick and fertile brain. Not only did he deal efficiently with the silver but it was really at his suggestion that Dr. Monygham carried out the brilliant idea of making Sotillo drag for it in the bay—wasting precious time in the one manner that could have appeared genuine to that rapacious and gloomy ruffian. And then, again, his ride across country to warn Barrios was a feat of genius. But the gnawing worm of discontent follows hard upon these immense material successes. Unable to extract the last ounce of recognition—the delicate flattery of unqualified fame—he feels all the bitterness of failure. He has got nothing out of it, nothing at all, neither glory nor money! Such thoughts open the path to his decline and fall. Brooding upon the injustice of society, upon their capacity to take all his abilities, his achievements, and his integrity as a matter of course, he comes to the slow conclusion that he will revenge himself by never revealing the fact that the silver is not really at the bottom of the sea, but hidden deep within the shelving sand of the Great Isabel—never revealing the fact but using his own knowledge to grow rich by stealth. Like Charles Gould, he, too, is the victim of an *idée fixe*. But our last glimpses of Nostromo are lighted for us by another flash of his former genius—the procuring of old Viola and his two daughters as keepers of the new lighthouse upon the Great Isabel. Betrothed to one daughter and secretly in love with the other, he can come there in future without comment—come to that lonely island on the border of the Placid Gulf, and abstract, one by one, the precious and haunting ingots of silver. Let me finish these words about Nostromo by giving this striking portrait of him:—

> Nostromo woke up from a fourteen hours' sleep, and arose full length from his lair in the long grass. He stood knee deep amongst the whispering undulations of the green blades with the lost air of a man just born into the world. Handsome, robust, and supple, he threw back his head, flung his arms open, and stretched himself with a slow twist of the waist and a leisurely growling yawn of white teeth, as natural and free from evil in the moment of waking as a magnificent and unconscious wild beast. Then, in the suddenly steadied glance fixed upon nothing from under a forced frown, appeared the man.
>
> (pp. 129-31)

And another very curious character is that of Dr. Monygham. He is one of these strange men who have drifted through every form of bitter degradation into a hopeless view of life, relieved only from despair by cynical hatred of his fellow-men. His atrocious sufferings under Guzman Bento, wherein in a moment of tortured weakness he has revealed the secrets which mean disaster and death to his friends, have filled his heart with an utter abasement of misery. He is like a lost soul wandering in the torments of hell. The biting sarcasm of his words conceals an agony of useless repentance. For Dr. Monygham is a man whose nobility of spirit has suffered an outrage from which it cannot recover of its own accord. He is a man who has lost all belief in himself. There is nothing more touching in Conrad than the way in which Mrs. Gould realises this in the exquisite tenderness of her compassion, and the way in which Dr. Monygham repays her by his pure devotion. To this outcast she has brought back the very breath of life.

Decoud, the Parisian mocker, the airy lover of Antonia Avellanos, the *flaneur* of the Boulevards, is another interesting study. It is not quite apparent, I think, what final impression of him Conrad means us to retain, but I should say it was the impression of a sincere patriot, who, like so many patriots, only half believes that there is anything in it all. He is the type of universal scoffer whose feelings are stronger than the reason which opposes them. His death on the Great Isabel is certainly one of the most thrilling passages in **Nostromo**. The psychology it reveals is marvellously subtle. The demoralising, mysterious effect of silence and insomnia has never before been presented with such intolerable power. (pp. 131-32)

And one of the most singular and vivid people in this book is Sotillo, the Colonel of the Esmeralda regiment, and a leader of the Montero revolution. In him is epitomised that spirit of cowardice, greed, and ruthless cruelty underlying a certain type of semi-educated South American. He has the soul of all the furies, pent up for most of his career beneath the languishing

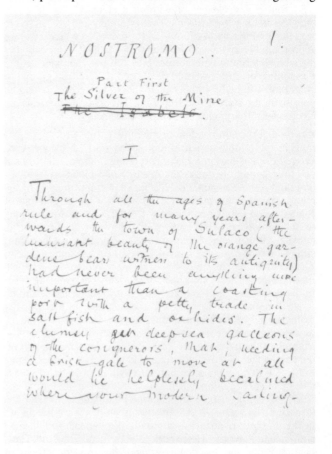

First manuscript page of Nostromo.

and irresistible exterior of a notorious ladykiller but let loose at last in an appalling avalanche of vicious cupidity and savage anger. The picture in which Conrad describes the shocking blackness of his heart is so striking that I will give it here . . .:

> Every time he went in and came out with a slam of the door, the sentry on the landing presented arms, and got in return a black, venomous, unsteady glance, which, in reality, saw nothing at all, being merely the reflection of the soul within—a soul of gloomy hatred, irresolution, avarice, and fury.
>
> (p. 133)

[Mrs. Gould] is one of the most pathetic figures in all literature. If Balzac had been a greater artist in words no doubt he would have made Père Goriot extraordinarily pathetic, but, as it is, there is not the sustained finish about his portrait that there is about Mrs. Gould's. I consider that this capacity for creating a quite beautiful and tender figure, who passes through the book radiating gentleness and understanding upon all the blind prejudice of life, reveals a very noble talent. . . . [There is] something intensely tragic about Mrs. Gould. She is not only powerless to avert the great sorrow of her life—the slow fading of Charles Gould's love—but she is at last, this fragile and pathetic figure, invaded by the poison of doubt. She who has succoured every one, is unable to succour herself, is filled in her loneliness by an awful misgiving as to her own power. As Conrad says, towards the end of the book:—

> Mrs. Gould leaned back in the shade of the big trees planted in a circle. She leaned back with her eyes closed and her white hands lying idle on the arms of her seat. The half-light under the thick mass of leaves brought out the youthful prettiness of her face; made the clear light fabrics and white lace of her dress appear luminous. Small and dainty, as if radiating a light of her own in the deep shade of the interlaced boughs, she resembled a good fairy, weary with a long career of well-doing, touched by the withering suspicion of the uselessness of her labours, the powerlessness of her magic.
>
> (pp. 147-48)

But even the bitterness of lost hope can but scratch the surface of her compassion, and that is why I am unable to believe that she would ever have used these words of biting cynicism to the fair Giselle, which Conrad puts into her mouth. I quote the scene here, not because it is striking in itself but because it seems to me the one false touch in this most beautiful of portraits:—

> "Console yourself, child. Very soon he would have forgotten you for his treasure."
>
> "Señora, he loved me. He loved me," Giselle whispered, despairingly. "He loved me as no one had ever been loved before."
>
> "I have been loved too," Mrs. Gould said in a severe tone.
>
> (pp. 148-49)

As Conrad remarks, it was "the first and only moment of cynical bitterness in her life"—but all the same I cannot bring myself to believe that she could have had such a moment: not even when I remember that she had just come from a last talk with Nostromo (Giselle's lover, wounded to death) about the

silver—the silver that had wrecked his life and had wrecked hers—the accursed silver of the mine. No, Mrs. Gould has cast her spell over me as she did, all unwittingly, over the characters in *Nostromo,* and I decline to believe that a word of cynicism ever escaped her lips. Her compassion was too genuine for her to have loosed from her heart the secret of her own unhappiness. As I said before, she is still—very still. She suffers deep within herself, keeping to the world her air of gentle wisdom and sympathy. It was Dr. Monygham alone, who, in his unbounded reverence for her, guessed all the darkness of her secret. (p. 149)

> *Richard Curle, in his* Joseph Conrad: A Study, *Doubleday, Page & Company, 1914, 245 p.*

JOSEPH CONRAD   (essay date 1917)

[*In the following excerpt, Conrad discusses the composition of* Nostromo *and notes the sources for some of the characters and background material of the novel.*]

Nostromo is the most anxiously meditated of the longer novels which belong to the period following upon the publication of the *Typhoon* volume of short stories.

I don't mean to say that I became then conscious of any impending change in my mentality and in my attitude towards the tasks of my writing life. And perhaps there was never any change, except in that mysterious, extraneous thing which has nothing to do with the theories of art; a subtle change in the nature of the inspiration; a phenomenon for which I can not in any way be held responsible. What, however, did cause me some concern was that after finishing the last story of the *Typhoon* volume it seemed somehow that there was nothing more in the world to write about.

This so strangely negative but disturbing mood lasted some little time; and then, as with many of my longer stories, the first hint for *Nostromo* came to me in the shape of a vagrant anecdote completely destitute of valuable details.

As a matter of fact in 1875 or '6, when very young, in the West Indies or rather in the Gulf of Mexico, for my contacts with land were short, few, and fleeting, I heard the story of some man who was supposed to have stolen single-handed a whole lighter-full of silver, somewhere on the Tierra Firme seaboard during the troubles of a revolution.

On the face of it this was something of a feat. But I heard no details, and having no particular interest in crime *qua* crime I was not likely to keep that one in my mind. And I forgot it till twenty-six or seven years afterwards I came upon the very thing in a shabby volume picked up outside a second-hand book-shop. It was the life story of an American seaman written by himself with the assistance of a journalist. In the course of his wanderings that American sailor worked for some months on board a schooner, the master and owner of which was the thief of whom I had heard in my very young days. I have no doubt of that because there could hardly have been two exploits of that peculiar kind in the same part of the world and both connected with a South American revolution.

The fellow had actually managed to steal a lighter with silver, and this, it seems, only because he was implicitly trusted by his employers, who must have been singularly poor judges of character. In the sailor's story he is represented as an unmitigated rascal, a small cheat, stupidly ferocious, morose, of mean appearance, and altogether unworthy of the greatness this opportunity had thrust upon him. What was interesting was that he would boast of it openly.

He used to say: "People think I make a lot of money in this schooner of mine. But that is nothing. I don't care for that. Now and then I go away quietly and lift a bar of silver. I must get rich slowly—you understand."

There was also another curious point about the man. Once in the course of some quarrel the sailor threatened him: "What's to prevent me reporting ashore what you have told me about that silver?"

The cynical ruffian was not alarmed in the least. He actually laughed. "You fool, if you dare talk like that on shore about me you will get a knife stuck in your back. Every man, woman, and child in that port is my friend. And who's to prove the lighter wasn't sunk? I didn't show you where the silver is hidden. Did I? So you know nothing. And suppose I lied? Eh?"

Ultimately the sailor, disgusted with the sordid meanness of that impenitent thief, deserted from the schooner. The whole episode takes about three pages of his autobiography. Nothing to speak of; but as I looked them over, the curious confirmation of the few casual words heard in my early youth evoked the memories of that distant time when everything was so fresh, so surprising, so venturesome, so interesting; bits of strange coasts under the stars, shadows of hills in the sunshine, men's passions in the dusk, gossip half-forgotten, faces grown dim. . . . Perhaps, perhaps, there still was in the world something to write about. Yet I did not see anything at first in the mere story. A rascal steals a large parcel of a valuable commodity—so people say. It's either true or untrue; and in any case it has no value in itself. To invent a circumstantial account of the robbery did not appeal to me, because my talents not running that way I did not think that the game was worth the candle. It was only when it dawned upon me that the purloiner of the treasure need not necessarily be a confirmed rogue, that he could be even a man of character, an actor and possibly a victim in the changing scenes of a revolution, it was only then that I had the first vision of a twilight country which was to become the province of Sulaco, with its high shadowy Sierra and its misty Campo for mute witnesses of events flowing from the passions of men short-sighted in good and evil.

Such are in very truth the obscure origins of *Nostromo*—the book. From that moment, I suppose, it had to be. Yet even then I hesitated, as if warned by the instinct of self-preservation from venturing on a distant and toilsome journey into a land full of intrigues and revolutions. But it had to be done.

It took the best part of the years 1903-4 to do; with many intervals of renewed hesitation, lest I should lose myself in the ever-enlarging vistas opening before me as I progressed deeper in my knowledge of the country. Often, also, when I had thought myself to a standstill over the tangled-up affairs of the Republic, I would, figuratively speaking, pack my bag, rush away from Sulaco for a change of air and write a few pages of the *Mirror of the Sea*. But generally, as I've said before, my sojourn on the Continent of Latin America, famed for its hospitality, lasted for about two years. On my return I found (speaking somewhat in the style of Captain Gulliver) my family all well, my wife heartily glad to learn that the fuss was all over, and our small boy considerably grown during my absence.

My principal authority for the history of Costaguana is, of course, my venerated friend, the late Don José Avellanos, Minister to the Courts of England and Spain, etc., etc., in his impartial and eloquent *History of Fifty Years of Misrule*. That work was never published—the reader will discover why—and I am in fact the only person in the world possessed of its contents. I have mastered them in not a few hours of earnest meditation, and I hope that my accuracy will be trusted. In justice to myself, and to allay the fears of prospective readers, I beg to point out that the few historical allusions are never dragged in for the sake of parading my unique erudition, but that each of them is closely related to actuality; either throwing a light on the nature of current events or affecting directly the fortunes of the people of whom I speak.

As to their own histories I have tried to set them down, Aristocracy and People, men and women, Latin and Anglo-Saxon, bandit and politician, with as cool a hand as was possible in the heat and clash of my own conflicting emotions. And after all this is also the story of their conflicts. It is for the reader to say how far they are deserving of interest in their actions and in the secret purposes of their hearts revealed in the bitter necessities of the time. I confess that, for me, that time is the time of firm friendships and unforgotten hospitalities. And in my gratitude I must mention here Mrs. Gould, "the first lady of Sulaco," whom we may safely leave to the secret devotion of Dr. Monygham, and Charles Gould, the Idealist-creator of Material Interests whom we must leave to his Mine—from which there is no escape in this world.

About Nostromo, the second of the two racially and socially contrasted men, both captured by the silver of the San Tomé Mine, I feel bound to say something more.

I did not hesitate to make that central figure an Italian. First of all the thing is perfectly credible: Italians were swarming into the Occidental Province at the time, as anybody who will read further can see; and secondly, there was no one who could stand so well by the side of Giorgio Viola the Garibaldino, the Idealist of the old, humanitarian revolutions. For myself I needed there a man of the People as free as possible from his class-conventions and all settled modes of thinking. This is not a side snarl at conventions. My reasons were not moral but artistic. Had he been an Anglo-Saxon he would have tried to get into local politics. But Nostromo does not aspire to be a leader in a personal game. He does not want to raise himself above the mass. He is content to feel himself a power—within the People.

But mainly Nostromo is what he is because I received the inspiration for him in my early days from a Mediterranean sailor. Those who have read certain pages of mine will see at once what I mean when I say that Dominic, the padrone of the *Tremolino*, might under given circumstances have been a Nostromo. At any rate Dominic would have understood the younger man perfectly—if scornfully. He and I were engaged together in a rather absurd adventure, but the absurdity does not matter. It is a real satisfaction to think that in my very young days there must, after all, have been something in me worthy to command that man's half-bitter fidelity, his half-ironic devotion. Many of Nostromo's speeches I have heard first in Dominic's voice. His hand on the tiller and his fearless eyes roaming the horizon from within the monkish hood shadowing his face, he would utter the usual exordium of his remorseless wisdom: "Vous autres gentilhommes!" in a caustic tone that hangs on my ear yet. Like Nostromo! "You hombres finos!" Very much like Nostromo. But Dominic the Corsican nursed a certain pride of ancestry from which my Nostromo is free; for Nostromo's lineage had to be more ancient still. He is a man with the weight of countless generations behind him and no parentage to boast of. . . . Like the People.

In his firm grip on the earth he inherits, in his improvidence and generosity, in his lavishness with his gifts, in his manly vanity, in the obscure sense of his greatness and in his faithful devotion with something despairing as well as desperate in its impulses, he is a Man of the People, their very own unenvious force, disdaining to lead but ruling from within. Years afterwards, grown older as the famous Captain Fidanza, with a stake in the country, going about his many affairs followed by respectful glances in the modernized streets of Sulaco, calling on the widow of the cargador, attending the Lodge, listening in unmoved silence to anarchist speeches at the meeting, the enigmatical patron of the new revolutionary agitation, the trusted, the wealthy comrade Fidanza with the knowledge of his moral ruin locked up in his breast, he remains essentially a man of the People. In his mingled love and scorn of life and in the bewildered conviction of having been betrayed, of dying betrayed he hardly knows by what or by whom, he is still of the People, their undoubted Great Man—with a private history of his own.

One more figure of those stirring times I would like to mention: and that is Antonia Avellanos—the "beautiful Antonia." Whether she is a possible variation of Latin-American girlhood I wouldn't dare to affirm. But, for me, she *is*. Always a little in the background by the side of her father (my venerated friend) I hope she has yet relief enough to make intelligible what I am going to say. Of all the people who had seen with me the birth of the Occidental Republic, she is the only one who has kept in my memory the aspect of continued life. Antonia the Aristocrat and Nostromo the Man of the People are the artisans of the New Era, the true creators of the New State; he by his legendary and daring feat, she, like a woman, simply by the force of what she is: the only being capable of inspiring a sincere passion in the heart of a trifler.

If anything could induce me to revisit Sulaco (I should hate to see all these changes) it would be Antonia. And the true reason for that—why not be frank about it?—the true reason is that I have modelled her on my first love. How we, a band of tallish schoolboys, the chums of her two brothers, how we used to look up to that girl just out of the schoolroom herself, as the standard-bearer of a faith to which we all were born but which she alone knew how to hold aloft with an unflinching hope! She had perhaps more glow and less serenity in her soul than Antonia, but she was an uncompromising Puritan of patriotism with no taint of the slightest worldliness in her thoughts. I was not the only one in love with her; but it was I who had to hear oftenest her scathing criticism of my levities—very much like poor Decoud—or stand the brunt of her austere, unanswerable invective. She did not quite understand—but never mind. That afternoon when I came in, a shrinking yet defiant sinner, to say the final good-bye I received a hand-squeeze that made my heart leap and saw a tear that took my breath away. She was softened at the last as though she had suddenly perceived (we were such children still!) that I was really going away for good, going very far away—even as far as Sulaco, lying unknown, hidden from our eyes in the darkness of the Placid Gulf.

That's why I long sometimes for another glimpse of the "beautiful Antonia" (or can it be the Other?) moving in the dimness of the great cathedral, saying a short prayer at the tomb of the first and last Cardinal-Archbishop of Sulaco, standing absorbed

A revised typescript page of Nostromo.

in filial devotion before the monument of Don José Avellanos, and, with a lingering, tender, faithful glance at the medallion-memorial to Martin Decoud, going out serenely into the sunshine of the Plaza with her upright carriage and her white head; a relic of the past disregarded by men awaiting impatiently the Dawns of other New Eras, the coming of more Revolutions.

But this is the idlest of dreams; for I did understand perfectly well at the time that the moment the breath left the body of the Magnificent Capataz, the Man of the People, freed at last from the toils of love and wealth, there was nothing more for me to do in Sulaco. (pp. xv-xxiii)

Joseph Conrad, "Author's Note," in his Nostromo: A Tale of the Seaboard, *1918. Reprint by J. M. Dent & Sons, Ltd., 1974, pp. xv-xxiii.*

[VIRGINIA WOOLF]   (essay date 1918)

[A British novelist, essayist, and short story writer, Woolf is considered one of the most prominent literary figures of twentieth-century English literature. Like her contemporary James Joyce, with whom she is often compared, Woolf is remembered as one of the most innovative of the stream of consciousness novelists. Concerned primarily with depicting the life of the mind, she revolted against traditional narrative techniques and developed her own highly individualized style. Woolf's works, noted for their subjective explorations of characters' inner lives and for their delicate poetic quality, have had a lasting effect on the art of the novel. A discerning and influential critic and essayist as well as a novelist, Woolf began writing reviews for the Times Literary Supplement *at an early age. Her critical essays, termed "creative, appreciative, and subjective" by Barbara Currier Bell and Carol Ohmann, cover almost the entire range of English literature and*

contain some of her finest prose. Along with Lytton Strachey, Roger Fry, Clive Bell, and others, Woolf and her husband Leonard formed the literary coterie known as the "Bloomsbury Group." In the following excerpt, Woolf discusses difficulties in the composition of Nostromo *and criticizes the novel for a lack of vitality and action.*]

To possess a fuller account of the processes which have produced some notable books we should be willing to offer their distinguished authors liberal terms in the shape of our gratitude, or, if it suited them better, promise to forgo a chapter here, a volume there, in return for the gift of a few pages of spiritual autobiography. It is no impiety. We are not asking that the creator should dismember his own creatures. We ask only to be allowed to look more closely into the creative process and see those whom we know as Nostromo, Antonia, or Mrs. Gould as they were before they came into the world of Sulaco, while they existed merely in the rarer atmosphere of their maker's mind.

For whatever we learn of their pre-existence undoubtedly adds to our understanding of them when they come before us as men and women of established character and settled destiny. An artist like Mr. Conrad, to whom his work is the life of his life, can only speak of his characters in the tone with which we speak of lives that have an existence independent of our own. There is a suggestive power in what he says about his intentions or his affections for these people which enables us to guess at more than is actually said. It is necessary to help out the words themselves with whatever power of intuition we may possess. In the Note [see excerpt by Joseph Conrad dated 1917], which is of course much too short for our satisfaction, Mr. Conrad tells us that after writing *Typhoon* there occurred

> a subtle change in the nature of the inspiration;
> a phenomenon for which I cannot in any way
> be held responsible. What, however, did cause
> me some concern was that after finishing the
> last story of the *Typhoon* volume it seemed
> somehow that there was nothing more in the
> world to write about.

It is for us to guess what this check in the course of his development amounted to. We should like to fancy that we see how it happened that when one conception had worked itself out there was a season of seeming emptiness before the world again became full of things to write about; but they were not the same things, and we can guess that they had multiplied in the interval. The knowledge of this crisis, if such we can call it, lends vitality to an old dilemma into which it is common to find people plunging when *Nostromo* comes up for discussion. Is it "astonishing," or is it a "failure," as critics according to Mr. Conrad variously term it, or can one hold that it is both?

In either case it is illuminating to know that it is the work of a writer who has become aware that the world which he writes about has changed its aspect. He has not got used to the new prospect. As yet it is a world in which he does not see his way. It is a world of bewildering fullness, fineness, and intricacy. The relations of human beings towards each other and towards those impersonal ideals of duty and fidelity which play so large a part in Mr. Conrad's scheme of life are seen to be more closely related and finely spun than had been visible to his youthful eye. From all this there results a crowding and suffocating superabundance which makes *Nostromo* one of those rare and magnificent wrecks over which the critics shake their heads, hesitating between "failure" and "astonishing," un-

able to determine why it is that so much skill and beauty are powerless to float the fabric into the main stream of active and enduring existence. The demon which attends Mr. Conrad's genius is the demon of languor, of monotony, of an inertness such as we see in the quiescence of the caged tiger. In *Nostromo* the tiger broods superb, supine, but almost completely immobile.

It is a difficult book to read through. One might even say, had he not in later books triumphantly proved himself master of all his possessions, that the writer would have been better served by slighter gifts. Wealth of every sort pours its avalanche from different tributaries into his pages. It would be difficult to find half a dozen thin, colourless, or perfunctory sentences in the length of the book. Each is consciously shaped and contributes its stroke to the building up of a structure to which we are sometimes tempted to apply terms more applicable to the painter's art than to the writer's. "... there was not a single brick, stone, or grain of sand of its soil that I had not placed in position with my own hands," he tells us in that passage of his *Reminiscences* where he records how for twenty months, "neglecting the common joys of life," he "wrestled with the Lord" for his creation. One may be aware, perhaps, of the extreme effort of this labour of construction, but one is also conscious of the astonishing solidity of the result. The sun is hot, the shadows profound, the earth weighted and veined with silver; the very plaster of Mrs. Gould's drawing-room appears rough to our touch, and the petals of her flowers are red and purple against it. But in a novel we demand something more than still life, and where the still life is thus superbly designed we want humanity as largely modelled and inspired by a vitality deep and passionate in proportion to the magnificence of the conception. As is apt to be the case with any work by Mr. Conrad, his characters have the rare quality of erring upon the side of largeness. The gestures with which they move upon his wide stage are uniformly noble, and the phrases lavished upon them are beautiful enough to be carved for ever upon the pedestals of statues. But when critics speak of the "failure" of *Nostromo* it is probable that they refer to something inanimate and stationary in the human figures which chills our warmer sympathies. We salute the tragedy with a bow as profound and deferential as we can make it; but we feel that nothing would be more out of keeping than an offering of tears.

> [*Virginia Woolf*], *"Mr. Conrad's Crisis," in* The
> Times Literary Supplement, *No. 843, March 14, 1918,
> p. 126.*

GUSTAV MORF   (essay date 1930)

[*In the following excerpt from an essay originally published in 1930, Morf relates characters and events in* Nostromo *to Conrad's life and to his enduring patriotic feelings for Poland.*]

A curious legend has formed around *Nostromo,* the legend that this novel is based mainly on Conrad's impressions received during a two days' visit to Venezuela, in 1876. The whole legend (for it is nothing else, as we shall see) has arisen from Conrad's own ambiguous statements, and has come to be accepted simply because of the insufficient knowledge of Conrad's Polish past, on which the novel is really built.

When Conrad was working on *Nostromo,* he wrote to R. B. Cunninghame Graham, in a letter dated 8th July, 1903:

> I am dying over that cursed *Nostromo* thing.
> All my memories of Central America seem to

slip away. I just had a glimpse twenty-five years ago—a short glance. That is not enough *pour bâtir un roman dessus*. And yet one must live.

The idea has been taken up by John Galsworthy, who wrote in his *Reminiscences of Conrad* (1925) that "in *Nostromo* Conrad made a continent out of just a sailor's glimpse of a South American port, some twenty years before."

This view does not stand a closer examination of the facts. Very few things in that novel can be called typically Central American, and even these Conrad might have got to know through his reading. All the really important facts, and, what is more, all the characters are taken from Polish or Mediterranean, reminiscences. The revolution theme itself, which might seem to be so characteristic of Latin America, reminds one distinctly of the struggle between Poles and Russians.

The key to the understanding of *Nostromo* can be found in its "Author's Note" where . . . Conrad states distinctly that Antonia Avellanos was modelled on that Polish girl ("my first love") who gave him, on his departure for France, a final hand-squeeze which he was to remember his whole life [see excerpt dated 1917]. If that be so, then Martin Decoud would be Conrad himself as a youth, for Antonia is to Martin Decoud exactly what her Polish model was to young Conrad. This supposition is fully confirmed by a close study of this curious character. Conrad has drawn a parallel between himself and Decoud in his "Author's Note," and a study of Martin Decoud throws a new light on his youth, his relations to Poland, and his patriotic sentiments.

Don Martin Decoud (so Conrad disguises himself), "a dilettante in life," "the adopted child of Western Europe," has been living in Paris for several years. There he had been "an idle boulevardier, in touch with some smart journalists, made free of a few newspaper offices, and welcomed in the pleasure haunts of pressmen." All this is closely modelled on Conrad's own life in Marseilles, as he describes it in *The Arrow of Gold,* and this manner of existence has the effect on Decoud's character it had had on Conrad's:

> This life induced in him a Frenchified—but most unFrench—cosmopolitanism, in reality a mere barren indifferentism posing as intellectual superiority.
>
> (pp. 198-99)

It is true that the young man does not then see himself as he is:

> He imagined himself French to the tips of his fingers. But far from being that *he was in danger of remaining a sort of nondescript dilettante all his life.*
>
> (p. 199)

Exactly as in Conrad's case, a more active life and a complete change of scene save him. He helps to sell arms to the silver mine in San Tomé and, moved by a curious impulse, decides to accompany the precious consignment to Sulaco himself. The cause of this unexpected zeal is the longing to see Antonia again, whom he "used to know when she wore her hair in two plaits down her back." . . . Eight years had passed since he had seen her for the last time, but he had never forgotten that "girl of sixteen, youthfully austere, and of a character already so formed that she ventured to treat slightingly his pose of disabused wisdom." This is most certainly a personal remi-

Conrad in 1873, just before he left Poland.

niscence, as a comparison with the "Author's Note" will show, and the same may be said of what follows:

> On one occasion, as though she had lost all patience, she flew out at him about the aimlessness of his life, and the levity of his opinions. He was twenty then, an only son, spoiled by his adoring family. This attack disconcerted him so greatly that he had faltered in his affection of amused superiority before that insignificant chit of a school-girl. But the impression left was so strong that ever since all the girl friends of his sisters recalled to him Antonia Avellanos by some faint resemblance, or by the great force of contrast.
>
> (pp. 199-200)

Once back in his native country, to which he had grown a stranger, his cosmopolitan superiority and superficiality soon gives way to patriotic feelings. He is "moved in spite of himself by that note of passion and sorrow unknown on the more refined stage of European politics." . . . *Passion* and *sorrow*, the very words one would be tempted to use when characterizing the Polish risings of 1831 and 1863!

Decoud had only meant to come on a short visit, but once landed, his country claims him irresistibly, and the very embodiment of that claim is the beautiful Antonia:

> But when the tall Antonia, advancing with her light step in the dimness of the big bare Sala

of the Avellanos' house, offered him her hand (in her emancipated way), and murmured, "I am glad to see you here, Don Martin," he felt how impossible it would be to tell these two people that he intended to go away by the next month's packet. . . .

The pressure of Antonia's hand was so frank, the tone of her voice was so unexpectedly unchanged in its approving warmth, that all he found to say after his low bow was:

"I am unexpressibly grateful for your welcome; but why need a man be thanked for returning to his native country? I am sure Doña Antonia does not think so."

(p. 200)

The importance of this passage cannot be overrated. It is, I think, *nothing less than the exact picture of what Conrad thought would happen to him if he returned to his native country,* a picture expressing, as do certain dreams, a definite psychological situation, namely his apprehension that a day would come when his country would claim him in the name of bonds which are stronger than practical resolutions.

So Decoud stays in Sulaco. He puts his talents as a journalist at the service of a patriotic cause by taking the direction of the newspaper *El Porvenir* ("The Future"). When the revolution breaks out, and the troops of the dictator Montero are approaching, he is the only one who urges resistance upon the frightened Sulaco notabilities, and who refuses to submit to the authority of the new ruler. This episode is very significant. With all the recklessness which youth and love can inspire, Decoud-Conrad steps into the middle of these weaklings and opportunists and pours out upon them all his scorn and contempt for their undignified behaviour.

The notabilities are assembled in a big room in Avellanos' house. Decoud comes in, asking bluntly: "What are you deliberating upon, gentlemen?" Several voices reply at once: "On the preservation of life and property," and Don Juste adds: "Till the new officials arrive." And then follows a great scene in which Joseph Conrad "dreams" that he is playing the heroic and patriotic part which it was not given to him to play in reality:

I walked up to the table blindly, as though I had been drunk. "You are deliberating upon surrender," I said. They all sat still, with their noses over the sheet of paper each had before him, God only knows why. Only Don José hid his face in his hands, muttering, "Never, never!" But as I looked at him, it seemed to me that I could have blown him away with my breath, he looked so frail, so weak, so worn out. . . .

"Do you know," I cried, "what surrender means to you, to your women, to your children, to your property?"

"I declaimed for five minutes without drawing breath, it seems to me. . . . And then for another five minutes or more, I poured *out an impassioned appeal to their courage and manliness,* with all the passion of my love for Antonia. For if ever man spoke well, it would be from a personal feeling, denouncing an enemy, defending himself, or pleading for what really

may be dearer than life. . . . I *absolutely thundered at them.* It seemed as if my voice would burst the walls asunder, and when I stopped I saw all their scared eyes looking at me dubiously. And that was all the effect I had produced! Only Don José's head had sunk lower and lower on his breast. I bent my ear to his withered lips and made out a whisper, something like, "*In God's name, then,* Martin, my son!"

(pp. 200-01)

Decoud-Conrad had insisted on action. He had exclaimed, alluding to a well-known proverb: "There is never any God in a country where men will not help themselves." . . . And now he is challenged by Don José himself to show the way. He is called to lead the people, to organize resistance, to lay the foundations of the new Occidental Republic!

Coming out of the assembly, he perceives Antonia in the gallery:

As I opened the door, she extended to me her clasped hands.

"What are they doing in there?" she asked.

"Talking," I said, with my eyes looking into hers.

"Yes, yes, but. . . ."

"Empty speeches," I interrupted her. "Hiding their fears behind imbecile hopes. They are all great Parliamentarians there—on the English model, as you know." I was so furious that I could hardly speak. She made a gesture of despair. . . . "It is a surrender," I said . . . "But it's more than talk. *Your father told me to go on in God's name.*"

. . . there is that in Antonia which would make me believe in the feasibility of anything. . . .

"*Your father himself,* Antonia," I repeated, "*your father, do you understand? has told me to go on.*"

(p. 201)

Martin Decoud *goes on* indeed, but the way he carries out his glorious mission is very Conradesque and very Polish. He is a true Korzeniowski. His real achievement stands in a strange contrast with his exalted plans. It is true that the Occidental Republic is formed in the end (obviously a creation of no stability), but even that little is done without Decoud. (pp. 201-02)

A few . . . details in the description of Decoud's suicide are such distinct reminiscences that their study actually throws fresh light on the character of Conrad himself and on his romanticism. Decoud cannot bear to be alone:

The brilliant "Son Decoud," the spoiled darling of the family, the lover of Antonia and journalist of Sulaco, was not fit to grapple with himself single-handed. Solitude from mere outward condition of existence becomes very swiftly a state of soul in which the affections of irony and scepticism have no place. *It takes possession of the mind, and drives forth the thought into the exile of utter unbelief. . . . In our activity alone do we find the sustaining illusion of an independent existence as against the whole scheme of things of which we form a helpless part*. Decoud lost all belief in the reality of his action past and to come. On the fifth day an immense melancholy descended upon him palpably. . . .

And now, as would a true romantic, Decoud *absorbs himself in his melancholy*. He derives from the painful analysis of his own state of mind a sort of sensuous pleasure, as certain people experience when ruminating over imaginary wrongs. He sees his mistake as if through a magnifying glass. He had believed in action, in effort, in a future for his country, in his own exalted mission. In the bustle of life, in the midst of persons who inspired him, who told him to go on, he had not seen the monstrosity of his audacity. But now that he was alone with himself, these illusions dispersed and he saw himself as he was, "a victim of the disillusioned weariness which is the retribution meted out to intellectual audacity" . . . , and the sense of the "utter uselessness of all effort" is brought home to him:

> . . . as if to escape from this solitude, he absorbed himself in his melancholy. The vague consciousness of a *misdirected life given up to impulses whose memory left a bitter taste in his mouth was the first moral sentiment of his manhood*. But at the same time he felt no remorse. What should he regret? *He had recognized no other virtue than intelligence, and had erected passions into duties. Both his intelligence and his passion were swallowed up easily in this great unbroken solitude of waiting without faith*. Sleeplessness had robbed his will of all energy, for he had not slept seven hours in the seven days. *His sadness was the sadness of a sceptical mind. He beheld the universe as a succession of incomprehensible images*. . . .

Three days afterwards he commits suicide. His last words are "It is done" (the very words in which Conrad had learnt the death of his father), and then the waves cover "the talker, the novio of Doña Antonia." (p. 204)

A few remarks may also be made on the fictitious Central American state that forms the scene of the novel. The word Costaguana is obviously formed on the model of Costarica, but the name is less flattering, since it is derived from guano. (It may be a mere coincidence that *guana* is the Polish genitive of *guano*). That Conrad should have chosen rather a contemptuous expression to design his fictitious state, may seem very questionable, since Costaguana stands for Poland, but the difficulty is more apparent than real. Conrad loved Poland as Antonia and Decoud love Costaguana (the latter actually dies for it), but he hated like poison the usurpers who ruled the country, together with the incapable and weak opportunists or the blind idealists and makers of new eras and new revolutions. And these types obviously formed the majority in Costaguana, as they formed the majority in the Poland of 1870, or, for that matter, of 1903. This character sketch of the Costaguanero, which Conrad puts into the mouth of Decoud, applies very well to the Poles:

> There is a curse of futility upon our character: Don Quixote and Sancho Panza, chivalry and materialism, high-sounding sentiments and a supine morality, violent efforts for an idea and

a sullen acquiescence in every form of corruption.

> (p. 207)

Eastern corruption, indeed, is not at all absent from Costaguana. Mr. Gould, on his arrival in the country, finds "circumstances of corruption . . . naïvely brazen." . . . Conrad even tells at length the complicated story of an attempt at bribery. The bribery could not succeed because its object preferred the satisfaction of a personal revenge to a pecuniary advantage. Mr. Gould had had the misfortune of offending the present Minister of Finance and

> it so happened . . . that the Finance Minister . . . was a man to whom, in years gone by, Mr. Gould had, unfortunately, declined to grant some small pecuniary assistance, basing his refusal on the ground that the applicant was a notorious gambler and cheat, besides being more than half suspected of a robbery with violence on a wealthy ranchero in a remote country district, where he was actually exercising the function of a judge. . . .

> (pp. 207-08)

Once in power, this man revenged himself by burdening Mr. Gould with a silver mine which, to an incompetent man like Mr. Gould, could only bring losses, especially as heavy taxes were immediately levied on it. Mr. Gould naturally tried to bribe the mistress of the Minister, but in vain:

> "Pas moyen, mon garçon," replied that florid person. "C'est dommage, tout de meme. Ah! zut! Je ne vole pas mon monde. Je ne suis pas ministre, moi! Vous pouvez emporter votre petit sac." . . .

Another Polish reminiscence seems to underlie Mrs. Gould's description of Sulaco:

> . . . we are very proud of it. It used to be historically important. The highest ecclesiastical court, for two vice-royalties, sat here in the olden time. . . .

Now, one has only to read the article *Cracow* in the *Encyclopaedia Britannica* to see at once the resemblance with Cracow. Cracow was once the most important town in Poland, the seat of the first bishopric, and the residence of several kings. After the partitions, it became the capital of Galicia, and the rallying point of the Polish patriots. (p. 208)

[Near the end] of *Nostromo* may be found another Polish reminiscence. Every year the owner of a famous coffee plantation sends three sacks of coffee beans to a patriotic society in remembrance "of the third of May," the date of an important battle. Now it so happens that the third of May (the only date mentioned in *Nostromo*) is one of the most important dates in Polish history, so important, indeed, that it is now the National Day. On that day, in 1791, the famous "Constitution of the Third of May" was adopted by the Diet, converting Poland into a hereditary limited monarchy with ministerial responsibility, and abolishing the *liberum veto* and other anomalies.

And finally, the "alien complex" is not absent from *Nostromo*. It is easy to imagine how often Conrad's Polish name must have been not only mispronounced but sneered at during his seafaring life. Conrad never says a word about it . . . , but this does not mean that he did not resent it. He did certainly mind it, since he adopted the name Conrad long before his first book was published. (John Galsworthy, who met him on board the *Torrens*, knew him as Mr. Conrad.) But if Conrad's resentment was repressed, it expressed itself all the better in an indirect way. The name *Nostromo* is a corruption of the Italian *Nostro uomo*, and it is an Englishman, Captain Mitchell, who is responsible for it. Conrad insists several times upon the fact:

> The Italian sailor, *whom all the Europeans in Sulaco, following Captain Mitchell's mispronunciation, were in the habit of calling Nostromo*. . . .
>
> *He whom the English called Nostromo*. . . .
>
> "You mean Nostromo?" said Decoud.
>
> *"The English call him so, but that is no name either for man or beast"*. . . .
>
> "*. . . the praise of people who have given you a silly name*—and nothing besides—in exchange for your soul and body." . . .
>
> "Who are you?"
>
> Already Nostromo had seemed to recognize Dr. Monygham. He had no doubt now. He hesitated the space of a second. The idea of bolting without a word presented itself to his mind. No use! *An inexplicable repugnance to pronounce the name by which he was known kept him silent a little longer*. At last he said in a low voice:
>
> "A Cargador." . . .
>
> (pp. 208-09)

Nostromo is not only a remarkable achievement from a literary point of view, but also full of significance for the psychologist. It is one of the best examples of the compensatory function of artistic creation. All the repressed Polish reminiscences, sentiments, aspirations and resentments, lying deep under the surface of the artist's conscious mind, had their day of rehabilitation when this book was written. Disguised in the robe of fiction, and speaking a different tongue (though not an unfamiliar language), they rose to the daylight to amuse the onlooker and to tell of things far off, long gone by, but never forgotten. Without them, there would be no *Nostromo*. (p. 209)

> *Gustav Morf, "On Nostromo," in* The Art of Joseph Conrad: A Critical Symposium, *edited by R. W. Stallman, Michigan State University Press, 1960, pp. 198-227.*

F. R. LEAVIS (essay date 1941)

[*Leavis is an influential contemporary English critic whose methodology combines close textual analysis with predominantly moral and social concerns and emphasis on the development of "the individual sensibility." Leavis views the writer as that individual who represents "the most conscious point of the race" in his or her lifetime. More importantly, the writer is one who can effectively communicate this consciousness. Contrary to what these statements may suggest, Leavis is not specifically interested in the individual writer per se, but rather with the usefulness of his or her art in the scheme of civilization. The writer's role in this vision is to eliminate "ego-centered distortion and all impure motives" from his or her work and to promote what Leavis calls "sincerity"—or, the realization of the individual's proper place in human society. Literature which accomplishes this he calls "mature," and the writer's judgment within such a work he calls*

a "mature" moral judgment. Although some scholars have been alienated from Leavis's work by what they consider his advocacy of a cultural elite, the vagueness of his moral assumptions, and his refusal to develop a systematic philosophy, he remains an important, if controversial, force in literary criticism. In the following excerpt from an essay which originally appeared in Scrutiny *in 1941, Leavis discusses the characters in* Nostromo *as well as Conrad's narrative technique.*]

[If Conrad's] most considerable work had had due recognition, it would be known as one of the great novels of the language. For *Nostromo* is most certainly that. . . . In *Nostromo* Conrad is openly and triumphantly the artist by *métier*, conscious of French initiation and of fellowship in craft with Flaubert. The French element so oddly apparent in his diction and idiom throughout his career (he learnt French before English) here reveals its full significance, being associated with so serious and severe a conception of the art of fiction.

The controlling conception of the novelist's art is severe, but the novel is luxuriant in its magnificence: it is Conrad's supreme triumph in the evocation of exotic life and colour. Sulaco, standing beneath snow-clad Higuerota, with its population of Indians, mixed-bloods, Hidalgos, Italians and English engineers, is brought before us in irresistible reality, along with the picturesque and murderous public drama of a South American State. This aspect of Conrad's genius in *Nostromo* has had full recognition; indeed it could hardly be missed. What doesn't seem to be a commonplace is the way in which the whole book forms a rich and subtle but highly organized pattern. Every detail, character and incident has its significant bearing on the themes and motives of this. The magnificence referred to above addresses the senses, or the sensuous imagination; the pattern is one of moral significances.

Nostromo has a main political, or public, theme, the relation between moral idealism and "material interests." We see the Gould Concession become the rallying centre for all in Costaguana who desire peace and order—the constitutionalists, the patriotic idealists, the Robin Hood of the oppressed, the representatives of the financial power of Europe and North America. The ironical end of the book shows us a Sulaco in which order and ideals have triumphed, Progress forges ahead, and the all-powerful Concession has become the focus of hate for workers and the oppressed and a symbol of crushing materialism for idealists and defenders of the spirit. This public theme is presented in terms of a number of personal histories or, it might be said, private themes, each having a specific representative moral significance.

The Gould Concession is in the first place the personal history of its inheritor, Charles Gould—and the tragedy of his wife. He, like the other main characters, enacts a particular answer to the question that we feel working in the matter of the novel as a kind of informing and organizing principle: what do men find to live *for*—what kinds of motive force or radical attitude can give life meaning, direction, coherence? Charles Gould finds his answer in the ideal purpose he identifies with the success of the Gould Concession:

> "What is wanted here is law, good faith, order, security. Anyone can declaim about these things, but I pin my faith to material interests. Only let the material interests once get a firm footing, and they are bound to impose the conditions on which alone they can continue to exist. That's how your money-making is justified here in the face of lawlessness and disorder. It is justified

because the security which it demands must be shared with an oppressed people. A better justice will come afterwards. That's your ray of hope.''

Charles Gould's faith is parodied by his backer, the American financier Holroyd, whose interest in furthering a ''pure form of Christianity'' and whose rhetorical faith in the manifest destiny of the United States cannot without irony be said to give ideal significance to his love of power. Charles himself is absorbed by the Concession that killed his father, and Emilia Gould, standing for personal relations and disinterested human sympathy, looks on in starved loneliness at the redeeming triumph that is an ironical defeat of the spirit.

Nostromo, picturesque indispensable to his patrons and popular hero, has no ideal purpose. He lives for reputation, ''to be well spoken of''—for his reflection in the eyes of others, and when, tempted by the silver, he condemns himself to clandestine courses the mainspring of his life goes slack. His return to find the new lighthouse standing on the lonely rock hard by his secret, and his consequent betrayal into devious paths in love, are magnificent and characteristic triumphs of symbolism. His appropriately melodramatic death is caused by the silver and occurs during a stealthy visit to it.

Martin Decoud, intellectual and ''dilettante in life,'' Nostromo's companion in that marvellously rendered night of the Gulf (it is one of the most vivid pieces of sensuous evocation in literature), also has no ideal purpose. The voice of sceptical intelligence, with ''no faith in anything except the truth of his own sensations,'' he enjoys conscious advantages, and has no difficulty in summing up Nostromo:

> Decoud, incorrigible in his scepticism, reflected, not cynically but with general satisfaction, that this man was made incorruptible by his enormous vanity, that finest form of egoism which can take on the aspect of every virtue.

He can also place Charles Gould, that ''sentimental Englishman'' who

> ''cannot exist without idealizing every simple desire or achievement. He could not believe his own motives if he did not make them first a part of some fairy tale.''

Decoud himself, contemptuously free from the ''sentimentalism of the people that will never do anything for the sake of their passionate desire, unless it comes to them clothed in the fair robes of an ideal,'' is frankly moved by his passion for Antonia Avellanos, and that alone, when he initiates the step through which the mine is saved and the aims of the patriots and idealists achieved. In this respect he provides a criticism of Charles Gould's subtle infidelity to his wife. Yet, even apart from his passion, he is not quite self-sufficient. At a moment when we might have expected him to be wholly engrossed in practical considerations we find him, significantly, illustrating an essential human trait:

> all the objectless and necessary sincerity of one's innermost life trying to react upon the profound sympathies of another's existence.

For

> In the most sceptical heart there lurks at such moments, when the chances of existence are involved, a desire to leave a correct impression of the feelings, like a light by which the action may be seen when personality is gone, gone where no light of investigation can ever reach the truth which every death takes out of the world. Therefore, instead of looking for something to eat, or trying to snatch an hour or two of sleep, Decoud was filling the pages of a large pocket book with a letter to his sister.

Marooned on the Great Isabel (site of the subsequent lighthouse) he discovers that his self-sufficiency is indeed radically qualified:

> Solitude from mere outward condition of existence becomes very swiftly a state of soul in which the affectations of irony and scepticism have no place. It takes possession of the mind, and drives forth the thought into the exile of utter unbelief. After three days of waiting for the sight of some human face, Decoud caught himself entertaining a doubt of his own individuality. It had merged into the world of cloud and water, of natural forces and forms of nature. . . .
>
> . . . He had recognized no other virtue than intelligence and had erected passions into duties. Both his intelligence and his passion were swallowed up easily in the great unbroken solitude of waiting without faith.

He shoots himself. The whole episode is given in painful immediacy.

Of all the characters the one nearest to self-sufficiency is Dr. Monygham, the disliked and distrusted, and he, for all his sardonic scepticism about human nature, does hold to an ideal. His scepticism is based on self-contempt, for his ideal (he is, in fact, a stronger and quite unequivocal Lord Jim) is one he has offended against; it is an exacting ideal of conduct. He offers a major contrast with Nostromo too, since his success in the desperate venture that saves the situation and rehabilitates him (in his own eyes—he expects death) depends upon his having no reputation except for ''unsoundness'' and a shady past, and his being ready to be ill-spoken of and ill-thought of. His ideal, of course, isn't merely personal—it is of the same order as the moral idea of the Merchant Service (he is ''an officer and a gentleman''): it owes its strength to a traditional and social sanction; and he has an outer stay in his devotion to Mrs. Gould. (pp. 231-35)

[A] negative point had better be made by way of stressing the distinctive nature of the impressiveness of **Nostromo**. The impressiveness is not a matter of any profundity of search into human experience, or any explorative subtlety in the analysis of human behaviour. It is a matter rather of the firm and vivid concreteness with which the representative attitudes and motives are realized, and the rich economy of the pattern that plays them off against one another. To suggest, as Edward Garnett does in his introduction to *Conrad's Prefaces*, that perhaps this or that character wouldn't really have behaved just as he does in the book is misdirected criticism. The life-like convincingness of Conrad's persons (which is complete as we read, and undisturbed by properly critical reflection) doesn't entitle us to psychologize them as lives existing outside the book. I am reminded of certain remarks of T. S. Eliot's:

A "living" character is not necessarily "true to life." It is a person whom we can see and hear, whether he be true or false to human nature as we know it. What the creator of character needs is not so much knowledge of motives as keen sensibility; the dramatist need not understand people, but he must be exceptionally aware of them.

It is an Elizabethan dramatist Eliot has in front of him; and it strikes me that there is something that recalls the strength of Elizabethan drama about the art of *Nostromo*—something Shakespearean, in fact. The keen sensibility and the exceptional awareness are apparent in the vividness with which we see and hear Conrad's persons, and there is nothing about them that, on reflection, we find untrue to human nature as we know it. But the seeing and hearing is adequate understanding: they are present to us and are plainly what they are; and to try, by way of appreciation or criticism, to go behind that is to misunderstand what the book offers us. There is plainly no room in *Nostromo* for the kind of illustrated psychology that many critics think they have a right to demand of a novelist (and of Shakespeare). Consider the number of personal centres of moral interest, and the variety of themes. Consider the number of vivid dramatic scenes and episodes. Consider the different strands that go to the totality of the action. There is the private tragedy of the Goulds; there is Nostromo's history, involving that of the Viola family; there is the story of Decoud and Antonia; there is that of Dr. Monygham and his self-rehabilitation; and all these and so much else are subsumed in the public historical drama—the study, concretely rendered, of the play of moral and material forces, political and personal motives, in the founding of the Occidental Republic.

Clearly, Conrad's study of motives, and of the relation between the material and the spiritual, doesn't depend for its impressiveness on any sustained analytic exhibition of the inner complexities of the individual psyche. The impressiveness lies in the vivid reality of the things we are made to see and hear, and the significance they get from their relations in a highly organized and vividly realized whole. It lies in such effects as that of the presence of Decoud and Nostromo in the lighter as it drifts with its load of silver and of Fear (personified by the stowaway Hirsch) through the black night of the Gulf; and that of the unexpected nocturnal encounter between Nostromo and Dr. Monygham, two sharply contrasted consciousnesses, in the vast deserted Custom House, and their discovery that the "shapeless high-shouldered shadow of somebody standing still, with lowered head" seen on the wall through a doorway, is thrown by the hanging body of the tortured Hirsch. (pp. 237-39)

Again, we have the symbolic pregnancy of Conrad's dramatic method in such a representative touch as this (the context is the flight of aristocrats and adherents of "law and order" to the protection of the "master of the Campo"):

> The emissary of Hernandez spurred his horse close up.
>
> "Has not the master of the mine any message to send the master of the Campo?"
>
> The truth of the comparison struck Charles Gould heavily. In his determined purpose he held the mine and the indomitable bandit held the Campo by the same precarious tenure. They were equals before the lawlessness of the land. It was im-

possible to disentangle one's activities from its debasing contacts."

There is—the adjective proposes itself at this point—something rhetorical, in a wholly laudatory sense, about Conrad's art in *Nostromo*. One might add, by way of insisting further on the Elizabethan in it, that it has a certain robust vigour of melodrama. The melodrama, of course, is completely controlled to the pattern of moral significance. Consider, for instance, how the climax of the public drama is given us: it is a thrilling nick-of-time *peripeteia*, but it is given in retrospect through the pompous showmanship and uncomprehending importance of Captain Mitchell ("Fussy Joe"). The triumphs of the Progress he hymns are already assured and commonplace, and already (a few pages on) Dr. Monygham is asking:

> "Do you think that now the mine would march upon the town to save their Señor Administrador? Do you think that?"

He has just pronounced:

> "There is no peace and no rest in the development of material interests. They have their law, and their justice. But it is founded on expediency, and it is inhuman; it is without rectitude, without the continuity and the force that can be found only in a moral principle."

This is only one instance of that subtle play of the order of presentment against the time-order which the reader finds himself admiring in the book as a whole—subtle, yet, once taken stock of, appreciated as inevitable. It is characteristic of Conrad's method, to take another instance, that we should have seen, in a prospective glimpse given us at the very opening of the book, the pitiable *débâcle* of the Ribierist dictatorship of "reform" before we are invited to contemplate the hopes and enthusiasms of its supporters at the inauguration.

It will probably be expected, after so much insistence on the moral pattern of *Nostromo,* that something will be said about the total significance. What, as the upshot of this exhibition of human motive and attitude, do we feel Conrad himself to endorse? What are his positives? It is easier to say what he rejects or criticizes. About the judgment on Decoud's scepticism we can have no doubt. And even Decoud concedes that the illusions "those Englishmen" live on "somehow or other help them to get a firm hold of the substance." To this concession we can relate the observations of the engineer-in-chief:

> "Upon my word, doctor, things seem to be worth nothing by what they are in themselves. I begin to believe that the only solid thing about them is the spiritual value which everyone discovers in his own form of activity—"
>
> "Bah!" interrupted the doctor.

The engineer has in mind Holroyd the millionaire and his preoccupation with a "pure form of Christianity." But although Dr. Monygham, himself devoted to a moral idea, is as such clearly not disapproved by the author, he is made to seem Quixotic, and it is difficult to feel that the ironic light in which the "spiritual values" discovered by the other main characters in their forms of activity are shown is less essentially dissociating than the irony focussed upon Holroyd. In fact, though Decoud is so decisively dealt with in the action, he remains at the centre of the book, in the sense that his consciousness seems to permeate it, even to dominate it. That consciousness is clearly very closely related to the author's own personal *timbre*, that which becomes representable in quotation in such characteristic sardonic touches as:

> They had stopped near the cage. The parrot, catching the sound of a word belonging to his vocabulary, was moved to interfere. Parrots are very human.
>
> "Viva Costaguana!" he shrieked. . . .

It is not a question of a "philosophy"; Conrad cannot be said to have one. He is not one of those writers who clear up their fundamental attitudes for themselves in such a way that we may reasonably, in talking of them, use that portentous term. He does believe intensely, as a matter of concrete experience, in the kind of human achievement represented by the Merchant Service—tradition, discipline and moral ideal; but he has also a strong sense, not only of the frailty, but of the absurdity or unreality, in relation to the surrounding and underlying gulfs, of such achievement, a sense so strong that it often seems very close to Decoud's radical scepticism, which is, in the account of those last days, rendered with such significant power. In fact, Decoud may be said to have had a considerable part in the writing of *Nostromo;* or one might say that *Nostromo* was written by a Decoud who wasn't a complacent dilettante, but was positively drawn towards those capable of "investing their activities with spiritual value"—Monygham, Giorgio Viola, Señor Avellanos, Charles Gould.

At any rate, for all the rich variety of the interest and the tightness of the pattern, the reverberation of *Nostromo* has something hollow about it; with the colour and life there is a suggestion of a certain emptiness. And for explanation it is perhaps enough to point to this reflection of Mrs. Gould's:

> It had come into her mind that for life to be large and full, it must contain the care of the past and of the future in every passing moment of the present.

That kind of self-sufficient day-to-dayness of living Conrad can convey, when writing from within the Merchant Service, where clearly he has known it. We are made aware of hostile natural forces threatening his seaman with extinction, but not of metaphysical gulfs opening under life and consciousness: reality on board ship is domestic, assured and substantial. "That feeling of life-emptiness which had made me so restless for the last few months," says the young captain of *The Shadow-Line,* entering on his new command, "lost its bitter plausibility, its evil influence." For life in the Merchant Service there is no equivalent in *Nostromo*—no intimate sense conveyed of the day-to-day continuities of social living. And though we are given a confidential account of what lies behind Dr. Monygham's sardonic face, yet on the whole we see the characters from the outside, and only as they belong to the ironic pattern—figures in the futilities of a public drama, against a dwarfing background of mountain and gulf. (pp. 240-43)

> *F. R. Leavis, "Joseph Conrad," in his* The Great Tradition, *Doubleday & Company, Inc., 1954, pp. 211-72.*

WALTER F. WRIGHT (essay date 1949)

[*Wright is an American educator and critic. In the following excerpt, he traces the destructive influence of silver on the lives of Charles Gould and Nostromo.*]

Nostromo . . . is not more profound than Conrad's other works, but it is perhaps, as he himself believed, his "largest canvas." There were good reasons for laying the story in Costaguana, the revolution-torn South-Central American republic. The country, whose boundaries only were imaginary, provided a striking juxtaposition of refinement and crudity, of aristocratic graciousness and exploitative violence. The spirit of material conquest, supported in part by foreign capital, gave an opportunity to show the power of an idea to captivate and corrupt the mind. The legendary curse of dragon hoards was for Conrad no fanciful myth. In making the San Tomé silver mine the villain of his novel, he was giving to an idea that sinister tangible embodiment which it assumes for the human mind.

Of the vast canvas it is impossible to cover all. There is Dr. Monygham, for example, who, under torture, once betrayed his friends. There is Martin Decoud, the skeptic, who loses faith in his actions and commits suicide. But principally there are the two men who are most directly the slaves of the mine—Charles Gould, partner and manager, and Nostromo, *capitaz de cargadores.*

Utterly free from greed and miserliness, Gould has noble ideals; he will improve the conditions of life in Costaguana. Far from glorifying himself as a hero, he is a hard working, unassuming man, who sees a practical task before him. There is disorder and there is poverty. The wealth from the mine can reduce the poverty and bring stability. But to do so, it must be safeguarded as the essential means. Its protection, Gould soon discovers, involves intrigue stretching to North America and Europe and also necessitates the bartering of money for influence in the entangled political affairs of Costaguana itself. Before long, men are for Gould commendable not because of character or aspirations for their country, but because of their alignment on the side that offers the greater protection to the mine. He is not lustful for power; yet he finds that only power will enable him to achieve his goal and only the mine, of course, will give him that power. He has certain principles of conduct. Government officials supported by the mine can be expected to return service for money, and Gould himself will adhere to the commitments which he has made. But the idea of the mine takes precedence over all else, even human life.

The depth to which Gould has sunk is not expressed in rashness or obvious brutality. Though thoroughly sick of the intrigue in which he has enmeshed himself, he remains outwardly self-possessed. The most serious devastation of spirit that he has experienced is, as we might expect in Conrad, revealed indirectly. Others, including his wife, may be unhappy, but their thoughts are about humanity, religion, love. It is precisely the absence of any real feeling of these, whatever giving of alms and insistence upon justice he may display, that makes Gould tragic. Intellectually he may stress the value of humane sentiments, as we might admit the value of a knowledge of the languages of Tibet, but all sensation of them has left him. He is like Godwin's St. Leon or Maturin's Melmoth the Wanderer, who even when they are making others happy are, through their supernaturalness, deprived of kinship in human feeling. Gould does not, like Macbeth, call life an idiot's tale, but he finds it, nevertheless, cheap and depressing.

Gould does not condemn himself, for his is a career very unlike Lord Jim's or Arsat's surrender to impulse. The process of his decline has been too gradual and too well justified. He has seen his problem as a two-horned dilemma. To enunciate a visionary ideal but reject all unpleasantness in its pursuit is to indulge in sentimental cant. Gould, as his wife points out, does cloak his motives in a "fairy tale" in order to believe in them; but he has, at the same time, chosen to be practical, "to stoop for his weapons." We should, of course, like to suggest a third alternative that he might have chosen, but that Conrad has not made easy. Gould is a politician in the broadest implication of the term, and he has shaped his life and interests not by philosophic meditation upon ultimate values, but by the making of specific commitments as practical problems have confronted him day after day. Were he without integrity, he would be the proper subject for satiric comedy. But the pressures upon him are much like those which confront all of us, and the tragic horror is accentuated by the fact that the victim, though finding life empty, is unaware of what he has excluded that might have been a part of his experience.

The tragedy of Nostromo, the *capataz*, develops with swiftness, but it, too, is no trick of impulse. While on a voyage to Mexico, Conrad heard of a man who had stolen a lighter of silver. Knowing nothing of the thief's motives and character, Conrad found a challenge to his imagination. He decided that to perform such a deed one would have to be resolute and reckless, and for his model in these respects he drew upon his old pirate friend Dominic de Cervoni. He concluded, too, that the act should result not in the quickening of conscience and desire for atonement, but in the corruption of the thief. In this part of Nostromo's history he had no one model, but the observations gleaned in half a lifetime.

The ways of Nostromo and Gould touch only superficially until the silver of the mine reaches out to ensnare even the bystanders. Among the dock workers Nostromo the "incorruptible" enjoys the prestige that easily comes to the man who is always daring and always successful. Both to his employers and to his associates he is "our man," to be paid and complimented for his risks, but to be treated with the same cavalier offhandedness with which he himself seems to regard his achievements. No one stops to ask whether he has a soul, for Nostromo does not wear his heart on his sleeve. He takes the risk, draws his pay, and distributes largesse to his admirers.

It is only when a lighter of silver is to be spirited from the harbour to prevent capture that Nostromo comes under the spell of the mine. The undertaking proves much harder than he has expected. He narrowly misses capture and death, and his having to content himself with only partial success by hiding the silver on an island amounts, for him, to failure. The experience daunts him and he feels betrayed. In order to rescue the silver he has been unable to take time to bring a priest to his dying benefactress. In rescuing it he has been jarred into the horrifying sensation of failure, a sensation contradictory to his whole experience. "This thing," he tells Decoud, "has been given to me like a deadly disease."

It is not until the bitter realization of his position overtakes him that Nostromo senses, still confusedly, what cold reason could have shown him in advance. Surely one is not to be accused of lack of ethical principles for saying that Nostromo actually owes little or no moral obligation to the owners of the silver. They have regarded him as a mere tool and yet have asked him to stake his life and peace of mind. Only by the figment of man-made laws does the silver belong to them; the bars of metal will, in fact, be small reward for his loss. What he does not realize is that in concealing them and then representing them as sunk in the harbor he has become their victim. As he ironically remarks before he yet knows the truth of his words, "there is something in a treasure that fastens upon a man's mind."

Had it been another man, . . . there would have been no such dilemma. The "perfect love of the work" would have seen him through without question as to the ownership and, of course, without the loss of self-respect. But Nostromo, even in his successes and despite his apparent indifference to praise, has never thought of a dangerous job for its own sake, but rather of Nostromo in the triumph of its accomplishment. He is not bitter toward himself . . . , for like Gould he has made no mistake from impulse. On the contrary, he has exercised both his ingenuity and his courage and yet has been defeated. (Decoud's purloining a bar to weight himself for drowning is a second blow and becomes an excuse for not returning the silver.) He is enraged at fate and cynical about humanity, and so there is no escape. For the silver he comes to sacrifice the happiness of the two girls who love him, and, in what amounts to a physical parallel of his spiritual destruction, he loses his own life. His submission to the power of the silver, confirmed by his cautious reflection "I must grow rich slowly," took for Conrad the symbolic pattern of legendary romance:

> And the spirits of good and evil that hover about a forbidden treasure understood well that the silver of San Tomé was provided now with a faithful and lifelong slave.

(pp. 137-41)

Besides being much better written than *Almayer's Folly* and *An Outcast of the Islands, Nostromo,* like *The Secret Agent* and *Under Western Eyes,* shows the intricate relationships by which the evil of one life reaches beyond it to take possession of the lives of others and then comes back augmented. Gould has become so engulfed in intrigue that, instead of ruling others, he is the victim of capitalistic exploitation and of political conspiracy. Nostromo, with no political or social views and with indifference to the prosperity of the mine, is caught in the scheme of corruption which, even beneath the urbane and cultivated exterior, pervades the society of Costaguana. Mrs. Gould, the two sisters who love Nostromo, and many others who escape with their souls still pay in suffering. An idea disguising itself as the materialistic benefactor of mankind has grown, dragonlike, until it has filled and then enveloped the castle that once housed it; and it has victimized not only its host, who naïvely welcomed it, but all within his feudal domain. (pp. 141-42)

Walter F. Wright, in his Romance and Tragedy in Joseph Conrad, *University of Nebraska Press, 1949, 217 p.*

ROBERT PENN WARREN   (essay date 1951)

[*Warren is considered one of the most distinguished men of letters in America today. Consistently in the intellectual vanguard of American scholarship, he began his career—with John Crowe Ransom, Donald Davidson, Allen Tate, and several others—as a member of the Fugitive group of Southern poets during the 1920s. The stated intent of the Fugitives was to create a literature utilizing the best qualities of modern and traditional art. After 1928, the four major Fugitives joined eight other writers, including Stark Young and John Gould Fletcher, to form the Agrarians, a group dedicated to preserving the Southern way of life and traditional Southern values. The Agrarians were concerned with social and political issues as well as literature; in particular, they attacked Northern industrialism as they sought to preserve the Southern farming economy. Warren, Ransom, and Tate eventually left Agrarianism and went on to become prominent founders of New Criticism, one of the most influential critical movements of the mid-twentieth century. Although the various New Critics did not subscribe to a single set of principles, all believed that a work of literature had to be examined as an object in itself through a process of close analysis of symbol, image, and metaphor. For the New Critics, a literary work was not a manifestation of ethics, sociology, or psychology, and could not be evaluated in terms of any nonliterary discipline. Warren's work is strongly regional in character, often drawing its inspiration from the land, the people, and the history of the South. The intensely metaphysical nature of his poetry and the experimental style of his fiction have brought him critical acclaim. While he often bases his themes on specific historical events, Warren successfully transcends the local to comment in universal terms on the human condition. Warren's deep interest in history and his conception that art is a vital force in contemporary society informs all of his work. In the following excerpt from an essay originally published in 1951 as the introduction to the Modern Library edition of* Nostromo, *he discusses Conrad's philosophical outlook as exemplified in that novel.]*

In [*Nostromo*] Conrad endeavored to create a great, massive, multiphase symbol that would render his total vision of the world, his sense of individual destiny, his sense of man's place in nature, his sense of history and society. (p. 48)

All readers of Conrad know the classic picture of imperialism at its brutal worst in *Heart of Darkness*, the degradation and insanity of the process, and remember the passage spoken by Marlow:

> "The conquest of the earth, which mostly means the taking it away from those who have a different complexion or slightly flatter noses than ourselves, is not a pretty thing when you look into it too much. What redeems it is the idea only."

In *Heart of Darkness* we see the process absolutely devoid of "idea," with lust, sadism, and greed rampant. In *Nostromo* we see the imperialistic process in another perspective, as the bringer of order and law to a lawless land, of prosperity to a land of grinding poverty. At least, that is the perspective in which Charles Gould sees himself and his mine:

> "What is wanted here is law, good faith, order, security. Anyone can declaim about these things, but I pin my faith to material interests. Only let the material interests once get a firm footing, and they are bound to impose the conditions on which alone they can continue to exist. That's how your money-making is justified here in the face of lawlessness and disorder. It is justified because the security which it demands must be shared with an oppressed people."

This passage and Gould's conception of his own role may be taken as the central fact of the social and historical theme of *Nostromo*. But how does Conrad intend us to regard this passage? Albert Guerard, Jr., in his careful and brilliant study of Conrad, says that the mine "corrupts Sulaco, bringing civil war rather than progress." That strikes me as far too simple. There has been a civil war but the forces of "progress"—i.e., the San Tomé mine and the capitalistic order—have won. And we must admit that the society at the end of the book is preferable to that at the beginning.

Charles Gould's statement, and his victory, are, however, hedged about with all sorts of ironies. For one thing—and how cunning is this stroke!—there is Decoud's narrative, the letter written to his sister in the midst of the violence, that appears at the very center of the book; and the voice of the skeptic tells us

how history is fulfilled. For another thing—and this stroke is even more cunning—old Captain Mitchell, faithful-hearted and stupid, the courageous dolt, is the narrator of what he pleases to call the "historical events." His is the first human voice we have heard, in Chapter II of Part I, after the mists part to exhibit the great panorama of the mountains, campo, city, and gulf; and in Chapter X of Part III, just after Nostromo has made his decision to ride to Cayta and save the Concession and the new state, the voice of Captain Mitchell resumes. He is speaking long afterward, to some nameless distinguished visitor, and now all the violence and passion and the great anonymous forces of history come under the unconscious irony of his droning anecdotes. We can say of Captain Mitchell what Conrad says of Pedrito Montero, inflamed by his bad novels read in a Parisian garret: his mind is "wrapped . . . in the futilities of historical anecdote." Captain Mitchell's view is, we may say, the "official view": "Progress" has triumphed, the world has achieved itself, there is nothing left but to enjoy the fruits of the famous victory. Thus the very personalities of the narrators function as commentary (in a triumph of technical virtuosity) as their voices are interpolated into Conrad's high and impersonal discourse.

But we do not have to depend merely on this subtle commentary. Toward the end of the book, at a moment of pause when all seems to be achieved on a sort of Fiddler's Green at the end of history, a party has gathered in the garden of the Casa Gould. They discuss in a desultory way the possibility of a new revolution, and the existence of secret societies in which Nostromo, despite his secret treasure and growing wealth, is a great force. Emilia Gould demands: "Will there never be any peace?" And Dr. Monygham replies:

> "There is no peace and no rest in the development of material interests. They have their law and their justice. But it is founded on expediency, and is inhuman; it is without rectitude, and without the continuity and force that can be found only in a moral principle. Mrs. Gould, the time approaches when all that the Gould Concession stands for shall weigh as heavily upon the people as the barbarism, cruelty, and misrule of a few years back."

The material interests have fulfilled their historical mission, or are in the process of fulfilling it. Even Charles Gould, long before, in defining his mission to bring order through the capitalistic development, had not seen that order as the end, only as a phase. He had said: "A better justice will come afterwards. That's our ray of hope." And in this connection we may recall in *Under Western Eyes* how, after hearing the old teacher of languages give his disillusioned view of revolution, Miss Haldin can still say: "I would take liberty from any hand as a hungry man would snatch at a piece of bread. The true progress must begin after." In other words, the empire-builder and hard-bitten realist Gould and the idealistic girl join to see beyond the era of material interests and the era of revolution the time of "true progress" and the "better justice." Somewhere, beyond, there will be, according to Miss Haldin's version, the period of concord:

> I believe that the future will be merciful to us all. Revolutionist and reactionary, victim and executioner, betrayer and betrayed, they shall all be pitied together when the light breaks on our black sky at last. Pitied and forgotten; for without that there can be no union and no love.

Emilia Gould, trapped in her "merciless nightmare" in the "Treasure House of the World," leans over the dying capataz and hears him say, "But there is something accursed in wealth." Then he begins to tell her where the treasure is hidden. But she bursts out: "Let it be lost for ever."

If in this moment of vision, Emilia Gould and (in a sense that we shall come to) Conrad himself repudiate the material interests as merely a step toward justice, what are we to make of revolution? We may remember that Conrad most anxiously meditated the epigraphs of his various books, and that the epigraph of *Nostromo* is the line from Shakespeare: "So foul a sky clears not without a storm." It is innocent to think that this refers merely to the "storm" which is the action of the novel, the revolution that has established the order of material interests in Sulaco. If the sky has cleared at the end of that episode, even now in the new peace we see, as Dr. Monygham sees, the blacker and more terrible thunderheads piling up on the far horizon.

Heart of Darkness and *Nostromo* are, in one sense, an analysis and unmasking of capitalism as it manifested itself in the imperialistic adventure. Necessarily this involves the topic of revolution. The end of *Nostromo* leaves the sky again foul, and in the years immediately after finishing that novel Conrad turns to two studies of revolution, *The Secret Agent,* begun in 1905 and published in 1907, and *Under Western Eyes,* begun in 1908 and published in 1911. These books are in their way an analysis and unmasking of revolution to correspond to the already accomplished analysis and unmasking of capitalism and imperialism. In the world of revolution we find the same complex of egotism, vanity, violence, and even noble illusion. As the old teacher of languages in *Under Western Eyes* puts it:

> A violent revolution falls into the hands of the narrowminded fanatics and of tyrannical hypocrites at first. Afterwards comes the turn of all the pretentious intellectual failures of the time. Such are the chiefs and the leaders. You will notice that I have left out the mere rogues. The scrupulous and the just, the noble, humane, and devoted natures; the unselfish and the intelligent may begin a movement—but it passes away from them. They are not the leaders of a revolution. They are its victims: the victims of disgust, of disenchantment—often of remorse. Hopes grotesquely betrayed, ideal caricatured—that is the definition of revolutionary success. There have been in every revolution hearts broken by such successes.

We could take this, in appropriate paraphrase, as a summary of the situation at the end of *Nostromo.* There is the same irony of success. There has been the same contamination of the vision in the very effort to realize the vision. As Emilia Gould reflects: "There was something inherent in the necessities of successful action which carried with it the moral degradation of the idea." (pp. 48-53)

The setting of [*Nostromo*], the isolation of Sulaco, is in itself significant. The serrated wall of the Cordillera, hieratic and snow-capped, behind the Campo, the Azuera and the Golfo Placido define a little world that comes to us as complete—as a microcosm, we may say, of the greater world and its history. Man is lost in this overwhelming scene. The story of the two gringos, spectral and alive, on the peninsula of Azuera is, of course, a fable of greed and of the terrifying logic of material

interests unredeemed. But it is also a fable, here at the threshold of *Nostromo,* of man lost in the blankness of nature. At the center of the book, to resume the same theme, we find the story of Decoud, who loses his identity into the "world of cloud and water, of natural forces and forms of nature." When he commits suicide, he falls into the "immense indifference of things." Then at the very end of the novel, in the last paragraph, Dr. Monygham, in the police-galley, hears the wild, faithful cry uttered by Linda, the name of Nostromo: "Never! Gian' Battista!"

> It was another of Nostromo's successes, the greatest, the most enviable, the most sinister of all. In that true cry of love and grief that seemed to ring aloud from Punta Mala to Azuera and away to the bright line of the horizon, overhung by a big white cloud shining like a mass of solid silver, the genius of the magnificent capataz de cargadores dominated the dark gulf containing his conquests of treasure and love.

This, too, is a fable: the passionate cry in the night that is a kind of triumph in the face of the immense indifference of things. It is a fable with a moral not unlike that of the second of Yeats's "Two Songs from a Play":

> *Whatever flames upon the night*
> *Man's own resinous heart has fed.*

Or to take another fable, one from Conrad's essay on Henry James:

> When the last aqueduct shall have crumbled to pieces, the last airship fallen to the ground, the last blade of grass have died upon a dying earth, man, indomitable by his training in resistance to misery and pain, shall set this undiminished light of his eyes against the feeble glow of the sun. . . .
>
> For my own part, from a short and cursory acquaintance with my kind, I am inclined to think that the last utterance will formulate, strange as it may appear, some hope now to us utterly inconceivable.

I have tried to define my reading of Conrad's work in general and of *Nostromo* in particular. In these matters there is not, and should not be, an ultimate "reading," a final word and orthodoxy of interpretation. In so far as a work is vital, there will continually be a development, an extrapolation of significance. But at any one moment each of us must take the risk of his sensibility and his logic in making a reading. I have taken this risk, and part of the risk is the repudiation, or at least criticism, of competing interpretations.

There is one view, not uncommonly encountered, that Conrad did not intend his fiction to have "meaning." We encounter, for example, the comment of Edward Crankshaw: "Bothering about what Conrad meant in *Heart of Darkness* is as irrelevant as bothering about what Mozart meant in the Haffner Symphony." Conrad himself gives some support to this view in his skeptical bias, in his emphasis on the merely spectacular value of life, and in not a few of his remarks on his literary intentions, particularly in the famous one: "My task which I am trying to achieve is, by the power of the written word, to make you hear, to make you feel—it is, before all, to make you *see.*"

All of this seems to me, however, to mean nothing more than that Conrad was an artist, that he wanted, in other words, to arrive at his meanings immediately through the sensuous renderings of passionate experience, and not merely to define meanings in abstraction, as didacticism or moralizing. Conrad made no split between literature and life. If anything, he insisted on the deepest inward relationship. As he put it about the writer in the essay **"Books":** "It is in the impartial practice of life, if anywhere, that the promise of perfection for his art can be found, rather than in the absurd formulas trying to prescribe this or that particular method of technique or conception."

Over and over again, Conrad implies what he says in the Author's Note to *Chance:* "But every subject in the region of intellect and emotion must have a morality of its own if it is treated at all sincerely; and even the most artful writer will give himself (and his morality) away in about every third sentence." And even to the famous sentence about his intention being, before all, to make us "*see*," we find an addition: "That—and no more, and it is everything." To seeing in its fullest sense, to "our sympathetic imagination," as Conrad says in **"Autocracy and War,"** we must look "for the ultimate triumph of concord and justice." (pp. 55-7)

The philosophical novelist, or poet, is one for whom the documentation of the world is constantly striving to rise to the level of generalization about values, for whom the image strives to rise to symbol, for whom images always fall into a dialectical configuration, for whom the urgency of experience, no matter how vividly and strongly experience may enchant, is the urgency to know the meaning of experience. This is not to say that the philosophical novelist is schematic and deductive. It is to say quite the contrary, that he is willing to go naked into the pit, again and again, to make the same old struggle for his truth. But we cannot better Conrad's own statement for the philosophical novelist, the kind of novelist he undertook, quite consciously, to be: "Even before the most seductive reveries I have remained mindful of that sobriety of interior life, that asceticism of sentiment, in which alone the naked form of truth, such as one conceives it, can be rendered without shame."

For him the very act of composition was a way of knowing, a way of exploration. In one sense this is bound to be true of all composition, but the matter of degree and self-consciousness is important in our present distinction, even crucial. We know a little of how *Nostromo* came to be, how it rose out of a feeling of blankness, how its composition was, in sober fact, an exploration and a growth, how the "great mirage," as Edward Garnett called it, took shape until it could float before us, vivid and severe, one of the few mastering visions of our historical moment and our human lot. (p. 58)

> Robert Penn Warren, " 'The Great Mirage': Conrad and 'Nostromo'," in his Selected Essays, Random House, 1958, pp. 31-58.

WINIFRED LYNSKEY   (essay date 1954)

[Lynskey is an American educator and critic. In the following excerpt, she analyzes the use of silver as a symbol in Nostromo.]

In Conrad's *Nostromo*, critics have failed to consider the rôle of the silver. The clear fact is that Conrad objectifies the evil he is concerned with. In *Victory*, for example, he presents a totality of evil, objectified in Jones (intellectual or conscious evil); in Ricardo (instinctive savagery); and in Pedro (brute

force). In *Nostromo* evil is objectified in the silver, incorruptible itself but capable of corrupting everyone who comes in contact with it, no matter what his attitude or motive may be.

In *Nostromo* Conrad creates a totality of moral or ethical attitudes toward the silver, the two extremes and the mean. At one extreme is Gould, the idealist, the man who erects illusions into convictions, who sublimates his passion for the silver mine into an act of abstract justice. At the other extreme is Decoud, the sceptic, the man without illusions, who knows well his own "sane" and cynical motives in serving the silver. The mean is Nostromo, the man of simple faith, who wants only to fulfill the obligations which life lays upon him, to live up to the trust people have in him. He is Conrad's answer to the problem of evil. He is a typical Conrad hero.

In *Nostromo* the evil (i.e. the silver) is the evil of material interests or capitalism, and it is invincible. Its power lies in its ability to exact its own conditions for its survival. Gould makes this power clear where he says, "Only let the material interests once get a firm footing, and they are bound to impose the conditions on which alone they can continue to exist." The conditions which the silver (or material interests) imposes in *Nostromo* are moral disaster for Gould, death for Decoud, and enslavement and death for Nostromo.

In the fate of his three main characters Conrad points to the powerful rôle of the silver. The silver becomes the mistress of Gould's thoughts, consumes him like a passion, destroys his love for his wife, and erects "a wall of silver bricks" between them. The despairing Decoud, marooned on the Great Isabel island, puts four ingots of silver in his clothing to carry him down in the water, and shoots himself. Thus, "weighted by the bars of the San Tomé silver," Decoud disappears. Nostromo, who has betrayed his faith and is morally dead, is shot, "creeping out of the ravine, weighted with silver."

None of these men had a personal interest in the silver for whose safety they were all ready to die. If none of these high-minded moral attitudes are proof against the silver, what of lesser men, who are motivated by greed and selfishness? Such men behave badly, and the novel exposes them all. But the real pessimism lies in the picture of the silver over-riding all human morality exemplified in Gould, Decoud, and Nostromo.

In his preface to the Modern Library edition of *Nostromo,* Mr. Robert Penn Warren does not mention the role of the silver (except on the simple plot level) nor weigh the moral attitudes. Failure to consider Conrad's analysis of the moral struggle against the silver can lead to complicated theorizing. It also eads to Mr. Zabel's reference to the "dramatic impenetrability" of *Nostromo*. In the light of Conrad's analysis, characters and motives are not impenetrable. Viola and Antonia, for example, are idealists. Dr. Monygham is a sceptic.

In the end, Mrs. Gould, who has the greatest insight in the book, says to the dying Nostromo, "Let it (the silver) be lost forever." Her statement is a recognition of the power the silver exerts over all human motives, whether good or bad. But her statement is no solution to the problem. Conrad's epigraph for *Nostromo* reads: "So foul a sky clears not without a storm." Obviously the foul sky, darkened by material and capitalistic interests, has not cleared through the storm of revolution in **Nostromo.** The silver has conquered or corrupted all who were drawn to it. The storm is yet to come. But the novel reveals what all of Conrad's novels reveal: that evil is too powerful for humanity, but humanity, nevertheless, possesses magnificent courage and moral stamina in its fight against evil.

Winifred Lynskey, "Conrad's 'Nostromo'," in The Explicator, *Vol. XIII, No. 1, October, 1954, Item #6.*

ALBERT J. GUERARD (essay date 1958)

[*Guerard, an American novelist and critic, has written extensively on Conrad, and his* Conrad the Novelist *(1958) is considered the standard critical interpretation of several of Conrad's works. In the following excerpt from that book, Guerard discusses the theme of skepticism in* Nostromo.]

Nostromo is . . . a philosophical novel: a meditation on politics, on history, on motivation. Is it, as I believe, a pessimistic and skeptical meditation; and therefore a true one? The instances are glaring of the generous-minded who have read into Conrad's narratives their own tenderness and faith. But the contrary danger exists that the disillusioned, reading as tendentiously, should discover only their own disillusionment with political process. *Nostromo*'s prophecies of 1904 would seem to have been confirmed to a remarkable degree, and not only in South America. Or does this mean that we misread its prophecies from the vantage point of our mid-century ruin? Robert Penn Warren's brilliant introduction to the Modern Library edition (which sees a less ironic treatment of "idealization" than I do, and a less pessimistic view of capitalism) has repeatedly led me to question my conclusions. And the essay has in fact led me to modify certain opinions on the novel's structure. But my view of the novel's ethics and politics remains unmodified: that *Nostromo* is a deeply skeptical novel.

To weigh the value of idealization and illusion means weighing, also, the value of skepticism and reality. And any definition of the novel's position or attitude must depend to a considerable degree on how we interpret Martin Decoud. The problem is a special one, to which we must presently return. But there are other skeptics in *Nostromo* besides Decoud, and others who place some faith in the efficacy of skepticism. There is first of all the omniscient narrator who (after commenting on Nostromo's reaction to Señora Viola's death) brings up the matter rather gratuitously: "The popular mind is incapable of skepticism; and that incapacity delivers their helpless strength to the wiles of swindlers and to the pitiless enthusiasms of leaders inspired by visions of a high destiny." The history of popular misfortune in Costaguana is a history of credulity, as generation after generation is taken in by slogan and glowing manifesto. "Liberals!" even Charles Gould complains. "The words one knows so well have a nightmarish meaning in this country. Liberty—democracy—patriotism—government. All of them have a flavour of folly and murder."

Does skepticism, protecting us from folly, also prevent us from acting at all? Such would seem to be the meaning of Decoud's death, and of the aphorism that holds action the enemy of thought and the friend of flattering illusion. But the general skepticism of Dr. Monygham and the political skepticism of Father Romàn do not prevent them from acting and acting loyally; and even the thought-paralyzed Decoud turns out to have accomplished a good deal. Characteristically, Conrad makes it difficult to know how to value the disillusionment of Father Romàn.

[He was] saddened at the idea of his flock being scattered or else enslaved. He had no illusions as to their fate, not from penetration, but from long experience of political atrocities, which seemed to him fatal and unavoidable in the life of a State. The working of the usual public institutions presented itself to him most distinctly as a series of calamities overtaking private individuals and flowing logically from each other through hate, revenge, folly, and rapacity, as though they had been part of a divine dispensation. Father Romàn's clear-sightedness was served by an uninformed intelligence; but his heart. . . .

The rhetorical uncertainties (clear-sighted but uninformed, from long experience not from penetration) suggest Conrad felt more sympathy with this nihilism than seemed to him proper. And what is his attitude toward Mrs. Gould (the novel's unequivocal heroine) when she reaches its most succinct skeptical recognition? "There was something inherent in the necessities of successful action which carried with it the moral degradation of the idea."

The history of Costaguana is largely determined by individuals, and by their idealizations as well as by their cupidities and lusts; men compose the state. Yet these seem to be, in *Nostromo,* two separate areas for inquiry: first, man's propensity to self-deception and his need to "idealize" his existence; second, the failure of institutions to work and the failure of history to make sense. The protagonists and their illusions stand a little to the forefront of a turgid and disordered congeries of event.

The meanings of the words "ideal," "idealize," and "ideal conception," whether used by Decoud or another, are by no means immutable. The sense in which Dr. Monygham made an "ideal conception of his disgrace" is dark and elusive, but at least it involves the "imaginative exaggertion of a correct feeling." It does not imply self-deception, much less self-flattery. But Decoud suggests (speaking of Charles Gould's idealization of the mine) both distortion of reality and unconscious moralistic self-deception. Gould "cannot act or exist without idealizing every simple feeling, desire, or achievement. He could not believe his own motives if he did not make them first a part of some fairy tale." He must, Decoud remarks, endow his "personal desires with a shining robe of silk and jewels"; must see life as a "moral romance." And Decoud's contempt for that "utter sentimentalist" Holroyd, the San Francisco financier, is grounded in his awareness of the man's need to moralize his game of power—who "would not drop his idea of introducing, not only justice, industry, peace, to the benighted continents, but also that pet dream of his of a purer form of Christianity." Decoud speaks as forcefully as anywhere in the novel when he refers to "the sentimentalism of the people that will never do anything for the sake of their passionate desire, unless it comes to them clothed in the fair robes of an idea."

How much credence are we to give this skeptical, attractive voice with its distinctly Conradian rhythm and rhetoric? The question is raised by Decoud's solitary vigil on the Great Isabel, and death. Thereafter he cannot speak for the author or anyone else. But someone does appear at once, the chief engineer, who can speak at least for Decoud. The degree to which he echoes Decoud suggests that Conrad shared no little of this skepticism; or, at least, could not "turn off" a congenial voice and flow of thought:

"The introduction of a pure form of Christianity into this continent is a dream for a youthful enthusiast, and I have been trying to explain to you why Holroyd at fifty-eight is like a man on the threshold of life, and better, too. He's not a missionary, but the San Tomé mine holds just that for him . . . Upon my word, doctor, things seem to be worth nothing by what they are in themselves. I begin to believe that the only solid thing about them is the spiritual value which everyone discovers in his own form of activity—''

''Bah!'' interrupted the doctor, without stopping for an instant the idle swinging movement of his legs. ''Self-flattery. Food for that vanity which makes the world go round.''

In daily life we may approve this tendency to moralize and idealize all impulse; or we may, as I do, find it deeply repugnant. What is the novel's attitude toward it? Warren's important discussion of this problem refers back to **Lord Jim**'s famous passage on the ''destructive element'' and on the dream into which man is born. ''By the dream Conrad here means nothing more or less than man's necessity to justify himself by the 'idea,' to idealize himself and his actions into moral significance of some order, to find sanctions.'' But does Conrad therefore approve this necessity under all circumstances, and even when it involves gross egotism and self-deception? To argue thus, and to suggest approval of the ''true lie'' at all times and even when directed toward oneself, is to destroy at one stroke Conrad's healing lucidity and irony. Warren remarks that we see the process of imperialism ''absolutely devoid of 'idea' '' in **Heart of Darkness** [see excerpt dated 1951]; presumably he refers to the pilgrims or ''explorers.'' But the grandiloquent moralizings of Kurtz, which feed his vanity in solitude, lead to conduct even more abominable. The ''idea'' and the very process of moralistic self-deception here corrupt. My own feeling is that Conrad does not limit our choice (as Warren implies) to an inhuman naturalism or a self-deceptive idealism, to animal savagery or ''illusion.'' **Nostromo** seems rather to distinguish between the self-deluding, self-flattering victim of his own illusions and the genuine clear-headed idealist; between, say, Charles Gould and his wife. But also I think the novel makes much more allowance than Warren does for those who do something ''for the sake of their passionate desire''; who without illusion but also without meanness pursue it. They need not be cynics, after all, nor mere healthy animals. I should even include Father Corbelàn among them, that passionate man—driven by something stronger than vanity and other than religious obligation.

The skepticism concerning historical and political process is less equivocal; it seems, at times, total. There is first of all a total distrust of political discourse, spoken or written. All governments however corrupt seek the ''peace,'' ''progress,'' and ''security'' of Sulaco; all journalism and all propaganda is deceitful. But **Nostromo** insists, as *1984* will, that the deception is often self-deception and the rhetoric self-intoxicating. Even the chief engineer is affected. ''It was as if something subtle in the air of Costaguana had inoculated him with the local faith in 'pronunciamentos.' '' For the young Goulds the passing of the silver escort to the harbor was ''like another victory gained in the conquest of peace for Sulaco''; their friend, the historian Don José, expatiates even in their presence ''upon the patriotic nature of the San Tomé mine.'' Conrad separates himself from the Decoud who repudiates patriotism because ''the narrowness of every belief is odious,'' but less so from the Decoud who says patriotism in this country was ''hopelessly besmirched . . .

had been the cry of dark barbarism, the cloak of lawlessness, of crimes, of rapacity, of simple thieving.'' I am not sure that he separates himself at all from the Decoud who feels political journalism is a degrading profession, and who dislikes evoking the enthusiasms which will send ignorant people out to die. The parrot's cry ''Viva Costaguana!'' defines the country's excited preoccupation; Decoud's *''Gran' bestia!''* defines the methods of its journalism. Amused or perhaps embittered by the ''boastful tumult'' and self-deceptions of the politicians gathered at the Casa Gould, he shouts it into the room—*''Gran' bestia!''* his journalistic epithet for Montero—''with all the strength of his lungs.'' But the politicians, not recognizing the irony, turn toward him ''with an approving expectation.''

The political skepticism of **Nostromo** goes much farther than this. In places it suggests, simply, that reason and good will are relatively powerless before dumb or hidden process; that history escapes man's intentions and his will. What are the true causes of ''history''? Pedro Montero's reading of light historical literature in the Paris garret is one; Decoud's love for Antonia is another. But there would be no thriving Occidental Republic without the eleven-story Holroyd building in San Francisco. Certain employees there suppose ''the Holroyd connection meant by-and-by to get hold of the whole Republic of Costaguana, lock, stock, and barrel.'' The truth is that Holroyd took up the country as a hobby, even took up the man Gould rather than the country, and made the journey south because his doctors insisted he take a vacation. Yet who can really know the truth? Holroyd's ancestry had given him ''the temperament of a Puritan and an insatiable imagination of conquest.'' So behind the individual's whim and moral heritage lies a nation's manifest destiny. The last sentence of Holroyd's remarkable prediction is the most important one:

> ''Of course, some day we shall step in. We are bound to. But there's no hurry. Time itself has got to wait on the greatest country in the whole of God's Universe. We shall be giving the word for everything: industry, trade, law, journalism, art, politics, and religion, from Cape Horn clear over to Smith's Sound, and beyond, too, if anything worth taking hold of turns up at the North Pole. And then we shall have the leisure to take in hand the outlying islands and continents of the earth. We shall run the world's business whether the world likes it or not. The world can't help it—neither can we, I guess.''

These then are some of the contradictory forces flowing together, in Costaguana, to bring forth the historical events: from one side chance, unpredictable dreams and illusions, whim, folly; from the other a vast predetermined economic movement. But the two conceptions of history that insist on them are not contradictory: they alike discount man's reason as a force and alike deny a rational orderly consecutiveness of event. The chronological dislocations and almost insoluble complications of the first part of the novel thus dramatize a theory of causality. They suggest too that since one manifestation is much like the next one, it little matters which ''came first.'' The main events of the Sulaco disorders (which we retrospectively discover lasted only a few days) give an impression of occuring over weeks or even months; conversely, events which occurred years apart seem contemporary. Costaguana is a country in which ''everything merely rational fails''; literally, then, its history is absurd.

It is inviting to universalize this country, which in many ways seems truer and more contemporary than the England of **The**

Secret Agent or the Geneva and Russia of *Under Western Eyes*. And it is reasonable to suppose that Conrad was thinking of lands as far removed from each other as nineteenth-century Paraguay and Carlist northern Spain and imperial Russia (as well as say Venezuela or some Central American republic) when he wrote of an endemic moral darkness breeding "monstrous crimes and monstrous illusions," and of the "indolence of the upper classes and the mental darkness of the lower" as "fundamental causes." But his thematic insistence is on the "moral romance of capitalism" (with its inherent tendency to confuse power and goodness, profit and welfare) as it affects a small, still undeveloped, and anarchic land. It is the fatality of the country, Decoud complains, to be exploited by foreign speculators while the natives cut each other's throats. But Charles Gould argues that only capitalism—"material interests"—can stop the throat-cutting:

> "What is wanted here is law, good faith, order, security. Any one can declaim about these things, but I pin my faith to material interests. Only let the material interests once get a firm footing, and they are bound to impose the conditions on which they alone can continue to exist. That's how your money-making is justified here in the face of lawlessness and disorder. It is justified because the security which it demands must be shared with an oppressed people. A better justice will come afterwards. That's your ray of hope."

The classic defense could hardly be put more succinctly. But what do the material interests actually accomplish, and by what methods? Granted that Holroyd looks upon God "as a sort of influential partner," and granted too Charles Gould's ambition to "redeem" the mine—the Gould Concession must work in an imperfect world of men and manners and must stoop for its weapons. The story is subtly equivocal. The Concession does bring a position of "privileged safety" to the miners, but at a cost of individuality and personal freedom. They live in the three numbered villages protected by an armory, an armed body of sereños, and under the benevolent absolute authority of Don Pépé. They are safe on visits to Sulaco, even have a relative immunity to arrest, but because they wear a kind of uniform, the colors of the mine. The San Tomé mine is a state within a state. Did it, with its bribes increase or diminish the overall corruption? The evidence . . . is ambiguous, since the chronology is obscure; we cannot be sure whether the mine profited from, reacted against, or contributed to the increasing cynicism. My guess is that Conrad intended a contrast between the naked cynicism and "brazen-faced scramble" for loot in the hinterland and the subtler methods practiced in an Occidental State controlled by the mine. The former killed all enterprise; the latter encouraged at least a nepotistic energy. There would thus be a choice of evils. But surely one evil is replaced by another evil (or at least by a dangerous precedent) when the Gould Concession finances the revolution which brought Don Vincente Ribiera into his five-year dictatorship with a mandate of reform.

So far as Dr. Monygham is concerned, and finally Mrs. Gould herself, there is a corruptive fatality in the "material interests":

> "No!" interrupted the doctor. "There is no peace and no rest in the development of material interests. They have their law, and their justice. But it is founded on expediency, and is inhuman; it is without rectitude, without the continuity and the force that can be found only in a moral principle. Mrs. Gould, the time approachs when all that the Gould Concession stands for shall weigh as heavily upon the people as the barbarism, cruelty, and misrule of a few years back."

And Mrs. Gould,

> There was something inherent in the necessities of successful action which carried with it the moral degradation of the idea. She saw the San Tomé mountain hanging over the Campo, over the whole land, feared, hated, wealthy; more soulless than any tyrant, more pitiless and autocratic than the worst Government; ready to crush innumerable lives in the expansion of its greatness.

These passages occur very near the end of the novel's chronological time. *The time approaches. . . .* In my interpretation they look forward to a period when—as in Guatemala yesterday, as in the Middle East today—the conflicts induced by captalist exploitation outweigh the benefits accrued. But according to Warren we may read them hopefully, keeping in mind Charles Gould's prediction that a better justice will come afterwards. "The material interests have fulfilled their historical mission, or are in the process of filling it. . . . The difference would seem to lie in how far the novel looks into the future. We can respect Warren's serious statement —"nothing is to be hoped for, even in the most modest way, if men lose the vision of the time of concord"—without admitting that *Nostromo* dramatizes or even implies it. The horizon offered by the book itself seems to me, simply, Dr. Monygham's dark one.

What are we to say of Sulaco within the dramatized lapse of time? Certainly the society at the end of the book is preferable to that at the beginning, as Warren argues, if we take as beginning the savage old days of Guzman Bento's tyranny and as end the quiet moment when Dr. Monygham makes his prediction. Or is the "end" that referred to by the narrator who momentarily speaks in the first person: a Sulaco with cable cars, foreign merchants with modern villas, a vast railway goods yard, warehouses, and "serious, organized labour troubles"? He remarks, of the earlier Sulaco, that the "material apparatus of perfected civilization which obliterates the individuality of old towns under the stereotyped conveniences of modern life had not intruded as yet. . . ." The old debate—the values of modern comfort against those of individuality and ancient culture—is suggested but not solved. On the large subject of "progress" even imagery offers an uncertain testimony:

> . . . the sparse row of telegraph poles strode obliquely clear of the town, bearing a single, almost invisible wire far into the great campo— like a slender, vibrating feeler of that progress waiting outside for a moment of peace to enter and twine itself about the weary heart of the land.

Martin Decoud remains to be dealt with; and no small part of the impression of skepticism left by *Nostromo* comes from him. His consciousness, as Leavis says [see excerpt dated 1941], seems to permeate and even dominate the book. And if the novel succeeds in "repudiating" Decoud with sufficient force, this must certainly affect our response to the over-all vision. Warren remarks that Conrad "repudiates the Decouds of this world'' and Leavis that ''we can have no doubt'' about the judgment on Decoud's skepticism. But both go on to recognize that the creative situation is more complex than this. Indeed it is! We cannot say that Conrad repudiates skepticism by repudiating Decoud; we cannot even say (without further qualification) that Conrad develops some creative sympathy for Decoud while disapproving of him. The characterization obviously belongs with those in which a writer attempts to separate out and demolish a facet of himself; attempts to condemn himself by proxy. But there are certain signs of an even more special relationship than this; *there is, generally, a marked discrepancy between what Decoud does and says and is, and what the narrator or omniscient author says about him.*This suggests that some of the irony is directed at a personage who is not fully in the book or not in it at all; a Decoud-self conceived but not dramatized. To put matters bluntly: Conrad may be condemning Decoud for a withdrawal and skepticism more radical than Decoud ever shows; which are, in fact Conrad's own. May we not alter Leavis' proposition—that *Nostromo* was written by a Decoud who wasn't a complacent dilettante and who was ''drawn toward those capable of 'investing their activities with spiritual value' ''—to say that it was written by an even more skeptical Decoud who recognized, to be sure, the immobilizing dangers of skepticism?

Critics have generally dwelt on what the narrator or author says about Decoud, if only because it is so quotable. The book's mannerism of recurrent ironic epithets is repeatedly directed against him: he is ''the boulevardier,'' ''the exotic dandy of the Parisian boulevard,'' ''the dilettante in life,'' ''the spoiled darling of the family,'' ''the brilliant Costaguanero of the boulevards,'' etc. And the account of his suicide includes a large amount of decisive repudiation. Decoud ''died from solitude and want of faith in himself and others''; he ''was not fit to grapple with himself single-handed''; the affectations of irony and skepticism had driven forth his thought ''into the exile of utter unbelief.'' And he died a ''victim of the disillusioned weariness which is the retribution meted out to intellectual audacity''; he ''disappeared without a trace, swallowed up in the immense indifference of things.'' Some of the force of Conrad's ''repudiation of skepticism'' may be taken away by that last phrase. If Decoud experiences a total cosmic skepticism, the surviving narrator here certainly shares it! It is useful to recall, too, that only ten days but 194 pages separate the Decoud we left on the Great Isabel and the Decoud who commits suicide. For how indifferent, inactive, and uncommitted is the real Decoud, whom Warren describes as thinking ''himself outside of the human commitments''? If we subtract the ironic epithets, authorial summaries, and solitary suicide, a quite different person emerges. So far from believing in or caring about nothing, he has an ideal of lucidity and of intellectual honesty, he is very much in love, and he is (quite apart from his love for Antonia or from his attitude toward the current political situation) a patriot. His bitter reaction to the slurring remarks of young Scarfe and his sudden ouburst to Don José are hardly those of an indifferent man:

> ''There is a curse of futility upon our character: Don Quixote and Sancho Panza, chivalry and materialism, high-sounding sentiments and a supine morality, violent efforts for an idea and a sullen acquiescence in every form of corruption. We convulsed a continent for our independence only to become the passive prey of a democratic parody, the helpless victims of scoundrels and cut-throats, our institutions a

> mockery, our laws a farce—a Guzman Bento our master! And we have sunk so low that when a man like you has awakened our conscience, a stupid barbarian of a Montero—Great Heavens! a Montero!—becomes a deadly danger, and an ignorant, boastful Indio, like Barrios, is our defender.''

How are we to weigh these impassioned tones against Decoud's claim that he is not a patriot, or against his desire (enunciated by the narrator once) to carry Antonia ''away out of these deadly futilities of pronunciamientos and reforms''? The paradox is like that of Conrad himself, though I offer it as illustration rather than ''source'': a deeply patriotic and even excited feeling toward Poland doubled by intellectual distrust of fanaticism. Decoud very properly sees propaganda journalism as ''a sort of intellectual death,'' yet becomes the editor of a local newspaper; he sees accurately enough that the political situation in Costaguana is comical, yet brings the small arms to Sulaco; he ridicules the excited discussions of the legislators in the Gould salon, yet fathers the Occidental Republic. ''Another revolution, of course. On my word of honour, Mrs. Gould, I believe I am a true *hijo del pays,* a true son of the country, whatever Father Corbelàn may say. And I'm not so much of an unbeliever as not to have faith in my own ideas, in my own desires.'' He is, to borrow his own words, one of those who *will* do something for the sake of his passionate desire, and even though it not come ''clothed in the fair robes of an idea.''

The creative situation is thus exceedingly complex, even if we put aside possible direct biographical connections. On the one hand there is a Martin Decoud who, in spite of the epithets, receives no little of his creator's sympathy and approval: the apparently idle and indifferent young exile who returns home to participate in inflammatory journalism, obeys his loved one's commands, and fathers a revolution, yet all the while (through his lucid insight into men's motives) maintains intellectual integrity. He is at once spectator and actor, and he achieves a kind of immortality in the commemorative medallion and Antonia's undying love. But there also has been present, perhaps all the time, the idea or image (though not in the events of the book itself) of another Decoud or another self: immobilized in total physical isolation and in the exile of utter unbelief, who sees no reason for action, who is virtually incapable of it. This is the dramatically invisible Decoud now and then belabored by epithet, and whose suicide we are allowed to witness: ''his sadness was the sadness of a skeptical mind.'' Is it hard to believe, in spite of Conrad's magnificent rhetorical evocation of his solitude, that the active and loving Decoud would commit suicide so soon? The remarkable thing is that we believe as much as we do. For the two Decouds are, indeed, two very different men, two different ''potential selves.'' (pp. 189-202)

> *Albert J. Guerard, in his* Conrad the Novelist, *Cambridge, Mass.: Harvard University Press, 1958, 322 p.*

E. M. W. TILLYARD   (essay date 1958)

> [*Tillyard was an English scholar of Renaissance literature whose studies of John Milton, William Shakespeare, and the epic form are widely respected. In the following excerpt, he remarks upon aspects of* Nostromo *which parallel traditional conventions in epic narrative.*]

[*Nostromo*] is unique among all the works of Conrad in its span, both of space and of time. It concentrates on an imagined small town in Central or South America but simultaneously it makes us aware of the whole world outside. The main action takes place within three days, but simultaneously is set in a great stretch of history with hints of prehistory or of the fabulous. These matters are vital in creating the epic effect. (p. 127)

Costaguana is much more than the self-contained and narrow setting which Conrad sometimes uses to correspond to and set off the stripped and fundamental conflicts of a few characters; a ship or the abandoned quay in *Victory*. Costaguana is full of a seething and varied life, and its fortunes are the concern of much of the world outside. It is ruthlessly faithful to the virtues and vices of Spanish America, but it is exposed to the inroads and the criticisms of some of the chief nations of the earth. Through these inroads and these criticisms Conrad not only tells us more of Spanish America but conveys a whole phase of Western European policy and thought. The following passage illustrates (as could a score of others) this double operation. It describes Charles Gould returning to his house at dawn of the third day of rioting at Sulaco:

> Charles Gould rode on, and turned into the archway of his house. In the patio littered with straw, a practicante, one of Dr. Monygham's native assistants, sat on the ground with his back against the rim of the fountain, fingering a guitar discreetly, while two girls of the lower class, standing up before him, shuffled their feet a little and waved their arms, humming a popular dance tune. Most of the wounded during the two days of rioting had been taken away already by their friends and relations, but several figures could be seen sitting up balancing their bandaged heads in time to the music. Charles Gould dismounted. A sleepy mozo coming out of the bakery door took hold of the horse's bridle; the practicante endeavoured to conceal his guitar hastily; the girls, unabashed, stepped back smiling; and Charles Gould, on his way to the staircase, glanced into a dark corner of the patio at another group, a mortally wounded Cargador with a woman kneeling by his side; she mumbled prayers rapidly, trying at the same time to force a piece of orange between the stiffening lips of the dying man.
>
> The cruel futility of things stood unveiled in the levity and sufferings of that incorrigible people; the cruel futility of lives and of deaths thrown away in the vain endeavour to attain an enduring solution of the problem.

That is Spanish America seen through the eyes of a certain Englishman; and many other eyes see it. But though it exists thus contingently, as it meets the outside world, it exists also, and as firmly, in its own rights. And that outside world too has the same double function. It serves first as background and influence. It is *there*, while the fierce action proceeds at Sulaco; and it intervenes to direct that action. But it exists in its own right too. It presents what were for Conrad the main political drifts of the late nineteenth century. Of these I shall write later. My present point is that by combining the closely inbred, the strictly documented domestic, with the ecumenical *Nostromo* achieves the kind of variety and amplitude propitious to the epic effect.

In point of time, though much of the action is transacted within the compass of three days, we learn a very great deal about roughly the amount of time (before and after those days) that a man could be conscious of in an ordinary lifetime. And into that time a whole revolution in the ways of life is compressed; feudalism yields to the pressure and the exploitations of modern capitalism, which itself becomes exposed to the beginnings of a communist movement. Such scope is impressive enough, but it is not the whole, for the revolution, propelled ultimately by western Europe with the help of North America and not by the Spaniards of the new world, repeats a pattern set up hundreds of years ago.

Conrad set the action of *Nostromo* in the context of history with engaging tact. He scarcely ever moralises like the historian, but works mainly through a judicious modicum of plain but pregnant facts about the condition of the land in the old colonial days. The road from Sulaco to Rincon and into the plain is still the old royal road, the Camino Real; and the gentle iteration of the name works secretly on our minds. And there is the statue of Charles IV at the entrance of the Alameda, now known to the ignorant simply as the Horse of Stone. The San Tomé mine itself had a long history. In the earliest Spanish days it was worked by slave labour, as in its latest phase it was to be worked by men nominally free but subject to different forms of compulsion. In the interval it was closed, and then reopened after the war of independence by English exploiters. These were murdered in the confused times after the death of Guzman Bento, the savage dictator. The new governments confiscated and owned the mine but could not work it, and one of them forced it on Gould's father in repayment for the loans it had wrung from him. Charles Gould, inheriting and working it, suffered yet another version of the slavery it had been destined to inflict from the day of its opening. He is but one of a number of historic victims. Nor were royal road and mine the only witnesses of a cruel past.

> The heavy stonework of bridges and churches left by the conquerors proclaimed the tribute-labour of vanished nations. The power of king and church was gone, but at the sight of some heavy ruinous pile overtopping from a knoll the low mud walls of a village, Don Pépé would interrupt the tale of his campaigns to exclaim—
>
> "Poor Costaguana! Before, it was everything for the Padres, nothing for the people; and now it is everything for those great politicos in Sta. Marta, for negroes and thieves."

Writing his letter to his sister about the progress of the riots, Decoud tells her that Viola's house, in which he writes, "may have been contrived by a Conquistador farmer of the pearl fishery three hundred years ago." And it is Decoud who utters the most explicit statement of history repeating itself. The Goulds and their party, which includes Decoud, are returning in their carriage from the harbour where they have seen Barrios and his troops (armed with the rifles Decoud has just brought from Europe) embark for Cayta. As the carriage passes through the "old gateway facing the harbour like a shapeless monument of leaves and stones," their ears are smitten by a "strange, piercing shriek," and the whole procession of people from the harbour turn their heads to see an empty construction train "returning from the Campo to the palisaded yards." The driver applies his brakes,

> and when the ear-splitting screech of the steam-whistle for the brakes had stopped, a series of hard, battering shocks, mingled with the clank-

ing of chain-couplings, made a tumult of blows
and shaken fetters under the vault of the gate.

These words end a chapter; and their emphatic place confirms
Hewitt's surmise that these fetters are symbolic of the grip on
the land of Costaguana maintained by the new railway, a principal instrument of those "material interests" whose triumph
is one of the themes of the book. Anyhow, immediately after,
in the next chapter, Decoud takes them as such. The carriage
passes through the gate: with the noise of whistle and of shaken
couplings in his ears he scanned

> moodily the inner aspect of the gate. The squat
> turreted sides held up between them a mass of
> masonry with bunches of grass growing at the
> top, and a grey, heavily scrolled, armorial shield
> of stone above the apex of the arch with the
> arms of Spain nearly smoothed out as if in
> readiness for some new device typical of the
> impending progress.

And the combination of sound and sight provoke him to remark
that the "sound puts a new edge on a very old truth." And
that truth is that Spanish America was subject from the first
to the invasions of the English. The new, English, railway is
a later version of an old story. Decoud explains:

> "Just imagine our forefathers in morions and
> corselets drawn up outside this gate, and a band
> of adventurers just landed from their ships in
> the harbour there. Thieves, of course. Specu-
> lators, too. Their expeditions, each one, were
> the speculations of grave and reverend persons
> in England. . . . But to return to my noises;
> there used to be in the old days the sound of
> trumpets outside that gate. War trumpets! I'm
> sure they were trumpets. . . . In those days this
> town was full of wealth. Those men came to
> take it. Now the whole land is like a treasure-
> house, and all these people are breaking into
> it, whilst we are cutting each other's throats. . . .
> It has always been the same. We are a won-
> derful people, but it has always been our fate
> to be exploited."

And in the end Charles Gould, who thought he had accepted
the burden of the mine from the highest motives (and was
indeed partly right in his thought), slips into the mood of an
adventurer, the English adventurer on foreign soil:

> After all, with his English parentage and En-
> glish upbringing he perceived that he was an
> adventurer in Costaguana. . . . He was pre-
> pared, if need be, to blow up the whole San
> Tomé mountain sky high out of the territory of
> the Republic. This resolution expressed the te-
> nacity of his character . . . and something, too,
> of the spirit of a buccaneer throwing a lighted
> match into the magazine rather than surrender
> his ship.

Like the English-staffed railway, Gould, in the end, "puts a
new edge on a very old truth."

Through this insistence on the setting of history, never obtruded
but beautifully contrived and sufficiently sustained, *Nostromo*
achieves a breadth and a dignity unique in Conrad's novels
and through that achievement shares in the virtues of the epic
kind.

But Conrad does not limit his sense of time to recorded history,
for *Nostromo* as well as being centred fiercely in the reality of
modern life is a fairy-tale; and the fairy-tale extends the options
of time through the whole span of datable human events to the
unknown or purely conjectural; it unites the nearest and the
farthest.

As far as I know, the fairy-tale element in *Nostromo* has passed
undetected: a surprising omission when one considers how
fashionable such a detection is. Anyhow, since it has so passed,
I had better go to some length in trying to establish that it is
indeed there. What first put me on to it was the behaviour of
General Montero, destined later to lead the revolt against the
Ribierist government, at the lunch given on board the *Juno* to
President Dictator Ribiera himself, others of his government,
and Sir John, who had come from Europe "to smooth the path
for his railway." Montero is incensed that he is not getting
enough attention. "Why was it that nobody was looking at
him?"—at him who had performed the "greatest military exploit of modern times." He is a sinister figure:

> The white plume, the coppery tint of his broad
> face, the blue-black of the moustaches under
> the curved beak, the mass of gold on sleeves
> and breast, the high shining boots with enor-
> mous spurs, the working nostrils, the imbecile
> and domineering stare of the glorious victor of
> Rio Seco had in them something ominous and
> incredible; the exaggeration of a cruel carica-
> ture, the fatuity of solemn masquerading, the
> atrocious grotesqueness of some military idol
> of Aztec conception and European bedecking,
> awaiting the homage of worshippers.

Like the railway and Charles Gould, Montero repeats early
South American history, but just as surely he is the malicious
fairy, slighted, resentful, and bent on mischief, at the christening feast of the infant railway. Once we see Montero in this
guise (and Conrad leaves us here to our own inferences) we
find the fairy theme, with its kin the ballad theme all over the
place, often explicitly mentioned.

The world of magic enters immediately after the opening paragraphs introducing the setting of Sulaco, for the barren peninsula of Azuera, which bounds the gulf on the north, "is deadly
because of its forbidden treasures." True, there is no dragon
guarding them, but they belong to the class that dragons used
to be interested in. And the devils and ghosts that do this work
are a satisfactory substitute. Many adventurers perished looking
for the gold, the latest being two foreign sailors, probably
American; and it matters that they should be so, for it is thus
that Conrad unites present reality with a fabulous past. This
opening legend is like a dumb show in Elizabethan drama,
shadowing future happenings, for the mine which Gould inherits is fabulous also, as is the boat-load of silver that corrupts
Nostromo. Gould's father, we are told, "became at once mine-
ridden. . . . It took the form of the Old Man of the Sea fastened
upon his shoulders. He began also to dream of vampires." His
letters to his son had the flavour of "a gruesome Arabian Nights
tale." Charles Gould, intellectually convinced that it is his
duty to take on the responsibility of working the mine for the
general good, retains a superstitious fear because in so taking
it on he goes against his father's wishes. As the mine is exploited, its wealth begins to grow fabulous: "there had never
been anything in the world to approach the vein of the Gould
Concession." It reminds one of the Cave of Mammon in Spenser. It ends by being far more than a big silver mine for "its

territory, containing gold, silver, copper, lead, cobalt, extends for miles along the foot-hills of the Cordillera.''

Charles Gould, the book's principal hero, is the exiled prince, the son of a king who has been robbed of his inheritance. When his father dies he returns to claim it. He succeeds, and the people habitually call him the King of Sulaco. Decoud, who stands outside the fairy-tale and lives in his intellect and in the single canalised appetite of love alone, dislikes Gould in his part of fairy prince and remarks of him that ''he could not believe his own motives if he did not make them first a part of some fairy-tale,'' and again that for Gould and by no means for himself life is a ''moral romance derived from the tradition of a pretty fairy-tale.'' If Montero is the wicked fairy at the feast, Mrs. Gould is the good fairy, as Conrad keeps telling us. For instance, this is how she appears, early in the book in her drawing-room:

> Mrs. Gould, with her little head and shining coils of hair, sitting in a cloud of muslin and lace before a slender mahogany table, resembled a fairy posed lightly before dainty philtres dispensed out of vessels of silver and porcelain.

But it is a fairy-tale with a tragic turn. The good fairy fails to get the reward due to her for helping the prince to his inheritance. A wall of silver encloses him and keeps them apart, and it has been ''erected by evil spirits.'' And in the end she suffers a species of defeat:

> Small and dainty, as if radiating a light of her own in the deep shade of the interlaced boughs, she resembled a good fairy, weary with a long career of well-doing, touched by the withering suspicion of the uselessness of her labours, the powerlessness of her magic.

And her defeat is made the more bitter by the fabulous wealth the prince's inheritance has brought her: she is ''wealthy beyond great dreams of wealth.''

If Gould is the exiled prince, Nostromo is the proletarian, the swineherd's son or the scullion, who achieves wealth by his courage and resourcefulness. But like Gould he deals with enchanted things and there is an initial curse on his traffic with the silver of the mine. He has nothing to do with the mine itself, but is brought in touch with a boat-load of silver from it. Once so brought, he is never free from its enchantment. He begins his dealings with it in the unnatural darkness that invests the Golfo Placido at night.

> The eye of God Himself could not find out what work a man's hand is doing in there; and you would be free to call the devil to your aid with impunity if even his malice were not defeated by such a blind darkness.

From the first Nostromo feels superstitiously about the load of silver. He tells the dying Teresa that he is needed to save it and that it is ''a greater treasure than the one they say is guarded by ghosts and devils in Azuera.'' He has to choose between fulfilling his promise to save the silver and obeying the request of the dying Teresa to fetch her a priest. In denying that request (as Gould disobeyed his father's order to keep clear of the mine), Nostromo corrupted his conscience and, becoming desperate, ended by selling his soul for the whole load of silver. The whole load; because, as Dr. Monygham remarked, ''for taking the curse of death on my back, as you call it, nothing else but the whole treasure should do.'' Actually, Nostromo

does not get the whole load, for Decoud took four ingots as weights to ensure his drowning when he jumped overboard. Conrad does not pursue this theme, but plainly, if he had wished to end the story of Nostromo happily, he could have used the missing ingots as a means of his escape. Not having received full payment, Nostromo could have repudiated his bargain and expelled the alien soul that had taken possession of him. Anyhow, the four missing ingots, as well as being the entirely realistic means of ensuring the death of an unenchantable character, come from the very heart of fairy-lore.

It would be tedious to list other references to fairies, ghosts, and enchantment. There are plenty more. Conrad's triumph is that he has integrated his fairy-lore so beautifully with the whole complex of the book that readers have deeply felt rather than consciously perceived it. I have said that by introducing the themes of the fairy-tale Conrad extended the dimension of his novel's imagined time; simultaneously he enriched the novel's content incalculably. (pp. 127-35)

> E. M. W. Tillyard, ''Conrad: 'Nostromo','' in his The Epic Strain in the English Novel, Chatto & Windus, 1958, pp. 126-67.

DOROTHY VAN GHENT (essay date 1961)

[Van Ghent was an American educator and literary critic. In the following excerpt, she discusses folklore motifs in Nostromo.]

The subject of Nostromo is the guardianship of a treasure, a simple and fateful subject common throughout folklore. In this novel, the material form of the treasure is the silver of the San Tomé mine, in the republic of Costaguana, on the west coast of South America. The mine belongs, as a permanent concession, to the English family of Goulds; but successive civil wars, which have laid waste the land, have destroyed the workings of the mine. Charles Gould, an experienced mining engineer, sets out to rehabilitate it with the aid of North American capital. It becomes a financial success, and its success brings about the peace and order necessary for sustained economic enterprise. But when the main action of the story opens, a new political revolution, motivated by greed for the mine's riches, threatens the established order with bloodshed and anarchy.

Conrad's most fertile invention in Nostromo is to adapt the legendary idea of the mysterious potency of a treasure to the conditions of a frontier country in a modern period of colonial imperialism. In folklore a treasure is always a powerful mana-object that tests the characters of men: it confers great benefits, but only those with the highest physical and moral courage, and the deepest spiritual insight, are able to recognize its true nature and to use it properly. In a story with a modern milieu, the treasure can be quite concretely the chief industrial resource of a country—a rich silver mine—and yet, through the way men interpret its potential uses, it can arouse the most violent and disparate human responses, from crude appetite to passionate idealism. Actually, everybody in Conrad's story has a different attitude toward the silver of the mine. To some it is an opportunity for loot. To others, it is the material ''fact'' that has made legal security and good government possible— possible, at least, until revolution again threatens. To Charles Gould, it has a very personal meaning. His father had been forced by corrupt and impotent governments to pay ruinous royalties on the then worthless property, and had died from outrage at such a perversion of justice. Gould has come under the fascination of the idea that if he can make a success of the mine, it will be a ''way of atonement'' for his father's death.

The development and protection of the mine are to him a moral necessity.

Part of the range of ambiguity in what the treasure of the mine signifies may be illustrated by those occasions when we see the silver ingots in somebody's hands. Mrs. Gould had received the first ingot from the reopened vein, and, in her devotion to her husband, the silver seemed to her to be the palpable expression of his idealism:

> . . . she had seen the first spungy lump of silver yielded to the hazards of the world by the dark depths of the Gould Concession; she had laid her unmercenary hands, with an eagerness that made them tremble, upon the first silver ingot turned out warm from the mould; and by her imaginative estimate of its power she endowed that lump of metal with a justificative conception, as though it were not a mere fact, but something far-reaching and impalpable, like the true expression of an emotion or the emergency of a principle.

The Goulds have no children. It is suggested that, with a subtle unfaithfulness to his wife, Charles Gould has allowed his redemptory idea of the mine to usurp her place in his emotions. The language in the passage above is that of a birth, of "emergence" from "dark depths." The "spungy lump," "still warm from the mould," lies in Emilia Gould's hands as a "conception," a truly immaculate conception and the only one she will know. The San Tomé mine is to make her married life barren.

Nostromo, foreman of the stevedores who load the silver for shipping north, also is seen with ingots in his hands. Nostromo's name has come to stand for absolute fidelity and incorruptibility. But in the last episode of the story, he has become a thief. He steals a few ingots at a time from the barge-load of silver he has buried on a desert island, and disposes of them secretly so that his good name will be protected while he grows rich. To Nostromo, the treasure of the mine has meant moral death, and the touch of the ingots is hateful to him. They bear "the smell of earth, of damp foliage," the smell of a dark rot in nature.

Martin Decoud, the young Creole intellectual, is the third person who is seen in physical contact with the silver. To Decoud, the treasure has finally no more meaning than any other dead weight which will help a man to drown. He puts a couple of the heavy ingots in each pocket before he commits suicide in the Golfo Placido.

In even so slight a sketch, more than one major folklore element may be seen. There is not only the treasure itself—which in myth and fairy tale may be a golden fleece, the golden apples of the Hesperides, a horse or hound with supernatural powers, the Holy Grail, or other variations on the idea of a treasure. There is also, in the part played by Charles Gould, the motif of the "stranger knight" who comes to a "waste land," and who, because of his moral purity, is able to rehabilitate the land. Gould is always described as extremely foreign-looking, with his thin, blazingly red face and fiery moustaches; he comes from abroad (his youth was spent in Europe); he rescues the treasure of the land from the forces of corruption, and thereby brings about peace and prosperity. In fairy tale, when the knight has accomplished his mission, he becomes the "good king" and reigns happily ever after. Gould is called the "king" of the province where the mine is located—El Rey de Sulaco. But he does not reign happily ever after. Apparently there was

something wrong with his interpretation of the use of the treasure, for the same old troubles of corrupt intrigue, war, and widespread ruin appear again in the land.

In fairy tales where a treasure is the central emblem, a fairy princess is almost always associated with it, so closely that she may be looked upon as an essential part of the treasure itself. The "stranger knight's" marriage with the fairy princess is the crown of his successes. Their union is a traditional image of union and communion between people. The motif of marriage is one significant indication that the treasure in the fairy tale is more than a material thing; it is a thing with spiritual powers, and one of its mysterious significances is fulfillment in human communion. Several times Conrad describes Emilia Gould as "fairy-like," with her masses of fair hair, the rich rings on her fingers and lace on her wrists, "gracious, small, and fairy-like, before the glittering tea-set." The sterile relationship between Charles Gould and his wife is one of the important variations Conrad makes on a legendary model. (pp. vii-x)

The "ordeal" is a constant element of stories formed on the kind of model we are considering. Mortal dangers must be gone through by the adventurer who would win the benefits that a treasure can confer. This motif is found in the most sophisticated literature—like Conrad's *Nostromo*—as well as in naive folklore, simply because it represents the arduous necessities of man's work in fulfilling his needs and desires. (p. x)

Let us trace the phases of the ordeal in *Nostromo*. Of evidently great importance in Conrad's design is the man Nostromo himself, who gives the title to the book, and whose name constantly occurs as leitmotiv even when he is not in the foreground of the action. That Nostromo's character and role should have primary importance seems, at first glance, out of keeping with Conrad's habitual concern with subtle problems of conscience, for Nostromo does not have any subtlety of conscience to make him psychologically interesting in the way Conrad's principal characters usually are. He is called the "natural man," the "Man of the People," and his lack of a cultivated conscience is precisely the reason for his importance in this novel that is broadly representative of the human condition: for the great multitudes of men everywhere are without benefit of the cultivated conscience. Nostromo presents in clear relief the first and elemental phase of the human ordeal, the facing of the primitive tests of nature. His great achievements lie in the world of nature, which he can master because he is virile and brave and physically skillful. These Adamic qualities are implicit in the poetic image of his awakening after his swim from the sunken barge:

> Nostromo woke up from a fourteen-hours' sleep and arose full length from his lair in the long grass. He stood knee-deep among the whispering undulations of the green blades, with the lost air of a man just born into the world. Handsome, robust, and supple, he threw back his head, flung his arms open, and stretched himself with a slow twist of the waist and a leisurely growling yawn of white teeth; as natural and free from evil in the moment of waking as a magnificent and unconscious wild beast. Then, in the suddenly steadied glance fixed upon nothing from under a forced frown, appeared the man.

But the world in which Nostromo lives is not the Adamic world, "natural and free from evil." It is, rather, a frontier world, where a sleepy, pastoral Campo has been invaded by industrialism, bringing with it all the complex energies, confusion of racial histories and attitudes, and moral anxieties that an industrial revolution introduces to a pastoral colonial people. In this frontier setting, the natural tests of manhood are still vitally necessary, and Nostromo passes these valiantly—tests of the sea and the mountains, and those which give a man command over the primitive passions and appetites of other men. But, tragically, ability to pass these tests is not enough.

Nostromo's superb natural gifts have their "ideal" and summary form in the virtue of fidelity—the virtue that relates him ethically to other men. But the men to whom he is bound in fidelity are men who belong to the invading industrial front—the San Tomé mine, the North American silver and iron interests, the European shipping and railway interests that have made capital investments in Costaguana. These men are involved in a vastly complicated enterprise whose potential for either good or evil is beyond the understanding of the "natural man," who has only instinct and virile pride to guide him. When revolutionary anarchy threatens the industrial interests, Nostromo is entrusted with a silver shipment, to be taken out to sea and beyond the reach of the rioters in the city. It is his great ordeal, the most "desperate affair" of his life, and he gives to it all his courage, all his skill, all his fidelity. But, afterwards, he learns that, in the complication of events, it actually mattered very little whether the silver was saved or whether it sank to the bottom of the sea. Nostromo had risked his life for nothing; his fidelity had meant nothing. His sense of the meaning of his own identity is completely baffled, for it has been undervalued by the men to whom he was faithful. Only the silver remains as a palpable fact to be trusted. Faithful to the silver, Nostomo becomes a thief.

He dies with "the bewildered conviction of having been betrayed"—as Adam himself, emerged without preparation out of the simple garden of nature into the human world of sin and death, must have died with the same sense of having been betrayed and "hardly knowing by what or by whom." The other figures in the novel, all caught in the "bitter necessities" of the frontier state, gain their plastic, significant relief from Nostromo's presense, the presense of the "natural man" whose primitive endowments are the base for any more evolved morality. Therefore his name is uttered again and again, as that of the "indispensable man" upon whom all the other characters are dependent in one way or another. Pacing slowly on his silver grey mare through the night streets, his face muffled mysteriously by his sombrero, he is the man in the background, whose ancestry is older than civilization, and who has not even a proper kind of Christian name.

Charles Gould has his own unquestionable courage, his skill as a mining engineer, and his authority in commanding men to his purpose. But he also has, as Nostromo has not, an understanding of the complexities of the frontier milieu where he has to do his work. To return to our fairy-tale paradigm, the actions of Gould correspond with that phase of the human ordeal which demands experience of psychological evil in others, in order that the treasure of life may be understood and properly used. And yet, as with Nostromo, Gould's particular gifts are not by themselves enough.

"Charles Gould was competent because he had no illusions," we are told. Nobody could be more aware of the murderous anarchism in Costaguana politics. One of his uncles had been elected President of the province of Sulaco and afterwards was put up against a wall and shot. His father had inculcated in him since childhood his own experience of the greed and corruption of Costaguana officials, the same type of officials with whom Gould has to deal in running the mine. He is also under no illusion about the motives of the North American financier who has made the working of the mine possible, the great Holroyd, the millionaire endower of churches, who expresses his faith in American capitalism this way:

> We shall be giving the word for everything—industry, trade, law, journalism, art, politics, and religion, from Cape Horn clear over to Smith's Sound, and beyond, too, if anything worth taking hold of turns up at the North Pole. And then we shall have the leisure to take in hand the outlying islands and continents of the earth. We shall run the world's business whether the world likes it or not. The world can't help it—and neither can we, I guess.

But Gould is not fooled into collaboration with anyone else's vast conceptions of destiny. The success of the San Tomé mine is an aim which is "definite in space and absolutely attainable within a limited time," and it makes the other man, Holroyd, with his "insatiable imagination of conquest," appear "as a dreamy idealist of no importance." Gould's experience prepares him to stoop for his weapons, both in using Holroyd's millions to get the mine working, and in dealing with Costaguana politicians and racketeers.

He stakes his character on the success of the mine; his moral identity is bound up with it. In this way, he feels that he has kept his own personal motive pure and independent—the motive of "atonement" for his father's death by redemption of the mine that had killed his father. For "material interest" alone he would not have touched the mine, but "material interests" have made success possible, and vaguely he recognizes certain social ideals that may be fulfilled along the way. "What is wanted here is law, good faith, order, security," he tells his wife.

> Only let the material interests once get a firm footing, and they are bound to impose the conditions on which alone they can continue to exist. That's how your money-making is justified here in the face of lawlessness and disorder. It is justified because the security which it demands must be shared with an oppressed people. A better justice will come afterwards. That's your ray of hope.

But all this—law and order, good faith, security and justice for an oppressed people—is merely incidental to Gould's personal obsession, and his sense of the sacrosanct purity of his own private intention has itself prevented him from submitting to the final ordeal of self-knowledge. His idea of father-atonement is a kind of adultery, subtly wooing him away from his wife, who is left in the isolation of a sterile marriage. At moments he seems dimly aware of this fact, but emotionally unable to face it:

> He bent over her upturned face very tenderly and a little remorsefully. . . . For a moment he felt as if the silver-mine, which had killed his father, had decoyed him farther than he meant to go; and with the roundabout logic of emotions, he felt that the worthiness of his life was

bound up with success. There was no going back.

In the legendary terms that we have been using to clarify the emblematic aspects of the novel, what Gould fails to recognize is that the "treasure" is worthless without the "fairy princess," and that in abusing his union with her he has refused the human communion that is an essential benison of the treasure. In his abstract, obsessional commitment to the father, he has lost touch with the feminine, maternal principle which cherishes for its own sake—as Emilia Gould does—"the past and the future in every passing moment of the present."

Dr. Monygham's part in the book corresponds with the third phase of the ordeal—that of self-knowledge. Long before the main action of the story starts, Dr. Monygham has suffered the experience of evil in himself—an experience analogous to that moment in the tale of Conn-Eda when the prince is called upon to kill his best friend, the little shaggy horse, and though he refuses to do so, finds that the knife nevertheless moves in his hand and the deed is done. In the time of the bloody dictator, Guzman Bento, Monygham had been tortured and confessions were extorted from him implicating some of his best friends, who were imprisoned and executed on that accusation. He bears testimony to his experience by the cicatrices on his cheeks, his damaged ankles and crooked feet. This battered personality, limping around Sulaco, has come under the spell of Emilia Gould—of "the delicate preciousness of her inner worth, partaking of a gem and a flower"—and the latent tenderness of his essentially loyal nature has unfolded to it. Whereas Charles Gould has abandoned his wife to loneliness because of his conviction that the "worthiness of his life" is bound up with the success of the mine, Dr. Monygham's sense of the *unworthiness* of his life leads him to an act of self-sacrifice by which he hopes to save Emilia Gould from a frightful disaster. In terms of our legendary model, Monygham, having learned by the ordeal of self-knowledge the helpless evil of which he is capable, has the humility to offer his life for another—and he offers it for the "fairy princess" who lives by giving herself wholly to others.

He deliberately adopts the character of a traitor. When menaces close around the mine—and not the least of these is Gould's decision to dynamite it sky-high to prevent it from falling into the hands of the revolutionary troops—he decoys a whole army out into the harbor, with the lie that Gould has sunk some of the silver there, for his own use, to be retrieved later by divers. The doctor is kept on the boat, with a noose around his neck, ready for hanging if the silver is not discovered. It is an act in which his damaged reputation serves him well, for the colonel of the army believes that Monygham would naturally betray Gould for a part of the loot. As the doctor tells himself, in bitter memory of his earlier ordeal, "I am the only one fit for that dirty work." But his ruse succeeds in relieving the besieged city.

In one way or another, for every character, the silver of the mine formulates the heart's "secret purposes," by the ordeal which each undergoes in relation to it. In Martin Decoud's case, we have something that escapes direct legendary parallel, except in an interpretive and revisionary way. What Decoud suffers may be "the greatest evil of all." . . . The greatest evil of all is lack of faith in the treasure. If the treasure is the good of life, then lack of faith in it is death.

When Decoud is alone with the barge-load of silver on the Great Isabel, one of the sterile spurs of rock in the Golfo

Placido, he discovers the "secret purpose" of his heart to be death. The principle of his life has been rationalism, the nineteenth- and twentieth-century heritage from the Enlightenment. For traditional rationalism, ultimate reality is the evidence of the senses, which is the raw material upon which reason works. What can reason do with the evidence of the senses, even with a pile of silver ingots beside one, on a desert island in the middle of an immense gulf where no ship passes? The Ancient Mariner had a similar problem:

> Alone, alone, all, all alone,
> Alone on a wide, wide sea!
> And never a saint took pity on
> My soul in agony.

One's senses, and what reason can make of them, become as indifferent as the sea and the sky and the rock and the silver itself. Decoud commits suicide in "the immense indifference of things." (pp. xii-xviii)

Unlike gold—which corresponds alchemically to the sun's fire, the light of day and reason—silver is a nocturnal metal, correspondent to the moon, to emotion and imagination. The "treasure," whose emblem is silver, is misprized if it is thought to be any abstract ideal or truth (as Charles Gould thought it to be), or any theory of history that one might try to find in the story. The book shows on a vast scale the recurrence of the human ordeal and the resurgence of desire. It ends in moonlight, the brilliance of the moon lying like a bar of silver on the horizon, and with a cry of faith into the night. (p. xxv)

Dorothy Van Ghent, in an introduction to Nostromo: A Tale of the Seaboard *by Joseph Conrad, Holt, Rinehart and Winston, 1961, pp. vii-xxv.*

STANLEY TICK (essay date 1964)

[*In the following excerpt, Tick discusses religious aspects of* Nostromo, *demonstrating that Conrad expressed many religious viewpoints throughout the novel without affirming any one of them over the others.*]

If, as I believe, Conrad was uneasy with the subject of religion, that would be explanation enough for its general absence from his fiction: his sympathy for those who felt the need to believe was likely to clash with his own developed ethic, although the religious "illusion" was not necessarily less worthy than most others: and repeatedly, including in *Nostromo,* Conrad assures us that illusions are of fundamental importance to the maintenance of well-being. This dilemma confronts all who, like Conrad, reject dogmas but profess ideals.

Any treatment of the religious theme in his fiction, then, would very probably produce unintended ambiguities. And I think that Conrad realized this. For when a context that would accommodate such treatment came to hand, Conrad included religion in considerable fullness. The suitable context was *Nostromo:* "[Conrad's] most complex historical and political drama, a comprehensive matrix of his moral and ethical sensibility, resonant of a profoundly riddled debate of moralities and creeds of conduct" [see M. D. Zabel entry in Additional Bibliography].

On the second and third pages of *Nostromo,* we are given the story of some legendary inhabitants of Azuera, the stony peninsula jutting into the Golfo Placido. This story, which functions as a prophetic prologue to the subsequent action, ends thus:

The impious adventurers gave no other sign. The sailors, the Indian, and the stolen burro were never seen again. As to the mozo, a Sulaco man—his wife paid for some masses, and the poor four-footed beast, being without sin, had been probably permitted to die; but the two gringos, spectral and alive, are believed to be dwelling to this day amongst the rocks, under the fatal spell of their success. Their souls cannot tear themselves away from their bodies mounting guard over the discovered treasure. They are now rich and hungry and thirsty—a strange theory of tenacious gringo ghosts suffering in their starved and parched flesh of defiant heretics, where a Christian would have renounced and been released.

Immediately two things impress us: the rich religious vocabulary, and especially the Christian insight offered as a conclusion; the remoteness of the narrator, who clearly does not credit the legend (his dissociation is also in evidence at the beginning of the narrative). But these two impressions contradict: why neatly embellish the story with "impious, sin, souls, heretics," and why draw the profound conclusion if one believes the story devoid of seriousness?

The resulting ambiguity, I believe, is basic to the method of Conrad in *Nostromo*. All the way through, Conrad is exploring and celebrating the nature of human and institutional forces so complex as to include their own expression and denial, self-contained dialectical entities. This, I take it, is what Morton Zabel means by "profoundly riddled debate," what Robert Penn Warren refers to as "elements . . . in suspension" [see excerpt dated 1951]; perhaps, too, this is why Dr. Leavis finds that the novel "has something hollow about it" [see excerpt dated 1954]. Certainly Conrad elsewhere indicated more than once his awareness of such a world. This statement, from *A Personal Record*, might stand as a commentary on *Nostromo:*

> "The ethical view of the universe involves us at last in so many cruel and absurd contradictions, where the last vestiges of faith, hope, charity, and even of reason itself, seem ready to perish, that I have come to suspect that the aim of creation cannot be ethical at all. I would fondly believe that its object is purely spectacular: a spectacle for awe, love, adoration, or hate, if you like, but in this view—and in this view alone—never for despair! Those visions, delicious or poignant, are a moral end in themselves."

The essential and necessary complexity unto contradiction that is the substance of *Nostromo* is revealed in the areas of personal, political and religious morality. And their manifestations are so intricately and elaborately linked, that to isolate one—as I intend doing—is to do some injustices to Conrad's superb organization. Yet for purposes of this analysis, I have concerned myself principally with the religious elements of the novel. As we might expect, these reveal the same kind of complexity that characterizes the novel's ethical and political actions.

I have found it helpful to divide my examination as follows: religion as a public force, asserting its claim impersonally; belief as a private sensibility, affecting the behaviour of individuals.

Although Conrad sub-titled *Nostromo* "A Tale of the Seaboard," every reader is impressed initially by the historical emphasis of the novel that begins: "In the time of Spanish rule, and for many years afterwards, the town of Sulaco. . . ." Most of the first section of the novel, and much of the second as well, are given over to what, in another context, would be called background material: recounting past events and current biographies. Included in the information about Sulaco is its ecclesiastical history. Mrs. Gould explains to Sir John, the chairman of the railway board who is visiting from London: "The highest ecclesiastical court, for two viceroyalties, sat here in the olden time." . . . To which the great magnate comments: "We can't give you your ecclesiastical court back again; but you shall have more steamers, a railway, a telegraph cable—a future in the great world which is worth infinitely more than any amount of ecclesiastical past." . . . But prophets make poor historians, and the questionable authority of this prophecy is revealed fully in the last section of *Nostromo*—when the present achievements and future hopes of Sulaco are related to us (with calculated irony on the author's part) by the obtuse Captain Mitchell.

These achievements and hopes are dependent upon the continued prosperity of foreign investments, notably Holroyd's silver mine and Sir John's railways. And these investments are threatened by precisely what Sir John thought had been replaced—the ecclesiastical court! Indeed, with a kind of subtlety we cannot appreciate on a first reading, Conrad had offered a presage of what might come only a few pages after Sir John's prophetic utterance:

> Afterwards, late at night, pacing to and fro outside, [Sir John] had a long talk with his chief engineer. . . . From the contact of these two personalities who had not the same vision of the world, there was generated a power for the world's service—a subtle force that could set in motion mighty machines, men's muscles, and awaken also in human breasts an unbounded devotion to the task. Of the young fellows at the table, to whom the survey of the track was like the tracing of the path of life, more than one would be called to meet death before the work was done. But the work would be done: the force would be *almost as strong as faith. Not quite, however.* In the silence of the sleeping camp upon the moonlit plateau . . . two strolling figures in thick ulsters stood still, and the voice of the engineer pronounced distinctly the words—

> *"We can't move mountains!"* . . . (italics mine)

The material prosperity of Sulaco, the silver mine, is located on a mountainside; and this mountain, like all mountains, may be "moved" by faith. At the novel's end, the well-being of Sulaco is severely threatened by several allied forces, all centered in the powerful, incorruptible leader of the church, Cardinal-Archbishop Corbelàn.

Dr. Leavis is only half-right, I believe, in calling Corbelàn "fanatical." We are told, rather, that he has a "fănatical and morose air." I feel certain that we are meant to credit the widespread rumor that "his unexpected elevation to the purple was a counter-move to the Protestant invasion of Sulaco." And Captain Mitchell has probably got it straight when he tells his listener that Corbelàn is highly thought of in Rome. In short,

Corbelàn, fanatical or not, is the recognized spokesman for the established church, and the force he represents is institutional as well as personal. (If one wished to argue that the church, itself, is fanatical, then it must be pointed out that its spokesmen and practices, in the context of the novel, are no more fanatical than those of the political or economic pressure groups. Therefore, the term "fanatical" has no special significance when applied to Corbelàn.)

We are left in no doubt of the proven and potential power of this religious force. In the past, Corbelàn had played a part in sponsoring and then undermining the Ribierist cause—even before he was a bishop and before he had powerful allies in and out of the church. Now he is a cardinal. And he has, in addition to church backing, several eminent converts. Chief among these is Hernandez, the distinguished and brave ex-outlaw who is now Minister of War and in control of the Army. It was Corbelàn who gave Hernandez the opportunity to demonstrate his responsibility; furthermore, Hernandez is a very pious man, a spiritual as well as political disciple of the cardinal. Antonia Avellanos is also conspiring with her uncle. And Nostromo, until his death, has been using his influence and his money for the same cause.

Dr. Monygham declares that they are conspiring for the invasion of Costaguana (from which Sulaco has become independent). And Monygham, though a cynical observer, is in no sense a fool. His discussion with Mrs. Gould, after Corbelàn departs, must be read as a corrective to Mitchell's prognostications delivered to a nameless, transient listener.

The complexities which define *Nostromo* are, in part, those which demonstrate the nature of political "causes." There appear to be many, more or less intimately related aspects of the cause which Cardinal-Archbishop Corbelàn is championing. In his parting words to Dr. Monygham, he stresses "the aspirations of the people" as opposed to the "material interests of the foreigners." . . . But Corbelàn is a man of the cloth as well as of the people, and there can be no doubt at all that part of the dire threat to Sulaco's future stems from the Catholic-Protestant antagonism, a new feature of that society and associated with its economic prosperity. Implicated in this institutional clash is the Holroyd organization.

Robert Penn Warren is surely correct when he declares that "Holroyd's concern with a 'pure form of Christianity' . . . serves as a mask and justification for his imperialistic thirst for power." Even Mrs. Gould realizes that Holroyd's was "the religion of silver and iron." But there is more to the American financier's Protestantism than that. For whatever reason, he does endow churches annually; additionally, and more to the point, he is rabidly anti-Catholic! So that his pet dream of introducing into Sulaco "a pure form of Christianity" doesn't end with his own disgust "at the tawdriness of the dressed-up saints in the Cathedral." He has taken the positive action of sponsoring missionaries in Sulaco, and of organizing "The Holroyd Missionary Fund." And this action must be understood to be in large part responsible for Corbelàn's dangerously subversive activities. The future of both Sulaco and Costaguana now depends to a very large degree on the actions of church-led forces. Sulaco's ecclesiastical court is not only back again, but it is in the process of determining the fate of Sir John's own vision.

The reader is not invited to pass judgment on the gathering conflict, however. For one thing, this religious controversy is only one note in a profound discord, the resolution of which seems beyond even conjecture. For another, and this I think

is of crucial importance, nothing that we have learned enables us to judge wisely even if we wish to do so. Concerning religious issues at any rate, Conrad is true to his personal skepticism as well as to the sense of his novel. The history of the established Catholic Church of Costaguana is as "riddled" as it is inconclusive. There is no more evidence to make us believe that the Church had been a force for good than there is to the contrary.

The commendable Father Roman is at least balanced by the unspeakably evil Father Beron. And while Corbelàn risked his life to convert savage tribes (itself a questionable achievement), the "trembling and subservient Archbishop" celebrated masses of Thanksgiving for the bestial dictator Guzman Bento. Nor is there any commentary, other than that they exist, about Holroyd's Protestant missionaries and their "purer form of Christianity"!

Conrad's treatment of institutional religion, then, reveals the ambivalence that concurs both with his own notion of its contribution to the world and with the demands of his novel. Like economic "growth" and political "progress," its value is manifestly ambiguous. The "spectacle" is more impressive than the ethic.

Where *Nostromo* fails to satisfy some critics is in its structure; the Nostromo-Viola story, they believe, is inferior to as well as poorly integrated into the main theme. My analysis of the religious component of the novel could be used to support this last contention.

The concept of "belief," as opposed to institutional religion, is treated only within this second ("minor") story. And I can not see that Conrad is using these two strands of religious implication in any kind of balanced or contrasted way. Whereas Viola's political views and Nostromo's self-delusion offer useful comparative links with the main story and its characters, the two religious aspects do not relate organically. In the novel, only Nostromo and the Violas are shown to be motivated by religious scruples, however vague. Their common Catholicism, however, is related to the State issue only at the very end of the novel, when we learn that Nostromo has been conferring with Corbelàn and has been using his resources to assist the Cardinal-Archbishop's cause.

Nevertheless, Conrad took considerable pains with this substory, and it contains what I think is Conrad's most elaborate and sympathetic study of supernatural (rather than psychological) forces—a wonderfully contrived account of religious faith and superstition that is brought to a conclusion with the inevitability of Divine Justice. This last comment perhaps ought to be emphasized, for however sentimentalized the episode of Nostromo's love and death may be, Conrad worked out the story with precise effect.

The legend of Azuera, as I earlier pointed out, is not credited by the narrator. His dissociation is evident in such phrases as "it is said" and "[they] are believed to be dwelling," and in the obvious irony of a passage like this: "The poor, associating by an obscure instinct of consolation, the idea of evil and wealth, will tell you that [the Azuera peninsula] is deadly because of its forbidden treasures. The common folks of the neighborhood, peons of the estancias, vaqueros of the seaboard plains, tame Indians coming miles to market with a bundle of sugar-cane or a basket of maize worth about three-pence, are well aware that heaps of shining gold lie in the gloom of the steep precipices cleaving the stony levels of Azuera." . . . Nostromo does not fit into any of these groups, but he is plainly intrigued by the legend. His first reference to it occurs when he is endeavoring to excuse himself from carrying out Teresa Viola's dying request. ''I am needed,'' he tells her, ''to save the silver of the mine. Do you hear? A greater treasure than the one which they say is guarded by ghosts and devils on Azuera.'' . . . Immediately after, he makes a lighthearted reference to the legend as he parts from Giorgio. Thereafter, he speaks of this same legend to Dr. Monygham . . . , and twice, towards the conclusion of the novel, Nostromo ponders the bizarre tale. . . . In these latter instances, he realizes the strong similarity between his own plight and the fate of the luckless gringos. The final paragraph of the novel, in addition to calling attention to ''silver'' (for which Conrad felt the need to apologize), also calls attention to the now completed reenactment of the old legend of Azuera.

In order to make Nostromo's story parallel the legend, Conrad was willing to risk some of the sense of the plot. There is no good reason, for example, why Decoud had to use ingots in order to ensure his suicide. Even more open to question is Nostromo's motivation for cashing in on the hidden treasure. He exclaims, ''How could I give back the treasure with four ingots missing?'' But surely he had long since demonstrated his honesty, and he knew that his word would be accepted by all the whites; moreover, he could have accounted for the missing silver (if need be, Decoud's body might have been recovered). Finally, and beyond any satisfactory explanation, Nostromo need not have stolen. He could have disposed of the silver, say by sinking it in the gulf, without stealing any of it.

Yet Conrad offers an explanation:

> A victim of the disillusioned weariness which is the retribution meted out to intellectual audacity, the brilliant Don Martin Decoud, weighted by the bars of San Tomé silver, disappeared without a trace, swallowed up in the immense indifference of things. His sleepless, crouching figure was gone from the side of the San Tomé silver; and for a time the spirits of good and evil that hover near every concealed treasure of the earth might have thought that this one had been forgotten by all mankind. Then, after a few days, another form appeared striding away from the setting sun to sit motionless and awake in the narrow black gully all through the night, in nearly the same pose, in the same place in which had sat that other sleepless man who had gone away for ever so quietly in a small boat, about the time of sunset. And the spirits of good and evil that hover about a forbidden treasure understood well that the silver of San Tomé was provided now with a faithful and lifelong slave. . . .

Conrad has carefully prepared the way for this by making the principals in the substory ''simple believers,'' as opposed to the sophisticated ''realists'' in the main plot. (But the fact that none of the Anglo-Saxons is a believer doesn't make the two stories any better related; the contrast is not significant, so far as I can see.) In addition, Conrad prepares us for his ending by lavishing on the setting for the final action—the Golfo Placido—a wealth of religious imagery.

The major dramatic impulse for the minor story comes from the interview between Nostromo and Teresa Viola. He is at the peak of his fame, about to set off with the silver for his most important adventure. She is dying. At great risk, Nostromo has brought a doctor (Monygham) to the wife of his only friend. '''I want a priest more than a doctor,' she said pathetically. . . . 'Would you go to fetch a priest for me now? Think! A dying woman asks you!''' Nostromo refuses: ''He did not believe in priests, in their sacerdotal character. A doctor was an efficacious person; but a priest, as priest, was nothing, incapable of doing either good or harm. Nostromo did not even dislike the sight of them as old Giorgio did. The utter uselessness of the errand was what struck him most.'' . . . But the narrator tells us that Nostromo felt ''uneasy at the impiety of this refusal.'' Before he can leave the room, Teresa utters a fearful prophecy: ''Your folly shall betray you into poverty, misery, starvation. The very leperos shall laugh at you—the great Capataz.''

The next day . . . , after his night adventure with the silver, Nostromo returns to the Albergo d'Italia Una. Uppermost in his mind are the padrona's grim final words to him: '''she has prophesied for me an end of poverty, misery, and starvation.' These words of Teresa's anger, from the circumstances in which they had been uttered, like the cry of a soul prevented from making its peace with God, stirred the obscure superstition of personal fortune from which even the greatest genius amongst men of adventure and action is seldom free. They reigned over Nostromo's mind with the force of a potent malediction. And what a curse it was that which her words had laid upon him!'' . . . Viola tells him that just before his wife died she called upon Nostromo to save her daughters. After a long silence, Nostromo murmurs ''gloomily'': ''God rest her soul!'' He silently vows to respect this dying wish, having refused her first one!

The great Capataz de Cargadores, who can credit the legend of Azuera, can also believe in curses. He determines, in order to overcome the curse, to marry one of the Viola girls. And, as the novel concludes, he appears to have avoided Teresa's prophecy—only to die under the greater curse attached to all stolen treasure. The affront to Christian belief, it seems, could be reconciled in a way that the evil spirits could not.

In what must be counted a masterstroke of deepening complexity, Conrad makes Viola the unwitting agent for rendering final retribution to the cursed Nostromo. The elderly man is, in matters of religion, mid-way between his wife's firm devotion and Nostromo's superstitious credulity. He believes in God, but not in ''saints, priests, or prayers,'' and he never enters a church.

With the kind of intrusive significance that Conrad felt acceptable in this plot, the Bible is made the old man's constant companion. Every night on the Great Isabel Island, the old man sits reading his Bible. He exchanges this companion only for ''his old gun,'' so that he can protect his honor should Giselle's wooer come. After he has killed Nostromo, Giorgio cannot be made to comprehend what has happened. Linda leads him back inside the house, and there Giorgio takes up his Bible again, and he reads until he falls asleep.

The setting for the novel's concluding action is Sulaco's harbor, which during the day can be compared to ''an enormous semicircular and unroofed temple open to the ocean.'' . . . But at night, ''the eye of God himself . . . could not find out what work a man's hand is doing . . . and you would be free to call the devil to your aid with impunity if even his malice were not defeated by such a blind darkness.'' . . . In this supernatural darkness occur the adventures which conclude with Nostromo's death and the reenactment of the legend: the hiding of the silver, the purloining of the ingots by Nostromo, and his meetings with Giselle. Neither Linda's light of love and duty nor the light by which old Giorgio reads his Bible can affect the darkness of evil whose spirits have marked out Nostromo for their own ends.

The story of Nostromo and the Violas is made to work itself out according to the legend of Azuera. It seems pagan rather than Christian, but I would suggest that here too Conrad's ambiguity is intended. Although old Giorgio's belief is beyond dispute, his murder of Nostromo is in no sense a victory for Christian morality. Had he even suspected who it was, Giorgio would never have fired. Besides, Nostromo's "sin" was being expiated, and the devout Teresa's prophecy had not been fulfilled. Save for conforming to the legend, then, the moral ends of this story are no more closed than are those of the main plot. Once again, the spectacle is all.

Dr. Leavis reminds us that Conrad "is not one of those writers who clear up their fundamental attitudes for themselves in such a way that we may reasonably, in talking of them, use that portentous term [philosophy]." This is probably truer for *Nostromo* than for any other of Conrad's works. This novel seems dedicated to morally ambiguous spectacle: it defies both simple and subtle elucidation in defense of any positive ethic. The only explicit credo offered in the novel is this: "In our activity alone do we find the sustaining illusion of an independent existence as against the whole scheme of things of which we form a helpless part." . . . I cannot think of a less committed novel of Conrad's than *Nostromo*. There is no saving Marlow, no celebration of discipline or tradition, no heroic realization (of a Jim or Razumov or Heyst). There are only the last words of Dr. Monygham to Emilia Gould: "The time approaches when all that the Gould Concession stands for shall weigh as heavily upon the people as the barbarism, cruelty, and misrule of a few years back." . . . That, and the final cry of Linda, uttered in "fidelty, bewilderment, and despair": "Never! Gian' Battista!" (pp. 17-26)

> Stanley Tick, *"The Gods of 'Nostromo',"* in Modern Fiction Studies, *Vol. X, No. 1, Spring, 1964, pp. 15-26.*

AVROM FLEISHMAN   (essay date 1967)

[*Fleishman is a literary historian and critic. In the following excerpt, he offers a Marxist interpretation of* Nostromo, *in which the character Nostromo is a tragic hero symbolizing the proletariat's awakening class conciousness and subsequent corruption through greed.*]

Nostromo has often been assumed to be a pathetic failure, rather than a tragic hero, because the critics have not identified him with the social movements in which he becomes engaged. By the same token, the final chapters of the novel, which depict Nostromo's melodramatic love and death, have been taken to be irrelevant because of a failure to see them within the symbolic pattern of the entire novel. In this pattern, Nostromo's career represents the history of an entire class, the proletariat— its enlistment and exploitation in the industrialization of the country, its entry into the separatist revolution (fighting for class interests not directly its own), its growth of self-consciousness and discovery of an independent political role, its temptation by the materialistic drives of capitalism, and its purgation by traditional idealists in its own camp.

The pattern is a tragic one, as we shall see, because it is founded on contradictions within the hero and his class, rather than on circumstance. As in classical tragedy, the hero is bounded by forces larger than himself, yet what happens to him is the expression of his own nature. Like classical drama, too, the novel connects the individual hero with a social group—which he represents not only symbolically but dramatically—in historical action. Conrad's special version of tragedy is that this very social rootedness of the individualist hero contains the contradictions which destroy him. The career and development of Nostromo follow a dialectic as incisive and ironic as one of the character studies of Hegel's *Phenomenology of Mind.*

Nostromo is to be understood as the symbol of a class. At the same time, and without avoiding the contradiction, he is an individual, a vigorous egoist, whose drives to maintain his gilded reputation and at the same time to become integrated in the making of a community cause him to oscillate between vigorous social action and almost total estrangement. Totally lacking in political sensibility, Nostromo joins the Waverley heroes in running the full gamut of political commitment. The climax of his career, in which he benefits society and establishes his highest honor, only leads to his deepest isolation. (pp. 163-64)

The title of *Nostromo* has been found wanting by many who take seriously its grand historical theme, but Conrad's choice of the name has something to tell us about his larger intentions. The hero who bears this name is not only a romantic individual but acquires dramatically the status of a complex symbol. On the meaning of this symbol, Conrad is more explicit than is elsewhere his practice:

> Nostromo does not aspire to be a leader in a personal game. He does not want to raise himself above the mass. He is content to feel himself a power—within the People. . . . He is a man with the weight of countless generations behind him and no parentage to boast of. . . . Like the People.

> In his firm grip on the earth he inherits, in his improvidence and generosity, in his lavishness with his gifts, in his manly vanity, in the obscure sense of his greatness and in his faithful devotion with something despairing as well as desperate in its impulses, he is a Man of the People, their very own unenvious force, disdaining to lead but ruling from within. Years afterwards . . . listening in unmoved silence to anarchist speeches at the meeting, the enigmatical patron of the new revolutionary agitation, the trusted, the wealthy comrade Fidanza with the knowledge of his moral ruin locked up in his breast, he remains essentially a man of the People.

> . . . Antonia the Aristocrat and Nostromo the Man of the People are the artisans of the New Era, the true creators of the New State . . . [See excerpt dated 1917].

It is thus the collective sense of his nickname—"our man" (like Lord Jim, "one of us")—and not its Italian meaning, "boatswain," that is emphasized in the title of the novel.

Nostromo's career, as outlined here, represents the exploitation of the proletariat in behalf of the various political forces that contend for the country without reference to the interests of its masses. He ultimately tries to emancipate himself and materially supports the proletarian revolution, but he does so through crime—the concealment of and slow theft from the silver hoard. Nostromo's corruption by silver, which is, in part, a complex symbol of "material interests," evokes the moral danger of taking on the values of the propertied classes that yawns before revolutionary movements.

Nostromo is, however, not only the dramatic representative of the people but an individual—indeed, an individualist, a stern foreman, a would-be popular hero. His existence is a more complex affair than its primary symbolic function; it involves the relation of the individual ego to the collective identity of the people. It is the unwillingness to see the hero in this double aesthetic role that has obscured for most critics his tragic stature.

The focus of *Nostromo* is not "material interests" and their representative, Gould, but the people and their representative, Nostromo. Permeating the novel, densely filling the interstices between characters, providing motive and meaning to their actions, are the people. Costaguana is the most palpable presence in *Nostromo* by virtue of the gross human fact of popular suffering. It is "a great land of plain and mountain and people, suffering and mute, waiting for the future in a pathetic immobility of patience. . . . On all the lips she found a weary desire for peace, the dread of officialdom with its nightmarish parody of administration without law, without security, and without justice." . . . The vision is Mrs. Gould's, and, despite her limited perspective (she finds, for example, that all Costaguanans look alike), she is able to perceive it because "having acquired in Southern Europe a knowledge of true peasantry, she was able to appreciate the great worth of the people." . . . (pp. 172-73)

The people stand in danger of that primary evil of industrialism: dehumanization. In the days before the revolution ("nobody had ever heard of labour troubles then") the naïve human spirit of the European-born Cargadores led them to strike every bull-fight day. Nostromo's role as foreman, master of labor, is to roust out the men on the mornings after from their "black, lightless cluster of huts, like cow-byres, like dog-kennels." . . . When he later rebels against his own exploitation, he becomes at the same time conscious of the proletariat over whom he has been boss: "What he had heard Giorgio Viola say once was very true. Kings, ministers, aristocrats, the rich in general, kept the people in poverty and subjection; they kept them as they kept dogs, to fight and hunt for their service." . . . (p. 173)

Nostromo's career is, then, a record of growing class consciousness. His offended egoism first leads to withdrawal: "What did he care about their politics? Nothing at all." . . . But egoism also turns him against his former employer; the mine "appeared to him hateful and immense, lording it by its vast wealth over the valour, the toil, the fidelity of the poor, over war and peace, over the labours of the town, the sea, and the Campo." . . . Finally, he reasserts his origins and his ties to his mentor, recognizing himself "a republican like old Giorgio, and a revolutionist at heart (but in another manner)." . . . (pp. 173-74)

The "other manner" is his acquisition of silver. It is not mere rationalization by which Nostromo explains it to himself: "The rich lived on wealth stolen from the people, but he had taken from the rich nothing—nothing that was not lost to them already by their folly and their betrayal." . . . The point is supported by the plot of the novel, for what provokes Nostromo to steal

is the businesslike complacency of his employers towards their loss. To them it is only money, well lost for political gains. To him it is labor, courage (facing the dangers he encounters), and pride—in short, the values of the work ethic and their just reward.

Nostromo takes up the silver, which Conrad has carefully designated as a symbol of capitalism by making it the mine's actual product, and acquires a secret taint on his erstwhile "incorruptible" character. The taint of wealth goes further: when the revolutionary party leader visits Nostromo at his deathbed in search of the bequest of his fortune to the movement, he claims it because "the rich must be fought with their own weapons." . . . It is, then, a mark of his dedication to the revolution that Nostromo does not answer, does not allow the curse to be passed on to the people.

And yet, for all his developing class consciousness, Nostromo remains bedeviled by the contradictions of his own character. An egoist whose pride has been hurt, he tries to identify himself with the people, but just when his egoistic desire for reputation is satisfied in the fullest measure, he is isolated by his guilty conscience and by his hidden crime. He then tries to take on another identity along with the old—that of Captain Fidanza, seaman-merchant and respectable patron of the radical party. How are we to regard this ironic mixture of alienation and integration, of individualism and social responsibility, of self-transcendence and self-destruction?

Nostromo's political career centers on four acts: the rescue of the escaping President Ribiera and the suppression of the rioting *Lumpenproletariat;* the "off-stage" secret mission to Hernandez; the removal of the silver from Sulaco to save it from the invading Monterist forces; and the summoning of General Barrios' army to defeat the Monterists and establish an independent Occidental Republic. In the first case, Nostromo's act is along strict class lines, favoring the aristocratic Blancos against the demagogic popular party. In the second, he is the emissary of Father Corbelàn, serving the efforts of the aristocracy (Corbelàn is of the Avellanos family) to put itself in league with its own peasantry, despite their "bandit" status. In the third, the interests of the mine—of the new capitalist order—are uppermost, but here Nostromo breaks with his role of upper-class factotum when he discovers his exploitation. In the last action, his guiding principle is the separatism of Decoud and is in the popular interest: to protect the community of Sulaco from the depredations of a ruthless military regime.

It is at this point that Nostromo identifies himself with the community most fully and most altruistically—at precisely the time of his greatest egoism, when he is already absorbed in his own plans to become rich. Individualism here fosters social action, but later, his social integration is eroded by personal preoccupations. This ironic relationship of communal identity and inveterate isolation is what gives Nostromo's career, like the larger historical action of the novel, its tragic character. Community and individual are found to be both interdependent and mutually exclusive: they create and they destroy each other— at least at this imperfect level of social development.

We are now in a position to justify the otherwise intolerably melodramatic conclusion of the novel, in which Nostromo, drawing off silver in order to "become rich slowly," is shot by his revolutionary mentor, Giorgio Viola, who takes him for the young worker, Ramirez, the unwelcome suitor of his daughter. Given the class conflicts and symbolic suggestions of the novel, the denouement reads like a myth of radical politics:

Viola, the old-guard Garibaldino, rejects Ramirez because he is a native of Sulaco and therefore lacking in traditional class consciousness. (It is the European element that forms the working-class elite and the native half-breeds who constitute the tools of the demagogues Gamacho and Fuentes. . . .) The idealist Viola fails to recognize Nostromo because of his both literal and symbolic poor vision. The faded radical is out of touch with the new proletariat and is himself ridden by class prejudices (e.g., those of the European workers against the natives).

Nostromo is, even without Viola's myopia, directly destroyed by the contradictions between self-seeking and class consciousness. He uses the silver, at least in part, for the support of the radical movement, but he keeps his secret so well that he becomes totally isolated. He is killed by that isolation, through Viola's ignorance of his identity and designs. As in **Lord Jim** and other Conrad fables of the individual's relation to the social organism, there is in *Nostromo* a residual resistance to complete assimilation with the people, and this heroic individualism accounts both for the hero's demise and for his stature.

Like every tragic figure, Nostromo cannot be held by the world any longer—cannot be contained, at least within its usual morality. Like every tragic figure, he takes on himself the burden of guilt (or at least the illusion of it): the guilt of failing to bring a priest for the dying wife of Viola, the guilt of leaving Decoud behind to die. Nostromo is the sacrifice that societies make in order to live, and thereby he is made awesome. His very self-sacrifice leads him to rid himself of the conventional social bonds—to be, with the aged Oedipus, beyond society. Like every tragic hero, he achieves freedom, a certain recklessness born of the infinity of possibilities which opens before him when he acquires the treasure and becomes alienated from all classes and all men. He becomes the benefactor of the people, but the new order he has brought about is repressive in its turn. He joins the revolutionary party, but he never becomes ideologically committed to social or political action.

He is now free of everything but the treasure, the very instrument of his flight to freedom. There remains only to rid himself of that bond and he will be free, so free that there remains for him only to die. "In the exulting consciousness of his strength, and the triumphant excitement of his mind, he struck a blow for his freedom." He tells his beloved, Giselle Viola, of the treasure and when she asks how he got it, "He wrestled with the spell of captivity. It was as if striking a heroic blow that he burst out: 'Like a thief!'" . . . In judging his own crime, Nostromo frees himself from "captivity," strikes a "heroic blow," fulfills himself as tragic hero. He points the way toward an ideal social hero who achieves full integration with his nation or his class. But he himself does not fulfill that ideal. He is, rather, another kind of hero, the tragic figure torn apart by the contradictions involved in his effort to transcend his historical situation and his own ego. This dialectical negation is as far as Conrad will go in leading our imagination toward the ideal of community. (pp. 174-76).

> *Avrom Fleishman, in* Conrad's Politics: Community and Anarchy in the Fiction of Joseph Conrad, *The Johns Hopkins Press, 1967, 267 p.*

DOUGALD McMILLAN   (essay date 1972)

[*In the following excerpt, McMillan offers a Christian allegorical reading of* Nostromo.]

More than in any other of Conrad's novels the reader needs some familiar pattern beneath the complex surface of events and details to help him see the structure of [*Nostromo*]. Both Dorothy Van Ghent and Claire Rosenfield have pointed out that Nostromo's acts follow the pattern of "the myth of the hero" as detailed in Joseph Campbell's *The Hero with a Thousand Faces*. Miss Van Ghent goes on to compare the novel with the Irish Fairy tale of Con-Edda, while Miss Rosenfield finds the folk legend of "The King and the Corpse" most instructive. Costaguana does labor under a curse like those of the old legends, and Nostromo is clearly the hero who undertakes a quest and undergoes an ordeal to save the people. But to see only the similarities of his actions to the large patterns of nearly all heroes is to perceive only a vague outline where Conrad has provided a distinct and remarkably intricate pattern to give form to his novel. The guilt and redemption which dominate the book are worked out specifically in terms of Christian myth and theology. To overlook this is to miss one of the most central sources of unity in the novel.

The silver of the San Tomé mine from which the curse upon the land emanates is a vastly powerful but ambiguous force. It has the potential to make Costaguana a kind of paradise, but on the other hand it is a strong temptation that drives men to cruelty and barbarism. There is no neutral point in the struggle between the two tendencies inherent in the mine. Like Eden, Costaguana must be a successful paradise or its inhabitants must be under a curse. It has not been a paradise since the first Europeans set foot there in search of treasure.

In the beginning of *Nostromo* the curse of the mine rests only upon the Gould family in the form of an unworked concession. But when Charles Gould and his wife Emilia decide to make the mine operative, they, like Adam and Eve, extend the curse to all of Costaguana. The dual nature of the mine's potential and the parallels with Eden are made quite specific in the physical description of the mine. It is a lush mountain garden with a pure waterfall later "dammed up above" . . . to make sluices for working the mine. Don Pepe, the overseer, calls it "the very paradise of snakes." . . . The allusion to Eden becomes unmistakable when Don Carlos Gould says to his wife, "It is no longer a paradise of snakes. We have brought mankind into it, and we cannot turn our backs on them to go and begin a new life elsewhere. . . ." But it is she who feels the responsibility for extending the curse beyond herself and more than Don Carlos seeks to ease the suffering it has brought. When she and her husband began their plans to make the mine operative, they thought they were making the cause of "an absurd moral disaster" into a "serious and moral success," . . . but the problem remains with them only on a much larger scale.

When the curse of the silver manifests itself in the form of the greed that leads to the Monterist revolution, Mrs. Gould's compassionate instincts come into conflict with her husband's attitudes. As Decoud explains in his letter to his sister, "Don Carlos's mission is to preserve unstained the fair name of his mine. . . ." . . . His idea of a "moral success" is law and order above all else. "Haunted" by the "fixed" idea "of justice," . . . he will do anything to keep the mine out of the hands of the corrupt Monterists. He is prepared, if necessary, to blow up the mine, out of the territory of the republic . . . , an action that will bring political reprisal and misery to Sulaco. So strong is his passion for justice that even his wife is not exempt from it. He is even willing to "bring heaven down piteously upon a loved head." . . . Mrs. Gould's mission is "to save him from the effects of that cold and overmastering passion.'' . . . This is only possible through the agency of Nostromo. Unless he is successful in keeping the most recent shipment of silver out of the hands of the Monterist revolutionaries and securing aid against them, her compassion cannot win out over her husband's rigid demands for justice.

Nostromo thus becomes the agent of mercy protecting vulnerable humanity caught between the opposed forces of corruption and stern justice. To save the mine and abort the revolution, Nostromo must take the curse of the silver, ''The curse of death'' . . . as he calls it, upon himself. Like Christ who undoes the curse brought upon the world by Adam and Eve, he performs an act of vicarious atonement.

The specific curse with which Nostromo is burdened as a direct result of his efforts to save Sulaco is not exclusively brought on by his own guilt. It originates from his involvement with other people. In choosing to go to sea with the lighter of silver rather than bring a priest for the dying Teresa Viola, Nostromo abandons her to death without confession. She dies believing that he has ''deprived her of Paradise.'' . . . In her despair she is the first to speak of the curse that will fall on him. In choosing to complete the salvation of Sulaco by bearing a message to the friendly general, Barrios, rather than returning to the Great Isabel, he leaves Martin Decoud to perish alone. Decoud might have survived, but he lacks the faith to wait even a few days for Nostromo's return. The manner of these two deaths and Nostromo's part in them are the direct cause of the curse under which he labors. He realizes in thinking how his fate has come upon him, ''the part he had played himself. First a woman, then a man, abandoned each in their last extremity, for the sake of this accursed treasure. It was paid for by a soul lost and by a vanished life.'' . . . (pp. 167-69)

By his later actions Nostromo assumes the guilt for both a failure to confess and a lack of faith. In his case they are combined in an act of secrecy which determines that he shall die like a thief. He has only to have enough faith in the reliability of other men to tell them what has happened to Decoud and the silver and he will avoid all the suspicion and guilt with which he is later surrounded, but he chooses instead to keep silent.

Nostromo returns from taking the silver out into the Golfo Placido to a scene dominated by confessions about the silver. The first person he encounters is Dr. Monygham, who is already infamous for one false confession and is in the process of making another. The body of Hirsch, the ox-hide merchant who has been killed because he ''confessed everything,'' . . . dangles in the background during their conversation, casting its large shadow over two living men. Both duty and love demand that Nostromo also make a kind of confession—that he give an account of his acts to Captain Mitchell out of duty and to Giorgio Viola out of friendship and a sense of community. But from his first waking moments on shore, the idea of betrayal destroys in him all faith in other men and works to prevent this confession.

Certainly Nostromo has been used by the Europeans and undoubtedly Decoud does betray him later, but the cries of betrayal which he makes at this point are founded more upon his own vanity than upon real grievances. Because there is no one to welcome him and applaud his great exploit publicly, he comes to see all those who have depended upon his great fidelity as enemies and betrayers. This mistrust aroused in him by the wound to his vanity leads him to reject mentally the idea of revealing the fate of the silver to Captain Mitchell or to old Viola. . . . (pp. 169-70)

While Nostromo's mistrust begins mentally, his first real opportunity to share his knowledge of the silver comes when he meets Dr. Monygham in the custom-house and his mistrust rapidly becomes centered in the doctor. Though Monygham thinks to himself, ''I must take him into my confidence completely,'' and does so, Nostromo makes no reciprocal gesture of faith. Instead he succumbs to the temptation to use Monygham's former weakness as a betrayer who has confessed to a conspiracy that did not exist as justification for his own destrust of other people. He expands his assessment of Monygham first to the San Tomé oligarchy, ''You fine people are all alike. All dangerous. All betrayers. . . .'' . . . Later at Viola's, he includes everyone in his judgment. ''There was no one to understand; no one he could take into the confidence of Decoud's fate, of his own, into the secret of the silver. That doctor was an enemy of the people—a tempter. . . .'' . . .

The attitude of secrecy established in the encounter with Monygham grows like an ever more binding spell cast upon him by the silver. Aboard the ship bringing Barrios back to Sulaco he is again given an opportunity to confess the secret of the silver but again he remains silent, ''under the influence of some indefinable form of resentment and distrust.'' . . . He thinks to himself that he will let Decoud tell the story ''from his own lips'' but even as this thought is going through his mind, Decoud is already dead. Nostromo's silence and lack of faith have assured that he will become a figure of guilt.

The nature of the curse of secrecy and the power it has over Nostromo may be seen in his near attempt at confession to Giselle. Softened by her love, he struggles against the spell of the silver which he feels like a ''weight as of chains upon his limbs, a pressure as of a cold hand upon his lips.'' . . . As he is able to confess that he has a treasure gotten ''like a thief,'' he feels that he has ''struck a blow for his freedom.'' . . . But when he forbids her to ask where it is hidden, we see that his confession is incomplete, that ''He had not regained his freedom.'' . . . (pp. 170-71)

In one sense Nostromo's sin of secrecy is Adam's sin of possessing forbidden knowledge. Though the knowledge of the silver is not in itself damning, Nostromo makes it so by turning it into a guilty secret in defiance of love and duty. In the scene in the custom-house when Nostromo makes his decision to keep his secret, he is presented as a guiltless Adam who becomes more and more Satanic as he becomes more committed to secrecy. At the beginning the emphasis is upon his innocence.

> Nostromo woke . . . from his lair in the long grass. He stood knee-deep among the whispering undulations of the green blades, with the lost air of a man just born into the world. Handsome, robust, and supple, he threw back his head, flung his arms open, and stretched himself with a slow twist of the waist and a leisurely growling yawn of white teeth; as natural and free from evil in the moment of waking as a magnificent and unconscious wild beast. . . .

From the reference to him as a beast in a ''lair,'' his serpentine movements and the ''lost air'' about him we may see his potential for evil but at this point it remains only a potential.

As he begins to experience the vanity which sets his mind against his fellow men, he is described in terms suggesting both Adam and Satan: "Nostromo tasted the dust and ashes of the fruit of life into which he had bitten deeply in his hunger for praise." . . . The fruit he eats suggests the forbidden fruit of Adam, but the taste is that of the dust and ashes which Satan is condemned to eat for his part in corrupting man. After he has met Monygham who further wounds his vanity by assuming the silver lost, his feelings are described in terms suggestive of Satan's fall. "The sense of betrayal and ruin floated upon his sombre indifference as upon a sluggish sea of pitch." . . . The mind of the previously innocent and incorruptible Nostromo has now become a kind of hell. In the necessity to come to grips with Monygham's plan to tell Sotillo that the silver is on the Great Isabel, he gives way to "hissing vehemence." . . . And finally, as he commits the first act of deceit to keep the silver a secret by offering the counterplan to tell that the silver has been lost in the sea, the process is complete: Monygham calls him a "Devil of a man!" . . . (pp. 171-72)

While Nostromo is depicted as Adam succumbing to temptation and assuming the characteristics of Satan, another undercurrent of suggestion keeps us aware that in assuming this sin he is atoning vicariously for all of Costaguana. His unexpected return to shore when "everything seemed lost in Sulaco" . . . is looked on as a miracle of rebirth bringing deliverance. Giorgio Viola experiences it as "a return to life." . . . Monygham calls it a "marvelous" reappearance . . . To him "Nostromo's return was providential. He did not think of him humanely, as of a fellow-creature just escaped from the jaws of death. The capataz for him was the only possible messenger to Cayta, the very man." . . . He says again later that Nostromo is "the only man." . . . Nostromo, himself, alludes to his accomplishment in saving the silver, saying, "if that silver turned up this moment. . . . That . . . would be a greater miracle than any saint could perform." . . . And he speaks of his arrival with Barrios as a "return in triumph." . . . (p. 172)

Despite the new hope that Nostromo's awakening brings to Sulaco, he himself experiences it as a kind of death. After we see him depicted first as lying "as if dead," "still as a corpse." . . . watched over by a vulture, we are told that for him awakening "was more like the end of things. The necessity of living concealed somehow, for God knows how long . . . made everything that had gone before for years appear vain and foolish, like a flattering dream come suddenly to an end." . . . As his old innocent life passes away and he feels "the burden of sacrilegious guilt descend upon his shoulders," . . . Nostromo undergoes a kind of passion which parallels his assumption of the qualities of Satan. In the sky the cloud bank is like "a floating mantle stained with blood." . . . In the ocean below the blood red of the sky is mingled strikingly with the water. In this atmosphere he experiences the "bitterness approaching that of death itself" . . . which overcomes him at the thought of his betrayal as physical thirst. "His mouth was dry . . . with heavy sleep and extremely anxious thinking. . . ." And he tries to reject the very praise for which he longs. "He tried to spit before him—'Tfui'—and muttered a curse upon the selfishness of all the rich people." . . . As he makes the mental decision that he can trust no one, an owl lets out an "appalling cry—'Ya-acabo! Ya-acabo!' (It is finished! It is finished!)" . . . Nostromo thinks that this cry is a sign that Teresa is dead and that the "unseen powers which he had offended by refusing to bring a priest to a dying woman were lifting up their voice against him," . . . but he does not realize

that it signifies the finality with which the curse he earned by the act has been settled upon himself.

Though Nostromo has assumed the guilt of others and suffered for it symbolically in the scene in the custom-house, the guilt with which the novel is charged is not purged until the end of the book. Before the curse can be removed permanently, Nostromo must find absolution, and those for whom the sacrifice is made must demonstrate their belief so that the vicarious atonement can be effective.

At his physical death Nostromo retains the role of sacrificial victim. He is shot while "weighted down with silver." . . . His wrongdoing is thus exposed, but he makes sure that no one shares with him the guilt of the knowledge of the treasure's hiding place. His first words to Mrs. Gould after she is summoned to his side are an attempt to ensure that Giselle will not be thought guilty. "She is innocent," he says, "She is innocent. It is I alone." . . . If he has not bought the golden crown for her brow or taken her to that paradise with a palace on a fertile hill crowned with olive trees, vineyards, and corn that he dreams for her . . . , he has at least kept her free from guilt in the eyes of others.

Nostromo's own sins are absolved by acts of confession and faith which parallel and counteract the events by which he assumed guilt. His request (carried out by Dr. Monygham) to have Mrs. Gould brought to him brings someone to perform an office of confession like that denied to Teresa Viola. When she arrives "cloaked and monastically hooded." . . . Mrs. Gould hears him confess that he is "Nostromo the thief." . . . (pp. 172-74)

This confession undoes half of the guilt. Mrs. Gould is the kind and gracious lady whose presence throughout the novel we experience as a constant force for good. When she responds to Nostromo's offer to tell her where the treasure is by saying "No capataz . . . no one misses it now. Let it be lost forever," . . . we feel that Nostromo has been forgiven and that the curse attached to the silver has been allowed to go out of the world. This impression is strengthened later when she silences Dr. Monygham's question about Nostromo's relationship to the treasure with "He told me nothing." . . . (p. 174)

Despite all this Mrs. Gould's response to Nostromo is ambiguous and insufficient to clear the air of all guilt. Her dismissal of his rescue of the silver is only one of many such dismissals, each of which Nostromo has regarded as a betrayal. Nostromo might have divulged his secret to Monygham, Viola, Captain Mitchell, and Don Carlos Gould and saved himself, but each of them encouraged his silence by assuming the silver lost and Nostromo incapable of retrieving it. Only moments before, Nostromo has reproached Don Carlos for saying, "It was nothing of importance. Let it go." . . . He reacts to her words by closing his eyes, saying "no word" and, making "no movement." This may be construed as a sign of relief from his burden, but it may also be seen as an indication of complete despair.

However we read Nostromo's response to the pardon bestowed on him by Mrs. Gould, it is clear that his absolution is incomplete, for she still believes him a thrall to the silver. Although she has heard him declare his love for Giselle and his faith in her and say that he could have torn himself away from the treasure for her . . . , she nonetheless says to Giselle, "Console yourself, child. Very soon he would have forgotten you for his treasure." . . . In her eyes he has found forgiveness for taking the silver but not for the faithlessness it aroused in him.

The guilt associated with Decoud's death is not yet purged, and even as he is confessing to Mrs. Gould, Nostromo denounces Don Martin as a betrayer.

The act of faith necessary to make salvation complete comes from Dr. Monygham. He accepts Mrs. Gould's assertion that Nostromo told her nothing as absolute pardon for Nostromo. As soon as she speaks, the light of the "temperamental enmity to Nostromo" goes out of his eyes. . . . Paradoxically, however, he does not give up his belief that Nostromo has somehow saved the silver that was lost. He alone believes that Nostromo has performed the "miracle greater than any saint could perform" and yet affirms his innocence. His act of faith not only completes Nostromo's absolution but provides the belief in the act of sacrifice that makes it effective.

It is significant that Monygham's forgiveness and faith come first when he has no cause for them. It is thus the counteraction not only to Decoud's suicide and the long series of failures to ask about the silver, but also to Nostromo's secrecy itself. In the custom-house Nostromo holds Dr. Monygham strictly accountable for his past, and thus begins the chain of events that leads to the dishonorable death. Monygham, in contrast, extends his forgiveness in spite of even more tangible evidence of Nostromo's guilt. (pp. 174-75)

Conrad demands from his readers the same faith based on extension of grace that is demanded of his characters. If we believe that either the popular revolution or imperialist expansion will change Costaguana, we do so in the face of vast evidence to the contrary. The history of Costaguana as it is given in the book, from the earliest Conquistadores through the reign of Guzman Bento and the Ribierist experiment down to the most recent attempted coup in Santa Marta, gives no reason to expect salvation from either end of the political spectrum. And yet if Conrad has been successful and if we respond to the prodding he gives in his author's note, we see Antonia Avellanos as a figure modeled on "the standard-bearer of a faith to which we all were born, but which she alone knew how to hold aloft with an unflinching hope!" . . . We do somehow disregard all the history which Conrad has shown us in such detail and suspend our judgment of men enough to hope at least that Costaguana can be reunified and the benefits of the mine extended to all. The faith demanded is not, however, merely optimism. It contains the awareness that all humanity is involved in a "desperate affair." Like Linda's cry—"Never Gian Batista"—with which the novel ends, it is a mixture of anguish at the impossibility of human perfection, unquestioning pardon for imperfection, and affirmation of a spirit of love that binds us together in spite of the infidelities we commit.

The presence of a theological structure unifying *Nostromo* not only helps us to order the threads of the plot, it also suggests a relationship between Conrad and the reader somewhat different from the one we are accustomed to thinking about. Encouraged by the dramatic presence of his famous narrators, Conrad's readers have for the most part been content to see themselves as listeners to a story. Their job has been the familiar one of judging character, weighing motives, responding to description, and following the action. To be sure most of them have felt the need to participate actively in the telling to evaluate testimony and correct the biases of the various points of view. But even in this complex process readers have involved themselves primarily in a transaction with the personae of the stories. Conrad's presence, except in the degree that he is equated with his narrators, is not felt. But as soon as the words we read begin to have suggestions about a larger structure of which the characters of the novels are themselves unaware a new element is present. When, for example, we read a phrase like "a very devil of a man" not as Dr. Monygham commenting idly on Nostromo's tenacity, but also as Conrad inviting us to share his knowledge of the order behind these events, we realize that we are more than listeners to a story related by the personae that inhabit Costaguana. We are dealing directly with the more complex literary mind of Joseph Conrad. From time to time as in the playful double entendre that allows us to read "damned up above" in "dammed up above" we get a relieving glance at the kind of sophisticated and sometimes humorous relationship Conrad has to his material. The feeling of discovery and the relief of the humor are in themselves important parts of the pleasure of the novel, but like most of the other elements of Conrad's technique they also serve the purpose of involving us more directly by fostering a sense of participation on a level of understanding shared only between us and the author. By making us his accomplices in discovery and by letting us smile with him in the playful superiority of our knowledge, Conrad forestalls our criticism of what he has to tell us and gains a kind of acceptance few novelists enjoy. (pp. 179-80)

Dougald McMillan, " 'Nostromo': The Theology of Revolution," in The Classic British Novel, edited by Howard M. Harper, Jr. and Charles Edge, The University of Georgia Press, 1972, pp. 166-82.

C. B. COX (essay date 1974)

[*Cox is an English nonfiction writer, educator, and critic. In the following excerpt, he proposes that an underlying philosophical opposition exists in* Nostromo *between the skepticism represented by Decoud and the humanity and morality represented by Emilia Gould.*]

Nostromo presents at least two irreconcilable points of view. At one extreme there is a profound scepticism which pervades the descriptions of landscapes and people, and which seems akin to that of Decoud when he commits suicide; at the other extreme this pessimism is countered by the human and moral claims most finely represented by Mrs. Emilia Gould.

In the opening chapter, Conrad describes how in Sulaco at midday the sun withdraws from the Placid Gulf the shadow of the mountains, and the clouds roll out of the lower valleys to blot out the peaks of the Sierra: "The Cordillera is gone from you as if it had dissolved itself into great piles of grey and black vapours that travel out slowly to seaward and vanish into thin air all along the front before the blazing heat of the day." This "as if" fancy imaginatively enacts a process of dissolution to which all the people and landscapes of the novel are forced at times to submit. Just as Higuerota is transformed into a bubble, so the characters become ghosts, or dissolve into shadows, as though human beings were no more than flickering images cast on a screen by some eternal cine-camera.

This pervading sense of human insubstantiality is particularly noticeable at moments involving crowds in times of crisis. The individual is caught up in an historical process which is determined to extinguish his identity. This is brilliantly symbolized in the fourth chapter, as Giorgio, the old Garibaldini, gazes across the plain where Nostromo is pursuing the rioters:

> On this memorable day of the riot his arms were not folded on his chest. His hand grasped the barrel of the gun grounded on the threshold; he did not look up once at the white dome of

Higuerota, whose cool purity seemed to hold itself aloof from a hot earth. His eyes examined the plain curiously. Tall trails of dust subsided here and there. In a speckless sky the sun hung clear and blinding. Knots of men ran headlong; others made a stand; and the irregular rattle of firearms came rippling to his ears in the fiery, still air. Single figures on foot faced desperately. Horsemen galloped towards each other, wheeled round together, separated at speed. Giorgio saw one fall, rider and horse disappearing as if they had galloped into a chasm, and the movements of the animated scene were like the passages of a violent game played upon the plain by dwarfs mounted and on foot, yelling with tiny throats, under the mountain that seemed a colossal embodiment of silence. Never before had Giorgio seen this bit of plain so full of active life; his gaze could not take in all its details at once; he shaded his eyes with his hand, till suddenly the thundering of many hoofs near by startled him. . . .

This game of killing is placed at such a distance it seems without purpose. Human beings in *Nostromo* are often reduced in size, to dwarfs as here, or to insects. Giorgio himself at the time of his wife's death is compared in his movements to a mouse, and Nostromo with Decoud on the lighter in the darkness of the Placid Gulf thinks they are like beetles. As he gazes on the animated scene, Giorgio, like the narrator of the novel, cannot take in all the details at once, cannot impose form on this confused tableau. The fallen rider vanishes as if he had never existed. Above, the white dome of Higuerota stands as a colossal embodiment of Nature's silent, unmoved response to the anguish of human beings.

Many other passages show how the people can make no indelible impression on the blank indifference of the landscape: "Men ploughed with wooden ploughs and yoked oxen, small on a boundless expanse, as if attacking immensity itself." Often the narrator's perspective, like Giorgio's, is deliberately placed at a distance so that the people are diminished in importance. From the plain the stamp sheds and the houses of the mine appear "like the nests of birds clustered on the ledges of a cliff": "The zigzag paths resembled faint tracings scratched on the wall of a cyclopean blockhouse." Similar effects to those in the scene on the plain watched by Giorgio occur when the aristocratic families are in flight to take sanctuary with the robber Hernandez. They pass a roadside rancho of woven rushes and a roof of grass which has been set on fire by accident:

Great masses of sparks mingled with black smoke flew over the road; the bamboos of the walls detonated in the fire with the sound of an irregular fusillade. And then the bright blaze sank suddenly, leaving only a red dusk crowded with aimless dark shadows drifting in contrary directions; the noise of voices seemed to die away with the flame; and the tumult of heads, arms, quarrelling, and imprecations passed on fleeing into the darkness. . . .

Often in *Nostromo* Conrad gives this impression that behind visible shapes hovers a ghost world, whose truth negates the conscious aims of the characters. Here the movements of the people are in fact far from aimless as they flee to save their lives. But the description transforms them into shadows, not

understanding their true purposes, and eventually drifting away into the darkness. There are many occasions when suddenly the colourful events appear to one character as unreal or dreamlike. As Decoud rides in the carriage after the troops of General Barrios have embarked, he gazes on the mass of people trudging along the road, all turning their heads in sombreros and rebozos, as a train passes quickly out of sight behind Giorgio's house:

And it was all like a fleeting vision, the shrieking ghost of a railway engine fleeing across the frame of the archway, behind the startled movement of the people streaming back from a military spectacle with silent footsteps on the dust of the road. . . .

This impression of a ghost-world mocking the illusions of the characters is fixed in our minds by the opening chapter. There we are told the story of the two wandering American sailors who, according to legend, organized an expedition to search for treasure in the peninsula of Azuera, but were never seen again. Their ghosts, now rich and hungry and thirsty, are supposed still to mount guard over their treasure, unable to tear themselves away. Their legend reflects most obviously the way the silver mine casts its spell on Charles Gould and Nostromo. The latter often compares himself to the American sailors, and as he eventually assumes guard over the stolen silver, appears in a sense to have merged his identity with theirs. Such ghosts reflect the inevitable futility of the projects of man. After Nostromo has returned to Sulaco leaving Decoud stranded with the silver, he meets Dr. Monygham, the eccentric sceptic whose pessimism has been tempered by romantic feeling for Mrs. Gould. As in the Custom House Dr. Monygham explains to Nostromo his scheme to bring back General Barrios to Sulaco, behind them the dead body of Señor Hirsch hangs from the roof, apparently listening attentively. He is a reminder of the absurd horrors involved in the movements of history. (pp. 62-4)

The determined historical processes are most clearly illustrated in the career of Charles Gould. Conrad detests the sentimentalizing of commercial power by a man such as the American captain of industry and finance, Holroyd, and shows how Gould ruins himself by allying himself with this fanatic. In his letters Conrad expressed his distrust of the rationalizations of American imperialism in Cuba and the Philippines: he believed that capitalism and imperialism destroy the individuality of people. The philosophy of progressive capitalism is explained by Gould to his wife in the early days of their love:

"What is wanted here is law, good faith, order, security. Any one can declaim about these things, but I pin my faith to material interests. Only let the material interests once get a firm footing, and they are bound to impose the conditions on which alone they can continue to exist. That's how your money-making is justified here in the face of lawlessness and disorder. It is justified because the security which it demands must be shared with an oppressed people. A better justice will come afterwards. That's your ray of hope." . . .

The failure of these ideals in the novel seems at times virtually total. When the Goulds first visit the mine, the narrator describes the waterfall and tree-ferns, a hanging garden above the rocks of the gorge, as "a paradise of snakes." The Goulds bring corruption into this natural wilderness. At first Mrs.

Gould is successful in establishing her hospitals and schools, and the mine provides peace and stability for the Indian workmen. But gradually other less fortunate influences are noticeable. The "material apparatus of perfected civilization" obliterates the individuality of old towns under the stereotyped conveniences of modern life. The railway disturbs the picturesque simple lives of the people, replacing with its yards the land previously used for popular festivals. The miners begin to lose their identities in Village One, Village Two and Village Three, places like Nostromo, without an inherited name. By interfering in Costaguana politics, the mine is responsible for another revolution, that of Montero against Ribiera. At the end Antonia and Father Corbelan are plotting to annex the rest of Costaguana for the new Occidental Republic, and we know that bloodshed and horror will return. History is proved to be cyclical, as the broken time scheme implies, not in accord with Gould's dreams of a progressive capitalism. Dr. Monygham is allowed the last word:

> "There is no peace and no rest in the development of material interests. They have their law, and their justice. But it is founded on expediency, and is inhuman; it is without rectitude, without the continuity and the force that can be found only in a moral principle." . . .

The novel might properly end with Mrs. Gould, alone in a garden, betrayed by her husband's obsession with the mine, stammering out as if in the grip of a merciless nightmare: "Material interests."

This historical process has a metaphysical dimension. Charles Gould is trying to conquer matter, and to make its hard intransigence his servant. If he succeeds, he will prove consciousness is not a passing shadow, but capable of imposing its values on the material world. He is promoting an industrial civilization which with its railways, roads and mines will make Nature conform to a human idea. As he listens to the growling mutter of the mountain pouring its stream of treasure under the stamps, he is listening to his own desire, and he imagines the noise must reach to the uttermost limits of the province. For both the Goulds in the early years of their marriage, each passing of the escort with the silver under the balcony of their house is like another victory gained in the conquest of peace for Costaguana. The silver passes through Sulaco at dawn; in the whole sunlit range of empty balconies along the street "only one white figure would be visible high up above the clear pavement—the wife of the Señor Administrador—leaning over to see the escort go by the harbour, a mass of heavy, fair hair twisted up negligently on her little head, and a lot of lace about the neck of her muslin wrapper." They are redeeming the land; this symbolic scene places her "high up," as if floating away in innocence and purity from the corruption of Costaguana. It is a new dawn, a dream of human justice, order and love. For Emilia at this time, the silver becomes an embodiment of her aspirations: "She endowed that lump of metal with a justificatory conception, as though it were not a mere fact, but something far-reaching and impalpable, like the true expression of an emotion or the emergence of a principle."

The faith of the Goulds is treated with bitter irony. According to Royal Roussel, Gould cannot escape from the fundamental process in Conrad's world whereby the source of life continually negates and reabsorbs its own creation. He is possessed by the mine, by matter, as after death the body itself must turn to dust. His consciousness solidifies, petrifies, so that his inhuman coldness can no longer respond to the tenderness of his wife. In the battle between matter and mind, the former always wins. In the last sentence of the novel, the white cloud shining like a mass of solid silver hangs over the Placid Gulf, symbolizing that all the creations of men will eventually be absorbed back into the elemental components of Nature.

This pessimism is certainly the main impression we take away from a first reading; we may concur with Dr. Monygham, who tells Emilia that the mine will eventually weigh upon the people as heavily as the barbarism, cruelty and misrule of previous years. Gould at the end seems to have been transformed into a ghost, like the American adventurers on Azuera. But some doubts remain. The paradise was *of snakes,* and we may remember that the Indians do achieve a happiness in their villages denied to them in their previous poverty-stricken existence. Although the total historical process may appear determined, a provisional freedom for short periods of time seems attainable, and by no means to be treated with disdain. Some of the Goulds' ideals are achieved, if only temporarily.

We may also wonder how far Gould's failure is a determined historical process, and how far it is the result of personal weakness. His submission to material interests is a developing process of irrationality. He becomes increasingly obsessed with the mine, until he is willing to blow it up to protect it from his enemies. At times this process seems an inevitable result of his mistaken confidence in the rational benefits of progressive capitalism, as well as of the war between mind and matter. But on other occasions we feel that Gould fails for psychological reasons, and that a different man would not have treated his wife so shamefully. Is there any universal reason why Gould's misplaced faith in capitalism should result in his apparent sexual frigidity? He is irrational in his attitude to the San Tomé mine largely because he is reacting emotionally to the career of his father. The tumult of words and passion poured out about the mine in his father's letters aroused in him a fascination:

> Mines had acquired for him a dramatic interest. He studied their peculiarities from a personal point of view, too, as one would study the varied characters of men. He visited them as one goes with curiosity to call upon remarkable persons. He visited mines in Germany, in Spain, in Cornwall. Abandoned workings had for him strong fascination. Their desolation appealed to him like the sight of human misery, whose causes are varied and profound. They might have been worthless, but also they might have been misunderstood. His future wife was the first, and perhaps the only person to detect this secret mood which governed the profoundly sensible, almost voiceless attitude of this man towards the world of material things. . . .

Presumably service of mines becomes a substitute for service of his father: he will slay the dragon that killed his father, and so prove his own manhood. His re-opening of the mine coincides with the first year of his marriage. His father died at the moment when he and Emilia were discovering their love, and so their devotion to the mine becomes, almost subconsciously for them, a way of repaying the father who never lived to hear of their engagement: "A vague idea of rehabilitation had entered the plan of their life. That it was so vague as to elude the support of argument made it only the stronger." Decoud argues that the eventual corruption of Charles results from this personal kind of engagement. He tells Emilia that

Charles is an Englishman, and therefore must idealize every simple feeling, desire or achievement: "He could not believe his own motives if he did not make them first a part of some fairy tale. The earth is not quite good enough for him, I fear." In his letter to his sister, Decoud describes how Gould's sentimentalism attaches a strange idea of justice to his work at the mine: "He holds to it as some men hold to the idea of love or revenge. Unless I am much mistaken in the man, it must remain inviolate or perish by an act of his will alone." Like other idealists in Conrad's novels, he is dangerous to other men because he will not face facts. He has grown to hate the bribing and intriguing necessary from the beginning for the preservation of the mine, and so he has interfered directly in politics, and supported the Ribierist faction. He is not satisfied by a provisional commitment, by a temporary state of order. He wants to conquer the whole land, to impose his spiritual idea on everything. In this, he imitates Holroyd. These desires have eaten away the true being of Gould, so that he is too confident in his own rectitude:

> For all the uprightness of his character, he had something of an adventurer's easy morality which takes count of personal risk in the ethical appraising of his action. He was prepared, if need be, to blow up the whole San Tomé mountain sky high out of the territory of the Republic. This resolution expressed the tenacity of his character, the remorse of that subtle conjugal infidelity through which his wife was no longer the sole mistress of his thoughts, something of his father's imaginative weakness, and something, too, of the spirit of a buccaneer throwing a lighted match into the magazine rather than surrender his ship. . . .

As he reflects on the riot, he is dominated by a fixed idea, and in the years that follow this brings untold suffering on his wife. The narrator's comment does not equivocate: "A man haunted by a fixed idea is insane. He is dangerous even if that idea is an idea of justice, for may he not bring the heaven down pitilessly upon a loved head?"

Is it not possible, therefore, that some other man might have succeeded in developing the mine without becoming so inflexible? We cannot attribute all the misfortunes of Emilia to the malign influence of "material interests." Certainly they cannot be blamed for the Goulds' failure to produce a child, though the barrenness of the marriage appears symbolic. If the suffering of Emilia is in some degree a consequence of personal weaknesses in her husband, then a possibility emerges that men do have some qualified freedom to escape from the determined processes of history. Conrad's comment on Gould's need for action has been quoted as a total summary of the scepticism of the novel: "Action is consolatory. It is the enemy of thought and the friend of flattering illusions. Only in the conduct of our action can we find the sense of mastery over the Fates." But action does influence events in *Nostromo,* and bring a temporary peace, as Dr. Monygham proves, when he courageously deceives Sotillo and so succeeds in altering the future history of Costaguana. Gould himself makes a great impact on the lives of many people. For several years they are given security, justice and order.

On some occasions, therefore, Gould appears morally responsible for his behaviour, and his actions change the course of history. At others he seems caught by inevitable historical and metaphysical processes. *Nostromo* is full of sadness at human suffering, but it does not convey a sense of unmitigated futility. There are possibilities available for meaningful action, at least in a limited context. There are also possibilities available for fidelity and passion.

Whereas Antonia Avellanos is depicted superficially, Mrs. Gould is portrayed with a depth rare in Conrad's treatment of women. What she represents is a "humanizing influence," and its lights cannot be entirely put out by the darkness of the Gulf:

> She kept her old Spanish house (one of the finest specimens in Sulaco) open for the dispensation of the small graces of existence. She dispensed them with simplicity and charm because she was guided by an alert perception of values. She was highly gifted in the art of human intercourse which consists in delicate shades of self-forgetfulness and in the suggestion of universal comprehension. . . .

She builds up a community, a living witness to human solidarity, which even seduces Decoud temporarily by its virtues. In her loneliness, her attitude to her husband's obsession is like that of a mother for the weakness of a son. On one occasion, she touches his cheek "with a light touch, as if he were a little boy." Her desolation is tragic, for her husband has betrayed the values of personal relations which are her own supreme possession. Conrad writes of "her unselfishness and sympathy":

> She could converse charmingly, but she was not talkative. The wisdom of the heart having no concern with the erection or demolition of theories any more than with the defence of prejudices, has no random words at its command. The words it pronounces have the value of acts of integrity, tolerance, and compassion. A woman's true tenderness, like the true virility of man, is expressed in action of a conquering kind. . . .

While her husband fails to impose his ideal order on matter, she *does conquer.* Her care for people gathers around her the best men of Sulaco, charmed by her warm affection and habits of consideration. Don Pépé, Don José, Dr. Monygham and Decoud find it easy to place confidence in her. While her husband grows increasingly obsessed with material interests, she develops her schools and hospitals. She resembles "a good fairy," "as if radiating a light of her own." At the end she feels her magic is powerless, as Charles drifts further away from her. Yet we remember the sick and dying men she cared for in her courtyard during the riot. We remember her countless acts of consideration and tact. Although she ends the novel deserted and alone, she has created something with which to oppose the Void.

Decoud and Nostromo have some things in common, for both are adventurers without real ties with one specific country. When Father Corbelan accuses Decoud of believing in nothing, "neither in stick nor stone," Decoud replies that in this he is at one with the Capataz of the Cargadores. In his letter to his sister, he tells her that Nostromo "like me, has come casually here to be drawn into the events for which his scepticism as well as mine seems to entertain a sort of passive contempt."

When Nostromo becomes aware of his lack of true relationships, of his existence solely in terms of reputation, his identity is destroyed, and he is reborn into a zombie-like way of life.

In contrast, Decoud is highly intelligent, and therefore continually aware that there is an element of pose in all the roles he assumes. This self-consciousness makes it impossible for him ever to commit himself entirely to human relationships, because he cannot rid himself of a self-mockery that watches his own antics cynically, as he plays out his part in the human drama. This double consciousness prevents him from ever achieving a fixed identity, for he cannot "idealize" any one kind of purposeful action. In Ian Watt's words about Conrad himself, he cannot "establish any real connexion between the alienation he felt and the commitment he sought." Because he cannot fix himself permanently in any one life style, his identity becomes like the clouds and the landscapes, something continually dissolving in a fluid manner from one moment to the next. His problem is summed up when he turns to the assembled throng in Mrs. Gould's house, who are talking of Montero, and shouts into the room with all the strength of his lungs: "Gran' bestia!" Is this just a piece of journalistic rhetoric as he himself supposes? Or is he being to some extent reborn into his true nature as a patriot? The doubtful status of this outcry is typical of his actions. When he falls in love, "his familiar habit of ironic thought fell shattered against Antonia's gravity." As patriot and lover, he does not know how far he is honest, how far he is a poseur. His thoughts, feelings and actions, as well as the opinions of other characters on him, accumulate into a pile of separate entities, but never coalesce into a vital organism.

This uncertainty makes Conrad's treatment of Decoud often seem contradictory. This is a problem that affects the whole novel. There is no Marlow through whose narration we see the events. The anonymous story-teller of *Nostromo* has no identity; we know that this person visited Sulaco on occasions, but we are not given any information about his character, not even his age. Yet he makes quite firm moral judgments on certain occasions, judgments which may not seem validated either by the events or by his choice of imagery. The fluid quality of Decoud's character, transmitted to us in this uncertain manner, seems to me in tune with the total imaginative impact of *Nostromo*. Decoud is the new man of the twentieth century, whose scepticism and alienation make him a "dilettante of experience," and about whom the reader is given no definitive judgment. Conrad leaves us in our "vertiginous stance."

Both Albert Guerard and F. R. Leavis argue that Conrad was too personally involved with Decoud, and that this is the cause of our uncertainties [see excerpts dated 1941 and 1958]. Guerard feels that Conrad was very much attracted towards scepticism, and that his condemnations of Decoud, including the decision to have him commit suicide, signify Conrad's subconscious desire to separate out and demolish a facet of himself, to condemn his own neurotic self-contempt by proxy: there is "a marked discrepancy between what Decoud does and says and is, and what the narrator or omniscient author says about him." Leavis thinks Decoud's consciousness dominates the novel: "In fact, Decoud may be said to have had a considerable part in the writing of *Nostromo;* or one might say that *Nostromo* was written by a Decoud who wasn't a complacent dilettante, but was positively drawn towards those capable of 'investing their activities with spiritual value'—Monygham, Giorgio Viola, Señor Avellanos, Charles Gould." My feeling is that just as Conrad will allow the reader no organizing image by which to understand Costaguana, so his treatment of Decoud is deliberately unclear. Decoud wavers between commitment and non-commitment, and we are not certain how to judge him. His honesty interferes with his ability to create satisfying hu-

man relations. When on the Great Isabel he is withdrawn from all contacts with people, in a silence unalleviated even by the song of birds, he feels, like Nostromo, that he is nothing, and must die.

Decoud's identity passes through three stages. He is introduced as an "idle boulevardier," an "exotic dandy," who has been living a worthless life in Paris. The anonymous narrator treats this period of his life with contempt. Decoud has assumed "a Frenchified—but most unFrench—cosmopolitanism, in reality a barren indifferentism posing as intellectual superiority." He imagines he is a Parisian to his fingertips, but he is in danger of remaining "a sort of nondescript dilettante" all his life: "He had pushed the habit of universal raillery to a point where it blinded him to the genuine impulses of his own nature." When he first appears in company with Antonia, his stylish cravat, round hat and varnished shoes suggest an idea of French elegance, yet, we are told, he is otherwise the very type of a fair Spanish creole, the type never tanned by its native sunshine.

But what are Decoud's "genuine" impulses? Is the French elegance a pose, or his Spanish birthright the key to his nature? In Sulaco, in the second stage of his development, Decoud's love for Antonia introduces him to genuine feelings which surprise him by their intensity. He prefers to believe that love is another form of illusion, but in company with Antonia his growing affection awakens in him a new sensibility: "He remained silent for a minute, startled, as if overwhelmed by a sort of awed happiness, with the lines of the mocking smile still stiffened about his mouth, and incredulous surprise in his eyes." His plan for the new Occidental Republic is not just a freak of fancy, for he is carried away by what, to some extent, must be rated a "genuine" enthusiasm.

Decoud's sceptical intelligence cannot be written off as merely "barren," for it enables him to reach a degree of understanding of the other characters beyond the scope of anyone else in the novel. His analysis of Gould's sentimentality seems definitive, and he perceives most clearly the nature of Nostromo's egotism. Such clarity of insight exemplifies an honesty of its own, and gives weight to his general observations on life. He himself has "no faith in anything except the truth of his own sensations." In his opinion, convictions are merely particular views of our personal advantage either practical or emotional: "It seemed to him that every conviction, as soon as it became effective, turned into that form of dementia the gods send upon those they wish to destroy." The career of Charles Gould appears to prove him right. The alternatives seem to be a barren, cold detachment, or a commitment, like that of Dr. Monygham for Emilia, which may prove highly dangerous to other people. The "fatal touch of contempt for himself to which his complex nature was subject" is a feature both of Decoud's honesty and of his inability to commit himself to a moral principle. (pp. 69-78)

> *C. B. Cox, in his* Joseph Conrad: The Modern Imagination, *J. M. Dent & Sons Ltd, 1974, 191 p.*

STEPHEN K. LAND (essay date 1984)

[*In the following excerpt, Land discusses the characters Gould and Nostromo as representatives of two types of Conradian hero.*]

In all of Conrad's earlier novels the actions turn unambiguously upon a single central figure to whom the other characters, however prominent, are from a structural point of view clearly subordinate. Even Kurtz, whose actual presence spans only a few pages, is unquestionably the hero of *Heart of Darkness*, because it is around him, and not the loquacious Marlow, that the action turns. These earlier heroes are not only mainsprings of action but also the focal points of the Conradian structural pattern; in them, or in their actions, lies the fatal paradox; the ambivalent compromise, at once both guilty and distinguished, lies in their past; and theirs are the powerful voices and reputations by which others are variously attracted and repelled. In *Nostromo,* however, there is no such single central figure. Much of the action turns upon Gould, not Nostromo, and both Decoud and Monygham also make specific and emphatically independent contributions to its evolution. Again, Nostromo is not the sole possessor of the qualities associated with such earlier hero types as Kurtz, Wait and Jim; he is a man of widespread repute who becomes paradoxically compromised over his dealings with the silver, but the same is true in a different way of Gould, while Monygham re-enacts a past "crime," and Decoud pursues a heroine representative of an ideal.

Even so, there remains a sense in which Nostromo is the most important, although not the sole hero of the novel. The very fact that his name provides the book's title suggests that this is so, for it was Conrad's frequent practice to name novels for their heroes, as in *An Outcast of the Islands, The Nigger of the "Narcissus," Lord Jim, The Secret Agent,* and *The Rover.* Nostromo, although a background figure through the first half of the novel, is none the less primary in that he alone stands conspicuously maintaining a precarious balance between the ideological extremes of his world. The other heroes in the story, Gould, Decoud and Monygham, make their respective compromises through a distinct commitment to some current of the politico-ideological stream which forms the story's plot; Gould allies successively with material interests, Ribierism, and Sulacan separatism; Decoud becomes first a Ribierist and then the leading spirit of the separatist movement; while Monygham, under Emilia's protection, enters Sulacan high society and risks his dubious respectability to preserve the safety of his patroness during the rebellion. Nostromo, however, makes no such commitment, acting to the end for himself alone. In this respect he prefigures the other heroes of Conrad's "political" novels, Verloc and Razumov, men who try in vain to steer an independent course of self-interest between the conflicting polarities of political ideas.

Nostromo thus introduces a new type of hero and a new approach to the Conradian structure. The heroes of Conrad's first mature phase are embodiments of paradox, men possessed of exceptional qualities which entail vitiating weaknesses. The paradox of these central figures then extends itself into their respective plots as their characters generate situations of self-defeating endeavour. The heroes of the political novels, on the other hand, are not significantly paradoxical in character, and their plots are not generated directly by any purposive action on their part. The anomalies of their stories arise rather from the heroes' attempts to *avoid* decisive action which would commit them to either side in a dualistic conflict. The paradox now lies not so much in the character of the hero as in the dualistic conflict of his world, which ensures, first, that he cannot maintain his stance of neutrality and, secondly, that having compromised himself by action on behalf of one side the hero will be met with extreme retribution from the direction of the other. The paradox in the novels of this phase might be said to be universal rather than psychological. The heroes themselves, instead of rare and striking figures like Wait, Kurtz and Jim, are now relatively colourless, naturally passive, and temperamentally mild figures, such as Verloc and Razumov. Nos-

tromo displays more verve than his immediate successors, but even he makes his object not to effect some change in the world around him, but simply to secure his own comfort while eschewing entanglement.

The hero who is not an ambitious idealist but rather one who seeks the easy option of neutrality in a universe of dualistic conflict is the distinguishing mark of Conrad's second mature phase, which includes *Nostromo, The Secret Agent, Under Western Eyes,* and a number of contemporaneous short stories. The change from a hero who provokes his nemesis by striving after a goal to one who desires primarily to avoid commitment further shifts the moral balance of Conrad's stories, continuing the direction of movement observed from Wait to Whalley in the first phase. The heroes of the second phase are generally forced into action against their own will and better judgment. The retribution they draw upon themselves seems therefore the less deserved. Where the heroes of the previous phase are men destroyed by their failure in some undertaking they have planned and embarked on for their own ends, the heroes of the second phase are victims of inequitable fate, punished in spite of their initial unwillingness to become involved in conflict.

Nostromo therefore marks several structural departures. It is on a much broader scale than any of the earlier novels—a broader scale, in fact, than Conrad was ever to attempt again—concerning itself not with the career of a single hero, but with the evolution of a whole society, and involving no less than four distinct characters, each of whom follows the course of a Conradian hero through compromise into paradox. At the same time, the novel abandons the hero type of Wait, Kurtz, Jim and Whalley, to present in Nostromo himself the first of a new type, Conrad's "political" hero, who typically aims not to create a world in conformity to an ideal, but to achieve his own comfort and security without committing himself actively to either side in the struggle which rages around him.

The framework of the universe presented in *Nostromo* is the familiar Conradian dualism, now rendered in an emphatically political mode. The earliest Malayan novels are worked out against the background of a broadly racial dualism in which political concerns are secondary. In both *Heart of Darkness* and *The Nigger of the "Narcissus,"* where the racial contrast still plays some part, the story turns towards an ethico-political dualism of licence versus control, anarchy against authority. This ideological conflict, held largely in abeyance through *Lord Jim* and *The End of the Tether,* reappears in *Nostromo.*

The history of Costaguana is a succession of revolutions, oscillating between the rule of a partly enlightened aristocracy and the tyranny of popular dictatorships. Into this situation come, initially, two men, Gould and Nostromo, Gould to take up his late father's mining concession, and Nostromo "to make his fortune." . . . The Gould Concession, granted to Charles Gould's father, reflects the political state of affairs, in a typically Conradian image, as at once a source of great wealth, being a rich silver mine, and a deadly burden, because of its exposure to the rapacity of Costaguana politicians. The father dies, having spent vain years attempting to make of the mine a working concern and having warned his son in the strongest terms against becoming involved in it. "He implored his son never to return to Costaguana, never to claim any part of his inheritance there, because it was tainted by the infamous Concession; never to touch it, never to approach it, to forget that America existed, and pursue a mercantile career in Europe." . . . The Concession, in short, presents a difficult and dangerous state of affairs which Charles Gould may either take up or leave alone.

Gould does not ignore his father's injunctions, but is, on the contrary, strongly influenced by the dead man and much affected by his fate. Yet he decides, none the less, upon disobedience. His father's death "filled his breast with a mournful and angry desire for action," for which action "the mine was obviously the only field." . . . Like the typical Conradian hero of the earlier novels, Gould is impelled by desire for action to make some mark upon the world. His action, moreover, is directed by a vague but strong idealism.

> Mines had acquired for him a dramatic interest. He studied their peculiarities from a personal point of view, too, as one would study the varied characters of men. . . . Abandoned workings had for him a strong fascination. Their desolation appealed to him like the sight of human misery, whose causes are varied and profound. They might have been misunderstood. . . .

The mine is inevitably the focus for Gould's action, and Gould is a man who (in Decoud's words) "cannot act without idealizing every simple feeling, desire, or achievement." . . . (pp. 108-12)

Gould sees the mine not simply as a material difficulty which might, if overcome, be turned to profit, but rather as a challenge to his sense of humanity. The Concession is to him a potential source of good, which has yielded so far only misery because of its entanglement with the corruption of politics in Costaguana. Gould's aim is to bring order out of this chaos by not only working the mine but also making it an instrument for the furtherance of civilization. The ravine beneath the mountain into which the mine is dug is called "the paradise of snakes." . . . Gould, with a glance at the story of Eden, later remarks that his operations there have "disturbed a great many" snakes and "brought mankind into it," . . . an observation revealing the extent of his idealization. He sees himself in the position of a creator bringing order and life into a world of chaos inhabited by forces of evil.

Gould's ideals are shared and reflected by Emilia, to whom, significantly, he proposes marriage at the very point when, having just learnt of his father's death, he decides to return to Costaguana. "His future wife was the first, and perhaps the only person to detect this secret mood which governed the profoundly sensible, almost voiceless attitude of this man towards the world of material things." . . . She shares with him his ambitions for the mine and is conspicuously at his side from the beginning of his work. In particular, she organizes the social functions of the Gould Concession, establishing medical and spiritual care for its employees and making herself the centre of society in the nearby town of Sulaco.

Emilia is the heroine of Gould's world, the female reflection of his ideals, who lives at the heart of his sphere of operations. The sphere is the mine and, more broadly, the political situation of Costaguana, from which the mine is inseparable. Like Wait before him and Verloc and Razumov after, Gould, in pursuit of his ideal, enters a world of dualistic political conflict, a world torn by the perennial strife between licence and authority. His compromise consists originally of a reluctant alliance with "material interests." In order to open up his mine Gould needs capital, for which he turns to Holroyd, an American millionaire who is prepared to back the operation as long as it proves itself profitable. Thus Gould, although personally interested in the mine as a sphere for the active realization of his ideal, is forced from the first to consider also its purely financial returns. "Charles Gould, on his part, had been obliged to keep the idea of wealth well to the fore; but he brought it forward as a means, not as an end. Unless the mine was good business it could not be touched. He had to insist on that aspect of the enterprise." . . . (pp. 112-13)

Holroyd, with whom Gould makes this compromising agreement, is an acute reflection of Don Carlos himself—an aloof, autocratic, wealthy man who idealizes the monetary power he commands. Holroyd's obsessive founding of Protestant churches in South America and his vacuous talk about the "destiny" of his nation function as a gentle parody on a somewhat larger scale of the Goulds' ideals, their missionary work among their employees and their visionary conception of the mine. The subtle bond of confidence between Gould and Holroyd, which has a vital function in the plot and which goes beyond the merely financial aspects of their bargain, underlines their alliance and personal similarity.

The immediate effect of Gould's compromising alliance with material interests is the discernible beginning of a rift, which subsequent moves will widen before the end of the story, between Charles and his heroine. After Holroyd's first visit to the Goulds in Sulaco, Emilia "wondered aloud why the talk of these wealthy and enterprising men discussing the prospects, the working, and the safety of the mine rendered her so impatient and uneasy, whereas she could talk of the mine by the hour with her husband with unwearied interest and satisfaction." . . . While never offering open opposition to her husband's course of action Emilia, unlike Gould, remains personally unaffected by the materialistic involvement of the mine and is even able at the end to repudiate this entirely when she allows the whereabouts of the lost silver to remain unknown. Speaking to her husband of their departed guests, she says, "But you have listened to their conversation? They don't seem to have understood anything they have seen here." To this Gould replies, with the practical outcome of the visit in mind, "They have seen the mine. They have understood that to some purpose." . . . At this point neither wife nor husband is aware of the incipient divergence of their attitudes, yet by the novel's end Gould's entanglement with material interests has left Emilia a virtual widow. (pp. 113-14)

The pattern of Gould's career . . . [follows] that of the early heroes Almayer and Willems, men whose purposive action places them in a world of dualistic conflict, in which every deliberate step they take towards their goal involves deeper compromise and further entanglement in the universal struggle. Like them, Gould identifies his ideal with a heroine, with whom, after an initial period of unison, he finds himself increasingly at odds; and like them he finds himself opposed in his efforts by a man from within the world he has selected for his sphere of operations, a rival whose enmity is provoked by the hero's very successes. We would therefore expect, all other things being equal, that towards the end of the story the growing tension would snap and Gould would be confronted, probably with fatal result, by the consequences of his compromises, as are Almayer and Willems and all the heroes of the intervening novels. Yet this does not happen in *Nostromo*. Not only does Gould survive the end of the story, but he defeats his rival, Montero, and succeeds in his separatist venture.

Gould's impunity does not mean that Conrad has changed his view of the human situation to allow his hero to evade the usual nemesis. Gould is still in action at the end of the story because *Nostromo* is uniquely structured among Conrad's works and because Gould is not the sole hero of the story. The end of the book centres not upon Gould but on Nostromo, who does complete the normal cycle from compromise to destruction, while Gould, after the decision to pursue separatism, is kept all but invisible in the background. *Nostromo*, furthermore, while taking its plot from a short slice of time, is full of both allusions to the past and hints of the future. It portrays, rather like the Wagnerian story, one turn of a cycle that might be indefinitely repeated. For this reason it is impossible to select a single event with which the story "begins"; the granting of the Concession, the decision of Charles Gould to disregard his father's warning, the alliance with Holroyd, the adoption or the failure of Ribierism could all be put forward for the position with more or less equal plausibility. In a similar way, although the story stops with the death of Nostromo, it does not really "end" there, as the main political sequence of events, in which Gould has become inextricably involved, is still very much in motion.

We are told, for instance, that after the political separation and the establishment of a government consistent with Gould's ideas there grows up a democratic opposition made up chiefly from Italians and natives, former employees of the railway and of the mine itself.... At the same time, some of Gould's political allies are saying that the logical and necessary conclusion of their work must be the annexation of the rest of Costaguana to the new state, and that the democratic party is lending its support to this view.... Clearly, as Monygham observes, "there is no peace and no rest in the development of material interests."... The silver of the mine is like Wagner's gold; it cannot allow the world in which it is at large to rest stable, but is always at work to keep the balance of forces swinging.

Gould will not, therefore, be allowed to enjoy for long the momentary success of his latest compromise. The new state is, by the time the story closes, already looking towards its next crisis, a choice between widespread internal discontent and a war of annexation, a selection of paths from which Gould will be unable to hold aloof. Gould's nemesis is not avoided, but merely suspended by the end of the novel.

In yet another sense, however, Gould pays the price of his concession to material interests even within the pages of the story, for towards the end he becomes plainly the prisoner of the mine rather than its master and has lost his relationship with Emilia. Emilia herself gives us the final picture of Gould.

> She had a clear vision of the gray hairs on his temples. He was perfect—perfect. What more could she have expected? It was a colossal and lasting success; and love was only a short moment of forgetfulness, a short intoxication, whose delight one remembered with a sense of sadness, as if it had been a deep grief lived through. There was something inherent in the necessities of successful action which carried with it the moral degradation of the idea.... He was perfect, perfect; but she would never have him to herself.... [S]he saw clearly the San Tomé mine possessing, consuming, burning up the life of the last of the Costaguana Goulds; mastering the spirit of the son as it had mastered the lamentable weakness of the father. A terrible success for the last of the Goulds....

Emilia sees, as in a way she has seen from the beginning, the fate towards which Gould is heading as a logical result of his decision to return to Costaguana and his willingness to compromise. (pp. 118-19)

There remains Nostromo himself, the first of a new line of heroes, which also includes Verloc and Razumov. The earlier heroes, including Gould and Decoud, are placed in situations of self-defeating endeavour. They are men of unusual abilities which are generally directed outwards in attempts to improve the world along the lines of the heroes' ideals. They fail because flaws in their own natures render the ideals impossible of achievement without vitiating compromise. The new line of heroes, which begins here with Nostromo, presents us with a man whose object is no longer to pursue any ideal beyond the bounds of self-interest, but rather to attain the largely negative goal of surviving in passive comfort without compromising involvement in the conflicts of the world around him. Such men are Verloc, playing off anarchists against reactionaries for his own profit; and Razumov, seeking only to pursue his studies and lead a quiet life without political entanglements.

Such, too, is Nostromo, the first of the line, who appears in the same story as Gould, the last and perhaps the most magnificent of Conrad's idealistic supermen. The combination shows us that *Nostromo* is not only the second chronological turning point in Conrad's literary career but also a brilliant piece of structural composition creating between two characters a contrapuntal relation which forms the chief axis of the novel. Decoud and Monygham, important as they are, figure only episodically in the story, which turns upon the antithesis of Nostromo and Gould, "the two racially and socially contrasted men, both captured by the silver of the San Tomé mine."... Gould is aristocratic, Anglo-Saxon, reserved and idealistic, while Nostromo is "a Man of the People,"... Italian, flamboyant and fundamentally self-centred. While Gould follows the established path of the early Conradian hero from idealism through compromise towards destruction, Nostromo, manifestly unidealistic and unconcerned with the state of the world at large, endeavours unsuccessfully to avoid precisely the kind of purposive action and moral commitment which is essential to Gould.

Nostromo, as he himself tells Decoud, has come to Costaguana "to make his fortune."... Here he finds himself in a land of violent political tensions between two extremes, with both of which he develops loose affiliations. On the one hand he is a man of plebeian origin with deep roots in the common people, among whom he has a high reputation and a large following. On the other hand his wish to make his fortune, combined with his initial political neutrality, leads him to place his abilities at the disposal of the Sulaco oligarchy, represented by Captain Mitchell and ultimately by Gould himself. At the beginning of the events of the novel, therefore, Nostromo stands between the opposing forces of popular discontent and authoritarian government and is, moreover, a vital factor in the precarious balance between them; it is through his agency that the European party controls an effective work-force in Sulaco and keeps a semblance of order among the factions of the populace. (pp. 131-32)

Nostromo keeps his options open by cultivating both the good opinion of his employers and popularity among the working classes. To commit himself to the democratic party or to adopt a normal plebeian level of existence would lose him the esteem of Mitchell and the Europeans, while to become an open supporter of the policies of Ribiera and Gould would deprive him of his popular support. Balanced between two worlds he occupies a unique position, on account of which he exercises considerable powers; his following among the people makes him an effective leader of the harbour work force, which in turn, as long as he steers clear of involvement in politics, makes him a valuable employee to Mitchell. Nostromo is thus the linch-pin upon which the cohesion of local economy depends, the channel of command between the European capitalists and the local workers. Yet he can function in this way only as long as he avoids open espousal of either popular or patrician values, and as long as he holds aloof from both wealth and domestic obscurity.

Nostromo at the beginning of the story is living on his reputation, his popularity with the people, which makes him an effective leader, and his good name with the Europeans as an efficient foreman. His reputation depends upon his avoidance of commitment, and he is therefore an essentially vague character, without defined motives or long-range plans. The thin sketching of his personality in the first half of the story, far from being a weakness of the novel, is integral to its purpose. Nostromo, at the beginning, is indeed little more than a name. "The only thing he seems to care for, as far as I have been able to discover," observes Decoud, "is to be well spoken of." . . . He is "a man for whom the value of life seems to consist in personal prestige." . . . The number and variety of his names is in keeping with the nebulosity of his character. He is known variously as Nostromo, the Capataz, Gian' Battista, Juan, Giovanni and, later, Captain Fidanza.

The crisis of Nostromo's career comes when he accepts the job of removing the consignment of silver from Sulaco by sea in order to keep the Monterists from capturing it and, if possible, to deliver it to pro-separatist forces outside. This undertaking is not of his choosing, but is pressed upon him. To the Europeans he appears the only man for the job, and his vanity, when the matter is so put to him, causes him to accept it, yet Teresa sees at once the implicit dangers of the venture.

> "They have turned your head with their praises," gasped the sick woman. "They have been paying you with words. Your folly shall betray you into poverty, misery, and starvation. The very leperos shall laugh at you—the great Capataz." . . .

After a little thought Nostromo begins to see that to take charge of the treasure is like "taking up a curse" upon himself . . . , and that, without seeing quite what he was doing, he has given up the neutrality and good name which was the basis of his eminent position.

The point, as he soon realizes, is that for as long as he has charge of the treasure he is a marked man, whom anyone would kill to take it from him. The silver therefore exiles him. Once he has put out to sea with it he cannot come back; to return without it would be to admit publicly to failure or worse, and to return with it would be courting death. (pp. 134-35)

His only course, having accepted charge of the treasure, is to deliver it as required to Barrios. Delivery of the treasure to Barrios, however, will virtually ensure the ultimate success of the separatists and, inevitably, make Nostromo one of the foremost heroes of their victory. From that point he will be largely identified with the governing party and will forfeit to that extent the following he has had among the people. Nostromo's acceptance of the job of delivering the silver occupies a point in his career exactly corresponding to the appearance of Haldin

in Razumov's rooms and to the order Verloc receives to blow up the Observatory. From this moment the hero finds himself in the position of having to either take sides or go to the wall. He has, against his will, accepted compromise and commitment.

There follow the unforeseen collision with Sotillo's troopship and the concealment of the silver on the Great Isabel. When Nostromo returns he learns from Monygham that, through Hirsch, Sulaco now believes the silver to have been lost in the Gulf and Decoud drowned. At this point, other things being equal, Nostromo might simply have confided the real whereabouts of the treasure to Gould and returned to his normal duties. What deflects him from this path is his meeting with Monygham who, unintentionally, upsets Nostromo greatly by showing him how little the supposed loss of the treasure really means to the European party, who were concerned chiefly to remove it from the rebels' clutches. Nostromo begins to take the view that his own interests, and quite possibly his life, have been put at risk very lightly by people who now show no concern for the outcome of his adventure.

> "Was it for an unconsidered and foolish whim that they came to me, then?" he interrupted suddenly. "Had I not done enough for them to be of some account, *por Dios*? Is it that the *hombres finos*—the gentlemen—need not think as long as there is a man of the people ready to risk his body and soul? Or, perhaps, we have no souls—like dogs?" . . .

In this frame of mind he returns to the home of the Violas to decide what he should do.

Teresa had died shortly after Nostromo's departure with the silver, killed by the sound of a shot fired by one of the rebels "as surely as if the bullet had struck her oppressed heart." . . . Nostromo feels particularly guilty on this score, because he had refused to fetch her a priest, as she had requested, in order to keep his appointment with the lighter of silver. By the time he gets back to shore, disgusted at the dangers to which he has been so lightly exposed by the Europeans, he is strongly inclined to accept both Giorgio's republicanism and Teresa's advice. "They keep us and encourage us as if we were dogs born to fight and hunt for them," he says of the rich. "The vecchio [Giorgio] is right. . . . Teresa was right too." . . . (pp. 135-37)

At the inn after his return Nostromo meets Giorgio, who advises him, for purely idealistic reasons, to do as Monygham has suggested and depart at once by train with a vital message for Barrios. Nostromo does so, having no time to pass on to anyone he trusts (he does not trust Monygham) the truth about Decoud and the silver. When he returns to the scene some time later, events have taken the decision out of his hands. With Decoud dead and four bars of silver gone with him to the bottom of the Gulf, Nostromo cannot tell the truth without incurring suspicion of theft and even murder. Yet Nostromo, like Gould, having compromised and taken risks, appears to have been successful. He has made his fortune.

His success, however, like Gould's, plunges him into a network of typical Conradian ironies. Although he now possesses a far greater personal fortune than he can ever have hoped for, he can reap only fractional benefit from it for fear of discovery. On him, as on Gould, material wealth has a deleterious psychological effect. A man accustomed to living openly and rejoicing in popular acclaim, Nostromo now becomes furtive and cut off from those around him.

> And to become the slave of a treasure with full self-knowledge is an occurrence rare and mentally disturbing. But it was also in great part because of the difficulty of converting it into a form in which it could become available. . . . The crew of his own schooner were to be feared as if they had been spies upon their dreaded captain. He did not dare stay too long in port. . . . To do things by stealth humiliated him. And he suffered most from the concentration of his thoughts upon the treasure.
>
> A transgression, a crime entering a man's existence, eats it up like a malignant growth, consumes it like a fever. Nostromo had lost his peace; the genuineness of all his qualities was destroyed. . . .

Once again Conrad uses dress to accentuate a change in the inner man. In his days of innocence Nostromo dressed naturally "in the checked shirt and red sash of a Mediterranean sailor," . . . but after he obtains the treasure we see "the vigour and symmetry of his powerful limbs lost in the vulgarity of a brown tweed suit." . . . The unsuitable clothing is the outward sign of the paradox of Nostromo's new situation as a rich man who must pretend relative poverty, a man of the people who must hide from public view, a sailor who dresses like a shopkeeper.

At a deeper level, however, Nostromo's situation remains much the same as it was. His object is still to "make his fortune," to use and enjoy the treasure which has now come into his possession. Against this object are the demands that he should enter into society, abandon his solitary, uncommitted way of life and undertake a proper measure of responsibility and public purpose. These demands, formerly voiced by Teresa Viola, are in the closing stages of the story represented by her elder daughter, Linda, the woman whom Nostromo is generally expected to marry. "Linda, with her mother's voice, had taken . . . her mother's place." . . . Nostromo has no particular desire to marry Linda, for he is attracted to her younger sister, Giselle, yet he cannot marry Giselle, because Giorgio would not permit the elder daughter to be so passed over, and neither can Nostromo carry her off, for fear of losing the silver.

The connection between the Viola girls and the treasure is established when a lighthouse is built on the Great Isabel where Nostromo has concealed the silver. He secures the appointment of Giorgio as keeper of the light, knowing that he himself will then be able to visit the island publicly as Linda's suitor. The silver thus prevents him from offending Giorgio by either repudiating Linda or running off with Giselle. To continue his visits to the treasure he is obliged to accept open betrothal to the elder daughter.

The two girls represent the paradoxical tension between Nostromo's goal, the satisfaction of his appetites, and the gravitational pull of social norms. The orthodox Linda, like Teresa, stands for public and approved domestic stability, whereas Giselle is licentious, passionate and thoroughly desirable in a definitely unconventional fashion.

> As time went on, Nostromo discovered his preference for the younger of the two. . . . His wife would have to know his secret or else life would be impossible. He was attracted by Gi-

selle, with her candid gaze and white throat, pliable, silent, fond of excitement under her quiet indolence; whereas Linda, with her intense, passionately pale face, energetic, all fire and words, touched with gloom and scorn, a chip of the old block, true daughter of the austere republican, but with Teresa's voice, inspired him with a deep-seated mistrust. . . .

The treasure itself dictates that Nostromo should prefer Giselle, for he could not reveal its secret to the "austere" Linda, who has inherited her parents' high and idealistic standards. Giselle, who embodies his desire for freedom and luxury, is quite compatible with his possession of the silver and is even entrusted with knowledge of its existence. The irony lies in the fact that, precisely because of the treasure, Nostromo cannot make his preference for Giselle publicly known.

We can recognize here a familiar Conradian theme and pattern. In the tension between Nostromo's desires and what is generally expected of him we see the old opposition of selfish freedom and social responsibility, of licence and control, previously explored in the stories of Wait and Kurtz. Each of the Viola sisters stands at one pole of this dichotomy, Giselle symbolizing the hero's personal will and desire, Linda his moral duties in the public domain. They therefore take on the roles of heroine and anti-heroine respectively in relation to Nostromo. Giselle is the heroine, the woman who stands at the centre of the world the hero desires to enter. Linda is the anti-heroine, the rival for the hero's affections who comes from the orthodox world he has deserted through his compromise. It is no accident that Linda becomes keeper of the lamp "that would kindle a far-reaching light upon the only secret spot of his life." . . . (pp. 137-39)

The ending of Nostromo's story is worked out in terms of the familiar pattern employed earlier for Willems and Kurtz. In pursuing his personal goals the hero turns his back on the world of moral orthodoxy and commits a crime. The new life he wishes to shape for himself is directed towards a heroine, a young and desirable woman, but the hero is still tied to the anti-heroine, who belongs essentially to the respectable, authoritarian world he has abandoned. His position is threatened by a rival, who advances a competing claim to the heroine's affections, and he is finally confronted with fatal consequences by a male figure, the nemesis of an offended orthodoxy, who exacts punishment for the original crime. (p. 139)

We have seen that Nostromo first appears as a hero of a different kind from Kurtz. Kurtz is one of the line of Conradian central figures, running from Wait to Whalley and Gould, who are embodiments of paradox, and whose careers are therefore models of self-defeating endeavour. Nostromo is the first of those whose object is not to achieve a positive ideal but to secure their own comfortable independence in worlds of conflicting extremes. His immediate successors are Verloc and Razumov, both of whom wish only to steer non-commital courses of safety between warring parties. The outstanding problem is why Conrad reverted, for his conclusion of *Nostromo,* to the structural pattern of the earlier stories, introducing several new characters in order to do so (for both Linda and Giselle, as well as Ramirez, are effectively new in the last two chapters of the book), returning to the highly-charged symbolic manner of the tales of Wait and Kurtz.

The result suggests a possible degree of uncertainty in handling the new heroic style or, more probably, a wish to keep the novel from growing disproportionately long. *Nostromo* is the only novel in which Conrad attempted to deal simultaneously with a plurality of heroes, and their careers within it are not entirely coterminous. As Gould's affairs are approaching what promises to be a cataclysmic resolution, Nostromo is still setting out on his attempt to balance a compromise between opposing forces. His act in appropriating the silver corresponds structurally to Verloc's attempt on the Observatory and to Razumov's betrayal of Haldin, both deeds which take place relatively early in their respective stories. Had Nostromo been accorded a development of plot proportionate to those of his successors, it seems fair to assume that his story would have been prolonged to something like twice its present length. It may be that, foreseeing this, Conrad opted for a quick ending, to achieve which he drew upon the fictional mechanisms he had already evolved for dealing more rapidly with the heroes of shorter stories. (pp. 140-41)

> *Stephen K. Land, in his* Paradox and Polarity in the Fiction of Joseph Conrad, *St. Martin's Press, 1984, 311 p.*

ADDITIONAL BIBLIOGRAPHY

Baines, Jocelyn. "Achievement without Success, I." In her *Joseph Conrad: A Critical Biography,* pp. 286-315. London: Weidenfeld and Nicolson, 1960.
  Speculates on autobiographical aspects of *Nostromo.* Baines asserts that "*Nostromo* is Conrad's most ambitious feat of imagination and is worthy of comparison with the most ambitious of all great novels."

Beker, Miroslav. "Virginia Woolf's Appraisal of Joseph Conrad." *Studia Romanica et Anglica Zagrabiensia,* No. 12 (December 1961): 17-22.
  Examines Virginia Woolf's review of *Nostromo* (see excerpt dated 1918).

Berthoud, Jacques. "*Nostromo.*" In his *Joseph Conrad: The Major Phase,* pp. 94-130. Cambridge: Cambridge University Press, 1978.
  Praises many aspects of *Nostromo.* Berthoud states that "with *Nostromo* and *The Secret Agent* we reach the summit of Conrad's achievement as a novelist."

Boyle, Ted E. "*Nostromo.*" In his *Symbol and Meaning in the Fiction of Joseph Conrad,* pp. 154-85. London: Mouton & Co., 1965.
  Analyzes symbolic roles which are enacted by the four primary characters in *Nostromo.* Boyle posits Charles Gould as "knight-savior," Nostromo as "boatswain," and Decoud and Monygham as "two aspects of nihilism."

Bradbrook, M. C. "The Hollow Men." In his *Joseph Conrad: Poland's English Genius,* pp. 41-8. Cambridge: Cambridge at the University Press, 1942.
  Discusses the thematic counterpoint of the separate plot lines in *Nostromo.*

Brewster, Dorothy, and Burell, Angus. "Conrad's *Nostromo:* Thirty Years After." In their *Modern Fiction,* pp. 65-83. New York: Columbia University Press, 1934.
  Analyzes Conrad's narrative technique and several important characters in *Nostromo.*

Coolidge, Olivia. "The Years of Aspiration." In her *The Three Lives of Joseph Conrad,* pp. 161-77. Boston: Houghton Mifflin Company, 1972.
  An account of the writing of *Nostromo.*

Cooper, Frederic Taber. "The Man's Novel and Some Recent Books." *The Bookman,* New York XX (November 1904): 216-21.

Contains a plot summary of *Nostromo* and a discussion of its complexity.

Curle, Richard. "*Nostromo—1904.*" In his *Joseph Conrad and His Characters: A Study of Six Novels,* pp. 67-107. New York: Russell & Russell, 1957.
  Traces the development and actions of several major characters in *Nostromo.*

Davidson, Arnold E. "Patterns in *Nostromo.*" In his *Conrad's Endings: A Study of the Five Major Novels,* pp. 31-53. Ann Arbor, Mich.: UMI Research Press, 1984.
  Examines the conclusion of *Nostromo.* Davidson writes that "even though various patterns become clear, the book does not really end. Dreams and revolutions will continue. In fact, the groundwork for yet another revolution is being laid in the last chapters of the novel, and this one is designed, appropriately, to undo precisely what the previous revolution accomplished."

Ford, Ford Madox. "Working with Conrad." In his *Return to Yesterday,* pp. 186-201. New York: Horace Liveright, 1932.
  An account of Ford's literary relationship with Conrad. Ford claims that he authored passages of Conrad's books, including twenty-five manuscript pages of *Nostromo* "at a time when Conrad was very ill and the next installment of the book, which was being serialized in *T. P.'s Weekly,* had to be supplied."

Galsworthy, John. "*Nostromo.*" In *A Conrad Memorial Library: The Collection of George T. Keating,* edited by George T. Keating, p. 138. Garden City, N.Y.: Doubleday, Doran & Company, 1929.
  A brief assessment of *Nostromo,* which Galsworthy describes as Conrad's "most considerable book," while stating that it "becomes melodrama towards the end."

Guerard, Albert, Jr. *Joseph Conrad.* New York: New Directions, 1947, 92 p.
  Makes several observations concerning *Nostromo* in the context of Conrad's work as a whole. Guerard's statements on *Nostromo* are frequently cited by later critics. Guerard later devoted a chapter of his seminal study *Conrad the Novelist* to *Nostromo* (see excerpt dated 1958).

Gurko, Leo. "Life and Death in Costaguana." In his *Giant in Exile,* pp. 119-43. New York: Macmillan Co., 1962.
  Discusses the disillusionment which the characters of *Nostromo* each experience.

Haugh, Robert F. "*Nostromo.*" In his *Joseph Conrad: Discovery in Design,* pp. 147-63. Norman: University of Oklahoma Press, 1957.
  Explication of *Nostromo* emphasizing the power of silver and the pattern of betrayal in the novel.

Hawthorn, Jeremy. "*Nostromo:* Materialism and Idealism." In his *Joseph Conrad: Language and Fictional Self-Consciousness,* pp. 56-71. Lincoln: University of Nebraska Press, 1979.
  Argues that Conrad was a materialist, a philosophical position which led him to a "pessimistic determinism" which he expressed in *Nostromo.*

Hay, Eloise Knapp. "*Nostromo.*" In her *The Political Novels of Joseph Conrad: A Critical Study,* pp. 161-216. Chicago: University of Chicago Press, 1963.
  Discusses Conrad's hostility toward both capitalism and the utopian ideologies which are placed in opposition to it.

Heimer, Jackson W. "Betrayal, Confession, Attempted Redemption, and Punishment in *Nostromo.*" *Texas Studies in Literature and Language* VIII, No. 4 (Winter 1966): 561-79.
  Examines betrayal in the lives of the four primary characters in *Nostromo.*

Hewitt, Douglas, "*Nostromo.*" In his *Conrad: A Reassessment,* pp. 46-69. Totowa, N.J.: Rowman and Littlefield, 1975.
  Analyzes the complexity and scope of *Nostromo.*

Hoffman, Frederick J. "Violence and Decorum." In his *The Mortal No: Death and the Modern Imagination,* pp. 23-93. Princeton: Princeton University Press, 1964.

Discusses the role of violence in *Nostromo*.

Inamdar, F. A. "*Nostromo*." In his *Image and Symbol in Joseph Conrad's Novels*, pp. 100-24. Atlantic Highlands, N.J.: Humanities Press, 1980.
Finds four groups of symbols in *Nostromo*: "(1) the San Tomé mine, silver, and the mountain ranges, (2) characters as symbols of savagery, (3) nature imagery, and (4) colour symbolism."

Jones, Michael P. "Conclusion: 'All the Past Was Gone'." In his *Conrad's Heroism: A Paradise Lost*, pp. 113-38. Ann Arbor, Mich.: UMI Research Press, 1985.
Analyzes the various critical viewpoints on *Nostromo*.

Karl, Frederick R. "The Significance of the Revisions in the Early Versions of *Nostromo*." *Modern Fiction Studies* V, No. 2 (Summer 1959): 129-44.
Discusses Conrad's revisions of *Nostromo* from magazine serialization to its ultimate publication in book form.

————. "*Nostromo*." In his *Joseph Conrad: The Three Lives*, pp. 529-68. New York: Farrar, Straus and Giroux, 1979.
An account of Conrad's life during the two years in which he wrote *Nostromo*.

Mégroz, R. L. "Plot and Imagination." In his *Joseph Conrad's Mind and Method: A Study of Personality in Art*, pp. 199-223. New York: Russell & Russell, 1964.
Examines the narrative complexity of *Nostromo*. Mégroz prefers straightforward chronological narration, and compares *Nostromo* to Marcel Proust's *A la recherche du temps perdu* and to James Joyce's *Ulysses*, both of which he considers marred by their non-chronological structure.

Moser, Thomas. "The Early Conrad's Anatomy of Moral Failure (1895-1912)." In his *Joseph Conrad: Achievement and Decline*, pp. 10-49. Cambridge: Harvard University Press, 1957.
Discusses fidelity, betrayal, and self-knowledge in Conrad's early fiction. Moser states: "If fidelity is the highest virtue of Conrad's moral code, its opposite—betrayal—is the central theme of the early period. . . . All the main characters of *Nostromo* betray their friends or their responsibility at some point."

Mueller, William R. "Man and Nature in Conrad's *Nostromo*." *Thought: A Review of Culture and Idea* XLV, No. 179 (December 1970): 559-76.
Examines the struggle of humanity against natural forces in *Nostromo*.

Newhouse, Neville H. "Man in Society." In his *Literature in Perspective: Joseph Conrad*, pp. 116-39. London: Evans Brothers, 1966.
Includes a general discussion of *Nostromo*, focusing on the multiple narrative viewpoints of the novel.

Payne, William Morton. Review of *Nostromo*, by Joseph Conrad. *The Dial* XXXVIII, No. 448 (16 February 1905): 126.
An early review praising *Nostromo* as a whole while faulting its structure.

Rapin, Rene. "Conrad's *Nostromo*." *The Explicator* XIII, No. 8 (June 1955): Item 50.
Refutes Winifred Lynskey's statement that "critics have failed to consider the role of the silver" in criticism on Nostromo (see excerpt dated 1954), citing Albert Guerard's 1946 study of Conrad (see Additional Bibliography).

Raskin, Jonah. "*Nostromo*: The Argument from Revision." *Essays in Criticism* XVIII, No. ii (n.d.): 183-92.
Argues that Conrad's revision of the serial version of *Nostromo* makes the book "more humane, more positive, more liberal in intention at any rate if not in total effect."

Rieselbach, Helen Funk. "*Nostromo*." In her *Conrad's Rebels: The Psychology of Revolution in the Novels from "Nostromo" to "Victory,"* pp. 9-35. Ann Arbor, Mich.: UMI Research Press, 1985.
Focuses on Conrad's characterization of the primary participants of the revolution of Costaguana in *Nostromo*.

Rosenfield, Claire. "*Nostromo*: Within a Paradise of Snakes." In her *Paradise of Snakes: An Archetypal Analysis of Conrad's Political Novels*, pp. 43-78. Chicago: University of Chicago Press, 1967.
Discusses the opposition of good and evil in *Nostromo* and links symbols used in the novel with the edenic myth.

Roussel, Royal. "*Nostromo*: The Ironic Vision." In his *The Metaphysics of Darkness: A Study in the Unity and Development of Conrad's Fiction*, pp. 109-51. Baltimore and London: Johns Hopkins Press, 1971.
Examines the symbolic force of darkness and ambiguity in *Nostromo*.

Said, Edward W. "Record and Reality." In *Approaches to the Twentieth-Century Novel*, edited by John Unterecker, pp. 108-52. New York: Thomas Y. Crowell Co., 1965.
General discussion of *Nostromo*, touching on its composition, symbolism, circuitous narration, and nihilistic perspective.

Saunders, William S. "The Unity of *Nostromo*." *Conradiana* V, No. 1 (1973): 27-36.
Argues that *Nostromo* lacks thematic unity but achieves another kind of unity through Conrad's detached attitude toward his themes.

Sherry, Norman. "'Gasbar Ruiz'," "The Garibaldino," "Nostromo and Decoud," "Sir John and 'Material Interests'," "Dr. Monygham and Don Jose Avellanos," and "Costaguana and Sulaco." In his *Conrad's Western World*, pp. 137-201. Cambridge: Cambridge at the University Press, 1971.
Discussion of possible sources for the characters and background of *Nostromo*.

Smith, David R. "Nostromo and the Three Sisters." *Studies in English Literature* II (1962): 497-508.
Centers on a group of three islands in *Nostromo* called "The Isabels," viewing them as symbolic of an archetypal group of three sisters who appear throughout folklore, mythology, and literature.

Tomlinson, T. B. "Conrad's Trust in Life: *Nostromo*." *The Critical Review*, No. 14 (1971): 62-81.
Asserts that Conrad affirms life rather than Decoud's pessimism in *Nostromo*.

Verleun, J[an] A. *The Stone Horse: A Study of the Function of the Minor Characters in Joseph Conrad's "Nostromo."* Groningen, The Netherlands: Bouma's Boekhuis B. V., 1978, 318 p.
Organized into separate chapters on the minor characters in *Nostromo*.

Verleun, Jan [A.], and de Vries, Jetty. "Conrad Criticism Today: An Evaluation of Recent Conrad Scholarship." *English Literature in Transition 1880-1920* 29, No. 3 (1986): 241-75.
Examines early 1980s criticism of Conrad's work.

Vidan, Ivo. "Perspective of *Nostromo*." *Studia Romanica et Anglica Zagrabiensia*, No. 13-14 (July-December 1962): 43-54.
Analyzes the complex philosophical perspective of *Nostromo*.

Warner, Oliver. "Greater Novels." In his *Joseph Conrad*, pp. 93-132. London: Longmans, Green and Co., 1951.
Examines the influence of silver on the lives of several characters in *Nostromo*.

Whitehead, Lee M. "*Nostromo*: The Tragic 'Idea'." *Nineteenth-Century Fiction* 23, No. 4 (March 1969): 463-75.
Discusses the view presented in *Nostromo* of the role of the individual in society.

Zabel, M. D. "Chance and Recognition." In *The Art of Joseph Conrad: A Critical Symposium*, edited by R. W. Stallman, pp. 19-35. East Lansing, Mich.: Michigan State University Press, 1960.
Examines several aspects of Conrad's work.

François Coppée

1842-1908

French poet, dramatist, novelist, and short story writer.

Coppée was one of the most popular and respected literary figures in late nineteenth-century France. Although he began his career under the tutelage of the Parnassian poets, whose central tenet was the absolute rejection of all forms of literary Romanticism, he later developed distinctly Romantic tendencies in his own works and focused in particular on the courageous endurance of the poor. Coppée's popularity was the direct result of this sympathetic treatment of the economically dispossessed, and while his diverse writings were critically acclaimed for their stylistic sophistication, he was known to the vast majority of his readers simply as ''the poet of the humble.''

Born in Paris, Coppée was the son of a civil servant whose meager income afforded the family only a marginal existence. The adversity of the poet's youth was further exacerbated by his poor health, and his education was frequently interrupted by severe illness. Coppée nevertheless completed his primary education and attended the Lycée St. Louis, where he developed a keen interest in poetry. After his father's death in 1862, Coppée was forced to accept a clerical position in the Ministry of War in order to provide for his mother and sister, but he continued to write poetry and to hope for a literary career.

In 1863, Coppée became acquainted with Catulle Mendès, a successful and flamboyant poet to whom he confided his literary aspirations. Although Mendès disliked the poems Coppée initially showed him, he offered the younger man some direction, believing him capable of much better work. In addition, Mendès introduced Coppée into the Parnassian circle, which included such prominent figures as Stéphane Mallarmé and Leconte de Lisle, the acknowledged leader of the group. Coppée's natural talent soon earned the respect of the Parnassians, and the 1867 publication of his first volume of poetry, *Le réliquaire,* brought the approval of the larger critical community. Popular success came two years later, when his verse comedy *Le passant* was performed at the *Théâtre Odéon* with Sarah Bernhardt in the starring role.

The majority of Coppée's subsequent works were equally well received, and in 1884 he was accorded the highest honor available to a French author: membership in the prestigious Académie Française. Having secured his reputation as a poet and critic, Coppée went on to publish novels and short stories, beginning in 1889 with the novel *Henriette.* Near the end of his life, Coppée underwent a religious conversion, and the works he published between 1897 and his death in 1908 reflect their author's strong Catholic faith.

Although Coppée created works in a wide variety of genres, he is best known for his popular poetry, his verse dramas, and his *contes en vers,* or verse tales. His early poems, collected in the volumes *Le réliquaire* and *Les intimités,* exemplify Parnassian ideals of rigid formalism, semantic precision, and objective response. Later, when Coppée had abandoned objective response in favor of a more emphatic approach to his subject matter, he nevertheless adhered to the primary stylistic tenets of the Parnassians. As a result, both his poetry and his prose

have been applauded for their simplicity and clarity, while his images are described as precise and powerfully realistic. Coppée's sentimental characterizations of the oppressed poor and his realistic depictions of Parisian life, most notably those of the verse collection *Les humbles,* have also been widely praised.

Coppée's literary reputation, however, does not extend beyond the borders of France. In part because of their reliance upon the subtleties of the French language for their style, few of his works have been translated into English, and many of the extant translations are considered markedly inferior to the originals. Within his own country, however, Coppée is praised for his skillful concretization of Parnassian literary theories as well as for his championing of the poor, and he is considered by many to be a major figure in the development of French poetry.

PRINCIPAL WORKS

Le réliquaire (poetry) 1867
Les intimités (poetry) 1868
La grève des forgerons (poetry) 1869
Le passant (drama) 1869
  [*The Passer-by,* 1885; also translated as *The Wanderer,* 1890]
Poèmes modernes (poetry) 1869

Deux douleurs (drama) 1870
Les humbles (poetry) 1872
Le cahier rouge (poetry) 1874
Une idylle pendant le siége (poetry) 1874
Olivier (poetry) 1875
Promenades et intérieurs (poetry) 1875
L'exilée (poetry) 1876
    [*L'exilée,* 1879]
Le luthier de Crémone (drama) 1876
    [*The Violin Maker of Cremona,* 1892]
Severo Torelli (drama) 1883
Vingt contes nouveaux (short stories) 1883
Les Jacobites (drama) 1885
Contes en vers et poésies diverses (poetry) 1886
Arrière-saison (poetry) 1887
Oeuvres completes de François Coppée. 10 vol. (poetry,
    dramas, short stories, and novels) 1888-92
Henriette (novel) 1889
    [*Henriette; or, A Corsican Mother,* 1889]
Ten Tales by François Coppée (short stories) 1890
Toute une jeunesse (novel) 1890
    [*The Days of My Youth,* 1890; also translated as
        Disillusion; or, The Story of Amedée's Youth, 1890;
        also *A Romance of Youth,* 1905]
Les paroles sinceres (poetry) 1891
Les vrais riches (short stories) 1892
    [*True Riches,* 1893; also translated as *Blessed Are the
        Poor,* 1894]
Rivales (drama) 1893
    [*The Rivals,* 1893]
Le trésor (drama) 1893
    [*The Treasure,* 1895]
Mon franc parler (journalism) 1894
Pour la couronne (drama) 1895
    [*For the Crown,* 1896]
Le pater (drama) 1896
    *[*Pater Noster,* 1915]
Le coupable (novel) 1897
    [*The Guilty Man,* 1911]
La bonne souffrance (essays) 1898
    [*Happy Suffering,* 1900]
Tales for Christmas, and Other Seasons (short stories)
    1900
Dans la prière et dans la lutte (poetry) 1901
Des vers français (poetry) 1906
Oeuvres de François Coppée. 6 vols. (poetry, dramas,
    short stories, novels) 1907

*This drama was also performed in the United States as *The Prayer.*

_____

BRANDER MATTHEWS (essay date 1890)

[*An American critic, playwright, and novelist, Matthews wrote
extensively on world drama and served for a quarter century at
Columbia University as professor of dramatic literature, the first
to hold that title at an American university. Matthews was also
a founding member and president of the National Institute of Arts
and Letters. Because his criticism is deemed both witty and informative, Matthews has been called "perhaps the last of the
gentlemanly school of critics and essayists" in America. In the
following excerpt, he assesses the quality of Coppée's works.*]

Like Molière, like Boileau, like Regnard, like Voltaire, and
like Musset, M. François Coppée was born in Paris, and more
than any other of the half-dozen is he a true child of the fair
city by the Seine, loving her more ardently, and leaving her
less willingly. The facts of his simple and uneventful career
have been set forth by his friend M. de Lescure in "François
Coppée: l'Homme, la Vie et l'Œuvre (1842-1889)." From this
we learn that the poet was born in 1842, that he was the
youngest child of a poor clerk in the War Department, that he
had three elder sisters, one of whom survives still to take care
of her brother, that he spent most of his struggling childhood
in old houses on the left (and more literary) bank of the Seine,
that he was not an apt scholar in his youth, that he began to
write verses very early in his teens, and that at last his father
died, and he succeeded to the modest position in the War
Department, becoming the head of the family at twenty-one.
In time he made acquaintance with other young poets, and was
admitted into the "Parnassians," as they were called—followers of Victor Hugo, of Théophile Gautier, of Théodore de
Banville, students of new and old rhythms, and seekers after
rich rhymes, as ardent in the search as the Argonauts of 'Forty-
nine. M. Coppée burned every one of his juvenile poems, and
wrote many another of more cunning workmanship; and of
these newer poems two volumes were published in the next
few years—*Le Réliquaire* and *Les Intimités*—but they did not
sell two hundred copies all told.

Then, in 1869, came the first golden gleam of fortune. *Le
Passant,* a little one-act comedy in verse, was acted one night
at the Odéon, and the next day the name of François Coppée
was no longer unknown to any of those who care for letters.
Le Passant is undeniably artificial, and at bottom it is probably
forced in feeling, if not false; but beyond all question the poet
believed in it and accepted its truth, and delighted in his work.
The sentiment is charmingly youthful, with a springlike freshness, and the versification is absolutely impeccable. For years
M. Coppée was called "the author of *Le Passant,*" until he
came almost to hate his first-born. But only one of his later
plays has rivalled it in popular acceptance; this is the pathetic
Luthier de Crémone, of which there are several adaptations in
English. A third one-act play, *Le Pater,* forbidden in Paris by
the stage censors, was, strangely enough, brought out here in
New York at Daly's Theatre shortly after as the *Prayer.* As a
dramatist, M. Coppée continues the romanticist tradition, now
a little outworn; and his longer plays lack the directness of his
later poems and prose tales. No one of them has had more than
a merely honorable success, and no one of them—with a single
exception only—has shown itself strong enough to stand the
perils of translation.

During the dark days of 1870 and 1871 M. Coppée did his
duty in the ranks, like many another artist in letters and with
the brush. Of course, he wrote war poems, both during the
fighting and after, neither better nor worse, most of them, than
the war poems of other French poets. Better than any of these
martial rhymes are the *Grève des Forgerons,* written just before
the war, and *Les Humbles,* a volume of verse written shortly
after peace had been restored. The *Grève des Forgerons* is a
dramatic monologue, in which a striking iron-worker explains
how it came to pass that he killed a man, and why he did the
deed. It suggests Browning in its mingling of movement and
introspection, but it is neither as rugged in form nor as swift
in action as the British poet would have made it.

It is in *Les Humbles* that there was first revealed the French
poet with whom we of Anglo-Saxon stock can perhaps feel

ourselves most in sympathy. The note which dominates the poems in that collection, and in most of M. Coppée's later volumes of verse, is less seldom found in English literature than in French. This is the note of sympathy with the lowly, with the unsuspected victims of fate. It is the note of compassion for those who struggle secretly and in vain, for those who are borne down beneath the burdens of commonplace existence, for those who have never had a chance in life. It is the note we mark now and again, for instance, in the deeper poems of Mr. Austin Dobson. Many of the foremost French authors of late years are mere mandarins, writing exclusively for their peers; they are Brahmins, despising all outside their own high caste; they are wholly without bowels of compassion for their fellowman. Compare, for example, again, the contemptuous and contemning attitude of Flaubert towards the creatures of his own making, whom he regards distantly, as though they were doubtful insects under a microscope, and the warmer tolerance George Eliot shows even for her least worthy characters.

M. Coppée is as detached from his humble heroes and heroines as any one could wish; he is too profoundly an artist ever to intervene in his own person; but he is not chill and inaccessible in his telling of their little lives, made up of a thousand banalities and lit by a single gleam of poetry, not cast by the glare of a great self-sacrifice, but falling from the pure flame of daily duties performed without thought of self. *Les Humbles* is but a gallery of pictures in the manner of the little masters of Holland—a series of portraits of the down-trodden in their every-day garb, with that suggestion of their inner life which illuminates every painting by an artist of true insight. In the old-fashioned sense of the word there is little ''heroic'' in *Les Humbles*; and there is absolutely nothing of the exaggerated larger-than-life-and-twice-as-natural manner of Victor Hugo, set off with violent contrasts and startling antitheses. Instead we have an accomplished poet telling us of the simple lives of the poor in the simple speech of the people. M. Coppée has a homeliness of phrase not unlike that of Theocritus, but perhaps less consciously literary.

Indeed, nothing more clearly shows the delicacy of his art than his extraordinary skill in concealing all trace of artifice, so that a most carefully constructed poem is seemingly spontaneous. To most of us French poetry is rarely interesting; it is obviously artificial; it strikes us as somewhat remote; possibly from the enforced use of words of Romance origin (which therefore seem to us secondary) to describe heartfelt emotion, expressed by us in words of Teutonic stock (which are therefore to us primary): Lowell has told us that it is only the high polish of French verse that keeps out decay. We do not feel this is reading the best of M. Coppée's poetry; it seems to us as natural an outgrowth almost as Heine's or Longfellow's. In another essay Lowell says that perhaps the great charm of Gray's ''Elegy'' is to be found ''in its embodying that pensively stingless pessimism which comes with the first gray hair, that vague sympathy with ourselves which is so much cheaper than sympathy with others, that placid melancholy which satisfies the general appetite for an emotion that titillates rather than wounds.'' That M. Coppée has put into French verse, unmusical as it is, the qualities which Lowell finds in Gray's ''Elegy'' is evidence that neither in manner nor in matter is he like most French poets.

But this acceptability of his poetry to ears attuned to more Teutonic rhythms has not been won by any accidental dereliction from the strictest rule of the Parnassians. M. Coppée

has besieged and captured the final fastnesses of French metrical art, and his work is completely satisfactory even to Banville, who bestrides his hobby of ''rich'' rymes as though it were Pegasus itself. M. Coppée early gave proof of remarkable skill at the difficult game of French versification, and he still plays it scientifically, and with great good luck. Of late years he has been called upon frequently to sing to order, to write verses for a celebration, and he has always been as ready as Dr. Holmes was once to lay a garland of rymes on the grave of a hero. The art of writing occasional verse which shall be worthy of the occasion is not a common gift. M. Coppée possesses it abundantly, and his many poems for feasts or fasts are always appropriate, adequate, and dignified.

Olivier is M. Coppée's most ambitious longer poem. But it is not in his longer poems that he is seen at his best. What he does to perfection is the *conte en vers*—the tale in verse. The *conte* is a form of fiction in which the French have always delighted, and in which they have always excelled, from the days of the *jongleurs* and the *trouvères*, past the periods of La Fontaine and Voltaire, down to the present. The *conte* is a tale something more than a sketch, it may be, and something less than a short story. In verse it is at times but a mere rymed anecdote, or it may attain almost to the direct swiftness of a ballad. The *Canterbury Tales* are *contes* most of them, if not all, and so are some of the *Tales of a Way-side Inn*. The freeand easy tales of Prior were written in imitation of the French *conte en vers;* and that likewise was the model of more than one of the lively narrative poems of Mr. Austin Dobson.

No one has succeeded more admirably in the *conte en vers* than M. Coppée. Where was there ever anything better of its kind than ''**L'Enfant de la Balle**''?—that gentle portrait of the infant phenomenon, framed in a chain of occasional gibes at the sordid ways of theatrical managers, and at their hostility toward poetic plays. Where is there anything of a more simple pathos than ''**L'Épave**''?—that story of a sailor's son whom the widowed mother vainly strives to keep from the cruel waves that killed his father. (It is worthy of a parenthesis that although the ship M. Coppée loves best is that which sails the blue shield of the city of Paris, he knows the sea also, and he depicts sailors with affectionate fidelity.) But whether at the sea-side by chance, or more often in the streets of the city, the poet seeks for the subject of his story some incident of daily occurrence made significant by his interpretation; he chooses some character commonplace enough, but made firmer by conflict with evil and by victory over self. Those whom he puts into his poems are still the humble, the forgotten, the neglected, the unknown, and it is the feelings and the struggles of these that he tells us, with no maudlin sentimentality, and with no dead-set at our sensibilities. The sub-title Mrs. Stowe gave to *Uncle Tom's Cabin* would serve to cover most of M. Coppée's *contes* either in prose or verse; they are nearly all pictures of ''life among the lowly.'' But there is no forcing of the note in his painting of poverty and labor; there is no harsh juxtaposition of the blacks and the whites. The tone is always manly and wholesome.

''**La Marchande de Journaux**'' and the other little masterpieces of story-telling in verse are unfortunately untranslatable, as are all poems but a lyric or two now and then by a happy accident. A translated poem is a boiled strawberry, as some one once brutally put it. But the tales which M. Coppée has written in prose—a true poet's prose, nervous, vigorous, flexible, and firm—these can be Englished by taking thought and time and pains, without which a translation is always a betrayal. Ten of these tales have been rendered into English by Mr. Learned, and the ten chosen for translation are among the best of the twoscore and more of M. Coppée's *contes en prose*. These ten tales are fairly representative of his range and variety. Compare, for example, the passion in the "**Foster-sister**"—pure, burning, and fatal—with the Black Forest *naïveté* of the "**Wooden Shoes of Little Wolff.**" Contrast the touching pathos of the "**Substitute,**" poignant in his magnificent self-sacrifice, by which the man who has conquered his shameful past goes back willingly to the horrible life he has fled from, that he may save from a like degradation and from an inevitable moral decay the one friend he has in the world, all unworthy as this friend is—contrast this with the story of the gigantic deeds "**My Friend Meutrier**" boasts about unceasingly, not knowing that he has been discovered in his little round of daily domestic duties—making the coffee of his good old mother, and taking her poodle out for a walk.

Among these ten there are tales of all sorts, from the tragic adventure of "**An Accident**" to the pendant portraits of the "**Two Clowns,**" cutting in its sarcasm, but not bitter; from the "**Captain's Vices,**" which suggests at once George Eliot's *Silas Marner* and Mr. Austin Dobson's *Tale of Polypheme,* to the sombre reverie of the poet "**At the Table,**" a sudden and searching light cast on the labor and misery which underlie the luxury of our complex modern existence. Like "**At the Table,**" the "**Dramatic Funeral**" is a picture more than it is a story; it is a marvellous reproduction of the factitious emotion of the good-natured stage-folk, who are prone to overact even their own griefs and joys. The "**Dramatic Funeral**" seems to me always as though it might be a painting of M. Jean Béraud, that most Parisian of artists, just as certain stories of Maupassant's inevitably suggest the bold freedom of M. Forain's sketches in black and white.

An ardent admirer of the author of the stories in the *Odd Number* has protested to me that M. Coppée is not an etcher like Maupassant, but rather a painter in water-colors. And why not? Thus might we call M. Alphonse Daudet an artist in pastels, so adroitly does he suggest the very bloom of color. No doubt M. Coppée's *contes* have not the sharpness of Maupassant's nor the brilliancy of M. Daudet's. But what of it? They have qualities of their own. They have sympathy, poetry, and a power of suggesting pictures not exceeded, I think, by those of either Maupassant or M. Daudet. M. Coppée's street views in Paris, his interiors, his impressionist sketches of life under the shadow of Notre Dame, are convincingly successful. They are intensely to be enjoyed by those of us who take the same keen delight in the varied phases of life in New York. They are not, to my mind, really rivalled either by those of Maupassant, who was a Norman by birth and a nomad by choice, or by those of M. Daudet, who is a native of Provence, although now for thirty years a resident of Paris. M. Coppée is a Parisian from his youth up, and even in prose he is a poet. Perhaps this is why his pictures of Paris are unsurpassable in their felicity and in their verity.

It may be fancy, but I seem to see also a finer morality in M. Coppée's work than in Maupassant's, or in M. Daudet's, or in that of almost any other of the Parisian story-tellers of to-day. In his tales we breathe a purer moral atmosphere, more wholesome and more bracing. It is not that M. Coppée probably thinks of ethics rather than esthetics; in this respect his attitude is undoubtedly that of the others. There is no sermon in his song, or at least none for those who will not seek it for themselves; there is never a hint of a preachment. But for all that,

I have found in his work a trace of the tonic morality which inheres in Molière, for example—also a Parisian by birth—and in Rabelais, too, despite his disguising grossness. This finer morality comes possibly from a wider and a deeper survey of the universe; and it is as different as possible from the morality which is externally applied, and which always punishes the villain in the fifth act.

It is of good augury for our own letters that the best French fiction of to-day is getting itself translated in the United States, and that the liking for it is growing apace. Fiction is more consciously an art in France than anywhere else, perhaps partly because the French are now foremost in nearly all forms of artistic endeavor. In the short story especially, in the tale, in the *conte,* their supremacy is incontestable, and their skill is shown and their esthetic instinct exemplified partly in the sense of form, in the constructive method which underlies the best short stories, however trifling these may appear to be, and partly in the rigorous suppression of non-essentials, due in a measure, it may be, to the example of Mérimée. That is an example we in America may study to advantage, and from the men who are writing fiction in France we may gain much. (pp. 182-95)

Brander Matthews, "Aspects of Fiction: The Prose Tales of M. François Coppée," in his Aspects of Fiction and Other Ventures in Criticism, 1896. Reprint by Literature House/Gregg Press, 1970, pp. 182-95.

ANATOLE FRANCE (essay date 1890)

[*France was a French novelist and critic of the late nineteenth and early twentieth centuries. According to contemporary literary historians, France's best work is characterized by clarity, control, perceptive judgment of world affairs, and the Enlightenment traits of tolerance and justice. In the following excerpt, France praises Coppée's prose works.*]

François Coppée is a born poet; verse is his mother-tongue. He speaks it with charming facility. But—and all poets are not thus endowed—he also writes, when he wishes, an easy, laughing, limpid prose. I would willingly believe that it was journalism that trained him as a writer of prose. He was for a time a collaborator of mine, and his happy period with *La Patrie* is not forgotten, when he replaced M. Édouard Fournier as dramatic critic. Journalism is not such a bad school of style as people make out. I have no knowledge of any fine talent being spoilt therein, and, on the contrary, I have seen some minds gain a suppleness and vivacity which was lacking in their earlier work. One learns to avoid the obscure, strained style into which the most artistic writers so often relapse when they write far removed from the public. Journalism, in fact, is like those baths in running water, from which we emerge all the more alert and agile.

However it may be with the singer of *Les Humbles,* and however he may have developed his talent for prose, one must, whilst recognizing that his primary place is in poetry, give him also a niche in the charmed circle of our story-tellers, between M. Catulle Mendès and M. André Theuriet, who, like himself, are both poets and story-tellers.

His recent novel, *Henriette,* is not yet forgotten; it is worked out with graceful simplicity, and he touches us by showing the work-girl's bunch of violets laid on the grave of the son of the family.

He now gives us a more extensive work; *Toute une jeunesse;* a kind of analytical novel, in which the author has been pleased to express only the purest and simplest sentiments. The title would incline one to think that it was an autobiography and a confession; and when it appeared in an illustrated magazine the illustrations were not calculated to turn us away from this idea, for the illustrator had given the hero of the book a likeness to M. Coppée himself. As a matter of fact, the author of *Intimités* has in no wise told his own story in this book. This youth is not his youth. It is sufficient to glance at M. François Coppée's biography to be sure of it.... [The] adventures—very simple, by the way—of young Amédée Violette, the hero of *Toute une jeunesse*, have no connection with M. François Coppée's real existence. Amédée Violette, the son of an inferior employé in a ministry, loses his mother while still quite a child. It is known that Mme Coppée saw the first glimmer of her son's celebrity. Friends of the good old days will remember, in that modest house in the Rue Rousselet, the joy beaming from the suffering face of that sympathetic woman, on the morrow of *Le passant*. They remember, not without emotion, the poet's mother, of the same delicate build as her son, pale and slender, sitting bowed beside the fire, held fast to her arm-chair by the nervous malady which made her daily look smaller, without effacing the smile of her eyes and the adorable grace of her devastated face. With her tongue half paralysed by this mysterious illness, she seemed to murmur, "I can die." She died, leaving in her place a second self.... This is enough to show that M. François Coppée has not lent his own recollections to his hero, and that we are dealing with pure fiction, when the modest and unhappy love affairs of Amédée Violette are unfolded.

Without telling her so, the young man loves Maria, the daughter of an engraver, half artist and half workman, a pretty and intelligent girl, who, having become an orphan, copies pastels in the Louvre for a livelihood, and has allowed herself to be seduced in a casual sort of way by the handsome Maurice, whose natural function is to be beloved of all women. On Amédée's urgent representations the handsome Maurice marries her, after which he fulfils his function by betraying her with women of the streets. He would have continued to do so, had he not assumed the cap of the mobiles in 1870, placed in his heart "like a flower in his rifle-barrel, the resolution to die bravely," and done his duty at Champigny, where he fell gloriously on the field of honour. It is only the bad eggs who have luck right up to the end.

Maurice dies in Amédée's arms, bequeathing to him Maria and the son he has given her. Amédée marries Maria, but she does not love him. She still loves Maurice, and the recollection of the dead man fills her peaceful heart.

Amédée asks nothing more of love; expects no more of life. One autumn evening, overwhelmed by monotonous boredom, he lets his silvered temples fall between his hands, and meditates: happiness is a dream, youth but a spark. The art of living is to forget life. The leaves fall! the leaves fall!

But imaginary as he is, and involved in imaginary adventures, Amédée Violette feels life as M. François Coppée felt it, when a child and a young man. The author does not conceal the fact, and the hero, according to his own statement, resembled him as the pensive child of Blunderstone, David Copperfield, resembles Dickens. So that, while fiction if taken literally, *Toute une jeunesse* is true in spirit, and it is not indiscreet to recognize in this young man, "brown, with blue eyes, and an ardent and melancholy expression," the happy but soon saddened author

of *Le reliquaire* and *Le passant*. And how avoid applying to the author himself what he says about Amédée, who, having learnt literature among the romantics, and having for some time followed the beaten track, suddenly finds an unexplored path, his own medium of expression?

> He had, some time before, thrown into the fire his first verses, clumsy imitations of favourite masters, and his 1830 drama, in which two lovers sang a passionate duet under the gallows. He found his way back to truth and simplicity by the scholars' way, the longest. Inclination and necessity simultaneously compelled him to express plainly and sincerely what he saw before his eyes, to display what he could of the humble ideals found among the ordinary people amid whom he had lived, against the melancholy landscapes of the Parisian suburbs where his youth had been spent; in short, to paint after nature.

M. François Coppée has not distorted his literary beginnings so far as to prevent our seeing certain likenesses therein. His first encounters with the Parnassians are described, and in Paul Sillery it is easy to recognize one whom he describes as an exquisite poet and an excellent comrade. I know M. Catulle Mendès to be of all men the most attached to letters in the whole of Paris, the greatest stranger to envy, as also to mean ambitions. Still, one must not judge the long-haired poets of 1868 by comparison with the rather black, satirical, and much too vague portraits which are to be found in *Toute une jeunesse*. If one were tempted to do so, M. Coppée would be the first to say:

> Take care! I have not put everything into this story, in which I sought only to explain a soul. Not in a psychological novel, but in my unrestrained everyday conversation, in my many newspaper articles, in the notices which I wrote for Lemerre's anthology, will it be seen whether I have not always paid tribute to my old companions in arms, Léon Dierx, Louis de Ricard, José-Maria de Heredia, and to their frankness and loyalty. No, they were certainly never envious. I shall never cut myself off from the poets amid whom I grew up, and it shall not be said that I denied either Stéphane Mallarmé or Paul Verlaine.

That is what M. François Coppée would reply to anyone who made the mistake of believing that he had forgotten the charming hours on Parnassus and the subtle conversations of his coterie.

Once more M. François Coppée gives us a "true" book, in which his "feeling" for life is vividly presented. He feels things as a poet and a Parisian. The whole of the first part of his *David Copperfield* expresses so deep and delicate an appreciation of our old faubourgs that however little of a Parisian one may be one is conscious of a kind of mystical tenderness, and one hears the very stones speaking. I am a Parisian, heart and soul, and I tell you truly that I cannot without deep emotion read these simple, unaffected sentences, in which the poet recalls the urban landscapes of his and our childhood: the following, for example:

> To the right and the left he saw the Rue Notre-Dame-des-Champs unfolding itself in a gra-

cious curve; one of the most peaceful streets of the Luxembourg quarter, a street then hardly half built; where the boughs of the trees overhung the wooden fences of the gardens; so quiet and full of silence that the solitary passer-by could hear the cage-birds singing.

It is with an indescribable pleasure that I follow the walks of the father and child, who wandered "on fine evenings amid the solitudes."

> They followed the beautiful outer boulevards of other days, where there were elms dating from Louis XIV, ditches full of weeds, and ruined palisades which permitted a view, through their breaches, of market-gardens, where the melon bell-glasses shone in the rays of the setting sun.... In this way they went far, far beyond the Barrière d'Enfer.... In these suburban deserts there were no more houses, but occasional tumble-down ruins, all, or nearly all, one story high. Sometimes a sinister-looking cabaret, painted the colour of wine-lees, or perhaps, at the junction of two deeply-rutted roads, under some acacias, a café garden with its arbours and its sign, a little wind-mill at the end of a pole, turning in the cool evening breeze. It was almost country. The grass, now less dusty, invaded the side-walks, and even crossed the road between the broken paving-stones. On the top of the low walls a poppy flourished here and there. There were few or no people passing, except some very poor folk; a good woman in a peasant's bonnet, dragging a weeping child, a workman with his tools, a belated pensioner, and sometimes, in the middle of the road, a flock of exhausted sheep, bleating desperately, bitten in the legs by the dogs, on their way to the slaughter-house. The father and son walked straight on until it grew quite dark under the trees. They then returned, their faces whipped by the keener air, while in the distant avenue, at great intervals, the old street lamps on brackets, the lanterns of the Terror, shone like yellow stars in the green twilight sky.

Dear Coppée! Every one of these words, whose meaning, or rather whose mysterious meaning I understand so well, gives me a thrill, and by this enchantment I am carried away to the delightful depths of my earliest recollections. Would I might tarry there! What greater praise can I give your book than to tell of the dreams it has afforded me?

In those days, my dear Coppée, we were two very good and intelligent little boys. Let me blend my brotherly recollections with your own. I was brought up on the Quays, where old books blend with the landscape. The Seine, which flowed before me, charmed me by the grace natural to water, the origin of things and the source of life. I ingenuously admired the delightful miracle of the stream, which carries boats and reflects the sky by day, and by night is covered with jewels and luminous flowers.

I used to wish that this beautiful water might be ever the same, for I loved it. My mother used to tell me that rivers flow to the sea, and that the flow of the Seine is unending; but I rejected this idea as very depressing. In that I lacked the scientific spirit,

but I nourished a dear illusion, for in the midst of life's evils nothing is sadder than the perpetual flux of all things.

And so, thanks to your book, my dear Coppée, I see myself once more as a little child, watching the boats pass from the Quai Voltaire, and breathing in life with delight; and that is why I say it is an excellent book. (pp. 277-84)

> *Anatole France, "François Coppée," in his* On Life & Letters, *third series, translated by D. B. Stewart, John Lane/The Bodley Head Ltd., 1922, pp. 277-84.*

E. PROTHERO AND **R. E. PROTHERO**   (essay date 1890)

[In the following excerpt, the critics discuss some characteristics of Coppée's poetry.]

[Coppée was ranked as one of the] *Parnassiens, Fantaisistes, Stylistes* or *Impassibles,* as the group of poets has been variously nicknamed. A common dislike, rather than a common object, formed their bond of union. By example, and not, like the *Cénacle* of 1825, by manifesto, they inaugurated a movement which powerfully influenced the subsequent tendencies of French poetry. Their *bête noire* was the *École de bon sens* of which Casimir Delavigne was the pontiff, and Ponsard the prophet. They protested against the popular canon, that there could be no genius without defective syntax, no passion without imperfect prosody. Sincerity did not, in their opinion, demand that strong feeling should find expression in weak rhymes, or real emotion in false grammar. They even dared to criticize Lamartine or Musset as bad models, possessed of more genius than art. In their eyes, Lamartine was a great amateur lyrist rather than a great lyrical poet. To their judgment, even the irony and passion, the tears and laughter, of Alfred de Musset could not atone for neglect of form, carelessness of language, incoherence of imagery. Still more strongly did they rebel against the faults of versifiers, who had no lawlessness of genius to excuse their slovenly workmanship, clumsy versification, grandiose confusion of thought, florid magnificence of language. They insisted on deference to rules of prosody, strict literary proportion, precision of language, clearness of outline, coherence of metaphor, exactitude of detail, variety of rhythmic movement. Their gospel was the *Petit Traité de Poésie française* of Théodore de Banville. Words must fit ideas with the closeness of a kid glove. Virtuosos of all that was rare and exquisite in literary style, sybarites who could not endure a crumpled roseleaf in the couch of the Muse, they adored their art with the passion of lovers for their mistress. Their ambition was to produce

> Quelque belle strophe étoilée
> Au rhythme bel et savoureux;
> Un fier sonnet, rubis, topaze,
> Ciselé de même qu'un vase
> De Benvenuto Cellini.

> [Some beautiful, shining strophe
> With beautiful and savory rhythm;
> A proud sonnet, ruby, topaz,
> Sculpted like a case
> By Benvenuto Cellini.]

A word robbed Baudelaire, the Brummel of literary dandyism, of sleep for a day, a phrase for a week, a page for a month; a volume deprived him of reason and of life. And if this worship be not carried to the extreme of pedantry or affectation,—if it remains a religion of art for art's sake, and does not degenerate into a religion of art for the sake of beauty,—who will make bold to say that the cult is excessive or misplaced? The clear-cut effigy on some disinterred coin reveals the features of a ruler, whose very existence history has forgotten; the sculptured marble outlives the city, whose palaces it once adorned. Yet even these are impaired by age. The clear-cut, sculptured phrase alone survives time and defies decay.

To this group of Parnassians François Coppée in his youth belonged; to its literary traditions he still remains faithful. But he has struck out an independent line. He has created a manner for himself. As the poet of Paris, his genius was moulded and coloured by the circumstances of his youth and childhood. It was the struggle of his early life, which shaped the distinctive features of his verse—his love for Paris, his pity for sorrow and suffering, his insight into the charm of quiet domestic life. (pp. 655-56)

Born in Paris of Parisian parents, Coppée is a *parisien parisiennant*, a Parisian of Parisians. Paris is his native place, his home, his mistress. He studies every aspect of her life with the ardour of a lover. Rarely absent for any length of time, to him *le meilleur du voyage est encor le retour* [the best part of the voyage is the returning home again]. In Paris his thoughts habitually dwell. Her streets are the stage on which are played his humble tragedies; each stone in her pavements is a friend; at every corner an association greets him; down every alley in her gardens flits some phantom of his youth; her trees sheltered alike his first loves and his first rhymes. Paris, as a whole, is to him a personal living being. Like his own *enfant du vieux Paris,* he loves to seek her outskirts, to distinguish the various sounds which create the booming hum of her busy life, catch her tired sigh of relief as twilight creeps across the sky or the evening breeze rustles in the grass, and watch her lights burst out, one by one, through the gathering darkness. He has made every detail of her humble life his own. He does not chaunt the glories of her great streets, or palaces. But, as in *Les Humbles,* he dedicates his genius to sing of the weak and forlorn, the pariahs on whom a gay society rarely bestows even a smile, the obscure heroes and unknown heroines whom his pity detects among her newsvendors, nurses, grocers, foundlings, and motherless child-mothers. Others have sung of Parisian life, but none have treated it in Coppée's peculiar vein. He does not, with Murger, hymn the melancholy and regrets of *la folle Bohême,* nor with Dupont, celebrate the artizan and the student as the *gais volontaires de Progrés*. Still less does he, as so many of the Parnassians were prone to do, ridicule the life of the *bourgeois*. French men of letters were, for the most part, soldiers of fortune, who came to Paris from the provinces. They knew nothing of her domesticity, but plunged into her Bohemianism, and despised her respectability. Coppée, to whom Paris was a home, rather than a stage for the pursuit of wealth or fame, adopts a totally different attitude. He is not only the poet of Paris, but the poet of her solid, unostentatious virtues. (pp. 656-57)

It is Coppée the poet, not Coppée the dramatist or prose writer, who forms the subject of our study. Most poets are but corridors *où passe le vent* [where passes the wind], statues of Memnon that are silent save when some passing wind woos them to music. Coppée forms no exception to the rule. His life . . . is the key to the interpretation of his verse. Chronologically his poetry falls into four groups, (1) 1864-69; (2) 1869-74; (3) 1874-78; (4) 1878-90, containing *Contes en Vers et Poésies diverses, Arrière-Saison,* and a number of smaller pieces, mostly consisting of verses written for special occasions which have not yet been collected into a volume.

The first group of poetry naturally takes its tone from the general character of the epoch, and from the personal surroundings of the poet. The period was not one when the storm rose high, vocal with great ideas, and noble enthusiasms. On the contrary, it was a time of decadence and disenchantment. Nor was Coppée's retired, domestic, life, with its narrow horizon darkened by premature anxieties, favourable to lyric or epic outbursts. His early verse is tentative, deficient in breadth and amplitude. It is uniformly subjective in character, for there was little in external events, or in his own career, to take him out of himself. Sometimes it is elegiac in tone charged with wistful regret for the past, a reliquary in which he lays the ashes of ideal loves and departed dreams. Sometimes it is erotic in character, dedicated to scenes, half-tragic, half-comic, of a boy's first passion, a mirror to reflect the fugitive lights and shades of hope and despair, jealousy and trust, which flicker over the heart in the spring-time of youth. But even in this early group of poems, narrative and dramatic elements more and more predominate, as the poet approaches the period when he produced *Le Passant,* and found the special field for the display of his poetic genius. In such poems as "Les Aïeules," "Angelus," "L'Adagio," "La Bénédiction," and *La Grève des Forgerons*, the subjective poet almost disappears. He turns from the contemplation and expression of his own feelings and experiences to observe the outside world, narrate stories of action, paint external scenes in the drama of real life. (pp. 658-59)

It was in the second group of poetry (1869-74) that Coppée first revealed his characteristic style. Told off to sentry duty on the ramparts during the siege of Paris, shut up within the walls of the city during the horrors of the Commune, and, after peace was restored, struggling hard to gain his livelihood, the poet grows depressed by national and personal misfortunes, distrustful of his talents, uncertain of his country's future. In a large part of the poetry written during this period, these events or feelings are reflected. His "Lettre d'un Mobile Breton," conveyed from Paris in a balloon, produced a prodigious sensation in the provinces. His "Plus de Sang" is a vigorous appeal to his countrymen against the internecine struggle of the Commune. His "Le Chien perdu," and "La Chaumière Incendiée" are touching reminiscences of the Franco-Prussian War. (p. 660)

It was in this stormy period, that Coppée discovered, and began to work, the rich vein which he was the first to quarry. In it he has created a style and manner peculiarly his own. *Les Humbles* contain some of his most characteristic verse. He saw that beauty does not reside only in what is rare. There is poetry, if the feeling is sincere and skilfully expressed, in a grocer's shop. In his vivid pictures of domestic life among shopkeepers, clerks, and artisans, he unites French grace with Dutch realism, the fidelity of Mieris with the grace of Watteau. The "East-End," and transpontine Paris are his stage. Here he finds his heroes and heroines. If Burns had written poems on humble city-life in exquisite modern English, instead of painting country scenes and character in Ayrshire dialect, or if Jasmin had used Parisian French instead of the *patois* of Agen, they would have anticipated Coppée's peculiar charm. To describe a life as homely, and as familiar as that which Burns or Jasmin describes, and to describe it in Parisian French instead of some homely provincial idiom, is Coppée's peculiar art. His realism is not the hard, unsympathetic realism of Crabbe who painted with a wire-brush pictures of which he did not see the poetry. Coppée is not only a realist, he is also a poet and a consummate artist. He has the rashness as well as the courage of an innovator. Sometimes in his frank realism and imperturbable truth, he oversteps the border line which separates the worlds of poetry and prose. But always his tone and style are exactly proportioned to their subject. In *Les Humbles* the poet gives vivid transcripts of what he sees, *and feels*, at his own door. Here are no circumlocutions or periphrases. Every thought is expressed with singular directness, in clear natural language which flows along without effort, and in simple, easy, rhythm, which charms without surprising or wearying the reader. Here are sympathy with suffering, genuine feeling, quick susceptibility to generous ideas. His little *genre* pictures of quiet interiors display his characteristic gifts, his honesty of observation and expression, sureness of touch, correctness of drawing, harmony of colour, and careful perfection of finish. In them he shows himself to be the poet of Paris—of the great, silent, toiling, domestic city, which underlies the scum and froth of the Paris of politicians and novelists. (pp. 660-61)

> *E. Prothero and R. E. Prothero, "The Life and Poetry of François Coppée," in* The English Illustrated, *Vol. 8, 1890-91, pp. 655-61.*

BERNARD SHAW   (essay date 1896)

[*Shaw is generally considered to be the greatest and best-known dramatist to write in the English language since Shakespeare. He is closely identified with the intellectual revival of the British theater, and in his dramatic theory he advocated eliminating romantic conventions in favor of a theater of ideas, grounded in realism. During the late nineteenth century, Shaw was a prominent literary, art, music, and drama critic, and his reviews were known for their biting wit and brilliance. In the following excerpt from an essay originally published in* Saturday Review, *7 March 1896, Shaw presents a negative appraisal of* For the Crown, John *Davidson's English adaptation of Coppée's* Pour la couronne.]

In order to write a true dramatic poem, one must possess very deep human feeling. In order to write historical drama in rhetorical blank verse, one only need possess imagination—a quite different and much cheaper article. Shakespeare had both in an extraordinary degree: consequently his rhetoric, monstrous as much of it is, is so quickened by flashes and turns of feeling that it is impossible to be bored by it; whilst his feeling expresses itself so spontaneously in rhetorical forms that at the climaxes of his plays rhetoric and poetry become one. And so, since his time, every poor wretch with an excitable imagination, a command of literary bombast, and metric faculty enough to march in step, has found himself able to turn any sort of thematic material, however woodenly prosaic, into rhetorical blank verse; whereupon, foolishly conceiving himself to be another Shakespeare, he has so oppressed the stage with yards upon yards and hours upon hours of barren imagery, that at last the announcement of a new historical play in verse at a London theatre produces an involuntary start of terror among the critics, followed by reassuring explanations that although it *is* a fifteenth-century business (more or less), it is really not so bad after all.

François Coppée, as a Frenchman, has not caught the rhetorical itch in its full Shakespearean virulence; but unfortunately the milder form in which it afflicts him is duller than the English variety by just as much as Racine and Corneille are weaker than our immortal William. (pp. 359-60)

Unfortunately for the liveliness of [*For the Crown*], M. Coppée's power of imagining ready-made heroic situations and characters is not fortified by any power of developing them. Bazilide and Michael Brancomir never get beyond the point at which they are first dumped on the stage: they keep saying the same things about themselves and one another over and over again until at last the spectator feels that the play would be greatly improved if most of it were presented by accomplished pantomimists in dumb show. The second act—the Lady Macbeth act—is especially wearisome in this way. A Turkish spy forces the hand of Bazilide by the masterly argument that if Michael Brancomir does not betray his country somebody else will—probably the scullion. Bazilide passes on the argument to Michael, improving the scullion into a horseboy. But poor Michael is quite unable to get any forwarder with his conventional compunction, whilst Bazilide is equally at a loss for any idea except the horseboy, on whom she falls back again and again, the whole conversation being strung up to concert pitch of absurdity by the monstrously tall talk in which it is carried on. The pair prance as if they were bounding over the Alps; but they do not advance an inch. One has only to think for a moment of Lady Macbeth tempting Macbeth, or Iago tempting Othello, to realize how comparatively stupid the poet is, and how, of all methods of marking time, the most futile is to mark it in blank verse. Even in the striking scene of the parricide, there is hardly a human note struck, except in the preliminary chat between the sentinel and the shepherd, which is a welcome relief after Bazilide's fustian. When the catastrophe approaches, father and son do not rise for a moment into any human relation with one another. The more terribly the emergency presses, the more literary do they become, taking it by turns to deliver tearing apostrophes to heaven, hell, honor, history, hope, memory, Christianity, the fatherland, the past and the future; each waiting with great politeness until the other has finished, the audience meanwhile watching patiently for the fight and the finish. In short, except as a display of rhetoric for the sake of rhetoric—a form of entertainment which is chiefly interesting as the only known means by which an author or speaker can make the public respect him for unmercifully boring it—the play has no value apart from the force of the main situation and the charm of the pretty love scenes between Militza and Constantine. (pp. 361-62)

> *Bernard Shaw, "The Return of Mrs. Pat," in his* Dramatic Opinions and Essays with an Apology, Vol. 1, *Brentano's, 1907, pp. 357-66.*

JOSÉ DE HEREDIA   (essay date 1905)

[*A Cuban-born French poet and critic, Heredia was a central figure in the Parnassians, a group of late nineteenth-century literary artists who, rejecting what they considered the semantic obscurity and excessive sentimentality of the Romantics, recommended the use of classic fixed forms and concise imagery in poetry. Heredia's own verse, written entirely in the form of Petrarchan, or Italian, sonnets, is collected in a single volume entitled* Les trophées, *and it is on this one volume that his considerable reputation as a poet rests. In the following excerpt, Heredia praises Coppée's poetry.*]

If as a poet we contemplate him, Coppée belongs to the group commonly called "Parnassiens"—not the Romantic School, the sentimental lyric effusion of Lamartine, Hugo, or De Musset! When the poetical lute was laid aside by the triad of 1830, it was taken up by men of quite different stamp, of even opposed tendencies. Observation of exterior matters was now greatly adhered to in poetry; it became especially descriptive and scientific; the aim of every poet was now to render most exactly, even minutely, the impressions received, or faithfully to translate into artistic language a thesis of philosophy, a discovery of science. With such a poetical doctrine, you will easily understand the importance which the "naturalistic form" henceforth assumed.

Coppée, however, is not only a marker of verses, he is an artist and a poet. Every poem seems to have sprung from a genuine inspiration. When he sings, it is because he has something to sing about, and the result is that his poetry is nearly always interesting. Moreover, he respects the limits of his art; for while his friend and contemporary, M. Sully-Prudhomme, goes astray habitually into philosophical speculation, and his immortal senior, Victor Hugo, often declaims, if one may venture to say so, in a manner which is tedious, Coppée sticks rigorously to what may be called the proper regions of poetry.

François Coppée is not one of those superb high-priests disdainful of the throng: he is the poet of the "humble," and in his work, *Les Humbles,* he paints with a sincere emotion his profound sympathy for the sorrows, the miseries, and the sacrifices of the meek. Again, in his *Grève des Forgerons, Le Naufrage,* and "L'Epave," all poems of great extension and universal reputation, he treats of simple existences, of unknown unfortunates, and of sacrifices which the daily papers do not record. The coloring and designing are precise, even if the tone be somewhat sombre, and nobody will deny that Coppée most fully possesses the technique of French poetry.

But François Coppée is known to fame as a prose-writer, too. His *Contes en prose* and his *Vingt Contes Nouveaux* are gracefully and artistically told; scarcely one of the *contes* fails to have a moral motive. The stories are short and naturally slight; some, indeed, incline rather to the essay than to the story, but each has that enthralling interest which justifies its existence. Coppée possesses preëminently the gift of presenting concrete fact rather than abstraction. A sketch, for instance, is the first tale written by him, "Une Idylle pendant le Siège." . . . In a novel we require strong characterization, great grasp of character, and the novelist should show us the human heart and intellect in full play and activity. In 1875 appeared also *Olivier,* followed by *L'Exilée* . . . ; *Recits et Elegies* . . . ; *Vingt Contes Nouveaux* . . . ; and *Toute une Jeunesse* . . . , mainly an autobiography, crowned by acclaim by the Academy. *Le Coupable* was published in 1897. Finally, in 1898, appeared *La Bonne Souffrance.* In the last-mentioned work it would seem that the poet, just recovering from a severe malady, has returned to the dogmas of the Catholic Church, wherefrom he, like so many of his contemporaries, had become estranged when a youth. The poems of 1902, *Dans la Prière et dans la Lutte,* tend to confirm the correctness of this view.

Thanks to the juvenile Sarah Bernhardt, Coppée became, as before mentioned, like Byron, celebrated in one night. This happened through the performance of *Le Passant.*

As interludes to the plays there are "occasional" theatrical pieces, written for the fiftieth anniversary of the performance of *Hernani* or the two-hundredth anniversary of the foundation of the "Comédie Française." This is a wide field, indeed, which M. Coppée has cultivated to various purposes.

Take Coppée's works in their sum and totality, and the world-decree is that he is an artist, and an admirable one. He plays upon his instrument with all power and grace. But he is no mere virtuoso. There is something in him beyond the executant. Of Malibran, Alfred de Musset says, most beautifully, that she had that "voice of the heart which alone has power to reach the heart." Here, also, behind the skilful player on language, the deft manipulator of rhyme and rhythm, the graceful and earnest writer, one feels the beating of a human heart. One

feels that he is giving us personal impressions of life and its joys and sorrows; that his imagination is powerful because it is genuinely his own; that the flowers of his fancy spring spontaneously from the soil. Nor can I regard it as aught but an added grace that the strings of his instrument should vibrate so readily to what is beautiful and unselfish and delicate in human feeling. (pp. vi-ix)

> *José de Heredia, in a preface to* A Romance of Youth *by François Coppée, 1905. Reprint by Current Literature Publishing Company, 1910, pp. v-ix.*

STUART HENRY (essay date 1921)

[*In the following excerpt, Henry assesses Coppée as a successful poet and superior dramatist.*]

In his first poems and tales [Coppée] reflected the life of the common people living along the southern edges of the Latin and art quarters of Paris. His volume *Les Humbles* made him known as the poet of the Humble. His verse was simple in effect, like his stories. It was written for plain people, and no other writer was then more widely read and beloved by the general French public.

But there appears, also, in his output an aristocratic strain or association, evidencing his cultivation of the nobility. Counts and marquises were fondled with an admiration which did not seem to conflict with his love and cult of the Humble.

He was avowedly Catholic. He became latterly one of the leading defenders of the church in its troublous days in France. He was anti-Republican, anti-Dreyfus. He stood against all that is making French history and progress. He was practically opposed to the larger and Republican liberties and opportunities of those selfsame humble classes whose virtues he sang of so tenderly, so compassionately.

This conflicting attitude or development appears similar in a way to Brunetière's. For Brunetière grew up as a revolutionary, scientific, intellectual agnostic and evolutionist. Then he suddenly went over to the Catholic church, becoming prominently identified as a worshiper of tradition, of conservatism, of sanctified authority, always harking back to the royalist, aristocratic centuries.

It is strange that though the name of Coppée was among the most *retentissants*—well-known—names in literary France, there exist two mistaken impressions about him. One is that he was a great poet and greatest as a poet. He was in fact, as indicated above, essentially light, weak, fragile, not only as a story writer but as a versifier (except in so far as his plays are verse). He approached neither Verlaine nor Maupassant. He was successful, but he discovered or felt nothing very new or different.

Far more important was he as a dramatist. He wrote effective and most admirable stage pieces, always in verse and lyrical by nature. *Le Passant* and others are little classics. His best drama is *Pour la Couronne.* His plays are of a more finished Romanticism than Hugo's. They were companions, in a sense, of Richepin's noble, sonorous dramas in rime, but more feminine. It must be remembered, however, that Coppée, ardent in his views on many public questions, created at times, like Sardou, veritable sensations on the boards and came into conflict with the political authorities.

The other mistaken impression about Coppée is that he was really a Parnassian. He identified himself with the Parnassians, it is true, and stood classed with them, yet he was nothing but a Romantic. He exhibited none of the leading Parnassian attributes—hard, impeccable virtuosity, adoration of impersonal beauty, fondness for the barbarous Exotic. On the contrary he was intimate, personal, sentimental, emphatically *emotional*—all Romantic qualities. He was a descendant of Hugo. Even his cult of the Humble was born direct from Hugo's verse and prose.

Coppée possessed neither the intellectuality, the ultra-refined sensibilities, the exclusive distinction nor philosophic training of Sully Prudhomme. Nor did he have anything of the mystic and musical mystery and genius of Verlaine, who fathered a school and whose original influence is fertile, fructiferous and increasing. Nor did Coppée display any of the glorious, unfeeling brilliance of Leconte de Lisle.

His fame will not grow. His plays, nevertheless, will remain for no little time a true and living adornment of the Paris stage. Unfortunately they will reach no other, for they lose all in translation.

Coppée's literary product is characterized by amiability, smooth-toned *lyrisme* and expansive generosity. A winning, popular, beloved figure, he appealed in his books to the hearts of men and women. He softened mankind. He left it more justly human through his emotionalism and through a certain simple and direct nobleness. (pp. 220-22)

> Stuart Henry, "*François Coppée*," in his French Essays and Profiles, *E. P. Dutton & Company, 1921, pp. 217-22.*

HUGH ALLISON SMITH (essay date 1925)

[*In the following excerpt, Smith discusses Coppée's dramatic works in the context of late nineteenth-century French theater.*]

François Coppée is a Romantic dramatist of the second generation, one not unaffected perhaps by the reaction of good sense and one living in the midst of realism, but a Romantic dramatist none the less. A Parisian, born of humble family and forced at an early age to earn his living, he always retained his sympathy for simple life and common people. The volume of his work is considerable and falls into several categories, but his fame is greatest as a lyric and as a dramatic poet. Despite his other work, he wrote a greater number of successful verse plays than any other French author of his day.

His really significant dramas may be classed in two groups: in the first he is above all a Romanticist and a disciple of Hugo and Dumas père, and in the second he is primarily the idyllic and lyric poet in pieces that recall Musset. In the first class are to be placed his more ambitious efforts, for the most part five-act, historic tragedies, such as *Severo Torelli, Les Jacobites,* and *Pour la Couronne,* and in the second are found especially a number of one-act plays, of which some have already become classics of the French theatre, such as *Le Passant, Le Luthier de Crémone, Le Trésor* and *Le Pater.*

In Coppée's longer historic pieces, we are inclined to see not only the outright Romantic playwright, but even something of the Romantic melodramatist, especially in subject matter. *Severo Torelli* is so extreme and horrifying in its premises and situations that only a Shakespeare could have fully mastered it; *Les Jacobites* has much of the violence and some of the crime of *Le Roi s'amuse;* and even in *Pour la Couronne,* probably the best of his tragedies, the Romanticist's love of striking situations has led him to create a dramatic dilemma from which

there is no escape without considerable damage to poetic justice.

This last play may be taken as a fair example of the class. In *Pour la Couronne,* Michel Brancomir, dominated by his young wife, is about to betray to the Turks the country he had so gloriously defended. His son, Constantin, is forced to kill him to save his country and his father's fame, and then tormented by remorse, Constantin allows himself to be accused of the intended treason and dies in disgrace. It is throughout an interesting and moving drama, but the third act especially, in which the father is killed, is notably effective. However, Coppée has done here what Hugo and others did so often; in order to create a strong situation, he has allowed himself to be enticed into an *impasse.* Constantin is entirely noble and sympathetic, but after the killing of his father he can neither live honored, with his own consent, nor die dishonored, with the consent of the audience.

As we have seen, dilemmas of this sort are frequent in Hugo and are usually exploited for their immediate pathetic and lyric effect; Coppée has exploited this one dramatically—and magnificently—but the rest of his play is badly compromised none the less. A very similar situation is to be found in *Severo Torelli.* The practice is obviously due to the desire to find a strong, overwhelming situation, and proper consideration has not been given in advance to the possibilities of liquidating this situation satisfactorily; in its inspiration, at least, this is a usage of melodrama.

With all this, Coppée is very far from having all the faults of Hugo's drama. Most of the absurdities and impossibilities of the latter have been eliminated. Coppée's plots and situations are, in general, properly motivated and do not rely on surprises and accidents. His characters especially are not the fatalistic Byronic types, nor are they simply built on antithesis, vacillating and moving in a circle. On the contrary, they are as a rule consistent, strong-willed and masters of their own fate, even in the terrific storms by which the author surrounds them. Coppée's dramas are consequently much changed from their Romantic prototypes, although not all of the possible modifications dictated by good judgment have been made. His is rather the work of Hugo corrected by Corneille, who was himself half a Romanticist in taste and spirit; it is an improvement dramatically over Hugo's plays, but while many faults are eliminated, some are applauded.

It is probably the short plays of Coppée that will live longest. *La Passant,* associated with the first great stage triumph of Sarah Bernhardt in 1869, has been a model for one-act lyric dramas since its time, and the others mentioned above have been favorites with some of the greatest actors of the French theatre. It is not that these modest pieces are remarkable in their psychology or thought; doubtless such types as those found in *Le Passant* and *Le Trésor* are now somewhat discredited; nevertheless, these little plays are flowers of sentiment and lyricism, and, although floral fashions change as do others, a true flower of nature is always beautiful. They are entirely genuine and even most characteristic of Coppée's genius.

In all the plays of Coppée the spirit of democracy and the interest in humble life and people are apparent. This popular element began with the Romanticists but is here much more in evidence, and Coppée has been called the realistic poet of the humble. Such passages as the following are numerous:

> "Non! mais j'ai bien assez réfléchi pour savoir
> Que tout droit en ce monde est doublé d'un devoir.
> Pour avoir trop usé de l'un sans remplir l'autre,

Ceux qui portaient des noms fameux comme le nôtre
Sont tombés, et leur plainte est perdue en l'écho
De ce canon vainqueur qui vient de Marengo. . . .
Moi qui dois désormais borner ma perspective
Aux trois ou quatre champs de blé que je cultive
Et demander ma vie au labeur de mes mains,
Je fais très bon marché de tous mes parchemins.''

[No! but I have reflected enough to know
That every right in this world is accompanied by a
    duty.
For having too much used the one without fulfilling the
    other,
Those who bore famous names such as ours
Have fallen, and their lament is lost in the echo
Of this conquering cannon which comes from
    Marengo. . . .
I who must henceforth limit my perspective
To three or four fields of wheat that I cultivate
And sue for my life with the labor of my hands,
I hold my titles cheaply.]

In any case, there is nothing of the aristocrat in Coppée, and this is to be seen in the motives of his characters. It is interesting to note the successive transformations of the aristocratic ideals in dramatic heroes. The Cid struggles over *points d'honneur* which are almost feudal, and in *Hernani* these points are Romantically chivalric, where they are not purely fantastic. Gérald's honor, in *La Fille de Roland,* involves primarily moral righteousness and Christianity. In **Pour la Couronne,** the dominating motive of Constantin is patriotism, rationalized and justified by the social welfare, by the desire to save the country and the people from the cruel reign of the Turk. It is a noticeable evolution toward realism in that most uncompromisingly chivalric and idealistic element of French character and of French literature, the *point d'honneur.* (pp. 68-72)

Hugh Allison Smith, "The School of Good Sense and Later Verse Drama," in his Main Currents of Modern French Drama, *Henry Holt and Company, 1925, pp. 59-75.*

ADDITIONAL BIBLIOGRAPHY

"Poems by François Coppée." *Appleton's Journal* VIII n.s., No. 13 (March 1880): 231-39.
    Translated excerpts of Coppée's poetry with a biographical introduction.

Blunt, Hugh Francis. "François Coppée." In his *Great Penitents,* pp. 148-68. 1921. Reprint. Freeport, N.Y.: Books for Libraries Press, 1967.
    Discusses Coppée's conversion to Catholicism.

France, Anatole. "Three Poets." In his *On Life and Letters,* pp. 134-45. London: John Lane/The Bodley Head, 1924.
    Favorable review of *Arrière-saison.*

Matthews, Brander. Introduction to *Ten Tales,* by François Coppée, pp. ix-xvi. 1891. Reprint. Freeport, N.Y.: Books for Libraries Press, 1969.
    Praises Coppée's achievements in the *conte*—the short story—noting especially his "little masterpieces of story-telling in verse."

"François Coppée." *Review of Reviews* XI, No. 1 (January 1895): 96-97.
    Describes the literary community of which Coppée was a member.

Schaffer, Aaron. "A Comparison of the Poetry of François Coppée and Eugene Manuel." *PMLA* XLIII, No. 4 (December 1928): 1039-54.
    Detailed analysis of themes in the work of Coppée and Manuel. Schaffer contends that Coppée was strongly influenced by Manuel's poetry, much of which predates Coppée's similar work.

Clarence (Shepard) Day (Jr.)

1874-1935

American memoirist, essayist, poet, critic, and illustrator.

Day, who gained critical recognition as an insightful satirical essayist early in his career, is best known as the author of *Life with Father,* anecdotal memoirs about his family that are particularly concerned with detailing the blustering attempts of Clarence Day, Sr., to rigidly systematize a normally chaotic household. This book and the similar volumes of reminiscences, *God and My Father* and *Life with Mother,* became best-sellers, and *Life with Father* inspired a successful stage production, a motion picture, and a television series. Critics attribute the popularity of these autobiographical works to Day's ability to present the universal subject matter of household conflicts with humor, candor, and perceptiveness.

Day was the oldest of four sons born to a Wall Street stockbroker and his wife. After graduating from Yale University in 1896, he served briefly in the United States Navy during the Spanish-American war. In 1897 he became a member of the New York stock exchange and joined his father's brokerage firm, but was soon forced to give up this career because of an arthritic condition that left him an invalid by 1900. Confined to his New York apartment and bedridden for increasingly long periods of time, Day maintained a nocturnal routine: breakfasting in the late afternoon, receiving guests in the evening, and following a midnight dinner with several hours of writing and sketching. Although he published essays of his own and also edited, illustrated, and wrote introductions to the works of other writers, Day was unable to earn a living from his literary efforts, and supplemented his income by speculating in the stock market. The stock market crash of 1929 left Day in severe financial straits; however, his growing popularity as an essayist soon enabled him to support his family comfortably through his writing. In the early 1920s Day had published his first books, the volumes of satirical essays *This Simian World* and *The Crow's Nest,* which sold poorly despite uniformly positive reviews. Throughout the twenties he had also published essays, criticism, and illustrations in such periodicals as *Harper's,* the *New Republic,* and the *New Yorker,* among others. It was in the *New Yorker,* during the early years of that magazine's publication, that Day's reminiscences about his family, which formed the basis of the "Father" and "Mother" books, first appeared.

This Simian World and *The Crow's Nest* are volumes of informal essays that comment on various aspects of human behavior. Despite their humorous nature, the essays are regarded as philosophically and anthropologically penetrating. Francis Hackett has compared Day's essays with those of Michel de Montaigne, whose sixteenth-century *Essais* are considered the foundation of the essay form in their utilization of a casual, familiar writing style and eloquently simple language to provide profound insight into the human condition. In addition to his volumes of essays, Day also produced *Thoughts without Words* and *Scenes from the Mesozoic, and Other Drawings,* collections of drawings and brief verses which are informed by what one critic called "savagely delightful" satire. In a style described in the *New Yorker* as "weirdly parabolical because they were a compromise between his genius and his arthritis,"

the drawings often depict powerless, small men dominated by women or intimidated by social obligations, and have been found by some critics to resemble the drawings of James Thurber in subject matter and execution. The humorous verses accompanying many of the drawings show a predilection for wordplay and allusions to the works of other authors.

The sketches Day wrote about his childhood in the New York of the 1880s were immediately popular with readers. *God and My Father, Life with Father,* and *Life with Mother* are written in the familiar style for which Day's essays were commended; however, many critics discern behind this seeming nonchalance keen observations of a family whose behavior is intrinsically ironic because its members lack self-knowledge. This inability or unwillingness to reflect on personal motives is epitomized in "Father," who persistently tries to subjugate not only his wife and children, but also an intractable world, to his will, ignoring the lessons of past experiences which foretell his almost certain defeat. Despite his tempestuous behavior, the senior Day is usually bested by his wife Vinnie, who triumphs in their many arguments about money, servants, and their children, owing to what one critic termed her unconquerable "combination of sweetness and ruthlessness." Day described the behavior of his family without explication, and this restraint has been cited by critics as one of the strongest elements of the "Father" stories, perhaps most notably by Louis Kronenberger, who indicated that it would have been an artistic error for Day to insert overt comment on his father's behavior, for "if you can't see what's wrong with Father just by looking at Father, you'll never learn by harking to the indictments of the son." Kronenberger has asserted that the "Father" books are also of value as accurate social documents of upper-middle-class New York society during the Victorian era, and asserts that they serve as a "casually terrible revelation of the entrenched bourgeois spirit" of that time and place. Nevertheless, critics note that Day was never savagely satirical or broadly farcical in his portrayal of his family: according to Hackett, Father was a "justly perceived being," and most commentators maintain that Day was interested in lovingly recreating his redoubtable parent and not in focusing upon his faults. Howard Lindsay and Russel Crouse, who produced the stage play *Life with Father,* offered the opinion that "Clarence Day wrote not just of his father and mother and family—but of all fathers and mothers and of all families. . . . The universal appeal of the simple saga of Clarence Day's family seems to prove again that the springs of human action transcend the boundaries of geography and race."

As an essayist and memoirist Day possessed honesty, intelligence, and an unpretentious humor that gained him a wide audience: critics believe that sophisticated readers appreciated his dry and impartial manner of presenting his material, while a less sophisticated readership vastly enjoyed the humorous material itself. *Life with Father* and Day's other books about his family were extremely popular with readers for more than two decades, and inspired the stage and movie adaptations that further captivated an even larger audience, confirming the universal quality of Day's familial anecdotes, which reportedly drew from people all over the world the insistent claim that his "Father" was also theirs.

(See also *Contemporary Authors,* Vol. 108 and *Dictionary of Literary Biography,* Vol. 11: *American Humorists, 1800-1950.*)

PRINCIPAL WORKS

This Simian World   (essays and drawings) 1920
The Crow's Nest   (essays, verse, and drawings) 1921; also published as *After All* [enlarged edition], 1936
Thoughts without Words (drawings and verse) 1928
God and My Father (memoir) 1932
Life with Father (memoir) 1935
Scenes from the Mesozoic, and Other Drawings (drawings and verse) 1935
Life with Mother (memoir) 1937
The Best of Clarence Day (memoirs, essays, verse, and drawings) 1948

ROBERT LITTELL (essay date 1920)

[*Littell was an American critic, journalist, and author. During the 1920s he worked as an associate editor of the* New Republic, *and as a drama critic and columnist for the* New York Evening Post *and the* New York World. *In 1927 Littell began a long association with* Reader's Digest, *becoming senior editor of that publication in 1942. In the following excerpt, he praises the style and content of* This Simian World.]

Few indeed have been the men who by a subtle regrouping of familiar words could draw an impersonal picture of our race. It is a talent rare among creatures whose firm belief in pre-destined world-empire and even in kinship with God, makes any attempt to view themselves from the impartial standpoint of an animal, a deity, or the inhabitant of another planet seem blasphemous or impossible. Just this rare quality of detachment, of complete independence from man's ancient myopia of self-esteem is the chief among the many high qualities of Mr. Clarence Day's *This Simian World.*

No less complete and varied than his estimate of man is Mr. Day's expression of it: a natural blend of wisdom with lightness, humour with profundity, hope with art, economy with abundance, kindliness with malice. The quality that makes possible such alliances is the one most infrequently granted to mortals: Mr. Day sees things as they are beneath accumulated centuries of appearances; he cannot, he will not be fooled. Given such an equipment, he may have had, but he did not require, biology.

Swift required no knowledge of biology to see that man would be less unlike his best self if he were more like a horse. And with no help from biology Anatole France saw the very close resemblance between men and penguins. The rest of us at some time or other feel dimly aware of "the beast with which we are crossed." It is an uncomfortable feeling, one we should like to forget, for what divides us most sharply from our fellow animals is an intense desire to become something else. Even if Darwin had never been born, we should have felt the chimpanzee stirring in our blood, and been angry, ashamed, and untruthful about it. So, Darwin or no Darwin, once Mr. Day had perceived that man is descended from or closely related to other animals, he would have seen for himself that if men's ancestors were the animals they most resembled in behaviour, these animals must have been monkeys.

Consider our civilization, says Mr. Day, were we descended from any other sort of creature. Ants, for instance. They lead "chaste and industrious lives." Too industrious, in fact: "The ant is knowing and wise, but he doesn't know enough to take a vacation." The vision of a super-ant civilization is highly distasteful to us simians: it would be "an orgy of work." (pp. 197-98)

Brief quotation . . . will show only a glimpse of his art. And quotation cannot translate the amusing, wistful, imaginative little drawings that all too seldom decorate the book. (p. 199)

Haphazard quotation cannot do justice to *This Simian World.* It must be read as a whole. Only then can one see how idea follows idea, how artfully and with what purpose Mr. Day varies the cadences of his prose, how skilfully he contrives now to make us go on with him and forget what has been said, now to make us hear the undertones when he wants the echoes of what he has been saying to be prolonged. Only from the book as a whole can one learn in what just proportions can be combined the casual and the profound; the light touch and the brief glimpse into chasms of darkness or into unknown heavens. Mr. Day sees our simian selves with a sharp eye, all the sharper because it is kind. He sees innumerable possible grounds for despair, yet he does not despair: he is gay. He avoids completely the peevishness of the satirist mocking a bitter world. He can feel—suggest—hope, infinite magnificent hope, a slow ignoble march toward an unutterable destiny, but this cannot make him even faintly sentimental.

In this slim book, which looks so unimportant and will live so long, a weary mind, pausing a moment from its frantic simian activity, will find a merciless, yet temperate portrait of his race. It is not a picture that need tempt him to discouragement, to transform to inaction his busy futility. Rather will he see that there are new ways of looking at himself, new things to discover about himself, and that both art and profit can result from the attempt. He will find, too, something uncommonly not human about the book, a detachment incompatible with the self-importance, the self-esteem of most humans, a suggestion of the wisdom and impersonal amusement of some kindly deity here on visit. (p. 200)

> *Robert Littell, in a review of "This Simian World,"
> in* The Dial, *Vol. LXIX, No. 1, August, 1920, pp.
> 197-200.*

FRANCIS HACKETT   (essay date 1921)

[*Hackett was a respected Irish-American biographer, novelist, and literary critic during the first half of the twentieth century. His reviews appeared in the* New Republic, *the* Saturday Review of Literature, *and other prominent American periodicals. In the following excerpt, Hackett discusses some strengths and weaknesses of individual essays in* The Crow's Nest.]

Clarence Day has a supreme quality among all the critics and essayists in America today—he thinks naturally, writes naturally, draws naturally. For this reason, of course, he is the enemy of his kind. What is the use of erudition and authority if Clarence Day can put all Maeterlinck in an eggshell? What is the use of going to Harvard and learning to be dove-colored if a blackleg like Clarence Day is to run loose? The profession of critic is gone, *spurlos versenkt*, if this creature is to be permitted to crow from his crow's nest like an ordinary bird living in direct relation with his feelings and his senses. We should rise against him, march to Riverside Drive and force the caitiff to confess that he is a disruptive influence in the pay of the Third Internationale.

Sometimes, I don't know why, he slips from his aware simplicity into a kind of bromidic simple-mindedness that is worthy of popular magazines. It comes, I think, when he feels it his duty to be light, judicious, sound and wise. At such times he writes like a sweet old gentleman leaning over the go-cart and trying to explain the choo-choos to a baby. He is capable of nodding his head and saying, "Ah, well, if we must romanticize something, it had best be the past." And, in another place, "Well, it's all very interesting. Will and Wisdom (capitalized by him) are both mighty leaders. Our times worship Will." He has an idea in this, though not very much of an idea, but the whole thing is in the style of the patient, benevolent teacher. I may whisper, too, that **"Improving the Lives of the Rich"** and **"The Revolt of Capital"** and **"The Man Who Knew Gods"** are also a little labored. Here the wingless critics have nothing to fear from C. D. Jr. The ideas are good enough. It's fairly funny to call Gary "President Albert H. Hairy," but the total effect is one of miscegenation, like a sermon turned sprightly or a library table that converts into a folding bed. If you felt that the author of the sermon (or the library table) couldn't help himself, it would be all right. But Clarence Day could have helped his **"Revolt of Capital."** That essay was sapped from his brain, it did not spring from his spirit.

But when he teases old Fabre, the man who loved insects, and says, "you can see he has insect blood in him, if you look at his photograph,"—here he is really enjoying himself. And,

like waiters or undertakers or dentists or kings, he does his work best when he is really enjoying himself. Mark Twain never wrote anything funnier than **"The Enjoyment of Gloom,"** the first four pages. But it isn't because Day is funny that this is so good. It is because he becomes all alive, personally incandescent and absorbed and wholly natural, in such a bit of narrative. He is equally natural a few pages later, writing of Conrad. Here he isn't trying to convert criticism into literary vaudeville for the gum-chewers. He is trying to condense all his own love of adventure, and fear of adventure, into a few luminous words. And how real, how secure, is the grip of Clarence Day's experience on our own inside experience which before had perhaps never met such an understanding:

> There's one great man now living, however, who has almost too much of this sense: this cosmic adventure emotion. And that man's Joseph Conrad. Perhaps in his youth the sea came upon him too suddenly, or his boyhood sea dreams awed too deeply his then unformed mind. At all events, the men in his stories are like lonely spirits, sailing, spellbound, through the immense forces surrounding the world. "There they are," one of them says, as he stands at the rail, "stars, sun, sea, light, darkness, space, great waters; the formidable Work of the Seven Days, into which man seems to have blundered unbidden. Or else decoyed." We all have that mood. But Conrad, he's given to brooding. . . .

Still, I like Clarence Day best when he takes things more in the wrong spirit. I like him about Kabir, about sex, about The Turmoil. Except that, as he gets weary, he gets wise and helpful. Then he peers into the reader's cradle and burbles, "So it goes, so it goes. And playing some game well *is* needful, to make a man of you. But once in a while you get thinking it's not quite enough."

These appealing homilies come from him when he is low-spirited. They never occur to him when he's writing of people or cockroaches, only when he is bravely trying to put an intellectual spit-ball across the plate, with every eye in the bleachers following him. In dealing with real people he becomes quite absorbed and absorbing, and this is when I like him best. Here his style is truly natural, informal, and to the point. If he is amusing here, it is not because he is afraid he won't hold his audience unless he is original and witty, but because he has really ripened and mellowed in the lovely perceptions and feelings out of which he speaks. **"Portrait of a Lady"** is superb, both as a likeness and as a painting. It is romantic, full of color, and true. **"Grandfather's Three Lives"** is a little ingenious but it is more to my taste than Strachey, and **"Story of a Farmer"** is a very pretty sketch, except for the last line. The last line has a kind of Hippodrome flourish, "His name was George Washington!!!" But the subject is one on which it would be enchanting to read fifty of Clarence Day's pages. . . .

He really convinces one that, without any stilts under him, he is able to see for himself. He sees very deeply. He sees more amusingly than our best fabulists. When he stands things on their heads, or reverses some customary viewpoint, I don't think he is seeing things for himself most naturally. He is best, I believe, in the straight portrait. But of course what one enjoys in these portraits, besides the rich play of sympathy, is the bright play of perception. "Whenever a parent feels blue, or is not making good, he immediately declares that his hopes are in his little son anyhow. Then he has a sad, comfortable glow at his own self-effacement.'' Such observations give one the delightful feeling of the living, unforced play of mind. The drawings add enormously to this result, being perfectly unstudied and personal in pattern. But ''unstudied'' is a poor word, suggesting that Clarence Day improvises. He does not improvise, he gropes around for a union between subject and spirit. When the subject comes right, then we see the spirit for what it is, in its serene wisdom, its honest simplicity, its even American temper, its gaiety, its beauty.

Francis Hackett, ''Clarence Day,'' in The New Republic, *Vol. XXIX, No. 369, December 28, 1921, p. 131.*

CARL VAN DOREN (essay date 1923)

[*Van Doren is considered one of the most perceptive critics of the first half of the twentieth century. He worked for many years as a professor of English at Columbia University and served as literary editor and critic of the* Nation *and the* Century *during the 1920s. A founder of the Literary Guild and author or editor of several American literary histories, Van Doren was also a critically acclaimed historian and biographer. Howard Moss wrote of him: ''His virtues, honesty, clarity, and tolerance are rare. His vices, occasional dullness and a somewhat monotonous rhetoric, are merely, in most places, the reverse coin of his excellence.'' In the following excerpt, Van Doren discusses Day's qualities as an essayist.*]

Clarence Day must have been born honest and he has, so far as I can see, never done anything to waste his birthright. The eyes with which he looks at things are as level as E. W. Howe's, but his language is lighter and his fancy nimbler. In ***This Simian World*** it was his fancy which perhaps did most to get him a hearing. In ***The Crow's Nest,*** without giving up his fancy, he ranges over more varied fields than in his first book and seems even wiser. He has a perfect temper. He has known pain but it has not soured him—or at least his book. He has known passion but it has left no visible ruts or hummocks in his mind. He has done all that a human being can do with his reason but he feels no resentment that reason at its best can do so little. Having a perfect temper he sits at ease in his crow's nest and surveys the deck, the sailors, rival ships, the waves, the horizon, and the sky, without heat, of course, but also without pride in his position or in his self-control. Having a perfect temper he is not harried into any violence of style by his instinct to express himself. As shrewd as a proverb, he never plays with epigrams. As much of a poet as he needs to be, he yet seems to have no need for eloquence. Such lucidity as his is both prudent and elevated.

He is primarily an anthropologist, as he showed in ***This Simian World.*** The race of man is for him ''a fragile yet aspiring species on a stormy old star.'' It has lived a long while and has gone a long way from its original slime, but plenty of the old stains still colour its nature. Its impulses are tangled with the impulses of the ape and with the inhibitions of the amoeba. ''The test of a civilized person is first self-awareness, and then depth after depth of sincerity in self-confrontation.'' By this test Mr. Day is thoroughly civilized. Nor does he merely search in his own mind and admit what he finds there. He observes others with the same awareness and the same sincerity. Hardy, he sees, takes his pleasure in portraying gloom. ''That's fair,'' says Mr. Day.

Shaw has had a vision of the rational life that men might lead and can never stop insisting that they lead it: a master of comedy when he paints the contrast and rather tiresome when he insists too much. Maeterlinck is king in the realms of romance he has created, like any other child; he is also a child when it comes to judging the ''real'' world. We know what Fabre thinks of wasps, but we wish we knew what the wasps think of Fabre. Mr. Day's ideas are never gummed together with their hereditary associations. He talks always as if he had just come into this universe and were reporting it for other persons as intelligent as he. What a compliment to mankind! And what a compliment to mankind, too, that he should find it quite unnecessary to lecture it! A whimsical fable, a transparent allegory, a scrap of biography, a few verses, a humorous picture—these are his only devices. (pp. 199-201)

Carl Van Doren, ''A Casual Shelf: Honesty Is a Gift,'' in his The Roving Critic, *Alfred A. Knopf, 1923, pp. 199-201.*

LEE WILSON DODD (essay date 1932)

[*Dodd was an American dramatist, novelist, poet, and critic. In the following excerpt, he notes the artistry that is masked by the ''deceptive simplicity'' of Day's prose style in* God and My Father.]

[***God And My Father***] is one of those rare creations likely to be cherished by the happy few long after it has been enjoyed and forgotten by the negligent many. And when I call it a rare creation, I may well do so in a double sense. All contemporary readers of discernment have crow after crow to pick with Clarence Day. He writes, *when* he writes, so supremely well; yet he comes so very near to not writing at all. He seems to be running a sort of race for the prize of reticence with Ralph Hodgson, the English lyric poet. Something, in both instances, should be done about it. Not since the poet Gray has so much talent produced so little copy. (p. 629)

However, here finally is another brief book by Clarence Day—and we have not been waiting in vain. Quantitatively, but in no other possible sense, it is disappointing. One would search far to find as much humor, shrewdness, character, ironic wisdom, and sheer good writing in an equal number of pages. This is a book not to borrow, but to own. It belongs on thoughtfully tended shelves, not too far from the *Essays of Elia* and the *Sentimental Journey*—neither of which small masterpieces it superficially resembles. But we are not in this review discussing the superficial.

If, by good fortune, like the present reviewer, you were brought up in the tranquilly provincial metropolis of New York some forty years or more ago, this book will do more than delight you—it will move you to secret tears. Clarence Day has recovered (and in so much less than nine volumes) the very form and pressure of that *temps perdu.* He has done it so casually, with such apparent (but deceptive) ease! For there must be no mistake as to the style of these seemingly artless pages—it is masterly. It has the cunning simplicity (minus the slightly archaic tone) of the prose style of Goldsmith. We could all, of course, write like that—if only we could write like that. But somehow we never can—or, at least, we never do. (pp. 629-30)

[Goldsmith and Clarence Day] are spiritually and artistically of the same family, in spite of some negligible differences of manner due to the passing of years. There is the same deceptive simplicity masking a shrewd, sly irony—an irony, however, which is never harsh, but always sympathetic, humorsome, humane. . . . I salute in ***God And My Father*** an unmistakable and, as I believe, a lasting work of art. (p. 630)

Lee Wilson Dodd, "Akin to Goldsmith," in The Saturday Review of Literature, *Vol. VIII, No. 37, April 2, 1932, pp. 629-30.*

E. B. WHITE (essay date 1935)

[White was an American essayist, poet, humorist, and author of books for children. He is often considered one of the finest American prose stylists of this century. White's essays, characterized by their wit, directness, and unrhetorical observation, have appeared regularly in the New Yorker *and* Harper's Magazine *for many years. In the following excerpt, White discusses the poems and drawings in* Scenes from the Mesozoic *and* Thoughts without Words.*]*

Vapors rise in a thin steady stream from Clarence Day's mind, curling upward till they meet a down-draft and settle in some monstrous shape on a piece of paper by his bedside. While the rest of us sleep, Mr. Day stews in his messes and finally delivers himself of a quatrain at half past four in the morning. The hideous afterbirth is a picture, lightly pencilled, vaguely illustrative of the poem. The most recent of these fascinating emanations are collected in a book called *Scenes from the Mesozoic*—amorphous, evil, disturbing. They are the product of as wicked and lovable a talent as one is likely to run across in the bookshops.

In 1928 Mr. Day brought out a volume of his drawings and verses called *Thoughts Without Words*. It was, and is, a strange book, containing an assortment of volatile matters—a memorable fragment of the decade. In it one encountered rare doings: the resurrection of Mrs. Eliza Bainwick Kelly, a side view of Original Sin, a New England professor guarding the glory that was Greece, an old librarian being separated from his books by the King of Worms, and a couple of under-exposed snapshots of God.

Scenes from the Mesozoic, much of which has already appeared in the *New Yorker*, the *Saturday Review*, and other magazines, is a sort of sequel to *Thoughts Without Words*. It dips into the age of the great beasts, and discovers you and your mate, up to your knees in slime, astonishing the skies with your noisy trouble. The author has always been preoccupied with anthropological affairs, and it is a matter of intense and living interest to him that Man, by some unaccountable accident, is descended from the simians, rather than—as might well have happened—from the Great Cats, or the lizards.

Mr. Day is fascinated by germinal things:

> Oh who that ever lived and loved
> Can look upon an egg unmoved?

he once wrote.

In his new book one finds the egg-shaped beginnings of many creatures, and zoölogical sports. He is faithful to Natural History in his fashion. He draws abortive animals and men, and they become the dreadful symbols of abstract qualities and human difficulties. On page 65 you find Middle Age. On page 66 Fidelity. On page 74 Rhythm. On page 76 Cynicism. Time, to Clarence Day, is virtually non-existent; early slime is coeval with today's gum wrappers. Likewise, he finds very little difference between a Saurian and a housepainter, but recognizes a great gulf between a female anything and a male anything. Like most male artists, Mr. Day comforts himself with the bitter assumption that his sex might get somewhere if it weren't for the Female. He is unusually ruthless and merry about this. When, on page 78, you discover Discipline holding back a Rover, it doesn't surprise you that Discipline is a woman. Evil (P. 61) is also a woman—not the Evil that Satan knew, but the *real* Evil, "darker, older, colder." Men, in Mesozoic times, were eager to love and part. But, writes Mr. Day—

> . . . surly, surly, late and early,
> Was the female heart. . . .

Who can bid farewell to the author on the last page without wincing? He pictures himself, a frog-eyed amiable little man, dragged off by the hand to seek the Holy Grail, he knows not why.

E. B. White, "Quatrains of Early Morning," in The Saturday Review of Literature, *Vol. XII, No. 3, May 18, 1935, p. 11.*

Thoughts on Bondage   [437

Who drags the fiery artist down?
What keeps the pioneer in town?
Who hates to let the seaman roam?
It is the wife, it is the home.

One of Day's "thoughts on bondage." From The Best of Clarence Day, *by Clarence Day. Copyright 1948 by Katherine B. Day. Reprinted by permission of Alfred A. Knopf, Inc.*

FRANCIS HACKETT (essay date 1935)

[In the following excerpt from a review of Life with Father, *Hackett commends Day's ability to depict his father with humor and candor without resorting to either savage satire or broad farce.]*

Old Mr. Day was a Wall Street broker of the past generation, and Clarence Day might possibly, in his dutiful youth, fresh from Yale, have written a brownstone biography of his father, filled with Parmlys, Johnsons, Ben Day, George Day. It would have been heavy going. But by divine accident Clarence Day lost his focus as a son of Eli and a son of Clarence. With no gross breach of tradition or even convention, the figure of his father has shifted just enough so that, remaining lovable and admirable and pretty terrible, he can be treated with insight: and a father who saw himself only as serious, whom others saw only as serious, who was serious, is now, to one's immense relief, allowed to be comic, with perfect fidelity to the importance of Wall Street and his family's loyal and pungent experience of him.

At the beginning, perhaps, in *Life with Father,* there was a hint of monkey shines, of Clarence Junior squaring accounts with the Patriarchs. There was a touch of revolt in the first lines of that portrait. But very soon the pure delight of an artist in a beautiful subject took the upper hand, and before Clarence Day's memories had rolled into the first score of episodes we had a male parent so well seen, so round, so original and yet so truly in character, that the piquant biographical aspect gave completely away to the absolutely joyous recollection of a living man. He roars. He swears. He carries on. Yet he is not a humoristic subject, not a potted parent, but one of those justly perceived beings who brim with life, who override others by sheer exuberance, so intent on living that they never mirror the other mind or the other will, getting their own way by tactics often hugely infantile, triumphing by irrationality over all about them, unless a wife oppose them by another irrationality, this time feminine, or else a David come along with the sling of comedy and lay the giant low.

But this Father is not a stuffed tyrant, a tedious over-blown Patriarch. It is a palpable man, full of humors and attractiveness. At times the situations spring out so characteristically that the book convulses one with laughter. Old Mr. Day is not only placed in his environment so as to make a convincing picture of a civilization, but the absurdities of that civilization break out when he behaves with irresistible naturalness. He is at times "pure act," like the late Theodore Roosevelt, and it is in this virile compulsion that the comedy consists, because of course poor little Clarence, the informant, is always acted upon by the overwhelming parent, and yet bobs up again after the hurricane, weak and resilient as grass. Old Mr. Day imposing music on Clarence is obviously funny. Clarence sees that, as Mark Twain might have seen it. But Clarence Senior opening Clarence Junior's letters and trying to fit the letters about false whiskers into the broker's life, Clarence Senior answering all telephone calls and trying to fit them to his measure, Clarence Senior revolting at his son's meekness about illness, refusing to have high blood pressure, declining to be killed—here is a richly amusing character, and when we understand him, when we admit the dreadful implications of the extravert Anglo-Saxon father, when the energy of the father in having his own way, in making Irvington give him ice, or the slow agency give him a cook, becomes fully developed, then we surrender and revel in him, with occasional twinges of the executive male in ourselves.

The literary problem, with a rich topic like this, is to keep the easy accent of life. If the humor is savage we go into satire and if it is broad we go into farce. By confining his topic solely to the unit of the family and keeping it inside the polite limits of Madison Avenue in the eighties and nineties, Clarence Day has never forced his note. He has amusingly recreated that plump era, with lunch downtown at Delmonico's and horseback riding up at Irvington, with a grim attitude about debts and a visit to the Chicago World's Fair. It is all candid and real, but Clarence Day is not the sort of realist who opens the vacuum cleaner for his material. He is an *enfant terrible,* but not an *enfant gaté.* And what he pours out is abundantly enjoyed, ripe in experience and feeling.

Those of us who have watched every scrap of his work for the past twenty years know that there is in him something of the musing wisdom of Montaigne. Like Montaigne he has kept

inquisitiveness, the active principle of wonder, while shedding every speck of myth-making, all the delight in bubble-blowing and dreaming that turns wonder into poetry at one end and into delusion and nonsense at the other. When he has let his imagination loose, as in his drawings, it has sometimes been rough stuff, with a kind of resistance against myth-making in it. It is the side of him that is not reconciled, and its force is rude. But Clarence Day is full of social tact and experience and feeling, of dry awareness and peculiar wise insight. What he needed was a medium where he could release all of himself without fabricating, and his father has given it to him. Here his comedy could have the dignity and warmth that his social instinct craves. It could have a simple style, like old Margaret's cooking, and be fertile and informal, just as American as Jane Austen is English, with everything honestly to scale. It could be democratic in the early sense, unpretentious and yet individualistic. All of this he has secured, in this quiet, abundant, warm, and devilish revelation of his father. So the book is a feast.

Francis Hackett, "Clarence Day's Father," in The Saturday Review of Literature, *Vol. XII, No. 14, August 3, 1935, p. 5.*

PHILIP LITTELL   (essay date 1935)

[*Littell was an American author, critic, and journalist. In the following excerpt from a reminiscence about his long acquaintance with Day that was originally published in the* New Republic, *11 September 1935, Littell praises Day's sympathetic portrayals of his family in* God and My Father *and* Life with Father.]

Clarence Day is a close inspector. He gets a lot of fun out of understanding things. Truth is the quarry he hunts with such zest. Or—in case he should read this—he would detest the word "truth" as too tall; suppose I tone it down into saying that what he is after is always a likeness? In his writing even wit, an uncommon office for wit to fill, often delineates character; just as his laughter, being a humorist's, is also a designer's, a composer's, a builder's. No humorist I can think of is at once so unsentimental and good-natured and hardheaded. There is hard-headedness in his wisdom, cordiality, sympathy and affection, all of which color and deepen his feeling toward the world of men and women. Both [*God and My Father* and *Life with Father*] . . . make us better acquainted with this feeling. They give life back to his parents, her beauty and youth back to his mother. They are acts of piety, and no other act of piety resembles them. They are done with affection and gusto, with here and there a touch of lovely, unsweetened tenderness, always with kind, unflinching eyes and the friendliest laughter. And while we read we also laugh, often uncontrollably, in outbursts, for these are two of the funniest books written in our time, and written in a prose whose ease is deceptive. It is written for the ear, it sounds like the best talk, it has a casual air, its nonchalance invites you to ignore the subtlety of its cadences. Delightful books they are, these two, books you like as though they were alive, books that are alive with energy and collisions and the running water of happiness.

In a book about the writer's own people there is always a risk that we may not see them quite as he sees them. The only part of *Life with Father* where I dissent from the author's view is the chapter called "Father Interferes with the Twenty-third Psalm." Here Clarence Day tells us how he felt as a small boy about the Bible in French. Among the French words that upset him and made him laugh was *"irrité"* where the English Bible says "wroth." Instead of the Lord being wroth, *le Seigneur* was *irrité*. The patriarchs were *irrité* when they ought to have been wroth. This was unsatisfactory. It lowered the patriarchs. It reduced their stature. "If they were full of mere irritation all the time," Clarence Day felt, "they were more like the Day family." I don't feel that way at all. What *Life with Father* shows us is not irritation. Nearly every chapter in the book does, I admit, lead us up to and into and then away from an outburst of temper. It is from explosion to explosion that the story moves on its quiet feet. Life in the Day family was a series of detonations. Mr. Day lost his temper often and tremendously. But he was not irritated. Men several sizes smaller, thin-lipped ungenial men, they are the ones who get irritated. Mr. Day was wroth. (pp. 236-37)

> Philip Littell, "Life with Father," in The Critic as Artist: Essays on Books 1920-1970, *edited by Gilbert A. Harrison, Liveright, 1972, pp. 233-37.*

LOUIS KRONENBERGER   (essay date 1937)

[*A drama critic for* Time *from 1938 to 1961, Kronenberger was a distinguished historian, literary critic, and author highly regarded for his expertise in eighteenth-century English history and literature. In an assessment of Kronenberger's critical ability, Jacob Korg states: "He interprets, compares, and analyzes vigorously in a pleasingly epigrammatic style, often going to the essence of a matter in a phrase." A prolific and versatile writer, Kronenberger also wrote plays and novels and edited anthologies of the works of others. In the following excerpt from a review of* Life with Mother, *Kronenberger commends Day's portrayals of his family and regards this work, together with* Life with Mother, *as inadvertent social documents testifying to the less appealing aspects of the milieu of which the Day family was a part.*]

Clarence Day has come to please the highbrows and the lowbrows alike, and it is not too difficult to see why. The highbrows have appreciated the severely honest, drily impartial way in which he has used his material, and the lowbrows have relished the material itself. Day took the measure of his parents with the same deadly thoroughness and calm that Jane Austen took the measure of her neighbors, and with a touch of the same tight, old-maidish wisdom. If his parents left him with scars, Day has obliterated them as perfectly as Jane Austen obliterated the county's snubs. His father, at once so dreadful and so funny, and, more than either, so human, is always granted the privilege of exposing himself; and so is his mother, with her petty notions, defiant determination, sympathetic impulses, and misleading Victorian helplessness.

Clarence Day could have been harsh toward his father and soft toward his mother, or he could have avoided being rancorous about the old man by being clownish. What he did, of course, was much better. Father, with his tantrums and prejudices and self-indulgences, is not even so much overtly satirized as, say, Squire Western. He is never cunningly paced toward a climax. He blows up and calms down, or holds himself in and explodes, or barks and bites, or barks and fails to bite. There is no pattern to his illogic, he has all the convincing changeability of the weather. . . .

However it once was, by the time Clarence Day came to describe these goings-on he had achieved a tranquility to match their tempestuousness. He no more emphasizes what is unpleasant than what is humorous, he no more condemns than he apologizes, he no more understates than he overstates. Father's rich crustiness, Mother's buzzing emptiness, the whole of Victorian family life, the whole of middle-class social life

must attract or repel by virtue of their own reality. Where Father always thrashed his arms about in anger, Clarence never even raises a finger in protest. He needn't have been an artist to be so dead pan about it all: if you can't see what's wrong with Father just by looking at Father, you'll never learn by harking to the indictments of Son.

Life with Mother is by no means so juicy a book as *Life with Father*—many of the episodes are so similar as to be monotonous—but the two books together have their value as social documents. Perhaps it is very serious-minded of me to insist that chronicles so full of entertainment have a sociological importance, but to me they are about the most casually terrible revelation of the intrenched bourgeois spirit that any historian could ask for. Behind the antics and the extravagances is as much bigotry and complacency and selfishness as any of our major novelists has ever scooped up; and however much of a problem grown-up Father may have been, we can't forget that Father and Mother were highly acceptable members of a correct society during two generations. Their treatment of servants, tradesmen, people beyond their world; their enmity to or ignorance of all liberal ideas are still interesting to observe. Clarence Day himself must have been a humane and gentle soul who never copied their tactics, but one is left wondering just how far he questioned the philosophy their tactics were built upon. One wonders even more in just what sense a lowbrow audience has enjoyed Father and Mother and sized them up. Certainly it must have recognized in these pages much that it had seen or heard about "at home." Have these books acted as a purge, leading people to the conclusion that they don't want Father around even when he is funny? Or have they been books to wallow in, because that's the way it was in our family, too, and Father's the image of dear old Uncle Walter, who left us $25,000 in his will?

> Louis Kronenberger, "Day at Home," in The Nation, *New York, Vol. 145, No. 8, August 21, 1937, p. 202.*

BROOKS ATKINSON   (essay date 1941)

[*As drama critic for* The New York Times *from 1925 to 1960, Atkinson was one of the most influential reviewers in America. In the following excerpt, he comments on the character of Father from the Howard Lindsay-Russel Crouse stage production of* Life with Father.]

[*Life with Father*] is the perfect American comedy with popular appeal. The joke on which it is based is the fundamental one of the "papa love mama?" comic strip. But there is nothing cheap or commonplace about *Life with Father*. Although the basic joke is an old one, father is a man worth respecting. He is logical, industrious, unselfish, fond of his sons, devoted to his wife, the backbone of America. He lacks humor and imagination, but he has in abundance the enduring virtues of the head of a family. As a matter of fact, he was the father of the late Clarence Day, who wrote sketches about him with humorous independence in the *New Yorker*. After Clarence Day's death, Howard Lindsay and Russel Crouse, who had previously collaborated on musical comedies, made a play out of the sketches and managed with great skill to preserve the good taste and mettlesome humor of the source material. Father is comic, but a real person. His anxiety over his wife's health is genuinely touching, which illustrates Bernard Shaw's thesis that no comedy is a good one unless it is also moving. . . . *Life with Father* has restored the era of good feelings to the stage. (p. xxi)

> *Brooks Atkinson, in an introduction to* Sixteen Famous American Plays, *edited by Bennett Cerf and Van H. Cartmell, Garden City Publishing Co., Inc., 1941, pp. xi-xxi.*

HOWARD LINDSAY AND RUSSEL CROUSE   (essay date 1944)

[*Lindsay was an American actor, dramatist, producer, and director. Collaborating with Russel Crouse, Lindsay wrote, produced, and directed numerous plays from 1934 until Crouse's death in 1966, making their's one of the longest and most successful collaborations in American theater. Crouse entered the theater in 1931 after a twenty-five-year career as a journalist. Life with Father, their 1939 play based on Day's stories, was among their most successful productions, and for five years of its eight-year run starred Lindsay and his wife Dorothy Stickney. Lindsay and Crouse's State of the Union was awarded the 1946 Pulitzer Prize for drama, and in 1959 the dramatists collaborated on the libretto for the popular Richard Rodgers-Oscar Hammerstein musical The Sound of Music. In the following excerpt, the playwrights attribute the success of their adaptation of Life with Father to the duplication of Day's universally recognizable characterizations.*]

As you read the . . . works of Clarence Day, Jr., you will find that many lines in our play are taken literally and bodily from the little white sheets he so painfully inscribed during his long illness. But that is not important. You will find the robust, if evanescent, spirit of a father and a mother and their family in those pages. That's why his stories gave him immortality. That's why *Life with Father,* the play, is a success. We put the same spirit on the stage. (p. ii)

Clarence Day wrote the story of his family out of his heart. It flowed through his crippled fingers with the ease and grace of truth. He may have been conscious of the fact that he was putting his own family on paper, but he could not have known that he was also capturing for a whole world a little something of everybody's family. That, however, is what he was doing. (pp. ii-iii)

The Days lived on Madison Avenue in New York, but these stories of recognition and identification have come to us from every Main Street in the nation.

That is not all. Clarence Day's canvas is not framed by the boundaries of one nation. Shortly after the play opened René Clair, the brilliant French motion-picture director, came to see it. After the play he asked to meet us. His first question was:

"Tell me, how and where did you know my father?"

We assured him we had never met his father. And then for an hour he regaled us with stories of Père Clair which Clarence Day might have written—which, indeed, he did write. . . . (p. iii)

We sat at dinner one night beside a Polish woman who demanded even before the soup was served a complete explanation of how we happened to know so much about Polish family life. Three beaming Chinese gentlemen appeared backstage one night to tell us that Father Day was also a part of that ancient sector of civilization. And only last week we had a mellow note from two Norwegian refugees who reported they had seen the play and had felt its nostalgia so deeply that they had gone quietly from the theatre to a bar where they had drunk far too many "Skols" to fond memories.

So it would seem that Clarence Day wrote not of just his father and his mother and his family—but of all fathers and mothers and of all families. To us there is great significance in that fact. For now there is in every heart the burning hope for world understanding from which alone can come a rich and everlasting peace. The universal appeal of the simple saga of Clarence Day's family seems to prove again that the springs of human action transcend the boundaries of geography and race. It is hopeful evidence that in some future day the human race can be a human family. (p. iv)

> *Howard Lindsay and Russel Crouse, in a foreword to* Life with Father *by Clarence Day, The Modern Library, 1944, pp. i-iv.*

NORRIS W. YATES   (essay date 1964)

[*Yates is an American critic and essayist with a special interest in humor and humorists. In the following excerpt, he discusses the personal nature of Day's essays and fiction.*]

In *This Simian World* . . . , the opening theme was that ours is a "simian civilization." Day's *persona* is a man who has not really made up his mind about human worth but is stirred to clarify his attitude by the pessimism of a friend. "I myself feel differently at different times about us human beings: sometimes I get pretty indignant when we are attacked . . . (for there is altogether too much abuse of us [humans] by spectator philosophers) and yet at other times I too feel like a spectator, an alien: but even then I had never felt so alien or despairing as Potter." Gravely the speaker examines the possibility that the ants and bees might have made better rulers of the earth; then he discusses the sort of overlords the cats, dogs, elephants, and other animals might have made. He reflects that man's origin as a simian is responsible for his gregariousness, energy, aimlessness, love of gabble, and above all, for his curiosity. Day (after the first few paragraphs the speaker and the author seem to become one and the same) has misgivings about this animal's ability to solve the problems raised by the excess of his inquisitiveness. "Each simian will wish to know more than his head can hold, let alone ever deal with. . . . It would stretch a god's skull to accomplish such an ambition, yet simians won't like to think it's beyond their powers."

Yet Day finally places himself with the optimists and, by implication, with the reformers rather than with the conservatives who carried on the tradition his Father stood for. We simians, Day says, lack appreciation of beauty, love, and creativeness, and yet, "This is no world for pessimists. An amoeba on the beach, blind and helpless, a mere bit of pulp,—that amoeba has grandsons today who read Kant and play symphonies. . . . This world, and our racial adventure, are magical still." Day's brand of Darwinism stresses the upward evolution of man rather than mere brutish conflict. There were essentially two ways of accepting Darwinism and of applying it to human society. Day is less like Herbert Spencer, Benjamin Kidd, William Graham Sumner, and H. L. Mencken, and more like Emerson, Whitman, and Sandburg. The former emphasized man's selfishness and the struggle for survival, and drew antidemocratic implications therefrom. The latter stressed man's evolutionary progress toward perfection and hence toward democracy. However, Day also resembled his fellow humorist in the reform movement, Finley Peter Dunne, in distrusting the slightest excess in either optimism or zeal among his Progressive colleagues. (pp. 231-32)

On controversial matters Day's view was consistently moderate, as in **"Sex, Religion and Business,"** where he compared free love as promoted in Mikhail Artsybashev's novel *Sanine* to asceticism as described in some poetry of India (probably by Tagore). Day stressed his own normal, middle position, saying, "I'm not starved at the moment; but I'm not getting all I want either." (At the time of writing this sentence, he was still single.) In one of his liveliest satires, **"The Revolt of Capital,"** Day knocks together the heads of both capital and labor, and advocates a compromise: labor should be represented on corporation boards of directors—"Both those who do the work and those who put in the money should rightfully be represented in these governing bodies." The proposal seemed radical at the time, and indeed, the principle that labor should help run the company has not yet been accepted in some quarters; however, labor's right at least to sit with management and with the public on arbitration boards was enacted into law with the creation of the Railroad Labor Board in 1920 and would gain yet further respectability under the New Deal. Citizen Day, like Walter Lippmann and others writing for the *New Republic,* was merely trying to find the most reasonable plan between the extremes of destructively competitive capitalism and stultifying control by government—searching, one might say, for a true norm in "normalcy."

Day's drawings deserve attention. They enliven *The Crow's Nest* and *After All* and furnish the main interest in *Thoughts Without Words* (into which, however, a few words crept, "Like flies, buzzing around each of the pictures") and in *Scenes From the Mesozoic.* . . . Though Day's cartoons have an over-all flavor wholly different from Thurber's, they share the same grotesque impishness and give the same impression of being childish scrawls instead of the little masterpieces of art they really are. Like Thurber too, Day sometimes drew the frequent spectator, bumbler, or henpecked husband with a face like his own—in his case, round and bespectacled; whereas Thurber's is lean and has a thin mustache. That there were limits to Day's

Day's illustration for "The Noblest Instrument," an essay on his early violin lessons.

"radicalism" is further suggested by the following jingle under a drawing in *Thoughts Without Words:*

> To Pacifists the proper course
> Of conduct is to sit on Force.
> For, in their dreams, Force can't resist
> The well-intentioned Pacifist.

FATHER AND SON

After the success of the play *Life With Father,* Harold Ross told Frank Sullivan that "if he had never printed anything except Clarence Day's stuff, it would have been enough." Thurber remarked that Ross probably didn't know that "the central theme of the play, the baptism of Father Day, was based on two stories that had appeared in *Harper's* and later in a book called *God and My Father."* The appearance of these two pieces in that magazine . . . offers an example of how a livelier sort of prose was penetrating the pages of the older quality monthlies. (pp. 233-34)

In many ways Father is an obtuse tyrant and bully. Why should the stage version of *Life With Father,* by Howard Lindsay and Russel Crouse—a version weakened in characterization and atmosphere and jazzed up with a teen-age romance—have had the longest continuous run of any play ever on Broadway? Brooks Atkinson has made some shrewd guesses; he was discussing the play, but his remarks also fit the subject of the present discussion, namely, the sketches of the Day family as first written by Clarence, Jr. Father, says Atkinson, has become "one of the representative American figures. . . . His family problems and his attitude toward them became the familiar experience of most fathers in the home" [see excerpt dated 1941]. Moreover, life was exciting in the Day household, even when nothing much was really happening. Yet Father's rages, in spite of their epic proportions, are often ineffectual; "Father is defeated in nearly every issue that is raised"—for instance, in his long but fruitless resistance to baptism.

One may add that the life of this family revealed as much affection as it did tension. The rages of Father Day clearly spring from what Clarence, Jr. calls a "thoroughly good-hearted, warm-blooded man." Father may have been arrogant and obtuse, but he was not mean or malicious.

Atkinson's phrase, "representative figure," needs fuller definition. The time-span covered by the sketches is roughly the last two decades of the nineteenth century, and Father is a personage around whom there hangs an air of quaintness because that figure—the stern masculine ruler of the family, the Victorian paterfamilias—had largely vanished from the American scene, along with the period environment of horsecars, coachmen in livery, massive furniture, ornate clocks, and china pug dogs in which all this human grandeur flourished. This environment was re-created by Day with affection and yet with criticism. . . . [He] tempered nostalgia with critical detachment. His discrimination is based on the difference between the baroque tastes of the upper-middle-class Victorians and the more restrained tastes of the somewhat less prosperous but more cultivated readers in his own generation for whom he was writing.

> Our hall had a solemnly dramatic atmosphere about it to all of us boys, because that was where the black hatrack stood, at the foot of our stairs, and it was usually there that we got spanked.

As this hatrack was the first thing that visitors saw when they entered, it had to be, and was, most impressive. It consisted of a long, black-walnut chest, low enough to sit down on, hidden away in which were all the family's galoshes and rubbers and two or three baseballs. Mounted on this chest was a mirror, seven feet high and five wide, in a fluted black-walnut frame, and this frame had a spreading carved canopy overhanging on top. At each side were some gleaming brass pegs, long and straight, on which hung Father's hats; and under these were two umbrella racks with deep brass pans underneath.

(pp. 234-35)

Dark red curtains hung in the windows. There was a thick red rug on the floor. The lower three or four feet of the walls was painted a deep chocolate color. Above that they were a dull bronze, with a Grecian pattern made of flat strips of felt molded on them in relief. Two gory battle scenes and a crayon portrait hung on these walls. The cheeriest thing in the room was the fireplace. It was a rather small one however, with a little brass grate in it, and the overhang of the mantelpiece dwarfed it.

The care with which each detail is recalled and presented betrays the nostalgia. The critical temper appears in the emphasis on the hatrack as an article of conspicuous consumption, the mention of the incongruous objects hidden within this fine black-walnut piece, the adjective applied to the battle scenes, and the ironic stress on the disproportionate smallness of the one cheerful fixture in the setting.

But what does Father himself represent? In his rocklike integrity no less than in his bewilderment at the contrariness of his family, Father is enough like Ade's husbands and Mencken's mask of the responsible citizen to qualify as a member of the elite imagined by these writers. However, the basic contrast is not between this elite and a mass of boobs, nor does the author identify himself with Father's type of man. Instead, Day views his Father with the detachment of a younger generation—but not of just any member of that generation; his *persona* is not one of Lardner's suburban yokels but a man of taste and reflection who has been freed by time from the visual grotesqueness and the social conservatism of the Victorian period but has not succumbed to the garishness and conservatism (or radicalism either) of the nineteen-thirties. There is little satire of his own time by Day in these sketches of his family, but possibly without realizing it, he personified a solid, rational citizen of his own generation, liberal in his social views and restrained in his aesthetic tastes, and not otherwise basically different from Father (with whom the son remained on affectionate terms until the older man's death, even though some of Clarence, Jr.'s sketches about Father Day had already been published and been read by their subject). Father's standards of independence, forthrightness, industry, thrift, and obedience were not so much abandoned as redefined, or remodeled, much as a man like Clarence, Jr. might have had a Victorian parlor remodeled to let in light and air without forfeiting the sense of sturdiness conveyed in that room. Father's ideals of integrity, chastity, and family loyalty were accepted without question. The only new ingredients added by his son were humor, detachment, and a more liberal view of the role of women.

Perhaps Clarence, Jr. went furthest from his Father in his interpretation of Mother's role in the household. In Lavinia Day's frequent triumphs over Father, one glimpses yet another phase of the war between men and women, a phase that is neither Ade's social climber corrupting her husband's simple tastes nor Thurber's female browbeating a pliant slave, but something in between that generates less tension and more laughter. Mother needs to assert herself, but she is no climber or cold-blooded schemer. The friction between Mother and Father over her carefree way with money shows all this. Their liberal son has little use for the Victorian subjection of women to the role of household serfs without money or property, and he suggests that his Mother's haphazard spending is the fault of her background—before her marriage ". . . she had never laid eyes on a ledger"—and from Father's habit of keeping the purse and paying all the bills himself, a habit quite customary at the time. . . . Day underscored his Mother's vague resistance to this legal and financial thralldom. She "seemed to have no great extravagances. But she loved pretty things," and because of the financial inexperience born of her economic dependence, she "was one of those persons for whom charge accounts were invented." Her own genuine confusion and Father's low boiling point usually frustrated his attempts to make her account for her erratic purchases, and eventually Mother absorbed enough of the New Woman's attitude from her younger friends to pry a regular monthly allowance out of Father—an enormous concession, for him. From this she even managed to save a little, secret nest egg, just to have some real money all her own. Concerning this inconsequential hoarding, her son says, "What she—and still less Father—didn't clearly realize was that she was half unconsciously groping toward a life of her own, in a random, haphazard, inactive way." To this end she could manipulate Father but had no wish to dominate him; indeed it was sometimes all she could do merely to offset his domination of her.

Day's stress on the ridiculous elements of the past, including Father's ineffectuality and Mother's "working" of him, does not lessen one's sense that Father Day was a fitting embodiment for the strong, solid values of his time and social group and that his cluttered but massive home was a fitting framework for these values. W. E. H. Lecky, British historian, wrote in 1896 of the middle class that it was "distinguished beyond all others for its political independence, its caution, its solid practical intelligence, its steady industry, its high moral average." Except for Father's "political independence," which may be estimated by his feeling that ". . . it was hard to see why God had made so many damned fools and democrats," Lecky's description fits Father like a driving glove.

When Clarence Day, Jr. wrote of the present, he often played the Little Man as philosopher and critic. When the economy went to smash in the early nineteen-thirties, Day turned to the past for his subject matter. In so doing he dropped his self-deprecatory role and, reversing the trend in American humor, assumed a firmer stance as a solid citizen of the present who upholds reason and taste. In this capacity he evoked a bygone atmosphere in which life was exciting but ordered, made challenging by duty but warm by love. In this environment he recreated, with amazingly few departures from literal fact, a father-type nearer to the self-made patriarchs of Ade's fables and to the more recent "Father Barber" of the radio perennial "One Man's Family" than to the other beleaguered husbands in the *New Yorker*. This essentially Victorian type was set off by a wife and mother who "got round" her husband only to the extent of making the father-image less formidable and more appealing. To the whole picture, Day added two elements in harmonious contrast: nostalgic respect for the middle-class Victorian atmosphere and values, and a cultivated, modern liberal *alter ego* suggesting how those values needed modification. (pp. 236-39)

> *Norris W. Yates, "Life with Clarence Day, Jr.," in his* The American Humorist: Conscience of the Twentieth Century, *Iowa State University Press, 1964, pp. 229-39.*

ADDITIONAL BIBLIOGRAPHY

Acheson, Dean. Introduction to *This Simian World*, by Clarence Day, pp. vii-ix. New York: Alfred A. Knopf, 1968.
> Calls *This Simian World* "satire of the purest Swiftian style, but gentler."

Adams, Franklin P. "All the Long-Lived Clarence Day." *The New York Times Book Review* (15 August 1948): 6.
> Review of *The Best of Clarence Day*, stating that in Day "America has a universal writer of great and largely unappreciated gifts."

Blair, Walter, and Hill, Hamlin. "Between World Wars." In their *America's Humor: From Poor Richard to Doonesbury*, pp. 388-459. New York: Oxford University Press, 1978.
> Discusses Day in a chapter outlining the early history of the *New Yorker* magazine.

Canby, Henry Seidel. "Who Was Who." In his *American Memoir*, pp. 300-14. Boston: Houghton Mifflin Co., 1947.
> Personal recollections of Day in a chapter discussing "the Americans I knew who seem to me now to have been in the midstream of the course of American literature." Canby characterizes Day as "that strange genius," "an unsparing realist with a kind heart."

Duffus, R. L. "A New Garland of Sketches and Verses by Clarence Day." *The New York Times Book Review* (23 August 1936): 5, 19.
> Review of *After All* in which Duffus examines Day's philosophy as expressed in his essays.

Knopf, Alfred A. "Publishing Clarence Day." *The Yale University Library Gazette* 55, No. 3 (January 1981): 101-15.
> Personal reminiscences by Day's longtime publisher.

Masson, Thomas L. "The Younger Set." In his *Our American Humorists*, revised edition, pp. 374-94. 1931. Reprint: Books for Libraries Press, 1966.
> Characterizes Day as a satirist of mature insight.

Paterson, Isabel. "A Fantastic, Irascible, and Lovable Father." *New York Herald Tribune Books* (4 August 1935): 1-2.
> Favorable review of *Life with Father*, including abridged selections from the book.

Poore, C. G. "Clarence Day's Forthright, Downright, Upright Father." *The New York Times Book Review* (4 August 1935): 2.
> Enthusiastically approbatory review of *Life with Father*, calling it a classic.

Saper, Edward. "When Words Are Not Enough." *New York Herald Tribune Books* (5 August 1928): 3.
> Finds in *Thoughts without Words* philosophy in which "humor healthily outweighs wit."

Watts, Richard, Jr. "Life with Mother" (1948). In *The Passionate Playgoer: A Personal Scrapbook*, edited by George Oppenheimer, pp. 572-74. New York: The Viking Press, 1958.
> Praises the Howard Lindsay-Russel Crouse stage production of *Life with Mother* as "every bit as delightful as its predecessor," *Life with Father*.

"This Simian World." *The Weekly Review* 3, No. 74 (13 October 1920): 306-07.
> Calls Day "an ingenious and thought-provoking satirist" on the strength of the essays in *This Simian World*.

William Henry Drummond

1854-1907

Irish-born Canadian poet.

Drummond was the author of extremely popular narrative verse written in the dialect of the French-Canadian inhabitants of rural Quebec, known as *habitants*. In such poems as "Leetle Bateese" and "The Curé of Calumette," Drummond attempted to reproduce the manner in which the *habitants* would tell their own stories to an English-speaking person. Although he did not intend to create caricatures of these people, the image of the *habitants* Drummond conveyed is nonetheless quaint and sentimental, and some critics consider his verse to be implicitly condescending to these French-Canadians. Nevertheless, other critics find that Drummond was sensitive to both the pathos and humor in the lives of his subjects, and believe that his poetry can still be appreciated by modern readers.

The son of an officer in the Royal Irish Constabulary and his wife, Drummond was born in Ireland and moved with his family to Canada in 1865. His father died soon after, leaving Drummond's mother to support their four children. Drummond attended private school in Montreal, but left at the age of fourteen to work as a telegraph operator on the Rivière des Praires in Quebec, where he first met the French-Canadian *habitants*. In 1876 he returned to school and ultimately received a degree in medicine from Bishop's College in 1884. Drummond maintained a country practice in two small Quebec towns for several years, living among the *habitants* and learning more about their life and customs. In 1895 he was appointed professor of medical jurisprudence at Bishop's College. For some time it had been Drummond's custom to entertain friends by reciting verses he had written about the *habitants,* and these friends persuaded Drummond to publish a volume of his poetry. When *The Habitant* was published in 1897 it became an immediate success. Drummond thereafter was much in demand for recitations of his poetry, and he published three more volumes during his lifetime. In 1905 Drummond became co-owner of a silver mine, which occupied most of his attention for the last years of his life. He died suddenly in 1907 of a cerebral hemmorrhage.

Drummond's poetry conveys his warm and sympathetic view of the *habitant* farmer and *voyageur,* or traveller. The title poem of *The Habitant,* for example, describes in a few verses the cycle of life of a French-Canadian farmer, a cycle which had been recurring for generations, while in "How Bateese Came Home," Drummond details his protagonist's experiences in the United States and his decision to return to the family farm, bringing back a new appreciation of the life he had left. Although many of his poems are humorous, Drummond also wrote on more serious subjects, especially those associated with his Roman Catholic faith. For example, the narrator of "The Curé of Calumette" describes with respect and admiration the tireless work of his parish priest, while in "The Last Portage" an old man nearing death dreams of his final journey. Some of Drummond's poems have been passed along orally and have become well known among people who have no knowledge of their origin. There exists in Canada to this day a popular image of the *habitant* farmer which is largely descended from Drummond's portrayal.

Although Drummond wrote a few poems in standard English and in Irish dialect, his fame rested on the verse written in the habitant dialect. The following lines are typical: "Mos' ev'ry day raf' it is pass on de rapide / De voyageurs singin' some ole chanson / 'Bout girl on de reever—too bad dey mus' leave her / But comin' back soon wit' beaucoup d'argent.'" Conscious that the poetry could be construed as mockery of the *habitants,* Drummond obtained an introduction to *The Habitant* written in French by Louis Frèchette, a prominent French-Canadian author who praised Drummond's work and emphasized that Drummond meant to celebrate the *habitants* rather than to make fun of them. Drummond himself wrote a preface emphasizing that point, stating: "I have not written the verses as examples of a dialect, or with any thought of ridicule. . . . I have endeavored to paint a few types, and in doing this, it has seemed to me that I could best attain the object in view by having my friends tell their own tales in their own way, as they would relate them to English-speaking auditors not conversant with the French tongue." Early critics praised Drummond's work, and few objected to his use of dialect. Nonetheless, the poetry eventually fell into obscurity, and when a selection of Drummond's poems was reprinted in 1960 as part of the New Canadian Library series, critics protested that the verse was sentimental and patronizing, perpetuating a stereotypical view of French-Canadians. Gerald Noonan has contended that the basis for interest in Drummond's poems when they were first published was an implicit condescension toward French-Canadians. Nevertheless, Noonan acknowledges that Drummond's intent was not to patronize the *habitants,* but to use their dialect as the most effective means of portraying their culture. According to R. E. Rashley, Drummond adopted the language of a certain group of common people in order to avoid the well-worn conventions of nineteenth-century poetry. The charge that the use of French-Canadian dialect is inherently condescending, Lee Briscoe Thompson has written, is purely political and merely reflects the attitudes of modern French-Canadians struggling for independence. Aesthetically, Thompson maintains, Drummond's poems remain a distinguished contribution to Canadian literature.

Drummond's use of dialect and first-person narrative eliminated an obtrusive authorial presence and allowed a close identification between the subjects of his poems and his readership. His work also introduced a previously neglected culture to English-speaking Canadians. Despite the controversy that surrounds his work, Drummond's poetry has become an important part of Canadian folk culture.

PRINCIPAL WORKS

The Habitant, and Other French-Canadian Poems   (poetry) 1897
Phil-o-rum's Canoe. Madeleine Vercheres.   (poetry)   1898
Johnnie Courteau, and Other Poems   (poetry)   1901
The Voyageur, and Other Poems   (poetry)   1905
The Great Flight   (poetry)   1908
The Poetical Works of William Henry Drummond   (poetry) 1912; also published as *Dr. W. H. Drummond's Complete Poems,* 1926

THE SPECTATOR   (essay date 1898)

[*In the following excerpt, the critic praises the dialect poetry of* The Habitant.]

[In *The Habitant*] Dr. Drummond has achieved the very difficult task of writing poetry, and real, if not great, poetry, in the broken French-English of the Canadian farmers. *The Habitants,* who live on the borders of the province of Quebec, or in parts where they come much in contact with their British fellow-citizens, have created a patois of their own which at first sight would seem quite impossible for the purposes of the poet. Dr. Drummond, however, has managed to move us to tears as well as laughter in this broken tongue. He has evidently a minute knowledge of, and keen sympathy with, the simple country folk of the Dominion, and he uses his knowledge and his sympathy to interpret for us the feelings and attitude towards life of the only white people on the North American continent who not only lead the life, but have the aspirations, of the true peasant,—men who do not want to go away and make their fortunes, and rise in life, and speculate in townlots, and buy shares and become rich, but who genuinely desire to live on a little farm by the river, exactly like their fathers before them, and also like their fathers, to be nothing but *Habitant* farmers. The following verses have a really miraculous power of painting the Canadian landscape of "woods, waters, wastes," and

of showing at the same time the spirit of the peasants of French origin who live among these scenes and love them so well:—

De place I get born, me, is up on de reever
   Near foot of de rapide dat's call Cheval Blanc
Beeg mountain behin' it, so high you can't climb it
   An' whole place she's mebbe two honder arpent.

De fader of me, he was habitant farmer,
   Ma gran' fader too, an' hees fader also,
Dey don't mak' no monee, but dat is n't fonny
   For it's not easy get ev'ryt'ing, you mus' know—

All de sam' dere is somet'ing dey got ev'ryboddy,
   Dat's plaintee good healt', wat de monee can't geev,
So I'm workin' away dere, an' happy for stay dere
   On farm by de reever, so long I was leev.

That is the mental attitude of a class, and a very large and interesting class, photographed in verse. But Dr. Drummond can do more than merely produce moral photographs. Here is his description of how, in the Canadian country, the spring comes with one precipitate bound, and how, "for one consummate hour" after the snow's retreat, the life of flowers and beasts and birds awakes with a rush as the Palace awakes in Tennyson's "Sleeping Beauty":—

O! dat was de place w'en do spring tam she's comin',
   W'en snow go away, an' de sky is all blue—
W'en ice lef' de water, an' sun is get hotter
   An' back on de medder is sing de gou-glou—

W'en small sheep is firs' comin' out on de pasture,
   Deir nice leetle tail stickin' up on deir back,
Dey ronne wit' deir moder, an' play wit' each oder
   An' jomp all de tam jus' de sam' dey was crack

An' ole cow also, she's glad winter is over,
   So she kick herse'f up, an start off on de race
Wit' de two-year-old heifer, dat's purty soon lef' her,
   W'y ev'rht'ing's crazee all over de place!

An' down on de reever de wil' duck is quackin'
   Along by de shore leetle san' piper ronne—
De bullfrog he's gr-rompin' an' doré is jompin'
   Dey all got deir own way for mak' it de fonne.

But spring's in beeg hurry, an' don't stay long wit' us
   An' firs't'ing we know, she go off till nex' year,
Den bee commence hummin', for summer is comin'
   An' purty soon corn's gettin' ripe on de ear.

Dat's very nice tam for wake up on de morning
   An' lissen de rossignol sing ev'ry place,
Feel sout' win' a-blowin' see clover a-growin'
   An' all de worl' laughin' itself on de face.

Any one who, when the winter is breaking in Switzerland, has seen the behaviour of the cows who have lived for six months in a dark stable and are suddenly turned out on to the village Alp, will appreciate Dr. Drummond's line:—

   W'y ev'ryt'ing's crazee all over de place!

We would gladly quote the whole of Dr. Drummond's pleasant poem did space allow. We can only say, however, that we have by no means picked out the plums, and that the verses not quoted are as good as those we have chosen. Though the rest of the volume contains some very interesting and very readable verse, the reviewer's obligation obliges us to say that there is nothing in it which comes up to the standard of **"The**

Habitant." The other poems cannot compare with it either in feeling or in poetic expression. Still, **"De Nice Leetle Cana-dienne"** is very charming, and there is a wonderful deal of interpretation as well as of charm in the poem called **"How Bateese Came Home."** Bateese is the *Habitant* farmer who goes to the States and becomes a smart Yankee, but in the end comes back and settles down on his father's old farm. Take the book as a whole, it is a most delightful one, and does exactly what Dr. Drummond evidently wants it to do,—*i.e.*, make us love the vigorous, wholesome, if rather reactionary, Canadian peasant. (p. 304)

> *"American Dialect Poems," in* The Spectator, *Vol. 80, No. 3635, February 26, 1898, pp. 303-04.*

THOMAS O'HAGAN (essay date 1903)

[*O'Hagan was a Canadian historian, poet, and critic whose works reflect his devotion to the Catholic Church. In the following excerpt, he discusses Drummond's portrayal of the French-Canadian* habitant *and evaluates several poems from* The Habitant *and* Johnnie Courteau.]

There is one quarter, one corner of Canada that has yielded rich and promising soil for the Canadian dialect poet—Quebec, the home of "Bateese," the French-Canadian *habitant*. Nova Scotia is differentiated but little from British Columbia, while the people of Manitoba are a fac-simile of the people of Ontario plus the wider vision and stronger ozone of the Western prairie. But Quebec stands alone—unique, the heir in its traditions, life, character, and customs of France under the *Old Monarchy* untouched by the torch, tremor or trumpet of the French Revolution, and maintaining its supremacy of faith and virtue amid every vicissitude of political life and fortune.

Naturally, French-Canadian life, fashioned for nearly three centuries under such conditions and with such environment, has produced character individual, indigenous, picturesque. Nay more, the descendants of the Norman Touraine and Guienne peasants who settled early in the seventeenth century in the land discovered and explored by their fellow-countrymen Cartier and Champlain, living for nearly two centuries in seigniorial relationship to their manorial masters, holding to the teachings of the church, to the word of the *curé*, with the fidelity of primitive Christians, could not but evolve a type of character not only unique but highly and truly ideal.

It is with this type of character of the French-Canadian *habitant* that Dr. William Henry Drummond, of Montreal, deals in his two admirable volumes of dialect poetry—*The Habitant* and *Johnnie Courteau*. It is not too much to say that Dr. Drummond has written himself immortally into these French-Canadian poems.

It requires but little talent to set the foibles of a people to metre, but it calls for genius in touch with the lowly and divine to gather up the spiritual facts in a people's lives and give these facts such artistic setting that both people and poems will live. This certainly Dr. Drummond has done.

The first French-Canadian dialect poem from the pen of Dr. Drummond to give promise of and shadow forth the genius of its author in this new and chosen field, was **"The Wreck of the Julie Plante: A Legend of Lac St. Pierre."** The tourist will remember the expansion of the St. Lawrence below Montreal known as Lake St. Peter. This is the scene of this ballad-legend so cleverly told in French-Canadian dialect verse by Dr. Drummond. A friend of mine once told me that he heard the Amer-

ican humorist Bill Nye recite it, down in Bermuda. It has gained favor everywhere—in the lumber shanties of Wisconsin and upper Michigan, in the drawing-rooms of New Orleans, among the cowboys out on the Western plains, and among exclusive clubmen of our metropolitan cities. It will be noticed that much of the humor in the poem is derived from pitching the story in such a high dramatic key. Never did ocean liner go down to her grave amid such foot-lights of tragedy as sank the wood scow "Julie Plante" in the historic waters of Lac St. Pierre. (pp. 523-24)

But to my mind the poem which exhibits Dr. Drummond's dialect gift at its best is neither **"The Wreck of the Julie Plante," "De Papineau Gun,"** nor **"How Bateese Came Home."** It is **"Le Vieux Temps,"** which as a piece of French-Canadian characterization gives a truer, deeper, juster, and more sympathetic insight into the very spirit and life of the French-Canadian *habitant* than anything that has yet been done in either verse or fiction. The great value attaching to Dr. Drummond's French-Canadian characterization is that it is not overdrawn. Truth is the basis of all his idealization. This gifted writer has gone among the peasantry of Quebec with an honest, open, and sympathetic mind ready to find the fragrance of virtue wherever the flower grew. He sees all things with a spiritual, not an intellectual eye, and so his judgments have about them something of the accuracy of heaven. We can never justly judge our fellow-man while our point of view remains earthy of the earth.

Next to **"Le Vieux Temps"** I should be inclined to rank **"Pelang"** as Dr. Drummond's finest French-Canadian dialect poem. I think this is the highest poetic conception to be found in either of his volumes, and is worked out most artistically. It is full of delicate imagery, as where he describes the night before the great snow-storm has enveloped Marie's lover on the *Grande Montagne:*

> I open de door, an' pass outside
> For see mese'f how de night is look.
> An' de star is commence for go couché,
> De mountain also is put on his tuque.

And surely, too, there is something touching and tender in these lines:

> An' I t'ink I hear de leetle bird say,
> "Wait till de snow is geev up its dead;
> Wait till I go, an' de robin come,
> An' den you will fin' hees cole, cole bed."

Dr. Drummond has a great command of pathos. Nor is it a maudlin pathos. He touches the minor chord of life with great surety and deftness and passes from humor to pathos, and from pathos to humor, with that ease of transition which is the especial gift of the Celt. (pp. 526-27)

It is said that art is born of the intellect and humor of the spirit. Humor, too, is generally unconscious, and consists frequently in a situation. Dr. Drummond shows a fine sense of humor in his French-Canadian dialect work. It is not coarse and vulgar buffoonry that he depicts when he gives us such poems as **"How Bateese Came Home," "De Stove Pipe Hole," "M'sieu Smit,'"** and **"The National Policy."**

"How Bateese Came Home" is certainly true to the life, as any one knows who has watched the evolution of a young French-Canadian *habitant* from the time he has left his father's farm on the banks of the St. Maurice to the time when he has reached the full stature of his ambition after a sojourn of some five years under New England skies.

Whether Dr. Drummond has reached a higher level of poetic work in his second volume *Johnnie Courteau* than in his first essay of French-Canadian characterization in *The Habitant*, may be questioned by critics. When the first volume appeared the field of French-Canadian characterization was comparatively new. It is true something had been done in fiction by Sir Gilbert Parker and E. W. Thomson, but it remained for the poet to give concrete setting to the inner life, character, hopes, joys, as well as daily dreams and visions, of the French-Canadian habitant.

There is one poem in Dr. Drummond's second volume, *Johnnie Courteau,* which to me at least is worthy of disputing for the first place among the productions of this gifted writer. It is true that the poem is largely a piece of individual characterization. Unlike **"Le Vieux Temps,"** which as a story touches French-Canadian life on many sides. **"The Curé of Calumette"** is the delineation of a single character—the good curé "Fader O'Hara" of Calumette. (pp. 527-28)

French-Canadian life and character are full of beauty and truth. It has blossom and fruit of rare fragrance and flavor. Its covenant and kinship are closer to heaven than earth. Dr. Drummond has discovered both blossom and fruit. Nor has he failed to build into his work the larger life of the French-Canadian *habitant*—his loyalty to his church, his simplicity of faith, his devotion, his goodness, and his love. (p. 531)

Thomas O'Hagan, "A Canadian Dialect Poet," in The Catholic World, *Vol. 77, No. 460, July, 1903, pp. 522-31.*

THE CANADIAN MAGAZINE OF POLITICS, SCIENCE, ART AND LITERATURE   (essay date 1905)

[*In the following excerpt the critic reviews* The Voyageur.]

Since the publication of *The Habitant*, the verse of Dr. William Henry Drummond has held a peculiar place in the estimation of Canadian readers. He has accomplished what is a rare achievement—has taken his public so completely into his confidence and has made us feel so much at home with "Leetle Bateese" and his people, that it is impossible to do more or less than be on the friendliest terms with all of them. In homely phrase and naive dialect he has interpreted the Habitant life so humanly that the critic can only smile back at these simple, gay, industrious folk and forget about problem novels and magazine articles concerning graft and guile as he feels the

> Win' that blows
> Over God's own boulevard.

The most pleasing feature about his work is that Dr. Drummond is not "writing himself out." His verse is fresh and vigorous with a deepening note in such poems as **"The Last Portage"** and **"Dieu-donné."**

The nearness to Nature as shown in the love of "reever" and lake appeals to every Canadian who has known his country's wealth of stream and forest. Who that has spent days in the great northern country where the lakes of cold steel-blue mirror

a cloudless sky can fail to understand the old fisherman's joy in **"Lac Souci":**

> Happy to leev an' happy to die dere—
> But Heaven itself won't satisfy me
> Till I fin' leetle hole off on de sky dere
> W'ere I can be lookin' on Lac Souci!

The first poem, **"The Voyageur,"** from which the volume takes its title, is buoyant and stirring as the Autumn breeze from a hill of pines and one almost hears the clink of glasses in the verse:

> I'm proud of de sam' blood in my vein,
> I'm a son of de Nort Win' wance again—
> So we'll fill her up till de bottle drain
> An' drink to de Voyageur.

There is red-veined humanity in the poems of the student of Habitant ways, and the reader is better and brighter for a glimpse of this simple, healthful life.

A review of "The Voyageur," in The Canadian Magazine of Politics, Science, Art and Literature, *Vol. XXV, May-October, 1905, p. 374.*

A. WYLIE MAHON   (essay date 1907)

[*In the following excerpt, Mahon discusses Drummond's use of dialect, his humor, and the spiritual quality of his later poetry.*]

Although Dr. Drummond did not publish his first volume of habitant verse until well on in life, few names in Canadian literature are so widely known to-day, and so well-beloved, as that of the author of *The Habitant, Johnnie Courteau,* and *The Voyageur.* Dr. Louis Fréchette, in an introductory note to *The Habitant,* calls Dr. Drummond "the pathfinder of a new land of song," a beautiful expression which Longfellow a good many years ago made use of with reference to Dr. Fréchette himself.

Dr. Drummond's poetry, like all Gaul in Caesar's immortal Commentaries, may be divided into three parts, first, the English poems, which are few in number but fine in flavour; and secondly, the Irish dialect poems, which are still fewer in number, but richly racy of the "ould sod," of that

> Most disthressful country that iver yet was seen,

where Drummond first saw the light in 1854; and thirdly, the French-Canadian dialect pieces, which constitute the principal and most characteristic part of the work of Canada's most popular poet.

Dialects have been cultivated in literature so assiduously of late that the most of us have longed at times for something English, something more easily understood, something more in accord with the grammatical genius of the language which we call our mother tongue, where the words have a more comfortable look when they have their heads on and their tails not off. Charles Sumner, the distinguished American statesman, when he tried to read James Russell Lowell's *Biglow Papers,* said: "It is too bad that they were not written in English." Many have felt in this way about some of the dialect literature of to-day.

But we must not forget that there are dialects *and* dialects. Some are classical. They have been made so by the character of the people who have spoken them, and by the genius of the writers who have employed them. The Scottish dialect, for example, is wondrously expressive because of the keenness of the Scottish intellect, and the richness of the Scottish character, and the genius of such writers as Burns and Scott and George Macdonald.

Still some critics have held that Burns' English poems are superior to his dialect pieces, and that there was no good reason why he should have made so much of his work difficult to understand and difficult to read, by putting it in the form of a somewhat barbarous brogue. There is no man with lowland Scotch blood in his veins who does not fiércely resent such criticism as this, who does not feel a profound sense of pity, mingled freely with contempt, for the poor body who holds such views. Criticism of this kind is both heresy of doctrine and heresy of heart.

Dr. Drummond's French-Canadian dialect poems have certain rich and charming qualities about them which have given them a popularity unprecedented in the history of Canadian poetry. They are not quite like anything ever produced before. Sir Gilbert Parker and Dr. Henry Van Dyke have made some use of the French-Canadian dialect in their stories, but they have done so with prentice hands. Dr. Drummond lived so long amongst the French, and entered so intimately into their lives and ways of thinking, that the language they spoke when trying to speak English became as familiar to him as his mother tongue. In the most sympathetic way he entered into the gay and simple life of the French-Canadian peasantry. He succeeded in a marvellous degree in converting himself into an habitant.

As an illustration of this sympathetic interpretation of French-Canadian life, I need refer only to that beautiful poem, **"The Curé of Calumette."** The profound reverence of the habitant for the parish priest, who is monarch of all he surveys, whose right there is none to dispute, who is medical and legal adviser as well as spiritual, is brought out very beautifully in this poem:

> I dunno if he need our prayer, but we geev' it heem
>   jus' de sam',
> For w'en a man's doin' hees duty lak de Curé do all de
>   tam,
> Never min' all de t'ing may happen, no matter he's
>   riche or poor,
> Le bon Dieu was up on de heaven, will look out for dat
>   man I'm sure.
> I'm only poor habitant farmer, an' mebby know not'ing
>   at all,
> But dere's wan t'ing I'm alway wishin', an' dat's w'en
>   I get de call
> For travel de far-away journey ev'ry wan on de worl'
>   mus' go,
> He'll be wit' me de leetle Curé 'fore I'm leffin dis
>   place below.

In many cases those who have gone amongst the simple farmers of Quebec have exercised their gifts in caricaturing what they have seen and heard, in making laughable pictures of ignorant priests and superstitious people; but there is nothing of this in Dr. Drummond's books. He lived amongst the French-Canadians till he had learned to love them, till he was able to interpret their life aright, till he was able to put himself in their place and look upon life as they do.

These dialect poems contain a delicate sense of humour which is most delightful. There is nothing whimsically extravagant about them, nothing to make any one laugh boisterously, nothing of Mark Twain's preposterous confusion of sense and non-

sense, and yet there is a flavour of humour about these short and simple annals of the poor which is charming. Dr. Drummond's English poems have no trace of this saving grace of literature. This leads us to wonder if the humour consists in the dialect, in the oddities of grammatical construction and expression. An American critic in deprecating the books written in the Scottish dialect says: "I wonder what would be thought of books like Wee McGreegor, and all the rest of the books of that kind, if they were translated into ordinary English." He thinks that they would lose all their humour and become flat, stale, and unprofitable.

Although Drummond's dialect enhances in many cases, and perhaps creates in some the happy sense of amusement which we get from the poems, we cannot fail to see that the humour nearly always goes deeper than the dialect. In **"The Habitant"** there is a good illustration of this kind. An evening in the kitchen is pictured in a most graphic and amusing way. We see the old man smoking his pipe in the corner, and the old woman sewing by the big stove her father had given her when she got married a long time ago. The cat is playing with the pup, and the old dog is snoring, and the big stove is roaring:

> Philomene—dat's de oldes'—is sit on de winder
>   An' kip jus' so quiet lak wan leetle mouse,
> She say de more finer moon never was shiner—
>   Very fonny, for moon isn't dat side de house.
>
> But purty soon den, we hear foot on de outside,
>   An' some one is place it hees han' on de latch,
> Dat's Isidore Goulay, las' fall on de Brulé
>   He's tak' it firs' prize on de gran' ploughin' match.
>
> Ha! ha! Philomene—dat was smart trick you play us;
>   Come help de young feller tak' snow from
> hees neck,
> Dere's not'ing for hinder you come off de winder
>   W'en moon you was look for is come, I
> expec'.

A scene like this would be humorous if expressed in any language. The humour goes deeper than the dialect. Sometimes Drummond's humour consists in making the habitant say amusing things all unconsciously, with the simplicity of a child, and I think this is the quality which predominates. (pp. 57-8)

Dr. Drummond's poetry is not all in a gay and humorous strain. In some of his later poems there is a spiritual note which is lacking in much of his earlier work. In **"The Last Portage,"** the old man who is nearing the end of life dreams that he is starting on his last journey. It is a dark night and the way is rough, and his heart is fearful; but there comes to him the sweet voice of his dear boy long dead to comfort him. Under the inspiration of the child's presence he can say:

> An' now no more for de road I care,
> An' slippery log lyin' ev'rywhere—
> De swamp on de valley, de mountain too,
> But climb it jus' as I use to do—
> Don't stop on de road, for I need no res'
> So long as I see de leetle w'ite dress.
>
> An' I foller it on, an' wance in a w'ile
> He turn again wit' de baby smile
> An' say, Dear Fader, I'm here you see,
> We're bote togeder, jus' you and me—
> Very dark to you, but to me it's light,
> De road we travel so far to-night.

All literature that helps us to be better citizens, better men and women, has in it a spiritual note which awakens earnest thought, and leads us to think sometimes of the last portage and what lies beyond. Dr. Drummond's poetry is not altogether lacking in this spiritual quality. As Dr. O'Hagan says: "It requires but little talent to set the foibles of a people to metre, but it calls for genius in touch with the lowly and the divine to gather up the spiritual facts in a people's lives, and give these facts such artistic setting that both people and poems will live forever." This Dr. Drummond has done. He has written himself immortally into these dialect poems, and has enabled Canadians of a different nationality and a different faith to understand more sympathetically the people of rural Quebec. (p. 59)

> A. Wylie Mahon, "The Poet of the Habitant," in
> The Canadian Magazine of Politics, Science, Art and
> Literature, Vol. XXIX, May-October, 1907, pp. 56-60.

THE EDINBURGH REVIEW (essay date 1909)

[*In the following excerpt, the critic discusses Drummond's patriotism, love for children, depiction of nature, and use of dialect.*]

The foundations of Drummond's nature studies were laid in the rambles of his boyhood; it was in those early days that his mind took the bent which made a nature poet, and more—a poet of human nature. Here he excels in portraiture, for his poems are all concrete productions and are never without human interest, and his sentiment always rings true. The metre of his verse is at times irregular and faulty, but a false or inharmonious note in the thought or feeling may be sought for in vain. Drummond is essentially truthful, and yet to a certain extent he idealises his habitant—he makes heroes of them all! History does not narrate the state of society which does not contain the coarse and vulgar, but Drummond was able to depict vulgar types without vulgarity, and his humour contains nothing of the grotesque. Sensitive to the simple life of the poor—their toil, their cares, their joys and loves—he pictures that labour lightened by love, the labour with which he is first of all occupied.

He also draws vivid yet delicate and truthful sketches of inanimate nature. The impression on the mind left from the study of English foliage, massed thickly before the low brooding, softly vaporous clouds of the island landscape, is that of imposing dignity, and the fine silhouette of spruce and balsam sharply etched against the brilliantly coloured background of Canadian sky seems somehow, by contrast, thin, cold, undeveloped. But again, where the river course is overhung with the thickly growing graceful birch and a luxuriant elm and maple growth, festooned and linked together with the wild Virginia creeper and clematis, the Canadian scene is strangely tropical. At the end of a toilsome day in canoe and over portages—'An' only 't'ing decen' you do all day is carry me on partage,' complains Phil-o-Rum's old canoe—the silent half-breeds quickly pitch the tents and make up beds of fragrant boughs before a cone of blazing logs, and, listening to the lonesome call of the loon and the thousand mysterious voices which speak at night in the wilderness, we softly sink to sleep. Such are the recollections which Drummond's verse conjures up for the hunter, and, as is to be expected, his volumes form a part of every camp outfit throughout Canada and the United States.

Neither will anyone forget Drummond's descriptions who has observed the low, long, many-gabled, broad-porched habitations scattered along the banks of the St. Lawrence which are characteristic of the dwellings throughout the Province of Quebec, housing families the old-fashioned numbers of which might well awaken the envy of their ancient fatherland. Could but France lay claim to-day to these large families!

> W'at's use de million acre, w'at's use de belle rivière,
>   Ant'ing lak dat if we don't have somebody leevin'
>   dere?
> W'at's make de worl' look out for us, an' kip de nation
>   free,
> Unless we're raisin' all de tam some fine large familee?

The character and suggestiveness of Drummond's work places it on a high level, and the form of dialect which he has made his own is admirably calculated to express his thought, and is as fascinating as original. His characters tell their own story, and tell it in the language to which they would resort in talking to an Englishman ignorant of French. This particular use of dialect, the least artificial of any form of literary expression, is typical of the man, and in all his verse he shows himself a modern in his use of plain diction. In a word, simplicity of form and strength of feeling are the chief characteristics of his style, and in them are contained his charm and his power. The simply descriptive emotional narrative evokes images pleasant to dwell upon; it always tells a story—a story at once pathetic and humorous. (pp. 481-82)

Patriotic, imperialistic, Drummond is, yet quite free from the bitter prejudice sometimes mistaken for patriotism, and he is far from the view-point of a certain Englishman who protests that, through patriotic motives, he travels only in countries which are under the British flag. In **"Two Hundred Years Ago"** it is not the Canadian, but a man with universal sympathy for all brave endeavour and fruitful accomplishment who points out to the neighbouring nation that which they owe to the French flag:

> So, ma frien', de Yankee man, he mus' try an'
>   understan'
> W'en he holler for dat flag de Star an' Stripe,
> If he's leetle win' still lef', an' no danger hurt hisself,
>   Den he better geev' anoder cheer, ba cripe!
> For de flag of la belle France, dat show de way across
>   From Louisburg to Florida and back;
> So raise it ev'ryw'ere, lak' de ole tam voyageurs,
> W'en you hear of de la Salle an' Cadillac—Hooraw!
>   For de flag of de la Salle an' Cadillac.

"The Voyageur" begins with a piece written in praise of the heroic *coureur de bois*, the pioneer of civilization. The ingenuity of the author and the ingenuousness of the hero in **"Pro Patria"** make it one of the most laughable among his pieces for recitation. In **"How Bateese Came Home Again,"** another popular favourite, an ambitious youth travels across the border in the hope of bettering his condition, but, made wiser by experience, John B. Waterhole disappears for ever and Bateese Trudeau returns to his former way of life, realising that higher pay does not necessarily signify more substantial gain. **"Ma Leetle Cabane"** contains the same wholesome lesson. (pp. 485-86)

The exceeding love Drummond bore little children also finds expression in his verse, and **"The Last Portage"** was written in commemoration of a young son from whose loss he never fully recovered:

> De night is dark and de portage dim,
>   Got plaintee o' log lyin' ev'ryw'ere,
> Black bush aroun' on de right an' lef',

A step from de road an' you los' yourse'f,
De moon and de star above is gone,
Yet somet'ing tell me I mus' go on.

An' off in front of me as I go,
Light as a dreef of de fallin' snow—
Who is dat leetle boy dancin' dere,
Can see hees w'ite dress an' curly hair,
An' almos' touch heem, so near to me
In an' out dere among de tree?

Nor is it altogether surprising that with his Celtic nature the poet had a vein of superstition, and did not disbelieve in occult influences. When his boy was dying, though absent, he declared he distinctly heard his voice calling him.

In *The Great Fight,* Drummond's posthumous work, **"The Calcite Vein," "The Boy from Calabogie,"** and **"Marriage,"** are the natural developement of his mining experiences, but, like the previous volumes, it is chiefly devoted to the habitant. The piece which gives the book its name has the strong religious sentiment of the habitant for its ruling purpose. A kiss given his pretty young wife is overlooked, but a derogatory word directed against his patron saint—and the "Great Fight" ensues. (p. 487)

Drummond has made the habitant better known to thousands of his fellow-citizens; he has revealed him to many in England itself. His verse touches upon universal experience, and appeals to the universal heart; he possesses the power, not only to bring forth a smile or a sigh, but to make us wiser and better men. To understand is to sympathise, and so he helps us to a better comprehension of the simple, gay, laborious, and religious character of one of the most lovable types which the Empire contains. (p. 488)

> *"Two Canadian Poets: Fréchette and Drummond,"*
> in The Edinburgh Review, *Vol. CCIX, No. CDXXVIII,*
> *April, 1909, pp. 474-99.*

HORATIO HART   (essay date 1912)

[*In the following excerpt, Hart reviews Drummond's collected works and comments on his portrayal of the French-Canadian habitant.*]

[*The Poetical Works of William Henry Drummond*] is a delightful book, even if it is not without its defects as a representation of the poet's genius. One could wish that some friend with the requisite critical judgment had exercised a discriminating supervision over the making of the volume, and had been given the right to exclude such poems as added nothing to its weight and interest. Dr. Drummond had a single vein. But like so many other poets of a *genre,* he was ambitious to develop his gift in other directions. Hence the very ordinary Irish dialect poems, and the quite conventional pieces in literary English, which should have been ruthlessly sacrificed, even had they been very much better than they are, if only for the sake of unity. Drummond is one thing, and one thing only: the interpreter of the life and character of the French Canadian people in a dialect which, just because it is crude and composite, the result of a perpetual creative effort, becomes an admirable vehicle for the expression of primitive sentiments and emotions. For the rest, Dr. Drummond was merely a very mediocre provincial poet whose thin celebrations of the Empire and of Canadian nationality strike a false and artificial note in a book so rich in the qualities of universality.

Even in his own field, however, he did not by any means invariably attain the highest level he was capable of reaching. He was not proof against the temptation to make a merely journalistic use of his gift and of his medium; and many of his verses in the French-Canadian dialect are nothing more than an attempt to put his comments on contemporary events in a piquant dress. If he had had the idea of creating a French-Canadian Mr. Dooley, he might have made his fortune from the newspapers; or if he had had the talent and perspicacity to conceive a series of French-Canadian *Bigelow Papers,* he might have left an exceedingly valuable political and historical document. As it is, his verses which contain the germs of such ideas are too trivial and desultory to be worthy of serious consideration, though it is but fair to add that there are few that do not contain at least some traces of his best manner in touches of tender pathos, and quaint humour, in brief, true, and effective traits of characterisation, and in that mingling of an unfailing sense of the picturesque with a kindly and affectionate understanding of the life and the people portrayed, which is all his own.

It is, however, only when, going straight to the heart of these people in what is the very substance of their lives—their joys and sorrows, their pastimes and vocations—whether as farmers along the shores of the broad St. Lawrence, as lumbermen working their rafts down the swift current of many a tributary stream, or as dwellers in the fastnesses of the great forests, that he becomes inspired with a real poem. Such a poem, one that remains among the very best, as it was one of the first, before its author began, to a certain extent, to manufacture subjects, is **"The Habitant."** To appreciate thoroughly this little masterpiece, which, in a few simple stanzas and through the idyllic method, sums up the cycle of the farmer's life as it has revolved through generation after generation for more than two centuries in a land of brief, ardent, laborious, summers, and long secluded patient winters, one must have seen for himself something of this life, and of the conditions climatic, economic, and moral, under which it is lived. Organised by the French seigneurs of the seventeenth and eighteenth centuries on a strictly feudal basis, it retains to-day marked traces of medieval structure and sentiment. Its essence is the element of piety and respect for the past which, strengthened by the clerical domination, scarcely undermined as yet by modern influences, causes these people, more perhaps than any other, to cling fast to their customs and traditions:

> De fader of me, he was habitant farmer,
> Ma gran'fader, too, an' hees fader also—

In these lines one gets close to the real religion of the people which makes them go on doing what their ancestors have always done before them, regardless of whether or not it is the best way. Thus, even to-day, they go on building their fences of wood, though wood is now comparatively scarce, while stones litter their fields or are built up in secular cairns in the midst of them. And akin to this traditionalism of the people, this regionalism, as we call it to-day, this sense of being rooted in the soil, and of growing there as a race, is a quality of gentle resignation—of contentedness rather, we might better call it, since there is little consciousness of any effort connected with it. The *habitant* is calm, quiet, and equable, taking life as he finds it without serious complaining and, indeed, with a good deal of blithe buoyancy, of simple spontaneous pleasure in the few unexciting incidents of his social life. Vain indulgences are frowned upon by the clergy—there is little or no dancing—and the family is itself the centre of rest and recreation, as it is of work. To "veiller," as they call it—that is, to visit from house to house and to sit in a large circle of men and women in the dimly lighted kitchen at night—this is the principal amusement, the only excuse for conviviality, when the bottle of "whiskey blanc" or Holland gin is brought from the cupboard and dispensed to the guests.

And tobacco is passed around, too, *tabac* (pronounced "tawbawc") *canayen* which, grown by every farmer for his own consumption and cured over the cowstalls in the *bâtisse,* will never be forgotten by any one who has ever tried to smoke it. Such tobacco gives the point to a story told in verse farther on in the book—a story that reads like a French-Canadian version of a legend once poetised by Rossetti in a Dutch setting. The Devil comes to get Louis Desjardins, who treats him to a smoke:

> Wan pipe is all I want for me—
>   We'll finish our smoke downstair',
> De devil say, an' it was enough,
> For w'en he tak' de very first puff
> He holler out, "Maudit, w'at stuff!
>   Fresh air! fresh air! fresh air!!!"

And the upshot was that as long as Louis kept on smoking, the devil could not get near him, and, pipe in mouth, he remains safe till this day.

Glimpses of this interior life are contained in **"The Habitant,"** which thus becomes, though on a slighter scale, the French-Canadian equivalent of such poems as "Snowbound" and "The Cotter's Saturday Night." Here, too, enters that courting element, so important a feature of all popular poetry. Love-making is carried on largely *coram publico.* Otherwise it presents few novel or unfamiliar features, and of course, as in all rustic communities where the women are heavily burdened with domestic work and childbearing, love seems like a cruel lure of nature to lead the young girl almost without transition into haggard middle age. Still the process is accompanied here with less seeming cynicism than in many places elsewhere, and there is much truth in those scenes of domestic sentiment pictured by Dr. Drummond where a faithful and active affection survives the passionate explosions of youth.

The brevity of youth in this Canadian land has its symbol and correspondence in the pathetic brevity of the spring under northern latitudes. The coming of spring, the breaking up of the long death of the winter, is the recurrent theme of all these poems, the point where they best attain rapture and ecstasy and where the poet accordingly reaches his highest poetic level:

> Oh! dat was de place w'en de spring tam she's
>   comin',
> W'en snow go away, an' de sky is all blue—
> W'en ice lef' de water, an' sun is get hotter,
>   An' back on de medder is sing de gouglou—
>
> W'en small sheep is firs' comin' out on de
>   pasture,
>   Deir nice leetle tail stickin' up on deir back,
> Dey ronne wit' deir moder, an' play wit' each
>   oder,
>   An' jomp all de tam jus' de sam' dey was
>   crack—
>
> An' ole cow also, she's glad winter is over,
>   So she kick herse'f up, an' start off on de
>   race
> Wit' de two-year-ole heifer, dat's pretty soon
>   lef' her,
> W'y ev'ryt'ing's crazee all over de place!

> An' down on de reever de wil' duck is quackin',
>   Along by de shore leetle san' piper ronne—
> De bullfrog he's gr-rompin' an' doré is
>   jompin',
>   Dey all got dier own way for mak' it de
>   fonne.

There is actually something Chaucerian in the simple joyousness (as well as occasionally in the language) of these animal pictures. But, as the poet continues:

> But spring's in beeg hurry, an' don't stay long
>   wit' us.
> An firs' t'ing we know, she go off till nex'
>   year,
> Den bee commence hummin', for summer is
>   comin',
> An' purty soon corn's gettin' ripe on de ear.

And summer is the season of hard work, how hard only he can know who has seen the *habitant* farmer rushing to get through in two or three months what the New England farmer has four or five in which to accomplish it. The season is one long race. "For," as Drummond writes in another poem:

> For de mos' fine summer season don't las' too
>   long, an' we know it,
>   So we're workin' ev'rybody, w'ile de sun is
>   warm and clear,
> Dat's de tam for plant de barley, an' de injun
>   corn we sow it,
>   W'en de leaf upon de maple's jus' de size
>   of squirrel's ear.

> *   *   *   *   *

> Yass, de farmer's offen worry, an' it sometam
>   mak heem snappy,
>   For no sooner wan job's finish, dan he got
>   two t'ousand more.

So, although Drummond makes his *habitant* farmer welcome the summer and glory in it, we suspect that most of these farmers themselves are rather glad when it is over and they can take life more easily by their kitchen fires.

Such, in its broad outlines, is the life that Drummond pictures in his poems. He embroiders his presentation with a thousand little details, all of them suggestive and all of them true, so far as one can judge who has seen the *habitants* only in towns, villages, and the farming sections. The poet has seen them everywhere, and that is what makes the value of his work as a social document. The book which has its historical and legendary background and its dramatic incidents, like that of the Rebellion of 1837, in **"The Papineau Gun"** is really an epic of the French-Canadian people, told in ballad and lyric. (pp. 323-25)

Horatio Hart, in a review of "The Poetical Works of William Henry Drummond," in The Bookman, *New York, Vol. XXXVI, November, 1912, pp. 322-25.*

E. K. BROWN (essay date 1944)

[*Brown was a Canadian critic and educator. Chief among his works is the critical survey* On Canadian Poetry, *in which Brown traced the development of Canadian poetry from its pre-confederation era to the notable achievments of its three major figures, Archibald Lampman, Duncan Campbell Scott, and E. J. Pratt. In the following excerpt from that work, Brown examines the*

Drummond . . . came to know the intimate life of French Canadians on the farm and in the village as no English Canadian but a physician could. He became aware how new to other English-speaking persons was the kind of material he was amassing in the course of his professional and social visits; and little by little he began to give it an artistic form. "It seemed to me," he says, "that I could best attain the object in view by having my friends tell their own tale in their own way, as they would relate them to English-speaking auditors not familiar with the French tongue." What this means is best made clear by an example:

> Mos' ev'ry day raf' it is pass on de rapide
>   De voyageurs singin' some ole chanson
> Bout girl down de reever—too bad dey mus' leave her
>   But comin' back soon wit' beaucoup d' argent.

There are more French words here than in most passages of this length; but the general mixture of French words, English words pronounced with a French twist, an occasional French construction, is representative of Drummond's verse as a whole. In 1897, when he had found by giving informal recitations that there was an audience for what he had written, he gathered together a sample of his work and had it published in New York under the title, *The Habitant and Other French Canadian Poems*. To make sure of a sympathetic reception from French Canada, he invited a preface from Louis Fréchette, the leading French Canadian poet of the day. Fréchette seized Drummond's artistic problem with real insight, and commented upon the novelty and difficulty of undertaking to present a group of characters who cannot read even their own idiom and who use a language which is not their own and which they have learned by hearing it spoken. He was concerned to point out that Drummond had no thought of ridiculing his subjects but was instead bent upon commending them to the respect and affection of English Canada.

It was wise of Drummond to obtain this preface; but it did not suffice. Many French Canadians have never forgiven him for putting a patois on the lips of his habitants, and insist—mistakenly—that the vulgar error in English Canada that French Canadians do not generally speak good French has its origin in Drummond's poems. The political shortcoming of his work—it was certainly no part of his intention to produce such an effect—is not so grave as its literary weakness. A stanza such as I have quoted aims at rigorous realism of diction; and this consorts well with the sly humour expressed. But when Drummond aims at pathos or tragedy—as he does not often do in his first collection—there is an inescapable incongruity between the medium and the substance.

For younger readers, despite his four volumes, Drummond is now scarcely a name, certainly no more; but almost every Canadian knows, usually without recalling who wrote it, the stirring ballad called **"The Wreck of the *Julie Plante*."** Lines like:

> De cook she's name was Rosie,
>   She come from Montreal,
> Was chambermaid on lumber-barge
>   On de Grande Lachine Canal.

or

> De win' can blow lak' hurricane
>   An' s'pose she blow some more,
> You can't get drown' on Lac St. Pierre
>   So long you stay on shore.

have become parts of the meagre treasure of our popular song. Their author will not always be so neglected as he has been during the last generation. (pp. 59-61)

E. K. Brown, "The Development of Poetry in Canada," in his On Canadian Poetry, *revised edition, 1944. Reprint by the Tecumseh Press, 1977, pp. 28-87.*

R. E. RASHLEY (essay date 1949)

[*In the following essay, Rashley examines Drummond's use of dialect as an attempt to express aspects of life which the conventional poetic styles of his contemporaries were not suited to convey.*]

The immediately striking feature of W. H. Drummond's work and the one that accounts for most notice of him, favourable and unfavourable, is his use of the Habitant patois, a kind of compromise on the borders of English and French. The speech is not in any way unique. The North American continent has absorbed many large groups of people and each has passed through its period of malaise with language and produced, for a time, a half-foreign variant. There have been many who have found literary material in these tongues. Arthur Stringer has written extensively in an Irish variant, and south of the border there have been many; Lowell's Yankee, Leland's German-English, Dooley's Irish, Milt Gross's Yiddish, and others. Apart from these there was always the example of Robert Burns and his numerous Canadian progeny. Time has not been kind to most of these writers. A partial language necessarily represents a loss in communication, both because its use is limited and because that limitation is proof of weakness in the language. One can only think as the language will permit, and this language is servant to the very ordinary needs of living, and only for unintellectual people. It is only the overlapping of the lives of the two peoples that requires expression. This is all the more true of Drummond's patois because both languages continued to flourish and the marginal area tended to die out rather than either of the true tongues. It seems almost certain, then, that Drummond will receive less and less notice. This may not be all to our advantage. It is not likely that a poet who is prepared to write several volumes of verse will choose an unconventional style without realizing some gains to compensate for his loss, or that nothing is to be learned from his adventure.

Since Drummond wrote verses in other manners and settled on the Habitant patois for the greater part of his work it is apparent that the patois satisfied a felt need, that its use was deliberate. That it brought gains is also evident. In his best work in "poetic" English Drummond appears as a dignified versifier roughly equivalent to most of the writers of the preceding period.

> O Spirit of the mountain that speaks to us tonight,
> Your voice is sad, but still recalls past visions of
>   delight,
> When 'mid the grand old Laurentides, old when the
>   earth was new
> With flying feet we followed the moose and caribou.

The movement is pedestrian and the language hackneyed with its "past visions of delight" and "flying feet", the caesuras fall patly, the metrical form is obvious, and the poetic background suggested by "mid" is wearisome. There is an improvement in the use of the couplet over some predecessors, perhaps, but it is still undistinguished verse, without colour or life. It lacks freshness, vigour, clarity, impact. It is part of a large body of early Canadian writing in a manner so ineffectual that one reads it unrememberingly. The erosion of many hands has rubbed down the distinguishing differences. It is a mode as common and fully formed as a dress suit and similarly donned for the occasion. It is practised very much as women crochet; there are a number of stock patterns available, the product is decorative, and there is a certain skill in the evenness and competence of the craftsmanship. The result is recognizable as poetry, not by the individual's contribution to it but by his relative success in reaching the convention. There is an occasional feeling of restriction, a suggestion of impatience as in Sangster and Mair, but the poems that win to freedom are rare. The style is a web that binds its victims under veiling folds and robs them of individuality and strength. This was the dilemma that faced Canadian poets. The material of the verse was adequate to life, and to a vigorous life, but it was not adequate to poetry. It was the style that was at fault.

It was just this inadequacy that was forcing the poets of 1860 to experiment in new uses of language, and in an unusually well-educated pioneer community it was inevitable that the direction should be along respectable lines of scholarship. We do not find an effort to translate the rude life into an equally rude verse with a possibility of equal vigour, but a longing for the polish and perfection of civilization. Lampman, through Keats, arrived at a brocaded decoration that is as much a defence against life as a transcription of life. Through it he was enabled to transmute a certain part of his sensibilities into a permanent and lovely form, like insects suspended in amber. Carman, won by the musical content of words, developed an enviable facility in running harmonies and lost that part of life which cannot be approached in terms of melodies. Duncan Campbell Scott's intellectual approach froze the sensibilities into a delicate hoar frost. These poets found adequacy of style in a rigorous winnowing of language. One feels in them that the eye is on the word rather than what the word stands for; the sort of thing apparent in Lampman's fondness for the word "creamy", or in Scott's "Opal fires weave over all the oval of the lake," and its repetition in "With oval spots of opal over all", or Carman's whippoorwill:

> night long
> Threshing the summer dark
> With his dim flail of song.

The attack on conventionality is an attack on the language itself, the persistent, and almost painfully persistent, effort to find in the varied ores of language some pure vein and free it from the taint of too common usage. It was true of Lampman, and must have been true of Duncan Campbell Scott, though probably much less true of Carman, that composition was very arduous and the pleasure of achievement rarely complete. The intention was so limited and resources so scant! Each achieved, in his own way, individuality and control of certain effects, but style is a master as well as a servant; it necessarily involves exclusions. Because they wrote as they did these poets were denied humanized substance. They did find release from the flowers-under-glass contemporary falsity, but at some cost. The persistent effort toward individual style brought them, through a change of direction, back to the dilemma, for an individual style, though it seems to give freedom, only reimposes its own limitations and denials. The more distinctive the style the more rigorous the selection and the narrower the possibilites.

Drummond's approach to the problem was also through style but with a difference. His affectionate understanding of the

Habitant suggested concrete expression, but the conventional terms at his disposal were not capable of creating the Habitant either concretely or affectionately. He decided to let the Habitant speak an approximation to his own tongue and was immediately freed to use the most commonplace terms as material for verse. Phrases worn down by repetition were renewed, cliches stopped being cliches, hackneyed rhythms borrowed a little freshness from the language, and even prepositions, conjunctions and words of one syllable won a small new individuality from the change. Even a term as commonplace as "the wild and stormy weather" gained some small freshness from the change to:

"T'roo de wil' an' stormy wedder from St. Pierre de Miquelon."

The convention is broken not by control of certain elements of language but by a refurbishing of the language through which words which had slipped too familiarly over the tongue reacquired flavour and substance by slight alteration of pronunciation and form. This was not done without the application of some intelligence on Drummond's part. He did not, as his Preface suggests, simply let his friends "tell their own stories in their own way." There was, of course, no "way"; the overlappings of the two tongues varied even in the individual from time to time and from subject to subject. Drummond found in the patois as it was spoken a new emphasis in words, an increment of sentiment, perhaps, or of humour, an animation that was attractive, and in working for these effects he took the patois as a guide but followed his own needs in creating his speech. Spellings and pronunciations, the percentage of French, and the degree of distortion vary from poem to poem and within poems. There is evidence of control. Arthur Stringer, in an early experiment with the French Canadian's English writes: "Wail, m'sieu, you hax me w'ere I got dat leetle gold compass wit' de diamon' an' de' pearl on heem!" The style is harsh and difficult. It requires something of an effort to read far into the story. This is not true of Drummond. With him the accent is softened, the explosive and emphatic elements of French are reduced, and what is retained is usually the slurred or broken consonants and the changed vowels; and, in his best poems, not in large proportion. He is the child of his time in that his tendency is toward softness. He has usually the simple statement in simple words, freshened and given a certain amount of impact by the change into patois. There is nothing comparable to Duncan Campbell Scott's

> His eyes were jewels of content
> Set in circles of peace.

Instead we have:

> Beeg feller, always watchin' on hees leetle weasel eye.

His language is incapable of Scott's kind of excellence, but it is also incapable of his kind of absurdity. He is not permitted effects which in Scott demand the use of "plangent", "brangle", "pulvil" and "alular" simply because in his patois the words do not exist, nor the need for them. His needs are certainly restricted, but he gains a style very adequate to those needs, and, indeed, much more adequate than his own English style. It is a freshened, renewed language, a genuine discovery and a successful escape from a predicament. It denied Drummond exactly what was achieved by the other poets of the period, grace, elegance, polish; but it gave him humanized substance, exactly what they were denied. It is a style just as legitimate as theirs and in just the same sense that theirs is a style. When Drummond writes:

But her sail's not blowin' out wit de warm breeze of de
    sout'
An' its not too easy tellin' w'ere de snowflake meet de
    foam
Stretchin' out on ev'ry side, all across de Gulf so wide
W'en de nor' eas' win' is chasin' de "Rose Delima"
    home.

he is not making any greater distortion of language than Duncan
Campbell Scott when he writes:

> How shall we transmit in tendril-like images,
> The tenuous tremor in the tissues of ether.

or than Carman writing:

> Golden Rowan of Menalowan.

He is doing no more and no less than they are doing, manipulating the language to obtain certain effects in accordance
with an artistic design. The motive in each case is the same,
escape from a damaging conventionality of language that had
reduced poetry to insignificance.

There is, of course, a great difference in result. If you open
one door you will not likely get into the same room as if you
had opened another, and Drummond's style led him away from
the members of the group of 1860 into its own freedom and
its own confinements. If we compare **"Little Lac Grenier"**
with "The Unnamed Lake" it is clear that the patois is not
adequate to the possibilities of the situation. In F. G. Scott's
poem, in spite of artificialities, the style is adequate to the
splendour and isolation of the object and the sense the observer
has of being an intruder, alien to a self-contained and sufficient
world:

> Along the shore a heron flew,
>   And from a speck on high,
> That hovered in the deepening blue,
>   We heard the fish-hawk's cry.
>
> Among the cloud-capt solitudes,
>   No sound the silence broke,
> Save when, in whispers down the woods,
>   The guardian mountains spoke.

If there is a failure here it is a failure of the individual. Compare
this with Drummond's:

> Leetle Lac Grenier, she's all alone,
> Up on de mountain high
> But she never feel lonesome, 'cos for why?
> So soon as de winter was gone away
> De bird come an' sing to her ev'ry day,
>
> Leetle Lac Grenier, she's all alone
> Back on de mountain dere,
> But de pine tree an' spruce stan' ev'ry where
> Along by de shore, an' mak' her warm
> For dey kip off de win' an' de winter storm.

The diminutive "leetle", the shortening of the words and alterations of pronunciation reduce and limit too severely the
sensitiveness of the reaction. It is a kind of experience that the
language cannot achieve. The refinements and subtleties of the
individual making over his reactions to the natural world into
a realizable pattern are simply not permitted. In a partially

similar poem, **"The Wind that Lifts the Fog"**, there is a much
more successful effort:

> Star of de Sout'—did you see de light
> Steamin' along dat foggy night?
> Poor leetle bird! anoder star
> Shinin' above so high an' far
> Dazzle you den, an' blin' de eye,
> W'ile down below on de sea you lie
> Anchor dere—wit' your broken wing
> How could you fly w'en de sailor sing.

Both poems are in similar ways a reaching out from Drummond's usual material toward something more personal, but
"The Wind that Lifts the Fog" is the individual's reflection
on a group activity, or, better, the reflection of an individual
who is part of a group and only partly an individual and only
for a moment, a sailor at the wheel for example. Hence, one
is led to speculate that it is only in communal material, in
situations where the group spirit is alive, where man is in
contact with man or with nature through the group senses, that
this style takes on life and becomes something more than broken English. This is in keeping with Drummond's usual practice. The restriction imposed is that Drummond can approach
his material only through a generalized concept, through the
group consent. When he describes a man he gives those characteristics that are obvious to others, the best common observation of the group. It is the individual differences that are
sifted out and the resemblances that remain. When he describes
a people he gives those aspects that are perceptible characteristics of the group; there is much in common with the Kipling
of the *Barrack Room Ballads*. In return, the authority of group
consent is given his observations. His people are real in the
sense that any man is real to the group of his friends; the
overlappings make the picture. There is a loss in the limitation
to moods and thoughts available to the group, but the gain is
simplicity and concreteness. He is easily accessible, and, within
his limits, authentic. The transcription of life is accurate, at
least in so far as one is able to compare with other transcriptions. For example, a large part of the significant content of
Maria Chapdelaine is already in Drummond. By selecting poems
one could block out most of the plot and wash on much of the
character and local colour. In fact, there is nothing in *Maria
Chapdelaine* that could not have been clear to a person fresh
from a reading of Drummond's poems. There is, however, an
element that could not have been expressed in Drummond's
style. His problem—the discovery of a freshened, objective
means to comment of humanity—is solved, but, as with the
others, he is returned to the dilemma, for the very means that
give him his escape limit him to material that is accessible
only to the group.

It is unlikely that Drummond foresaw the most unfortunate
results of his choice of style: his being considered a cheap
humourist, and the loss of effect through incongruity. He has
always had a genial manner and was often simply the humourist
but certainly did not expect that the patois would be treated as
a humourous device even when the intention was serious. The
simplicity with which he obtains his effects is a witness of the
sincerity with which he uses the patois. He has humour, certainly, but at its general level it is humour of character and it
springs from affectionate understanding. The humour that seems
to spring from language alone is as much a defect of the reader
as of the style. However, there was the other risk involved,
and the flaw remains. E. K. Brown calls attention to the "inescapable incongruity between the medium and the substance."

The charge is unanswerable to any who agree with it, and there must be many who do. A poem exists only as a reaction to a group of words on a page. If an unforeseen reaction occurs there may be simply a bad poem. If the patois can be accepted as a live speech the pathos of "**The Hill of St. Sebastien**" and "**De Bell of Saint Michel**" is real enough and the language satisfyingly adequate. The tone of affectionate good humour that enriches "**Johnnie Courteau**" and "**Leetle Bateese**" seems to spring quite naturally from the language used. The poignancy of the longing of old Captinne Baribeau for the sea, so excellent in its kind, is native to the tongue:

An now he's lyin' 'dere, w'er de breeze is blow hees hair,
An' he's hearin' ev'ry morning de "Rose Delima" call,
Sayin', "Come along wit' me, an' we'll off across de sea,
For I'm lonesome waitin' for you, Captinne Paul.

The mood is at least as sensitivly expressed as in Masefield's "Sea Fever" and the sensitiveness is not there in spite of the language; it is a freshness, a spring air that drifts in occasionally on the words. A good test of the flaw of style would be "**Bateese de Lucky Man.**" If the incongruity between the medium and the substance is to appear, it will surely be pronounced in this poem. If it does not intrude, then the poem stands as an affectionate, artless tribute, a bit violently expressed, perhaps, but deliberately so, and achieving, even because of its contrast and exaggeration, a very human comment on death and love. In fact, the sense of incongruity does not need to intrude. If "**Bateese de Lucky Man**" is read together with O'Hagan's "The Freckled Boy at School," where the subject is identical, it will be obvious that Drummond's is the better poem. A similar comparison with Duncan Campbell Scott might be more effective. "**The Wreck of the *Julie Plante***" and "After a Night of Storm" resemble each other in subject. It is difficult to believe that "**The Wreck of the *Julie Plante***" is not the better poem.

Five groupings of Drummond's work are possible: his interpretations of the spirit of the Habitant, his essays in character, his handful of ballads, his purely humourous poems, and his poems in other styles. Of these the first three are significant, and in each of them the poet achieves success. His skill in discovering and recording the cohesions, the points of contact in the Habitant group has already received comment. "**Le Vieux Temps**" and "**De Bell of Saint Michel**" are specimens in this field. "**Johnny Courteau**," "**Leetle Bateese**" and "**Bateese de Lucky Man**" are similar successes in the second grouping. "**The Wind that Lifts the Fog**" is very nearly a success of a different kind. In it are a checked, controlled movement, and a feeling of strain and incompleteness that suggest that Drummond was trying to break from the limitations of his style but was defeated by them. The ballads are the most poetic achievement. "**The Wreck of the *Julie Plante***" is well enough known. Three ballads might be grouped with it; "**The Windigo**," which is the best of them, "**Phil-O-Rum Juneau**," the most imperfect, and "**The 'Rose Delima'.**" In these four poems Drummond approaches a little toward the old English ballads. There are a terse introduction, which sets the mood, a rapid dramatic narrative, told plainly but skillfully, rapid transitions from speaker to speaker, and certain phrases that are reduced to conventions. In "**The 'Rose Delima'**" there are stanzas that seem carelessly worked up, but the two love stories, that of Pierre and Virginie and that of Captinne Baribeau and his ship, are charming. The nostalgia of the old sailor for the sea is sensitively expressed

and there are one or two bits of suggestive description. "**The Windigo**" is a longer ballad, concise and complete in structure, admirably developed in form, controlling its narrative devices with confidence and ease. It is a presentation of the pressure of the unknown upon human life. E. J. Pratt at his best has a more sustained, but never a better, narrative skill. As in all Drummond's work, there are no quotable lines. The effect is in the whole, and it is one of artistry. It is odd that the poem has not found its way into more than one anthology.

These poems are the achievement of a man whose artistic tenets were sound, however limited their scope. He is one with Carman, Lampman and Duncan Campbell Scott in his perception of the problem of style, and his need for escape. His escape into the patois and the conventionalized group-reaction is just as legitimate, artistically, as Lampman's escape into a formal style, or Carman's into music, or Duncan Campbell Scott's into austerity. There is a division in Canadian poetry about the time of Confederation. The "respectable" poets digress into styles that lead them further and further away from the needs of a flesh-and-blood world to the borders of humanity. Drummond is somewhere nearer the centre, and his success constitutes a useful criticism of theirs. A poetry of power should have wider inclusions than either. The two are divergences, complementary as well as contemporary, and are each equally a demonstration of the dilemma of style. (pp. 387-96)

R. E. Rashley, "W. H. Drummond and the Dilemma of Style," in The Dalhousie Review, *Vol. 28, No. 4, January, 1949, pp. 387-96.*

GEORGE WOODCOCK (essay date 1960)

[*Woodcock is a Canadian educator, editor, and critic best known for his biographies of George Orwell and Thomas Merton. He also founded Canada's most important literary journal,* Canadian Literature, *and has written extensively on the literature of Canada. In the following excerpt, Woodcock objects to Drummond's inclusion in the New Canadian Library (edited by Malcom Ross), considering him outdated and overly sentimental.*]

[Drummond's **Habitant Poems**] are interesting literary curiosa; they tell us much about popular Canadian taste in those happily past days when the public recitation of bad verse was a recognised form of entertainment. But to treat Drummond seriously as more than an outdated popular versifier, or to suggest that his grossly sentimental fake-dialect "poems" tell us anything penetrating about French-Canadian life, is just about as absurd as to uphold *Uncle Tom's Cabin* as good American writing or a really authentic picture of American society. In fact, this volume raises very sharply the question whether the literary historian in Dr. Malcolm Ross may not have triumphed over his critical *alter ego* in determining his selections for the New Canadian Library. (pp. 74-5)

George Woodcock, "Venture on the Verge," in Canadian Literature, *No. 5, Summer, 1960, pp. 73-5.*

LEE BRISCOE THOMPSON (essay date 1980)

[*In the following excerpt, Thompson asserts that Drummond fell into obscurity for largely political reasons, due to the supposed condescension toward French-Canadians exhibited in his work.*]

A. M. Klein, in his fine poem "Portrait of the Poet as Landscape," describes the condition of the poet in slick modern times. No longer a powerful and revered figure, the poet has become "in a shouting mob, somebody's sigh," "a Mr. Smith in a hotel register,—incognito, lost, lacunal." Klein is speaking of poets generally, supplanted by scientists, tycoons, orators, jazz musicians, actors and other imposters. A "shelved Lycidas": the phrase recurred forcibly when I reached last semester for my trusty Klinck and Watters *Canadian Anthology*—third edition—to read aloud in class a snippet of William Henry Drummond's habitant verse. Not there! Somewhere between the first and third editions, Drummond had been discreetly excised, shelved. Was it a purge of popular writings? No; Robert W. Service had acquired *additional* selections; and the anonymous ballads were still there. Well, were pieces of primarily historical rather than literary merit being dropped? No; Joseph Stansbury, Standish O'Grady, Haliburton's "Prince de Joinville's Horse" had survived. It had to be something else.

My thoughts flashed on the ludicrous removal of "Royal" from Canadian mailboxes and the Royal Canadian Mounted Police; the well-meaning, expensive mismanagement of the Bilingualism and Biculturalism Commission recommendations; the hundreds of lipservice concessions to Quebec, about which the average Quebecois could not have cared less. Overlaid upon these thoughts were my observations of U. S. white liberal responses to newly militant blacks—the generalized guilt at past bigotry, brutality and abuses; the rapid, conciliatory shedding of symbols perceived to be condescending: Aunt Jemina, watermelons, theories of natural rhythm, Otis jokes, Kakewalks, even (in some circles) Br'er Rabbit.

Politics appeared to be the link. Drummond, I suspect, has been quietly dropped from public view because he has become an embarrassment to a modern English Canada which is trying to show how equal and worthy the French-Canadian is in Anglo eyes. It is feared, no doubt, that Quebec will be offended by this turn-of-the-century English-Canadian portrait of the rural-Canadian as "un pauvre illettre," "a speaker of broken English, an illiterate country hick. Such fears, while perhaps realistic, are the product, in part, of a modern unfamiliarity in both cultures of Canada with the times, with the intent (perceived and expressed) of the author, and with the actual content of the poems. (pp. 682-83)

Critical response to [Drummond's] habitant poetry, generally deemed far superior to his regular English poems or his Irish dialect verses, was invariably laudatory, dwelling upon his Wordsworthian celebration of the common man and his eye for details of daily life, his kindliness and sincerity, his lilting rhythms and lively humour. Certainly criticism has toughened in subsequent decades, and critics are now inclined to find fault with his excessively cheerful portrait of the French-Canadian psyche and with his reinforcement of a stereotypic view of French Canadians as simple hewers of wood and drawers of water. Yet even recent critics acknowledge his "unique" benevolence, "transparent goodwill" and choice of themes which "have never lost their appeal." One thinks, for example, of **"Little Bateese"**:

> You bad leetle boy, not moche you care
> How busy you're kipin' your poor gran'pere
> Tryin' to stop you ev'ry day
> Chasin' de hen aroun' de hay—
> W'y don't you geev' dem a chance to lay?
>
> > Leetle Bateese!

Off on de fiel' you foller de plough
Den w'en you're tire you scare de cow
Sickin' de dog till dey jomp de wall
So de milk ain't good for not'ing at all—
An' you're only five an' a half dis fall,

> Leetle Bateese!

• • • • •

But leetle Bateese! please don't forget
We rader you're stayin' de small boy yet,
So chase de chicken an' mak' dem scare
An' do w'at you lak wit' your old gran' pere
For w'en you're beeg feller he won't be dere—

> Leetle Bateese!

J. F. Macdonald goes so far as to argue that this poem will still be read 300 years from now.

> It is fast rooted in the fundamentals of life which do not change with the centuries. . . . The theme of the poem is perennial, and there is nothing in its treatment that would make it anything but delightfully humorous and poignantly pathetic even in a future age. But when that anthology of the twenty-third century is made and "little Bateese" is in it, we'll "not be dere." The dialect of Drummond's poems may come to be, I suppose inevitably will come to be, regarded as an historical curiosity. The critic of that time, however, if he understands his art, cannot fail to recognize that William Henry Drummond was, if not a great, at least a genuine poet who touched the heart of his own generation.

In his introduction Louis Frechette accurately characterized both Drummond's verse and the poet himself: "a good person, gentle, amiable, honest, intelligent and upright, a wide-awake spirit, a heart full of a natural gift for poetry stimulating his patriotism, casting a glowing beam into his modest soul, lulling his dreaming hours with distant and melancholy memories." Frechette, no Uncle Tom, acknowledged the danger of Drummond's verse falling into buffoonery, vulgarity, the grotesque or burlesque; but also noted that he had been able to detect *nowhere* the taint of carciature but *everywhere* "l'expression d'une ame amie" ("the expression of a friendly spirit"). Like Drummond's widow, Frechette felt that the poet's accomplishment was not solely artistic but significantly patriotic, for it would produce "a desirable growth in the esteem of our English-speaking compatriots." The poems "cannot help but cement the union of heart and spirit which ought to exist among all the groups which make up the large Canadian family called upon to live and to prosper under the same law and the same 'flag." Drummond and Frechette, it must be remembered, were writers out of the decades of Canada First and the Confederation Dream; they were simply reflecting, as art usually does, the temper—in this case the optimism—of the times, and what the wildly popular Ralph Connor was doing in fiction, Dr. Drummond was doing in popular verse. Post-Quiet-Revolution, we may find the perspective naive, but we can hardly fault the vision of peace, harmony and equality that prompted it.

What of the so-called "habitant dialect" Drummond used? Linguists point out that it is not pure in the sense of Robbie Burns' Scottish dialect, for Burns' speech largely clung to the Anglo-Saxon vocabulary and pronunciations abandoned by the mainstream of Anglophones and was therefore closer to the roots of the language. Drummond's "dialect," by contrast, is technically a corruption or "broken English," that was pieced together by Francophones in lumbermills and hunting camps, factories and tourist traps. It is English rendered phonetically, in halting phrases, with syntactic, vocabulary and idiomatic borrowings from the mother tongue, French. I can verify the authenticity of Drummond's renderings from my own childhood in Montreal and Quebec City, from the speech patterns of one of my aunts-by-marriage, from recent travels in the upper Ottawa Valley, and from some television commercials still beamed to Vermont by Montreal stations—the Dorion Suit ads being among the best illustrations. J. F. Macdonald offers similar testimony, telling of reading Drummond's **"The Habitant"** to the predominantly Quebecois lumberjacks in camps in the Algoma district of northern Ontario. He reports:

> After we got acquainted, they would correct my pronunciation of the French phrases when my Ontario French offended their ears, and sometimes one of them, who was a good raconteur, would launch into a tale suggested by the last poem read. It was obvious they felt that the language was true to life, and believed that the poems were those of a kindly friend who understood and loved them.

Drummond viewed his role as documenter of a passing way of life and a language variant, and as that of intermediary between English Canada and a lesser known segment of French Canada. (pp. 684-86)

And what of the portrait Drummond presents of the French-Canadian? It is somewhat idealized, skirting the dark side of human nature, emphasizing a simple, sunny, sensible philosophy. But tragedy, deprivation and frustration also appear and Drummond's view of the universe, via his characters, must be considered more pragmatic, common sense than ivory-tower or isolationist. His characters know about the world outside, speak of Roosevelt and the Philippines, Edward VII, and industrialization, with an irony that matches the vision of "Ringuet's" much later novel, *Thirty Acres* (1938). Unlike "Ringuet's" characters, Drummond's rural figures are able to choose among the delights and disasters of the early 20th century. Their consistent option for hearth and home values is rendered in a way that Drummond probably hoped would offset the English-Canadian stereotype of the habitant as a backwoods, church-ridden, foot-dragger who perversely refused to leave the 17th century. The average Western Canadian of 1979 knows almost as little about the average Quebecois (and vice versa) as did their forbears in 1899. Set in the historical context, then, the poems still stress basic values to which the average Canadian and *Canadien* continue to subscribe.

Drummond, despite his rejection by current Canadian and Quebec intellectuals, fought for the recognition of the unique gifts, culture and identity of rural French Canada. He feared that *Canadiens* would be swallowed up by the boom and expansion of English Canada (see, for example, **"National Policy"**) and he took advantage of every occasion to remind not only English Canada but *also French Canada herself* of past glories and her worthy contributions to this continent:

> Remember when these tales you read
> Of rude but honest "Canayet."
> That Joliet, La Verandrye,
> La Salle, Marquette, and Hennepin

Were all true "Canayen" themselves—
And in their veins the same red stream
The conquering blood of Normandie
Flowed strong, and gave America
Coureurs de bois and voyageurs
Whose entrail extends from sea to sea!

He also warned as energetically as any parish priest against the losses to be sustained by a move to the glittering U.S. of A. In one poem **"How Bateese Came Home,"** Bateese succumbs to the lure of Yankee dollars and heads for the States despite a friend's warning that

> . . . she's not so healtee place, an' if you
>   mak' l'argent,
> you spen' it ju' lak Yankee man, an' not
>   like habitant.

When the friend meets Baptiste fifteen years later, the exile confesses:

> . . . I forget mos' all ma French since I go
>   on de State.
> Dere's 'noder t'ing kip on your head, ma
>   frien' dey mus' be tole
> Ma name's Bateese Trudeau no more, but
>   John B. Waterhole!

The poem ends happily and humorously, but that's simply Drummond's sugar-coating of a pill as bitter as the one "Ringuet's" expatriate *Canadien* must swallow in the final scenes of *Thirty Acres*.

Even if one concedes the falsity of the folk peasant society concept of habitant life that Drummond promotes (and I do not *entirely* so concede) and even if one argues that Drummond's pure Quebecois peasant is drawn from an irrepressibly Anglo point of view, it would still be part of Canada's history of ideas, representing a stage of development in North American culture.

To deny that phase would be futile and foolish. In Canada the implications for national unity of such denial are actually very serious, for Canada is a country built upon ambiguity, upon a myth of hyphenation and transcendence of categories, upon an ideal of one's capacity to encounter, tolerate and rejoice in more than one culture, in a mingling of cultures. If one removes from a standard Canadian literary anthology a writer of immense popularity who sought, albeit in an ingenuous and deliberately unsophisticated way, to play with humorous hybrids and promote mutual understanding and respect between Canadians and *Canadiens*, what is the effect? It is unconscious cooperation with that destructive either-or thinking which denies the viability of being both Quebecois and Canadian, which rejects the myth of the Mosaic.

The shelving of Drummond is, significantly, an English Canadian response to the pressures of an emerging group, for the Quebecois are a people in the midst, not at the end, of the struggle to acquire recognition. Unlike post-recognition Hispanic Americans and post recognition Black Americans, French Canadians are still too much in that transitional stage—the uncertain stage between the past and future "special status" or even independence—to tolerate much joking. For many members of the Parti Quebecois nothing could be more distasteful than the image, however good-natured, of a linguistic merger. Their attitude is admittedly even handed; they are as repelled by the English Candian's imperfect French as by Drummond's broken English. To a Canadian federalist, however, Drummond's flaws pale before the importance of his attempt to unite the two solitudes of Canada in "cheerful and kindly laughter." Once the political destinies of Canadians and *Canadiens* have come to pass, perhaps this shelved Lycidas will be restored to his place in Canada's and North America's popular literature. If so, the inscription on William Henry Drummond's gravestone on the side of Mount Royal will be fulfilled:

> Youth's for an hour
> Beauty's a flower
> But love is the jewel that wins the world.
>
> (pp. 686-88)

Lee Briscoe Thompson, "The Shelving of a People's Poet: The Case of William Henry Drummond," in Journal of American Culture, *Vol. 2, No. 4, Winter, 1980, pp. 682-89.*

GERALD NOONAN (essay date 1981)

[*In the following excerpt, Noonan surveys the critical reception of Drummond's poetry.*]

On April 8, 1907, in its obituary tribute to Dr. William Henry Drummond, The Montreal *Daily Star* cites "the quaint humor and tender pathos of his poems." That summary phrase, with one major exception, typifies almost the complete canon of critical analysis devoted to a poet . . . whose dialect verse was read with interest and delight in the United States, England, and, according to the newspapers, across the length and breadth of Canada. The sensitivity of the interest and the nature of the delight were not an issue to Anglo-Saxon readers in Drummond's era; they were eager, from all reports, for the habitant stereotype. At a Drummond reading in Massey Hall, December 20, 1905, President Loudon of the University of Toronto "said he would rather be the author of **'Johnny Courteau'** than the owner of the richest silver mine in Cobalt." To be sure, Louis Fréchette, the best-known of the French-Canadian poets, assured readers (in a French Introduction to Drummond's first volume) that Drummond's representation of "my unlettered compatriots" was "accurate" and without "the faintest stroke of the caricaturist." Moreover, he went on to say that Drummond "cannot fail to benefit them [the habitants]—and consequently their countrymen—with a most desirable increase of esteem on the part of our English compatroits who have not studied them so clearly as Dr. Drummond."

In retrospective view, however, Fréchette's leap of esteem from habitant "consequently" to all French-Canadians is surely suspect; the Montreal *Star's* obituary tribute labels Drummond the "Poet Laureate of French Canadians," a designation that obliterates in one phrase the work of Fréchette and all his French compatriots. Toronto's *Mail and Empire* obituary comment praises Drummond's receptivity "to the silent appeal of a primitive people"—i.e., French-Canadians. And the New York *Evening Sun* managed to extend the pejorative sweep slightly by its declaration that Drummond put into his books "everything that was characteristic of the most interesting side of the old life of the Dominion."

About Drummond's "close study" of the habitant, even the contemporaneous obituary articles express divergent opinion. The Montreal *Star*, whose editor had been a friend of the poet, noted that Dr. Drummond's medical practice had been in Montreal mostly, that his scant country experience "was not among the French-Canadians but among the Highland Scottish."

He spent some time among the lumber camps and in the woods, but it is said that in those places he did not come in contact with the people he described with such perfect fidelity. Therefore, it must be said that Dr. Drummond, like all true poets, was inspired.

In far-off England, nonetheless, the London *Spectator* was able to inform its readers: "Both the matter of his poems and the manner of their diction were collected and collated during the never-ending journeys of a country-doctor in Quebec." And in Boston, an unidentified newspaper declared: "They [the poems] were originally scribbled on a block of paper held on the author's knee, often by a campfire. . ."

Irrespective of the way they came about, the responses to Drummond's poems and to the stereotype of the habitant were overwhelmingly positive. The Boston newspaper that evoked the campfire muse was basically accurate in reporting: "later, begged, borrowed or purloined by friends, many of them [the poems] drifted into print and became popular without the author's name and with no trace of their parentage. It was the poet's wife who carefully collected all these earlier poems . . . and so made possible one of the best-selling books of poetry in recent years."

The popularity of the poems encouraged public comment which in its breadth of enthusiasm tends to reveal various biases of the time that otherwise would be unnoticed or unrecorded. Surprisingly, however, the summation of the poet's significance for his own era, and perhaps ours, is generally consistent throughout an amalgam of Drummond's press clippings, the unpublished biography of his wife, and the most sustained academic analysis of Drummond's verse (by R. E. Rashley in the *Dalhousie Review,* 1949 [see excerpt above]).

Perhaps it was the sheer popularity of the poems that preserved them from what seems now to be the questionable associations of their exponents. The Folklore Club of Montreal, for example, for its meeting of January 16, 1896, matched "Dr. Drummond's reading of seven new poems" with a "Dr. Johnson" (Montreal *Star*) talking "on superstitions of the Negro race" in Africa and Jamaica. In a brief report, the Montreal *Herald* said: "Every distinctive trait and characteristic of this people [the French-Canadian] was shown to perfection by Dr. Drummond and splendidly rendered." As for the talk by "Dr. Johnston" [*sic*] the subheadline told of "caterpillars a favourite diet, and the doctor had to eat them." Further afield, an example of selective reading provides an interesting imperialistic inversion of **"The Habitant's Jubliee Ode."** In the poem, the habitant advocates regarding England as a foster mother: "Is it right you don't call her moder, is it right you don't love her too?" A British comment in a letter, from Lees Knowles, in the *Cambridge Review,* is reprinted in Toronto's *The World,* June 16, 1907: "The poem which, I think, appealed to us most was **'The Habitant's Jubilee Ode'** which beautifully describes the kindly feeling of England towards the French-Canadians. . . ." Selectivity of another kind is practised by the Boston *Globe* which, for a conclusion to its obituary feature, believed it fitting to quote the kindly feelings of one of its feature writers who had once toured Quebec's habitant area and reported the praise of a village priest, an Irishman, for Drummond:

No other man has ever pictured the real habitant, no one has understood the simple, trusting, childlike nature of these people, their love of the river, the rapids, the birds, and all the beautiful things about them. Those poems have been an inspiration to me. I know them by heart, every one, and I'll venture to say that you can't visit the room of a village priest throughout the province of Quebec without finding Dr. Drummond's poems somewhere about the place.

What in 1907 the *Globe* omitted was the distinction that its writer, Ellene Foster, had made in the original article six years earlier (April 19, 1901), a distinction between the picture of "the real habitant" she obtained in her pleasant tour of rural Quebec and the experience of the French-Canadians "who find employment in the factory towns of New England." Of these latter, she says:

> We have studied his characteristics, we are familiar with his patois, and when the habitant is mentioned we shrug our shoulders. Ah, that is where we are mistaken, for as widely different as the time-honored chalk is from the cheese are the habitant and the French-Canadian in our mills.

A gloss on the village priest's view of the habitant, as quoted by Ellene Foster, is provided, for those who wish it, by another Irish priest, "Rev. Father Frank O'Sullivan" who told the Catholic Literary Association of Peterborough:

> The French-Canadian farmer belongs to the good old Catholic stock that came out with Champlain . . . He may not know very much, it is true, about geometry, trigonometry, zoology and the other ologies that our Ontario educationalists try to cram into children's heads before they can read and spell, but I will venture to say that he can tell more about God and his own immortal soul, and say his prayers better, than many a graduate of our Collegiate Institutes.

A politican-journalist of the time is one of the few commentators to betray some sensitivity, initially at least, to the French fact. In a column in the Toronto *Sunday World* (January 2, 1897), about Drummond's first volume, **The Habitant,** he begins:

> I do not know that all my French-Canadian fellow-countrymen will give me the credit of being more than friendly to their race and a lover of their province. They have seen me and others with me, from the English provinces, opposing the passage in Parliament of an act regarding education coercive of Manitoba.

Before getting to his review, however, he says, "Let me tell a story"—a story, as it turns out, about meeting a New Englander on a sleeper train to Montreal who said he liked "Lower Canada . . . because you can get there a sixteenth-century civilization with a feudal service. . . . The people are so different and yet so hospitable and friendly." The writer, one "W.F.M." goes on blandly:

> The statement, "a sixteenth-century with a feudal service" was certainly a striking offhand deliverance and made a great impression on me, partly by reason of its force, partly as confirming my own observations.

Drummond's focus on the habitant, whether as feudal or angelic, was a breakthrough in Canadian literature. As the *GLobe* of Toronto said on February 16, 1899 (and as Professor R. E. Rashley would argue more extensively and specifically fifty years later):

> he succeeds in making a most charming picture of materials hitherto despised as far as literary purposes are concerned. His habitant speaks the broken English dialect, helplessly and hopelessly incorrect in its grammar and syntax, but in the hands of Dr. Drummond an admirable instrument for the realistic delineation of the character of his types.

That Drummond's characters were types—special cases in particular circumstances—and not *the* type of French-Canada was discerned more readily in Quebec than elsewhere in the world. An editorial in the *News and Advocate* of St. Johns, Quebec (February 3, 1899), noted:

> Dr. Drummond has given us a type, but a passing type. It is local and temporary, and is dependent upon boundary and atmosphere and environment. It is fascinating to a degree, and we owe the doctor a debt of gratitude for his charming studies, which are at once whimsical and pathetic and undeniably veracious.

The editorial writer proceeds to find fault not with the potential for misconception in Drummond's portraits but with their regional limitations:

> What we should seek for is the abiding type which will stand for the vital features of a single nationality. How long must we wait for this common type which, whether limned in prose and verse, shall be instantly and universally recognized as standing for what is essentially Canadian! Are we singing localities while awaiting that amalgam which shall create the strong national figure . . .—courageous, facing the future with confidence, containing within itself the best features of the Celtic and the Anglo-Saxon, and illustrating, in physique and mentality, the grandeur of our mountains, the poetry of our lakes and rivers, the wholesomeness, (moral as well as physical), of our bracing climate!

This nationalist opposition to "singing localities" was, one suspects, not widespread; Goldwin Smith's comment in a letter to Drummond (July 16, 1902) gives the counter-view. After praising Drummond's poetry for its creation of interest in a small nationality, Smith says: "I believe in variety and free development, not in having everything rolled flat."

Comments in the French-language press of the time focus much more precisely on the linguistic and racial issues. "Mme. Dandurand" in *La Patrie* (December 15, 1901) says of the habitant characters of Drummond:

> There is, it seems, this fear that the language used by them will by its nature create for outsiders a false impression. This very special language is confined to a particular group in our population (which is) merged in common employment with workers of the English race lack-

ing the ability or the will to understand the French language. (my translation)

The point, obvious but unacknowledged in the English press, is still not pressed home here: the habitant—"unable to read his own language," as Fréchette's Introduction says, "helplessly and hopelessly incorrect" in English as the *Globe* said—nonetheless had learned to be understood by his Anglo companions, whereas the Anglo incompetence was total. From this, Mme. Dandurand ultimately draws the conclusion that "cet idiôme bâtard" ["that bastard idiom"] is a victory of a kind since it has invaded and "crippled the language of the conqueror":

> This jargon has for the ear a strange fascination and a certain musical fantasy and parody. It has the attraction of the comedy of travesty. It should be said that nothing in the world is less classical. Now the extraordinary vogue of the books of M. William H. Drummond in the United States as well as in Canada causes some of us to fear lest everyone impute to the mass of French people in the province of Quebec that bastard idiom.
>
> Sincerely we believe there is no place for alarm on that subject. The crippling of the language of the conqueror—after a century and a half of contact—by Jean Baptiste Canayen, marks instead the inalienability of his French spirit, his faithful attachment to the speech of his brothers.

Mme. Dandurand sees Drummond's work as an attention-getter: for the French in North America, and, therefore, an opportunity for New France writers to extend the Anglo-Saxon's education:

> Suffice it to say that the sympathetic heroes and heroines of *The Habitant* and of *Johnny Courteau* call to American [attention] the existence of the French-Canadian people. Since the days when the name of the French-Canadian nation rang in the four corners of the continent like a thunderbolt which accompanies the light of a formidable sword, there has been a period of obscurity. Our ancient rivals may have thought that we also had sunk into obscurity or had been assimilated. The wall of forgetfulness and indifference which the years have raised between us and them, M. Drummond attacks with a noble gesture. The popular stories of New France open hearts for us, conquer sympathies for us. The breach is now open; it is for us to enlarge it. It is for us of the French with our works and our masterpeices to follow the friend of the French-Canadian.

After Drummond's death, *La Patrie* is quoted (presumably in translation) by the Toronto *News* (April 13, 1907), and again there is greater precision about Drummond's subject matter and more restraint in the praise:

> It is interesting to note the opinion of the French-Canadian press. *La Patrie* says of his work: "He succeeded in sketching in verse, half-English, half-French, some of the better types of our country people, showing their frankness,

sincerity and ability in his truly French-Canadian heroes. A great admirer of our race, he exhibited in his verse their attractive qualities and their inexhaustible good-nature and vivacity. For this we owe him certainly an acknowledgement."

A stronger note of grateful appreciation runs through a general-summary article by "Pierre Lorraine" that appeared in a series of installments in *Le Journal de Francoise*. The article emphasizes the general notion that Drummond's dialect verse was his best:

> each time that he was unfaithful to the bizarre language that he had created initially; each time that he wished to clothe his more general ideas in a more chastized form, the spirit of his subject matter is lost; and he does not gain in elegance that which he has lost in emotion and picturesqueness. The same thoughts are there, but the expression that refurbishes them no longer moves us. It is as if a marvelous bagpipe-player who controls at will our tears and laughter undertook to execute the same melodies on an instrument with which he is not familiar; we remain unwarmed.
>
> The English poems of Drummond are certainly beyond the ordinary, but if he had written only that, he would remain in amateur's clothing instead of that of a national poet. (my translation)

In the only major analysis of Drummond's work that I located, R. E. Rashley, in a 1949 *Dalhousie Review* article, similarly upholds the value of Drummond's use of habitant patois, suggesting that the poet's deliberate choice and sustained practice demonstrates "that the patois satisfied a felt need." The carefully controlled manipulation of the patois enabled Drummond "to translate the rude life into an equally rude verse with a possibility of equal vigour." The result was an "escape from a damaging conventionality of language that had reduced poetry to insignificance.". . . Rashley argues that poets such as Carman, Lampman and Duncan Campbell Scott escaped from the limitations of the era's dignified poetic conventions in ways "that led them further and further away from the needs of a flesh-and-blood world to the borders of humanity." He cites "Lampman's escape into a formal style . . . Carman's into music . . . Duncan Campbell Scott's into austerity."

Drummond's escape into patois, Rashley says, is accompanied by a focus on "the conventionalized group-reaction":

> it is only in communal material, in situations where the group spirit is alive, where man is in contact with man, or with nature through the group senses, that this style takes on life and becomes something more than broken English. . . . The restriction imposed is that Drummond can approach his material only through a generalized concept, through the group consent.

The biography of the poet written by his widow corroborates in the main Rashley's implications about Drummond's predilection for the group spirit, and, perhaps, the distancing he achieved by patois. The biography reports that for a number of years, Drummond, as an independent adult and medical doctor, shared adjoining houses in Montreal with his mother and two married brothers. His immersion in habitant and voyageur language and lore appears to have begun when he was fifteen and was stationed as a summertime telegrapher at Bord-à-Plouffe. He worked there six summers and, one can speculate from casual scattered references in his later letters and from a phrase or two of May Drummond's that expressions in dialect became a playful mode of domestic discourse. (In a letter from Vancouver, September 3, 1901, for example, he tells his wife of meeting a man who "I remember when I was a 'small boy on de farm'"; and when his popularity as a writer forced a decision as to whether he continue as a doctor May Drummond writes that "he must choose, as he himself said: 'which side de cat she jomp on de fence'."

Nevertheless, a number of references make clear that, like most writers, Drummond wrote from personal experience and emotion—even when the resultant poem is alive with habitant language and setting. "'**Little Bateese**', almost as popular as the famous **'Wreck'**, was inspired by his son Barclay, a mischievous youngster of five who was also the prototype of '**Dominique**'...." The account in **"The Last Portage"** of a lumberman being led by the ghost of his son through a dark night to "de boss on de camp" was written after "our little son William Harvey died of tubercular meningitis at the age of three and [a] half years. The blow almost broke his father's heart, for he worshipped the beautiful child, so quiet, gentle and affectionate." The little boy, according to his mother, had "shadow playmates" with whom he played and talked. "He was always surprised when I was unable to see the 'little blue girl' who accompanied him on all his walks, or the other children with whom he played games on the floor."

> 'An' oh! mon Dieu! w'en he turns hees
>   head
> I'm seein' de face of ma boy is dead—
> Dead wit' de young blood in hees vein—
> An' dere he's comin' wance more again
> Wit' de curly hair, an' dark-blue eye,
> So lak de blue of de summer sky—
>   **("The Last Portage")**

A dog owned by William Henry Parker, Drummond's partner in a hunting and fishing club in the Laurentians, was named "Boule"; "beloved of the Commodore [Parker] it was despised by the Doctor by whom it was nevertheless immortalized in the poem of the same name."

"Le Vieux Temps" (of which the *Midland Review*, Louisville, Kentucky, said, "For truth, sincerity, simplicity and idealization no such poem as this has ever been written in America"), "was composed during my convalescence from a serious illness which... lost us our first child, a boy." **"Little Lac Grenier,"** of the poem so entitled, was Drummond's own favourite fishing spot, even though the fish there were small. His widow thought he liked, more particularly, the solitude and the setting—"a tiny sheet of water set like a gleaming jewel on the summit of a high hill. Surrounded by tall pine trees...."

Along with Drummond's sincerity in a number of his poems, the biography offers evidence about his sincerity, and consequently identity, as a Canadian. He emigrated from Ireland with his parents at the age of 10; but it was thirty-eight years later, 1902, before Drummond, as a poet and physician of some eminence, took advantage of an offer of a free passage to visit England (for the Coronation), Scotland and Ireland. In his letters to his wife, he expresses dislikes of most things English: the meat, the mushrooms, the peaches (too expensive), London's Strand—"all pleasure and vice... My God, what a beautiful thing purity is, or even comparative purity"—the railway accomodation—"the worst, I think, in the world"—and the silent unhelpful passengers. In Scotland, he admired the vigorous health of the men, though not the general humourlessness, and found all the women ugly. Ireland was "priest-ridden to an extent I never dreamed of.... I can't go any further touring, not even to my own birthplace; would be too painful—let me dream of it as it seemed in my boyhood days."

As Drummond summed it up in one letter: "the trip will have taught me a lot, but all the same *Je dis Canada pour moi,* and you can tell that to anybody you like." In another letter, he said:

> I don't believe the English people will ever appreciate my things—they are really very slow to see humour in anything outside England. Clever people too, these Londoners, and just as eager to grasp a dollar as any Yankee, but in some way they are behind the times.

"I am glad we live in Canada," he said—"haven't seen any place on this side I prefer to Montreal and I'd rather have my boys brought up in a country where for practical purposes all are equal."

After his death, Drummond was praised—perhaps undeservingly, since he earned his living as a physician—by a Toronto newspaper for not moving to the United States "as, alas, so many of our Canadian writers have done, moving over to the great republic to be nearer their nourishment." For Drummond, it seems clear, the nourishment for his poetry came from all the things in his life that he prized. In general, there was Canada, the outdoor life, and the independent unlettered farmers and lumbermen on the Quebec frontier, his paternal concern for his own young family and his physician's concern for all human beings. In particular, there was the patois he heard in the summers of youth at Bord-à-Plouffe as well as the emotions he experienced in common with all races and classes. It seems not too much to say that the consensus of Rashley's academic analyses, May Drummond's biography, and the obituary notices in newspapers at home and abroad agrees with E. W. Thompson's line in his commemorative poem which labels the poet "Everybody's friend." That Drummond also managed to produce some enduring poems is a pleasant testimony that literature and life can draw strength from each other without either delving deeply into anguish.

Drummond's general theme was described in the "Book and Beaver" column in the *Montreal Standard* (April 30, 1907) as "man, and the primary sanctities of the home" in contrast to the "note of refinement in Lampman, Roberts, Carman, Campbell, the Scotts..." "and their theme generally is nature-worship, pure and simple, the delight of the few."

> That is why his (Drummond's) verse comes home to the business and bosoms of all men. He has the sympathetic insight that comes from the true brotherly affection of a living man for living men. He has humor, that presence of sanctity and balance, whereas our Canadian muse is too dignified or too sad to glance in the direction of Burns' old crony, Fun.... The "net result" is that **"The Wreck of the *Julie Plante*"** gives pleasure to thousands, for whom (Lampman's first volume, 1888) *Among the Millet* is

a book with seven seals. It would be a narrow-minded critic who could think this a matter of regret.''

Whether Drummond himself would agree with the priority in this summation is doubtful. According to his wife, the doctor was reluctant to consider himself a literary man. ''He often expressed regrets that Archibald Lampman was obliged to slave in a government office instead of employing all his time and genius to the glory of literature.'' Nonetheless, the widespread popularity of Drummond's verse—miners in Cobalt could quote poems from memory—made its own contribution by helping to break up the stereotype of poetic convention at the beginning of the twentieth century. Although Drummond and his poems may not have moved critics to much comment, both were front-page news at his death and both broadened the general public's notion of poetry and extended for many readers their receptivity to literature. (pp. 179-86)

> *Gerald Noonan, ''Drummond—The Legend & the Legacy,'' in* Canadian Literature, *No. 90, Autumn, 1981, pp. 179-87.*

ADDITIONAL BIBLIOGRAPHY

Review of *The Voyageur*. *The Bookman* 29, No. 169 (October 1905): 44.
  Praises the themes and subjects of the poems in *The Voyageur* while disparaging the dialect in which they are written.

Burpee, Lawrence J. ''W. H. Drummond.'' In *Leading Canadian Poets*, edited by W. P. Percival, pp. 71-8. Toronto: Ryerson Press, 1948.
  A biographical sketch and a recapitulation of earlier critics' assessments of Drummond.

''Dr. Drummond's Last Work.'' *The Canadian Magazine* XXXII (November 1908—April 1909): 480.
  A laudatory review of *The Great Fight*.

Craig, Robert H. ''Reminiscences of W. H. Drummond.'' *The Dalhousie Review* 5, No. 2 (July 1925): 161-69.
  Relates several anecdotes about Drummond.

Drummond, May Harvey. ''William Henry Drummond.'' In *The Great Fight*, by William Henry Drummond, pp. 3-48. New York: G. P. Putnam's Sons, 1908.
  A biographical essay by Drummond's wife.

Macdonald, J. F. *William Henry Drummond*. Toronto: Ryerson Press, n.d., 129 p.
  An anthology of Drummond's best known poems, with a biographical introduction and an appreciation discussing Drummond's use of dialect and commenting on the poems included in this volume.

Munro, Neil. ''William Henry Drummond.'' In *The Poetical Works of William Henry Drummond*, pp. v-xx. New York: G. P. Putnam's Sons, 1912.
  Laudatory biographical essay.

Review of *The Habitant*. *The Nation* LXVI, No. 1718 (2 June 1898): 426-27.
  Praises Drummond's dialect poetry as ''uproariously jolly.''

''The Habitant Poet.'' *The New York Times Review of Books*, (20 October 1912), 616.
  A laudatory review of *The Poetical Works of William Henry Drummond*.

Noonan, Gerald, ''Perceptions of Drummond, 'Cet Idiome Bâtard,' and the French Canadian *Pastorale*.'' *Essays on Canadian Writing* 27 (Winter 1983-84): pp. 35-40.
  Discusses the stereotype of the *habitant* conveyed in Drummond's poetry.

O'Hagan, Thomas. ''A Canadian Dialect Poet.'' In his *Intimacies in Canadian Life and Letters*, pp. 83-94. Ottawa, Canada: Graphic Publishers, 1927.
  Appreciation of Drummond's life and works.

Osborn, E. B. ''Drummond and His Habitants.'' In his *Literature and Life: Things Seen, Heard, and Read*, pp. 116-23. Freeport, N.Y.: Books for Libraries Press, 1922.
  Praises Drummond's life and poetry.

Pacey, Desmond. Review of *Habitant Poems*. *Queen's Quarterly* 68, No. 1 (Spring 1961): 179-80.
  Disparages *Habitant Poems* as sentimetal.

Rhodenizer, V. B. ''William Henry Drummond.'' *The Canadian Bookman* 9, No. 2 (February 1927): 35-36.
  Discusses Drummond's life and the circumstances of his first publication.

———. ''William Henry Drummond.'' In his *A Handbook of Canadian Literature*, pp. 243-50. Ottawa, Canada: Graphic Publishers Ltd., 1930.
  Discusses Drummond's place in Canadian literature and quotes extensively from his poetry.

''The Poet of 'Les Habitants'.'' *The Spectator* 98, No. 4112 (April 20, 1907): 609-10.
  A laudatory reminiscence of Drummond.

Joseph Furphy

1843-1912

(Also wrote under pseudonyms Tom Collins and Warrigal Jack)
Australian novelist, poet, short story writer, and essayist.

Furphy is chiefly remembered as the author of *Such Is Life,*
considered one of the most important novels by an Australian
author. Like the works of his younger contemporary Henry
Lawson, Furphy's novel expresses nationalist sentiments, socialist ideals, and a profound understanding of life in the Australian bush in the late nineteenth century. Rejecting the romantic conventions of fiction of the era, Furphy sought to
present a realistic and humorous account of provincial life while
offering his views on various philosophical questions, the art
of fiction, and the future of Australia. Among the most admired
aspects of *Such Is Life* are its sophisticated experiments with
the novel form and vivid character portraits, particularly that
of the novel's narrator, Tom Collins. For these and other
achievements, *Such Is Life* is considered a classic of Australian
literature. According to American critic C. Hartley Grattan:
"As the years pass . . . , *Such Is Life* continues to fascinate,
to wax in power, and more and more obviously demonstrate
that it has the qualities which make for permanence."

Furphy was born near Yarra Glen, Victoria, nearly three years
after his parents emigrated to Australia from County Armagh
in Northern Ireland. His early education was conducted at home
by his mother, who used the Bible and the works of Shakespeare as textbooks for her children, but he later attended school
when the family moved to Kangaroo Ground and subsequently
to Kyneton. A large, literate, and inventive family, the Furphys
contributed humorous verses and prose works to a family literary album and continued to write for one another's amusement well into adulthood. According to Furphy, his teens were
spent "in dodging out of farm work, and in learning to mis-
manage various kinds of portable engine plant." He left home
at an early age to work as a miner, but at twenty-two he
returned, and at twenty-three he married Leonie Germain, a
sixteen-year-old French immigrant. In 1868 Furphy and his
wife moved to a selection—a farm on land offered by the
government for settlement—in the Lake Cooper district of Victoria, where Furphy's family had also relocated. He later described their life there as "four or five years' occupation of
the worst selection in Rodney." Abandoning the farm in pursuit
of a more substantial income for his family, he became a
teamster, or "bullocky," transporting wool and other goods
by oxcart from remote stations to railway lines and market
centers; *Such Is Life* is based largely on his experiences as a
bullock driver during this period. In 1883, the year in which
Such Is Life is set, Furphy was forced to sell his bullocks due
to a severe drought which devastated the entire region. He
accepted a position at his brother John's foundry in Shepparton
and, for the first time in his life, worked regular hours and
enjoyed ample leisure in which to write. In the evenings he
worked on *Such Is Life,* eventually producing well over one
thousand pages of manuscript. Upon its release in 1903, the
novel was greeted with enthusiasm by Australian critics. Appreciative reviewers recognized the historical value of its realistic portrayal of Australian bush life in the late nineteenth
century, and in 1956 novelist Miles Franklin described the work

as the "first novel of magnitude to deal so inherently with the
landscape" of Australia. Some critics, however, considered
Such Is Life too politically oriented, noting in it numerous
lengthy digressions expressing Furphy's socialist and nationalist ideals. Furphy's subsequent novels, *Rigby's Romance* and
The Buln-Buln and the Brolga, were less successful both artistically and commercially than *Such Is Life.* In 1905 Furphy
and his wife moved to Western Australia to be near their three
children. He died there in 1912 after suffering a cerebral hem-
orrhage.

Furphy's reputation rests primarily on *Such Is Life,* which he
published under the pseudonym "Tom Collins." Submitting
the manuscript to editor A. G. Stephens of the *Bulletin* in 1897,
Furphy wrote: "I have just finished writing a full-sized novel,
title, *Such Is Life,* scene, Riverina and Northern Vic.; temper,
democratic; bias, offensively Australian." Although Stephens
required extensive revisions in the lengthy manuscript, he confidently published *Such Is Life,* believing that it would become
"an Australian classic, or semi-classic." The work presents a
purportedly random selection of diary entries written in 1883
by Tom Collins, a government "Deputy-Assistant-Sub-
Inspector" whose job brings him into contact with a wide range
of bush types, including selectors, station managers, boundary
riders, bullock drivers, and swagmen. Collins's journal entries

form a series of loosely connected minor episodes in themselves, while incidentally revealing the underlying plot of the novel—the "romance" of Molly Cooper and "Warrigal" Alf Morris—a plot to which Collins himself is blind. According to Furphy: "The studied inconsecutiveness of the 'memoirs' is made to mask coincidence and cross purposes, sometimes too intricate," and critics consider this experimental structure representative of Furphy's sense of "how things happen." He held that knowledge does not come to us complete, believing rather that we comprehend it casually and coincidentally. This concept is central to the art of Furphy's fiction and to his vision of life. The story of Mary O'Halloran, an Australian child who is lost in the bush for several days and dies only moments before a rescuer discovers her whereabouts, is often cited by critics as exemplary of Furphy's view of the accidental and arbitrary nature of human life. Collins, and through him the reader, learns the details of Mary's life and death over several chapters, with each new piece of information affording further insight into the tale. As in the story of the missing child, coincidence and chance seem to play a large part in the world of the Australian bush dweller and Collins concocts the "one controlling alternative theory" in a personal attempt to understand the nature of the universe. He suggests that people are allowed a limited number of decisions in life, and that the choices made at these junctions determine their lives until another opportunity to choose arises. Collins sees the theory as a compromise between free will and determinism, but most critics have recognized that the events of the novel expose his philosophy as ultimately fatalistic.

While the structure and philosophy of *Such Is Life* have been the subjects of extensive critical debate, most critics agree on Furphy's comic genius. This quality is most notably embodied in the ironic misperceptions and predicaments of narrator Tom Collins, which often form the basis of Furphy's parody and satire. His humor ranges from the subtle rendering of immigrant dialects, to substitutions such as "(adj.)" or "(compound expletive)" for the obscenities pervasive in the conversation of bushmen, to the hilarious episode in which Collins lands trouserless in the midst of a Sunday school picnic. A favorite target of Furphy's satire is the popular literature of the era, and he especially attacked the conventional romanticism of such novels as Henry Kingsley's epic *The Recollections of Geoffrey Hamlyn* (1846).

The chapters deleted from *Such Is Life* at the request of Stephens were later reworked by Furphy into two less comprehensive works, *Rigby's Romance* and *The Buln-Buln and the Brolga*. As excisions, they are often studied coordinately with the published versions of *Such Is Life*. In *Rigby's Romance* Collins relates the story of American Jeff Rigby, who functions as a spokesperson for Furphy's Christian Socialist views. Rigby is pursued in Australia by a woman he had loved and left forty years earlier, and critics often compare this romance to that of Molly Cooper and "Warrigal" Alf Morris in *Such Is Life*. Furphy believed that *Rigby's Romance* contained his best work, but few critics have agreed with this assessment. In *The Buln-Buln and the Brolga*, the European, romantic tradition in literature and the bush tradition of oral storytelling compete in a series of campfire tall tales told by the Buln-Buln ("lyre bird"), Fred Falkland-Pritchard, and the Brolga ("native companion"), Barefoot Bob. Although these novels have received decidedly less critical attention than *Such Is Life*, most reviewers have recognized their importance to Furphy scholarship. For example, critic Joseph Jones has studied Furphy's socialist philosophy as it is presented in *Rigby's Romance* and

has concluded that "out of context, *Rigby's Romance* is scarcely more than a well-sugared political prescription, but recalled as part of the original design [of *Such Is Life*] it shows us how seriously the author took his political theory."

Unlike some early critics who viewed the novel as an autobiographical document, modern critics regard *Such Is Life* as an elaborately conceived, intricately structured experimental novel. Later scholars have concentrated on the complex structure and philosophy of the work, with critical comment since the 1960s focussing primarily on narrator Tom Collins and the ironic philosophical separation between him and Furphy. Since the republication of *Such Is Life* in the 1940s and the posthumous release of Furphy's two shorter novels, Furphy's works have steadily gained an audience both popular and academic. John K. Ewers has remarked that "in recent years *Such Is Life* has been more often critically dissected and analyzed than any other Australian novel. And more than any other Australian novel, each criticism of it affirms its quality." According to H. M. Green: "*Such Is Life* is what Stephens said it was fit to become: 'an Australian classic, or semiclassic.' Along with Lawson . . . Furphy represents the Australia of his day, and for good and ill he stands, more than Lawson or any other writer, for 'aggressive Australianism'."

PRINCIPAL WORKS

Such Is Life [as Tom Collins]   (novel)   1903; abridged edition, 1937
Rigby's Romance [as Tom Collins]   (novel)   1905-06; published in journal *Barrier Truth;* unabridged edition, 1946
Poems   (poetry)   1916
The Buln-Buln and the Brolga   (novel)   1948
The Buln-Buln and the Brolga, and Other Stories   (novel and short stories)   1971
Joseph Furphy   (novels, short stories, poetry, essays, and letters)   1981

JOSEPH FURPHY   (essay date 1903)

[*In the following review originally printed in the* Bulletin *in 1903, Furphy appraises Australian literature and provides a synopsis and evaluation of* Such Is Life. *When this review was published it was not known by the general public that Furphy was the author of* Such Is Life.]

Nowhere is literary material more copious in variety, or more piquant in character, than in legendless Australia. Off the well-beaten tracks of the spurious-picturesque and the unconditional-hoggish, lie spacious areas of subject-matter, irreverently challenging the Biblical axiom, that "there is no new thing under the sun". And countless types of character, evolved by the industrial, social and territorial conditions of heretofore inarticulate activities, confront the seeing eye and await the graphic pen. For tragedy, humour, pathos, fancy, however indissolubly linked with human nature, must assume unhackneyed aspects in a continent which resembles Europe or North America only inasmuch as there is a river in both.

The fictional literature of Australia—scanty at most, and uneven at best—has advanced by orderly gradation from Anglo-Australian, through Colonial, to National. The successional replacement of the immigrant, with his old-world ideals, by the impressionable representative of a new type has made such a transition inevitable. But the mass of our literature is British: and book-begotten sentiment dies hard, except amongst pioneers of opinion. Conventionality persists in viewing Australian characteristics and deviations as more or less exotic; whilst to the fully emancipated native-born, these stand as self-established units of comparison, as normal and legitimate phenomena, in opposition to the hearsay conditions of moister and less home-like lands. The corresponding penalty of this National consciousness is a certain narrowness of outlook, a spontaneous impression that the sun rises over the Barrier Reef, and sets behind the Leeuwin. When darkened by stolidity, such focalized regard is sometimes amusing, sometimes regrettable—which, however, doesn't signify much, as it seldom reaches the dignity of print. Shrivelling into provincialism, it becomes contemptible; and, festering into the imperial-cum-provincial sentiment, it becomes obscene.

But when illuminated by intelligence, the same insular survey crystallizes into far-sighted patriotism. When further reinforced by acute observation, and cast into literary form, it invests with interest the minutest details of National life. Add humour, sympathy, and felicity of phrase, together with that rarest of mental qualities, *initiative,* and the subtle touch of nature is achieved. Such fiction may be truer than truth itself, since the latter, often anomalous and untypical, is always part-hidden from view. But here a new light of significance is flashed on the commonplace; a shade of actuality softens the bizarre; and each scene, action or colloquy, carrying authenticity on its face, becomes an indispensable accessory to the completed work. This describes Tom Collins—at his best.

At his worst, he displays an immoderate egotism, apparently undisciplined by controversy, and evidently fostered by solitary self-communion. The outcome is a pedantic cock-sureness of conclusion, a literary arrogance which blandly accepts hypothesis (his own, always) as demonstration. To be sure, this particular vice has its virtue, in outspoken contempt of fetish, in calm Australian sufficiency, and in disregard of hostile opinion. Less excusable, perhaps, is an affected mannerism which wantonly, and often profusely, weaves into the text quotations and inferences, more or less apt, but too recondite for the casual reader.

Tom Collins can condense when he chooses—but that is not always. However, as his antithesis to brevity is discursiveness, rather than prolixity, he never drags. There is interest, if not relevancy, in every sentence. The style is attractive—lucid, vigorous, half-scholarly, half-slangy, and occasionally graceful; carrying the frank personality of the writer through every paragraph.

Apart from the historical value of the book, as seizing and fixing pictures of Riverina life, necessarily transitory, the portraiture deserves notice. Here the author is unconsciously at home. Rarely is a character revealed by verbal description, each speaks for himself; and clean-cut individuality, consistent in its human inconsistency, is thrown on the page. Isocratic rather than democratic in tone, these sketches present each individual—squatter or sundowner—as a document of special interest, yet bearing the common seal. Hence the silhouette of any passer-by shows sharp and distinct as the finished portrait of a familiar.

Beyond all other Australian writers, Tom Collins is a master of idiom. There is no confusion of patois, nor exaggeration of grammatical solecism in his dialogue. As in actual life, the education of each speaker is denoted by his phraseology; the dialect of each European bespeaks his native locality; and, above all, the language of the most unbookish bushman never degenerates into "coster".

Originality is a characteristic of *Such Is Life;* and this is attained, to begin with, in the simplicity of the scheme. Setting out with an unpremeditated purpose of amplifying the diary-memoranda of one week—the book naturally falls into seven chapters. The first date is taken at hazard, from a series of filled-up pocket diaries. This random text introduces five typical bullock-drivers, with three or four assorted nomads. The day is uneventful, but the night's camp (a risky grass-steal) is enlivened by Outback topics. The scene is on the Lachlan plains.

Then for sufficient reasons, the diary-records cease to be consecutive, and are henceforth separated by monthly intervals. The scene of chapter II is placed in the Lachlan-Darling scrub country, amongst local station hands. Chapter III opens on the Murray, between Echuca and Albury. Chapter IV displays the Lower Lachlan, with actors proper to the scene; and chapter V falls in an adjacent locality, with all accessories widely dissimilar. Chapter VI returns to the vicinity of chapter I but the aspect is squattocratic, not nomadic. Chapter VII is arbitrarily built on a date six or seven weeks subsequent to that of its forerunner, in order to serve as a sequel.

Underneath this obvious dislocation of anything resembling continuous narrative, run several undercurrents of plot, manifest to the reader, though ostensibly unnoticed by the author. For example: an incidental camp fire yarn, in chapter I, casually furnishes the key to some strong character-painting in chapters IV and VI. In fact, the studied inconsecutiveness of the "memoirs" is made to mask coincidence and cross purposes, sometimes too intricate. (pp. 405-07)

> *Joseph Furphy, in a review of "Such Is Life," in his* Joseph Furphy, *edited by John Barnes, University of Queensland Press, 1981, pp. 405-07.*

THE ATHENAEUM   (essay date 1904)

[In the following excerpt, the critic discusses the strengths and weaknesses of Such Is Life.*]*

Such Is Life is . . . long, extraordinarily long, close packed with reflection, realistic in most of its grim detail, clever, undisciplined, pseudo-philosophical, and genuinely bitter; a really remarkable book, and well worth the rather serious effort which is required to peruse it from end to end. Truly the author says: "I am no romancist. I repudiate shifts, and stand or fall by the naked truth." If he does not always see the whole truth, he at least states nakedly enough what he does see, and assuredly he is no romancer. He is a great deal too bitter to be the philosopher he thinks himself, and too furiously a partisan and an enthusiast to see as far into life as he thinks he sees. He is intolerant of stupidity, and, should he happen upon a dense, slow-moving mind, must needs lash it with scorpions of sarcasm and vituperation. Hence he is absolutely unable to see anything of the sterling virtues, the solid merits, which frequently accompany these mental shortcomings. The vanity, mock gentility, and pinchbeck pride of the wastrel remittance-man have mortally offended this ardent son of the colonies, and he is unable to see that any Englishman, other than a tradesman, is of the slightest use in Australia, to himself or to any one else. Yet he knows something of the history of his own country and, if not blinded by his cynicism and bitterness, would be forced to admit that the generation which preceded that of the "native-born" achieved a great deal more for themselves and for Australia than their successors have done. He has met some sterling characters among men of lowly origin, and some ne'er-do-weels among men of another class. So he must needs revile the whole body of gentlefolk, and assume that no gentleman can ever really hold his own outside a drawing-room or a tennis-court. It is clear that he is maddened by the sight of incompetent persons of the kind. But one hastens, in the interests of sweet justice, to admit that his madness is frequently both plausible and entertaining, and that in his lucid intervals Mr. Collins gives ample evidence of close and penetrating observation, of good and even kindly feeling towards his fellow-man, and vivid ability to depict the rough and strenuous up-country life. But, as in his country itself, so in Mr. Collins as a writer and a thinker, a lamentable lack is shown of the salutary influences of discipline. For example, Mr. Collins aims avowedly at nothing short of the grimmest and most undeviating realism in his pictures of bush life, and he attains it when dealing with his own people, with the rough-hewn kind of men he most admires. But let him step aside for one moment to point a jibe or an argument against the sort of people he does not understand, and that very moment his vaunted realism crumbles into stuff as remote from truth as the rhapsodies of the latest favourite of the circulating libraries. He is sketching a party of bullock-drivers, whose manners and habits are savagely primitive. Among them is one Willoughby, born an English gentleman, who has long been a wastrel of the wastrels, and a swagman in the bush. To give point to his assertion that men so reared must needs prove sorry fools in the rough-and-tumble world of pioneering, the author so shamelessly forsakes his realism as to make Willoughby talk like this, over the camp fire:—

> "Precisely, Mr. Collins," replied the whaler. "Nature produces such men expressly for rank and file; and I should imagine that their existence furnishes sufficient rejoinder to the levelling theory." . . . "Well, to quote Madame de Stael," replied Willoughby, "he abuses a man's privilege of being ugly."

And this in conversation with men who are feeding him, and who themselves talk like this:—

> "No, by Cripes! Not me. That cove's an (adj.) liar. He don't give a dam, s'posin' a feller's soul gits bashed out. Best sight I seen for many a day was seein' him gittin' kicked. If the mean beggar'd only square up with me, I'd let summedy else do his work."

The author learns from camp-fire conversation among bushmen (and to the reviewer's own knowledge bushmen are only to be excelled by sailors in the matter of the extraordinary and impossible yarns that pass current among them for facts) that Burke the explorer carried a special receptacle among his baggage for a silk hat or a cocked hat. Upon the strength of this alone, one sees that the author despises the explorer's memory, and expects his reader to go with him so far. "Of what use could such a man be as a pioneer?" he asks in effect. "Any native-born bullock-driver could have done far better."

Mr. Collins has evidently done a deal of reading in his time, but in this, as in everything else, he suffers from want of discipline. His active mind appears to be a receptacle crammed almost to bursting with a mass of unclassified, undigested knowledge—a chaotic jumble, the hopeless confusion of which robs him of all sense of perspective, and shows him no one thing in its true relation to other things.

We pay more notice than usual to Mr. Collins's book because we are inclined to think that he is in many ways a typical Australian writer, whose riotous tendencies in thought have been aggravated by the influence of the *Sydney Bulletin.* As to our hopes for his future, that depends very largely upon his present age, of course. If *Such Is Life* is written by a young man, it shows promise of fine work to come. If it is the book of a man past maturity, we can only regret that the early influences of his life did not make more for mental discipline, concentration, and open-minded study of his fellows. In any case, the book as it stands is purely Australian and exceedingly interesting; and we trust that its great length and somewhat wearisome faults of intolerance and verbose bitterness—not to mention the sheer rudeness of passages which lead one to hope and believe the author is a young man—will not prevent its receiving the consideration of thoughtful readers. (pp. 43-4)

> *A review of "Such Is Life," in* The Athenaeum, *No. 3976, January 9, 1904, pp. 43-4.*

C. HARTLEY GRATTAN (essay date 1937)

[*An American economist as well as a social and literary critic, Grattan was a prolific contributor of articles to national magazines and was considered a well-informed judge of literature. His literary career began in 1924, when one of his essays appeared in H. L. Mencken's* The American Mercury; *afterward, like Mencken, he earned a reputation as an outspoken opponent of the moralistic New Humanism movement in American letters. Throughout much of his career, Grattan was also a recognized authority, through his many lectures and writings, on Australia and the southwest Pacific. In the following excerpt, he favorably appraises* Such Is Life *as a significant contribution to Australian literature and examines Furphy's political and social ideals.*]

As the years pass and lesser Australian books fade from memory or assume a purely antiquarian interest, *Such Is Life* continues to fascinate, to wax in power, and more and more obviously demonstrate that it has the qualities which make for permanence. (p. 68)

[Furphy] wrote a highly personal book of which it can truly be said that whoever touches it touches a man. There is nothing in Tom Collins's variety of "speculatism" that suggests the struggles for an absolutely impersonal point of view which obsessed certain of the French writers of the latter part of the nineteenth century. It is not only that he intrudes into the book as an actor; but it is also that nothing is transacted in the book, whether of the mind or of the body, which is not subtly transmuted by the author into something rich and strange. It is impossible to think of the book apart from the author or the author apart from the book. The one is the guarantee of the immortality of the other. Yet to seal this identity required the "death" of Joseph Furphy, and when he wrote to A. G. Stephens, then editor of *The Bulletin,* on the 4th of April, 1897, he was announcing not the completion of a book simply, but rather the birth of Tom Collins. What he said was:

> I have just finished writing a full-sized novel, title, *Such Is Life,* scene, Riverina and Northern Vic.; temper, democratic; bias, offensively Australian.

Seldom has an author found it possible so accurately to describe what it is he has put on paper. Furphy's book was freighted with the wisdom of a lifetime. (p. 69)

The form of *Such Is Life* is perfectly adapted to the incurable digressiveness of the author. Pretending to take up a diary kept in very abbreviated form, Collins decides to expand the entry for the ninth day of every month during the year 1883. Sometimes circumstances make it necessary for him to take in happenings of the eighth day and, to complete a story, to advance to the tenth day. Characters recur in different entries, but it is not necessary that they do so and apparently it was not consciously planned to practice this economy of invention. What any single "entry" will contain is impossible to predict and the reader has to the full the pleasure of surprise. He may be treated to a long conversation, to an adventure of Collins's, to a series of yarns told around a single theme, to a discursive essay on any one of the various subjects to which Collins gave attention in his miscellaneous reading, or to a combination of all of these things.

While the form is the loosest possible and the subject matter in the truest sense a potpourri, the book is integrated by a sustained point of view. "The fact is," wrote Collins, "that I object to being regarded as a mere romanticist, even as a dead-head speculator, or dilettante reporter, of the drama of life. You must take me as a hard-working and ordinary actor on this great stage of fools; but one who, nevertheless, finds a wholesome recreation in observing the parts played by his fellow hypocrites. (The Greek 'hupokrisis', I find, signified indifferently, 'actor' and 'hypocrite'.)" That was his *literary* attitude. Much more important for any true understanding of *Such Is Life* is a clear conception of Collins's outlook on life and that, in turn, can only be understood in relation to the setting in which it was developed.

The year 1883 marks no outstanding event in Australian history around which Collins might have built his book; it was merely one in the interminable procession. Yet a recurring note in the work is that a crisis is facing the Australian people and another is that it behoves them to think well of the line of action to be taken to protect the future. Less than a century old, Australia had already passed through several evolutionary phases and the diseases of the Old World were appearing on the continent. By encouraging the development of sheep stations, the early governors had unconsciously planted a seed which in time made impossible the use of the continent as the seat of penal settlements. . . . In spite of some aristocratic opposition inspired by fear of losing a cheap labor supply, the agitation against the convict labor grew so strong that by the early 1850's transportation to the Eastern colonies ceased. In the early fifties also, gold was discovered, a vast horde of fortune-seekers poured into the country, and Australian society was once more made fluid.

With the decline of gold production the assimilation of the ex-miners became an acute problem, a political issue of the first magnitude. The cry was to unlock the lands, since much of the desirable acreage, both as to location and fertility, was in the hands of the squatters. Collins remarks that it had been "purchased or stolen . . . in the good old times." The unlocking of the lands was accomplished in the sixties and a new class, or at least a vastly expanded class, appeared, the farmers. References to the struggle are fairly frequent in *Such Is Life*: to the tricks played by the squatters to defeat the law; to the hardships endured by the farmers after they had acquired the land. (pp. 69-71)

In the sixties also, David Syme, who had been a leading advocate of unlocking the lands, began to agitate for protection in his newspaper, the Melbourne *Age,* ostensibly to provide employment for the laboring class. As a result the foundations of Australian industry were laid and a new menace to Collins's ideals took root. When the Commonwealth was established Victoria's protection was adopted as a national policy and the drive for "secondary" industries proceeded on a national scale.

By 1883 these significant changes were being digested and in *Such Is Life* the new situation is reflected in an amazingly complete fashion. It should be noted that Collins's own life covered the crucial years of Australian history and that as Joseph Furphy he either directly or indirectly engaged in or experienced the successive changes: he was born in 1843 before transportation ceased, worked on the gold fields, tried farming, turned to bullock driving in the back country, and ended his life as an employee of a "secondary" industry. When he came to write his book, Collins, either with clairvoyant insight or by extraordinary good luck, chose central characters from a group which still retained elements of independence based on the possession of property but which, nevertheless, lacked land and was, moreover, at the mercy of a dominant class, the squatters. He chose to write his book around bullock drivers, men engaged in trucking wool out of the back country to the railway (which would eventually pretty much displace them) and manufactured goods and food supplies in to the stations. It was gruelling work in the hot, dry country, but it gave plenty of scope for the development of personality and abundant time for reflection. The nightly camp of the "bullockies" is a favourite setting in *Such Is Life*. The rambling talk around the camp fire justifies the rambling structure of the book. (pp. 71-2)

It was a cruel country for man and beast, this in which *Such Is Life* is set. . . . But, alas, such a land is subject to the same possibilities as any other and Collins is forced to raise his voice in warning:

> As day by day, year by year, our own fluid Present congeals into a fixed Past, we shall do well to take heed that, in time to come, our own memory may not be justly held accursed. For though history is a thing that never repeats itself—since no two historical propositions are alike—one perennial truth holds good, namely, that every social hardship or injustice may be traced back to the linked sins of aggression and submission, remote or proximate in point of time.

What did the men Collins so lovingly studied—bullock drivers, boundary riders and other station hands, "swaggies" (itinerant workers, some down and out)—have to do with all this as they met on the road or around camp-fires? Woven into their yarns of adventure, heroic and grotesque, were weighty reflections on the themes announced above. . . . Throughout the book there is an undercurrent of fear that the country will be completely conquered by a plutocracy and that a supine citizenry will regard it as a "divinely instituted sponge for the absorption of every desirable thing the world can produce."

The cause? Individualism encouraged by Samuel Smile's "pig philosophy" and the gospel according to Poor Richard! The full panoply of a dominant class is being developed. The traditional Vested Interests (the capitals are Collins's) have appeared. Evidences on all sides illustrate the "profound cunning of a propertied class operating with sinister purpose on the

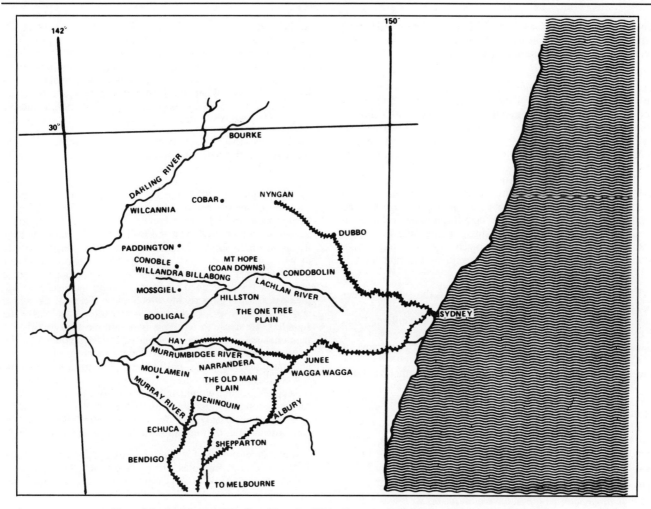

Map of the Riverina and Northern Victoria, 1883. Courtesy of University of Queensland Press.

inevitable flunkeyism of a dependent class.'' The church is an instrument in the struggle and Collins's anti-clericalism is pervasive. He speaks of "noblemen, gentlemen, *clergymen,* and intermediary pimps of substantial position." He speaks of the "silky loyalty to the law and the profits" of the church. The only clergyman in the story suffers an ignominious defeat in argumentation, worsted by an illiterate and an educated bullocky in about equal degree. Even literature, Collins saw, though he loved it—Shakespeare especially, and Milton, Goethe, Dante, Spenser, Thomson, Cowper, Crabbe, Walt Whitman, Pope, Byron, Longfellow and the Bible are freely and appositely quoted—is also a weapon of oppression. Gray, Cowper and Crabbe are shown to be hostile to the "men of no property" while Burns and Tom Paine are cited as their champions. (To a friend Furphy remarked, "I hate Sir Walter Scott as the incarnation of the British Tory.") Nothing that will contribute to the defeat of the common man has been neglected by the partizans of privilege.

The consequences? "In this pandemonium of Individualism, the weak, the diffident, the scrupulous, and the afflicted, are thrust aside or trampled down." "The best of all possible worlds remains under the worst of all possible managements." "We find that sort o' thing means the survival of the greediest."

The remedy? "Restraint's the thing we want now. . . ." It is to the socialists that Collins turned, writing ironically of "the

nefarious Socialist movement, poisoning the public mind with aspirations for a state of things which would make life worth living." Even in those days, Australian labor unions were on their feet, the socialists were agitating and the peculiar non-Marxist socialism, "socialisme sans doctrines" as a French observer called it, was in the making. *Such Is Life* is a primary document for any student of the history of Australian attitudes. However severe the reverses suffered, however distorted they have since become, Collins's ideas and ideals still animate the Australian masses in some degree. Insofar as they do, they are a source of health. (pp. 72-4)

It would be a distinct disservice, however, to give the impression that the bare bones of Collins's ideology, which I am sure he felt to be "offensively Australian", and that of the Australian common man, protrude from *Such Is Life* as in some crude proletarian novel of 1934. The ideology is an integral part of the book, the dynamic element indeed, and the way in which it infuses the total structure illustrates excellently the difference between an ideology derived from hard experience and long reflection and one learned by rote and applied without understanding.

The quotations I have made are in "literary" English, but equally relevant citations could be found couched in the extraordinary dialects of some of the characters. For while long passages in the book are in Collins's own style which was decidedly personal and flavorous, though somewhat labored, when conversations are recorded the language is that of the characters depicted. The correspondence is exact and lovingly carried out. Only one concession is made. Collins was a bit of a Victorian and could not bring himself to write—much less print—two words which occur in the conversation of the "dinkum Aussie" hardly less frequently than commas and periods on the printed page: hell and bloody. His device for indicating their occurrence is rather amusing: "'You're a (adj.) liar!' 'Who the (adj. sheol) do you think you're talking to?'" Otherwise the authentic speech comes through clear and ringing, as direct as the actions being depicted, or the thoughts being conveyed.

Peppered with hells and bloodies, then, the men tell of their adventures, their encounters with the squatters in the struggle for grass and water (the only things, according to their code, it was not wrong to steal), their bad luck and its causes, the ironies of fate to which they had been subjected, tell of children lost in the trackless bush, of loads burned by grass fires, of sickness in isolation, of fantastic gambling, of incredible fortitude in adversity. High humor and pathos, grandeur and misery, generosity and meanness, fellow feeling and misanthropy find their place. And then again the men merely stand and wait. That also is part of the record.

For such is life! The refrain which Collins found covered all possible contingencies and finally chose as his title, is well-worn now and a bit banal to sophisticated ears, but it serves with complete accuracy, which is important, to designate a superb book. It is a book which speaks directly to those men of no property to-day who, even in countries with traditions of democratic equality, are faced with the consequences of aggressions supinely submitted to by their ancestors. It is, in fact, a book full of "dangerous thoughts" and for that reason not least a (adj.) fine book for the present generation. (pp. 75-6)

*C. Hartley Grattan, "To Collins's 'Such Is Life',"
in The Australian Quarterly, Vol. IX, No. 3, September, 1937, pp. 67-76.*

VANCE PALMER (essay date 1937)

[In the following excerpt from his preface to the abridged edition of Such Is Life, *Palmer directs his general commentary at a non-Australian readership.]*

For over thirty years [*Such Is Life*] has been held in high regard by Australians. They have been attracted by its pervasive comedy, its authentic dialogue, its eye for character, but perhaps, more intimately, by its note of robust egalitarianism, recognizing this as the spirit of the country. There are homely qualities, family jokes, that endear a book to a particular audience; *Such Is Life,* however, does not depend on those. English readers will find this abridged version of it just as comprehensible as, say, Mark Twain's *Life on the Mississippi,* a work that in some ways it resembles.

The Riverina, that stretch of pastoral country north of the Murray, was Joseph Furphy's Mississippi. He had trudged its long tracks behind a bullock-team, fighting, like the men in his book, for grass and water. Around its scattered campfires he had shared in the tale-telling, the endless argument on bushcraft, politics or general ideas. The salt of all such talk must be humour. That Furphy had his own original brand of it is evident all through *Such Is Life,* but particularly in the third chapter with its pursuit of an outrageous situation to its logical

end, the overflowing farce never obliterating human character. . . .

As a boy he must have been aware of the great change taking place in the country, the tumult that followed the discovery of gold in Ballarat and Bendigo, the tide of newcomers pouring in, ships lying deserted in Port Phillip, canvas-towns springing up along one creek bed after another. (p. 11)

But the gold boom, with its promise of wealth for all, was soon over. The world into which Joseph Furphy plunged as a youth was peopled by unsuccessful miners who had dreamt of Eldorado and had awakened to find a pastoral country divided into great holdings thinly filled with cattle and sheep. It was a world where most of the workers had to be nomads, moving from one job to another, with little hope of attaining independence. The sharp, ironic contrast between dream and fact brought to birth ideas which have coloured Australian life ever since.

Furphy's struggling teamsters, unsettled station hands, sundowners, knockabout bushmen, are the sons of those unlucky gold-seekers and hopeful immigrants. They are a mixed lot, but beneath their sardonic, slipshod talk can be found the thread that unites them. This is their belief in "mateship," a passion for social equality. . . . Joseph Furphy writes not only of these people but for them; not only for them but as one of them. For all his Irish love of the long word, the literary allusion, he is no professional author keeping one eye on the oddities of his subject matter, the other on his middle-class audience. This attitude of his gives *Such Is Life* an unusual flavour, even to-day when proletarian writing is no longer rare.

As to the form of the book, a word of warning is needed. The declared artlessness of the author, as a mere "annalist of stern veracity" setting out in "these scrappy memoirs" and by the elaboration of a week's diary to find what life means, is a device that conceals unremitting literary guile. Does that first chapter, for instance, seem in the main a long and rambling dialogue round a campfire, leading nowhere? Not a word of it can be missed, for it is significantly veined with minor cross-currents of plot and motive. What may seem a digression of the author or a mere ejaculation of some character will prove to be part of the book's complex framework. What is life? asks Joseph Furphy. He pulls with strong, sensitive fingers at the end of thread nearest to him; and finds himself led to traverse the whole of his intimate experience; such is life. (pp. 12-13)

Vance Palmer, in a preface to "Such Is Life": Being Certain Extracts from the Diary of Tom Collins *[pseudonym of Joseph Furphy] by Tom Collins, edited by Vance Palmer, Jonathan Cape, 1937, pp. 11-13.*

A. G. MITCHELL (essay date 1945)

[In the following excerpt, Mitchell examines the philosophical and moral questions considered in Such Is Life *and analyzes the novel's structure.]*

Furphy has indicated that *Such Is Life* is more than a meaningful and appropriate title. It is a theme followed out not only in separate parts but also in the whole fabric of the book.

Such Is Life is trite, and we need not suspect that Furphy had any delusions about its orginality. He had as quick an eye as the next for "original remarks". . . . But the expression has, in Furphy's use of it, the more significance for being well worn.

In its common use "Such Is Life" is merely an expression of surprise at odd happenings, and there are plenty of events and situations in *Such Is Life* that invite the remark. Things happen contrary to or in even apparent mockery of what the most careful forethought plans or allows for. . . . The example from *Such Is Life* that remains most vividly in the memory is the story of the wanderer who died near Rory's house. As Collins approaches Rory's house he sees a man, apparently wriggling himself into a more comfortable position beneath a vine-covered tree. Collins' first impulse is to approach the man with a friendly greeting, but he checks himself. It is two hours before sunset, and the proper time for a swagman to approach the house is at sunset, when it is too dark for work on the wood-heap. So Collins decides he will allow the swagman to choose his own time. In the morning he asks Rory whether he sees many swagmen about. Rory tells Collins he had heard of a man half-blind with sandy blight making for Ivanhoe. He adds that a week or ten days before he had found a swag and noticed some tracks, and felt sure that both belonged to the man with the sandy blight. Collins asks Rory immediately to come with him to the creeper-covered tree. There he finds the swagman dead, "not of thirst alone, but of mere physical exhaustion, sealed by the final collapse of hope." "Such is Life," says Collins, "and such is death." There is an appalling incongruity between the trivial, light-hearted reason for Collins' checking his natural impulse to speak to the man, and the consequences of his action. The difference between life and death for the wanderer was a five minutes' space of time: "Likely he had heard the cocks crowing at your place before daylight, and was making for the sound, only that the light beat him, and he gave it best five minutes too soon." Five minutes and a seemingly unimportant decision amount to the difference between life and death.

Such Is Life abounds in incidents of this kind, on larger and smaller scales; happenings which not only mock the most careful judgment and patient forethought but which twist themselves into stranger shapes than invention could contrive.

Or we may meet an unexpected coincidence so pat to the circumstances that it seems to have been contrived by a watchful deity for his own amusement and the moral correction of the persons concerned, "a conjuncture, in fact, which for the moment threw us both staggering back on the theology of childhood." . . . But these are only parts of the larger puzzle, the "engaging problem," life. As we read on "such is life" takes on, as I have no doubt Furphy intended, a deeper significance.

Every man, using whatever powers of perception and reasoning he possesses, tries to find a hypothesis which will explain his own experiences and those of others. He brings to the test of his experiences hypotheses which claim to offer a satisfying solution. Furphy makes it increasingly clear that no single hypothesis of which he knows will explain more than part of the complex pattern of experience as he observes it. Those who rely upon a single philosophical or religious explanation are compelled either to imagine that there must be reason and regularity where none can be observed or to shrug the shoulders at happenings which defy their principles of judgment.

Take, for example, the question of providence, which constantly exercises Furphy's mind. There are three rather obvious qualities attributed in literature to the spirit or force sustaining and governing the universe in its relationship to man, benev-

olence, malevolence, indifference (the impersonal "It" of Hardy). There is a fourth described by Shakespeare:

> As flies to wanton boys, are we to the gods;
> They kill us for their sport.

Furphy represents all four ideas, either explicitly through one of his characters or implicitly through a series of events seen against a background of individual character, motive, responsibility, intention. (pp. 43-5)

But the effect is much more powerful when one or other of these ideas emerges as the possible explanation of an event or set of circumstances. The explanation is not given directly by Furphy; it emerges from the narrative. The outstanding example of this is the affecting story of the lost child, in which one hypothesis is suggested at a certain stage in the story, is rejected in favour of another through succeeding events, and asserts itself again at the end. Furphy carries us through the whole range of possibilities in one story which defies full explanation on any supposition. He invites us to make what we can of it.

Rory's little girl, five years old, sets out in search of her father, taking with her some milk and half a loaf of bread. She is lost for over 72 hours and wanders for 25 miles. She is in constant danger. There are fences to become caught in, holes to fall into, dingoes prowling round her at night. Her food is exhausted and the billy thrown away. Yet for 72 hours the child is unharmed, and, only for her growing weakness, would have been found alive. A merciful providence? But the child was not found alive in spite of the most frantic efforts on the part of the searchers. A malevolent providence then? But if providence had ordained simply that the child should die and the efforts of the searchers should be in vain, why was she not brought to her end sooner through one of the many dangers that hourly confronted her? Why keep her unharmed just long enough to cheat and mock the efforts of the searchers. . . . If she had died five or six hours before they found her their minds would not have been tormented by the thought that a little more speed on their part might have brought them to her before she died. But what are the facts? The child is kept safe for over 72 hours, and the time between her death and their finding her is less than half an hour. Again the reader, though Furphy says nothing directly, thinks back over the whole series of events in the search and shares the torment that must have been in the minds of the searchers. The difference between life and death is less than half an hour, less than half an hour gained by the searchers or lost by the child in her wanderings. If only the alarm could have been raised sooner, if the dogs had followed the tracks, if a black-tracker could have been found sooner, if the child had not removed her shoes and so made her tracks harder to follow, if she had slept a little longer or walked a little more slowly or rested more often—the possibilities crowd into the imagination and every one a torment and a mockery. Was it, then, the gods who kill us for their sport? Then when we seem to have touched the limit of calculated cruelty in the dealings of providence with man, we hear Stevenson speaking:

"'This Dan has much to be thankful for', remarked Stevenson, with strong feeling in his voice. 'Suppose that thunderstorm had come a few hours sooner—what then?'" If the thunderstorm had come a few hours sooner the tracks would have been obliterated and the child might never have been found. Stevenson then relates the story of his younger brother, lost and never found. The mental torment of imagining what might have happened to him had killed his mother, driven his father insane and cast a shadow over his own life. Was the fact that the child was found at all a benevolent dispensation of providence? (pp. 45-7)

As with the dealings of providence so with the validity and the application of the moral law. Virtue is rewarded and wrong punished, it is said. Furphy would like to believe it. But he knows, from the evidence of his own eyes, that the innocent suffer and the wrong-doer prospers. He cannot pretend that the moral law is simple and straightforward in itself or uniformly just in its application. Furphy is concerned to show how blind hasty and conventional moral judgments may be, how much we are inclined, because we are lazy or too easily satisfied or dishonest, to take into account only a convenient selection of the facts. In order to reveal this one-sidedness of judgment he uses his technique of the ''back elevation.'' . . . He invites us not merely to look inside the building as well as at the façade, but to look at the back which was not intended for inspection. He applies this technique to good effect. For example we like to suppose that in our system of society the thrifty, the industrious and the righteous prosper, the shiftless and the lazy go to the wall. That is the front elevation. The rear elevation shows us the greedy, the selfish and the unscrupulous prospering, while ''the weak, the diffident, the scrupulous, and the afflicted are thrust aside or trampled down.'' Stewart prospered partly because he was well respected, a shrewd judge of cattle and a good organiser, but *mainly because his manna never failed.* On the whole Furphy sees prosperity and hardship distributed without any reference at all to moral worth. To come by grass and water for bullocks outside the limits allowed by law is stealing. That is the front elevation. But what if grass and water is not to be had otherwise? And do not the squatters depend upon the services of bullockies whom they treat as outlaws? (pp. 47-8)

As no single philosophical or religious hypothesis can compass the whole of observed experience so no single and consistent set of principles can embrace all problems of moral responsibility and desert. All are assailable; ultimately all who think honestly and directly are rounded up ''on the one unassailable bit of standing-ground, namely, that such is life.'' That is where Furphy finds himself. But he rejects emphatically the despairing conclusion that life is formless and meaingless or meaningless though not formless, that the moral law is invalid and ineffective or ineffective though not invalid. Furphy has certain fundamental beliefs which he holds unassailable, respect for the dignity of all men, selflessness, sincerity, willingness to help others, and he would reject any philosophy which called these in question. (p. 48)

Let us keep the title in mind. Furphy asks us to believe that the book is simply a record of experience on certain days of his life. It is not fiction. Obviously he must claim that he is a chronicler and not a romancer. If he admits that he is writing fiction he lays himself open to the charge of manipulating events to suit his theories. . . . We must play the game as Furphy intended and believe the book as free of Furphy's imagination as if, apart from the philosophy and comment, it had been set down by a recording angel, though we know that in fact it was most artfully contrived. We observe, for example, certain connections between parts of the narrative; in the last chapter certain threads are taken up and woven together. Collins asks us to believe that he didn't design these connections. They simply happened to be there and he is in no better position than the reader to discover them. This claim is not merely a literary pose. Unless we concede it we miss the point of the book.

Here then, says Furphy, is a mere record of events on eight widely separated days of one man's life. On the surface the record is chaotic and formless, broken up into a number of disconnected stories. To find a single line of narrative running through one day is as much as we can expect. From one day to the next there can, on the face of it, be no connection except the reappearance, in fact or by report, of familiar persons and places. But as we read we discover connections between one part of the book and another. We find a thread of narrative, dropped earlier, being taken up again, puzzling events and characters explained after a long interval, a series of happenings which seemed susceptible of one obvious interpretation, shown later to have had a quite different meaning. Ragged ends are taken up and woven into the fabric of the book. And such is life. On the surface it is formless and chaotic, showing a well defined pattern only in small isolated fragments. But when we look more closely we trace effects back to causes which at first we did not recognise, we discover seemingly isolated happenings falling into relationships with one another that suggest a pattern, a direction and cohesion if not quite an inner logic and a purpose. The more one looks at life the more clearly this vague pattern takes shape. The more one thinks about *Such Is Life* the more its organisation becomes apparent. (pp. 50-1)

Such Is Life is more than a novel in being less than a novel. Its structure is remarkable not merely for its novelty, or for its variation from the conventional form of the novel, but also for its significance. Much of the meaning of *Such Is Life* is conveyed by its structure alone.

There is a purpose behind everything that Furphy does. (p. 52)

Furphy intends that the reader should discover the connections in the book for himself. He gives no help. He simply gives the evidence, the mass of fact and event. The reader has to trace the threads running through the narrative for himself, and far from helping him, Furphy slyly tries to throw him off the scent. There is, for instance, the story of Warrigal Alf and his Molly running right through the book. The reader has to connect the clues given in Cooper's story of his sister, in Warrigal Alf's confessions made during his illness, in Collins' visit to Nosey Alf and in the subsequent report that Nosey Alf has been seen wandering the country in which Warrigal Alf was last reported to have been seen. When the reader gathers together the loose ends of four distinct sections of the book, widely separated, he has the outline of a continuous tragic story, running from end to end of the book.

Furphy asks us to interpret the evidence, to pick up and relate the clues which he lays before us not only in a connected story like this of Alf but in smaller matters. The more we read the book the more we admire the artfulness with which he leaves the clues. They are hidden with just sufficient cunning to make their discovery an enjoyable mental exercise, but not so heavily disguised as to make their discovery and connection discouragingly difficult. He has a way of raising questions without an accompanying answer. The reader knows there must be an answer and sets out in search of it. Sooner or later he has the satisfaction of discovering the answer through some small hint ten or even a hundred pages removed from the question. For example when Collins asks Rory O'Halloran's little girl her name, Mrs. O'Halloran breaks in with: ''She's got no name'' (p. 89). Why? the reader asks. Is she illegitimate? This is impossible. The parents were married and the mother was fearsomely proper. We know there is the deepest of gulfs between Rory and his wife in religion. This question remains at the back of our minds, not quite settled. It is answered on p. 241.

When Thompson finishes the story of the lost child he tells how she was taken into Hay for burial: "Catholic priest in Hay sympathised very strongly with him, he told me, but couldn't read the service over her, on account of her not being baptised." So that was it. The religious difference between the parents prevented them from agreeing upon the baptism of the child. And this, to her severely religious mother, meant that she had no name. The reader feels that he will not soon come to the end of these connections. Bob and Bat are reported dead in Chapter I. Bob later turns up and explains the truth. The dog that came down to Solliker from heaven was the "Monkey" lost by Thompson. Small remarks connect one chapter with another by recollection or anticipation. "My watch is at the bottom of the Murray," connects Chapters 3 and 4 by recollection "I had enough of your doctoring at the yellow tank, bust you," from Warrigal Alf in his sickness, connects Chapters 4 and 6 by anticipation. The reader acquires a technique of reading Furphy. Whenever a remark seems inexplicable or a character unfamiliar he holds it in mind for later clarification. (pp. 54-5)

Part of the fun is that there is more than one way of tracing the clues. The solution may be more or less laborious than the one we have outlined. But Furphy very cleverly makes the solution not so obvious as to deprive the reader of satisfaction in reaching it, and not so difficult as to deter him. . . . To half conceal and half reveal and to dispose . . . numerous clues with such adroitness that the reader is coaxed and teased into hunting and relating them requires at least as much artful planning as is to be found in the most deftly articulated mystery novel. (p. 56)

In ordaining that the reader should find and interpret the clues on his own without help from the narrator, Furphy created a formidable problem for himself. Is he to pretend that Collins, who is forever commenting upon events and persons, is so dull as to miss the clues? If Collins does not miss the clues he must interpret them because it is against his nature not to do so, and the reader will be spared the trouble which Furphy intends he shall take. Furphy not only overcomes the difficulty. He turns it to humorous account.

Take, for example, the way in which Collins misses the clues in the story of Warrigal Alf, and toils his way to a quite wrong interpretation of the story. When Collins misinterprets the story to Stewart we feel that perhaps we can forgive him for failing to connect Cooper's story with the hints given by Alf in his delirium. He takes Alf's remarks about his wife and about Cooper's sister Molly as referring to the same person. He gets it into his head that Alf's wife was a tawny-haired tigress. Where did he get such an idea, we wonder? Then we remember that he had been reading an Ouida romance and had sunk deeper and deeper into a romantic trance from which Mosey had great difficulty in stirring him—"What a sweet, spicy, piquant thing it must be to be lured to destruction by a tawny-haired tigress with slumbrous dark eyes." When he meets Stewart he goes on with this rigmarole. He is keen on working out the whole anatomy of Alf's misanthropy. He wants to argue from the effect, through the circumstances, which he imagines he knows, to the cause, namely Alf's character. He is so intent upon this complex web of theory that he misses what is under his nose. The reader at this point has the satisfaction of being miles ahead of Collins, while suspecting that Furphy is slyly trying to throw him off the scent. Collins goes blundering on when he meets Nosey Alf, who is the Molly of Cooper's story and Warrigal Alf's confession of his "one deliberately fiendish and

heartless action." The indications that Nosey Alf is a woman are plentiful. But more significant is her anxiety to learn something about Warrigal Alf without appearing curious. Collins' obtuseness causes him to inflict the most terrible mental anguish on Nosey Alf. He cannot understand her being upset when she learns that Warrigal Alf had actually been duffing in her paddock. This torture, unwittingly inflicted, reaches its climax when, replying to a remark made by Molly about her disfigurement. Collins says: "It's pure effeminacy to brood over such things, for that is just where we have the advantage of women. A woman's first duty is to be beautiful." At this "The boundary man laid down his pipe, rested his forehead in his arm upon the table, and for a minute or two sobbed like a child." In the intervals between Alf's "fits" Collins is very busy spinning theories about the effect of moonlight and the midnight hour upon the mentally unstable. When he takes leave of her in the morning he remarks: "I can see through you like glass. I could write your biography." Collins' obtuseness seems incredible. But Furphy has taken great pains to explain it by carefully establishing Collins' inordinate love of the most tortuous and laboured processes of reasoning. (pp. 57-8)

When Andrew Glover tells his story of the burnt haystack Collins confesses to only a vaguely fancied recognition of him. Surely, we think, this is too much. He could hardly fail to recognise Andrew with his bad eyes and bad hearing, and the deep impression left on his mind by the painful adventure associated with the burnt haystack cannot have been obliterated. But Collins has a theory: "With the circumspection of a seasoned specialist, I had bracketed two independent hypotheses, either of which would supply a satisfactory solution. One of these simply attributes the whole matter to unconscious cerebration. But here a question arose: If one half of my brain had been more alert than its duplicate when the object first presented itself—etc." Collins is on his way, so bemused by his theories that he cannot see what is under his nose. He must gather all the evidence, sift and arrange it, gather his precedents and analogies, then submit the whole mass to the most tedious and toilsome process of analysis and reasoning that he can devise. The more laborious it is the more he enjoys it. It is a pity to interrupt him. Collins has a reasonable chance of getting to the right solution eventually, but he will be plodding contentedly along miles behind the reader. Thus Furphy contrives it that the reader may beat Collins every time in interpreting the facts laid before us without having to attribute an improbable and unexplained degree of stupidity to Collins. It is an ingenious and amusing solution to a really formidable problem. (p. 59)

A. G. Mitchell, " 'Such Is Life': The Title and the Structure of the Book," in Southerly, Vol. 6, No. 3, 1945, pp. 43-59.

JOHN K. EWERS (essay date 1956)

[*Ewers is an Australian fiction writer, poet, historian, and critic. In the following excerpt, he appraises* Such Is Life *and briefly compares Furphy to Henry Lawson.*]

Wherein lies the . . . value [of *Such Is Life*] for Australian literature?

In the first place, it is a starting-point for the really Australian outlook in the longer form of the novel. Here at once is a revolt away from the tear-dimmed, exile wistfulness of Kingsley, Clarke, Boldrewood and company. Furphy addresses himself to his own Australian people. They are his audience. That they were, in effect, an exceedingly thin audience does not in any way qualify the sincerity of his intention.

Furphy's second value is his early recognition and statement of Australian egalitarianism. C. Hartley Grattan has called him "the great Australian literary philosopher of the common man," and has described his book as "a primary document for any student of Australian attitudes."

In this respect Furphy has much in common with Henry Lawson. But his own individual contribution to our literature is a prose that for polish, balance, precision and vigour stands alone in the pioneering stages of our writing, and, indeed, has few peers in English. True, there are occasions when Furphy seems to intoxicate himself with words, but analysis shows them to be words of full savour and rich meaning. He can use them to devastating effect when attacking an abuse; he can pile them like stone on stone to build an edifice of unchallengeable argument; but he never makes the mistake of misusing them in the conversations of his homely bush characters. (pp. 52-3)

I believe that he, more than any other, sounds the note and points the way for future generations of writers. Not that they should imitate his technique, for that was something that arose out of the peculiar circumstances of his life and his approach to writing. Gavin Casey, in an address at the Furphy Centenary celebrations in Perth, on September 26, 1943, made the distinction clearly when he likened all writers to men who drew from the wells of experience. Most drew a bucketful at a time, acquiring skill in the process, until after a while the bucket began to grow rusty. Furphy drew but one, huge voluptuous bucketful, and if in the very nature of things its contents were varied and apparently lacked selection, at any rate the bucket did not grow rusty in the process.

It is possible to make comparisons and contrasts between Furphy and Lawson. Both preached a fervent Australianism. There is little distinction between their attitudes on this point. Both were disciples of the current creed of socialist egalitarianism. But, whereas in Lawson the rights of the common man found expression in many a ringing line of verse, in many a masterly story, yet when fulfilment tarried his enthusiasm gave place to despair. Furphy was not emotional about socialism; he was too well read not to know the tremendous forces opposing it; his strength lies in that he recognized the difficulties, but refused to admit that they were insuperable. In style, there are great contrasts. Lawson never aspires to Furphy's verbal oratory, but Furphy's simple narrations told in the plain speech of his nomad characters rival Lawson at his best. In technique Lawson was undoubtedly the superior. He mastered the art of writing the sort of short story he chose to tell; Furphy's technique was ambitious and subtle and it very nearly mastered him. For that reason, it is doubtful whether he will ever command the same wide audience that Lawson does. A. G. Stephens said that *Such Is Life* was a book that would be relished a hundred years hence. If the gathering interest and approval of Furphy's work is any indication, this may well be so. In recent years *Such Is Life* has been more often critically dissected and analysed than any other Australian novel. And more than any other Australian novel, each criticism of it affirms its quality. (pp. 54-5)

> *John K. Ewers, "The Beginnings of the Novel," in his* Creative Writing in Australia: A Selective Survey, *revised edition, Georgian House, 1956, pp. 51-6.*

MILES FRANKLIN (essay date 1956)

[*An Australian novelist and autobiographer, Franklin is recognized for her vivid portrayal of life in Australia at the turn of the century. Displaying vigor, a pervasive feminism, and the strong nationalism that was developing in Australia at the time, her first novel,* My Brilliant Career *(1901), was enthusiastically received by critics. Aside from that novel, written when Franklin was sixteen years old, her most significant work is* All That Swagger *(1936), a saga spanning more than a hundred years in the lives of a family of European immigrants to Australia.* All That Swagger *and the series of novels she wrote under the pseudonym "Brent of Bin Bin" helped to popularize the saga form in Australian writing. In the following excerpt, Franklin praises* Such Is Life *as a truly Australian novel and compares Furphy with Henry James.*]

Such Is Life is our first novel of magnitude to deal so inherently with the landscape. It is our only one in which the main characters are bullock-drivers, perhaps the only one in the world by a bullock-driver about the practice of his trade. And such a bullock-driver! The *Adelaide Register* observed, "Imagine a writer, who apparently has the whole range of literature at his fingers' ends, living the life of the bush, and caring for no other." He knew and followed his craft as Conrad knew his, and had comparable ability in presenting it. His books—book really—are set almost entirely out of doors, a rooflessness natural to the nomads of animal transport and to Furphy:

> Mile after mile we go at a good walk, till the dark boundary of the scrub country disappears northward in the glassy haze, and in front, southward, the level black-soil plains of Riverina Proper mark a straight sky-line, broken here and there by a monumental clump or pineridge. And away beyond the horizon, southward still, the geodesic curve carries that monotony across the zone of salt-bush, myall, and swamp box; across the Lachlan and Murrumbidgee and on to the Victorian border—say, two hundred and fifty miles.
>
> Just about mid-day, the station track I was following intersected and joined the stock route; and against the background of a pineridge, a mile ahead, I saw some wool-teams. When I overtook them, they had stopped for dinner among the trees. . . .
>
> There were five bullock-teams altogether: Thompson's twenty; Cooper's eighteen; Dixon's eighteen; and Price's two teams of fourteen each.

Skilful characterization is in the teamsters' dialogue, saltiness in Tom Collins's commentaries on them, pathos in the finely rounded story of the lost child, tragedy in the ill-mating of her parents, irony in the swagmen's death within reach of help because of Tom Collins's delicacy in leaving his presence unmentioned. The slapstick comedy of the lost trousers appeals widely to men readers. The dog, the horses, the bullocks each has personality. Tom Collins, the narrator invented for convenience, like the diary entries, often acts as clown-chorus, "feeder" as it is termed in the theatre. At times he is perspicacious, or conceited, at others he exposes strands of the design of which he is ostensibly and stupidly unaware of himself. (pp. 123-24)

Furphy had his quirks such as the assertion that the Australian girl is distinguished by an incipient "mo," a theory allowing of a different twist had Furphy seen the number of darkened upper lips on young Latin beauties. And he had sharp prejudices for one who was a monument of tolerance and magnanimity.

Henry Kingsley nauseated him by the glorification of English squatters with schoolboy mentality. He wrote to his friend Cathels that he hated that beggar, and that "Mrs. Beaudesart was intended to serve as a sequel to Geof-Ham." He takes over Maud Buckley, whom we saw as a laughing girl returning with her family to England at the end of *Geoffry Hamlyn,* and reintroduces her as a middle-aged widow in the job of house-keeper at Runnymede, a big station where Tom Collins hangs around. Maud is here Mrs. Beaudesart, or old Mother Bodysark in station argot; she is indigent, if not a decayed gentlewoman, and virulently snobbish:

> Mrs. Beaudesart possessed a vast store of De-brett-information touching those early gentle-men-colonists whose enterprise is hymned by loftier harps than mine, but whose sordid greed and unspeakable arrogance has yet to be said or sung.

Mrs. Beaudesart is allowed good looks, but no other redeeming quality, and is exhibited in a clash with Ida, selected as slavey for the male staff because she is like a Hogarth drawing. Ida is a poignant figure who has been through as much punishment from life as an unlucky soldier. The Bodysark is somewhat caricatured, but this is an interesting reappearance, like the finishing of Jane Austen's novel or the sequel to *Dombey and Son,* as evidence of gathering moss on our literary tree.

This slow and subtle process of transplanting the inner life of a people from ancient cultures to raw soils is illustrated by divergences and parallels in the cases of Joseph Furphy and Henry James. Both were born into English-speaking communities, of British origin, but behind James settlement from the home lands had continued for more generations, was of more heterogenous composition, and had undergone the drastic divorce of war to establish separate nationality. . . . Both men were remarkable as writers of their day, both of unusual natural endowments, each persistent towards a goal, yet very differently fashioned and compelled by circumstances to the final outcome and sum-total of their manhood and work.

James was born in 1843, five months before Furphy, and lived till 1916, Furphy till 1912. There one parallel ends. One was a man who ran away, and one a man who stood his ground: the finespun and the homespun: a writing man and a man who wrote. (pp. 124-25)

Furphy . . . was free from inherited nostalgia. He rooted so soundly in his native soil that he felt no intransigence in its rawness as material for a masterpiece. With sturdy self-reliance, he trued-up to his own pole of integrity as a writer. This made him a founding father of the Australian novel and invincible inside his circumstances, but having worked in obscure isolation he remains unknown beyond his native back paddocks except to a few intrepid explorers. (pp. 126-27)

Furphy . . . was fully assimilated to his milieu. He was antagonistic to the European taboos of aristocratic superiority, alert against reproduction of such pretensions in Australian life, and he attacked them in pioneer fashion with an axe, where James traced their refinements with a pencil. Furphy was the healthy upsurge of the successors of the "dregs of humanity" who in chains had laid the foundation of settlement, and of those who hoped for a social and economic system free from tyranny and degrading poverty. Furphy had no doubts about the common humanity of man. He practised as well as preached brotherhood. He recognized humorously that no exclusiveness can ensure that kingly qualities will appear more regularly in the offspring of a monarch than of a blacksmith. Inference of universality is in his declaration that the ignoble blood of Dixon, magnificent specimen, has crept through scoundrels since the flood. He chronicled his own as readily as the other fellow's discomfitures: he comprehended the grief as well as the mirth in laughter: he had a precipitate of the inspired humour of the great clowns, the laughter-makers who tickle the fools but sober the thoughtful, the humour that scores without corrosion. The ridicule of louts amused him as he realized that the gap between the savant and the savage is not worth conceit. Stephens said he came late and lonely to scholarship: he was intellectually lonely all his life, but, as set forth in the biography, he began early, and this bush boy's acquaintance with recondite writers was as remarkable as any precocity of the teen-age Henry James.

Furphy and James each had a heavy overloading to his gift of story-telling. Furphy was a born tractarian, James a natural psychiatrist. Furphy openly preached. James, the dissector of implication, allowed his bent too full rein. (pp. 128-29)

Such a mind and character as Furphy's, combined in a spokesman for "hitherto inarticulate activities," naturally resulted in something hitherto unknown among novels. Philosophy, humour, irony, farce, tragedy, pathos, sesquipedalianism, dialects, a quiz kid's bag of miscellaneous information, spice the rich compound: a complex conception in artistic craftsmanship and spiritual content. So many theories could be concocted to explain its intricate construction that it is not exhausted by many readings. Virile, free from neuroses, where is there another to match it among unusual novels?

The book had a *succès d'estime* among critics here. There were only one or two dissentient voices, but there was no discovery overseas except by the critic of the *Athenaeum* [see excerpt dated 1904]. This gentleman was somewhat outraged—as well he could have been—at the rude way Furphy trounced established society and the members of it who drifted here as remittance men; but that did not deflect the critic from acclaiming the literary merit of the work. (pp. 129-30)

When *Such Is Life* reached publication in America, Henry Seidel Canby, Ph.D., Litt.D., ranked it among the best "frontier" novels in the English tongue. This from a man of such academic standing is promotion, though "frontier" is not rightly applied to the work. (p. 130)

Furphy's chronicle of the eighties was nearer to a social novel than a frontier tale though it was of teamsters and station hands, swagmen, remittance men, clergymen and others met on the Great Stock Routes, or around the homesteads large and small. The big station homes were run on English lines with every current amenity. Furphy observed: "Social status, apart from all consideration of mind, manners, or even money, is more accurately weighed on a right-thinking Australian station than anywhere else in the world."

To question "frontier" may be a quibble, but Australians did not use the word for their back paddocks and Never-Nevers, which had a glory and lure not yet adequately grasped by outsiders, and writers aware of their land are conscious of nuances in literary presentation.

The bush and the conditions familiar in Furphy's day have gone. When *Such Is Life* reappeared in 1944 it met a new and divided audience. Discussions during the revival showed fewer who admired or understood the literary worth of the book than who were pleased by its politics. In the present chaos there is a demand for novels with a concrete message, and Furphy meets this. While not a revolutionist, his stand for equality is uncompromising. His political philosophy, though trite through garbling, retains urgency and is still far from general acceptance. How long this interest will float the book cannot be gauged. A factor to make it archaic to the average lay reader is the insertion of dialects, always too difficult for the uneducated or for the beginners in a new language. The Irish brogue, one of the easiest and most popular, has grown out of ordinary understanding in the United States, and that will follow here inevitably. Furphy's work, however, is increasingly a subject of academic attention, completely withheld during his lifetime when recognition of his achievement would have watered his arid loneliness, though its absence did not ruffle his equanimity. He set spoors for later pedants, easily missed at a first or second reading. Rarely can a man have been so aware of every treasure he tucked in his hamper or so content with the probability of posthumous renown. (pp. 131-32)

> Miles Franklin, *"The New Century: The Established Trend," in her* Laughter, Not for a Cage, *Angus and Robertson, 1956, pp. 118-38.*

CHRIS WALLACE-CRABBE (essay date 1961)

[*Wallace-Crabbe is a prominent Australian poet, novelist, and critic. In the following excerpt, he discusses the structure and philosophy of* Such Is Life.]

One of the problems, a source of doubts and difficulty among readers tackling *Such Is Life* for the first time (for it is a book which gains in impressiveness and coherence with successive readings), is the uniqueness of Furphy's mode, its remoteness from any familiar *genre*. Even his affinities with the eighteenth-century novelists are fairly tenuous, when all is said and done. How, for example, is a reader going to react to a novel which includes in its first half-dozen pages such different passages as the following?

> Whilst a peculiar defect—which I scarcely like to call an oversight in mental construction— shuts me out from the flowery pathway of the romancer, a co-ordinate requital endows me, I trust, with the more sterling, if less ornamental qualities of the chronicler. This fairly equitable compensation embraces, I have been told, three distinct attributes: an intuition which reads men like signboards; a limpid veracity; and a memory which habitually stereotypes all impressions except those relating to personal injuries.

and

> Mile after mile we go at a good walk, till the dark boundary of the scrub country disappears northward in the glassy haze, and in front, southward, the level black-soil plains of Riverina Proper mark a straight sky-line, broken here and there by a monumental clump or pine-ridge. And away beyond the horizon, southward still, the geodesic curve carries that monotony across the zone of salt-bush, myall, and swamp box; across the Lachlan and Murrumbidgee, and on to the Victorian border—say, two hundred and fifty miles.

and even

> "It's this way," said Mosey imperatively, and deftly weaving into his address the thin red line of puissant adjective; "You dunno what you're doin' when you're foolin' with this run. She's hair-trigger at the best o' times, an' she's on full cock this year. Best watched station on the track. It's a risk whatever way you take it. We're middlin' safe to be collared in the selection, an' we're jist as safe to be collared in the rampaddick. Choice between the divil an' the dam. An' there's too big a township o' wagons together. Two's enough, an' three's a glutton, for sich a season as this."

To appreciate *Such Is Life*, the reader must be ready to respond to these differences in tone, to regard them as integral to the book's development. And in doing this he will begin to realize the significance of the gap between Furphy and Collins.

Tom Collins is a substantial and active character, for all his Deputy-Assistant-Sub-Inspector's aloofness. The distance maintained between him and Furphy is an important technique of comment-by-implication throughout the book, and is one of the chief vehicles of a balanced vision which does not always appear on the surface. Admittedly Collins often propounds views which are manifestly the author's own (for example, the denunciations of the "novelist's" distorted view of the world, the Meerschaum Pipe dissertation on hardship and Christian civilization in Chapter III, and the aside on English notions of fair play, inspired by the pompous bully, Folkestone, in Chapter VI), but Furphy keeps distancing himself effectively by making his narrator sound portentous or pedantic, as well as by revealing considerable disparity between Collins's benevolent, egalitarian ideas and his ability to put them into practice. His fantastic over-ingenuity, combined with a real incapacity for seeing beyond the end of his nose, results in the imprisonment of poor, harmless Andy Glover and, almost certainly, in the death of the lonely swagman, George Murdoch, while his preoccupation with the "tawny-haired tigresses" of Ouida blinds him repeatedly to evidence of the Warrigal Alf-Molly Cooper relationship.

Tom Collins's theories are seen in fact as hopelessly limited and arbitrary, if not downright absurd; and in this they are representative of all our attempts, whether in terms of religion, metaphysics or politics, to account for the complex tragi-comedy which is life. Here is a view of life in which comfortable dogmas can play no part. Like Collins we can only grin and bear it. . . . (pp. 51-2)

However comic its manner, *Such Is Life* is, as I have already suggested, a serious experimental work based on a distinctive theory of the novel. Furphy is not seeking to tell a story of purpose and logical sequence, nor to generate a series of developments through the dramatic interaction of characters, but to give a sense of how things actually happen: the pattern of life itself. This is why his book is so specifically an "anti-novel," why so much stress is placed on the haphazard selection of dates from Collins's pocket diary, and why the author so obviously delights in the piecemeal, oblique development of his veins of narrative. If the parts of this narrative fit together like the pieces of a large-scale jigsaw puzzle, it is because this is how things are generally revealed to us in real life. In this way, *Such Is Life* can be seen as a profoundly realistic novel; but its realism is not the realism of character, nor is it a Social Realist's view of the commonplace events of Riverina life in the eighteen-eighties (Collins's diary is dated 1883). A kind of realism emerges which undermines romantic assumptions, literary conventions and even political ideals, demanding instead our assent to the proposition that people and events remain quite individual, quite unpredictable. The artistic unity of *Such Is Life* resembles the haphazard and precarious unity we impose on our own experience.

It is significant that Furphy, like Xavier Herbert after him, writes an ambitious, original novel in a deliberately comic mode. However, it seems to me that their types of comedy are almost diametrically opposed—quite apart from the consideration that Furphy's approach is consciously "literary" in a way that could never be suggested of Herbert. In the more Dostoievskian world of *Capricornia* (the analogy is not entirely paradoxical) an irrevocably tragic pattern of life includes a great deal of comedy; in *Such Is Life,* on the other hand, a predominantly comic world manages to encompass the tragedies of such people as Mary O'Halloran, George Murdoch and Andy Glover without demanding a grimly stoical response. Both, however, would appreciate the view represented in Auden's lines:

> About suffering they were never wrong,
> The Old Masters: how well they understood
> Its human position; how it takes place
> While someone else is eating or opening a window or
>   just walking dully along.

It is more than personal idiosyncracy that makes Tom Collins respond to the unpredictable twists and turns of fate with his frequently reiterated "such is life." This mildly sardonic acceptance of things is demanded by the whole development of the novel. For Furphy, both through and outside Collins, offers a basically determinist interpretation of the way things happen. Like the twentieth-century Existentialists, he sees man's existence as composed of a series of instantaneous, unguided choices, but unlike them he attaches no particular value to the notion of choice. An important analogy, presented in Chapter II after Collins has avoided speaking to the reclining George Murdoch, is that of a locomotive speeding along a line where it is suddenly faced with unheralded junctions; at each of these, with little or no guiding information, the locomotive must suddenly make a choice of lines, and in each case this choice will affect the remainder of its journey. Collins's choice on Goolumbulla Station, prompted solely by an overscrupulous sense of bush courtesy, leads to the death of Murdoch and, less directly, to that of Mary O'Halloran. The result is out of all proportion to the apparent implications of his choice.

For all this, a comic response is demanded by the way men vainly, ridiculously seek to systematize, generalize, moralize and theologize. In *Such Is Life* these human vanities are constantly being deflated; Collins's theories, whether of social democracy or of the fantastic science of Nomenology, are mocked by his actual performance; Willoughby's university education is grotesquely useless to him in the Riverina, and Sollicker's credulous faith is easily shown up in all its stupidity. One of the purposes of Furphy's remarkable range of national and occupational types is to stress the role played by environment and circumstances in forming men's opinions. For example, every bullocky sees the crucial issue of grass-stealing as perfectly natural and every squatter, even a decent, tolerant man like Montgomery, opposes it: apart from the curious case of Stewart of Kooltopa, only Collins, from his independent position as a minor government official, really looks at both sides of the question and he remains morally indifferent. Even Rory O'Halloran's Catholicism is seen as a geographical accident,

a result of his having been born in Ireland. There is no shade of belief or doctrine which receives approval.

The only possible response to the vagaries of life that can gain Furphy's assent is a warm, untheoretical concern for other men. This is most fully exemplified in Stewart of Kooltopa, a squatter but an "(adj.) Christian," who, after voicing his moral disapproval of Warrigal Alf at some length, proves willing to care for Alf through his illness. But Stewart is only a minor character in the book, and is seen as exceptional.

Life is a complex thing and no final answers are presented. Furphy's aim is neither to despair nor to rejoice but to take up the kind of attitude we find in the last paragraph of *Such Is Life,* where individual lives are seen as isolated and ridiculous, and yet as retaining some real value:

> Now I had to enact the Cynic Philosopher to Moriarty and Butler, and the aristocratic man with a "past" to Mrs. Beaudesart; with the satisfaction of knowing that each of these was acting a part to me. Such is life, my fellow-mummers—just like a poor player, that bluffs and feints his hour upon the stage, and then cheapens down to mere nonentity. But let me not hear any small witticism to the further effect that its story is a tale told by a vulgarian, full of slang and blanky—signifying—nothing.

SUCH IS LIFE

BEING CERTAIN EXTRACTS FROM THE DIARY

OF

TOM COLLINS

SYDNEY, MCMIII—THE BULLETIN NEWSPAPER COMPANY, LIMITED, PUBLISHERS

Title page to Such Is Life.

Whatever may be arbitrary and chaotic in life as we know it, that last injunction is essential to a balanced view: Furphy's response to life is a comic, not a cynical one.

The comic mode of *Such Is Life* manifests itself in a variety of ways: first of all, of course, in the general presentation of Tom Collins, with its continual contrast between theory and performance; secondly, in the elaborate self-parody and word-play of many of Collins's "philosophical" monologues (though some of these could profitably be cut); thirdly, in a great deal of purely literary reference and burlesque; fourthly, in some excellent scenes of high comedy (Tom's nude Odyssey along the Murray on the night of the Sunday School picnic is extraordinarily funny and well-sustained: imagine what Steele Rudd would have made of the same theme!); and, lastly, in much comedy of manners, involving some pretty devastating accounts of station etiquette, together with a wide range of exotic dialects. *Such Is Life* offers stoic humour as the only response to an unpredictable fate and the terrible arbitrariness of personal decisions: it is seen as the only response which will both protect us in adversity and allow us to retain the humility which is demanded of us.

But if this prevailing attitude is honest and in some ways engagingly clear-sighted, it also has disturbing limitations. For one thing, we all know that men do live by the beliefs and ideologies which Furphy spoofs so amiably; that these become powerful motivating forces in many people's lives; and that they often provide moral sustenance where nothing else is available. We cannot demand that Furphy should acquiesce in this human peculiarity, but a book which is called *Such Is Life* should at least take account of it as a significant fact. Even the doctrine of Mateship, however sentimental it became at times, could become a real source of personal conviction: some of Lawson's stories exemplify this. Yet the scene in Chapter I where the camped bullockies systematically destroy the reputation of each man who goes to fetch water puts paid to any idealized notion of Mateship. In such things as this, Furphy's realism may involve leaving out rather too much of life. We must ask ourselves whether the book offers us enough in the way of positive human values to compensate for this kind of exclusiveness.

But there is another, more serious limitation apparent in the moral achievement of *Such Is Life* (the book somehow demands that one should bring moral criteria into play). This is brought out most strongly in the beautifully handled discussion of lost children. The bullockies are yarning in the evening. Steve Thompson, Collins's old friend, tells the story of Mary O'Halloran's death in the bush. This moving tale, which brings indirect responsibility home to Collins himself, is immediately followed by the parallel, yet significantly different stories of Saunders and Stevenson. Finally, as the bullockies are falling asleep, Collins asks Thompson a question which indicates that he is aware of the degree of his own responsibility; but Thompson is asleep. Collins muses about the O'Hallorans for a while, but then drifts off into the generalized rambling of "Deepest pathos lies only in homely things, since the frailness of mortality is the pathetic centre, and mortality is nothing but homely." Soon Collins is asleep also, and the O'Hallorans are all too easily forgotten.

A. A. Phillips has praised this passage highly for its emotional control [see Additional Bibliography] and we can easily see why. Nevertheless, when we take it in the context of the whole book, we find Furphy's irony drifting too close to sheer heartlessness. Collins may be a fantastic bumbler, but he is meant to be a likeable one. It is constantly being suggested that his heart is in the right place. And yet, both in this passage and elsewhere, he is allowed to escape from any lasting sense of responsibility for his fellow men. An amiable egocentric he may be, but given his role in the novel, it is disturbing that his human deficiencies are allowed to go unreproved. Far more than any question of structural over-ingenuity or an occasional excess of garrulousness, this tendency to simply acquiesce in an amoral and fatalistic universe seems the important weakness of *Such Is Life*.

In the last resort, Furphy's reputation must stand or fall by *Such Is Life*. (pp. 52-6)

For this reason, one must concentrate on *Such Is Life* and on the effectiveness of its unique brand of realism. I have done no more here than to hint at Furphy's realism in a narrower, but still important sense: to the broad range of his picture of Riverina life, to the convincing detail with which he portrays the activities of bullockies and stationhands, to his remarkably concrete presentation of vegetation and topography, and to the strong impression he gives of physical space and distance. It is these strengths which provide a basis for the more ambitious achievements of *Such Is Life*. For Furphy's choice of the Riverina as a setting had not much political or nationalistic significance; its importance for him lay in the fact that it was a self-contained and thoroughly familiar society—a microcosm in which he could detect the patterns and operations of life itself. (p. 56)

> *Chris Wallace-Crabbe, "Joseph Furphy, Realist,"*
> *in* Quadrant, *Vol. V, No. 2, Autumn, 1961, pp. 49-56.*

H. M. GREEN (essay date 1961)

[*An Australian poet and critic, Green is the author of the comprehensive critical study* A History of Australian Literature: Pure and Applied *(1961). In the following excerpt from that work, he examines* Rigby's Romance *and* The Buln-Buln and the Brolga.]

Rigby's Romance, of which Furphy hoped, and thought, so much, is in every respect inferior to *Such Is Life*, of whose river it is, as Stephens called it, "an anabranch"; he also called it "another planet of the benevolent afternoon sun"; if we regard *Such Is Life* as a planet of the sun at the height of noon this remark hits the centre. Furphy had had, and no wonder, enough of *Such Is Life* and of the infinite trouble that it had caused him, apparently to little purpose: he naturally did not want to be regarded as a man of one book, and that a book that would not sell; he concentrated upon the other and hoped for better things from it. As printed in the *Barrier Truth* the burden of the story was a long sermon on state socialism by the principal character; a considerable part of this was omitted when the story first appeared in book-form, but it has been restored in the recent edition. According to Lloyd Ross, in its serial form the story "was read eagerly by the miners" and "served as a text for many an argument on socialism, free thought, and the coming of the social revolution"; it is hard to imagine it successful as a serial for any but political reasons: apart from the sermon, it is an entertaining story, but the fact is that what may have attracted the doctrine-hungry miners not only spoils the book from a literary point of view, but is poor stuff in itself. Furphy intended *Rigby's Romance* as a novel of purpose; he told Cathels that he was no admirer of that kind of novel and would have preferred his treatise in treatise form, but he wanted to make sure that it was read, so he "sugarcoated" what he described as "the last word on the moral aspect of'' socialism with the ''sweetest romance you ever struck.'' *Rigby's Romance* may be regarded either as a sermon with a story wrapped round it, or as an expanded short story with a disproportionately long sermon embedded in it. The sermon is actually a rambling and platitudinous identification of socialism with Christianity; it is expressed in such a manner as to give the effect, sometimes, of windy sawdust, but it is interrupted here and there by something interesting when Furphy feels that Rigby's audience could not have been expected to stand any more without a break: at its worst it is like this:

> If the idea of sharing can be preserved, the parties are brought abreast and mutually elevated by the primitive virtue of the principle. Whereas, the eleemosynary idea, interpreting a similar act, brings the parties into contact vertically, not laterally, and the benefaction, materially good, is poisoned by its implication.

In either version, the book reads like one of those sequels that recreate something of the atmosphere of the original, making it rather thinner, however, and without attaining anything like its vitality; for this there are three probable reasons: the story is not an excerpt from the larger book but an expansion of one of its chapters, and expansions are almost always thin; there is, even apart from the sermon, too much talk and too little action; and when the book was written Furphy may well have been a tired man. The gist of the story is this: twenty-five years earlier, Rigby had been passionately in love with Kate Vanderdecken, but had left her after a quarrel; she still loves him and comes out from America to hunt him up; they arrange to meet one evening, and since she is described as still ''exquisitely lovely,'' it looks as though she will not have come out for nothing. But along with Collins and others Rigby goes out fishing, and what with the yarns and the discussions that arise out of their social intercourse, and most of all Rigby's own contribution, he forgets his appointment: this in spite of Collins's occasional hints and one or two other things that might have acted as reminders; Kate goes off and Rigby follows her too late and misses her again. Of Rigby, Furphy had as high and mistaken an opinion as of the book as a whole; he told Kate Baker that Rigby was

> . . . humanly perfect—courteous, magnanimous, of clean and blameless life, replete with everyday capability, scholarly, humorous, unselfish; and I did my little possible to make him an intellectual giant.

This sounds like an adolescent ideal, and in fact there is a touch of the adolescent about Furphy when he returns from the real to the ideal world, in spite of his wide experience and worldly wisdom, and in spite of his subtlety. As a matter of fact Rigby is little more than a courteous but sentential wraith, as long-winded and polysyllabic as Furphy at his worst, but without the vital and individual quality that make Furphy what he is: like Furphy, he can turn his hand to most things; he has Furphy's pedantic scholarship but scarcely any of his humour; his ''clean and blameless life'' appears to be due not to self-control but to a tepidity which is hard to reconcile with his former passion; and as for being an intellectual giant, Furphy was not that himself and he had never known one, and in any case he would, like other writers, have found it difficult to create one in fiction. When, as a result of a final prod by Collins, Rigby does remember his appointment he is filled with remorse, not because he has any feeling left for Kate, but merely because he has shown her a discourtesy; it turns out that he had entirely

forgotten her, though now at last he seems to remember that he had ''made love to that woman once.'' Not that he had not been impressed by her at their meeting, but he ''fairly shuddered at the thought of having such a flower of womanhood for a wife'': because of the time he would lose if he lived in such an atmosphere! As for the other characters in the book: the echo of Collins, which has been referred to, is even more of an onlooker than the Collins of *Such Is Life;* Dixon has taken over from Willoughby a number of Latin quotations, which he combines with his natural expletives in an extremely entertaining manner, and his account of his researches into Biblical history is equally entertaining, but it is rather too obvious that he has been introduced merely as comic relief; Thompson also is a little thinner, though one of the new characters, the boy Sam, is as good as any of the casual strollers through *Such Is Life.* The only real women in the book are Mrs. Ferguson and the others we catch sight of at the Coffee Palace; Kate Vanderdecken and her travelling companion are purely literary characters, shadowy pendants of a slightly less unsubstantial shadow. (pp. 624-26)

Furphy's third book, *The Buln-Buln and the Brolga* is as far inferior to *Rigby's Romance* as that is to *Such Is Life;* to carry on Stephens's metaphor, the afternoon sun has now become the evening sun, and the planet that *The Buln-Buln* represents is not only in all senses smaller than *Rigby* but a planet of a different kind: *The Buln-Buln* also represents a ''segregated chapter'' from the huge original, but, as with *Rigby,* the prototype has been expanded and grown thinner and less vital thereby. The original title was *The Lyre Bird,* and the original idea was that, ''loosely federated'' with *Rigby's Romance,* the two should have made a single book; but this idea was abandoned, and in Western Australia, after the serial publication of *Rigby,* Furphy turned himself intermittently, in the intervals between building fowl-houses and tank-stands, to rewriting and elaborating this section of the original version of *Such Is Life* as he had rewritten and elaborated the others. The Buln-Buln or Lyre bird is, by one of Furphy's characteristic puns, his ideal liar, Fred Prichard, an old schoolfellow of Furphy's who does not appear in either of the previous books; the Brolga, the long-legged native companion, is the long-legged bushman, Barefooted Bob, of Chapter V of *Such Is Life;* and other male characters are Thompson and Collins himself. The book begins by telling how Collins meets Bob and Fred, and harks back to the days of their boyhood: in those days Fred had been a limp and cowardly little butt, distinguished only by a marvellous talent for romantic mendacities, in which he always figured as the hero he would have liked to be; he is now Frederick Falkland-Pritchard, a portly and distinguished person with an adoring wife and three children, who has travelled abroad and developed his one talent, and is conscious of indisputable preeminence. The rest of the book is occupied by an exchange of reminiscences between him and Bob; Bob's are simple and here and there almost credible bush furphies; Fred's are elaborate and cosmopolitan Munchausenisms. Yet the truth of all the yarns is taken for granted, except by Collins, and Fred's are received, not only by the simple bushman, Bob, but, so at least she makes it appear, by Mrs. Pritchard, who, incidentally, must have heard most of them before, with an extreme of credulous fascination. Bob, who appears only in the second part of the book, gains nothing by his elaboration here, and Thompson, who appears only in the first part, gains little. Collins is, except as a schoolboy, the thinner echo of himself that he had become in *Rigby's Romance;* even more the mere onlooker, but with the old Furphy-Collins' parade of learning; the same prejudice against the ''upper classes''; the same tendency, though in this far smaller book much less is made of it, to divagation; and the same pretension to psychological insight, which is shown as usual to be ludicrously mistaken. It is on Fred that the interest centres, and it is by reason of his yarns and their reception that the book becomes different in kind from the other two. Collins's schoolday recollections are vigorous accounts of country boyhood as real as Norman Lindsay's, and not unlike them, as has been pointed out [by Douglas Stewart in the *Bulletin* (26 January 1949)], and Fred's childish and youthful mendacities fit in naturally with the boyish life described. But those of the second part of the book, in which Fred's one talent has developed, with experience, a larger scope and an extremer fantasy, cannot be measured by realistic standards, and the tales themselves are not more incredible than the language in which Fred clothes them: in one yarn, before making a single-handed attack upon a pirate vessel, he "darted into my cabin, and slipped on an undress uniform, together with a splendid sword, presented to me by the Emperor of the French"; and he afterwards refuses a colonel's commission in England because "I had sworn allegiance to the French flag, and no man of my race ever sold his sword to the highest bidder." Here Furphy no doubt intended to parody the heroic utterances in the romances of adventure that he loathed, but they come out more like second-rate thrillers of his day. This part of this book may be taken as a satiric fantasy founded on fact; as such it is an amusing trifle, well worth publishing as a work of Furphy's and as throwing some light on the boyhood of the character in whom Furphy put much of himself, but otherwise, though sometimes lively and amusing, of small literary importance.

Whatever his defects and deficiencies, Furphy stands by himself and no real comparison can be found for him. Like Borrow, and in a quite different way like Sterne, he is self-conscious, prejudiced, wandering, idiosyncratic to the point of mannerism; and like them he has a highly individual sense of humour and doesn't give a tinker's damn, or dam, for literary forms and conventions, writing the sort of thing he wants to write because he happens to want to write it. But fundamentally he is as far apart from either of these as Australia from England: as an artist he is inferior to Borrow and infinitely to Sterne, being an inhabitant of a much less civilized and cultivated world, whose narrowness and crudity deform him, but from which he has drawn freshness and power. He has been compared with Mark Twain, with whom he has in common an easy-going and satiric humour, but nothing more, and his humour is of a different sort; *Such Is Life* has been compared with *Moby Dick,* but the philosophic divagations that interrupt the two stories are quite different in kind, and Furphy's, perverse or platitudinous though they may be, are entirely his own, while Melville's owe a great deal to Carlyle; and, though Melville has a finer art and a far wider range, at least if we take into account his other books, in *Moby Dick* he is further removed from actual life than Furphy, being thoughout a dealer in the bizarre. . . . On the whole, what oversea affiliations may be found in Furphy are with the literature of the eighteenth or early nineteenth century; among Australian writers he has something, though not much, in common with O'Dowd. He represents one of the peaks in Australian literature, and if beyond his own country his value is confined mainly to his reflection of its life, that is to some extent due to limitations which were imposed upon him from without, and from which it was largely family love and loyalty that prevented him from breaking free. *Such Is Life* is what Stephens said it was fit to become: "an Australian classic, or semi classic." Along with Lawson, though in a very different manner, Furphy represents the Australia of

his day, and for good and ill he stands, more than Lawson or any other writer, for "aggressive Australianism." (pp. 631-33)

H. M. Green, "Self-Conscious Nationalism: Novels of the Countryside, Furphy," in his A History of Australian Literature: Pure and Applied, 1789-1923, *Vol. I, Angus and Robertson, 1961, pp. 609-33.*

BRIAN KIERNAN (essay date 1971)

[*Kiernan is an Australian critic and educator whose works reflect his interest in Australian and American literature of the nineteenth century. In the following excerpt, he presents an extended analysis of the varied functions of "Tom Collins" as narrator and protagonist of* Such Is Life.]

Through the narrator's digressions on novels and novel-writing, and Furphy's own play with a novelettish plot that remains undetected by Collins, *Such Is Life* itself indicates the author's artistic concerns and his departure from the established conventions of colonial Australian fiction. Tom Collins as the putative author is an anti-artist. His derision for "the flowery pathway of the romancer," the alterations he makes to his original selection of extracts from his diary, and his denial that the life he describes has any plot, reveal his preference for life before art. His aim is to record life as he has experienced it, rather than to romanticize it as have the novelists he has read, especially those dealing with Australian life. Henry Kingsley, whose *Geoffry Hamlyn* is a compendium of most of the clichés of the colonial novel, is his chief target, and the life of Kingsley's Major Buckley is continued and concluded by Collins in his account of Mrs. Beaudesart's earlier life. The literary parody is amusing but beneath it lies a serious concern of the real author. Those conventions of the colonial romance which Furphy, through Collins, objects to—"The outlawed bushrangers; the lurking black-fellows; the squatter's lovely Diana-daughter, awaiting the well-bred greenhorn. . ."—were the stereotypes Australia evoked in the English literary imagination. (pp. 1-2)

Collins rejects these conventions of what he calls "romance," and of the colonial Australian romance particularly, in favour of the realistic device of a selection of extracts from his diary.

> SUN. DEC. 9. *Dead Man's Bend. Warrigal Alf down. Rescue twice. Enlisted Terrible Tommy.*
>
> Now what would your novelist rede you from that record, if he had possession of my diary? Something mysterious and momentous, no doubt, and probably connected with buried treasure. Yet it is only the abstract and brief chronicle of a fair average day; a day happy in having no history worth mentioning; merely a drowsy morning, an idle mid-day, and a stirring afternoon. Life is largely composed of such uneventful days; and these are therefore most worthy of careful analysis.

The rejection of "the mysterious and momentous" for a "careful analysis" of everyday life is a partial statement of Furphy's own concerns, though like Collins he is concerned not only with provincial Riverina life but also with "Life," with that "engaging problem" and "ageless enigma." But a "careful analysis" is what Collins fails to make here and he remains oblivious of the significance of the events he records. . . . He remains unaware that the life he has chronicled contains in the Warrigal Alf-Molly Cooper plot the most improbable of melodramas. The fact that Collins is so busily engaged in *not* writing a novel, a "romance," that he is blind to this novelettish plot in his own chronicle implies Furphy's ironic detachment from Collins' faith in documentary, slice-of-life naturalism as a means of achieving "a fair picture of Life."

Such Is Life reveals ironically that even in a "record" the disjunction between literature and life cannot be as absolute as Collins assumes. The stock comic situations of mistaken sexual identity show that the life Collins encounters is more like romance than he realizes or allows. Jim Quarterman and Nosey Alf are women; Cleopatra is a stallion; and the awful possibility occurs to Collins that the traveller he is attempting to debag on the banks of the Murray may be a woman. Things are not always what they seem and may prove to be closer to fiction, or farce, than to the factual world that Collins trusts. Furphy's parodying of the aristocratic bias of Australian romances by his introduction of the caricatures Willoughby, Folkestone and Maud Beaudesart into Collins' factual record reveals the consciousness of itself as literature with which *Such Is Life* faces life. Objections to the introduction of these unrealistic "aristocratic" caricatures seem to have been made by critics who share Collins' belief that a novel should be consistently true to life. Furphy's concern, however, goes beyond the realistic depiction of the normal and everyday; he is as much concerned with art as he is with life, or, rather, he is concerned with art as a means of perceiving the complexity of reality.

Although Furphy's known love of eighteenth century English literature (discernible in his "Sterne-like palaver" and literary parody "à la Fielding-Richardson") doubtless affected his conception of the novel, these influences are not inconsistent with the comparisons made with Conrad, James and Joyce by the critics who first seriously considered *Such Is Life* as a novel. Fielding's and Sterne's explicit concern in their novels with the relationship of artifice to reality reveals their awareness of a problem that recurs in the modern novel—how to contain life within the confines of fiction. The comparisons which have been made between Furphy's theory of the novel and those of other modern novelists draw our attention to the originality of Furphy's concern with form at the time he was writing. In what seems to have been almost complete isolation from contemporary European literature, Furphy can be seen experimenting with a "new" novel with some similarities to those written by James and Conrad, writers who like Furphy were contemptuous of the conventional novel, who developed their ideas of the novel as art, and used the technique of the involved narrator, so creating a centre of consciousness separate from their own to provide a "point of view." (pp. 3-5)

Collins is Furphy's means of presenting life in all its immediacy and confusion and, at the same time, providing the detachment and shaping significance of art. Collins is immersed in the flux of experience. The fact that he is writing up his experiences from scanty notes in a diary (a "nonfictional" form) does not destroy the illusion of immediate experience but adds to it the further dimension of Collins' awareness as both "hero" and "author." It presents Collins' awareness of himself, and shows him also as doubly unaware—at the time of the event and at the time of his imaginative re-creation of it. In thus using Collins to present the "untransmuted," raw experience of life while himself remaining invisible, Furphy presents the life he knows, and simultaneously engages the reader with his problem of how the random pattern of everyday events can be both rendered and illuminated. How better than by dramatizing his narrator's comic attempts to demonstrate the "suchness of life?" (p. 5)

Collins is the anti-hero as author, and his role as the anti-hero could be defined as his consciousness of his failure to live up to what he imagines the expectations of the reader of fiction to be. But his conscious playing of the parts of the "author" and the "hero" are only two aspects of his role-playing. He sees life as the playing of a part, and the Shakespearean metaphor of life as a stage becomes this "Hamlet-man's" defence against life. In his encounters with others Collins preserves his integrity and self-esteem by allowing them to see only that side of his personality he chooses to unmask. His awareness of others allows him to respond to their expectations, to manifest the response he anticipates will be most sympathetically accepted by them, and yet enables him to retain an ironic reserve in his dealings with them. This art of taking the measure of his man is apparent in all his dealings with others—though it is not always successful. It brings out the "aristocrat" in him in his conversation with Willoughby, the "lawyer" in him in his interview with Quarterman over the burning of the haystack, the "Scotsman," the "Anglophile" and the white supremacist in him in his encounters with Tom Armstrong, Sollicker and Paul Sam Young. To Maud Beaudesart's self-ideal of long-preserved gentility he responds with the pretence of his own respectable lineage. His role-playing is constant and various, but it is seen through by others. (pp. 6-7)

Collins' image of himself as a peripatetic philosopher makes him a figure of fun around Runnymede. Far from being a typical bushman, he is a comic centre of consciousness whose mind is sicklied o'er with thoughts of a speculative, metaphysical cast. As an author he may be a know-all, but he is not as omniscient as he pretends to be. He can be unperceptive and forgetful: for example, he fails to see that Hungry M'Intyre was the real father of Sollicker's "son"—a fact which undercuts his musings on race, heredity and "the coming Australian"—and his introduction of Rory O'Halloran reveals that he had met Rory twice before without realizing that he was the same man. He is, however, of the "artistic" type—detached, concerned more with speculations about "Life" than with the life before him, conscious always of himself before an audience. Despite his deprecations of romances and Romanticism, he has much of the romantic Wanderer about him as he moves freely through this society encountering the paradoxes of life—or so he would like to see himself. We meet him debating one metaphysical alternative; we leave him debating another. In between he has interfered considerably in the lives of a number of people without being fully conscious of this and without becoming involved in any relationship other than a farcical flirtation with Mrs. Beaudesart. The main "action" of the novel is Tom Collins' response to the life he records, both at the moment of experiencing it and at the later stage of presenting it to us. He does not provide us with a flat realistic portrayal of Riverina life (as he intends) but with that "oblique and indirect view" Henry James aimed at: we see Tom seeing life. (pp. 7-8)

Tom Collins is a digressive writer who will seize any opportunity to hold up the narrative so that he can express his opinions, air his erudition and reminisce. In these digressions are found those passages that are frequently quoted as examples of Furphy's expression of the idealism of the period. In them we do find a complex of attitudes that express the nationalistic culture of the eighties and nineties, ideas which derive ultimately from a European radical tradition. But it is not only Furphy's sensibility we discern in them (and this is distorted anyway by being transmitted through Collins); it is the sensibility of the age. The opposing ideas presented by Collins reflect the intellectual controversies of the period, especially the conflicts between sceptical, scientific attitudes and Christian beliefs. Tom does not resolve these conflicts—as Furphy attempts to resolve those between Christianity and socialism in *Rigby's Romance*—nor does Furphy demonstrate any of Collins' alternatives as being superior to another. Rather, what we are presented with is Tom's conceptual framework through which he views life, and this is far from being a consistent schema. In manner the digressions are distinguished from the didactic expression of similar ideas in *Rigby's Romance,* or in the journalism of the period, by the general air of abstraction with which Collins delivers them and his indifference to the political—a manner which expresses the escapist nature of much of Collins' cerebration.

The loose logic of the digressions, their associative structure and manic verbal play present Collins in the process of thinking in his dual role as "author" and "hero." Through his digressions the "author" both expands the significance of his story, by introducing into "scenes of provincial life" transcendental speculations on the ultimate meaning of Life (which also enable Furphy to draw attention to his own concerns), and at the same time makes a fool of himself. Maundering over a bewildering range of topics, the digressions have in common the sort of reasoning Collins himself is amused by in Rory O'Halloran's *A Plea for Woman*—reasoning directed to reconciling contradictions in the Bible and Shakespeare, reasoning that soars from the flimsiest of factual bases to the boundless realms of abstraction. Rory's discourse on women is only an exaggeration of Collins' own reasoning in his contradictory explanations of life, and as Rory's discourse seems a sublimated response to his own marital situation, so Collins' philosophizing often refers covertly to his own situation. (pp. 8-9)

[A. D. Hope in a review of Miles Franklin's *Joseph Furphy*] saw Furphy, like Joyce, conceiving his novel in terms of a philosophy of life and saw the digressions as central to the novel—most of all the digression on alternatives which Collins delivers as he recalls his discovery of the swagman sleeping in the shade near Rory's hut. To Hope this digression stated the philosophy Furphy intended, but failed, to demonstrate in the novel. It seems to me that a reader today, alerted to the novel's dramatic structure by Hope and other critics, would see Collins' "mere afterthoughts" (interpolated between his descriptions of the swagman and of his resumed approach to the hut) as a defensive rationalization of a decision he has learnt to regret. The fault would then appear to be not that the novel fails to demonstrate this philosophizing but that this digression should seem to be a statement of Furphy's intentions. The weakness of this digression as of that on bigotry (also in Chapter Two), or that on music which Collins delivers later in Nosey Alf's hut, is that they are prolonged beyond their plausibility as passages of Collins' consciousness and become boring displays of erudition in which Furphy himself is engaged. (pp. 9-10)

Furphy's dramatic presentation of his narrator should make us wary of accepting Collins' Utopian musings and egalitarian inclinations at their face value. The two meetings with Andrew Glover point to the sometimes barefaced incongruity between the ideals of Christian socialism which Collins elaborates in his digressions, and his own actions. Similarly, there is a discrepancy between the optimistic democratic ideals he professes and the real society in which he moves. His digressions present the moral ideal of social relationships "deduced" from democratic and Christian principles, but in the rest of the novel he presents concrete moral situations—such as those that enable us to judge Collins himself. *Such Is Life* reveals the ways in which a society "works" by showing us the network of everyday relationships and how these appear to the individual within the net. Collins as a roving bureaucrat is well situated to observe the formal and informal patterns that social relationships take, and much of what he shows us undercuts his own idealism. Instead of this society justifying his democratic Utopianism, the Riverina is revealed as a pastoral extension of Australian society at large in that it shares the same broad stratification on the basis of wealth, the same class conflicts between "wage-slaves" and "monopolists" and the same class consciousness. (pp. 11-12)

Throughout, the novel weighs Collins' generalizations against particular social situations and contrasts ideal and actual social values. Collins' own status as a Deputy-Assistant-Sub-Inspector in the Central Office of Unconsidered Trifles (an office that implies the interference of a remote and inscrutable bureaucracy in local life) is at odds with his matey egalitarianism. His "mateyness" is a mask: he falls readily into conversation with those he meets on his travels, is generous in lending a hand or sharing his tobacco, but his only constant companion is a kangaroo dog. The paramount social value of mateship which expresses the solidarity of the lower classes emerges from the first chapter as a convention governing the casual and impersonal relations between men in a semi-nomadic society. . . . Collins at the very beginning of the chapter warns the reader that prudence is needed in dealing with men in the Riverina, and the events of the chapter confirm the justice of his remark. Warrigal Alf gains his revenge on Mosey for selling him Pilot; Dixon helps his mate Bummer steal a horse; and M'Nab ingratiates himself with Montgomery by informing him that the bullocks are camped on his land. Collins himself in his inspection of Cleopatra whilst bargaining with M'Nab reveals little of that open-handedness the myth of mateship would lead us to expect.

Despite his narrator's Utopian leanings, so often quoted out of context, Furphy's vision is not of an Australia Felix, whether that prophesied in the nationalistic dreams of a coming Australia or in those earlier dreams of Australia as an antipodean Arcadia in which the country gentry or the yeomen of England could be re-established. . . . Kingsley, whose Major Buckley leads the life of an English country gentleman in Australia, begins his description of the Australian landscape in *Geoffry Hamlyn* by apostrophizing—"A new heaven and a new earth!"; Collins' opening description is of "hot, black clay, thirsting for spring rain and bare except for inedible roley-poleys, coarse tussocks, and the woody stubble of close-eaten salt-bush," a realistic appraisal of the land's potential for grazing. The other aspect of the immigrants' dream, the hope of establishing a closely settled and self-sufficient yeoman class, is even more tellingly exposed as a delusion. . . . The nearest the novel comes to presenting the dream of simple rural contentment is with Rory and his family, and Sollicker with his. But both are employees of a station rather than independent farmers, and their domestic lives fall short of the bucolic idylls depicted in romances. (pp. 12-14)

The significance of the novel is achieved through Collins' attempts to define the "suchness" of life. It is a comic significance in that life is seen as greater and more varied than the rational schemata men seek to reduce it to. No resolution of the contradictory viewpoints embodied in the characters (and in Tom's *ad hoc* philosophizing) is possible: each sees life from his own conditioned point of view, none sees it whole; the comedy is in their attempts, especially Collins', to explain how and why things happen as they do. Throughout, Furphy's awareness is fuller than Collins' and is guiding our judgement of him. What this judgement amounts to is not something that can be extracted from the novel and called a "philosophy"; it is rather the continual weighing of Collins' responses to life. Life is found in the tragi-comedy of Collins' experiences, not in his attempts to explain them. For every explanation life throws up an exception and preserves its inscrutable variety. Constantly the inadequacy of Collins' response is revealed. Through his evasion of moral issues we are made conscious of them and their resolution in everyday life. We see that injustice is done and that the sky does not fall. This is one aspect of the sense in which *Such Is Life* can be called a comic novel: it faces things as they are with equanimity and an amused awareness (often Collins' own) of the discrepancy between the ideal and the actual "suchness" of life. (p. 19)

Tom Collins may assume the mask of the cynic most frequently, but beneath it he manifests an engagement with life which cannot be given full recognition if we see him as merely responding stoically to a meaningless existence. Life may appear absurd, an ultimately futile, senseless pantomime, but it does engage all of Collins' perplexed attention. He reveals an exuberant resilience in the face of fortune's blows—the resilience of a philosopher who sees life *sub specie aeterna,* but also of the clown. There is a rhythmic movement that grows out of Collins' responses to life which is more important than the concealed plots in giving the work an organic unity. This is the rhythm of Collins' emotional fluctuations between pessimistic dismay and manic inspiration; and it is upon the exuberant note of the latter that the novel ends. When we read the novel through there is comic relief from the tragic aspects of life. The tragic note is present in the figure of Andrew Glover but it is outweighed by the comedy of Collins' masquerading. With his closing words we are conscious not of the end of the action but of its continuation beyond the limits of the novel. These, it seems, are only some strands from the patchwork web of life and it will continue to be woven—for good or for bad. The comic vitality Collins displays at the end expresses more than simply acquiescence in an ironic world and an imperfect society. However inadequate his response may be in terms of his own avowed ideals, his comic vitality gives the work a positive force. It exults in the unpredictability of events which relieve the monotony of life, the idiosyncrasies which make other people tolerable, the sharing of adversity that can bridge the gulf between individuals and make life bearable. It is this which gives colour, warmth and variety to the drama of everyday events played out against the inhospitable Riverina background: without it life would be unendurable, "signifying nothing." (p. 20)

> *Brian Kiernan, "Joseph Furphy: 'Such Is Life',"* in *his* Images of Society and Nature: Seven Essays on Australian Novels, *Oxford University Press, Melbourne, 1971, pp. 1-20.*

BARRY ARGYLE (essay date 1972)

[*In the following excerpt, Argyle examines the treatment of social and political conflicts in* Such Is Life.]

When *Such Is Life* is read for the first time, it immediately impresses as a sprawling novel, linked only by the narrator's constant presence, accounted for by his assertion that he is writing no romance, with plot and denouement, but a chronicle of extracts taken with more or less arbitrariness from his "twenty-two consecutive editions of Letts Pocket Diaries." Its sprawl, like its arbitrariness, is more apparent than real. It first appears to be a picaresque novel, a series of loosely-connected anecdotes of the sort which talkative, semi-literate men might tell round a camp-fire. It is this picaresque quality plus a carefully-fostered suggestion of literary wilfulness that has led to the novel being compared with *Tristram Shandy.* There is also of course the "philosophical" temper of its narrator, and even the presence of an equally "philosophical" pipe, which seems to have been inherited from Uncle Toby. More important, there is a comparable prurience and furtive vulgarity.

But so much appearance and protestation mask a carefully constructed plot, to which the circumscribed locality offers a clue. Nearly everyone in the novel knows, has known, or is invited to know, everyone else. That bullock teams, and Collins, go from station to station across the Riverina, camping and yarning, provides the restless quality of a picaresque novel, but they never go where they are unknown. The success of the novel, like the success of their business, depends upon the treading of worn tracks. Beneath the literary wilfulness lies the story-teller's well-trodden but well-constructed path.

The novel opens with Collins taking the reader into his confidence, discussing the philosophical implications of his recent dismissal, an event which provides him with the time and the excuse for his writing, and immediately introduces a verisimilitude which the philosophizing heightens by contrast. Referring to the first of his diaries, he introduces his bullockies camping on, or not far off, the track—a piece of allegory which finds its explanation in the title to the novel. (pp. 180-81)

By the reappearance throughout the novel of the same characters riding its boundaries or driving along, or not far off, its main tracks, Furphy creates an air of casual, or fortuitous unity. (p. 182)

The talkative, camping bullock-drivers, besides linking the main contrasted themes of Warrigal Alf and Nosey Alf, and Collins and Madame Beaudesart—which . . . leads into an avowed literary critique—also epitomize, and voice, what many consider, with Furphy's encouragement, to be his main purpose in writing: to express his "democratic bias." Squatters and bullock-drivers were two interdependent communities. Without the one, the other could not have existed. Bullocks, however, had to feed, but the well-used tracks they travelled between homesteads were usually eaten out and waterless. To overcome this, teams camped off the track, in the squatters' paddocks; and this, as Folkstone, one of Furphy's typical English aristocrats, points out, is trespass. Thomson, a bullock-driver, early presents the problem and makes clearer what Furphy sees as implicit in this continuous struggle between the two classes:

> If you want a problem to work out, just consider that God constructed cattle for living on grass, and the grass for them to live on, and that, last night, and to-night, and to-morrow night, and mostly every night, we've a choice between two dirty transactions—one is, to let the bullocks starve, and the other is to steal grass for them. For my own part, I'm sick and tired of studying why some people should be in a position where they have to go out of their way to do wrong, and other people are cornered to that extent that they can't live without doing

wrong, and can't suicide without jumping out of the frying-pan into the fire. . . .

Remembering what Furphy says about such a region being the one where Australians gain a consciousness of their own nationality, we realize that he is here isolating what he and many others in the nineties saw as the political struggle, the struggle between "them," who locked up the land even against bullock-drivers, and "us." Collins, who deals with "them" and camps with "us," is the striving middle-class whose concern is promotion to a higher grade and whose fear is the sack. As the Sydney official in the bush, he also represents the settled—or inclined-to-settle—city man that Furphy discounts. His easy meaningless job is to distribute lettered forms to squatters; his function in the novel is to observe and record the actions of others, actions which, though without the impetus of encouragement or the distraction of fear, are more intelligible than his own. By making him, at the time of writing, one of the unemployed, however, Furphy blurs what objectivity—to give it a kind name—such a man might in such circumstances be thought to possess. Presented in this way, the class war assumes a simplicity more touching than earlier writers had thought possible. Its simplicity is in every sense pastoral, and even today is not without its devotees. Furphy encourages them thus: "between the self-valuation of the latter-day squatter and that of his contemporary wage slave, there is very little to choose. . . . Either the anachronistic tradition must make suicidal concessions, or the better-class people must drown all plebeian Australian males in infancy, and fill the vacancy with Asiatics." In other words, the choice is between social revolution and mass coloured immigration. What happened was much more prosaic: the petrol engine was developed and two-thirds of Australia's population chose to live in the cities and townships. Joseph Furphy, the bullock-driver who like Holy Dan lost his team through drought and pleuro-pneumonia, was among the first to go. The land in Australia, as in Scotland, remained locked up in large holdings because it was better economics for everyone that it should be that way. And Australia remained as aggressively "white" as Furphy could have desired. As a social prognostication, *Such Is Life* was already out of date when it was written.

But the contemporaneity or political importance of Furphy's book is of secondary importance. . . . What does concern us is the way in which *Such Is Life*—fabricated in "near-isolation," as one critic once asserted—links with the by then established Australian literary tradition, and the way that tradition continued to show, even to depend on, its European origins. Indications of this link are apparent in the extracts already quoted. The first is in the emphasis Thomson, the bullock-driver, gives to the inevitable criminality there is in his job, a fact of life which parallels the literary convention embodied in the Byronic hero, and which Furphy exploits. The second is in the reference to Asian immigration and Furphy's fear of it, which had its original social parallel in those convict opinions most notably shared by Governor Macquarie and acknowledged in Rowcroft's *Tales of the Colonies*. Australia was the "convict country," a prison; and one of the functions of prison walls is to keep people out. Both find support in Furphy's elaborated concern for the "real" gentleman, and for those walks of life in which the gentleman has traditionally interested, and perhaps defined, himself. . . . As H. J. Oliver has pointed out . . . [Furphy's] general theme is perhaps "responsibility." Having chosen his audience of fellow pilgrims whose lives were more sedentary than his own—in other words, the city-man—he states in the book's last paragraph what the object of that

responsibility is: "Such is life, my fellow-mummers—just like a poor player, that bluffs and feints his hour upon the stage, and then cheapens down to mere nonentity. But let me not hear any small witticism to the further effect that its story is a tale told by a vulgarian, full of slang and blanky, signifying—nothing." What he is attacking is the orthodoxy of the cultured, represented by the phrase "cheapens down to mere nonentity," which recalls Sir Thomas Browne's "The greater part must be content to be as though they had not been, to be found in the Register of God, not in the record of man." What he is proclaiming is the unorthodoxy of the uncultured, whose representative, for Furphy, is always Shakespeare, who had little Latin and less Greek. Thus the battle is a simplified extension of the simplified political battle. To wage the same war on two fronts is the book's purpose. It turns out to be another phoney war as soon as the terms of the conflict are examined; for what Furphy is saying is that the vulgarian is as good as the cultured man, and he is good in the same ways. He is learned though untaught; he is a Christian though no church-goer; he will flatten an enemy though he is no soldier; he is a nationalist though no imperialist; history is what will be made in the future, not what has been done in the past; literature is a chronicle with a love interest, not a love story with a feature interest; while, to persuade and convince, Furphy employs, even in the puns and alliteration on the first page, the devices of rhetoric—ironically, it is true; but irony is defensive, half in love with what it half condemns. Furphy thus upholds the same orthodoxy among different believers. (pp. 182-87)

As the book's last paragraph makes clear, Furphy's intention is to show that ordinary men are worth writing about, a fact which Dickens, for instance, had assumed was self-evident. Collins's "philosophical" pipe earlier argues the reasons, and explains the difficulties:

> the man who spends his life in actual hardship seldom causes a trumpet to be blown before him. He is generally, by heredity or by the dispensation of Providence, an ornament to the lower walks of life; therefore his plea, genuine if ungrammatical, is heard only at second-hand, in a fragmentary and garbled form. Little wonder, then, that such a plea is received with felicitous self-gratulation, or passed with pharisaical disregard, by the silly old world that has still so many lessons to learn—so many lessons which none but that unresisting butt of slender-witted jokers can fitly teach, and which he, the experienced one, is usually precluded from teaching by his inability to spell any word of two syllables. Yet he has thoughts that glow, and words that burn, albeit with such sulphurous fumes that, when uttered in a public place, they frequently render him liable to fourteen days without the option.

Although "glow," "burn," "sulphurous fumes," and "fourteen days without the option" introduce what might be called the "Satan-convict" idea, the main point is that it is difficult for the common man either to write a book or to be made the hero of a book. These are the tasks Furphy sets himself. To overcome the problem of reproducing the common man's burning language, he adopts the literary convention of replacing such words as "hell" and "bloody" with euphemisms, but by making the substitutes rather more esoteric than, for instance, Boldrewood's "by Jove," and by extending the con-

Letter from Furphy to his mother.

vention to include such possible indelicacies as ''bed'' and ''trousers,'' he pokes fun at it. By poking fun at it, however, the power of the convention is acknowledged; irony is not the weapon with which conventions are destroyed; and by choosing irony, Furphy suggests that he was not keen to see it go. To write the kind of realistic novel in which a spade is called a spade, he would have had to forego many of his knowing laughs; and, to those who admire the novel, such laughs are a great part of its attraction. As much in literary method as in political theory, Furphy was a conservative. Like Boldrewood, he favoured modification, not change. To fire literary squibs was his way of dealing with the hotheads. (pp. 189-90)

Neither Furphy's literary nor his political conservatism is surprising. Both imply a wish for a respectability comparable with that traditionally said to be possessed by the originator of the colony's literature and political system, namely Britain, so that Australian nationalism can begin to compete with Britain's imperialism. If the colony altered the terms under which she would compete, there could be no competition. Furphy goes to great lengths to ensure that they are the same. His heroes drink less and wash more often than any Englishman, he says, evidently believing, like Samuel Smiles, that cleanliness is next to godliness, and drunkenness an abomination. It is a remarkable claim, when almost every previous writer had noted there was more alcohol than water in the land. Furphy's heroes are thus having their virtues exaggerated at the same time as the

viciousness is withdrawn from their vices. They are heroes not of the sixteenth or eighteenth century, but of the nineteenth. (p. 194)

To the extent that she is a hero and not a heroine, Nosey Alf is presented in . . . Byronic terms. Because of her accident, she is without a nose. Addressing the reader, Collins says: ''Your nose, in all probability, is your dram of eale—your club foot—your Mordecai sitting at the king's gate—but you would look very queer without it.'' As she is musically gifted, Collins assures her that ''if [a person is] an artist, as you are, what might otherwise be a disfigurement becomes the highest claim to respect and sympathy.'' This may be another example of Collins talking rubbish for the sake of Furphy's irony, but Furphy is also using the injury to help hold the reader's ''respect and sympathy.'' Thus he is employing the convention which equated the artist with the Byronic hero. Artist, she certainly is. Besides her playing, which ''was both a mystery and a revelation,'' she has a voice ''rich, soft, transcendent, yet suggesting ungauged resources of enchantment unconsciously held in reserve,'' while the ''tendency of her songs was toward love, and love alone.'' Collins—or Furphy—then adds, ''chaste, sensuous, but purely human love.'' The deformity is Byron's, but the love is Scott's. And we are to believe that ''such is life!'' (p. 198)

Collins says: ''I always make a point of believing the best where women are concerned,'' but his tone, as well as his behaviour, converts the remark into yet another of Furphy's ironies. Apart from Warrigal Alf's jilting one girl, and leaving another, there are the three stories he tells in which women are tragically unfaithful in the way that the convict origins of Australia had encouraged them to be. None of these three women was married to a convict—for Furphy ignores the convict era—but the habits of that era seem to have persisted. Old Sollicker's wife was one whose loyalties were early mixed, or mixed for her. Rory O'Halloran's wife—whose title of "Mrs." is conspicuously frequent and therefore suspect—is a shrew who, though "married" to a darling of a man, has yet "explored the profound depths of masculine worthlessness." Cooper's half-admiring complaint has a different source. He has found that women "can't suffer to be idle, nor to see anybody else idle." He realizes that woman's "settlement of the empty spaces of Australia" involves not only a willing self-sacrifice, but also a willingness to sacrifice the "up-country" man's dream of himself. Settlement would also change those empty spaces, "so grave, subdued, self-centred," as much as it would change the matching mood of man. The only men in *Such Is Life* who find women desirable are Sunday-School teachers and Willoughby, the Englishman, all of whom are objects of Furphy's contempt. Willoughby "was detected—ha-ha! *Sua cuique voluptas*—in a liaison with a young person who resided with [his] uncle's wife." The reader is evidently intended to shudder; and the reader might very well oblige, if he were given less ambiguous encouragement of this kind:

> There is nothing dainty or picturesque in the presentment of a naked character washing himself; yet how few of our later novels or notes of travel are without that bit of description. . . . It would be much more becoming to wash our dirty skins, as well as our dirty calico, in private.
>
> We might advantageously copy women-writers here. Woman, in the nature of things, must accumulate dirt, as we do; and she must now and then wash that dirt off, or it would be there still. (Like St. Paul, I speak as a man). But the scribess never parades her ablutions on the printed page. . . . Woman must be more than figuratively a poem if she can promenade a dusty show-yard for a long, hot afternoon without increasing in weight by exogenous accretion; but her soulfulness, however powerless to disallow dirt, silently asserts itself when that dirt comes to be shifted.

There is prudery in all this, and only a writer obtuse in the manner of Saint Paul could liken dirty skins to any kind of dirty calico. In attacking writers like Kingsley—who allowed his characters a "tubbing" almost as frequently as Furphy allows Collins a bathe in a stagnant water-hole, where he always seems to "lose his virility" in what can only be a lonely orgasm among the duckweed—Furphy switches to attack those women-writers who coyly leave their characters clean but unwashed. He thus introduces a prurience in the service of what he takes to be a sort of "no nonsense" realism, the sort that calls a spade a bloody shovel. "Exogenous accretion" may be an ironic euphemism; but what about Furphy's own coyness in depriving his characters of their sexuality? Most civilizations have considered a bed more important than a bath; and it might be thought that in Australia, where people are as scarce as water, it would be more realistic to increase the one while conserving the other.

Furphy's hearty but limited, and therefore unhelpful, vulgarity—if that is what it is—is apparent in the frequency with which he has his characters untrousered. Rory O'Halloran is the first to appear thus, out of forgetfulness; Collins is the next, out of carelessness. And Ida, Madame Beaudesart's good but ugly allegorical maid, who "had a straggly goatee of dirty white, with woolly side-boards of the same colour," says with some truth to Collins: "I picked up this little buckle aside o' your b-d; it's come off the back of your tr—rs. I'll sew it on for you any time, for I notice you're bothered with them slippin' down." What is one to make of so many naked men and bearded trousered women?

This seaside-postcard stuff has been described as "comic variation"; yet its comedy is slight, and its variation none. (pp. 199-201)

[It] must be said again—as so many have said before—that the book has, in the words of H. J. Oliver, "a most subtle and original plan." Similarly, its verbal intricacies have long provided cause for comment. "Irony" has been the word most on scholars' lips; it could equally well have been "vulgarity." There is, for instance, the water tank known as Faugh-a-ballogh, which is pronounced by one bullock-driver as "Fog-a-bolla"—an approximation to what in Australian speech (lately called "Strine") would be "Fuck a bullock." Under the influence of the same accent, the name of the noxious English aristocrat, Folkstone, would become "Fuckson"; while the obsequious English peasant, "old Sollicker," who believes that "orders is orders," would be "arse-'ole licker." These are isolated examples. There may well be others.

Englishmen are, on the whole, the most hated among Furphy's hates. For him, they epitomize that orthodoxy which he attacks on the first page. They are victims of his satire, not of Collins's irony. They are foolish and pretentious, unloved and unloveable. The Chinese, whom Collins always addresses in the Australian variant of "black-feller talk," are the most despised. They are "our lowest types," "the Turanian horde," "partners with opium and leprosy," "joss devotees," whose greatest fault is to be considered "cheap and reliable" by employers. The Irish have a "noxious innocence and all-round ineptitude." Germans, appearing in their traditional literary role of scientists, are dullards and possessors of handkerchiefs. They have a "vivid interest in bushrangers and blackfellows," unaware that Australia in 1883—the year Collins purports to be recording—had freed herself from fears of such people. To establish Australia's respectability—or new orthodoxy, which Boldrewood had felt historical truth could not imperil and might perhaps enhance—Furphy is thus content to ignore the fact that Ned Kelly was bushranging in 1880. Like Mark Twain, he has much fun reproducing German English, unwilling to acknowledge, as Kingsley and Boldrewood were not, that two languages are better than one. Furphy's Germans are true sons of "the microbe-laden atmosphere of Europe." His Scotsmen are mean and "impracticable," though Stewart of Kooltopa is the exception. He is the Australian equivalent of Scott's John, Duke of Argyle. There is a deal of racial theorizing in the book which Furphy may have caught from Zola, one of whose novels turns up as Collins's "swapping-book." Collins later repudiates the habit as practised by "Marcus Clarke, or Trollope, or Froude, or Francis Adams," but concludes that "The coming Australian is a problem," a remark which Compton Mackenzie in his *Gallipoli Memories,* writing of the Australian troops, almost echoes, though with a handsome and no more than just qualification: "They really were rather difficult; and so, no doubt, was Achilles.'' With so much evidence of Furphy's unpleasant nationalism, it is puzzling that he continues to be seen as ''supremely right—seizing on'' what is called ''this sense in the best of us that we are equals.'' It is said to be his ''deepest theme.'' But some of us seem to remain more equal than others. (pp. 202-03)

Barry Argyle, ''Joseph Furphy: 'Such Is Life','' in his An Introduction to the Australian Novel: 1830-1930, *Oxford at the Clarendon Press, Oxford, 1972, pp. 178-207.*

JOHN BARNES (essay date 1981)

[*Barnes is an Australian critic and educator. In the following excerpt, he discusses* Such Is Life, Rigby's Romance, *and* The Buln-Buln and the Brolga.]

Such Is Life consists of a number of variations on given themes. Furphy tended to see people as types and to analyze situations in terms of their basic patterns. Part of the sense of amplitude which *Such Is Life* gives comes from his habit of seeing a situation as containing different possibilities. The simplest examples of this patterning are sequences of stories told around a camp fire, as in chapters I and V, or a sequence told by one man, as in chapter IV. On a smaller scale are the somewhat mechanical patterns, like stage routines, which Furphy introduces into conversations, such as in chapter I the comments of the assembled group on each person who goes over to the wagon for a drink. Sometimes, the patterning is no more than a joke of a familiar kind, such as Collins's titles for Mr Q—, and Mr Q—'s variations on Collins's name. Sometimes a joke has much larger implications, and is pursued in an extraordinary variety of forms, as for instance the variations on the theme of confused sexual identity.

The sex joke is first introduced when Collins gets the horse named Cleopatra in a deal in chapter I. He doesn't change the horse's name ''though, afterwards, men of clerkly attainment took me aside and kindly pointed out what they conceived to be a blunder.'' (pp. xix-xx)

Collins's encounter with Nosey Alf is more significant. . . . Collins's failure to recognize that she is a woman stems not from lack of observation (the descriptive detail is very precise) but from his habit of mind. ''I was interested in this boundary rider and resolved to know his history.'' . . . Collins's version is that Nosey Alf (Collins knows ''by a kind of incommunicable intuition, that he was a Sydney-sider, and had been in some way connected with the drapery-business'') is an artistically gifted man, suffering from melancholia and hiding away from the world because of his disfigurement and his hopeless love of a woman. His attempt to rally Alf by appealing to masculine pride—''It's pure effeminancy to brood over such things, for that's just where we have the advantage of women''—reduces Alf to tears; but Collins, confident that he has the right interpretation, doesn't reflect upon his own logic and draw the obvious conclusion about Alf.

The realism of Furphy's novel is severely strained here, and the elaborate display of Collins's obtuseness does some violence to the characterization, making Collins seem heartless and insensitive in the extreme. The pathos of Nosey Alf is filtered through the genial incomprehension of Collins. The character of the woman still in love with the man who abandoned her is a sentimental conception; and although the portrait of Warrigal Alf, sullen and remorseful, is shrewdly drawn, the

interest is limited. In the handling of the Alf-Molly ''romance''—which in the original was set against the ''romance'' of Rigby and Kate, and the burlesque romance of Collins and Mrs. Beaudesart—Furphy focused on the narrator's misunderstanding of the situation rather than the situation itself. (pp. xx-xxi)

But while Collins is self-deceived, as it were, by his own mental processes, he is also a deceiver of others. ''I am not what I am'' is an age-old theme of comedy, and in the course of the novel Collins plays many parts. His talent does run ''in the line of low-comedy acting,'' as Stewart tells him with some asperity after hearing of his impersonation of a Scotsman. Furphy endows Collins with his own wit and intelligence in the encounters with the boundary riders (though Collins is shown as being so bemused by theory that he misses the truth of Roddy's parentage). Collins's performance as a Scotsman is something of a *tour de force*, and is the most extreme instance of his disguising himself (on this occasion it is a purely linguistic disguise). Throughout the novel Collins takes on different roles, and acting becomes a metaphor for life as Collins (and Furphy) conceives of it. In the Proem to *Rigby's Romance* he tells the reader: ''You must take me as a hard-working and ordinary actor on this great stage of fools; but one who, nevertheless, finds a wholesome recreation in observing the parts played by his fellow-hypocrites. (The Greek *hupokrisis*, I find, signifies, indifferently, 'actor' and 'hypocrite'.)'' The role a man plays is how he chooses to let himself be seen by his fellows. Collins is something of a chameleon, taking on the appropriate colour according to the occasion, always under the illusion that he is in command of the circumstances.

At the end of *Such Is Life* Tom Collins takes his leave of the reader with a reflection on his role-playing:

> Now I had to enact the Cynic philosopher to Moriarty and Butler, and the aristocratic man with a ''past'' to Mrs Beaudesart; with the satisfaction of knowing that each of these was acting a part to me. Such is life, my fellow-mummers—just like a poor player, that bluffs and feints his hour upon the stage, and then cheapens down to mere nonentity. But let me not hear any small witticism to the further effect that its story is a tale told by a vulgarian, full of slang and blanky, signifying—nothing.

The tone of this leaves one uncertain what weight it is meant to have. Certainly, it carries some disturbing implications about life and its possibilities. The extent to which Furphy is to be identified with Collins varies during the novel. In some crucial passages, such as this, the role of Tom Collins seems to enable Furphy to evade the responsibility of committing himself, or even perhaps acknowledging openly what is deeply felt. Collins is genial and seemingly indestructible, but the picture that he gives is of lonely, unfulfilled and fragmented lives. Much of the strength of *Such Is Life* comes from the sense it gives of an imaginatively complete world; and in that created world human relationships do not involve the deepest self, nor do they offer the possibility of growth and fulfilment. What we are left with finally is a deeply felt sense of individual aloneness that is at odds with the expressions of belief in human solidarity. (pp. xxi-xxii)

Furphy's fascination with modes of speech is obvious in his phonetic representation of foreign speech; and in his own review [see excerpt dated 1903] he quite fairly praised himself as a "master of idiom." *Such Is Life* is a kind of treasury of colloquial speech and prose styles. Tom Collins himself has more than one style, and displays a facility with language that others cannot match. For the present-day reader his fondness for puns and his mingling of phrases from literature and history can be baffling and certainly indigestible. It is almost, at times, as if Collins is erecting a linguistic barrier between himself and the reader; but Furphy's intention was the opposite. Collins can hardly be separated from his creator, stylistically, although one must say that when Furphy writes as Collins he writes as a man with a licence to display his wit and his learning. Through Collins Furphy intends to appeal to *the reader's* wit and learning, but he does not always judge very happily what the reader will recognize—and with the passage of time much has become less comprehensible. Even when the reader cannot follow the allusions, though, Collins's very playfulness prevents his being a bore. (pp. xxii-xxiii)

Furphy could not match Lawson for ease and naturalness of expression. When he did not employ the *persona* of Tom Collins—or in passages where the Tom Collins manner is minimal—his prose in which he sets forth his thinking tends to be formal, dignified, and rhetorical, as for instance in the passages affirming his sense of nationality and his view of Mary O'Halloran as Young Australia. In *Rigby's Romance* Rigby shows none of Collins's redeeming liveliness, and his voice is indistinguishable from that of Furphy at his most earnest. There are incidental verbal felicities in *Rigby's Romance*, such as Dixon's retelling of the story of Moses . . . , but Rigby's "sermon," which dominates the book, does not show Furphy at his most creative. Although Furphy was careful to suggest some critical views of Rigby, and although the events reflect upon Rigby, the character exists primarily as a mouthpiece for Furphy's beliefs, and the human comedy is inhibited by the didactic purpose.

Within the ironic perspectives of the original *Such Is Life,* Rigby's exposition of Christian Socialism would have been more telling than it is on its own in an expanded form. It is a period piece now, but one should not underestimate the craftsmanship with which Furphy pursued his purpose, or the energy of mind which is displayed in the handling of ideas. Although Furphy cannot be considered an original or independent thinker, it is a demonstration of an intellectual strength. He did not live in a current of ideas, except as they reached him through the *Bulletin:* that was his lifeline, his point of reference, his fixed centre so far as contemporary thinking was concerned. The controversies within its pages on such topics as the *New Australia* movement, or the future of the federation, or the relevance of the Bible engaged him, and he occasionally contributed. . . . In *Rigby's Romance* he was ambitious to give a more permanent and more comprehensive form to his thoughts on the individual in society. There was a strain of the preacher in Furphy (hardly surprising, given his background), and in *Rigby's Romance* he voiced his deepest convictions about the purpose of man's life.

Rigby's Romance finds its readers mainly among those who have already enjoyed *Such Is Life* and want to have more of Furphy. *The Buln-Buln and the Brolga,* on the other hand, has attracted more and more readers in recent years, and is for many their first introduction to Furphy. It is more immediately accessible than *Such Is Life,* it is comparatively short, and it is consistently entertaining. In revising the original chapter II of *Such Is Life,* Furphy cut out an extended burlesque of romantic fiction . . . and re-cast the chapter as an amusing study

of two kinds of fiction. The "buln-buln" (Aboriginal word for the lyre-bird) is Fred Falkland-Pritchard, whose stories of his own exploits are pure invention, fabricated out of stock romance materials. The "brolga" (or native companion, as the bird is familiarly known) is Barefooted Bob, whose stories are a re-working of actual experiences. A restrained Tom Collins is present to record the "lies" of the two men, and to tell the reader of boyish adventures with Fred, which are neatly interspersed to expose (only to the reader) Fred's fantasizing of his life.

The Buln-Buln and the Brolga has a greater ease and confidence about it than the two more substantial books. It seems to indicate that Furphy, as a stylist, was more sure of himself, more relaxed, when he came to write this little work; and also that, following his success with the "yarns" in the revised chapter V of *Such Is Life,* he was attracted by the possibilities of the "yarn" as a form of fiction. Disappointingly, no substantial work followed *The Buln-Buln and the Brolga.* The individual stories he wrote in later years do not have the impact of the yarns he told in the novels. Furphy's imagination was most alive when he was working within a large framework, a structure which allowed him scope to create patterns of meaning.

The great endeavour of Furphy's life had been "to write a book": once *Such Is Life* was published, there was no comparable impulse, no comparable conception to work towards. For a time he hoped that *Such Is Life* represented a beginning, but during his final years in Western Australia he came to recognize that there would not be another book. When Furphy died in 1912 the man and his work were little appreciated by the Australian public, and it was left to later generations to discover the measure of his achievement. (pp. xxiii-xxiv)

> *John Barnes, in an introduction to* Joseph Furphy, *edited by John Barnes, University of Queensland Press, 1981, pp. xi-xxv.*

JAMES WIELAND   (essay date 1985)

[*Wieland is an Australian educator and critic. In the following excerpt, he discusses the composition and revisions of* Such Is Life *and notes the importance to Australian literature of the existentialist outlook expressed by Furphy in that novel.*]

Before it was published in 1903, *Such Is Life* underwent three revisions, designed to hone it down to a commercially viable length. Of these, the 1901 revisions, initiated by A. G. Stephens, were major: the present Chapters Two and Five, the O'Halloran story, were substituted for longer chapters, which were subsequently published as *Rigby's Romance* and *The Buln-Buln and the Brolga.* These revisions were carried out regardless of the fact that four years before Furphy had felt that it was "fix[ed] . . . , for better or worse, as a unit." Earlier, he had said, "Quality apart, I don't think the jumble of incident, dialogue, reflection &c. (Such *is* life) is too long."

As John Barnes points out [in *Joseph Furphy*], the effects on the novel of these revisions were manifold. They

> reduce[d] the element of literary parody, and . . . [gave] less prominence to Furphy's Christian Socialist beliefs (which he had put into the mouth of Rigby). In the two new chapters he introduced the O'Halloran family, and expanded the theme of the lost child—an incidental reference in the original text—into the most moving situation of the novel.

For many readers, the Mary O'Halloran incident alters the whole tone of the novel, forcing us to take seriously the element of nihilism which Harry Heseltine locates in the work [see Additional Bibliography]. The "new" Chapters II and V, says Barnes, have "altered the relationship between the narrator and the reader." For, whereas originally, the "philosophic point" of the narrative was "the failure of the narrator to recognize the patterns in his own narrative," in the new chapters Tom becomes "less of a comic figure, more a conduit of feeling than he is elsewhere in the novel." He "is not required to become obtuse at critical moments to sustain Furphy's design" and Furphy's earlier bland summary of the narrative distance no longer holds: "Also you will notice that a certain by-play in plot and éclaircissement is hidden from the philosophic narrator, however apparent to the matter-of-fact reader." For a moment, Collins joins the reader in a position of privileged insight and his feelings, like ours, are aroused. One of the gaps in the narrative is closed:

> Soon a disquietude from another source set my mind at work in troubled calculation of probabilities. At last I said:
>
> "Would you suppose, Steve, that the finding of George Murdoch's body was a necessary incitement among the causes that led to the little girl's getting lost?"

But the others are asleep and Tom quickly deflects his anxiety. And yet, the change has altered the texture of the novel, complicating both its network of ideas and the narrative structure.

The neatly written manuscript which Furphy sent to Stephens in 1897, then, was a radically different work from its published version. The original text has become three, the nature of the narrator become more conjectural, and what was a passing incident in the manuscript version—the lost child—has been so expanded that it alters the way in which we respond to the questions of Free Will and Determinism. By considering the effect on the original *Such Is Life* of Stephens, and on the published novel of Nettie and Vance Palmer in the Cape abridgement, it may be seen that the method of printing or publishing a work carries cultural and aesthetic significance for the work itself.

Because the Cape edition was to be directed at an English audience Edward Garnett suggested that "a great deal of verbose and redundant matter" should be cut. But it is just this "matter"—the digressions, such as the Willoughby business—that helps capture the spirit of the novel's time and place, at the same time as exposing the narrator. The abridgement caused an uproar and Vance Palmer was attacked comprehensively by the Nationalists, the most vociferous of whom were Miles Franklin and P. R. Stephenson. They felt that the "botched" novel was an emblem of Australia's colonial status, that it was a "gesture of contempt for Australia by Cape" (Stephenson), and that we were once more being "lectured by our patronising overlords from England" (Franklin). We can sympathise with their position but Palmer had believed that an abridged novel might expand Furphy's audience. The point of the example is that, rather than the fundamental nature of the work being determined in its own right, it can be distorted by the decisions, actions, and motivations of particular people at a certain time.... (pp. 19-21)

In a similar way, to study a work's reception through time is to understand that, while the text may be sanctioned by a philologist, the work is subject to the changing expectations of readers, and is thus reread according to its text and the expectations of these readers; it takes its place in a changing aesthetic, social and cultural milieu and performs different functions for its different readers. In the case of *Such Is Life,* there was nothing, at first, to suggest that it would fulfil Stephens' forecast and become an "Australian classic." In its first decade of publication it sold just over 1100 copies. By 1947, however, it had achieved classic status....

The interest shown in Furphy in the 1940s stands in marked contrast to that taken in his death in 1912, which went almost unnoticed. This progress was, at first, carried by Kate Baker and a small group of enthusiasts, from which it was swept forward on an emotive wave—you're not Australian until you've read *and* enjoyed *S'Life*—and, then, in the 1940s the criterion became one of craft, while, from the 1960s, the metaphysical potential of the work has been tapped. The history of the reception of *Such Is Life* mirrors the reception of Australian Literature as a discipline, and the readings which the novel initiates instruct us as much about the changing culture as they do the work. (p. 21)

By transposing Furphy's novel forward in time, and by ignoring the tone, it is possible to read the final paragraph as [Heseltine does in his essay "Australian Image: The Literary Heritage" as] "a nihilistic summation of the meaning of existence":

> Now I had to enact the Cynic philosopher to Moriarty and Butler, and the aristocratic man with a "past" to Mrs. Beaudesart; with the satisfaction of knowing that each of these was acting a part to me. Such is life, my fellow-mummers—just like a poor player, that bluffs and feints his hour upon the stage, and then cheapens down to mere nonentity. But let me not hear any small witticism to the further effect that its story is a tale told by a vulgarian, full of slang and blanky, signifying—nothing.

The paragraph is central to our literature. But it is so not simply because it ends with the word "nothing," it is because of the tensions between tone and sense—the conjunction of geniality and despair, which underwrites existence in Australia—and because of the ambiguities implicit in "nothing." On the one hand, it carries its full complement of existential inference, this is its present significance; on the other hand, its particular characteristics are distinctively Australian, not European. If we place the word correctly in the text, and then in its material context, we can begin to map out our Australian "nothingness" and understand where it meets, or converges from European existentialism or explorations into nihilism: they are not the same at their source, nor in their implications.

Heseltine nudges Tom towards Prufrock but although Tom is a dissembler, distorting things through his clouded opthalmic glasses, the ironies and ambiguities in *Such Is Life* lie as much in the tension between the ideals of Socialism and the self-interest of the individual as in the divided sensibility of the protagonist.

One of the endearing features of the novel to a Modern is that it is experimental and self-conscious about its form in the way that many contemporary works are, but, from Fielding's and Sterne's explorations into the Novel's potentialities and shortcomings, we see the novelist continually confronting the technical problems of realism. Such a preoccupation with form is understandable in someone, such as Furphy found himself, trying to unshackle novels written in Australia from English models and expectations: "... the book is not like any other that I know of," wrote Furphy. And while, thematically, Furphy is concerned with life lived and life speculated about, he is not, as many twentieth-century writers are, affronted by the possibility of a meaningless reality, even as he recognizes its relativity and complexity. We understand, in the same way that we do in reading *Tristram Shandy,* that we have to put the plot together, that we have to make choices about it; that Tom is fallible; and that the randomness, which is suggested by Tom's decisions about what to include and omit from the story, is modified by the web of connections which, when we have learnt to read the novel, take cognizance of its directions and indirections, gives a coherence to the work that consolidates Furphy's thematic preoccupation with Choice. We can despair that life signifies nothing, or we can accept this absurdity as the reality, without succumbing to it: either way, we are not coerced into a position. Furphy can see the alternatives, Tom would rather ignore them: he would rather "not hear any small witticisms ... signifying—nothing." Such *is* life: we can submit to it, or make do; see it through "clouded glasses" as Tom does, or face it in its complexity. (pp. 23-5)

> *James Wieland, "Australian Literature and the Question of Historical Method: Reading Lawson and Furphy," in* Journal of Commonwealth Literature, *Vol. XX, No. 1, 1985, pp. 17-35.*

ADDITIONAL BIBLIOGRAPHY

Barnes, John. "The Structure of Joseph Furphy's *Such Is Life.*" *Meanjin* XV, No. 4 (December 1956): 374-89.
  Attacks many of the views presented by Arthur Phillips in his essay "The Craftsmanship of Joseph Furphy" (see Additional Bibliography). Barnes argues that *Such Is Life* represents an intricately contrived, loose "federation" of stories and suggests that because of the structure of the novel "Furphy's 'philosophy' seems rather nebulous."

————. *Joseph Furphy.* Melbourne: Oxford University Press, 1979, 46 p.
  Biographical and critical study.

Croft, Julian. "'Who Is She?' The Image of Woman in the Novels of Joseph Furphy." In *Who Is She?,* edited by Shirley Walker, pp. 1-11. New York: St. Martin's Press, 1983.
  Asserts that two levels of narration coexist in Furphy's works, one realistic and the other romantic. According to Croft: "The values and status of the heroes of the first level are treated comically, while those of the heroes of the second level are taken seriously. The true hero of *Such Is Life* is Molly Cooper, of *Rigby's Romance* Kate Vanderdecken, and of the *The Buln-Buln and the Brolga* Mrs. Falkland-Pritchard.

Douglas, Dennis. "Joseph Furphy and the Picaresque: A Generic Reappraisal of *Such Is Life.*" *Overland* 73 (1978): 15-17, 19-24.
  Concludes that "the universality and the distinction of *Such Is Life* resides in its use of elements that reflect the continuity of narrative traditions from the sixteenth century to the present day."

Dutton, Geoffrey. "The British and Us II—Gentlemen vs. Liars." *Quadrant* IX, No. 1 (January-February 1965): 14-20.
  Examines the depiction of the English gentleman in Australian literature, noting that "one of [Furphy's] main purposes in *Such Is Life* is to explore the connections between three different sets of ideals, that of the gentleman, with his behavior code, that of the educated man, with his range of response to life, and that of the democratic, practical man, with his ability to *do* things."

Ewers, John K. "*Rigby's Romance:* Its Social Significance for Today." *Southerly* 8, No. 1 (1947): 40-3.
  A favorable review of *Rigby's Romance.* According to Ewers: "Furphy will be honored as one who gave the wheel of social evolution an (adj.) good shove in the right direction."

————. "No Ivied Walls." *Westerly: A Quarterly Review* No. 4 (December 1969): 60-8.
  Compares the lives and careers of Furphy and Henry James.

Franklin, Miles. *Joseph Furphy: The Legend of a Man and His Book.* Sydney: Angus and Robertson, Ltd., 1944, 190 p.
  Detailed account of Furphy's life and career. Franklin reprints numerous letters, personal reminiscences, and photographs of Furphy, his family, and friends.

Glass, F. Devlin. "Joseph Furphy's Novels: Naked Capers in the Riverina." In *The Australian Experience: Critical Essays on Australian Novels,* edited by W. S. Ramson, pp. 73-96. Canberra: Australian National University, 1974.
  Compares the characterization of "Tom Collins" in Furphy's three novels.

Grattan, C. Hartley. *Australian Literature.* Seattle: University of Washington Book Store, 1929, 39 p.
  Maintains that "[Collins] is the nearest approach to a Herman Melville that Australia has produced. ... He has the same capacity of mingling the most abstruse speculation—discursive essays in history, sociology, morals, anthropology, and Shakespearean criticism—with veridic glimpses of actuality."

Hadcraft, Cecil. "The New Century: First Harvest of Fiction." In his *Australian Literature: A Critical Account to 1955,* pp. 145-68. London: Heinemann, 1960.
  Brief introductory survey of Furphy's works. Hadcraft claims *Such Is Life* is "the most unusual book in Australian literature" and notes that "the erudition and the reflections and the style can be a facade, with underneath a wavering unease. In Furphy may reside the pathos of the self-educated man."

Hamer, Clive. "The Christian Philosophy of Joseph Furphy." *Meanjin Quarterly* XXIII, No. 2 (June 1964): 142-53.
  Examines the moral philosophy underlying *Such Is Life,* concluding that "Furphy's response to life is not cynical nor nihilistic; but neither is it merely comic. It is realistic; and it is Christian."

Heseltine, H. P. "Australian Image: (1) The Literary Heritage." *Meanjin* XXI, No. 1 (1962): 35-49.
  Maintains that "*Such Is Life* is, in effect, concerned with the discrepancy between what we are and what we appear to be, and with the futility of human endeavour."

Howarth, R. G. "Joseph Furphy." *Southerly* 12, No. 2 (1951): 72-8.
  Discussion of *Such Is Life, Rigby's Romance,* and *The Buln-Buln and the Brolga.*

Jones, Joseph. "Australians: Socialism Rampant: Adams, Furphy." In his *Radical Cousins: Nineteenth Century American and Australian Writers,* pp. 96-107.
  Traces Furphy's socialist philosophy as presented in *Rigby's Romance.* According to Jones: "Out of context, *Rigby's Romance* is scarcely more than a well-sugared political prescription, but recalled as part of the original design [of *Such Is Life*] it shows us how seriously the author took his political theory."

Knight, Nina. "Furphy and Romance: *Such Is Life* Reconsidered." *Southerly* 2, No. 4 (1969): 243-55.
  Examines the Molly Cooper/Alf Morris "romance" and challenges the prevailing critical view that "one of Furphy's purposes in writing [*Such Is Life*] was to react against the sentimental stereotyped and 'unrealistic' novel produced by the popular writers of the nineteenth century."

Mares, F. H. "Such Is Life." *The Australian Quarterly* XXXIV, No. 3 (September 1962): 62-71.
  A general appraisal of *Such Is Life.* According to Mares: "Furphy had the technical skill as a writer to construct a large and ambi-

tiously comprehensive novel on an entirely new scheme. He was able to control the interweaving of plots and minor episodes, and to strike and maintain an exact idiom for a large range of very varied characters.''

McDougall, Robert L. *Australia Felix: Joseph Furphy and Patrick White*. Canberra: Australian National University Press, 1966, 17 p.
Compares ''created worlds'' in the works of Furphy and the Australian writer who won the Nobel Prize for literature in 1973.

McKenzie, K. A. ''Joseph Furphy, Jacobean.'' *Australian Literary Studies* 2, No. 4 (December 1966): 266-77.
Discusses Furphy's use of allusions and quotations drawn from the Bible and the works of Shakespeare.

Moore, T. Inglis. *Social Patterns in Australian Literature*. Berkeley: University of California Press, 1971, 8 ff.
Includes numerous references to Furphy, his philosophy, and his works.

O'Dowd, Bernard. ''*Such Is Life* and the Liver Thereof.'' *Southerly* 14, No. 2 (1953): 127-30.
Reprints an excerpt from a paper delivered before the Institute of Arts and Literature in Melbourne, 7 September 1922. O'Dowd maintains that ''[*Such Is Life*] is very likely to take a similar place in our past—when we earn a past—to that which Montaigne's *Essays* take in the past of France. There is something similarly catholic and universal about *Such Is Life* and about the *Essays*, and something as singularly individual about Tom Collins as about Montaigne.''

Oliver, H. J. ''Joseph Furphy and 'Tom Collins'.'' *Southerly* 5, No. 3 (1944): 14-18.
Praises the form and style of Furphy's works of fiction.

Phillips, Arthur. ''The Craftsmanship of Joseph Furphy.'' *Meanjin* XIV, No. 1 (March 1955): 13-27.

A close analysis of the structure of *Such Is Life*.

Pringle, John. ''A Classic Novel of the Australian Wilds.'' *The Times Literary Supplement*, No. 2951 (19 September 1958): 532.
An introductory essay praising *Such Is Life* and offering brief assessments of *Rigby's Romance* and *The Buln-Buln and the Brolga*.

Richters, Z. P. ''The Moral History of Tom Collins.'' *Southerly* 39, No. 3 (September 1979): 246-64.
Sees the moral decline of Tom Collins as ''the central and possibly the unifying subject of *Such Is Life*.''

Scheckter, John. ''The Lost Child in Australian Fiction.'' *Modern Fiction Studies* 27, No. 1 (Spring 1981): 61-72.
Compares the lost child scenario in Henry Kingsley's *The Recollections of Geoffrey Hamlyn* (1859), Marcus Clarke's ''Pretty Dick'' (1869), and Furphy's story of Mary O'Halloran from *Such Is Life*.

Southerly 6, No. 3 (1945): 1-64.
''Furphy'' issue containing three of his short stories, criticism of his works, and personal reminiscences written by several of his friends.

Thomson, A. K. ''The Greatness of Joseph Furphy.'' *Meanjin Papers* 2, No. 3 (Spring 1943): 20-3.
Seminal essay assessing Furphy's craftsmanship in *Such Is Life* and praising Furphy as a versatile stylist and a highly original humorist and philosopher. According to Thomson, Furphy's ''greatness seems . . . to lie in the fact that he could see the uncommon in the most common of men, and that he could see the common humanity that is in all men.''

Wilson, Robert R. ''Bushmen in Porcelain Palaces: Knowing and Mistaking in 'Such Is Life','' *Southerly* 39, No. 2 (June 1979): 123-42.
Studies Furphy's examination of the nature of knowledge in *Such Is Life*.

(Francis) Bret(t) Harte

1836?-1902

American short story writer, novelist, poet, and dramatist.

Harte was one of the most celebrated and influential American writers of the nineteenth century. In such classic short stories as "The Luck of Roaring Camp," "The Outcasts of Poker Flat," and "Tennessee's Partner," he nostalgically portrayed the mining camps and ethnic groups of California during the gold rush of 1849. Featuring melodramatic incidents, far-fetched coincidences, and sentimental endings, Harte's stories made him one of the most popular authors in America. Although Harte's fiction lost much of its popularity later in his career, elements of his work—especially its regional flavor and his creation of such stock characters as the seedy prospector, the cynical gambler, and the frontier prostitute—influenced his contemporaries and later writers of popular Westerns.

Harte was born in Albany, New York, to a schoolteacher and his wife. An unhealthy child, he was tutored at home, where he read such authors as Charles Dickens, Edgar Allan Poe, and Washington Irving. When Harte was nine years old his father died, and his family moved to New York City. When Harte was eighteen his mother remarried, and the family moved to San Francisco; shortly thereafter Harte left home. Over the next decade he held several jobs, most significantly that of apprentice printer for the journal *Northern Californian*, where he was eventually given editorial responsibilities. After his marriage in 1862, Harte supplemented his income as a journalist by serving as a government clerk at the San Francisco mint. In 1865 Harte became editor of the *Californian*, where he commissioned Mark Twain, who was then a relatively unknown author, to write a weekly story for the journal. Regarding Harte's editorial influence, Twain later remarked that it was Harte who "trimmed and schooled me patiently until he changed me from an awkward utterer of coarse grotesqueness to a writer of paragraphs and chapters." Harte became editor of the *Overland Monthly* in 1868, and during his tenure with the journal his ballad "Plain Language from Truthful James" (also called "Heathen Chinee"), as well as such stories as "The Luck of the Roaring Camp," appeared in its pages and inspired what his biographer George Stewart termed a "literary epidemic" of imitations. Afterward Harte received offers of editorial positions from across the country. In 1871 he signed a one-year contract for $10,000 with the *Atlantic Monthly*, which gave the magazine exclusive rights to a minimum of twelve stories and poems and made Harte the highest paid American writer of the time. However, he was careless about fulfilling his contract, and it was not renewed. In need of a new source of income, he went on a lecture tour from 1872 to 1875, but the proceeds barely covered his expenses and the demands of creditors became an increasing problem. In a further attempt to recover his financial solvency, Harte collaborated with Twain on an adaptation of "Heathen Chinee" as the play *Ah Sin*. Performed in 1877, the drama was a failure. Later that year, Harte called on contacts in political circles who helped him obtain a consulate in Crefeld, Germany, and, two years later, in Glasgow, Scotland. He remained a prolific writer for the last twenty-two years of his life, publishing a volume of short stories almost yearly. Supported by a wealthy

patron named Mrs. Van de Velde, Harte moved to London in 1885 and became a favorite in literary and social circles. He died in London in 1902.

In his stories Harte offered a sentimental depiction of the gold-rush era of 1849, finding favor with the reading public through sensationalistic fiction that featured grotesque or idealized characters and a strong appeal to sentiment, qualities which earned him the title "Dickens among the pines." Just as Charles Dickens had created larger-than-life caricatures who became standard representations of English types, Harte invented such standard frontier types as the seedy prospector Kentuck, the hard-bitten gambler Jack Hamlin, and the dance-hall girl, characters whose outward churlishness is essential to Harte's most familiar plot formula: to expose the "heart of gold" beneath a coarse or depraved exterior. Thus, the callous miners in "The Luck of Roaring Camp" become the sensitive and self-sacrificing guardians of a child born to a prostitute, and the cynical Jack Hamlin reveals an underlying concern for others in "An Heiress of Red Dog" and "Mr. Jack Hamlin's Meditation." Reversing the formula, Harte portrayed corruption disguised as innocence in *M'liss*, a novella in which a schoolgirl becomes a pubescent seductress, and contrasted apparent respectability with actual viciousness in "Heathen Chinee," a ballad relating how two Anglo-Saxon Americans scheme to cheat, but are instead outwitted by, a Chinese immigrant. Perhaps the most outstanding example of the typical Harte story is "Tennessee's Partner." Presenting an idealized view of friendship between two miners, the story contrasts the uncouth and untutored appearance of Tennessee's partner with his extremely virtuous magnanimity toward Tennessee. Not only does the partner forgive Tennessee for seducing his wife, but he also tries to save Tennessee from execution during a trial for robbery. Loyalty is further celebrated by the story's sentimental ending, in which the two men are pictured embracing after death as they meet at heaven's gate. Although Harte occasionally experimented with different characters and settings, his stories of American frontier life in the mid-nineteenth century are considered his most typical and important works.

Early in his career, Harte received virtually undisputed acclaim as a short story writer, with critics offering similar praise for his skill as a humorist. After 1880, however, reviewers began to criticize Harte's fiction for its reliance on coincidence, romantic situations, and melodramatic prose. Mark Twain, whose talent Harte had discovered and fostered, was one of the earliest and most outspoken detractors of Harte's fiction. Applying the criteria of realism, with its demand for a faithful rendering of details, Twain noted egregious flaws in Harte's work, including inaccurate representations of frontier vernacular, faulty observation, and subservience of fact to sentiment. Despite such criticism, critics have noted that Twain was indebted to Harte; as Twain scholar Margaret Duckett suggests, the technique in "Heathen Chinee" of employing a naive narrator to reveal information and attitudes of which he is unaware influenced Twain's method in *Adventures of Huckleberry Finn*. Other critics concurred with Twain's judgments, emphasizing the maudlin emotional responses Harte solicited in even his best stories. In spite of the decline of his critical standing in the United States, Harte continued to please audiences abroad and became especially popular in England, where his fiction was favorably compared with that of Dickens. Nevertheless by 1943, when Cleanth Brooks and Robert Penn Warren wrote a derisive appraisal of "Tennessee's Partner," the view of Harte as a Victorian sentimentalist was widely held.

In the last three decades, however, some critics have begun to reassess the strengths and modernity of Harte's fiction. J. R. Boggan, for instance, contends that the sentimentality of the narrator of "The Luck of Roaring Camp" is intended to be ironic rather than sincere, and Charles E. May finds the behavior of the partner in "Tennessee's Partner" essentially sardonic and not motivated by loyalty, as most critics have assumed, but by revenge. Others note that Harte's influence as a preeminent regionalist writer and creator of standard American character types helped further the evolution of an American literature independent of European influence. In describing Harte's influence, Granville Hicks wrote: "Harte, though he may not have been in any strict sense the founder of American regionalism, was the first writer to gain popularity after the Civil War by the exploitation of sectional peculiarities, and there is little doubt that his example directly inspired many of the writers of the seventies, eighties, and nineties." For this achievement Harte remains an important figure in the development of American literature.

(See also *Contemporary Authors*, Vol. 104; *Dictionary of Literary Biography*, Vol. 12: *American Realists and Naturalists*; and *Something about the Author*, Vol. 26.)

PRINCIPAL WORKS

Condensed Novels, and Other Papers   (parodies)   1867; enlarged edition, 1871

The Lost Galleon, and Other Tales   (poetry)   1867
The Luck of Roaring Camp, and Other Sketches   (short stories)   1870; enlarged edition, 1871
Poems   (poetry)   1871
Stories of the Sierras, and Other Sketches   (short stories)   1872
M'liss   (short story)   1873
Mrs. Scaggs's Husbands, and Other Sketches   (short stories)   1873
Idylls of the Foothills   (short stories)   1874
Tales of the Argonauts, and Other Sketches   (short stories)   1875
Gabriel Conroy   (novel)   1876
Two Men of Sandy Bar   (drama)   [first publication] 1876
Ah Sin   (drama)   [first publication] 1877
Thankful Blossom, and Other Tales   (short stories)   1877
The Twins of Table Mountains, and Other Stories   (short stories)   1879
In the Carquinez Woods   (short story)   1883
California Stories   (short stories)   1884
On the Frontier   (short stories)   1884
Maruja   (short story)   1885
The Crusade of the Excelsior   (novella)   1887
Cressy   (short story)   1889
A Sappho of Green Springs, and Other Stories   (short stories)   1891
Colonel Starbottle's Client, and Some Other People   (short stories)   1892
A Protegee of Jack Hamlin's, and Other Stories   (short stories)   1894
Barker's Luck, and Other Stories   (short stories)   1896
The Writings of Bret Harte. 20 vols.   (short stories, novel, and poetry)   1896-1914
Three Partners; or, The Big Strike on Heavy Tree Hill   (short stories)   1897
Tales of Trail and Town   (short stories)   1898
Mr. Jack Hamlin's Meditation, and Other Stories   (short stories)   1899
Trent's Trust, and Other Stories   (short stories)   1903

THE ATLANTIC MONTHLY   (essay date 1868)

[*In the following excerpt, the critic reviews* Condensed Novels, and Other Papers.]

Of the novelists condensed [in *Condensed Novels, and Other Papers*], Mr. Dickens, who must have been one of the most difficult to do, seems to us the best done. The parody of Captain Marryat is very good; but that of Charlotte Brontë is not so happy as the imitation in the "Orpheus C. Kerr Papers." Mr. Harte has an admirable burlesque of Michelet, and has condensed a good deal of Victor Hugo's manner and social philosophy in this bit of moralization: "Fantine loved Tholomyes. Why? My God! what are you to do? It was the fault of her parents, and she hadn't any. How shall you teach her? You must teach the parent if you wish to educate the child. How would you become virtuous? Educate your grandmother!"

Mr. Harte's miscellaneous essays given in this volume are imbued with so much original humor, that we have all the more to regret a tendency in them to imitation of the author whom he has best parodied in his acknowledged burlesques. We find no other fault with essays inspired by the multiform and interesting life of California, and depicting San Francisco with all the advantages of local color.

> *A review of "Condensed Novels, and Other Papers,"*
> *in* The Atlantic Monthly, *Vol. XXI, No. CXXIII, Janu-*
> *ary, 1868, p. 128.*

THE NATION   (essay date 1868)

[*In the following excerpt, the critic reviews* The Lost Galleon and Other Tales.]

Perhaps by itself [*The Lost Galleon, and Other Tales*] would not give one so distinct an impression of Mr. Harte as is given by his volume of parodies on popular novels [*Condensed Novels and Other Papers*], but it confirms the pleasant impression which one gets from that agreeable little book. In his serious pieces, which are all patriotic, Mr. Harte does not shine, though he is always the man of sense and of considerable delicacy of taste, and shows to advantage beside the mass of his rivals, wholly evading one, and escaping unruined from the other of the two besetting dangers of patriotic poetry—which is pretty sure to be not poetry at all, and which is apt to make one sincerely hate his native land. In the most successful of the serious pieces; however, there is at least a touch of the comic; **"How Are You Sanitary?"** we call the most successful. And it is in the pieces purely comic that we find Mr. Harte at his best. He is then exercising the special faculty in which he excels, probably, a very large majority of all the human beings now in existence; whereas in the production of more than passable little sentimental matters, many thousands of his contemporaneous fellow-denizens of earth are as good as he, and some thousands, we dare say, are better. So that it seems as if he would do best for himself and his readers if he would forswear unmixed sentiment and make satire and fun his mainstay. His comic verses, some of them, are labored, as if done at short notice for the newspapers; and some of them, as **"The Lost Galleon,"** are labored and apparently have not the excuse of short notice; and some of them depend for their effect on nothing more humorous than a parody of the obvious characteristics of Poe or some other grave writer; and almost none of them is filled full of fun. But most are funny in places; as witness this, which is from some remarks on Alaska:

> Where the short-legged Esquimaux
> Waddle in the ice and snow,
> And the playful polar bear
> Nips the hunter unaware.

And we laughed at the idea of calling a pony's tail its "back-hair." **"The Pliocene Skull"** we liked also. It relates to the skull which was found two miles from Angel's, in Calaveras county, California, at a depth of one hundred and fifty-two feet below the surface of the earth. The newspaper savants of California promptly decided that man must have existed in that State years before the mastodon was created. But after a long address, in a highly scientifc strain, delivered by Mr. Harte, the skull explains as follows, using the mining dialect of the present century:

> Which my name is Bowers, and my crust was busted
> Falling down a shaft in Calaveras county.

> *A review of "The Lost Galleon, and Other Tales,"*
> *in* The Nation, *New York, Vol. VI, No. 147, April*
> *23, 1868, p. 335.*

THE NATION   (essay date 1870)

[*In the following review of* The Luck of Roaring Camp, and Other Stories, *the critic charges Harte with sentimentality.*]

Mr. Bret Harte's **Luck of Roaring Camp,** of which Messrs. Fields, Osgood & Co. are the publishers, is a republication in the sense of being largely, if not wholly, made up of articles that have previously appeared in the magazines. In noticing the magazines from month to month, we have had occasion to speak of these pieces, and there is little or nothing that it remains for us to say. We find them like other republished magazine articles, in that they do not show quite so well by themselves and intrinsically considered, as when the reader was involuntarily making comparison of them with the stories and sketches on the average magazine level, which, as our magazines go, is a low one, and one which a writer may transcend, and transcend with apparent triumph, and with the loud applause of the magazine public, while yet he has done nothing capable of giving permanent pleasure. That what Mr. Harte here offers us is incapable of giving permanent pleasure, or at least pleasure for a long time, it would not, we think, be true to say. **"Tennessee's Partner"** seemed to us very good on a second reading; we were, perhaps, rather clearer in mind than we had been before as to the badness of the last part of it; but we were equally sure, at last and at first, that all the essential portion of the story was admirable for vigorous sketching of an odd character, for unforced and unexaggerated humor, and for pathos kept excellently well in hand and devoid of sentimentalism. It is a fault of Mr. Harte's that his pathos very often runs into sentimentality, and that he apparently needs all his sense of the humorous and all his turn for analyzing and satirizing his own feelings to prevent a lapse into the falseness and mawkishness of sentimentalism. The death bed scene of Tennessee's partner is weak by reason of this fault; the **"Luck of Roaring Camp,"** good as that is, has traces of it which interfere much with one's enjoyment, and the inferior pieces— these two being the best in the book—indicate it so often as to make one doubt if strength of fibre be not wanting in a writer who likes the lachrymose so well, and if we have not all been expecting from him rather more than we shall get. . . .

The better work, however, was well worth saving. It makes it plain that we have a new writer of decided abilities as a sketcher of the character and scenes of the strange life of the Far West; a man who is at least enough of a humorist to delight in observing and to excel in catching for us the native humor, conscious or unconscious, that abounds on the Pacific Coast and on the Plains; a man of sympathies so quick as to forbid his merely drawing the outsides of his oddities; and to compel him to enter into their hearts and minds, thus causing his figures to live and glow with something of the inner truth of portraiture; a man, finally, of skill in the management of his materials, and of a pleasant style, which, however, shows ease and a taste for refined elegance in detail rather than solidity or strength; but which, on the other hand, if sometimes verging towards too much polish, is sometimes as racy as Burns's Scotch, and never is polished to the extent of Burns's provincial English. Against this list of merits are to be set the fault we have mentioned of sentimentalism; a leaning towards self-sacrificing gamblers, women of easy virtue, and, in general, towards people with some sort of decidedly melodramatic turn to their goodness and their badness; allied to this a little leaning towards sensationalism in his incidents—though that, no doubt, he has in his capacity of Californian quite as much as personally. The substantial and distinctive praise, however, that he is a humorous observer, with an eye to see inside as well as to see thoroughly well the outside, remains to him. Whether or not he was fortunate in having his lines cast in California may, perhaps, be doubted. He has at least been aided to begin by the temptation of the strongly-marked figures around him; and to have made a beginning is much. It is to be hoped that as years bring him thought and study, he may be seen working on a larger canvas, and produce enduring works as good of their kind as these sketches.

A review of "Luck of Roaring Camp," in The Nation, *New York, Vol. XI, No. 268, August 18, 1870, p. 108.*

THE NATION   (essay date 1871)

[*In the following excerpt, the critic reviews* Poems.]

In this volume [*Poems, by Bret Harte*] Mr. Harte has collected not all but most of his pieces in verse, and all we think that have any claim to remembrance. Not that all of the poems that are in this volume have any good claim to remembrance, and would not have been better omitted. Almost all of the serious poems are of a kind not materially different from the pieces which appear in such numbers in the magazines. Sometimes, for instance, they are imitative to a degree which, to say nothing of its often lowering the reader's estimate of the author, is apt to interfere with the reader's pleasure. (p. 42)

THE

LUCK OF ROARING CAMP,

AND

OTHER SKETCHES.

BY

FRANCIS BRET HARTE.

BOSTON:
FIELDS, OSGOOD, & CO.
1870.

Title page of The Luck of Roaring Camp.

Good, among the serious pieces, and above any but the highest magazine level, is **"The Reveille."** And good, in a somewhat too pretty way, perhaps, is **"Relieving Guard;"** though this is hurt by the memory which it recalls of an exquisitely pretty passage in Longfellow's "Hyperion," where when "sweet Emma of Ilmenau" begins her misfortunes, a star falls out of the evening heaven. As being, on the whole, a fair specimen of Mr. Harte's abilities as a serious poet working after the usual methods, we quote this **"Relieving Guard."** It is prefaced by these initials and words: "S.T.K. Obiit March 4, 1864."

> Came the Relief. "What, Sentry, ho!
>   How passed the night through thy long waking?"
> "Cold, cheerless, dark—as may befit
>   The hour before the dawn is breaking."
>
> "'No sight? no sound?'" "No; nothing save
>   The plover from the marshes calling,
> And in yon Western sky, about
>   An hour ago, a Star was falling."
>
> "A star? There's nothing strange in that."
>   "No, nothing; but, above the thicket,
> Somehow it seemed to me that God
>   Somewhere had just relieved a picket."

Of the jocose poems, too, there are a number that one would have thought their author would leave out of this volume—the second, we believe, in which they have appeared. What, for example, is there worthy of preservation in this very cheap fare? A **"Geological Madrigal"** is the title of it:

> You wished—I remember it well,
>   And I loved you the more for that wish—
> For a perfect cystedian shell
>   And a *whole* holocephalic fish.
> And O, if Earth's strata contains,
>   In its lowest Silurian drift,
> Or Paloeozoic remains
>   The same,—'tis your lover's free gift.

Both the wit and the grammar might well have been dispensed with, as fitter for once appearing in a newspaper than for any other publishing. And pretty much the same thing, barring the remark about the grammar, might be said of the **"Tale of a Pony,"** and which is in J. G. Saxe's worst style, being farcical in wit and vulgar in two senses of that word; of **"The Ballad of the Emeu,"** and of all the parodies. (pp. 42-3)

Where our author really deserves hearty praise is in his "Poems in Dialect." They are less often poems, strictly so-called, than humorous character-pieces illustrative of the wild life and the strange personages of the early Californian days. In some of these pieces—as in that which treats of the "heathen Chinee"; and of the sudden revulsion of feeling in the breast of Mr. Nye when he finds that the Chinee who was to be cheated is not altogether guileless, but can himself violate the moral law with a skill, effect, and sinfulness sickening to Mr. Nye's Caucasian moral sense; and of the instant discovery and assertion by Mr. Nye of the politico-economical truth that "we are ruined by Chinee cheap labor"; and of the promptness and thoroughness with which he vindicates the moral and the economical law—in this and some of the other pieces, Mr. Harte not only jumps luckily with the popular thought and feeling of the moment, but proves himself a satirist with a keen eye, and a humorist with a light and sure hand, and a fine power of expression. Perhaps it is in this piece that he gives most unequivocal evidence of an ability to accomplish more than he has yet accomplished. The skilful presentation of personages with dialectic oddities—with what ought to be called dialectic oddities of thought, manner, and experience, as well as of phraseology—is a good thing to do, and one not too easy to do, but still is a thing so often done well, and so often done well by writers who cannot think, and who have only a species of mimetic skill, that it can hardly be taken as giving promise that a writer has more than a capacity for giving momentary pleasure. To be sure, Mr. Harte has the advantage over most of these character-painters in that he gives us his material not in an amorphous mass of prose, but crystallized into short pieces of verse, from which everything is excluded except the personage whom he wishes us to see; and he has the further advantage of dealing with personages who are now very fresh and interesting.

Again, it is usual to find that the mimetic skill of which we speak is united with a considerable degree of power of touching the common sentiments, and united, too, with a fondness for moving them and a habit of doing so which seem to argue sentimentalism in the writer, and make one dubious as to his or her future. Excellent, then, as they are, very touching as some of them are, one is inclined to say of the **"Heathen Chinee"** that it gives more certain promise of better things, has more thought, and is on a higher plane of literature, than the extremely skilful, objective, unsentimental **"Chiquita,"** or the pieces like **"Cicely," "Jim,"** and **"In the Tunnel,"** where we have an objective handling of the subjects, and of subjects which are pathetic. (p. 43)

"Bret Harte's Poems," in The Nation, *New York, Vol. XII, No. 290, January 19, 1871, pp. 42-4.*

E. S. NADAL (essay date 1877)

[*Nadal was an American critic. In the following excerpt, he evaluates Harte's work as a short story writer, novelist, and dramatist.*]

The scenery and the society of this continent have found perhaps in the works of no writer of the land such graphic expression as in those of Bret Harte. It is true that Mr. Harte's books describe the life of a remote region and of a rude frontier people. But that life was an extravaganza of the traits of our whole democratic society. It is the scenery and the society of the country, then, which are expressed in Mr. Harte's books. Mr. Harte is a bad critic of his own writings; his humor is often feeble; he is very melodramatic; he writes an ill-conditioned style; he applies the phrases of the magazines to thoughts good enough to be well expressed. But he is a writer of marked genius, and has produced works which are as certain as any of his time and country to be read in the future. (p. 81)

The short stories of Mr. Harte are his best works, and it is likely that short stories are the best things he can write. He catches well a special phase of character and conduct, but he has not the ability to hold a character before the eye of the reader. This is very evident in *Gabriel Conroy.* (pp. 82-3)

The leading male character in *Gabriel Conroy* is so drawn as to appear one man at one time and another man at another time. Mr. Harte gives you a lively glimpse of a person at a particular moment, and he does this often by some piece of external description. In the **"Idyll of Red Gulch,"** the "white cuffs and collars," "the chaste skirts," paint us a charming picture of a Puritan schoolmistress amid the Sierras. (In Mr. Harte's recent play at Wallack's, by the way, this girl, who should have been the pink of Puritanical neatness, was made

a dowdy.) The cuffs and collars do very well in a sketch. But suppose she had to be carried through two hundred pages of a novel. Mr. Harte would try more cuffs, more collars, and more "chaste skirts," but they would not eke out a character. The Donna Sepulvida, in *Gabriel Conroy,* is one of Mr. Harte's best female characters; by a single sentence, descriptive of a mark upon her cheek, we obtain an instant impression of a weak, amiable, and charming woman: "The late Don José Sepulvida's private mark—as well defined as the brand upon his cattle—was a certain rigid line, like a grave accent, from the angle of this little woman's nostril to the corners of her mouth." The Donna Sepulvida, indeed, is well described throughout the book. But then she is seen but little, and has to do nothing by which she might cease to be herself and become another. Mr. Harte is very clever at describing a trait of interesting inferiority. His imagination seizes it with precision, and he expresses it happily. The Donna Sepulvida and Clytie Morpher are very real. Mliss, to whom Clytie Morpher is the foil, is a clever and vivid fancy. That is a pretty scene in which Mliss in the wood runs up the bough of a fallen tree and hides among the leaves at the approach of the Schoolmaster. But, owing to Mr. Harte's want of reticence, the *naïveté* of Mliss is sometimes strained. Clytie Morpher is rather more real. It is curious to see the means by which he insinuates into the mind a picture of this dull and haughty girl. A few phrases and a scene or two are sufficient to make the young girl as real as some fungous growth of the night in the depths of the rainy woods, as real as the monk's-hood which the teacher discovers among the flowers in the lap of Mliss. Clytie would not do in a novel; she could not last. The heroine in *Gabriel Conroy* appears twice; and the second description of her is most interesting. But there is no identity between the subjects of the two descriptions. We have the author's assurance that Grace Conroy and the woman who appears later in the story are one and the same, but we should never have known it if we had not been told so.

The gifts of Bret Harte are vivid imagination, color, dramatic dialogue, power to attract and power to entertain, a good sense of nature, a lively and daring humor, and considerable keenness of perception. His power of dialogue is surpassed by no living writer. The similitude of the talk of his characters to real speech is apparent in all his books. A few words sketch for us Miggles as his vivid fancy sees her, and then she sits down and talks exactly as such a woman would talk. **"The Rose of Tuolumne"** is one of his best stories. The color and the sense of nature in this story are brilliant, and the dialogue is dramatic. It is a beautiful story of youth and love. Mr. Harte has filled it with moonlight which perhaps only a California moon may yield. The place is the Sierras, and the time those small hours of the night which the old never see and which valetudinarians have forgotten. That is a good passage which describes the appearance of Marley's Hill the morning after the hanging of **"Tennessee's Partner."** An account of the execution had been printed in the **"Red Dog Clarion."** "But," says Mr. Harte, "the beauty of that midsummer morning, the blessed amity of earth and sky and air, the awakened life of the free woods and hills, the joyous renewal and promise of nature, and, above all, the infinite serenity that thrilled through each, was not reported, as not being part of the social lesson. And yet, when the weak and foolish deed was done, and a life with all its possibilities and responsibilities had passed out of the misshapen thing that dangled between earth and sky, the birds sang, the flowers bloomed, the sun shone as cheerily as before; and possibly the **'Red Dog Clarion'** was right." But why "weak and foolish"? Self-defence is the only principle upon which we can take the life of men; and what society has a better right to act upon it than that in which there are no laws or none that can be enforced?

The humor of Mr. Harte is often overworked and often falls into a feeble and wearisome mannerism; but the best of it is full of audacity and delight. He has conceived the thought with surprise and pleasure, and is in haste to tell it. His ghost-stories contain some amusing fancies. The Devil haunts the road to the Mission Dolores in the shape of an old whaler armed with a harpoon. One night the fat Padre Vicentio, riding along in constant terror of the apparition, hears a shout of "There she blows!" The Padre swoons, and wakes to find himself in a boat, being rowed away from shore by a ghostly crew of rowers. That is a good piece of grotesque fancy in which Mr. Harte makes one of them "catch a crab": "A one-eyed rower, who sat in front of the Padre, catching the devout father's eye, immediately grinned such a ghostly smile, and winked his remaining eye with such diabolical intensity of meaning, that the Padre was constrained to utter a pious ejaculation, which had the disastrous effect of causing the marine Cocles to 'catch a crab,' throwing his heels in the air and his head into the bottom of the boat. But even this event did not disturb the gravity of the ghostly crew." Among his funny and delightful things is that tender and regretful remark of one of his rude characters upon a little boy whom he loved greatly: the little boy was not well; the man said, pensively, that he had changed very much since he used to see him standing on the bluff and "heavin' rocks at Chinamen." In **"Lothaw"** there is a good instance of his fun and spirits. The family of the Duke and Duchess are in the habit of sitting round the breakfast-table with their coronets on. Their brother-in-law, the good-humored St. Addlegourd, a radical, having a rent-roll of $15,000,000, and belonging to one of the oldest families in Great Britain, says: "'Pon my soul, you know, the whole precious mob looked like a ghastly pack of court cards, you know."

Mr. Harte has been thought to have some new sentiments which are his own, and to be to a certain degree a moralist. His lesson of sentiment is that rough men may have a great deal of virtue and kindness, and that much good feeling may be found even in the breasts of wicked men. This is no doubt true, and respectable people need to be reminded of it. But Mr. Harte's taste does not seem strong enough to enable him to distinguish between the natural and the affected, the genuine and the melodramatic. **"The Outcasts of Poker Flat"** is very nearly spoiled by the absurd manner of Oakhurst's death and the foolish inscription on his shingle. Mr. Harte shows his want of judgment by admiring his characters in the wrong places. His heroes are men whom all women adore; and Mr. Harte is apt to become vulgar when he touches upon this subject. The subject is not necessarily foolish. Fielding, for instance, writes of it as it is according to nature, and therefore modestly and rightly; but the irresistibleness of Oakhurst and Poinsett is in very bad taste. Poinsett in *Gabriel Conroy* is frequently admired in the wrong place. When he gratuitously tells the Donna Slavatierra that he is the lover of Grace Conroy and the father of her child, the author evidently thinks that he is making the young man cut a fine figure, whereas he is making him strut in a very silly manner. In the meeting between Poinsett and Dumphy, in which Poinsett is supposed to exhibit to Dumphy the superiority of a well-bred man over a churl, the young man does not act like a gentleman in the least. Mr. Harte's description of Poinsett makes it plain that he is not able to sustain a character under the stress of the reader's long intimacy with him. *Gabriel Conroy* is indeed a bad failure. A more industrious attention might have straightened the story out; as it now is, it seems to be the hopeless product of a desperate inattention. But Mr. Harte is not the only author among us who cannot write long works. Nearly all of our younger writers are very short-winded, and, what Mr. Harte is not, very slight. Why is it that no American author nowadays can write a long, workmanlike, and stupid tale like Cooper's *Deerslayer*? This inability of our young writers is due perhaps to the weakness which comes of self-consciousness; they never finish anything till they have first looked at it from without; they start at their own shadow when they catch sight of it on the wall; a sentence not in perfect dress is recalled and made fit to appear in company. Indeed, the best contemporary writers both here and in England are rather exact than full. The epistles to the cantos of *Marmion*, for instance, contain descriptions which would seem very loose and vague to a modern artist, and perhaps are so; but Scott was full of generous and lovely sentiments, and it is these the reader feels through, and perhaps in spite of, his careless phrases.

In the play which Mr. Harte brought out last autumn in New York the author did not of course mean to produce a work which should rival the masterpieces of Goldsmith and Sheridan. But, of course, he wished to write a play which people would like to go to see. Now any comedy must have at least one pair of lovers whom the audience desire to have married. Mr. Harte's play had two or three pairs of lovers, but each of them was so presented that nobody cared whether they were married or not. Lovers in plays must be unexceptionable. There are certain ideal, perhaps sentimental and conventional, requirements to which they must be made to conform. A hero who would do very well in a novel might not do at all on the stage. Young ladies are much more particular concerning lovers in plays than lovers in novels, infinitely more particular than they are concerning their own. Mr. Harte's lovers did not conform at all to the ideal requirements. One would fancy that it could not be difficult to have in a play a pair of lovers to whom some kind of languid interest would attach. The interest need not be very great; if the audience would rather have the play end well than badly, it would be enough. The Chinaman was very funny, and Starbottle was amusing; a few more of the people in **"M'liss"** and **"The Outcasts of Poker Flat"** could have been brought in; but the thread of the story should have been given to a few characters drawn solely with a view to have the audience interested that the play should end well. A great many things were in the play which Mr. Boucicault would have left out. It is one of Mr. Boucicault's principles, I am told, that an audience should not be surprised, and he refrains from doing this for the very good reason that they do not like to be surprised. The coming point must not be made too plain, but the audience must be prepared for it and permitted to suspect it. When a surprise is sprung upon them, they think the new point arbitrary and unnatural. In *Two Men of Sandy Bar* the audience were at no time able to judge what was coming; they were often surprised, and always bewildered; there was no story, or one which it would have been as hard as a sum in algebra to get straight; the aim appeared to be to get in everything, and to contrive a plot which would be a thin and intricate theory of the conduct of the characters. The play, of course, made no pretensions to be a literary effort; I only speak of it here because it showed the same want either of judgment or of industry which is shown in *Gabriel Conroy,* the same confusion and helplessness when the author sits down before a long story and a great many facts.

The style of Mr. Harte is very incorrect and imperfect. This is a much graver fault than the want of ability to sustain a character through a prolonged description. Mr. Harte is not under the least obligation to write long stories; but he cannot write at all without using words. Why should he choose to express himself in the shabby style of the newspapers? He has not a proper sense that his fine thoughts deserve to be expressed with perfection. It would seem to be only necessary to perfectly conceive a thought to be able to express it well; the thought should be the thread by which one should be able to find his way out of the labyrinth of a bad style. Why should Mr. Harte use such a phrase as "moral atmosphere" to denote a thought which could be so much more elegantly expressed by plain words? No kind of phrase is so poor and feeble as an exploded figure of speech; unless a figure can be used which will express the thought with novel truth, the thought should be expressed in plain words. Those figures of speech which people have forgotten are usually inelegant, and often indicate that the writer does not know quite what he would say. A newspaper writer in haste for a phrase may seize one of them gratefully; but one who is writing a page containing a conception which he thinks worthy to be perfectly expressed should avoid them. But Mr. Harte's thoughts are so good, the images in his mind are so original, that his works are certain to fascinate the reader in spite of the slovenly mannerism of his writing. One of the bad results of an inferior style and of a want of proper reticence in a writer is that the reader who has read but a little of him is likely to conceive a mean opinion of him. It is necessary to read a great deal of Mr. Harte to have a right opinion of his works. They form together a picture of the life, landscape, and society which the author saw in his youth; the picture lies in the author's mind as a whole, and should so lie in the reader's mind; a thought or image of Mr. Harte's which, taken by itself, might appear to be of no great significance, will become much more interesting when it is seen as part of this picture. (pp. 84-90)

E. S. Nadal, "Bret Harte," in The North American Review, *Vol. CXXIV, No. CCLIV, January, 1877, pp. 81-90.*

WILLIAM ERNEST HENLEY (essay date 1879)

[*Henley was an important figure in the counter-decadent movement of the 1890s and the leader of an imperialistic group of young British writers—including Rudyard Kipling, H. Rider Haggard, and Robert Louis Stevenson—who stressed action, virility, and inner strength over alienation, effeminacy, and despair: characteristics they attributed to the decadents. In the following excerpt, Henley provides an ambivalent review of* The Twins of Table Mountain.]

Of late Mr. Bret Harte has produced but little that is worthy of his old reputation. Indeed, with the exception, perhaps, of **"The Heiress of Red Dog,"** he has written little or nothing that recalls the hand that gave us **"The Outcasts of Poker Flat"** and **"How Santa Claus Came to Simpson's Bar."** Judged by the standard of his highest work, **"The Twins of Table Mountain"** is not of extraordinary merit; but it is a great improvement on his later stuff, and will be read with pleasure, if without emotion. To say that its story is vague in itself, and made more vague in the telling, is no more than to say that Mr. Bret Harte is the author; and to add that the types it introduces are in a certain sense familiar, and of an old and well-worn strain, is to add no more than the truth. But if the story is loose and flimsy, it is excellently written and full of passionate suggestiveness and clever dramatic dialogue; if the types are old, they are presented to us under a new aspect; the effect of the whole thing is good, and there are passages in it of great merit. Altogether, it should prove a pleasant surprise to the large circle

of readers who have faith in Mr. Harte, and whose faith, it may be, has had of late to bear up under a good many trials.

William Ernest Henley, in a review of "The Twins of Table Mountain," in The Academy *n.s. Vol. XVI, No. 387, October 4, 1879, p. 243.*

OSCAR WILDE (publication date 1889?)

[*Wilde was an Anglo-Irish dramatist, novelist, poet, short story writer, and critic. Identified with the nineteenth-century "art for art's sake" movement, Wilde defied the contemporary trend that subordinated art to ethical instruction. In contrast to the traditional cult of nature, Wilde posed a cult of art in his critical essays and reviews. In the late 1880s he crusaded for aestheticism as a book reviewer and as the editor of* Woman's World. *In the following excerpt, Wilde praises* Cressy *as Harte's finest achievement.*]

Mr. Bret Harte has never written anything finer than **"Cressy."** . . . It is one of his most brilliant and masterly productions, and will take rank with the best of his Californian stories. Hawthorne re-created for us the America of the past with the incomparable grace of a very perfect artist, but Mr. Bret Harte's emphasised modernity has, in its own sphere, won equal, or almost equal, triumphs. Wit, pathos, humour, realism, exaggeration, and romance are in this marvellous story all blended together, and out of the very clash and chaos of these things comes life itself. And what a curious life it is, half civilised and half barbarous, *naïve* and corrupt, chivalrous and common-place, real and improbable! Cressy herself is the most tantalising of heroines. She is always eluding one's grasp. It is difficult to say whether she sacrifices herself on the altar of romance, or is merely a girl with an extraordinary sense of humour. She is intangible, and the more we know of her, the more incomprehensible she becomes. It is pleasant to come across a heroine who is not identified with any great cause, and represents no important principle, but is simply a wonderful nymph from American backwoods, who has in her something of Artemis, and not a little of Aphrodite. (pp. 82-3)

Oscar Wilde, "Some Literary Notes (4)," in his Essays, Criticisms and Reviews, *n.p., 1901, pp. 75-86.*

FRANK NORRIS (essay date 1897)

[*Norris was an American novelist, short story writer, and essayist who is recognized as one of the first important Naturalist writers in American literature. In the following sketch, which originally appeared in the* Wave *in 1897, Norris parodies Harte's stock characters, typical plots, and prose style.*]

Mr. Jack Oak-hearse calmly rose from the table and shot the bartender of Tomato Can, because of the objectionable color of his hair. Then Mr. Oak-hearse scratched a match on the sole of his victim's boot, lit a perfumed cigarette and strolled forth into the street of the camp to enjoy the evening air. Mr. Oak-hearse's face was pale and impassive, and stamped with that indefinable hauteur that marks the professional gambler. Tomato Can knew him to be a cool, desperate man. The famous Colonel Blue-bottle was reported to have made the remark to Miss Honorine-Sainte-Claire, when that leader of society opened the Pink Assembly at Toad-in-the-Hole, on the other side of the Divide, that he, Colonel Blue-bottle, would be everlastingly "——ed if he didn't believe that that ——ed Oak-hearse would open a ——ed jack-pot on a pair of ——ed tens, ——ed ef he didn't." To which Miss Ste.-Claire had responded:

"Fancy now."

On this occasion as Mr. Jack Oak-hearse stepped in the cool evening air of the Sierra's from out of the bar of the hotel of Tomato Can, he drew from his breast pocket a dainty manicure set and began to trim and polish his slender, almost feminine finger nails, that had been contaminated with the touch of the greasy cards. Thus occupied he betook himself leisurely down the one street of Tomato Can, languidly dodging an occasional revolver bullet, and stepping daintily over the few unburied corpses that bore mute testimony to the disputatious and controversial nature of the citizens of Tomato Can. He arrived at his hotel and entered his apartments, gently waving aside the half-breed Mexican who attempted to disembowel him on the threshold. The apartment was crudely furnished as befitted the rough and ready character of the town of Tomato Can. The Wilton carpet on the floor was stained with spilt Moet and Chandon. The full-length portrait of Mr. Oak-hearse by Carolus Duran was punctured with bullet-marks, while the teakwood escritoire, inlaid with buhl and jade, was encumbered with bowie knives, spurs, and Mexican saddles.

Mr. Oak-hearse's valet brought him the London and Vienna papers. They had been ironed and scented with orris-root, and the sporting articles blue-penciled. "Bill," said Mr. Oak-hearse, "Bill, I believe I told you to cut out all the offensive advertisements from my papers; I perceive, with some concern, that you have neglected it. Your punishment shall be that you will not brush my silk hat next Sunday morning."

The valet uttered an inarticulate cry and fell lifeless to the floor.

"It's better to stand pat on two pair than to try for a full hand," mused Mr. Oak-hearse, philosophically, and his long lashes drooped wearily over his cold-steel-blue eyes, like velvet sheathing a poignard.

A little later the gambler entered the dining-room of the hotel in evening dress, and wearing his cordon of the Legion of Honor. As he took his accustomed place at the table, he was suddenly aware of a lustrous pair of eyes that looked into his cold gray ones from the other side of the catsup bottle. Like all heroes, Mr. Jack Oak-hearse was not insensible to feminine beauty. He bowed gallantly. The lady flushed. The waiter handed him the menu.

"I will have a caviar sandwich," affirmed the gambler with icy impassivity. The waiter next handed the menu to the lady, who likewise ordered a caviar sandwich.

"There is no more," returned the waiter. "The last one has just been ordered."

Mr. Oak-hearse started, and his pale face became even paler. A preoccupied air came upon him, and the lines of an iron determination settled upon his face. He rose, bowed to the lady, and calmly passed from the dining-room out into the street of the town and took his way toward a wooded gulch hard by.

When the waiter returned with the caviar sandwich he was informed that Mr. Oak-hearse would not dine that night. A triangular note on scented mauve paper was found at the office begging the lady to accept the sandwich from one who had loved not wisely but too many.

But next morning at the head of the gulch on one of the largest pine trees the searchers found an ace of spades (marked) pinned to the bark with a bowie knife. It bore the following, written in pencil with a firm hand:

> Here lies the body of
> JOHN OAK-HEARSE
> who was too much of a gentleman
> to play a Royal-flush
> against a Queen-full.

And so, pulseless and cold with a Derringer by his side and a bullet in his brain, though still calm as in life lay he who had been at once the pest and the pride of Tomato Can. (pp. 185-87)

Frank Norris, "'A Hero of Tomato Can by B——t H——te'," in American Literature in Parody: A Collection of Parody, Satire, and Literary Burlesque of American Writers Past and Present, *edited by Robert P. Falk, Twayne Publishers, 1955, pp. 185-87.*

HENRY JAMES   (essay date 1898)

[*An American novelist, James is valued for his psychological acuity and complex sense of artistic form. Throughout his career, James also wrote literary criticism in which he developed his artistic ideals and applied them to the works of others. Among the numerous conceptualizations he formed to clarify the nature of fiction, he defined the novel as "a direct impression of life." The quality of this impression—the degree of moral and intellectual development—and the author's ability to communicate this impression in an effective and artistic manner were the two principal criteria by which James estimated the worth of a literary work. In the following excerpt, James speculates on the relationship of Harte to his subject matter.*]

Do I come late in the day to invoke from Mr. Bret Harte such aid as may be gathered—in the field in which he has mainly worked—toward the supposition of a "school?" Is not Mr. Bret Harte perhaps, after all, just one of the chiefs I am in search of? No one probably meets more the conditions. I seem, with a little ingenuity, to make out his pupils—to trace, in his descendants, a lineage. If I take little time, however, to insist on this, it is because, in speaking of Mr. Bret Harte, a livelier speculation still arises and causes my thought to deflect. This is not the wonder of what others may have learned from him, but the question of what he has learned from himself. He has been his own school and his own pupil—that, in short, simplifies the question. Since his literary fortune, nearly thirty years ago, with **"The Luck of Roaring Camp,"** sprang into being full-armed and full-blown, he has accepted it as that moment made it and bent his back to it with a docility that is, to my sense, one of the most touching things in all American literary annals. Removed, early in his career from all sound, all refreshing and fertilizing plash, of the original fount of inspiration, he has, nevertheless, continued to draw water there and to fill his pitcher to the brim. He has stretched a long arm across seas and continents; there was never a more striking image—one could almost pencil it—of the act of keeping "in touch."

He has dealt in the wild West and in the wild West alone; but to say as much as this, I immediately feel, is to meet, in regard to the total feat, more questions than I shall find place or answer for. The essence of them is, after all—in the presence of such a volume as *Tales of Trail and Town*—the mere curiosity of the critic. It is, none the less, just the sense of such encounters that makes, I think, the critic. Is Mr. Bret Harte's supply of the demand—in an alien air, I mean, and across the still wider gulf of time—an extraordinary case of intellectual discipline, as it were, or only an extraordinary case of intellectual sympathy, sympathy keeping alive in spite of deterrent things? Has he continued to distil and dilute the wild West because the public would only take him as wild and Western, or has he achieved the feat, at whatever cost, out of the necessity of his conscience? But I go too far: the problem would have been a suject for Browning, who would, I imagine, have found in it a "psychological" monologue and all sorts of other interesting things. (pp. 511-12)

Henry James, "American Letter," in Literature, *Vol. 2, No. 28, April 30, 1898, pp. 511-12.*

THEODORE WATTS-DUNTON (essay date 1902)

[*Watts-Dunton was an English novelist, poet, and critic. In the following excerpt, he compares Harte's fiction to that of Charles Dickens.*]

It is easy to be unjust to Bret Harte—easy to say that he was a disciple of Dickens—easy to say that in richness, massiveness, and variety he fell far short of his great and beloved master. No one was so ready to say all this and more about Bret Harte as Bret Harte himself. For of all the writers of his time he was perhaps the most modest, the most unobtrusive, the most anxious to give honour where he believed honour to be due.

Harte in 1890. Culver Pictures, Inc.

But the comparison between the English and American story-tellers must not be pushed too far to the disadvantage of the latter. If Dickens showed great superiority to Bret Harte on one side of the imaginative writer's equipment, there were, I must think, other sides of that equipment on which the superiority was Bret Harte's.

Therefore I am not one of those who think that in a court of universal criticism Bret Harte's reputation will be found to be of the usual ephemeral kind. It is, of course, impossible to speak on such matters with anything like confidence. But it does seem to me that Bret Harte's reputation is more likely than is generally supposed to ripen into what we call fame. For in his short stories—in the best of them, at least—there is a certain note quite indescribable by any adjective—a note which is, I believe, always to be felt in the literature that survives. The charge of not being original is far too frequently brought against the imaginative writers of America. What do we mean by "originality"? Scott did not invent the historic method. Dickens simply carried the method of Smollett further, and with wider range. Thackeray is admittedly the nineteenth-century Fielding. Perhaps, indeed, there is but one absolutely original writer of prose fiction of the nineteenth-century—Nathaniel Hawthorne. (p. 658)

Surely those who talk of Bret Harte as being "Dickens among the Californian pines" do not consider what their words imply. It is true, no doubt, that there was a kind of kinship between the temperament of Dickens and the temperament of Bret Harte. They both held the same principles of imaginative art, they both felt that the function of the artist is to aid in the emancipation of man by holding before him beautiful ideals; both felt that to give him any kind of so-called realism which lowers man in his aspirations—which calls before man's imagination degrading pictures of his "animal origin"—is to do him a disservice. For man has still a long journey before he reaches the goal. Yet though they were both by instinct idealists as regards character-drawing, they both sought to give their ideals a local habitation and a name by surrounding those ideals with vividly painted real accessories, as real as those of the ugliest realist.

With regard to Bret Harte's Argonauts and the romantic scenery in which they lived and worked, it would, no doubt, be a bold thing to say whether Dickens could or could not have painted them, and whether, if he had painted them, the pictures would or would not have been as good as Bret Harte's pictures. But Dickens never did paint these Argonauts; he never had the chance of painting them. Bret Harte did paint them, and succeeded as wonderfully as Dickens succeeded in painting certain classes of London life. . . .

Every one is born with an instinct for loving some particular kind of scenery, and this bias has not so much to do with the birth-environment as is generally supposed. It would have been of no avail for Bret Harte to be familiar with the mighty cañons, peaks, and cataracts of the Nevada regions unless he had had a natural genius for loving and depicting them; and this, undoubtedly, he had, as we see by the effect upon us of his descriptions. Once read, his pictures are never forgotten. But it was not merely that the scenery and atmosphere of Bret Harte's stories are new—the point is that the social mechanism in which his characters move is also new. And if it cannot be denied that in temperament his characters are allied to the characters of Dickens, we must not make too much of this. Notwithstanding all the freshness and newness of Dickens's characters they were entirely the slaves of English sanctions.

Those incongruities which gave them their humorous side arose from their contradicting the English social sanctions around them. But in Bret Harte's Argonauts we get characters that move entirely outside those sanctions of civilization with which the reader is familiar. And this is why the violent contrasts in his stories seem, somehow, to be better authenticated than do the equally violent contrasts in Dickens's stories. Bret Harte's characters are amenable to no laws except the improvised laws of the camp; and the final arbiter is either the six-shooter or the rope of Judge Lynch. And yet underlying this apparent lawlessness there is that deep "law-abidingness" which the late Grant Allen despised as being "the Anglo-Saxon characteristic." To my mind, indeed, there is nothing so new, fresh, and piquant in the fiction of my time as Bret Harte's pictures of the mixed race we call Anglo-Saxon finding itself right outside all the old sanctions, exercising nevertheless its own peculiar instinct for law-abidingness—of a kind.

We get the Anglo-Saxon beginning life anew far removed from the old sanctions of civilization, retaining of necessity a good deal of that natural liberty which, according to Blackstone, was surrendered by the first human compact in order to secure its substitute, civil liberty. We get vivid pictures of the racial qualities which enable the Anglo-Saxon to paint his roots and flourish in almost every square mile of the New World that lies in the temperate zone. Let a group of this great race of universal squatters be the dwellers in Roaring Camp, or a party of whalers in New Zealand when it is a "no man's land," or even a gang of mutineers from the Bounty, it is all one as regards their methods as squatters. The moment that the mutineers set foot on Pitcairn Island they improvise a code of laws something like the camp laws of Bret Harte's Argonauts, and the code on the whole works well.

Therefore I think that, apart altogether from the literary excellence of the presentation, Bret Harte's pictures of the Anglo-Saxon in these conditions will, even as documents, pass into literature. And again, year by year, as nature is being more and more studied are what I may call the open-air qualities of literature being more sought after. This accounts in a large measure for the growing interest in a writer once strangely neglected, George Borrow; and if there should be any diminution in the great and deserved vogue of Dickens, it will be because he is not strong in open-air qualities.

Bret Harte's stories give the reader a sense of the open air second only to Borrow's own pictures. And if I am right in thinking that the love of nature and the love of open-air life are growing, this also will secure a place in the future for Bret Harte.

And now what about his power of creating new characters— not characters of the soil merely, but dramatic characters? Well, here one cannot speak with quite so much confidence on behalf of Bret Harte; and here he showed his great inferiority to Dickens. Dickens, of course, used a larger canvas—gave himself more room to depict his subjects.

If Bret Harte's scenes and characters seem somewhat artificial, may it not be often accounted for by the fact that he wrote short stories and not long novels? For it is very difficult in a short story to secure the freedom and flexibility of movement which belong to nature—the last perfection of imaginative art. (p. 659)

Theodore Watts-Dunton, "Bret Harte," in The Athenaeum, *No. 3891, May 24, 1902, pp. 658-60.*

JOSIAH ROYCE (essay date 1909)

[*Royce was an American philosopher whose works included* The Religious Aspect of Philosophy *(1885) and* The Conception of God *(1897). In the following excerpt, he argues that Harte's fiction presents a misleading portrayal of the social conditions in nineteenth century California.*]

As a Californian, I can say that not one childhood memory of mine suggests any social incident or situation that in the faintest degree gives meaning or confirmation to Bret Harte's stories. It is true that, when I came to consciousness, in the early sixties of the last century, the earlier California of Bret Harte's stories had, of course, passed away. But it is also true that Bret Harte himself never saw the mines in '49 and '50, and that, years later, he collected the chance materials of his stories from hearsay. It is also true that the social order which Bret Harte depicts is an order that never was on sea or land, and that his tales are based upon a deliberately false romantic method. What concerns me here, however, is that Bret Harte's stories err very notably just in this, that they depict the early California mining camp as if it were more or less of an established institution and portray the miners as if they already possessed a sort of provincial consciousness. For Bret Harte the early miner is already a definable social type,—with a dialect, with a set of characteristic customs and manners, with a local consciousness almost such as a peasantry or a Highland clan might possess.

In fact, however, no Americans who went to California in 1849 knew beforehand anything about mining. Everybody was there, so to speak, by accident. Nobody at first intended to make his permanent home anywhere in the mines. There were dialects of course,—Yankee, southern, western,—but there was no ruling dialect. There were customs, good and bad; but they were such as individuals brought with them,—such as our villages and our frontiers had in various ways developed all over our country. And—herein lay the essential matter—nobody regarded his customs or his dialect or his ideals as especially fitting to this new community. One's memories, and usually one's hopes, lay elsewhere. One owed at first no loyalty to the place, or to its social order. One's heart and one's social ideals, if one had such, generally clung to the old home. One meant, by lucky mining, to collect quickly the means to pay off the mortgage on the New England farm, or to make a fortune wherewith to grow old in one's native place. Meanwhile one felt quite free of foot. Home was not here. If hard times came, one moved on to another mining camp.

How hard it is to depict the social life of just such a community as this. Bret Harte cannot accomplish the feat. One needs a social background for the characters of a story. Bret Harte creates this social background by conceiving his mining community in distinctly provincial terms. An unprovincial community seems something indescribable, senseless.

By the time when I myself began to look about me, this earliest stage of the mining life had indeed quite passed away. The community was not yet possessed of the consciousness of a province. But it was indeed rapidly *becoming* provincial. What I was privileged to see in my childhood was, as I now know, the *second* stage of frontier social life,—the struggle for and towards a provincial consciousness. This second stage,—this, and the motives which made it in California so critical and so momentous a stage for social health, have taught to me personally something of the true value of provincialism. (pp. 233-34)

Josiah Royce, "Provincialism: Based Upon a Study of Early Conditions in California," in Putnam's

Magazine, *Vol. VII, No. 2, November, 1909, pp. 232-40.*

HENRY SEIDEL CANBY (essay date 1909)

[*Canby was a professor of English at Yale and one of the founders of* The Saturday Review of Literature, *where he served as editor in chief from 1924 to 1936. He was the author of many books, including* The Short Story in English (1909), *a history of that genre which was long considered the standard text for college students. Despite the high acclaim his writings received, Canby always considered himself primarily a teacher whose declared aim was "to pass on sound values to the reading public." In the following excerpt, Canby maintains that Harte's short story technique was particularly well-suited to his time and place.*]

Bret Harte was certainly not the author of the best English stories of the nineteenth century, but it is a question whether, on the whole, his tales have not been the most widely read. Hawthorne never has been *widely* read in his short stories, except as the cumulative processes of time and the agencies of school-English have piled up the numbers of his readers. Poe's following in America has always been a large one, but in England, until recently, his success has been, at most, one of esteem. Bret Harte, however, was, and is, pretty generally known by all the reading classes, and very nearly as widely on one side of the water as the other. Thus, if we regard those years when the new short story was just getting a foothold, he appears as an advance agent of a fiction of American life for Englishmen, as well as of California habits for the Easterner, with an audience evenly distributed through much of the English-speaking world. (p. 288)

Bret Harte's technique ... is, roughly, Poe's. The volume published at Boston in 1870, *The Luck of Roaring Camp, and Other Sketches,* includes what are probably the three very best stories he wrote, **"The Luck," "The Outcasts of Poker Flat,"** and **"Tennessee's Partner."** Strangely enough, they are called "sketches," in contra-distinction to the "stories," which, beside **"M'liss,"** embrace two very inferior narratives. Each of these three early masterpieces begins with the matter in hand, moves quickly to its conclusion, and emphasizes the climax by direction of narrative, by proportion, and by selection of incident. Each has unity of tone, and perfect unity of impression. Indeed, there is no better example of this last than **"Tennessee's Partner."** Whether Bret Harte learned this technique from Poe, or from the exigencies of journalism, is comparatively unimportant. He had to learn it, as the earlier **"M'liss,"** which, for all its pathos, suffers for lack of good telling, and other early narratives show.

Now this fashion of arranging one's materials was particularly well adapted to bring out contrasts in life, singular associations, vivid situations. The earlier American story-tellers, each in his way, negatively or postively, had demonstrated that. But it was just such contrasts, associations, and situations in real life that the young Harte was ambitious to turn into literature. No distinctly Californian story had been written on the coast. *The Overland Monthly* wanted one. California life: the romance of the Argonauts, the revelry, chivalry, pocket-finding, shooting, love, hate, and sudden friendship of Roaring Gulch and Sandy Bar, it was all chiaroscuro, it was rapid, it had little past, and an unseen future, it was compounded of the strangest contrasts. The settled orders of the old world had broken rank and flung themselves in social confusion upon the gold-fields, and the society that resulted was like that of the farce-comedy, kaleidoscopic, capable of anything, a society in which a remark-

able situation could instantly develop and give place as quickly to another. The novel as a beaker for so turbulent a mixture would never have succeeded; the life was too new, confusing, transient. The old and simple tale might have swept up certain episodes, but it would have lost the glitter, the brilliance, the vivid transitoriness of the unexpected situation. But the new short story, with its emphasis upon the climax, and that climax the heart of a situation, was the very means. Read these fine stories, compare them with the "local color" sketches of Bret Harte's contemporaries, and one sees why, to use his own language, he "turned the trick."

In this fortunate application of a method of telling to a life which only so could best be told, Bret Harte advanced upon Mr. Hale's first stories, where the grasp of a strong situation, rather than any way of emphasizing it, attracts attention; advanced upon [Fitz-James] O'Brien, whose skill was scarcely equal to his imagination, and became a pioneer by virtue of the new realms he conquered for the short story. But it is impossible to sum up his achievement without more consideration of the content of these short stories. It was the fresh life depicted in them which his contemporaries hailed, and although it is probable that if his California novelties had not been exhibited in just the proper show-case, to wit, the short story, they would have gained a hearing that at most was contemporary, yet it is erroneous to suppose that his triumph, like Poe's, was a triumph of technique. Tennessee's Partner, John Oakhurst, Yuba Bill, Kentuck are as long-lived, seemingly, as any characters in nineteenth century fiction. Mliss would join them if Harte could have given her an equally good narrative; the New England schoolmarm in the Sierras must be added, although she appears under too many names to be individual. What gives these characters their lasting power? Why does that highly melodramatic tragedy in the hills above Poker Flat, with its stagy reformations, and contrasts of black sinner and white innocent, hold you spell-bound at the thirtieth as at the first reading? Why does Tennessee's partner make you wish to grasp him by the hand? Bret Harte believed, apparently, that it was his realism which did it. He had put the Western miner into literature as he was—hence the applause. He had compounded his characters of good *and* evil as in life, thus approximating the truth, and avoiding the error of the cartoon, in which the dissolute miner was so dissolute that it was said, "They've just put the keerds on that chap from the start." But we do not wait to be told by Californians, who still remember the red-shirt period, that Roaring Camp is not realism. The lack of it is apparent in every paragraph describing that fascinating settlement. The man who would look for Yuba Bill at Sandy Bar, would search for Pickwick in London, and Peggotty on Yarmouth Beach. Not the realism, but the idealization, of this life of the Argonauts was the prize Bret Harte gained. After all, the latter part of the introduction to his first book was more pertinent than the first, which I have just been paraphrasing, for, at the end, he admits a desire to revive the poetry of a heroic era, and to collect the material for an Iliad of the intrepid Argonauts of California.

In this attempt, Harte sought out novel characters, and then idealized the typical and the individual which he found in them. So doing, he sat at the feet of a greater writer, one not more fortunate in materials, but far stronger, more versatile, more poignant in grasp. The debt which Bret Harte owed and acknowledged to Dickens has been often remarked upon, yet in no way can the value of these pictures of the gold-fields be better estimated than by emphasizing it again. What Dickens did in England, the ever-living personalities which he created by imagining English cockneys, English villains, English boys, with all their energies devoted to an expression of what was most individual, peculiar, and typical in them, just this Bret Harte endeavored to accomplish with his Californians. The truth by exaggeration was his art also. And the melodrama which accompanies contrasts more violent than life, the falsity which follows an attempt to make events illustrate a preconceived theory of human nature, were his faults as well. He looked upon the strange life about him with the eye of an incurable romancer, and gave us a Poker Flat which is just as false to the actual original in the Sierras, as it is true sentimentally. In this, his error, if you are foolish enough to call it so, was again the error of Dickens. But Mr. Pickwick is more valuable than any actual gentleman of his period, Kentuck will outlive the John Smiths of the California historical society. The sentimental romancer, when he is not banal, nor absurd, is an inestimable boon to the race he describes. He inspirits with the emotions which live for ever the body of contemporary verisimilitude: clothing, manners, speech, morals, which, without a soul, must die with their generation. Dickens did this for his London, and Harte, in his footsteps, performed a like service for the golden days of California.

It would be pedantic and wearisome to prove by analysis the likeness in methods between master and pupil, for all readers of both must feel it. Harte confessed his obligation by constant praise of the older writer. Dickens recognized it; went so far as to find in **"Roaring Camp"** and **"Poker Flat,"** so Forster says, "such subtle strokes of character as he had not anywhere else in late years discovered; the manner resembling himself, but the matter fresh to a degree that had surprised him." The best proof of the connection lies in comparison, for, as the Middle English proverb has it, "Trundle the apple never so far, he comes from what tree he came." I do not mean, however, to insist too much upon this influence. In such a criticism as this, Dickens is to be regarded, not as an author, but as a point of view; and there is divergence in plenty between the two writers. Age could not wither nor custom stale the infinite variety of the Englishman. But if Harte's mine never ceased yielding, the rich pocket was soon exhausted, and the vein he followed beyond produced ore that was seldom of a bonanza quality. In his innumerable later narratives the same character types appear with wearisome frequency. The virginal dew is dried from the cheeks of his untamed women; the Argonaut no longer glows with the colors of a dawning civilization. And although his biographer, T. Edgar Pemberton, strenuously asserts that the stories in other fields prove that he was not graveled for matter when he left California, still **"Unser Karl,"** **"The Desborough Connections,"** and his other old-world tales are no more than good magazine work. The classic aura is not upon them. For the situation must be very novel, very fresh, very significant of those human traits which can be seen in the lightning flash, "which doth cease to be ere one can say 'It lightens,'" else this kind of short story loses its place in great literature. In the narrowness of his genius which could not add new provinces when the old ones were exhausted, Harte was inferior to his master. He was far inferior in humor, far inferior in the breadth as well as the length of his creative powers. In pathos alone does he even approach an equal level.

On the other hand, it is exceedingly improbable that Dickens could have immortalized the Forty-niner. The short story was the only tool that was capable of such magic. Sandy Bar was no novelist's spoil; its life was too rapid. Nor would "sketches," like those by "Boz," have caught the day of the Argonauts; if one missed its vivid contrasts, one missed more than half.

The new short story was the tool, and Dickens, it is quite certain, could never have restrained himself to its limits. In spite of his one experiment, "The Signal-Man," the feat was against nature. But Harte, of a race keen to see the significance of events, quick of perception beyond comparison among Anglo-Saxon peoples, inclined to be superficial, inclined to hurry, inclined to be pleased with a novelty and to advertise it; Harte, with the view-point of Dickens, his own sense of form, and a genius for sympathetic study, was the man to turn into five talents the sum he had been lent.

And so, at the end, one is inclined to agree with Harte's own conclusion, as expressed in his *Cornhill* essay. He was certainly wise in coming to his own world for characters, for plot, and for setting. And one agrees, also, that to this step toward truth of portraiture is due much of the strength of the modern short story. But we must add to these statements. It was the use of the new short story that made Harte's shift to local subjects so fruitful in result; it was the high color, the novelty, the rich contrasts of California life, which put upon his success an emphasis that advertised the short story. It was his good fortune to look upon this variegated life with eyes which Dickens had opened to see personality, with senses by this insight made keen to feel the old primeval emotions stirring in unexpected places, with a resultant power to make poetry of that from which the realist made prose. In every way Bret Harte was a fortunate man.

Finally, he completes that development towards a popular form for the short story which, after the passing of Poe and of Hawthorne, O'Brien had begun. While the novel life of California was peculiarly get-at-able by means of the short-story technique, novel situations, unusual contrasts, strange contradictions everywhere could be exploited by the same method. Harte's stories raised a crop of "wild life" tales after them, but they were also followed by an equally flourishing growth of narratives in which the striking situations provided by the most civilized life were written into some kind of literature. In the decade after his first success, the short-story form became a usual, not the extraordinary tool. And as the peculiarly geographical development of our civilization, and the general shifting of social standards and social orders, which marks the end of the nineteenth century, proceeded, more and more fields were opened up for its use. So, after all, Harte was right; it was the treatment of life, as it was here in America, which began the vogue of the short story. (pp. 291-98)

> *Henry Seidel Canby, "The Mid-Century in America," in his* The Short Story in English, *Henry Holt and Company, 1909, pp. 280-98.*

HENRY CHILDS MERWIN   (essay date 1911)

[In the following excerpt, Merwin examines Harte's method of characterization and use of humor.]

Bret Harte's faculty was not so much that of imagining as of apprehending human character. Some writers of fiction, those who have the highest form of creative imagination, are able from their own minds to spin the web and woof of the characters that they describe; and it makes small difference where they live or what literary material lies about them. Even these authors do not create their heroes and heroines quite out of whole cloth,—they have a shred or two to begin with; but their work is mainly the result of creation rather than perception. (p. 293)

A few great novels have indeed been written by authors who did not possess this faculty, especially by Dickens, in whom it was conspicuously lacking; but no long story was ever produced without betraying its author's deficiency in this respect if the deficiency existed. *Gabriel Conroy,* Bret Harte's only novel, is so bad as a whole, though abounding in gems, its characters are so inconsistent and confused, its ending so incomprehensible, that it produces upon the reader the effect of a nightmare.

In fact, the nearer Bret Harte's stories approach the character of an episode the better and more dramatic they are. Of the longer stories, the best, as everybody will admit, is **"Cressy,"** and that is little more than the expansion of a single incident. As a rule, in reading the longer tales, one remembers, as he progresses, that the situations and the events are fictitious; they have not the spontaneous, inevitable aspect which makes the shorter tales impressive. **"Tennessee's Partner"** is as historical as Robinson Crusoe. Bret Harte had something of a weakness for elaborate plots, but they were not in his line. Plots and situations can hardly be satisfactory or artistic unless they form the means whereby the characters of the persons in the tale are developed, or, if not developed, at least revealed to the reader. The development or the gradual revelation of character is the *raison d'être* for the long story or novel.

But this capacity our author seems to have lacked. It might be said that he did not require it, because his characters appear to us full-fledged from the start. He has, indeed, a wonderful power of setting them before the reader almost immediately, and by virtue of a few masterly strokes. After an incident or two, we know the character; there is nothing more to be revealed; and a prolongation of the story would be superfluous.

But here we touch upon Bret Harte's weakness as a portrayer of human nature. It surely indicates some deficiency in a writer of fiction if with the additional scope afforded by a long story he can tell us no more about his people than he is able to convey by a short story. The deficiency in Bret Harte was perhaps this, that he lacked a profound knowledge of human nature. A human being regarded as material for a writer of fiction may be divided into two parts. There is that part, the more elemental one, which he shares with other men, and there is, secondly, that part which differentiates him from other men. In other words, he is both a type of human nature, and a particular specimen with individual variations.

The ideal story-writer would be able to master his subject in each aspect, and in describing a single person to depict at once both the nature of all men and also the nature of that particular man. Shakespere, Sterne, Thackeray have this power. Other writers can do the one thing but not the other; and in this respect Hawthorne and Bret Harte stand at opposite extremes. Hawthorne had a profound knowledge of human nature; but he was lacking in the capacity to hit off individual characteristics. Arthur Dimmesdale and Hester, even Miriam and Hilda, are not real to us in the sense in which Colonel Newcome and Becky Sharp are real. Hawthorne's figures are somewhat spectral; they lack flesh and blood. His forte was not observation but reflection. He worked from the inside.

Bret Harte, on the other hand, worked from the outside. He had not that faculty, so strong in Hawthorne, of delving into his own nature by way of getting at the nature of other men; but he had the faculty of sympathetic observation which enabled him to perceive and understand the characteristic traits that distinguish one man from another.

"Barker's Luck" and **"Three Partners,"** taken together, illustrate Bret Harte's limitations in this respect. Each of these stories has Barker for its central theme, the other personages being little more than foils to him. In the first story, **"Barker's Luck,"** the plot is very simple, the incidents are few, and yet we have the character of the hero conveyed to us with exquisite effect. In **"Three Partners"** the theme is elaborated, a complicated plot is introduced, and Barker appears in new relations and situations. But we know him no better than we did before. **"Barker's Luck"** covered the ground; and **"Three Partners,"** a more ambitious story, is far below it in verisimilitude and in dramatic effect. In the same way, **"M'liss,"** in its original form, is much superior to the longer and more complex story which its author wrote some years afterward, and which is printed in the collected edition of his works, to the exclusion of the earlier tale. (pp. 293-96)

We have his own testimony to the fact that his genius was perceptive rather than creative. In those Scotch stories and sketches in which the Consul appears, very much in the capacity of a Greek chorus, the author lets fall now and then a remark plainly autobiographical in character. Thus, in **"A Rose of Glenbogie,"** speaking of Mrs. Deeside, he says, "The Consul, more *perceptive* than analytical, found her a puzzle."

This confirms Bret Harte's other statement, made elsewhere, that his characters, instead of being imagined, were copied from life. But they were copied with the insight and the emphasis of genius. The ability to read human nature is about the most rare of mental possessions. How little do we know even of those whom we see every day, and whom, perhaps, we have lived with all our lives! Let a man ask himself what his friend or his wife or his son would do in some supposable emergency; how they would take this or that injury or affront, good fortune or bad fortune, great sorrow or great happiness, the defection of a friend, a strong temptation. Let him ask himself any such question, and, in all probability, he will be forced to admit that he does not know what would be the result. Who, remembering his college or schoolboy days, will fail to recognize the truth of Thoreau's remark, "One may discover a new side to his most intimate friend when for the first time he hears him speak in public!"

These surprises occur not because human nature is inconsistent,—the law of character is as immutable as any other law;—it is because individual character eludes us. But it did not elude Bret Harte. He had a wonderful faculty both for understanding and remembering its outward manifestations. His genius was akin to that of the actor; and this explains, perhaps, his lifelong desire to write a successful play. Mr. Watts-Dunton has told us with astonishment how Bret Harte, years after a visit to one of the London Music Halls, minutely recounted all that he had heard and seen there, and imitated all the performers. That he would have made a great actor in the style of Joseph Jefferson is the opinion of that accomplished critic.

The surprising quickness with which he seized and assimilated any new form of dialect was a kind of dramatic capacity. The Spanish-English, mixed with California slang, which Enriquez Saltello spoke, is as good in its way as the immortal Costigan's Irish-English.

> "To confer then as to thees horse, which is not—observe me—a Mexican plug. Ah, no! you can your boots bet on that. She is of Castilian stock—believe me and strike me dead! I will myself at different times overlook and af-

front her in the stable, examine her as to the assault, and why she should do thees thing. When she is of the exercise I will also accost and restrain her. Remain tranquil, my friend! When a few days shall pass much shall be changed, and she will be as another. Trust your oncle to do thees thing! Comprehend me? Everything shall be lovely, and the goose hang high.''

Bret Harte's short stay in Prussia, and later in Scotland, enabled him to grasp the peculiarities of nature and speech belonging to the natives. Peter Schroeder, the idealist, could have sprung to life nowhere except upon German soil. ''Peter pondered long and perplexedly. Gradually an explanation slowly evolved itself from his profundity. He placed his finger beside his nose, and a look of deep cunning shone in his eyes. 'Dot's it,' he said to himself triumphantly, 'dot's shoost it! Der Rebooplicans don't got no memories. Ve don't got nodings else.' ''

What character could be more Scotch, and less anything else, than the porter at the railway station where the Consul alighted on his way to visit the MacSpaddens. '' 'Ye'll no be rememberin' me. I had a machine in St. Kentigern and drove ye to MacSpadden's ferry often. Far, far too often! She's a strange, flagrantitious creature; her husband's but a puir fule, I'm thinkin', and ye did yersel' nae guid gaunin' there.' ''

Mr. Callender, again, Ailsa's father, in **''Young Robin Gray,''** breathes Scotch Calvinism and Scotch thrift and self-respect in every line.

> ''Have you had a cruise in the yacht?'' asked the Consul.
>
> ''Ay,'' said Mr. Callender, ''we have been up and down the loch, and around the far point, but not for boardin' or lodgin' the night, nor otherwise conteenuing or parteecipating.... Mr. Gray's a decent enough lad, and not above instruction, but extraordinar' extravagant.''

Even the mysteries of Franco-English seem to have been fathomed by Bret Harte, possibly by his contact with French people in San Francisco. This is how the innkeeper explained to Alkali Dick some peculiarities of French custom:

> ''For you comprehend not the position of *la jeune fille* in all France! Ah! in America the young lady she go everywhere alone; I have seen her—pretty, charming, fascinating—alone with the young man. But here, no, never! Regard me, my friend. The French mother, she say to her daughter's finacé, 'Look! there is my daughter. She has never been alone with a young man for five minutes,—not even with you. Take her for your wife!' It is monstrous! It is impossible! It is so!''

The moral complement of this rare capacity for reading human nature was the sympathy, the tenderness of feeling which Bret Harte possessed. Sympathy with human nature, with its weaknesses, with the tragedies which it is perpetually encountering, and above all, with its redeeming virtues,—this is the keynote of Bret Harte's works, the mainspring of his humor and pathos. (pp. 297-99)

There is often in Bret Harte a subtle blending of satire and humor, notably in that masterpiece of satirical humor, the **''Heathen Chinee.''** The poet beautifully depicts the naïve indignation of the American gambler at the duplicity of the Mongolian,—a duplicity exceeding even his own. '' 'We are ruined by Chinese cheap labor!' ''

Another instance is that passage in **''The Rose of Tuolumne,''** where the author, after relating how a stranger was shot and nearly killed in a mining town, records the prevailing impression in the neighborhood ''that his misfortune was the result of the defective moral quality of his being a stranger.'' So, in **''The Outcasts of Poker Flat,''** when the punishment of Mr. Oakhurst was under consideration, ''A few of the Committee had urged hanging him as a possible example and a sure method of reimbursing themselves from his pockets of the money he had won from them. 'It's agin justice,' said Jim Wheeler, 'to let this yer young man from Roaring Camp—an entire stranger—carry away our money.' But a crude sentiment of equity residing in the breasts of those who had been fortunate enough to win from Mr. Oakhurst overruled this narrower local prejudice.''

Even in these passages humor predominates over satire. In fact,—and it is a fact characteristic of Bret Harte,—the only satire, pure and simple, in his works is that which he directs against hypocrisy. This was the one fault which he could not forgive; and he especially detested that peculiar form of cold and calculating hypocrisy which occasionally survives as the dregs of Puritanism. Bret Harte was keenly alive to this aspect of New England character; and he has depicted it with almost savage intensity in **''The Argonauts of North Liberty.''** Ezekiel Corwin, a shrewd, flinty, narrow Yankee, is not a new figure in literature, but an old figure in one or two new situations, notably in his appearance at the mining camps as a vender of patent medicines. ''That remarkably unfair and unpleasant-spoken man had actually frozen Hanley's Ford into icy astonisment at his audacity, and he had sold them an invoice of the Panacea before they had recovered; he had insulted Chipitas into giving an extensive order in bitters; he had left Hayward's Creek pledged to Burne's pills—with drawn revolvers still in their hands.''

Even here, however, the bitterness of the satire is tempered by the humor of the situation. But in Joan, the heroine of the story, we have a really new figure in literature, and it is drawn with an absence of sympathy, of humor and of mitigating circumstances which is very rare, if not unique, in Bret Harte. (pp. 300-01)

California humor was, therefore, in one way, the reverse of ordinary American humor. In place of grotesque exaggeration, the California tendency was to minimize. The Pioneer was as euphemistic in speaking of death as was the Greek or Roman of classic times. ''To pass in his checks,'' was the Pacific Slope equivalent for the more dignified *Actum est de me* [''It is all over for me'']. This was the phrase, as the Reader will remember, that Mr. Oakhurst immortalized by writing it on the playing card which, affixed to a bowie-knife, served that famous gambler for tombstone and epitaph. He used it in no flippant spirit, but in the sadly humorous spirit of the true Californian, as if he were loath to attribute undue importance to the mere fact that the unit of his own life had been forever withdrawn from the sum total of human existence.

Of this California minimizing humor, frequent also in the pages of Mark Twain and Ambrose Bierce, there is an example in Bret Harte's poem, **''Cicely'':—**

I've had some mighty mean moments afore I kem to
    this spot,—
Lost on the Plains in '50, drownded almost and shot;
But out on this alkali desert, a-hunting a crazy wife,
Was r'aly as on-satis-factory as anything in my life.

There is another familiar example in these well-known lines
by Truthful James:—

Then Abner Dean of Angels raised a point of order,
    when
A chunk of old red sandstone took him in the abdomen,
And he smiled a kind of sickly smile, and curled up on
    the floor,
And the subsequent proceedings interested him no
    more.

This was typical California humor, and Bret Harte, in his stories
and poems, more often perhaps in the latter, gave frequent
expression to it; but it was not typical Bret Harte humor. The
humor of the passage just quoted from **"How Santa Claus
Came to Simpson's Bar,"** the humor that made Bret Harte
famous, and still more the humor that made him beloved, was
not saturnine or satirical, but sympathetic and tender. It was
humor not from an external point of view, but from the victim's
point of view. The Californians themselves saw persons and
events in a different way; and how imperfect their vision was
may be gathered from the fact that they stoutly denied the truth
of Bret Harte's descriptions of Pioneer life. They were too
close at hand, too much a part of the drama themselves, to
perceive it correctly. Bret Harte had the faculty as to which it
is hard to say how much is intellectual and how much is emotional, of getting behind the scenes, and beholding men and
motives as they really are. (pp. 304-05)

> *Henry Childs Merwin, in his* The Life of Bret Harte:
> With Some Account of the California Pioneers,
> *Houghton Mifflin Company, 1911, 362 p.*

EDWARD J. O'BRIEN (essay date 1923)

[*O'Brien was an American poet and critic who also edited numerous collections of short stories, including the well known
annual volume of* The Best Short Stories *(1914-1940). In the
following excerpt, O'Brien assesses Harte's achievement as a
short story writer.*]

What . . . is the merit of Bret Harte? Well, he is the typical
"man of feeling," and at his best he combines sense and
sensibility in his work. We also find swift and vivid narrative,
unity rising to effective climax, and a worthy subject matter
for a romantic epic. Pioneer life is rendered vividly for the
first time. In an article entitled **"The Rise of the Short Story,"**
he pleaded that his wish was to accept life as he found it, and
to record it faithfully without provinciality and without passing
a moral judgment. He implied that he believed himself to have
been eminently successful in achieving this absence of provinciality, and seems to have considered that in this respect
his work showed a marked improvement over the work of
Hawthorne and Poe. There is a false glitter about his general
plea, and not a little fatuousness, but I believe that his first
intentions were thoroughly honest, and that for a short time
they were successfully realized.

He built upon Poe's structure, but sought the unexpected rather
than the marvelous. The feeling of this contrast has led critics
to call him a realist, which is true if we allow for considerable

qualification. He was conscious of the art with which Poe and
Hawthorne utilized tone color for their effects, but he could
seldom subdue his color to its appropriate place in the background. There is usually a glare, and I dare say this accounts
for some of his popularity. One also feels that he was a little
too anxious to present America with a literature which it would
readily acknowledge, to question the value either of his methods or of his achievements. (pp. 108-10)

[He] was fond of Dickens, and from Dickens he learned the
effectiveness of caricature in the portrayal of human nature.
Harte did not realize, however, that the secret of Dickens is
his manner of selecting one tiny but characteristic detail and
heightening it discreetly, while in his own method he heightens
the whole picture till everything stands out in relief and there
is no shadow. To ask of him the Shakespearean sense of comedy which Dickens possessed would be unfair. True comedy
is born of suffering and rich human sympathy. It is not bestowed upon those who follow consistently the line of least
resistance.

The parallel between the naked light of California and the lack
of penumbra in Harte's short stories has not been pointed out,
so far as I know. The two facts would appear to be related as
cause and effect. His later stories, written under English skies,
while he recalled the California of his youth, have sharper and
sharper outlines. In his earlier stories, the fault is less noticeable, and occasionally, as in **"Tennessee's Partner,"** his sense
of nature becomes almost pantheistic, so that the forest plays
the part of a sympathetic Greek chorus to the action of the tale.

What conflict was Harte called upon as an artist to resolve? It
was the essential conflict of pioneer society in new settlements
which no writer who has experienced it has ever successfully
sublimated, though it is a possible achievement. "It was, in
one sense, a free life," says Van Wyck Brooks, half-para-
phrasing Bret Harte.

> It was an irresponsible life, it implied a break
> with civilization, with domestic, religious and
> political ties. Nothing could be freer in that
> sense than the society of the gold-seekers in
> Nevada and California as we find it pictured in
> *Roughing It*. Free as that society was, never-
> theless, scarcely any normal instinct could have
> been expressed or satisfied in it. The pioneers
> were not primitive men, they were civilized
> men, often of gentle birth and education, men
> for whom civilization had implied many re-
> straints, of course, but innumerable avenues
> also of social and personal expression and ac-
> tivity to which their natures were accustomed.
> In escaping responsibility, therefore, they had
> only placed themselves in a position where their
> instincts were blocked on every side. There
> were so few women among them, for instance,
> that their sexual lives were either starved or
> debased; and children were as rare as the "Luck"
> of Roaring Camp, a story that shows how hys-
> terical, in consequence of these and similar
> conditions, the mining population was. Those
> who were accustomed to the exercise of com-
> plex tastes and preferences found themselves
> obliged to conform to a single monotonous rou-
> tine.

Now there was a magnificent opportunity here for a literary artist to sum up in a great gesture the whole pioneer conflict between suppressed instinct and environment, and to resolve and sublimate the struggle. Bret Harte admirably portrayed the picturesque side of this life, and showed no little sentimental sympathy with it in doing so, but he missed its epic tide, and to this day the pioneer west awaits its great chronicler. Such a man must possess all the narrative qualities of Bret Harte, all the human depth of Mark Twain, and a capacity for testing and transcending experience which both men lacked. Melville could have done it, but his life found expression in other channels. It has not been done in Australia, where the same opportunity offered. Now it is perhaps too late, for the chance would seem to have passed. Jack London had the experience, but he succumbed to the public, as most of Bret Harte's successors have succumbed.

In fact, Harte was a perfect type of the literature which was to follow him. Sharp-sighted, eager, nervous, superficial, anxious for quick results, and with a sentimental faith in his star, he may be taken to represent a common American ideal of the happy warrior. His heroism finds wish-fulfillment only in his writings, and it finds fulfillment there only in a fundamental romantic evasion of reality. The short story is in the marketplace as soon as he publishes his first tale, and it is only a step to "O. Henry" and his school of protective coloration. Harte is far from being the greatest of American story writers, but he is probably the most representative of the characteristic qualities and weaknesses, and historically he may prove to have been our most influential man. (pp. 110-13)

> *Edward J. O'Brien, "Bret Harte and Mark Twain,"*
> *in his* The Advance of the American Short Story,
> *Dodd, Mead and Company, 1923, pp. 98-116.*

LUDWIG LEWISOHN   (essay date 1932)

[*Lewisohn was a German-born American novelist and critic. In the following excerpt from his critical survey* Expression in America, *he derides Harte's formula fiction for its second-rate emotional effects.*]

Of the sectionalists to gain a broad reputation the earliest was, of course, Bret Harte. He had the initial advantage of a section already romanticized in every American's heart by its natural splendor and by that release from the dictates of moral order which had accompanied the gold-rush to the West coast and was, with similar literary results, to accompany the later gold-rush to the Klondike. All the elements were given out of which the ingenious talent of Bret Harte wove the pattern of the typical American short story, the story of O. Henry and of the popular magazines, the story with the happy ending which editors are still seeking and still buying. (p. 282)

The formula invented by Bret Harte and since repeated with a thousand variations of content introduces the reader to a world of romance in which the ordinary restraints are loosened. Vicariously the reader can now rove and gamble and shoot and lynch and consort with outcasts and prostitutes. But the reader has not only this lawless individual self; he has another, a social self, a self that is crammed with terror and that answers to every liberation with a feeling of guilt. Hence it must be clear to this reader from the start—otherwise his reaction would not be one of pleasure but one of moral indignation, that is to say, of inner guilt projected on others—that he will be able to pay for his vicarious release by being present, at the end of

First page of the manuscript for "Captain Jim's Friend."

the story, at the triumph of virtue and goodness and the moral order, the conversion of the recalcitrant and the noble death of gambler and harlot, the repentance of the erring and the reward of virtue. He must know, in other words, that his social self will be able to pay and overpay the debt incurred by the vicarious libertinage of his revery self. It is for this reason that "the work of regeneration began in Roaring Camp," that the gambler of Poker Flat dies a sacrificial death, that the glasses are charged for "Miggles, God bless her!" that Tennessee and his "pardner" meet in heaven and that the harlot hands over her son to the school-teacher with the words: "Help him to—to—to forget his mother!" It would be futile to continue with other of the famous stories or to show how the anecdotical poems of Bret Harte, which still linger in anthologies, follow the same pattern from the pseudo-release of pent-up impulse to the happy ending. It may be as well to add here, in connection with the origin of the American short-story, that the notorious happy ending is bad not because it is happy, but precisely because it is not. A happy ending to a human story profoundly rooted in both character and fate, were it attainable in such a world as the present, would be of an inestimable preciousness. The meretricious happy ending of the conventional short-story from Bret Harte to the present has no relation to such an one. It is, rather, a feebly propitiatory gesture; an *absit omen;* it is a sop to the slightly neurotic and wholly muddle-headed who ask of art as of life not reality but feigning, not catharsis but confirmation in immaturity, not cure but drug. (pp. 285-86)

> *Ludwig Lewisohn, "The Soil and the Transition,"*
> *in his* Expression in America, *Harper & Brothers,*
> *Publishers, 1932, pp. 273-309.*

GRANVILLE HICKS (essay date 1935)

[*Hicks was an American literary critic whose famous study* The Great Tradition: An Interpretation of American Literature Since the Civil War (1933) *established him as the foremost advocate of Marxist critical thought in Depression-era America. Throughout the 1930s, he argued for a more socially engaged brand of literature and severely criticized such writers as Henry James, Mark Twain, and Edith Wharton, who he believed failed to confront the realities of their society and, instead, took refuge in their own work. Hicks was shocked by the effects of the Great Depression and believed that events demanded a new commitment on the part of writers to clearly understand and express their times. In Marxist terms, this meant that all American artists should comprehend the growth of capitalism and its negative side effects, such as war, periodic depressions, and the exploitation and alienation of the working class. Thus, the question Hicks posed was always the same: to what degree did an artist come to terms with the economic condition of his or her time and the social consequences of those conditions? He believed that it was the task of American literature to provide an extremely critical examination of the capitalist system itself and of what he considered its inherently repressive nature. After 1939, Hicks sharply denounced communist ideology, which he called a "hopelessly narrow way of judging literature," and in his later years adopted a less ideological posture in critical matters. In the following excerpt, Hicks contends that Harte's career established the pattern for later American regional writers.*]

California was waiting for Bret Harte, who, as editor of the newly founded *Overland Monthly*, announced in 1868 that it was the duty of the magazine to print material pertaining to its own state, and then, in illustration of his theory, published **"The Luck of Roaring Camp."** This young man, thirty-two years old when the story appeared, had taught school, worked in a drug store, and set type. He had also served a brief term as Wells Fargo express messenger and perhaps had done some mining. But his background was academic and his aims were literary, and the decade before the appearance of **"The Luck of Roaring Camp"** had been chiefly devoted to writing. He had written sketches, burlesque novels, and an occasional story for the *Golden Era* and the *Californian*, edited a collection of state verse, and published a volume of prose and one of poetry. He had been given a comfortable sinecure as secretary of the California mint, and his choice as editor of the *Overland Monthly* indicated public recognition of his talents. Already he had outstripped his friends and colleagues—Charles Warren Stoddard, Mark Twain, Charles Henry Webb, and the rest—and when the amazing popularity of **"Plain Language from Truthful James"** followed in 1870 the success of **"The Luck of Roaring Camp,"** he was a national figure.

Harte had, he later said, a "very early, half-boyish but very enthusiastic belief" in the possibility of "a peculiarly characteristic Western American literature." Whatever that phrase may have meant to him, many of his sketches of Californian scenery and his adaptations of Spanish legend obviously owed more to his reading of Washington Irving than to any immersion in the life of the frontiersman. And it is clear that the same appreciation of the picturesque determined the themes of his short stories. If one examines the tales collected in the volume called *The Luck of Roaring Camp,* one notices not only the use of an amusing and perhaps inaccurate dialect, the reliance on bizarre details, and the emphasis on eccentricities of character; one notices also that the theme of each is the emergence of fine qualities in some character whose rough exterior gives no promise of such virtues. The very basis, then, of his stories is the picturesque contrast between superficial uncouthness and inner nobility, and he was far more interested in stating this contrast dramatically than he was in analyzing the true character of the pioneer.

Moreover, the California of the gold miners was being rapidly transformed, at the time he wrote his stories, into the California of the business men, and this change may have had something to do with his admiration for the miners. We know that he had once regarded these men as vulgar and unworthy of literary attention, and we know that his subsequent respect for them accompanied the growth of a bitter hatred for the money-grubbing spirit. As a boy he had worshipped the heroes of Froissart's *Chronicles,* Dumas' romances, the sea-stories of Marryat, and the *Leatherstocking Tales* of Cooper; and his own character, in its impulsiveness and even irresponsibility, was closer to the hearty good nature of the first settlers than it was to the well-mannered ruthlessness of the entrepreneurs. And this antipathy alone would have prevented him from following, in his fiction, the development of California from the pioneering to the commercial stage.

There were, then, two obstacles to the growth of the realistic elements in his stories, and when he added a third by leaving for the East he was forever committed to the romantic, sentimental tale of the mining camps. He went East both because he dreamt of living a free, idealistic life among men of literary aims and because he wanted to escape from the commercialism of his San Francisco contemporaries. He discovered that Boston had changed, just as California was changing, and the tranquil life of its men of letters did not blind him to the power of the new Boston, the city of factories and brokers' offices and struggling immigrants. Longfellow still seemed to him the embodiment of quiet nobility, and he venerated him accordingly; but the younger men of letters he distrusted. Having to make a living, he continued to write stories, tried his hand at plays, wrote one novel, and suffered on the lecture platform. Seven years passed, and at last, unhappy and poor, he accepted, from a government that he hated for its subservience to commercial interests, a minor post in Germany. Thence, in 1880, he went to Glasgow, and when he lost his post there five years later, he settled in London. America he never revisited.

Reading carefully the letters Harte wrote to his wife during those long years abroad, one detects the tragic note. Though he seems to have found life in London pleasanter than life elsewhere, and though he appreciated the prestige he enjoyed there and the larger income he was able to earn, he found much to distress him in his adopted home, and his affection for the United States grew with absence. As for his own work, it was cheap and he knew it. His writing was pure drudgery. "You," he wrote his wife, "cannot possibly hate pen and ink as I do who live in it and by it perpetually." "Sick or not," he said, "in spirits or out of spirits, I must work, and I do not see any rest ahead." So he went on, grinding out story after story about the golden hearts of profane miners and quick-shooting gamblers. Yet sometimes, in a story such as **"A Protégée of Jack Hamlin's"** or **"Colonel Starbottle's Client,"** a little of the old vigor returned, as if memory suddenly woke in him and he found himself back in frontier California. The life there, it must have seemed to him, was after all the best he had known, and he may not have been wholly sorry that popular demand forbade him to desert his one great theme.

Bret Harte's literary career ended, to all intents, when he left California in 1871, and it is possible that even his early work has been too highly esteemed. He has been called a stylist of distinction, a master of the short story, and a penetrating student of human nature. Yet it is easy to find flaws in his style, to expose the superficiality of his characterization, and to list many short story writers more dextrous than he. Even his own claim, that he founded a peculiarly western literature, will not bear scrutiny, for he owed much to picturesque writers of other regions, and he portrayed only so much of California life as happened to fit his formula. Yet it is impossible to deny that there is power in his early work, and that something of the frontier does live in these romantic tales. Harte did not found a peculiarly western literature, but he did make a beginning. And then, with the beginning scarcely made, he turned his back on the West and on the hope of literary growth. What he had written, out of a real desire to express the spirit of the region he knew, was, he discovered, merely entertainment for his readers. He accepted—harassed, one must admit, by personal difficulties and financial troubles—the rôle of entertainer, and as an entertainer survived for thirty years his death as an artist.

Harte, though he may not have been in any strict sense the founder of American regionalism, was the first writer to gain popularity after the Civil War by the exploitation of sectional peculiarities, and there is little doubt that his example directly inspired many of the writers of the seventies, eighties, and nineties. It is, therefore, striking that the pattern of his life should be the pattern, to a great extent, of the regional movement in American literature. Writer after writer began with a sincere desire not merely to portray the life of a particular section but to express its spirit; writer after writer ended as a mere entertainer, providing formularized amusement for an appreciative nation. Individual careers varied, but the fundamental pattern scarcely changed: the writer did not grow with his section. The region that appeared in his books was always the region as he had known it when he began writing, or even when he was a child. Often he left the region, and thus freed himself to live with memories of what it had been. In any case nostalgia and often sentimentality filled his tales. Again and again the tragedy of Bret Harte in London repeated itself. (pp. 34-8)

> *Granville Hicks, "A Banjo on My Knee," in his* The Great Tradition: An Interpretation of American Literature Since the Civil War, *revised edition, Macmillan Publishing Company, 1935, pp. 32-67.*

CLEANTH BROOKS, JR., ROBERT PENN WARREN AND JOHN THIBAUT PURSER (essay date 1936)

[*In the following excerpt from their 1936 edition of* An Approach to Literature, *the critics discuss sentimentality in* "The Luck of Roaring Camp."]

The theme of [**"The Luck of Roaring Camp"**] is, to put it broadly, that within the most violent and degenerate man there remains some element of decency and tenderness, some aspiration toward the kind of life and the set of values which he has, apparently, repudiated. . . . Bret Harte's story is concerned with the regeneration of the citizens of Roaring Camp, the awakening of their apparently lost impulses to decency, through the influence of the child of the dead prostitute. Now a reader may hold, with Harte and Stevenson, that to every man, no matter how degraded, some human worth and dignity still attaches. But a story on this theme is not necessarily good because the theme of the story seems to involve a truth about humanity. Many people judge literature merely on the basis of the ideas expressed or implied. If the idea seem "true" or "noble" or "useful"—that is, if the piece of literature flatters their own

preconceptions—they are inclined to believe that the piece of literature is therefore good. But in such a case, the readers are not reading the piece of literature. The idea is satisfactory to them, no matter in what form it is cast, or what treatment it receives.

The chief defect of **"The Luck of Roaring Camp"** is sentimentality. . . . [Sentimentality] arises from a writer's attempt to claim a greater emotional response on the part of the reader than is actually justified by the materials and treatment of the piece of work. . . . That is, such a writer relies on the reader's stock responses to gain his effect, and not on his own understanding and presentation of the materials of his story, poem, or novel. . . . This story is sentimental because it over-simplifies the situation; it makes the regeneration of Roaring Camp too easily achieved. The change in the life of the miners is too sudden and too complete. The reader feels that human character is more complex than is indicated by Bret Harte, that habits of conduct and attitudes of mind usually change gradually. For instance, we are told that the miners who brought "clusters of wild honeysuckles, azaleas, or the painted blossoms of Las Mariposas" and fragments of quartz and bright pebbles to The Luck, "suddenly awakened to the fact that there were beauty and significance in these trifles, which they had so long trodden carelessly beneath their feet." The more tough-minded reader may ask himself this question: How often have I known a man whose whole life and point of view were so completely changed even by his own child? And Harte has the change affecting a whole camp. He does not allow for differences in character and temperament among the men; the regeneration touches all of them in the same way, and almost at the same time. In other words, there is no presentation of the inevitable conflict of attitudes and feelings among the men. The story would be more convincing if Harte had taken one character, Kentuck, for example, and had indicated, in some degree, at least, the actual psychological process of the change in him; that is, if he had given some presentation of the inner conflict which the change would, necessarily, involve.

There are some details of the story which can be related to the basic sentimentality. For example, in describing the birth of the child, Harte writes: "The pines stopped moaning, the river ceased to rush, and the fire to crackle. It seemed as if Nature had stopped to listen too." Now, we could admit that the pines might have stopped moaning, because of a lull in the breeze; but we know perfectly well that the river did not cease to rush, and that, if the sound of the pines had stopped, the sound of the river would have been more readily heard than before. Harte is deliberately falsifying his scene in order to play on the reader's emotions and to prepare him, thereby, to accept the regeneration of the camp. Or the last paragraph of the story might be analyzed to prove the same point. Harte is straining for his effects, and . . . sentimentality always involves just this kind of strain. . . . (pp. 86-7)

> *Cleanth Brooks, Jr., John Thibaut Purser, and Robert Penn Warren, in a discussion of "The Luck of Roaring Camp," in* An Approach to Literature, *Cleanth Brooks, Jr., John Thibaut Purser, Robert Penn Warren, eds., third edition, Appleton-Century-Crofts, Inc., 1952, pp. 86-7.*

CLEANTH BROOKS AND ROBERT PENN WARREN (essay date 1943)

[*Brooks and Warren are considered two of the most prominent figures of the school of New Criticism, an influential movement in American criticism that also included Allen Tate and R. P. Blackmur. Although the various New Critics did not subscribe to any single set of principles, all believed that a work of literature had to be examined as an object in itself through a process of close analysis of symbol, image, and metaphor. For the New Critics, a literary work was not a manifestation of ethics, sociology, or psychology, and could not be evaluated in the general terms of any nonliterary discipline. In the following essay, they discuss ''Tennessee's Partner,'' finding Harte's portrayal both unconvincing and sentimental.]*

[**''Tennessee's Partner''**] is a story about the loyalty of one man for his friend, Tennessee, a man who, by all commonly accepted standards, could have no claim on loyalty. On two counts Tennessee has forfeited all reasonable claim on his friend's loyalty: first, he has stolen his friend's wife, and second, he has been caught red-handed, given a fair trial, and convicted of highway robbery. But in spite of this forfeiture his partner tries to save him from execution and when he fails in this, claims the body and buries it with his own hands.

Tennessee's Partner, the author makes plain, is a simple, untutored, and rough man, a member of a community which, taken as a whole, is simple, untutored, and rough. His act of loyalty is all the more touching since it springs from such an unpromising background, a background which, at first glance, would appear to offer no encouragement for tenderness and sensitivity. There is an element of surprise, consequently, in the author's revelation of this idealism in Tennessee's Partner. This surprise is obviously a part of the author's intended effect. The use of the unlikely background and of the rough, simple character, gives several related effects: a rebuke to moral snobbery; an emphasis on the pathos inherent in the situation; a guarantee of the genuineness of the emotion—Tennessee's Partner is too simple and uncouth to adopt a pose.

The use of such a contrast between the idealism of the hero and his roughness, is in itself, of course, perfectly legitimate. The contrast derives from one of the basic facts of human nature: the fact that goodness and decency are not confined to the cultivated and educated members of society. Many writers have made use of this special type of contrast and for the same complex of effects for which Bret Harte strives here. The poet Wordsworth, for instance, constantly affirms the basic goodness and sensitivity of common human nature, and makes the unexpected revelation of it the focal point of many of his poems. Or, to take an instance from contemporary writers, the student may consider the work of Ernest Hemingway in which his ''tough'' and ''hard-boiled'' characters reveal a sensitivity which belies their apparent callousness.

There is nothing wrong, we may judge, either with the general idea in itself (the theme), or with the particular situation in which Bret Harte finds the theme embodied. But neither theme nor situation as such can guarantee the success of a story. Other factors must be considered. For instance, we are entitled to ask ourselves whether Tennessee's Partner is credible in the action which he performs. In asking ourselves whether his character as portrayed is convincing, it is not enough to decide that such persons have performed such acts in real life. Rather, we must decide whether the character of Tennessee's Partner, as Bret Harte has delineated it for us in this story, is actually convincing in the magnanimous action which he is made to perform. That is, we must decide whether Bret Harte has made us understand the psychological steps by which the man arrives at his action, an action which, we discover, comes with some surprise to the other members of the community.

What is Tennessee's Partner like as he first appears in the story? We do not even know his name, but this situation was not uncommon in a society where many were trying to conceal their past lives. He is merely **''Tennessee's Partner.''** But early in the story occurs an incident which ordinarily strains partnerships past the breaking point. Tennessee runs off with his partner's wife. A little later, when the wife deserts Tennessee for another man, the two friends renew their partnership as if nothing had happened, even though the whole town had turned out for the expected shooting.

Why does Bret Harte use this incident? He obviously uses it to prepare for the scene which he considers to be the climax . . . of his story—the scene of the ''funeral service.'' Certainly, if Tennessee's Partner can so readily forgive Tennessee for stealing his wife, he may be expected to perform the easier task of burying his friend. So far as character is concerned, then, the funeral scene is really an anticlimax. But why does Tennessee's Partner forgive Tennessee so easily for the wife-stealing? The matter is never explained, and we learn nothing of the state of mind which led the partner to the decision. In other words, Bret Harte has dodged the real psychological issue of his story: the conflict in the mind of the partner between his affection for Tennessee on the one hand, and, on the other, his attachment to his wife and his outraged honor which the primitive community expects him to avenge with bloodletting.

One might defend the motivation of the story by saying that Bret Harte simply was not interested in dealing with the wife-stealing incident in detail, but *was* interested in the burial of Tennessee. This is all very well, in one sense: an author does have the right to select the incidents on which he cares to focus attention. But his selection must have its basis in some logic, and, in this case, it is a logic of character; that is, Harte is dealing with the partner's attitude toward the perfidious Tennessee. Apparently, Bret Harte's intended strategy was this: by touching lightly on the wife situation he hoped to lull the reader into an acceptance of an easy solution of the psychological problem involved in it, and then hoped to use the reader's acceptance of it as a preparation for the climax. But if a reader does not accept the easy solution of this problem, then the rest of the story will seem false.

What else does Bret Harte give us in preparation for the climax? He gives us the scene of the attempted bribery. The purpose of this scene seems to be to indicate a certain characteristic of the partner: his naïveté with regard to the conventions of society, to the nature of law, and even to the concept of abstract justice itself. Apparently, he honestly sees the situation into which Tennessee has fallen as one which can be settled by a money payment. The stranger will be compensated for his losses and will be given something for his trouble. Perhaps there is the implication that he is attempting to bribe the court; certainly, the violent reaction of the bystanders would indicate this assumption, though the judge apparently realizes the childlike nature of the man's mind. Indeed, the judge proceeds to give the man a lecture on the nature of law: ''The man was made to understand . . . that Tennessee's offense could not be condoned by money.'' But another purpose of the scene is to develop the idea of the partner's fidelity; he is willing to sacrifice his ''pile'' for his friend. Furthermore, the fidelity suggested by the scene is a kind of doglike devotion which takes no account of abstract matters such as the moral character of Tennessee or the nature of his offense.

But does this incident represent a real development of the idea first suggested to the reader by the incident of the partner's forgiveness of Tennessee for the wife-stealing? One would be inclined to suppose that it is more credible that a man should put up money to help a friend than that he should sacrifice his wife to his friend's pleasure and accept smilingly the insult to his personal honor. If this is true, then the court incident is again anticlimactic; it does not represent a true progression. Moreover, if the partner is a man who sees things in very concrete personal terms (as the bribery incident indicates), does this court scene afford any real clarification of the forgiveness of Tennessee for the wife-stealing? For, presumably, the relation of the man to his wife is also a personal, concrete relation, not merely an abstract and conventional relation. Moreover, if one rationalizes the whole incident of the forgiveness, by saying that the partner regarded his wife as merely a chattel (and remember the author has given us no basis for making this supposition), then the whole meaning of his act of forgiveness is lost, for the conflict—between personal affection for his friend on the one hand, and personal honor and personal affection for his wife on the other—disappears from the situation.

For what, after all, does this court incident intend to prepare us? It is, of course, not merely for the incident of the burial, as such. For someone among the rough citizenry would have buried the hanged man in any case, and perhaps with a kind of elemental pity. (Tennessee, has, for instance, certain qualities which would extort special admiration in this primitive community—a courage and coolness, which are dramatized several times in the story.) The intended high point in the story is the funeral oration, which Tennessee's Partner delivers to the camp. It is here that our full sense of the pathos is supposed to emerge.

But if such pathos is to emerge to the full, and is to be meaningful, the author must have convinced us (1) that it is logical for this particular character to deliver the oration under the circumstances and (2) that this oration brings to focus elements of interpretation and meaning implicit in previous incidents.

But there are more difficulties. First, would the partner, as his character has been prepared for in earlier pages of the story, have made such a speech to the members of the community who had turned out, purely from curiosity, to see what he would do? A man whose life had been dominated by a merely personal attachment to his friend and who had been completely incapable of understanding why his friend had to be hanged (as indicated by the bribery scene), would more probably have felt a sullen resentment against the men who had done his friend to death for, in his eyes, no good reason. At least, he would probably have wanted privacy for his sorrow. (He can be under no illusion that the spectators have come out of love for Tennessee.)

Second, assuming that the partner would have delivered the oration, would he have said what Bret Harte makes him say? For example, would he have apologized to the spectators and have thanked them for their trouble? (Notice that Bret Harte does not intend for us to take this as the bitter irony of a hurt man, but as a manifestation of a kind of Christlike forgiveness. The partner is almost too good to be true.) And notice, further, in this connection, what Bret Harte has the partner say in his delirium as he dies of a broken heart. Here, even the language becomes unrealistic; it is entirely out of the partner's idiom. For example, would he have said: "There, now, steady, Jinny,— steady, old girl. How dark it is!" Isn't it more likely that he would have said: "It's dark as hell." Or: "God-a-mighty, it's dark!" Why does Bret Harte break out of the partner's idiom?

Because Bret Harte is straining for a highly emotional effect, and feeling that the realistic language is not good enough, he resorts to "poeticizing" the character. In other words, he is not willing to let the case rest on its own merits. The same thing is true of the symbolic reference, in the dying speech, to the pine tree on the top of the hill.

But other examples of such strain are to be found earlier in the story—take, for example, the description of nature as the partner carries the body to the place of burial: "The way led through Grizzly Cañon, by this time clothed in funereal drapery and shadows. The redwoods, burying their moccasined feet in the red soil, stood in Indian file along the track, trailing an uncouth benediction from their bending boughs upon the passing bier." Nature, apparently, is sympathetic with the partner's grief. Like him, it can give only an "uncouth benediction," but it expresses its brooding sympathy as best it can. One recognizes that a writer may legitimately use description of nature as a device for defining the atmosphere of a piece of fiction, or may even use it as specific symbolism. But it should be quite clear that Bret Harte here is not using it legitimately. It is used here to give a false heightening to the pathos of the scene, and the language in which the description is couched is as "poeticized" as is the language of the partner's dying speech. For example, the description of the redwoods "burying their moccasined feet in the red soil" is completely irrelevant and represents an attempt at fanciful decoration; it is another instance of the author's straining for effects which, he seems to feel, are not adequately supported by the situation in itself.

The presence of this straining for an emotional effect is one of the surest symptoms that one is dealing with a case of sentimentality. . . . In its general sense sentimentality may be defined as an emotional response in excess of the occasion. We speak of a person who weeps at some trivial occurrence as being sentimental. Such a person lacks a sense of proportion and gets a morbid enjoyment from an emotional debauch for its own sake. When we apply the term to a piece of literature, a story, for instance, we usually mean that the author intends for the reader to experience an intense emotion which is actually not justified by the materials of the story.

One symptom of sentimentality is, as we have said, the author's straining to heighten and prettify and poeticize his language quite apart from the dramatic issues involved in the story.

A second symptom frequently to be found is "editorializing" on the part of the author—pointing out to the reader what he should feel, nudging the reader to respond—devices which would not be necessary if the story could make its own case. (For example, Bret Harte comments on the hanging of Tennessee as follows: "And yet, when the weak and foolish deed was done, and a life, with its possibilities and responsibilities, had passed out of the misshapen thing that dangled between earth and sky, the birds sang, the flowers bloomed, the sun shone, as cheerily as before. . . .")

A third symptom is the tendency to dodge the real issues which should prepare for the final effect of a story. That is, an author who is primarily concerned with giving the emotional effect may not be too scrupulous about the means adopted to that end. For example, in this story Bret Harte is so thoroughly obsessed with the pathos of the partner's loyalty that he has devoted no thought to the precise nature of the basis of that loyalty. As has already been pointed out, he does not bring the wife-stealing episode into real focus. Either he was so little interested in the psychology of the situation that he did not investigate it, or he was aware that the issues involved were too complicated for him to handle in terms of the scheme which he had laid down for the story.

The reading of this story raises some such question as this: Has not Bret Harte taken a theme which, perhaps, he had seen successfully employed for pathetic effects in other fiction, and attempted to trick it out with a new romantic setting, touches of local color (such as descriptions of the community and bits of dialect), and poeticized writing, without ever grounding the story in a presentation of the real psychological issues involved? (pp. 214-20)

> *Cleanth Brooks and Robert Penn Warren, in an interpretation of "Tennessee's Partner," in* Understanding Fiction, *edited by Cleanth Brooks and Robert Penn Warren, Appleton-Century-Crofts, Inc., 1943, pp. 205-20.*

ALLEN B. BROWN (essay date 1960)

[*In the following excerpt, Brown offers a Christian reading of "The Luck of Roaring Camp," examining possible biblical parallels to the events in the story.*]

"Bret Harte's **'The Luck of Roaring Camp,'** whatever one may think of its merits, must be admitted to be the most influential short story ever written in America." So states Fred Lewis Pattee in *The Cambridge History of American Literature*. This story has been and still is reprinted in many anthologies and textbooks of American literature. Edward J. O'Brien included it in *The Twenty-five Finest Short Stories*. . . . Any novelty it once had cannot account for the continued life of this story, first published in 1868. Powerful appeal to the subconscious of most of its readers can.

A long period of overestimation was inevitably followed by detractions. One of the most severe is in Brooks, Purser, and Warren's *An Approach to Literature* [see excerpt dated 1936]. Harte is criticized for an excess of editorial comment, a hackneyed theme, oversimplifying characters and situation, and, above all, for sentimentality. Knickerbocker and Reninger in their *Interpreting Literature* have done their best to refute these charges by claiming that the characters *are* representative, that Harte did possess accurate information about California miners, and that their actions are sufficiently motivated. However, Knickerbocker and Reninger admit that the ending is too contrived. Pattee claims that Harte is less sentimental than Dickens . . . , his favorite author.

My contention is that these well-known critics have missed the chief point, that **"The Luck of Roaring Camp"** is not primarily an early realistic story but a romantic, symbolic story akin to Hawthorne and Kafka and therefore of a type that can be respectably admired by today's scholars. George R. Stewart, Jr., Bret Harte's latest and most complete biographer, states that Harte was thoroughly grounded in the Bible. **"The Luck of Roaring Camp"** certainly bears this out. Harte's father was a Roman Catholic teacher of Greek in an Albany, New York, seminary; and Pattee has noted that Harte was a bookish boy who had read all of his father's considerable library, that some of his earliest stories are "pure Hawthorne" and even the style is sometimes like Hawthorne, and that "he had read much in the French." Harte has frequently been said to show the influence of Victor Hugo; and the subject matter, the teaching, the symbolism employed, the "unpadded, finely calculated" clear-cut style is not unlike some of the work of Maupassant.

The story is familiar. The son of the disreputable Cherokee Sal is the first child born in Roaring Camp. The hundred men there adopt the orphaned baby, contribute to its support, suckle it by an ass, hold a formal christening at which they name him Thomas Luck, and proceed to regenerate themselves under his beneficent influence. They vie in attending the child, and Nature herself is "his nurse and playfellow." Roaring Camp is unusually prosperous and becomes a model mining community. About a year later, a flash flood kills the three principal characters (The Luck, Stumpy, and Kentuck), but not before Kentuck is convinced that he will accompany the dead baby, that his salvation is secure.

Harte records in his introduction to ***The Luck of Roaring Camp and Other Tales*** that the printer of *The Overland Monthly*, a deacon, protested to the publisher that "The Luck of Roaring Camp" "was so indecent, irreligious, and improper that his proofreader—a young lady—had with difficulty been induced to continue its perusal." . . . A number of other people agreed with the publisher and the printing department. After the story was published, over their united protests, a religious magazine strongly objected to it as "unfavorable to immigration" and "the investment of foreign capital." But let us look at the story itself. If it can be shown that this story has closely interwoven Christian symbolism as well as disreputable characters and hints at profanity—Christ himself preferred the company of the disreputable to the scribes and Pharisees—it may be easier to understand why this story laid tremendous hold upon all its readers and stirred many to subconscious resentment. They felt it a sacrilege.

The story has many Christian echoes and parallels. Roaring Camp, its miscellaneous inhabitants drawn even from distant Australia, is destroyed by flood and may easily represent the world in miniature. That the Son of God came to redeem our world, to all believers in Him, is the luckiest thing that ever happened. The Luck seems to have been born about Christmas Eve 1850. "A fire of withered pine boughs" and "staring red flannel" coupled with the gifts brought to the baby may suggest Christmas. Christ's function in the world, regeneration, is mentioned twice; and the miners and their surroundings are changed almost beyond recognition. They keep out all strangers and the legend arises that "they worship an Ingin baby." Theirs is a "pastoral happiness," which Cockney Simmons calls "'evingly.'"

The Luck's mother, moreover, like the mother of Our Lord, is a disgraced virgin and again, like the Lady of Sorrows, suffers "martyrdom" fulfilling "the primal curse" and "punishment of the first transgression" and so "expiates her sin." Stumpy, who stands godfather to the child, is also like St. Joseph in being the head of two families. The men who attend her lying-in are as contemptuous as were the people of Bethlehem, and the new baby receives as rude a cradle, most appropriately for this "light of the world" a candle-box. Harte says The Luck is "introduced *ab initio*," the same words that begin the Latin New Testament. There is another Biblical echo in calling Roaring Camp "a city of refuge." The hundred men, who act as a unit and as modern wise men, bring, along with many inappropriate things, considerable gold, and a Bible that Harte may intend as a clue to his whole story. Principally they illustrate that appearance may be the opposite of reality. I find it highly suggestive that one has a Raphael face and another is like Hamlet, often said to be a kind of Christ. Harte's calling attention to three fingers and one eye can suggest the holy Trinity and the Masonic emblem for God. Further use of the mystic three is the triangular shape of the valley, which lies between two hills and a river, the age-old symbol of life and death. The resolve to secure outside help is postponed for three months and The Luck's lullaby has ninety stanzas. The only outlet to the valley is a steep trail that is "lost in the stars above." As she dies, Cherokee Sal is said to leave "Roaring Camp, its sin and shame, forever" by that trail.

Now comes the passage that Brooks, Purser, and Warren find particularly objectionable and oversentimental. "The pines stopped moaning, the river ceased to rush, and the fire to crackle. It seemed as if Nature had stopped to listen too." They object:

> Now, we could admit that the pines might have stopped moaning, because of a lull in the breeze; but we know perfectly well that the river did not cease to rush, and that, if the sound of the pines had stopped, the sound of the river would have been more readily heard than before. Harte is deliberately falsifying his scene in order to play on the reader's emotions and to prepare him, thereby, to accept the regeneration of the camp.

The whole camp is regenerated (or at least improved) because, despite Brooks, Purser, Warren, Knickerbocker, and Reninger, the baby *is* a miracle worker. Here Harte makes use of the well-known legend, so beautifully expounded in Milton's hymn from "On the Morning of Christ's Nativity" (stanzas III-VII), that all nature held its breath when the Prince of Peace was born. Later, the baby, like St. Francis, talks to the birds; and, as Stumpy says, they were "'a-jawing' . . . like two cherry-bums."

The donkey, so often associated with Jesus, is mentioned several times. There is a hint at resurrection or the continuity of life in laying out the dead mother on the left (evil side) and the newly born on the right. The men all uncover to show their respect, and rough old Kentuck, who has some similarity to the Apostle Peter, is delighted with the infant's holy touch when The Luck wrestles with his finger as the angel did with Jacob. "The d—d little cuss!" exclaims Kentuck, a euphemism which Harte may well intend to mean doomed as well as damned in this world. Kentuck tries to demonstrate his unconcern by whistling, but pauses at a large redwood tree, which might represent the cross of Christ, and returns to join Stumpy beside the baby. The suggestion that the baby be sent to Red Dog, a hell compared to the regenerated Roaring Camp, forty (a favorite Biblical number) miles away is summarily rejected. No other region can share their new faith. Most appropriately, finery for the child, including a rosewood cradle, perhaps an allusion to love or the mystic rose, is ordered from Sacramento (twice forty miles away).

The men are superstitious, and it is felt that "a fresh deal" is called for. The christening is complete with choir, music, procession, banners, and altar. Stumpy ends their service by declaring, "'I proclaim you Thomas Luck, according to the laws of the United States and the State of California, so help me God'," as if "under a Christian roof." Kentuck, who had regarded his garments as a kind of snake's skin (long a symbol of regeneration and resurrection), becomes admirably clean and changes his shirt every day. "Nor were moral and social sanitary laws neglected." The baby, always surrounded with pine boughs or other evergreens, lies above as the men work below, receives gifts of every beautiful thing that they can find (they

had never noticed Nature's beauty before), and becomes as grave, tractable, and quiet as we imagine the Baby Jesus must have been. Roaring Camp is "inviolate" and completely closed to strangers, although some think it would be best to extend his influence to others. This is comparable to the early Jewish Christians' attitude toward the Gentiles. Like Jesus, the baby ("the hope . . . of Roaring Camp") disappears but reappears with Kentuck (Peter), who has withstood the trial by water and now ventures confidently into the Unknown.

I have attempted to demonstrate that Harte was steeped in the Bible and Christian tradition, almost certainly patterned **"The Luck of Roaring Camp"** on earlier moral writers, that it is the suggestion of sacrilege which horrified his earliest readers and his religious teaching which charmed the rest. When one is aware of the dominance of the multitude of Christian symbols closely interwoven throughout the story, the action is never questionable and the ending is inevitable. Bret Harte's masterpiece has long puzzled readers and even many otherwise acute critics because it is stated not in inartistic allegory but in highly suggestive symbols. (pp. 629-33)

> *Allen B. Brown, "The Christ Motif in 'The Luck of Roaring Camp'," in* Papers of the Michigan Academy of Science, Arts and Letters, *Vol. XLVI, 1961, pp. 629-33.*

FREDERICK ANDERSON (essay date 1961)

[*In the following excerpt, Anderson discusses the collaboration between Harte and Mark Twain on the play* Ah Sin.]

The existence of a text of *Ah Sin,* Bret Harte and Mark Twain's play set in a mining camp on the Stanislaus River, has only recently become known. The production of the play in 1877 was a failure, the work was never published, and scholars have relied on contemporary reviews for information about the only collaborative venture by two of the West's foremost writers. Even a casual reader will discover the cause for this neglect, since while *Ah Sin* is not the poorest work by either man, it is not far from it. Nevertheless, a play about the West by two authors whose experiences in the area provided material for some of their most effective writing deserves examination. The work assumes additional importance when one realizes that it was written just after the apex of Harte's literary career and just before the peak of Mark Twain's. (p. v)

Although Clemens was responsible for the final revisions [of *Ah Sin*], much, perhaps most, of the initial material in the play came from Bret Harte. The names and to some extent the characterizations of all the figures in the play except Silas Broderick, Ferguson, and the Tempest family were already known to Bret Harte's readers. For example, Ah Sin is the name of "the heathen Chinee" in Harte's **"Plain Language from Truthful James,"** and similar comic Chinese figures appear often in Harte's works. In his play, *Two Men of Sandy Bar,* the Chinese character called Hop Sing is clearly an antecedent of Ah Sin. In fact, the performance of Charles T. Parsloe as Hop Sing in 1876 had been such a popular success that the present play was conceived as a vehicle for Parsloe.

The Plunkett family had appeared in Harte's **"A Monte Flat Pastoral,"** but the transformation of Plunkett from a pathetic derelict and the elaboration of the roles of the female Plunketts substantiate Clemens's claim for them when he praised "my old Plunkett family" as being "wonderfully coarse & vulgar on the stage." The raffish Plunkett family, despite Mrs. Plunkett's obvious descent from Mrs. Malaprop, are the most vigorously realized characters in the play.

Clemens's chief contribution to *Ah Sin* was his effort to render accurately the rhythms and vocabulary of actual speech since Harte's dialogue in this play, as in most of his writing, was conventionally stilted and romantic. Clemens's skill in the use of the vernacular was seriously tested by Harte's rhetoric, as is shown by the evolution of the following passage. Harte originally had Judge Tempest remark, "I know not what to say." Clemens revised this specimen of unlikely speech to "Well, I don't know of anything further to say." Such revisions permeate the fragments of the early manuscript and repeatedly show Mark Twain's efforts to move from the formalized speech of the nineteenth century stage toward realistic language and characterization. These efforts were too few and made too late to salvage a play which was written well within the dramatic conventions of the period and however considerable Clemens's revisions may have been, his statement that he had "left hardly a foot-print of Harte in it anywhere" is exaggerated.

The uneasy and sporadic collaboration between Harte and Clemens is reflected in the play's chaotic and sometimes incoherent succession of events, the implausibly feeble motives which bring these events about, and the sketchily developed characterizations. Moreover, since neither man was a trained dramatist, their conception of the enterprise wavered from tragedy and melodrama to comedy and farce with no successful attempt to develop or sustain a consistent mood. (pp. x-xii)

> *Frederick Anderson, in a preface to "Ah Sin": A Dramatic Work by Mark Twain and Bret Harte, edited by Frederick Anderson, The Book Club of California, 1961, pp. v-xvi.*

MARGARET DUCKETT   (essay date 1964)

[*In the following excerpt, Duckett traces the influence Harte's fiction had on the writings of Mark Twain and later American authors.*]

Literary historians and critics of the past thirty years have been apt to deny emphatically that Bret Harte had any influence on Mark Twain's work. . . . [One] exception was the late Van Wyck Brooks. Another exception is Walter Blair, whose thorough and illuminating study of the genesis and maturation of *The Adventures of Huckleberry Finn* suggests that Mark Twain's writings about the South may have been influenced by Bret Harte, that Colonel Grangerford was a blood relation—almost an identical twin—of Colonel Starbottle, and that Harte had "prepared the way for Huckleberry Finn as a leading character." Referring to what is generally regarded as the "Harte formula" of "good in the heart of an outcast," Professor Blair wrote: "Twain, eager for acceptance by the literary elite, hardly would have ventured to make Huck the center of a novel if the trail had not been broken by Harte."

Although I question some of his conclusions concerning Bret Harte's influence on Mark Twain's writings about the South, Professor Blair seems to me to come much closer to the truth than those critics who deny that Bret Harte had any influence on the writings of Mark Twain. Most significant is the recognition of Harte's influence on the "sound heart" of the outcast that won over the "deformed conscience" of the social conformist in Huck Finn (p. 312).

Occasionally, elements appearing earlier in the fiction of Mark Twain can be recognized in the fiction of Bret Harte. For example, certain elements of *Huckleberry Finn* are dimly discernible in Harte's **"Cressy"** and **"Three Vagabonds of Trinidad."** But these resemblances hardly indicate that Harte had

a flair for plagiarism, although they may indicate that Bret Harte was exploiting interest in Mark Twain's themes as Twain in *Roughing It* had exploited interest in Harte's. Harte's little-known story **"Ali Baba of the Sierras"** seems to owe more to *Tom Sawyer* than to the Forty Thieves. Its small-boy hero and his sweetheart appear shoddy imitations of Tom Sawyer and Becky Thatcher; Spanish Pete was obviously another Injun Joe (who disguised himself as a deaf and dumb Spaniard in a serape) and like Injun Joe was trapped at the mouth of a cave where treasure was hidden. The very title is suspect as an elaboration of an allusion to the *Arabian Nights* in *Tom Sawyer*.

But before becoming too sure that Bret Harte was now working a claim staked out by Mark Twain, one should read closely Harte's own revised and lengthened version of the once-popular **"M'liss,"** first appearing in 1860 in shorter form as **"The Work on Red Mountain."** At the urgent request of the editor, Harte reluctantly tried to expand the story, and the result—which he never liked—was published in serial form in the *Golden Era* in 1863, a year before Mark Twain left Nevada for San Francisco and thirteen years before the publication of *The Adventures of Tom Sawyer*.

> "Now, where on earth can that child be?" said Mrs. Morpher, shading her eyes with her hand, as she stood at the door of the 'Mountain Ranch,' looking down the Wingdam road at sunset.
>
> "With his best things on, too. Goodness!— what *were* boys made for?"

Thus begins a chapter entitled **"The Trials of Mrs. Morpher,"** and although the dialogue is much less skillful than the famous beginning of *The Adventures of Tom Sawyer*, Mrs. Morpher's speech as well as her trials are a good deal like Aunt Polly's:

> "Tom!"
>
> No answer.
>
> "Tom!"
>
> No answer.
>
> "What's gone with that boy, I wonder?"
>
> You Tom!"
>
> No answer.
>
> The old lady pulled her spectacles down and looked over them about the room; then she put them up and looked out under them. She seldom or never looked *through* them for so small a thing as a boy.

The small boy Mrs. Morpher was looking for bore the impossible name of Aristides. He shared Tom Sawyer's resentment against the restraint of new clothes and cleanliness, and with feverish excitement he collected such treasures as a ravished jay's nest and a dead hare. He wore his hat on the back of his head, his trousers were too large for him, and he liked to burrow his bare toes luxuriously in cool, loose dirt. He practiced whistling shrilly between his fingers (instead of whistling melodiously with his tongue tapping the roof of his mouth, as did Tom Sawyer). (pp. 320-22)

Harte's interest in children as subjects of fiction was probably stimulated by his admiration for Dickens, but Harte's sympathy for children and his understanding of child psychology seemed largely intuitive. Even before **"M'liss,"** whose small boy fought, fell in love, met death, and ran away from home in 1863, such slight journalistic features as **"Sufferings of a Small Person"** (*Golden Era,* February 3, 1861) and **"With 'Buster,'"** (*Golden Era,* April 14, 1861) reflect Harte's interest. They demonstrate his awareness of and sympathy with the point of view of a child, his defense of the disorderly small boy, and his condemnation of didactic fiction which falsified life in order to emphasize the horrible retribution in store for the Bad Boy. As editor of the *Overland Monthly,* Harte reviewed with particular attention and discrimination the current books being published for children.

Harte's concern with the theory and practice of writing juvenile fiction was further evidenced by a letter written on May 1, 1874, to Mrs. Mary Mapes Dodge, editor of *St. Nicholas Magazine for Boys and Girls,* which was about to publish Harte's **"Baby Sylvester,"** a bear story. In this letter Harte expressed admiration for the art, "which none values more highly than myself," of writing for children, but on grounds that it would be writing down to his readers, he rejected the editor's suggestion that he modify his language for childish minds. He insisted that an author should respect a child's taste, his judgment, and his ability to recognize a lie in fiction. Although he continued to try to write stories for children, Bret Harte lacked Mark Twain's ability to *become* the child about whom he was writing. Children often liked his stories, but finally Harte's fiction maintained the point of view of an imaginative and affectionate adult observing the child. Bret Harte's use of this perspective (which obtrudes in less successful passages of *Tom Sawyer*) may partly explain Mark Twain's difficulty in making up his mind whether he intended his first book about boyhood to be read by children or adults. To Mrs. Dodge, Harte professed his own belief that he lacked the art of writing juvenile fiction.

There can be no doubt that Mark Twain was aware of Bret Harte's interest in fiction for and about children. The influence of **"M'liss"** on Mark Twain's work was, I believe, more specific and detailed than has heretofore been noticed. My hypothesis that the shabby little M'liss with her friend Risty stood, recognized or unrecognized, in the shadowy backgrounds of Mark Twain's mind when he was writing *Tom Sawyer* and *Huckleberry Finn* is altogether compatible with Bernard De Voto's conclusion that with Tom Sawyer, Mark Twain found the theme best suited to his interest, his experience, and his talents. And it does not dim in any way an appreciation of Mark Twain's artistic achievement in writing his two most famous books. (pp. 328-29).

Today the influence of Bret Harte on the development of American literature is underestimated. But in the lifetime of Bret Harte and Mark Twain, it was overestimated. Bret Harte knew it and Mark Twain resented it. The year 1870 was recognized as a turning point in American literature. And 1870 was Bret Harte's year. In the years that followed American critics commented on the deterioration of Harte's work but continued to compare him with Turgenev and to insist that what he had already produced would "always remain a vigorous, brilliant, original contribution to American literature." According to Henry Adams, "the fateful year of 1870" marked the close of a literary epoch, "when quarterlies gave way to monthlies; letter-press to illustrations; volumes to pages. The outburst was brilliant. Bret Harte led, and Robert Louis Stevenson followed. Guy de Maupassant and Rudyard Kipling brought up the rear, and dazzled the world.

Nineteenth-century critics frequently listed Mark Twain among

the followers of Bret Harte. The main reason was that Harte's writing about California stimulated the fictional exploration of other regions so that in 1872, Howells would prophesy that gradually but surely the "whole varied field of American life" would be observable in American fiction. This idea generated Mark Twain's *Atlantic* essays, later expanded and published as *Life on the Mississippi.* But the best of all regional studies in fiction are those marvelous Mississippi Valley scenes in *Huckleberry Finn:* the camp meeting, the Grangerford home, Peter Wilks's funeral, the Arkansas town where loafers laughed as dogs chased an old sow and where a mob gathered for a lynching bee. The fact that the middle chapters of *Huckleberry Finn* are much more than local color does not alter the fact that it was Mark Twain's interest in recreating the life of the Mississippi River Valley which he knew so well that led him to abandon the idea of taking Jim to freedom. The resulting chapters were not only the greatest in the book but the greatest writing Mark Twain ever produced.

Bret Harte was the first to recognize the effectiveness of Mark Twain's attacks on social ills. Aware of Twain's sensitiveness about assertions that he had imitated Harte, time and again Bret Harte reiterated his own early dictum that Mark Twain stood alone as the most original humorist that America had yet produced: "He alone is inimitable." **Ah Sin,** Mark Twain's bitter words, Mark Twain's triumphs, and Bret Harte's own disappointments and frustrations never changed Harte's critical judgment of Twain's work. In 1899, the year Hamlin Garland interviewed both Harte and Twain in London, Bret Harte was asked to write for *Cornhill* magazine an essay on **"The Rise of the 'Short Story.'"** In this essay Harte again rebuked critics who, mistakenly attributing to him the invention of the local-color genre, applied the term "imitators" to such writers as Joel Chandler Harris, George Washington Cable, Mary E. Wilkins Freeman, Constance Fenimore Woolson, and "Mark Twain in 'Huckleberry Finn.'" The term "imitator," Harte said, "could not fairly apply to those who cut loose from conventional methods and sought honestly to describe the life around them." For himself, Harte added, he could claim only "to have shown them that it could be done." Bret Harte had considerable right to that claim.

"Waves of influence run from the man," wrote Henry Seidel Canby in 1926, "and indeed the literary West may be said to have founded itself upon the imagination of Bret Harte." Bret Harte's influence was not nearly so bad as "The Modest Club" would have us believe. That Harte's **Condensed Novels** "brilliantly satirized the falsification of life by sentimental novelists" has been recognized by Everett Carter [in his *Howells and the Age of Realism*]. But as I have attempted to demonstrate, even Harte's inferior works include seminal elements for better fiction. When Bret Harte, portraying a small town in the wake of the Gold Rush, commented that the teacher who came to "Riches are deceitful" in a pupil's copybook elaborated the noun "with an insincerity of flourish that was quite in the spirit of his text," Harte knew a good deal about Hadleyburg. And when Harte's popular stories exhibited the effects of close observation and detailed reporting of a particular region, with all his romanticism, Harte was encouraging narrative techniques that led to realism.

Instead of attributing to Bret Harte a "flair for plagiarism," it seems more just to accord him a respected place in America's literary history because his techniques and his ideas stimulated the development of superior techniques and the expression of more profound thought. (pp. 330-32)

Margaret Duckett, "The Question of Influence," in her *Mark Twain and Bret Harte,* University of Oklahoma Press, 1964, pp. 312-32.

J. R. BOGGAN   (essay date 1967)

[*In the following excerpt, Boggan questions the standard Christian reading of "The Luck of Roaring Camp," finding its use of Christian symbolism essentially ironic.*]

Bret Harte tells us that when, despite the warnings, the protests, of both his printer and publisher, he went ahead and published **"The Luck of Roaring Camp,"** with its abandoned, outcast mother (the prostitute Cherokee Sal) and its innocently realistic language (that of his 1850 California miners), he was denounced by conservative and conventional reviewers as being either "improper" and "corrupting" or "singular" and "strange."

That Harte considered these criticisms provincial is obvious, for he goes on to speak of the "secret" of the American short story which is, in part, he says, to treat "characteristic American life . . . with no more moral determination except that which may be the legitimate outcome of the story itself. . . ."

And yet for us to decide just what the moral outcome of Harte's position is in **"The Luck of Roaring Camp"** is certainly more of a complicated matter than many may have sentimentally thought. Is it true, for instance, as one reader has recently stated [Roy R. Male, *Types of Short Fiction*], that Harte is taking no position at all here, is being involved with "nothing in particular—except telling an entertaining story"? Or is it true, as other readers have suggested [see Brooks, Warren, and Purser excerpt dated 1936], that Harte fails here in his attempt to write a realistic local color tale—fails because he falsifies his story treatment in order to force the reader into an emotional acceptance of Christian regeneration and redemption? Or is it true, as at least one other reader has argued—a reader who rightly recognizes that the story is primarily symbolic rather than realistic [see Brown excerpt dated 1960]—that Harte, having perhaps charmed a number of early readers with his "religious teaching," is undeniably taking a Christian point of view, and that, in order to understand this, one has only to consider "the multitude of Christian symbols" therein?

That there are, of course, a number of Christian allusions and Biblical echoes in the story is plain to see. Obviously, for example, the child born of Cherokee Sal at the beginning is, in one sense, the Christ child, the Saviour. Needing a foster father, he is born, if not in a manger, in a rude cabin, and if he does not receive the most valuable gifts of the Wise Men he does receive the most valuable gifts of the men of Roaring Camp. Moreover, in supposedly regenerating these men, he comes to be worshipped by them, and in dying in the flood at the story's end he can, at least in the person of Kentuck, inspire man's faith in the hereafter.

Having granted this obvious parallel, however, I intend in this essay to show that the ironic voice that tells us the story and intrudes to comment freely if somewhat ambiguously on the happenings in Roaring Camp is really *not* the voice of a Christian believer and that, despite the coming of little Luck, the men of Roaring Camp are *not* really regenerated. (pp. 271-72)

That the storyteller seems to be committed to Christianity, but is not, might be inferred again and again. Consider, for example, the following complementary passages:

The camp lay in a triangular valley between two hills and a river. The only outlet was a steep trail over the summit of a hill that faced the cabin, now illuminated by the rising moon. The suffering woman might have seen it from the rude bunk whereon she lay—seen it winding like a silver thread until it was lost in the stars above . . . for whether owing to the rude surgery of the camp, or some other reason, Cherokee Sal was sinking fast. Within an hour she had climbed, as it were, that rugged road that led to the stars, and so passed out of Roaring Camp, its sin and shame, forever.

The only way out of this small "city of refuge" (though not that kind of city unfortunately for Cherokee Sal lying in her rude cabin on the outer edge of the clearing, as much an outcast here as she might well have been in any society anywhere), the only way out for one living in Roaring Camp—or nearby Red Dog, or anywhere else in California, or the West, or the world—is the difficult, winding climb of life to the "summit" (if such it be) of death. The trail winds, one might say, like a "silver thread"—or an umbilical cord—to death. Dying there in her bunk, Sal "might" have looked at the sky, might have followed the trail until it was "lost in the stars"—lost, as we know, because the trail that goes down over the hill never really gets to the heavenly stars in the first place.

In a manner of speaking, then, Cherokee Sal, "sinking fast," paradoxically climbed "that rugged road . . . and so passed out of Roaring Camp, its sin and shame forever." Roaring Camp, then, having lost its outcast "very sinful woman," was left with its own sin and shame—perhaps its sense of the wrong its men had done her. In any event, the birth of the child was something the very nature of the men were ready and waiting for. There had been too many worthless killings; this was something "novel" to engage their attention, to excite their curiosity, to bet on. One could see very early, perhaps that these men might be willing to gamble their all. The congregation outside Sal's rude cabin rose to their feet as one man before the sharp cry of their god-child, while inside his candle-box the swathed infant lay, awaiting the "procession," the offertory of the Camp's collective conscience to begin.

Later, when it comes time for the christening ceremony (the life-giving waters, the sacrament of Baptism) Stumpy proclaims the child "Thomas Luck"—so help him God. Whether, of course, God does help Stumpy or whether that "helpless bundle" of Luck does ever go back on Stumpy are questions for the future. Right now it's enough to say that the men have been transformed from doubting Thomases into doting disciples and that Tommy was christened "as seriously as he would have been under a Christian roof, and [not that perhaps it did much good] cried and was comforted in an orthodox manner."

No sooner, though, had the men become regenerated, no sooner had they begun worshipping their child-god, idolizing him, giving him whatever little attentions they could, than there came to them, "forewarned" (as much as Noah ever was) by Red Dog under water, the unexpected deluge. Stumpy, eager for the water to put more gold into the gulches, loses his cabin and the tabernacle of his life, and Luck dies in the arms of his undying believer, Kentuck.

A smile lit the eyes of the expiring Kentuck. "Dying!" he repeated. "He's a-takin' me with him. Tell the boys I've got the Luck with me now''; and the strong man, clinging to the frail babe as a drowning man is said to cling to a straw, drifted away into the shadowy river that flows forever into the unknown sea.

Again Harte suggests the conventional idea of a Heaven but does not commit himself to it. Just as, before, Cherokee Sal was "sinking fast," so now is a man drowning; just as, before, Cherokee Sal "passed out" of Roaring Camp, perhaps to follow a trail that was "lost in the stars," so now a man drifts away "into the shadowy river that flows forever into the unknown sea." For all we know, Cherokee Sal in her most secret moments might yet have been a believer; the regenerated Kentuck, we know, is. In terms of the analogy chosen by the narrator, however, the "frail babe" is of no more help to the dying man than a piece of straw. Of course, that's with regard to continuing his life in this world. As for the heavenly life to come (up out of the "unknown sea"), that's another matter.

Perhaps we're to infer that that flood isn't so destructive after all? Perhaps the same God who justly destroyed the wicked in Noah's time now justly rewards the good? Perhaps the baptismal waters, having been sprinkled over the Luck, now splash over his disciples? And yet we have no more reason to think that from evil (Eve, Cherokee Sal experiencing the "primal curse") comes good (the new Adam, the little child that shall lead them) than from good (the infant innocence of Luck) comes evil (the destroying flood). Just because the men of Roaring Camp—for various reasons: to ease a guilty conscience, to find relief from boredom, to seek excitement in a different kind of gamble, to experience paternal love for their flesh-and-blood child—feel the need to adopt themselves to this god of a candle-box, does it necessarily follow that this helpless little bundle, hanging on with a cry of pain to Kentuck's finger, is going to grow up tomorrow to be their protector-saviour? Moreover, if, as the storyteller seems to infer, Christ failed in his attempt to regenerate man, is that any reason to suppose that this infant child will do any better? Luck is the child of a reckless gambling man, and his name, after all, is not that of the supposed far-seeing Christ child but, rather just the opposite, that of blind Chance.

Of course, the child of luck cannot be compared exclusively with the Christ child. In fact, he need not be thought of as a child of organized religion at all. He need not be thought of, for instance, as those in the nearby society of Red Dog think of him—as some superstitious North American Injun god. He need not be thought of, though he is taken down and put beside the gold gulch, as Mammon, god of the riches of this world. He need not be thought of, there in his bower—"serenely happy, albeit there was an infantine gravity about him, a contemplative light in his round gray eyes"—as the Buddha who achieved his enlightenment under the bo tree. He need not be thought of as a Hindu holy man, practicing yoga though, as the narrator ironically says, "it is recorded" that he dropped over a bank "on his head in the soft earth, and remained with his mottled legs in the air in that position for at least five minutes with unflinching gravity."

Indeed, the whole upside-down point of all this is that Tommy Luck need not be thought of as representing any one of these religions, Christian or otherwise. To the storyteller one is no more superstitious, lucky or unlucky, than another since all are unbelievable. "I hesitate to record," he says, with mock concern, "the many other instances of his [Luck's] sagacity,

which rest, unfortunately, upon the statements of prejudiced friends. Some of them were not without a tinge of superstition." Indeed—though maybe, like Saint Francis, little Luck can talk with the birds: "... and dern my skin," says the unconsciously irreverent Kentuck, "if he wasn't a-talkin' to a jaybird as was a-sittin' on his lap ... [them] a jawin' at each other just like two cherrybums."

Although it may not have seemed that way to us at first, we can now begin to see, perhaps, that the child of luck is surely as much the pagan child of Nature as he is the Christ child. On the day of the christening, the "procession ... marched to the grove with music and banners," and the child was "deposited before a mock altar." Later, the men fix him up a "bower" and decorate it "with flowers and sweet-smelling shrubs" and such beautiful minerals as mica and quartz. The woods and hillsides yield treasures which, if they would not do for all high priests, "would do for Tommy." He was surrounded "by playthings such as never child out of fairyland had before"—which is not to say, of course, that he, or, for that matter, the Christ of the Magi, *was* a child out of fairyland—he might not have been.

Was it a myth, like many another, that "Nature took the fondling to her broader breast," that in that "rare atmosphere" some "subtle chemistry ... transmuted ass's milk to lime and phosphorous"? "Strange to say" was it, that "the child thrived"? That "Jinny," the ass, could successfully nurse the Luck, says the storyteller, "was no less problematical" than that Romulus and Remus could be suckled by a she-wolf (and, he might have added, that Romulus could build up Rome and be made divine). In other words, Harte implies that, if the reader doesn't believe that little Luck could have survived under such maternal conditions, then he can't very well believe in the literal reality of any myth, pagan or Christian. Or, to put it another way, *is* the reader to believe in the literal reality of the story? Is he to read **"The Luck of Roaring Camp"** as a realistic (and consequently a sentimental) local color tale of the West? "Strange," indeed, that the child "thrived," for, if, on the day of his birth, all Nature seemed to stop in awe to listen to his cry, if for him "she would let slip between the leaves golden shafts of sunlight that fell just within his grasp," if for him she sent "wandering breezes," so, too, was it for him she sent the roaring flood. The pathetic fallacy is that one could believe blind, indifferent Nature to be benevolent.

Repeatedly, then, it seems to me that Harte in no way commits himself to the idea that life, this one or the supposed hereafter, is worth looking forward to. Consider, for example, the deliberate juxtaposition of the dead Cherokee Sal (lying in her cabin under the blankets, on a shelf, waiting to be "committed to the hillside") with her new-born infant, "the d—d little cuss," the "last arrival at Roaring Camp" (lying in his box, swathed in "staring red flannel"). Thus, after several exhausted hours, in which the "sharp, querulous cry" of the child is heard, Stumpy, during the gift-giving ceremonies, is shown to be maintaining "a silence as impassive as the dead on his left, a gravity as inscrutable as that of the newly born on his right." Then, as Kentuck bends over the candle-box, the child turns and "in a spasm of pain" catches hold of his finger, much as if he wants now, in this life, the same kind of help that Kentuck, holding on to the helpless drowned babe, will want later, in the next.

In might be argued that, because the men's eyes have been "cleared and strengthened" to the beauties of Nature, to the mica and quartz, for example, that had heretofore been thought "trifles," a sense of the beautiful comes to those who worship. It might also be argued that, because the men embrace religion, they become better and so learn to love not only the Luck but their neighbor. But that Nature has beautiful things for an observer to see, that the one and only world we know yields up more treasures than ever "child out of fairyland had before," is scarcely proof that a hereafter exists or that the storyteller thinks it does. And though Stumpy the lounger accepts the responsibility of staying up all night in Sal's cabin, and though Kentuck, finger held high, repeats again and again his embarrassing refrain, is that any sign that either of them are better men than they were before? Stumpy, after all, wants religiously to be the proprietor of an office, while Kentuck, in the carelessness of his large nature, shows no more sentiment than what, presumably, he's felt all along.

If, however, Kentuck is a believer, perhaps we can infer that Tommy Luck, like the dying Christ, has worked his regeneration, has left his disciples, his myth, behind him? And yet, just as some unsentimental people may argue that the world today is little better for having had Christ or his religion in it, so Harte may argue that the men of Roaring Camp are little better for having had Luck and having worshipped him. If, in other words, the Camp felt it had to isolate itself from, say, the strangers in Red Dog in order for its men to be "saved," this need not suggest that the Luck had a divine mission but only that all men are dying.

The first "spasm of propriety" (coming the day after "the spasm of pain" felt by the infant child) was "the first symptom of the camp's regeneration." This sudden, temporary contraction into decency—as if such a thing were purely involuntary, not to be helped—was accounted for only by a harsh "unkind allusion" to the defunct Cherokee Sal, namely, that Roaring Camp, so one man speaking for the rest had said, didn't want any more of her kind. And in such communities as Roaring Camp "good and bad actions are catching," says the narrator, as if, either way, he were talking of a disease. Thus when that first man in line enters—(what?)—the makeshift funeral parlor of Sal's rude cabin to see her lying starkly outlined under a sheet—or the lying-in hospital of her no longer used brothel to pay curious homage to her infant child—when that first man enters with his hat on, he uncovers himself and so "unconsciously" sets an example for the next man. But whether this action is good or bad depends solely on whether the majority in the society approves of such a custom as, say, a man (though not a woman) taking off his hat before going into a church, or Kentuck showing openly his unmanly sentiment for "the d—d little cuss," or on whether a man can forget himself for a moment and show himself touched by a woman's sufferings, or on whether a man can read his Bible in peace.

Consequently, if, despite their physical imperfections, the "aggregate force" of Roaring Camp, or of any other place, approve of one god over another, it is wise for one, unless he intends to become an outcast and consequently an evil person, "to bow to the majority"—much as Stumpy was "wise enough" to do when the crowd appointed him "extempore surgeon and midwife" to Sal (with the result, incidentally, that he soon won society's reward, could with priestly "authority and *ex-officio* complacency" suggest the hat be passed, as it were, for an acceptable offering). Right from the beginning, then, the Roaring Camp that smoked its pipe and literally awaited "the issue" was the Camp that rose as one man, as one congregation, to later fiercely put down Sandy Tipton's individual

notion that they should send the infant to Red Dog "where female attention could be procured."

> "Besides," said Tom Ryder, "them fellows at Red Dog would swap it, and ring in somebody else on us." A disbelief in the honesty of other camps prevailed at Roaring Camp, as in other places.

And so, despite the distrust that remained to follow that first "spasm of propriety," the "work of regeneration began in Roaring Camp." Now many of these rehabilitated, spiritually reborn men got into the habit of "lounging in at Stumpy's," and this forced the rival establishment of "Tuttle's grocery" to import the kind of carpet and mirrors one might find in a rehabilitated saloon. Moreover, now that these people who, before, had been against a show of sentiment even when some of them felt it, were taking a good look at themselves, "the appearance of Roaring Camp tended to produce stricter habits of personal cleanliness. Thus Kentuck, though in the carelessness of his large nature being anything but prudish, had quickly to slough off his decaying, snake's-skin-like garments for "certain prudential reasons." That is, he, too, was wise enough to bow to the majority, to the "subtle influence of innovation," and to begin to appear regularly at the Luck's "in a clean shirt," his face "still shining from his ablutions."

But although "moral and social sanitary laws" were put into effect, how much really had the men changed for the good? Before, they had a "natural levity," now they smoke with "Indian gravity." Before, when their luck wasn't so good, they would habitually say, "D—n the luck!" and "Curse the luck!" Now, when the luck is with them, they don't say that anymore. Before, the men drank, now their eyes are "cleared and strengthened," now they sit around "drinking in the melodious utterances," the lugubrious lullaby of "Man-o'-War Jack," who has so decked out the exploits of the "*Arethusa,* Seventy-Four" (into ninety would-be comforting stanzas, each ending with a prolonged dying fall) that, as the infant Luck is about to close his eyes, the men are looking happily ahead to the future. "An indistinct idea that this was pastoral happiness pervaded the camp. 'This 'ere kind o' think . . . is 'evingly'," said the Cockney Simmons. Of course (since gods and heavens are as persistently changeable over the years as the here and there emergent waters of the Arethusa or the rise and fall of the stanzas about the exploits of the ship that bears its name), one thinking man's pipe dream of a heaven on earth is apt to be different from another's; Simmons was reminded, as we, in a different time and place might not be, of Greenwich.

If, then, the men were content, "it is to be hoped that Tommy was." At any event, this was "the golden summer" of Roaring Camp. And yet, because their "claims had yielded enormously," because the Luck was with them, the Camp "was jealous of its privileges and looked suspiciously on strangers. Possessively the men begin to preempt the land around them, and, instead of giving encouragement to immigration (aside from the eminently respectable idea of inviting one or two "decent" families to "reside" with them), attain a "proficiency with the revolver." The "reserve" of Roaring Camp is thus kept "inviolate," is no longer the uncivilized "city of refuge" it was before—not by a long shot.

Thus, whether the Luck was not content after all and so did go back on Stumpy, or whether Stumpy himself was too concerned about the flood waters putting more gold into the gulches and so got more than he bargained for, the logical outcome of the story is that, like the good citizens of Harte's well-known Poker Flat (experiencing, at the expense of the outcasts, "a spasm of virtuous reaction, quite as lawless and ungovernable as any one of the acts that provoked it"), the men of Roaring Camp are no more regenerated, no more spiritually reborn, than is the Christ child in the person of little Luck. (pp. 273-80)

J. R. Boggan, "The Regeneration of 'Roaring Camp'," in Nineteenth-Century Fiction, Vol. 22, No. 3, December, 1967, pp. 271-80.

DONALD E. GLOVER (essay date 1973)

[Glover is an American educator and critic. In the following excerpt, he argues that Harte experimented in his later work with new themes, more realistic treatment of setting and character, and greater emotional restraint.]

Harte's career conveniently falls into two major periods: the brief, glittering success of 1868-1872, and the long exile in England from 1880 to his death in 1902. These periods reveal the basic dichotomy and paradox which control his art and the critical response to his work as a whole. The majority of critics suggest that the important period in Harte's life and work ends with the production of "The Outcasts of Poker Flat" in 1869. His later career is tantalizing for the mystery surrounding his twenty year separation from his wife and his relationship with Mme. Van de Velde, but the scores of short stories that constitute his later works are traditionally thought of as sad and negligible repetitions of an earlier style and themes.

However, it was after 1878 that Harte won at least partial acceptance of his own image, the image of a Victorian man of taste who happened to have been "out West." This image led him on an Easterly course from the crude response in San Francisco to the brief plaudits of New York, and finally to acceptance in London—Mecca for American writers of that day. Harte was an expatriate more by necessity than by real inclination or choice, but like all artistic expatriates, he was looking for an audience which would appreciate his writing and flatter his artist's ego. In England, he met Hardy and George Eliot. He was the frequent guest of the Duke of Northampton; Sullivan asked for a libretto; the Prince of Wales requested an introduction. Harte even had the temerity to criticize Henry James, whom he had just met, for being "un-American."

Met Henry James, Jr. the American novelist, who is creating quite a reputation here. He looks, acts, and thinks like an Englishman, I am sorry to say, excellent as his style is. I wish he had more of an American flavor.

Public and private interest was such that Harte was asked to lecture at Oxford and to present the "Response" to the Royal Academy Toast to Literature; magazines deluged his agent with requests for stories.

Feeling successful in Europe, for the first time Harte stopped writing about California, choosing German ("The Legend of Saamtstadt") and later Scottish locales (the "St. Kentigern" stories narrated by an urbane consul) drawn from his experiences in Crefeld and Glasgow. More secure financially, and approved by his audience as something more than a local phenomenon, he wrote what he wanted: a disastrous series of plays (The Luck of Roaring Camp and Thankful Blossom, both in 1882) adapted from earlier successful stories. Here we see the paradox in his career. Although contemporary criticism in En-

gland showed that Harte was fully appreciated for his skill as a technician and wit, the English reader clearly wanted only local color stories dealing with the romantic Gold Rush era. The irony of Harte's dilemma now becomes apparent. The conflict is no longer between his own view of himself as artist and an unappreciative audience, but between his desire to escape the old materials and his English reader's insistence that he continue with stereotyped California materials. By 1890, the strain shows through in a letter to Mrs. Florence Henniker, daughter of Lord Houghton and Harte's literary protégé.

You are quite right; I have been "working hard" lately, but I fear that the "numbness at the back of the head" will be reserved for my readers. My writing lately has revealed to me hitherto unknown depths of weariness and stupidity! (Harte's italics)

He tried to escape the boredom by writing more plays (unsuccessful); by experimenting with various themes, such as racial prejudice and the social outcast; and by completing the libretto for an opera, The Lord of Fontenelle, which was set to music by Emanuel Moōr, but left unperformed. Harte frequently escaped from London to the country estates of friends like James Anthony Froude or Geraldine Webb and even made one trip to Switzerland. But sheer financial necessity forced him to write for the only audience who would pay—the very sort of story which he undoubtedly wrote best and which American critics now thought him incapable of writing because of his distance from the source of inspiration.

What then of the later work, by far the bulk of his creative output? A study of these stories uncovers several factors that help put the total work in critical perspective. First, Harte continued to follow the pattern established in the early work: use of local color materials (now German, Scottish, English, and Californian), humor-tempering sentiment, melodramatic endings, simple characters and plot lines. Second, the development of his later writing was dictated by the reaction of his audience. During the period 1882-1885, he wrote for both American and English readers. By the late 1880's, he had turned, through financial necessity, almost entirely to an English public. The late stories clearly reflect the reactions of his readers and their effect on any innovations in technique and theme which he attempted. Third, between 1882 and 1902, Harte experimented with many other story types using appropriately developed styles. He returned to the theme of social criticism, especially attacking prejudice against minority groups in stories presented with increasing realism; he attempted international stories along the lines of James and Howells; he used a new, urbane tone with the consular narrator of the St. Kentigern stories. Each experiment met opposition from his readers and their continued demand for the favorite California Gold Rush story. Finally, forced by his financial dependence on a receptive audience, Harte adjusted his style and technique to produce highly colored, melodramatic stories combining humour, sentiment, and pathos with a strong dash of not always factually accurate local color.

The process of adapting his style to the demands of an English audience was a slow one for Harte, and one he frequently rebelled against, but it was this adaptation which brought into being a quite different kind of western story from that which he had produced in America in the 1870's. By observing selected works from the later period, we can recognize the process of change and its end product.

"**In the Carquinez Woods**" (1882) best serves as the example of Harte's indecision about his audience and his treatment of materials as he began adjusting to new demands from an English audience. The English magazine reader was, like his American counterpart ten years earlier, receptive to the glamour of the Golden West, but as Boynton points out, "So far as it [the reading public] was English, it had a pretty vague notion of the veracity of his replicas of the early California sketches."

As his first work commissioned by a major magazine in two years, "**In the Carquinez Woods**" represents an active return to magazine writing after the failure of the dramatic adaptation of "**The Luck of Roaring Camp**," a production on which Harte had mistakenly placed high expectations. Critical reception of "**In the Carquinez Woods**" was mixed; most critics praised scene depiction and plotting, while the *Spectator* disliked its lack of moral force. The *Spectator* review, however, notes the appeal of "novel scene" and "novel states of society," personified by the hero, the half-breed Indian botanist Low, and the half-breed Mexican gypsy, Teresa.

The plot of this romance is incredible. L'eau Dormant, popularly known as Low Dorman, lives in a hollowed-out redwood tree. He saves the runaway Teresa from jail by stabbing her lover. They set up housekeeping in the tree. Low's ex-sweetheart, Nellie Wynn, frivolous daughter of the bigoted local minister, plays with the affections of Teresa's former lover, Sheriff Dunn—who in turn is Low's unknown father. In the *dénouement* of this intricate plot, a cataclysmic forest fire conveniently burns Low and Teresa to death.

Unlike the earlier stories, "**Carquinez Woods**" was conceived on a grand scale, appearing in four weighty installments. Long sections are devoted to developing the grandeur of the local setting, which critics are quick to point out is inaccurately portrayed as a redwood forest rather than the grassy plain it is in fact. These "slips" give presumed further evidence of Harte's fading memory. The description, however, clearly shows Harte manipulating his memories and materials for an effect to be produced on an audience unfamiliar with the actual geography of California.

The characters and plot, as well as setting of "**Carquinez Woods**" are intensified. Such characters are uncommon even in the context of "**The Outcasts of Poker Flat**" or "**The Luck**," where local color figures are set against an indigenous background. In England, removed from the demands for local realism, Harte places his highly exaggerated characters before a vivid backdrop. The major characters are least credible; at times they are noble savages living in a pastoral setting. But they swiftly become merely savages living in a tree. As sensational personalities, however, they were eminently successful with English readers.

Although this story touches on the theme of social ostracism, one which appears throughout Harte's work and perhaps relates to his own father's position as the unrecognized son of a wealthy Jew, social inequality here is hidden by a sensational overlay of sentimental love and intrigue. It is quite unlike Harte's harsh and stark treatment of the same theme in "**Three Vagabonds of Trinidad**" (1900).

"**Maruja**"(1885) marks Harte's commitment to a new audience. Although he had used California-Mexican and Spanish materials earlier, he had never used these materials extensively, nor used a woman of aristocratic Spanish background as the heroine in such an extended plot. The intricacy and length of the plot required certain changes in Harte's technique.

He arouses interest by using a legendary curse, a picturesque heroine (based on Majendra Atherton, a woman known by the Hartes), a down-trodden hero, and an insane villain. The sensationalism of plot, with its dramatic encounters between father and abandoned son, its violent deaths, and its passionate love scenes, contributes to what the *Athenaeum* called a "quite new picture of old Spanish life." Harte manages to use the unwieldy materials well, combining them into fast-moving melodrama. The characters, however, remain stiff and inconsistent, Maruja, for example, shifting abruptly from heartless coquette to tender lover. There is less wrenching of coincidence for effect, although the chance meeting of West and his son strains credibility.

"**Maruja**" shows Harte moving a step away from the simple tales of the early seventies, from the integrated local color of setting, character, and action, toward the more artificial, albeit more dramatic, presentation of picturesque characters in a heightened California setting. Characters are more important and more fully developed, as seen in a comparison of Maruja and Teresa. Serial publication helped to enforce more rigid control of plot and suspense than in earlier, shorter works, and "**Maruja**" moves rapidly and smoothly to its conclusion with all the plot elements integrated.

Comparing Harte stories of the early seventies and mid-eighties, one sees that the tone of the early work, bordering on broad farce and sentimental melodrama, becomes more sophisticated as Harte's lovers move into polite society. Gone are the rude, grizzled miners and tawdry, golden-hearted prostitutes. A tone of refinement pervades all dialogue indicating both Harte's desire to meet his audience on their own level and his awareness of the success of the stories of his countrymen, Howells and James.

By 1889, with American criticism of his catering to English taste on the rise, Harte began, on commission, the first story in a trilogy: "**A Waif of the Plains**" (1889), "**Susy**" (1893), and "**Clarence**" (1895). This trilogy marks the high point of his later career. These three stories reveal a new sense of realism, a controlled use of coincidence and sentiment, and a fully developed grasp of effective dramatic scenes.

The major reviews of "**A Waif**" repeat the trans-Atlantic critical dichotomy. The *Nation* commented that the later work showed "aimless incompleteness." Strachey of the *Spectator* captured the essence of Harte's appeal to the typical English reader.

> In none of his previous work . . . has Bret Harte exhibited more powerfully his rare faculty of bringing a scene vividly before us, or more skillfully his delicate appreciation of character in old and young alike.

Taking his traditional outcast orphan as central figure, Harte convincingly depicts Clarence Brant as a sensitive and independent boy rejected by those on whom he has an honest claim. His youthful enthusiasm and discouragement, however reminiscent of Oliver Twist, are handled with more realism. The setting gives ample local color material; yet, Harte shows restraint by depicting only scenes integral to plot movement. Local setting is carefully used for dramatic and realistic effect, as in the children's early sighting of an Indian for the first time, and later in a child's realistic view of the bloody bodies of savagely massacred whites. There is less coincidental and sensational matter, and greater realism in descriptions of death without the usual pathos and sentimentality. There are faults with the inconsistent characters and incomplete ending, but clearly Harte has developed the technical skill of narration well beyond the level of "The Luck."

"Susy" added sub-themes of squatter's rights, problems of Spanish land grants, and Mexican superstitions, and "Clarence" incorporated the Civil War as background effectively. Taken together, they indicate that Harte was equipped to meet the demands of novel writing as he had not been in 1875. More interesting, however, is the new realistic treatment of setting and character, the interest in new themes, and the new emotional restraint which diminishes his usual sentimentality.

Harte attempted to return to Scottish material in "The Heir of the McHulishes" (1893), and "A Rose of Glenbogie" (1894). Once again, the critics rejected his bid for a new subject matter. And, compared with other stories of this period which have an American setting, the Scottish stories do seem flat and artificial. Harte's talent was for action and natural description, not for recording social dialogue. His works are invariably dullest when two characters are placed face to face in a drawing room and required to talk. His style is most effective where it deals with dramatic episodes, characters in action, the humor of situation or event, and broad, sweeping melodrama; all of which Hollywood took from his stories into the silent Western movie and then into our era via television.

Although Harte continued to use the themes of social injustice and racial prejudice, and experimented with combinations of old and new material, only two stories during the last nine years of his career, "An Ingénue of the Sierras" (1893), and "Dick Boyle's Business Card" (1899), stand out as significant in this discussion. In "Ingénue," Harte resurrected Yuba Bill, the irrepressible stage driver of the early stories. The dialect and humor are perfect as the plot moves to a surprise ending of O. Henry smoothness. There are no improbable actions forced upon the reader, who enjoys Bill's silent consternation as he slowly realizes that the ingénue he has been duped into helping is in fact a "she-devil." Harte united character with plot using local color only as a necessary background. Unlike his earlier successes, there is no hint of sentimentality; humor and irony remain the central focus.

"Dick Boyle's Business Card" stands at the end of Harte's career as evidence of the considerable achievement of his mature style. A traveling salesman rides with an Army Commandant's daughter, who is secretly conveying needed arms to a nearby fort. Indians attack while the soon-to-be lovers fall behind the wagon in conversation, and the hero kills an Indian and of course wins the lady. The story succeeds because Harte keeps tight rein on the emotional element. The narrative shifts deftly from the lovers to the Indian attack. The characters and situations are credible. Harte infuses the story with realism and humor and escapes the usual sentimental clichés of his earlier love stories.

We are left with essentially two views of Harte's later writing. One suggests that, ". . . he lived quietly in London, an overworked hack, scraping the bottom of the California barrel to turn his thousand words a day. . . ." The other states,

> California was all the subject he ever needed rather than the only subject he could think of, and the limitations of his accomplishment are rather those of his art than of the opportunities of his material. . . . His range was small, his heights and depths neither lofty nor profound,

his mind not richly stocked with intellectual goods. But he has not been surpassed in what he did best. This is enough to guarantee his permanent place in American letters.

I prefer the second view. It avoids the pitfalls of the "native writer-spontaneous creation" trap and does justice to Harte fairly on his own ground. Early critics overestimated Harte as a literary artist who displayed great originality, sensitivity, and descriptive genius in his early stories, and whose later years were a tragic descent into despair, penury, and hackwork.

Perhaps his English readers assessed him more nearly at his real level. For them, he was not primarily a nationalistic writer; he was a *raconteur*. His fame rested neither on his personality nor on his anticipated novel. In England, free from the constricting demands for accurate local description, he allowed his inclination to bend realistic local color for the purpose of excellent story telling. (pp. 143-51)

> *Donald E. Glover, "A Reconsideration of Bret Harte's Later Work," in* Western American Literature, *Vol. VIII, No. 3, Fall, 1973, pp. 143-51.*

CHARLES E. MAY   (essay date (1977))

[*May is an American educator, editor, and critic. In the following excerpt, he challenges the standard reading of "Tennessee's Partner" as a sentimental story, contending that the sentimentality in the story is ironic and serves to disguise its theme of revenge.*]

Every student of American literature knows that Bret Harte wrote banal and sentimental short stories. The only point of debate seems to be which of his best-known sketches—"The Luck of Roaring Camp," "The Outcasts of Poker Flat," or "Tennessee's Partner"—is the most banal and sentimental. Since 1870, indiscriminate readers have wept over the death scene of Kentuck with the "cold and pulseless" babe in his arms, have softened at the sacrifice of Mother Shipton for Piney Woods, and have marveled at the forgiveness that passes all understanding of Tennessee's Partner. T. Edgar Pemberton, an early Harte admirer, has asked of "Tennessee's Partner": "Will anyone with the soul to understand it ever forget the exquisite pathos of the ending of that beautiful story?" Of those more critical readers who might answer his question with a disgusted and superior snort, Pemberton says, "Such people will always exist, and, most happily for humanity, Bret Harte does not appeal to them, but to the 'great heart of the nation'."

Thirty years later in his career, after all the excitement of the epoch-making volume, *The Luck of Roaring Camp and Other Sketches,* had died down, Harte himself felt that he had not only spoken to the great heart of the nation, but he had also spoken of the habits of mind of its people. Although humbly denying that he had originated the short story in America, he was quite willing to accept credit for helping establish the "American short story." Poe and Hawthorne had written short stories, Harte says in his 1899 essay in the *Cornhill Magazine,* but they had not written stories "characteristic of American life, American habits nor American thought."

And, indeed, serious scholars of American fiction have conceded that Harte's influence has been considerable. Arthur Hobson Quinn has said that Harte taught nearly every American writer of short stories some of the essentials of his art. And Fred Lewis Pattee places him second only to Washington Irving in his influence on the form [see *TCLC,* vol. 1]. Although Quinn admires Harte, especially for his "realistic . . . probing beneath the surface for the more profound causes of human conduct,'' while Pattee has reservations about Harte's work being more "extravaganza" than truth, both realize that Harte's most important saving grace was a sense of humor. Pattee says that without it, Harte would have been as sentimentally extreme as Dickens, his master; Quinn says that his sense of humor "preserved in him that sense of proportion which was one of his great gifts to the development of the short story." Harte would have been happy to accept this as his major contribution, for in his *Cornhill* article he singles out humor as the factor which finally diminished the influence of English models on the short story in America:

> It was *Humour*—of a quality as distinct and original as the country and civilization in which it was developed. It was at first noticeable in the anecdote or "story," and after the fashion of such beginnings, was orally transmitted. It was common in the barrooms, the gatherings in the "country store," and finally at public meetings in the mouths of "stump orators."

Pattee has noted that in **"Tennessee's Partner,"** Harte records an important clue to his appeal—that in the gulches and barrooms of early California, "all sentiment was modified by a strong sense of humor." Without humor, Pattee observes, the funeral scene in **"Tennessee's Partner"** would have been "mere gush." Even then, however, he adds, the last paragraph is "mawkish sentimentality." Pattee is not the only one who has noted Harte's sense of humor, but not found it strong enough in **"Tennessee's Partner."** In fact, most critics, even those who have called it the best of all Harte's stories, say that its chief effect is not humor at all, but pathos. Henry Childs Merwin, in an early biography of Harte, says the story's pathos results from the fact that Tennessee was unworthy of his partner's devotion:

> Had Tennessee been a model of all the virtues, his partner's affection for him would have been a bestowal only of what was due. It would not have been, as it was in fact, the spontaneous outpouring of a generous and affectionate character.

Of course, it is just that "spontaneous outpouring" which has caused more cynical or more critical readers of Harte's story to reject it as psychologically invalid, unrealistic, and just plain incredible.

An interesting early cynical response to the story was reported a few years ago by Bradford A. Booth, who had access to the first edition of *The Luck of Roaring Camp and Other Sketches* from the library of one of America's most famous cynics: Mark Twain. Twain's annotations on the story focus on the central problem:

> But does the artist show a clear knowledge of human nature when he makes his hero *welcome back* a man who has committed against him that sin which neither the great nor the little ever forgive? & not only welcome him back but love him with the fondling love of a girl to the last, & *then* pine and die for the loss of him?

The problem has been stated in more detail since by those forerunners of a whole generation of close, critical readers— Cleanth Brooks and Robert Penn Warren [see excerpt dated 1943]. After asserting the usual theme of the story—"a man's intense loyalty to his friend"—Brooks and Warren proceed to question the credibility of many of Tennessee's Partner's actions. Would a man, they ask, who sees things in such concrete terms that he has no concept of abstract judicial law forgive Tennessee for stealing his wife? Would a man who felt that the townspeople had hanged his friend for "no good reason" actually invite them to the funeral and thank them for their trouble? Brooks and Warren's most serious question, however, is the most damaging one to Harte: "Has not Bret Harte taken a theme, which, perhaps he had seen successfully employed for pathetic effects in other fiction . . . without ever grounding the story in a presentation of the real psychological issues involved—without, in other words, trying to understand his main character?" A serious charge, indeed, and one that perhaps needs more careful examination. Perhaps it is the critics who have not understood.

Brooks and Warren base their judgment on the fact that Harte dodges the psychological problem of the reconciliation between the two partners by failing to bring into focus and make believable the wife-stealing episode. This episode, which Brooks and Warren say is one of the important psychological steps by which Tennessee's partner arrives at his subsequent actions, is simply not made credible. As a result the whole story loses its point. Of course, that depends on what one takes the point of the story to be. But Brooks and Warren go on confidently to suggest the reasons why Harte fails:

> By skimping it and moving away from it toward the final effort at pathos, Bret Harte has made the whole story seem anticlimatic and illogical. Either he was so little interested in the psychology of the situation that he did not investigate it, or he was aware that the issues involved were too complicated for him to handle.

Although it is obvious that Brooks and Warren think the latter reason is true, the story itself supports the former one. But regardless of the reason, whether the skimping of the scene makes the story anticlimatic and illogical depends not so much on the critic's viewpoint as it does on the storyteller's point of view, for it is his moral perspective which should direct the reader's response to the story. And this story has a dramatically defined narrator with a voice and purpose of his own.

After relating how Tennessee's partner went to San Francisco for a wife and was stopped in Stockton by a young waitress who broke at least two plates of toast over his head, the narrator says that he is well aware that "something more might be made of this episode, but I prefer to tell it as it was current at Sandy Bar—in the gulches and barrooms—where all sentiment was modified by a strong sense of humor." It is from this point of view—sentiment modified by humor—that the narrator also tells the episode which Brooks and Warren criticize. The incident of Tennessee's running off with his partner's wife is related in the same flippant phrases and in the same intonation as that of Tennessee's partner's somewhat hazardous wooing. But more importantly, it is this barroom point of view which dominates the whole story. And once we are willing to accept it, the story takes on a new and not so pathetic dimension. The narrator fully intends for this story to be, not the occasion for tears, but for sardonic laughter.

The first clue to the ironic discrepancy in the story comes in the title and in the first line in which the narrator explains the title's significance: "I do not think we ever knew his real name.'' The narrator then devotes the first full paragraph to a discussion of men in Sandy Bar being christened anew with names indicative of some aspect of dress or character. This should not be taken as gratuitous local color; for the whole story centers around a man who *seems* to have no character except in relation to his devotion to his partner, and who *seems* to have no name except a relative one.

The fact is, however, Tennessee's partner does have another name, a name that, from the barroom point of view, indicates his real character in the story. In the crucial courtroom scene, after Tennessee's partner has unsuccessfully tried to bribe the judge and jury, Tennessee himself calls his partner by another name: "For the first time that evening the eyes of the prisoner and his strange advocate met. Tennessee smiled, showed his white teeth, and saying 'Euchred, old man!' held out his hand.'' Knowing that euchre is a card game and that the capture and trial of Tennessee has been described in the terminology of cards, and knowing that the verb form of the word ''euchre'' is a colloquial expression which originated in American English around 1845 and which means to get the better of someone by scheming, we begin to suspect that there is something more in this story than the straining for pathetic effect.

The name that Tennessee calls his partner is the past tense form of the verb ''euchre.'' That Tennessee's partner was not euchred is obvious. He was not beaten by scheming. Tennessee simply ran off with his wife. No, the euchred one in the story is Tennessee himself who has been beaten by his partner by quiet scheming and a poker face. In fact, it is probable that Tennessee himself gives his partner the name at that very moment during the trial because he has realized what his partner has done. This would not only explain Tennessee's understanding smile, but it would also explain his partner's nervous mopping of his face as he lets Tennessee's hand fall from his passively and withdraws without another word. The title of the story, had it been named after the true character of the central figure, might have been ''Euchred,'' but that, of course, would have given the game away. It is little wonder that Harte considered this one of his favorite stories, for in it his typical American humor of the barroom and country store has euchred readers for a century—even Mark Twain, who knew cards and storytellers well enough to know better.

Brooks and Warren are certainly correct when they say that Tennessee's partner is a man ''who evidently sees everything in very concrete and personal terms.'' When he loses his wife he takes it ''simply and seriously.'' When Tennessee returns from his escapade and all the boys who gather in the canyon are ''naturally indignant'' that there is no shooting, Tennessee's partner looks at them in such a way as to indicate ''a lack of humorous appreciation.'' In fact, the narrator gives us another clue here which should tip us off to the partner's potential for silent, yet deadly, revenge; for he is a ''grave man, with a steady application to practical detail which was unpleasant in a difficulty.'' Tennessee's partner's steady application to practical detail proves unpleasant indeed to Tennessee in his difficulty at the trial. For surely, the partner, in his serious and practical way, knows that his attempt to bribe the judge and jury will clinch the case against Tennessee, knows that it will be the final trump in the card game which began with Tennessee's capture. The narrator tells us that the insult of the bribe attempt on Judge Lynch—''who, whether bigoted, weak, or narrow, was at least incorruptible—firmly fixed in the mind of that mythical personage any wavering determination of Tennessee's fate.''

Further clues to the sardonic potential of the partner are suggested by the imagery with which the narrator describes him during the courtroom scene. When he enters the court, we note, with foreboding perhaps modified by humor, that his face is ''sunburned into a preternatural redness,'' his trousers are ''streaked and splashed with red soil,'' and he is mopping his face with a ''red bandana handkerchief, a shade lighter than his complexion.'' Before we are tempted to pass this off as gratuitous caricature, we should note that Tennessee's partner's preternatural redness is referred to again in the story after the funeral oration when the men look back and see him sitting on Tennessee's grave, ''his face buried in his red bandana handkerchief.'' This image of sorrow and pathos is ambiguously mixed with demonic humor, for ''it was argued by others that you couldn't tell his face from the handkerchief at that distance, and the point remained undecided.'' Is Tennessee's partner lost in grief, his face in his red bandana? Or is his face glowing with that preternatural redness of his sardonic revenge?

Additional elements of the sardonic humor in the story point the way to its real meaning. For example, not to be missed in that scene of the partner sitting on Tennessee's grave is the fact that the grave itself is in a rough enclosure, ''which in the brief days of Tennessee's partner's matrimonial felicity, had been used as a garden, but was now overgrown with fern.'' Harte makes use not only of colloquial expressions but colloquial pronunciation as well to indicate his satiric purpose. That the partner, when he comes to ask for the body, asks for the ''diseased,'' that he says, ''when the gentlemen were done with the 'diseased,' he would take him,'' is not to be ignored. For Tennessee has been a ''disease,'' not only to his partner, but to the body politic of Sandy Bar as well. Furthermore, the partner invites the men to the ''fun'l,'' and afterwards says, ''the fun'l's over; and my thanks, and Tennessee's thanks, to you for your trouble.'' The ''fun'' that is the funeral is a sardonic fun, indeed, more serious and more complicated than we at first imagine.

When Tennessee's partner invites the men to the funeral, the narrator says, ''Perhaps it was from a sense of humor, which I have already intimated was a feature of Sandy Bar—perhaps it was from something even better than that, but two thirds of the loungers accepted the invitation at once.'' That ''something better,'' which sentimental readers have always been willing to accept as an indication of sympathy and perhaps regret on the part of the men, might be seen instead as the final necessary act in the ritual of complicity between the partner and the town in their vigilante justice on Tennessee. The ''popular feeling'' which had grown up against Tennessee in Sandy Bar could end no other way. At the trial, the narrator makes it abundantly clear that Tennessee's fate was sealed, that the trial is only to justify ''the previous irregularities of arrest and indictment.'' The men have no doubt about his fate; they are ''secure in the hypothesis that he ought to be hanged on general principles.'' It is this very knowledge that they are going to hang Tennessee not so much for a concrete wrong as on general principles that makes them begin to waver until the partner, who has suffered a concrete wrong by Tennessee, enters the game with his attempted bribe. As a result of his taking a hand, the town helps Tennessee's partner avenge himself on Tennessee, and the partner helps the town get rid of a bothersome blight on the body politic. The complicity here between the serious, slow partner and the townspeople is similar to that between the slow-witted idiot and the town to rid themselves of an obnoxious practical joker in Ring Lardner's ''Haircut.''

One final problem remains to be dealt with—the pining away and dying of Tennessee's partner at the conclusion. It can be understood more clearly now that we know the true psychology of the main character. He is a serious and simple man, with a steady application to practical detail. As Brooks and Warren well note, he sees things in very concrete terms. He takes the loss of his wife quietly and seriously. He accepts Tennessee back in the same manner. In his simple and serious way, however, he knows he must avenge himself. This is not to say that he is not close to Tennessee; they have been partners for four years. After his scheming has achieved his purpose, he cannot escape his responsibility for Tennessee's death. As he says to the men at the funeral, "You see, it's sort of rough on his pardner." That he begins to fail in health and seems to pine away and die for the loss of Tennessee out of simple dog-like devotion would indeed be psychologically incredible. It is surely hard to believe, as it was for Mark Twain, that Tennessee's partner would die of "rampant adoration," but not so hard to believe he would die of grief-stricken guilt.

The economical use of detail in the story as well as its combination of sardonic humor and moral complexity is similar to Poe's masterpiece, "The Cask of Amontillado." In its use of a narrator who quietly and cleverly controls his satiric intent, it is surely as well done as Ring Lardner's "Haircut" or Mark Twain's "Celebrated Jumping Frog." One brief incident in the story, typical of those details which many readers have passed over as gratuitous, but which really reflect on the true purpose of the story, takes place on the way to the "fun'l": "Jack Folinsbee, who had at the outset played a funeral march in dumb show upon an imaginary trombone, desisted from a lack of sympathy and appreciation—not having, perhaps, your true humorist's capacity to be content with the enjoyment of his own fun." Bret Harte surely exhibits the "true humorist's capacity" in **"Tennessee's Partner."** Because of the lack of reader appreciation, he has had to be content with the enjoyment of his own fun for over a hundred years. (pp. 109-17)

Charles E. May, "Bret Harte's 'Tennessee's Partner': The Reader Euchred," in The South Dakota Review, *Vol. 15, No. 1, Spring, 1977, pp. 109-17.*

PATRICK D. MORROW (essay date 1979)

[*Morrow is an American educator and critic. Regarding his writings, Morrow has commented: "I consider myself primarily a critic—of life, culture, human relationships, and art. To me the primary function of criticism is explication and not attack. My ideal critic strives to make clear what is obscure, not to pass moral judgements from on high. I strive for the personal voice and vision that the shared experience of reader and writer under these terms makes all concerned better able to understand life and cope with it." In the following excerpt, Morrow discusses Harte's literary criticism, distinguishing the ideas and attitudes expressed in his critical writings from those in his fiction.*]

Harte's fiction is at least known, if not always well respected, through a handful of perennially anthologized pieces, but his literary criticism is virtually unrecognized. No standard work on American literary criticism even mentions Harte as a critic, and only two aspects of his critical career are at all widely known. Anthologies and handbooks frequently note that Harte was the editor of and book reviewer for the *Overland Monthly* (1868-1871). And, Harte is commonly chided for being one more Victorian too stuffy to appreciate the "barbaric yawp" of Walt Whitman. In 1870, editor Harte rejected Whitman's "Passage to India" as "a poem too long and too abstract,"

interestingly a view that Roy Harvey Pearce also holds in his highly acclaimed modern study, *The Continuity of American Poetry.*

In addition to numerous reviews, essays and prefaces, Harte wrote critical commentary in letters to a variety of people. He also wrote parodies of topical poems, **Condensed Novels,** and literary advice to aspiring novelists. Harte's parodies and **Condensed Novels,** satiric burlesques of popular writers including Poe, Longfellow, Hugo, Cooper, Dickens, and Reade, were such careful distortions of the originals that they constituted a dimension of literary criticism. An anonymous critic in the *North American Review* of April, 1866, considered Harte "a parodist of such genius that he seems a mirror into which novelists may look and be warned."

There are two diverse explanations that may account for the neglect of this body of literary criticism. First, *all* of Bret Harte's writings have been obscured because a dual stream of literary criticism has developed around him. Criticism of Harte is characterized by a pair of mutually antagonistic types—the amateur enthusiasts and the moral elitists. Both types of critics reduce Harte to mere caricature. The amateur enthusiast simply enjoys sentimentality, which Harte's writings contain in bountiful amounts. Dramatic chronicler of the Mother Lode, Harte moves the amateur enthusiast's powerful feelings to overflowing, for such a person sees Harte's local color as a kind of nationalism of region, making him a Booster with a gift for words. It is hard to take the amateur enthusiast very seriously though, because he wilts when faced with factual knowledge and rational observation. Actually, Harte was much more an Eastern Dude than a Western Rotarian. Previous to his *Overland* stories, Harte's references to miners, the Gold Rush, California in general, and even the sainted San Francisco in particular had been almost totally abusive. He had frequently lambasted the area for its earthquakes and foggy climate, and the people for their barbaric cultural depravity. Harte's experience in, and enthusiasm for the Gold Country was—to be generous—of a limited sort, as his **"How I Went to the Mines"** vividly and hilariously shows. If Harte came to write glowingly of California from being converted to new beliefs, then this should be considered a literary change, not the enthusiastic voice of experience. The amateur enthusiast may tell us much about his own interest in high-pitched drama and tourism, but he gives little insight concerning the complex writer that was Francis Bret Harte.

Conversely, elitist literary critics with ethical and financial investments in editing and explicating "The Great Works" could hardly have conjured anything better than Bret Harte, prototype of the minor author. His writing is usually devoid of paradox, ambiguity, and stylistic complexities, while filled with sentimentality and stereotyped characters, orchestrated in what Mark Twain intimated was a "mincing" style. Worse, Harte wrote volume upon volume for the frank purpose of making money, a veritable strip-mining of his long-gone fame and milieu. Where is that well-wrought novel of personal agony, the fiction of rage and outrage, however suppressed, or the testimony of a labyrinthine vision that would render him at least some redeeming moral value? Nowhere to be found. No wonder Bret Harte is often dismissed as "merely of historical interest" or "of secondary importance." Besides idolizing great writers, moral critics frequently attack "inferior" writers, and in making such clear distinctions they aim to establish *themselves* among the elite. Harte is a set-up for ready-made moral judgments in terms of his life (the money, women, and drinking scandals) and his writing (who *could* seriously rank Harte above Hawthorne, Faulkner, Melville, James, or even Howells?). Perhaps the most devastating single blow to Harte's reputation came with long-time friend Mark Twain's vicious, prolonged, and largely unsubstantiated personal and literary attacks, culminating in the posthumous volume *Mark Twain in Eruption*. So to the moral elitists, sometimes led by self-righteous Twainians, Harte is not worthy of serious study, and anyone who thinks he is, is suspect. Both the elitists and the enthusiasts have a deep commitment to their cause, and Harte serves as unwitting grist.

In addition, much of Harte's criticism—his "other side"—has been scattered, sometimes not even readily identifiable, in obscure California newspapers, defunct magazines, or rare books. Harte never gathered his critical theories, or ways of reading literature into a definitive essay; nor did he make an effort to collect his own criticism. Unlike such contemporaries as William Dean Howells or E. P. Whipple, Harte for most of his life was not an armchair critic, operating as the literary voice of an influential magazine. The expository criticism Harte wrote was typically occasional: book reviews, prefaces, essays on topical figures, or close readings of authors specifically contracted by journals. Harte established no new school in literary theory. While we can associate "beauty" with Poe, "realism" with Howells, "romance" with the early James, and "veritism" with Garland, no such term can be associated with Harte. "Local color," "satire," and "humor" describe Harte's fiction, but his criticism was not written from the vantage point (or precipice) of defending or demanding some particular critical ideal. Schooled in the tradition of journalism and little magazines, Harte was a practical critic. He searched for incompetence and affectation, and stressed a just analysis above judgment by taste.

Harte always thought of himself as a creative writer rather than a literary critic. Yet in letters spanning almost the length of his adult life, he demonstrated a penchant to estimate and evaluate literature, although he typically seemed embarrassed, even apologetic, for this "fault." A Harte letter in 1869 to William Dean Howells concluded a discussion of the latter's fiction by saying: "But what I meant to say before I fell into this attitude of criticism. . . ." Twenty-four years later, Harte wrote a long letter of critical comment to Mrs. Mary Boyd about novels, romances, and "real" characters, and then ended the letter with a highly self-conscious paragraph: "That's all! Please, Ma'am, may I go out and play now? I am very busy today and am dining out, or I should try to tell you all of this by word of mouth."

His contemporaries considered Harte not only a fine writer but a fine critic, and several important authors turned to him for help with their own writings. Ambrose Bierce, Henry George, Joaquin Miller, Prentice Mulford, Artemus Ward, Charles Warren Stoddard, Orpheus C. Kerr, and especially Mark Twain gathered around Harte for literary advice. According to Margaret Duckett, "The lively young writers on 'San Francisco's Literary Frontier' . . . acknowledged Harte as their leader and recognized in him an uncompromising critic of his own work as well as of the work of his companions." (pp. 7-10)

A writer most grateful for help from Harte was Mark Twain. Mark Twain once stated that Bret Harte "trimmed and trained and schooled me patiently until he changed me from an awkward utterer of coarse grotesquenesses to a writer of paragraphs and chapters that have found a certain favor in the eyes of even some of the very decentest people in the land." Sydney J.

Krause in *Mark Twain as Critic,* a book which scrupulously avoided overpraising Harte, felt that: "This was the highest tribute Twain paid Harte. In fact, on the matter of help, Twain paid no one as high a tribute, not even Howells. . . ." Harte's criticism also led to friction with Mark Twain. In a letter of November 26, 1870, Mark Twain explained to Charles Webb how Mark and Bret were now "off." But this same letter also mentioned Harte's part in helping to shape the enormous text of the "Quaker City Letters" into *The Innocents Abroad:*

> Harte read all the MS of the "Innocents" & told me what passages, paragraphs & chapters to leave out—& I followed orders strictly. It was a kind thing for Harte to do, & I think I appreciated it. He praised the book so highly that I wanted him to review it *early* for the *Overland,* & help the sale out there.

Besides acting as a strong influence on a number of important writers with whom he came in contact, Harte also in a sense "discovered" Mark Twain, the most important one. Harte's widely-read column in the *Springfield Republican* (1866) singled out Mark Twain's comic brilliance and brought "the Washoe Giant" to the Eastern readers' attention. With frequent mention of Mark Twain and his work in essays, lectures, and reviews, Harte helped establish him as the most important American humorist. Paul Fatout in *Mark Twain on the Lecture Circuit* stated that Harte recognized Mark Twain's greatness "a generation before many critics discovered that Mark Twain was more thoroughly American than Lowell or any other."

In his own time Harte gained considerable recognition as a critic for his reviews in the *Overland Monthly.* Many Eastern journals, including *Putnam's, Knickerbocker, The North American Review,* and even the *Atlantic,* praised the *Overland's* "Current Literature" section for its independent literary judgment and it became known to many as the most worthwhile part of the magazine. Harte's criticism continued to be in some demand throughout the rest of his life. In 1874 he prepared a lecture on **"American Humor"** and in 1882 wrote a long "Preface" to his first collected works. During the later English years he was asked to write critical pieces for publication by such magazines as the *New Review* and *Cornhill.* Although his popularity as a fiction writer far eclipsed his reputation as a critic, Harte continued to write criticism and to act as a literary advisor to several aspiring writers, particularly Mrs. Florence Henniker. In these later years, Harte became an important apologist for popular fiction and drama, writing on Dumas, Anthony Hope, Kipling, and others.

To understand Harte's literary criticism we must first understand something of his fiction, for the two are both interrelated and opposed in some important ways. In Harte's heyday of popularity, the early 1870's, many readers regarded his fiction as a whole new and strange world. Actually, Harte's strange new world was often nothing more than a new set and stage to dramatize the values of his East Coast reading public. Today, most critics believe that Bret Harte's fiction declined in quality as the author got older and farther removed in time and space from California. But this may be a misreading of Harte's work. In "A Reconsideration of Bret Harte's Later Work," Donald E. Glover makes the fascinating assertion, backed by illuminating analysis, that Harte's later stories are *qualitatively* very similar to his earlier ones [see excerpt dated 1973]. If this is true, Harte may not have been writing increasingly inferior art, but creating the same product for a changing audience, one that became increasingly less sophisticated. This could explain why in the 1870's Harte was publishing in the *Atlantic, Lippincott's,* and a handful of the most respected literary journals, but why in 1895 he was for the most part publishing in such slick and conservative illustrateds as *Weekly Graphic, Windsor Magazine, The Strand,* and *Cosmopolitan.* The sophisticated *literati* had moved on to new forms and ideas. Over a thirty-year period Harte's successful, essentially unchanged literary product increasingly appealed to those who wanted familiarity instead of discovery. It is perhaps not coincidental that in the last decade or so of his life Harte published numerous stories in magazines intended for children or adolescent girls.

At this point we need to make some distinctions between high or serious literature and formula fiction, realizing that these two exist on a continuum and are not two separate and mutually exclusive forms. Serious literature is usually considered to be the development and statement of a brilliant individual's consciousness delivered into artistry through great skill with words and mastery of form. Serious literature gives us a philosophical sense of the world, articulates new possibilities and perspectives, and often makes moral statements showing us the difference between good and evil, the genuine and the spurious. Typically, great writers tend to change, to mature and develop; witness Mark Twain, James and Faulkner. Formula writers tend to repeat the successful performance of a product; witness, to go outside literature, the portraits of Sir Joshua Reynolds or Lawrence Welk's homogenized arrangements of any song his orchestra plays. Formula literature reinforces an audience's values and expectations, often with the skillful manipulation of cliche, stereotype, convention and predictable plot. By means of formula art an audience can find both a justification of its covert and overt values and a dramatization of wish-fulfillment. Formula literature often restates old myths in new ways, creating a product that shows how people feel about issues and values at a given time. For example, Peter Bogdanovich took Larry McMurtry's scathing but unpopular anti-small-town novel, *The Last Picture Show,* and turned it into a black and white film of bittersweet 1950's nostalgia that helped articulate a rising national feeling. Most of Harte's stories work in a similar way: They dramatize an audience's feelings and values far more than they show an artist's "world picture" and personal vision. The literary critic, then, must try to uncover in a formula work the why and how of its success. Questions about a formula work's "quality" are secondary, since by definition its audience is convinced that it is "good entertainment."

With this distinction between formula and serious literature in mind, let us examine one of Harte's most famous stories, **"The Luck of Roaring Camp."** **"The Luck"** forms the prototype for Harte's most famous fiction. This story has been attacked, like many of Harte's tales, for being facile, filled with slick language, overdrawn in sentiment, and riddled with cliches. Roy R. Male delivers a typical critical judgment:

> Harte's tone is uneven, insecure, and facile.... The reader is apparently intended to take the smooth rhetoric of these comments [about Cherokee Sal] seriously, but after the author's earlier flippancy he cannot. The same is true of the idyllic passages in which Nature sympathizes with the infant.... This is what John Ruskin called the pathetic fallacy in a rather slick and sentimental form. Harte strains for effect, as he does again in the ending, with its cliche about the drowning man and its pale euphemisms concerning death.

These statements contain much truth; and, Male is perceptive enough to see the story as an essentially mythic one about a mysterious stranger. But he, following Brooks and Warren in *Understanding Fiction* as well as others, measures Harte's fiction against the standard of high art and serious literature, making failure and dismissal inevitable. Justifications of the story as a piece of sophisticated literature have proved to be less convincing than arguments attacking the story. For example, J. R. Boggan sees in this story a narrator of "ironic voice that tells us the story and intrudes to comment freely if somewhat ambiguously on the happenings in Roaring Camp..." [See excerpt dated 1967]. But there is no indication that Harte saw in the story any ambiguity or irony. On the contrary, there is every indication that he took the sentiment of **"The Luck of Roaring Camp"** most seriously. In a letter dated August 29, 1879, Harte wrote to his wife, Anna: "Do you remember the day you lay sick in San Jose and I read you the story of **'The Luck'** and took heart and comfort from your tears over it, and courage to go on and *demand* that it should be put in the magazine (the *Overland*)?"

I am inclined to follow Allen B. Brown who views the story as a Christian parable of redemption [see excerpt dated 1960]. Seeing **"The Luck"** as a "parable" instead of a "short story" explains the lack of realism (except for touches of detail), psychological motivation, and organization around a central conflict. Parables are designed to illustrate truths, reinforce an audience's expectations, or reaffirm an audience's ideal values. They are not typically well-wrought statements from an artistic consciousness. Read as parable, much formula literature may be seen not as "escapist," but as a disguised intensification of typical experience. *Gone With the Wind* has been convincingly interpreted as an uplifting parable about the Great Depression. Similarly, *The Exorcist* and *Jaws* have been interpreted as achieving vast popularity through their veiled commentary on Richard Nixon's Presidential administration. Bret Harte recognized his debt to the parable form in the "Preface" to his first **Collected Works**. There Harte related that he "will, without claiming to be a religious man or a moralist, but simply as an artist, reverently and humbly conform to the rules laid down by a Great Poet who created the parable of the 'Prodigal Son' and the 'Good Samaritan'...." But Allen Brown, I believe, mistakes the motif for the message. To me, the **"Luck"** parable, although outfitted with Christian trappings, primarily illustrates the triumph of Victorian civilization over the anarchistic wilderness.

Using a mixture of picturesque and realistic details within a Romantic setting, this particular parable depicts the ultimate nobility of all (white) men, especially in times of crisis. The story is mythic, not realistic, and presents the age-old convention of a Mysterious Stranger as a rescue figure. The characters are carefully stereotyped into external villains and internal saints. Roaring Camp is an outpost, a "city of refuges," and clearly these lawless types need to be saved—regenerated—repatriated to civilization. Cherokee Sal, of course, must succumb to the conventions of nineteenth-century melodrama, but it is a shocker that in 1868 a woman of such "low vartue" would even be "on-stage" for so long. Her role as perverse madonna, who brings forth in miracle and mystery the faith-giving Tommy Luck, flouts decorum and propriety; but in a striking way she reaffirms Harte's keystone belief that potentially everyone has some good. Complete with creche and adoring bucolics (the miners), Tommy is born as "the pines stopped moaning, the river ceased to rush, and the fire to crackle. It seemed as if Nature had stopped to listen too." Of course this is a cliche bedecked in purple prose—but consider the audience. They want a reconfirmation that their cultural beliefs hold validity. The Luck is sent to redeem men fallen from a worthy civilization, and Harte concentrates not on developing the title figure, but on portraying his effect on other characters.

James Folsom in *The American Western Novel* indignantly berates Harte for turning the story into an "Eastern." Indeed, Folsom is correct. After the Luck arrives, Roaring Camp goes Middle Class. Stumpy turns from a profane miner into a devoted house-husband, lovingly cooing at the infant and calling him "the d—n little cuss." According to Harte, the Luck makes the camp regenerate by returning to civilized ways, as the miners take on parental roles, tidy up sleazy cabins, hold a christening, build new living quarters, and "produce stricter habits of personal cleanliness." Somewhat as in *Snow White and the Seven Dwarfs*, hard work and lyrical adoration create a chosen community during a halcyon summer. The luck is with them; gold claims yield enormous profits, and the "town fathers" want to move in "respectable families in the fall." Says the area's mail carrier: "They've a street up there in Roaring that would lay over any street in Red Dog. They've got vines and flowers round their houses, and they wash themselves twice a day. But they're mighty rough on strangers, and they worship an Ingin baby." . . . These strangers have not reached that "highly civilized" plateau of "Roaring's" denizens who regard the white settlement of the area as an ideal goal, symbolized by the baby. How could anyone ask for a tale that more beautifully renders the myth of Manifest Destiny recovered?

One serious problem with the mysterious stranger story, as Roy R. Male notes in *Types of Short Fiction,* is what to do with the stranger once his function is completed. If he lingers, he may move to the position of protagonist, and the story becomes something else, in the case of **"The Luck of Roaring Camp"** possibly a *bildungsroman.* Such a complication would also change the parable into a more involved piece of fiction. Male, and probably most contemporary readers, considers the story's ending ineptly comic bathos. But to the Victorian audience, with its very different values and expectations, the ending was tinged with high pathos. What Harte regarded as sentiment (deep, valid feelings), we would likely regard as sentimental (gratuitous, sham feeling). Like his mother, Tommy is killed by a literary convention, a flood, which also drowns several miners, including Stumpy and Kentuck. These men receive some redemption in that they died better men than they were before The Luck's arrival. But Harte's real pitch is for repatriation, and is made to the audience. The story should regenerate *us* by providing renewed purpose, optimism, faith, belief in human potential, and if we are Victorian enough, a good cry. Serious literature produces a theme, but parables and Western Union—with luck—deliver messages.

Similarly, **"Tennessee's Partner"** should not be dismissed as merely a mawkish story of implausible events and psychologically invalid characters cohabiting in a world of melodramatic conventions. **"Tennessee's Partner"** is a parable about the power of brotherly love. Harte treats the subject with high pathos and obscures some of the issues the story raises by plating them with his golden rhetoric. He tends to substitute dramatic effect for character development. The brotherly love theme fascinated Harte, and among his other treatments of the partner relationship are **"Barker's Luck," "In the Tules,"** and **"Uncle Jim and Uncle Billy."** The custom of partnership was firmly rooted in mining camp folkways, as contemporary jour-

nals and historical studies have shown. Like so many of Harte's tales, **"Tennessee's Partner"** has a realistic basis carefully crafted into a romantic scenario that portrays man's goodness.

Numerous other Bret Harte stories follow this parable formula. **"The Outcasts of Poker Flat"** shows that in a crisis, there is good in even the worst people. This tale has a fair sampling of Harte's famous colorful and picturesque characters, including the slick gambler, the whore with a heart of gold, the ingenue, and "the innocent." **"Outcasts"** has little to do with realistic conventions such as character motivation. Rather, the tale describes the conversion of several characters from evil to good when they are isolated by a blizzard in the High Sierras. **"Brown of Calaveras"** is a parable that demonstrates the nobility of duty over desire. This tale marks the first appearance of Jack Hamlin, whose masculine objectivity and laconic stoicism Harte used in some twenty other works. **"How Santa Claus Came to Simpson's Bar"** is a parable with the theme of "never give up." The town's miners, a rough but chivalrous bunch, contrive to rescue a deprived boy from having a solitary and disillusioning Christmas. On the edge of despair, the boy is emotionally resurrected by Dick Bullen, who, after a torturous mountain ride to a far-away town, returns with a present. Harte's use of parables spanned his career, and they may be found in his children's stories, and even in his few fictional works with settings other than California.

By writing formula stories, however innovatively, Harte frequently boxed himself into the role of satisfying an audience's demand for very predictable and superficial conventions. With overuse, these conventions have become hallmarks of familiar cliches—the happy ending, the sentimental tryst, the gentleman gambler, the melodramatic incident, the amazing coincidence, and, of course, the whore with a heart of gold. Despite his use of realistic detail, Bret Harte was seldom what *we* would call a truly realistic artist; that is, someone who perceives, with a shock of recognition for the reader, an in-depth view of the calamities, conflicts, incoherencies, and particular characteristics of a people and their area. Rather, Harte saw California in mythic and archetypal terms and wrote parables which showed the Eastern reading public that picturesque Western scenes really were a part of universal experience and truth. (It is an axiom that the farther away from California's shores an audience is, the more likely they will respond favorably to Harte's mythic view of the West.)

It would be wrong, of course, to say that Harte merely wrote simple parables. In addition to literary criticism, his stories sometimes contained social criticism and complex statements about the human condition. Margaret Duckett has noted Harte's concern with race relations. She regards **"Three Vagabonds of Trinidad"** (1900) as a story which condemns the idea of Manifest Destiny, an historical concept which Harte celebrated some thirty years before in **"The Luck of Roaring Camp."** Professor Duckett in an article on Harte's novella, *The Crusade of the Excelsior,* points to Harte's historical perspective in the story to show that he attacks social and racial injustice. The story protests militarism and exploitation, through the Church and government, of the gentle, pastoral Mexicans. The parable has some ironic twists in its obvious moral, "honesty is the best policy," for the individuals who follow this moral in *Crusade* have their rights curtailed by a Church desperately trying to maintain orthodoxy. Another Harte story, **"The Right Eye of the Commander,"** also explores moral and social issues. Harte occasionally ranged far beyond the parable framework in stories about men-women relationships, as Jeffrey F. Thomas's article "Bret Harte and the Power of Sex" so clearly demonstrates [see Additional Bibliography]. (pp. 12-20)

However much Harte emphasized the formula parable or masked his true meanings, a definite schism is apparent between Harte the critical thinker and Harte the story writer, profitably producing for a philistine audience. In several stories Harte expresses not only his characteristic liberal and humanitarian beliefs, but criticism against social practices, criticism directed *at* his audience. Furthermore, Harte's stories contain virtually no direct autobiographical incidents. Perhaps this omission was simply Victorian diffidence, but as numerous letters and the recollections of others reveal, Harte led a far more interesting life than most people. Like his idol, Longfellow, Harte may have found his experiences at odds with his ideals, and chose to portray a vision of man's humanity to man in the hope that with enough good examples, this ideal would become truth.

Whatever the case, readers should notice in Bret Harte's fiction the consistent use of a third person narrator, not merely to establish a sense of distance, or as author intrusion, but as authorial control. Harte's narrators manipulate and withhold information to the point of condescension. At his most extreme, Harte's narrators separate themselves so much from their story that a distinct archness divides action, reader and narrator. Harte's narrator not only tells a story but interprets it—giving his version, obscuring or emphasizing material, analyzing the scene, characters and audience with a penetrating sophistication.

Occasionally, Harte places directly in the story some literary analysis, as happens in "Who Was My Quiet Friend?" where a madman quotes his favorite author, Charles Dickens. Or, in "A Ward of the Golden Gate," Harte portrays a humorously strained version of *Uncle Tom's Cabin*. He even delves into self-satire in "Jinny," a story on the order of "The Luck of Roaring Camp" except the birth of a mule substitutes for the birth of a child. More frequently Harte can be seen in the role of author as director, manipulating character and scene in the third person. . . . Sometimes Harte's narrator moves to the first person, as in "The Man on the Beach." "Whether this arose from a fear of reciprocal inquiry and interest, or from the profound indifference before referred to, I cannot say." But even here, the narrator is not the action's central figure. Other stories, such as "Maruja," contain footnotes, Harte stressing here the validity of his factual data, the reliability of his narrator, sometimes disguised as a sensitive, "literary" country editor. Other stories, "The Heritage of Dedlow Marsh" or "A First Family of Tasajara," for example, reveal subtle, covert narrative manipulation. The narrator's high diction too stresses the distance between himself and the story. Harte sees the function of the narrator and literary-cultural critic as one, a joining of roles sometimes further emphasized by the narrator's comments about literature. The use of a narrator who assumes the *persona* of a literary critic suggests Harte's commitment to this perspective. My purpose here has been to suggest *types* of narrative hold, not list numerous examples, although this would be easy enough to do as anyone who has read much Harte fiction knows very well. In all his writings, Harte is at his best and most comfortable posing as the concerned and witty man of taste evaluating these unusual manifestations of American culture, instructing his audience as to their meaning and value.

The weaknesses of Bret Harte's short stories point to some strengths in his literary criticism. Harte's stories are typically schematic rather than visionary, with a strong sense of authorial control or narrative hold. This, taken with his use of high diction and dense metaphors frequently obscures or hides meaning. But in his criticism, the narrator as detached man of taste becomes the voice of an objective, logical critic, an explicator with a talent for insightful, imaginative phrases. As a critic, Harte had more freedom than in his role of formula fiction writer; he could analyze much more objectively and to his own taste instead of catering to the demands of an audience and being bound by formulaic conventions. . . . [Critic] Harte roundly condemned sentimentality, a lack of realism, and weak characterization, all faults of his own fiction. Unlike his typical fiction, Harte's criticism is full of inquiry and experimentation. (pp. 21-3)

> *Patrick D. Morrow, in his* Bret Harte: Literary Critic,
> *Bowling Green State University Popular Press, 1979,*
> *193 p.*

WARD B. LEWIS (essay date 1980)

[*In the following excerpt, Lewis examines the fiction Harte wrote while living in Germany.*]

In July 1878 Bret Harte, with literary successes behind him such as **"The Luck of Roaring Camp"** . . . and **"The Outcasts of Poker Flat,"** . . . found himself in Germany—not as the consequence of a grand tour of the continent, but as a representative and employee of the United States government. Thus began a period which the author termed his "exile from home," a span of two years which played an important role in his life and is reflected in his work from those days, writing which has never been considered in this context.

The year before had seen a low point in Harte's career; his work was sporadic and received little critical acclaim; his income was little, and he stood in debt; the attempt was being made to support a family of six. Fortunately friends in the U.S. Department of State under President Rutherford B. Hayes succeeded in garnering for him an appointment as the United States Consul, or more accurately Commercial Agent, to the town of Crefeld, Germany at about $2,500 per annum. (p. 213)

Long before Harte visited Germany in 1878 his work was known there. An introduction had been made by Ferdinand Freiligrath to the German reading audience six years previously, and the acquaintanceship had deepened since that time. Five issues of the weekly *Die Gegenwart* had carried a half-dozen poems translated by Freiligrath and accompanied by his extended commentary under the title "Aus Californien. Lieder eines Goldgräbers" ["From California. Songs of a Gold Miner"]. Hailed by the editors as "etwas Frisches, Naturwüchsiges und höchst Eigentümliches" ["something fresh, natural, and utterly special"] . . . , the poems deal with figures such as a miner who sacrifices his life to save a comrade underground and a Mexican-American girl whose father is unknown. Freiligrath praises Harte's ability "mit wenigen kecken Strichen ein Bild, eine Situation, ein Erlebnis scharf und greifbar hinzuwerfen" ["to dash off a sharp and tangible portrait, situation, or episode with a few bold strokes"] . . . and in the American's language finds himself confronted with a challenge to which he is not always equal. Dialect must, of necessity, be ignored, and slang on occasion goes misunderstood. (pp. 214-15)

From the time of Freiligrath's introduction of Harte to Germany through the first year of the author's residence in Crefeld a large number of his works appeared in that country. Among these were seven in English for the series "Collection of British Authors" of the Tauchnitz publishing house in Leipzig, six titles in the "Universal-Bibliothek" of Reclam, and a total of at least thirty collections of his prose and poetry, including a half dozen translations of the novel *Gabriel Conroy*.... (pp. 215-16)

The critical reception afforded these works was cordial indeed. Hailed as the American successor to Longfellow and Poe in the hearts of his audience, the author is seen as fresh, bold, and unconventional by European standards. (p. 216)

In 1880 an extended critical essay on Harte appeared with the dateline "New York" beneath the name of Udo Brachvogel, a friend of Carl Schurz and a German-American, who had emigrated in 1867. Brachvogel, the translator of Longfellow and other authors for German readers, describes Harte as a "Weltschriftsteller" ["world author"], irresistible in his depiction of humanity; although the critic describes the novel *Gabriel Conroy* as undisciplined, exaggerated, and contrived ..., he finds that such faults receive more than sufficient compensation in the two overriding strengths of the work. These are to be found both in that wider vista of California which Harte now provides—confining his attention no longer to just mining camps but extending it to the metropolis of San Francisco and old Spanish California—and in the sense of history conveyed by the depiction of the state's first European settlers.... Brachvogel attempts to whet his reader's appetite in conclusion when it is speculated that Harte may be working currently on something based in his experiences in Europe, or Crefeld in particular.... (pp. 216-17)

After Harte's literary appearance in Germany for an entire decade his works were published in greater numbers than those of any other American author. The reception he was accorded equaled that which had been granted Hawthorne, Melville, Whitman, and Mark Twain; moreover the author's popularity continued long after it had subsided in the U.S. In this century the number of his works published in Germany reached 109 by 1912, and they still appear currently. (p. 217)

Five prose stories from Harte's Crefeld period, the German sketches, reflect a common technique. Described by one scholar as "charming," the stories consist of the extended presentation of vivid contrasts. These are evoked by the juxtaposition of one culture to another—the German to the American—or the representatives of the two cultures to each other. The reader is introduced to the remarks of a foreign observer, encounters the American traveling abroad, or meets a German immigrant to this country. (pp. 218-19)

The author employs a number of techniques to enhance the German background of his tale ["**Unser Karl**"]. The most obvious consists of the use of German terms, as for example in the reference to "this eternal Kriegsspiel" ["war game"] in which the soldiers in town indulged themselves.... Further, Harte attempts to reproduce those characteristics in the English of native German speakers, which he heard or thought he heard. Thus, German "d" and "p" replace English "th" and "b" respectively. Karl exclaims, "But all Shermany is mine volks,— de whole gountry.... Pet your poots! How's dot, eh?" (pp. 219-20)

A more intricate technique is evidenced when the author uses German syntax in English, not to reflect the inadequate nature of the English rendered by a foreigner but rather to suggest that the German employed bears a resemblance to English. A parody of German syntax provides the implication that the

German written was influenced by English structure. This effect is obtained when the counsel writes a note to General Adlerkreutz "in his own American German":

> If he [the consul] might have the temerity to the undoubted, far-seeing military authority of suggestion making here, he would suggest that Karl was for the commissariat fitted! Of course, he still retained the right, on production of satisfactory proof, his discharge to claim....

More amusing are the instances in which Harte comments upon a feature of the language as part of his objective description of events. There is, for example, the dinner where the health of the consul is toasted formally by Adlerkreutz; one hears "a neat address of many syllables containing all the parts of speech and a single verb."... The American, bracing for his response, rises to reply "tremulous with emotion and a reserve verb in his pocket."... (p. 220)

It is not only the juxtaposition and contrast between different language cultures which occupies the central focus of Harte's "**Peter Schroeder**," where the main figure is a member of a particular breed of German immigrants to America, the Forty-Eighters. These numbered about four thousand and consisted of well-educated, politically conscious idealists disappointed by the failure of the Revolution of 1848. In the United States they supported broad social legislation including the abolition of slavery and the enfranchisement of women and blacks, both goals which accounted for their support of the Republican party. In their educated, middle-class background and their political activism the Forty-Eighters distinguished themselves from earlier German immigrants.

An influential member of this wave of new-comers was Carl Schurz, who eventually became the U.S. Senator from Missouri and with whom the character Schroeder identifies himself.... By Rutherford Hayes Schurz was appointed to the Presidential Cabinet as Secretary of the Interior (1877-81), and from this position he assured Bret Harte of his ultimate selection by Hayes for a post in Europe, that which materialized at Crefeld.

The story "**Peter Schroeder**" is composed in first person narration at the introduction and the conclusion, thus providing a "frame" about the corpus of the tale, which is narrated in the third person by an omniscient voice. Of central importance is a German visitor from the Rhineland, known affectionately as "Dutch Pete", and characterized by "old, simple, blundering slang" ("You dakes your money and you bays your schoice."....) Harboring a profound sense of patriotism and belief in American political institutions, Schroeder abandons mining after striking gold and joins the forces of the Union in the Civil War. With the armistice he retires to Germany and lives sustained by his wealth, his memories, and his sense of idealism in his advancing years.

The scene in Germany is one of tedium: "Troops parading night and morning before his window"; "the monotony of five meals a day seriously considered and dutifully performed" followed by "that digestive glow known in the rich vernacular of his analytical nation as Essfieber ..." ["eating fever"]. (pp. 220-21)

In the absence of his wife, who is attending a "soul-friend," ... Schroeder is visited by Americans in whose behavior he notes "an instance of that republican simplicity and social freedom which he admired in theory; but he was conscious that his next life had brought with it responsibilities to other customs." . . .

Schroeder's guests are shown in a most unfavorable light. They are overly familiar, assuming, callous, and preoccupied with the newest fashions. Distinctly impressed by German military uniforms and the hint of titled nobility, the Americans are engaged in sightseeing, "heading up the Rhine to tackle some of them ruined castles." . . .

The visitors mock the American mementos Schroeder keeps in his room—a large flag, a picture of Lincoln, the cap and blouse to his Union army uniform. To this reaction he responds, "Der rebooplicans don't got no memories. Ve don't got nodings else." . . . Such an utterance as well as Schroeder's decision to dedicate himself to the establishment of a republic in Latin America where he is ultimately executed by a firing squad contributed no doubt to the description of the tale by one critic as "rather too consciously pathetic."

Less a sketch or tale with a discernable plot line and more a collection of random observations assembled with no apparent structure, **"Views from a German Spion"** takes its name from that mirror placed along the casement of the narrator's window, which reflects activity upon the outside street into the room where the author presumes to record "the impressions made upon two thirds of American strangers in the larger Towns of Germany." . . . Remarks are made upon the gravity of children, the reverence they show adults, and young German women with "that frank, clear, honest, earnest return of the eye." . . . A cause of "fresh and active resentment" is found in the use of a dog as a beast of burden . . . ; and the celebrations of Karneval unleash "a half-melancholy, half-crazy absurdity." . . . (p. 221)

Both censure and praise are meted out as the author directs his attention first one way, then the other. Harte makes reference to "this elsewhere discarded, uncouth, slowly-decaying text known as the German Alphabet, that plucks out the bright eyes of youth." . . . As in the sketch **"Unser Karl"** German syntax evokes Harte's satire when he writes that he as an American must grope his way "through a blind alley of substantives and adjectives, only to find the verb of action in an obscure corner." . . .

The typical German maid-servant is lauded to the skies. She is intelligent, clean and neat, obedient without being servile, polite without attempting to flatter, willing and accommodating without the expectation of immediate reward.

> Heaven bless thee, child, in thy early rising and in thy later sittings, at thy festive board over-flowing with Essig and Fett, in the mysteries of thy Kuchen, in the fullness of thy Bier, and in thy nightly suffocations beneath mountain-ous and multitudinous feathers! Good, honest, simple-minded, cheerful, duty-loving Lenchen!

While Harte was still in Germany one of his sketches appeared before readers there as a result of his agreement to do a series for the *Berliner Tageblatt*. This was **"The Legend of Sammts-tadt,"** which remained the only work published under this arrangement. The tale presents a variation on Washington Irving's "Rip van Winkle," in which the central figure falls asleep after a glass of wine and is transported through time, in this case backwards, to the middle ages, awakening as a swash-buckling cavalier granted the favor of the young lady from whose hand he received the glass. To be sure a "romantic little tale," as it has been called. . . .

The reception of this sketch by Harte's fellow residents of Crefeld was, however, strongly unfavorable. In Harte's words they were "very much annoyed" . . . and behind the misspelling of the German in the title detected their own "Velvettown" described further as "not a quaint nor romantic district, only an entrepôt for silks and velvets." . . . (p. 222)

The major figure in the sketch and the object of Harte's satire is the American James Clinch—stuffy, self-important, and excessively efficient; "The guide-books had ignored Sammtstadt and he was too good an American to waste time in looking up uncatalogued curiosities." . . . (pp. 222-23)

Such lines might well have been expected to find offense in Crefeld, even when intended quite obviously by the author to constitute primarily a commentary on the American. A similar case is presented by Clinch's pompous observation that a country such as Germany "that stops business at midday to go to dinner, and employs woman-servants to talk to businessmen is played out." . . . That Harte attempts here to convey an image of Clinch as a chauvinist philistine is clear upon comparison with remarks from another sketch based on the author's experience as consul, with whom servant girls conducted the affairs of their employers: ". . . there was a grave serious business instinct and sense of responsibility in these girls of ordinary peasant origin which, equally with their sisters of France, were unknown to the English or American women of any class." . . .

The sketch is in part didactic in effect. The reader observes Clinch in the process of gradually acquiring knowledge and understanding beyond his national experience, of becoming more cosmopolitan. The character frequently pauses and checks his speech, while considering conditions similar or comparable to those in his own country—ones which he had always taken for granted until now when they are perceived in a different light.

The tale conceived as one of a "series of frank, outspoken 'impressions' of Germany" . . . evoked such resentment among his readers that Harte pursued no longer his agreement with the *Berliner Tageblatt*. "Writing them for a German paper and living in a German community," the author confided, "and above all holding a half-diplomatic position here, cramps my pen." The readers of Crefeld interpreted "the extravagant speeches I put in C.'s mouth as my own utterance," he continues and describes his readership as "thin-skinned with the fear of truth before my eyes." . . . (p. 223)

Harte's family never joined him in Crefeld, where the author suffered intensely under the self-inflicted pains of hypochondria (rheumatism, hay fever, dyspepsia, bad teeth), convinced that this condition would become terminal should he not resettle elsewhere. The decision to leave and accept a post in Glasgow in 1880 provoked sharp comment from the German press—scurrilous remarks from Berlin and rebukes from Cologne. In this city a poem appeared consisting of four stanzas of nine unrhymed lines each, where is asserted that Germany as the source of truth and inspiration is more appropriate to Harte's elevated, creative nature than is England with its ignoble wealth. . . . Although his works were exceedingly popular at this time and there is no evidence that the writer felt neglected by his German public, lines are intended to console the readership for its loss by suggesting that the American was an ingrate. (pp. 223-24)

The works of Bret Harte's residency in Germany are not masterpieces. However, when considered in the light of his correspondence, his experiences there, and his various attitudes, they reveal a great deal of the relationship of an eminent American author to his European host country. With him Harte brought little worldliness nor an acquaintance with things German; indeed, he was already beset by some strange, ingrained prejudices before he ever set foot outside the U.S. To what he observed the author reacted with wide-eyed wonder in letters to his children, superficial appreciation, and at times, exaggerated admiration. Harte was perhaps not sufficiently aware that his enormous stature in Germany lent great weight to his remarks and might transform an offhand observation into a slight, however unintentional. It may also be supposed that the American was more brash and tough-skinned than many of his readers. When Harte took it upon himself to leave, his German audience reacted with understandable defensiveness. (p. 224)

> Ward B. Lewis, "Bret Harte and Germany," in Revue de littérature comparée, *Vol. LIV, No. 2, April-June, 1980, pp. 213-14.*

ADDITIONAL BIBLIOGRAPHY

Review of *The Luck of Roaring Camp, and Other Stories,* by Bret Harte. *The Atlantic Monthly,* XXV, No. CLI (May 1870): 633-35.
  Surveys the stories included in *The Luck of Roaring Camp,* finding "The Outcasts of Poker Flat" to be the best in the collection.

Barnett, Linda D. "Bret Harte: An Annotated Bibliography of Secondary Comment." *American Literary Realism* 5, No. 3-4 (Summer-Fall 1972): 189-484.
  Comprehensive annotated bibliography of writings about Harte.

Boynton, Henry W. *Bret Harte.* New York: McClure, Phillips, and Co., 1903, 117 p.
  Early biographical and critical study.

Buckland, Roscoe L. "Jack Hamlin: Bret Harte's Romantic Rogue." *Western American Literature* VIII, No. 3 (Fall 1973): 111-22.
  Traces the development of romanticism in the characterizations in Harte's Jack Hamlin stories.

Burton, Linda. "For Better or Worse: Tennessee and His Partner—A New Approach to Bret Harte." *Arizona Quarterly* 36, No. 3 (Autumn 1980): 211-16.
  A reading of "Tennessee's Partner" that sees a homosexual relationship between the two main characters.

Chapman, Arnold. "Voices of the Frontier." In his *The Spanish American Reception of United States Fiction 1920-1940,* pp. 185-88. Berkeley: University of California Press, 1966.
  Traces the Spanish American critical response to Harte's fiction, finding it mostly favorable.

Conner, William F. "The Euchring of Tennessee: A Reexamination of Bret Harte's 'Tennessee's Partner.'" *Studies in Short Fiction* 17, No. 2 (Spring 1980): 113-20.
  Rejects the standard interpretation of "Tennessee's Partner" as a sentimental tale of loyalty, suggesting instead that the sentimentality is only there to mask the real theme of frontier gamesmanship. According to this reading, the reader is tricked by Harte in the same way that Tennessee and the town's onlookers are tricked by Tennessee's partner.

Harlow, Alvin F. *Bret Harte of the Old West.* New York: Julian Messner, 1943, 307 p.
  Romanticized account of Harte's life, with an emphasis on the early years.

Howells, William Dean. "A Belated Guest." In his *Literary Friends and Acquaintances: A Personal Retrospect of American Authorship,* pp. 289-305. New York: Harper and Brothers, 1900.
  Reminiscence of Harte highlighting a week-long visit to Boston. Howells also focuses on Harte's temperament and his attitude toward Eastern writers.

Krause, Sydney J. "Bret Harte: The Grumbling Realist's Friend and Foe." In his *Mark Twain as Critic,* pp. 190-224. Baltimore: Johns Hopkins Press, 1967.
  Details Mark Twain's marginal notes in his personal copies of Harte's work.

Kuhlmann, Susan. "To the West." In her *Knave, Fool, and Genius,* pp. 33-48. Chapel Hill: The University of North Carolina Press, 1973.
  Study of the confidence man as a fictional type, with references to Harte's characters John Oakhurst, Jack Hamlin, and Yuba Bill.

Matthews, Brander. "Bret Harte and Mr. Howells as Dramatists." In *The American Theatre as Seen By its Critics, 1752-1934,* edited by Montrose Moses and John Mason Brown, pp. 147-48. New York: W. W. Norton and Co., 1934.
  Brief review of Harte's play *Two Men of Sandy Bar.* Matthews writes: "*Two Men of Sandy Bar* has been tried in the light of the lamps and found wanting. It has no unity of plot. There is no singleness of purpose—no definite aim held firmly from the first scene to the last: all is veering and shifting. Faults like these are fatal to dramatic effect."

Morrow, Patrick D. "Parody and Parable in Early Western Local Color Writing." *Journal of the West* XIX, No. 1 (January 1980): 9-16.
  Sketches Harte's influence on other writers while he served as editor of the *Overlander.*

Review of *The Luck of Roaring Camp, and Other Stories,* by Bret Harte. *The New York Times* (30 April 1870): 11.
  Praises Harte for his characterization and his humor.

O'Connor, Richard. *Bret Harte: A Biography.* Boston: Little, Brown and Co., 1966, 331 p.
  Stresses the paradoxical and contradictory nature of Harte's life.

Pemberton, T. Edgar. *The Life of Bret Harte.* New York: Dodd, Mead and Co., 1903, 358 p.
  Biography written by Harte's friend and collaborator that quotes extensively from Harte's letters to family members, friends, and acquaintances as well as from some of Harte's poems and tributes to other writers.

Quinn, Arthur Hobson. "Bret Harte and the Fiction of Moral Contrast." In his *American Fiction: An Historical and Critical Survey,* pp. 232-242. New York: Appleton-Century-Crofts, 1936.
  Praises Harte's artistry as a fiction writer, particularly his sympathetic portrayal of disreputable characters. Quinn states that Harte "remains a world artist not merely because of his depiction of the gold rush of California, but because he discovered that other, richer vein, the sympathy which even the most puritanical feel for the sinner who leads them vicariously into the paths of adventure which they have shunned, but of which they love to read in the pages of fiction."

Scherting, Jack. "Bret Harte's Civil War Poems: Voice of the Majority." *Western American Literature* VIII, No. 3 (Fall 1973): 133-42.
  Examines Harte's Civil War poems from a cultural perspective as reflecting attitudes and concerns of Californians toward the war in progress.

Stewart, George R. *Bret Harte: Argonaut and Exile.* Port Washington, New York: Kennikat Press, 1935, 385 p.
  Considered the definitive account of Harte's life. Stewart avoids the romanticizing tendency of earlier biographers.

Thomas, Jeffrey F. "Bret Harte and the Power of Sex." *Western American Literature* VIII, No. 3 (Fall 1973): 91-109.
  Overview of sexual relationships in Harte's fiction.

Twain, Mark. *The Autobiography of Mark Twain*, edited by Charles Neider, pp. 123-29, 289, 294-309. New York: Harper and Row, 1917.
 Twain's reminiscence of his youthful friendship and later disillusionment with Harte.

Vedder, Henry C. "Bret Harte." In his *American Writers of Today*, pp. 212-29. Freeport, N.Y.: Books for Libraries Press, 1894.
 Biographical discussion of Harte, including some assessment of his work, which Vedder finds essentially melodramatic and sentimental.

Ward, Alfred C. "Bret Harte: 'The Luck of Roaring Camp.'" In his *Aspects of the Modern Short Story*, pp. 45-59. London: University of London Press, 1924.
 Examines theme, characterization, and style in Harte's fiction.

Julian Hawthorne

1846-1934

(Also wrote under pseudonym of Judith Hollinshed) American novelist, short story writer, biographer, journalist, and essayist.

Hawthorne, the only son of the celebrated American author Nathaniel Hawthorne, was a prolific writer best known during his lifetime for popular romantic novels which frequently incorporated elements of Gothic fiction. Throughout his career, the younger Hawthorne was challenged by critics to duplicate the superior literary achievements of his father, and his failure to do so resulted in harsh appraisals of his fiction. More highly regarded were Hawthorne's biographical and critical works, which include several important studies of his father's life that are still considered invaluable by scholars.

Hawthorne was born in Boston but spent much of his childhood abroad, traveling to England, Germany, and Italy with his parents and two sisters. During these travels, he was tutored by his mother and father, a governess, and others in the family's employ, and his early lessons comprised an eclectic mixture of subjects ranging from dance to classical languages. Hawthorne began his formal education at the prestigious Sanborn School in Concord, Massachusetts; he later attended Harvard University and, after his father's death in 1864, studied engineering in Germany.

Returning to the United States in 1870, Hawthorne married and secured a position as a hydrographic engineer for the city of New York. Shortly afterward, he began to write short stories as a means of supplementing his income. Hawthorne's first stories sold quickly, due in part to his father's reputation, and his work appeared in *Harper's, Harper's Weekly, Appleton's,* and other periodicals throughout 1871 and 1872. Encouraged by these successes and by his mentor, Robert Carter, a family friend and former editor of *Appleton's,* Hawthorne published his first novel, *Bressant,* in 1873. Reviewed more favorably in England than in the United States, *Bressant* was generally assessed as imaginative but stylistically flawed, with many critics attributing its shortcomings to the author's inexperience and its strengths to hereditary genius. Although Hawthorne himself was less than pleased with the novel, he was disturbed by the critics' obvious readiness to compare his work to that of his father, and he recorded in his journal that "people are rather desirous than otherwise that I should prove worthy the name I bear: and will cling as long as possible to the belief that I yet may. . . . I can never reproduce nor even imitate the simple grandeur and pure intuition of that man. And so I shall wisely walk in as divergent a path as possible, consistently with self-respect and truth." Despite such intentions, critics discerned in Hawthorne's second novel, *Idolatry,* many similarities to the romances of Nathaniel Hawthorne, and in a scathing review Henry James asserted that these similarities elicited "the feeling of a broad burlesque of his father's exquisite fantasies."

Throughout the next two decades, Hawthorne published two or three novels per year, in addition to a number of short stories, essays, biographies, and histories. From 1874 to 1881 he also worked as a staff reviewer for the *London Spectator.* After 1900, Hawthorne worked exclusively as a journalist, contrib-

uting to a number of major periodicals. Although he cultivated personal and professional relationships with many renowned contemporaries, he also alienated others in the literary establishment by indulging in several highly publicized arguments with fellow members of the Authors' Club, with his brother-in-law Robert Lathrop, who was also a Nathaniel Hawthorne biographer, and with the eminent poet James Russell Lowell, Hawthorne's former tutor and a close family friend. The dispute with Lowell, which arose late in 1886 when Hawthorne published an interview which Lowell insisted had been intended as a purely private conversation, was particularly damaging to Hawthorne since it led to questions concerning his professional ethics, and he was thereafter considered a journalistic malefactor by many.

The most humiliating event in Hawthorne's life, however, occurred in 1913, when he was sentenced to serve one year at the Atlanta State Penitentiary for his part in a mail fraud scheme. Still proclaiming his innocence, he nevertheless accepted his lot and took an active part in prison life, becoming editor of the penitentiary's newspaper. Drawing upon this experience, Hawthorne later wrote *The Subterranean Brotherhood* as a denunciation of the entire penal system, proposing that the practice of imprisonment be abolished because it was "not only dangerous, but wicked." After his release from prison, Hawthorne traveled for several years, settling finally in California, where he wrote for the *Pasadena Star News* until his death in 1934.

Despite Hawthorne's avowed intention to walk a "divergent path" from his father, themes and characterization in many of his novels show the direct influence of Nathaniel Hawthorne's fiction. The novel *Garth,* for example, treats the hereditary transmission of sin, a consistent concern in the elder Hawthorne's work and the major theme of *The House of the Seven Gables.* Similarly, conflicts between love and ambition, which figured prominently in Nathaniel Hawthorne's fiction, inform several of his son's novels, including *Bressant* and *Sebastian Strome.* Nevertheless, Julian Hawthorne did develop themes not found in his father's work, most significantly that of the inherent conflict between sacred and profane love. In his exploration of this last theme, Hawthorne included comparatively frank discussions of human sexuality, and, as a result, his novels were denounced as obscene by many nineteenth-century critics. More often, however, Hawthorne's literary contemporaries objected to the composite nature of his fictional techniques, finding his attempt to unite the conventions of Gothic fiction with elements of scientific naturalism clumsy at best. This aspect of Hawthorne's fiction is most clearly exemplified in the novel *Archibald Malmaison,* in which he combined the traditional secret passageways and undisclosed lineages of Gothic romance with character portrayals drawn from modern psychological theory.

In contrast to his fiction, Hawthorne's biography *Nathaniel Hawthorne and His Wife* is recognized by critics as a well-written and perceptive work, valuable for the insight it provides into the eminent author's personality and for its candid revelations concerning the events of his life. In addition to this biography, Hawthorne produced several other highly-regarded works on related topics, including *Nathaniel Hawthorne and His Circle.*

Acutely aware of his own artistic limitations, Hawthorne wrote fiction primarily to entertain the reading public, and he was highly successful in this endeavor. Several of his novels were extremely popular and the majority sold well. Moreover, recent critical reassessments which consider Hawthorne's fiction independently from that of his father have judged his work to be less flawed than previously thought, and critic Maurice Bassan attempted to put his literary career in perspective when he wrote that "in an age of giants like Clemens and James—to speak only of his American contemporaries—Hawthorne was a pygmy. . . . Yet, surprisingly, there are quite genuine if rare treasures scattered here and there in the works of the younger Hawthorne, treasures that ought to be recovered unapologetically."

PRINCIPAL WORKS

Bressant (novel) 1873
Idolatry (novel) 1874
Saxon Studies (essays) 1876
Garth (novel) 1877
Archibald Malmaison (novel) 1879
The Laughing Mill, and Other Stories (short stories) 1879
Sebastian Strome (novel) 1879
Ellice Quentin, and Other Stories (short stories) 1880
Yellow-Cap, and Other Fairy Stories for Children (short stories) 1880
Prince Saroni's Wife, and Other Stories (short stories) 1882

Beatrix Randolph (novel) 1883
Dust (novel) 1883
Fortune's Fool (novel) 1883
Nathaniel Hawthorne and His Wife [2 vols.] (biography) 1884-85
Love—or a Name (novel) 1885
Noble Blood (novel) 1885
John Parmalee's Curse (novel) 1886
An American Penman (novel) 1887
Confessions and Criticisms (essays and criticism) 1887
The Great Bank Robbery (novel) 1887
A Tragic Mystery (novel) 1887
An American Monte Cristo (novel) 1888
Another's Crime (novel) 1888
David Poindexter's Disappearance, and Other Tales (short stories) 1888
A Dream and a Forgetting (novel) 1888
A Miser of Second Avenue (novel) 1888
The Professor's Sister (novel) 1888; also published as *The Spectre of the Camera; or, The Professor's Sister,* 1888
Section 558; or, The Fatal Letter (novel) 1888
A Messenger from the Unknown (novel) 1892
Six-Cent Sam's (short stories) 1893; also published as *Mr. Dunton's Invention, and Other Stories,* 1896
A Fool of Nature (novel) 1896
The Golden Fleece (novel) 1896
Love is a Spirit (novel) 1896
Hawthorne and His Circle (memoir) 1903
The Subterranean Brotherhood (essays) 1914
Shapes that Pass: Memories of Old Days (memoir) 1928
The Memoirs of Julian Hawthorne (memoir) 1938

THE NATION (essay date 1873)

[*In the following review, the critic condemns* Bressant *on moral and artistic grounds.*]

"Psychical analysis" is, we believe, the name that is given to the exceedingly distasteful quality which marks Mr. Julian Hawthorne's novel, *Bressant,* and which is to be found in many French novels of various grades, as well as in the yellow-covered literature of other times and countries. It is called analytic because it discusses a problem, the problem being the way in which a man loves two women at the same time, one with a sort of brute-like ferocity, and the other with all the purity and tenderness of a lofty nature. This complex man is Bressant; the diverse objects of his devotion being two sisters, Cornelia and Sophie, the daughters of a slipshod recluse, Professor Valeyon. Bressant, we are given to understand, is "a child in the world of affections"; he has received from his father a singular education; and when he finds himself an orphan at the age of twenty-three or four, he makes his way to Professor Valeyon, nominally to study theology—which, so carefully has he been taught, he thinks is a profession, very much as civil engineering is—but really to develop his remarkable talent for bigamy. One evening he walks in the garden with Cornelia, the beautiful but bad sister, and while there the following incident takes place. In a pause in the conversation she kills a mosquito that is biting his hand:

Bressant felt the soft, warm fingers strike smartly, and then begin to remove, cautiously and slowly, because the mosquito was possibly not dead after all. What was the matter with the young man? His blood and senses seemed to quiver and tingle with a sensation at once delicious and confusing. In the same instant he had seized the soft, warm fingers in both hands and pressed them convulsively, almost fiercely. Cornelia very naturally cried out, and sprang to her feet. Bressant, it would seem not so naturally, did the same thing, and with the air of being to the full as much astonished and startled as she.

"What do you mean, sir? How dare you?" she said, paling after her first deep flush.

He looked at her, and then at his own hand, on which the accommodating mosquito was artistically flattened, and then at her again, with a slight, interrogative frown.

"How did it happen? What was it? I didn't mean it!"

The next appearance of this simple-minded student of divinity is at a village ball, and although his dancing had hitherto been as much neglected as his affections, he, "beautifully as she danced, was no whit her inferior. They moved in complete accord. Years of practice could not have made the harmony more perfect." On his way home with Cornelia, Bressant stops a horse which is running away with his prospective father-in-law, but thereby he breaks his collar-bone. He staggers on, groaning, to the front steps and then faints. Soon Cornelia is obliged to go away to see fashionable life, and Sophie's turn comes. She reads to him, and in a few days they are engaged. This is kept a secret from Cornelia, who returns and is somewhat dismayed at the turn things have taken. She has become a mass of worldliness in her absence, and the French novels she has read have found her an apt pupil in ways of guile. Not unjustly, she had considered Bressant as good as engaged to her when she went away, and she is soon successful in winning the inexperienced young man back to the adoration of her charms. Then, too, if he married Cornelia he would be rich; if he married Sophie he would be only a poor country clergyman. Cornelia wins the day, Sophie dies of a broken heart, complicated by typhoid pneumonia, and so the story ends. If this were all, if there were no other faults to be found with the book than that the plot is awkward, the study of character crude, the telling of the story unskilful, the novel might be dismissed with very few words. It would be simply a poor novel. But the truth is that it is a very bad thing. It is bad because it lacks decency. In the place of genuine study of human beings, it gives us a morbid fingering of unclean emotions. After an experience of many centuries, society has agreed that there are certain subjects which shall not be talked about by its members, and which are eschewed even by intimate friends, and hence one cannot help regarding with even greater dislike a book which is to have wide circulation among inexperienced readers, who get a very great part of their knowledge of the world—to call it knowledge—from what they read, and which will give such persons so inaccurate and misleading an idea of what they themselves and other people are.

A review of "Bressant," in The Nation, *New York, Vol. XVII, No. 419, July 10, 1873, p. 27.*

THE SATURDAY REVIEW, LONDON   (essay date 1874)

[*In the following excerpt from a review of* Idolatry, *the critic compares Hawthorne's skill as a novelist unfavorably to that of his father, condemning the former for his failure to develop his inherited talent.*]

If Mr. Julian Hawthorne's second book were not his second, one would be inclined to think far more highly of its author's capacities and probable future. His first work, ***Bressant,*** was full of extravagance, but full also of promise. His present performance cannot be said to fulfil that promise. That the younger Hawthorne is gifted with a power which, judged by the standard of ordinary novels, is great, cannot be doubted. Nor can it be doubted that he has misused that power. It is a common enough experience that the consciousness of strength leads its possessor into extravagance; and this can be pardoned in the case of a novice. The extravagance may be removed while the power will remain. Thus it is with the singer who is endowed with a strong voice. He will delight in producing a mere volume of sound until experience has taught him that natural force must be educated and tempered by art. Thus it is also with the young writer who feels that he has ideas beyond the general scope, and words apt to embody them. There is, unfortunately, this difference between the two cases. Were the singer to reject the experience of professors, and insist on trusting merely to his natural gifts, the experience of the public would soon convince him of his error. But to the mass of the reading public the most obvious want of training and attention to art in the making of a fiction appears to be no objection. It is enough for them if there are some touches of strength or originality in the book, some qualities which will bring a new sensation to their novel-jaded minds. Sometimes indeed it is enough if there are none. Whether this state of things indicates an increasing want of ideas among readers or writers or both, or whether it is more happily only a passing form of fashion, is a question capable of discussion. It is possible that it is an instance on a large scale of that extravagance springing from power which is exemplified individually in ***Idolatry.*** It is but a short time ago in the history of civilization that the capacity and taste for reading became universal. Perhaps the indiscriminate greed for fiction is analogous to the chest notes which the scarce taught singer hurls forth. One effect of such a condition of affairs is that an author of any unusual ability can choose between the success of securing an immediate, if momentary, attention and the more real success which is dear to the true artist. Mr. Hawthorne has apparently chosen the former of these alternatives.

The lesser seems to have inherited the love which distinguished the great Hawthorne, of relieving the workaday aspect of the tangible world by casting over its actors and events a mist borrowed from realms fantastic, imagined, or even supernatural. He takes the same delight which his father did in imagining such combinations as might, so far as the laws of physics are concerned, take place in everyday life, but which as a matter of experience never do. He has the same perception of the fine irony of circumstances which was used with so much effect by the author of the *Marble Faun.* For the possession of these qualities, which are as likely to be inherited as imitated, it would be unfair to quarrel with the writer of ***Idolatry.*** It is not unfair to blame him for the use to which he has put them. The delicate impalpable veil with which the father was wont to hint rather than to establish a connexion between the real and the fanciful world becomes gross, and therefore incredible, in the hands of the son. Upon those doubtful points of eerie imagination which the father was wont to glide lightly by, as if half doubting their existence himself, the son makes an appreciable pause, and thus at once destroys his reader's belief. And as soon as the improbability of circumstances and characters hitherto unknown is made clear and manifest their charm is dispelled. Such a comparison as that which we have instituted would be unfair were not the likeness and unlikeness between the two writers so patent that they cannot escape observation. It is not only in the details of his work, but in its very essence, that Mr. Julian Hawthorne's too heavy hand produces a disagreeable impression. To build a romance upon utterly improbable events is the acknowledged privilege of the novelist, so long as he can decently disguise their improbability. When he chooses subjects which are not only unlikely, but also revolting, he exceeds his prerogative.

Mr. Hawthorne makes a considerable demand upon his reader's power of accepting the improbable at the very beginning of his book in the matter of one of its characters. . . . [The] conversion of an Egyptian youth into an American clergyman is curious enough. More curious still is the fact that he is adopted by an eccentric gentleman, the Master Hiero Glyphic . . . , with a perfect craze for everything that is Egyptian, so that he builds an Egyptian temple out of one half of his house. Standing at an altar in this temple the Rev. Manetho Glyphic [, the Egyptian,] performs the marriage service for Thor Helwyse, an Americanized Dane, great of limb and voice, and Helen, sister to Hiero Glyphic, with whom Manetho is desperately in love. Most curious of all, however, is the attempt at portrayal of Manetho's character. With the malice and all but the capabilities of Mephistopheles he combines the patient cunning of Iago and the tender susceptibilities of Werther. It would be difficult to find a more impossible monster. Of this the author himself seems to have become in some sort conscious, for he has scattered hints throughout his story that the Rev. Manetho was more than a little mad. This is but a weak device, however, and rather increases than lessens the impossibility of the character. The author's intention seems to have been to produce a great effect by depicting a character full of hitherto unprobed contrasts. The intention is neither ill conceived nor impossible of execution. But the author has failed to execute it. The means he has employed are too violent and inartistic. In contrasts of character there must be a certain coherence, just as in music there are certain discords which may, and certain others which may not, be properly employed. The author has resorted to a merely mechanical trick to heighten his effect by speaking of Manetho as "the clergyman" whenever he is employed upon any peculiarly fiendish piece of wickedness.

Far better drawn is Balder, the son of Thor Helwyse, Manetho's old rival. If he is not perfectly real, he is at least not perfectly impossible and monstrous. There is a brightness and cheerfulness about him which is an agreeable relief to the murky extravagance of Manetho and the solitary castle which he inherited from his old patron with the ridiculous name. Balder may be supposed to typify a form of modern faith or unfaith, as Manetho does one of older growth. The idolatry to which each of the chief characters in the book has given him or herself up takes in Balder Helwyse the form of an inordinate belief in self, springing from much successful dealing with the world, and the knowledge of the manners and cities of many men. From this idolatry Balder is converted by the softening influence of failure and trouble, just as the other personages are converted each from their own special worship in a special way. The representation of a character true and noble, but hardened by success into surpassing egotism, which is dissolved by an apt series of events, would be well enough. Only

one seems to have read of a certain Raphael Aben Ezra, and a certain Tom Thurnall in the writings of Mr. Charles Kingsley, who have forestalled Balder Helwyse both in his egotism and his conversion. The parallel may of course be accidental. In that case we can only be . . . sorry for Mr. Hawthorne. . . . (pp. 540-41)

Manetho's whole being after he has married Thor Helwyse to the woman whom he himself adores becomes absorbed in the idea of vengeance. This idea he proceeded to carry out by kidnapping, as he thinks, Balder Helwyse's twin-sister and carrying her off to his solitary castle. Here with a devilish ingenuity he conceives the plan of educating her so that she shall mistake good for evil and evil for good, and returning her to her supposed father when her education is complete. The latter part of this plan is frustrated by the death of Thor Helwyse, the former by the innate goodness of Gnulemah, by which remarkable name the girl is known. The study of a girl brought up entirely sequestered from all human influences save one, and that one of so appalling a kind as Manetho's, is a new idea, and here and there there are indications that the excellence of its execution will correspond to its novelty. The hopes raised by such indications are doomed to disappointment. The author manages always to fall short of the mark. If he failed altogether to approach it, the effect would not be nearly so irritating. This is one of the weaknesses of human nature which a writer should weigh well before setting himself a difficult task. He should remember that readers will have much less toleration for him who does that which is nearly good than for him who does that which is in no way good. In the latter case their attention is not seriously disturbed. In the former it

Pencil sketch of Nathaniel Hawthorne drawn by Julian in 1861.

is aroused only to be disappointed. That which most nearly approaches to goodness in this part of *Idolatry* is the first meeting between Balder and Gnulemah. What follows hard upon this—the supposed catastrophe on which the revenge of Manetho turns—is so horribly revolting that one is astounded at Mr. Hawthorne's dealing with such an incident in the pages of a romance. Mr. Leslie Stephen in his last book said, with picturesque terseness, ''Poe was a kind of Hawthorne and delirium tremens.'' The latter part of the younger Hawthorne's book recalls this expression. The final and real catastrophe of *Idolatry* is a most lame and impotent conclusion, for which it is most difficult to assign any reason beyond the unworthy one of a desire to finish the novel with a startling effect. If such was the writer's object, he would have been wise to employ a less hackneyed incident.

There is one character in *Idolatry* described with a skill and delicacy which are almost worthy of the author of the *Scarlet Letter*. Unfortunately this character [Mr. MacGentle] has nothing to do with the movement of the book, and is merely introduced as a picture by the way, so that it is possible to draw the inference that the success of the effort is due to its not being sustained. . . . Mr. Hawthorne has capacities for humour and observation which he would do well to cultivate, in place of the ill-ordered fantasies which he has indulged in. . . . Were the whole of Mr. Hawthorne's work equal in merit . . . , we might rejoice in the advent of a new writer of romance. As it is, we can only be sorry that he did not put away *Idolatry* for a year or two before he thought of publishing it. (p. 541)

A review of ''Idolatry,'' in The Saturday Review, *Vol. 38, No. 991, October 24, 1874, pp. 540-41.*

[HENRY JAMES]   (essay date 1874)

[*As a novelist James is valued for his psychological acuity and complex sense of artistic form. Throughout his career, James also wrote literary criticism in which he developed his artistic ideals and applied them to the works of others. Among the numerous dictums he formed to clarify the nature of fiction was his definition of the novel as ''a direct impression of life.'' The quality of this impression—the degree of moral and intellectual development— and the author's ability to communicate this impression in an effective and artistic manner were the two principal criteria by which James estimated the worth of a literary work. James admired the self-consciously formalistic manner of contemporary French writers, particularly Gustave Flaubert, which stood in contrast to the loose, less formulated standards of English novelists. On the other hand, he favored the moral concerns of English writing over the often amoral and cynical vision which characterized much of French literature in the second half of the nineteenth century. His literary aim was to combine the qualities of each country's literature that most appealed to his temperament. James's criteria were accepted as standards by a generation of novelists that included Ford Madox Ford, Joseph Conrad, and Virginia Woolf. Hawthorne attended school with James's younger brothers and the two had a common publisher. However, they had no contact until 1879, when James consulted Hawthorne in preparation for writing* Nathaniel Hawthorne *(1879) in the ''Men in Letters'' series. Hawthorne aided James in this project but harbored resentment because the publisher had not asked him to write the work about his father, and because James had written harsh reviews of the younger Hawthorne's novels. In the following excerpt, James provides an uncomplimentary review of* Idolatry.]

It has been more than once remarked that, on the whole, the penalties attached to bearing an eminent name are equal to the privileges. To be the son of a man of genius is at the best to be born to a heritage of invidious comparisons, and the case is not bettered if one attempts to follow directly in the paternal footsteps. One's name gets one an easy hearing, but it by no means guarantees one a genial verdict; indeed, the kinder the general sentiment has been toward the parent, the more disposed it seems to deal out rigid justice to the son. The standard by which one is measured is uncomfortably obtrusive; one is expected *ex officio* to do well, and one finally wonders whether there is not a certain felicity in having so indirect a tenure of the public ear that the report of one's experiments may, if need be, pass unnoticed. These familiar reflections are suggested by the novel lately published by Mr. Julian Hawthorne, a writer whose involuntary responsibilities are perhaps of an exceptionally trying kind. The author of *The Scarlet Letter* and *Twice-Told Tales* was a genius of an almost morbid delicacy, and the rough presumption would be that the old wine would hardly bear transfusion into new bottles; that, the original mold being broken, this fine spirit had better be left to evaporate. Mr. Julian Hawthorne is already known (in England, we believe, very favorably) as author of a tale called *Bressant*. In his own country his novel drew forth few compliments, but in truth it seemed to us to deserve neither such very explicit praise nor such unsparing reprobation. It was an odd book, and it is difficult to speak either well or ill of it without seeming to say more than one intends. Few books of the kind, perhaps, that have been so valueless in performance have been so suggestive by the way; few have contrived to impart an air of promise to such an extraordinary tissue of incongruities. The sum of *Bressant*'s crimes was, perhaps, that it was ludicrously young, but there were several good things in it in spite of this grave error. There was force and spirit, and the suggestion of a perhaps obtrusively individual temper, and various signs of a robust faculty of expression, and, in especial, an idea. The idea—an attempted apprehension, namely, of the conflict between the love in which the spirit, and the love in which sense is uppermost—was an interesting one, and gave the tale, with all its crudities, a rather striking appearance of gravity. Its gravity was not agreeable, however, and the general impression of the book, apart from its faults of taste and execution, was decidedly sinister. Judged simply as an attempt, nevertheless, it did no dishonor to hereditary tradition; it was a glance toward those dusky psychological realms from which the author of *The Scarlet Letter* evoked his fantastic shadows.

After a due interval, Mr. Hawthorne has made another experiment, and here it is, rather than as applied to *Bressant*, that our remarks on the perils of transmitted talent are in place. *Idolatry*, oddly enough, reminds the perspicacious reader of the late Mr. Hawthorne's manner more forcibly than its predecessor, and the author seems less to be working off his likeness to his father than working into it. Mr. Julian Hawthorne is very far from having his father's perfection of style, but even in style the analogy is observable. ''Suppose two sinners of our daylight world,'' he writes, ''to meet for the first time, mutually unknown, on a night like this. Invisible, only audible, how might they plunge profound into most naked intimacy, read aloud to each other the secrets of their deepest hearts! Would the confession lighten their souls, or make them twice as heavy as before? Then, the next morning, they might meet and pass, unrecognizing and unrecognized. But would the knot binding them to each other be any the less real, because neither knew to whom he was tied? Some day, in the midst of friends, in the brightest glare of the sunshine, the tone of a voice would strike them pale and cold.'' And elsewhere: ''He had been accustomed to look at himself as at a third person, in whose faults or successes he was alike interested; but although his present mental attitude might have moved him to smile, he, in fact, felt no such impulse. The hue of his deed had permeated all possible forms of himself, thus barring him from any stand-point whence to see its humorous aspect. The sun would not shine on it!'' Both the two ideas, here, and the expression, will seem to the reader like old friends; they are of the family of those arabesques and grotesques of thought, as we may call them, with which the fancy that produced the *Twice-Told Tales* loved so well to play. Further in the story the author shows us his hero walking forth from the passionate commission of a great crime (he has just thrown a man overboard from the Boston and New York steamer), and beginning to tingle with the consciousness of guilt. He is addressed caressingly by a young girl who is leaning into the street from a window, and it immediately occurs to him that (never having had the same fortune before) her invitation has some mysterious relation to his own lapse from virtue. This is, generically, just such an incident as plays up into every page of the late Mr. Hawthorne's romances, although it must be added that in the case of particular identity the touch of the author of *The House of the Seven Gables* would have had a fineness which is wanting here. We have no desire to push the analogy too far, and many readers will perhaps feel that to allude to it at all is to give Mr. Julian Hawthorne the benefit of one's good-will on too easy terms. He resembles his father in having a great deal of imagination and in exerting it in ingenious and capricious forms: but, in fact, the mold, as might have been feared, is so loose and rough that it often seems to offer us but a broad burlesque of Mr. Hawthorne's exquisite fantasies. To relate in a few words the substance of *Idolatry* would require a good deal of ingenuity; it would require a good deal on our own part, in especial, to glaze over our imperfect comprehension of the mysteries of the plot. It is a purely fantastic tale, and deals with a hero, Balder Helwyse by name, whose walking costume, in the streets of Boston, consists of a black velveteen jacket and tights, high boots, a telescope, and a satchel; and of a heroine, by name Gnulemah, the fashion of whose garments is yet more singular, and who has spent her twenty years in the precincts of an Egyptian temple on the Hudson River. This is a singular couple, but there are stranger things still in the volume, and we mean no irony whatsoever when we say they must be read at first-hand to be appreciated. Mr. Hawthorne has proposed to himself to write a prodigiously strange story, and he has thoroughly succeeded. He is probably perfectly aware that it is a very easy story to give a comical account of, and serenely prepared to be assured on all sides that such people, such places, and such doings are preposterously impossible. This, in fact, is no criticism of his book, which, save at a certain number of points, where he deals rather too profusely in local color, pursues its mysterious aim on a line quite distinct from reality. It is indiscreet, artistically, in a work in which enchanted rings and Egyptian temples and avenging thunderbolts play so prominent a part, to bring us face to face with the Tremont House, the Beacon Hill Bank in School Street, the Empire State steamboat, and the ''sumptuous residence in Brooklyn''—fatal combination!—of Mrs. Glyphic's second husband. We do not in the least object, for amusement's sake, to Dr. Glyphic's miniature Egypt on the North River; but we should prefer to approach it through the air, as it were, and not by a conveyance which literally figures in a time-table. Mr. Hawthorne's story is purely imaginative, and this fact, which by some readers may be made its reproach, is, to our sense, its chief recommendation. An author, if he feels it in him, has a perfect right to write a fairy-tale. Of course he is bound to make it entertaining, and if he can also make it mean something more than it seems to mean on the surface, he doubly

justifies himself. It must be confessed that when one is confronted with a fairy-tale as bulky as the volume before us, one puts forward in self-defense a few vague reflections. Such a production may seem on occasion a sort of *reductio ad absurdum* of the exaggerated modern fashion of romancing. One wonders whether pure fiction is not running away with the human mind, and operating as a kind of leakage in the evolution of thought. If one decides, as we, for our part, have decided, that though there is certainly a terrible number too many novels written, yet the novel itself is an excellent thing, and a possible vehicle of an infinite amount of wisdom, one will find no fault with a romance for being frankly romantic, and only demand of it, as one does of any other book, that it be good of its kind. In fact, as matters stand just now, the presumption seems to us to be rather in favor of something finely audacious in the line of fiction. Let a novelist of the proper temperament shoot high by all means, we should say, and see what he brings down. Mr. Hawthorne shoots very high indeed, and bags some strangely feathered game; but, to be perfectly frank, we have been more impressed with his length of range than with his good luck. *Idolatry*, we take it, is an allegory, and the fantastic fable but the gayly figured vestment of a poised and rounded moral. We are haunted as we read by an uncomfortable sense of allegorical intention; episodes and details are so many exact correspondences to the complexities of a moral theme, and the author, as he goes, is constantly drawing an incidental lesson in a light, fantastic way, and tracing capricious symbolisms and analogies. If the value of these, it must be said, is a measure of the value of the central idea, those who, like ourselves, have failed to read between the lines have not suffered an irreparable loss. We have not, really, the smallest idea of what *Idolatry* is about. Who is the idol and who is the idolizer? What is the enchanted ring and what the fiddle of Manetho? What is the latent propriety of Mr. MacGentle's singular attributes, and what is shadowed forth in the blindness of Gnulemah? What does Salome stand for, and what does the hoopoe symbolize? We give it up, after due reflection; but we give it up with a certain kindness for the author, disappointing as he is. He is disappointing because his second novel is on the whole more juvenile than his first, and he makes us wonder whether he has condemned himself to perpetual immaturity. But he has a talent which it would be a great pity to see come to nothing. On the side of the imagination he is distinctly the son of his illustrious father. He has a vast amount of fancy; though we must add that it is more considerable in quantity than in quality, and finer, as we may say, than any use he makes of it. He has a commendable tendency to large imaginative conceptions, of which there are several noticeable specimens in the present volume. The whole figure of Balder Helwyse, in spite of its crudities of execution, is a handsome piece of fantasy, and there is something finely audacious in his interview with Manetho in the perfect darkness, in its catastrophe, and in the general circumstances of his meeting with Gnulemah. Gnulemah's antecedents and mental attitude are a matter which it required much ingenuity to conceive and much courage to attempt to render. Mr. Hawthorne writes, moreover, with a conscience of his own, and his tale has evidently been, from his own point of view, elaborately and carefully worked out. Above all, he writes, even when he writes ill, with remarkable vigor and energy; he has what is vulgarly called ''go,'' and his book is pervaded by a grateful suggestion of high animal spirits. He is that excellent thing, a story-teller with a temperament. A temperament, however, if it is a good basis, is not much more, and Mr. Hawthorne has a hundred faults of taste to unlearn. Our advice to him would be not to mistrust his active imagination, but religiously to respect it, and, using the term properly, to cultivate it. He has vigor and resolution; let him now supply himself with culture—a great deal of it. (pp. 746-48)

> Henry James, in a review of "Idolatry," in The Atlantic Monthly, *Vol. XXXIV, No. CCVI, December, 1874, pp. 746-48.*

[HENRY JAMES]   (essay date 1876)

[In the following excerpt, James objects to the tone and content of Saxon Studies, *finding Hawthorne's remarks concerning German culture shallow and frequently petty.]*

Mr. Hawthorne is decidedly disappointing. He strikes us as having inherited a certain portion of his father's genius. He writes with vigor and vivacity, and his style has a charm of its own; but he perpetually suggests more than he performs, and leaves the reader waiting for something that never comes. There is something masculine and out of the common way in his manner of going to work, but the use he makes of his talent is not characterized by a high degree of wisdom, and the reader's last impression is of a strange immaturity of thought. *Saxon Studies* is such a book as a very young man might write in a season of combined ill-humor and conscious cleverness; but it is a book which most young men would very soon afterwards be sorry to have written. We suspect that this intelligent compunction will never be Mr. Hawthorne's portion, and the feeling makes us judge his volume with a certain harshness. The author fairly convinces us that he is not likely ever to understand why the tone in which he has chosen to talk about the worthy inhabitants of Dresden is not a rational, or a profitable, or a philosophic, or a really amusing one. Mr. Hawthorne spins his thread out of his own fancy, and at the touch of reality it would very soon snap. He had a perfect right, of course, to produce a faithful book about Dresden; but such a book, as it gives our imagination some trouble, is more than usually bound to justify itself. It must have a graceful, agreeable, and pliable spirit to reward us for the extra steps we take. But Mr. Hawthorne has quite violated this canon and has been fanciful only to be acrimonious, and reflective only to be—it is not too strong a word—unwholesome. He has written a *brooding* book, with all the defects and none of the charms of the type. His reveries are ill-natured, and his ingenuity is all vituperative.

He declares, in an amusing preface, that "his interest in Saxony and the Saxons is of the most moderate kind—certainly not enough to provoke a treatise upon them. They are as dull and featureless a race as exists in this century, and the less one has to do with them, the better. But the plan of his work requiring some concrete nucleus round which to group such thoughts and fancies as he wished to ventilate, and the Saxon capital chancing to have been his residence of late years, he has used it rather than any other place to serve his turn in this respect." This strikes us as an explanation after the fact. In so far as *Saxon Studies* had a "plan," we suspect it consisted of the simple desire on the author's part to pour forth his aversion to a city in which, for several years, he had not been able to guard himself against being regrettably irritable and uncomfortable. Dresden has served his turn, and enabled him to write his book; he ought at least in fairness to admit that there was something to say about her. But in truth, of what there was to say about her, even for ill, Mr. Hawthorne strikes us as having made but little. Of "plan" his volume contains less than the pardonable minimum; it has little coherency and little definiteness of statement. It is taken for granted in the first few pages, in a off-hand, allusive manner, that the Saxons are an ignoble and abominable race, and this note is struck at desultory intervals, in the course of a good deal of light, rambling talk about nothing in particular, through the rest of the volume; but the promise is never justified, the aversion is never explained, the story is never told. Before we know it we have Mr. Hawthorne talking, as of a notorious fact, about "the cold, profound selfishness which forms the foundation and framework of the national and individual character in every walk of life, the wretched chill of which must ultimately annul the warmth of the most fervent German eulogist," etc. This is a sweeping but an interesting charge, and the reader would have been glad to have the author go a little into the psychology of the matter, or at least into the history of his opinion—offer a few anecdotes, a few examples of Saxon selfishness, help us to know more exactly what he means. But Mr. Hawthorne is always sweeping and always vague. We can recall but two definite statements in his volume—that bearing upon the fact that the Germans, indoors, are pitifully ignorant of the charms of pure air, and the other upon the even more regrettable circumstance that they condemn their women to an infinite amount of hard labor. (p. 214)

In spite of Mr. Hawthorne's six years' residence in Dresden, his judgments appear to be formed only upon those matters which limit the horizon of a six weeks' sojourner—the tramways, the cabmen, the policemen, the beer-saloons. When he invites us to penetrate into a Dresden house, we find he means only to gossip rather invidiously about the parties, and to talk about the way the doors open and the rooms are distributed. The most successful pages in his volume are an extremely clever and amusing supposititious report, from a local newspaper, of the appearance of the first street-car, and a charming sketch of a beer-maiden, or waitress in a saloon, who invites the author and his friend to be her partners at a ball. These are the only cases we can recall in which Mr. Hawthorne's humor is not acrid and stingy. For the rest, he gives us no report of his social observations proper, of his impressions of private manners and morals; no examples of sentiments, opinions, conversations, ways of living and thinking. Upon those other valuable sources of one's knowledge of a foreign country— the theatre, literature, the press, the arts—Mr. Hawthorne is entirely dumb. The only literary allusion that his volume contains is the observation that the relation of Schiller and Goethe to the Germans of the present day may be described as sublimity reflected in mud-puddles. The absence of those influences to which we have alluded makes *Saxon Studies* seem unduly trivial and even rather puerile. It gives us the feeling that the author has nursed his dislikes and irritations in a dark closet, that he has never put them forth into the open air, never discussed and compared and intelligently verified them. This—and not at all the fact that they *are* dislikes—is the weak point of Mr. Hawthorne's volume. He had a perfect right to detest the Saxons, and our strictures are made not in the least in defence of this eminent people, but simply in that of good literature. We are extremely sorry, indeed, that so lively an aversion should not have been better served in expression. Even if Mr. Hawthorne had made the Saxon vices much more vivid, and his irritation much more intelligible, we should still find fault with his spirit. It is the spirit which sees the very small things and ignores the large ones—which gives more to fancy than to observation, and more to resentment than to reflection. (pp. 214-15)

> [Henry James], in a review of "Saxon Studies," in The Nation, *New York, Vol. XXII, No. 561, March 30, 1876, pp. 214-15.*

JOHN NICHOL (essay date 1882)

[*Nichol was a Scottish biographer, critic, and poet. In the following excerpt, he considers Hawthorne's choice of his father's profession audacious and assesses his work as uneven in quality, remarking in particular upon the improbability of his plots and the heavyhanded style in which they are frequently presented.*]

It is boldness in Julian Hawthorne to write novels at all: the height of daring, to write them, as he habitually does, in the metaphysical manner: an almost incredible audacity, that he should take for his recurring text the ruining or regenerating results of sin, and illustrate his theories of transmitted qualities by reference to popular superstitions. The ghost of Napoleon I. was, at the commencement of the Franco-German war, represented, in political cartoons, as warning away from the gulf the wearer of his name. Julian Hawthorne has only rashness in common with the prisoner of Sedan; but, in dealing with the supernatural, and endeavouring to make it throw light on moral problems, he should recall the line—

Within that circle none dare walk but he.

It is as if a son of Spenser had attempted to complete the *Faërie Queene*, or a son of Bacon the *Novum Organum*. Nature, however, will have her way, and perhaps the only literary lesson now worth reading is not to tax her energies by vainly endeavouring to do too much.

Julian Hawthorne's works, as those of the majority of his compeers, consist of [short] sketches, representing situations or episodes; and of more elaborate, though, in his case, seldom highly-finished, romances—generally tragedies—of a whole life. In the preface to his best volume of the former he boldly justifies the frequent unreality of the atmosphere in which they are steeped. "What is called the human interest, in fiction, is doubtless more absorbing than any other—but the marvellous always possesses a fascination, and justly. . . . He who would mirror in his works the whole of man must needs include the impossible along with the rest. . . . *Tom Jones, Adam Bede,* and *Vanity Fair* are earth without sky . . . the sky of Shakespeare and Dante, of Goethe and George Sand. A reader with a healthy sense of justice feels that an occasional excursion mysteryward is no more than he has a right to demand. And such excursions are wholesome for literature no less than for him. For the story-teller, sensible of the risk he runs of making his supernatural element appear crude and ridiculous, exerts himself to the utmost, and his style and method purify and wax artistic under the strain." This is precisely what Nathaniel Hawthorne has—what Julian has not—done. The latter has paid too little attention to his style, as a comparison of the above with any of his father's prefaces will show: it is rarely inaccurate, but often crude: his finest sentences seem constrained into beauty or power by the terseness or truth of the thought; but he never exerts himself to avoid repetition: consequently few who have written so well have also written so ill. His only considerable humorous sketch, *Mrs. Gainsborough's Diamonds,* which he slights as "a mere *jeu d'esprit,*" is, in matter and manner, rarely excellent, strange enough yet perfectly credible, satirical and dramatic—a little in the style of N. P. Willis, but on a higher level. In the same volume **"The Laughing-Mill"**—a ghastly misnomer—is as powerful as *Ethan Brand,* and the pathetic **"Christmas Guest"** is no way inferior to *Lily's Quest* or the *Sister Years* of the elder Hawthorne. But when Julian attempts to combine the manner of the last-named, of Edgar Poe and of G.P.R. James, as in the murderous **"Kildharns Oak,"** the result is ludicrous. The incidents of the duel with Red Beard; the planting of the tree; the man rolled down

the cliff; the torn hand; the Sybil of ninety years blown away with the oak in a storm,—are less worthy of the *Castle of Otranto* than of a third-rate theatre. A more interesting example of this writer's tendency to trip, and fall on the wrong side of the line, is **"Ellice Quantin"**; a story in which occasional flashes of insight and touches of subtilty traverse and sometimes redeem the almost nonsensical basis. Ellice loves Geoffrey Herne, keeps him from going to Australia, and, "her eyes glowing with luxurious light, the curving of her lips being eloquent of refined enticement," says, "Be sure you make me love you enough. Do I overflow your heart?" Her father suddenly inherits a fortune. She meets Geoffrey, and wishes him to make her safe by an off-hand marriage. But he, being law-abiding and honourable, recoils. She replies, "Well, it is fate," and writes next day giving him up. Herne, after the fashion of disappointed men, gets on at the bar. Subsequently, he, at a garden party, meets Ellice, now the wife of Mr. Amidon, "a youngish-looking man, with a flaxen moustache and pale grey eyes rather red round the edges," who opens his mouth, only once, to exclaim, "Capital punch, upon my soul." Mrs. Amidon tells Geoffrey that she cannot do without him, and only "wears her husband as she wears her hat." "She was a woman who wanted much; but who was not, perhaps, willing to go all lengths to get it. . . . A woman who has achieved a position before the world will hesitate profoundly before abandoning outward conventionality for avowed outlawry. Compromises are more convenient. But how if a stubborn man persists in refusing to stoop to compromise?" Geoffrey does so; but she gives him a "white rosebud," puts it in his button-hole, and says, "Before this fades." She drives to his hotel, sees him at the window reading a paper, murmurs, "If he looks out and recognises me, I will go to him." He does not; so she returns to Mayfair in the same hansom. Two years pass: Herne is morosely neglecting his work. "What is the odds what a man does? The devil is at the bottom of it all." Meanwhile Ellice, having determined to divorce her husband, comes to her lover, having in vain written for him. "Your rose is withered," she cries, "but it may not be too late to make it bloom again." "We cannot," he answers; "I am going to be married." She asks to see the lady; and at last his virtue succumbs. "Oh, Ellice, if you only say so I will come without her." But she has a grain of conscience, and demurs, in her turn, to the suggested treachery. The betrothed pair pay a visit to the old love: she brings in three glasses of wine. Gertrude and Geoffrey choose safely: Ellice drains the one poisoned cup and dies, leaving the survivors in a somewhat unpleasant position. Such outlines are apt to be travesties; and, here as elsewhere, apology is due for omission of the delicate shades and lurid lights which impassion, if they do not vitalise, the story. But there is no defence of the melodramatic conclusion. In another tale, of about the same length, the author's success is as decided as is his failure in the above, to make us believe in his stage and sympathise with his actors. The introduction to *Archibald Malmaison* contains a few sentences of characteristic pessimism, at least as true as the glib optimism which it challenges—

When I was a child I used to hope my faery stories were true. . . . The knowledge of maturity, which has discovered that nothing that is true (in the sense of being existent) can be beautiful, deprecates truth beyond everything. What happens, we find, is never what ought to happen, nor does it happen in the right way or season. In palliation of this hardship, the sublime irony of fate grants us our imagination. . . . Your hearer's life and those of his friends are enough true stories for him; what he wants of you is merciful fiction. . . . To bully him with facts is like asking him to live his life over again; and the civilised being is yet to be found who would not rather die than do that. . . . I have now to reconcile this profession of faith with the incongruous fact that the following story is a true one.

The exceptional character of the facts, in the history of the Malmaisons—whom he represents as an old Sussex family of the Huguenots—may have reconciled Mr. Hawthorne to their reality. . . . The opportunities afforded by this tragedy are put to a masterly use in a tale of terror, love, violence, and mystery where, granting the postulate of the strange pathology, there is nothing incredible. The manner in which, in critical moments, Malmaison bounds back into life and authority frequently reminds us of the old nobleman's reappearance in the burning castle of Victor Hugo's *Quatrevingt-Treize.*

The same artistic and other features—sombre views, penetrative power, and limited range of vision, a large demand on our credulity, great inequality of style, a passion for the anomalous, with general disdain for the conventionalities of life—appear in the author's longer works. Of these, *Sebastian Strome* has the best-constructed plot and most freshness, if not originality, in its characters. The good Vicar himself is a model type of unaggressive Stoicism, the "incarnation," as he is described, "of self-forgetting enthusiasm," keeping "through all the stress and strain of manhood the guileless candour and ingenuousness of a child," the sternness of his devotion constantly softened by a charity that endures all things but treachery; a man of whom we hardly need to be told that "confidence went to him as metal to the lodestone." Talking of the poor girl, his parishioner, who has been led astray, he "seems holding out protecting arms to her through the crowd," but when she will not give her betrayer's name he exclaims, "I'm glad I do not know him, wife. I could not keep my hands from taking him by the throat; the man's heart must be flint." "Surely," rejoins the silver-haired old lady, "her sin is as great." But the husband is of another mind, and, resolving to go to London in search of Fanny, says, with fine tact, "It is a man's work to bring her here, not yours." The task is ultimately devolved upon their son and idol, Sebastian, who is in the metropolis studying for the ministry, and is engaged to a noble, though impulsive, country heiress, his old playmate. He is a gambler, an atheist, and, as the novel-initiated reader from the first divines, the criminal. His moral redemption, the central theme of the book, is wrought out through a series of vicissitudes and calamities, probable and improbable; the main agents being the remorse caused by the death of his father (who is killed by the revelation of his son's guilt) and love for his child, with whom he lives for some years, as a wood-carver, in the slums of London. . . . The author, under difficulties, succeeds in making us ultimately forgive the younger Strome. He fails to reconcile us to *Bressant*—the hero of an earlier novel, woven on thinner strands—for the inherent selfishness of this social innovator and trifler with hearts, over which he wields a fickle lordship, by the sheer audacity of a handsome giant, is unredeemed by any final sacrifice. Valeyon is a weaker forecast of the vicar, hardly made more interesting by the mystery that surrounds him. Here, as elsewhere, in the two women, Cornelia and Sophia, we have the hereditary contrasted female types: the text of the *Marble Faun* is set forth too plainly in the dialogue. "B.—'To do anything there must be a whirl in the blood. . . . It would be better to commit a deadly crime than

to dribble out like that fountain.' S.—'Even to speak of sins doing good is a fearful and wicked thing.' B.—'I think anything is better than to be torpid.'"

The excessive intricacy of *Garth* makes special criticism, in our space, impossible. It is the author's only considerable romance, the scene of which is laid in America, and it gives occasion for his most vivid descriptions,—as the passage of the torrent, or the race on skates at the rescue,—and it has some historical interest. The story in this case turns on transmitted qualities,—the hero having inherited a disposition to commit murder, against which he successfully struggles,—and on a blood-feud, not, as in the *House of Seven Gables,* between families, but between races; the one represented by the half-caste Indian Kineo, the other by Garth, who is a Puritan Anak with the soul of a *Sintram.* The opposed female types reappear, in their weirdest and wildest forms, in Madge Denver and Elinor. The *dénoûement* is both terrible and perplexing; but, in isolated incidents, the author has never been so dramatic. Julian Hawthorne's depth of insight, passion unchilled by philosophy, determination to cleave through the crusts of society to the lava reservoirs of the heart, observing and reflective powers undimmed by the storms and gusts of feeling he represents and seems to share, catholic breadth with profound purpose,—these qualities indisputably stamp him as a man of genius; but his talents are inadequate, his work frequently chaotic, often recklessly sensational, and he is perpetually playing

Hawthorne with his sisters, Una (left) and Rose, in 1861.

variations of the same tune on the same old Stradivarius. No one requires to be more continent of speech; or, if he desires them to live, more careful in his creations. He has hitherto, in his conceptions and plots, followed too closely the example set by the glory of his name: he is in danger of forgetting to follow it in one essential. There is little that may not be hoped from him, if he be content to disdain the bad precedents of contemporary light literature, and write one novel in two years: there is nothing that may not be feared if, bitten by the tarantula activity, against which Nathaniel Hawthorne unceasingly protested, he perseveres in the foolish feat of issuing two in one year. (pp. 380-88)

> John Nichol, "American Novelists, 1850-1880," in his American Literature: An Historical Sketch, 1620-1880, *Adam and Charles Black, 1882, pp. 353-401.*

THE ATLANTIC MONTHLY   (essay date 1883)

[*In the following review, the critic considers* Dust *clever and well-written, but notes flaws in the novel's plot.*]

Mr. Julian Hawthorne, by virtue of a patient endurance of England, has given us not only a novel [, ***Dust,***] wholly English in its circumstance, but one which deals with a historic England. He has chosen the period of the first quarter of the present century, and by so doing has rid himself quite completely of all temptation to insert any Americanism. The England of that day and the United States were farther apart in their mutual influence than they had been before or have been since. There is nothing, therefore, in the form of the book to give the slightest hint of any other than an English nativity; and yet one may amuse himself by detecting, now and then, a note which suggests that the writer is viewing England, and is not himself of the soil. To be sure, the very attitude of a historical romancer is necessarily a little outside of his subject; and perhaps this helps to confirm the illusion we are entertaining,—that the American, however long he may remain away from his native soil, never quite loses the native accent.

Be this as it may, we doubt if an Englishman would detect the subtle presence of America in the book any more readily than an American. Mr. Hawthorne has the artist's rather than the historical student's faculty, and he has helped himself to the tone and color of the life which he depicts with a quickness of perception and a deftness of touch which make mere historical treatment seem lumbering and ineffective. He has not, it would appear, given himself the trouble which Thackeray took to preserve the *vraisemblance* of an earlier period, but he has not been betrayed into too great anxiety for historical effect. He has allowed his story to move on its way unencumbered by an excess of antiquarian baggage, and the result is a freedom which constantly makes the reader forget that he is reading a story, and persuades him that he is listening to a veritable narrative.

It certainly is an admirable art which does this, and Mr. Hawthorne has secured his success by asking the reader's interest in the persons of his drama, and not in the stage properties among which they move. The principal characters are not many, and they are all involved in the plot of the story. A young man, who figures as a very self-conscious and self-analytic poet; an old man of singularly marked features, who yet moves about apparently unrecognized in a circle to which he returns, after a sudden disappearance under a cloud a score of years or more before; a rascally banker; a cold-blooded solicitor; a young

woman of a somewhat heavy cast, but very vigorous in nature; a young woman of brilliant parts and passionate caprice,—these are not singularly new to fiction, and when one reviews the story he almost fails to discover why he became so much interested in the movement of these characters.

Yet interested most will become, and it is this vitality in the book which is a mark of strength in the author. He tells his story with a will, and one is carried along by the very force of the action. This is the more noticeable that the resolution of the author is expended upon a fictitious moral. The *motif* of the book is self-sacrifice, and by a careful concealment of the nature of this sacrifice until the story is nearly completed, the author succeeds in developing the plot without injury. (pp. 704-05)

Mr. Hawthorne would have us believe that Sir Francis Bendibow . . . and Mr. Charles Grantley . . . were associated in business when young men; that Mr. Grantley discovered Sir Francis to be a gambler of the deepest dye, who had misappropriated the funds of the bank; that, in order to shield Sir Francis, Charles Grantley placed all his money in his partner's hands to make good the loss of the bank, left his wife and young daughter in the gambler's care, and fled to India, to begin life over again,—his expectation being that his own name would thus be stained, and his partner's cleared. (p. 705)

Where the plot is so intricate as it is in this book, it is not easy to make a brief statement serve as explanation, nor is it quite fair to attempt this; but the point we would emphasize is the nonsensical nature of the self-sacrifice which Mr. Grantley makes, and upon which the whole development of the novel turns. Self-sacrifice is a fine thing, but it must be allowed a justifiable motive. To shield a villain, when every indication points to the villainy being ingrained, one does not part with his good name, and at the same time bestow upon his daughter the inheritance of felony. He does not leave his daughter to be piously brought up by the villain who has wronged him, and go off to India to make his fortune, and bring it back for the benefit of another young woman, his landlady's daughter.

There comes, through this misapplication of morality, to be a certain air of unreality about the monetary transactions of the book. This great banking house, a rival of Childs', is built on the bottomless pit of a gambling hell; the poet receives a check for eleven hundred and fifty pounds . . . ten days after his great Southeyan poem of Iduna is published. Nothing in the book is more unreal than these eleven hundred and fifty pounds: an English publisher makes his accounts more exact than that; there should be some odd shillings, pence, and half-pence. The twenty thousand pounds which Mr. Grantley leaves dance about from hand to hand, with the alacrity of counterfeit coin; and finally, when the hero has got into a pecuniary scrape, where his own and his wife's integrity have placed him, he is pulled out by a lucky five thousand pounds, left him by a nebulous ducal uncle. Money, indeed, in this book, has an air of legerdemain about it, which makes it curiously volatile. We begin to want a little of it.

In one respect we may commend the author, that he has shown a reserve in using his heroine's capacity for second sight. She employs it twice quite effectively, but we are very glad she does not use it again. As a delicate piece of machinery in a novel, such a contrivance may work well, but only when carefully handled. In spite of the central fault of the book, there is so much cleverness about it, so much good writing, and so many skillful touches that one cannot help admiring the author's faculty. No one who throws so much vitality into his work can be blamed for writing novels as often as he wants to. (pp. 705-06)

A review of "Dust," in The Atlantic Monthly, Vol. LI, No. CCCVII, May, 1883, pp. 704-06.

THE CRITIC AND GOOD LITERATURE (essay date 1884)

[*In the following excerpt, the critic asserts that* Beatrix Randolph *shows improvement over Hawthorne's previous novels.*]

Mr. Julian Hawthorne, in his latest novel, **Beatrix Randolph,** restricts himself to ordinary human nature and the present generation in the selection of his characters; the preposterous element, without which, probably, no Hawthorne could write a story or a book, being supplied by the plot, according to which a New York impresario, disappointed by a cablegram in losing the services of a famous European singer, supplies her place by a young girl from a village in central New York, who has, it is true, a very fine voice, but who has never been on the stage, or even sung in a concert room. Her stage presence, and her acting, however, prove all that could be desired, even on the opening night, and the public never discover that she is not the Great Marana, whose name, as well as whose place, she had taken. Having assumed the situation, Mr. Hawthorne treats it with much cleverness. . . . The story is interesting, though not a pleasant one. It deals largely with people who, to say the least, are disagreeable, even the heroine having very mixed moral convictions; while the problem of an innocent, though not lofty, soul voluntarily basing success upon a falsehood and being suspended in a moral snare from which the reader can foresee no possible escape, is not alluring. But the book abounds in graceful, thoughtful and wise paragraphs; and a striking characteristic of the work is, that while dealing almost wholly with people who have false conceptions of life, and love, and duty, the impression made upon the reader is one to elevate the dignity, the sweetness and the responsibility of life and its opportunities. Mr. Hawthorne's work is always interesting; not always interesting in itself, but as giving greater promise, in each successive novel, that each ebullition of his "fiery and untamed" genius is leaving a clearer and finer residue of moral conviction, of deep and tender thought, and of sympathetic insight; while he is turning his really fine imagination to finer uses in letting it color with meaning the possibilities of actual life and human nature, than in bidding it invent impossible conditions, unreal circumstances, and elfish souls. In other words, each successive novel proves more certainly that the author has the literary instinct which impels one to write aside from the question of fame or money; and although it is curious to see the genius of the elder Hawthorne,—crystalline, pure, flawless from the beginning, so that it never suggested in its earliest efforts the possibility of improvement,—succeeded by the lawless talent that at first suggested little but that it might be capable of improvement, it is a pleasure to see the latter yielding, consciously or unconsciously, to the training which is making it all of which it contained the possibility.

A review of "Beatrix Randolph," in The Critic & Good Literature, n.s. Vol. 1, No. 6, February 9, 1884, p. 64.

JULIAN HAWTHORNE (essay date 1887)

[*In the following excerpt from his* Confessions and Criticism, *Hawthorne takes a humorous, self-deprecating attitude toward his accomplishments as a fiction writer.*]

[**Bressant**] was received in a kindly manner by the press; but both in this country and in England some surprise and indignation were expressed that the son of his father should presume to be a novelist. This sentiment, whatever its bearing upon me, has undoubtedly been of service to my critics: it gives them something to write about. A disquisition upon the mantle of Nathaniel Hawthorne, and an analysis of the differences and similarities between him and his successor, generally fill so much of a notice as to enable the reviewer to dismiss the book itself very briefly. I often used to wish, when, years afterwards, I was myself a reviewer for the London *Spectator,* that I could light upon some son of his father who might similarly lighten my labors. Meanwhile, I was agreeably astonished at what I chose to consider the success of **Bressant,** and set to work to surpass it in another romance, called (for some reason I have forgotten) **Idolatry.** This unknown book was actually rewritten, in whole or in part, no less than seven times. *Non sum qualis eram.* For seven or eight years past I have seldom rewritten one of the many pages which circumstances have compelled me to inflict upon the world. But the discipline of **Idolatry** probably taught me how to clothe an idea in words. (pp. 11-12)

I began another novel, **Garth,** instalments of which appeared from month to month in *Harper's Magazine.* When it had run for a year or more, with no signs of abatement, the publishers felt obliged to intimate that unless I put an end to their misery they would. Accordingly, I promptly gave Garth his quietus. The truth is, I was tired of him myself. With all his qualities and virtues, he could not help being a prig. He found some friends, however, and still shows signs of vitality. I wrote no other novel for nearly two years, but contributed some sketches of English life to *Appleton's Journal,* and produced a couple of novelettes,—**Mrs. Gainsborough's Diamonds** and **Archibald Malmaison,**—which, by reason of their light draught, went rather farther than usual. Other short tales, which I hardly care to recall, belong to this period. I had already ceased to take pleasure in writing for its own sake,—partly, no doubt, because I was obliged to write for the sake of something else. Only those who have no reverence for literature should venture to meddle with the making of it,—unless, at all events, they can supply the demands of the butcher and baker from an independent source.

In 1879, **Sebastian Strome** was published as a serial in *All the Year Round.* Charley Dickens, the son of the great novelist, and editor of the magazine, used to say to me while the story was in progress, "Keep that red-haired girl up to the mark, and the story will do." I took a fancy to Mary Dene myself. But I uniformly prefer my heroines to my heroes; perhaps because I invent the former out of whole cloth, whereas the latter are often formed of shreds and patches of men I have met. And I never raised a character to the position of hero without recognizing in him, before I had done with him, an egregious ass. Differ as they may in other respects, they are all brethren in that; and yet I am by no means disposed to take a Carlylese view of my actual fellow-creatures.

I did some hard work at this time: I remember once writing for twenty-six consecutive hours without pausing or rising from my chair; and when, lately, I re-read the story then produced, it seemed quite as good as the average of my work in that kind. I hasten to add that it has never been printed in this country: for that matter, not more than half my short tales have found an American publisher. **Archibald Malmaison** was offered seven years ago to all the leading publishers in New York and Boston, and was promptly refused by all. Since its recent appearance here, however, it has had a circulation larger perhaps than that of all my other stories combined. But that is one of the accidents that neither author nor publisher can foresee. It was the horror of *Archibald Malmaison,* not any literary merit, that gave it vogue,—its horror, its strangeness, and its brevity. (pp. 12-15)

I cannot conscientiously say that I have found the literary profession—in and for itself—entirely agreeable. Almost everything that I have written has been written from necessity; and there is very little of it that I shall not be glad to see forgotten. The true rewards of literature, for men of limited calibre, are the incidental ones,—the valuable friendships and the charming associations which it brings about. For the sake of these I would willingly endure again many passages of a life that has not been all roses; not that I would appear to belittle my own work: it does not need it. But the present generation (in America at least) does not strike me as containing much literary genius. The number of undersized persons is large and active, and we hardly believe in the possibility of heroic stature. I cannot sufficiently admire the pains we are at to make our work—embodying the aims it does—immaculate in form. Form without idea is nothing, and we have no ideas. If one of us were to get an idea, it would create its own form, as easily as does a flower or a planet. I think we take ourselves too seriously: our posterity will not be nearly so grave over us. For my part, I do not write better than I do, because I have no ideas worth better clothes than they can pick up for themselves. "Whatever is worth doing at all is worth doing with your best pains," is a saying which has injured our literature more than any other single thing. How many a lumber-closet since the world began has been filled by the results of this purblind and delusive theory! But this is not autobiographical,—save that to have written it shows how little prudence my life has taught me.

. . . . .

I remember wondering, in 1871, how anybody could write novels. I had produced two or three short stories; but to expand such a thing until it should cover two or three hundred pages seemed an enterprise far beyond my capacity. Since then, I have accomplished the feat only too often; but I doubt whether I have a much clearer idea than before of the way it is done; and I am certain of never having done it twice in the same way. The manner in which the plant arrives at maturity varies according to the circumstances in which the seed is planted and cultivated; and the cultivator, in this instance at least, is content to adapt his action to whatever conditions happen to exist.

While, therefore, it might be easy to formulate a cut-and-dried method of procedure, which should be calculated to produce the best results by the most efficient means, no such formula would truly represent the present writer's actual practice. If I ever attempted to map out my successive steps beforehand, I never adhered to the forecast or reached the anticipated goal. The characters develop unexpected traits, and these traits become the parents of incidents that had not been contemplated. The characters themselves, on the other hand, cannot be kept to any preconceived characteristics; they are, in their turn, modified by the exigencies of the plot.

In two or three cases I have tried to make portraits of real persons whom I have known; but these persons have always been more lifeless than the others, and most lifeless in precisely those features that most nearly reproduced life. The best results in this direction are realized by those characters that come to

their birth simultaneously with the general scheme of the proposed events; though I remember that one of the most lifelike of my personages (Madge, in the novel *Garth*) was not even thought of until the story of which she is the heroine had been for some time under consideration.

Speaking generally, I should suppose that the best novels are apt to be those that have been longest in the novelist's mind before being committed to paper; and the best materials to use, in the way of character and scenery, are those that were studied not less than seven or eight years previous to their reproduction. Thereby is attained that quality in a story known as atmosphere or tone, perhaps the most valuable and telling quality of all. Occasionally, however, in the rare case of a story that suddenly seizes upon the writer's imagination and despotically "possesses" him, the atmosphere is created by the very strength of the "possession." In the former instance, the writer is thoroughly master of his subject; in the latter, the subject thoroughly masters him; and both amount essentially to the same thing, harmony between subject and writer.

With respect to style, there is little to be said. Without a good style, no writer can do much; but it is impossible really to create a good style. A writer's style was born at the same time and under the same conditions that he himself was. The only rule that can be given him is, to say what he has to say in the clearest and most direct way, using the most fitting and expressive words. But often, of course, this advice is like that of the doctor who counsels his patient to free his mind from all care and worry, to live luxuriously on the fat of the land, and to make a voyage round the world in a private yacht. The patient has not the means of following the prescription. A writer may improve a native talent for style; but the talent itself he must either have by nature, or forever go without. And the style that rises to the height of genius is like the Phœnix; there is hardly ever more than one example of it in an age. (pp. 15-20)

> *Julian Hawthorne, "A Preliminary Confession," in his* Confessions and Criticisms, *Ticknor and Company, 1887, pp. 9-30.*

CHARLES F. RICHARDSON　(essay date 1889)

[*Richardson, an American journalist, poet, and literary historian, was best known for his pioneering studies of American literature. In the following excerpt from the second volume of his* American Literature, 1607-1885: American Poetry and Fiction *(1889), he calls Hawthorne the finest living romance writer. Although Richardson notes faults in language, construction, and characterization in Hawthorne's fiction, he asserts that the novels nonetheless display power and originality.*]

To the smaller novelists as well as the greater there sometimes comes that ideal vision, that clearer insight, which peers to depths and heights of life unseen before. If the thought and the power be those of romance, the resulting life-picture need not be less true because less commonplace or familiar.

Such life-pictures are not hard to find in the tales, novels, and romances of the younger Hawthorne. Over his broad field hang both European and American skies, but they are not seldom illumined by "the light that never was on sea or land." Internationalism, in his method, is but a convenience in the portrayal of minor character; it is not a mere matter of external amusement. "Analysis" he reserves for such essays as those printed in *Saxon Studies*; soul he deems a thing somewhat deeper than may be shown by mere study of attitude or lesser act. His studies in stories are of life, not of society; and he prefers to create rather than to record. The soul and its struggles, deep sin and grim inexorable penalty, inner loveliness and spiritual triumph, are his higher themes; and though he occasionally writes some compact tale of mere crime and discovery, he usually turns to subjects far more intricate and psychological. His lighter tales are long-removed from the intense romance called *Sinfire* or the original creation of *Archibald Malmaison*; yet even in the former there sometimes appears the romancer's profound impression of the depth and half-guessed meaning of the mystery of life, and his constant search for some utterance of that impression.

The careless opulence of which I have just spoken, as a sign of the strength and the weakness of later American fiction, finds no better illustration than in Julian Hawthorne's books. They crowd upon each other in their rapid appearance; their construction and language are too often so faulty that they almost seem wayward; and now and then the figures are blurred upon the mental retina. *Archibald Malmaison* seems to me the most original and the strongest of the author's books, a remarkable example of the romance pure and simple; yet even here, where the elaboration of the peculiar plot demands the utmost nicety, are occasional signs of haste. Julian Hawthorne has not yet applied to fiction the constructive art and the gravely decorative detail which make his *Nathaniel Hawthorne and his Wife* the best biography written in America. In *Sebastian Strome,* which is not unable to endure mention beside *Adam Bede,* of which it is a sort of unintentional counterpart, the author shows his most sustained strength. I prefer, however, to find in the general, rather than the particular, those qualities which led a living critic [Richard Henry Stoddard]—a critic thoroughly familiar with the work of Nathaniel Hawthorne and Edgar Allan Poe—to declare that Julian Hawthorne "is clearly and easily the first of living romancers."

None knows better than Mr. Hawthorne himself the perilousness of so confident a statement as this. But it is certain that his published books display the originality and power of genius. (pp. 445-46)

Charles F. Richardson, "Later Moments in American Fiction," in his *American Literature: American Poetry and Fiction, 1607-1885,* Vol. II, *G. P. Putnam's Sons, 1889, pp. 413-50.*

LIONEL STEVENSON (essay date 1931)

[*A respected Canadian literary critic, Stevenson was also the author of five biographies, each highly acclaimed for its wit, scholarship, and clarity. In the following excerpt, Stevenson finds that the fusion of Gothic romanticism and scientific naturalism in Hawthorne's fiction reflect a transitional period in literature, noting in addition the moral and aesthetic prejudices that prevented late nineteenth-century critics from performing objective analyses of his work.*]

[Julian Hawthorne's] place in American literature has never been intelligently considered. His first works were regarded with preconceived opinions based on his father's reputation, and later he was subjected to other prejudices, arising out of his forcible opinions, his professed commercialism, his fecundity and versatility. Later, when a truer perspective might have been expected with the ceasing of professional competition and its attendant jealousies, the literary fashion had so changed that Julian Hawthorne and his contemporaries, except three or four Titans, were not evaluated at all, but were ignored as outmoded. Now, perhaps, it is time for him to emerge from

that inevitable limbo through which every writer must pass between current acclaim and secure historic recognition.

His only books to have retained a steady position are his biographical studies, *Nathaniel Hawthorne and His Wife,* published in 1884, and *Hawthorne and His Circle,* twenty years later. Now, after another quarter-century, has come a third to put beside them, *Shapes that Pass.* The first draws a vivid and detailed picture of Nathaniel Hawthorne with particular attention to his home life and his wife's influence; the second sketches his relations with the other interesting people of his time, both at home and in England; while the third gives a similar survey of English literary men a few years later, when the son was received into the writing fraternity of London.

The manner and method of these books are agreeable; intimate glimpses of private life, touches of irony in character delineation, lack of reverence in allusions to celebrities, all the qualities which grieved the readers of the first book, have come to be regarded as virtues. The titles are enough to show that he avoided the dulness of an official "Life and Letters." On the other hand, he was skilful in handling the difficulties inherent in his relationship to the subject: he did not display unthinking adulation, yet he contrived to indicate a genuine sympathy and admiration for his father which implies credit to both of them. Similarly, his recent reminiscences could not be more self-effacing: he tells little about his own achievements and ideas, he does not record what he said to Browning or Swinburne nor any flattering remarks which they made to him; he brings them all to very human life without parade of the showman.

In any estimate of his literary significance, however, these books must be set aside; and along with them should go *Saxon Studies*—a pleasant record of his Dresden days, sometimes showing kinship with *Innocents Abroad* in its shrewd touches, but free from the responsibility of being persistently comic—and *Confessions and Criticisms,* an assemblage of the comments which made him spectacular, and sometimes unpopular, when they appeared in the Reviews of the eighties. So-called "creative writing" has to be the final basis of permanent literary values, so the eventual reputation of Julian Hawthorne must depend on his works of fiction.

Their chief importance in literary history will probably be that they reflect with remarkable clearness an important transition which affected the whole of human life and thought everywhere, and in the United States with particular intensity. The concluding third of the nineteenth century witnessed the triumph of the scientific spirit over all adversaries. Science, both theoretical and applied, having become the determining influence in daily life and in methods of thought, inevitably pierced to the very foundations of literature. Theoretical science showed itself not merely in the immediate controversy of dogmatic religion and agnostic materialism, but also in the application of scientific methods to the observing of human character and human relationships, with the resulting new sciences of psychology and sociology; applied science began to replace the "crusted characters" and "local color" of the old dispensation with the standardized types developed by mass-production of commodities and by easy travel.

Since it was not humanly possible for anyone to perceive how comprehensive the revolution was to be, the instinctive efforts to harmonize the new outlook with the old were bound to cause contradiction and paradox. In Julian Hawthorne's novels the struggle to assimilate the new elements without rejecting the old is plainly visible is many directions.

Primarily, it would seem, he was a devotee of the Gothic romanticism which, after culminating in England with Scott, Byron, and their contemporaries, had crossed the Atlantic and found a second blooming in Poe, to say nothing of playing an important rôle, in spite of the repressions imposed by Brook Farm transcendentalism, in the work of Hawthorne the elder. Its distinguishing features are to be discerned in every one of the younger Hawthorne's novels, and not as superficial trimmings but always innate in the very heart of the story. Chief of these traits are fondness for the supernatural and the horrible, violence in the depiction of uncontrolled emotional frenzy, selection of a hero who is a superman in physique, intellect, and passion, and indulgence in what Ruskin dubbed the "pathetic fallacy" of natural phenomena as responsive to human moods. Admitting that these elements were largely responsible for his popularity with the circulating-library public, which is always romantic in its tastes, one yet must hesitate to suggest that he chose them for that reason, for they are handled with gusto and often seem to be the very embryo of the plot.

On the other hand, he clearly recognized and admired the new tendencies. He championed the naturalism of Zola and his colleagues; he was personally acquainted with Meredith, Hardy and other English writers of the new dispensation, and was writing in competition with them; he hailed the superiority of James and Howells among his own compatriots. The whole method and outlook in his books were consistent with this radicalism: he devoted much space to analysis of psychological problems, placing heavy emphasis on sex; he admitted material which would have been condemned as ugly, sordid, or indelicate by his fastidious predecessors; he enjoyed the accumulation of familiar commonplace detail; and he introduced earnest discussions of the ethical and social problems which the situations implied. In all of these respects he was an enthusiastic disciple of the changed world.

The result was that he did not fully satisfy any faction. The prudish censured him for immodesty, as when the *Nation* said of his first book: "'Psychical analysis' is, we believe, the name that is given to the exceedingly distasteful quality which marks *Bressant* and which is to be found in many French novels of various grades.... It is a very bad thing because it lacks decency. In the place of a genuine study of human beings it gives us a morbid fingering of unclean emotions. After an experience of many centuries, society has agreed that there are certain subjects which shall not be talked about" [see excerpt dated 1873]. This blast was called forth by the fact that the story investigated a youth in love with two girls at the same time. His second novel, *Idolatry,* annoyed the London *Athenæum* by suggesting, though not actually presenting, the theme of incest: "There are passages a woman should hardly read aloud." Four years later the same journal called *Sebastian Strome* "worse than painful" because it began with the hero seducing a servant-girl and proceeded with the heroine marrying a pervert; and after another six years we find the *Critic,* in discussing *Love— or a Name,* applying the favorite *cliché* of prudery: "The reader lays down the book in disgust. Mr. Hawthorne throws an implied slur on what is supposed to be respectable young womanhood as a class.... It is merely a book to leave an unpleasant taste in the mouth."

On the other hand, the more advanced critics complained of the fanciful supernatural touches, the premonitions, second sight, ancestral curses, and so forth, that appeared in almost every book. The *Saturday Review* found in *Bressant* "a superstitious element of what we may call magnetico-mesmerico-

spiritualism which, to our mind, is very silly." Of *Garth,* in an otherwise favorable review, the *Atlantic Monthly* declared, "He could do better if he would not encumber himself with so much legendary matter. He has made his tradition so florid, and his reproduction of the past in the present so obvious, that he comes to the verge of destroying verisimilitude." The same magazines disliked *Dust* because the action at several points turned on the clairvoyance of the heroine, and *Fortune's Fool* because the hero was suddenly able to play the banjo without previous training. Similar objections were raised against many of the other books.

Meanwhile, the devotees of romance and fantasy complained that the supernatural phenomena were injured by too close a contact with familiar realistic details, as when the dying heroine of *Bressant* sent out her spirit in pursuit of the hero and found him in a train in which "the brakeman came in, took the poker and opened the stove door with it, peeped into the red-hot interior a moment, grasped a solid chunk of wood from the pile, and popped it in cleverly." *Idolatry,* the most fantastic of all his stories, was full of enchanted rings and Egyptian necromancy and avenging thunderbolts, yet the Nilotic temple of horrors was situated on the Hudson, and the action occurred in such places as the Tremont House, the Beacon Hill Bank in School Street and the *Empire State* steamboat. The more sentimental romance readers were cheated of happy endings in some of the stories, such as *Fortune's Fool,* which closed with the chief male character being murdered under the stage of a burning theatre while the heroine committed suicide on the stage above by playing Cleopatra with what was practically a real live asp. In general, the brutality of the villains throughout the books was recounted with a relish which made the tender-minded squirm, although the addicts of blood-and-thunder melodrama grumbled that they had to plod through too much meticulous analysis in order to reach the thrills. In short, the only stories of Julian Hawthorne to win anything like universal approbation were those of that indeterminate length, longer than short stories but shorter than novelettes, in which the mixing of incongruous ingredients was not apparent. Tales of abnormality and horror, like *Archibald Malmaison,* and of crime and detection, like *Mrs. Gainsborough's Diamonds,* evoked a unanimous praise never accorded to the long novels.

Every one of his outstanding traits can be readily traced to the conflict between Gothic romanticism and scientific naturalism. His heroes, with their defiance of convention, their potentialities for great evil as well as great good, their frenzied inward conflicts, are in the authentic succession from Byron, but they are not portrayed merely as superhuman monsters. Every element of heredity and environment, every subconscious byway, is explored. The phenomenon of genius particularly fascinated him: the hero of *Garth* is a painter, of *Dust* a poet, of *Fortune's Fool* a sculptor, and the heroine of *Beatrix Randolph* a singer. Most of these geniuses are introspective and temperamental, so the author has full opportunity of anatomizing them. Other psychological problems are equally prominent in other books. The hero of *Bressant* is shown at the age of twenty-three, the product of an experimental education which has made him a physical and intellectual prodigy but kept him entirely ignorant of love, and the story is devoted to his sexual awakening. The hero of *Sebastian Strome* is a fanatical seeker for absolute truth, who goes through all the throes of sin, crime, and religious infidelity, and emerges triumphant by reason of inward integrity. Byronic though all these beings may be, they are decked out in the livery of Comte and Dalton.

Then again, his handling of the supernatural lacks the pristine assurance of the Gothic tales of terror, from Mrs. Radcliffe to Poe. The second half of the nineteenth century witnessed the first invasion of mesmerists, mediums, mahatmas, who are still with us, having brought the practice of black magic up to date by investing it with a technical vocabulary and expounding it in abstruse treatises. In short, even superstition had to follow the new fashion and become scientific. Julian Hawthorne, therefore, whenever he introduced an apparition or a spell or a curse into his story, felt impelled to comment upon it in the best scientific terminology. The *Saturday Review* remarked, "A broomstick pure and simple, an old hag riding on it, and her black cat, we might perhaps stand; but the laws of the mysterious processes of a broomstick are too much for us."

Another great change which came over the novelists during the nineteenth century was their discovery of their influence over the public mind. Where their predecessors had been content to entertain with a good story, satisfied if they aroused laughter, shudders, or tears, as the case might be, the Victorian writers felt a solemn duty to turn this power to higher things. Whether in preaching morality, or propagating social theory, or suggesting some philosophical interpretation of existence, nearly all the major novelists were using their stories for ulterior purposes, and Julian Hawthorne caught the infection. No matter how romantically bizarre and intensified his stories might be, he was always ready to expatiate on current social or intellectual problems. The familiar paraphernalia of dastardly villains and angelic heroines, of disguised benefactors and exchanged infants and missing wills, must have felt astonished to find themselves so unwontedly sicklied o'er with the pale cast of thought. Even *Idolatry,* in which of all his books the romantic traits of wonder and escape from actuality were most fully developed, was an intermittent allegory of the soul's ordeal, accompanied by arguments about the necessity of sin, and so on. *Garth* is concerned with the relationship of art and morality, and *Sebastian Strome* plunges into the greatest controversy of its era, the free-for-all between religious faith and scientific agnosticism.

Were it only for the insight which they give us into the mental transition from which our present epoch emerged, Julian Hawthorne's novels would repay the attention of modern readers; but in addition they have intrinsic merits to recommend them. There is a sort of primitive vigor about them, a contagious joy in physical action and the exercise of the senses. The ideas are positive and individual, the events are stirring, the characterization boldly impressionistic. The literary style, while uneven in some of the more rapidly written books, is seldom without a touch of distinction, and frequently rises to real beauty. His robust virility is very unlike what we usually associate with the Victorian era, and yet there is a certain indefinable guilelessness, a hint of fairy tales and make-believe, in even his most morbid episodes, which offer a charming contrast to the conscientious sophistication of today.

Many characteristics which the writing profession now cultivates—avoidance of hierarchic pretension, admission that the financial returns of an author's work have some significance to him, assumption that an author may experiment with any subject and method he pleases—can be traced back to Julian Hawthorne. He had to parry many of the blows which innovation provokes. He helped to carry American literature through an awkward age, and to maintain its reputation both at home and abroad. Deserving respect for his energy, determination, and versatility, he asks for it no more in his eighty-fourth year

than he ever asked for it before, and that is all the better reason why it should be accorded him. (pp. 168-72)

Lionel Stevenson, "Dean of American Letters: Julian Hawthorne," in The Bookman, Vol. LXXIII, No. 2, April, 1931, pp. 164-72.

GEORGE KNOX (essay date 1957)

[*In the following excerpt, Knox discusses Hawthorne's literary, social, and political ideas, particularly as expressed in his writings for the* Star-News *during the late period of his life spent in Concord, California.*]

[We] should realize [Julian Hawthorne's] position as the son of a great man, and sympathize with all the difficulties he inherited when trying to succeed on the great man's own ground. Nathaniel was a specter constantly before him in memory, an image of achievement which he never really hoped to equal, an image which his contemporaries, moreover, would never allow him to equal. This image of a glorious past was an awesome edifice in the shadow of which Julian's present was but pigmy imitation and simulacrum. He had constantly to confess his own limitations. Writing once of Mrs. Henry Wood, author of *East Lynne* Julian reflected: "If I enjoy a superiority over her, it is that when I come across some of my own rubbish, I know it," and he added that she, fortunately, had not possessed any such torturing self-consciousness and sense of inferior talent as his own.

He also confessed once in *Lippincott's* that he had never found the literary profession, in and for itself, entirely agreeable. (pp. 19-20)

From time to time describing the receptions accorded to various of his works, he inclines to recall the disparities between intention and execution, between the originating stimulus and the subsequent exigencies, such as the perversities of language and the pressures of editors. In the case of *Bressant,* he recounted the kindly reviews but lamented the usual pose which critics took anent the presumptuous son of a genius. But he characteristically tried to allay his bitterness with bland irony.

> This sentiment, whatever its bearing upon me, has undoubtedly been of service to my critics: it gives them something to write about. A disquisition upon the mantle of Nathaniel Hawthorne, and an analysis of the differences and similarities between him and his successor, generally fill so much of a notice as to enable the reviewer to dismiss the book itself very briefly [see excerpt dated 1887].

As a result of such extrinsic criticism Julian often turned to his diaries and journals for self-questioning and out-pouring of uneasiness about a literary career, private fears to which the readers of his rather off-hand columns would never penetrate.

One of the lengthiest of these can be found in his diary of November, 1883, where he swears he will not undertake another novel and ascribes the failure of his fiction to various causes, one being his inability to cater to popular tastes. He also realized something of the anomalous nature of his work as a sport or hybrid product, a strange cross between the Gothic and the Realistic. Another reason was his own inability to believe in his characters and his proneness to treat them capriciously. Further, he felt that he really had no deep regard, only a theoretical one, for people. Failing to "create" (being inspirationist he distrusted the "creative" concept) any convincing character in the dozen or more volumes he wrote, Julian was willing to chalk it up to his dominant interest in "complication" rather than in what his father would have called problems of the human heart. He was never, taking his reminiscences as a whole, an accurate observer in the sense that James was, although some of his most vigorous descriptions resulted from his attempts to capture the spirit of James. He knew too much theoretically and not enough practically. This forced him to think of people abstractly and to create fictional characters thrice-removed from "real life."

Posing as a student and portrayer of character he suffered the inner conviction that he was trying to speed successfully in a direction he was least fitted to go. Consequently, he also recognized that for his lack of emotional sympathy he had to overcompensate by coaching an "indolent, cold, and indifferent imagination." Julian's big trouble, I should insist, was that according to his inspirational esthetic, he felt guilty (insincere) when he had to contrive what at the moment of writing he did not deeply feel. Thus, in moments of disappointment he could accuse himself bitterly: "I am too certain, too flippant, too indifferent to everything, truth included. I have no reverence for anything, and would sacrifice anything, truth included, for the sake of a startling or picturesque effect."

And when Julian indulged his down-spiraling self-examinations he inevitably levelled out on the plateau of self-effacement, of Gide-like assuming of masks and roles, but without the self-conscious artistry in self-portraiture that Gide possessed.

> I notice, in my association with men that I very seldom—I may almost say never—show more than one facet of myself. Why not? The reason is, a shyness, connected with vanity and with timidity. I desire to be thought a superior person, and I desire to be on genial terms with those I meet; but I'm invariably conscious of not being so much a man as I would fain appear. But this disingenuousness and acting in me, so monopolises my care and attention, that I am able to spare very little for my interlocutor; in preventing him from getting a square look at me, I prevent myself from getting a square look at him; and the crisp of the joke . . . is, that, after all, people estimate me at pretty nearly what I am worth; failing to appreciate some good points, but, on the other hand, ignoring many successfully-conceded bad ones. I know this, and yet I keep up the masquerade. And the result is, that men are to me either fools or foes, according to the degree of their strength and penetration. I get on much better with women, because I can more easily and completely subdue them; and also for other reasons . . . but neither do they know me.

Whether or not we accept such probings as attempts to avoid the real issue,—realization that he lacked solid genius—and to create a more complex personality than he actually had, we do see the pervasive feeling of aloneness. His isolation was not, however, like his father's, which was cultural and esthetic more than psychological.

Julian could, in spite of his self-dramatizations, analyze the works of the great novelists with sound results, and from a number of such analyses he could deduce a paradigm of the great novel; but he was annihilated because he couldn't write one himself. He could not represent life in its roundness and completeness, but in some one-sided advocate's view, something contrived for the moment. How could he ever achieve that balance between spirit and mystery on one side and flesh-and-blood and realistic matter-of-factness on the other? Striving to emulate Nathaniel's "romance" he erred toward mystery, mystification, and grotesquerie. His own pre-occupation with self-analysis led him to work up characters who were case studies in "complexes." Trying scientifically to explain the fantastic and the bizarre, he constructed gargoyles.

Yet, as he grew older he became resigned to being merely the son of Nathaniel Hawthorne and not an estimable writer in his own right or one who might someday be great. (pp. 20-2)

For Julian, no complete expression was possible without "inspiration," and this constitutes the basic message of [his] *Star-News* columns, insofar as they offered advice to aspiring writers. He inherited the Tolstoian theory of sincerity, which came into American criticism, probably, through Howells, Emerson, and Crane and continues to modern times in I. A. Richards. To Julian, "he who is the subject of the inspiration can account no better than any one else for the result which art accomplishes through him. The perfect poem is found, not made; the mind which utters it did not invent it." Emerson was his favorite poet and he never tired of comparing him with the moderns, who, of course, fell miserably short. With Emerson he associated the windharp which was fixed in a tree in front of the house. Julian had often listened raptly to the moaning of the winds through this romantic instrument, and as a writer held himself up analogously in function, a receiver of the infusions from Concord. In his literary criticism he claimed to exalt the search for "spirit," which gives art "universality"; and consonant with this stand he bemoaned photographic realism, the "new gospel of the auctioneer's catalogue, and the crackling of thorns under a pot. He who deals with facts only, deprives his work of gradation and distinction." He scorned those who "adopt the scientific method of merely collecting and describing phenomena" and made a plea for "structure," "controlling idea," and "underlying emotional maturity" as the cohesive architectural elements in all writing.

Adapting his father's theory of romance and adherence to truths of the "heart," Julian strove to implant the need of "ideality" in the practice of his contemporaries. He held that:

> Ideality and imagination are themselves merely the symptom or expression of the faculty and habit of spiritual or subjective intuition—a faculty of paramount value in life, though of late years, in the rush of rational knowledge and discovery, it is fallen into neglect . . . It undoubtedly belongs to an abstruse region of psychology; but its meaning for our present purpose is simply the act of testing questions of the moral consciousness by an inward touchstone of truth, instead of by external experience or information.

Although training to think like a scientist, Julian defected toward fantasy. He had listened too long to the oracles of Concord and had drunk the transcendental milk of paradise. For him, literature was always best defined as "the written communications of the soul of mankind with itself." The Emersonian-Carlylean esthetics emerged in his definition of art as "the imaginative expression of a divine life in man.'' It depended for its worth and veracity, not upon adherence to scientific exactitude or verification of literal fact, but upon ''its perception and portrayal of the underlying truth, of which fact is but the phenomenal and imperfect shadow.''

Although he made a case for the vigor of American Literature as much as or more than any one of his time he felt that America was not the ideal place to stimulate ''romance.'' There was, on the other hand, plenty of stimulus in America for the realist, limited though it might be in comparison with the possibilities for a realism of manner in Europe. But in addition to the faithful and objective study of nature, the novelist must aim for a loftier reality, and this must be evolved from an adequate knowledge of nature itself. This imaginative process was in a way itself scientific for it doubted and rejected the lifeless and the insincere. But it was precisely in being *merely* scientific that American realists were inadequate. As much as he disliked certain aspects of Zola, the Goncourts, and continental realists generally, he was constantly defending them as craftsmen, as being more aware and mature artists than American realists. . . . Even in Howells and James, whom he more admired than condemned over the years, he found more ''realism of texture'' and less of ''form and relation.'' Such realism encouraged near-sighted reading instead of comprehension. Howells, he said, had ''produced a great deal of finely wrought tapestry; but does not seem, as yet, to have found a hall fit to adorn it with.''

If Julian too often came close to the Sunday Supplement kind of romance in his own practice, he never condoned it as a critic. He particularly deplored modern sentimental excursions into half-imaginary past events which masquerade as historical novels. He denounced the mass of ''false and sentimental and tawdry rubbish'' that has been ''foisted upon us under the guise of historical romance'' for ''The accents of the literary huckster are heard in every line indited by the authors of these lifeless mongrels.'' He castigated his contemporary critics and novelists for seeing too much agnosticism and for not having strong convictions. Ironically, for the same reason, his own ''romances'' rang false. The attempts by late 19th century and early twentieth century realists to ''portray existence in its naked and unconsecrated lineaments,'' he evaluated as transient productions, although ''normal.'' We must not decry such writing as bad or a waste of time, but condition our taste so that we detect counterfeits and beware of them, whether counterfeit realists or counterfeit romances.

When he could not admire Howells he condemned him; Howells succeeded because of his foibles and because of his mediocre contemporaries as much as for the innate greatness of his works. Even Thackeray was too much occupied with minutiae and topical matters. D. H. Lawrence's failure lay in his inability to show the spiritual side except through the too fleshly, and by the same token, the popularity of his books was a symptom of the defect in the moral tone of our civilization. In the typically wry mood of the Pasadena days, he pled that he and other ''old fogies'' of literature might not ''clutter the paths of Olympus trodden by the aspiring feet of our joyous choir of Gertrude Steins and Ernest Hemingways.'' Yet, hard as he could be on the ''moderns'' Julian was unflagging in his attacks on anyone who recommended they be censored or suppressed.

If in his own fiction Julian tried to command two fronts, in a great degree incompatible,—a superficial dramatic and narrative similitude and completeness, and a unity of eerie impressionism—he was nevertheless able to recognize the proper balance in others. In Howells and James he saw ''texture'' brought to a fineness never surpassed. Moreover, they had ''discovered charm and grace in much that was only blank before.'' They had ''detected and described points of human nature hitherto unnoticed, which, if not intrinsically important, will one day be made auxiliary to the production of pictures of broader as well as minuter veracity than have heretofore been produced. All that seems wanting thus far is a direction, an aim, a belief.'' In his remarks on James we find the problem of realism vs. ideality being dealt with quite soundly.

In some of James's earlier tales, such as ''The Madonna of the Future,'' he found a balance of the realistic, the fanciful and the ideal. (pp. 24-7)

Starting from James and Howells he envisioned an American literature which would ''rest neither in the tragic gloom of Turgenieff nor in the critical composure of James, nor in the genteel deprecation of Howells.'' A new, strong American Literature should demonstrate that the weakness of man is the motive and condition of his strength. Consequently, it would not flounder in the despair and immature cynicism of naturalism.

> It will not shrink from romance, nor from ideality, nor from artistic completeness, because it will know at what depths and heights of life these elements are truly operative. It will be American, not because its scene is laid or its characters born in the United States, but because its burden will be reaction against old tyrannies and exposure of new hypocrisies; a refutation of respectable falsehoods, and a proclamation of unsophisticated truths.

He saw his responsibility as a literary-page critic to be the proclamation of a doctrine of cleansing and renewing. He also pled for a professional seriousness, for a sturdy ideal of craftsmanship. But mere hack work, which he found Trollope sometimes guilty of, could never insure artistic satisfaction or enlighten public taste. (pp. 27-8)

Julian's own work, his detective stories, for instance, ever fell short of his critical standards. His Byronic heroes with twentieth century ''complexes'' did not satisfy him.

Yet Julian was honest. He admitted his faults and admonished the writer to turn wherever he might find his métier. American literature needed everything it could ingest and assimilate. Americanism was a point of view, a way of thinking; and Julian, in this contention, is important in tempering the tradition of nationalism in American criticism.

> Let us not refuse to breathe the air of Heaven, lest there be something European or Asian in it. If we cannot have a national literature in the narrow, geographical sense of the phrase, it is because our inheritance transcends all geographical distinctions. The great American novel may not be written this year, or even in this century. Meanwhile, let us not fear to ride to death, whatever species of Pegasus we can catch. It can do us no harm, and it may help us to acquire a firmer seat against the time when our own, our very own winged steed makes his appearance.

Readers of Julian's criticism will find him objectivist, for he asserted that fiction should tell us, not what ought to happen, but what, as a matter of fact does happen. If this seems to go against his romancer and idealist tendencies, we should see that he is also anti-moralist. From his critical position, "the God of the orthodox moralist is not the God of human nature."

Although he never became a Swedenborgian, he flirted with Swedenborgian thought. Although not an orthodox socialist, in theory he espoused politically libertarian principles. Although never an advocate of immorality, he proposed "unmorality" to the more legalistic Victorian critics. He found that "art dwindles in direct proportion as the moralizing deity expatriates; in fact, they are incompatible." So, instead of pleading that art should be moral, he pled that all true morality is art, and that art is finally the testing ground of our morality. (pp. 28-9)

Julian was . . . a competent judge of style and he refused to trace simple causal lines between author and work. Rather, he looked to the work in order to make inferences about the author's method and thought. "My Aunt Lizzie was a Christian whether she knew it or not; her life proved it."

His literary theory carries us over easily and naturally into his political writing, both being supported by Emersonian and Carlylean tenets. This is not to equate Emerson and Carlyle, but I think a quotation can clearly illustrate the fusion, or admixture. He felt that a literary work is not merely a revelation of the author, for:

> No artist worthy the name ever dreams of putting himself into his work, but only what is infinitely distinct from and other than himself. It is not the poet who brings forth the poem, but the poem that begets the poet; it makes him, creates in him the poetic faculty. Those whom we called great men, the heroes of history, are but the organs of the great crises and opportunities.
>
> (pp. 29-30)

[In] a review of *Discourses of Keidansky,* entitled "Society at a Pregnant Moment" Julian reveals the germ of his sociological-esthetic, or metaphysical theory of society.

> Society is at an interesting and pregnant moment now; and an order of things radically new is about to appear. A double movement is going on;—that of God, moving toward the co-operative brotherhood of the race, but on a plane not reached by the consciousness of the individual, and therefore not constraining his free-will; and that of man, the creature, self-conscious, obstructive, perplexed, finite, but unawares carrying out God's purpose. It is the function of a true seer not to abuse but to discriminate and to detect the deep and all controlling sweep of the tide from underneath the surface currents and wind-flurries.

Thus, to Julian, who was of the Utopian-Socialist cast, socialism was "a truly universal posture of the human mind (in the not remote future)," and a means, furthermore, of "relieving us of most of the burden of laboring for the bare means of subsistence" so that we have the "opportunity to study the arts which beautify and ennoble life."

One overcomes selfhood both as artist and as citizen. Individuality and identity mean different things, for the achieving of one's identity is the achieving of consubstantiality with all men and with the continuum of art. The individual, Julian felt, suffers a delusion when he thinks of himself absolutely a unique integer.

Therefore, the overcoming of self-consciousness is a stage in arriving at artistic objectivity. One lets "inspiration" realize itself in overcoming the social ego and allowing society to evolve "naturally" towards Socialism. (pp. 30-1)

As in his notions about what constituted an American Literature, his Socialism reflected a kind of Blakean proposition, i.e., that "America" is a state capable of being incarnated anywhere. But, practically, he felt that "spiritual democracy" had its best chance of fulfillment in the United States. Following a Whitmanesque cue, he contended that America began with "soul," with the generating motive of communal selflessness, or, in short, with a socialistic "idea" of government.

> The soul of the true America is now, as at first it was, Socialism—or I don't mind calling it Industrial Democracy, if you prefer—and though during the past century or two we have grown upon our clean body all manner of goitres, carbuncles, and cancers, leprosies and smallpox pustules, outcome of our spiritual sins of capitalism, oligarchies, trusts, bosses, civic indifferences, and the like, that true and inalienable soul will at last avouch itself, and restore our primitive healthy complexion. The nation, being a soul, was bound like individual souls to pass through hell on its way to regeneration; but is even more certain than the individual soul to get there. For the individual soul is subject to free-will, but the national soul is under unconscious and therefore inevitable Divine guidance, and must come out right anyway.

Stated as a formula, Julian's concept might be simply: Americanism is an idea, and that idea is emerging Socialism. (p. 31)

Julian's Socialistic thinking was as full of paradoxes as Jack London's, but typically it held something peculiar for him alone. This was a concept of personal liberty translated in terms of an artistic-oriented community. Marx he rejected rather summarily, in preference for what might be called a concept of Christian unmoralism. Here he dressed up his spontaneity, or voluntaristic esthetic, again. He thought in terms of a Christlike rebellion against the letter-of-the-law kind of obedience, conceiving the Decalogue as a stage in man's evolution toward a lawless community. He avoided the term "morality" in his theory because that implied a pawnbroker God, and a legalistic minded citizenry who think that by devotion to state-sanctioned precepts that they inherit everlasting blessedness. Instead of enlightened selfishness he advocated "enlightened selflessness." A spontaneous and unmoral man would be the vessel of art and virtue, for

> the life of man under Socialism must not be virtuous, self-conscious, or moral, nor immoral, of course, either, but unmoral, spontaneous, unselfconscious, selfless, realizing self only in others, and, therefore, really for the first time in history *good.* If Socialism were to be a sort of paternalized morality, it would produce a worse hell upon earth than has ever yet been known here—and that is saying much. . . .

However, inspirationalists and voluntarists are notoriously reluctant, or unable, to "explain" how an art work or the social millennium evolves. Having traced his theories from under Emersonian templates, he diverged farther and farther from Nathaniel's thinking.

In his later days he was thus able to extend his esthetic into a political dimension, seeing art as one of the great social functions of mankind, appreciation being a kind of ownership. In pious transport, he began asking artists to grow big enough and the citizenry humane enough to qualify for his semi-religious brand of socialism. His role as a writer for socialism was to foment the sense of brotherhood through art. Artists put themselves automatically in harmony with "natural law" and hence can never be anarchistic; only the student of art, the dilettante, and the poseur can be anarchistic.

> Persons of true artistic temperament are at bottom (or at top) socialists, as soon as they think it out. Art may be regarded as the good of the individual universalized for the good of the many. The artist gets his personal impression of beauty in a subject, and he plucks out its soul, and represents it as a work of art, which others, seeing it, and consulting their own personal experience, recognize as beautiful and true, only elevated somewhat above what they have personally felt and seen.

Thus he attempted to conjoin a political philosophy with an artistic purpose, and if the attitudes sound a bit too coached, the gestures look a bit too stagey, it betokens Julian's guilelessness. He was not dishonest.

Nor was he always naive. He was a man of paradoxes, as the incidents connected with his mining promotion (taken together with his professed Socialism) reveal. But in purely literary matters he was more sound. If we follow the *Star-News* columns from December 28, 1925, we see, for example, how he took strong issue with Lowes' assumptions about Coleridge's imagination, recognized the value of Norman Foerster's *American Criticism*, repeatedly justified the complexity of James's style, and made judgments of Howells that square with such estimable critics as Lionel Trilling. Quiescent yet circumspect in those California sunsets, he carried on steadily the fight for high standards in American literature, acidly attacking the easy biographers, translators who posed as original artists, and the hucksters who he felt were producing most twentieth century literature.

Nearby, he could see the great Hollywood mills of ersatz glamor and artistic pretentiousness. He could demolish this world by holding it up to the reflections of Concord, a world whose bright emanations were dulled by the dark glasses the hucksters had fit readers with. He felt that the Hollywood world was promoting patterns of mediocrity, of unimaginative uniformity. Unfortunately, American art seemed drifting toward such stultification and Americans increasingly lured on by the lotus blossom, eternal youth images of the cinema. . . . And so he wrote in those days for the people who are still glad to reminisce about Julian Hawthorne, and of his endless excursions into the past; who reminisce about the days when Julian sat with Hamlin Garland and talked of their youth and their conversations with Tennyson and Browning, of Margaret Fuller and Louisa May Alcott. For others, who were children when their parents knew him, the memories are dimmer. Logan Wilshire recalls that in his childhood he knew Julian Hawthorne as "a Jovian char-

acter, remote and unapproachable, and somewhat shabby in the genteel tradition. There was a sadness at the back of his eyes and little was left of the Harvard oar and blood. Yet, he remained a noble ruin." (pp. 32-4)

> George Knox, "Julian Hawthorne: Concordian in California," in The Historical Society of Southern California Quarterly, *Vol. XXXIX, No. 1, March, 1957, pp. 14-36.*

MAURICE BASSAN   (essay date 1970)

[*Bassan is an American editor and literary critic. In the following excerpt from his* Hawthorne's Son: The Life and Literary Career of Julian Hawthorne, *Bassan examines stylistic and thematic elements of Hawthorne's early short stories, their culmination in his first novel,* Bressant, *and appearance in subsequent novels.*]

The short stories written in the first years of [Julian Hawthorne's] apprenticeship (1871-73) seem singularly different from the important modes of writing in the period. In the first place, Julian Hawthorne's fiction does not seek to exploit the new vein of local color being richly worked by Bret Harte, Sarah Orne Jewett, and George Washington Cable. Although his settings range from quiet New England towns to New York City, from Cape Ann in Massachusetts to the Dead Sea in Palestine, Hawthorne never explores the life and folkways of a single regional setting. More important, his settings do not bear an integral relation to the themes of the tales. Third, the realistic mode of fiction, as coming to be defined by Edward Eggleston and Howells, is deliberately eschewed in favor of rather old-fashioned romance, with, frequently, a supernatural twist. . . . Perhaps at first Hawthorne had really been interested in catching the flavor of contemporary life; such, at any rate, seems to be the main point of his parable **"The Real Romance,"** . . . in which the only character in his story that the fictional author finds not to be a "mis-formed, ill-balanced, one-sided creation" is the housemaid, whom he had patterned after a real person. This is theory, certainly, but not the kind that Hawthorne could live up to; for fifteen years later he was to write:

> In two or three cases I have tried to make portraits of real persons whom I have known; but these persons have always been more lifeless than the others, and most lifeless in precisely those features that most nearly reproduced life. The best results in this direction are realized by those characters that come to their birth simultaneously with the general scheme of the proposed events.

Indeed, **"The Real Romance"** is completely fanciful, does not exhort by example, and is quite as much concerned with poking fun at romantic stereotypes as in advocating a realistic mode. (pp. 69-70)

It was to the romantic and supernatural mode rather than to the realistic that Julian Hawthorne turned in these first years of short-story writing. His imagination in his early tales, even the humorous ones, was directed to the mysterious, the spiritual, the fanciful; and he made extensive use of romantic coincidences. He looked to the past for his inspiration—in particular, to that segment of literary past dominated by his father—rather than to the present or the future. (p. 71)

In **"The Mysterious Case of My Friend Browne,"** Hawthorne takes up the Gothic properties of an old manuscript, a poisoned ring, and even a palpable ghost escaped from Trinity Church-yard to wreak his revenge on the descendant of a man who had wronged him. In this story there is a precise reenactment in present-day New York of events that had occurred one hundred and fifty years earlier; and this very theme of deliberately created "wonder" is exploited again in the fantastic narrative **"Mrs. Suffrin's Smelling-bottle,"** in which the characters play out in modern dress a tragedy that had taken place fifty centuries earlier at the destruction of Sodom. The phenomenon of clair-voyance, which had fascinated Nathaniel Hawthorne in *The Blithedale Romance,* makes its first appearance in two bizarre tales, **"Dr. Pechal's Theory"** and **"Mr. Maximilian Mor-ningdew's Advice."** In the former, Dr. Pechal, a "frowzy precise foreigner," has "evolved the law which regulates the time, place, and circumstances, of the death of every human being"; but his attempt to stave off his own death succeeds only through a lucky coincidence. In the latter story a youth is deeply troubled by a dream in which his immediate future has accurately been foretold. Hawthorne does not focus on whatever sense of wonder can be extracted from this rather stale situation; he merely requires us to accept the fact of the revelation and proceeds to recount the lad's disillusionment at the hands of the cynical Mr. Morningdew. **"The Strange Friend"** foreshadows a whole rash of later stories in which a skeletal plot is made to serve as a springboard for extended meta-physical speculations, in this case on the distinction between earthly and heavenly love. The humorous tales of this period, **"Why Muggins Was Kept"** and **"The Mullenville Mystery,"** show an ingenious handling of the surprise ending, but even these are not free of romantic improbability. Much more suc-cessful than any of the tales so far mentioned is **"A Picturesque Transformation,"** which deliberately recalls the father's story **"The Prophetic Pictures."** Tremaine, a penniless painter, is in love with Hildegarde, who is also loved by her rich guardian, the Professor. Tremaine paints a great picture, and the Pro-fessor, seeking to exploit his rival's cupidity, offers to pay him handsomely for copies of the original. The painter performs this work for two years, meanwhile postponing his marriage to Hildegarde; and as time goes on, the three faces in the picture become changed, hardening into the portraits of "three con-demned souls." Seized with horror at the change, Tremaine offers to forfeit the Professor's money if Hildegarde will marry him; but she and her guardian have become engaged, and, it is implied, the Professor's punishment will swiftly follow. In all these stories Julian Hawthorne does not explore very deeply the sense of horror possible in the melodramatic incidents he contrives; nor does he effectively use the supernatural as a means of moral insight. He scarcely dwells upon his ghosts, in fact, and the "unvariegated hue of common circumstance" (a phrase from **"The Real Romance"**) is freely mixed with the wilder fantasies. Even **"A Picturesque Transformation,"** with its symbolic concern about the evils of the prostitution of artistic talent, is weakened by its melodramatic and mechanical struc-ture.

More serious and carefully wrought than the above tales are **"Star and Candle," "The Bronze Paper-Knife,"** and **"The Minister's Oath,"** which are linked both by their attempt to study the consequences of sin and by the use of unduly melo-dramatic incidents to further this attempt. **"Star and Candle,"** which was the seed of the long novel *Sebastian Strome* . . . , presents a hero whose selfishness is gradually transmuted into self-abnegation. Honslow, the sinner in **"The Bronze Paper-Knife,"** finds that his bastard son Jim is stalked by the ghost of his friend's wife, who had died believing her own husband to be Jim's father. Alice, the woman's daughter, grows up a

peculiar child, very much recalling Pearl in *The Scarlet Letter:* she was, Hawthorne writes, "an exquisite monstrosity as re-garded mankind." She has a strange predilection for the paper-knife that Honslow had presented her mother, as if the "cold and bitter soul of that lady, when it left her body, had slipped into the hard, metal image, and perhaps found it quite as con-genial an abiding-place." When Alice sees the branded letter "H" on Jim's forehead, she is impelled by some supernatural force to stab him; but she is forestalled by Honslow, who burns the dagger and banishes the curse. The concern with the con-sequences of sin is scarcely central to this long story. Haw-thorne seems more interested in the figure of the revengeful mother, in Alice's inherited hatred for Jim, and in the sym-bolism of the knife: that is, in the melodramatic, rather than the moral, elements of the tale.

With some modification the same point may be made of Haw-thorne's most ambitious story of 1871-73, **"The Minister's Oath,"** which seems deliberately to invite comparison, on the basis of the title alone, with the elder Hawthorne's "The Min-ister's Black Veil." The heroine, Ellen Barret, jilts Harry Pel-more at a ball; and even though he quickly forgets his vow of eventual revenge, his former fiancée does not. Years later, Ellen is married to Pelmore's former rival, the young minister Frank Morley. Their son falls ill, and Pelmore, now a physi-cian, is called in to attend him. When the child dies, the wife, convinced that Pelmore had deliberately murdered him, makes her husband swear to kill whoever injures her, even though she never reveals her suspicions of Pelmore to him. Years again pass, and a girl has been born to the Morleys. One night, as the minister completes a sermon on "Sudden Death," Ellen seeks to have him withdraw his oath, but Morley refuses. The mother, going in to her baby girl, meets "sudden death" when a pair of scissors clasped by her child pierce her brain in the dark. Her husband becomes deranged at the sight of his dead wife and bloodstained child, and, true to his oath, attempts to kill the baby. But before any injury can be done, his brain weakens completely. The years again pass. Pelmore has raised his own son with Sallie Morley and has lived near the insane minister. The two youngsters chance upon the old sermon, and Morley, hearing Sallie read it, is seized with his old frenzy. His renewed attempt to kill the child is thwarted by Pelmore, who loses his life in the process, while Morley recovers his sanity.

The original oath itself, the motivating force of the story, seems absurd, for the husband did not vow to punish the "murderer" of his son but only whoever harmed Ellen. This seems a trans-parently obvious "setting up" for the events to follow, like the misunderstanding at the heart of **"The Bronze Paper-Knife."** The violent passages of time in a reasonably short story are likewise troubling; the materials here seem more than sufficient for a novel, and no single emotion or idea is long sustained. Hawthorne again seems most concerned with the melodramatic surface of his tale: the terrible night scene when the mother dies and the child plays in her blood, and the pathetic murder attempt at the close. The author does attempt to do something—very little, to be sure—with the effect of the oath on the min-ister's character; and the reader feels that surely here, if any-where, the primary interest of such a story must lie. Hawthorne, however, merely describes something of this effect:

> His whole life, since the night he took the oath,
> had been an unnatural and morally unhealthy
> one. Human and divine love had been at con-
> tinual war within him, and he had beheld the

demoralizing spectacle of the divine continually worsted in the struggle. To one of such exceptional fineness and delicacy of feeling as he nothing could be more destructive of all balance and proportion. . . . The integrity, purity, and truth of the minister's nature were deeply compromised, the corruption having eaten into the very weapons and armor with which alone he could have hoped to keep corruption away.

This sort of analysis is good as far as it goes. But Hawthorne has not yet developed the ability to go beyond melodrama, to dramatize such internal conflicts, or even to focus his narrative properly upon them as static forces, a model for which is a chapter Hawthorne knew well: "The Interior of a Heart," in *The Scarlet Letter*. Too much plot gets in the way, and the final impression one has is an incoherent blur of merely sensational events. If **"The Minister's Oath"** is a decided failure as a short story, it is nevertheless not a serious failure for an imaginative young writer who has yet to learn to compress his tale and to satisfy his readers' aroused expectations for a narrative of conscience. Although Hawthorne continued writing short stories to the end of his life, he learned to structure his more abundant fancies into novels and romances.

The impression is inescapable that in the twenty tales and sketches written between 1871 and 1873, Julian Hawthorne was deliberately working the vein that had, in the elder Hawthorne, produced fiction of great power and beauty. To invite, even challenge, comparison on his father's own ground was, at this point in his career, foolhardy. To begin with, his style was hasty, slapdash, and, in diction, inexact. He lacked, and was indeed never to acquire, the historical imagination that had produced such tales as "The Gray Champion." Some of his themes seemed either unnecessarily crude or unbearably sentimental. Finally, his compulsive supernaturalist fancies were frequently handled carelessly or with a rather vulgar humor: almost, sometimes, as if young Hawthorne scarcely believed in them and scarcely expected the reader to.

The difficulty in interpreting these early tales is not one of evaluation. One may state at the outset, categorically, that with one or two exceptions Julian Hawthorne's best stories are not as good as Nathaniel Hawthorne's poorest. But evaluation aside, the question of deliberate imitativeness remains puzzling. Two answers suggest themselves. The first is that Julian Hawthorne was attracted by a reasonably easy way of making a living; if magazine editors and publishers expected a Nathaniel Hawthorne-esque story of his "father's son," then that was what he would supply them. The second, more flattering, and equally probable answer is that the young writer produced his tales as a form of homage to his father's name and memory. Perhaps both answers are in some measure true; to the end of his life it may be said that Julian Hawthorne both revered his father's name—and exploited it.

The romantic directions apparent in these early stories were momentarily, in the writing of Hawthorne's first novel, *Bressant* . . . , to be bypassed in favor of a stricter realism. In his second long work, *Idolatry* . . . , however, the Gothic and supernatural reasserted themselves; and for the next twenty years, the fiction of Julian Hawthorne evidenced this dichotomy between the realistic and the supernatural modes, in his "novels" and in his "romances." (pp. 72-7)

The genesis of his first novel was recalled by Hawthorne in *Confessions and Criticisms*:

I finished it in three weeks; but prudent counselors advised me that it was too immoral to publish, except in French; so I recast it, as the phrase is, and, in its chastened state, sent it through the post to a Boston publisher. It was lost on the way, and has not yet been found. I was rather pleased than otherwise at this catastrophe; for I had in those days a strange delight in rewriting my productions; it was, perhaps, a more sensible practice than to print them. Accordingly, I rewrote and enlarged *Bressant* . . . but—immorality aside—I think the first version was the best of the three.

Bressant's lineage is Byronic, and he is endowed with strange magnetic powers. When he appears at the opening of the novel, he is a dedicated and ascetic young intellectual, unsophisticated and almost primitive in his social relationships. His mentor, Professor Valeyon, finds him a product of a theory of education that "aimed rather to give the man power in whatever direction he chose to exercise it, than to store his mind with greater or less quantities of particular forms of knowledge. The only faculty to be left uncultivated . . . was that of human love— this being considered destructive, or, at least, greatly prejudicial, to progress and efficiency in any other direction." At first Bressant regards love only as a "delicious weakness," refusing to believe that it can coexist with lofty aims and strenuous effort; but before the end of the narrative, he declares: "Love is study enough, and work enough, for a lifetime. Mathematics, and logic, and philosophy—all those things have nothing to do with love, and couldn't help me in it. . . . It has laws of its own." Bressant's emotional and sexual awakening is dramatized in his alternating love for Valeyon's two daughters: the "earthly," dark, sensual Cornelia, and the fair, "spiritual" Sophie—the latter, in name, invalidism, drawing skill, and spirituality of temperament recalling to the reader the young Sophia Peabody [, Julian Hawthorne's mother]. Although the stress on the redemptive power of love recalls a recurrent theme of Nathaniel Hawthorne, Julian Hawthorne's concurrent stress on the power of sexual attraction is both coarser and more frank and worldly than anything to be found in the elder Hawthorne's novels.

Bressant presents three themes that are to be dominant in the major fiction of the ensuing decades. The first is the primacy of love over selfish intellect. Hawthorne's heroes, beginning with Bressant, are afflicted with the Faustian lust for knowledge and power, boundless ambition, and an egotistical contempt for their fellow creatures that isolates them from humanity. Julian seems to have taken for his text his father's often-repeated views about the dangers of intellectual ambition, which had been expressed as early as his first volume of short stories. Discussing the painter in "The Prophetic Pictures," Nathaniel Hawthorne had written:

Like all other men around whom an engrossing purpose wreathes itself, he was insulated from the mass of human kind. . . . His heart was cold. . . . It it not good for man to cherish a solitary ambition. Unless there be those around him by whose example he may regulate himself, his thoughts, desires, and hopes will become extravagant, and he the semblance, perhaps the reality, of a madman.

There appears in Julian Hawthorne's heroes the same grave imbalance between head and heart that afflicts such familiar figures as Aylmer, Chillingworth, and Ethan Brand. In the younger Hawthorne's stories, these heroes tend to begin their lives in quest of learning in a serious profession; they are scientists, divinity students, or, very commonly, artists. Their intellectual self-absorption inevitably fades, however, as they learn, through the development of their affections, to accept a humble lot. One may view this thematic material as a by-product of an overly sentimental interpretation of standard Christian doctrine, especially if one views humility as a poor substitute for unfettered rational inquiry.

A related theme dramatized in *Bressant* is the necessity for a choice between sacred and profane love, a problem that Hawthorne had first explored in **"The Strange Friend,"** and that was later to face such characters as Lancaster in *Dust,* Boardwine in *A Dream and a Forgetting,* and Merlin in *The Professor's Sister.* Artistically, however, Hawthorne was unmoved by the spectacle of the "good" women, his nominal heroines, who, from Sophie in *Bressant* onward, are unmitigated bores. Women with a little bit of the devil in them, on the other hand, like Cornelia, stir his pen to individualizing creativity. Cornelia, the beautiful, passionate sister, is the lineal antecedent of such brilliantly portrayed Hawthorne women as Madge Danver in *Garth,* Mary Dene in *Sebastian Strome,* and Perdita Grantley in *Dust.* Unfortunately, Hawthorne's use of the dual-heroine convention as a dramatic form for his investigation of sacred and profane love is not successful. It results generally in a sacrifice of dramatic force, in a vapidity of treatment; one wishes that his heroes would not always wind up in the arms of the fair, and patently insufferable, angel.

A third theme introduced in *Bressant* and repeated unvaryingly in every succeeding novel and romance is the contrast between the purity and innocence of small-town life and the wickedness and corruption of the big city. Hawthorne was not, of course, a reformer complaining of the evils of urbanization; his view is sentimental rather than intellectual, and falls into the stereotype that was only rarely to be questioned before the appearance of Ed Howe, Hamlin Garland, Edgar Lee Masters, and Sherwood Anderson. The village town in *Bressant* is portrayed with the deep affection we may expect from a writer who grew up in Concord; and the country scenes of such novels as *Garth, Fortune's Fool,* and *Beatrix Randolph* are handled with the same loving attention to detail. The evil contrast in this first novel is supplied by New York, where Cornelia is exposed to wicked society life. Even granting Hawthorne's easy adoption of a literary convention, one may question his sincerity here, even more than in the use of the themes discussed above, or certainly more than in his use of supernatural themes. He loved society, adventurous women, and life in such great cities as New York and London. On the other hand—and again granting the convention—one may suspect in this glorification of simple country life a sincere but suppressed longing for the recovery of his childhood.

Hawthorne's own copy of *Bressant* (preserved in the Julian Hawthorne Collection at the University of California, Berkeley) contains scores of the author's changes penciled into the text—changes that, it would appear, were designed for a second edition in 1875 that never was published. Not only is the language tightened and many trite passages omitted in this revision but the melodramatic plot (as distinguished from the narrative of the hero's emotional development in contact with the sisters) is greatly altered and improved. As the plot stands, Professor Valeyon, at whose parsonage Bressant is studying for the ministry, believes the young man to be the son of Abbie, his old

love, who had left her husband and now keeps a boardinghouse in the nearby village. Bressant learns the truth from his real mother, the New Yorker Mrs. Vanderplanck, however: that he is her illegitimate son, who had replaced Abbie's dead child in his father's household. In the most powerful scene in the novel, which anticipates the soon-to-be fashionable truth-telling scenes of Ibsen, Bressant savagely berates Abbie for her life of supposed purity, which, he declares, has been the fraudulent cloak of her unforgivable sin in abandoning her sickly child in order to live independently.

Bressant, who had planned to marry Sophie and become a country parson, finds that in order to fulfill his plans he would have to give up his claim to his father's fortune. Ashamed of his own brutal motives, and shamed even more by the revelation of his true birth, he decides to run away to Europe with Cornelia, who has won his love by "dishonorable intriguing and reckless self-desecration." On the train to New York, a young lad talks to him, and when the boy evidences a mystic acquaintance with the situation, and even goes so far as to point out the lessons of the tale, Bressant realizes that it is the spirit of Sophie, who is lying gravely ill at home, speaking to him. He returns to the parsonage; and although Sophie has died, a ray of sunshine descends from heaven at the close and shines on him, presaging better days. These days will be spent, after all, with Cornelia, for the spectral boy had proclaimed: "Let it be the work of your lives—a work of penitence and punishment—to elevate and refine your love, which has been degraded, until it becomes worthy of the name of love, in its highest sense. You have lowered each other, and now each must help to raise the other up."

Yet *Bressant* is a surprisingly unsentimental work of fiction, despite its "ideal" portraits of Sophie Valeyon and her absent-minded old father, and its tedious conclusion. The unabashed carnality of the love between the hero and Cornelia; the attack upon hypocrisy; the exploration of the phenomena of innocence and sophistication: all of these mark the work's considerable originality. The psychology of love interested Hawthorne, and even though its dramatic form is fairly primitive, its manifestations in the sexual and emotional awakening of Bressant are recounted with great power. Certain scenes, also—Cornelia's rage at losing Bressant's love, Bressant's attack on Abbie—indicate artistic skill in tracing the subtleties of emotional states. These are valuable things to find in a first novel. But the defects of *Bressant* are at least as obvious as its virtues. The style is undistinguished; the ponderousness of Bressant's utterances is rarely offset by the author's wit or anything that can be called a sense of humor. The mechanical contrasts of character, the overly involved and melodramatic plot, the disfiguring elements of the marvelous that enter at the most inappropriate moments, betray an immaturity of dramatic treatment that marks the novel's distinct failure as a work of art. (pp. 78-83)

> *Maurice Bassan, in his* Hawthorne's Son: The Life and Literary Career of Julian Hawthorne, *Ohio State University Press, 1970, 284 p.*

MARTHA MAYES PARK　(essay date 1974)

[*In the following excerpt, Park discusses conventional Gothic elements in* Archibald Malmaison, *which she considers Hawthorne's best novel.*]

In 1879 *Archibald Malmaison,* Julian Hawthorne's contribution to the Gothic genre, was published by R. Bentley of London after having been offered to and turned down by all the leading publishers in New York and Boston. Hawthorne, the second child and only son of Nathaniel Hawthorne, had previously relied upon superstition, oral tradition, and supernatural trappings in his earlier novels, *Bressant* . . . , *Idolatry* . . . , and *Garth* . . . , and in several of his short stories; but for the first time he fused in *Archibald Malmaison* the romantic and the real to produce the desired effects of horror. In fact, he united them so effectively and dramatically in his novelette that the real intensifies the horror.

Before looking at the Gothic machinery of the novelette, however, a summary of *Archibald Malmaison* may prove helpful. The tale turns upon Archibald's malady, a type of dual personality in which he has seven years of near idiocy followed by seven years of normalcy. For example, during his first seven years Archibald was a fat, lazy, untalkative child who scarcely paid attention to anything, except a cat. Upon the cat's death, he refused to eat and passed into a coma. Upon his recovery, he started sucking again at the wet nurse's breast and remembered nothing occuring before his illness. Gradually and then rapidly, he passed through infancy and made up the accomplishments of the lost years.

This progressive state lasted for seven years, during which time Archibald found the entrance to the secret chamber of Malmaison house, a room for which Hawthorne had previously prepared the reader. Perhaps the excitement of that discovery prompted the relapse which followed, during which he forgot the people he had known earlier, even Kate Battledown, whom he had adored. During this stage of his simplemindedness, Kate agreed to marry Richard Pennroyal, for she thought Archibald would never be anything other than what he was then, a man with a child's mind. Following the marriage ceremony for Kate and Pennroyal, Archibald, who had ironically been best man, underwent a third change. Upon his arousing from the dizziness, he asked what the occasion was, remembered Pennroyal and told him he looked old, and asked Kate if it were not to be their own wedding.

With the situation thus complicated, a feud later developed between the Malmaisons and the Pennroyals after Pennroyal had declared that the late Sir Clarence Malmaison, Archibald's father, had been illegitimate and that the Malmaison estate was his own as the result of his earlier marriage to Sir Clarence's sister. Archibald's brother Edward had a duel with Pennroyal and died from the wounds, leaving Archibald as Malmaison heir. After what may have been an accidental meeting, Kate and Archibald renewed their friendship by other secret meetings. With her love to encourage him and his desire for revenge, Archibald brought forth papers from the secret chamber and proved during a court hearing that his father was legitimate and Pennroyal an impostor. Fiendishly, however, the penniless and by now nearly alcoholic Pennroyal gloated over having Kate as his wife, for he knew Archibald would have given all his fortune for her. Thus Pennroyal begged her one winter evening to promise she would never marry Archibald when she became a widow.

Ironically, however, Kate and Archibald had planned a meeting for that same night, after which Archibald would take her home to the secret chamber decorated as a luxurious bridal suite but suggesting more an ancient vault. As Kate left, Pennroyal, drinking and musing upon the past, thought he saw Jane, his demented dead wife, beckoning to him; he followed the shape which led to the fish pond where she had drowned. Suddenly he realized the figure was not Jane; it was Kate, being embraced and kissed by Archibald, his enemy. The two men fought with

pistols, and Archibald killed Pennroyal and sank his body in the pool. His remark that the water would freeze over that night and the body would be eaten by fish is dramatically successful because of its horror and terseness.

The "two pallid and haggard" figures returned to Malmaison house and entered the secret chamber. Archibald seated Kate and covered her with a satin cover from the bed, gave her some wine, reassured her of his love, locked the door securely, and went to see his mother, a feeling of sluggishness overcoming him as he went. His first words to his mother were, "Mama . . . where is Kate?" Dr. Rollinson came, for "Sir Archibald had gone daft" again. One night seven years later, Archibald, in possession of his faculties again and happy in the thoughts of a future life in another country for several years, returned to the chamber to find Kate. He remembered how disturbed she had been when he left her less than an hour ago and wondered why she had let the fire and the light go out. He saw her kneeling with her face resting on a chair. She remained still and silent when he called; he thought she had fainted and grasped her shoulder, disturbing her head and discovering the terrible secret: she had been dead for years. Dr. Rollinson came and attended Archibald during the eight or nine months he lived after that horrible night.

In *Confessions and Criticisms,* Hawthorne referred to *Archibald Malmaison* as a novelette which "went rather farther than usual" because of its "light draught." The book came, he confessed, during the period when he had already ceased to write for the pleasure of writing and wrote instead for money. According to his own estimate in 1887, it had probably had a larger circulation than all his other stories combined. . . . Hawthorne thought it was "its horror, its strangeness, and its brevity and not any literary merit" that made the tale popular. (pp. 103-05)

Hawthorne furnished "A Chapter of Afterthoughts" for the 1899 edition. Also included as an appendix . . . are the opinions of six prominent physicians regarding the malady of Archibald. In his twenty-four pages of introductory remarks, Hawthorne may have been consciously imitating Poe's "Philosophy of Composition." However, seemingly serious at first, these afterthoughts contain pert humor not evident in Poe's piece. If Hawthorne were imitating Poe, his imitation included parody as well, shown by such impudent explanation as those of Archibald's birthday and the Malmaison name. It is an interesting speculation at least and one that enriches both Hawthorne's comments and the novelette. For the story itself, in addition to being a successful Gothic tale, has hanging over it a kind of indescribable, grotesque humor.

In these introductory remarks, Hawthorne lays bare his feelings regarding the contemporary age's concern for "occult science"; hypnotism "has become an absolute nuisance"; the study of subliminal consciousness reveals that an individual may have three or more distinct personalities living on hostile terms among themselves; "mental healing" now alarms no one except the Health Board; new concepts regarding the soul and God are rampant; a modern jargon, or "new Thought," has arisen to express the ideas of the age; and on an ordinary walk, a person is "liable to be waylaid by a materializing medium, a psychometrist, a palmist, and an astrologer, who incidentally suggest to you that nothing is except what does not appear." After all these things, Hawthorne said it is then comforting to enter a hash-shop or perform some physical act "by way of comforting yourself for the insupportable burden of so much transcendental phenomena."

He declared that in 1878, however, when he wrote *Archibald Malmaison,* it was a different age. "The conception upon which the story was based, namely, that there may be two contrasted personalities in a man (or woman), tho of course it was very far from being an original conception, was by no means so widely accepted as it now is; and could not be called a hackneyed motive in fictitious literature." . . . Or more wryly, at that time, "the transcendental incubus had not so much as loomed definitely upon our horizon, much less rolled over and over us, and flattened us into imbecility. The faculty of innocent wonder had not yet died within us from overfeeding." . . . (pp. 105-06)

But more important, *Dr. Jekyll and Mr. Hyde* had not been written then; this "unpretending little narrative had its chance" and "had novelty enough for that unsophisticated age to arouse a good deal of indignant or sceptical criticism in certain orthodox quarters." . . . (p. 106)

The story was quickly and easily written, the hardest problem being to refrain from including "too much psychological speculation, which, however meritorious in itself, all but one reader in a hundred would be certain to skip." Hawthorne admitted that he was glad he had deleted one whole chapter of metaphysical reflections from the completed story and thought perhaps that it contained too much still. A writer, he said, should digest and assimilate such material before he begins to write, and then the reader can find a moral and meaning for himself if he wishes. In addition, too much analysis of any sort indicates the writer's weakness or laziness; and he himself often had been accused, not unjustly, of being a "psychologico-analytic novelist." Nature dissected, he continued, becomes lifeless; but a reader can see truth through the forms, "the way it was meant to be seen." As material nature suggests that God teaches human souls, storytellers should be satisfied with a comparable method of suggestion. . . .

Hawthorne said that he had written many things which seemed better than this novelette, but that there is no reason why an author is the best judge of his own work. He supposed the work's popularity was due to the "interest aroused by the oddness of the incidents, by the sequence of development, and particularly by the "strong human sympathy felt for the hero and heroine in their terrible fate—which overtook them precisely in the spot where they had hoped to enjoy their greatest felicity." Their tragedy saved their sin from coarseness and allowed a reader to pity rather than condemn them. Hawthorne remarked that the story conforms to the requirements of ethics and art, but that the theme is "crudely and imperfectly" worked out. He wished for "the sake of literature" that the tale had been written by Robert Louis Stevenson, the author of *Dr. Jekyll and Mr. Hyde.* . . . (p. 109)

Even allowing that his hindsight of twenty years may have been somewhat indulgent and capricious about the planning and writing of *Archibald Malmaison,* Hawthorne furnishes a good insight into some basic aspects of the novelette. That he planned the work as an inoffensive horror tale having verisimilitude is noteworthy, for the fusion of horror and probability in this neo-Gothic tale illustrates the trend already established in his earlier fiction. The mixture here is considerably more effective than that of *Bressant* or *Idolatry.* An explanation may be that Hawthorne used fewer incredible artifices of the *Idolatry* type and that the conventional Gothic aspects are presented as historic, somewhat as they were in *Garth.* Within such a framework, the horror of the tale becomes so real and appropriate

that the ordinary awkwardness usually evident in Hawthorne's mixture of the two modes is hardly apparent. (p. 111)

Archibald Malmaison is . . . a terror tale using Gothic conventions, and Hawthorne succeeded in his plan to write an "historical" tale which can be read in one sitting. The planned attendant horror is certainly effective. The descriptive, but casual, picture of the Malmaison place as a type of Gothic castle is appropriate in view of the family's past. Likewise, a reader can quite easily accept the narrator's position, which is reminiscent of that often used by Washington Irving, Edgar Allan Poe, and Nathaniel Hawthorne. The first person narrator, or a dramatized Hawthorne, is never directly involved in the story, but relates an occurrence told to him by Dr. Rollinson. He reminds the reader several times that he is retelling "history" and cannot analyze Archibald's mental state as he could if he were writing a "created" novel. Moreover, the reader is reminded that he can find full details of the case elsewhere if he is curious and is specifically referred to *The Morning Post* of March 7, 1821, for the details of Kate and Pennroyal's wedding.

Also the occasional references to the "wise folk" who had their own predictions about Archibald's case enhance the natural and probable setting and add background humor as well, as shown by the following comment: "Some said he would lose what little wit he had; others that he would become an acknowledged wizard; others, again, that he would never wake up at all. In short, like other prophets, they foretold everything except that which was actually to happen; and they would have foretold that too, if they had thought of it in time." . . . And as a type of doting and anxious mother, Lady Malmaison is realistically and humorously shown as she tries to soften the account of Archibald's condition in order not to ruin his chances for receiving Aunt Tremount's fortune.

Against the background of Malmaison and its believable and type characters, Hawthorne adds an ample supply of details common to Gothic novels. In addition to the Gothic castle itself, the east chamber occupied by Archibald was the one from which his ancestor had magically disappeared in 1745. The room contained his great-grandfather's portrait, and that ancestor had a forefinger pointing mysteriously downward. The author also said the room probably contained some of Mrs. Radcliffe's romances. Here Archibald, in his thirteenth year, by following the direction of the pointed finger, found the entrance to the secret chamber by discovering a rod hidden in a crack of the floor. Inside the dark secret room, Archibald saw romantic trappings: life-size figures painted on the walls, gold and silver plate, a suit of sixteenth-century armor, and most frightening of all, a mirror in which he saw himself and imagined a goblin was present. Later Archibald was to save his family's honor by papers found in the room.

The secret chamber and Archibald's personality are the chief elements around which the final horror revolves. But to aid the general background and sinister tone, still other Gothic and romantic features are liberally sprinkled throughout the tale. For example, Pennroyal's first wife, Jane Malmaison, was insane and drowned herself in the ornamental fishpond near the edge of the Pennroyal estate. There are, however, subtle hints that Pennroyal consciously allowed her to drown. His uneasy feelings are evident when her ghost visits him; he sees or imagines he sees reproach in her glances. Two other deaths are also included: Sir Clarence died of apoplexy as a result of alcoholism and anger, and his son died as a consequence of dueling wounds.

Yet the center of interest, as well as of horror, for the romance is Archibald. The hints about his peculiar ancestors add the desired background for Archibald's even stranger peculiarities. The "wise folk" considered him strange and mad and, even perhaps, a wizard or companion of the devil. His own history enveloped him in a shroud of mystery and set him apart from others, for whom he felt no human sympathy. He was of "remarkable personal beauty, which in moments of anger or energy gleamed out with an almost satanic intensity"; . . . "men shrunk from meeting the stern inquisition of his black eyes, and for women his glance possessed a sort of fascination unconnected with his beauty." . . . (pp. 112-13)

At least twice, once to Kate Battledown and later to a servant, Archibald mysteriously appeared from nowhere. The reader knows, of course, that he came from his secret chamber into the east room, but no one else knew of the forgotten room, and the circulated stories invested Archibald with the power of making himself invisible at will. There is, as a result, a kind of effective dramatic irony running throughout the tale. The reader sees and knows more than Archibald's family and neighbors; at the same time, Archibald's own peculiarities are best seen through the other characters' impressions. . . . The reader has also the dramatic tension of wondering exactly when the next alternation will occur, and thus a superiority over Archibald, who is not aware of his own curious changes.

Not so subtle as the irony, but nevertheless effective, are the various suggestions that Archibald may ultimately harm Pennroyal. Pennroyal liked to amuse himself by questioning Archibald about his "enlightened period," of which he remembered nothing. Of this practice, the narrator comments: "The Honorable Richard Pennroyal was not the first man who has failed to see whence his greatest danger was to be expected." . . . Later the narrator, or more likely Hawthorne himself intruding, wonders whether Archibald should in one part of his "being" be held responsible for a crime committed in the other stage. And again, the reader is reminded before the court hearing that Archibald hated Pennroyal "heartily" and thought him "responsible for all the ills that had fallen upon Malmaison and upon himself; and he was evidently not the man to suffer a grudge to go unrequited." . . . Likewise, the fact that Archibald's animosity for Pennroyal and his love for Kate appear in the same phases foreshadows an impending crisis as both the hatred and love increase proportionally.

In fact, the only real flaw, if it is one, that mars the dramatic effectiveness of the novelette is that a reader may question Archibald's memory of people and events as the story moves nearer and nearer the final horror. After the first two changes, there is little carry-over except for subliminal consciousness, but later Archibald remembers certain events and people as evidenced by his remark about Pennroyal's age and his asking for his father who had died earlier. Actually, though, the pace of the work and the mystery are such that the question of consistency in this one instance hardly matters. Hawthorne succeeds in getting a reader's rapt attention until Archibald leads him to the final discovery. It is not so much, however, that the reader does not know what he will find in the chamber as that he wonders how and when Hawthorne will reveal what is there. (pp. 113-14)

[The characters] are flat characters, but for the purpose of the tale—horror—all a reader needs of them is there. More emphasis is placed on setting than on characters, but I find the focus effective. Malmaison house, like the usual castle for a

Gothic novel, needs to be prominent to prepare for the ultimate terror in its secret chamber.

The tale is . . . blunt, bold, and horrible. The first two qualities increase the horror as Hawthorne intended they should; the relation, while offensive to that critic, nevertheless, seems to me to fascinate because of Archibald's alternating stages. The sense of mystery controls as a result of the suggestions already pointed out, and Hawthorne's holding back Archibald's final stage and the disaster as long as possible created the climactic horror desired for a tale filled with other Gothic apparatus. Rather than offensive and revolting, the tale has an appropriate and natural conclusion.

The tale is blunt, but dramatic. The narration is largely telling rather than showing. One example of the terse and effective style is the narrator's account of Archibald and [his brother] Edward's understanding of each other before Edward's death: "Again the brothers grasped hands, looked in one another's eyes for a moment or two, and then Archibald went out; the day passed, and the evening fell. At midnight he was Sir Archibald of Malmaison." . . . The use of narrated scenes rather than conversation is natural because of the frame of the story. In the final two paragraphs following the scene of terror, the narrator, or author (it is in first person and can be either, or both), remarks again that facts were closely followed throughout, although some conversations were "imagined, but always on an adequate foundation of truth or logical inference. All the dates and 'coincidences' are genuine. But, indeed, I prefer fiction, and am resolved never in (the) future to make an excursion into the crude and improbable regions of reality." . . . (pp. 114-15)

Hawthorne succeeded in mixing the supernatural and the real in *Archibald Malmaison*. The success lies chiefly in his making the unnatural seem natural, so natural that he can say he will hereafter stick to fiction. The artifices are acceptable here as believably belonging to the real, and the real itself seems the "earthly" rather than any reflection of "loftier reality," as Hawthorne usually intends for it to be. To look at the situation from another angle, the novelette succeeds because Hawthorne was not, as in *Idolatry,* trying to write two different books at one time, one realistic and one romantic. He harmonized the romantic and the real by making the former seem a part of history that a reader can accept as probable.

Perhaps another reason for the story's effectiveness is that there are fewer authorial comments and less philosophizing and moralizing than in *Bressant, Idolatry,* and *Garth.* While the earlier novels have intrusions that often are neither very interesting nor valuable within themselves and are also detrimental to the prevailing tones of the stories, *Archibald Malmaison* has few intrusions and the sense of mystery holds the reader's attention throughout. A reader can, as Hawthorne suggested, find a moral here if he wishes, but the chief concern is interest rather than morality. Kate and Archibald commit a crime; and punishment will, as a reader knows, follow; but the concern is not so much with their receiving a conventional punishment as with wondering when and how it will come.

Altogether, *Archibald Malmaison* is Hawthorne's most successful work in fiction. The ingredients for it are comparable to those of his other novels and romances, a mixture of romantic elements and the actual. It is the quantity rather than the ingredients that varies. There are more Gothic features than in any other romance except *Idolatry,* or perhaps *Garth,* but the elements are so harmonized with the real that the union is artistically and dramatically successful. The bluntness of the tale also intensifies the terror and dramatic effect. Hawthorne frequently succeeded in uniting the two modes in short pieces, but he never again in a novel or romance mixed the romantic and the real skillfully and sustained a unified tone as well as he did in the Gothic novelette, **Archibald Malmaison.** (p. 115)

> *Martha Mayes Park, "'Archibald Malmaison': Julian Hawthorne's Contribution to Gothic Fiction," in* Extrapolation, *Vol. 15, No. 2, May, 1974, pp. 103-16.*

ADDITIONAL BIBLIOGRAPHY

James, Henry. Review of *Garth*, by Julian Hawthorne. *The Nation* XXIV, No. 625 (21 June 1877): 369.
  Assesses *Garth* as an improvement upon Hawthorne's first two novels, but finds it immature, crude, and provincial.

Knox, George. "The Hawthorne-Lowell Affair." *The New England Quarterly* 29, No. 4 (December 1956): 493-502.
  Discussion of the dispute between Hawthorne and James Russell Lowell arising from the former's publication of an interview, which Lowell insisted was a private conversation. Knox provides published letters by both men defending their positions, and representative samples of the ensuing argument over the issue, which was vigorously debated in the American and British press.

Pancost, David W. "Henry James and Julian Hawthorne." *American Literature* 50, No. 3 (November 1978): 461-65.
  Discusses the personal and professional relationship between the two writers.

Pattee, Fred Lewis. "Shifting Currents of Fiction." In his *A History of American Literature Since 1870*, pp. 385-415. New York: The Century Co., 1917.
  Disparages Hawthorne as a writer, finding that he "lacked seriousness, conscience, depth of life, knowledge of the human heart. . . . No literary career seemingly so promising has ever failed more dismally."

"An American Visitor." *The Times Literary Supplement* (4 October 1928): 706.
  Positive appraisal of *Shapes that Pass,* calling Hawthorne's memories of his father and other prominent people affectionate and insightful.

Weber, Carl J. "Lowell's 'Dead Rat in the Wall'." *The New England Quarterly* 9, No. 3 (September 1936): 468-72.
  Results of some early research into the dispute between Hawthorne and Lowell, reprinting the texts of letters from, to, and about Lowell commenting on the affair.

———. "More About Lowell's 'Dead Rat'." *The New England Quarterly* 9, No. 4 (December 1936): 686-88.
  Reprints letters from Lowell to a Boston newspaper representing his side of the dispute with Hawthorne.

Gaston Leroux

1868-1927

French novelist, dramatist, and short story writer.

Leroux is recognized as a highly original contributor to two specialized areas of literature: the detective novel and the horror story. In *Le mystère de la chambre jaune* (*The Mystery of the Yellow Room*), the first of his novels featuring the reporter and amateur detective Joseph Rouletabille, he created a classic figure in the annals of crime fiction, as well as what many commentators believe is the finest example of a "locked room" mystery. With *Le fantôme de l'opéra* (*The Phantom of the Opera*) he originated an avatar of horror that captured, and continues to hold, the popular imagination.

Leroux was born in Paris, the only child of financially secure shopowners. After leaving school he found a clerical position with a firm of lawyers, and when not occupied by his official duties or the usual pursuits of the boulevardier, he began writing essays and short stories which occasionally appeared in magazines and newspapers. In 1890 Leroux became a full-time journalist, parlaying his legal background into the post of legal chronicler for a Paris newspaper. Besides reporting on the more sensational court cases of the day, he also began writing theater reviews. His growing interest in the stage inspired him to write plays of his own; of these only a few, coauthored with other dramatists, were successful. Just before the turn of the century Leroux became a newspaper correspondent. He embarked on several years of world travel, despatching to Paris accounts of international escapades with Leroux himself at the center of the action. When he began writing novels in the early 1900s, they featured the same kind of exciting incident that had figured in his foreign correspondence. These novels were often serialized in French periodicals or weekly newspapers, and sometimes in English and American publications, before appearing in book form.

Leroux had his first major success with *The Mystery of the Yellow Room,* which has been characterized by Howard Haycraft "as one of the classic examples" of the "locked room" mystery. While not the first detective novel to exploit the plot device of a seemingly insoluble crime committed in a sealed chamber, it is commonly regarded as one of the earliest and best of all such novels. *The Mystery of the Yellow Room* also features a confident amateur sleuth who is always several steps ahead of the authorities in solving the crime, and a surprise denouement revealing a hitherto unsuspected character as the malefactor. While one early reviewer criticized Leroux for thus concealing the culprit's identity, this narrative ploy has since become a commonplace of detective, crime, and mystery fiction, and at the time *The Mystery of the Yellow Room* appeared another reviewer found this device "as original as it is fascinating." The novel's sequel, *Le parfum de la dame en noir* (*The Perfume of the Lady in Black*), though well received, met with the reservation that it did not represent any improvement over the first Rouletabille mystery, and none of the subsequent "aventures extraordinaires de Joseph Rouletabille" were as popular as the first, which critics agree represents Leroux's best work in this genre.

In 1910 *The Phantom of the Opera* began appearing as a serial shortly before its publication as a novel. The book's moderately

successful sales in Europe and the United States, however, did not give the mysterious denizen of the Paris Opera House his world fame; that happened in 1925 when the novel was made into a silent movie by Universal Pictures. This movie not only made the phantom well known, it also advanced the career of the vaudeville comedian Lon Chaney, who enacted the phantom on the screen; however, the movie did little to advance Leroux's renown as the creator of this horror archetype. The popular image of the phantom derives largely from this and subsequent filmed versions, each of which varies in some degree from Leroux's original, somewhat convoluted account of how a mysterious masked figure came to dwell in hidden passages and chambers of the massive Paris Opera House. Because he suffered from a lingering illness for the last two years of his life, Leroux may never have seen a movie version of *The Phantom of the Opera.* He continued to write and publish almost to the time of his death in 1927.

Familiarity with the eponymous "phantom" of Leroux's classic horror novel has come to many more moviegoers than novel readers. In fact, early reviews of *The Phantom of the Opera* were unenthusiastic, characterizing it as inferior to Leroux's first novel. One critic deplored the melodramatic nature of the story and the use of a well-worn plot: a hideously ugly protagonist falls in love with a beautiful young woman and abducts her; another critic called *The Phantom of the Opera* "the wildest and most fantastic of tales,'' one that would lose readers because "when the phantom ceases to be a phantom, and things begin to be accounted for, one's interest sensibly weakens.'' In a later appraisal of the novel, however, Drake Douglas maintains that the opposite is true: "Despite later explanation, it is not always completely clear just how the phantom manages his little artifices.'' Other commentators discussing the novel have deplored the stilted narrative, unskilled characterizations, and unbelievable behavior of the characters. Douglas, however, contends that these are not flaws "of the writing itself, but of the time in which the writing was executed,'' and, putting these objections to the novel's style aside, concludes that "in his picture of life in the Paris Opera, particularly in the dark nether regions known only to the initiate, Leroux has composed a fine brooding work of horror.'' Although Leroux has never been widely known for either of his most famous creations—the Phantom or Rouletabille—aficionados of horror and detective fiction consider him an important contributor of classic works to these fields of literature.

(See also *Contemporary Authors*, Vol. 108.)

PRINCIPAL WORKS

La maison des juges (drama) 1907
Le mystère de la chambre jaune (novel) 1907
    [*The Mystery of the Yellow Room*, 1908]
Le parfum de la dame en noir (novel) 1908
    [*The Perfume of the Lady in Black*, 1909]
Le lys [with Pierre Wolff] (drama) [first publication]
    1909
La fantôme de l'opéra (novel) 1910
    [*The Phantom of the Opera*, 1911]
Le fauteuil hanté (novel) 1911
    [*The Haunted Chair*, 1931]
L'homme qui a vu le diable (drama) 1911
Alsace [with Lucien Camille] (drama) [first publication]
    1913
L'épouse de soleil (novel) 1913
    [*The Bride of the Sun*, 1915]
Chéri-Bibi (novel) 1914
Chéri-Bibi et Cecily (novel) 1916
    [*Cheri-Bibi and Cecily*, 1923]
L'etranges noces de Rouletabille (novel) 1916
Le coeur cambriolé (novel) 1922
    [*The Burgled Heart*, 1925; also published as *The New Terror*, 1926]
Le crime de Rouletabille (novel) 1922
La machine à asassiner (novel) 1924
    [*The Machine to Kill*, 1935]
La farouche aventure; ou, la cocquette punie (novel)
    1925
    [*The Adventures of a Coquette*, 1926]
Mister Flow (novel) 1927
    [*The Man of a Hundred Faces*, 1930]
The Gaston Leroux Bedside Companion (short stories)
    1980

THE NATION (essay date 1908)

[*The following is a favorable review of Leroux's* The Mystery of the Yellow Room.]

For sheer originality and ingenuity we reckon [*The Mystery of the Yellow Room*] the best detective story published for some time. A scientific investigator and his daughter are living in a lonely house outside of Paris. The daughter is nearly murdered in a room from which there appears to have been no mode of exit for the criminal; a young newspaper reporter, who has his friendly "Dr. Watson,'' solves the mystery in the face of the official detectives. As stated the plot is familiar enough, being compounded one might say of "The Murders in the Rue Morgue'' and of any one of Sherlock Holmes's adventures. But the peculiar manner of sustaining the uncertainty to the end, while suspicion is thrown upon this and that person, not without hints of some mystical force of nature discovered by the scientist, is as original as it is fascinating. Not often does a detective story end with so total a surprise, which, nevertheless, when known, seems logical and natural. The writing of the book is above the average, although the translator has allowed a few gallicisms to slip in. And the characters are more than commonly interesting for the *genre*.

> *A review of "The Mystery of the Yellow Room,'' in* The Nation, *New York, Vol. LXXXVII, No. 2247, July 23, 1908, p. 75.*

RUPERT RANNEY (essay date 1909)

[*In the following excerpt,* The Perfume of the Lady in Black, *Leroux's sequel to* The Mystery of the Yellow Room, *is favorably reviewed.*]

Those persons who found entertaining **The Mystery of the Yellow Room** when it appeared last summer are not likely to have any cause for complaint against its sequel. To state the matter sweepingly, **The Perfume of the Lady in Black** is no better than its predecessor, and it is no worse; which implies neither high praise nor serious disparagement. The faults and merits of one book are the faults and merits of the other. Joseph Rouletabille has not changed in the least. He is just as long winded and snivels as much as ever. On the other hand, his creator shows the same unusual ingenuity and sense of the dramatic that made **The Mystery of the Yellow Room** the *feuilleton* sensation of Paris when it was appearing in *L'Illustration*.

M. Leroux is taking it for granted that every one who reads **The Perfume of the Lady in Black** is acquainted with the events of the earlier story. (pp. 199-200)

The grim story plays itself out at the Fort of Hercules, a feudal castle built upon a rock jutting out into the Mediterranean. There are gathered all the principal characters in the story. . . .

With a stage setting like this M. Leroux's ingenuity has free play. . . . The reader's suspicions are constantly being diverted from one person to another, and it is Rouletabille alone who holds the key and furnishes the final explanation. Whether this explanation will be found satisfactory the present reviewer does not venture to say. That the creator of Rouletabille should have ventured to offer it is to the credit of his temerity and perhaps to his ingenuity. (p. 200)

> *Rupert Ranney, in a review of "The Perfume of the Lady in Black,'' in* The Bookman, *Vol. XXIX, No. 2, April, 1909, pp. 199-200.*

THE NATION (essay date 1911)

[*In the following review of* The Phantom of the Opera, *the critic notes that the novel is both ingenious and suspenseful, but ex-*

presses a wish for more detective fiction from Leroux in the vein of his earlier The Mystery of the Yellow Room.]

It is a long drop from M. Leroux's **Mystery of the Yellow Room** to this fantastic piece of nonsense [**The Phantom of the Opera**]. The former was one of the best-constructed and most exciting detective stories of recent years; the present tale is enormously ingenious, but melodramatic *à outrance,* and runs in places pretty close to the ridiculous. A man of great powers, but born diabolically ugly (the old and wearisome *âme damnée* of the romanticists), becomes one of the contractors for building the opera house at Paris, constructs a secret dwelling for himself in the cellars, with all sorts of trap-doors, hidden passages, etc., through the edifice, and there, unseen and unknown, lives and makes himself felt by a thousand mysterious pranks and crimes. Of course, he falls in love with a young singer; in fact, the plot of the story hangs on the combat of this unseen wooer and an ordinary young man for the fair soprano. Despite the incredibility of the whole situation, M. Leroux succeeds in piquing the reader's curiosity, and the last search for the demon through the dark cellars of the opera is not without moments of what is called "breathless suspense." The audacity of the writer almost deprives the reader of his judgment. But M. Leroux owes to the world another detective story as good as **The Mystery of the Yellow Room** and better than **The Perfume of the Lady in Black.**

> A review of "The Phantom of the Opera," in The Nation, *New York, Vol. XCII, No. 2380, February 9, 1911, p. 142.*

THE NEW YORK TIMES BOOK REVIEW   (essay date 1911)

[*In the following review of* The Phantom of the Opera, *the critic finds Leroux unable to sustain the emotion of horror throughout the novel and criticizes as "cheating" the nonsupernatural nature of the phantom.*]

The wildest and most fantastic of tales is **The Phantom of the Opera.** . . . The scene is laid in the vast Opera House of Paris, the characters wandering from the lyre of Apollo that tops its seventeen stories to the mysterious lake beneath its five cellars. So long as it is a ghost story, it holds the reader as ghost stories do, but when the phantom ceases to be a phantom, and things begin to be accounted for, one's interest sensibly weakens. It is, moreover, far too long for that literature which the brilliant author of *L'Ame des Anglais* declares to be "a manifestation purely English—the literature of fear." Poe understood that horror is an emotion which must be quickly captured and as quickly released, and, as our French author recognizes, he is supreme in the "literature of fear." Mr. Leroux, on the contrary, permits the "goose-flesh" to subside; the blood to resume its normal flow; nay, the reader to become slightly bored, long before the phantom is laid. Moreover, do we ever forgive a writer for cheating us into shudders? If we are introduced to a ghost, let him be a ghost to the end—no less. Despite these faults, however, the book is effective. Its style is picturesque and vivid, and its descriptions of the great Opera House give the story a real value. There is a far cry, however, from the author's thrilling **Mystery of the Yellow Room** to this elaborately constructed melodrama.

> "An Opera-House Phantom," in The New York Times Book Review, *February 19, 1911, p. 90.*

Cover of a French edition of The Phantom of the Opera. *From* The Gaston Leroux Bedside Companion, *edited by Peter Haining. Victor Gollancz Ltd, 1980.*

THE NATION   (essay date 1912)

[*In the following review,* The Man with the Black Feather *is characterized as a sensational but unsuccessful novel.*]

[**The Man with the Black Feather**] is a shilling shocker from the hands of the man who wrote that excellent tale, **The Mystery of the Yellow Room.** There is comparatively little mystery here, but sensation enough to satisfy the least fastidious taste. Many of our readers, for instance, have read in history of the amiable Renaissance practice of cutting off a man's ears. But how many modern readers have actually seen the thing done? It is done in M. Leroux's book, and with a wealth of detail that is quite fatal to one's appetite for supper. The main idea of the story is simple enough. The soul of Cartouche, a brigand who attained notoriety under the Regency in France, and a man of a hundred murders, finds reincarnation in the body of M. Theophrastus Longuet, retired manufacturer of rubber stamps, resident in the suburbs of Paris. M. Longuet, impelled by this metaphysical motive power within him, casts aside his green umbrella at regular intervals to reproduce under modern conditions the career of eighteenth-century Cartouche. Now and then the thoroughly consistent way in which the scheme is worked out produces its effect. But the author was evidently hard put to it to spin out a volume of atrocities, and so pads out his story with a rather silly and tedious chapter of mesmeric wonder-working, a journey in the catacombs of Paris, and a bit of detective ratiocination quite in the vein of *The Mystery of the Yellow Room.*

A review of "The Man with the Black Feather," in The Nation, *New York, Vol. XCIV, No. 2440, April 4, 1912, p. 339.*

THE NEW YORK TIMES BOOK REVIEW (essay date 1915)

[*In the following review,* The Bride of the Sun *is described as a typically entertaining Leroux novel.*]

To have read any one of Gaston Leroux's previous novels, *The Perfume of the Lady in Black, The Mystery of the Yellow Room,* or some other of equally romantic title, is to know beforehand the character of story to expect—rapid action, much exciting incident, more or less mystery, and a generally romantic atmosphere in which outlines grow sufficiently vague to disguise any belying of the possible which may take place in the narrative. All the elements of just such a galloping, entertaining story are indeed here [in *The Bride of the Sun*], but with a setting and a theme sufficiently unusual to make the book, for people who enjoy that kind of a book, more than usually absorbing and exciting.

The scene is in Peru and the plot is concerned with the religious mysteries practiced by the Indians, whereby they require a beautiful girl of the white race to bury alive in the ruins of the ancient palace as a bride for the last Inca, a "bride of the sun." The girl whom they have chosen for the sacrifice is the daughter of an English mother and a descendant of one of Pizarro's Captains. The author makes all the stronger the contrast between the ancient rites by portraying her as a very modern young woman, manager of the big business interests with which her mother had enriched her father's title. There is much vivacious account, woven into the story so skillfully that it becomes a vital factor, of the history and the remains of the ancient civilization, while the religious rites of its modern descendants, in which the plot of the story reaches its climax, have a detailed and colorful description. There is some mild humor in the account of an attempted "revolution" which helps the development of the tale. The author manages quite cleverly the growing suspense and horror of his story until he nears the end, when he plunges with a crash into anti-climax.

A review of "The Bride of the Sun," in The New York Times Book Review, *February 21, 1915, p. 58.*

CAROLYN WELLS (essay date 1929)

[*Wells was an American novelist, poet, and critic who was considered the foremost female humorist in the United States during the first two decades of the twentieth century. She wrote over 170 books, including dozens of volumes of parody and light verse, and several crime novels. In the following excerpt from her* The Technique of the Mystery Story, *Wells discusses Leroux's contribution to the genre of the detective novel. Unexcerpted passing references throughout the book also mention Leroux's handling of such mystery and crime story devices as footprints, disguises, unique murder weapons and techniques, and complex plots.*]

Among the best of the detective stories of this time are two by Gaston Leroux, *The Mystery of the Yellow Room* and *The Perfume of the Lady in Black*. In these stories two detectives figure. Though they are professional and amateur, they are not

opposed, as is so often deemed necessary for dramatic effect, but have a far subtler contrast. Rouletabille is a delightful character and satisfactory in his procedure, while Larsan is a genius. (p. 157)

Rouletabille appreciated the dramatic value of what Poe called the pungent contradiction of the general idea. In *The Mystery of the Yellow Room* . . . the following conversation occurs:

> "Have you any idea as to the murderer's station in life?"
>
> "Yes," he replied; "I think if he isn't a man in society, he is, at least, a man belonging to the upper class. But that, again, is only an impression."
>
> "What has led you to form it?"
>
> "Well,—the greasy cap, the common handkerchief, and the marks of the rough boots on the floor," he replied.
>
> "I understand," I said; "murderers don't leave traces behind them which tell the truth."
>
> "We shall make something out of you yet, my dear Sainclair," concluded Rouletabille. . . .

[This] young man was not infallible; but his author made him this way for the same reason. Because he figures in a novel, and the infallible detective must do his work in a short-story.

Rouletabille's strong card is pure reason.

> "How did you come to suspect Larsan?" asked the President.
>
> "My pure reason pointed to him. But I did not foresee the drugging. He is very cunning. Yes, my pure reason pointed to him."
>
> "What do you mean by your pure reason?"
>
> "That power of one's mind which admits of no disturbing elements to a conclusion. The day following the incident of 'the inexplicable gallery,' I felt myself losing control of it. I had allowed myself to be diverted by fallacious evidence; but I recovered and again took hold of the right end."

Again, he says:

> "M. Sainclair, you ought to know that I never suspect any person or anything without previously having satisfied myself upon the 'ground of pure reason.' That is a solid staff which has never yet failed me on the road and on which I invite you all to lean with me."

His pure reason is of the subtlest variety, and his fine work throughout the book commands always the admiration of the connoisseur. In a seemingly inexplicable situation he exclaims:

> "Let us reason it out!"

And he returned on the instant to that argument which had already served us and which he repeated again and again to himself (in order that, he said, he should not be lured away by the outer appearance of things): "Do not look for Larsan in that place where he reveals himself;

seek for him everywhere else where he hides himself.''

This he followed up with the supplementary argument:

''He never shows himself where he seems to be except to prevent us from seeing him where he really is.''

And he resumed:

''Ah! the outer appearance of things! Look here, Sainclair! There are moments when, for the sake of reasoning clearly, I want to get rid of my eyes! Let us get rid of our eyes, Sainclair, for five minutes—just five minutes—and, perhaps, we shall see more clearly.''

Rouletabille's subtlety of reasoning rose almost to clairvoyance. (pp. 225-27)

There is nothing imitative about this young detective. His methods are unique. His pure reasoning is most subtle; and though the farthest possible remove from realism it presents a semblance of reality that is entirely convincing. (p. 228)

> *Carolyn Wells, in her* The Technique of the Mystery Story, *edited by J. Berg Esenwein, revised edition, The Home Correspondence School, 1929, 435 p.*

WILL CUPPY   (essay date 1935)

[*In the following favorable review of* The Machine to Kill, *the critic notes reasons for continued reader interest in Leroux.*]

M. Leroux's compositions grow no less wild and weird as the years roll on. This one [*The Machine to Kill*] is about Gabriel, an automaton constructed by old M. Norbert, a watchmaker, and his beauteous daughter, Christine. Dr. Jacques Cotentin supplied Gabriel with a brain taken from the executed Benedict Mason, the Bluebeard of Corbilieres, and the fat was in the fire. Gabriel ran amok, taking Christine with him, and you wouldn't believe the fantastic things that went on hither and yon. Instead of talking, Gabriel, writes notes, such as ''If you value your life, keep silent,'' and ''Have you a mirror wardrobe in your home?'' Christine talks to him in the deaf and dumb language and writes notes to her father about how agonizing it all is. There is a certain who's-looney-now flavor to M. Leroux's books which not a few fans crave; others try them at their own risk. They are exciting, in a way—that's why M. Leroux keeps his devoted customers.

> *Will Cuppy, in a review of ''The Machine to Kill,'' in* New York Herald Tribune Books, *August 18, 1935, p. 10.*

HOWARD HAYCRAFT   (essay date 1941)

[*Haycraft is an American editor and critic who has written extensively on mystery and detective fiction. In the following excerpt, he characterizes* The Mystery of the Yellow Room *as a classic ''locked room'' detective mystery, although one with major flaws of plot and narration that render Leroux's writing unappealing to modern readers.*]

[Gaston Leroux] was already well known as a journalist and author of popular fiction when he turned in 1907 to the detective story with *Le Mystère de la Chambre Jaune (The Mystery of the Yellow Room)*, the first of half a dozen ''aventures extraor-

dinares'' featuring Joseph Rouletabille, reporter. But the only one of the succeeding novels to approach the popularity of the initial volume was its immediate sequel, *La Parfum de la Dame en Noir.*

The Mystery of the Yellow Room is generally recognized, on the strength of its central puzzle, as one of the classic examples of the genre. For sheer plot manipulation and ratiocination—no simpler word will describe the quality of its Gallic logic—it has seldom been surpassed. It remains, after a generation of imitation, the most brilliant of all ''locked room'' novels. The author's use of the official detective as the culprit (though an outworn device to-day) was also in its time a highly original conception. Moreover, Leroux, unlike most of his compatriots, played religiously fair with his readers.

But on the debit side, one regrets to say, the score is also high. The author's narrative method can be compared only to the serial thrillers of early moving-picture days. The dialogue stems directly from the ''Hist!'' and ''Aha!'' school. The aged theme of family scandal is dragged from its mothballs to serve once again. The characters are still the incredible puppets of [Emile] Gaboriau's feuilletons. (One wonders, in passing, if Leroux's employment of the name Stangerson for two of his chief actors was an intentional or an unconscious tribute to Conan Doyle: see *A Study in Scarlet;* he openly borrowed Doyle's Watson convention, giving Rouletabille his admiring Sainclair.) Disguises and aliases abound; the long arm of coincidence is stretched beyond all credibility; and mere probability is ever the least of the novelist's anxieties. We are expected, for example, to believe that Rouletabille was little more than sixteen years old at the time of the *Yellow Room* problem—and that he could interrupt a criminal trial and virtually take over its conduct from the constituted officials of justice. As a crowning touch, the chubby hero is revealed (in the second novel of the series) as the *son* of his arch-foe!

No, for all his excellence as a contriver of adroit puzzles, Leroux is simply not the modern reader's dish. He was an influence and an important one, but his position is chiefly historical and technical. (pp. 104-05)

> *Howard Haycraft, ''The Continental Detective Story,'' in his* Murder for Pleasure: The Life and Times of the Detective Story, *D. Appleton-Century Company, Incorporated, 1941, pp. 103-111.*

DRAKE DOUGLAS   (essay date 1966)

[*In the following excerpt, Drake offers a discussion of* The Phantom of the Opera. *Unexcerpted portions of the essay contain plot exposition and discussion of the major motion picture versions of the novel.*]

Although he is little read today [Gaston Leroux] secured a form of immortality through his most famous work about the opera phantom, still a favorite with readers of old-time mystery and horror. The book first appeared in 1911, sixteen years before the death of the author. Although it is no longer easily available today, the character of the protagonist is, by way of various film versions, as well known today as when he first made his appearance on the literary scene.

The story of *The Phantom of the Opera* is placed almost entirely in the huge, rambling Paris Opera beginning on the night that the two managers of the opera, Debienne and Poligny, are entering into retirement and handing over control to two other gentlemen, Moncharmin and Richard. The principal characters of this somewhat involved tale are the lovely singer, Christine Daaé, her lover Raoul de Chagny and his brother Philippe, who is the Comte de Chagny, the two new managers, and the mysterious phantom, Erik, generally referred to as the opera ghost. (p. 200)

The writing is often stilted, generally naïve, the characters are caricatures of life. Christine is impossibly pure and wholesome, a typical example of the long-lost breed of helpless, defenseless women; Raoul is irritatingly patient and understanding. The Age of Chivalry still shines through this work. Raoul, in spite of his consuming passion, would never think of taking advantage of Christine, even in the most advantageous circumstances. The phantom is incomparably evil, yet even he, while he has Christine imprisoned in his underground palace, respects the purity of womanhood and spends most of his time on his knees pouring out his love and pleading for understanding and compassion. It is difficult to conceive of any present-day villain behaving with such regard for feminine chastity; perhaps modern emancipated woman does not rouse such chivalrous feelings. It might also appear that Christine was more highly conscious of her honor than women are today; she could have saved the situation in the underground lair by merely pretending agreement to marriage, but it seems this never occurred to her. Though under duress, she had given her word to marry the phantom, and she was a woman of her word.

These flaws, again, are not necessarily of the writing itself, but of the time in which the writing was executed. Europe was in a state of ferment and indecision, but the First World War had not yet erupted when Leroux penned his story. It was still a world of gentility and propriety, a world in which good always prevailed and evil was inevitably overcome. Four letter words were not permitted in polite society, either in spoken or in printed form. The more intimate possibilities between the sexes were not mentioned by writers; if some daring author should be so careless and improper, "the right kind" of people certainly would not read him—at least, not openly. Vulgarity in

Lon Chaney as the Phantom. Culver Pictures, Inc.

speech or action had no place in literature; love was a spiritual longing, never to be confused with animal lust.

Leroux's story is often confusing and sometimes difficult to follow. Despite later explanations, it is not always completely clear just how the phantom manages his little artifices. His monumental passion for Christine is also somewhat difficult to understand, for she seems in every way quite an ordinary, rather dull, young lady.

But in his picture of life in the Paris Opera, particularly in the dark nether regions known only to the initiate, Leroux has composed a fine brooding work of horror. The Opera House becomes a world of secret panels and passageways, of long, dark stone corridors, peopled by unknown wraiths and monster rats, of underground lakes and waters, of an existence lived in complete darkness, made all the more mysterious by the fantastic world of glitter and color upon the stage directly above these mysterious depths. The phantom, with his ghost appearances and half-appearances, his horrifying death's head, becomes a chilling figure of unknown evil.

In many monsters, we find something to pity. We can feel with deep sympathy the longing of the Frankenstein monster for friendship and understanding, the agony of Lawrence Talbot during his transformation into a wolf. Perhaps we can even, just a little, pity Dracula for his endless battle against the forces which would destroy him, and Karis for his attempts to prove undying love and devotion. There are times, also, when we can feel a surge of pity for the Phantom of the Opera—the little boy who was so hideous that his own mother forced him to wear a mask. The home he erected for himself beneath the Opera House of Paris was merely another mask, another attempt to conceal his own hideousness from the eyes of the world that rejected him, as it does monsters of all kinds. There is in the phantom, in his loneliness, his alienness, much of the Frankenstein monster. When one such as he falls in love, we can find time for sympathy. His constant weeping and crawling at the feet of his goddess may be repugnant to us, but we cannot help but be moved by the depth of such a love. And in his final scenes with the Persian, in which Leroux's writing reaches its finest emotional peak, when Erik speaks of the wonder of being looked upon without fear by a beautiful woman, of actually feeling the warmth of a woman's kiss on his horrible face, surely then we cannot feel too much fear and hatred for this monster who had the misfortune to be born with a great heart and a terrible ugliness.

It is difficult to avoid comparison between the phantom's hopeless love for Christine and the great passion of Quasimodo for the gypsy girl, Esmeralda. Leroux, in fact, was obviously strongly influenced by Victor Hugo's classic *The Hunchback of Notre Dame*. Hugo had his cathedral, his monster, his air of love and loneliness, his beautiful girl; all these elements are present in Leroux's less important work. Even the conclusion is the same—as the phantom's body was found in the depths of the Opera long after the end of the tale, so was Quasimodo's skeleton later discovered in the vault of Montfaucon.

In his final release of Christine, the phantom, perhaps, does not behave entirely true to form. After what we have seen of the intensity of his longing and passion, his soul-searing loneliness, it may seem somewhat unlikely that Erik would so relax his hold on Christine after she has finally succumbed to his importunings and given her word to be his forever. But we have, fortunately, never been in quite the same position in which Erik found himself; possibly we can not quite realize the effect of a woman's kiss on the face of a man who had never before known the meaning of tenderness and compassion. Then, too, at the time Leroux wrote his tale, novels were the pastime of women, and they would not have expected any other ending—or accepted it—but one in which Christine and Raoul lived happily ever after. (pp. 209-12)

> Drake Douglas, "The Phantom," in his Horror! 1966. Reprint by Collier Books, 1969, pp. 196-220.

PETER HAINING   (essay date 1979)

[*Haining is an English editor and critic who has compiled dozens of anthologies of horror and fantasy fiction. In the following excerpt, he offers an overview of Leroux's career.*]

[In] the early 1900s [Leroux] started to write a series of unashamedly sensational yarns, all heavily laced with mystery and terror. Early works like *La Double Vie de Théophraste Longuet,* a kind of French *Dr. Jekyll and Mr. Hyde,* and *La Bataille Invisible,* about a madman's scheme to rule the world, revealed him as a storyteller of ingenuity and excitement.

In 1907 he scored his first major success with the publication of *Le Mystère de la Chambre Jaune,* which introduced to the public the brilliant young detective Rouletabille and his admiring chronicler, Sainclair, who is reminiscent of Dr. Watson. Howard Haycraft, the expert on crime fiction has underlined the achievement of this book in his *Murder For Pleasure: The Life and Times of the Detective Story* [see excerpt dated 1941]:

> *The Mystery of the Yellow Room* is generally recognised, on the strength of its central puzzle, as one of the classic examples of the genre. For sheer plot manipulation and ratiocination—no simpler word will describe the quality of its Gallic logic—it has seldom been surpassed. It remains, after a generation of imitation, the most brilliant of all "locked room" novels. The author's use of the official detective as the culprit (though an outworn device today) was also in its time a highly original conception.

Despite this praise, Mr. Haycraft goes on to say the book has numerous faults, including poor characterisation and undue reliance on coincidence, and he believes that Leroux's importance today is "chiefly historical and technical." None of the other books he wrote about Rouletabille enjoyed anything like the success of *The Mystery of the Yellow Room,* which was swiftly translated into English and published with resounding success on both sides of the Atlantic.

The second and most important milestone in Leroux's literary career came in 1911, when he published *La Fantôme de l'Opéra,* although this did not receive the immediate acclaim which the Rouletabille novel had done. It did, however, sell well in volume form, and was serialised in French, English and American newspapers. Leroux had got the idea for the novel during one of his many visits as a critic to the Paris Opera House. He heard the legend of a mysterious man who was supposed to live in the subterranean depths of the building and had been responsible for some strange deaths. His reporter's instinct told him that here was a very special story and he busied himself researching all the facts he could find. (pp. 13-14)

The enormous edifice of the Opera House which had been conceived during the glorious days of the Empire, in 1861, but not completed until 1879, was a marvellous background for Leroux's story. He made the most of its seventeen floors, vast maze of stairways and corridors, innumerable dressing rooms to cater for over five hundred performers, and the dozens of storage cellars for scenery and costumes. The fact that the lower levels of the place were vast and empty, rarely visited or explored, made the tale that he spun around the mysterious phantom all the more intriguing and exciting. It was clearly a unique creation, and the only surprise is that its importance was some time in being appreciated, and that its reputation was made on the screen rather than in print.

With *The Phantom of the Opera* Leroux reached the height of his literary powers, and although he developed another fascinating figure, Chéri-Bibi, the magician, who appeared in several novels between 1916 and 1923 [including *Les Cages Flottantes; Chéri-Bibi et Cecily; Palas et Chéri-Bibi* and *Fatalitas!*], nothing quite matched that one book. He did produce several more grim and exciting novels in the same vein, such as *Balaoo, The Man with the Black Feather* . . . and *The Man Who Came Back from the Dead* . . . , both about reincarnation; *The Secret of the Night* . . . , and *Bride of the Sun* . . . , two imaginative fantasies; and the posthumously published works, *Man of a Hundred Faces* . . . , and *The Haunted Chair.* . . . He also wrote a small number of really outstanding macabre and weird short stories which are even less well-known and more neglected than his novels. . . . (p. 15)

Most of these stories were written in the early 1920s when Leroux's popularity was at its peak, and the demands for his work were never-ending. As a thoroughly professional journalist and a man never afraid of hard work, he did not like refusing requests, and drew on his seemingly bottomless well of ideas for the stories. All are the equal of, if not actually superior to, most of his longer novels.

A group of these tales takes the form of adventures related by five old sea captains who meet in a café at Toulon to try and outdo each other with yarns from their past ["**A Terrible Tale,**" "**The Mystery of the Four Husbands,**" "**The Inn of Terror,**" "**The Woman with the Velvet Collar,**" and "**The Crime on Christmas Night,**" . . . . other] stories demonstrate Leroux's mastery of three other areas of fiction which particularly fascinated him: historical subjects ("**In Letters of Fire**"), the mixture of romance and terror ("**The Gold Axe**") and a macabre drama woven around the Paris he knew and loved ("**The Waxwork Museum**"). (pp. 15-16)

Fashions in both the detective and the horror novel seem quickly to leave behind both his Rouletabille stories and *The Phantom of the Opera,* and it was some years before *The Mystery of the Yellow Room* was recognised as a classic *tour de force,* and the story of the masked man appreciated as one of the greatest contributions to the genre of macabre fiction. In my contention Gaston Leroux was more than just a brilliant writer of weird fiction, he was a master of Grand Guignol. (p. 16)

> Peter Haining, "The Master of Grand Guignol," in The Gaston Leroux Bedside Companion, *edited by Peter Haining, Victor Gollancz Ltd., 1980, pp. 7-16.*

ADDITIONAL BIBLIOGRAPHY

Anderson, Isaac. Review of *The Machine to Kill,* by Gaston Leroux. *The New York Times Book Review* (18 August 1935): 14.

Acidulous review of *The Machine to Kill* by a critic who expresses "regret that duty compelled us to read it."

Review of *The Octopus of Paris*, by Gaston Leroux. *The Boston Evening Transcript*, No. 207 (7 September 1927): 4.

Favorable review of *The Octopus of Paris*, noting that "for the past twenty years a novel by Gaston Leroux has been regarded as the trademark of a good mystery story" and naming *The Phantom of the Opera* as Leroux's best work.

"A Detective Story." *The New York Times Book Review* 14 (20 March 1909): 160.

Calls *The Perfume of the Lady in Black* "a cleverly contrived and . . . well-written detective story."

"A French Detective." *The New York Times Book Review* 19 (10 May 1914): 230.

Review of *The Secret of the Night*, finding that "in the tangling of its scheme and the rapid succession of incidents and mysteries the most devoted lover of detective yarns could hardly ask for more."

"Murder in Paris." *The New York Times Book Review* (12 September 1926): 19.

Review of *The Phantom Clue*, which is held to be "entertainingly written, colorful, and convincing. . . . As detective stories go, it is well above the average in construction, character, and atmosphere."

Stark, Beverly. Review of *The Mystery of the Yellow Room*, by Gaston Leroux. *The Bookman* 27, No. 6 (August 1908): 603-04.

Severely criticizes the denouement of *The Mystery of the Yellow Room* for revealing as the villain a hitherto unsuspected character. The critic praises Leroux's ability to sustain interest throughout the narrative.

Van Dine, S. S. Introduction to *The Mystery of the Yellow Room*, by Gaston Leroux, p. vii. New York: Charles Scribner's Sons, 1929.

Characterizes *The Mystery of the Yellow Room* as one of the six best novels "from the entire field of detective fiction . . . both as to their powers of thrilling and dramatic entertainment, and as to their importance in the development of detective fiction."

Frederic Manning

1882-1935

(Also wrote under pseudonym of Private 19022) Australian-born English novelist, poet, essayist, biographer, and critic.

Manning is chiefly remembered as the author of *Her Privates We,* considered one of the most important fictional accounts of daily life in the British infantry during World War I. Often called a classic of modern war literature, *Her Privates We* is recognized as a unique historical portrait of the lower ranks during the Somme and Ancre battles of 1916-17. Its realistic examination of the horrors of trench warfare, its sympathetic rendering of camaraderie among the soldiers, and its perceptive criticism of military policies have led critics to favorably compare *Her Privates We* with more famous novels of the first World War, including *All Quiet on the Western Front* (1929) by Erich Maria Remarque and *The Spanish Farm Trilogy* (1927) by R. H. Mottram. According to C. Kaeppel: "*Her Privates We* is the greatest work in any language that the Great War has as yet produced," and Mark Taylor has stated that "it is unimaginable that any novel by a participant in the war of 1914-18 has more to tell us of the reality of the Western Front, or can tell it more faithfully." An aesthete and classicist, Manning also wrote a highly regarded collection of philosophical essays and several volumes of traditional poetry.

Manning was born in Point Piper, an affluent suburb of Sydney. His father, Sir William Manning, was an accountant and politician of Irish Catholic descent who had served in the legislature and as Lord Mayor of Sydney for several terms. An asthmatic whose schooling was often interrupted by illness, Manning attended Sydney Grammar School until he discontinued formal education to travel to Europe in the company of a tutor, Arthur Galton. Galton, an Anglican minister and biographer whose friends included Matthew Arnold and Lionel Johnson, had been serving as secretary to the governor of New South Wales when he was hired by the Mannings. He acted as Manning's tutor and guide, instructing him in the classics, romance languages, and modern European literature as they visited the continent together. Upon their arrival in England, Galton introduced Manning to his many literary acquaintances in London and Oxford, and for the next several years Manning lived with his tutor in a vicarage near Bourne in Lincolnshire. His literary career began modestly when *The Vigil of Brunhild,* his first volume of poetry, was published in 1907; *Scenes and Portraits,* a collection of historical dialogues, followed in 1909. Now considered his most important early work, *Scenes and Portraits* received favorable reviews upon publication and brought Manning many literary admirers, including T. E. Lawrence and Ezra Pound.

After the outbreak of the first World War, Manning enlisted in the King's Shropshire Light Infantry, although serving in the infantry was considered beneath his social position and his military superiors pressured him to accept a commission. He adamantly refused to leave the ranks, however, reasoning that he had no experience in the management of men and that he lacked the usual public school education of the officer class. He eventually accepted a commission in May 1917, after serving with the K.S.L.I. at the Somme and Ancre fronts. Transferred as a subaltern to the Royal Irish Regiment in Tip-

perary, Manning was troubled by shell-shock. He resigned his commission in early 1918 but remained in Ireland until November of that year. On the eve of the armistice he returned to England, where he found the adjustment to civilian life difficult. Spending much of his time on the continent, he traveled restlessly in pursuit of health and solitude. He visited Australia twice, but found that it held little interest for him. In 1929 Manning's friend and publisher Peter Davies convinced him to write a novel based on his experiences with the infantry in World War I. The result of six months work, *The Middle Parts of Fortune*—later published in an expurgated edition titled *Her Privates We*—was recognized as a classic work of war fiction. At Manning's request it was published anonymously as the work of "Private 19022," but T. E. Lawrence, an avid admirer of *Scenes and Portraits,* recognized Manning's prose style in the preface and the author's identity became known. Never in strong health, Manning died in 1935 following a bout with pneumonia.

Manning's unique portrait of the common soldier was welcomed by reviewers deluged with novels written by former officers. Critics recognized at once the historical value of *Her Privates We* as a record of daily life in the infantry, and they praised the insight and honesty of its author. Attempting to show that "war is waged by men; not by beasts, or by Gods," Manning produced a novel that the *Times Literary Supplement* called "a fine tribute to the British soldier and a notable record for ages to come." Unlike many war novels, *Her Privates We* contains few battle scenes, although confrontations with the enemy provide the novel's frame. Opening with an unsuccessful skirmish at the end of the battle of the Somme, the action of the novel follows an English battalion through a period of relative calm in an area behind the frontline, and then back into battle at Ancre. While critics have praised his realistic portrayal of trench warfare, they note that Manning did not sensationalize combat as some of his fellow novelists did. Recommending Manning's account, Arnold Bennett wrote: "I have read no book which gives so complete, fine, and true a picture of military life in the trenches before an attack, and of military life 'over the top' and through the enemy's wire, than this book represents." Manning borrowed the name for the central character of the work—known to the reader only as Bourne—from the village in Lincolnshire in which he had lived with Galton, and the protagonist resembles Manning in many ways. He is not English by birth and has nothing in common with the other men socially or intellectually, but he refuses a commission for the same reasons that Manning did. While Bourne is recognized as a portrait of Manning and the action of the novel is based on events that actually occurred, *Her Privates We* is not autobiography. The secondary characters in the novel are wholly fictitious, although Sergeant-Major Tozer and Bourne's comrades—Shem, Martlow, and young "Weeper" Smart—represent types that Manning encountered in his Shropshire regiment. In his preface he wrote: "I have drawn no portraits; and my concern has been mainly with the anonymous ranks, whose opinion, often mere surmise and ill-informed, but real and true for them, I have tried to represent faithfully." Borrowing a title from *Hamlet* and heading each chapter with a

Shakespearean quote, Manning attempted to place their story within a universal framework, and critics have agreed that he rendered the points of view of his fellow soldiers perceptively. Scenes depicting the loss of men as a result of negligent or incompetent leadership, such as Manning's description of troops being shelled while ordered to wait in line for breakfast in plain view of the enemy, are considered representative of the criticism of military bureaucracy and decision-making implicit in much of *Her Privates We*.

Of Manning's other works, *Scenes and Portraits* is generally considered the most important. A collection of philosophical debates in dialogue form, the volume has been praised for its elegant prose style and inventive blend of history, philosophy, and fiction. Appraising the work, Richard Aldington wrote: "Dissatisfaction mingled with an exquisite appreciation of beauty, the irony of [Anatole] France wedded to the aesthetic perceptions of Pater—that is the book's character." Manning's poetry, traditional in form and classic in content, drew praise from contemporary reviewers but is little read today. However, the war poems included in his 1917 collection *Eidola* are often mentioned in connection with his war novel.

Manning's renown in his own lifetime was slight, although he was well known in literary circles and his early works were greatly admired by Bennett, Pound, T. E. Lawrence, and E. M. Forster, among others. His anonymously published war novel won high praise but brought him no personal fame, and following strong initial sales due to the vogue World War I literature was enjoying at the time of its publication, *Her Privates We* declined in popularity. An edition that listed Manning as the author was not published until 1946, and the unexpurgated edition was not readily obtainable in the United States until the late 1970s. Now available in several editions, *Her Privates We* has fulfilled the expectations of Lawrence, who wrote to Manning in 1930: "Your book [will] be famous for as long as the war is cared for—and perhaps longer, for there is more than soldiering in it."

PRINCIPAL WORKS

The Vigil of Brunhild (poetry) 1907
Scenes and Portraits (dialogues) 1909; also published as
    Scenes and Portraits [enlarged edition], 1930
Poems (poetry) 1910
Eidola (poetry) 1917
The Middle Parts of Fortune [as Private 19022] (novel)
    1929; also published as *Her Privates We* [abridged edition], 1930

EZRA POUND (essay date 1909)

[*Pound, an American poet and critic, is regarded as one of the most innovative and influential figures in twentieth-century Anglo-American poetry. He was instrumental in obtaining editorial and financial assistance for T. S. Eliot, Wyndham Lewis, James Joyce, and William Carlos Williams, among other poets. His own Cantos, published throughout his life, is among the most ambitious poetic cycles of the century, and his series of satirical poems* Hugh Selwyn Mauberly (1920) *is ranked with Eliot's* The Waste Land (1922) *as a significant attack upon the decadence of modern culture. In the following excerpt, Pound praises* The Vigil of Brunhild.]

It is something in this age (when even Chaucer finds readers with difficulty) to write a narrative poem of sixty-odd pages that shall be readable, be constantly interesting. Manning, in his [*The Vigil of Brunhild*], has done not only this, but has given us a poem full of "the mellow juice of life," not perhaps as Bliss Carman meant it in his delightful lyric beginning: "Now the joys of the road are chiefly these," but he, Manning, has given us the last "Vigil of Brunhild" in vigorous colors and has drawn his characters humanly.

Neither a redaction of the story, nor yet the selections which follow, will give you the idea of the poem which I wish to convey, but for lack of better means I must give you the book in this manner until you are fortunate enough to come upon the full text.

Briefly, then, the scene and story are: Brunhild, at last taken by her enemies and condemned to death, is visited in prison by the priest, and to him, yet not as a confession but rather in a soliloquy, that only now and then notes his presence, reviews the glory and sorrow, the war, life, lust, love, and all the varied splendor of that life of hers, of whom his poet Fortunatus says at the triumph:

"Lo, what a pearl Spain gave unto the world!" I give you the opening passage:

> Brunhild, with worn face framed in withered hands,
> Sate in her wounded royalty; and seemed
> Like an old eagle, taken in the toils,
> And fallen from the wide extended sway
> Of her dominion, whence the eye looks down
> On mountains shrunk to nothing, and the sea
> Fretting in vain against its boundaries.

And looking down upon her mountains shrunk to nothing, she tells how that sea-soul of hers had striven against the boundaries of her time.

I think you will grant me that if at some points the poem shows reminiscence of other poets (though at no time unrefreshed by a very individual and personal flavor), and if the author does overwork his splendid simile of the eagle, using it four times, and if in some places the metric is not polished to the verge of extinction, yet the lines reach out into senses beyond the literal and show the working of a very delightful quality of thinking intelligence behind them.

Again I must recall Coleridge's remark, that the charm of the real poet is not a charm of particular gaudy passages, but of the general undercurrent of feeling: and with this give you these stray lines recalling to you that they are but typical fragments.

Brunhild, speaking of her own voyage into that ". . . vast, unfathomable, angry sea, broken by no white gleam of friendly sails," says:

> I go untrammelled by mere selfishness,
> Conscious that many hopes converged on me,
> Till I became a symbol in men's eyes;
> And still more conscious of the silent strife
> In mine own spirit when two courses lay
> Before me, and a voice cried: "Choose the best!"
> By what I choose now let my soul abide.
> One thing I learned, which is a part of hope
> With me: God knows how willing is man's soul,

Yet how his life is clouded o'er with doom,
And hindered with innumerable things;
So He will never judge by what I did,
But read my soul, and know thence what I was,
As no man knows me. Yet with tears I go;
For I have loved the green lap of the earth,

Later she repeats poetically what I have quoted in the introduction:

But in this little moment which is mine,
While all my foes are sleeping drunkenly,
Among the dying lights, the broken meats
Which the dogs tear upon the rush-strewn floor,
While even the moonlight sleeps upon the hills,
I build again, out of my memories,
The storm and splendour of my troubled life.

Past the middle of the poem, in her dialog with Gregory of Tours, she says:

I have been blinded by the tears of Love,
Lulled into heavy slumber with his wine,
Till life slipped by me, fugitive as dreams,
While I lay drowned in an excess of joy,
Fed but unsated, and insatiable.
Ah! this interminable stress of life
Intruding on the splendid pageantry,
Wherein is decked the gaudy press of dreams,

and later

I am but half a dreamer, and can shut
My purpose close unto the narrow view,
To seize the nearest opportunity,
Weaving it into this strange web of life,
As now I make the fate of Merow mine.
Yet am I compact of so many moods,
That a great yearning comes on me at times
For an illimitable night of stars.

So much for the selections. I know not "what porridge had Frederic Manning," but he has caught much of the old Saxon vigor and some of that mediaeval glamour that lies as April dew upon the works of William Morris, and I feel sure that I shall get nothing but thanks from such of you as through my measured praise are led to reading him. (pp. 620-21)

> *Ezra Pound, "The 'Brunhild' of Frederic Manning,"*
> in The Book News Monthly, *Vol. 27, No. 8, April,*
> *1909, pp. 620-21.*

RICHARD ALDINGTON (essay date 1914)

[*Aldington is perhaps best known as the editor of the Imagist periodical the* Egoist *and as an influential member of the Imagist movement, whose other members included Hilda Doolittle, Ezra Pound, and Amy Lowell. Aldington's work with the Imagists was cut short by World War I, after which he virtually gave up writing poetry and took up prose. As a novelist he achieved some success with angry yet honest attacks on war and on his native England, while as a literary critic and biographer, he combined his skills as a poet, his sensitivity as a reader, and his personal reminiscences to produce criticism that is creative as well as informative. In the following excerpt, Aldington discusses Manning's critical writings in* Scenes and Portraits.]

As far as I can see we have three men to-day who might, without arrogance, pretend to the title of critic. These are Ford Madox Hueffer, Sturge Moore and Frederic Manning. . . . Mr.

Manning is the youngest of these three; if he is the least original in manner, he is not the least fertile in ideas. And he has fascination. It is true, he has kept something of the University attitude; the pale shade of Pater dims some of his best pages, and not all the delicate irony, which he has inherited from modern France, can purge his pages of perilous Paterisms.

But—and this is a large but—the fact that Mr. Manning has been bold enough to adopt and even embellish the Epicurean attitude is remarkable at a time when such an attitude is in great discredit with all young men of parts. It is absurd and ignorant to say that Mr. Manning is a repetition of the "nineties"; he has simply read the books of more languages and centuries, looked at more pictures, heard better music and thought more imaginatively than most of his contemporaries.

"Ataraxia, a withdrawing, a folding of the hands," a standing-aside from the great noisy concourse of the world—that is the key-note of Epicureanism. . . . "To contemplate with appropriate emotions the spectacle of life"—that, or something like it, is the Epicurean attitude.

If, by chance, that were read to Mr. Manning, he would probably say that it was nonsense, that it was not Epicureanism at all, least of all his Epicureanism. A *chacun sa philosophie* is the motto to-day, for "all that we know is that we know nothing"—and even that is not certain.

Still, Mr. Manning's *Scenes and Portraits* are, we may take it, a series of studies in chronological order putting forth the critical attitude of the modern Epicurean towards life and literature. Towards literature largely, for though Mr. Manning discusses contemporary theories with great insight, he does so a little languidly and seems to be much happier when he is speaking of the people of books, like all Epicureans who seem to derive the vicarious happiness promised by their philosophy through the contemplation of literature rather than through the contemplation of life. It is that fact which explains the extraordinary hatred of Epicureanism among the middle classes and among the writers of literary reviews.

As a literary critic Mr. Manning is fascinating. There is not the faintest suspicion of charlatanism—with which so many of our writers are tainted—in any of his essays. He is always perfectly sincere, his views are mostly in accord with his main philosophy—I mean that he has no incoherences, no blatant contradictions, signs of fundamental insincerity—and he is often as original as a man can be in a world where nothing is new. At least one of his critical remarks, namely, where he says that the little genre pictures at the beginning of the cantos of the Divine Comedy are like large illuminated letters, has become classic among a small circle of his admirers. Indeed, his whole criticism of Dante is admirable. In a dialogue between Machiavelli and Thomas Cromwell—more in the manner of Pater than of Landor or Lucian—he criticises the political, religious and poetical aspects of Dante's poetry, and has some new appreciation, some new view-point for each of them. His décors are exact, and therefore beautiful. The villa at San Casciano is delicately described, unintentionally, as it were, by hints and casual remarks. The minds of Machiavelli and of Cromwell are indicated as much by their unconscious movements, by their clothes, by their jewellery even, as by their spoken words. And Mr. Manning, in each of his "scenes" has reproduced the manner of his period—a virtue our historical novelists cannot claim. For instance, the letter written by Cromwell to his friend is, barring the spelling, so nearly like a piece of prose of the reign of Henry VIII. that it might have been written by the Blessed Sir Thomas More himself.

Mr. Manning must be content to hear himself called an Epicurean, but the difference between his Epicureanism and that of Pater is that the latter seems always perfectly self-satisfied while Mr. Manning appears to suffer from a perpetual dissatisfaction. He seems to be struggling always towards something else, towards something more satisfying than Lucretius, but it looks as if he were damned by irony, the mark, the pleasure, and the curse of distinguished minds. (p. 375)

Indeed, with all its charm and beauty, Mr. Manning's book reads like a commentary on the most famous quotation from Ecclesiastes. Merodach, Protagoras, Serenus—the friend of Paul—Cromwell, Machiavelli, Francis of Assisi, Innocent III., Rénan, and Leo XIII.—through what Gourmont-like irony is it that Mr. Manning makes all these great men and their works seem vain and foolish? Perhaps it is not Ecclesiastes, perhaps he has only—like France, like Gourmont, like so many brilliant men of to-day—brooded something too deeply over the words of the "Master," as Mr. Manning calls him, over the tremendous lines of Lucretius. A book remains to be written on the influence of Lucretius on our time. In Mr. Manning's case the influence is shared by Plato among the ancients and Renan and France among the moderns. Perhaps **"The House of Euripides"** contains too many reminiscences of the divine dialogues, perhaps **"The Friend of Paul"** reminds one a little too much of the early part of *Sur la Pierre Blanche,* but one easily passes these trifles over in admiration for the general structure of Mr. Manning's book and for the many brilliant thoughts it contains.

Dissatisfaction mingled with an exquisite appreciation of beauty, the irony of France wedded to the aesthetic perceptions of Pater—that is the book's character. Few people have loved more than Mr. Manning the poetry, the charm, the beauty of the life of Francesco Bernadone. But at the same time none of his lovers has so clearly realised the essential defects of the Franciscan movement. **"The Jesters of the Lord"** reads like an extract from the Fioretti, accompanied by a slightly ironical criticism. I do not recall anything I have read which was at once more beautiful, more pathetic and more ironical than the end of this exquisite essay. Francis and his followers returning gladly from Rome with permission to found the new order fall fainting by the roadside in the heat of the sun. A young man going by in a cart finds them and revives them with wine. When they got to Orte that night, Francis suddenly said, "That was an angel who succored us." And they marvelled that they had not known it sooner. "They were twelve fools," said the young man to his sweetheart. . . .

[Mannings prose] is, at least to certain tastes, a little too ornate, too finely chased, too precious. That is the inevitable result of the Epicurean attitude. But it is most certainly never cheap prose, and if we do not always hear Mr. Manning's own voice in his writing, if he gives us something which is less austere and restrained than the speech of "one gentleman talking to another" he has at least an academic grace of expression finer than any living Englishman and a felicity of epithet as mellifluous as that of Pater if not as precise as that of Anatole France. (p. 376)

Richard Aldington, "The Prose of Frederic Manning," in The Egoist, *Vol. I, No. 19, October 1, 1914, pp. 374-76.*

HARRIET MONROE (essay date 1919)

[*As the founder and editor of* Poetry, *Monroe was a key figure in the American "poetry renaissance" that took place in the early twentieth century.* Poetry *was the first periodical devoted primarily to the works of new poets and to poetry criticism, and from 1912 until her death Monroe maintained an editorial policy of printing "the best English verse which is being written today, regardless of where, by whom, or under what theory of art it is written." In the following excerpt, Monroe praises Manning's poems collected in* Eidola.]

Over here we don't know what this English poet looks like, but somehow [*Eidola*] suggests a young Narcissus in the trenches. It is shot full of beauty and sorrow, the beauty of a Greek clarity and the sorrow of an austere shapeliness. The book should be read backward, for the earlier poems are printed at the end, among them the lovely **"Simaetha,"** finely curved as a vase, which *Poetry* printed in ancient days before the war. Even though these runs an undercurrent of sorrow, as if the beauty of life were too keen for joy.

But Narcissus is not blasted in the trenches; no shell destroys him—thank heaven!—and even his ecstasy in beauty survives, suffering a sea-change under the alchemy of war.

> But the mean things of the earth hast thou chosen,
> Decked them with suffering,
> Made them beautiful with the passion for rightness,
> Strong with the pride of love.

Exalted by the "passion of rightness" and the "pride of love," he finds beauty even here—the horror has no power over him. **"The Sign"** is an expression of spiritual triumph:

> We are here in a wood of little beeches:
> And the leaves are like black lace
> Against a sky of nacre.
>
> One bough of clear promise
> Across the moon.
>
> It is in this wise that God speaketh unto me.
> He layeth hands of healing upon my flesh,
> Stilling it in an eternal peace.
> Until my soul reaches out myriad and infinite hands
> Toward him;
> And is eased of its hunger.
>
> And I know that this passes:
> This implacable fury and torment of men,
> As a thing insensate and vain:
> And the stillness hath said unto me,
> Over the tumult of sounds and shaken flame,
> Out of the terrible beauty of wrath,
> *I alone am eternal.*
>
> One bough of clear promise
> Across the moon.

Yet there are vividly realistic pictures of a soldier's life—in **"Grotesque," "Leaves," "The Trenches," "A Shell," "The Transport"** full of the splendor of two stallions, and that bitterly tragic detail of death, **"The Face."**

It would be unfair to quote only from the war poems if some of the best of the earlier ones were not familiar to our readers. **"Ganhardine"** is a lovely song in rhyme, and **"To Saï"** gives us the very soul of a little child. (pp. 281-82)

Harriet Monroe, "Narcissus at War," in Poetry, *Vol. XIII, No. 5, February, 1919, pp. 281-82.*

FREDERIC MANNING   (essay date 1929)

[*The following is Manning's prefatory note to* The Middle Parts of Fortune.]

While [*The Middle Parts of Fortune* is] a record of experience on the Somme and Ancre fronts, with an interval behind the lines, during the latter half of the year 1916; and the events described in it actually happened; the characters are fictitious. It is true that in recording the conversations of the men I seemed at times to hear the voices of ghosts. Their judgments were necessarily partial and prejudiced; but prejudices and partialities provide most of the driving power of life. It is better to allow them to cancel each other, than attempt to strike an average between them. Averages are too colourless, indeed too abstract in every way, to represent concrete experience. I have drawn no portraits; and my concern has been mainly with the anonymous ranks, whose opinion, often mere surmise and ill-informed, but real and true for them, I have tried to represent faithfully.

War is waged by men; not by beasts, or by gods. It is a peculiarly human activity. To call it a crime against mankind is to miss at least half its significance; it is also the punishment of a crime. That raises a moral question, the kind of problem with which the present age is disinclined to deal. Perhaps some future attempt to provide a solution for it may prove to be even more astonishing than the last.

> Frederic Manning, in a preface to his The Middle Parts of Fortune: Somme & Ancre, 1916, *1929. Reprint by St. Martin's Press, 1977, p. iii.*

THE TIMES LITERARY SUPPLEMENT   (essay date 1930)

[*In the following review, the critic offers a favorable appraisal of* Her Privates We.]

The private soldier has never been vocal, and thus we have not many pictures of warfare from his point of view. Even in the case of Rifleman Harris the splendid story comes to us from a highly educated man and skilful writer, to whom the old warrior related it as he sat at his shoemaker's bench. So in that of *Her Privates We,* probably the best and honestest description of life in the ranks during the Great War that has yet appeared in English, the narrator has chosen for his principal personage—and obviously to represent himself—a man of antecedents, education and sentiments very different from those of his fellows and even of his closest friends. Private Bourne does not speak in the first person, but the War is seen through his eyes; and on the rare occasions when other men discuss him in his absence we feel that the author has momentarily lapsed from his high standard. This method does not on the face of it appear likely to produce a faithful representation of the ordinary member of the rank and file, but in fact it is in this respect triumphant.

"Private 19022" is a very able writer, but he lacks that power—which, indeed, few seem to have possessed since the days of the great Victorian novelists—of crowding a stage with characters and giving every one of them, even the merest super, a distinct and easily recognizable personality. Some of his supers are supers only. But Bourne's friends, Shem, Martlow, "Weeper" Smart, the Regimental Sergeant-Major—what an original, happy and convincing portrait is this, Sergeant-Major Tozer!—are all clear-cut. Bourne himself is really masterly. He is a man who in days of peace would never have found anything in common with the bucolic Shem or the *gamin* Mar-

tlow. He is a cool, intelligent soldier, who would make an excellent platoon commander, but he dislikes the notion of taking a commission. The long period of association with the others has given him something of their outlook, and he feels that he will never acquire that of the officer. And yet between him and them there is a gulf, bridged by good fellowship on both sides, but never filled in. Even with Shem and Martlow, the other two of a trio of inseparables, the link is, as he explains to the Chaplain, comradeship rather than friendship. "It is different: it has its own loyalties and affections; and I am not so sure that it does not rise on occasion to an intensity of feeling which friendship never touches. It may be less in itself, I don't know, but its opportunity is greater." Here, then, we see the private soldier as Bourne, his mate, his comrade and half but only half his kin, sees him. The picture is not only unforgettable but convincing. There are few War-books of the truth of which one feels so certain from first to last. Not only the characters of individuals but the spirit of what must have been a very good battalion are brought out. We have met many defeatists and "lead-swingers" in recent fiction. This book helps to remind us that men of that type are not representative, though they did exist. For all their foul language, their grumbling, their criticism of authority, their cynicism, Bourne and his friends are determined to win the War, though the only hope any of them has of seeing the end is by the aid of a wound. They have none of the optimism of certain of their superiors. "Oh, we'll win all right, Sir," says one of them to his officer, "but not yet." And for almost every one of them whom the comfortable "blighty" avoided that "not yet" meant "not in my time."

If the atmosphere is realistic, the mode of life appears equally so. Those of us who served only as officers can say no more than "appears" of certain aspects, though of others we can declare that they are definitely true. The old Army tradition remained unchanged by the War: officers were expected to know as much of their men's lives as would conduce to their comfort and happiness and the discipline of the unit, but not to search for more. The smuggled bottle of whisky, the quiet gamble, the knuckle-fight in a cowshed, one shut one's eyes to them if one could; and the sensible commanding officer looked without favour on the Paul Pry who brought them to light, even while he faithfully dealt out punishment. But so much is the very essence of War-time existence that one can take the writer on trust for the rest, especially as it is all so convincing. The feasts in the various cafés may have been unusual in their luxury, but that was because Bourne was a man of means as private soldiers went. The scenes in the trenches and that of the terrible abortive attack on the Ancre are as good as any that have yet appeared. The book has faults, chiefly lack of proportion, but it is a fine tribute to the British soldier and a notable record for ages to come. So many books have been written about the Great War that it were rash to prophesy undying fame for this; we can at least say that any similar book on a former war would have taken its place as a classic of its kind. We all of us pray that there may never be a repetition of those years, but we may also venture to hope that we may never be without men of the greatness of heart of Shem and Martlow.

> A review of "Her Privates We," in The Times Literary Supplement, *No. 1459, January 16, 1930, p. 40.*

ARNOLD BENNETT   (essay date 1930)

[*Bennett was an Edwardian novelist who is credited with bringing techniques of European Naturalism to the English novel. His*

A trench scene at the Somme, 1916. Courtesy of The Trustees of the Imperial War Museum, London.

reputation rests almost exclusively on The Old Wives' Tale *(1908) and the Clayhanger trilogy (1910-16), novels which are set in the manufacturing district of Bennett's native Staffordshire and which tell of the thwarted ambitions of those who endure a dull, provincial existence. In the following excerpt from a review that originally appeared in the* Evening Standard *in January 1930, Bennett lauds* The Middle Parts of Fortune *as a valuable document of war literature.*]

I have just read another war-novel: ***The Middle Parts of Fortune***. For some reason the author neither divulges his name nor employs a pseudonym. He prefers to be strictly unknown. His identity, however, is certain sooner or later to emerge; for his book is one of the big novels of the war. So he might as well confess at once and save us from bad guessing. The title is explained by a well-known passage from *Hamlet*. It is not a satisfactorily descriptive title—save in a sense savagely ironic—and can only be attributed to the secondary effect of a poor pun. Never were men less in the favours of fortune than the heroes of this book.

But what an inspiring and beautiful book! Assuredly I have read no book which gives so complete, fine and true a picture of military life in the trenches before an attack, and of military life "over the top" and through the enemy's wire, than this book presents. The author knows what goes on in men's minds. And he knows all the smells, sounds, mud, and sights of warfare to the least particular. And he puts the whole thing down.

So much and such various detail of the British soldier's life by day and by night has not before, to my knowledge, been got without crowding into one book.

The result is a quiet and utterly convincing glorification of the common soldier. The tale is full of horrors, cruelties, stupidities, grossnesses; but it is also full of nobility. It is a wreath laid on the innumerable tomb, known and unknown, visited and unvisited, of the war's victims. It compels in the reader a reluctant belief that war is glorious after all. The tale is of privates. That is to say, the mind and sufferings of the private are described from the inside, whereas the mind and sufferings of the officer are described from the outside. The chief character, Bourne, is a gentleman-ranker, who lives philosophically in most intimate contact with the ordinary ranker—and profoundly understands and esteems him.

I would not mislead you. The book is not grandiose; it has no ingeniously calculated "effects"; it has indeed here and there a dull page or so; the best thing in it, after the culminating, futile, fatal attack (Somme and Ancre, 1916), is a long recital of an alcoholic and extremely earthy jollity. It has little or no "serial interest" in the usual significance of the term. Indeed to serialise it would be to ruin it. It depends for its moral magic on a continuous veracity, consistent, comprehending, merciful, and lovely. It is admirably written. ***The Middle Parts of Fortune*** will be remembered when *All Quiet on the Western Front*, with all its excellences, is forgotten. It goes deeper. It is bound to survive as a major document in war-literature. (pp. 341-42)

Arnold Bennett, "A Tale of the Private's War," in his Arnold Bennett: The "Evening Standard" Years, "Books and Persons," 1926-1931, *edited by Andrew Mylett, Archon Books, 1974, pp. 341-43.*

T. E. LAWRENCE (letter date 1930)

[*Popularly known as Lawrence of Arabia, Lawrence was an English autobiographer and translator. He is perhaps best known for his dramatic personal life, which is revealed in his masterpiece* Seven Pillars of Wisdom *(1922), an epic documentation of the Arab Revolt during World War I. Lawrence, a long-time admirer of Manning's work, was the first to correctly identify the author of* Her Privates We. *Manning responded in a letter to Lawrence dated 11 February 1930 asking: "Was it some uncanny flair, that led you to me; or did Will Rothenstein tell you that he has some letters from me with my regimental number on them, 19022? I have been rather anxious lest he should discover it." In the following excerpt from his reply dated 25 February 1930, Lawrence offers his initial impressions of Manning's novel.*]

No, it wasn't Rothenstein. . . . As for the authorship of [**Her Privates We**]—the preface gives it away. It is pure **Scenes & Portraits**. How long, I wonder, before everybody knows? You need not worry at their knowing. It is a book everyone would have been proud and happy to have written.

Of course I'm ridiculously partial to it, for since 1922 my home has been in the ranks, and Bourne says and thinks lots of the things I wanted to have said. But don't imagine that I'm anything like so much of a lad as he was. The R.A.F. is as gentle as a girls' school, and none of us drink.

I have read too many war books. They are like drams, and I cannot leave them alone, though I think I really hate them. Yours, however, and Cummings' *Enormous Room* and *War Birds* [by Elliott Springs] seem to me worth while. *War Birds* is not literature but a raw sharp life. You and Cummings have produced love-poems of a sort, and yours is the most wonderful, because there is no strain anywhere in the writing. Just sometimes you seem to mix up the "one's" and "his's": but for that, it is classically perfect stuff. The picture about ⅔ through of the fellows sliding down the bank and falling in preparatory to going up for the attack, with the C.O.'s voice and the mist—that is the best of writing.

I have read **Her Privates We** twice, and **The Middle Parts of Fortune** once, and am now deliberately leaving them alone for a while, before reading them again. The airmen are reading the **Privates,** avidly: and E. M. Forster . . . has **The Middle Parts.** Everyone to whom I write is loudly delighted with the **Privates.** I hope the sales will do you good.

Peter Davies is trying to use my dregs of reputation as one more lever in the sales. Do not let that worry you. Adventitious sales and adventitious advertisements are very soon forgotten: the cash will remain with you, and your book will be famous for as long as the war is cared for—and perhaps longer, for there is more than soldiering in it. You have been exactly fair to everyone, of all ranks: and all your people are alive. (pp. 682-83)

[Thank] you for the best book I have read for a very long time. (p. 683)

T. E. Lawrence, in a letter to Frederic Manning on February 25, 1930, in his The Letters of T. E. Law-

rence, *edited by David Garnett, Jonathan Cape, 1938, pp. 682-83.*

A. C. WARD (essay date 1930)

[*In the following excerpt, Ward questions the possibility that any "educated and imaginative" author can accurately render the experience of British privates in World War I, while praising* Her Privates We *as an excellent work in its own right.*]

Private 19022 wrote **Her Privates We** and Private X wrote *War is War*, but the British private soldier's tale of himself between 1914 and 1918 is still untold. A man of letters does not become a private soldier by the simple step of enlisting, nor can he do it in any other way. He remains throughout an educated and imaginative man to whom the War was an experience different from that which the uneducated unimaginative passed through; and however socially mixed the army may have been, the latter type is properly meant by the term "private." Unless it should chance to be done almost casually through the medium of slow and fragmentary dictation, it is probable that the British private's view of the War will never be given at length. (p. 164)

Except what may be learnt from the War-time songs, literature so far provides only *external* pictures of the private in the War. . . . **Her Privates We** is, so far, undoubtedly the finest book of its kind which has come out of the War—and possibly, in its kind, nothing finer can be done. It is full, honest, and written with the utmost literary skill: its prose is at once exalted and solidly earthy. Companionship and courage take their proper place, and the soldier's life is represented "in the round." From the very first sentences it is clear that this is to be a book which penetrates beyond blood and clamour to the spiritual resistances that give whatever meaning there is to the tragedy of war. The central character, Bourne, though a private, belongs to the officer class, and is about to receive a commisssion when he is killed. His companion privates are excellently drawn, in their good and bad qualities alike. But again it must be said that an educated man, and especially one who can draw five-pound cheques at will upon the chaplain, does not experience quite the same war as the common "full private" knows. There is nothing in the text of **Her Privates We** so bitter and tormentedly savage as the title. When their exact implication is realized those three words seem a vituperative curse hurled at war-makers. (pp. 165-66)

A. C. Ward, "The Unhappy Warriors," in his The Nineteen-Twenties: Literature and Ideas in the Post-War Decade, *Methuen & Co. Ltd., 1930, pp. 140-67.*

BONAMY DOBRÉE (essay date 1931)

[*An English historian and critic, Dobrée distinguished himself both as a leading authority on Restoration drama and as a biographer who sought, through vivid description and an attention to prose style, to establish biography as a creative form. In all his writings, Dobrée's foremost concern was to communicate to the reader his aesthetic response to the work under discussion. In the following excerpt from a review of the enlarged edition of* Scenes and Portraits, *he discusses dialogue and structure in that collection.*]

There are some unlucky and misguided people who say that they cannot abide the dialogue form, thus shutting themselves out from some of the most delightful things in literature—Plato, Lucian, the Essay of Dramatick Poesy, Fontenelle, Berkeley, Landor, and Mr. Lowes Dickinson; and they will miss another delight in not being able to read Mr. Manning. Not that *Scenes and Portraits* . . . is written in the strict dialogue form; it is on the Platonic rather than the Berkeleian model. . . . In this form of essay we are allowed to do more thinking for ourselves than we are in the monologue; we do not cower before opinions hurled at us, nor feel that we are being forced or persuaded into a trap. The author permits us to watch him thinking round a question; he does not give us his product ready-made; and he convinces us of his intelligence by showing us both sides of a matter; for a fool, as Halifax remarked, is one "that hath no dialogue within himself." Mr. Manning is not didactic; he gives us two points of view, and enables us to see the ground between. Moreover, the method is peculiarly suited to what he has to say, for he is concerned with attitudes towards life which seem incompatible with each other. Thus he is able to bring aspects together in a way which would be difficult in a narrative, and impossible in the direct essay.

Mr. Manning himself appears to be an Epicurean Roman Catholic; and if this may seem to be trying to get the best of both worlds, the answer is that Mr. Manning in reality gets little of either, since he is that very agreeable thing, a happy sceptic. This, I trust, is not to injure him in these days of discreet "enthusiasm." His affinities are—and here again are strange bedfellows—Pater and Anatole France, and he has admitted to Loisy. But he writes like none of these, and here his affinity is the glorious one of Landor: like Landor he can use what in other writers would be an affectation, without its seeming to be such. Thus, he writes "hath" for "has" where it makes for euphony and distinction, as before another sibilant. In the matter of form he is finished and rounded, like M. Paul Valéry: he does not leave us at the end of a dialogue with the last words echoing on the empty air. We get a complete "scene" as well as a "portrait," set about a discussion or a tale; and as we finish a conversation we are satisfied, neither left hungry, nor given more than we can digest.

All the chapters are good: they carry us along, not only by the interest we take in the people and their ideas, but also by their style; for Mr. Manning is that increasingly rare thing, a conscious stylist with a recognizable manner. . . .

The conversations range from Adamite times almost to our own, for the last is between Leo XIII and Renan (himself no mean writer of dialogues), who meet in the Paradise of the Disillusioned: it is the only Dialogue of the Dead. In the first, the least perfect in form, we meet a charming philosopher, the Bernard Shaw of his day, but without Mr. Shaw's facile optimism. The next is a conversation **"In the House of Euripides,"** where we hear Socrates bring out the views of Protagoras, who believes in God much as the modern scientists do:

> We are not concerned with the existence of the gods, but with our knowledge of their existence. It would be equally foolish for us to deny, as to affirm, their existence. There may be a supreme reason acting on the world, whose ends we cannot understand, whose actions we cannot comprehend. It may be, that the world exists for some other purpose than the realization of our dreams. Perhaps we are only the superfluities, the parings of ivory, the winnowed husks from the threshing, by-products in the creation of something more perfect; and perhaps the confused and obscure sense of the ideal, which works in us, and is at once our

desire and our despair, is a dim consciousness of the growth of this beauty, a desire and despair of being one with it.

"The Friend of Paul" is an enchanting story of an old Roman Epicurean, who meets Paul of Tarsus at Corinth; he is drawn by the power of the man, but does not feel that his philosophy can add anything to what he has already got; the new ideas permeate every philosophy, and Paul's is only another version of them. In **"The Jesters of the Lord"** we meet St. Francis of Assisi, and assist at an interview with the Pope, where the sweetness of the would-be monk over-persuades the watchful administrator. At San Casciano we listen to Thomas Cromwell and Machiavelli saying to each other many things which are applicable at the present day; but that is the test of all good dialogues between people who lived long ago, a test which these survive triumphantly, to be as full of meaning for the present as they pretend to have been significant in the past. But this dialogue is not only political, for the friends discuss Virgil and Dante as well as Luther, and the government of princes. All the dialogues bring us into the presence of living men, and take us back to their times which seem so like our own; for all of them are concerned with something new coming into the world, at epochs, which like ours, seem ready for some great change, when men feel that 'tis well an old age is out, and time to begin a new. . . .

[I] would not leave the impression that these conversations are entirely philosophic; they deal also with the mind clogged by its agreeable frame of flesh: and if they are philosophic, they are so in the only form which is palatable to one reader at least. If there are some who cannot read dialogues at all, there are others for whom philosophy can be read only in dialogue: and for these Mr. Manning has provided a volume which will be read and read again with very great pleasure.

> Bonamy Dobrée, "Imaginary Conversations," in The Spectator, Vol. 146, No. 5349, January 3, 1931, p. 21.

C. KAEPPEL (essay date 1935)

[*In the following excerpt, Kaeppel favorably appraises* Her Privates We *and discusses that novel in the context of World War I fiction.*]

Of the great books dealing with old time wars—*War and Peace* is the outstanding example—nearly all were written many years after the events they treat of; so perhaps the greatest book of the late War is still to come. Certainly if we compare *Her Privates We* with its colossal predecessor we shall note the absence of certain characteristics of Tolstoi's masterpiece. There is not, e.g., the historical background, the causes of the war, nor are the characteristics of the warring nations, save only Britain, portrayed; also we would have liked to have heard more of the antecedents of the central character, Bourne, undoubtedly the author himself. But beyond question, *Her Privates We* is the greatest work in any language that the Great War has as yet produced, imperishable in its courage, fidelity, and artistry, and one reader at any rate doubts whether its plan could have been altered without surrendering some of the peculiar excellencies. (p. 47)

We have had various excellent books by gifted men who played an honourable part in the War. There are, e.g., "Blunden's" *Undertones of War*, Thompson's *These Men, Thy Friends*, or Mottram's *Spanish Farm* Trilogy. They are beautiful, well proportioned, books with something of genius in them; but they are all the work of [officers. What the reading public has lacked is] . . . the real record from a private's point of view, a work not simply photographic, but with the imaginative insight to realise and portray what lay behind all happenings. Now it has got it, from an author who was at once soldier, scholar, and artist. It is significant that every chapter is headed with a passage from Shakespeare . . . ; there, if ever, was a poet who understood war and soldiers, and by his felicitous quotations, to speak of nothing else, Manning shows that he had much of the Shakespearean outlook.

Her Privates We is not a novel, neither is it an exact record. It gives the history of a platoon and a battalion on the Somme and Ancre fronts with typical characters and conversations fundamentally true. In the author's own words [see excerpt dated 1929]:

> While . . . the events described actually happened; the characters are fictitious. It is true that in recording the conversations of the men I seemed at times to hear the voices of ghosts. Their judgments were necessarily prejudiced; but prejudices and partialities provide most of the driving power of life. It is better to allow them to cancel each other than attempt to strike an average between them. Averages are too colourless, indeed, too abstract in every way to represent concrete experience. . . . my concern has been mainly with the anonymous ranks, whose opinion, often mere surmise and ill informed, but real and true, I have tried to represent faithfully.

The last ten years have given us a plethora of so called warbooks, with an outlook the reverse of Shakespearean, books whose sole value is pathological as illustrating certain tendencies in the post-War world, in that, while boring or antagonising the normal fighting man, they are eagerly bought up by the adolescent and by those who have never smelt so much as a Chinese cracker fired in anger. They are books in which characters are neurotic and the circumstances abnormal, both alike picked out for their special horror and beastliness, and presented as normal and typical. This tendency to concentrate on strain and agony, dirt and beastiality, is found in the "warbooks," of all nations, markedly so in Germany with *All Quiet on the Western Front* as a typical example, about which Sir John Squire has acutely remarked that had the German Army been anything like what it is represented to have been in most of the German war-novels, the Allies would have been through it in a week. Whether that loathsome note is struck for pathological or for commercial reasons, or for both, does not concern us here; the point is that to come upon Manning's work after such things is like coming out of a sewer into the sunlight.

A special feature of the *All Quiet* type of book is the "strong" language—a feature that has made for much of their circulation. Well, the adolescent smut-hound, male or female, will find that "Private 19022" has strong language in plenty, and an abundance of words, for all natural functions. But our adolescent will be disappointed; for the language in *Her Privates We* is neither titter of prurience nor neurotic challenge; it is a natural part of the robust, albeit unrefined, conversation that one hears every day in the pub, in the ring or traffic block, and forgets the moment after.

Sentimentalism and brutality are but the obverse and reverse of the same thing and Manning is neither sentimental nor brutal.

He burks nothing. He shows slaughter and anguish; but he shows too rest and enjoyment, escape and repose. In fine, in his own words, he shows that "war is waged by men; not by beasts or gods."

To this stupendous merit we must add an absolute naturalness of dialogue, together with a simple and beautiful style. (pp. 48-50)

[Manning] has shown how war appears to a normal soldier, for he was at once a normal soldier and a genius, and, showing this, he strikes that note which is to be heard in all great English literature—that there are many things worse than death. (p. 50)

> *C. Kaeppel, "Frederic Manning, Soldier, Scholar, Artist," in* The Australian Quarterly, *Vol. 7, No. 26, June, 1935, pp. 47-50.*

EDMUND BLUNDEN   (essay date 1964)

[*Blunden was associated with the Georgians, an early twentieth-century group of English poets who reacted against the prevalent contemporary mood of disillusionment and the rise of modernism by seeking to return to the pastoral tradition exemplified by the poetry of William Wordsworth. In this regard, much of Blunden's poetry reflects his love of the sights, sounds, and ways of rural England. However, Blunden is also one of the more prominent war poets of his generation—he was badly gassed while serving in World War I and the horror of war is a major theme in his work. In the following excerpt, he praises* Her Privates We.]

Among the large number of prose works on the first World War by those who took part in it—and far more achieved original excellence than perhaps can now be easily discovered—Frederic Manning's [*Her Privates We*] . . . was at once seen on its first appearance to be of a very high order. It was an instance of new literature not at war with the centuries of thought, feeling and form which had preceded it, but qualified for the attention of the coming race by the author's deep regard for the creative past and his observation of and reflection on his own world. If he had not been, what Peter Davies called him, "an intellectual of intellectuals" and a master of many classics [see Additional Bibliography], I doubt if he could have written such a modern classic; but he was obviously of that heroic make which even in most frightful and startling actions and sufferings can notice what is going on all round, to be recorded later in the urgent yet governed style of *Her Privates We* from beginning to end.

"Fastidious almost to the point of foppishness" is another memory of Manning set down by Peter Davies. . . . I wonder if even at the worst moments, supposing one could ever say "the worst," Manning in common khaki was not still fastidious, still something of the dandy; a touch of impertinence and brilliance, brevity too, might often make the troops happier, and himself known as a real leader.

The comment arises also from the character Private, and very briefly Lance-Corporal, Bourne whose story is told, interspersed with remarkable psychological and philosophical essays or annotations, in this richly varied book. Bourne must to some extent be an anagram, shall we say? of the author. Bourne's presents of champagne and cash to some of his penurious and unambitious companions were evidently not the reason why he could live with them and tell them exactly what he thought. After all he could tell the Regimental Sergeant-Major and even some of the officers exactly that. A triumph, this.

Manning meanwhile was constantly though not mechanically studying as individuals alike officers and other ranks. He disclaims being anybody's biographer: "the characters are fictitious," "I have drawn no portraits." Yet his scenes are, in sorrow and in joy, occupied by remarkably real people. He almost contradicts himself in the moving words, "In recording the conversations of the men I seemed at times to hear the voices of ghosts." The point of it all may be that these are mediums for the spirit of those times and places and the ever mysterious, unpredictable Great War; and yet the old soldier even now on his way to the bowling-green or public library might look up and say concerning one or another of Manning's figures, "Why, that *must* be so and so of B Company" as another ancient comes along.

The grotesque savageries and the tremendous storms of steel of those days are suggested in their first impacts in this book. Anything more difficult in the writer's art than to convey the monstrous and complex circumstances of destruction, not only that of the battlefield, but that of peacetime calamities, I do not soon imagine. *Her Privates We* is as near success in this as any of the other great unveilings of war as it was. There are moments, too, of loveliness; moonlight was one of our Muses, his and ours, transforming even the Somme battle—until the wonted roar was up again among the gun-thrashed woods.

Among war books of its period, Frederic Manning's has a time-scheme which assists in its powerful unity of movement. It all belongs to the "Somme offensive" of 1916, and a few diversions to places a little away from the Somme battlefield do not alter the sense of a current of destiny, in which Bourne and his companions were plunged that July. High summer moved along, the great battle also, and at last wet, clammy or frosty winter came over the world of Western Front servicemen. An age of death had passed. Some felt that this would be enough, but no: the strange process of more obliterations ran into the New Year, by which time many front-liners like Bourne, though not many personalities so unusual in an infantry company, had done their duty. "It was finished," said C.S.M. Tozer, when Bourne was extinct. He would never forget him; nor shall we, loving his fellow-men, and not expecting much. (pp. v-vi)

> *Edmund Blunden, in an introduction to* Her Privates We *by Frederic Manning, Peter Davies, 1964, pp. v-vi.*

C. N. SMITH (essay date 1976)

[*In the following excerpt, Smith presents a close study of the structure and plot of* Her Privates We.]

The quality of *Her Privates We* was recognised widely when it was first offered to the public at large in 1930, and though it never enjoyed the huge sales of such works as *All Quiet on the Western Front* and *The Spanish Farm* it has been reprinted several times. Its place among the more significant novels attempting to come to terms with the horrors of experience on the Western Front in the First World War is now assured. In much of its detail it is realistic and honest, and this is a precondition of success in this sort of war fiction. But Manning goes beyond the squalor and the horror and sees the richness of human life in appalling circumstances. His focus is on Bourne—that remarkably complex, intellectual private—and the small group of soldiers with whom he is associated. But just as Manning knows better than to reduce this human diversity to average or typical figures, so too he appreciates that

a convincing and fair evocation of so great a conflict must take into account the nature of the military formations in which the men serve. There are, in fact, few war novels written from the angle of the private soldier which are more scrupulous in their attitude to commanders at every level, though Manning is certainly no apologist for a hidebound officer caste.

Even more remarkable is the carefully thought-out response to war itself. Manning makes a distinction—a valuable one—between the individual's response to the grave dangers of battle and the rather different way men react to the multiple pressures of army life when the battalion is withdrawn from the front line. In both situations Manning finds positive values. He is not a militarist or an enthusiastic soldier; he does not come, as Jünger does in his *Storm of Steel*, to prize conflict as a unique, tonic experience. But in *Her Privates We* there is a complex portrait of the infantryman's lot in the First World War which goes some way to explain how they managed to endure while, as R. H. Mottram put it, the Great Powers maintained "during years, a population as large as that of London, on an area as large as that of Wales, for the sole purpose of wholesale slaughter by machinery" (Preface to *Sixty-four, Ninety-four*). With so much First World War fiction conveying a deep loathing for war and all things military, it is no wonder that Manning's more dispassionate weighing of positives and negatives should have been welcomed as something valuable.

"By the time he had picked himself up again the rest of the party had vanished . . . the world seemed extraordinarily empty of men, though he knew the ground was alive with them." . . . These words from the opening of *Her Privates We* convey the essence of Manning's appreciation of the experience of extreme danger. The novel begins with an abortive attack and, after quite a long period for rest and refit following that initial mauling, ends with Bourne killed and the group of his chums broken up, at the start of a new offensive. Though safety is never more than relative when the battalion is pulled back, the risks that are daily run are different in nature from those in the front line. Placing the first battle scene at the very start of the book makes an immediate impact, and the device of Bourne's nightmare is indicative of Manning's method: the deliberate pause for reflection is as characteristic of this novel as the graphic account of events, either major or minor. The lengthy preparations for the next big push permit a gradual increase in tension and foreboding before the final attack. In this way Manning keeps to the fore the basic fact which every infantryman had to accept: one day he would have to quit whatever uncomfortable shelter the trenches afforded and, in response to orders from superiors in whom he did not feel unlimited confidence, go over the top. For commanders, the infantry are tactical units—brigades, battalions, companies—and the operational order that the men were not to pause to help wounded comrades is indicative of their conviction that human emotion was best discounted. The staff had made suitable arrangements for the treatment of casualties and having made this concession to humanitarianism felt free to order the men to stifle their instinctive desire to linger to do what they could for their chums. . . . But in *Her Privates We* there is not only a protest against such attitudes. In fact it is significant that the protest is voiced, not by Bourne, but by Weeper Smart.

Through Bourne's actions in the two assaults Manning offers an analysis of that resurgence of individuality, that heightened awareness of the self which results when men are thrust into extreme peril even in large masses. The events themselves might have no obvious significance, and Manning does not endeavour to set them into a context of history or invoke grand concepts of political causality to rescue them from absurdity. What discussion there is of the wider issues takes place behind the lines . . . and is apparently forgotten when the danger is greatest. Yet, doing as he must, acting as his military training dictates, Bourne has accepted the role that has been thrust upon him. "It had seemed impossible to relate that petty, commonplace, unheroic figure, in ill-fitting khaki and a helmet like the barber's basin with which Don Quixote made shift on his adventures, to the moral and spiritual conflict, almost superhuman in its agony, within him." . . . Bourne's heroism is not conventional fire-eating any more than it is the gay insouciance of so many soldiers in propaganda novels to which Weeper Smart's glum realism is a riposte. But in the portrayal of acute self-awareness, with a little momentary exhilaration to carry a man through initial apprehensiveness, there is an interpretation of the experience of battle, not only in the First World War, but in any other, which contrasts strikingly with talk of a doomed generation going to die as cattle.

The sense of heightened individuality, though real, is fleeting. The appearance of a subaltern or of the Company Sergeant-Major is enough to begin the process of re-integrating Bourne. Shem is discovered resting in a dug-out, and the difficulty Bourne has in communicating with him at first is indicative of the strains to which their human relationships have been subjected. . . . The soldiers are called out, make their way uncertainly along the trenches, an officer—not named yet, which is significant—gives his orders in a voice "cracked and not quite under control." . . . But gradually the soldiers become a group— a unit, as army parlance, for once selecting the *mot juste*, would call it. As they come up to the tents a shell falls, but now it hardly disturbs them. Captain Malet calls them to attention, as the camp details look on "tactfully aloof; for there is a gulf between men just returned from action, and those who have not been in a show, as unbridgeable as between the sober and the drunk." . . . But the collective will that holds the group together is still relatively weak. Manning adroitly doubles the dispersal of the group and the dissolving of sense of oneness as the men dismiss with Bourne's dream that night. In this way Manning indicates that though the men apparently return to normal rapidly the change is in fact slow, and this helps to emphasise the magnitude of the experience they have been through.

Soldiering does not, however, consist solely—or even mainly— of taking part in great battles, a point often stressed by military historians who argue that First World War fiction tends to falsify front line experience by making heavy fighting an almost daily occurrence. Placing battle scenes at the beginning and end of the novel gives due stress to the supreme test. But the remainder of *Her Privates We* explores the related, but significantly different topic of army life. As Bourne is detailed off for work in the orderly room and then, after rejoining his chums, detached for a spell of training as a signaller, opportunities are created for depicting a number of aspects of the work of a battalion. It might be felt that Manning has made things a little too easy for himself by giving Bourne a quite exceptional capacity for getting on well with a personage so elevated in the military hierarchy as an R.S.M. without souring his relationship with his chums or incurring the suspicions of the N.C.O.s. But, this implausibility apart, *Her Privates We* provides a remarkably comprehensive reflection of the life of a battalion on active service. This is done without recourse to the techniques of the "group" novel, as exemplified by C. S.

Forester's accomplished Second World War propaganda novel *The Ship,* and without turning Bourne into a mere observer or making him go through a gamut of experiences like a picaresque hero.

In the depiction of army life there is a strong element of criticism, though it is stretching a point to interpret the title of *Her Privates We* as an explicit attack on the supposed survival of Victorian attitudes in the forces. The whole episode of Bourne's period as an extra clerk in the orderly room is an expression of the common soldier's distaste for those who regulate his existence without fully sharing in the risks, and it is notable that Bourne feels as strongly about the injustices suffered by the junior officers at the adjutant's hand as about the absurd errors that imperil the privates. Exasperation at the army's inability to cope with the situation comes across in a whole series of incidents. For instance, after men needlessly lose their lives when parading outside the orderly room, the devious and disingenuous way those in charge shuffle off responsibility is described with scathing irony. When Scottish troops are caught in a similar situation as they queue up for rations the implication that the army as a whole is steadfastly unwilling to learn from experience hardly needs stating. Two other incidents skirt farce, though the laughter is always bitter. The chain of command principle is admirably ridiculed in the matter of Bourne's damaged steel helmet . . . , while the episode when an irate Frenchwoman halts the advance of the brigade on manoeuvres additionally makes a deeply felt ironic comment on the whole business of rehearsals before a big show. . . . Sober military historians may well protest that the attitudes expressed in such episodes are less than fair. But it is hardly to be wondered at if soldiers snatching a little rest after a mauling and before being thrown into battle once again failed to appreciate the administrative achievement, great though it was, that kept them supplied and the military policies which, even if not for the time being conspicuously successful, at least staved off disaster through months of warfare on an unprecedented scale.

Yet *Her Privates We* is not by any means a diatribe against the army, despite Manning's strictures. Indeed, he even permits Bourne to make a somewhat improbably eloquent speech in defence of the High Command. . . . None of the inadequacies of headquarters can escape scornful mention from the soldiers. But Bourne insists it is only fair to give the general a chance: "he's not thinking of you or of me or of any individual man, or of any particular battalion or division. Men, to him, are only part of the material he has got to work with . . . It's not fair to think he's inhuman." Bourne's whole appreciation of the system is summed up in his realisation that it is the task of H.Q. to plan and that "once we go over the top it's the colonel's and the company commander's job. Once we meet a Hun it's our job." Among the officers and N.C.O.s with whom he comes into contact, some—the new colonel of the battalion, for instance, and Captain Malet—are singled out for almost starry-eyed adulation. As for the troops' attitude to their superiors, it is summed up when, after no end of apparently futile preparations for the next big push, culminating in the bizarre business about wearing greatcoats *en banderole* which would have had the effect of virtually making it impossible for them to move their arms, they are ordered to have leather bars nailed across the soles of their boots: "it was characteristic that the men did not grumble at this latest order, as they saw at once its utility, and the precaution seemed to give them some confidence." . . .

If *Her Privates We* must be judged somewhat deficient in its portrayal of the rigid hierarchy of a battalion on active service,

A caricature of Manning by Max Beerbohm. Reproduced by permission of Eva Reichmann.

and particularly in the depiction of relations between corporals, sergeants and C.S.M.s and R.S.M.s, where matters of status assume great importance, this is offset by the sympathetic portrayal of the private soldiers. Asked about the motives that led them to volunteer, Bourne's chums are somewhat embarrassed. The phrases of high-flown patriotism do not come to their lips, and treaty obligations never meant much to these artisans and farm workers, while a spell on the Continent has not increased Martlow's love of the Belgians. . . . The call of duty could hardly be given a less prepossessing expression than Weeper Smart's glum account of the pressures that finally compelled him to take a step he never ceases to profess to regret, and on Bourne's decision to join up we are left to draw our own conclusions. But these questions all refer to the past, to a period before the army and the war imposed a new perspective. A little information is provided about the past of some of the major characters, though not all, for it is the exigencies of the moment that really matter. When we learn about somebody's background here it is most often a means to emphasise what he is cut off from. Among Bourne and his chums something new is developing. It is not, as he insists, friendship, for conditions are too unstable and disparities too great. . . . Regimental pride, by which the Regular Army set such store, hardly seems to count though the Battalion plainly has some awareness of corporate existence. More important psychologically is the sense of mutual responsibility that gradually forms between Bourne and his chums. The group is disparate, and changes a little in the course of the novel, with Weeper Smart joining it quite late on and Shem disappearing just before the end. Humphreys approaches its fringe, but receives no welcome: his exclusion, simply as a matter of course, and not as a consequence of any thought out plan, emphasises the solidarity of the group. Already nearly complete when the narrative begins, so that the reassertion of its pull can convey Bourne's return from the loneliness of going over the top, its dissolution provides an aesthetically satisfactory conclusion to a novel which, since its focus is on individuals, not on nations, could not convincingly end any other way. Manning stresses the aleatory turning of events, and it is not just a desire to avoid conventional heroics that leads him to portray Bourne's death as the immediate result of quite commonplace decisions in an insignificant skirmish. Yet the implication is plain. Weeper's decision to volunteer for the patrol, his "Ah'll not leave thee," . . . is the last expression of the group's cohesion. It counts for a lot. But Bourne knows that in dying men are alone. "It was finished," . . . and the words echo another sacrifice.

Thinking over Bourne's death, Tozer reflects that he was "a queer chap." . . . Older, better educated, from a different social class, Bourne certainly contrasts with his chums, and the difference is emphasised by the technique of interpreting most events through his reactions, as well as using his experiences as the basis for the narrative. The introduction of Weeper Smart, that highly sensitive, if uncouth character, half-way through the novel has, however, the effect of offsetting any impression that Bourne alone appreciates the full import of circumstances, just as the episodes with the deserter Miller are a counterpoint to the acceptance of duty. It has been assumed by critics from the outset that there is a lot of Manning in Bourne. (pp. 174-79)

In fact, though there is no doubt that **Her Privates We** has a basis in reality, though the operations of the 7th K.S.L.I. [King's Shropshine Light Infantry] form the background to the novel, though, despite the author's assurance that the characters are fictitious, old soldiers of the Battalion claimed to be able to recognise some of them, Bourne is only a partial self-portrait of Manning—and a somewhat idealised one at that. Bourne's origins, like those of the other soldiers, are never fully explained. In part this is for artistic reasons, as a means of portraying the strange relationships with all their intimacies and reservations that constitute comradeship, rather than friendship. But plainly Manning did not wish to use his novel for a public discussion of his own decision to join the army and the problems he must have faced in the ranks of an English county regiment. . . . It is only by piecing together the evidence that the reader becomes aware that Bourne, like his creator, is an Australian, but the fact, like the reference to his being of a different religion . . . , is not developed. Bourne's impatience with any insistence on needless class-distinctions . . . is sometimes supposed to reflect his origins, but the point is not stressed by Manning. When Australians are mentioned, no opportunity is created for Bourne to show his own personality fully; rather, tribute is paid to a national archetype with which he—like Manning—is temperamentally incapable of conforming.

There is, of course, no reason whatever why a novelist should not develop personal experience as he wishes provided the derivative is convincing, and Sassoon's observation that Sherston [in *Siegfried's Journey*] is a simplified version of his openair self, uncomplicated by the particular problems besetting authors applies to much First World War fiction. It is, however, only at the cost of certain implausibilities that Manning re-fashions his material. Through the figure of Bourne and his chums he conveys admirably his interpretation of the nature of battle, but in the depiction of army life the relationships of his hero with other privates as well as with his superiors are made too blithe, while the matter of sexual deprivation is treated with such delicacy that it resembles a daydream. . . . Bourne is an exceptional figure with privileges and idiosyncrasies, and the more clear-sighted of his chums recognise that it is inevitable that he will be obliged to try for a commission. Significantly Manning, who says little about the initial formation of the group, does not explore the psychological strains to which Bourne would have been subjected had his superiors' plans for him come to fruition. Death spares him that problem.

Written and published when the war novel boom was at its height, *Her Privates We* invites and merits attention in the first place as a depiction of experience at the front and as an interpretation of the impact of war and army life on individuals. Comparisons between Manning and Bourne add a dimension, making the novel a fascinating human document which is perhaps more revealing than its author appreciated. Attention has already been drawn to the narrative skill which, by avoiding both the over-ingenious mechanism of a well-made plot and the temptations of trying to present a grand historical sweep from Mons to the Armistice or a full account of Manning's military career, concentrates on essentials and indeed in itself conveys something of the private soldier's sense of beng deeply involved in matters which personally he cannot fully comprehend. One side of Bourne's character is reflected, though only obliquely, in the field of allusion created by the Shakespearean quotations that give the work its title and serve as epigraphs for the chapters. Though perhaps less out of key than Bourne's sudden recall of a Latin tag . . . , contrivance is, however, rather too obvious, and the irony, like that of the grim paraphrase of a line from Gray's *Elegy* . . . , is heavy-handed. Such artifice, like the somewhat routine references to moonlit nights, does not show Manning at his best as a literary artist. He has, however, two great gifts of which the Wardour Street preciosity of his pre-war writings had given little hint. Occasionally he slips, as when he speaks of "that thin wood known as three-ply". . . and puts supercilious inverted commas round "chips" . . . or when he overworks the subjunctive and the pronoun "one." But the use of precise terminology to create an impression of actuality is a feature of a novel which breathes reality without becoming heavy with detail or relaxing its psychological grip through pausing for needless description. Even more impressive is the command of dialogue styles. The group of Bourne and his chums comes into contact with many other characters, some playing a considerable part in the novel, others, like god-like Agamemnon at the exercises . . . making only a brief, but vivid appearance. With a few words of dialogue, again and again Manning creates a vivid impression. He can capture the more elegant idiom of the commanders to a nicety, but his greatest triumph is the differentiation of the privates by their manner of speech. The original version of the novel, privately printed under the title *The Middle Parts of Fortune*, had been less inhibited in its use of four-letter words than *Her Privates We*. But little is lost by bowdlerisation, except that Bourne is less clearly differentiated from his chums when they have to make do with the conventional euphemisms. The cussing, however, combines with a sprinkling of soldiers' Anglo-Indian words and a regular use of regional dialect to produce the indispensable medium for the expression of the human interaction, especially when drink loosens everybody's tongue and lets each man cast aside momentarily some of his reserve.

Her Privates We is a complex work, expressing primarily through the deep character of Bourne responses to the War more subtly differentiated than are found in much First World War fiction. Inconsistencies and loose ends do exist, and it would be special pleading to account for all of them as expressions of the relationships which, under the conditions prevailing, could never become complete. Nonetheless, even after another World War and half a century it is not difficult to see what qualities in Bourne and in *Her Privates We* led Eric Partridge, himself an old soldier, to claim that the book was "uncontradictably the best English war novel" [see Additional Bibliography]. (pp. 180-82)

C. N. Smith, "The Very Plain Song of It: Frederic Manning, 'Her Privates We'," in The First World War in Fiction: A Collection of Critical Essays, edited by Holger Klein 1976. Reprint by Barnes & Noble Books, 1977, pp. 174-82.

BERNARD BERGONZI   (essay date 1980)

[*An English novelist, scholar, and essayist, Bergonzi has written extensively on the works of H. G. Wells, T. S. Eliot, and other major figures in twentieth-century literature. In the following excerpt from his* Heroes' Twilight: A Study of the Literature of the Great War, *he discusses* Her Privates We.]

By any standards, *Her Privates We* is a fine novel, with a timeless quality that contrasts with the period flavour that now characterizes so many books about the Great War. For all its concentration on detail and narrow range, *Her Privates We* rises in places to the universality that distinguishes major literature. Unlike most other literary records of the war, Manning's novel is written from the point of view of the ordinary private soldier; it is centred on a small group of infantrymen serving on the Somme during the late summer and autumn of 1916. The most usual kind of war writing was the work of young infantry officers, and reflected the anguished isolation and self-awareness of such a position; they shared and were yet separated from the experiences of their men, occupying an uneasy place between the mass of the other ranks and the higher military command. . . . Nevertheless, the infantryman's was the truly common experience of the war, even though it was rarely given articulate expression. When it was, as in *Her Privates We,* one has a momentary insight into a massive universal process, as opposed to the necessarily particularized and individual quality of the junior officer's response. Everything, in the end, rested on the private soldier; as Manning sardonically remarks at one point: "That is what is called, in the British Army, the chain of responsibility, which means that all responsibility, for the errors of their superior officers, is borne eventually by private soldiers in the ranks."

Her Privates We is marked by its austere concentration on the troops' existence at or near the Front, to the exclusion of any other kind of life; in this respect, it resembles *Undertones of War*. Unlike most writers who wrote retrospective accounts of the war, Manning does not establish any kind of contrast between the realities of battle and a nostalgically recalled England. Apart from one or two unflattering remarks about the home front, he does not even dwell on the alienation of soldiers from civilians. He shows the soldiers as immersed in a totally self-contained world with its own laws and values, in which civilian attitudes are best forgotten, and in which the only reminder that there is another kind of life comes with letters and food-parcels from home. Having established this world, Manning shows its workings with a wealth of convincing detail;

in particular, he possessed a fine ear for dialogue, and a sensitive awareness of the various unexpected ways in which human qualities can appear in conditions of stress. At the same time, his use of Shakespearian chapter-headings indicates his desire to place the story on a universal plane, to underline the continuity of experience between the British troops on the Somme in 1916 and Henry V's battered army at Agincourt. *Her Privates We* is not an anti-war book; Manning does not flinch from rendering the brutality and bloody waste of battle, but he accepts the war as a total and inescapable experience and does not speculate about the possibility of things being otherwise. In his reflective passages, he has something of the tragic vision of some existentialist philosophers:

> It was not much use telling them that war was only the ultimate problem of all human life stated barely, and pressing for an immediate solution. When each individual conscience cried out for its freedom, that implacable thing said: "Peace, peace; your freedom is only in me!" Men recognised the truth intuitively, even with their reason checking at a fault. There was no man of them unaware of the mystery which encompassed him, for he was a part of it; he could neither separate himself entirely from it, nor identify himself with it completely. A man might rave against war; but war, from among its myriad faces, could always turn towards him one, which was his own.

In his preface to the novel [see excerpt dated 1929], Manning wrote: "War is waged by men; not by beasts, or by gods. It is a peculiarly human activity. To call it a crime against mankind is to miss at least half its significance; it is also the punishment of a crime."

Manning uses as his centre of consciousness a private called Bourne; we know nothing of his antecedents, nor even his Christian name, but he is obviously an educated man, a lover of good food and, particularly, of wine, and he seems to be fairly well off. At the same time, he is a good mixer and is thoroughly at home in the ranks; he is very popular with his comrades and the N.C.O.s, though rather less so with some of the officers, who resent the fact that a man of their own class and education should be serving as a private. He is urged to apply for a commission, but he is reluctant to leave the ranks, and only towards the end of the novel does he agree. Bourne is an interestingly complicated figure: an intellectual of a philosophical turn of mind, he is also, in the way of private soldiers, an expert scrounger, and possesses an Odysseus-like cunning; above all, he manages to be totally detached from his surroundings. Bourne has, in fact, elements of a type that has become familiar in more recent writing as the hipster, traveling light through the world. *Her Privates We* describes the adventures, in the trenches or in billets, of Bourne and his two comrades, Shem and Martlow; in essentials, Manning's novel is an exploration of comradeship, which, as so many writers testified, emerged as the supreme value amongst fighting men. As Manning insists, it was not the same as friendship; Bourne, Shem, and Martlow were very different types who would have had little in common in peace-time; but the shared experiences of war form a close union between them, which endures until it is bloodily broken.

Comradeship as an existentially lived value was meaningful to the men, whereas they were indifferent to all forms of patriotic and idealistic exhortation:

> When at last Mr. Rhys left them, they relaxed into ease with a sigh. Major Shadwell and Captain Malet they could understand, because each was what every private soldier is, a man in arms against the world, a man fighting desperately for himself, and conscious that, in the last resort, he stood alone; for such self-reliance lies at the very heart of comradeship. In so far as Mr. Rhys had something of the same character, they respected him; but when he spoke to them of patriotism, sacrifice, and duty, he merely clouded and confused their vision.

Manning reveals another of war's "myriad faces" in his portrayal of Weeper Smart, a superbly realized character: Smart is a lugubrious and shambling soldier who is an embodiment of envy, discontent, and defeatism. His attitude to fighting is an exact anticipation of Joseph Heller's Captain Yossarian: "'All that a says is, if a man's dead it don't matter no more to 'im 'oo wins the bloody war,' said Weeper." On the face of it, Weeper is a thorough coward, and yet Bourne feels "that in any emergency he would not let one down, that he had in him, curiously enough, an heroic strain." And in the event, Weeper does prove himself capable of heroic behaviour. He is contrasted with the deserter, Miller (though even he has the energy and ingenuity to escape several times from captivity).

Her Privates We concentrates firmly on a small, clearly defined area of front-line life, and is saturated in that life: it avoids the significant contrasts posited by other novelists, and does not attempt to illustrate the decline in English civilization as a whole. And yet it treats of war with a Shakespearian inclusiveness, concretely presenting the humour as well as the horror and the pathos. Manning's close-textured prose maintains an effective balance between the salty vigour of the colloquial exchanges of the soldiers, and Bourne's probing, existential reflections; Manning's philosophical concern provides an additional dimension and unifies the novel's disparate realistic observations. This blend of the particular and the universal gives the book, at times, a certain epic flavour. (pp. 190-93)

> *Bernard Bergonzi, "Retrospect II: Fiction," in his*
> Heroes' Twilight: A Study of the Literature of the
> Great War, *second edition, The Macmillan Press
> Ltd., 1980, pp. 171-97.*

KAISER HAQ (essay date 1985)

[In the following excerpt, Haq surveys Manning's poetry collections.]

There are three easily identifiable phases in Manning's poetic development, conforming fairly closely to his three books of verse, though with the inevitable overlaps. Manning's earliest poetic efforts were lyrics but his first book, [*The Vigil of Brunhild*], is a rare example in our time of a long narrative poem. This, together with two pieces from *Poems*, "Theseus and Hippolyta" and "Helgi of Lithend," comprises his narrative phase. These poems belong to the tradition of narrative poetry that includes Tennyson, Browning, Morris, Swinburne and Arnold, But the dominant influence is Morris, whom Manning admired for his "extraordinary power of narrative, the clear brightness and simplicity of his style" and his rootedness in reality. Tennysonian influence, too, is recognizable in *Brunhild* and "Helgi." Both these poems employ a supple blank verse, have an elegiac quality and are set at turning points in history. Like many creative and discursive works of our time they embody a cyclical view of civilization. It is interesting to note that Manning's abandonment of narrative verse coincides with the writing of *Scenes and Portraits,* which is the most memorable expression of his historical vision. Aestheticism is predominant in *Poems* and spills over into *Eidola,* where, however, the most significant feature is the evolution of a distinctly modern idiom. . . . [Pound] and the Imagism he espoused were decisive influences behind this development. (p. 2)

Brunhild takes us back to the violent world of sixth-century France. Sigebert the Merovingian King married Brunhild, daughter of the King of the Wisigoths of Spain. This aroused the jealousy of Sigebert's brother Hilperik, who after having three sons—Theodebert, Merow and Clovis—by his first wife Andovere, had repudiated her and was living with a servant woman, Fredegonde. He now dismissed Fredegonde and won the hand of Brunhild's elder sister Galswith. But Fredegonde still had a hold on him and a few days later Galswith was found strangled in bed; Hilperik then married Fredegonde. Sigebert prepared for war to avenge his sister-in-law but others intervened and imposed a mediated peace which cost Hilperik the lands he had received as Galswith's dowry. This only postponed the civil war, which finally broke out after six years, in 573. Sigebert emerged victorious and entered Paris with Brunhild, her daughters and son, Hildebert. Sigebert was proclaimed ''King of all the Franks'' but he was murdered at his investiture .by two slaves sent by the deposed brother. The tables were turned, Brunhild and her daughters were taken prisoner, though a loyal duke whisked off the son to Metz, where he was recognized King. Brunhild was taken to Rouen, where Hilperik's son Merow, struck by her beauty, fell in love with her and eventually married her secretly. He helped her escape and put her in the care of the priest who had married them, but he was soon discovered by Fredegonde's hired assassins and murdered. Brunhild mustered an army but was defeated and taken prisoner. She was tortured for three days, handed over to the army's outrages and finally tied to horses and dismembered limb from limb.

In a brief Introduction Manning explains that his choice of subject arose from an interest in women whose imperious intervention in history is attended by tragedy; Lady Macbeth and Cleopatra are well-known examples. He concedes that such subjects fall naturally under the purview of the dramatist's art, ''narrative poetry being a smoother and easier texture, allowing more scope to the subjective play of ideas,'' but precisely for this reason he avoids the dramatic form, which, he feels, would force him ''to limit her [Brunhild's] personality, to define her character, to treat only a part of her various and complex psychology.'' His intention is to give full attention to the qualities the dramatic form would suppress, so he sets the poem when the action is practically over, the gruesome finale only remaining, and captures Brunhild's tragedy through ''the pageantry, the splendour, the romance of a past which her memories evoke and clothe with faint, reflected glories.'' Hence the poem is in a sense Brunhild's *recherche de temps perdu.* Her audience is a compassionate priest who visits her in prison and tries to persuade her to repent and accept absolution. She is impenitent, her sole regret that she cannot live her life over again. He suggests that in her memory she is highlighting the glory of past events while ignoring ''the dross, that was a part of them'' and consequently her moral perspective is impaired; she cannot judge herself as strictly as she would judge others. Brunhild repudiates the universal validity of the priest's viewpoint and makes a forceful statement of the existential predicament of man, thrown amidst the turmoil of events he can only

partially control, forced to live by rough and ready rules he has to fashion without help and for which he alone is responsible:

> Ye, who are sheltered from the world O priest,
> . . . have time to pause
> Ere your minds fix the measure of pure truth
> And perfect justice; but our windy life
> Loses no time on niceties: for me,
> I gave such justice as I look to now;
> I swung a hammer on mine enemies,
> To forge the world anew unto my mind;
> My cause was justice in mine eyes, and those
> Who stood against me, enemies of God.

When Brunhild begins the story of her life the reader feels a tension between the necessity to keep the narrative flowing and the somewhat incompatible attempt to render psychological states. The strength of the poem, as one would expect from the author's introductory remarks, lies in the latter. Besides being a forceful political ally of Sigebert, Brunhild reveals herself as a woman of vision, who hoped to shape his barbarious people—she comes of a more refined society—into a civilization. Sigebert's assasination ruins her dreams and ends the first movement of the narrative. . . . (pp. 3-4)

The affair with Merow that now develops gives fresh impetus to the narrative. This is a suitably romantic liaison for a tragic tale (by contrast, Brunhild's relationship with Sigebert had been staid). The thrilling account of the lovers' escape is laced up with the additional *frisson* of love-making during a halt in the woods:

> But on a sudden Merow took my hand
> In his, and looked at me with pleading eyes.
> I dropped my gaze, and silent plucked a flower.
> But even closer drew that yearning face;
> And his hand grew more amorous, his mouth
>   Closed upon mine; nor was I hard to win . . .

In the final section Brunhild rises to philosophic eminence with her apologia. She accepts the rhythm of life, which determines that generations shall succeed each other, one that comes after having the choice of carrying on from where the efforts of the previous ones had failed. She recounts the panorama of history, the rise and fall of nations, Babylon, Egypt, Greece, finally Rome whose decline had left a lacuna that she had fondly hoped to fill by raising her adopted country to the state of high civilization:

>   I dreamed to raise
> An engine on the ruins of the old,
> Whose seat should be the Rhine. I was a voice
> Crying within the wilderness. Alas!
> The vision is for the appointed time.
> These eyes shall see it not. But even now
> There are moves among the people a desire
> For some firm order. Like the blind they grope,
> Or those who walk in darkness. . . .

Brunhild's historical position, amidst chaos haunted by the ghost of a recently fallen great civilization, is analogous to what many consider to be ours. This view of modern society Manning shared with the major writers of his time, and herein lies the profound significance of Brunhild's fascination for him.

Poems divides neatly into two sections, the second a sequence of twenty-two poems titled ''Les Heures Isolées,'' while the first section includes the two narrative poems already mentioned and fifteen others, among them a few that refuse the book's aestheticist label, for instance **"April Dance-Song,"** a compact, intricately rhymed love lyric:

> Out of all the skies, dies
>   Light, and only stars shine:
> Stars to me her wise eyes,
>   And her face a light.

Quite a different view of love is presented in the aestheticist **"Tristram,"** reminiscent of the frank sensuality of Dowson and Symons:

> But mine hands crave for her touch, mine eyes for her
>   sight,
> My mouth for her mouth, mine ears for her footfalls
>   light,
> And my soul would drink of her soul through every
>   sense,
> Thirsting for her, as earth, in the heat intense,
> For the soft song and the gentle dropping of rain.

There is a similar contrast between two aubades, **"After Night,"** which is, incidentally, technically interesting for its short un-rhymed lines, and the aestheticist **"L'Aube"** from "Les Heures Isolées." In the former there is a total identification with the cycles of nature (Dawn comes "As a flower awakens in Spring") and a divine order ("we labour for God / Unwittingly"); dawn is a creative force to be celebrated.... **"L'Aube,"** on the other hand, is informed with a sense of *fin-de-siècle* exhaustion and sadness at the coming of dawn and carries a fatalistic view of love:

> Yea, it is dawn, alas!
> Gray is the earth, and cold;
> Swift was our night to pass;
>   . . . . .
> The light falls on thine hand
> And trembles in thine eyes
> From which the dreams have fled.
>   . . . . .
> Love burnt us up like grass

Three poems in the first section (**"La Toussaint," "The Soul of Man"** and **"Song of the Soul"**) and four in the second (**"Revanants des Enfants," "Ad Cinarem," "Death and Memory"** and **"Death and Nature"**) betray a concern with mortality and posthumous existence. They are infused with a belief in the indestructibility of the soul, so that after death everything we have experienced will live on in our immortal memory. A curious corollary to this is that the living are constantly in the company of ghosts!

> But softer than love, and deeper than longing
> Are the sweet, frail voices of drifting ghosts;
> In the soul of man they are floating, thronging
> As wind-blown petals, pale, flickering hosts.
>   (**"The Soul of Man"**)

In these poems the Symbolist quest for a truer reality underlying the surface of everyday life takes on a preternatural turn and in this respect they are comparable to the work of Yeats's occultist phase.

"Kore" is probably the best known of Manning's poems, as a result of its inclusion alongside Pound's reply to it in Pound's *Provença* (1910) and in Eliot's edition of the latter's *Selected Poems*. (pp. 5-7)

both **"Kore"** and Pound's "Canzon: the Yearly Slain," like many other pieces in *Poems* and *Eidola*, show the power of myth on the imagination of early twentieth-century poets, due no doubt to the inherited tradition of using myth in poetry. The mythic subject of this pair of poems, for instance, was used memorably in a number of Victorian poems: Tennyson's "Demeter and Persephone" and Swinburne's "The Garden of Proserpine" and "Hymn to Proserpine."

Since Pound's reply was in the tradition, originally medieval, of answering or amplifying one poem with another, a comparison with it should better enable us to put **"Kore"** in the right perspective. Though Pound claims that like Manning he also knows "the Yearly Saint," it is doubtful if they "know" the same figure, since the poems reveal her with different faces. Manning's Kore is a weary woman, seemingly past her prime, who, having "blessed the earth," goes into winter's dark

> With slow reluctant feet, and weary eyes,
> And eyelids heavy with coming sleep,
> With small breasts lifted up in stress of sighs,
> She passed, as shadows pass, among the sheep;
> While the earth dreamed, and only I was ware
> Of that faint fragrance blown from her hair.

In Pound's poem she is a maiden. The event of her return to the underworld accompanies disaster, but is nonetheless beautiful.

In a third and final stanza Manning sketches the desolation following Kore's departure:

> The land lay steeped in peace of silent dreams;
> There was no sound amid the sacred boughs,
> Nor any mournful music in her streams

In other words nature hibernates, dreams, and is blissfully unaware of the cause of its desolation. Only the unique consciousness of the poet sees the mythic reality behind the phenomena of nature:

> Only I saw the shadow on her brows,
> Only I knew her for the yearly slain,
> And wept; and weep until she comes again.

In Pound we find nature herself hastening the change into the bleakness of winter; and Kore is mocked as she flees. The evocation of nature as an active process even in dissolution prepares the ground for the chief point of Pound's reply, the symbolic identification of the seasonal cycle with love.... The "Yearly Slain" in Pound's poem is therefore a symbolic composite embracing the Persephone myth of the seasonal cycle and a despairing view of earthly, human love. Manning, by contrast, speaks in the tone of an unshakeably enthralled lover, conforms closely to the original pagan myth and without stepping outside it succeeds in evoking a rich picture of nature's cycle of bloom and decay, which in itself is sufficient to sustain his romantic and elegiac response.

"Canzone," whose form betrays Pound's influence, was first published . . . under the title **"Hecate,"** the Greek goddess of magic who is here the object of a swooning declaration of love. Having seen her the speaker finds "that no more in my sight / Are mortal women lovely." A significant twist is given to the myth when the magic wrought by Hecate is presented as the source of the passing things in the phenomenal world. She becomes, as it were, a guardian of a Platonic world of forms:

>   among
> Her spools of weaving threads, her dreams beget
> Life, from nimble fingers and quick wit,
> Mirrored in mortal life, which fades and dies.

The poet's sensual rapture thus becomes an expression of mystic union with ultimate reality.

The aestheticist strain in the first section of *Poems* is predominantly transcendental, imbued with an anguished longing for a higher reality which is, in the finest pieces, embodied in mythological figures. "Les Heures Isolées" explores another aestheticist mode, the celebration of the transitory, which is seen as a momentary embodiment of a higher reality. Its doctrinal basis was provided by Pater in *The Renaissance,* where he identifies modernity with the consciousness of reality as something inconstant. Consequently a traditional *carpe diem* attitude is yoked with a modern scepticism that refuses to subordinate experience to any theory, because there is no way in which one can be certain of the latter's validity. Pater recommended that rather than look for abstractions and theoretical validity one should delight in and "refine and purify [one's] sensations and impressions." In poetry this led to emphasis on the short lyric that captures transient loveliness. This trend culminated in our century in a more strenuous quest for perfect "images" and "epiphanies." (pp. 7-9)

["The Pool,"] delineates the Paterian position and the anguish consequent upon the irruption of the hurrying world on the aesthete's reveries. His "soul is like a lake" that

> Holds but visions, unsubstantial things,
> Transient, momentary; and the feet
>   Of winds that smite the waters, blur the whole,
>   Shattering with the hurrying pulse of wings
>   That crystal quiet, which hath grown so sweet
>   With fragile reveries.

The exhortation to come to terms with transience by delighting in beautiful moments finds noteworthy expression in "**Tout Passe,**" "**Love's House,**" "**The House in the Wood**" and "**Soleil Couchant.**" Of these "**Love's House**" is also notable for the vitality of a relatively spare diction:

> Build not a house to last;
> Perish every flower
> When Autumn once is past
>
> Build for this little hour.

Of the other poems, "**The Crystal Dreamer**" deserves mention as a beautifully wrought symboliste—in fact rather Mallarméan—poem embodying a complex statement on art and its relationship to life. The poet is a votary of the "Sweet white mother of rose-white dreams." . . . The "Sweet white mother" being, like Hecate, guardian of a higher reality, it is a consummation devoutly to be wished to be absorbed into it:

> Cover me over with wide white wings,
> Prison my life in thy crystal sphere,
> As a clear globe prisons the golden light,
> Sweet white mother of dreams rose-white.

The immediate context in which *Eidola* appeared was that of the growing body of war poetry, and the fact that the seventeen odd war poems in it are placed at the beginning indicates that this was the context poet and/or publisher aimed at. The bulk of the collection, however, is made up of pre-war pieces. Aestheticism is very much in evidence, but so are the signs of "modernization." Even some of the aestheticist poems employ free verse, while in a good handful the use of free rhythms together with spare and precise diction and imagery signals Manning's modern phase, though there isn't, unfortunately, a clean break with the earlier mode, at least not till the mature war poems that round off the author's poetic career.

The most tenacious of outmoded elements are archaisms of diction—"art," "ye," "thee," "thou," "thine," the suffix "-eth," etc.—which frequently occur in otherwise quite modern poems. Their presence in the first of the two verse paragraphs of "**The Mother**" . . .—"She hath such quiet eyes" . . . "And level sunlight streameth"—sets it apart from the latter paragraph, which is wholly modern in diction and delicately modulates the free verse to capture the spontaneous drama of mother and child:

> But the child, gazing upward,
> Sees the glory of the apple-blossom suddenly scattered,
> As a bird flies through the branches;
> And he reaches toward the soft, white fluttering petals
> That light upon his face, and laughs; and she
> Stoops over him quickly with sudden hot, passionate
>   kisses,
> Smiling for all her tears.

More thoroughly modern in idiom and an altogether superb poem is "**To Sai,**" where the elfish elusiveness of a child's spirit is subtly captured in a delicate, organic free verse that D. H. Lawrence, I daresay, would have felt proud to have written. Sai is first presented at play among butterflies before the speaker enters the scene with her in the third and final paragraph:

> I shall not look at her,
> Lest she should hide from mine eyes
> In the shadow.
> I bring her pale honey in a comb, apples
> Sweet and smelling; and leave them beside me;
> Then comes she softly.
> There is a bee in the willow-weed,
> From flower to flower it climbs, and I watch it
> Till the honey and apples are eaten.
> Sai is quite close to me; now she has gone
> She has forgotten me,
>
> Sai is small,
> But a little child.

"Mine" in the second line above is the sole archaism in the poem.

Of the war poems at least one, "**Sacrifice,**" was written before Manning had any experience of the trenches. . . . Not surprisingly, the poem is too generalized and abstract to be effective; combatants are incongruously decked out in medieval armour and there is a facile assertion of the value of their "sacrifice" in terms of a fertility ritual. In a few pieces, like "**Bois de Mametz**" . . . , "**Reaction,**" and "**Wind,**" there is a partially successful attempt to deal with the intensities of war, "**Reaction**" has a few effective realistic touches: the mud the men scrape off their boots is "half human"—a telling epithet—and then they "are killing the lice in our shirts" or "Roaring our songs in estaminets," but the extended use of myth—Aphrodite is present with the soldiers, filling their "eyes with the wine of your vision"—is indulgent and detracts much from the overall impact. The flaw in these poems, which J. T. Laird rightly characterizes as "old-fashioned rhetoric" [see Additional Bibliography] reflects the inadequacy of the tradition that Manning inherited to deal with the shock of war. This is a problem all war poets had to face. (pp. 9-12)

Despite his drawback Manning succeeded in turning a fair number of poems that deserve a place in the canon of memorable Great War poetry. It is quite surprising, incidentally, that even when he came to be widely acclaimed as a war novelist he remained virtually unknown as a war poet. This is all the more surprising in view of the otherwise generous critical attention accorded to war poetry. (p. 12)

Manning is unique among the maturer war poets — as distinct from jingoistic versifiers—in his belief that human nature is responsible for war's irrational violence.... [This] idea is powerfully expressed in **"The Guns"**:

> But the torn and screaming air
> Trembles under the onset of warring angels
> With terrible and beautiful faces;
> And the soul is stilled, knowing these awful shapes,
> To be but the creatures of its own lusts.

Such philosophic acceptance of the cataclysm enables him in **"Autarkia"** to express a sober patriotism based on an existential notion of commitment; it is incomparably more reasonable and humane than the strident patriotism of, say, Brooke.

> I am alone; even ranked with multitudes:
> And they alone, each man.
>   So we are free.

Manning's war commitment affirms his unique relationship with his country (adopted in his case) and the Deity:

>   this England which is mine
> Whereof no man has seen the loveliness
> As with mine eyes: and even too, my God
> Whom none have known as I: for these I fight,
> For mine own self....

It is perhaps because of this philosophic quality that Manning, in a perfect little imagistic poem, **"A Shell,"** can combine realism with humour:

> Here we are all, naked as Greeks,
> Killing the lice in our shirts:
> Suddenly the air is torn asunder,
> Ripped as coarse silk,
> Then a dull thud....
> We are all squatting.

There are sharp, realistic portrayals of the Front in a number of poems which can be compared to the work of Read, Owen, Rosenberg or Sassoon. In **"The Trenches,"** there is a detailed description of the troglodyte world of the millions of fighting men:

> Endless lanes sunken in the clay.
> Bays, and traverses, fringed with wasted herbage,
> Seed-pods of blue scabious, and some lingering blooms;
> And the sky, seen as from a well,
> Brilliant with frosty stars.

"Transport" makes effective use of mythic allusions to point up the telling contrast between two magnificent stallions and their unattractive setting:

> ... two gray stallions
> Such as Oenetia bred;
> Beautiful as the horses of Hippolytus
> Carven on some antique frieze.
> And my heart rejoices seeing their strength in play,

> The mere animal life of them
> Lusting,
> As a thing passionate and proud.

> Then again the limbers and grotesque mules.

In **"The Face"** Manning brings off the difficult task of portraying the tragedy of an individual death.... [He] succeeds by focussing delicately, with pity and compassion, on a specific instance of a youth killed in action:

> Out of the smoke of men's wrath,
> The red mist of anger,
> Suddenly,
> As a wraith of sleep,
> A boy's face, white and tense,
> Convulsed with terror and hate,
> The lips trembling.
> Then a red smear, falling....
> I thrust aside the cloud, as it were tangible,
> Blinded with a mist of blood.
> The face cometh again
> As a wraith of sleep:
> A boy's face delicate and blonde,
> The very mask of God,
> Broken.

"Grotesque" stands out in the entire body of war poetry on account of its compact blend of literary allusion, "sardonic mockery" and realistic detail:

> These are the damned circles Dante trod,
> Terrible in hopelessness,
> But even skulls have their humour.
> An eyeless and sardonic mockery:
> And we,
> Sitting with streaming eyes in the acrid smoke,
> That murks our foul, damp billet,
> Chant bitterly, with raucous voices
> As a choir of frogs
> In hideous irony, our patriotic songs.

This poem stands at the climax of Manning's poetic development. Two points need to be made in summing up. That Manning's poetry bears the impress of the momentous transition that ushered in the modern age in literature. And that he has left a good handful of poems which deserve the attention of both the general reader and the critic. (pp. 12-16)

> *Kaiser Haq, "The Poetry of Frederic Manning," in* Journal of Commonwealth Literature, *Vol. XX, No. 1, 1985, pp. 1-16.*

ADDITIONAL BIBLIOGRAPHY

Aiken, Conrad. "Narrative Poetry and the Vestigal Lyric: John Masefield, Robert Nichols, Frederic Manning." In his *Scepticisms: Notes on Contemporary Poetry*, pp. 170-77. New York: Alfred A. Knopf, 1919.

> Includes an ambivalent review of *Eidola* in a discussion of contemporary poetry. According to Aiken: "*Eidola* ... shows an attempt to change the lyric method, but not so much by addition as by refinement. It cannot be said to be very remarkable. The work suggests that of [Richard] Aldington, but is more jejunely precise and very much less vivid."

Davies, Peter. Introduction to *Her Privates We*, by Frederic Manning (Private 19022). London: Peter Davies, 1943.

Praises Manning and his work. According to Davies: *"Her Privates We* is, and always will be, not only a noble memorial of the 1914-18 war, but a profound and truthful picture of the ordinary Englishman standing up to the perennial ordeal of war."

Drolet, Gilbert. "In the Painful Field." *Queen's Quarterly* 88, No. 2 (Summer 1981): 289-97.
Compares and contrasts the portrayal of soldiers on the front line in Manning's *The Middle Parts of Fortune,* Farley Mowat's tale of Canadian infantrymen in World War II, *—And No Birds Sang,* and *A Rumor of War,* a novel of the Vietnam war by Philip Caputo.

Eliot, T. S. "A Commentary." *The Criterion* XIV, No. LVI (April 1935): 431-36.
Concludes with an obituary tribute to Manning. According to Eliot: "[Manning's] passion for perfection became almost indistinguishable from a passion for destruction of his own work; even *Her Privates We* might never have been written, I believe, without the insistent urging of the friend who published it. . . . [He] was without ambition for notoriety, and had a style of writing, and a frame of mind, suited to a more cultured and better educated age than our own."

Fussell, Paul. "Barrack-Room Ballads." *The New York Times Book Review* (23 October 1977): 26.
Review of *The Middle Parts of Fortune* by a World War I scholar. According to Fussell: "Manning is excellent at understanding the way the mind in extremity defends itself by holding contradictory opinions at once and equally excellent in recognizing death in war as merely a figure for the death-sentence which is life."

Haq, Kaiser. "Forgotten Fred: A Portrait of Frederic Manning." *London Magazine* 23, No. 9810 (December 1983-January 1984): 54-78.
Biographical and critical essay surveying Manning's principal works. Haq concludes that "we owe it to ourselves to put [Manning] in a place of honor among writers of our time."

Hemingway, Ernest, ed. Introduction to *Men at War: The Best War Stories of All Time,* pp. xi-xxvii. New York: Crown Publishers, 1955.
Lauds *Her Privates We* in a discussion of World War I literature. According to Hemingway: "It is the finest and noblest book of men in war that I have ever read. I read it over once each year to remember how things really were so that I will never lie to myself nor to anyone else about them."

Hergenhan, L. T. "Some Unpublished Letters from T. E. Lawrence to Frederic Manning." *Southerly* 23, No. 4 (1963): 242-52.
Reprints nine letters written between March 1930 and November 1934.

———. "Novelist at War: Frederic Manning's *Her Privates We.* *Quadrant* 14, No. 4 (July-August 1970): 19-29.
Traces autobiographical elements in *Her Privates We* through an examination of the letters Manning wrote to Will Rothenstein during the war.

———. "Ezra Pound, Frederic Manning, and James Griffyth Fairfax." *Australian Literary Studies* II, No. 3 (May 1984): 395-400.
Examines Manning's expatriation as it influenced his works and affected his acquaintance with the American expatriate Pound and Fairfax, an expatriated Australian poet.

Klein, H. M. "The Structure of Frederic Manning's War Novel *Her Privates We.*" *Australian Literary Studies* 6, No. 4 (October 1974): 404-17.
Provides an extensive analysis of the plot and structure of Manning's novel. Klein concludes that "the whole book and all the people in it, including Bourne . . . , are kept firmly on the level of the there and then, the concrete situation."

———. "In the Midst of Beastliness: Concepts and Ideals in Manning's *Her Privates We.*" *The Journal of Commonwealth Literature* 12, No. 2 (December 1977): 136-52.

Concludes that "[Manning's] novel has a fixed world of values and opinions which are presented as absolute norms. They do not . . . amount to a glorification of war. . . . But they are one form of propaganda, and perhaps a more efficient one than the outbursts of pacifists which are much more easily ridiculed and discredited."

Laird, J. T. "Australian Poetry of the First World War: A Survey." *Australian Literary Studies* 4, No. 3 (May 1970): 241-50.
Includes a brief appraisal of *Eidola.* According to Laird: "Although in his weaker poems there is much old-fashioned rhetoric, there is less of it in his best work, where we can appreciate the virtues of his sparse masculine language, with its vivid and precise images of light, color, and sound, and its free rhythms."

Lawrence, T. E. *The Letters of T. E. Lawrence,* edited by David Garnett, 536 ff. London: Jonathan Cape, 1938.
Includes numerous references to and brief comments on Manning's works.

Macdonald, Lyn. Introduction to *Her Privates We,* by Frederic Manning. London: The Hogarth Press, 1986.
Describes the social climate surrounding World War I, the life of military personnel at the front, and the subsequent war fiction that attempted to tell the true stories of those involved in the fighting.

Man, Leonard. "Australian in Battle." *Overland* 4, No. 31 (Autumn 1965): 47-8.
Focuses on Manning's democratic outlook in *Her Privates We.*

Manning, Frederic. "Frederic Manning: 1887-1935." In *Letters to T. E. Lawrence,* edited by A. W. Lawrence, pp. 127-48. London: Jonathan Cape, 1962.
Includes eighteen letters from Manning to Lawrence written between March 1922 and Christmas 1934.

McDougal, Stuart Y. "Toward an Empyrean of Pure Light: The Radiant Medieval World." In his *Ezra Pound and the Troubadour Tradition,* pp. 70-101. Princeton: Princeton University Press, 1972.
Compares and contrasts Manning's "Kore" with Pound's reply poem, "Canzon: The Yearly Slain."

Monroe, Harriet. "Farewell to Two Poets." *Poetry* 46, No. 4 (July 1935): 219-22.
Obituary tribute to Manning and Nathan Haskell Dole. Monroe writes that Manning's "entire tribute to the art he loved best would make a very small volume, but one of a quality so fine that it will not soon be forgotten by the more exacting lovers of poetry."

Partridge, Eric. "The War Continues." *The Window* 1, No. 2 (April 1930): 62-85.
Declares that *Her Privates We* is "uncontradictably the best English war novel; it is considerably better than [*All Quiet on the Western Front*]. . . ."

Pound, Ezra, "A List of Books." *The Little Review* 4, No. 11 (March 1918): 54-58.
An appreciative review of *Scenes and Portraits,* which Pound recommends as a book "not to be neglected by the intelligent reader."

Taylor, Mark. "Bourne Again." *Commonweal* CVI, No. 1 (19 January 1979): 26-7.
Offers an approbatory review of *The Middle Parts of Fortune* on the occasion of its first publication in the United States.

"Three Books in Verse." *The Times Literary Supplement* No. 441 (23 June 1910): 224.
Includes a favorable review of Manning's *Poems.*

Van Zyl, J. A. "Falstaff and Frederic Manning." *Theoria* 27 (October 1966): 47-54.
Examines Manning's attitude toward war as it is presented in *Her Privates We.*

Edgar Lee Masters

1868-1950

(Also wrote under pseudonyms Dexter Wallace, Webster Ford, Harley Prowler, Elmer Chubb, Lute Puckett, and Lucius Atherton) American poet, novelist, dramatist, biographer, autobiographer, and essayist.

Masters is primarily remembered as the author of *Spoon River Anthology,* a collection of poems that exploded myths about the serenity of small-town life and that experienced popularity, renown, and even notoriety almost unprecedented for a work of American poetry. In these free verse poems, which take the form of epitaphs for the long-dead or recently deceased inhabitants of a rural midwestern town, Masters dealt explicitly with both admirable and ignoble aspects of life. For this innovative format, the use of then-controversial free verse, and the employment of subject matter that was considered inappropriate for poetry by many traditionalists, *Spoon River Anthology* became a widely discussed phenomenon in American poetry, and the collection made Masters famous. However, he never again approached this fame during the rest of his prolific career, which lasted more than a quarter of a century after the appearance of *Spoon River.*

Masters was born in Garnett, Kansas, and moved with his family to Lewistown, Illinois, on the Spoon River, when he was eleven. The semiautobiographical novels *Mitch Miller* and *Skeeters Kirby,* which share the settings of Masters's boyhood, recount Huck Finn-like adventures that some commentators maintain represent more of a homage to Mark Twain than an accurate retelling of the author's youth. Masters grew up greatly admiring his father, who worked as a grocer and schoolteacher before becoming a lawyer, and after a year of classes at Knox College, the younger Masters began to study law while working in his father's law office. During this time he contributed poems and sonnets to magazines and newspapers. After he was admitted to the Illinois bar in 1891, he moved to Chicago, where he worked for a time as a bill collector before entering a law partnership with Clarence Darrow. He continued to place poems in various journals, and his first book, *A Book of Verses,* appeared in 1898, the year of his marriage to Helen Jenkins. While living in Chicago Masters published several more volumes of poetry, using pseudonyms for fear that renown as a poet would hurt his law practice; however, these early collections were undistinguished and attracted little attention. He also wrote and published a number of plays, none of which were produced.

Masters's private life was seldom tranquil: he was involved in an affair with the sculptor Tennessee Mitchell (later to be Mrs. Sherwood Anderson), tried to obtain a divorce from his wife, and dissolved his partnership with Darrow in a bitter dispute over the division of legal fees, all at about the time he began writing the Spoon River poems. He originally intended to present a history of the Spoon River area by describing the interconnected lives of its inhabitants in a novel, which, he told his father, would be his only extended work of fiction. Several of Masters's acquaintants, including Harriet Monroe and Eunice Tietjens of *Poetry* magazine, maintain that the impetus to tell the story of Spoon River and its inhabitants in free verse came from Masters's friend William Marion Reedy, who in-

spired him to write the epitaphs after rejecting much of his more conventional poetry for publication in the periodical *Reedy's Mirror.* The poems appeared initially under the pseudonym Webster Ford, but within a year Reedy had revealed the actual author and the poems were gathered and published to immediate and widely varied critical response. Writing and publishing *Spoon River Anthology* marked a decisive period in Masters's private life as well as in his career. He became ill upon completion of the book and was bedridden for some time. Upon his recovery, his notoriety as a poet led to the loss of many of his legal clients, and he was forced to attempt to earn his living by writing. During this period, he separated from his wife, and the publicity surrounding their bitter divorce ended what remained of his law practice. He left Chicago for New York in 1923, his property and finances lost in the divorce settlement, and began to associate with other authors and with artists, editors, and publishers. In 1926 Masters married a teacher thirty years his junior. He died in 1950.

Spoon River Anthology was "an immediate and popular success," according to Robert Narveson, "the first thing of its kind and a phenomenon in American literature," according to May Swenson. The *Anthology* contains over two hundred brief poetic monologues, which appear under the names of the buried dead in Spoon River's cemetery. Each person reveals the facts of his or her death and, usually, a concealed fact of his or her life as well. Thus, a crusading prohibitionist admits that he died of cirrhosis of the liver caused by drinking; the heir to a fortune, that he killed to inherit it; husbands and wives, that they despised their spouses. Here, wrote Narveson, "came Masters's ghosts, avowing the presence of vice, corruption, greed, and pettiness" in the American small town, and these revelations made *Spoon River* something of a *succès de scandale*. However, as Amy Lowell noted, "the book would not be worth commenting upon, and Mr. Masters would in no sense rank as the poet he does, if its sensuality were not counteracted by other and great qualities." According to Narveson, "the portraits were strongly ironic, pathetic, heroic, comic. . . . Along with the notoriety due to scandal, came a fame based on the book's solid virtues," and *Spoon River* became "an established American classic." Many critics commented especially on the particularly American quality of the Spoon River epitaphs. Ezra Pound, for example, proclaimed Masters the first American poet since Walt Whitman to remain in his country and to treat themes unique to America in innovative poetry. *Spoon River Anthology* appeared at a time when literary traditionalists were questioning the value of the free verse and Imagist movements in modern poetry and the realistic and naturalistic tendencies in prose fiction. William Dean Howells, who decried many of these trends, averred that what Masters had written in *Spoon River* was not poetry at all, but "shredded prose." A few years after the volume appeared, T. S. Eliot referred to Masters as "a distinguished . . . talent," but expressed regret that Masters had "not perceived the simple truth that *some* artificial limitation is necessary" to poetry. Other commentators, who did not object to the free verse form of the *Spoon River* epitaphs, complained instead of the overwhelmingly negative picture that Masters presented of small-town American life. However, some critics have pointed out that many of the most famous poems from the *Anthology*, including "Lucinda Matlock," "Sarah Brown," and "Rebecca Wasson," are joyous celebrations of life rather than bitter or ironic comments upon it.

Although Masters continued to write for the rest of his life, he never equalled the achievement of *Spoon River Anthology*. Masters himself wrote that he did not want to produce a similar book for fear of being dismissed as "having but one set of strings," but in his desire to produce something markedly different, critics contend that he never again wrote anything as good. The editor of *Poetry*, Harriet Monroe, reported that she "was aghast at discovering" that his selections for *Songs and Satires*, the volume to follow the *Anthology*, included many poems written before *Spoon River*, and recalled "the puzzled look on his face" when she urged that he publish "only recent poems of his best quality" to "confirm or strengthen the acclaim which had greeted *Spoon River*." Without knowing when the individual poems from *Songs and Satires* had been written, Amy Lowell wrote that "one would prefer to hope" that they had predated the *Spoon River* epitaphs, and found it "strange that he should have considered them worth resurrecting." Following the enormous impact of *Spoon River*, Masters was warned by Edward C. Marsh that "the critics are sharpening their pencils. They won't let you repeat the success of *Spoon River* if they can help it," but in fact, several of Masters's subsequent poetic works were initially hailed as superior to *Spoon River*. Jessie B. Rittenhouse, for example, contended that *Toward the Gulf* represented such an advance in poetic themes as to make *Spoon River* seem "a juvenile entertainment" by comparison. Such assessments, however, represented a minority view even when they appeared, and are altogether dismissed by contemporary critics. Although Masters himself believed that the long narrative poem *Domesday Book* and its sequel, *The Fate of the Jury*, surpassed *Spoon River*, commentators assessing the whole of Masters's work concur that *Spoon River* is his premier work of poetry as well as his chief literary accomplishment.

Louis Untermeyer was among the commentators who found major faults in *Songs and Satires*, listing "juvenile prettiness," "verbosity," "banalities," and "flabby desuetude" among them, further maintaining that these faults multiplied in subsequent works of poetry. After the appearance of Masters's first several novels, however, Untermeyer wondered if what he perceived as "the debacle of a poet" was leading to "the rise of a novelist." Masters's seven novels, however, have never received much critical or popular attention. John T. Flanagan (see *TCLC*, Vol. 2) found that they exhibit a lack of sustained dramatic power and display the author's inability to provide prolonged character development—flaws of Masters's longer narrative poetry as well. Of the novels, *Mitch Miller*, *Skeeters Kirby*, *Kit O'Brien*, and *Mirage* are examined primarily for their autobiographical elements. These four novels are set largely in the Spoon River area of Illinois and contain thinly disguised portraits of Masters and members of his family. In these works, according to Robert Herrick, Masters "revived in a tender, reminiscential mood the associations of his earlier years, with their homely, intimate, quite American background." While the novels *The Nuptial Flight*, *Children of the Market Place*, and *The Tide of Time* also contain autobiographical elements, they are more noted for their exploration of sociological and historical themes. John H. Wrenn and Margaret M. Wrenn have pointed out that much of Masters's fiction, like his poetry, represented "an attempt to portray America through a faithful depiction of her representative men and women, towns and cities, realities and illusions," and this tendency was further exploited in the volumes of biography that Masters produced late in his career. His biographies of Abraham Lincoln, Walt Whitman, and Mark Twain reflect his intense interest in "representative" American figures, while *Vachel Lindsay: A Poet in America* is considered his finest effort in biographical writing, both for his insights into his friend Lindsay's character and his understanding of Lindsay's poetry.

Masters's autobiography, *Across Spoon River*, has been called a difficult work to assess. Completed in 1936, the work ends with the events of mid-1917, when the initial response to *Spoon River* was still strong. Characterized by the Wrenns as "a rationalization of his career, which he saw as a struggle between will and fate, with himself making his way through sheer determination," Masters's autobiography has been termed essentially "self-serving and incomplete," especially in view of Masters's own conviction that most autobiographies are "fakes because no one can really penetrate the web of motive in himself." Masters remains a complex and enigmatic figure in American letters, an amazingly prolific poet who produced many works in other genres but, the Wrenns wrote, "never recovered from the success of *Spoon River Anthology*. And he never fully understood it." The *Anthology* remains a brilliantly original approach to the recreation and representation of an archetypal American small town, and many of the individual poems from the collection are considered among the finest works of American poetry.

(See also *TCLC*, Vol. 2; *Contemporary Authors*, Vol. 104; and *Dictionary of Literary Biography*, Vol. 54: *American Poets, 1880-1945*.)

PRINCIPAL WORKS

A Book of Verses   (poetry)   1898
Maximilian   (drama)   [first publication] 1902
The New Star Chamber, and Other Essays   (essays)   1904
The Blood of the Prophets [as Dexter Wallace]   (poetry)   1905
Althea   (drama)   [first publication] 1907
The Trifler   (drama)   [first publication] 1908
The Leaves of the Tree   (drama)   [first publication] 1909
Eileen   (drama)   [first publication] 1910
The Locket   (drama)   [first publication] 1910
Songs and Sonnets [as Webster Ford]   (poetry)   1910
The Bread of Idleness   (drama)   [first publication] 1911
Songs and Sonnets, Second Series [as Webster Ford]
     (poetry)   1912
Spoon River Anthology   (poetry)   1915
The Great Valley   (poetry)   1916
Songs and Satires   (poetry)   1916
Spoon River Anthology [expanded edition]   (poetry)   1916
Toward the Gulf   (poetry)   1918
Starved Rock   (poetry)   1919
Domesday Book   (poetry)   1920
Mitch Miller   (novel)   1920
The Open Sea   (poetry)   1921
Children of the Market Place   (novel)   1922
The Nuptial Flight   (novel)   1923
Skeeters Kirby   (novel)   1923
Mirage   (novel)   1924
The New Spoon River   (poetry)   1924
Selected Poems   (poetry)   1925
Lee   (poetry)   1926
Kit O'Brien   (novel)   1927
Jack Kelso   (poetry)   1928
The Fate of the Jury: An Epilogue to Domesday Book
     (poetry)   1929
Lichee Nuts   (poetry)   1930
Lincoln: The Man   (biography)   1931
The Serpent in the Wilderness   (poetry)   1933
Richmond   (poetry)   1934
Invisible Landscapes   (poetry)   1935
Vachel Lindsay: A Poet in America   (biography)   1935
Across Spoon River   (autobiography)   1936
The Golden Fleece of California   (poetry)   1936
Poems of People   (poetry)   1936
The New World   (poetry)   1937
The Tide of Time   (novel)   1937
Whitman   (biography)   1937
Mark Twain   (biography)   1938
More People   (poetry)   1939
Illinois Poems   (poetry)   1941
Along the Illinois   (poetry)   1942
The Sangamon   (nonfiction)   1942
The Harmony of Deeper Music: Posthumous Poems of
     Edgar Lee Masters   (poetry)   1976

EZRA POUND   (essay date 1915)

[*An American poet and critic, Pound was "the principal inventor of modern poetry," according to Archibald MacLeish. He is chiefly renowned for his ambitious poetry cycle, the* Cantos, *which he revised and enlarged throughout much of his life. These poems are noted for their lyrical intensity, metrical experimentation, literary allusions, varied subject matter and verse forms, and incorporation of phrases from foreign languages, including Chinese ideographs and Egyptian hieroglyphs. History and politics greatly interested Pound, and many of his poems and critical writings reflect his attempt to synthesize his aesthetic vision with his political, economic, and cultural ideals. Pound considered the United States a cultural wasteland; his series of satirical poems* Hugh Selwyn Mauberly (1920), *has often been ranked with T. S. Eliot's* The Waste Land (1922) *as a significant attack upon the decadence of modern culture. Pound is also noted for his instrumental role in the encouragement of other authors: he obtained editorial and financial assistance for Eliot, William Butler Yeats, James Joyce, and Wyndham Lewis, among others. Pound's pro-Fascist activities during World War II led to his indictment for treason and for a time diminished his reputation as one of the most innovative and creative artists of the twentieth century. In the following excerpt, Pound enthusiastically hails "Webster Ford" (the pseudonym under which Masters wrote* Spoon River Anthology) *as the first American poet since Walt Whitman to treat American themes in vigorous poetry.*]

At last! At last America has discovered a poet. Do not mistake me, America that great land of hypothetical futures has had various poets born within her borders, but since Whitman they have invariably had to come abroad for their recognition. "Walt" seems to have set the fashion. . . .

At last the American West has produced a poet strong enough to weather the climate, capable of dealing with life directly, without circumlocution, without resonant meaningless phrases. Ready to say what he has to say, and to shut up when he has said it. Able to treat Spoon River as Villon treated Paris of 1460. The essence of this treatment consists in looking at things unaffectedly. Villon did not pretend that fifteenth-century Paris was Rome of the first century B.C. Webster Ford does not pretend that Spoon River of 1914 is Paris of 1460.

The quality of this treatment is that it can treat actual details without being interested in them, without in the least depending upon them. The bore, the demnition bore of pseudo-modernity, is that the avowed modernist thinks he can make a poem out of a steam shovel more easily and more effectively than out of the traditional sow's ear. The accidents and detail are made to stand for the core.

Good poetry is always the same; the changes are superficial. We have the real poem in nature. The real poet thinking the real poem absorbs the *decor* almost unconsciously. (p. 11)

I have before me an early book by Webster Ford, printed in 1912, and much more old fashioned than [the eighth-century Chinese poet] Rihoku. Nineteen-twelve was a bad year, we all ran about like puppies with ten tin cans tied to our tails. The tin cans of Swinburnian rhyming, of Browningisms, even, in Mr. Ford's case, of Kiplingisms, a resonant pendant, magniloquent, Miltonic, sonorous.

The fine thing about Mr. Ford's **Songs and Sonnets, Second Series,** is that in spite of the trappings one gets the conviction of a real author, determined to speak the truth despite the sectionised state of his medium. And despite cliches of phrase and of rhythm one receives emotions, of various strength, some tragic and violent. There is moral reflection, etc., but what is the use discussing faults which a man has already discarded.

In the **Spoon River Anthology** we find the straight writing, language unaffected. No longer the murmurous derivative, but:—

My wife hated me, my son went to the dogs.

That is to say the speech of a man in process of getting something said, not merely in quest of polysyllabic decoration.

It is a great and significant thing that America should contain an editor (of the St. Louis Mirror) with sense enough to print such straight writing, and a critic sane enough to find such work in a "common newspaper" and quote it in an American review (*i.e. Poetry*).

The silly will tell you that: "It isn't poetry." The decrepit will tell you it isn't poetry. There are even loathsome atavisms, creatures of my own generation who are so steeped in the abysmal ignorance of generations, now, thank heaven, fading from the world, who will tell you: "It isn't poetry." By which they mean: "It isn't ornament. It is an integral part of an emotion. It is a statement, a bare statement of something which is part of the mood, something which contributes to the mood, not merely a bit of chiffon attached. (pp. 11-12)

I have read a reasonable amount of bad American magazine verse, pseudo-Masefieldian false pastoral and so on. Not one of the writers had had the sense, which Mr. Ford shows here, in calling up the reality of the Middle West by the very simple device of names. . . . (p. 12)

> Ezra Pound, "Webster Ford," in The Egoist, *Vol. II, No. 1, January 1, 1915, pp. 11-12.*

FLOYD DELL   (essay date 1915)

[*An American novelist and dramatist, Dell is best known today as the author of* Moon-Calf *(1920), a novel which captures the disillusioned spirit of the Jazz Age. For several years he was a member, along with Carl Sandburg, Ben Hecht, Theodore Dreiser, and others, of the Chicago Renaissance, a group of writers who legitimized the American Midwest as a source of artistic material and achievement. A Marxist during his early career, Dell moved from Chicago to New York in 1914, and served as editor of the socialist periodical the* Masses *and its successor, the* Liberator, *for ten years. During the 1920s, Dell was associated with the bohemia of Greenwich Village and, through a series of novels and one-act plays, became known as a spokesman for society's rebels and nonconformists. His socialist sympathies softened over the years, although he remained an outspoken leftist throughout his career. In the following excerpt, Dell commends* Spoon River Anthology *for the inclusiveness with which it treats small-town life and inhabitants.*]

It is laid up as a charming fault against many if not most poets that they are chiefly interested in themselves. . . .

But when the poet appears who cannot but see in the faces of men and women the half-confessed secrets of pride and passion, who cannot but observe and reflect upon the course of their loves and hatreds, and who if he searches his own heart does so to discover what these other people are like—when such a poet appears, we mix our affectionate admiration with a deeper respect. For if we seek in his pictures, as we are said to seek instinctively in all literature, for our own likeness, we find it mirrored against a more significant background, moving to sterner and more ironic destinies. It is for that reason that we concede to such poetry, almost against our preferences, the title "great."

And it is for that reason that we are likely to find a strange impressiveness, akin to greatness, in the ***Spoon River Anthology*** of Edgar Lee Masters. It is the work of a man who has seen much of life with curious eyes, brooded much upon its subtle and ironic patterns, and traced those patterns for us with grave candor. It is a book which, whether one likes it or not, one must respect.

There are excellent reasons for disliking the ***Spoon River Anthology.*** For one thing, it is couched in free verse which many will find harsh and unmelodious. For another, its language is curt and factual often to the point of baldness, and is almost entirely lacking not merely in rhetorical adornments but in the imaginative and atmospheric use of words. It is indeed almost wanting in the ordinary properties of verse—though here and there a beautiful cadence, a striking simile, or a richly imaginative phrase appears, like a rose suddenly flowering out of one of those stone-fences that shoulder their way between raw-furroughed New England fields.

But in this curt, undemonstrative language there is set forth the history of an Illinois town, its lives, its passions, its aspirations, its failures. Sordid and splendid, pathetic and obscene, the life of Spoon River reveals itself. The way in which Mr. Masters has put this life before us is in a series of epitaphs—such epitaphs as were never carved on any gravestone. Sometimes it is as though the dead, with the clear light of perfect understanding flooding in upon their still warm passions, spoke for the first time truly of their lives. But for the most part these speaking shades still keep their old illusions, and are what they were in life save in one thing only: they look back and not forward. Quietly or with a shadowy anger, tenderly or ironically, but always briefly, they tell of themselves, adding their tag of ghostly wisdom, or some message to the living, or some comment on the world that still wags on. (p. 14)

We are presently to hear the story of Old Bill Piersol, and of the judge who sentenced Hod Putt; of the judge's son and daughter, and of those they loved; of the village puritan, who is indignant that lovers' kisses should be exchanged over his grave; of the saloonkeeper that was put out of business by the puritan; of the men who found happiness in drink, and their wives; of the preacher, and the village atheist; of the girl who ran away from home, and the one who came back to her father's house to nurse an old grief; of those who loved books, and had visions; of those who beat life at her game, and those whom life cheated.

Gradually the story of Spoon River takes shape in one's mind. Figures pass and repass, seen from the angle of this man or that woman. Secrets are revealed. The whole life of the community in thought and action, high intention and tawdry accident, is unrolled. The feeling that we are in touch with actuality comes to compensate for the intensity and beauty which we are accustomed to expect as the knock to which we open our sympathies. Against these emotions, so bluntly and yet so truly represented, we feel that we have no right to shut our hearts. . . .

And at the end one has not only been made to respond to the varying passions of these people of Spoon River, but has been cast under the spell of the author's own attitude toward life, which is deeply ironic. If we share, as most of us do, the cheerful American romanticism about life, a romanticism in which the disturbing fact of death cannot be said to have any place, it is something of a triumph for the author's art to have made us feel, even if only for a little while, that it is toward death that life leads, and that this is the final secret of life.

Whether the art of this book has any relation to the art of poetry is a delicate question. The theory of free verse has been expounded of late with obscure precision by the professors of

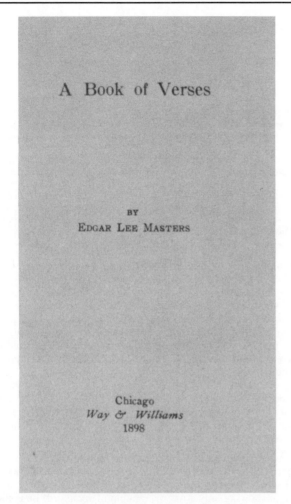

A Book of Verses

BY
EDGAR LEE MASTERS

Chicago
Way & Williams
1898

Title page of Masters's first book.

unacademic art, and its rules laid down with enthusiastic severity. One would not like to contradict them, and still less would one desire to repudiate, even in the interest of such a work as this one, the honorable tradition of verbal beauty and intensity in poetry. It is perhaps more profitable to consider whether the author's point of view is not in one respect a serious limitation. Every artist is entitled to his own philosophy. But in reading the *Spoon River Anthology* one feels that its author's high ironic attitude toward life cuts him off from appreciation of what is perhaps the most fundamental and characteristic thing in America—a humorous faith, a comedic courage, a gay and religious confidence in the goodness of things. A poet immersed in this American romanticism would give a more complete account of American life; and would be perhaps the better philosopher. (p. 15)

> *Floyd Dell, "Spoon River People," in* The New Republic, *Vol. II, No. 24, April 17, 1915, pp. 14-15.*

CARL SANDBURG (essay date 1915)

[*Sandburg was one of the central figures in the Chicago Renaissance, an early twentieth-century flowering of the arts, which vanquished the myth that the Eastern cities were the only centers of legitimate creativity in America and established the Midwest as the home of major writers, sculptors, and painters, as well as an important source of artistic subject matter. A lifelong believer* in the worth of the common, unsung individual, Sandburg expressed his populist beliefs in poetry and songs, and in his Pulitzer Prize-winning biography of Abraham Lincoln. In the following excerpt, he praises the highly personal nature of the poems in the Spoon River Anthology.]

I saw Masters write this book [the *Spoon River Anthology*]. He wrote it in snatched moments between fighting injunctions against a waitresses' union striving for the right to picket and gain one day's rest a week, battling from court to court for compensation to a railroad engineer rendered a loathsome cripple by the defective machinery of a locomotive, having his life amid affairs as intense as those he writes of.

At The Book and Play Club one night Masters tried to tell how he came to write the *Anthology*. Of course, he couldn't tell. There are no writers of great books able to tell the how and why of a dominating spirit that seizes them and wrenches the flashing pages from them. But there are a few forces known that play a part. And among these Masters said he wanted emphasis placed on *Poetry*, voices calling "Unhand me," verses and lines from all manner and schools of writers welcomed in Harriet Monroe's magazine.

Once in a while a man comes along who writes a book that has his own heart-beats in it. The people whose faces look out from the pages of the book are the people of life itself, each trait of them as plain or as mysterious as in the old home valley where the writer came from. Such a writer and book are realized here.

Masters' home town is Lewiston, Illinois, on the banks of the Spoon River. There actually is such a river where Masters waded bare-foot as a boy, and where the dead and the living folk of his book have fished or swam, or thrown pebbles and watched the widening circles. It is not far, less than a few hours' drive, from where Abraham Lincoln was raised. People who knew Lincoln are living there today.

Well, some two hundred and twenty portraits in free verse have been etched by Masters from this valley. They are Illinois people. Also they are the people of anywhere and everywhere in so-called civilization.

Aner Clute is the immortal girl of the streets. Chase Henry is the town drunkard of all time. The railroad lawyer, the corrupt judge, the prohibitionist, the various adulterers and adulteresses, the Sunday School superintendent, the mothers and fathers who lived for sacrifice in gratitude, joy,—all these people look out from this book with haunting eyes, and there are baffled mouths and brows calm in the facing of their destinies. (pp. 42-3)

In the year 1914 Masters not only handled all of his regular law practice, heavy and grilling. Besides, he wrote the *Spoon River Anthology*. There were times when he was clean fagged with the day's work. But a spell was on him to throw into written form a picture gallery, a series of short movies of individuals he had seen back home. Each page in the anthology is a locked-up portrait now freed. . . .

There is vitality, drops of heart blood, poured into Lee Masters' book. He has other books in him as vivid and poignant. Let us hope luck holds him by the hand and takes him along where he can write out these other ones. (p. 43)

> *Carl Sandburg, "Notes for a Review of 'The Spoon River Anthology'," in* The Little Review, *Vol. II, No. 3, May, 1915, pp. 42-3.*

RAYMOND M. ALDEN (essay date 1915)

[*In the following excerpt, Alden offers a negative assessment of* Spoon River Anthology *in an essay unfavorably examining Imagism, vers libre, and other aspects of "new poetry."*]

[The] *Spoon River Anthology* of Mr. Edgar Lee Masters . . . might be called the *reductio ad absurdum* of certain of the new methods,—such as the abandonment of conventional form and the fearless scrutiny of disagreeable realities. There is nothing here, to be sure, of the vaporings of some of our imagists, but a stern virility to which one might warm were it not so deliberately unlovely. The contents of this "anthology" is a series of *monologues d'outre tombe,* supposed to be spoken by the inhabitants of the Spoon River cemetery, who one by one tell us something of what they did and felt while living, and in many cases how they met their end. Whether Spoon River is meant to be viewed as typical of Illinois villages—for it appears to be in the vicinity of Knox College and Peoria—or to be a place peculiarly accursed, doth not clearly appear. In either case it furnishes an extraordinary study in mortuary statistics. From the first half of the volume, or thereabouts, there may be culled such characters as these: a person who was hanged for highway robbery and murder; a woman who was slain by the secret cruelty of her husband, the details not revealed; an inventor who was bitten by a rat while demonstrating a patent trap; a woman who took morphine after a quarrel with her husband; another who died in childbirth, the event having been foreseen by her husband; a boy who was run over while stealing a ride on a train; another boy who contracted lockjaw from a toy pistol; a woman whose lockjaw was due to a needle which had pierced her while she was washing her baby's clothes; a citizen who fell dead, presumably from apoplexy, while confessing a hidden sin to his church; a trainer who was killed by a lion in a circus; a greedy farmer who died from eating pie and gulping coffee in hot harvest time; a rural philosopher who was gored by a cow while discussing predestination; an innocent man who was hanged on a trumped-up charge; a courtesan who was poisoned by an Italian count; and a prohibitionist who developed cirrhosis of the liver from over-drinking. Enough—though the half has not been told. Under most of these tragedies lurk a grim pathos, and an irony due to such causes as the total misunderstanding by his fellows of the life (and often the death) of the ghostly speaker. A really remarkable series of character-studies, though the half would be much better than the whole; but for poetry—*cui bono?* Mr. Masters has shown before this that he knows what verse is; how then can he perpetrate, and endure to see in type, trash like this:

> If even one of my boys could have run a news-stand,
> Or one of my girls could have married a decent man,
> I should not have walked in the rain
> And jumped into bed with clothes all wet,
> Refusing medical aid.

(In passing, note this method of suicide, perhaps the most original, because the most indirect, of those described in the collection.) It can only be because he was resolved to portray—in the words of one of his own characters—a

> wingless void
> Where neither red, nor gold, nor wine,
> Nor the rhythm of life are (*sic*) known.

In two or three of the monologues only is the rhythm of life heard sounding underneath the tragedy—as it always is in actual poetry and real tragedy. . . . (p. 28)

Raymond M. Alden, in a review of "Spoon River Anthology," in The Dial, Vol. LIX, No. 697, June 24, 1915, pp. 28-9.

AMY LOWELL (essay date 1917)

[*Lowell was the leading proponent of Imagism in American poetry. Like the Symbolists before her, whose work she examined in* Six French Poets *(1915), Lowell experimented with free verse forms. Under the influence of Ezra Pound, Lowell's poetry exhibited the new style of Imagism, consisting of clear and precise rhetoric, exact rendering of images, and greater metrical freedom. Although she was popular in her time, modern evaluations of Lowell accord her more importance as a promoter of new artistic ideas than as a poet in her own right. In the following excerpt, she discusses* Spoon River Anthology *as Masters's best work, placing Masters at the head of the "middle era" of a three-part movement toward a native school of purely American poetry.*]

I think it is not too much to say that no book, in the memory of the present generation, has had such a general effect upon the reading community as has [*Spoon River Anthology*]. Every one who reads at all has read it. Its admirers are not confined to those who like poetry, people who have never cared for a poem before are enthusiastic over *Spoon River,* while professed poetry lovers stand, some aghast and some delighted, but all interested and amazed. Even its enemies admit it to be extraordinary. It has been characterized as an American "Comédie Humaine," but I think Dostoevsky in *vers libre* would be more accurate. Mr. Masters' habit of thought is more akin to the Russian than to the French. In fact, Mr. Masters is in some ways closer to the Swede, August Strindberg, than to any other modern writer.

Of course, analogies of this kind must not be pushed too far. If Mr. Masters resembles Balzac in the fecundity he shows in inventing characters and lives to fit them, he is also like Strindberg in showing only a narrow stratum of society. If he is like Balzac in confining his *mise en scène* in a small compass, he is again like Strindberg in being primarily interested in one important phase of life—that of sex. Balzac was no poet, but he realized that man is impelled by many motives; in Strindberg, the actions of the characters are all dependent upon their sex impulses. (pp. 139-40)

Mr. Robinson and Mr. Frost represent various things in the "new movement"—Realism, Direct Speech, Simplicity, and the like. They represent also the first stage of the progression I have been analyzing. Mr. Masters, who also stands for other things as well, embodies the second stage. I have put him and Mr. Sandburg together principally for that reason, although they have other points of contact besides this one. We may regard the work of these two poets as being the most revolutionary that America has yet produced. (p. 142)

Poetry published many *vers libre* poems during the first years of its existence, and Mr. Masters has often said that it was these poems which opened for him the way to *Spoon River.* In fact, they gave him the clue to just what he needed—freedom from the too patterned effects of rhyme and metre, brevity, and conciseness. Such a form seemed absolutely made for his purpose. Substance he had never lacked, fitting his substance to these short, sharp lines gave him a perfect instrument.

What suggested the idea of the anthology, I do not know, possibly he took it from the *Greek Anthology.* . . . The idea of epitaphs grew naturally out of the succinct brevity of the form, much in little, and in this very brevity Mr. Masters has found his happiest expression. Of course, a *vers libre* poem is not necessarily short, it may or may not be, as the author chooses. But the first poems in this form published by *Poetry* happened to be so, and that was fortunate for Mr. Masters. Had he attempted long poems in this medium in the beginning, I fear he would have wrecked *Spoon River* at the start. He has written many long *vers libre* poems since, but none of them has attained the rounded strength of the shorter, earlier pieces. (pp. 160-61)

Spoon River purports to be a small town in the Middle West. It is said that Hanover, Illinois, served as its prototype. The poems are supposed to be the epitaphs in the cemetery of this town. Or rather, it is as if its dead denizens arose, and each speaking the truth, perforce, revealed his own life exactly as it had been, and the real cause of his death. When I add that there are two hundred and fourteen of these people, we can see what a colossal study of character the book is. The mere inventing of two hundred and fourteen names is a staggering feat. How many names Balzac invented, or Scott, or Shakespeare, or Molière, I have not an idea, but the work of these men extended over a lifetime; Mr. Masters' two hundred and fourteen were all collected in one year.

The quality of the book already stands revealed in these names. They are uncompromising in their realism; hard, crude, completely local. Mr. Masters permits himself no subterfuges with fact. He throws no glamour over his creations. We hear of no Flammondes, no Bokardos, instead are Hannah Armstrong, Archibald Higbie, Bert Killion, Faith Matheny, Jennie M'Grew, Reuben Pantier, Albert Schirding, George Trimble, Oaks Tutt, Zenas Witt, and a host of others. What are these names? Some are Anglo-Saxon, some are clearly German; one, "Russian Sonia," tells of an origin, if not distinctly national, at least distinctly cosmopolitan; another, "Yee Bow," is as obviously Chinese.

We do not find German, French, Chinese names in Mr. Frost's books. Here, therefore, at once, in the table of contents, we are confronted with the piquant realism of locality. The highest art is undeniably that which compromises the farthest flights of imagination, but next to that, the most satisfying is the one which holds within it the pungency of place, undiluted. (pp. 162-63)

[The] difference between Mr. Frost and Mr. Masters is not only that they write about different parts of the country, it is a profound divergence of points of view. Mr. Frost . . . belongs to the first stage of the "new movement"; Mr. Masters to the second. Mr. Frost records with quiet sympathy; Mr. Masters is mordant and denunciatory. Mr. Frost is resigned, smilingly thinking resistance futile; Mr. Masters resists with every fibre of his being. Mr. Frost's work gives us the effect of a constant withdrawal; Mr. Masters' of a constant pushing forward.

Spoon River is a volume which should be read from the first page to the last. (Always excepting the final poem, "**The Spooniad**," a dreary effusion, which fits but slightly into the general scheme, and should never have been included.) No idea of its breadth and variety can be gained from fragmentary quotations. Each poem is a character, and as the characters multiply, the whole town is gradually built up before us. Other authors have given us characters, other authors have given us cross-sections of a community. But in most books we have a set of primary characters, and the others are forced more or less into the background by the exigencies of the case. We see the life from this or that angle, we do not get it entire.

In *Spoon River*, there are no primary characters, no secondary characters. We have only a town and the people who inhabit it. The Chinese laundry-man is as important to himself as the State's Attorney is to himself. None are forced back to give others prominence, but all together make the town. (pp. 163-64)

It is true, as has been said, that Mr. Masters sees life from the standpoint of a novelist. The material which the novelist spreads out and amplifies is condensed to its essence in these vignettes of a few lines. In them, Mr. Masters gives us background, character, and the inevitable approach of inexorable Fate. . . . (p. 169)

Mr. Masters has humour of a kind, a robust and rather brutal kind, it must be admitted, but still the quality is there. (p. 170)

Mr. Masters, with all his sociological tendencies, does not deify the working-man as Mr. Sandburg and many other sociological poets do. He sees life in too rounded a compass for that. (p. 173)

It cannot be denied even by Mr. Masters' most convinced admirers that, with all his vitality and courage, with all his wealth of experience and vividness of presentation, his point of view is often tortured and needlessly sensual and cruel.

Undoubtedly this element added to the immediate notoriety of *Spoon River*. But the book would not be worth commenting upon, and Mr. Masters would in no sense rank as the poet he does, if its sensuality were not counteracted by other and great qualities. (p. 176)

Spoon River undoubtedly errs on the side of a too great preoccupation with crime and disease. But it would be unfair to its author not to remark the occasional bursts of tenderness throughout the book. One [is] "**Emily Sparks**." . . . But there is another which is to me the most beautiful and most tragic poem in the volume. ["**Doc Hill**"] is real tragedy, not the tragedy of sordid giving way to inclination, but the tragedy of circumstance nobly faced, the tragedy of success out of failure, of joy denied and yet abundantly received. . . . (p. 178)

[It] had been stated that Mr. Masters was indebted to Mr. Robinson for his idea of these short sketches of men's lives. As a matter of fact, I know it to be true that, at the time he wrote *Spoon River*, Mr. Masters had not read a line of Mr. Robinson's poetry. It is only the most superficial observer who could ever have supposed one to be derived from the other. The whole scheme upon which the two poets work is utterly different. Mr. Robinson analyzes the psychology of his characters to the minutest fraction, he splits emotions and subsplits them. His people are interesting to him because of their thought-processes, or as psychic reactions to environment. Indeed, the environment is frequently misty, except where it impinges upon personality. Mr. Masters reveals the character of his *dramatis personæ* chiefly through their actions. What they do is, of course, the outcome of what they think, but it is usually the doing which the poet has set down on paper. His people are elementary and crude, carved on broad, flat planes.

The Tilbury Town of Mr. Robinson's books belongs more to the realm of mental phenomena than to actual fact. It is a symbol of certain states of mind. We feel it, but we do not see it. Spoon River, on the other hand, is indubitably and geographically a place. We know it even better than we do its inhabitants. Just as a person is a whole to us although made up of parts—eyes, ears, hands, nose, hair, etc.—so Spoon River is a whole, although constructed out of the life-histories of two hundred and fourteen of its citizens. We can see the cemetery, the Court House, the various churches, the shops, the railroad station, almost with our physical eyes.

It is not only that Mr. Robinson and Mr. Masters employ a different method of approach, an absolutely different technique; it is that fundamentally their ideas, not only of art, but of life, differ. To one, fact is the vague essence through which the soul of man wanders; to the other, man is a part, usually a tortured part, of a huge, hard, unyielding substance, the unalterable actuality of the world he inhabits.

If Mr. Masters has a prototype, that prototype can best be found in some of the poems in the *Greek Anthology*. (pp. 180-82)

Indeed, humanity varies very little throughout the ages. It is just this which makes *Spoon River* so remarkable—its humanity. These are not artificial personages, these two hundred men and women, they are real flesh and blood, with beating hearts and throbbing brains, revealing themselves to us with all their foibles and weaknesses, and their occasional grandeur. If, heaped one upon another, this monument of mid-Western American life errs on the side of over-sordidness, over-bitterness, over-sensuality, taken each one for itself, we have a true picture. It is never the individual characters who are false to type; it is only in the aggregate that the balance is lost by a too great preponderance of one sort of person.

It has been insisted over and over again, since the publication of *Spoon River,* that here was the great American poet, this verse was at last absolutely of America, that not since Whitman had anything so national appeared in print. The importance of *Spoon River* can hardly be overstated, and its dominant Americanism is without doubt a prime factor in that importance; but, because Mr. Masters' work is thoroughly local, is not to deny the same quality to work of quite a different kind. Was Poe less American than Whitman?—is a question which may very pertinently be asked here. Was Shakespeare less English because he wrote "Hamlet"? Was that arch-Englishman, Matthew Arnold, false to his birthright because he published "Empedocles on Etna"? How foolish this point of view is when so stated, is apparent at a glance. Nationality is so subtle a thing that it permeates all a man says and does. He cannot escape it, no matter what subjects stimulate his imagination. (pp. 183-84)

Mr. Masters is a thoroughly American poet, but not because he deals exclusively with American subjects. Truth to tell, he does not, as we shall see when, in a moment, we consider his later books. No, Mr. Masters is American because he is of the bones, and blood, and spirit of America. His thought is American; his reactions are as national as our clear blue skies.

The poets of the New Movement are all intensely national; they are not, as I have already pointed out, what the older generation were, followers of an English tradition. . . . When Mr. Masters is intensely moved, he becomes blatant. He keeps nothing to himself, out it comes on a swirl of passion. So this Americanism of his is a very obvious thing. It is a sort of *leitmotif* appearing again and again, and preferably on the trumpets. The symbol of this Americanism is the figure of Lincoln.

Washington and Lincoln are the two great symbols of American life. But to deal adequately with Washington needs a historical sense, a knowledge of the eighteenth century, which few of our poets yet possess. . . . It is therefore to Lincoln that our poets turn as an embodiment of the highest form of the typical American, the fine flower and culmination of our life as a separate nation. (pp. 184-85)

[With] Mr. Masters, Lincoln is a man first of all, but a man who, in his actual life, typifies a national aspiration. He is conceived as boldly, as surely, as any other of Mr. Masters' characters, and although venerated and loved with unchanging ardour, it is always as a man, neither conventionalized by tradition, nor flung by a powerful imagination into the realm of legend.

There is one little touch of Lincoln in *Spoon River,* a very beautiful touch, although only a collateral one. It is the epitaph of Ann Rutledge, the girl whom Lincoln loved, but who died before they could be married. (p. 186)

Just one year after the publication of the *Spoon River Anthology,* appeared another book from Mr. Masters' pen, a new volume of poems, *Songs and Satires*.

It has been hinted that many of the poems in this volume are reprinted from those earlier books which have slipt into oblivion. One would prefer to hope so, for it seems inconceivable that the author of the stark, vigorous *Spoon River* poems could afterwards perpetrate such a banality as ["**When Under the Icy Eaves.**"] (p. 187)

Here are all the old *clichés*: doves grieving for their lost mates, young lambs at play, swallows who *herald* the sun, winds that *bluster,* snows which *pass* over *tawny* hills, even the *spirit of life* awaking by a *lake* bordered with *flags*. . . . It reads like a parody; yet it is not intended as a parody, but as a serious and beautiful lyric. It gives us more than an insight into the reasons for Mr. Masters' early failures.

It would be unfair to the volume, however, to give the impression that all the poems are as bad as this. There are a number of weak lyrics scattered through the book, however, which no admirer of Mr. Masters can do other than deplore. And there are narrative poems on such hackneyed subjects as "**Helen of Troy**" and "**Launcelot and Elaine,**" in which the treatment does nothing to add freshness to the themes. (pp. 187-88)

There are ghastly attempts at an old English diction in ["**The Ballad of Launcelot and Elaine**"]. We have "trees of spicery," "morn's underne," "spake with a dreary steven."

That Mr. Masters should have written these poems among his early four hundred is not strange, what is strange is that he should have considered them worth resurrecting after he had written *Spoon River*.

Mr. Masters is seldom original when he writes in regular forms. It seems as though some obscure instinct of relation set his mind echoing with old tunes, old words, old pictures. Sometimes the result is a parody of the verse of the past; sometimes only a copy, quite beautiful, were it only his own. (p. 189)

What makes the book such a jumble is that these ancient ditties are interspersed with perfectly modern poems like "**The Cocked Hat,**" "'**So We Grew Together,**'" "**All Life in a Life,**" and the underworld studies: "**Arabel,**" and "**Jim and Arabel's Sister.**" But, in these modern poems, Mr. Masters has deserted the brevity of the *Spoon River* pieces, and his doing so has lost him much and won him nothing. When he allows himself a free hand, he does not know when to stop. In "'**So We Grew Together,**'" he takes nine pages where in *Spoon River* one would have sufficed. "**Arabel**" is six pages in length, "**The Cocked Hat**" is seven, and none of these poems gains anything, either in vigour or analysis, by the change.

"**The Loop**" is a descriptive sketch of the heart of Chicago. But there is no quick flash of vision here, no unforgettable picture imposed upon the mind in a few words. Instead, the poem enumerates long catalogues of objects, one after the other. They have neither form, colour, nor relation. They are not presented poetically, pictorially, not even musically (as the older verse counted music), for the poem is marred by such false rhymes as "current" and "torrent." They are just lists, as dreary as an advertisement from a department store. (pp. 189-90)

There is one poem in the book which shows Mr. Masters assuming a new rôle, or rather an old rôle in a new manner. **"In Michigan"** has a lyric quality very unusual to the poet's work. Most of his lyrics are couched in regular metres, and, for some strange reason, Mr. Masters does not seem able to think his own thoughts in conventional verse. Not only his expressions, his very ideas, run merrily back into the old moulds. On the other hand, Mr. Masters' free verse poems are singularly devoid of the lyricism of either sound or vision. So much so, indeed, that certain critics have declared him to be a novelist rather than a poet. **"In Michigan"** proves this verdict to be but partially true. . . . (p. 192)

If **"The Loop"** is without poetical images, **"In Michigan"** shows that the poet is really sensitive to beauty, and at times possesses the power to catch that beauty in a phrase:

> . . . a quiet land
> A lotus place of farms and meadows

gives the sleepy, lost quality of the landscape excellently well. (p. 193)

He speaks of the "misty eyelids" of "drowsy lamps," of a moon sinking "like a red bomb," of a land-spit running out into the lake until

> . . . it seemed to dive under,
> Or waste away in a sudden depth of water.

But even in this free-verse lyric, echoes of the older poets haunt him, and not to his advantage:

> . . a star that shows like a match which lights
> To a blue intenseness amid the glow of a hearth

challenges a comparison, which proves Browning's

> blue spurt of a lighted match

to be infinitely finer.

The haste with which Mr. Masters has followed up the success of *Spoon River* has undoubtedly been his undoing. Temporary, let us hope, but for the time, a fact. Eight months after the publication of *Songs and Satires,* his third book, *The Great Valley,* made its appearance.

The Great Valley is of course that flat stretch of continent between the Alleghany Mountains and the Rockies. It is a paraphrase for what we commonly call the Middle West. In other words, these are again poems of a locality. The book is a sort of extended *Spoon River.* The place is no more a little provincial town, but Chicago and the country adjacent. The horizon of place and character is wider than *Spoon River,* the poems are longer and more detailed; but, as in the long poems in *Songs and Satires,* the stretching out of his stories has not worked to the poet's advantage. Had *Spoon River* never been written, *The Great Valley* would have been a remarkable book. Unfortunately, it is still surpassed by the earlier volume. One of the most interesting traits of *Spoon River* was its homogeneity; the volume was a whole, as closely related within

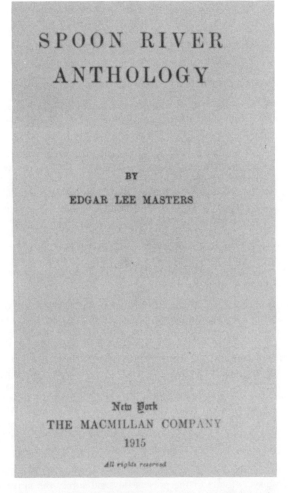

Title page of the first edition of Spoon River Anthology, *by Edgar Lee Masters. Macmillan, 1915. Courtesy of Macmillan Publishing Company.*

itself as is a novel, or a volume of essays grouped about a central theme. I have called *Songs and Satires* a jumble, Mr. Masters' taste again fails him in *The Great Valley.* What have such classical subjects as **"Marsyas," "The Furies," "Apollo at Pheræ,"** to do with the shouting Americanism of the rest of the book?

The truth is that in the back of the poet's heart, he still longs for that atmosphere of poesy which . . . [was] the unappeased desire of his adolescence. These poems represent the nostalgia of beauty. It eludes him still. He is the poet of the real, the absolute. He cannot break his bonds. Co-ordination is an integral part of beauty; in art, we call this co-ordination—taste, and of this particular kind of taste Mr. Masters has not a particle. The classic poems are thrown pell-mell among the others so carelessly that one wonders if Mr. Masters really arranged the book at all. One of the most unpleasant of the author's modern sex-tragedies is printed immediately after **"Apollo at Pheræ."**

There is one new note in the volume, a sort of tinkling sneer. As though a funeral march were to be played on the *glockenspiel.* This kitchen lyric is excellent in technique, but whether the sort of thing is worthy of a man who could produce some of the *Spoon River* poems is another question. (pp. 194-96)

*Amy Lowell, "Edgar Lee Masters and Carl Sand-
burg," in her* Tendencies in Modern American Poetry, *1917. Reprint by Haskell House Publishers Ltd.,
1970, pp. 139-232.*

JESSIE B. RITTENHOUSE   (essay date 1918)

[In the following excerpt, Rittenhouse favorably reviews Toward
the Gulf, *calling it Masters's most serious and thoughtful poetic
work.]*

Unless one wishes to think and to face all the consequences
of thinking, he should let quite alone Edgar Lee Masters's new
book, *Toward the Gulf.* This is not a book for entertainment.
The publishers mislead one when they say on the cover that it
is "a successor to his first and very popular work." *Spoon
River* was a juvenile entertainment as compared with *Toward
the Gulf.* In *Spoon River* Mr. Masters could laugh at life, even
when he found it in the sorriest plight. He was still on the
surface of things. In each succeeding book he has gone deeper
and deeper until, as I have said, one who follows him *Toward
the Gulf* does so at his own risk.

This title obviously applies to the course of the Father of Waters, which flows through Mr. Masters's poetic domain, "The
Great Valley," but if it be not symbolical, then no poet ever
had a truth within a symbol. Every one of these poems is a
look into the gulf, the impenetrable depth of life, and depths,
as we know, are dark and forbidding. One who looks into them
is disquieted, and from long looking, returns, blinking and
uncertain, to the light. Exactly this effect follows the reading
of *Toward the Gulf.* One comes back to the common day a
little bewildered and looks upon his companions with surprise
and incredulity, as if to say, "Do you, too, conceal so much?
are you, too, as inscrutable as this?"

Edgar Lee Masters is, in short, the most penetrating and merciless psychologist of the present day and surely the bravest.
He withholds nothing. Witness such a poem as **"Samuel Butler
et Al,"** where one indicts his mother for a life of recreance to
the finer duties of motherhood, while he pictures with pitiless
exactness the whole panorama of her life. This might be inex-
cusable, were it not true. We have all seen this woman and
observed every detail that Mr. Masters depicts. Indeed this
book is full of firsthand studies, of minute observation. These
souls under a microscope, however they might wish to escape,
can withhold nothing. One marvels continually at the relentless
analysis which probes deeper and deeper, seeking for the hidden springs of action. Only the trained mind, the legal mind,
could pursue such clues and arrive at such unappealable decisions. Heredity has an irresistible fascination for Mr. Masters, and it appears and reappears in his latest work. In **"Excluded Middle"** its effect upon a whole family is shown, in
the light of that ever-baffling preoccupation of Mr. Masters—
cross-currents of sex, and parental inharmony. In **"Botanical
Gardens"** it appears as an analogy between the life of man
and the plant, both of which strive and grow and crowd and
dispossess until, with the human species, it brings war. But
nature is equally pitiless and prodigal and complacently "scat-
ters life into the maws of death."

In **"Neanderthal,"** he turns to evolution, seeking the skull of
the first man that dreamed above the brute, only to show the
heavenward flight of the human mind that could at length
realise itself in Shelley. Under so forbidding a title as **"Dr.
Scudder's Clinical Lecture,"** which begins in a purely scientific treatise on heredity, comparing and weighing authorities

as one might in the classroom, he gives us the story of a spiritual
illumination which unfolds like a great yellow rose, laying bare
more and more of the beauty and mystery of the soul. Of
course, to Doctor Scudder, the case upon which he dilates is
paranoia, since the subject thinks he has had a direct revelation
from God.

So much for heredity, though this by no means exhausts the
list of the poems in which it appears. But what do these poems
show? An immense, consuming preoccupation with life, life
that constantly transcends itself, life that is prophecy hardly
yet hinted. Indeed before one gets through with Mr. Masters's
book he sees that just so far as he has looked into the gulf, he
has looked beyond it, and that the one vision has by no means
destroyed the clearness of the other. It is evident that the immense contrasts of life, the brute and the angel in man, Neanderthal and Shelley, engross his thought and struggle to be
reconciled. Indeed, if we have both a penetrating and a luminous thinker in modern American poetry, it is Edgar Lee
Masters, and one says this with full recognition of the fact that
it is not always pleasant to follow him in his penetrations.

There is no question that the psychologist in Mr. Masters often
gets the better of the poet, particularly in the more elaborate
studies in his last two volumes. One misses the pith and pungency of *Spoon River* and the gayety, even if a sardonic gayety,
that enlivened the earlier pages. His entire mood has changed,
he is intent upon the deeper truth of life and does not hesitate
to sacrifice poetic effect to philosophical speculation. While
beauty is by no means absent from the work, it is secondary.
We know it was secondary to Browning, in a great mass of
his work—and the Browning influence is strongly apparent in
the later work of Edgar Lee Masters—but as near to Browning's
period as we still are, we have come to see that he will live
almost solely by that portion of his work where beauty triumphs
or where philosophy and beauty are one. Mr. Masters strikes
off so many fine, imaginative flashes, one comes so frequently
upon passages of both power and beauty, that he is constantly
impressed with the fact that if the art side appealed to the poet
as strongly as the philosophical side appeals, he could fuse the
two more completely and give us work more certain of its
future place as sheer poetry. Yet even this may be undue cav-
illing. So much modern poetry is mere prettiness, one reads
so many volumes of gracefully turned verse that scarcely differ
an iota, one from another, and show no valid reason for being—
that it is invigorating to come upon a work in which one feels
a sense of mass and force; a work which calls forth definite
opinions, even though they be of resistance. There is something
of the Titan in Edgar Lee Masters, something that makes many
other poets seem puny beside him. He is a thinker, and, as we
know, thinkers are not let loose every day upon the earth.
(pp. 201-03)

*Jessie B. Rittenhouse, in a review of "Toward the
Gulf," in* The Bookman, *New York, Vol. XLVII, No.
2, April, 1918, pp. 201-03.*

CARL VAN DOREN   (essay date 1922)

*[Van Doren is considered one of the more important critics of the
first half of the twentieth century. He worked for many years as
a professor of English at Columbia University and served as
literary editor and critic of the* Nation *and the* Century *during the
1920s. A founder of the Literary Guild and author or editor of
several American literary histories, Van Doren was also a critically acclaimed historian and biographer. In the following excerpt, Van Doren characterizes the* Spoon River Anthology *as*

the first example of "the newest style in American fiction," characterizing it as an example of "revolt from the village" literature.]

The newest style in American fiction dates from the appearance, in 1915, of *Spoon River Anthology*, though it required five years for the influence of that book to pass thoroughly over from poetry to prose. For nearly half a century native literature had been faithful to the cult of the village, celebrating its delicate merits with sentimental affection and with unwearied interest digging into odd corners of the country for persons and incidents illustrative of the essential goodness and heroism which, so the doctrine ran, lie beneath unexciting surfaces. Certain critical dispositions, aware of agrarian discontent or given to a preference for cities, might now and then lay disrespectful hands upon the life of the farm; but even these generallly hesitated to touch the village, sacred since Goldsmith in spite of Crabbe, sacred since Washington Irving in spite of E. W. Howe.

The village seemed too cosy a microcosm to be disturbed. There it lay in the mind's eye, neat, compact, organized, traditional. . . . Mr. Howe in *The Story of a Country Town* had long ago made it cynically clear—to the few who read him—that villages which prided themselves upon their pioneer energy might in fact be stagnant backwaters or dusty centers of futility, where existence went round and round while elsewhere the broad current moved away from them. Mark Twain in "The Man that Corrupted Hadleyburg" had more recently put it bitterly on record that villages which prided themselves upon their simple virtues might from lack of temptation have become a hospitable soil for meanness and falsehood, merely waiting for the proper seed. And Clarence Darrow in his elegiac "Farmington" had insisted that one village at least had been the seat of as much restless longing as of simple bliss. *Spoon River Anthology* in its different dialect did little more than to confirm these mordant, neglected testimonies.

That Mr. Masters was not neglected must be explained in part, of course, by his different dialect. The Greek anthology had suggested to him something which was, he said, "if less than verse, yet more than prose"; and he went, with the step of genius, beyond any "formal resuscitation of the Greek epigrams, ironical and tender, satirical and sympathetic, as casual experiments in unrelated themes," to an "epic rendition of modern life" which suggests the novel in its largest aspects. An admirable scheme occurred to him: he would imagine a graveyard such as every American village has and would equip it with epitaphs of a ruthless veracity such as no village ever saw put into words. The effect was as if all the few honest epitaphs in the world had suddenly come together in one place and sent up a shout of revelation.

Conventional readers had the thrill of being shocked and of finding an opportunity to defend the customary reticences; ironical readers had the delight of coming upon a host of witnesses to the contrast which irony perpetually observes between appearance and reality; readers militant for the "truth" discovered an occasion to demand that pious fictions should be done away with and the naked facts exposed to the sanative glare of noon. And all these readers, most of them unconsciously no doubt, shared the fearful joy of sitting down at an almost incomparably abundant feast of scandal. Where now were the mild decencies of Tiverton, of Old Chester, of Friendship Village? The roofs and walls of Spoon River were gone and the passers-by saw into every bedroom; the closets were open and all the skeletons rattled undenied; brains and breasts had un-

locked themselves and set their most private treasures out for the most public gaze.

It was the scnadal and not the poetry of *Spoon River,* criticism may suspect, which particularly spread its fame. Mr. Masters used an especial candor in affairs of sex, an instinct which, secretive everywhere, has rarely ever been so much so as in the American villages of fiction, where love ordinarily exhibited itself in none but the chastest phases, as if it knew no savage vagaries, transgressed no ordinances, shook no souls out of the approved routines. Reaction from too much sweet drove Mr. Masters naturally to too much sour; sex in Spoon River slinks and festers, as if it were an instinct which had not been schooled—however imperfectly—by thousands of years of human society to some modification of its rages and some civil direction of its restless power. But here, as with the other aspects of behavior in his village, he showed himself impatient, indeed violent, toward all subterfuges. There is filth, he said in effect, behind whited sepulchers; drag it into the light and such illusions will no longer trick the uninstructed into paying honor where no honor appertains and will no longer beckon the deluded to an imitation of careers which are actually unworthy.

Spoon River has not even the outward comeliness which the village of tradition would possess: it is slack and shabby. Nor is its decay chronicled in any mood of tender pathos. What strikes its chronicler most is the general demoralization of the town. Except for a few saints and poets, whom he acclaims with a lyric ardor, the population is sunk in greed and hypocrisy and—as if this were actually the worst of all—complacent apathy. Spiritually it dwindles and rots; externally it clings to a pitiless decorum which veils its faults and almost makes it overlook them, so great has the breach come to be between its practices and its professions. Again and again its poet goes back to the heroic founders of Spoon River, back to the days which nurtured Lincoln, whose shadow lies mighty, beneficent, too often unheeded, over the degenerate sons and daughters of a smaller day; and from an older, robuster integrity Mr. Masters takes a standard by which he morosely measures the purposelessness and furtiveness and supineness and dulness of the village which has forgotten its true ancestors.

Anger like his springs from a poetic elevation of spirit; toward the end *Spoon River Anthology* rises to a mystical vision of human life by comparison with which the scavenging epitaphs of the first half seem, though witty, yet insolent and trivial. It is perhaps not necessary to point out that the numerous poets and novelists who have learned a lesson from the book have learned it less powerfully from the difficult later pages than from those in which the text is easiest.

Mr. Masters himself has not always remembered the harder and better lesson. During a half dozen years he has published more than a half dozen books which have all inherited the credit of the *Anthology* but which all betray the turbulent, nervous habit of experimentation which makes up a large share of his literary character. There comes to mind the figure of a blindfolded Apollo, eager and lusty, who continually runs forward on the trail of poetry and truth but who, because of his blindfoldedness, only now and then strikes the central track. Five of Mr. Masters's later books are collections of miscellaneous verse; during the fruitful year 1920 he undertook two longer flights of fiction. In *Mitch Miller* he attempted in prose to write a new *Tom Sawyer* for the Spoon River district; in *Domesday Book* he applied the method of *The Ring and the Book* to the material of Starved Rock. The impulse of the first

The Hill

Where are Elmer, Herman, Bert, Tom and Charley,
The weak of will, the strong of arm, the clown, the
    clown, the boozer, the fighter?
All, all, are sleeping on the hill.

One passed in a fever,
One was burned in a mine,
One was killed in a brawl,
One died in jail,
One fell from a bridge toiling for children and wife—
All, all are sleeping, sleeping, sleeping on the hill.

Where are Ella, Kate, Mag, Lizzie and Edith,
The tender heart, the simple soul, the loud, the
    proud, the happy one?—
All, all are sleeping on the hill.

One died in shameful child-birth,
One of a thwarted love,
One at the hands of a brute in a brothel,
One of a broken pride in the search for heart's desire,
One after life in far-away London and Paris
Was brought to her little space by Ella and
    Kate and Mag—
All, all are sleeping, sleeping, sleeping on the hill.

Manuscript page of "The Hill" from Spoon River Anthology, *by Edgar Lee Masters. Macmillan, 1915. Courtesy of Ellen C. Masters.*

must have been much the same as Mark Twain's: a desire to catch in a stouter net than memory itself the recollections of boyhood which haunt disillusioned men. But as Mr. Masters is immensely less boylike than Mark Twain, elegy and argument thrust themselves into the chronicle of Mitch and Skeet, with an occasional tincture of a fierce hatred felt toward the politics and theology of Spoon River. A story of boyhood, that lithe, muscular age, cannot carry such a burden of doctrine. The narrative is tangled in a snarl of moods. Its movement is often thick, its wings often gummed and heavy.

The same qualities may be noted in *Domesday Book.* Its scheme and machinery are promising: a philosophical coroner, holding his inquest over the body of a girl found mysteriously dead, undertakes to trace the mystery not only to its immediate cause but up to its primary source and out to its remotest consequences. At times the tale means to be an allegory of America during the troubled, roiled, destroying years of the war; at times it means to be a "census spiritual" of American society. Elenor Murray, in her birth and love and sufferings and desperate end, is represented as pure nature, "essential genius," acting out its fated processes in a world of futile or corrupting inhibitions. But Mr. Masters has less skill at portraying the sheer genius of an individual than at arraigning the inhibitions of the individual's society. When he steps down from his watchtower of irony he can hate as no other American poet does. His hates, however, do not always pass into poetry; they too frequently remain hard, sullen masses of animosity not fused with his narrative but standing out from it and adding an unmistakable personal rhythm to the rough beat of his verse. So, too, do his heaps of turgid learning and his scientific speculations often remain undigested. A good many of his characters are cut to fit the narrative plan, not chosen from reality to make up the narrative. The total effect is often crude and heavy; and yet beneath these uncompleted surfaces are the sinews of enormous power: a greedy gusto for life, a wide imaginative experience, tumultuous uprushes of emotion and expression, an acute if undisciplined intelligence, great masses of the veritable stuff of existence out of which great novels are made. (pp. 146-53)

> Carl Van Doren, "New Style: The Revolt from the Village," in his Contemporary American Novelists: 1900-1920, *The Macmillan Company, 1922, pp. 132-76.*

ROBERT HERRICK   (essay date 1924)

[*In the following excerpt, Herrick reviews two of Masters's novels,* The Nuptial Flight *and* Mirage, *comparing both unfavorably with the earlier novels* Mitch Miller *and* Skeeters Kirby.]

When Mr. Masters first turned to prose as his medium, he reverted also to the scene of his *Spoon River Anthology.* In *Mitch Miller* and *Skeeters Kirby* he revived in a tender, reminiscential mood the associations of his earlier years, with their homely, intimate quite American background. Such sophistications as his verse had achieved by broadening out from Sangamon County to Chicago and the great midland valley were forgotten, especially in *Mitch Miller,* which has a limpid style, a boylike fancifulness, and a clean objectivity unlike anything else that Mr. Masters has written. And the nature of the subject, in this first prose book, precluded an exclusive preoccupation with the sex impulse, whether treated analytically or "epically" or "philosophically."

The Nuptial Flight is not a continuation of the histories of these first two prose books, although the background largely remains the same. It is a survey of three generations of the Houghtons from 1849, when William Houghton and Nancy Creighton came by different paths from Kentucky to meet at Whitehall, Illinois, until the present day. The mood, at least at the start, is epic; there is nothing better in Mr. Masters's prose than the biblical simplicity of Father William and Mother Nancy—the one happily endowed pair—who prospered, begat children, and watched the unfolding tragedies of their descendants. . . . But Mr. Masters's preoccupation is less with them than with their unfortunate children and grandchildren, and in his presentation of their characters and their marital infelicities he is forced to abandon the simple epic strokes of his opening, to paint in detail, and it soon becomes evident that Mr. Masters for all his specifications and his will to blink nothing unpleasant is not a realist. He cannot draw a figure in the round. . . . For all its frequent lapses of technique, for all its heavy sordidness in detail, *The Nuptial Flight* has scope, fecundity and vitality. The epic significance called for by the title is not [to] be discovered in this collection of domestic infelicities, neither in the uncertain descent of Nancy nor in the nature of men and women. It is popular romantic biology to attribute to a possible Spanish strain of blood impulsive and passional imprudencies in mating. Nor is every woman an exploiter and every man an exploited. These things are not so easily disposed of!

As if aware of the failure in his epic treatment of marital disharmony Mr. Masters chose for *Mirage,* his last prose volume, one instance of disaster . . . for a more intensive treatment. Here he resumes the story of Skeeters Kirby, reveals restrospectively his ruined marriage and his entanglement with a Circe, and his struggles to emancipate himself and achieve emotional stability and self-understanding. It is a simpler picture, a more definite theme. The story of Kirby's emergence through the sordidness of blackmail and our barbaric divorce customs to a realization of the tawdriness of his Circe for whom he has striven in vain may be verified in any daily newspaper. But in the vulgar quagmire such as Kirby's life became, the fine flower of spiritual achievement may be grown. Whether the state of soul to which the man finally arrives will seem such a fine flower, is a matter of personal judgment. But the process of his growth as pictured in *Mirage* in sufficient literal detail is not a promising one: finally convinced of his Circe's casual infidelities and general unworthiness, Kirby, nevertheless, returns to plead, perhaps humanly, that "all be forgotten and forgiven" and another disastrous marriage begun between them. But when finally disillusioned—and incidentally repulsed—he goes forth from the hectic and alcoholic scene of renunciation to the arms of a woman in a neighboring hotel suite with whom he had scraped acquaintance on a railroad train a few days previously, as a second step in the cleansing of his soul embraces on presentation one of those studio divinities with whom the author interleaves the more serious engagements of his hero, then sends for a secretary he had formerly employed in the hope that a woman—any one—will do the trick for him and make him sound, lives with her, breaks her heart and returns for final consolation to an amour with the studio divinity, who is now living an emancipated life with gentlemen friends—one questions. All this promiscuity may be pathologically true of the wounded male soul, but Mr. Masters is not sufficiently equipped as a realist to give his pathological version either significance or credibility. It may be true, but what of it?

In these days style is both such a negligible and such a debateable matter that in saying that the style of *The Mirage* is the worst that Mr. Masters has ever written in verse or in prose

I am conscious of expressing merely a personal reaction. The style of *The Mirage* is a long, long way from the restraints of the *Spoon River* etching, from the flexible vigor of *Domesday Book,* from the self-effacing simplicity of *Mitch Miller.* It is just bad style. Subtly, perhaps unconsciously, it reveals that degeneration in taste, in grip upon life, that the people of Sangamon County suffered in their pilgrimage eastward to the metropolis of New York! They were at home in Sangamon County and however plain and common their life was, it was not vulgar. They do not realize themselves in the luxuries and sophistications of their new environment. (pp. 138-39)

> *Robert Herrick, "Mr. Masters's Prose," in* The New Republic, *Vol. XXXIX, No. 499, June 25, 1924, pp. 138-39.*

HENRY VAN DYKE   (essay date 1929)

[*In the following excerpt, Van Dyke maintains that* Spoon River Anthology *is neither original in conception nor particularly well-written; that it is not, in fact, even poetry.*]

A dark lantern is a very handy thing, serviceable both in the commission and in the detection of crime. (p. 93)

[Acquit me] of any intention to write scornfully or even slightingly of the poetical dark lantern. On the contrary, I mean to praise it for its usefulness, and to acknowledge gratefully the debt which we owe to it for its services! Only when it is acclaimed as a celestial luminary and saluted as a new star in the literary firmament, do I draw the line and withhold my feeble voice from the roaring Hallelujah Chorus. (p. 95)

[The] better things in current literature are not the things most vehemently puffed by the critics who abound in "prejudices" but have no standards. Their effort seems to be, not to commend a dark lantern for its usefulness, as it deserves, but to bully the world into believing that it is a new star of the first magnitude. I take as an example . . . a book called *Spoon River Anthology,* published in 1915, and supplemented in 1924 by *The New Spoon River.*

That this work was intended to be taken as a contribution to American poetry is evident from the use of the word "anthology," and from the fact that it is printed in broken lines, with a capital letter at the beginning of each line. Further evidence there is none.

Of the author's life I know little more than can be found in the red tome of *Who's Who,* and will say less. He was educated in high school and Knox College, studied law, wrote for newspapers, was married and divorced. I do not doubt that he is an estimable person. His first step into the limelight of fame was through the waters of *Spoon River,* and that is what I wish to consider; first, because the book has been praised as highly original and American, second because it has been set up as a model for the new poetry.

Understand, if you please, I should be the last to deny the real value of this book as throwing a light upon subterranean and microbic life in the Middle West of America. Is is a keen, piercing, ruthless illumination. But it is the light of a dark lantern, not of a new star.

The claim of novelty and absolute originality for *Spoon River* can not be sustained. (pp. 97-9)

[Consider] the ground plan of *Spoon River Anthology.* It is supposed to be a collection of imaginary epitaphs for the grave-

yard of that village. Compare it with the record of burials in *The Parish Register,* written by George Crabbe in England, 1807. Crabbe, who was an anti-romantic, realistic poet, was ahead of the Spoon Riverman in his plan by more than a hundred years, and more than that in the quality of his verse. (p. 101)

I think you will agree with me that Crabbe writes better verse and has a more pungent wit than his American disciple, who has added a new terror to death by the way in which he describes it.

But bad as Spoon River is as a place to die in, it must be still more awful to live there. If its necrologist is a truthful person, a real realist in poetry as he professes himself to be, his fellow villagers, take them by and large, must be a group of very undesirable citizens. Murder, seduction, bigamy, avarice, hypocrisy, drunkenness, and cruelty to children seem to be among their common habits. The exceptional qualities of honesty, kindness, chastity, and gentle manners are usually represented by the necrologist as the possession of weak-minded persons who suffer for their virtues. Their old-fashioned faith in the wisdom and goodness of God is shrewdly suggested as rather a good joke on them. This is a view of life, to be sure, but it is a dismal view, and I doubt whether it really is a true view. (pp. 104-05)

It would be foolish to deny the sharp, penetrating quality of some of these sketches. They flash into hidden places precisely like the ray of a dark lantern, revealing vermiform secrets and showing now and then a chrysalis from which a frail butterfly of hope is emerging to be crushed. They are full of shocks and surprises. They are valuable as an antidote to the smooth American self-complacency whose slogan is "stand pat," and whose secret watchword is "keep the lid on." A book which takes the lid off, even if it be as unmannerly as the novel called *Revelry,* or as dismal as the anthology called *Spoon River,* serves its useful purpose and deserves its meed of praise. But this does not entitle it to a place in the celestial regions of literature,—not even among the moons and minor satellites.

Two barriers exclude the anthologist of Spoon River from the starry company of poets. First, he has not a gleam of that cosmic vision which Matthew Arnold praises in Sophocles,

> Who saw life steadily and saw it whole.

Second, his ear for verbal music is defective, if not entirely lacking. Free verse is not a bad thing, provided it is really verse,—that is to say, provided it has a measurable movement, a rhythm, a cadence of its own, even though it may not fit into any of the recognized, orthodox metres. English poetry has a right to make metrical experiments and adventures in search of new rhythms. Often the result has been something quite wonderfully musical, like some of Milton's and Tennyson's new metres; like the unrhymed verses of Charles Lamb . . . ; like the subtle harmonies of Whitman in his inspired moments when he escapes from the fetters of his own theory of formlessness.

But the free verse of the Spoon Riverman has not this fortunate quality. In fact it is chop-stick prose,—knock-kneed, splay-footed, St. Vitus prose, compared with which the Charleston in its most dislocated spasms is a graceful and enchanting dance. Take this:

> To be an editor, as I was.
> Then to lie here close by the river, over the place
> Where the sewage flows from the village,
> And the empty cans and garbage are dumped,
> And abortions are hidden.

If this is poetry then a steam-riveter is a musical instrument, and the smell of decayed sauerkraut is a sweet perfume.

It is true that the Riverman has written other volumes in which the ancient rules of metre and rhyme are followed. But in truth they are less interesting than *Spoon River.* Some of them are flippant parodies of Bible stories, not sparing even the Holiest of All. Others, (and these rather the best of the lot,) are two-step versions of the Tale of Troy and the Arthurian legends. Still others are very blank verse settings of scenes in American history. The last . . . is called *Lee, A Dramatic Poem.* It gives a sound view, I think, of that noble and tragic hero's character and conduct. But it does not add much to the story either poetically or dramatically. And it is greatly confused and bewildered by the introduction of two mythical personages called Ormund and Arimanius. These I suppose the Riverman, in his childlike way, means to represent the ancient deities of Persian dualism, whose names were Ormuzd and Ahriman. They stand around and talk a good deal; but I can not see that they do anything about it. They are theatrical idols. It is astonishing how superstitious some of these modern unbelievers are!

However, that is a matter of opinion. The point on which this essay turns is that *Spoon River Anthology* is not a new planet swimming into our ken, but simply a dark lantern. (pp. 108-11)

> Henry Van Dyke, "A Dark Lantern," in his The Man Behind the Book: Essays in Understanding, *Charles Scribner's Sons, 1929, pp. 91-111.*

FRED LEWIS PATTEE (essay date 1930)

[*An American literary historian, critic, poet, and novelist, Pattee was a pioneer in the study of American literature. He believed that literature is the popular expression of a people, rather than the result of the work of an elite. Pattee reputedly held the first chair in American literature in the United States. In the following excerpt, he characterizes* Spoon River Anthology *as "the sensation of its period," a work important because of its uniqueness and its effect upon subsequent works.*]

By 1914 the free-verse movement was in full career. . . . Something had happened to American poetry. Freedom had come, said Miss Amy Lowell of Boston. Verse had freed itself from age-old chains. "Free verse" was now the battle cry, or "vers libre," which was a step beyond in emancipation. (pp. 283-84)

Elaborate volumes of the new verse began to pour from the presses so lately obsessed with fiction, some of them approaching best-seller figures. (p. 284)

Then in 1915 came the sensation of the period, the *Spoon River Anthology* by Edgar Lee Masters, the most talked of, perhaps the most influential, book of poems since *Leaves of Grass.* A purely Western thing it seemed, a Chicago thing by a Chicago man. (p. 285)

The book was unique, at least in English. It purported to be made up of the epitaphs in a prairie cemetery as they would be written could the persons come back from the dead and tell in briefest compass the actuality of their lives. According to the author, its purpose was "to analyze society, to satirize society, to tell a story, to expose the machinery of life, to present a working model of the big world." Certainly the collection does all this—and more.

The first shock and the first wave of best-seller popularity came from the very realistic sex revelations in the epitaphs. Even Amy Lowell, who had defended Sandburg, had no stomach for realism to this degree: "The pages of Mr. Masters and August Strindberg read like extracts from the Newgate Calendar. Everything that is coarse and revolting in the sexual life is here. *Spoon River* is one long chronicle of rapes, seductions, liaisons, and perversions. It is the great blot upon Mr. Masters's work. It is an obliquity of vision, a morbidness of mind, which distorts an otherwise remarkable picture."

The second shock came from their ruthlessness, their atmosphere at times of blasphemy, of sneering at the world-law. The dead R. F. Tanner, for instance, returning to compose his epitaph, runs off into a pessimistic bit of philosophy much in the vein of the living Clarence Darrow: Life is a trap, he reveals. The monstrous ogre Life watches you nibble his bait, and when you have sprung the infernal trap, he comes to—

> . . . stare with burning eyes at you,
> And scowl and laugh, and mock and curse you,
> Running up and down in the trap,
> Until your misery bores him.
>
> (pp. 286-87)

"Here are my two hundred and forty-four men and women," (not Browning's figures) enough people to make up a Main Street village, and like Lewis's work, exhibited to show the rawness and uncouthness of Western life. And yet it is not necessarily *American* life that is exhibited; very little local color here. It is life universal: it is a satire on human life generally. Two-score of these epitaphs illustrate "life's little ironies"— Daisy Fraser's fines, for example, that went toward educating the children of the village; dozens of them are law cases each condensed into ten lines; dozens more are scenarios; many of them are founded on facts brought out in police courts; some are variations of the *Ring and the Book* plan—the wife's story, then the husband's, the murderer's story, and then that of the murdered, the criminal's story and then the town's. Some have a trend of brightness and optimism—especially is this noticeable toward the end of the series; but the accent is strongest on the coarse and the sinful. To live in a town peopled by these two hundred and forty-four would be intolerable.

Little attempt is there at characterization, little at description. It is exposition in story form. Braithwaite, reviewing the volume a few weeks after its first appearance, called it "a novel

Chicago home where Masters wrote much of Spoon River Anthology. *Courtesy of Ellen C. Masters.*

in verse." Rather is it the fragments of an exploded novel—a novel broken into short-story episodes and each worked into a unity by itself. The epitaph centers always in a single situation: never is it the *whole* life. Seldom is there realistic study—the facing of all the facts and all the phases. These dead are not speaking in character, though they purport to do so. It is Masters who is talking, not Hod Putt. Hod Putt and Daisy Fraser could not talk like this. It is the conception not of a poet but of a legalist. The writer sums up the case like a criminal court advocate stressing only the evidence that he wishes to stress. Many of them are short stories, with what Jack London called a "snapper" at the end; most, however, are briefs of legal cases, mostly criminal cases.

During the early years of the volume praise went to an extreme that, in the light of to-day, seems incredible. (pp. 287-88)

Time has not only rebuked such critics, but has made them ludicrous. Masters's fame has been a diminishing thing. One is reminded of Stockton's tale "His Wife's Deceased Sister." At the one moment when such a thing was possible, inspired by a thrill in the air, a moment of expectation, the rush of a great movement, the culmination of a period, he struck thirteen, as it were, and was ruined. For never was he able to do it again, to strike twelve or even eleven. His later poetry has, for the most part, been on the level of his pre-*Spoon River* volumes.

He lacks the singing quality; he lacks the magic, the haunting expressiveness, the tingling atmospheres of poetry on the heights of poetry. He is a man with no "ear" and little voice trying to sing—any choir-leader can tell of that tragedy. Intellectual the poems are, good exposition, excellent narrative—but they are baldly prosaic and should not wear the masks of poetry. (pp. 288-89)

The value of the *Spoon River* volume lies in its originality of design, its uniqueness, its effect upon its times. Its colossal success started a choir of young poets. Whether we condemn or praise, we must accept it as a major episode in the history of the poetic movement in the second decade of the new century. (pp. 289-90)

> *Fred Lewis Pattee, "The Prairie Poets," in his* The New American Literature: 1890-1930, *D. Appleton-Century Company, 1930, pp. 270-92.*

HARRIET MONROE (essay date 1932)

[*As the founder and editor of* Poetry, *Monroe was a key figure in the American "poetry renaissance" that took place in the early twentieth century.* Poetry *was the first periodical devoted primarily to the works of new poets and to poetry criticism, and from 1912 until her death Monroe maintained an editorial policy of printing "the best English verse which is being written today, regardless of where, by whom, or under what theory of art it is written." In the following excerpt, she calls Masters an epic poet on the strength of what she considers his best poems.*]

Edgar Lee Masters, whatever else one may say of him, has size. He bulks large, and it may be that in that "next age," to which we accord the ultimate accounting, he will make a number of other figures now conspicuous look small. He has, not unnaturally, the faults that go with size—careless technique, uncritical sanctionings, indelicacies of emotional excess, far-sightedness which misses obvious imperfections of detail. The world will sift out and throw away many poems in

his numerous books of verse; and much of his prose—not all—will go into the discard. But when hurrying time has done its worst, enough will remain to prove a giant's stature and other attributes of power in this Illinois lawyer-poet of a changing age. (p. 46)

A Book of Verses, published under the author's own name in 1898, was almost as mild an affair as Byron's *Hours of Idleness*—indeed, these two poets offer many proofs of kinship. But Masters developed more slowly; already thirty years old when this first book appeared, he had reached thirty-four, with his sense of humor still in abeyance, when he put out a solemn blank-verse tragedy [*Maximilian*] on the subject of that be-whiskered busy-body of pitiable history, Maximilian, so-called emperor of Mexico.

Of course there was a drama in Mexico at that moment, but it did not follow academic lines. One would have expected a modern mind to find it, but Masters' theories of poetic art were intensely academic, and even eight years later, in 1912, when he issued *Songs and Sonnets* under the pseudonym of Webster Ford, we find him writing such things as an **"Ode to Fame"** in the most approved all-hail-to-thee style. This book also fell flat, of course; and its author, at forty-four a failure as a poet, was in danger of becoming embittered when even his friend Bill Reedy sent back his classic poems; for he could contrast the silence around him with the réclame which was beginning to salute the imagists and other free-versifiers during 1913.

One can almost see the satiric smile with which he said to himself, "If that's what they want, I'll give it to them!" But *Spoon River,* begun as a more or less satirical challenge to "the new movement," soon caught him up and carried him out to the depths. For the first time he found a theme which drew upon his humor as well as his knowledge and fervor and sympathy; and a form which made him forget old-fashioned prejudices, and thereby freed his art. By the time the world found him he had found himself. And it was a big discovery.

It is hardly necessary to repeat certain things that were said of this book in the first flush of its success. It fulfilled the old time-honored principle: present a local group completely, in its heights and depths and averages, and you present the race as it is in every time and clime. *Spoon River,* with its humors and tragedies and commonplaces, its strange interweavings of destiny, is precisely central Illinois, the very heart of Middlewest America; yet Lucretius or Omar or Li Po would recognize its types and incidents, and probably the poets of the twenty-fifth century will still pronounce it true. And not only true but beautiful, for the form of those terse little epitaphs is not only a perfect fit but that triumphant completion and fulfillment which marks the masterpieces of all the arts.

Spoon River classed its author as essentially an epic poet—that is, a poet whose chief urge is to tell the tale of the tribe. And although Mr. Masters has written fine lyrics, most of his best poems emphasize the epic quality of his vision. There be critics who aver that he has done nothing since *Spoon River,* but such a myopic verdict can come only from minds groping for details and blind to mass effects. Since *Spoon River* the very titles of his books have spread a large canvas; he has travelled down the Mississippi in *The Great Valley, Toward the Gulf, Starved Rock* and *The Open Sea,* with *Domesday Book* crossing the Atlantic and accepting the immensities of the World War; and finally he has given us *The New Spoon River,* with its philosophical development of the earlier subject. And although each of these volumes needs weeding out, each of them, except perhaps *The Open Sea,* contains a few essential and memorable poems which help to symmetrize and complete this poet's record of our time and place.

Throughout one is swept along by the man's impassioned quest of truth. In this quest he is absolutely sincere and uncompromising; yet, though he admits humanity's crimes, and lashes our smug and faulty civilization with laughter or even fury, one feels always the warmth of a big-hearted wistful sympathy with all God's sorely tried and tempted creatures as they move about among illusions and are ignorantly stirred by appearances and dreams. He is the attorney for the defense before the bar of ultimate justice, admitting the strong case against his client but pleading the sadness and bitter irony of man's endless struggle between good and evil, between beauty and sordidness.

If he plies the whip on Thomas Rhodes and Editor Whedon, and stings with laughter Bryan and Mrs. Purkapile and the Reverend Percy Ferguson, he has a sympathetic smile for Daisy Frazer and Roscoe Purkapile and ''dear old Dick,'' a wrench of the heart for Doc Hill and the pair at Perko's, and a splendid burning candleflare of beauty for Anne Rutledge and Lucinda Matlock . . . , and a few other simple and loyal souls. And always one feels these more or less imperfect creatures cast into their true perspective by the poet's ever-present, clear-sighted sense of humor. It is a humor enormous, like Swift's, in its satirical sweep and power, but more genial than that of the Queen Anne cynic. It permeates all his work, of course, and helps to make his portraits so intensely and sympathetically alive. But his sense of pity is just as keen, and the two in perfect unison sometimes combine to produce a masterpiece of portraiture as incisive as Velasquez, like **"Slip-shoe Lovey,"** **"Archibald Higbie"** or **"Fiddler Jones."**

Indeed, the human tenderness of this often harsh poet, in his handling of such a battered bit of flesh and blood as Elinor Murray of the *Domesday Book,* cannot be too highly praised: in spite of her manifest and numerous slips and sins, he reveals her as nobody's slave—a free and generous spirit capable of heights as well as depths, and escaping vulgarity by a certain inner flare of something like a hidden and hunted love of truth. The poet turns more lights on her than Browning on Pompilia in *The Ring and the Book,* indulging too far his lawyer's love of presenting the complete and voluminous testimony of many witnesses. But, however over-laden, the book is a powerful modern epic of democratic human averages; an episode of the eternal struggle of the race to save its soul, like Browning's and every other epic that ever was written. To complain that much of it is prose masquerading as bad blank verse, and that even its best passages are guilty of excruciating banalities of style and technique, is as idle as criticism of a mountain. The mountain is there, imperfect in line, rough and craggy in detail; but massive and mighty as it rests broadly on the solid earth and lifts its brow into the clouds.

His capacity for fierce living and hard thinking is what gives size and depth to this poet's work. One pictures his imagination as a battle-ground of ecstasies and agonies—more completely than with most poets his puppets' feelings become his own. His philosophy therefore is built on human examples—abstract reasoning apart from life is impossible to him. It is an epicurean philosophy, no doubt, one which follows earthly paths and finds happiness a sufficient aim; but beyond this immediate goal lies the remote horizon of mystery. Mr. Masters may be a realist, but we are constantly reminded that his realism transcends mere fact, that the finite and the infinite are equally real to him and equally of the tenuous stuff of dreams. He makes **"Elza Ramsey"** say:

Do you know what makes life a terror
And a torture, Spoon River?
It is due to the conflict between the little minds
Who think life is real,
And who therefore work, save, make laws,
Prosecute and levy wars—
Between these and the big minds
Who know that life is a dream,
And that much of the world's activity
Is pure folly, and the chattering of idiots.

Again and again he chants the praise of life—this splendid garment of happiness which is offered so often in vain, and which most of us, at the best, wear so clumsily:

O life, O unutterable beauty!—
To leave you, knowing that you were
    never loved enough,
Wishing to live you all over,
With all the soul's wise will!

The desecration of life—that is the unpardonable sin which he lashes in countless poems. The magnificence of the opportunity and the insignificance of our response to it—that is the gods' food for laughter, and the poet's stuff of satire. Mr. Masters does not predict, though he does not deny, that some future life may give us another chance; in his mind that is irrelevant to the immediate and important issue—our unworthy and inadequate use of the life we have.

And of course our efforts at religion are the chief of our inadequacies. His **"Sarah Dewitt,"** receiving her husband as a gift of God and then finding his ''just a thief,'' says:

Friends, it is folly to prison God
In any house that is built with hands,
In man or woman, in passionate hopes,
In the love of Truth, or the Rock of Ages. . . .
For God is Proteus, and flies like magic
From earth to heaven, from hope to hope.
You never can catch Him, and this is the reason:
The game of the soul is never to find,
The game of the soul is to follow.

Indeed, it is the narrow and self-righteous patterns of respectibility whom Masters whips with his sharpest satire, the static immovable human clods who obstruct the path of the adventurers, of the free and open-minded children of light. Perhaps **"Emmett Burns,"** in *The New Spoon River,* sums up most keenly his feeling about this blundering world:

Passer-by, do you know who are the slickest schemers
And the most excellent despots?
They are those who say this is right and this is wrong,
And who ascend the throne of what they call the right
And then hedge the right with a law.
Is there no way to beat these shallow souls?
Follow me, passer-by:
Be young, be wise,
Be indifferent to good and evil
And the laws they make—
Seek only the truth,
And die!

(pp. 47-53)

Mr. Masters has little patience with the ''Europe-blinded.'' Here at least is a poet who makes full use of our rich ''epic material.'' If he satirizes the republic and its individual citizens, he also glorifies them. He makes no apologies to the past or the far-away, he deals with the stuff of his own time and place, and he is absolutely fearless and sincere. At the heart of his philosophy is love of the race and a fierce desire for its "pursuit of happiness" and reasonableness; but with humor putting all this in perspective and tempering his bitter wrath with a laugh.

If this poet is fundamentally epic in the sweep of his vision, his prolific art indulges also other moods. Certain fine poems of more or less cosmic motive are epic corollaries, no doubt—such things as **"The World's Desire," "The Loom," "The Star," "Silence," "Worlds."** And many poems about real or typical characters—**"Autochthon," "William Marion Reedy," "Cato Braden," "Widow La Rue," "Emily Brosseau," "Sir Galahad"** and others—as well as out-door poems like **"Grand River Marshes," "The Landscape,"** and the supremely joyous **"Lake Boats,"** may be classed as details of that story of his place and people which is his chief legacy to art.

Sometimes his prolific genius is tempted by the past, and we have monologues from Shakespeare, Byron, Voltaire, and others. These are always interesting, whether one agrees or not with the poet's analysis of motives. But such excursions are tangents from the main curve of his orbit, and when they are pursued too deliberately, as in certain dialogues in **The Open Sea,** which elaborate the Brutus theme through the centuries, they become the most ineffective chapter of Mr. Masters' artistic history. Occasionally, however, one finds an intensely vivid study of remote and alien character, as in that rather early lyrical ballad **"Saint Francis and Lady Clare,"** which has all the emotion of a personal song.

Now and then he utters a real lyric cry. One would like to quote such poems as **"I Shall Never See You Again," "Song of Women," "Poor Pierrot," "Recessional," "My Light With Yours," "Sounds Out of Sorrow," "The Sign"**—poems which make a strong bid for remembrance because their intense rhapsodic passion burns away all imperfections and sweeps the reader along in its flame of beauty unstudied and sincere. Even the poet's technique, so often slipshod, has nobilities of its own at ecstatic moments. Perhaps the great thing about him is that he is *capable* of ecstasy, that he lives hard and deep, and knows the extremes, the agonies. Thus his art is sincere, convincing; one never doubts the emotion behind it. And to a poet who believes, who feels to the utmost, much may be forgiven. (pp. 53-5)

> Harriet Monroe, "Edgar Lee Masters," in her Poets and Their Art, *revised edition, Macmillan Publishing Company, 1932, pp. 46-55.*

EDGAR LEE MASTERS (essay date 1933)

[*In the following excerpt, Masters reminisces about writing* Spoon River Anthology.]

About 1904 I began to see copies of the St. Louis *Mirror;* and soon I met its editor, William Marion Reedy, and we became fast friends. He had had a classical training under the Jesuits, and was an acute judge of literature, a book-taster of the surest sense. He filled his weekly with his own remarkable comments, and with original verse, and verse copied from English journals, and translated from the French and the Russian. Before the tango started, when jazz was fumbling to an emergence, before American free verse was heard of, he was publishing the prose poems of Turgenev, and those of the French Symbolists. (pp. 47-8)

There was nothing new about free verse except in the minds of illiterate academicians and quiet formalists like William Dean Howells, who called **Spoon River** "shredded prose" [see Additional Bibliography]. Reedy understood all these things as well as I. He knew that Imagism was not a new thing, though he kept urging me to make the **Anthology** more imagistic, and I refused, except where imagism as vivid description in the Shakespearean practice was called for. I had had too much study in verse, too much practice too, to be interested in such worthless experiments as polyphonic prose, an innovation as absurd as Dadaism or Cubism or Futurism or Unanimism, all grotesqueries of the hour, and all worthless, since they were without thought, sincerity, substance.

Reedy was always referring to the classics, to rich old books like the *Greek Anthology,* and I used to buy these books as he brought them to my attention. He used to present me with books; he may have given me the *Greek Anthology.* I remember distinctly his references in the *Mirror* to it, from which I gathered that I could have Plato and Simonides and Theocritus in one book. At any rate, I read the *Greek Anthology* about 1909.

Along these years I was publishing poems in the *Mirror,* in rhyme, in standard measures. All the while there was implicit in Reedy's criticisms the idea that I should do something distinctively American, that my experience and background should not go unexpressed, and should not be smothered under verses of mere skill, which did not free what was really within me. I may have told him that I contemplated a novel with Lewistown as a microcosm; I don't remember now. But he did not suggest that I use this material for poetry, though he implied in all that he said that I should use life for poetry. I was trying to do that; I was doing it, but not in the way I did in the Anthology. He did not tell me to use epitaphy as a form. He merely acted like a friend who thought I could do something more distinctive than I was doing, somehow, some way, but without telling me how to do it.

But when I sent him the first pieces of the **Anthology**—"The Hill," and two others, **"Fletcher McGee," "Hod Putt,"** I think,—back came a letter immediately saying that this was the stuff. I was astonished for reasons too numerous to be briefly covered, and his extravagant praise seemed like irony. When I wrote these first pieces, and scrawled at the top of the page **Spoon River Anthology,** I sat back and laughed at what seemed to me the most preposterous title known to the realm of books. Hence when I saw that he really liked the work I wanted to change the title to *Pleasant Plains Anthology;* but he dissented so earnestly that I yielded to his judgment. (pp. 48-9)

I could go into the matter of the prosody of the **Anthology** if I were writing a technical exposition. I could refer to the bald stark prose of the Bohn *Greek Anthology,* and then parallel it with rhythmical pieces like **"Thomas Trevelyn,"** and **"Isaiah Beethoven,"** and in this connection I could cite the fact that the "Spooniad" is in blank verse, quite conventional enough; and that the "Epilogue" is in rhymed lyrics. I could show that there are sixty-seven pieces which are both rhythmical and metrical; and that I invented a rhythmical pattern for such pieces as **"Henry Tripp,"** which are distinctive of the book and expressive of the mood which created it. I could appeal to Aristotle's *Poetics,* which laid down the dictum that the difference between poetry and prose is the difference between literature which imitates action and emotion, and literature which imitates nothing, like arguments and the like. I could as justification for the freedom I took, and the rebellion I asserted against technical groves and academicians, appeal to Goethe's instruction to use in poems alliteration, false rhymes and assonance, which in 1831 he said he would do if he were again young.

However, I did not know of Goethe's doctrines on that subject at the time. Nor did I know of Saint Beuve's words that "the greatest poet is not he who has done the best, but he who suggests the most," not he who writes the *Æneid*, but he who gives to the world that which most stimulates the reader's imagination, and excites him the most to poetize himself, which remote things like the *Æneid* cannot so much do. I could go into all this to repel the savage attacks that were made on the *Anthology* at the time and since to the effect that it was prose, and bald prose, that it was without harmony and beauty, that in a word it was not poetry at all. I shall do none of these things here; but I shall refer to some matters of substance before resuming the history of the *Anthology* and of myself during its composition.

There are two hundred and forty-four characters in the book, not counting those who figure in the "Spooniad" and the "Epilogue." There are nineteen stories developed by interrelated portraits. Practically every ordinary human occupation is covered, except those of the barber, the miller, the cobbler, the tailor and the garage man (who would have been an anachronism) and all these were depicted later in the *New Spoon River*. What critics overlook when they call the *Anthology* Zolaesque, and by doing so mean to degrade it, is the fact that when the book was put together in its definitive order, which was not the order of publication in the *Mirror*, the fools, the drunkards, and the failures came first, the people of one-birth minds got second place, and the heroes and the enlightened spirits came last, a sort of Divine Comedy, which some critics were acute enough to point out at once.

The names I drew from both the Spoon river and the Sangamon river neighborhoods, combining first names here with surnames there, and taking some also from the constitutions and State papers of Illinois. Only in a few instances, such as those of Chase Henry, William H. Herndon and Anne Rutledge and two or three others, did I use anyone's name as a whole. (pp. 49-50)

As the Fall of 1914 came along, and as my memories of the Sangamon country and the Spoon river country became more translucent and imaginative under the influence of pale sunlight and falling leaves, I departed more and more from the wastrels and failures of life and turned more and more to gentle combinations of my imagination drawn from the lives of the faithful and tender-hearted souls whom I had known in my youth about Concord, and wherever in Spoon river they existed. As December came I was nearing exhaustion of body, what with my professional work and the great drains that the *Anthology* were making on my emotions. The flame had now become so intense that it could not be seen, by which I mean that the writing of the pieces did not seem to involve any effort whatever; and yet I should have known that I was being sapped rapidly. I had no auditory or visual experiences which were not the effect of actuality; but I did feel that somehow, by these months of exploring the souls of the dead, by this unlicensed revelation of their secrets, I had convoked about my head swarms of powers and beings who were watching me and protesting and yet inspiring me to go on.

I do not mean by this that I believed that I was so haunted; I only mean I had that sensation, as one in a lonely and eyrie room might suddenly feel that someone was in the next room

spying upon him. Often, after writing, during which I became unconscious of the passing of time, and would suddenly realize that it was twilight, I would experience a sensation of lightness of body, as if I were about to float to the ceiling, or could drift out of the window without falling. Then I would go out of the room and catch up one of the children to get hold of reality again; or I would descend for a beer and a sandwich. These nights I was playing on the Victrola the Fifth Symphony of Beethoven, out of which came the poem **"Isaiah Beethoven,"** and such epitaphs as **"Aaron Hatfield," "Russell Kincaid,"** and **"Elijah Browning."**

I might have made the *Anthology* fuller and richer and longer at this time except for my professional distractions, and if I had not been begged to stop by some of my relatives, who said that the work was long enough. If I had not been at this time descending rapidly to a sick bed, I should have gone on despite every obstacle, and so long as the spirits swarmed. (pp. 50-1)

For myself, now that I am writing about the book, I may say that if I had any conscious purpose in writing it and the *New Spoon River* it was to awaken that American vision, that love of liberty which the best men of the Republic strove to win for us, and to bequeath to time. If anyone is interested in my cosmology let him read **"Clifford Ridell"** in the *New Spoon River*. I think my poems, **"Mournin' For Religion,"** and **"The Mourner's Bench,"** are as much in the genre of America as anything in either anthology; that I have written many poems better than anything in either *Spoon River*, and that both *Domesday Book* and its epilogue, *The Fate of the Jury*, surpass them. (p. 55)

Edgar Lee Masters, "The Genesis of Spoon River,"
in American Mercury, Vol. XXVIII, No. 109, January, 1933, pp. 38-55.

JOHN COWPER POWYS (essay date 1937)

[*An English novelist, essayist, and critic, Powys is best known for a series of four novels set in Wessex county, a fictional region developed by Thomas Hardy as the setting for such novels as* Tess of the D'urbervilles *(1891) and* Jude the Obscure *(1895). Like Powys's other works of fiction, these novels employ a mythical and supernatural backdrop for examining the mysteries of human nature, most prominently its spiritual and sexual aspects, and for exploring the relationship of human consciousness to a transcendent order of being. As a critic, Powys presents a similarly eccentric image, and deliberately so. As he asserts in his study of Fedor Dostoevski: "The temperamental peculiarities of an honest critic are the tools of his trade. . . . The secret essence and innermost virtue of an author can only be wrung out of him by hate or love." Thus, Powys's critical writings are considered of a piece with his fiction, revealing as much about himself as they do the authors he discusses. In the following excerpt, he praises Masters's poetic achievement.*]

True critics of Edgar Lee Masters' work will think of him in after times as one who handed on, amid alien and hostile voices, the true tradition of that emotional-magical-dramatic inspiration in which, and in which alone, the purpose of poetry is fulfilled. Poetry, according to Matthew Arnold is "Criticism of Life," holding fast to the "highest Truth" and the "deepest Seriousness"; and to touch the human soul to its depths such poetry, as Milton said, must be "simple, sensuous and passionate."

Like Milton himself, and indeed like Matthew Arnold in many of his philosophical poems, Masters loves to substitute a singularly downright and lucid "free-verse" for those rhyming tags that so often "set off wretched matter and worse metre." He is deft enough and ingenious enough in his use of rhyme when something essentially lyrical in his subject seems to call for it; but the whole weight of his verse and all the intangible atmosphere that surrounds it follows the old poetic tradition in concentrating on the two grand elements of our human story—the soul of man struggling with chance, accident, and evil, in the presence of the unchanging elements. The first of these is the *dramatic* note, the second the *magical* note, and it has always been in these, from Shakespeare and Milton and Keats to our own time, that poetry has upheld, enlightened, transported us.

Masters is modern enough in his use of "free-verse" and in his powerful introduction of savage and sardonic details, but where he refuses to yield to the fashionable tendency of the hour is his persistent return to the magic of Nature and the ape-like tricks of humanity against that magical background. (pp. 88-9)

Like the old great poets Edgar Lee Masters retains a firm grip upon the austere harrow of destiny, as it drives forward, changing the face of nations and customs and codes and creeds under the urge of the unseen Power. In these later volumes of his poetry—in *Invisible Landscapes*, in *Poems of People*, in *The New World*—you are aware of a mind that "sees life steadily and sees it whole," a mind with the majestic weight of a true historian of the tumultuous drama, and yet a mind that can abandon itself, in that brooding passivity of which Wordsworth made so much, to the indescribable overtones and undertones of the secret backwaters. . . .

False and malicious and shallow are the carping critics of the hour that cannot catch, in this more recent poetry by the hand that wrote the first *Spoon River*, the same old, authentic and unique quality. . . . [How] refreshing it is in the midst of the convoluted mental labyrinths of modern verse, verse that would seem to be written by one clever "intellectual" for another clever "intellectual," to come once again upon Masters' symbolic and yet so engagingly realistic trick of introducing the actual names of his Middle-Western "dramatis personæ." And with the introduction of these homely names how there comes flowing in upon us again—upon us who know that most typically and purely American region of all the regions of America—all the scents and sounds and silences of those Illinois plains, those Indiana uplands, those secluded valleys of Missouri, those cornfields of Iowa, those interminable horizons of Kansas!

The most simple, the most unsophisticated, the most homely regions of the whole continent they are, free from the contorted asperities of New England, free from the sinister blood-stains of the South. And Edgar Lee Masters is still their poet, and being their poet he is still the poet of what is most porous in them to those great winds of voyaging mystery against which our mental cleverness and the fitful fevers of our perverse disillusions choke up the natural senses.

And with the familiar names of these people of the soil there come back to us in *Invisible Landscapes* the yet more familiar names of the places they inhabit. . . . (p. 90)

Sometimes the spirit of *Invisible Landscapes* makes you think of Wordsworth, but much more often of Thomas Hardy. . . .

Deep indeed would a person have to dive into the silt and ooze at the bottom of human nature, or into the aboriginal sand at the bottom of American human nature, to discover the reason why the critical coteries of today do so much less than justice

to Masters' recent poems. I yield to none in my admiration for the first *Spoon River*; but I confess that a poem like the one entitled "Tirzey Potter" in *Poems of People* touches me more than any single epitaph in that renowned anthology. "Tirzey Potter" is a poem quite as poignant, quite as homely, quite as evocative of those "thoughts that lie too deep for tears" as any of those obstinately under-stated vignettes, deliberately and grotesquely childish, with which Wordsworth outraged his sophisticated critics. (p. 91)

Poetry has become the specialty of a sophisticated class, and it has developed on two parallel lines, on the line of difficult aesthetic experiment, and on the line of political revolution.

Now Mr. Masters, as a born historian, has his own peculiar angle of historic interpretation, but this is not a theoretical or a doctrinaire *point d'appui*; it is a dramatic and evolutionary one, and its values are spiritual and emotional rather than ethical or æsthetic. The simple poignance of this "Tirzey Potter" type of poem has nothing to do with social revolution or with artistic experiment. It has to do with the old recurrent tragic-comedy of our existence as it goes on in the intimacies of human life whether the outer currents of events be reactionary or the reverse. . . .

Let any reader who can remember that unequalled symbol of the primitive hospitalities of the Middle West, the old "frame hotel," read the poem in *Poems of People* entitled "Hotel at Alpena, Michigan." For the conjuring up of an atmosphere that holds the palpable and breathing life of an America that is passing too quickly away this poem is a masterpiece of miraculous evocation. I know no poem like it! It is a "genre" by itself. No one but Masters could have written it and from start to finish, tone upon tone, image upon image, impression upon impression, it brings back to me, as an old pedlar of "culture" in such rural places, something that approaches an actual nostalgia for the land that was never mine.

There are many fine historic pictures of the great ones of the past in *Poems of People*, but I confess the portions of this book that stir me most are those that deal with the old Bars, the old Cafés, the old Resorts, and the quaint unreturning human characters that frequented these genial places. . . . (p. 92)

And who but Edgar Lee Masters could have pageanted and portrayed, as he does in *The New World*, the whole wild story, mumming in its tragic-comic motley the life of these States, from the dawn of time to the present hour? (p. 93)

There will be, no doubt, those to whom *The New World* will seem too plain, too blunt, too colloquial, too stripped of all the conventional poetic appeals. To such critics I would say consider Blake's *Prophetic Books*, for there also you have a simplicity that skates on the "outer edge" of oracular prose. The astonishing thing about this poem is the mixture of what you might call Tellurian learning with what you might call Bodleian learning. And exactly there you find the clue to its power. No ordinary poet, no *other* poet that I have ever heard of, has the whole history of a continent at his finger-tips! And you feel that Masters is writing, not as ordinary scholars would do—as Carlyle, that great *prose-poet* of history did—with the books at his elbow, but, as a real poet, in his bones. In fact you feel as if "the old eternal Genius," as Emerson would say, "who builds the world" gave to this Socrates of Illinois the privilege of a joy-ride down the highway of Time on his own divine-diabolic back, so that from his seat on the Hobby-Horse of celestial Whimsies he might measure aright the idols of normal human sentiment!

A Masters family portrait. Edgar Lee Masters is at the top right; his grandmother Lucinda Masters, on whom he based "Lucinda Matlock" of Spoon River Anthology, *is in the center of the bottom row. Courtesy of Ellen C. Masters.*

What we get in *The New World* is the genius of the most American poet since Whitman, and the most honest poet since Whitman, and the poet who arouses the same love and hate as Whitman, exposing in poetry, just as Swift exposed in prose, the multitudinous humbug of the rulers of half a hemisphere. (pp. 93-4)

What is it that gives its magic to Masters' stark, bitter stripping of the bruised bones of what is called History? Two main spiritual urges, it seems, drive him forward cutting his remorseless furrow through the rank undergrowth of luxuriant lies. The first is a deep, sick, angry awe, in the presence of what *looks* like demonic "miching mallecho" in the hidden Power behind the universe; but which *may* be something else! The second is an infinitely wistful and desperate faith in the unconquerable spirit, baffled and thwarted but ever "gathering a new mind for fresh struggles" of average humanity.

For all the leaders of our modern world this great poet has nothing but heart-weary contempt. It is their false prophesying, their treacherous lies, in league it may be, or may *not* be, with the dark inscrutable Power at the back of it all, who lead the blind, helpless, well-meaning People into illusion after illusion, disaster after disaster!

His *New World* begins with the movements of warriors Westward over waves and graves; and it closes in the Great War

with the movements of warriors Eastward over waves and graves! Everlasting movements after the *Fata Morgana* of peace and happiness, over the waves that engulf, over the graves that are silent. . . .

Like certain other great poets, but not like all, Masters finds his sole consolation in the natural benedictions of earth and sky and in the kindliness and courage of the common people. (p. 94)

> *John Cowper Powys, "Edgar Lee Masters' Recent Poetry," in* University Review, *Vol. IV, No. 2, Winter, 1937, pp. 88-94.*

MAY SWENSON (essay date 1962)

[Swenson is an American poet and educator. In the following excerpt, she discusses the biographical background and the polemical and technical elements of Spoon River Anthology.*]*

Edgar Lee Masters' *Spoon River Anthology* was the first thing of its kind and a phenomenon in American literature when it appeared in 1915. It is not less so today. Originally conceived as a novel, having the ingredients of a fatalistic drama as well as those of a tract on social injustice, the *Anthology* is a series of poetic monologues by 244 former inhabitants (both real and imagined) of Spoon River, an area near Lewistown and Petersburg, Illinois, where Masters spent much of his boyhood. All in the cast are dead—"all, all are sleeping on the hill" of a Midwestern cemetery—and from their graves they speak their own epitaphs, discovering and confessing the real motivations of their lives; they reveal the secret steps that stumbled them to failure, or raised them to illusionary triumphs while alive; it is as if the darkness of the grave granted them reveletory eyes for a recognition of their own souls.

Masters' conceptual frame for the work was as startling to American readers of the time as was his form—a blunt free verse considered graceless by many of his critics. The scandalous behavior of some of his characters, several of whom, under disguised names, were recognizable as influential figures lately dead or still living in the region, caused the book to become a notorious success—in fact, the first edition made more money for its author and its publisher than any previous volume of American poetry.

Born in Garnett, Kansas in 1868, Masters was in his middle forties when he began the *Anthology*. He had published eleven books of verse, plays and essays without gaining attention. Later evaluators agreed that his early work reflected a too obvious and energetic worship of Keats, Shelley, Milton, Swinburne and Whitman. He was to see published a total of over fifty volumes—of poetry, fiction, biography, drama—before he died in 1950, none of them up to the mark of the *Anthology*. With the encouragement of his publishers, Masters attempted a sequel to his masterpiece, and *The New Spoon River* appeared in 1924; it pictured the community as metropolized; although called a failure by many critics, it, too, was a best seller.

With Carl Sandburg and Vachel Lindsay, Masters forms the third pillar of the "poetic renaissance" as it arose in the Middle West during the second decade of the twentieth century, Chicago being the focus point. . . . In contrast to Sandburg, who found his poetic materials there, Masters hated the city, distrusting its decadent influences. Believing in agrarianism as the only healthy way of life, he would have dismissed urbanization from the earth, had he been able. Because his character encompassed a curious blend of the psychologist, the muckraker and reformer with the dramatist, poet and intellectual, and because of his law experience and ardent interest in political and economic issues, Masters was constantly faced in his writings with the task of reconciling conflicting impulses. He was acutely aware of the tragic weaknesses in human beings, the ironic contrasts between their ideals and their actions, and he was constantly angered at injustice, exploitation, industrialization. In respect of being born seventeen years before Ezra Pound, he might be called the earliest Angry Man in American Poetry.

In the *Spoon River Anthology* Masters fortunately found a way to amalgamate his intuitions with biographical facts by presenting, as if on a metaphorical witness stand, the "closed cases" of the citizens of Spoon River—the obscure and ordinary as well as the prominent, the criminal, the eccentric, the elect—on all of whom life had passed its unexceptional sentence and consigned to the same grassy prison. He has them testify, as if the tombstones had voices, and he defends them clairvoyantly—not against their sins, petty or great, for these they readily confess themselves—but against the inscrutable punishments and inequalities life fixes upon us all.

In his autobiography, *Across Spoon River* . . ., Masters wrote that the notion behind the *Anthology* first occurred to him eight years before he began it, and that he planned it to be a long work in prose. Meanwhile, among other things, he was industriously contributing verse to *Reedy's Mirror* of St. Louis, and the story goes that one day in 1913 its editor, William M. Reedy, gave him a copy of the *Epigrams from the Greek Anthology*, suggesting he read it for its realism and compression of style. Subsequently, in the May 29, 1914 issue of *Reedy's Mirror* there appeared the first published monologue, **"The Unknown"** under the pseudonym Webster Ford, which Masters later placed in the middle of his collection. Actually, the only significant points of convergence between the Greek Epigrams and the *Spoon River Anthology* are the ironic and extremely objective attitudes given to the characters, and the admirable brevity of the epitaphs. (pp. 5-7)

[He] made up a number of the names, giving suggestive clues to certain personalities in his ghostly cast, or to the attitudes he intends us to take toward them, for instance: Voltaire Johnson, Hamlet Micure, Minerva the Village Poetess "with her cock eye and rolling walk. . . ." John M. Church is an attorney and crook, Georgine Sand Miner is an aggressive and vindictive woman, Ida Chicken a vain and silly one, Silas Dement is an arsonist who gleefully sets fire to the courthouse, Zilpha Marsh is a medium. As one of his noble and "enlightened spirits" Masters included the epitaph of his grandmother under the pseudonym of Lucinda Matlock. She represents his ideal of the undaunted pioneer woman, who gave birth to twelve children, remained faithful to her husband, and lived to a ripe age.

Although there are a number of upright or modest monuments in his provincial community of the dead, Masters placed most of them at the back of the graveyard, so to speak—that is, toward the end of the book—and, quite naturally, it is the rakish, tumble-down headstones and the hypocritically ostentatious ones that most intrigue us. Hod Putt, robber and murderer lying side by side with his victim, is the first voice in the book. Chase Henry, the village drunkard, congratulates himself on lying beside a banker; Judge Somers bewails the injustice of his neglected grave while the drunkard has a marble stone and urn. Daisy Fraser, a loose but good-hearted woman of the town, (whom her biographer seems rather to admire than deplore) figures in several of the interlocking histories, including that of the arch villain of the drama, Deacon Thomas Rhodes, who "ran the church as well as the store and the bank." This portrait of an unscrupulous small town plutocrat, emerging through more than a dozen dead mouths of Rhodes' various victims, is vividly convincing. Rhodes' own defiant epitaph, exposing his rock-like egotism even in death, is a good example of Masters' contempt for the self-centered rich man, abuser of power and economic oppressor. Masters took the opportunity in the *Anthology* to inveigh against all that he despised—political swindling, graft, veniality, enforced poverty—and at the same time, by implication, to place himself on the liberal side of certain controversial issues of the day such as prohibition, anarchism, women's rights, free will, free love, membership in "The Social Purity Club." He makes Henry Phipps, the Sunday School superintendent, confess his hypocrisy while indicating his (Masters') own anti-pietistic, pro-social-change philosophy.

There is evidence that he intended us to find facets of himself in certain of his characters; he seems to stand behind the mask of Jefferson Howard—a suggestive name, for Thomas Jefferson was his idol—in the lines of that epitaph which read: "Foe of the Church with its charnel darkness, / Friend of the human touch of the tavern. . . ." Masters hated asceticism, emulated liberalism throughout his life. Nevertheless, in the *Spoon River* poems he clearly defines a strongly independent moral code. (pp. 7-9)

He was both a Yea-sayer and a Nay-sayer; his tract-writing proclivities frequently fought with the genuine poet in him; he had a canny and prophetic eye that surveyed the basically simple inner natures of men as well as the whole outward tangle of their existence. It may be that Edgar Lee Masters deliberately inserted his own epitaph into the *Anthology* under the apt name of Percival Sharp. This is a striking and significant poem in which a spirit observes his gravestone carved with a pair of clasped hands: "Are they hands of farewell or greeting, / Hands that I helped or hands that helped me? / Would it not be well to carve a hand / With an inverted thumb, like Elagabalus?" The spirit of Percival Sharp comments ironically on the symbols on other tombs: ". . . anchors for those who never sailed / And gates ajar—yes, so they were; / You left them open and stray goats entered your garden. / And an eye watching like one of the Arimaspi . . . And angels blowing trumpets . . . / It is your horn and your angel and your family's estimate." And he concludes:

> It is all very well, but for myself I know
> I stirred certain vibrations in Spoon River
> Which are my true epitaph, more lasting than stone.

"Certain vibrations" are stirred in any reader of this ingenious, multi-layered, dramatic, socio-historic, intuitive collection of lives-in-death; today and tomorrow they will continue to stir, and we do not have to accept Masters' prejudices or polemics often displayed in his other voluminous works in order to appreciate the *Anthology* as unique. Taken as a whole, this book, too, is flawed: It is bigger, more inclusive than need be. It is as if he became obsessed with his resurrection of souls; his graveyard is overpopulated, and some of the headstones seem repetitious. There is a stiffness to some verses that their free form does not entirely counteract, a statement-like recitation and formality of posture (like Grant Wood portraits) sometimes unintentionally ludicrous. Masters felt impelled to include every example he could think of, of the common and uncommon man or woman. By this, it is true, he reminds us of the grisly "togetherness" and multiplicity that death as well as life imposes—the leveling, the erasure of discriminatory features. There is great compression in his many excellent individual life histories; with few exceptions the poems do not go past a page in length (as if the dead disdained to babble) and the brevity he imposes on each voice is a lucky thing. But then, he adds **"The Spooniad"** after the epitaphs, an unfinished summary of the same material in derivative blank verse, and follows this with another coda, the **"Epilogue,"** a further re-iteration in play form that begins like *Faust* and ends a "mish-mash."

Masters wrote the chronicle of several generations and of a whole community, something not again attempted in either American poetry or drama until some twenty years later in Thornton Wilder's *Our Town*. In *Spoon River* we find the town Marshal, Judges, bankers, doctors, tradesmen, professional men, editors, churchmen, artists, Petit the Poet, Fiddler Jones, Andy the Nightwatch, the Village Atheist, Dora Williams the hatmaker, Russian Sonia, Ippolit Konovaloff from Odessa, Mrs. Kessler the laundress, Tom Beatty the gambler, Shack Dye, a Negro, Yee Bow, a Chinaman, Anne Rutledge, first love of Abraham Lincoln, and Hannah Armstrong who kept a boarding house in which Lincoln once lived; there are all the undistinguished citizens of Spoon River, partly factual and partly imag-

ined, who die accidental or violent or unnoticed deaths; there are the soldiers and the suicides and, finally inevitably—the stone mason and the undertaker "all, all sleeping on the hill." (pp. 9-10)

[Masters'] best poetic gifts and perceptions had been expended in the *Anthology*. Of the prodigious volumes of narrative poetry that followed, *The Domesday Book* and *The Fate of the Jury* are best-known, but both are closer to dogmatic novels in verse. In *Achievement in American Poetry 1900-1950*, Louise Bogan said that in his later writings Masters never equalled "either the power or the appeal" of *Spoon River*, and that "a shadow of bitterness and of rather small-minded iconoclasm clouds his many subsequent books" [see Additional Bibliography]. More than one biographer has suggested that the success of the *Anthology* was "an accident"—that Masters set out to write "a crude satire upon the uncouth productions of the vers-librists"—thus implying apparently that the direct, unembellished "common speech" flavor of the monologues was fortuitously mistaken by early critics for a new free verse technique. To this writer the interpretation seems hasty and imperceptive, to say the least. It is true that Masters tried to be classicist and modernist, reformer and poet, villager and city man, sophisticate and innocent Arcadian. Partly, he failed in all. But the *Spoon River* compilation impresses one as arising from the most genuine creative springs. On the basis of internal evidence it is neither something purely contrived, nor "an accident," but rather a spontaneous synthesis, generating naturally from a deep psychological, as well as inventive, core in Masters.

The only near parallel of note in poetic drama that comes to mind, written since the *Anthology*, is Dylan Thomas' play for voices, *Under Milk Wood*, set in a sleeping Welsh town; in scope, at least, Masters was the more daring, not to say extravagant. His ghosts freely gossip about each other and themselves, as well as about the private lives of neighbors still alive in their village. Masters let them be fearless in their sex revelations, and by this he branded himself as the Kinsey of his day. Few of the ingredients of human corruption and vulnerability are missing from the depositions of these underground witnesses, and the *Anthology* remains fascinating if for nothing else than to untangle the lurid web of small town scandal provocatively placed before us. Much more than this, it can be read as a sociological treatise that graphically depicts the effects of industrialization on village life in late nineteenth and early twentieth century America. But it is on the level of his having evolved a new vehicle of poetic expression that Edgar Lee Masters should earn our most important respect. (pp. 11-12)

In *Spoon River*, Masters borrowed the mouths of the dead to give outlet to all his grudges, beliefs, indignations, insights, prophesies, discoveries of glaring injustice, revelations of life's mysteries and paradoxes—and his own eccentric philosophy. Miraculously he also created and bequeathed to us a world in microcosm, new in form, timeless in essence. (p. 13)

> *May Swenson, in an introduction to* Spoon River Anthology *by Edgar Lee Masters, Collier Books, 1962, pp. 5-13.*

STANLEY EDGAR HYMAN (essay date 1963)

[*As a longtime literary critic for the* New Yorker, *Hyman rose to a prominent position in American letters during the middle decades of the twentieth century. He is noted for his belief that much of modern literary criticism should depend on knowledge received from disciplines outside the field of literature; conse-*

quently, many of his best reviews and critical essays rely on his application of theories gleaned from such disciplines as cultural anthropology, psychology, and comparative religion. In the following excerpt from an essay originally published in the New Leader *in 1963, Hyman discusses some reasons for the initial popularity and the enduring appeal of* Spoon River Anthology.]

Back in the days when poets had three names, in 1916, Edgar Lee Masters' *Spoon River Anthology* appeared, and scandalized the nation. I doubt that after almost half a century it will scandalize anyone. Yet it retains an odd sort of power despite its quaintness, like grandmother's pearl-handled revolver.

Spoon River Anthology consists of almost 250 epitaphs, all but two or three of them spoken by the deceased. Their composite picture of the Illinois town of Spoon River is thoroughly repulsive. Julia Miller married an old man to legitimize her unborn child, then took a fatal dose of morphine anyway. Nellie Clark, at eight, was raped by a 15-year-old boy, and the disgrace pursued her ever after and wrecked her life. Yee Bow was killed by a sneak punch from the minister's son. Oscar Hummel, drunk, was beaten to death by a fanatic prohibitionist. The amount of hidden crime would shame Singapore, and its quantity is equalled only by its nastiness.

The town's pervasive hypocrisy is worse than its crimes. From the epitaph of Daisy Fraser, the town whore, we learn that only she is honest in her whoredom: the newspaper editor takes bribes to suppress the instability of the bank; the judge is on the payroll of the railroad; the clergymen speak or keep silent as their masters command. Deacon Taylor is a prohibitionist and secret drinker who confesses that the true cause of his death was cirrhosis of the liver; and one after another all the hyprocrites and whited sepulchres confess.

Unhappiness is endemic in Spoon River. "A bitter wind . . . stunted my petals," cries Serepta Mason. "Sex is the curse of life," says Margaret Fuller Slack, who might have been a great novelist if she had not had eight children. The cemetery is strewn with the wreckage of dreams and hopes. Only a handful of the dead are happy: a dedicated old maid schoolteacher, a blind mother of sighted children, a fiddler who had no worldly ambition, a loving old couple, a dancer whose final placid years were spent living in sin in Spoon River, a reader of Proudhon who murdered his rich aunt and got away with it, a man whose wife loves him and mourns him, several people who were inspired by knowing Lincoln, and a few others.

As poetry, *Spoon River Anthology* is wonderfully old-fashioned now and was wonderfully old-fashioned when it appeared. By 1916 Pound had published eight volumes of poems and translations, and Eliot had published most of the poems in *Prufrock and Other Observations*, but Masters was writing in an older tradition. He took that tradition to be that of the *Greek Anthology*, and his poems are full of references to Hades, Furies, Fates and other Grecian properties, but his true tradition is Browning, Whitman and the native ironies of Yankee gravestones.

The world of the poems is more remote from us than Mycenae. Wickedness is summed up by "I was drinking wine with a black-eyed cocotte" in Paris, or "I killed the son / Of the merchant prince, in Madam Lou's." (pp. 91-2)

The style is fittingly archaic. "But thou grievest," Masters writes, or "Thou wert wise." Many of the poems end with exclamation points, and one ends with a little thicket of them:

> The loom stops short! The pattern's out!
> You're alone in the room! You have woven a shroud!
> And hate of it lays you in it!

The form is free verse. Sometimes it becomes almost metrical, falling into lines mostly anapaestic ("I know that he told that I snared his soul / With a snare which bled him to death") or mostly iambic ("'O, son who died in a cause unjust! / In the strife of freedom slain!'"); and sometimes it approximates rhyme ("Go out on Broadway and be run over, / They'll ship you back to Spoon River").

Masters' figures of speech are ponderous: labored similes ("She drained me like a fevered moon / That saps the spinning world") or interminable metaphors (Dippold the optician sees the afterlife as an eye examination, Joseph Dixon the tuner will be retuned by the great Tuner). In the much-anthologized **"Petit, the Poet,"** Masters mocks the ticking of Petit's little iambics "While Homer and Whitman roared in the pines." There are several Homeric similes in the book, but I am afraid that despite his self-identification, Masters ticks irregularly more than he roars.

The touch is very unsure, and *Spoon River Anthology* is full of failures, many of them in endings. One poem ends with a true whimper: "Refusing medical aid." A good poem in which a tethered cow is a metaphor for the limited freedom of the will is ruined when the metaphoric cow pulls up its stake and gores the homespun philosopher to death. Masters overdoes everything. In a typical poem, he is not content with blind Justice; her eyes must suppurate under the bandages. The mock epic and play with which the book concludes are worse than the worst of the lyrics.

To balance these there are considerable successes. We encounter fine single lines ("Toothless, discarded, rural Don Juan") and fine similes ("While he wept like a freezing steer"). There is an eloquent impression of a rattlesnake ("A circle of filth, the color of ashes, / Or oak leaves bleached under layers of leaves") and a vivid mean description of a woman:

> She was some kind of a crying thing
> One takes in one's arms, and all at once
> It slimes your face with its running nose,
> And voids its essence all over you;
> Then bites your hand and springs away.
> And there you stand bleeding and smelling to heaven!

Two of the poems seem to me, in their different fashions, completely successful. One is **"Roscoe Purkapile,"** a slight comic poem about the ironies of marriage. The other is Masters' most famous poem, **"Anne Rutledge,"** where his Lincoln worship somehow found its proper voice, the eloquence of understatement, and something that really does rival the spare beauty of the poems in the *Greek Anthology* was achieved.

The enormous popularity of *Spoon River Anthology* on its appearance warrants some discussion. One obvious explanation is *succès de scandale*—it was the sex-shocker, the *Peyton Place*, of its day. Knowing that childbirth would kill his wife, Henry Barker impregnated her out of hatred. The only feeling Benjamin Pantier inspired in his wife was sexual disgust. Old Henry Bennett died of overexertion in the bed of his young wife. Hamilton Greene is really his father's child by the German maid, as her epitaph confesses, although his own epitaph blindly boasts his "valiant and honorable blood." There is even a touch of sodomy. We have not advanced that much further in half a century.

Another feature that would have attracted readers in 1916 is the book's sour socialism. Its pervasive fable is the easy fable of Populism: that the pioneers built the land by their labor and

Masters relaxing in work clothes, 1933. Courtesy of Ellen C. Masters.

endurance but that it was all stolen from them by "the bank and the courthouse ring." **"English Thornton"** appeals to the descendants of the veterans of the Revolution and the Indian wars to rise up and battle the descendants of the profiteers and the thieves, to recover their inheritance. After Lincoln, Masters' heroes idolize Altgeld, Bryan and Henry George. Matching this Populist politics is the religious iconoclasm of the village atheist. "The reason I believe God crucified His Own Son," Wendell P. Bloyd explains, "is, because it sounds just like Him." Another hero is "Foe of the church with its charnel dankness."

The total effect of bitterness and frustration that *Spoon River Anthology* gives is greater than the sum of its poems. The dead really seem to be trying to tell us something about the quality of American life, something ugly yet essential to our knowledge. These are truths from the grave, thus *grave* truths. In his epitaph, the Town Marshal exults that Jack McGuire was not hanged for killing him, since he had first attacked McGuire. "In a dream," he says triumphantly, "I appeared to one of the twelve jurymen / And told him the whole secret story." But McGuire's epitaph on the next page explodes that inspirational account. McGuire really escaped hanging, he explains, because his lawyer made a crooked deal with the judge.

The most important factor in the appeal of the book, I believe, is that, as in *Winesburg, Ohio,* some larger vision of life shines

through all the pettiness. The terms in which this is put are mostly inadequate. "I thirsted so for love! / I hungered so for life!" says the shade of the poetess Minerva Jones, raped by a bully and dead of an illegal abortion. Frank Drummer tried to memorize the Encyclopaedia Britannica. Mrs. Williams doesn't think Spoon River would have been any worse had its people "been given their freedom / To live and enjoy, change mates if they wished." Mrs. Charles Bliss pleads from her experience that divorce is far better for the children than a bad marriage. "Love of women," Ezra Bartlett argues, may lead one to the divine. Harmon Whitney has been wounded by his wife's "cold white bosom, treasonous, pure and hard." Edmund Pollard pleads boldly for hedonism and joy.

It is almost inarticulate, and much of it is silly, yet some suggestion of the good life, a richer and fuller life than Americans knew in 1916, is there. Masters never understood the reasons for his success in *Spoon River Anthology,* and he never attained it again. He is not a great writer, nor even a good one. But he confronted the spiritual poverty of his America—which is still our America—without blinking, whereas Sinclair Lewis in *Main Street* ultimately turned away, and Thornton Wilder in *Our Town* never looked at America at all, merely sat down to copy *Spoon River Anthology* in a sculpture of fudge. (pp. 92-6)

> Stanley Edgar Hyman, "Truths from the Grave," in his The Critic's Credentials: Essays and Reviews, edited by Phoebe Pettingell, Atheneum, 1978, pp. 91-6.

ERNEST EARNEST　(essay date 1967)

[*Earnest is an American educator and critic. In the following excerpt, he discusses the initial impact of* Spoon River Anthology *on American poetry and analyzes the style, themes, and technique of the poems in the volume.*]

It is over fifty years since Edgar Lee Masters' *The Spoon River Anthology* first appeared in book form. It is safe to say that no other volume of poetry except *The Waste Land* (1922) made such an impact during the first quarter of this century. (p. 59)

Now, when Eliot's reputation has far surpassed that of Masters, it may seem strange to mention them in the same breath, but this was not always the case. In 1915 Ezra Pound congratulating Harriet Monroe on the publication of *Prufrock* wrote that among contemporary poets Eliot and Masters, "are the best of the bilin." . . . During the fifteen years following [the] publication [of *Spoon River*] almost every discussion of American poetry gave Masters a central place.

Many critics of the period, even while praising *Spoon River,* objected to its pessimistic tone; those hostile to it attacked it for indecency. In fact Mencken argued that its popularity "was chiefly due to the notion that it was improper." At a time when the legitimacy of free verse was being much debated, a number of critics used the work as an example of prose masquerading as poetry.

However, the chief reason for the decline of the reputation of *Spoon River* may well have been the appearance of *The Waste Land* which, along with Eliot's critical writing, changed the direction of modern poetry. The pervasive influence of Whitman was displaced by the courtly muses of Europe; realism gave way to symbolism. (pp. 59-60)

After Eliot, poetry became learned, filled with literary allusion and abstruse symbols; its techniques became complex and sophisticated. Certainly today the repertorial, often flat, statements in *Spoon River* seem naive in an era nurtured on Eliot. Masters' rhythms lack the polish and intricacies we have learned to appreciate. Masters' structure has much of the do-it-yourself architecture of a midwestern balloon framed house; Eliot's has the borrowed luxury of Mrs. Jack Gardner's Fenway Court.

But in other ways these two disparate works have odd similarities—the most important being that each represents modern society as a wasteland. Both by means of a series of vignettes present a panoramic view of that society. Both Eliot and Masters contrast a more vital past with an enervated present. Thus Lucinda Matlock, a character based on Masters' grandmother, after telling of her vigorous, happy life of ninety six years, addresses the present generation as

> Degenerate sons and daughters
> Life is too strong for you—
> It takes life to love Life.

The photographer Rutherford McDowell contrasting the faces of the pioneers in the old ambrotypes with those of the present:

> Freely did my camera record their faces too,
> With so much of the old strength gone,
> And the old faith gone,
> And the old mastery of life gone,
> And the old courage gone
> Which labors and loves and suffers and sings
> Under the sun!

It is the sort of contrast which Eliot gives in a very different way between Cleopatra in her barge and the bored modern woman in the expensive boudoir; between Spenser's nymphs gathering flowers along the Thames and the modern nymphs who leave empty bottles, sandwich papers, silk handkerchiefs, cardboard boxes and cigarette ends.

Both poets might be accused of glamorizing a somewhat mythical past at the expense of the present. In Spenser's England there were certainly the equivalents of the modern untidy nymphs, and London pubs with characters like Lil, Doll Tearsheet, Pistol, and Mistress Quickly were contemporaries of Elizabeth and Essex. And among the women Masters knew or knew of were Jane Addams, Harriet Monroe and Willa Cather—women as admirable as the rural Lucinda Matlock of an earlier generation.

The difference between the poets is one of technique. Masters' material is in the poem itself, whereas Eliot's is often outside the poem as witnessed by his own elaborate notes. For anyone familiar with Eliot's sources, his poetry is rich in connotation: the ''Sweet Thames run softly till I end my song'' brings to the reader whose mind is stored with pictures from the *Prothalamion* the idyllic atmosphere of the poem. On the other hand the symbolic significance of Thomas Rhodes' bank emerges from its impact on a variety of characters in *Spoon River.*

There is also an important difference in the uses of the past by the two poets. Eliot's is a mosaic past with fragments of Greek legend, Arthurian romance, Frazer's *Golden Bough,* Dante, Shakespeare, Spenser, Wagner, and many others. One of Eliot's avowed aims was to return literature and life to a tradition. But he specifically rejected the tradition of liberalism and Protestant pluralism in which he had been born. Instead he tried to create one based on classicism, royalism, and Anglo-Catholicism. As Northrop Frye points out, ''One cannot both accept a tradition and decide what it is to be.'' Furthermore a tradition is not the same thing as a mosaic of traditions.

By contrast, Masters is very much a part of a tradition, the Jeffersonian tradition of free inquiry, humanitarianism, equalitarianism. Unlike Eliot's drawn from the library, Masters' was absorbed through his pores. The names that echo through the minds of his characters are Atgeld, Jefferson, Lincoln, Grant, Bryan; Valley Forge, Starved Rock, Missionary Ridge; there are memories of the hanged anarchists in Chicago, of war in the Philippines, of Lincoln speaking on the courthouse steps.

To a degree that is not always recognized, Masters gives the colors and feel of the American countryside. Thus Hare Drummer asks,

> Do the boys and girls still go to Siever's
> For cider, after school in late September?
> Or gather hazel nuts among the thickets
> On Aaron Hatfield's farm when the frosts begin?

He remembers

> Stopping to club the walnut tree
> Standing leafless against a flaming west
> Now, the smell of autumn smoke,
> And the dropping of acorns
> And the echoes about the vales . . .
> Bring dreams of life.

(pp. 60-2)

Of course what made *Spoon River* immediately popular was the shock of recognition. Here for the first time in America was the whole of a society which people recognized—not only that part of it reflected in writers of the genteel tradition. Like Chaucer's pilgrims, the 244 characters who speak their epitaphs represent almost every walk of life—from Daisy Frazer, the town prostitute, to Hortense Robbins, who had travelled everywhere, rented a house in Paris and entertained nobility; or from Chase Henry, the town drunkard, to Perry Zoll, the prominent scientist, or William H. Herndon, the law partner of Abraham Lincoln. The variety is far too great for even a partial list: there are scoundrels, lechers, idealists, scientists, politicians, village doctors, atheists and believers, frustrated women and fulfilled women. The individual epitaphs take on added meaning because of often complex interrelationships among the characters. Spoon River is a community, a microcosm, not a collection of individuals.

It is ironic that the early discussions of Masters emphasized the sexual element in *Spoon River,* for it is far less obsessed with sex than is *The Waste Land.* Only about 38 of the 244 epitaphs are primarily concerned with the sexual experiences of the speakers. In Masters' picture the sterility of modern society is not merely a matter of frustrated or loveless sex; it is a complex product of sexual, social, religious, economic, and political forces. *Spoon River* is essentially a picture of a society maimed by puritanism, materialism, narrow religion and hypocrisy. At times, however, an epitaph echoes Lear's cry against the gods. Thus Schofield Huxley, after telling of man's achievements, asks of God:

> How would you like to create a sun
> And the next day have worms
> Slipping in and out between your fingers?

There is at times a transcendental note, not the serenely optimistic one of Emerson, but the questioning one of Melville and Emily Dickinson. For instance Davis Matlock advises one to live "like a god, sure of immortal life, though you are in doubt," and

> If that doesn't make God proud of you
> Then God is nothing but gravitation,
> Or sleep is the golden goal.
>
>   (p. 63)

Another element that is often overlooked in *Spoon River* is that despite its essentially realistic method it contains a considerable amount of symbolism. Just as Thoreau saw in a freight-car of torn sails "proof sheets which need no correcting" and telling "a story more legible and interesting now than if they should be wrought into paper and printed books," so Mrs. Kessler, the village laundress, reading the lives of the owners in the soiled and torn clothes brought to her, thinks that Life too is a laundress and that every face she saw in a coffin "looked like something washed and ironed." Abel Melveny, after buying every kind of farm machine that is known, and watching it rust away because he could not house it all and did not need it, saw it as a symbol of himself, "a good machine / That Life had never used."

This was of course the symbolic technique of Melville, who saw the monkey rope as the symbol of man's interdependence and the whale lines coiled about the men in the boat as analagous to the invisible forces that enmesh us all. It is also the method of Frost, who used such symbols as a farm wall, a tuft of flowers, or an apple harvest.

The advantage of the method is that it makes a more accessible poetry than one steeped in symbols derived from esoteric sources. Its dangers are flatness and literalness, as in Wordsworth's less successful poems. On the other hand this kind of poetry does not so easily overinflate an experience or an emotion by endowing it with some mythic significance. Not every gallant stand is a Thermopylae, not every downed airman an Icarus, nor every wanderer an Odysseus, every garage mechanic a Hephaestus. This method of Wordsworth, Frost, and Masters is less in danger of relying on the rehearsed response, the Pavlovian reaction to a borrowed line from Spenser or Donne, or a reference to Chartres or Knossos. (p. 64)

As Louis Untermeyer demonstrated by taking one of them and printing it as a prose passage without Masters' line divisions, the original structure is functional: it produces a kind of musical pattern. In a less eccentric manner it achieves some of the effects of Cummings' typography: the arrangement of the lives introduces a rhythm of its own. In *Spoon River* this rhythm is well suited to the meditative, reminiscent content of the epitaphs, usually ending with an aphoristic summing up. Very possibly it is a verse style unadapted to other purposes, but in *Spoon River* it was effective. However, even those critics who disliked the technique tended to agree that *Spoon River* had vitality. If it is not great poetry, it is certainly the stuff of poetry to a degree not always present in a lot of verse since its time. The dilemmas and emotions are those of real people; there is none of that tendency to overinflate the meaning of a fish, a red wheelbarrow, a dead groundhog, an ant, or a spider. *Spoon River* may lack intellectual or musical subtlety, but it has a robust, earthy quality that has been rare in the poetry since its time. (p. 65)

> *Ernest Earnest, "Spoon River Revisited," in West-ern Humanities Review, Vol. XXI, No. 1, Winter, 1967, pp. 59-65.*

JOHN W. CRAWFORD   (essay date 1968)

> [*Crawford is an American critic and educator. In the following excerpt, he characterizes the* Spoon River *poems as naturalistic, representing "a striking reaffirmation of the correlation of life and literature" illustrating "the deterministic interpretation of life." This view is challenged by Ernest Earnest (see excerpt dated 1968). In a subsequent essay, Crawford responded to Earnest's remarks (see Additional Bibliography).*]

Edgar Lee Masters' *Spoon River Anthology* purports to be a collection of epitaphs from the graveyard of a village called Spoon River. These are not merely the usual epitaphs, however, but true autobiographical obituaries, written as though the dead themselves had risen and stripped their lives of secret and falsity.... The book has an organic unity based on the experiences and environment common to all the personalities of Spoon River.

It seems to have been Masters' intent to portray the salient features of the whole American civilization by depicting accurately its most representative unit, the American small town. He hoped to give a world view drawn on the scale of a village, to show man in society stripped of the veils and subterfuges which usually hide his real life. Masters himself envisaged his intentions in this way:

> I had a variety of things in mind in writing the *Anthology*. I meant to analyze character, to satirize society, to tell a story, to expose the machinery of life, to present to view a working model of the big world and put it in a window where the passer-by could stop and see it run. And I had in mind the creation of beauty, and the depiction of our sorrows and hopes, our religious failures, successes and visions, our poor little lives, rounded by a sleep, in language and figures emotionally tuned to bring all of us closer together in understanding and affection.

In order to be as objective as it was his desire to be, Masters portrayed, in so far as it was possible, both sides of a single human case history. This objectivity was impossible if the primal passions and the actual conditions of human existence were to be obscured beneath heaps of euphemisms, and, in *Spoon River Anthology*, sex, economics, religion, government, and the whole scale of social values were regarded with a frankness hitherto unknown in American literature. The *Anthology* represents, then, a striking reaffirmation of the correlation of life and literature. (p. 6)

It was after a talk with his mother about these old citizens of the villages along the Spoon River that Masters wrote the introductory lyric of *Spoon River Anthology*, "The Hill." It is redolent of the futility and the frustration of Spoon River's inhabitants.

> Where are Elmer, Herman, Bert, Tom and
>   Charley,
> The weak of will, the strong of arm, and
>   clown, the boozer, the fighter?
> All, all, are sleeping on the hill.

Common names of common people are in evidence. Also buried in Spoon River's cemetery are Ella, Kate, Mag, Lizzie, and Edith. They had not been brought to the hill after lives gloriously spent, but the accidents which actually occur in the lives of most people occurred to them:

> One died in shameful child-birth,
> One of a thwarted love,
> One at the hands of a brute in a brothel,
> One of a broken pride, in search for heart's
>   desire,
> One after life in far-away London and Paris
> Was brought to her little space by Ella and
>   Kate and Mag—
> All, all are sleeping, sleeping, sleeping on the
>   hill.

Here in the prologue is rejected the tragedy of lives spent in "a village of little minds." What followed was revolutionary in American poetry. The dead of Spoon River are vocalized, the unique accomplishment and the lasting original vein of the book, and they are permitted, removed as they are from any hope of gain by deceit, to comment on their lives. Some are bitter, disillusioned, and hurt by life; some rise above life and achieve a sort of exaltation; some have caught a glimpse of an answer to the life riddle; some see life as a trap; others, as a game; still others, as an animal existence lacking in meaning and purpose. From the lips of these people, thwarted and wasted by life in Spoon River, come indictments of the profit motive and of the conventional moral code, indictments of the wanton and needless cruelty of life, denunciations of those who have blocked the way of the people in their struggle to fulfill the American dream.

The distinguishing mark of naturalistic literature is its philosophical interpretation of life. Like the realist, the naturalist looks at life and attempts to represent it in art without regard to his private prejudices, but in addition the naturalist is attempting to demonstrate the existence of universal determinism. His conviction, based on his knowledge of economic and biological determinism, is that all phenomena may be explained on the basis of determinable causes. He portrays man caught in the midst of circumstances which continually act on him, from without and within, and which are absolutely unmanageable from his standpoint. The naturalist implies, even though he may not actually cite instances, that the flux of circumstance is due to knowable causes, and these causes are in turn products of other causes, ad infinitum. This concept of determinism, which is the central doctrine of naturalism, causes the naturalist to delineate the impotence of man, and, as a consequence, to assume a general tone of pessimism. Thus, it is easy to see why many naturalists have conceived of man as trapped by life and used the figure of the trap in stating the nature of life.

Among the first epitaphs of *Spoon River* are those of characters low in the social scale, "the fools, the drunkards, and the failures," says Masters. There seems to be no particular reason for their fates; they did not will to be shoved into the world originally, and from birth on the creaking machinery of fact and circumstance, cause and effect carried them ineluctably toward their end. Hod Putt likens the disastrous end of his life to taking bankruptcy. Hod had become desperate with poverty and had robbed a man and killed him

> . . . unwittingly while doing so,
> For the which I was tried and hanged.
> That was my way of going into bankruptcy.
> Now we who took the bankrupt law in our
>   respective ways
> Sleep peacefully side by side.

Then follows **"Ollie McGee"** and its companion piece, **"Fletcher McGee."** These two poems are an example of Masters' presentation of both sides of the problem. Ollie complains of "secret cruelty never to be told," and Fletcher, reminiscent of Strindberg's misogyny, declares,

> She took my strength by minutes,
> She took my life by hours,
> She drained me like a fevered moon
> That saps the spinning world.

> • • • • •

> My secret thoughts were fingers:
> They flew behind her pensive brow
> And lined it deep with pain.

Three lives have passed in review; three lives have suffered unmerited pain. What is the nature of this "monstrous ogre life" that imposes such anguish of body and spirit on helpless man? In the fourth poem Robert Fulton Tanner has an answer; he says life is like a trap:

> You enter the room—that's being born;
> And then you must live—work out your soul,
> Aha! the bait that you crave is in view:
> A woman with money you want to marry,
> Prestige, place, or power in the world.
> But there's work to do and things to
>   conquer—
> Oh, yes! the wires that screen the bait.
> At last you get in—but you hear a step:
> The ogre, Life, comes into the room,
> (He was waiting and heard the clang of the
>   spring)
> To watch you nibble the wondrous cheese,
> And stare with his burning eyes at you
> And scowl and laugh, and mock and curse
>   you,
> Running up and down in the trap,
> Until your misery bores him.

Here is the naturalistic conception of life, the conception being brooded over by great and inexorable forces in comparison with which man's strength is utterly insignificant. Like other analyses of life by naturalists, **"Robert Fulton Tanner"** imputes no particular intelligence or purpose to the cosmic design.

Tanner, portraying man living in the midst of an indifferent or even hostile environment, is representative of a recurrent theme in Spoon River, and his is not a rare or exceptional opinion. . . . Even if those who have arrived at some analysis of life do not see man actually bound, they perceive that he is waging a losing battle from the beginning. There is Tom Beatty, a lawyer, who tried the rights of property as if by lamplight. He asseverates that

> Life's a gambler
> Head and shoulders above us all.
> No mayor alive can close the house
> And if you lose, you can squeal as you will;
> You'll not get back your money.
> He makes the percentage hard to conquer;
> He stacks the cards to catch your weakness
> And not to meet your strength.

Not all the late citizens of Spoon River are capable of an abstract appraisal of the nature of life; many have interpreted life simply and in the terms of their own meager experiences.

Mrs. Kessler believes that life is a laundress, finding out the secrets of her customers from the patches, stains, and decay which time puts in their lives, and that death is the result of too many washings:

> You are submerged in the tub of yourself—
> And I, who went to all the funerals
> Held in Spoon River, swear I never
> Saw a dead face without thinking it looked
> Like something washed and ironed.

And Widow McFarlane, who wove the carpets and rugs for the village, feels in her own loom the mystery and a symbol for life—life, the weaver of shrouds:

> For the cloth of life is woven you know,
> To a pattern hidden under the loom—
> A pattern you never see!

Each tends to make his own experiences the measure of all things. Griffy, the cooper, thinks of most men's lives as tub-sized in scope:

> You are submerged in the tub of yourself—
> Taboos and rules and appearances,
> Are the staves of your tub.
> Break them and dispel the witchcraft
> Of thinking your tub is life!

But here in **"Griffy the Cooper"** is struck a new note, and one is led to wonder if it is possible that there is a part of man which is forever untouched by life, as essence inviolable, which could gather strength from desire and burst the onerous confines of life? No, this urge, seemingly divine, is but a part of the diabolical scheme, an *élan vital* goading man on that he may the more surely be frustrated. It is a part of the ironic joke of cosmic size.

It is evident from the examples cited and from other poems in the *Anthology,* poems such as **"Harold Arnett," "Carl Hamblin," "Harmon Whitney," Shack Dye,"** and **"Many Soldiers,"** that Masters did follow the naturalistic tendency to show man in society caught in a web of circumstances which conspire to defeat his potential development. Since man's life is visualized in this, there is throughout *Spoon River* a strong bias toward pessimism.

Throughout all these epitaphs which illustrate the deterministic interpretation of life, there is an ancient and haunting sense of the poignancy of human disappointment and defeat. (pp. 6, 8)

> *John W. Crawford, "Naturalistic Tendencies in 'Spoon River Anthology'," in* The CEA Critic, *Vol. XXX, No. 9, June, 1968, pp. 6, 8.*

ERNEST EARNEST (essay date 1968)

[*In the following excerpt, Earnest disputes John W. Crawford's interpretation of* Spoon River Anthology *"as an expression of naturalistic philosophy" (see Crawford excerpt dated 1968). Earnest draws from his own earlier discussion (see excerpt dated 1967) and cites additional examples from the* Anthology *to demonstrate his contention that Crawford misrepresents the work by isolating only one theme.*]

In *The Critic* for June 1968 John W. Crawford deals with *Spoon River Anthology* as an expression of naturalistic philosophy [see excerpt dated 1968]. He is of course right in pointing out that element in the work, but like so many commentators on it, he misrepresents it by isolating a single theme. In the Mencken

era the book was represented as sensationally sexy despite the fact that only about 38 of the 244 epitaphs are primarily concerned with the sexual experiences of the speakers. Crawford in his naturalistic interpretation of *Spoon River* gives an equally one-sided view. He states that ". . . the naturalist is attempting to demonstrate the existence of universal determinism. His conviction, based on his knowledge of economic and biological determinism, is that all phenomena may be explained on the basis of determinable causes." Crawford then goes on to cite epitaphs which support this interpretation of life.

However, as I pointed out in "Spoon River Revisited" [see Earnest entry dated 1967] . . ., part of the greatness of the work lies in the variety of its responses to life. The views of almost every one of the characters can be matched by the opposing views of another. In fact the structure of the work is very often that of antithesis: *e.g.*, Cooney Potter who kills himself trying to expand his 40 acres to 2000, versus Fiddler Jones who played with life all his ninety years and ended up with 40 acres,

> . . . a broken fiddle—
> And a broken laugh, and a thousand
> memories
> And not a single regret.

Similarly, as opposed to those characters who take a deterministic view of life—very often as an excuse for their own failures—there are a considerable number who express a transcendental vision. These and some others show an almost Wordsworthian aesthetic feeling for nature. It is worth noting that Masters apparently attempted to give the nature-lovers and the transcendentalists the most poetic language in the epitaphs.

In a kind of epiphany like those of Wordsworth's boyhood, Dillard Sissman describes the wind in the pasture where he lies, watching his kite above the wind:

> And the hills sleep.
> And a farm-house, white as snow,
> Peeps from green trees—far away
> And I watch my kite,
> For the thin moon will kindle herself
> ere long,
> Then she will swing like a pendulum
> dial
> To the tail of my kite.
> A spurt of flame like a water dragon
> Dazzles my eyes—
> I am shaken as a banner!

Faith Matheny, describing Tintern-Abbey-like visions, speaks of ". . . catching a little whiff of the ether / Reserved for God Himself." (p. 8)

The theme of the transcendency of spirit over flesh appears in several of the epitaphs. Thus Sarah Brown says, ". . . through the flesh / I won Spirit, and through spirit, peace." Tennessee Claflin Shope tells of mastering the *Bhagavad Gita*, which "cured my soul." Ernest Hyde is essentially Emersonian in saying, ". . . the soul makes the world at one with itself." The Village Atheist, after reading the *Upanishads*, concluded:

> Immortality is not a gift,
> Immortality is an achievement;
> And only those who strive mightily
> Shall possess it.

Nor is The Village Atheist alone in his talk of immortality. Blind Jack, killed when two drunken men overturn a buggy, tells of his new world:

> There is a blind man here with a
>   brow
> As big and white as a cloud.
> And all we fiddlers, from the highest
>   to the lowest . . .
> Sit at his feet
> And hear him sing of the fall of Troy.

Possibly this may be taken merely as metaphor, but Joseph Dixon's experience as a piano tuner gave him "proof"

> Of an Ear that tuned me, able to
>   tune me over
> And use me again if I am worthy
>   to use.

It would seem that Masters is nearly as much in the tradition of Wordsworth, Emerson, and Whitman as of Darwin and Herbert Spencer. Perhaps Davis Matlock is as good a spokesman as any for Masters' blend of skepticism and transcendentalism:

> Well, I say to live it like a god
> Sure of immortal life, though you
>   are in doubt,
> Is the way to live it.
> If that doesn't make God proud
>   of you
> Then God is nothing but gravitation,
> Or sleep is the golden goal.

Similarly, Alfonso Churchill, who taught astronomy at Knox College,

> . . . preached the greatness of man
> Who is none the less a part of the
>   scheme of things
> For the distance of Spica or of the
>   Spiral Nebulae;
> Nor any less a part of the question
> Of what the drama means.

In the light of all this it would seem dangerous to pigeonhole Masters as simply a naturalist who, in Crawford's words, believes "that all phenomena may be explained on the basis of determinable causes." Whatever the limitations of *Spoon River Anthology,* it dealt with life on many levels. It is far from being merely a naturalistic exposé of village life; it comes closer to being a quest for meaning. (p. 9)

> *Ernest Earnest, "A One-Eyed View of Spoon River,"*
> *in* The CEA Critic, *Vol. XXXI, No. 2, November,*
> *1968, pp. 8-9.*

BARRY GROSS   (essay date 1977)

[*In the following excerpt, Gross maintains that* Spoon River Anthology *is not an example of "revolt from the village" literature.*]

We are to derive no comfort from the discovery that our critical elders—and betters—did not see clearly, that, however cultivated and refined their critical sensibilities, they were biased and their biases blinded them to what was there. (p. 4)

For decades our understanding of *Spoon River Anthology,* *Winesburg, Ohio* and *Main Street* has been conditioned by their early reception. They were widely and generally interpreted as works which endorsed—and even initiated—what came to be called "the revolt from the village," interpreted that way by critics who themselves wanted to see the village revolted from, who were convinced that provincial life, especially in the Middle West, condemned America to the status of second-class culture.

Eastern and urban, they knew nothing about the village or the Middle West except what they wanted to know and they found in the literature that came out of the Middle West before, during and after World War I confirmation for what they already believed. Paul Rosenfeld, one of the major literary critics of the decade, called the city "the rhythm of the age," and most of the other major critics agreed. For them the Middle West village was synonymous with Puritan repression and Victorian gentility, with middle-class convention and middle-class hypocrisy, with provincialism and tastelessness, with bourgeois monotony and conformity; the American waste land was not Eliot's "Unreal city" but the plains and the prairies that started west of the Hudson River and continued on to California. For them the revolt was from the village to the city, a city synonymous with art and culture, experience and sophistication, possibility and diversity, freedom and individualism, the new and the real.

Masters, Anderson, and Lewis *were* in revolt, but not from the village. They were in revolt from the *myth* of the village as the great good place, as simple and innocent, pure and virtuous, democratic and egalitarian. In revolt from that myth, they espoused others: the traditional myths of the frontier and agrarianism, the contemporary myths of modern decadence and the corrupt city. Their point of reference was a nineteenth century preindustrial Midwest which they saw as morally superior to the present, as a time when the village *was* the great good place.

It is not surprising that the critics misunderstood Edgar Lee Masters. Even now it is difficult to assimilate his peculiar blend of Jeffersonianism and Hellenism and Midwest Transcendentalism, even now it is difficult to read those thesis novels he wrote in which he attempted to demonstrate the spiritual superiority of the preindustrial Midwest. But Masters always believed, as he wrote in *Across Spoon River,* that "the city is facts, hard reality, lifeless stone. The country is the haunt of something universal and deathless and infinite which broods upon the earth and reflects itself in it. In communion with nature we can wrest from the gods ideas identifying life with eternity, and death which stalks the city with images of horror." He told August Derleth,

> (The critics) never knew Spoon River or Gopher Prairie or any of those places, but they pretended to know all about them and about us. There are poems in my Spoon River books about faithful and loving hearts, about kind and generous and hopeful people, but they don't seem to have read them. The best years of my life were spent back there in Illinois. To say that I was in revolt against village life . . . is being just about as silly as you can get. . . . There never was anything to this revolt from the village business. We didn't do any such thing. Maybe Lewis was backing away from something that hurt him, but he wasn't rebelling against the American small town any more

than I was [see Derleth entry in Additional Bibliography].

Masters speaks of his Spoon River *books* and it is *The New Spoon River,* published in 1924, that best summarizes Masters' positions. Consider this bitter defense of the farmer:

Is the ground cursed for the sake of man?
Are thorns and thistles a curse?
And is it a curse to eat your bread
In the sweat of your face?
Well, anyway what a race believes
They put as a curse in the mouth of God.
And you couldn't expect us to be farmers
With the Bible that curses the land and the work,
And a stock behind us that loved the bank,
Prospering in the city.

Masters says he spent the best years of his life back there in Illinois. . . . (pp. 4-5)

> Barry Gross, *"The Revolt That Wasn't: The Legacies of Critical Myopia,"* in The CEA Critic, *Vol. XXXIX, No. 2, January, 1977, pp. 4-8.*

ROBERT NARVESON (essay date 1980)

[*In the following excerpt, Narveson discusses the principal themes and the structure of* Spoon River Anthology.]

From its beginnings in *Reedy's Mirror* and on through the expanded, definitive edition of 1916, the *Spoon River Anthology* was an immediate and outstanding success with both critics and public. People were shocked, scandalized, indignant, delighted. The muckrakers had been busily exposing the shame of the cities, President Roosevelt and others had denounced malefactors of great wealth, but the small town was still the official haven of innocence and virtue. Now came Masters' ghosts, avowing the presence of vice, corruption, greed, and pettiness in the American Arcadia. Their sexual behavior was scandalous; their frank candor violated strong taboos; their conventional religious views were masks for meanness; their genuine religious feelings were heterodox; and the language and the verse form in which they couched their sentiments were appropriately unconventional.

On the other hand, the portraits were strongly ironic, pathetic, heroic, comic; the quest for the good life and the good society, the god-seeking, the love of nature were on a level of high seriousness; a fundamental affection for traditional agrarian values informed the whole volume. Along with the notoriety due to scandal, came a fame based on the book's solid virtues. Ever since its first public prominence it has continued to lure new readers. Often reprinted, translated, and adapted, it has had the vitality to survive the times that gave it birth; and is by now an established American classic.

Judged by its setting and characters, the *Anthology* may be seen to illustrate the realist's dictum that one writes best about what one knows at first hand. Masters knew the life of central Illinois in the last third of the 19th century. (p. 53)

The subject was complex, and not to be separated from the poet's attitude toward it. The *Spoon River Anthology,* as he later wrote, was born out of long meditation upon the life of two Illinois small towns in which his immediate ancestors had lived since the early days of the state and in which he had spent most of his first twenty-two years. An equal number of years in Chicago had not effected his youthful experiences, nor

had the years taken the edge off his memories. However much his perspective had been broadened, he still found that his early years had provided him with a point of view for interpreting all human existence.

The towns of Petersburg and Lewistown lie on opposite sides of the Illinois River in the central part of the state. Petersburg lies two miles north of New Salem, remembered as Lincoln's home in the 1830's. . . . There Edgar Lee grew up amid legends of Lincoln and the pioneer days. He enjoyed long visits to the Masters farm, where the domestic atmosphere was more tranquil than in the home of his temperamentally mismatched parents. In 1880 the family moved fifty miles northward to Lewistown. The transplanting was not easy. The father's struggle for an adequate practice cast an unpleasant shadow over the first few difficult years. Eventually he did succeed; he became a leading citizen of Lewistown, was several times elected its mayor, and ofter served as a delegate to state and national Democratic caucuses.

In later years Masters remembered Petersburg with affection, but he wasted no love on Lewistown. Powerful elements in Lewistown opposed his father in political, religious, and economic principles, and the son remembered the life there as one of more or less constant strife. Then, too, the discord within the family was increasingly galling as he grew older. Eventually his father's opposition to his literary ambitions, among other things, led to the young man's departure. He went in the classic American manner to the big city—in this case Chicago—to make his own way as best he could. There he settled to the practice of law, hoping to gain the leisure to write. (pp. 54-5)

[Masters] soon concluded, he said, that the great world of the city and the smaller world of the rural town were essentially alike. This idea was to become his guiding theme in the *Anthology.*

He began, he said, with "casual experiments in related themes" and ended by creating "an epic rendition of modern life." His first few poems were free imitations of ancient lyrics from the *Greek Anthology.* As the influence of his American setting gained ground over that of his classical model, he began more and more insistently to write into the epitaphs the familial and community interrelationships that give most of the dramatic force to his creation. . . . Until one fourth of the way through the series, the author seems to have resisted naming forthrightly the village on which his imaginary community centered. Though he employed other place-names drawn from his native region—Chandlersville, Thompson's Lake, Clary's Grove, Proctor's Grove all turn up in the early epitaphs—nowhere did he mention either town in which he had lived as a boy. Characters based on memories of each community spoke instead of "the village." His problem seems plain. His fictional community had to represent *both* Lewistown and Petersburg. Eventually "the village" became "Spoon River," and in it the differing tendencies that Masters associated with the two historical towns were settled in disharmony. It was a simple solution to a problem that has never existed for his readers but for personal reasons was very real to Masters.

Masters appreciated the advantages of his solution. From the point of its introduction, the specific application of "Spoon River" to the village occurs in epitaph after epitaph. In rearranging the epitaphs for the first edition he saw to it that the town of Spoon River was mentioned in the early pages. . . . Even the extensive rearrangement in the first edition did not reflect strongly enough Masters' interest in the town as a corporate entity, and in the first fourteen pages of the second edition he added three epitaphs, **"Constance Hately,"** **"Harry Carey Goodhue,"** and **"Kinsey Keene,"** each of which mentions the town of Spoon River, the last two in great particularity. Harry Carey Goodhue lists specifically a number of the issues that divide the town: prohibition, taxes, public utilities. Kinsey Keene names the men who personify the institutions, dominating the town:

> . . . Thomas Rhodes, president of the bank;
> Coolbaugh Whedon, editor of the Argus;
> Rev. Peet, pastor of the leading church;
> A. D. Blood, several times Mayor of Spoon River;
> And finally all of you, members of the Social Purity
> Club—

With the advantages of such epitaphs, today's reader need not repeat the error, made even by Masters' close friend Reedy, of overstressing the individual portraiture, important as that is, at the expense of the dramatic battle over the form that community life should take. So striking is the portraiture that even the . . . Broadway adaptation of *Spoon River* emphasized the nostalgic mood of recollection with which Masters began ("Where are Elmer, Herman, Bert, Tom, and Charlie—"). But it was Masters' satirical critique of contemporary America that soon became his central theme. In such epitaphs as Kinsey Keene's the acrimonious feuds of Lewistown between the liberals and "the party of law and order," as Masters satirically has people call it, are fought out once more. Not until later epitaphs does he emphasize the mellower spirit that he associated with Petersburg and the older pioneer generation.

Though the battle in Spoon River has many petty manifestations, the basic issue is momentous. Masters is writing of that transitional period in our history when a predominantly rural society adhering in principle to Jeffersonian-agrarian ideals was in the throes of change into the urban-dominated society we know today. He portrays society as an arena in which conflicting ideals battle to become institutionalized. The issue is joined; society is in flux, the outcome uncertain. The central question is whether social institutions shall favor the many or the few, whether the forms of life shall permit each person the largest possible freedom to work out his own destiny or whether those forms shall limit individual options. For him to do this required that he make his village society mirror the issues of the nation at large; this led him to portray village life in a way that was for his times little short of heretical. (pp. 55-7)

Masters' simple assertion of common nature and motives in city and country people was not only shocking but liberating, helping to give his poems a scandalous reputation.

The perspective of years has made it plain that Masters' love for his rural society led him to excoriate its evils the more bitterly. Petit the Poet sings of

> Life all around me here in the village
> Tragedy, comedy, valor and truth,
> Courage, constancy, heroism, failure. . . .

In this he speaks for Masters himself. The individual portraits portray the gamut of human emotions, desires, compulsions; and petty viciousness in one character is balanced by grandeur of soul in another. Far from repudiating the American pastoral myth, Masters made it central in his thought; but he was aware that the agrarian ideal differed from the actual condition of life in his times. Both sides of a dichotomy in American thought were present even in the rural community. Basically this dichotomy was between the urge to freedom, which he associated with Jefferson, and the urge to repression, which he identified with Hamilton. He did not limit his polarity to economics and politics; he saw it influencing attitudes toward religion and morality as well. One can see the polarity in the epitaph of Kinsey Keene, already quoted. It is present just as explicitly in **"Jefferson Howard,"** who speaks of "my father's beliefs from old Virginia: / Hating slavery, but no less war," and lists his opponents "here in Spoon River, with its dominant forces drawn from New England, / Republicans, Calvinists, merchants, bankers." Such a formulation of the issue extends the scope of *Spoon River Anthology* in space and time. The golden age of the Republic lies in earlier days, before the Civil War brought about the dominance of Hamiltonian impulses. The battle, though a losing one, continues.

Masters' Jeffersonianism shared the pragmatic spirit of the Progressive era. For him, freedom was quintessential to human life. Truth required continual testing in action and a man had to be free to seek his own truth because no received truth could be trusted to point the way. The inadequacy of convention in sexual mores and economic affairs was for him proved by its manifest failures to achieve order and justice. The libertarian position receives support by inference whenever the rules for life laid down by "preachers and judges" fail. The lives of people in the *Anthology* contradict conventional wisdom at every turn. Hod Putt, highwayman and inadvertent murderer, asserts his kinship to the rich man who used law to achieve ends that the law should rightly oppose. Of course Hod Putt is a guilty man; he recognizes it. More significant, however, than the question of his guilt is his interest in justice. If society values justice, but does not so order itself that justice is the rule, then it is as guilty of moral failure as Hod Putt the murderer; and that is what The Circuit Judge himself asserts. Editor Hamblin makes the same point generally and figuratively in attacking perversion of justice in the Haymarket case. Justice, proverbially blind, and no respecter of persons, is now too often no respecter of guilt or innocence. Sometimes the blindness of convention may be not legal but moral, as in the case of the Charles Blisses, whose incompatible marriage was continued on the urgings of Rev. Wiley and Judge Somers ("preachers and judges"), to the irreparable harm of the children. By the pragmatic test of results, the inadequacy of conventional views of marriage is evident.

The attack on provincial dogmatism is conducted with the village's own favorite weapon—the specific example. By the equally pragmatic test of mutual fulfillment, the Matlocks demonstrate that for some at least marriage is indeed a sublime institution. Therefore, the purport of one epitaph or group of epitaphs may be contradicted by one equally as convincing. Who could unreservedly uphold dogmatic views in the light of such confusing evidence? The welter of cases supporting every sort of conclusion does not, however, lead to complete skepticism. Masters' own moral bias is clearly on the side of the greatest possible freedom for each man to seek in his own way the meaning of life; and the best social organization is that which enhances personal freedom to the fullest extent. The Village Atheist states, "Immortality is not a gift, / Immortality is an achievement; / And only those who strive mightily / Shall possess it." The ideal form of life will least inhibit the quest.

Knowing both small town and city, and critical of both, Masters found the illustrations for his themes in the fabric of nineteenth century life. It is clear enough, from the shock of repudiation in the communities concerned, that Lewistown and Petersburg furnished a wealth of individual touches for the portraits. It is not so easily noticed that Chicago too contributed numerous characters and incidents. The Chicago Haymarket affair enters under its own name, and Lambert Hutchens refers directly to the giveaway by the Illinois legislature of the Chicago lake front to the Illinois Central Railroad. . . . Would the attacks on the small town plutocrat Thomas Rhodes, or the prostitute journalist Coolbaugh Whedon have been so vehement if they had not been the representatives of so much that Masters hated in industrial Chicago? Chicago, Masters knew, represented the shape of things to come, the final disappearance of the heroic pioneer era. The sense of loss, of life and vitality slipping away, that often seems like a paradoxical nostalgia for the communities of his youth (and later, in his glorification of Petersburg, became just that), is far more the expression of emotional involvement in a battle largely lost in Chicago but still raging in Spoon River.

This battle of a pre-industrial way of life now on the wane against the advancing era of the megalopolis, as Masters called it, was a rearguard action which Masters knew must result in defeat. In 1924, ten years after writing *Spoon River,* Masters returned to the subject and style in *The New Spoon River.* Much of the lesser dramatic power in the later book results from the loss of tension between rival value systems, for Chicago has won, and Spoon River is no longer the largely autonomous community it once had been: it has instead become "a ganglion for the monster brain Chicago." Megalopolis has triumphed.

Even as the epitaphs were appearing in the *Mirror,* Reedy noted that the poems were partly an elegy "of the country's declining heroic age, of the age in which came to first acuteness the personal problem of life multiplying complications." Since the Civil War, Reedy went on, "materialism came into rule and more and more idealists in Spoon River and elsewhere went down to dusty defeat." This may sound like an exceptional view from a liberal editor in 1914, just two years after Woodrow Wilson had led triumphant progressivism into power. But both populism and progressivism, for all their reformist tendencies, were basically holding actions, attempting to keep alive the cherished pre-industrial way of life by counteracting the forces that were destroying it. Nostalgia and a sense of loss were the other side of the energetic, hopeful progressive coin. Even as the poems were appearing, war had broken out in Europe, and soon the glorious faith in progress was to disintegrate, under the pressure of world-wide devastation, into the cynicism and selfishness of the 1920's. Therefore, even in its twilight mood the *Spoon River Anthology* is a faithful reflection of its era, recording hopes and fears, successes and failures, confidence and bewilderment, of a time which an historical cataclysm was bringing to a dismaying end.

Because Masters was what he was, the book can be this record of a particular moment in history and at the same time an intensely personal book. Not only had Masters the wealth of intimate knowledge of the life he portrayed; he had also felt in a personal way the peculiar qualities of desperation and resignation that inform the book and catch so authentically an emotional-intellectual mood of that historical moment. The anguish of the defeated souls is Masters' own anguish; the joy of the fewer victorious souls, and the serenity of the "enlightened spirits" on their rarified level above the battle, are Masters' compensatory vision. The tone of ironic mockery, which Masters mistakenly allowed to become dominant in the weak "Spooniad" and much weaker "Epilogue," is in part the self-mockery of a man who measures the slight worth of petty daily struggles at which he expends his best energies, knowing all the while that these struggles cannot be abandoned. Rarely is a book so truly the distilled essence of a personal experience that includes so much of the experience of its times.

It is curious that many of America's best books fit uneasily in recognizable genres. *Walden, Moby Dick, Leaves of Grass,* and the *Education of Henry Adams* are only the most illustrious examples. The *Spoon River Anthology* is another of these unique works. This uniqueness begins with the table of contents, with its alphabetical listing, like a town directory. The first poem, "The Hill," sets up an ironical relationship with traditional high culture by echoing the *ubi sunt* ["where are"] formula, which goes back to antiquity. The well known Rosetti translation of Villon's "Ballade of Dead Ladies," with its melancholy refrain, "Where are the snows of yesteryear?" is echoed by Petit the Poet: "The snows and roses of yesterday are faded, and what is love but a rose that fades?" But the highly conventional form of the ballads contrasts sharply with the free verse stanzas of Masters' poem, just as the highborn ladies who are the poetically suitable subject matter of the older poem contrast with the commonplace villagers of whom Masters writes. One is poetry of an elite, educated class; the other, poetry of comparatively classless democratic society. Through these contrasts Masters demands for his subjects the dignity reserved by ancient convention for more exalted figures.

The body of the work sustains this demand. The chief literary dept is to the lyrics of the classical Greek Anthology. Here again, the very name Masters chooses—*Spoon River Anthology*—raises ironic echoes of an old tradition; but does the echo imply a flattering comparison or a mocking contrast between the insignificant modern community and the great civilization of antiquity? Masters' poems purport to be epitaphs spoken by the dead subjects themselves, just as the confessional epitaph is a chief mode in the older collection. The brevity and concentration of his epitaphs follows the epigrammatic convention of the Greek poems. Indeed, some of the poems, like "The Unknown" and "Alexander Throckmorton," read almost like direct translations from the older work. Even the names assigned to some of the speakers, names such as Cassius, Amanda, and Ollie, raise classical echoes, not only because of obvious Latin etymologies but because as printed in the *Mirror* a number of them stood without surnames, suggesting an older practice of naming rather than the contemporary American practice. There was also a touch of an older practice in the use of generic names, such as Griffy the Cooper, Theodore the Poet, Schroeder the Fisherman, and The Town Marshal. (pp. 58-63)

Though most readers are impressed by the freedom of the verse in the *Anthology,* Masters moved progressively toward the use of conventional metrics, lines, and stanzaic patterns. Such a poem as "Petit the Poet" is in four-stress lines throughout, and if one observes the end punctuation one finds divisions into quatrains and a couplet, much as in a conventional sonnet. Similarly, "Fletcher McGee" is in traditional English ballad stanzas, and lacks only the rhymes to be conventional verse. A large number of the poems are in a fairly regular iambic tetrameter or pentameter, but the overall impression is still of free verse.

While the length of his epitaphs tended to increase beyond the limits of the epigrammatic convention, many of the later ones running a full page and more, the epigrammatic nature of Masters' models may have encouraged him to employ a sort of sharply worded summation, usually made more emphatic by a falling cadence in the last line, achieved by shortening it a foot or more. Ami Green concludes:

> . . . the much-sought prize of eternal youth
> Is just arrested growth.

Alexander Throckmorton says:

> But my weary wings could not follow my vision—
> Genius is wisdom and youth.

An outstanding example, because it also shows Masters employing a rare degree of alliteration and assonance, is the ending of **"William H. Herndon"**:

> As the cawing crows winged their way to the wood
> Over my house-top at solemn sunsets,
> There by my window,
> Alone.

Such devices, often effective in themselves, in their recurrence create the uniformity of tone pervading the volume.

In the individual poems, little attempt is made to adapt the style of the speech to the station and character of the speaker. There is even a certain monotony of diction that makes prolonged reading in a single sitting somewhat tedious. Yet this slightly monotonous language of the plain-spoken lawyer's brief is extremely functional; blunt and unbeautiful, it carries an air of conviction that a suaver diction probably would not. The very matter-of-factness contributes to the intensity of feeling. The speech is authentically Midwestern, though not in the idiomatic vernacular fashion of Mark Twain or Ring Lardner. It is rather the language of the public record, found in newspaper and court report. The touches of an older stock poetic diction ("Behold," "lo!," "O soul," "Ye living ones") may seem intrusions in this speech, yet can be justified as remainders of the ironical relation these poems bear to the poetic tradition. They sound, not inappropriately, like the clumsy attempts at literary language of people not fully at home with it. The frequent use of sturdy home-grown metaphor and simile, earnest, intense, and groping rather than graceful, precise, or pleasing, keeps the speech concrete and vivid, and avoids the diffusion and abstraction of ordinary newspaper or official prose. Toward the end, the opposite fault of murky and imprecise symbolism is less defensible.

While the characters speak, one is hardly conscious of the manipulations of the author. Only when Masters carries certain devices too far or repeats them too often do we lose the sense of authenticity. In poetry, and even in life, names may suggest character, but how far one wishes to indulge Masters' fondness for such names is a matter of taste. Excessively obvious parallels such as **"Robert Fulton Tanner"** (an inventor), **"Margaret Fuller Black"** (a would-be writer), and **"Jonathan Swift Somers"** (a satirist) are fortunately fewer than names formed by recombining the names of actual people of the communities in which he grew up. The "occupation analogy" is another device that is too transparent to bear much repetition, and there are a good many of these analogies. The dentist, the laundress, the weaver, the gardener, the chicken farmer, the piano tuner, the cooper, and many others use the language of their callings to interpret the meaning of life. Despite these and a few other traces of writing to formula, the book as a whole teems with individual life.

If their language is largely undifferentiated, the characters speak out of their own personal experiences as interpreted through their own individual outlooks. They come from every station in the life of their time and place, from nearly every occupation, sect, racial background, and level of society. The actors who dramatized Spoon River portraits on the Broadway stage occasionally employed slurred endings and local accents to make "characters" out of some of them. It made effective drama, but it allowed a condescension toward certain speakers that the leveling effect of Masters' constant diction does not encourage. In the *Anthology* all the speakers share a passionate concern with life that gives them all—the wise, the foolish, the good, the vicious—a seriousness demanding respect. They step forward as before the final bar of judgment, and they speak their inmost thoughts in recognition of the awesome finality of their pleas. We feel, not that they necessarily speak truth, but that they necessarily speak what they believe to be truth. They lack the slightest trace of the duplicity that unavoidably attends speech among the living. Where the truth lies is for the reader himself to judge. If the book is regarded as a novel in verse, as some early reviewers called it, it illustrates the illusion of objectivity for which Henry James praised the dramatic point of view.

However moving individual pieces in the *Anthology* may be, they do not show to best advantage when removed from the context of the collection. One epitaph supports and modifies another as chord modulates chord in symphonic music. The connections are various. There is first the circumstance that all the characters are or have been in some sense part of the same nineteenth century mid-American community called Spoon River, so that each contributes to the complex definition of that place and time. Beyond that, groups of characters are "interlocked by fate," as Masters said, in more intimate fashion. A group of connected epitaphs may tell a story, as in the case of the Pantiers, the Merritts, or Lambert Hutchins and his daughter. Epitaphs placed side by side may gain ironic power through contrast, as with Albert Schirding and Jonas Keene, or epitaphs refer to the same incidents, showing how events ramify and touch many lives, as in the case of the bank failure. Sometimes a series of epitaphs seem to form a colloquy, searchingly examining a topic from a number of viewpoints, as in the case of Henry Phipps, Harry Wilmans, John Wasson, and **"Many Soldiers,"** who discuss, directly or by implication, the nation's adventures in war. The passionate concern with finding meaning in their own lives and in life in general serves as the common denominator uniting an amazing range of material.

Not all of the characters conduct their search for meaning on the same level. Masters distinguished a three-fold division among his creations, claiming that as the portraits are arranged in the book, "the fools, the drunkards, and the failures came first, the people of one-birth minds got second place, and the heroes and enlightened spirits came last, a sort of Divine Comedy. Unfortunately, no simple three-fold arrangement is discernable in the book. This does not mean, though, that we should dismiss Masters' remark. In fact, there does seem to be a subtle progression, and by the last pages a change is obvious. Toward the end we do find a concentration of "heroes and enlightened spirits," just as he said. The overall progression could perhaps be described as moving from pettiness of vision to largeness of vision, and consequently from agitation and discord to serenity and harmony of soul. If Masters did have in mind an increasing breadth of vision, his "fools, drunkards and failures" might include those who think primarily in petty personal terms, his "people of one-birth minds" those who view human life in the context of the social world, and his "heroes and enlightened spirits" those whose vision transcends the personal and social to reach the universal. (pp. 64-7)

One must avoid emphasis on any one of these levels at the expense of the others. Early critics concentrated on the first level, and therefore likened the book to village gossip. Masters himself seemed to be aware of the danger of this, since the epitaphs added to the second edition tend in a number of cases to strengthen the second level by emphasizing the public issues in the early pages. The third level, on which most readers seem to find the book least impressive, is nevertheless prominently displayed in the final section of the book, and demonstrates that Masters wished to place the personal and the social in a perspective that denied them the final importance in life. An enviable calm pervading the final section contrasts sharply with the agitation that runs through the rest of the book. The "heroes and enlightened spirits" seem to have achieved a high degree of harmony with the essential nature of things. (p. 68)

Since the *Anthology* proper does end on this comparatively elevated plane, what can be said for the "Spooniad," which concludes the first edition, and what indeed for the "Epilogue," added at the end of the second edition? The "Spooniad" does, to be sure, draw in its burlesque fashion the line dividing the community into two contending camps, and it may be, as has been claimed, a parody of Milton's war in heaven in *Paradise Lost*. Most readers nevertheless find it heavy handed as well as unnecessary. Even worse is the "Epilogue," a relapse into the Shelleyesque conventions of Masters' earlier verse, bad as poetry and contradictory in implication to the epitaphs taken as a whole. (p. 69)

> Robert Narveson, " 'Spoon River Anthology': An Introduction," in MidAmerica, Vol. VII, 1980, pp. 52-72.

JOHN H. WRENN AND MARGARET M. WRENN (essay date 1983)

[*Margaret M. Wrenn is an American critic; John H. Wrenn is an American critic and educator. In the following excerpt from their biographical and critical study of Masters, they discuss the poetry that followed* Spoon River Anthology.]

On 15 January 1915, Edgar Lee Masters published his own epitaph as "Webster Ford" in *Reedy's Mirror*. *Spoon River* was finished: a few days later Masters was desperately ill with pneumonia. (p. 68)

Masters recovered in a few months from his pneumonia. But he never recovered from the success of *Spoon River Anthology*. And he never fully understood it. While the praises and approbation of the book were still building, Masters was objecting to his friends that he could do better, nay had done better, in a direction quite different from *Spoon River*.

Almost immediately the publishers were clamoring for another book.... Masters soon obliged with *Songs and Satires* and *The Great Valley*. At the time, he was writing additional *Spoon River* poems and the epilogue for the definitive edition. His close friend Eunice Tietjens remembers: "He would always in those days pull out a few more *Spoon River* sketches from his pocket and read them to us. And he used to look at me with a puzzled expression showing through his very justifiable pride, and ask: 'But why are these so much better than my other things? What makes people praise these and pay no attention to the others?' I tried to explain, but even then I could see it was no use. He could not understand" [see Additional Bibliography].

Harriet Monroe, writing her memoirs at the same time as Tietjens, had similar recollections: . . . "After the success of *Spoon River* . . . (when) he came to our office to show me the proofs of a proposed second book, I was aghast at discovering that he proposed to open it with the Launcelot and Elaine narrative of his ineffectual earlier period. My protest was emphatic. I can still see the puzzled look on his face" [see Additional Bibliography]. This second book . . . , *Songs and Satires*, indeed took a quite different direction from *Spoon River*—the direction of "his ineffectual earlier period." Half its poems he had published before 1912. Heeding Harriet Monroe's pleas, Masters opened the book with the poem "Silence." . . . (pp. 68-9)

"Silence," a Whitmanesque poem of seventy lines, sounds more like one of Sandburg's better poems than like the best of *Spoon River*. And it ends somewhat sententiously with "the silence" of those who have died and the lesson that it "shall be interpreted" to us as we "approach" our own deaths. In "The Vision," as early as page eighteen of *Songs and Satires*, we have a stream flowing "amidst our well beloved vale," and we are off not only in a different direction but in a different century of the past. If we persevere, we come near the end to the Launcelot narrative, written in imitation of medieval diction, with which Masters proposed to introduce his book. The knight visits the dead queen, kisses "the ceréd cloth," observing in "his woe" the perfection of her features, for "her nose was clear as snow." We forbear further comment.

The critics' disappointment is no surprise, though Masters's deep resentment is. As a man of his time, Masters evidently agreed with the critics who disliked *Spoon River* that poetry should generally adhere to a regular metric, such as the blank verse and ballad stanza of the two poems mentioned just above; that rhyme is desirable; that the diction should be "poetic," including frequent inversions. Masters's surprise at Reedy's acceptance of his first epitaphs and his perplexity at the critics' preference for his *Spoon River* poems was quite genuine. To him the *Anthology* really was in a direction quite other than what he considered his natural bent as a poet.

Nevertheless, with its publication he had crossed Spoon River, as imposing a stream figuratively as Caesar's Rubicon. He could not turn back. He was right in assuming that his gaining a reputation as a poet would ruin his legal practice. After *Spoon River* he had one large case; that was all, though he maintained a law office in the Loop in Chicago until 1920. The success of *Spoon River* committed him to a role as poet. He now turned his prodigious energy to filling the role and to finding the other direction in which his true talents lay. In the succeeding quarter century he published twenty volumes of poetry, seven novels, seven biographies (if we include studies of Whitman and Emerson, in which he allows his subjects to speak largely for themselves), and wrote at least twelve plays (two of them performed at colleges), and two historical studies. All of them were competent and none was much more than that.

Masters himself . . . preferred *Domesday Book* and its sequel *The Fate of the Jury* to his famous *Anthology*. The novel *Mitch Miller* was the book closest to his heart. (pp. 69-70)

[By] 1919 he had published not only the expanded "definitive" edition of the *Anthology*, but *Songs and Satires*, and a two-volume contribution to a Midwestern epic, *The Great Valley* and *Toward the Gulf*. Like their successors, they develop a unity of theme principally in the water imagery of their titles. The successors are *Starved Rock* . . . , *The Open Sea*, and *The New Atlantis*, published as *The New World*. Some of the poems of each develop the history of the area and its people. The last in particular is a sustained and unified historical narrative of America from pre-Columbian discoveries to the 1930s. But it lacks a protagonist and dramatic intensity, and it is unified chiefly by Masters's anger at the greed for gold. It was his last attempt at a long narrative poem. The four others are collections of poems, some of regional history, some lyrics, some character descriptions (more elaborate versions of the *Spoon River* genre), with a certain amount of political, social, and religious satire, often with a scientific or psychological emphasis. Especially in the lyrics, but in many other poems as well, the reader who knows Masters's autobiography will be on familiar ground. In fact this autobiographical thread can add a certain interest to otherwise unprepossessing volumes. (pp. 71-2)

The year after *The New Spoon River* Masters published his *Selected Poems.* The volume ends with twenty poems from *Spoon River* and eighteen from *The New Spoon River*, but nearly 400 preceding pages offer poems largely in conventional metrics with a wide range of mood and subject, grouped under such headings as "Dramatic Portraits," "Stories in Verse," "Lyrics and Sonnets," "Dithyrambs," "Poems of Reflection." Again the new directions are a return to the . . . older traditions of poetry. (pp. 72-3)

In 1933 came a small volume, *The Serpent in the Wilderness.* Its principal piece, **"Beethoven's Ninth Symphony and the King Cobra,"** is a long prose-poem which may owe something—in subject, metrics, and point of view—to D. H. Lawrence's poem "The Snake," published a decade earlier. A number of critics found it an impressive treatment of the problem of evil, symbolized by the monism of the cobra as opposed to the dualism of man. It narrates the responses of a caged cobra to the music of Beethoven played on the radio. Like the majority of Masters's poetry after *Spoon River* and like many of the later, added *Spoon River* poems, the set of poems in *The Serpent in the Wilderness* might be called opinion-poems or idea-poems, presenting rather direct conclusions from the poet's thought, such as his faith in science, his hatred of the Judaeo-Christian ethic as opposed to the Greek, his paradoxical love of nature and attraction to the city, his consciousness of evil, usually symbolized by the venomous snake. *Invisible Landscapes* continues these preoccupations, particularly nature-worship, including nostalgic reminiscences of Masters's childhood—**"New Salem Hill," "Concord Church," "Sandridge," "The Old Farm."** Here again the central poem is **"Beethoven's Ninth Symphony and the King Cobra."**

In *Poems of People*, published the same year as *Across Spoon River*, and in *More People*, which followed three years later, Masters returned to the portrait genre of *Spoon River.* In about one fifth of the poems in *More People*, he returned even to *Spoon River* events and persons. . . . (p. 73)

Domesday Book, takes a different direction from these other post-*Spoon River* collections of poems. It is a long dramatic narrative, or rather a series of dramatic monologues, in blank verse telling a single story. Its origin is an unpublished story from Masters's Lewistown days concerning the differing accounts of witnesses to a suicide. (p. 74)

The story centers on the death of Elenor Murray, whose body is discovered by a hunter on the shore of the Illinois River, much as a woman's body is discovered by Mitch Miller and his friend Skeeters in the novel *Mitch Miller*, also published in 1920. . . .

The story emerges somewhat in the manner of the *Spoon River* narrative, insofar as it is a narrative of intertwined lives and events. The coroner, Merival, speaking for the author, decides to create his own "Domesday Book" through which he can reveal the nation's "tenures spiritual" . . . , as King William's Domesday Book contained a tabulation of his kingdom's assets and resources, human and material. All those who can be found who knew Elenor testify in a series of monologues giving a composite picture of her life and of the American scene from about 1890 to 1920. The monologues are considerably longer than those of *Spoon River*, which gives them and the narrative a certain diffuseness never overcome by the single subject, the life and death of Elenor Murray. Actually, there is more than a single subject, since Elenor's story is intended, even by the coroner, to represent America's "tenures spiritual." (p. 75)

The characters Masters presents as heroes or heroines of all his narratives, poetic and fictional and dramatic, are in many ways typically American and quite believable. They are usually first presented, like the archetypal Huck Finn, as oppressed by circumstance and by the avarice, hypocrisy, ill will of others. All of them struggle to break out, to find their own "beauty" or "peace" through self-expression. Some of them find a tentative or transient satisfaction, usually in premarital or extramarital love. Somewhat in contrast to the few saved souls in *Spoon River*, almost none of the characters of Masters's fiction achieve fulfillment. Most of them, particularly the protagonists, seem to seek sensation rather than peace or beauty, and they indeed find it. But, and here we are closer to *Spoon River* again, only the pioneers and those who follow the old life-style find true fulfillment. It is as though order and discipline had disappeared from American life with the generation of pioneers, and even Masters, who acutely felt the loss of these fundamental values, could not recapture them. In *Domesday Book*, and in its sequel, *The Fate of the Jury*, there are none of these pioneers.

The Fate of the Jury is one of Masters's many epilogues. One might say even that he had a weakness for the epilogue—a concluding section intended to round out the design and clarify the meaning of the work. Hence the blank verse mock-heroic **"Spooniad,"** which concluded the first edition of *Spoon River* in 1915, and the second afterthought, actually entitled **"Epilogue,"** added to the definitive edition of 1916. Hence *The Fate of the Jury*, which follows the lives of the coroner's jury which had meticulously examined the life and death of Elenor Murray and the "riffles," or impingements, of her life on others. Seven of those others are now seen to be the jurors themselves and the coroner Merival, whom her death has brought together. (pp. 76-7)

The plot of the book is to have each jury member reveal, before his death, the controlling secret of his life—a continuation of the confessional character of *Domesday Book* and of *Spoon River.* (p. 77)

Intrinsically *The Fate of the Jury* has less to recommend it to the nonspecialist reader than *Domesday Book*. As a coda to the earlier work, it cannot quite stand alone. The blank verse is sustained but regular in tone: all the characters speak with the voice of Edgar Lee Masters, and act out much of his biography as well. (p. 79)

John H. Wrenn and Margaret M. Wrenn, in their Edgar Lee Masters, *Twayne Publishers, 1983, 144 p.*

ADDITIONAL BIBLIOGRAPHY

Bishop, John Peale. "The Intelligence of Poets." In his *The Collected Essays of John Peale Bishop*, edited by Edmund Wilson, pp. 263-69. New York: Charles Scribner's Sons, 1948.
    Discusses E. A. Robinson, Ezra Pound, and Masters as poets skilled in bringing "humor, irony, and incisive knowledge of life" to their poetry.

Bogan, Louise. "The 'American Renaissance,' 1912-1917." In her *Achievement in American Poetry, 1900-1950*, pp. 33-48. Chicago: Gateway Editions, 1951.
    Places Masters in relation to other figures of the Chicago Renaissance of the early twentieth century, praising *Spoon River Anthology* as his best work.

Burgess, Charles. "Masters and Some Mentors." *Papers on Language and Literature* 10, No. 2 (Spring 1974): 175-201.
    Notes some biographies, histories, and works of local fiction that may have influenced Masters in writing the Spoon River books.

———. "Ancestral Lore in *Spoon River Anthology:* Fact and Fancy." *Papers on Language and Literature* 20, No. 2 (Spring 1984): 185-204.
    Examines the extent to which Masters drew from his own family's history in composing some of the Spoon River poems.

Crawford, John W. "A Defense of 'A One-Eyed View'." *The CEA Critic* XXXI, No. 5 (February 1969): 14-15.
    Response to the Earnest essay of 1968 excerpted in this volume. Crawford emphasizes that he has only identified naturalistic tendencies in *Spoon River Anthology*, and has not labelled Masters a naturalist poet, although he maintains that the *Spoon River* poems display "a strong bias toward naturalism."

Derleth, August. "Edgar Lee Masters." In his *Three Literary Men: Sinclair Lewis, Sherwood Anderson, Edgar Lee Masters*, pp. 37-56. New York: Candlelight Press, 1963.
    Anecdotal account of Masters's life and career containing many transcribed conversations between Derleth and Masters.

Deutsch, Babette. "Returning to Realism." In her *This Modern Poetry*, pp. 33-56. New York: W. W. Norton & Co., 1935.
    Cites *Spoon River Anthology* as an example of "the rebirth of poetry" in the early twentieth century.

Duffy, Bernard. "Edgar Lee Masters: The Advent of Liberation." In his *The Chicago Renaissance in American Letters: A Critical History*, pp. 143-70. Westport, Conn.: Greenwood Press, 1954.
    Biographically oriented discussion of the works Masters produced while living in Chicago.

Eliot, T. S. "Reflections on *Vers Libre*." *The New Statesman* VIII, No. 204 (3 March 1917): 518-19.
    Maintains that vers libre is not a genuine verse form. In the essay Eliot briefly mentions that in *Spoon River Anthology* Masters was wrong not "to have perceived the simple truth that *some* artificial limitation is necessary" to poetry.

Flanagan, John T. *Edgar Lee Masters: The Spoon River Poet and His Critics*. Metuchen, N.J.: Scarecrow Press, 1974, 175 p.
    Surveys the critical reception of Masters's poetry and prose.

Frank, Waldo. "Chicago." In his *Our America*, pp. 117-47. New York: Boni and Liveright, 1919.
    Lyrical description of Chicago with brief mention of Masters as a member of the "generation which has found passionate voice" after coming to the city from the farmlands of the American Midwest.

Gilman, Lawrence. "Moving-Picture Poetry." *North American Review* CCII, No. 717 (August 1915): 271-76.
    Describes the "free verse" of *Spoon River Anthology* as "the cinematographing of narrative-verse," "a kind of moving-picture in the form of fictional verse."

Gosse, Edmund. "Domesday Book." In his *More Books on the Table*, pp. 353-58. New York: Charles Scribner's Sons, 1923.
    Very negative review of the long narrative poem *The Domesday Book*.

Hartley, Lois. *Spoon River Revisited*. Muncie, Ind.: Ball State Monograph Number One, 1961, 30 p.
    Description of the structure and content of *Spoon River Anthology* with some discussion of critical reaction.

———. "Edgar Lee Masters, Political Essayist." *Journal of the Illinois State Historical Society* LVII, No. 3 (Autumn 1964): 249-60.
    Descriptive and analytical discussion of Masters's political writings in *The New Star Chamber, The Constitution and Our Insular Possessions*, and individual contributions to various periodicals.

———. "The Early Plays of Edgar Lee Masters." *Ball State University Forum* VII, No. 2 (Spring 1966): 26-38.
    Finds Masters's plays "of limited and specific interest" to a full understanding of Masters as an important early twentieth-century literary figure, primarily because they contain themes that recur in his later work.

Hertz, Robert N. "Two Voices of the American Village: Robinson and Masters." *The Minnesota Review* II, No. 3 (Spring 1968): 345-58.
    Discusses the differences in perception of small-town life that are evident in the Tilbury Town poems of E. A. Robinson and the Spoon River poems of Masters.

Hilfer, Anthony Channell. "Masters and Anderson." In his *The Revolt from the Village: 1915-1930*, pp. 137-57. Chapel Hill: University of North Carolina Press, 1969.
    Contends that *Spoon River Anthology* and *Winesburg, Ohio* are both books built "around isolated characters . . . unified by their reflection of the spiritual quality of the town, by the common theme of the buried life, and by the tone of naturalistic pathos qualified by irony," adding that "the major difference between the books is that while Masters' characters hide their feelings, Anderson's inarticulate characters hardly know what their feelings are."

Howells, William Dean. "Editor's Easy Chair." *Harper's Magazine* CXXXI, No. DCCLXXXIV (September 1915): 634-35.
    Terms much modern poetry "shredded verse" and finds that it is only "when the strong thinking of Mr. Masters makes us forget the formlessness of his shredded prose that we realise the extraordinary worth of his work" in *Spoon River Anthology*.

Masters, Hardin Wallace. *Edgar Lee Masters: A Biographical Sketchbook About a Famous American Author*. Rutherford, N.J.: Fairleigh Dickinson University Press, 1978.
    Series of brief sketches of incidents in Masters's life written by his oldest son.

Masters, Hilary. *Last Stand: Notes from Memory*. New York: McGraw-Hill Book Co., 1982, 210 p.
    Reminiscence by Masters's son by his second marriage, combining Hilary Masters's own memories with accounts of family history told to him by his parents and grandparents.

Mencken, H. L. "The New Poetry Movement." In his *Prejudices: First Series*, pp. 83-96. New York: Alfred A. Knopf, 1919.
    Scathingly pronounces Masters "already extinct," disparaging the popular success of *Spoon River Anthology* and terming Masters's subsequent poetry "empty doggerel."

———. "Edgar Lee Masters." *The American Mercury* II, No. 6 (June 1924): 250-52.
    Mixed review of Masters's novel *Mirage:* "one of the most idiotic and yet one of the most interesting American novels that I have ever read."

Monroe, Harriet. "Combat and Company." In her *A Poet's Life: Seventy Years in a Changing World*, pp. 362-85. New York: Macmillan Co., 1938.
    Chronicles the second year of *Poetry*'s publication, with references to Masters's involvement with the magazine. Monroe explains why she believes Masters never equalled the poetic accomplishment of *Spoon River Anthology*.

Primeau, Ronald. *Beyond "Spoon River": The Legacy of Edgar Lee Masters*. Austin: University of Texas Press, 1981, 217 p.

Reassessment of Masters's place in American literature focusing on his neglected works.

Schreiber, Georges, and Masters, Edgar Lee. "Edgar Lee Masters." In *Portraits and Self-Portraits,* edited by Georges Schreiber, pp. 91-4. Boston: Houghton Mifflin Co., 1936.

Portrait of Masters by Schreiber, together with a brief autobiographical essay by Masters.

Untermeyer, Louis. "Edgar Lee Masters." In his *American Poetry since 1900,* pp. 113-32. N.Y.: Henry Holt and Co., 1923.

Maintains that all of Masters's poetry preceding and following *Spoon River Anthology* is vastly inferior to it: "With *Spoon River Anthology* Masters arrived—and left. . . . In that one extended burst, Masters accomplished greatness; he wrote not only a powerful book but a popular one."

Wells, Henry W. "Varieties of American Poetic Drama." *The Literary Half-Yearly* XIV, No. 2 (July 1973): 14-46.

Discusses Masters's contributions to socially conscious verse drama.

Wright, Willard Huntington. "Mr. Masters' 'Spoon River Anthology': A Criticism." *The Forum* LV (January 1916): 109-13.

Blasts *Spoon River Anthology* as aesthetically and philosophically inadequate, unrealistic, and lacking in originality.

Yust, Walter. "Edgar Lee Masters: An Interview." *The Double Dealer* II, Nos. 8-9 (August-September 1921): 79-83.

Transcription of a casual interview with Masters interspersed with details about his career.

S(amuel) E(dward) K(rune Loliwe) Mqhayi

1875-1945

South African poet, biographer, novelist, short story writer, lyricist, autobiographer, and translator.

Mqhayi is recognized as a leading Xhosa-language poet and prose writer. He is remembered primarily for his *izibongo*, traditional African lyric poems that gained him the title *imbongi yesizwe*, equivalent to poet laureate of his people. Hailed by Albert S. Gerard as "perhaps the last of the great tribal bards" for his contributions to Xhosa poetry, Mqhayi is also credited with introducing the Western genre of prose fiction into Xhosa literature in the early twentieth century. According to R.H.W. Shepherd: "His contributions to Xhosa literature . . . were outstanding in quality, and by them and in other ways he helped in no small measure to stabilize and purify the Xhosa language."

Mqhayi was born in Gqumahashe (or Gqamahashe) in the Victoria East District of Cape Province. He attended school in Evergreen from 1882 to 1885, when his family moved to Centane in the Transkei, where Mqhayi's great-uncle Ngonzana (or Nzazana) was a local chieftain. Mqhayi took great interest in the official activities he witnessed at his uncle's judicial court, the "Great Place," and he later wrote: "I thank my father for taking me to Centane, for it was the means of my getting an insight into the national life of my people." After completing a teaching course, Mqhayi worked as an educator and journalist for several years. During that time he contributed to influential Xhosa newspapers and periodicals, including *Izwi labantu* and *Imvo zabantsundu*, which he edited from 1920 to 1922. He retired from education in 1922 to assist in programs designed to standardize Xhosa grammar and syntax and the Xhosa-language Bible. In 1925 Mqhayi settled near King William's Town in a hilltop retreat named Ntab'ozuko, or "Mount of Glory." From there he traveled widely among the Xhosa-speaking peoples, who acknowledged him as the "poet of the race." He died at home in 1945.

One of Mqhayi's earliest prose works, the novel *U-Samson*, presents an adaptation of the Biblical story of Samson, imaginatively rendered to critique South African society in the era following the Anglo-Boer War. However, another biblically inspired work, the novella *Ityala lamawele*, has received considerably more critical attention. Published in 1914, though written several years earlier, *Ityala lamawele* is based on the biblical story of Tamar's sons in Genesis 38: 27-29 as well as on Mqhayi's memories of Ngonzana's law court at the "Great Place" in Centane. In the novella, Mqhayi related the tale of twins whose dispute over their birth order—and thus, inheritance rights—is decided through the native justice system, demonstrating the capabilities and practicality of the traditional administration. According to Gerard, "it was Mqhayi's aim [in *Ityala lamawele*] to vindicate traditional native justice threatened by the colonial administration." Another major prose work is the utopian novel *U-Don Jadu*, which describes a culturally and racially integrated Christian society in twentieth-century South Africa that utilizes the best of European and African cultures.

While Mqhayi's prose works are highly regarded by critics, it is as a poet that he is chiefly remembered. Working in the oral

tradition of tribal court bards, he composed many *izibongo*, traditional praise poems that proclaimed the accomplishments of chiefs and other public figures, celebrated cultural holidays, or commented on current events. These poems are not purely laudatory; A. C. Jordan has explained that tribal bards "had not only to praise the chief but also to criticize him." Mqhayi has been noted for treating modern themes in this ancient traditional form: some of his *izibongo* discuss British colonialism in Africa, and several are addressed to British royalty and administrators, albeit often ironically. Late in his career, Mqhayi experimented with European forms unfamiliar in Xhosa poetry, such as the sonnet and the heroic couplet, but most critics have expressed disappointment with these attempts to force Xhosa into foreign forms, especially noting the flatness of his rhymes. Most critics concur with Wandile Kuse that "Mqhayi was at his best when he wrote or recited poetry in the oral tradition."

While a lack of translations has hampered Mqhayi's international reputation, his work is beloved and renowned among Xhosa-speaking peoples, and has received high praise from other South African writers. Novelist A. C. Jordan attested to Mqhayi's literary achievement when, in an obituary tribute, he wrote: "Mqhayi takes the highest place in Xhosa literature. He has done more than any other writer to enrich Xhosa. In his hands it receives a fresh impress, and he has revealed all its possibilities as a powerful medium of expression of human emotion.''

PRINCIPAL WORKS

U-Samson   (novel)   1907
Ityala lamawele   (novella and short stories)   1914; also published as *Ityala lamawele* [enlarged edition] (novella, short stories, and poetry) 1931
U-Sogqumahashe   (biography)   1921
I-Bandla laBantu   (poetry)   1923
U-bomi bom-fundisi uJohn Knox Bokwe   (biography)   1925
Isikumbuzo zomPolofiti u-Ntsikana   (biography)   1926
Imihobe nemibongo yokufundwa ezikolweni   (poetry)   1927
"Nkosi sikelel' iAfrika''   (lyric)   1927; published in journal *Umteteli waBantu*
U-Don Jadu   (novel)   1929
U-Mhlekazi u-Hintsa   (poetry)   1937
U-Mqhayi wase-Ntab'ozuko   (autobiography)   1939
I-nzuzo   (poetry)   1943
Mqhayi in Translation   (abridged autobiography and novel) 1976

*Comprises seven stanzas of the African National Anthem. The first stanza was composed earlier by Enoch Sontonga.

D.D.T. JABAVU   (essay date 1943)

[*Jabavu was a South African poet, political activist, journalist, and critic who wrote in Xhosa and English. For much of his career he edited* Imvo zabantsundu, *an influential newspaper founded by his father, John Tengo Jabavu. In his works Jabavu examined race relations and the influence of European culture on native Africans. In the following excerpt, he offers a favorable appraisal of* I-nzuzo.]

S.E.K. Mqhayi, from whose numerous Xhosa productions the present poems [in *Inzuzo (rain)*] have been chosen explains that the title is designed to indicate "things rare and profitable."

This claim is justified by the contents because the author is without a peer among writers of Xhosa poetry, living or dead, when judged by the quantity and calibre of his output. . . . (p. 174)

The arrangement of the poems in this book is in five sections: 1. Didactic poems on subjects like Truth, Hope, Love, and so forth. 2. The passing of the old years and advents of new ones. 3. Obituary eulogia. 4. Praises of Africans who have travelled overseas. 5. Miscellaneous poems.

It is rare indeed to find other good poetry written in Xhosa on some of the subjects named, but with Mqhayi it is characteristic and it has deservedly earned him the popular appellation of *"Imbongi yesizwe"* (equivalent to Bantu Poet Laureate). Many of the poems are informative, and indeed "profitable" because informative, e.g. "**Amagama omCebisi**" in appreciation of the bi-monthly agricultural journal published at Umtata by the Bunga. The topic of the expiration of one year and the incoming of a new one is almost Mqhayi's annual exercise and monopoly, and he does it with gusto. The variety of stanza forms in this selection inevitably invites comparison with *Inkondlo kaZulu* by B. W. Vilakazi . . . but in the Zulu language. Both authors

employ forms definitely imitative of English rhymes such as the long and short metres, the sonnet and the heroic couplet. Both excel in their infinite variety of rhymes and rhythmic movement such as is also to be found in *Um Yezo* by J.J.R. Jolobe. (pp. 174-75)

With regard to diction, Vilakazi frequently uses archaic and extraneous words imported from the neighbouring South African tongues. But Mqhayi in the pieces included in this book employs archaic words with a moderation that just obviates their getting in between the reader and the subject matter as an obstacle, and he makes very few excursions into non-Xhosa words. This moderation, however, is absent in many of Mqhayi's poems outside of this volume.

Mqhayi is indeed a master of variety of phrase. He meticulously avoids the boredom of repeating any particular idiom beyond necessary limits. . . .

For sheer eloquence the poem "**Amagama om Cebisi**" is probably the most fascinating in this book, closely followed by "**U Jujuju kwelakwa-Nyawuza**"; but even these are easily surpassed by other poems by the same author which are not yet published in book form.

This book has the merit of displaying Mqhayi in his excellence in pieces polished with the delicate touch of Jolobe as well as pieces typical of the vigorous martial African manner as witnessed in the Sotho *Lithoko tsa Marena* (Praises of Chiefs) or the Zulu poetry poems by M. J. and C. Mpanza, while there are many other types between.

It is this versatility and copiousness that give Mqhayi his unrivalled place in Xhosa poetry, and possibly in all Bantu poetry. (p. 175)

> *D.D.T. Jabavu, in a review of "Inzuzo," in* African Studies, *Vol. 2, 1943, pp. 174-75.*

A. C. JORDAN   (essay date 1945)

[*Jordan is a South African novelist, short story writer, educator, and critic, whose novel* Inggoumbo yeminyanya (1940) *is considered a classic of Xhosa literature. In the following excerpt from a biographically-oriented memorial tribute written at Mqhayi's death, he discusses* Ityala lamawele, U-Don Jadu, *and Mqhayi's poetry.*]

Mqhayi was born on the banks of the Tyhume on the 1st of December, 1875. He attended school at Evergreen, in the Tyhume Valley, at the age of seven. During the three years at this school he met three of the men who were destined to influence his whole life and career. These were the Rev. E. Makhiwane, the Rev. P. J. Mzimba and Mr. J. Tengo Jabavu. In 1885 he accompanied his father to his new home in Centane (Kentani) and remained there for six years. Then he came to attend school at Lovedale where he received some training as a teacher before he went into the world. His literary career began in East London, when, with the encouragement of Dr. Rubusana, and Messrs N. C. Mhala, A. K. Soga, and G. Tyhamzashe—all of them distinguished leaders of the time— he began to contribute *izibongo* (praise poems) and historical information to the periodical *IZwi labaNtu* (The Voice of the Bantu). Later on he became sub-editor of this paper, but circumstances compelled him to return to teaching, and for many years he served as a teacher among the Ndlambe people. Then he became editor of the *IimVo zabaNtsundu*, but even this he had to give up after some time and go back to teaching. This time he was offered a post at his *Alma Mater,* Lovedale, but during the few years in the world Mqhayi's views on South African history and how it should be taught in African Schools had undergone such modification that he found himself compelled either to be false to his own convictions and teach history as the authorities would have him teach it, or to give up teaching altogether. He decided on the latter. On leaving Lovedale he went to make his home on the "summit" of Ntab'ozuko—a Mount Helicon whence he descended in his impressive kaross on great tribal or state occasions to sing the praises of important personalities. (pp. 105-06)

We owe a great deal to the six years in Centane. For it was during this time that Mqhayi began to understand the culture and history of his people. It was there that he saw *imidudo, iintlombe, intonjane, imiyeyezelo, amadini,* etc. As he relates, he used to sit spell-bound, listening to *inkundla* orations. It was there that he first listened to *izibongo* and himself began to "lisp in numbers," praising favourite oxen, other boys or himself. It was there that he began to appreciate the beauty, dignity and subtleties of Xhosa, and to acquire the amazingly wide vocabulary that even Tiyo Soga would have envied. (p. 106)

Because [Mqhayi] was nurtured in Christian culture and in the primitive culture of his own people at the same time, Christianity was for him not an "escape from the City of Destruction," but a mode of life abundant that was not irreconcilable with his native culture. Small wonder then that Tiyo Soga's translation of *The Pilgrim's Progress* should have had such an appeal for him that at the age of thirteen he was able to recite its first chapter with such feeling and expression that many who listened to him at an elocution competition at the Station School at Lovedale feared that "much learning hath made him truly mad."

To discuss all his writings is impossible. We shall therefore refer to his masterpiece, *ITyala lamaWele,* to his prose work *UDon Jadu,* and lastly to his poetry in general. *ITyala lamaWele* includes fiction, history and poetry. The book owes its title to the novelette that covers its first half—the lawsuit of the twins. The plot of this novelette is suggested by Verses 28-29 of the 38th Chapter of the Book of Genesis. As the author states in the preface, the purpose of the story is to give a picture of legal procedure among the Xhosa people, and to show the democratic spirit in which it is carried out. A civil dispute has arisen between Babini and Wele, twin-sons of Vuyisile, born under circumstances similar to those described in Genesis, Chapter 38. Having lived at a headman's kraal for six years as a boy in Centane, Mqhayi is conversant with legal procedure. The stating of the case by the plantiff, his cross-questioning by the councillors, the calling-in of witnesses, the *hlonipha* language used by the mid-wives in submitting evidence, the declamation of the bard at the end of each session, the reaction of the men to *izibongo,* the unassuming manner of the sage Khulile as he makes an exposition of the principles underlying the law of primogeniture, the pronouncement of the verdict and Chief Hintsa's sympathy with the senior twin in pronouncing it, the humble but dignified manner in which Babini receives the verdict given against him—all these give a beautiful picture of social life among the Xhosa during the reign of Hintsa. It is these and the beauty and dignity of the language that give this novelette its fascinating power and such a high place in Xhosa Literature. Mqhayi is not a great creator of individual character. Hardly any character stands out in this story, and consequently the impression left in the reader's mind is the collective dignity and refinement of the chief and his subjects.

In the latter half of the book, fiction and fictitious characters disappear, and we have true history. The "death" of Khulile synchronizes with the arrival of the Fingos from the east and of the news of a white race coming "from the sea." The relations between the Xhosa and these new-comers, the diplomacy exercised by the White men in driving a wedge between the Xhosa and the Fingos on the one hand and between the two rival sections of the Xhosa on the other, the mutual jealousies and the bitter rivalry that broke the unity of the Xhosa and contributed towards their downfall—all these are related with commendable restraint by Mqhayi. In beautiful style he traces the fortunes of the Xhosa people beyond the "emancipation" of the Fingos, beyond the death of Hintsa, beyond Sarili's exile, beyond Maqoma and Sir Harry Smith, right up to the acceptance of the new loyalties and to the disaster of the *Mendi,* by which time the subject is no longer the Xhosa alone, but the Bantu of South Africa in general. The book closes with short biographies of the new leaders of the "reaction to conquest." An interesting feature is the bard's own development. The poetry in this book punctuates the prose, each piece being appropriate to the incident under consideration. In the lawsuit as well as in the early chapters of the history, the versification, in keeping with the theme, is in the style of the traditional *izibongo,* but with the acceptance of the new loyalties by his people towards the close of the book, the bard himself begins to experiment in modern versification. Therefore, to be fully appreciated, *ITyala lamaWele,* though partly fact and partly fiction, partly verse and partly prose, must be viewed as a whole. Then it has the effect of a great epic drama in which the bard, like a Greek Chorus, comments upon, or predicts, the fortunes of his people.

Next to *ITyala lamaWele,* Mqhayi's most important prose work is *UDon Jadu.* Through the influence and guidance of Don Jadu, a highly educated African, the *amaRanuga* (detribalized Africans) of the Eastern Province acquire land of about the area of the Transkeian Territories. All kinds of industry begin to spring up in this new province of Mnandi (Sweetness). As a result, in a few years the population is double that of the Transkei. The Union Government becomes interested, and vote large sums of money to promote the scheme. Self-government is granted to the people of Mnandi and, the Union Government having disappeared from the scene, Great Britain assumes guardianship. Don Jadu is the first president.

There is neither racialism nor isolationism in Mnandi. Immigration is encouraged, and experts of all races and shades of colour come from the four corners of the earth to make a permanent home there. There is full social, economic and political equality. According to the constitution, women are free to go into parliament, but the sensible women of Mnandi decline this offer on the grounds that there is enough work for them to do at their homes! Mnandi is a Christian state, and Christ is the "President" of the Ancestral Spirits. Ministers of religion are officers of state, and their stipends come from the general revenue. Magistrates and ministers of religion work in close co-operation. In fact, Church and State are so closely knit together that there is no distinction between the police and deacons' courts. Education is compulsory. Xhosa is the first language, but English is such an important second language that no one who is not strictly bilingual may hold an office of state. Baby boys are baptized and circumcised in the Temple eight days after birth, and Holy Confirmation forms part of an initiation ceremony held in the Temple between the ages of fifteen and twenty. All these ceremonies are supervised by the magistrate and the minister of religion together. The marriage ceremony is conducted by the magistrate and subsequently blessed by the minister of religion. Divorce is prohibited by law. The importation or sale of liquor is prohibited by law. Home-brewing is allowed, but anyone found drunk in public places is locked up in a lunatic asylum, dressed in the uniform of the asylum and is for seven days subjected to the same treatment as the legitimate inmates of that institution. People who are sentenced to penal servitude receive wages for their labour. There are no prisons.

UDon Jadu makes very interesting and thought-provoking reading. It is true that in constructing a "bridge" between our present South Africa and his Utopia, the author idealizes away a few hard facts, but—

> its soul is right,
> He means right,—that, a child may understand.

If we turn to his poetry, we find that Mqhayi, though perhaps possessing more talent, is nevertheless more limited in scope, than some of the younger Nguni poets. Essentially a poet of the traditional type, for theme he is almost wholly confined to concrete subjects, usually human beings. He is confined to lyrical verse, chiefly odes and elegies. Even historical themes he was never able to put into narrative verse. If he had been able to write narrative poetry, we can almost be sure that the poem entitled **"UmHlekazi uHintsa,"** instead of consisting of eight cantos disappointingly lacking in unity, should have been an epic. Again, it is a pity that in his later writings he decided to break entirely with the diction and artistic formlessness of *izibongo* in favour of modern versification. With his limited knowledge of prosody it was only natural that he should not be able to go much further than discover rhyme—of all the artificial ornaments of Western versification the most obvious, and yet to Bantu the least desirable. A sense of effort and strain is always with us when we read his rhymed verse, and very often we feel that in order to observe rhyme, the poet has sacrificed sense, virility and easy flow of language. His favourite rhyme scheme is the heroic couplet, and because he invariably writes end-stopped lines, his rhymed verse makes dull and monotonous reading.

But if we judge Mqhayi by what he has achieved instead of judging him by what he has failed to achieve, then there is no doubt that his best poetry is of a high order. To understand him, let us remind ourselves that one of the essential qualities of *ubumbongi* was true patriotism, not blind loyalty to the person of the chief, but loyalty to the principles that the chieftainship does or ought to stand for. On public occasions *imbongi* had not only to praise the chief but also to criticise him by means of those epithets and metaphors that make such an interesting characteristic of *izibongo*. Obviously then only a man who took genuine interest in the social welfare of his people can be *imbongi*. Mqhayi possessed this quality, hence his being known as *ImBongi yesiZwe Jikelele*, which title was conferred upon him by a Zulu in Johannesburg. But Mqhayi had a double loyalty. As a Xhosa he was loyal to the Xhosa chiefs and their ancestors, and as a British subject he had to be loyal to the British king. A poem written during the Boer War in the *IZwi labaNtu* of March 13th, 1900, shows how very sincerely Mqhayi had accepted British guardianship. Each stanza has a refrain, *"SingamaBritani!"* (We are Britons!). Nurtured in Christianity and in the policy of the "Old Cape Liberals," he believed that the conquest of Southern Africa by the British was the working out of a Divine Purpose. After the

defeat in 1879, he makes the Zulus say in the poem **"ISandlwana":**

Wozani, maBritani, sigezan' izingozi;

(Come, ye Britons, let's bathe one another's wounds!)

Then the Zulus go on to tell the British that their own defeat was the working out of God's purpose, so that from the British, the Zulus might receive a new life, a new birth, a new learning, and see the Love of the Son of the Great-Great, and fight His battles.

But the Act of Union drove the "Old Cape Liberals" to the background, and representations to Britain did not receive the usual kind of reception. Britain was forgetting that she had "children" in Africa. So the poem written in praise of the Native Labour Contingency of 1916, **"umKhosi wemiDaka,"** opens with the significant lines:

> Awu! Ewe, kambe, siyabulela,
> Lakuth'ikokwethu lisicinge,
> . . . .
> Ngexesha lalo lokuxakeka.

(O yes! We must feel honoured, I suppose, that our father has remembered us in his time of need.)

But Mqhayi has not quite lost faith in the British connection. In the elegy written on the disaster of the *Mendi*, though bemoaning the loss of the flower of Africa, he reminds his people that some such worthy sacrifice had to be made if they truly loved Britain; he reminds them how God sacrificed His own Son, the Messiah. Again the working-out of a Divine Purpose! If the ties with Britain are not to break, as they threaten to do, this sacrifice must be.

> Ngoko ke So-Tase! kwaqal' ukulunga!
> Le nqanaw' uMendi namhlanje yendisile,
> Naal' igazi lethu lisikhonzile.

The last word in the second line, *yendisile,* is very eloquent. *Ukwendisa* is to give one's daughter in marriage, and those who know the mutual obligations between the families involved in a marriage-contract as Mqhayi understands marriage, will understand how strong should have been the ties, according to him, between Britain and the Africans after the disaster of the *Mendi*. But the Victorian Days were gone, never to return, and, if anything, Post-Union South Africa was threatening to undo all the good that Mqhayi had seen in the Victorian Policy. It is therefore in true *imbongi* spirit, and as a patriot praising and criticising a chief in public, that in praising the Prince of Wales in 1925, Mqhayi, after a succession of metaphors and similes, in which he likens the prince to all the mighty fabulous animals of Bantu Folklore, should utter words which may be translated as follows:

> Ah, Britain! Great Britain!
> Great Britain of the endless sunshine!
> . . . .
> You gave us Truth: denied us Truth;
> You gave us *ubuntu:* denied us *ubuntu;*
> You gave us light: we live in darkness;
> Benighted at noon-day, we grope in the dark.

Mqhayi has written several religious poems, on Christmas, on the Gospel, and on kindred subjects. Perhaps the best illustration of his deep-seated religion is to be found in the closing lines of a poem entitled **"In Taba kaNdoda,"** written in praise of a little mountain peak near King William's Town. A poem of forty lines, it closes as follows:

> Would that I had tongues, O Mount of my home
> O footstool of the God of my fathers,
> Thou, whose brow, facing the setting-sun,
> Is smitten by the rays of the closing day.
> So would I, protected, sing thy praise;
> So would I, forsaken, fly to thee,
> And kneel in humble prayer by thee,
> Who art the stepping-stone between me and my God.
> Still shall the aliens stare not understanding,
> While, praying, on this slope I build a ladder,
> And scale the vast fatiguing heights, to kiss
> The Feet of God the Father—Creator, Most High.

"Nature for Nature's sake" hardly has a place in *izibongo* of the old type, and Mqhayi's nature poems are on the whole disappointing. But this does not mean that he was blind to the beauties of nature. Scattered here and there are couplets that reveal not only his sensitiveness to the beauties of nature, but also his genius for the "precious word":

> Imizi yalo mlambo niyayibona na
> *Ukutyityimba* yakombelelwa yingxangxasi!
> (Lo, how the rushes on the waterside
> Thrill to the music of the cataract!)
> Kunqanqaza oonogqaza emathafeni,
> *Kukhenkceza* iinyenzane equndeni.
> (Grass-warblers clinking in the fields,
> Cicadas shrilling in the meads)
> Ndee *ntshoo-o!* ntshobololo-o-o!
> Ndaxel' inkwenkwez' ingen' elifini.
> (Sliding away, sliding away I go,
> Like a meteor swimming into a cloud.)

If this article has shown that Mqhayi was the soul of his people, and that to understand him is to understand their hopes and aspirations, then it will have served its purpose. Mqhayi takes the highest place in Xhosa literature. He has done more than any other writer to enrich Xhosa. In his hands it receives a fresh impress, and he has revealed all its possibilities as a powerful medium of expression of human emotion. His prose as well as his poetry contains expressions that became proverbial long before his death. If much of his verse will soon be forgotten, and for many generations to come, his prose style will remain something for younger writers to emulate. (pp. 107-16)

A. C. Jordan, "Appendix: Samuel Edward Krune Mqhayi," in his Towards an African Literature: The Emergence of Literary Form in Xhosa, *University of California Press, 1973, pp. 103-16.*

ALBERT S. GÉRARD (essay date 1971)

[*Gérard is a Belgian essayist and scholar who has contributed to surveys of African literature and to literary journals in South Africa and the Congo. In the following excerpt from his* Four African Literatures: Xhosa, Sotho, Zulu, Amharic, *Gérard examines the place of Mqhayi's prose and poetry within African literature and culture.*]

It was not until the beginning of the twentieth century that the Western genre of imaginative prose fiction was introduced into Xhosa literature, most prominently by a man who—somewhat paradoxically—was also perhaps the last of the great tribal bards.

Samuel Edward Krune Mqhayi was the great-grandson of Mqhayi, a one-time councillor of Chief Ngqika, who was killed by the English in 1835. (p. 53)

Mqhayi, while attending school intermittently, acquired a remarkable knowledge of his people, their history, and their language. "It was there," Jordan writes, "that he first listened to *izibongo* (praise-poems), and himself began to 'lisp in numbers,' praising favourite oxen, other boys or himself. It was there that he began to appreciate the beauty, dignity and subtleties of Xhosa, and to acquire the amazingly wide vocabulary that even Tiyo Soga would have envied" [see excerpt dated 1945]. He used to listen to the stories of the wars that the old men of the village told in the evenings. He learned how to extemporize praise songs in honor of his cows, his dogs, and his friends. And he also watched with fascination the judicial proceedings at the court of Chief Nzanzana. (p. 53)

After training as a teacher, he taught for a time in East London. But he was not really interested in teaching, and he soon left to become secretary of the congregation of the Reverend Rubusana, who fostered his growing concern with social and racial problems. He contributed . . . to Mhala's newspaper, *Izwi Labantu,* and later became one of its editors. After a new stay at Kentani, he resumed his work on *Izwi Labantu* but the journal had to stop publication for lack of funds and because of differences of opinion among the editors. Mqhayi again went to East London as a teacher, and assisted Jabavu in the editing of *Imvo Zabantsundu* from the turn of the century until Jabavu's death in 1921. His first poems were printed there.

Mqhayi's poetic talent soon caused him to be known as "the poet of the race." As a result of his linguistic abilities, he had been appointed in 1905 a member of the Xhosa Bible Revision Board. At that time, Dr. William Govan Bennie (1868-1942) was chief inspector for Native Education in the Cape. He sought Mqhayi's help in standardizing Xhosa spelling and in codifying Xhosa grammar. From then on, the young man devoted himself mainly to writing. His first published book was *U-Samson,* an adaptation of the Bible story of Samson.

Mqhayi's first original work was *Ityala lama-wele (The Lawsuit of the Twins),* which was printed in 1914, quite some time, he claims in his autobiography, after he had actually composed it. As a result of this publication, Z. K. Matthews writes, Mqhayi "sprang into fame at once as one of the best Xhosa writers, to be classed with men like Soga and Rubusana." The story takes place during the reign of Hintza, chief of the Gcaleka Xhosa, who was killed while attempting to escape from British imprisonment in 1835. The plot was suggested by the story of the birth of Thammar's twins in Genesis 38:27-29. It concerns a legal dispute between twins over who is the elder and therefore entitled to their father's inheritance. Mqhayi's memories of Nzanzana's court enabled him to provide, as Alice Werner pointed out, "a very illuminating picture of native judicial procedure." But Mqhayi's purpose was by no means merely ethnographic or antiquarian. The theme of justice is an important one in all literatures, as justice and law are the very foundation of the social order. A large portion of early narrative writing in Europe focuses on the theme of revenge. The trial of Ganelon in the *Chanson de Roland,* the *Njalssaga,* for example, illustrate the conflict between the primitive practice of private vengeance on the one hand, and the social and religious requirements of impartial and impersonal justice on the other hand. This was still a major theme in serious drama of the Renaissance and of the seventeenth century throughout Western Europe. Other aspects of justice preoccupied African writers during the early years of the twentieth century. . . . [It] is important to notice that there is considerable difference in approach between [Lesotho writer Azariele] Sekese and Mqhayi. The former, living in a British Protectorate where the native judicial system was not threatened by the European authorities, felt free to criticize its abuses from inside. The situation was by no means the same in South Africa. By the end of the nineteenth century, Xhosa chiefs in the Ciskei had seen their authority and their judicial privileges eroded by the setting up of district councils whose members were appointed by the Cape authorities. Whereas Sekese wanted to criticize the chiefs' courts in the hope of improving them, it was Mqhayi's aim to vindicate traditional native justice threatened by the colonial administration. He made this clear in the foreword to *Ityala lama-wele:* "Although I am no kind of expert on the legal affairs, I have, however, the conviction that the legal system of the Xhosas is not in the slightest degree different from that of the enlightened nations. When the white races came to this country, they found that the people of this country are virtually experts—all of them—in legal procedures." He even goes so far as to claim that "the white races took for themselves a considerable share of the customs and laws of the Xhosas." The chief virtue of Xhosa law, he says, is that it is based upon jurisprudence. Consequently, he goes on, "in this short tale I am endeavouring to show the efforts, the pains, and the time that the Xhosas take when they research into the origin of law, for they are trying to base it upon precedent." In the story itself those efforts, described in minute detail, come to nothing since the case appears to be one for which there is no precedent, even in the memory of the oldest man of the tribe. In his foreword, Mqhayi further claims that he is trying to show "that the king is not the final arbiter of affairs by himself, as foreigners believe is the case with us." Actually, in the tale it is the chief who makes the final decision, a highly subtle and ambiguous one, although he first has all the evidence gathered and listens to the advice of all the notables. At the end of the trial, the author describes the reactions of the people as follows:

> And concerning the judgement, some were mumbling, finding fault, and seeing many errors. But the majority did not forget a case that had proceeded with decorum and justice, and that had been spoken well, in which all aspects had been examined, and the judgement given with great skill.

The second part of the volume contains a historical account of the Xhosa nation through the nineteenth century and up to the famous *Mendi* episode, when a ship loaded with South African soldiers was sunk by a German submarine in the early months of World War I. By this time, as Jordan rightly observes, "the subject is no longer the Xhosa alone, but the Bantu of South Africa," one more interesting example of the growth of intertribal solidarity in the early decades of this century. (pp. 54-6)

In 1925 [Mqhayi] published *UBomi buka J. K. Bokwe (Life of J. K. Bokwe),* a biography of the Reverend Bokwe. This was followed in 1927 by a collection of poems for children, . . . *Imihobe nemibongo (Songs of Joy and Lullabies).*

In 1929 Mqhayi produced his second important work of prose fiction which is also the first Xhosa utopia, *U-Don Jadu.* This book, which provides the writer's picture of an ideal South African society, has been usefully summarized and discussed by Jordan in his article on Mqhayi [see excerpt dated 1945]. (p. 56)

It is interesting to compare Jordan's analysis with the harsh judgment passed upon *U-Don Jadu* by a European critic, John Riordan:

> In *UDon Jadu* the hero passes from town to town, solving all problems overnight, and leading raw tribesmen from a primitive state to an advanced civilization in a matter of weeks. . . . Thus does Mqhayi allow his imagination, fostered by a repulsive hunger for self-glorification, to run riot and escape into a world of pure fancy, where probability is grossly violated and logical development unknown. True, Mqhayi's imagination is colourful and productive, but it is not disciplined. His mastery of language is undoubted, but he blatantly tries to impress by playing with big words and archaisms. His glittering facade of words is unsupported by any real substance and so we go away unsatisfied [see Riordan entry in Additional Bibliography].

Obviously, Riordan had expected what Mqhayi never intended to give: a realistic, social, and psychological novel of the Western type. Jordan too recognizes that "Mqhayi is not a great creator of individual character," and that "hardly any character stands out in this story." This is a critique frequently leveled at the African novel in general, whose failure in character depiction must be ascribed to two main causes. First, concern with the individual personality is not a feature of traditional oral literature any more than it is of traditional tribal society. The individual apprehends himself first and foremost as part of the group, rather than as a separate personality endowed with its own rights and privileges. Literature is a public activity dealing with matters of public interest, and purely private experiences and emotions are seldom deemed worthy of literary treatment. Second, this particular trend in the native culture was further reinforced by the historical situation. In his autobiography, Mqhayi explains that the idea for *U-Don Jadu* can be traced back to his school years at Lovedale. He used to make frequent visits to his father in Grahamstown, and during those trips, he had to pass through the little town of Alice. There it was, he tells us, that he became aware for the first time of the antagonism between black and white. So far, he had lived a sheltered life at the court of his great-uncle and in the quiet multiracial seclusion of Lovedale. But in Alice, he witnessed how Xhosa cattle was requisitioned out of the common pastures to make room for the white people's cattle, and he realized the growing hostility between both racial groups. As cattle was the foundation of Xhosa economy, and therefore of Xhosa society, this was a problem of life and death for the Xhosa nation as a whole. *U-Don Jadu* grew out of these experiences and this realization. It was not meant as a realistic description of a situation that every one knew anyway. It was designed as a blueprint for the future coexistence of both races in South Africa. And it was conceived in a spirit of compromise and syncretism. There are only three things that Mqhayi forcefully rejects: the South African government, the prison system, and imported hard liquor as opposed to the native home-brewed beer. His ideal state is not a preliminary study in Bantustan. It is a multiracial society that places a high premium on education and progress, and it is a Christian society that has incorporated many of the beliefs and customs dear to African hearts. In the elaboration of this Bantu utopia, Mqhayi exhibits uncommonly powerful intellectual imagination. (pp. 57-9)

Mqhayi's next book was a biography of the Gold Coast scholar and advocate of Pan-Africanism, Dr. J.E.K. Aggrey, whose visit to South Africa in 1921 had initiated, if we are to believe Vilakazi, "a new spirit of co-operation and understanding between Africans and Europeans." (p. 59)

Mqhayi published a collection of eight cantos on Chief Hintza, *U-Mhlekazi U-Hintsa* (*Hintsa the Great* . . .). At the same time, he was writing his autobiography, which was first published in German, in Diederich Westermann's collection, *Afrikaner erzähler ihr Leben* . . ., before it appeared in Xhosa under the title *U-Mqhayi wase Ntab'ozuko* (*Mqhayi of the Mountain of Beauty* . . .). His last volume was one more collection of poems, entitled *I-nzuzo* (*Reward* . . .). In the late twenties, Mqhayi had settled on Tilana's Hill, near Berlin. He had renamed the place "Ntab'ozuko" (The Mountain of Beauty). This was on the territory of the Ndlambe clan, and at the same time that he established a model farm for the benefit of the Xhosa peasants, Mqhayi acted as poet laureate and secretary to the Ndlambe chieftain. (p. 59)

It was perhaps as a poet that Mqhayi was chiefly valued by the Xhosa audience, not least because he had completely mastered the form and the spirit of the traditional praise poem (*izibongo*) while adapting it to modern circumstances and topics. He was known as *imbongi yesizwe* ("Poet Laureate"), and Vilakazi calls him "the Father of Xhosa poetry," because "he is responsible for a transition from the primitive bards who sang the *izibongo*." The main function of the tribal bard (*imbongi*) was to strengthen the cohesion of the group, usually by celebrating the glorious figures of the past and extolling the authority of the reigning chief. Mqhayi's volume on Hintza is an example of this, as are the obituary eulogies of local figures in *I-nzuzo*. But since the central preoccupation of the izibongo in its purest form is to promote the prosperity and the greatness of the group, it does not deal solely with the chiefs, but also with any public events that may be significant in that respect. Hence Mqhayi's poetic treatment of topics that, to the European reader, sound hardly promising: *I-nzuzo* contains a poem written in appreciation of the bimonthly agricultural journal published at Umtata! Throughout the year, seasonal festivals offer opportunities to remind the tribe of its past achievements and to advise it for the future; therefore, the many New Year poems that Mqhayi composed. As Jabavu wrote, "the topic of the expiration of one year and the incoming of a new one is almost Mqhayi's annual exercise and monopoly, and he does it with gusto." But Mqhayi's inspiration also reached beyond the traditional tribal basis, and he wrote abundantly, in poetry and in prose, about prominent Africans of past and present. Further, his Christian beliefs merged into the edifying and societal purposes of traditional poetry in moralizing pieces dealing with such abstract subjects as Truth, Hope, and Love. If we are to believe Vilakazi, Mqhayi's attempts at innovation were not always successful. His poems dealing with nature, the Zulu critic says, are "dull," and those on religious subjects are "mere oratorical exercises" when compared with those of his successor Jolobe. Mqhayi "excelled in heroic poetry of the traditional type, and showed great skill in weaving his people's customs, legends, and myths into his poems."

The imbongi's role was not simply to praise the chief. As his major concern was with the welfare of the nation, he often felt called upon to criticize any abuses by the powers that be. On this score, too, the tradition was modified and enlarged by Mqhayi in the light of a historical situation where actual authority was vested in European hands. When the Prince of Wales (later Edward VIII) visited South Africa in 1925, the poet was entrusted with the privilege of delivering an izibongo of his composition. Jordan informs us that the poem began in the usual fashion, with "a succession of metaphors and similes, in which he likens the prince to all the mighty fabulous animals of Bantu Folklore." Then comes a section that is here quoted in Jordan's translation:

Ah, Britain! Great Britain!
Great Britain of the endless sunshine!

She hath conquered the oceans and laid them low;
She hath drained the little rivers and lapped them dry;
She hath swept the litle nations and wiped them away;
And now she is making for the open skies.

She sent us the preacher: she sent us the bottle,
She sent us the Bible, and barrels of brandy;
She sent us the breechloader, she sent us cannon;
O, Roaring Britain! Which must we embrace?

You sent us the truth, denied us the truth;
You sent us the life, deprived us of life,
You sent us the light, we sit in the dark,
Shivering, benighted in the bright noonday sun.

Jordan quotes this passage to show "that the idiom, style and technique of the traditional praise-poem can be applied most effectively to modern themes." But in its own right, it is a little masterpiece of irony and conscious artistry. It may be pure coincidence that the translation appears as a sort of inverted Elizabethan sonnet, with the couplet at the beginning instead of the end. But the structure of the poem is as carefully devised as that of a sonnet. It falls into two main parts, each of which is announced by an apostrophe ("Ah, Britain!" "O, Roaring Britain!"), and each of the three quatrains is a clearly distinguishable step in a continuous process of heightening tension. The first quatrain, describing Britain's universal power, is in the third person, objective and impersonal in tone, although a note of subdued irony creeps in as Britain's victories over nature (oceans, rivers) appear as an icon of her conquest of men (nations), and as the effects of her might are couched in increasingly destructive terms (oceans laid low, rivers lapped dry, nations wiped away). The last line is probably designed as ambivalent, referring both to the physical skies conquered by air power, and to the way the British manipulate the heavenly Gospel for purposes of their own. This, at any rate, is suggested by the mention of "the preacher" at the beginning of the second quatrain.

This third stanza has a more direct personal character ("She sent *us* the preacher") and refers to the particular experience that Mqhayi and his people have gained of British power. This experience is tersely described in its fundamental ambivalence: while England sent the Africans the light of Christianity, she also introduced them to liquor and firearms, both of them agents of destruction. The modulation in the second apostrophe ("Roaring Britain" instead of "Great Britain") contains an ominous, although hidden and implicit, answer to the question in the quatrain's last line. The main attribute of England, the source of her political greatness and power, is not the "sunshine" of Christian civilization, but the roaring, destructive might of artillery. It is not likely that Mqhayi, a devout member of the Presbyterian church, wanted to invite his people to use violence as a response to violence. The interrogative form of the line suggests the pathetic perplexity of the African in general, and intimates how tempting it is for him to conclude that only armed power, not the Christian faith, can redeem the African from the quandary where Britain herself placed him.

The gradual heightening of emotion reaches its climax in the last stanza, where Britain is now directly and aggressively apostrophized: the "you-us" relation replaces the "she-us" of the second quatrain and the impersonal "she" of the first. At the same time, the poet relinquishes metaphorical language and indicts Britain in straightforward terms, for bringing the truth of religion in theory and ignoring it in practice, and for bringing the light of progress and civilization while depriving the black population of its livelihood. The last two lines of the poem revert with deadly irony, to the light imagery of the beginning. Although Britain, the land where the sun of Christianity and modern civilization shines endlessly, sent the light to Africa, the African remains in the cold and the darkness of oppression, with only his native, physical "bright noonday sun" to console him. The translation can only preserve the bare bones of the poem's structure. There is little doubt that a study of the musical and connotational values of the Xhosa original would enhance our appreciation of this brief masterpiece, the quality of which certainly suggests that more of Mqhayi's work should be made available to an international audience. (pp. 59-62)

> *Albert S. Gérard, "Xhosa Literature," in his* Four African Literatures: Xhosa, Sotho, Zulu, Amharic, *University of California Press, 1971, pp. 21-100.*

O. R. DATHORNE   (essay date 1974)

[*Dathorne is a Guyanese-born novelist, short story writer, and critic whose fiction satirically examines the lives of expatriate black people in England and Africa. In the following excerpt from his study* The Black Mind: A History of African Literature, *he discusses the novel* Ityala lamawele, *the poetry collection* I-nzuzo, *and an individual, later poem that, combining elements of African and European literature, "initiated a literature of protest in Xhosa."*]

Although Sotho writing was firmly stabilized and developed in the first decade of the twentieth century, not until the twenties did a similar development take place in Xhosa. (p. 131)

S.E.K. Mqhayi . . . is the most important writer of this period. His *Ityala lama wele (The Case of the Twins)* is considered by D.D.T. Jabavu to be "an original effort to give a picture of Xhosa court life before the advent of the Europeans." The story is a kind of extended riddle—who is the elder of the two twins who are claiming the right of chieftainship? The whole trial, which adheres to a strict routine, is dramatized. The first twin complains that his brother, They-are-Two, is usurping his place. His brother replies to these charges, and then the midwives have to be called in. Finally the court is cleared so a decision can be made.

Although from the onset Mqhayi tried to get away from mission-school writing, he did not involve himself with recreating the oral literature. Instead he worked fairly closely with oral sources (in addition to indigenous idioms, his work is full of the precision of one directed but not hamstrung by a tradition) and his story emerges as another exercise in the attempt to establish individuality. Mqhayi makes the "case" even more difficult by presenting the contestants as twins. Who could claim to be different? His story, ostensibly about the right to rule, concerns the dubious assertion of individuality. The mere fact that they are twins not only heightens their similarity, but makes their case for separate recognition futile and ridiculous. The author asserts the predominance of the tribe, since it is an old tribal member who finally helps the court to decide. (pp. 131-32)

What Mqhayi did was to establish the artist's independence from the patronage of religious bodies. This does not mean that he was ahead of his time, for as late as 1942 when he published *I-nzuzo (Gain),* a collection of verse, the sections into which he divided the poems were along fairly conventional lines. For instance, the selection includes poems on "truth," "hope," and "love," on the "passing of years," on death, and perhaps, nearest to the tradition, poems of praise for Africans who had gone overseas. He imitated English rhyme as well as the sonnet and heroic couplet. But his poetic gifts were not entirely dissipated in producing conventional laudations. He expressed the new individual consciousness through satire and in the manner of the Sotho writer Azariel Sekese he even attacked royalty. One of his most successful pieces is his "praise song" to the then Prince of Wales, composed in 1925:

> Ah Britain! Great Britain!
> Great Britain of the endless sunshine!
> She hath conquered the oceans and laid them low;
> She hath drained the little rivers and lapped them dry;
> She hath swept the little nations and wiped them away;
> And now she is making for the open skies.
> She sent us the preacher, she sent us the bottle,
> She sent us the Bible, and barrels of brandy;
> She sent us the breechloader, she sent us cannon;
> O, Roaring Britain! Which must we embrace?
> You sent us the truth, denied us the truth;
> You sent us the life, deprived us of life;
> You sent us the light, we sit in the dark,
> Shivering, benighted in the bright noonday sun.

The last line is too obvious and does not accord with the unspoken suggestions in the rest of the stanza. The poem is remarkable in many ways: written in a European sonnet form it makes use of various devices of the African praise song— an important technical development. It also initiated a literature of protest in Xhosa. (pp. 132-33)

> *O. R. Dathorne, "Written Indigenous Literatures," in* The Black Mind: A History of African Literature, *University of Minnesota Press, 1974, pp. 89-140.*

WANDILE KUSE   (essay date 1975)

[*In the following excerpt, Kuse offers a brief survey of Mqhayi's principal works.*]

When Mqhayi wrote his first two poems for *Izwi LabaNtu* (The Voice of the People) in 1897, he was immediately acclaimed as *Imbongi yakwaGompo neyeSizwe Jikelele*. In these two poems the two main themes of Mqhayi's life's work are delineated, viz:

(a) In **"Izwe IakwaNdlambe" ("The Domain of the Ndlambe People"),** he declared his unshakeable loyalty and fidelity to the polity and traditions of his people.

(b) In **"UNtsikane"** he portrayed his quest to transcend local and ethnic considerations by heroising the first notable Xhosa convert to Christianity. Christianity and the values of Western European civilization had become the vehicles of "progress" in the eyes of Mqhayi's generation of writers. They were, however, not uncritical of proselytizers to the new ways of the alien civilization. (p. 183)

The evolutionary development of Mqhayi's attitudes is reflected in his contributions to two publications in particular: *Izwi labaNtu* and *Imvo zabaNtsundu*. He became editor of the former within the first year of it's existence, but funding dried up and the journal collapsed in 1910. Mqhayi then became editor of *Imvo zabaNtsundu* which was being produced in King William's Town. The various columns to which he contributed included ''Abantu'' (''People''), ''E ZaKomkhulu'' (''News from the Court'') and ''Incoko'' (''Conversation''). . . .

During the Anglo-Boer War (1899-1902) and World War I (1914-1918), Mqhayi wrote poetry which alluded to the hostilities between the Europeans in South Africa and in Europe. The significance of these wars of the ''natives,'' his countrymen, is elaborated upon in the body of the poems. His ideas were further elaborated in his prose fiction. His first novel, an adaptation of the Biblical story of ''Samson and Delilah'' entitled *USamson* . . ., offered a critique of South African society in the years following the Anglo-Boer War. He conceived of the ''natives'' as the impotent ''sleeping giant'' who, in the words of Shakespeare's Mercutio, willed and wished ''a plague on both your houses.'' The image was sustained by the Titan's act which brought to ruin the edifice constructed by the collusion of liberal white men and reactionary racists at the expense of the indigenous peoples of South Africa. Mqhayi was always aware that the intrusion of Europeans into the patterns of behaviour and politics of Africans was not always gentle and altruistic.

Mqhayi's name is, of course, pre-eminently associated with his epoch-making classic *Ityala Lamawele (The Lawsuit of the Twins)*. *Imvo* . . . quotes Professor Z. K. Matthews as saying that Mqhayi ''sprang into fame at once as one of the best Xhosa writers, to be classed with men like Soga and Rubusana.'' The negative posture of *USamson* led Mqhayi, in dialectical fashion, to the positive assertion of indigenous values in *Ityala Lamawele*. This book is a compendium of various styles: the opening is dramatic and thereafter the prose is punctuated by heroic poetry, historical and biographical sketches as well as legend and mythology. Here Mqhayi projected his image of men and women of culture who propagated the best ideas of their time. His heroes and heroines encompassed the representatives of tradition as well as men and women educated in the ways of the West. The first part of the work is an exciting portrayal of the ways of tradition while the latter part is a series of biographical sketches and historical situations.

Mqhayi's next work of fiction, *uDon Jadu* appeared in 1929. This book is both a utopia and an allegory. Its themes are parallel to two other books by Mqhayi and demonstrate the dynamic relationship between fiction and social reality. The *persona* (the narrative is in the first person singular) is an amalgam of the hero of the autobiography, *UMqhayi waseNtabozuko* and the author's free translation of C. Kinglsey Williams' *Aggrey of Africa—uAggrey umAfrika*, a work inspired by the visit to South Africa of Aggrey, the Ghanaian as a member of the Phelps-Stokes Commission on Education in Africa. Excepting the autobiography, Mqhayi's last two books underline the fact that he was pre-eminently a poet—a veritable traditional oral bard whose awareness and sensitivity to the great issues of his times as well as his responsiveness to the creative impulse led him to experiment often with European

modes of rhyme and rhythm—not altogether successfully. In 1937, Mqhayi wrote **''UMhlekazi uHintsa,''** (a poem in eight cantos). On the hundredth anniversary of the assassination of the Paramount Chief of the Xhosa, he felt the urge to reassert his credentials as the royal bard of old times. His composition won the May Esther Bedford Competition First Prize. It is a poem that sustains the viability of the oral techniques of praise poetry in the written format. Mqhayi's last book of poems, **Inzuzo,** sugggests that he was both an oral and literate poet who was socially aware and was well steeped in the techniques and content of the oral culture of his people while experimenting with English Romantic forms.

Mqhayi was at his best when he wrote or recited poetry in the oral tradition. My favorite poem by Mqhayi is his praise of a Ndlambe chief entitled **''Aa! Silimela!''** It is not included in any volume of Mqhayi's corpus of written works. The music of his poetry communicates even if one does not understand the words. However, there is a translation of the first paragraph of the poem Mqhayi wrote on the occasion of the recruitment of the ''Black Brigade,'' a black South African contingent in the First World War. If one has seen the film *Patton* one can sympathize with Mqhayi's sentiments in response as it were to Patton's saying, ''When your grandchildren expectantly ask you what you did in the great world war, you would not like to have to say 'you were shovelling shit in Louisiana'.'' Mqhayi introduces the poem **''Umkhosi WemiDaka''** in this manner:

Awu! Ewe kambe siyabulela
Lakuth' ikokwethu lisicinge
Ngokuya kusebenz' emazibukweni
Ngexesha lalo lokuxakeka.
Be singobani na thina boomthina?
Ukuba singanced' ukumkani weBritain
Ingangalale' engatshonelwa langa
Int' elawul' umhlaba nolwandle!
Kungoku nesibhakabhak' isingxamele!

Niyeva ke, madodana, niphakamile
Isizwe senu sisemqulwini wezizwe.
Ze niguye, ze niqambe;
Nenje nje, nenje nje! Nenje nje, nenje nje!
Nenje nje, nenje nje! Nenje nje, nenje njeya.

We are indeed grateful and impressed
That His Britannic Majesty
Should think of asking us to come
And work as stevedores
At a time when he is under pressure.
Who were we?
To even think of lending a hand
To the King of Britain
On whose empire the sun never sets.
His dominions extend over land and sea
As things now stand
He is ready to colonize the heavens.

Listen now fellows!
Your people now belong to the Commonwealth of Nations.
You should celebrate and dance
And act like this and this and that!

This bitterly satirical poem goes on to say that some good is bound to come out of the sacrifice by Africans for others. (pp. 183-84)

Wandile Kuse, "Mqhayi: Oral Bard and Author," in The South African Outlook, *Vol. 105, December, 1975, pp. 183-84.*

ADDITIONAL BIBLIOGRAPHY

Review of *U-Mqhayi wase-Ntab'ozuko. Bantu Studies* XIV (1940): 203-04.

Favorable appraisal of Mqhayi's autobiography. According to the critic: "The language of the book is clear and pleasing, colloquial but dignified, forming a model on which young writers of Xhosa might well mould their own style."

Kuse, Wandile. "Mqhayi through the Eyes of His Contemporaries." *South African Outlook* 105 (1975): 185-88.

Discusses poetic tributes to Mqhayi by J.J.R. Jolobe, Yali-Manisi, Adolphus Z. T. Mbebe and St. J. Page Yako, and Lettie G. N. Tayedzerhwa.

Opland, Jeff. "Praise Poems as Historical Sources." In *Beyond the Cape Frontier: Studies in the History of the Transkei and Ciskei,* edited by Christopher Saunders and Robin Derricourt, pp. 1-37. London: Longman, 1974.

Compares and contrasts the works of *imbongi* (praise poets), including Mqhayi.

———. "Two Unpublished Poems by S.E.K. Mqhayi." *Research in African Literature* 8, No. 1 (Spring 1977): 27-53.

Xhosa transcriptions and English translations of a recording of the poems "Ah Velile" and "A! Silimela!" made by Mqhayi in the 1930s. Opland includes some critical comment on the texts.

Riordan, John. "The Wrath of the Ancestral Spirits." *African Studies* 20, No. 1 (1961): 53-60.

Includes a brief negative assessment of *U-Don Jadu* in an appreciative review of A. C. Jordan's novel *Inggoumbo yeminyanya* (1940). According to Riordan: "Mqhayi's imagination is colorful and productive, but it is not disciplined. His mastery of language is undoubted, but he blatantly tries to impress by playing with big words and archaisms. His glittering facade of words is unsupported by any real substance and so we go away unsatisfied."

Scott, Patricia E. *Samuel Edward Krune Mqhayi, 1875-1945: Bibliographic Survey.* Grahamstown, S. A.: Rhodes University, 1976, 31 p.

Includes comprehensive bibliographies of Mqhayi's journalism, anthologized works, translated poetry, unpublished manuscripts, and works about Mqhayi.

Shepherd, R.H.W. "S.E.K. Mqhayi: His Life." *South African Outlook* 105 (1975): 191.

A brief, appreciative biography. According to Shepherd: "Few men have been more honored among African people than was S.E.K. Mqhayi. . . . His contributions to Xhosa literature as poet, historian, biographer, and translator were abundant and outstanding in quality, and by them and in other ways he helped in no small measure to stabilize and purify the Xhosa language."

Tom Redcam

1870-1933

(Pseudonym of Thomas Henry MacDermot) Jamaican poet and novelist.

Redcam is known as "the father of Jamaican literature." Writing at a time when his country's art forms were dominated by European influences, Redcam explored uniquely Jamaican themes in his fiction and celebrated Jamaica's natural beauty in his poetry. Although his works have been overshadowed by those of later, more technically adept Jamaican authors, they remain important as prototypes of a native literature.

Redcam was born in Jamaica, one of five children of an Anglican cleric who died young, leaving his family impoverished. Redcam was nevertheless able to attend school, although the extent of his educational background is not known. As a young man he taught school and worked as a journalist, becoming editor of the *Jamaica Times* in 1904. His position on the newspaper brought him some degree of influence among Jamaicans, and he encouraged his young readers to write and to publish their own works. In 1923 Redcam moved to England for health reasons. At the time of his death ten years later, the Poetry League of Jamaica was preparing to name him Jamaica's first Poet Laureate; the title was conferred posthumously.

Redcam's first published works were his three novels, *Becka's Buckra Baby, One Brown Girl and . . .*, and *Martha Brae*, all of which explore problems specific to Jamaican life. Critics agree, however, that the novel was not the best vehicle for his literary talents and that while his works in this genre display great sensitivity, they are marred by serious technical imperfections. Conversely, critics consider the expression of fervent patriotism in Redcam's lyric and narrative poetry so vigorous and imaginative as to render formal considerations unimportant. The longest of Redcam's narrative poems, *San Gloria*, relates with power and originality the poet's vision of the founding of Jamaica and has become the classic folk history of the island.

While Redcam's works no longer enjoy great popularity, many of his poems survive as the lyrics of patriotic songs. Moreover, his importance lies not so much in the reputation of his own works as in the response they inspired among succeeding generations of Jamaican writers who, building upon Redcam's achievements, brought Jamaican literature to the attention of the world.

PRINCIPAL WORKS

Becka's Buckra Baby (novel) 1903
One Brown Girl and . . . (novel) 1909
Martha Brae (novel) 1918
San Gloria (drama) 1920
Orange Valley, and Other Poems (poetry) 1951
Brown's Town Ballads, and Other Poems (poetry) 1958

J. E. CLARE McFARLANE (essay date 1956)

[*In the following excerpt, McFarlane praises Redcam's poetry.*]

Any consideration of the poetry of Jamaica must, of necessity, begin with Tom Redcam (Thomas Henry MacDermot). He laid its foundations, he did much toward the rearing of its superstructure. There may have been—indeed there were—writers in Jamaica before his time whose work possessed some merit as literature; but of the poetry that is undeniably Jamaican in its impulses, that draws its life and colour from Jamaica's sun and air, its streams, its blue skies, its wooded hills, and flower-filled valleys, Tom Redcam is the founder. Through the barren, dreary years he stood almost single handed as its defender and preserver, until a few spirits, touched with a kindred fire, joined him in service.

That he claims this distinguished position in our literature is hardly to be wondered at when one considers the intensity of his patriotism as manifested in his work, both as a poet and as an editor. Such whole-souled love when associated with more than ordinary mental powers is bound to issue in achievement of a distinctive nature. In his poetry the history of Jamaica lives in a light not of the common day, but such as is found only in the wonderland sacred to romance and to dreams; and over it all is cast the magic spell of the Antillean Queen; the beauty of form and face that bewitches all who gaze upon it.

In most of the poet's work this living "Presence of the Past" is to be found intimately interwoven with a contemplation of the natural features of his country:

> The billowing tides of Life outpour,
> The generations pass;
> Made void by time, the woodland fails
> As dies the bladed grass.

Such observations are characteristic of his spirit and temper. Orange Valley, St. Ann, with its great ceibas and golden-tinctured fields of grass on the one side, and on the other its "distant muted tides" and foam-white reefs, is to the poet a fitting stage on which to re-enact the past, and to trace the modifications, which man and nature have imposed upon each other with time as the common arbiter of their fate. The gray walls amid green boughs over which "long-stretched creepers climb" and whose guardians are "great cedars and the wind-worn palms," to the eye of imagination present a scroll upon which the history of the centuries is recorded.

> This loop-hole, wide in angle-room
> Speaks spacious Spanish days,
> When the brown Arawak went by
> On leaf-dark forest ways.

The panorama of life unfolds:

> The Spaniards pass, the Indians die,
> Like mists that fade afar.

and the British soldier holds the stage! Upon the scroll presented may be found the evidences of British occupation:

> Between these walls now rough with age
> Men talked of Benbow's fight,
> And Rodney's fame the courier told
> Who crossed Diablo's height,
> And at the tavern quaffed a glass;
> And hard by Huntley spurred,
> Till far Trelawny from his lips
> The news of victory heard.

So too, in the poem **"San Gloria"** addressed to Columbus, an appeal is made to the memory of the great discoverer. Does he recall these details of natural scenery, which to the poet seem themselves to hold memories of a past in which he was the central figure? Can it be—for this is the poet's unrecorded thought—that the spirit of man is less permanent than the environment in which it works and which in some measure it creates?

> San Gloria's wood-carved mountain frieze
> In the blue bay is mirrored now,
> As when thy white sail wooed the breeze.

There is infinite pathos in this suggestion of the greatness, albeit the possible transiency, of the human soul.

> Dost thou remember things like these
> Where thy great soul inhabits now?

The question remains unanswered; it is addressed, not merely to the man who discovered a new world, but also to the reason behind the universe; to the logic which shaped so marvellous a thing as human life and gave it a world for its setting. Tom Redcam is rarely deliberately philosophic; but in the great moments of his poetry there is to be found a well defined conception of man's exalted place in the scheme of things.

To his task as Jamaica's interpreter and chronicler the poet brings a developed musical sense and a happy gift of phrasing. His lyrical poems, many of which have been set to music, are too well known to need introduction here; **"Jamaica Marches On"** has been sung countless times to the tramping feet of little children, and **"We Are Marching to Conquer the Future"** is, I believe, known to every school boy in Jamaica—and to every school girl too. Tom Redcam is by nature a singer, and he spares no opportunity to tell of the beauty of his native land.

> I sing of the cloud-reaching height
> Of the roar of the wind-waving wood,
> Of the torrent descending in might,
> Of the sweep of the swift-gleaming flood.

And the effect of his singing, as I have said, is heightened by his gift of phrasing; almost any poem will illustrate his command of new and arresting word combinations; but perhaps **"Thou Hast Done Well,"** an ode on the death of Edward VII, is more remarkable than any other in its effective employment of words. In a short article to the press some years ago, I pointed out the significance of the use of the word "formless" in the couplet—

> A lamp of the eternal with its light
> On empty space and realms of formless night.

In employing this word instead of "boundless", say, the poet succeeded in conveying not only the idea of an infinitude of darkness, but also the mysterious, unknown quality of that darkness. But the whole poem is wrought with consummate skill:

> Blossoms of life death culls from failing lips
> In those last hours when end in deep eclipse
> All we accounted glory—

These lines are surpassingly beautiful; and in the two short lines which occur at the end we hear the deep booming of the bell which seems to break in upon our reverie and to remind us that "All is over now." The rhyming of the penultimate line with the first line of the poem gives to the piece a striking touch of finality which could hardly be achieved in any other way.

But neither his patriotic fervour, nor his command of musical measures, nor his artistry in words, would by themselves have entitled Tom Redcam to the position he has won. To these qualities must be added the reach of the man's soul, the range of his spirit. For the appraisal of this, his purely lyrical poems and such as are devoted to patriotic themes, or written to commemorate some episodes of the Great War—which brought added stimulus to our poet as it did to every other writer—offer fair opportunities. Among these may be mentioned **"The Ensign Streameth Red, Killed"** (written on hearing of the death of Capt. Arthur George Cecil MacDermot, the poet's cousin) and **"England, All Hail."** But it is to his longer poems that we must go for anything approaching the full measure of his stature. The narrative poem **"A Legionary of Life,"** which tells the tragic story of a man who, defeated by fear, failed in the hour of her peril the one dearest to him, and the drama *San Gloria* which deals with the shipwreck of Columbus on this Island—these reveal qualities to be found nowhere else. There is a spaciousness about them; a breadth of philosophic thought and vision for which lyrics, however excellent, offer no scope whatsoever; and it is on such as these that a final appraisal of his merit must rest.

Perhaps at this stage the reader may be thinking: "You are all praise; is there nothing with which to find fault?" I could evade such a question by replying that so little notice has been taken of Jamaica's poetic literature that an enthusiast may be forgiven if he keeps a blind eye for faults. But Tom Redcam's work needs no such apology. Such faults, or rather failings, as it possesses, arise for the most part out of the man's character. He may be said to have one passion: and that is Jamaica and her history. Of other phases of passion he appears to know very little. He is comparatively weak and unconvincing when he writes about love; the darker byways and subtler influences of desire seem to be entirely beyond his ken. On this account one misses in his work a certain tenderness; his music is more strong than sweet.

But Tom Redcam is a great poet. In Jamaica we are afraid to ascribe greatness to any of our fellows. We seem to believe that greatness is the exclusive right of peoples other than ourselves, and we are inclined to discourage even the aspiration toward it. Well, I have said that Tom Redcam is a great poet, and I am prepared to abide by it; more, I challenge anyone with equal knowledge of the facts and equal, or better, ability to judge, to contradict me successfully. Tom Redcam possesses the capacity of soul and the powers of intellect that would have made him a world poet; but our blind scheme of things decreed otherwise. It is little short of a crime that a man of his powers should have been compelled by circumstances to spend himself in editing and directing a weekly paper. The thoughts that he had no leisure to think are lost to us; the beauty that he might have created, but for the press of little duties we shall never see. But do we care for these things?

The death of Tom Redcam on the 8th October, 1933, brought formally to its close a life which had been spent in the service of its fellowmen. But his work as a man and a poet had ended some eleven years earlier, when failing health had compelled him to leave Jamaica and to take up residence in England.

And yet it is not quite correct to say that his work as a poet ended with his departure from Jamaica. It is characteristic of the man that he wrote one of his most beautiful lyrics from his sick bed in London, a poem of wistful yearning for the sights and sounds of his native land:

O little green Island in far-away seas,
Now the swift Tropic shadows stride over thy leas;
The evening's elf-bugles call over the land,
And ocean's low lapping falls soft on the strand.
Then down the far west, towards the portals of night,
Gleam the glory of orange and rich chrysolite.
Day endeth its splendour; the night is at hand;
My heart groweth tender, dear far-away land.

In this poem is epitomised the ruling passion of his verse: loyalty to Britain and love for Jamaica. In the pattern of his soul and of his poetry these two affections so blend into a harmony of sound and colour as to be incapable of a separate existence. Here we are reminded of an ideal whose outlines have been blurred by the clamour and short-sightedness of these opportunist years. Amidst the menacing shadows we have lost the faith we knew, and the vision seems no longer true. Yet who would willingly predict that the star of faith will never shine again?

For England is England, the strong and the true,
Whose word is her bond in her march through the blue;
For England is England, who mothers my soul,

Truth, bare in its glory, with her deep self-control . . .
But my little green Island, far over the sea,
At eve-tide, Jamaica, my heart is with thee.

His very last poem was a song, **"I Am in Love with Life."** It was very fitting that he to whom spiritual values had always been paramount should have flung the challenge of life in the face of death. The material world was falling away from him; but what of it? He possessed the permanent and the real:

I am in love with life;
Pride's bright insignia, all the gauds of power,
Ambition's lure and pleasure's fevered hour—
Ah, let them lie; here in the sunlit air,
I pass with one, immortal, young and fair:
I am in love with life.

(pp. 1-9)

J. E. Clare McFarlane, "Tom Redcam," in his A Literature in the Making, *The Pioneer Press, 1956, pp. 1-11.*

KENNETH RAMCHAND (essay date 1970)

[*In the following excerpt, Ramchand discusses Redcam's importance in the development of Jamaican literature.*]

In an article of 1899 entitled **"The Present Condition of Jamaica and Jamaicans,"** MacDermot wrote: "Today we lead; tomorrow we advise; and on the day following we are co-workers together with our black countrymen. It is as our actions and opinions relate to them that they will stand applauded or condemned by the future historian." As editor of the *Jamaica Times* between 1904 and 1923, his comments on public affairs, according to [W. Adolphe] Roberts, pointed to an ideal of Jamaica as a recognized entity, there being "an unhappy note in his writing when he thought that his native country was being treated as a step-child."

Although MacDermot was not the first Creole nationalist in the West Indies, he was the first Creole who practised as a literary man. In his second novel *One Brown Girl And . . .* he sets up the brown girl Liberta Passley as a likely centre of interest. She had been "handed over to Mother England to grow and to be trained among her sturdy sons and strong-limbed health-glowing daughters." Now that she has returned she is cut off from her people and she is heavy with the real and "inner Liberta Passley" waiting to be released. To put it like this is to draw attention to the similarity between Redcam's opening situation, and those developed with skill and concentration by George Lamming in *Season of Adventure* (1960), and Claude McKay in *Banana Bottom* (1933).

But Redcam does not become imaginatively involved in this significant West Indian dilemma. Liberta is reduced to peripheral status as the novel turns earnestly but ineptly to other social issues. The invoking of an exceptional Negro in contrast to the mass is in the tradition of anti-slavery novelists, but the White West Indian author also seems to look forward to much more recent attitudes. A physical description of Fidelia Stanton, a Negro girl employed in a Portuguese household, leads into a celebration of slave rebellions:

The unadulterated blood of her tribe ran in her veins and she was a Coromantee, daughter that is of the bravest of all the tribes that were brought to our shores during the eighteenth century, from the West Coast of Africa. They came as slaves; but the Coromantees, brave enduring, haughty and resolute, made bad bondsmen. Men whom nature had made free in soul, their fellow men found it no easy task to fetter. Through their brief periods of quiet submission they worked wonderfully well, inspired by their pride of race to show their powers; but they sprang into rebellion as surely as the rays of the midday sun, passed through the burning glass, kindle fire: and those rebellions which the Coromantees led. . . .

(One Brown Girl And . . .)

This is followed by an explicitly "corrective" view of the African past:

It is the conventional idea that the black men brought to the West Indies as slaves came from a life wholly savage and barbarous; through which there ran not a single vein of coherent organisation; a life unredeemed by a single spark of nobility and unsustained by aught of organised government, law or order. The truth however is that in some cases these men and women came from tribes which maintained a system and code of unwritten law that embodied for the tribe at least, more thoroughly and efficiently than Christianity has yet succeeded in doing for the whole race in the West Indies, a great number of those moral obligations that are elemental and are vital to the wellbeing of a people.

(One Brown Girl And . . .)

These essays are intrusions from an artistic point of view, but they are worth noticing: they help to show how close European romantic attitudes to the African are to the sentiments of later Négritude writers from the Caribbean.

When Redcam returns to describe the master's improper advances and Fidelia's human thumping reply, there is a classic example of the difficulty of the writer who feels he must express an African personality in his Negro characters, although he himself is more familiar with another system:

Fidelia Stanton was a full-blooded Coromantee though she knew nothing of the history of her tribe. None had ever told her of the valiant deeds of her grandfathers and of their sires; but the pure tribal blood flowing in her veins was a conducting chain along which thrilled mighty but irresistible forces that connected her in moments of emergency with that race and that past in Africa to which she belonged.

(One Brown Girl And . . .)

It is consoling to think that Fidelia's violent refusal of John Meffala was not due to the solid middle-class prudery her White West Indian author arms her with; on the other hand, it is disappointing to begin to feel that the whole thing was just a rush of the warrior blood.

Redcam's poetry and fiction are disappointing, but his activity helps to illustrate the connection between national feeling and the growth of a literature. He remains an important figure in our literary history because of the attempt he made to encourage writing and to create a book-buying public in Jamaica in the early years of this century. (pp. 51-4)

> *Kenneth Ramchand, "New Bearings," in his* The West Indian Novel and Its Background, *Barnes & Noble Inc., 1970, pp. 51-62.*

ADDITIONAL BIBLIOGRAPHY

Bennett, Wycliffe. "The Jamaican Poets." *Life and Letters,* 57, No. 28 (April 1948): 58-61.

Characterizes Redcam as Jamaica's "first national poet, father of our poetic literature and first Poet Laureate of Jamaica" and calls *San Gloria* "the quintessential statement on the discovery of Jamaica."

Jones, Joseph, and Jones, Johanna. "Thomas H. MacDermot." In their *Authors and Areas of the West Indies,* pp. 38-9. Austin: Steck-Vaughn Co., 1970.

Recounts a conversation between Jamaican authors Victor S. Reid and Peter Abrahams in which they "talked about Jamaican literature. . . . 'It began with Redcam,' Reid said."

Mark Rutherford

1831-1913

(Pseudonym of William Hale White; also wrote under pseudonyms Reuben Shapcott and Peter Bulkley) English novelist, short story writer, and essayist.

Rutherford was a late-Victorian author whose works explore English Protestantism, or Dissent, in the nineteenth century. In *The Autobiography of Mark Rutherford, Dissenting Minister* and *Mark Rutherford's Deliverance,* both semi-fictionalized accounts of his own life, he describes his upbringing in a stern, Calvinist environment and his subsequent disillusionment with religious orthodoxy. Later, in his novels, Rutherford broadened the scope of his narratives to include the Protestant community at large, denouncing the hypocrisy and affectation of many of its members. Profoundly influenced by Baruch Spinoza's concept of rational conduct and William Wordsworth's religion of nature, Rutherford was concerned primarily with moral and spiritual questions, and while critics note that his novels contain stylistic and technical flaws which make them unsuccessful as fiction, they agree that the philosophical sophistication of his ideas and the clarity with which they are presented mark his work as an important contribution to Victorian literature.

Rutherford was born in the predominantly Protestant town of Bedford, where his parents were members of the church once led by one of England's most renowned Dissenters, John Bunyan. Although Rutherford's father, a bookseller and political journalist, fostered a spirit of intellectual curiosity in his children, an appropriate atmosphere of piety was also vigorously maintained in the household, and Rutherford later reported that from an early age he felt oppressed by his parents' religious observances. Nevertheless, he outwardly complied with the dictates of their faith throughout his childhood and adolescence, even going so far as to enroll in the Protestant seminary at Cheshunt when he was seventeen years old, although he secretly wished to attend Oxford University. After three years at Cheshunt, during which he claimed to have learned nothing, Rutherford transferred to the seminary at New College, now part of London University, but he was promptly expelled when he manifested clear indications of anathematized doctrinal doubt in his first round of examinations.

Rutherford spent much of the next year experimenting unsuccessfully with a variety of careers, including teaching and ministry. Settling finally in London late in 1852, he secured an editorial position on the *Westminster Review,* where he met and worked closely with George Eliot, then an unknown writer. Rutherford quickly became enamored of Eliot, yet his extreme diffidence in social interactions prevented their relationship from developing beyond the point of professional camaraderie. Eliot's personal qualities, however, profoundly influenced Rutherford's conception of the ideal woman, and when he began to write fiction many years later it was her character that served as the model for his most sympathetically portrayed female protagonists.

Rutherford had accepted the position with the *Westminster Review* primarily because of his great admiration for the paper's freethinking, agnostic editor, John Chapman; but he soon tired of what he termed Chapman's ''cold negativism,'' and he left

the *Review* in 1854 to accept a civil service post. Two years later, he was assigned to the Admiralty, where he continued to work for nearly three decades. Rutherford's life during this period is described by biographers as a dreary cycle of hardship and despair: his wife suffered from a degenerative nerve disorder that rendered her an invalid, and he was forced to work long hours at an unrewarding job and to accept extra clerical assignments in order to support his large family. The adversity of his situation was further exacerbated by his struggle with chronic, severe depression. Despite the many obstacles to his well-being, however, Rutherford frequently submitted philosophical and political essays to various journals, primarily in the hope of maintaining his link with London's literary and intellectual communities. In 1880, he began to write a somewhat fictionalized record of his life, because, he stated, his experiences had brought him knowledge which might help others by serving as ''an antidote to the despair which . . . besets a man in his progress through the world.'' The work was published in 1881 as *The Autobiography of Mark Rutherford* and was followed by *Mark Rutherford's Deliverance,* in which Rutherford used fictional elements more freely in attempting to define the meaning of his life

The critical acclaim with which the *Autobiography* was greeted encouraged Rutherford to continue his philosophical crusade, and he published four novels and several collections of essays in the years that followed. During this latter portion of his life, his circumstances improved considerably; with the royalties from his writings and his Admiralty pension, he was able to live comfortably, and although his wife died in 1891 after years of suffering, he was solaced by the affection of his four surviving children. In 1911, at the age of eighty, Rutherford remarried, and the happiness of his final years is documented in his young wife's *Groombridge Diary*. He died in 1913.

Despite clear affinities with other late Victorian novels, Rutherford's work is generally regarded as an expression of the religious reaffirmation which began early in the nineteenth century with the nonsectarian transcendentalism of the English Romantics. Like George Eliot and George Gissing, Rutherford frequently focused on social problems in his work, yet the solutions he proposed involved personal moral regeneration rather than secular institutional changes. Rutherford explained in his *Early Life* that he was profoundly affected by his reading of Wordsworth's *Lyrical Ballads* at a time when he had begun to rebel against the "arid theology" of Calvinism, and that he eagerly embraced the idea of achieving a more personal communion with the divine will through contact with the natural world. It was not, he asserted, that Wordsworth's religion of nature supplanted all of his previous theological beliefs, but that the wider perspective he thus gained made it impossible for him to accept the orthodoxy of organized churches. As a result, Rutherford's fiction satirizes those Protestants whose religious faith is unexamined or superficial, a condition he invariably associated with intolerance and intellectual ossification, while it creates sympathetic and compelling portraits of characters whose spiritual crises are alleviated by some natural event, leaving them with renewed moral convictions. The enlightenment thus gained typically allows Rutherford's protagonists to endure with courage and honor what he considers the inherent baseness of human existence, and it is this spiritual prescription which Rutherford wished to communicate to his readers.

Although Rutherford's fiction has been frequently criticized for what many critics consider his inability to handle even the most rudimentary aspects of the novel form, his style was in fact the product of his conscious decision to subjugate medium to message. Considering the philosophical content of his works to be supremely important, he wrote, "if truth is of the slightest importance to us, we dare not obstruct it by phrasemaking." Consequently, the function of his narratives is to illustrate his moral precepts, and his plots frequently fail to conform to the conventions of fiction. In addition, his desire to state ideas succinctly and forcefully results in a bare prose style which, according to Irvin Stock, "resembles . . . the speech of a man who must speak coldly between clenched teeth lest he be overmastered by emotion." While such departures from literary tradition have led a number of critics to dismiss his work as simply inept, others have found his methods entirely valid, and several recent commentators have argued that his fiction is not nearly as flawed as was originally thought.

Despite conflicting assessments of the quality of his work, critics generally agree upon Rutherford's importance in English literature. As sincere and highly intelligent expressions of loss of faith during the Victorian period, *The Autobiography of Mark Rutherford* and *Mark Rutherford's Deliverance*, like the essays of Leslie Stephen and the poetry of Matthew Arnold, provide insight into a critical phase in the development of Western thought. In addition, some scholars judge his fictional persona to be an innovative literary technique, differing markedly from the subterfuges of other pseudonymous authors in its complex relation to his own life. Most often, however, Rutherford's work is praised for its perceptive portrayal of the human condition, which is given its veracity by his profound comprehension of the lessons of his own life.

(See also *Dictionary of Literary Biography*, Vol. 18: *Victorian Novelists after 1885.*)

PRINCIPAL WORKS

The Autobiography of Mark Rutherford, Dissenting Minister (fictional autobiography) 1881
Mark Rutherford's Deliverance (fictional autobiography) 1885
The Revolution in Tanner's Lane (novel) 1887
Miriam's Schooling (short stories) 1890
Catharine Furze (novel) 1893
Clara Hopgood (novel) 1896
An Examination of the Charge of Apostasy Against Wordsworth (essay) 1898
Pages from a Journal with Other Papers (essays) 1900
John Bunyan (biography) 1904
More Pages from a Journal with Other Papers (essays) 1910
The Early Life of Mark Rutherford (autobiography) 1913
Last Pages from a Journal (essays) 1915
Letters to Three Friends (letters) 1924

THE ATHENAEUM (essay date 1881)

[*In the following excerpt, a reviewer finds* The Autobiography of Mark Rutherford, Dissenting Minister *"remarkable" in its powerful portrayal of an unhappy life.*]

[*The Autobiography of Mark Rutherford, Dissenting Minister*] is certainly remarkable. It is short, and that in itself is a merit in these days of weary three volumes. It is incomplete, breaking off with a half promise from the editor, as he calls himself, that if more papers are found they shall be given to the world. It is the story of a mental struggle, in parts so powerfully told that it cannot be wholly fictitious. It is sad and gloomy in tone, yet not utterly hopeless, for the writer, in the midst of his drawn battles with unbelief and despair, manfully strives to "accept life as God has made it," and goes on fighting again and again. But the battle is always drawn, as the writer admits, and therein lies the tragedy of the tale. Mark Rutherford, born and brought up in the straitest sect of Calvinistic Independents, in early manhood becomes a minister. Before long the bonds of dogma fret him, he breaks away, drifts into Unitarianism, and then into a No-man's Land, where we reluctantly leave him. For the man, with his passionate longing after love, human and divine, is certainly worthy of some happier fate than that which befalls him, perpetually "perplexed by many problems I have never solved; disturbed by many difficulties I have never surmounted; and blotted by ignoble conceptions which are a constant regret."

A review of "The Autobiography of Mark Rutherford, Dissenting Minister," in The Athenaeum, *No. 2791, April 23, 1881, p. 555.*

WILLIAM DEAN HOWELLS (essay date 1886)

[Howells was the chief progenitor of American realism and the most influential American literary critic during the late nineteenth century. The author of nearly three dozen novels, Howells successfully weaned American literature away from the sentimental romanticism of its infancy, which earned him the popular sobriquet "the Dean of American Letters." Through realism, a theory central to his fiction and criticism, Howells sought to disperse "the conventional acceptations by which men live on easy terms with themselves" that they might "examine the grounds of their social and moral opinions." To accomplish this, according to Howells, the writer must strive to record detailed impressions of everyday life, endowing characters with true-to-life motives and avoiding authorial comment in the narrative. Criticism and Fiction *(1891), a patchwork of essays from* Harper's Magazine, *is often considered Howells's manifesto of realism, although, as René Wellek has noted, the book is actually "only a skirmish in a long campaign for his doctrines." In addition to his perceptive criticism of the works of his friends Henry James and Mark Twain, Howells reviewed three generations of international literature, urging Americans to read the works of Emile Zola, Bernard Shaw, Henrik Ibsen, Emily Dickinson, and other important authors. In the following excerpt, Howells praises the sincerity and objectivity of* The Autobiography of Mark Rutherford *and* Mark Rutherford's Deliverance.]*

[We] have read within the year two English books by an unknown hand which may yet mark a new era in English fiction. We hardly know, indeed, whether to call them fiction, they carry so deep a sense of truthfulness to the reader, they are so far in temper from any sort of mere artistry, so simply and nobly serious. The books are the *Autobiography of Mark Rutherford* and *Mark Rutherford's Deliverance,* the one being the rather unsatisfying sequel to the other. Yet it is unsatisfying only as the incompleteness, the brokenness of life, which it perfectly counterfeits, is unsatisfying. There never were books in which apparently the writer has cared so little to make literary account of himself, cared so little to shine, to impress, wished so much to speak his heart plainly out to the heart of his reader. There is absolutely no study of attitude, no appeal to the dramatic or the picturesque, no merely decorative use of words. When you have read the books you feel that you have witnessed the career of a man as you might have witnessed it in the world, and not in a book. We could not give too strong an impression of this incomparable sincerity.

The history is that of an Englishman of the lower or lowest middle class, who is bred to the ministry, but who is constrained by lapses of belief first to abandon his evangelical pulpit, and then to give up a Unitarian parish, and who at the close of his autobiography is the clerk of an atheistical bookseller in London. *Mark Rutherford's Deliverance,* which appeared last summer, four years after the publication of the *Autobiography,* takes up his story at the point where he becomes the Parliamentary correspondent of two provincial newspapers, and follows him through the failure of this employment, his marriage with the woman to whom he had been betrothed in his youth, and his final toil at hateful work under a hard master, to his sudden death. There is no "incident" in the story; there is neither more "plot" nor less than there is in the experience of God's creatures generally, so generally ignored by "imaginative" writers in their "powerful" inventions. It can not, therefore, find favor with readers who like to be "amused," and to "have their minds taken off themselves." We warn them that the story of Mark Rutherford will fix their "minds" all the more intensely upon themselves, and will stir them deeply, without in the least "amusing" them. Or rather it will

do this with readers who can think and feel; and the other sort had better go to the theatre and see a modern play.

Nothing of Mark Rutherford's error or weakness is concealed in these extraordinary books, and in him we have more distinctly got rid of that barbaric survival, the "hero," than in any other figure of fiction—if he is really fictitious. If you pity him, and even love him for his truth and purity and right endeavor, it is because you are sufficiently mature, sufficiently civilized, to see the beauty of these things in their union with tremulous nerves, irresolute performance, vague aspiration, depression, frequent helplessness, faltering faith. He is only one of ten or twelve other persons drawn with the same wise faithfulness, and presented to us with the belief that we shall have enough inconsistencies in them. When the author has to tell us that a certain man of clear, strong, disciplined mind is a journeyman printer, he seems not to feel bound to explain the fact that he can be both one and the other, and he has no excuses to make for asking us to be interested in the psychological experience of a waiter, a salesman, a porter, who are never at all romanced, but are considered simply in their quality of human beings, affected in due degree by their callings. But such a man as Marden, living and dying in gentle, serene, patient, agnosticism; such a man as McKay, groaning over the misery of London, and inventing out of his own poverty and helplessness a way to help it some little, however little; such women as Mary Marden, Theresa, and Ellen, taking quietly, strongly, unspectacularly, their share of the common burden of common life, have more of consolation and encouragement in them than all the "ideal" figures that ever "helpless fancy feigned" out of proportion to the things that are. The story where they move naturally, from real impulses and with genuine interests, is not gloomy, with all its unrelenting seriousness, and it would be very unjust to leave the reader with the notion that it is inimical to religion. It is very religious. We do not see how Christianity could be more subtly and profoundly comprehended, and throughout his doctrinal stumblings and gropings Mark Rutherford finds his happiness only in that highest good which Christ taught in the highest degree— good to others. This is the key-note of his story, touched throughout, but never with maudlin pathos or rhetorical flourish.

People who like genteel company in novels will not find him in it; there is not a "gentleman" or a "lady" in either of the books, and the plain, poverty-bound lives which they have to do with are considered as inapologetically in their struggles with real sorrows and troubles as if they were all so many gentlemen and ladies of leisure longing to get married or unmarried. If there is no false shame in depicting these common people and conditions, neither is there any boastfulness, or anything of the foolish superstition that there is merit in narrow circumstances of themselves. Perhaps the self-respectful attitude in regard to this material is kept so well because it is the inner life of these men and women that is portrayed—that experience so sweet, so bitter, so precious, of almost any human soul, which we should always be better and wiser for knowing, but which we so often turn from in the stupid arrogance of our cultures and respectabilities.

At times the author seems to have no art in presenting his facts, he does it so barely and bluntly, but he never fails to make you understand just what he means, and he never offends against that beautiful "modesty of nature" which, when one has once really valued it, one can not see offended in literature without a sense of outrage. (pp. 485-86)

William Dean Howells, in a review of "Autobiography of Mark Rutherford," and "Mark Rutherford's Deliverance," in Harper's New Monthly Magazine, *Vol. LXXII, No. CCCCXXIX, February, 1886, pp. 485-86.*

THE SPECTATOR   (essay date 1894)

[*In the following review of* Catharine Furze, *the critic provides an essentially positive assessment of that work.*]

In Mark Rutherford's earlier works, the author seems to be his own subject, and more or less consciously sets before his readers the struggle of a soul in an anguish of doubt and difficulty. In *Catherine Furze* the artist is more evident, and the judgment passed upon human life is calmer and less personal. In each work, however, the scene is kept within the limits of the provincial town. But if provincial life seems unexalting to the observer, it is vividly real to those who live it, and the very narrowness of the horizon intensifies the human joys and sorrows within it. It is such elements as these that furnish the interest of *Catherine Furze,* and a difficult problem that might make shipwreck of any life is treated with both force and delicacy. Catherine is the daughter of an ironmonger in a well-to-do Midland town; and there is much pathos in the faithful picture of the apparently unvarying smallness of aim and imagination which is to be found in that particular stratum of life. In Catherine herself there is a revolt, both of thought and speech; but it is of the kind that represses itself and works inwardly. Whereas a wilder nature might have broken away from all restraint, Catherine has a power of endurance that comes very near to being genuine nobility of soul. In Eastshorpe the lines are rigid and the barriers firm. The aim and effort of her mother was to rise a few inches in the social scale. So usual is this desire, that it is difficult to imagine how such a commonplace position can be anything but weariness to read about. But the quiet intensity of the reality carries us forward by main force. If there is no romance in Mrs. Furze's struggles and Mr. Furze's weak resistance after all, they are in their nature the mainsprings of action. Progressive desire rules the world, and the Furzes are only fulfilling their natural law in their little circle at Eastshorpe. Then follow the inevitable consequences—the ever-eluding attainment and the merciless chastisement for false steps taken in the pursuit. The honest sow's ear of Furze baffles all his wife's efforts to make it a silk purse. Refinement combined with want of education makes a sorry mixture, as far as happiness is concerned. Furze's shirtsleeves are always asserting themselves, and his gift for saying the wrong thing never fails him. The resistance of Catherine to her mother's views is more decided. She will not aim at what she knows to be worthless, and openly, and even defiantly, prefers her humble but faithful farmer friends to all the ladies of brewers or doctors who may please to call for a subscription to a local charity. But all this is only the setting to the real romance. To hold her own in the higher circles of Eastshorpe society Mrs. Furze realises that Catherine is inadequately equipped, and she is sent to the boarding-school of the neighbourhood, kept by the representative of local refinement and conventionality. Here for the first time Catherine comes under the influence of a mind that commands her own. Brought up as a Dissenter in a small provincial town, she has had little or no chance of encouragement in any breadth of reading, but under the protecting wing of the Miss Ponsonbys she makes friends with Mr. Carden, the vicar of the parish, and his wife, and so enters into a wholly different circle of ideas.

The character of Mr. Carden constitutes one of the main interests of the story, and is summed up by the old-fashioned doctor with acute common-sense. "A remarkable man in many ways, and yet not a man I much admire. He thinks a good deal, and when I am in company with him I am unaccountably stimulated, but his thinking is not directed upon life." His difficulties. . . . . . "are to a great extent artificial, and all the time spent upon them is so much withdrawn from the others which are real. He goes out into the fields reading endless books containing records of persons in various situations. He is not like any of those persons, and he never will be in any one of those situations. . . . . . I have known Carden to do very curious things at times. I do not believe for one moment he thought he was doing wrong, but nevertheless, if any other man had done them, I should have had nothing more to say to him." Such a character coming in contact with the repressed nature of Catherine could not fail to be as spark to tinder. All the intellectual force which underlaid the poverty of expression in her life blossomed at once in the genial atmosphere of Carden's literary speculations. With delicate and unconscious flattery, he drew out her opinions and developed her ideas. Married to a clever, but somewhat uncongenial wife, he found in Catherine both an apt pupil and an interesting study. The situation is a simple one, but all the more dangerous as the motives are good, and the intellectual gain tends to conceal for some time in what direction matters are going. Under the circumstances, it is impossible for Catherine to withdraw herself from his company. The gradual growth of his influence is well drawn; and though Catherine's upright simplicity never wavers, we are made to feel that the contest is an unequal one for Catherine. Her emotions are keener as well as more unselfish; and her life, apart from his sympathies, is dry and insipid. No doubt all this is far from being original,—indeed, when considered carefully, the cleverness and reality of the work lies in the treatment of the commonplaces of life; and this is the case with all the works of "Mark Rutherford." The minor characters of the book are fully as well drawn as the principal ones. The side-plot of Tom Catchpole is skilfully if somewhat melodramatically worked in, and gives rise to the wholly imaginative theories of Mrs. Furze which work such dire consequences. Good material of all kinds abounds in the book, and though it will never be a popular novel, it is full of the study of human nature. (pp. 830-31)

A review of "Catherine Furze," in The Spectator, *Vol. 72, No. 3442, June 16, 1894, pp. 830-31.*

THE ATHENAEUM   (essay date 1896)

[*In the following review of* Clara Hopgood, *the critic praises some characterizations in the novel but finds its structure severely flawed.*]

[*Clara Hopgood*] might be described as an inchoate mass of good material. It is a pity that the form of the book is so poor, for though the characters wander about, saying and doing things without any particularly obvious object, and the story divagates hopelessly, in themselves the characters are out of the common, and have the rare merit of appearing at first sight conventional and yet being really very suggestive. The description, for example, of Madge's gradual perception of the superficiality, mental and moral, of her first lover, is done with much subtlety, and even faintly suggests Mr. Meredith's penetrative glance into the emptiness of the conventional man. The Jew, Baruch

Cohen, with the mingled seriousness and volatility of his amative disposition, is also a character of great interest; for it is one outwardly very commonplace, and yet the author just manages to reveal the bit of human personality underlying the crust. Clara, who is presumably meant to be the heroine, is not adequately expounded; she remains a mysterious figure with a suggestion of interest about her which is not elaborated. The work of an original thinker is evident here, but it loses much of its force by the almost careless want of directness and unity in the mechanism.

A review of "Clara Hopgood," in The Athenaeum, *No. 3590, August 15, 1896, p. 220.*

THE ACADEMY   (essay date 1899)

[*In the following essay, the critic applauds Rutherford's perceptive depictions of the lives and personalities of provincial Dissenters in his novels.*]

Why are the novels of Mark Rutherford like none others that we know? Why do we place them on the same shelf as Spinoza's *Ethic,* and refer to them a good deal oftener? Because they are informed with a wisdom austere and sweet, a magnetic sympathy, an altruism which rejoices in contact with life. Because without them the blacks and duns of life remain for us untranslated, affronting the eye with mere dowdiness. In these stories, unmoulded by plot and ungilded by epigram, there is yet a fine symmetry and a flashing insight. Every sentence is perfectly clear, and this clarity extends to the exhibition of character and landscape, the working out of the incidents and the effect of the whole. Moreover, the clearness is a natural clearness—it does not mean deprivation of atmosphere, sentiment, eloquence; but it means that there is no "negligible quantity" in the novels, it means that a selective instinct of a high order has assisted at their production. Observers of character know that the *cliché* of custom lies so strongly on individuals that it is only in one action out of twenty that the average man expresses his own idiosyncrasy in a recognisable form. Mark Rutherford's novels evince the talent that recognises the typical action, and so is able to present the type. When Zachariah, in *The Revolution in Tanner's Lane,* under stress of emotion informs his guests that unless they believe God's Word they are lost, his wife says: "My dear, will you take any more tea? . . . Major Maitland, may I give you some more tea?" Nothing could repel us more effectually from the chilling nature of this ordinary woman. Mr. Hexton, of whom a similar anecdote is told in *The Autobiography of Mark Rutherford,* is a being of the same stamp. He did not beat his wife; but he told her to take her books down from the shelf in her sitting-room because they were shabby, and "he wanted a stuffed dog there." Mrs. Jane Coleman and Mr. Hexton are depreciators, the most formidable of the non-criminal community. It is a class against which Mark Rutherford is specially qualified to direct his deadly camera. Mr. Furze, the ironmonger, belongs to it. He gets a young man—whose benefactor he regards himself—to write difficult letters with which he is incompetent to deal. "Ten minutes after the letters were posted (he) was perfectly convinced that he had foreseen the necessity of each one—that he had personally and thoroughly controlled the whole day's operations, and that Tom had performed the duties of a merely menial clerk." As an illustration of the pathos of the depreciated, nothing can be finer than Baruch Cohen's experience when, in a moment of supreme danger, he sees his son Benjamin—once so devoted to him—leave him to his fate in order to rescue his sweetheart. As an illustration of the pathos of the depreciator nothing more beautiful can be found than the story of Miriam, whom the stars and the dawn taught to love her husband.

In the provincial world of shopkeepers, the industrial and "dissenting" world to which Mark Rutherford introduces us, the depreciator is, it must be understood, only one of many subsidiary types, each presented with memorable distinctness, though it be for only a few minutes. Generous and sympathetic people are not rare. Witness Theresa Wollaston (a true comforter), M'Kay (the Drurylane philanthropist), Mrs. Caffyn (who gave a rector a lesson in charity), and Mrs. Joll, to name no more. Mrs. Joll stands before us in a portrait which no canter—and which of us has not canted at some time in his life?—can contemplate without wincing. She was

> a rude, stout, hard person . . . fond of her beer, rather grimy, given to quarrel a little with her husband, could use strong language at times, and was utterly unintelligent so far as book learning went. Nevertheless . . . in her there was the one thing needful—the one thing which, if ever there is to be a Judgment Day, will put her on the right hand; when all sorts of scientific people, religious people, students of poetry, people with exquisite emotions, will go on the left, and be damned everlastingly.

Although they afford a unique exhibition of the types to be met with in "dissenting circles," and show a reverent regard for, and a deep knowledge of, the Scriptures, it were vain to seek in the novels a specific announcement of religious faith. It is not for Mark Rutherford to depreciate the value of pure living and the pursuit of noble purposes by giving them letters of credit on a divine exchequer. "Virtue," says Spinoza, "is to be desired for its own sake; nor is there anything more excellent or more useful to us than virtue, for the sake of which virtue ought to be desired." Integrity of the loftiest kind is the ruling passion of Mark Rutherford's eponymous heroines, of the before-mentioned Zachariah and of himself. Note his career: he breaks his engagement with Ellen because he doubts his own love; he relinquishes his Independent pastorate because his heterodoxy brings him into conflict with his flock; he resigns his appointment as preacher to a Unitarian chapel because "the desire for something like sympathy and love absolutely devoured" him; he tasted the bitterness of poverty and semi-serfdom, but he saw "the Kingdom of God through a little child"; and not too late in his gray and weary life recognised the authentic voice of love in his own heart, and found it Ellen's voice after all.

Mark Rutherford was "delivered"; but Death was not the deliverer, though Death came while his tyrant was apparently dominant. He had learned to command the depths of himself, to pay, not with blood, but the Gethsemane sweat exacted of him who would save even himself, for the truth that was wider than creeds, richer than explanations, being, as it were, both light and ultimate peace. Zachariah, the Calvinist, a "friend of the people," sentenced to imprisonment for complicity in that most sadly comic of failures the march of the Blanketeers in 1817, is led straight by loyalty to an indefinite future in America. "It is not known"—wrote the only authority on that subject to the writer of this article—"and most probably never will be known, what became of Zachariah and Pauline." This we know: they were arrows—bound to go straight. Zachariah's first wife was an incidental victim to the imperious command of his loyalty. We feel him so dutiful that it is natural not to be detained either in his Cimmerian dark of captivity or in his Elysian field of second marriage. We enter and are dismissed from both in half a page. As with the heroes, so with the heroines. In Catharine Furze and Clara Hopgood, a fixity of intention towards a free and pure spiritual life is as evident as in Mark Rutherford. To my mind nothing in literature is more touching than the relations between Catharine and the Rev. Theophilus Cardew and his wife. Here we have passion awakening in a girl of heroic honesty for a man of less indelible nobleness. We see a divine interposition in the girl's favour, one of those accidents more subtle than miracles, and the man is withdrawn from her ere he has wronged by some perfidy of anarchic love the warm-hearted woman wedded to him, whose commonplace echo of himself he disdains. It is not more strange than credible—such is the novelist's persuasiveness—that, in their love for each other, Catharine and the clergyman were both saved: she taught him, by one of those revelations that come to us when the great gray cliff holds us up above and against the surging sea of our desires, to love his wife and to bear with her, and to be simple in his teaching. Over **Clara Hopgood** the public that speaks of books as "edifying" or "unedifying" has loudly mourned. What a departure! What dangerous, if not wicked counsel! Why? Because Madge Hopgood is a seduced girl who refuses to marry the father of her child on the ground that she no longer loves him. Madge's sensual error is presented with an economy of circumstantial evidence which should satisfy the sensitiveness of all ordinary people. Surprise at the view of marriage put forward is unintelligent. It embodies Miss Arbour's energetic advice to Mark Rutherford, and that principle of sincerity to oneself and others which influenced his own conduct. It is noteworthy that the book is called after the elder sister, **Clara Hopgood**. Clara deliberately stood aside at the crucial moment, that the man whom she loved and who loved her might transfer his love to her embarrassed sister. He did so, knowing her history, and his name was Baruch, Spinoza's Jewish name. Clara we leave in Italy, dead in Mazzini's cause, her name living on her niece's lips. With such fine delicacy does Mark Rutherford subordinate the iconoclastic to the heroic. While a scandalised section of his readers are wrangling over Madge with enthusiastic "Individualists" the novelist is thinking all the time of Clara.

There are other imaginative writings by Mark Rutherford. An apology for Saul, supposed to emanate from Rizpah, is a wonderful *tour de force*. "David turned everything into songs"—how powerful is the sneer!—"my lord never sang nor danced, nor played; it was as much as he could do if he smiled." In this and other theological writings we perceive the strength of the born novelist as much as in the novels. For, after all, it is the faculty of adoption that separates the man of imagination from the mere parrot-perceiver. Not that the mere parrot-perceiver were not great in comparison with the numbers of cleverish novelists who falsify or neglect real happenings to chime with a gross optimism, for at least he is a reporter of facts. But in Mark Rutherford's novels we have much more, we have the submission of facts to the irresistible movement of souls determined on uprightness and sincere in strife. The trumpet of this world is not needed to confirm the imperfect, but authentic, felicity they ascribe to two or three, and would be an impertinence in that dark labour-world of which the fullest and most documentary of them—their putative author's own narratives—gives us such harrowing glimpses. To accept the light in the novels and reject the shadows, on the ground of progress made since the epoch of which they treat, were vain. The millennium is still Himalayan in its aloofness. The "Thing" is no more; and demonstrators are not fired upon. But, with multitudes of pinpricks and little agonies long drawn out, the strike between superciliousness and philanthropy, capital and labour, sect and sanctity, still goes on. Some of the blacks are now gray, but till the grays vanish before the theophany of paramount day Mark Rutherford's lantern will be a helpful guide. (pp. 161-62)

"The Art of Mark Rutherford," in The Academy, *Vol. CVI, No. 1396, February 4, 1899, pp. 161-62.*

W. J. DAWSON (essay date 1905)

[*In the following excerpt, Dawson discusses the theological uncertainty which informs* The Autobiography of Mark Rutherford.]

The characteristic note of [**The Autobiography of Mark Rutherford, The Revolution in Tanner's Lane,** and **Catherine Furze**] is a certain sad lucidity of vision. They are the confessions of an over-sensitive mind, for which the riddle of existence has proved too hard. They depict the struggles of a human soul in search of truth and faith; the wish to believe, at war with the conditions of belief; the martyrdom of a fine nature, too scrupulously honest to purchase peace by those conventional casuistries which rule commonplace minds; the tragedy of a superior nature, forced by the hand of fate into association with natures either mean or narrow, or dull and unillumined, which are capable of no response, and indeed of no vital contact with his own. Mark Rutherford, with all his capacity for both delicate thought and passionate emotion, is thrust into the narrowest of worlds. It is useless to declare his real thoughts, for no one would understand them. He is supposed to have been trained for the ministry, in a college where not a single problem of faith or religion has ever been stated honestly. His instructor was an elderly gentleman, with a pompous degree of Doctor of Divinity—"a gentleman with lightish hair, with a most mellifluous voice, and a most pastoral manner, reading his prim little tracts to us, directed against the shallow infidel. About a dozen of these tracts settled the infidel, and the whole mass of unbelief, from the time of Celsus downwards."

He becomes the minister of a stagnant church in a stagnant little town, where the only person who can afford him the least degree of intellectual comradeship as an atheistic printer. He drifts from this to a yet more stagnant Unitarian chapel; finds that the longer he preaches the less he has to communicate; plunges at last into the vortex of London life, enduring all the indignities of the poor and unconsidered; attaining at last just enough faith in altruistic ideals to attempt a little social work for the outcasts of Drury Lane. This is the brief story of the **Autobiography;** but it is told with such extraordinary intensity, it abounds in such vivid sketches of character, it is so pregnant with emotion, so exquisitely phrased, so rich in subtle analysis of the most secret passions of the heart, at once so frank, subtle, and sympathetic, that it possesses an incomparable charm, and ranks with the highest works of imaginative genius.

"No theory of the world is possible" is the last word of Rutherford's message. With perfect frankness he admits that he has erred in attempting to grapple questions too big for him, and he counsels men against the folly of too exorbitant curiosity. His only positive counsel is the old counsel of stoicism. There is no condition of life from which a man may not extract some grains of happiness, if he does not retain his fortitude and the readiness to find joy in simple pleasures. Men constantly make the mistake of asking too much of life. They expect ideal affections, and scorn the plain bread of human love. The woman whom Rutherford despised for her intellectual limitations be-

The Bedford Meeting, where Rutherford attended services in his youth.

comes in the end his honoured wife. Some natures, and especially natures of unusual depth and sweetness, never reveal their riches except in the hour of trial. If any justification can be found for what seem the senseless sufferings of human life, it is that these sufferings do liberate the best elements of fine characters. One of the most tender passages in the *Autobiography* describes the process by which a young girl, whom he loved little because he thought her dull and stupid, becomes a perfect nurse to his sick wife:

> Faculties unsuspected grew almost to full height in a single day. . . . I remember once going to her cot in the night as she lay asleep, and almost breaking my heart over her with remorse and thankfulness,—remorse, that I, with blundering stupidity, had judged her so superficially; and thankfulness that it had pleased God to present to me so much of His own divinest grace. . . . My love to Marie was love to God Himself as He is—an unrestrained adoration of Him, adoration transfigured into love, because the revelation had clothed itself with a child's form. . . . I had seen the Kingdom of God through a little child.

He who can thus misread his fellow-creature may well ask himself whether he has not also misread God. If no theory of the world is possible, there may nevertheless exist enough of hint and suggestion to encourage hope, or at least to make a wise man diffident in denial.

> The proper attitude, the attitude enjoined by the severest exercise of the reason is, "I do not know"; and in this there is an element of hope, now rising and now falling, but always sufficient to prevent that blank despair which we must feel if we consider it as settled that when we lie down under the grass there is an absolute end.

It may be doubted if any writer has ever rendered mental agony with such power as Mark Rutherford. Doubt is for him not a philosophic balancing of probabilities; it is a cruel force which rends his heart in twain. And his doubt goes very much beyond the questioning of this or that assumption of orthodox faith; it arraigns the whole scheme of things. He is unable to discern any sign that the "soul of the universe is just." He uniformly represents the comfortable rewards of life as falling to the unworthy, or at least to persons of featureless character. He pictures person after person, lavishly equipped with fine faculties of thought or affection, either denied the opportunity of their development, or put into a position which makes *these* very faculties a means of torture. He himself is a case in point. There should have been some place in society which he might have occupied with content and honour, but he never found it. He has an immense capacity for friendship, he would gladly have died for a friend; but he finds repeatedly that the ardour is all upon his side, that he calls thrice upon a friend for once that his friend calls on him, that he has stooped even to the point of shame and humiliation to give a love which no one values. He is made to feel that he is a superfluous person, nearly useless to the world. The agony of loneliness is sometimes too great for endurance. Yet something remains to him; for the Gospel of Christ reinterpreted by the conditions of his own life comes back to him with new emphasis and consolation. Christ also was lonely. His Gospel is particularly designed to be the gospel of the lonely and the despised. It has nothing to say to the prosperous whom the world suffices.

> The story of Jesus is the story of the poor and the forgotten. He is not the Saviour of the rich and the prosperous, for they want no Saviour . . . but every one who has walked in sadness because his destiny has not fitted his aspiration; every one who, having no opportunity to lift himself out of his narrow town or village circle of acquaintance, has thirsted for something beyond what they can give him; everybody who, with nothing but a dim daily round of mechanical routine before him, would welcome death if it were martyrdom for a cause; every humblest creature, in the obscurity of great cities or remote hamlets, who silently does his or her daily duty without recognition,—all these turn to Jesus and find themselves in Him. . . . There is no Saviour for us like the hero who has passed triumphantly through the distress which troubles us. Salvation is the spectacle of a victory of another over foes like our own.

It may be objected that reflections of this kind are better suited to the essay than to the novel, and it must be admitted that in the strict sense of the term the *Autobiography* is doubtful fiction. Much of it is but thinly disguised personal confession; perhaps, if the truth were known, there is not a single invented incident in the entire book. Yet the hand of the creative artist is visible in every line. Whether the people he pictures are idealised types or portraits of known persons—and perhaps they are something of each—it is certain that they are rendered with extraordinary vividness.

No extract, and no series of extracts, can do justice to the writings of Mark Rutherford. They have qualities which give them a place apart in later literature. He speaks as one who has greatly suffered, and hence he speaks as no other can to the suffering heart. He is the interpreter of inarticulate natures. The actual message which he has to deliver may be brief, but it is vital because it has been tested and sanctified by experience. He writes also with a curious pregnancy of phrase. His style is austere and simple, shorn of all redundancy, of all deliberate eloquence or laboured novelty, yet it is the most suggestive of styles. It is a triumph of severity and compression. Those who read his books once find themselves returning to them again and again; they hold the mind with an incomparable charm; they quicken thought, they reveal the deep things of life, and, in spite of their quiet rejection of orthodox faith, they have a strange power of creating that larger faith which is based, not on dogma, but on the universal instincts of humanity. Other writers of religious fiction represent certain phases of thought and feeling peculiar to their time; Mark Rutherford deals with the great secular thoughts of humanity. Sincere and accomplished as a writer like Mrs. Humphrey Ward may be in the examination of religious problems, yet her message seems shallow and almost insincere in comparison with the message of Mark Rutherford. For here is authentic suffering—here is spiritual tragedy which goes to the very roots of life; and hence the influence which Mark Rutherford exercises over minds that are sympathetic with him is unique. It is perhaps more perilous to forecast the future of books than of nations; but it would not be surprising if the writings of Mark Rutherford, or at least his *Autobiography,* should take rank with the famous classics and the imperishable treasures of English literature.

> W. J. Dawson, ''Religion in Fiction,'' in his The Makers of English Fiction, *Fleming H. Revell Company, 1905, pp. 268-89.*

H. N. MacCRACKEN   (essay date 1913)

[*MacCracken was a prolific American author and critic. In the following excerpt, he discusses the place of Rutherford's work in English literature and the possibility of Rutherford attaining a similar place in America, comparing aspects of his fiction with that of George Gissing and of George Eliot.*]

In England, though for years a leader, Rutherford outlived his time. In America he never lived. From the critics came a few notes of recognition, and the *Fortnightly* welcomed him as it had welcomed Francis Thompson. Elsewhere, silence complete; and yet in the literary history of the last quarter-century his place is as secure as any man's. Born into Bunyan's heritage, nourished upon the hopeful romanticism of Wordsworth and Carlyle, eager to share in the large freedom of the soul which was to come in a great mid-century, Rutherford found that place at last among the little company who strove—how hopelessly!—to reconcile their youthful vision with the epic poverty of London slums. Overwhelmed, and yet not quite overwhelmed, his gentle if somewhat nervous courage found refuge in spiritual self-reliance, viewing in rescued calm from the strong donjon of Mansoul, the evidences of God's transcendent world. He founded the school of perilous optimism. (pp. 189-90)

Six slender narratives, all labelled ''fiction'' in the public library, and shabbily rebound,—this is his gift to us. The [*Pages from a Journal*] . . . add little to his fame, though they complete, in a way, his remarkable self-revelation. But ''fiction'' is scarcely the word for Rutherford's stories. *The Autobiography of Mark Rutherford* and *Mark Rutherford's Deliverance* are absolute transcripts from life. We follow in these little booklets—they would not fill two hundred pages of a *Jean Christophe*—the growth of a real soul. Away from Bedford, the seminary, and the provincial congregations, we walk with Rutherford to London and the deliverance. We meet his friends, Mardon and his daughter Mary, with their enfranchising skepticism. We learn to know Ellen, his first love and his wife; and Theresa, the ''modern'' woman, strong, self-controlled, radiating confidence and resolution. Characters nod to us casually, like McKay who roared so loudly, in a purely professional way, down the columns of provincial Tory papers. The desperate little mission in Drury Lane, doomed to failure at it was, sounded the reveille to whole armies of social workers of to-day. Out of it all, the man's soul struggles to the light, passionless and serene, and yet deeply, intensely human.

The Revolution in Tanner's Lane, though cast as an historical novel, is almost equally revealing. The story curiously repeats Rutherford's relations with Mardon and Mary, in the life of Zechariah Coleman, a dreamy Calvinist of Clerkenwell, whose friendship with Jean and Pauline Caillaud involves him in the Blanketeer riots of 1814. Zechariah, in turn, guides George Allen out of narrow ways of thinking into spiritual revolution, and final freedom. But however subjective the treatment of the tale, no episode in the century's history is more vividly described in fiction than the rising of the Blanketeers.

Upon this group of narratives of intimate confession Rutherford's fame will chiefly rest. And yet there is much that is fascinating about the other three novels; George Eliot's characters live no more completely than Clara Hopgood, Catharine Furze, or the unforgettable Miriam of *Miriam's Schooling.* As a story, this last is almost flawless. A great passion suddenly inflames a big, dark-haired, black-eyed girl, inexperienced and impulsive; a passion for an unworthy lover. She learns his true nature in a midnight scene too poignant to repeat; but through all the tragedy of betrayal goes the discipline of a spiritual nature. If any of Rutherford's heroines live—and his sensitive pen caught women best—it will be Miriam; so tender, so bitter, so intense is the portrayal. There is poetic allegory, too, serving as accompaniment, where the girl finds forgetfulness in study of the silent stars; a note recalling the novelist's master, Bunyan.

Catharine Furze, the second in his studies of women, presents in a subdued key, and relieved with many rays of quiet humor, the tragedy of mismating and the spiritual cost of heroic renunciation. A curious Slav subjection to feeling, accompanied by paralysis of the will under a flood of skepticism, runs through the story. One feels also the equally Russian lack of inevitability in the final catastrophe. Compensation for these defeats is made in the searching characterization, and the simple truthfulness of a style that seems almost artless.

Clara Hopgood, Rutherford's last novel, is a wonderful study of the "single woman," self-denying and self-suppressing, who gives up all life holds to serve her loved ones. Casual readers, interested in the more commonplace romance of Clara's sister Madge, will miss the real point of the story. High-minded as Madge was, in her somewhat theatrical views of the world, she never thought of her sister. Clara, on the other hand, never thought of herself. It is, indeed, part of her tragedy that one's interest must follow Madge, the individualist, and her "problem," which just now usurps the stage everywhere. Madge has broken the social code; the man's caste and hers are not the same; what shall be done? Henry Arthur Jones, in *The Hypocrites,* lashes an insincere aristocracy to on unconvincing repentance; John Galsworthy, in *The Eldest Son,* storms along the same road; St. John Ervine, in *The Magnanimous Lover,* St. John Hankin, in *The Last of the De Mullins,* and Stanley Houghten in *Hindle Wakes* assert the entire independence of women from the necessity of a protecting social bond. In this solution, if it be one, they were long anticipated by Rutherford. And Madge Hopgood is appealing; her sisters of the theatres repel. With her the great refusal comes not of high spirits or of defiance, but of inspirational truth. Throughout her trial, the sublime courage never wavers. One is reminded of a similar situation in *Middlemarch.* Madge's single vision of duty, like the one upon the Damascus road, suffices for the convictions of a lifetime. Here, as again and again in his novels, Rutherford holds fast to faith in this instant inner light.

I have mentioned George Eliot's work as a basis of comparison; and in the lens-like intensity of vision that accompanies the narrowness of field which each focuses upon, there is, perhaps, some truth in the likeness. In the emphasis upon moral outcomes the two are also close. But with the man Rutherford, as revealed in his autobiography, there are literary affinities much closer and more interesting than this. One cannot read much of Rutherford without encountering the face of Gissing. Their best work was written side by side. With vastly greater output, and with more skill in the technique of the story, Gissing's quality is not so fine. Both knew London slums and provincial barrens; both write out of their hearts; both fight with all the bitter weapons the novelist can command against the narrow and inconsistent intolerance of English sectarianism; both are rather interested in women than in men; both are terribly oppressed with poverty, and its sad work in robbing the great English heritage of some of its best and highest traits. More than this, both feel a great spiritual conflict within themselves, the end of which they cannot see. Gissing's soul is torn by the conflict of culture and circumstance; Rutherford's by the similar struggle of religion with new criticism. Gissing's heroes break down before the social barriers of caste; Rutherford's characters come to disaster and repose through the loss and recovery of spiritual confidence. Of the two, Gissing's theme is broader, and his fame must wax; while the other will wane, as Calvinism ceases to be a living doctrine to us. In subtlety of design and in moral strength, however, Rutherford's world is as far above Gissing's as his own life was better governed than that of his fellow-craftsman.

A very different name is also inevitable, in seeking out standards by which to measure Rutherford. In his hack-work of articles, translations, and editions, the one title of peculiar significance is *The Life of John Bunyan.* Rutherford was well fitted to tell this life. His father was a trustee of the famous Bunyan Meeting at Bedford, and Bunyan's books were his childhood companions in the dingy printing-shop. All the spiritual intensity, all the miserable period of doubts and fears, self-torture and melancholy, ill-health and depression that we read of in "Grace Abounding" were repeated in this humble disciple. Bunyan's spiritual conflict and his return to repose in faith were a part of Rutherford's experience. Beyond this, however, Bunyan's power of depicting his own states of mind, his intimate spiritual confessions, written without a trace of self-consciousness or pose, and his way of suggesting a world beyond the bare recital were inherited by Rutherford. He was even like Bunyan in the composition of earnest but execrable verse, as if unaware that in prose he had an instrument exactly suited to him. He had all Bunyan's love of allegory, which gives significance to more than one of his stray pieces in the *Pages from a Journal.* There is the story of the clockmaker of Cornhill ("**Faith**"), of whom people used to say, "Ah, if you can only get one of the watches he used to make." He was caught once on a spit of land, surrounded by the incoming tide. Unable to swim, he should be drowned if the water rose past the hour of nine. All his security of mind depended on the faithfulness of his watch, the product of his own faithful work:

> Again and again he tried to repeat the reasons in favor of his watch. They were overwhelming, but his nerves shook, his brain was in confusion, and he made sure he should faint and drop. A ghastly dread such as he had never known in his life, paralyzed him. He pictured himself lying in the sand down there; and then

he saw himself carried home in a cart to-morrow.

The stars had now appeared. There was the great Boötes sloping silently to the west, and there was Arcturus. . . . With all his might he fought; he stiffened himself, and drew his arms rigidly down beside him. Lo! in an instant his faith was restored; the flutter of his heart ceased; the adversary spread his wings and was seen no more. . . . At 9.15 he heard the beat of oars. . . .

If you ever see a Parsons watch, buy it. Sell something for it if you have not got the ready money. When you have bought it, stand by it; train yourself by never doubting it. Do not alter it on the authority of any other watch nor of any clock; no, not even if it be church or cathedral.

Will Rutherford live? It must be admitted that some serious defects militate against this. His curious subtlety and love of ingenious contrivance, which led him to edit his own novels under the second pseudonym of Reuben Shapcott; his inability to construct elaborate plots; his absorption in the spiritual and religious; and the constant struggle with Giant Despair and Mrs. Diffidence which makes up the bulk of his writings, must narrow his appeal to the public. Only a cult can rescue him from the avalanche of fiction which now devastates our libraries. There are signs that in England at least a circle of admirers is thus at work for his fame. His novels have run through a dozen editions, and some have even attained the dignity of the shilling form.

In America, however, it will take all the explosive eloquence of the little cult that recently exploited the over-rated *Marie-Claire* to obtain a hearing for Rutherford with our full-fed novel readers. Such a hearing and such a public he would have been the first to deprecate. Within a small circle of artists in literature he is sure to become to us what he has been for a generation in England—one of the strong formative influences of our day. (pp.190-4)

> *H. N. MacCracken, in a review of "Pages from a Journal, with Other Papers" and "More Pages from a Journal, with Other Papers," in* The Yale Review, *n.s. Vol. III, No. 1, October, 1913, pp. 189-94.*

HENRY WILLIAM MASSINGHAM   (essay date 1923)

[*Massingham was an influential English critic who edited the London* Nation *from 1907 to 1923. In the following excerpt, he considers those aspects of Rutherford's fiction which render it both prophetic and enduring.*]

There has of late been a revival of interest in a writer who, in fact, has never gone out of fashion with his lovers. I mean "Mark Rutherford." This renewal of affection is an experience in men's literary as in their personal lives. Who that has ever been in love with Byron ever quite forgets him? And how quickly revives the passion for Shelley, grown cold maybe over some dissatisfaction with his form! "Mark Rutherford," indeed, carries more over from his period into ours than most of the Victorians. He is nearer to us, not in time only, but in substance and manner. He is melancholy and sceptical in our way even more than in that of his earlier contemporaries. For he saw what was coming, and had indeed partly come, in the

later years of his long life, the hard, shallow, material life of the great industrial city, which he had seen at its worst—the London of the 'sixties and 'seventies—the dissipating, distracting influence of the popular Press, the loss of faith and of the sense of beauty. Like Arnold, he lacked high spirits, and like him, was contemptuous of politics and journalism, the two English substitutes for the popular religion which he had studied in the decadent Nonconformity of the middle and later Victorian periods. So he appears, apart from his peculiar and most attractive artistry, as a father and prophet of our time, unaware of its greater calamities, but with a brooding sense of their arrival. He is even in touch with its troubles. Some pages of the *Deliverance,* for example, give a striking picture of the frightening effect of unemployment. And "Mark Rutherford" can look back as well as forward. *The Revolution in Tanner's Lane* is the one novel I know which combines a magnificent sketch of the revolutionary scene with an heroic study of the revolutionary temperament. *A Tale of Two Cities* is a fine book, with one or two strokes of absolute genius. But, in the main, it is a re-writing of Carlyle. *The Revolution in Tanner's Lane* is as original as *Henry IV* or *The Canterbury Tales*. It is a piece of imaginative history, unsurpassed in our literature for liveliness and concentration of effect.

But "Mark Rutherford" is not to be claimed for any school of political thought. He is the artist, throwing out, through the medium of his beautiful prose, the depth and the simplicity of his thought and the intensity of his feeling about life. It is hard to define very closely his exact place in literature. Perhaps he may be called one of the sad humanists. His main subject is somewhat remote. Born and brought up in the Eastern Midlands, he is especially the historian of the little chapel, of the lesser township and the small trading folk who dwelt in it, the men and women of sixty years ago, who rarely read anything, and whose mental relaxations were the "Dorcas Meeting" and the gossip of the local conventicle. You can see the country he describes in a railway journey between London and Bedford or Huntingdon. As for his soul journeys, they were made by thousands of our fathers and mothers, and by some of us who have reached the middle passage. Does the scenery seem strange to younger eyes? It may, to a world of "jazzing" and cinemas.

But I imagine that Rousseau's *Confessions* are still read, and that such themes as the unrest of genius, and the travail of fine natures in hard and commonplace surroundings, can stir even the modern mind. Moreover, "Mark Rutherford" is extraordinarily full of passion. It is suppressed; for an extreme delicacy of expression marks his Puritan upbringing, and, in some degree, maybe, his temper. With one exception, his heroes are rebels only in thought. But the loves of Pauline and Zachariah Coleman, and the sorrows of Miriam and Catharine, are of the things, exquisite in structure and suggestion, which will not die in men's souls as long as the love of literature lives. Catharine Furze is to me as lovely a figure as Hardy's Tess or Meredith's Lucy—as human and as finely arrayed. The detail, indeed, is not elaborated, as in our hard, curious, modern writing, with its auctioneer's zeal for cataloguing things that do not matter. More is left to fancy. The hand is that of an artist to whom one stroke of needless brushwork is an offence. (pp. 165-67)

But Hale White's chief subject, like Byron's, is himself. Not a little of the setting of the *Autobiography* and the *Deliverance* is stuff taken from his own experience as a young divinity student expelled from College for doubting the orthodox canon, and as a vagrant in mid-Victorian London, living by the hackwork of London-Letter writing, and by canvassing for John Chapman's "infidel" books. This is not exactly the Byron atmosphere, and there are other differences. Byron's egoistic melancholy was unlighted by religious faith, by any deep feeling for humanity, or by a definite sense of his times and their significance in the changing story of man's life. All these qualities are present in Hale White's pictures of middle England and of Victorian London. The atmosphere is rather still and unillumined, for White has no touch of Blake's fiery and entranced vision. And the faith is by no means unwavering. White's feeling about life is crossed with irony, or even with a shade of despair. Something in the London that he knew as he paced its mean streets after his flight from the St. John's Wood College seemed "insoluble." "Our times," he says in the **Deliverance,** "are answerable for the creation and maintenance of the masses of dark, impenetrable, subterranean blackguardism with which we become acquainted. The filthy gloom of the sky, the dirt of the street, the absence of fresh air, the herding of the poor into huge districts which cannot be opened up by those who would do good, are tremendous agencies of corruption." He had no theory as to means of rescue. Socialism, as a spiritual idea for the government of society, appeared to him to be in the way of progress, but he thought it might fail and ruin us all. Christ's teaching seemed a draught of pure idealism, a true manual of the "heavenly law to which everything strives." But how small its power to break down the hard practice of the world, the tyranny of master over man, the terrors of unemployment, the rule of the petty-minded, the incurably selfish mass! His early Calvinism seemed to stereotype this fatalist view. Many might be called; few could in any case be chosen. "Mark Rutherford" himself, with all his sensitiveness, is a hero of spiritual endurance; amid the strain and drive of his employment he keeps his personal refinement, his sacred circle of home affection. But he sinks under the lash of a slave-driver's tongue, which brings on a fatal heart attack. "The next morning his salary up to the day of his death came in an envelope to his widow, without a single word from his employers save a request for acknowledgment. Towards midday his office coat, and a book found in his drawer, arrived in a brown paper parcel, *carriage unpaid.* " In this last word of contempt the author of the **Deliverance** sums up the coarseness of the industrial system, as he glimpsed it through the London fog and filth.

But Hale White's thought is rarely continuous; it is the mixed work of the philosopher's and the artist's temperament. And of the artist you may ask anything but consistency. So you may quote Rutherford-White for Calvinism, and against it; for the life of ideas, and the impassioned protests that it were better to be "a carpenter or a bricklayer in country air" than to waste existence in bothering about what is beyond you. "One-fourth of life is intelligible, the other three-fourths is unintelligible darkness; and our earliest duty is to cultivate the habit of not looking round the corner." If this seems a last word, it may be countered by others, which preach the "absolute monarchy of the soul." Intellectual peace is a different thing. Who can know God? Life may contain exquisite consolations for the refined and the temperate, but not a key to the ultimate purpose of things. "The world is immense," he writes in his wonderful analytical sketch of the Book of Job, "constructed on no plan or theory which the intellect of man can grasp. It is transcendent everywhere." So, through the delicate reactions of a personality like "Mark Rutherford," the eternal battle goes on.

Great writers are dateless. They seem to die for one generation and to be reborn in the next. So with Hale White. The corner

Rutherford at the age of 24.

of Nonconformist England of which he writes is known now only to a few grey-haired men and women, and the little brown-red chapels of its lanes and by-streets are sinking fast into spiritual decay. But these tales make them live again, much as Shakespeare's Mantua or Arden live. For through them walk the unresting ghosts of man's loves and contentions. (pp. 168-70)

> *Henry William Massingham, " 'Mark Rutherford',," in H. W. M.: A Selection from the Writings of H. W. Massingham, edited by H. J. Massingham, Jonathan Cape Ltd., 1925, pp. 165-71.*

ARNOLD BENNETT (essay date 1923)

[*Bennett was an Edwardian novelist who is credited with bringing techniques of European Naturalism to the English novel. His reputation rests almost exclusively on* The Old Wives' Tale *(1908) and the* Clayhanger *trilogy (1910-16), novels which are set in the manufacturing district of Bennett's native Staffordshire and which tell of the thwarted ambitions of those who endure a dull, provincial existence. In the following excerpt, Bennett notes that Rutherford's novels contain very fine prose but flawed construction and narrative style.*]

I said some years ago that Mark Rutherford's prose was almost the finest modern prose.

I still think his prose is generally very fine, but it is rather untutored: he is not safe from bad grammar, or from indefensible phrasing. Also he makes his characters talk wonderful prose, even the lower middle-class characters. His characters are chiefly lower-middle class, and upper labouring or artisan class, with a sprinkling of professionals. They are chiefly dissenters and atheists. The atheists are the sheep, and the dissenters the goats. His places are small towns or large villages in the Eastern midlands, and sometimes the inner lower-class suburbs of London—Clerkenwell, Brondesbury, etc. His interests as a novelist are chiefly spiritual and intellectual, that is, strictly religious and philosophical. He explains his characters' "views" usually before anything else. And they argue with each other at length. The sisters Hopgood argue with astounding skill in beautiful sentences, using a vast vocabulary. He simply cannot construct. *The Revolution in Tanner's Lane* is the worst example of this (perhaps his best novel). It is really two separate novels, joined by a mere accident of relationship between a girl in one and a girl in the other. There is no sign of the revolution in Tanner's Lane until nearly the end of the novel. I think that he must have constructed as he went along. *Clara Hopgood* is not about Clara Hopgood at all, but about her sister Madge Hopgood, and Clara is only dragged in at the end. Throughout Madge is the principal character. (Cf. *Rhoda Fleming*, which is really a novel about Dahlia Fleming.)

He is fond of sudden deaths, generally caused by chills following on getting wet through. Also he seems to get tired of a story and compresses the important part towards the end into a page or two. He can be slyly amusing. Thus (beginning of *Catharine Furze*): The Bell Inn's "handsome balcony on the 1st floor, from which Tory county candidates, during election times, addressed free and independent electors and cattle." (He had referred to the cattle pens, a permanent feature of the marketplace and high street.) Also (same place) about "half a dozen old skulls" found in a gravel pit. "As it was impossible to be sure if they were Christian, they could not be put in consecrated ground; they were therefore included in an auction of dead and live stock, and were bought by the doctor." There is quite a lot of this kind of thing imbedded in the sombre narratives. He is always getting new, original wisdom, observations on life, character, manners. The love interest is always there, but seldom the chief interest. He deeply understands and knows small dissenting provincial communities, and such things as free-thought political clubs.

He always moves his plot on by means of pure accidents—often by flood and field, sometimes by people forgetting something and turning back; also by death or narrow escape from death. In fact his incident-invention is childish—and hasty. There are two deaths from consumption in *Catharine Furze,* one of his best books if not his best. Also he is too hard on his unsympathetic characters. The conversion of Orkid Joe in *Furze* is comic in its wording. Some of his wordings seem to show that he does after all believe in orthodox Christianity, despite his gibes at professing Christians and his sympathy for atheists.

His best contributions to literature are his spiritual stimulation, and his singular wisdom about the conduct of life. All his books are full of both. (pp. 750-51)

Arnold Bennett, "1923," in The Journal of Arnold Bennett: 1896-1928, *The Viking Press, 1933, pp. 748-753.*

JOHN MIDDLETON MURRY (essay date 1924)

[*Murry is recognized as one of the most significant English critics and editors of the twentieth century. Anticipating later scholarly opinion, he championed the writings of Marcel Proust, James Joyce, Paul Valéry, D. H. Lawrence, and the poetry of Thomas Hardy through his positions as the editor of the* Athenaeum *and as a longtime contributor to the* Times Literary Supplement *and other periodicals. As with his magazine essays, Murry's book-length critical works are noted for their unusually impassioned tone and startling discoveries; such biographically centered critical studies as* Keats and Shakespeare: A Study of Keats' Poetic Life from 1816-1820 *(1925) and* Son of Woman: The Story of D. H. Lawrence *(1931) contain esoteric, controversial conclusions that have angered scholars who favor more traditional approaches. Nevertheless, Murry is cited for his perspicuity, clarity, and supportive argumentation. His early exposition on literary appreciation,* The Problem of Style *(1922), is widely revered as an informed guidebook for both critics and readers to employ when considering not only the style of a literary work, but its theme and viewpoint as well. In it Murry espouses a theoretical premise which underlies all his criticism: that in order to fully evaluate a writer's achievement the critic must search for crucial passages which effectively "crystallize" the writer's innermost impressions and convictions regarding life. In the following excerpt, Murry finds the most important aspect of Rutherford's work to be the essential veracity of his vision.*]

I have been reading the newly published volumes of Mark Rutherford's letters, and I have been struck once more (for it is now a dozen years since *Pages from a Journal* first wove their quiet spell about me) by the extraordinary "quality" of the man—of the man rather than the mind or the work; for the first element to be insisted on, were one to attempt the almost impossible task of defining this "quality," would be the manifest oneness of Mark Rutherford. His letters, his novels, his journals, are radiations from a single living centre, functions—to use a mathematical term—of one unchanging soul. Unchanging, do I say? Unchanging, in the sense that all true organic growth is essentially contained in the seed from which it springs, or as the compass-needle through shocks and storms quivers always towards the pole. Unchanging, yet ever flexible, as must be the soul of a man who is wholly turned towards the discovery and the service of a living truth, and is sufficiently attuned to it to know that it will not be found in definitions, but rather in the note of a strange, still voice, which needs to be listened for, in men and works and the world.

Mark Rutherford, who could listen for the voice, could also use it. By the patience of his quest for truth, he became true. And we, in reading him, are made continually aware of the beautiful veracity: with what is true in ourselves we respond to it, and if that is our business, we try (as I am trying now) to communicate some sense of it to others. It is not easy: I grope for a word, and as sometimes happens, one recurs again and again to my mind. Mark Rutherford's writing is *suffused* with the beauty of truth. There is in him no brilliant, blinding flame; no flash of lightning; but a gentle and steady glow. And again this suffused light of his is somehow cool: though he struggled with questions which have fevered men, no trace of feverishness remains. Assuredly he had felt the fevers—for they are impossible to escape—but he waited for utterance till they were past. It was necessary to him that what he said should have the endorsement of his whole being, the imprimatur of his enduring self. Until that was given, his lips were locked.

To-day we begin to feel what is the reward of his impassioned integrity. (Impassioned may appear to some eyes a strange epithet for Mark Rutherford: but that will be because they do not see below the surface. Reticence like his is bought at a price: it is not, it is utterly different from, the conventional device of under-statement, with which amusing tricks can be played, but nothing more: this reticence is achieved only by a passion for true statement, by an unflinching suppression of the momentary ego in favour of the enduring self.) As he was single, his work also is single; the various parts cohere into one whole: and now that the turbid tides of popular applause and popular reaction which surged about the great figures of the nineteenth centry have begun to ebb, Mark Rutherford's work remains, not gigantic, perhaps not even great, but secure against decay, because it was moulded by a true man after his own image. In his work, Mark Rutherford was himself, the more surely because he knew how hard a thing that is to be. He digged down to the bedrock in his soul, and his works rest unshakable upon that firm foundation. (pp. 260-62)

> *John Middleton Murry "The Religion of Mark Rutherford," in his* To the Unknown God: Essays towards a Religion, *Jonathan Cape Ltd., 1924, pp. 260-275.*

ANNE FREMANTLE (essay date 1932)

[*In the following excerpt, Fremantle favorably assesses the quality of Rutherford's fiction.*]

[William Hale White] never wrote anything until he was nearly fifty: his first book, published in 1880, under his own name, was a translation of Spinoza's *Ethics*. In 1881 he published **The Autobiography of Mark Rutherford** which is largely an account of his own life, "thinly disguised," in 1885 appeared **Mark Rutherford's Deliverance** and in 1887 **The Revolution in Tanner's Lane**. These three novels attracted no little attention: for the first time Dissent, at whose expense Dickens was pleased to make so merry, found a champion: a writer who treated of it sympathetically, and who took it seriously. Hale White owes, it has been said, "his literary eminence to the powerful studies of domestic, social, moral and theological problems contained in this remarkable trilogy of novels."

The *Autobiography* is indeed a strange book. Published ten years later than Hardy's *Desperate Remedies*, six years after *Far from the Maddening Crowd*, and later than Pater's *Renaissance*, the style, technique and content are as unaffected by any of these as is the subject matter, or the general handling of the theme. White was only three years junior to Meredith, Ibsen and Tolstoi, yet from his writings it is possible to conclude that he never "heard on any o' them." He is, as far as he goes, unique, and his isolation, if not splendid, is at least interesting. The chief, indeed the only, problem in the *Autobiography* or the *Deliverance* is the relation of the individual soul to a personal God: both these novels show how all struggles to do without God lead to moral instability, yet do not make the idea of surrender to the, nor indeed to any, Divinity, very attractive. "With no Church, no philosophy, no religion" Mark Rutherford complains "the wonder is that anybody on whom use and wont relax their hold should ever do anything more than blindly rove hither and thither, arriving at nothing." But Mark, although he loves his childhood's faith, is led back to God through Nature, the Bible, and his own loneliness. His poverty and depression lead him to a "sorrowing Savior." "The healthy, active and well-to-do need Him not," he explains, "they require nothing more than their own health and prosperity. But everyone who has walked in sadness because his destiny has not fitted his aspirations, turns to Jesus, and finds himself in Him." This curious vision of Christ as the Prince of Failures, in many ways agrees with Huysman's dictum *Dieu n' habite pas les corps sains* [God does not inhabit healthy bodies]. White has, indeed, many points of resemblance with the author of *Sainte Lydwine*. The one crawled to God from the depths of mental despair and hyponchriacal despondency, the other from the sloughs and quagmires of sin:

neither are normal, nor ever happy: neither, in these first stages of their recovery, can join the sons of God in their "shouting for joy." But Rutherford had already realised, through Wordsworth, the affinity between Nature and her God: "Christianity," he affirms, "in strange historical fashion is an expression of nature, a projection of her into a biography and a creed," and the *Autobiography* abounds in lovely descriptions of the countryside. The following accounts of midday in September and of noon by the sea, are good examples:

> At midday the stillness was profound. We sat down on a floor made of the leaves of last year. The silence was broken only by the softest of whispers descending from the great trees which spread over us their protecting arms. Every now and then it died down almost to nothing, and then slowly swelled and died again, as if the gods of the place were engaged in divine and harmonious talk.

This breathes the calm of autumn; the second extract suggests a more complete repose:

> so still was the great ocean, so quietly did everything lie in it, that the wavelets which licked the shore were as pure and bright as if they were a part of the mid-ocean depths. Some fishing boats were becalmed just in front of us. Their shadows slept, or almost slept, upon the water, a gentle quivering alone showing that it was not complete sleep, or if sleep, that it was sleep with dreams.

The Revolution in Tanner's Lane opens with an admirable description of the 20th April, 1814, the day Louis XVIII was welcomed in London by the Prince Regent. It is a very lively and absorbing novel, and Pauline, the heroine, is an excellently well drawn character. She is the daughter of a Frenchman, named Dupin, and of Victorine, his mistress, a brave and gallant woman, who saved her unworthy lover from the guillotine. She and her adopted father, Caillaud, enter into the lives of Zachariah Coleman, a Calvinist printer, and of his wife. They all become friends of a certain Major Maitland, and through him become involved with the "Friends of the Poor." The story ends sadly with the hanging of Caillaud, who shot the Major's murderer during the march of the Blanketeers. Zachariah suffers two years' imprisonment for being involved in the fray. On his release, as his wife is now dead, he marries Pauline, but she dies in childbirth. The characterisation is very well done: the frigid, pious Mrs. Coleman, flattered by the Major's attentions yet miserably jealous of her husband and Pauline, is a very alive person, whilst the impetuous Pauline, the meetings of the "Friends of the People," and the condition of Manchester in the early nineteenth century, are all made very alive. But perhaps the most striking thing about the book is its rage against the uselessness of all "the undisciplined wildness and the feebleness of the attempts made by the people to better themselves." The latter part of this novel, from Pauline's death onwards, forms a kind of epilogue: but like Christiana's progress, or *Paradise Regained,* it does not compare with the first part. Of White's later novels, **Miriam's Schooling** may be dismissed as a poor attempt to prove that although women should be educated above their class, they should be content to remain in it, nor seek to "better themselves." It was published in 1890 and was followed in 1893 by **Catharine Furze.** This opens with a very powerful picture of a country town, which is anticipatory of the early chapters of Arnold Bennett's *Old Wives' Tale*. Here is the Bell inn:

> in the centre was the Moot Hall, a quaint little building, supported on oak pillars, and in the shelter beneath, the farmers assembled on Market Day. All around the Moot Hall, and extending far up and down the street, were cattle pens and sheep pens which were never removed. Most of the shops were still bow-windowed, with small panes of glass, but the first innovation, indicative of a new era at hand, had just been made. The druggist, a man of science and advanced ideas, had replaced his bow windows with plate glass, and had erected a kind of balustrade of stucco, so as to hide as much as possible of the attic windows, which looked over, meekly protesting. Nearly opposite the Moot Hall was the Bell Inn, the principal inn in the town. There were other inns, respectable enough, such as the Bull, a little higher up, patronised by the small commercial travellers and farmers, but the entrance hall to the Bell had sand on the floor and carriers made it a house of call. Both the Bull and the Bell had market dinners, but at the Bell the charge was three and sixpence, and sherry was often drunk. There the steward to the Honourable Mr. Eaton, the principal land owner, always met the tenants. The Bell was Tory and the Bull was Whig.

Catharine herself is a delightful child, and Eastthorpe an amusing, scandal-mongering little town. Catharine's love affair with a married clergyman is most discreet: she dies, and the clergyman as a result is more than usually amiable to his own very charming wife. *Clara Hopgood* is a less attractive girl: Mr. White, it would seem, is trying to give the story more "pep" when he introduces a clandestine love affair and its inevitable result. This novel, published in 1896, is a not very successful study of two "intellectual" women. White delighted in "brainy" girls: in **"Mrs. Fairfax"** he describes his ideal type; in Priscilla Broad he decries his pet aversion, the pretty, feckless creature who becomes merely "pretty little Mrs. Allen." Yet he could ridicule the blue stocking very effectively, and does so in **"George Lucy's Grandchild."** He believed women should develop their intellects, but not, however, at the expense of their womanliness: rather at that of their femininity, if such a distinction may be made. He wanted them not less wives and mothers, because companions, but less bird-like, less silly and frivolous. Quiet girls with thoughtful foreheads, who were good sick nurses, yet read *Epictetus:* such were the types he admired. But *Clara Hopgood* does not quite justify nor explain itself: the Dido and Aeneas scene between Miriam and her admirer is weak: Miriam's reasons for refusing to marry the father of her illegitimate child are even weaker, and it is unfortunate that she should get the plum she does not deserve and her sister covets, in the shape of an elderly Jew named Baruch. Clara goes off broken hearted to Italy with Mazzini, and dies there. In 1898 White published an essay entitled *An Examination of the Charges of Apostasy Against Wordsworth* in which, after affirming "I think we must admit that, so far as the French revolution was concerned, Wordsworth did not turn traitor"— he goes on to say "solemn institutions are at the present time more than ever necessary; we suppose that literature can take their place, that they were the device of an age which had no books, but it is possible that it may be wise to preserve them,

just because we have so many books and because there is so much to be learnt. We are beginning to see that the merest fragment added to the stock of beliefs which enable us to live in peace and hope is of more value than profitless rebellion." The author of *The Revolution in Tanner's Lane* had travelled far, farther even than his admired Wordsworth, and in how few years, along the road of conservatism. The *Pages from a Journal* contain many good things, amongst them this lovely recollecting of an early morning in January:

> A warm, still morning, with a clear sky and stars. At first the hills were almost black, but as the dawn ascended, they became dark green, of a peculiarly delicate tint which is never seen in the day time. The quietude is profound, although a voice from an unseen fishing-boat can now and then be heard. How strange the landscape seems! It is not a variation of the old landscape; it is a new world. The half moon rides high in the sky, and near to her is Jupiter. A little further to the left is Venus, and still further down is Mercury, rare apparition, just perceptible where the deep blue of the night is yielding to the green which foretells the sun. The east grows lighter, the birds begin to stir in the bushes, and the cry of a gull rises from the base of the cliff. The sea becomes responsive, and in a moment is overspread with continually changing colour, partly that of the heavens above and partly self contributed. With what slow, majestic pomp is the day preceded, as though there had been no day before it and no other would follow it.

In 1905 he wrote his *John Bunyan,* a very sympathetic study of the Bedford Dissenter, to whom he, spiritually, had some resemblances, although he was entirely without the divine gift of imagination which lifted Bunyan from his prison cell to the Delectable Mountains from whence the celestial City might be seen. White was a good critic: his essay on Byron, Goethe and Matthew Arnold, is a masterly piece of work, and all he says about Milton is worth reading. (pp. 282-85)

His literary affinities were few, and his literary indebtednesses even fewer. Of his contemporaries, he is near only to George Gissing and George Macdonald, and he owes more to Macdonald than to Gissing, for the *Ryecroft Papers* are of a different mettle than the "moderate Calvinism" which suited White best. His theology is far, but his temper is near, that of the author of *David Elginbrod;* though he never came near *Phantastes, Lilith* or *The Golden Key* he had much of Macdonald's sweet earnestness. Dissent has produced little great talent: Bunyan and Cowper are perhaps its solitary laureates, but White was always faithful to his father's creed, and can be claimed as one of Calvinism's novelists, if not of her genii. Although in some ways broadminded, he remained always a stern Puritan. "We must face the fact that we cannot read the Elizabethan dramatists and Thomas à Kempis," he told Dorothy Smith, and in the *Autobiography of Mark Rutherford* he is categorical enough:

> above all, there must be no toying with passion, no books permitted, which are not of a heroic turn. When the boy becomes a man he may read Byron without danger. To a youth he is fatal.

Yet himself he was a passionate devotee of Byron, as was his father before him! For over fifty years he spent the hours between 5.30 and 8.0 each morning reading the Bible, or Shakespeare, and no man was more convinced than he of the essential difference between good and evil: principles were to him "all in all" and he even went so far as to say "men who are totally at variance ought not to be friends." But there was another side to him, a very human side which sympathised with Saul's concubine, Rizpah the Horite, and loathed "that dancing David, who took Uriah's wife, and basely murdered Uriah, and was said to be a man after God's own heart." He tried always to attain to that way of life which Wordsworth recommended so wholeheartedly, whose object was

> The virtue to exist by faith
> As soldiers live by courage.
>
> (p. 286)

It is a little difficult to find Hale White his niche, either among his contemporaries, or in relation to posterity: his great originality lay in his writing of the Dissenting lower middle classes, of the country-town tradespeople, at a time when *The Importance of Being Earnest* was drawing crowded houses, and the *beau monde* was reading the old Ibsen or the young Shaw. The second Mrs. Hale White, who understood him better than anyone, has perhaps said the last word about him: "here you have got the commonplace, real commonplace, which is nothing more than it proposes to be, and moves only in circumscribed spheres." (p. 287)

> Anne Fremantle, "A Hero to His Valet," in The London Mercury, *Vol. XXV, No. 147, January, 1932, pp. 280-87.*

WILFRED STONE (essay date 1954)

[*Stone is a distinguished American critic who is best known for his perceptive study of E. M. Forster,* The Cave and the Mountain *(1966). In the following excerpt, he discusses Rutherford's prose style.*]

To come upon Hale White's prose after knowing the oratorical effects of Macaulay, Carlyle, and Meredith, or the elaborate refinements of Pater, Ruskin, and Swinburne, is to experience something like a cold shower after a milk bath. For in Hale White we find none of that phrasemaking, none of that impulse to decorate, burnish, and inlay which embellished the pages of Hale White's contemporaries until, as Oliver Elton has said, "you cannot see the page for the phrase." Hale White's pages were few and visible, and his sentences lucid and even austere. He worked and did not play with language; words were to him as precious as men's souls and like men's souls must be purified by their intensity, simplicity, and honesty. "If the truth is of serious importance to us," he writes, "we dare not obstruct it by phrase-making: we are compelled to be as direct as our inherited feebleness will permit."

This moral impulse made Hale White a conscious stylist and gave to his writing many of those same qualities which recommend him to us as a man. Much of his own life was dedicated to a search for absolutes, but the direction of his endeavor was always toward reducing complexity to the absolute of simplicity. With a scientific passion for precision and clarity he looked for the unity of life in particulars, for truth in the hard facts, and he disciplined his prose to be almost the perfect vehicle for such a search. "Painted glass is very beautiful, but plain glass is the most useful as it lets through the most light"

was a quotation used by his father, and it was a principle to which Hale White gave assent in nearly every line he wrote. We shall look far to discover another writer whose prose style was a more direct expression of his own personality. We have already looked through that clear glass to see the man behind it, and have discovered a remarkably clear and undistorted picture. The quality which he admired in Milton—"the power to keep in contact with the soul of man"—was his supreme gift as well, and he seldom lost contact with himself or the concrete stuff of his own deeply felt experience. Hale White had, therefore, no theory or practice of art which was not part of his theory and practice of life, and the reader who is attracted to his style must inevitably have some sympathy with the nature of its creator, for they are the same. And if we discover unevenness in that style—an oratorical quality sometimes competing with a cold austerity—it is only because in his own personality the public and private man never completely came to terms.

A rewarding approach to this study is to examine Hale White's habits of composition and revision. The original manuscripts of his novels were all, unfortunately, destroyed by the author, and we are told little about the conditions surrounding their composition except that the first of them was done at "extraordinary high pressure" and was often worked on at four o'clock in the morning. But there is abundant evidence that his normal habit was to write slowly and painstakingly, revising carefully before publication. When an article for *The Nation* was printed with a minor error in it, before he had been given a chance to see the proofs, he was extremely upset and "danced about the bed and swore." W. Robertson Nicoll wrote to Mrs. D. V. White that Hale White always "made the alterations himself" in his articles and that "he was extremely careful and punctilious in all his work." His advice to at least one of the young feminine authors who gathered about him in his advancing years was drawn from his own rule book. The manuscript under discussion was manual of instruction for teachers of arithmetic being prepared by Mabel Marsh:

> I speak from experience. My counsel remains the same. Do *not* begin to rewrite for a twelvemonth. Read every work on which you can lay your hands that bears on the subject . . . Ask nobody's opinion till your MS. is complete . . . Your facility in writing will be rather a hindrance than a help . . . You will have to curb your eager longing for results . . . You must *not* be anxious to see the thing done. Each page must be an end in itself.

The systematic precision of method which he advocated for others was evident in all his own work, even in his letters. The original of the letter partially reproduced above, for example, gave signs of careful proofreading. The word "work" had been substituted for "book," and elsewhere on the page "should prepare and outline" had been changed to "were to prepare an outline" and "I thought it failed rather in completeness of plan" had been altered to read, "I thought you failed rather in plan." These are small matters, but they indicate a concern for point and accuracy which never left him. As his first son wrote, "He hated shoddy," and the manuscripts of his letters have the same careful interlineations that his manuscripts for publication bore. (pp. 199-200)

Hale White never tired of criticizing the stale phrases and hypocritical verbiage which he was forced day after day to listen to in the House. The changed language of the House in the latter half of the century was to him an indication of its changed character and a symptom of the nation's moral decay. This was the language of the myrmidons, who had schooled themselves in the phrases of the popular newspaper instead of those of the Bible or an earlier political oratory. In *The Norfolk News* of August 1, 1874, he writes:

> We have got members who speak the English of Mrs. Gamp, and now it appears we have one who speaks that of the cheapest penny-a-liner. I heard a gentleman speak this week—not reported with accuracy—who in a few minutes brought in the following choice and original expressions—"Were launched into eternity," "mutilated remains," "hecatomb of victims," "primeval sentence of our race," "scene of the catastrophe," and many others which I have forgotten. We were also introduced to the sword of Damocles, which in the next sentence "descended like an avalanche scattering ruin." Radical as I am, I must own to a touch of sorrow as I sat and listened. It is significant of a good deal—not, mind you, of the popularisation of the House (that we should not regret), but of its growing wealth. It is not the genuine working man who talks this rubbish, but the millionaire. Mr. Burt and Mr. Macdonald are loyal to our native Saxon; it is the cotton-spinner and colliery-owner who murder it.

(pp. 204-05)

Now we might suppose that such an artistic conscience brought to the writing of novels would produce prose of a level sameness, lacking in color and sparkle, and—while free of jargon—reducing things and people alike to the crystalline purity of abstraction. To some degree this is true, but we need to remember that Hale White always worked *through* fact and experience to his generalizations and that, while the moralizing habit was never abandoned, he often found himself stuck fast in the fact itself. He first tried to see the particular clearly and whole, whether it was a sunset, a flower, a person, or an event. He often could not construct a general hypothesis from such data, but he always took it as his duty to examine the data to the limit of his capacity. And through such methods he has given us line drawings which, though sparse, have nevertheless often a terrible intensity and a shocking beauty. His imagination was almost entirely visual; he seldom describes for us a smell, or touch, or sound, for the world of soundless, odorless, bodiless spirit embodied in the concrete was what most interested and lured him, and the eye and the brain afforded the most direct and trustworthy entrance to such a world.

But his writing is not, therefore, lacking in emphasis or contrast. He draws his characters with an eye on their insides more than their outsides, but occasionally he gives us a sensuous detail, a lighted eye or a lovely fold of hair—so unusual, so lightly and justly sketched in—that the picture shocks and excites us. It is the pleasure of seeing a lovely woman in the company of starched old maids reading their prayer books. The escape to a sensuous delight becomes so urgent for the reader that he flies to embrace it, and it is magnified by the restraint and discipline with which it is surrounded. With the masterly touch of a few brilliantly chosen details, Hale White says in this passage all he has to say about the beginning of a passionate relationship:

> He stooped down, picked up a leaf, smoothed it between his fingers, and then raised his eyes. They met hers at that instant, as she lifted them and looked in his face. They were near one another, and his hands strayed towards hers till they touched. She did not withdraw; he clasped the hand, she not resisting; in another moment his arms were round her, his face was on hers, and he was swept into self-forgetfulness.

This reminds us almost of the close of *Paradise Lost,* the beginning of human love and the beginning of a long atonement, and the modulation shows something of the same repressed excitement as the great adventure begins. Such artistry is achieved not by conscious striving after effect, but by the determined omission of everything irrelevant or tangential to the *idea,* the moral idea at the center of Hale White's thought and art. "The long apprenticeship has ended . . ." he writes in *More Pages.* "How much I might have gained had I taken life as an art I cannot say." In his terms, being truly serious about life and being "artistic" were two different things. This scene, therefore, is not given us for its own sake. It is simply a necessary adventure on a spiritual pilgrimage, and it must be seen swiftly and precisely, for there is still much to learn and a long way to go.

Hale White was aware of a world "infinite both ways," the awesome immensity of the universe and the limitless mystery of *this* thing or *this* individual. We have seen this duality before. We have heard him advising us to "cease the trick of contrast," for in exercising it one provokes the comparison between what is and what might be, the reality and the ideal. To bring them into union was his lifelong ambition. But Hale White could never cease making such comparisons, and it is that fact more than any other which often makes him a brilliant satirist. Of all Hale White's critics, A. L. Morton has most perceptively detected this quality in his writing:

> There is an evenness, a fusing of the plain and heroic, an apparent monotony, that deceives us into thinking it is dull until we turn a corner and a flash of irony or a quietly perfect phrase reveals to us that we have climbed a hill, that, inconsiderable in itself, gives us a wide view over a country that is certainly not romantic but nevertheless infinitely desirable. . . . Like the country, the style becomes rich by refusing to spend itself upon extravagances, and in this both style and country are at the very heart of the English Puritan tradition.

The lives of his characters are for the greater part spent in suffering the passage of day after day "in unbroken, level succession" and not in exciting adventures, and Hale White's style shares a tempo and mood appropriate to the matter he is presenting. But in those moments when we ascend from the plain, we are often given unforgettable views across the prospect of human life and society, and it is then that the heavens and the world of men seem at the same time to be most alien and most closely joined.

We might expect, therefore, that those characters whose lives never "touched the universal"—like the Snales, Broads, and Hextons—would provoke Hale White's richest contempt. He was a student of the ways the divine and human could meet in living men, and when they did so meet he could not be ironical, for the very contrasts out of which irony is made disappeared. And to him there were ''very few . . . of God's creatures to whom the supernatural does not in some way present itself. . . . But when he had to deal with a character who was not so illumined and who showed no signs of amendment, his capacities for subacid satire were freely exercised. Mr. Thomas Broad met these requirements perfectly. He was the son of the man we identified earlier as the Reverend Mr. Jukes, the Bedford preacher. One of the habits of Mr. Jukes's fictional prototype was that on the day following the Sabbath he normally professed to feeling a little ''Mondayish.'' His son Thomas, who was also preparing for the ministry, proved himself an able apprentice by telling a young lady after his *first* attempt at preaching that he too felt ''a little Mondayish.''

But a later episode in Thomas Broad's career provoked from Hale White a more telling criticism. The young man had in his repertoire one sermon, based on the text, ''The carnal mind is at enmity with God,'' and furbished with ideas from his college lecture notes. Before he preached this sermon a second time, however, an unfortunate event occurred. He had tried to seduce a young lady (none other than the high-minded daughter of Pauline and Zachariah) and had had his wrist slashed with scissors for his pains. He appeared in the pulpit the following Sunday, however, and found the sermon on the carnal mind still appropriate.

> The accident was a little inconvenient on the following Sunday, when he had to preach at Hogsbridge Corner; but as he reproduced the sermon on the carnal mind, which he knew pretty well by heart, he was not nervous. He had made it much simpler, in accordance with the advice given on a former occasion. He had struck out the metaphysics and had put in new head—''Neither indeed *can* be.'' ''The apostle did not merely state a fact that the carnal mind was not subject to the law of God; he said, 'Neither indeed *can* be.' Mark, my brethen, the force of the *neither can.*''

Sometimes, after striking such satirical blows, Hale White feels called upon to append an explanatory comment, but this is left where it should be, without footnotes, permitting the dramatic irony to speak for itself. Hale White seldom gains his effects by raising his voice, but as we mark the force of the ''*neither can*'' we are reminded that his calm manner is deceptive and that there is often a surprising power in his low tones.

A dualistic habit of mind is an inevitable breeder of comparisons and contrasts. It is rather strange, therefore, that Hale White is so sparing in his use of simile and metaphor. The explanation lies in the fact that the most fundamental dualism of his life was the conflict between monism and dualism itself—between his longing for unity and his keen awareness of multiplicity. His effort to resolve this dualism manifested itself in an attempt to see the person or thing in itself and not in terms of comparisons which in turn needed explanation:

> By the third, which is neither ourselves nor the object, do we recognise it. The third is the celestial light.

With few exceptions, when he employs metaphor at all, he fines his standards of comparison in the elemental forces of nature, and draws his illustration as closely to the central nerve of life as words and his own insight will permit him.

Catharine's new birth is thus described:

> It was with her as we can imagine it to be with some bud long folded in darkness which, silently in the dewy May night, loosens its leaves, and, as the sun rises, bares itself to the depths of its cup to the blue sky and the light.
>
> (pp. 205-09)

Hale White's comparisons are usually of this kind, brought in when nothing else will do, when his consciousness of human separateness is most acute and the individual must double up in a relationship with forces beyond himself in order to be relieved of his own isolation. Here, if the powers of nature are not in actual sympathetic correspondence with Catharine's emotions, they at least awaken in her, and in the reader, the awareness that she is part of an elemental unity. Hale White spent more effort in seeing the thing as it is in itself than as it compares with something else, but when he does detect comparisons or identifications he draws them with just precision. Simile and metaphor did not, however, come easily to his pen. . . . [He] saved and served up Pauline's likeness to a ''wild seagull in a farm-yard of peaceful, clucking, brown-speckled fowls'' on two occasions, and we remember the passage because such comparisons are unusual in his work. In general, it may be said that he uses these devices when he is dealing with either the very high or the very low, when he is moved by the almost wordless wonder of a deep spiritual experience, or moved to almost speechless disgust at a temporal world which must be satirized. Thus with the preacher at Zoar ''The Calvinistic creed was stuck in him as in a lump of fat''; but he can say of Mrs. Carter, ''Her presence was like the southwest wind and sunlight after long north-easterly gloom and frost.''

While there is no radical change between his early and later books, a tendency to get away from the sermonizing essay style to a more dramatic and objective recording of experience is apparent. Hale White's first two books are, presumably, written by a Dissenting minister from whom a pulpit vocabulary and a didactic attitude might be expected. Here we find, indeed, ''prose of the center''—the colorless, sober, well-filed instrument for self-examination and spiritual surgery. While even the casual reader would not doubt that the later books were also written by Mark Rutherford, he would nevertheless see the preacher becoming increasingly emancipated from his old pulpit habits and prejudices. There is a growing tendency to let the lesson be acted out without sermonizing about it, without telling the reader quite so obviously where to cast his attention. There is a noticeable movement from the pious vocabulary of an orthodox Calvinist in favor of less parochial language. And there is, above all, a tendency to let dialogue carry a larger share of the dramatic burden. In *Clara Hopgood*, for example, roughly seventy-two of its one hundred eighty-eight pages are dialogue and, though much of its talk is bookish and lacking in the vernacular flavor we find in the *Revolution* and *Catharine Furze*, it often has great dramatic effectiveness. When the child, Madge, and her roommate, Selina, discuss the problem of election at their boarding school, we can hear the words and phrases of their parents being parroted in quite realistic fashion. Selina speaks:

''I suppose your father is a foreigner?''

''No, he is an Englishman.''

''But if he is an Englishman you must have been baptised, or sprinkled, or immersed, and your father and mother must belong to church or chapel. I know there are thousands of wicked people who belong to neither, but they are drunkards and liars and robbers, and even they have their children christened.''

"Well, he is an Englishman," said Madge smiling.

"Perhaps," said Selina timidly, "he may be—he may be—Jewish. Mamma and papa pray for the Jews every morning. They are not like other unbelievers.''

"No, he is certainly not a Jew."

"What is he then?"

"He is my papa and a very honest, good man."

"Oh my dear Madge! honesty is a broken reed. I have heard mamma say that she is more hopeful of thieves than honest people who think they are saved by works, for the thief who was crucified went to heaven, and if he had been only an honest man he never would have found the Saviour and would have gone to hell. Your father must be something.''

"I can only tell you again that he is honest and good.''

And following this exchange there is a paragraph of comment, but it is all part of Selina's stream-of-consciousness and not conspicuously the author's. In the *Autobiography* or *Deliverance,* however, Hale White would have surrounded this parable with editorial comment. (pp. 209-10)

But in general it must be admitted that, while Hale White's prose was capable of both great organ tones and sharp incisiveness, its range was normally not wide and its character not, in the deepest sense, poetic. It was, rather, the conversational language of a fastidious, painstaking man. Even his ''copperplate'' handwriting was a reflection of his cautious, businesslike intensity. While he could respond to ''preachments in tones'' he could seldom, in his own writing, rest until those preachments were reuttered in plain prose. He had poetic impulses but could never be a poet, for he lacked the moral confidence to be content with suggestiveness. He could, like a poet, let his characters, events, and descriptive sketches suggest meanings beyond themselves, but then—afraid of ambiguity and pressed on by the urgency of his message—he would normally destroy the suggestiveness by a prosaic examination of it. The poetic qualities we have seen in his work are fragments and not characteristic of the whole—brief ripples on a level lake. On those few occasions when Hale White tried to write poetry, the labored self-consciousness he brought to the task is obvious. He could not sing, but had to talk. Among the papers Mrs. D. V. White found after his death was this partially finished attempt. We reproduce it here with its corrections as a demonstration of his addiction to the prose-writing habit and as a self-evident confession that this man could be only a passing visitor on Parnassus.

> I wandered idly on the waste sea shore
> And saw with careless eyes a dull, green ~~stone~~ stain
> Upon a stone I picked up with disdain
> For I believed it worthless for my little store

Of minerals which glittered colours wore.
I broke it on the rock where it had lain.
And when I turned it o'er I found no vein
~~Of~~ Rarer ~~worth~~ than that which lies in thousands more
Dragged down and then rejected by the waves
Rounded & smooth and in to sameness worn.
I look again—one fragment chides my scorn
With purest tint of sea in sunlit caves
Of that which underneath a dark cloud laves
A tempest cleansed sky in early morn.

"Tempest cleansed sky" and "sunlit caves" show something of a Wordsworthian perception of natural beauty, but such fragments find small service in the total conception.

André Gide has said. "The work of art is the exaggeration of an idea," and the symbol of that idea is "the thing around which a book is composed." Whereas Hale White would doubtless have agreed with this pronouncement, he would have had to confess that he achieved such central unity in paragraphs rather than in whole books and that, as he has revealed in his poem, he was prone to become almost hypnotically fascinated with fragments of experience. He once wrote in his *Black Notebook:* "The deeper the emotion, the greater the need of symbolism as a means of expression. Religion: love are examples." This was with him, however, a *principle* and not a statement of his artistic practice. The structure of his books is linear rather than nuclear. They are not plotless nor do they lack thematic unity, but they incline to what we might call the *spiritual picaresque*—the records of pilgrimages made up of many single events which are remembered, cherished, and preciously registered, as if for use at some future time when suffering modern man can find one and not many symbols for the meaning of life.

His meaning is seldom imparted as the single blow of a closed fist, where emotion and conviction become part of a single action and become clear through the action itself. The action is used to interpret a philosophy or an idea. While few Victorian writers were more aware of the psychological complexity of man's moral life, and while few avoided oversimplification more effectively than he, his characters nevertheless play their parts for the sake of something outside themselves. Hale White does not have D. H. Lawrence's ability to make this exterior force seem the same thing as the characters' bone and flesh; they all grow toward such union, but they never seem to *be* that union. They cannot just speak and say the truth, they must always consult some oracle. And even when that oracle is their own conscience, it does not seem completely native to what would ordinarily be considered their personality. Hale White invented the action of his characters to illustrate the power and working of this monitor, but there was always a dualism between the monitor and the character. And because the action served such a purpose, Hale White always remained essentially a descriptive and not a dramatic artist; he tended to use his characters as means towards ends rather than ends in themselves. The essayist in Hale White has not, therefore, been completely metamorphosed into the perfect novelist. The abstracted idea has the final say, and we know at last that Hale White loves God more than people and wants us to do the same. The dramatic fist never quite closes.

One's liking or disaffection for Hale White's style is largely a matter of taste. Some critics have been chiefly aware of its chilling quality, and one felt that it had the effect of "lowering (his) blood pressure," calling Mark Rutherford the "apostle of low spirits, of masculine vapours, of matured green sickness.'' But most have warmed to its strength, vigor, and austere beauty.

But whatever one's reaction may be, Hale White's originality cannot be questioned. He belonged to no school and played the ''sedulous ape'' to no models, but spun these words, phrases, and paragraphs out of his own inner needs and compulsions. He was a greedy borrower of his own day—Tennyson, Wordsworth, Carlyle, and Ruskin were his particular heroes—and knew intimately such earlier writers as Virgil, Montaigne, Milton, Bunyan, Bacon, and—most especially—the authors of the Bible. But he cannot be said to have modeled himself after any one of them exclusively. That peculiar combination of scientific accuracy with moral earnestness gives his style, at times, a striking similarity to Bacon's; but in its more passionate moods it captures qualities reminiscent of Milton. And his mind was so thoroughly saturated with the vocabulary and syntax of the Bible that there is no telling where its influence begins or leaves off. He shaped his own vehicle of expression out of what may be said to have been a double impulse: to capture something of the oratorical tone and manner of past heroic age, and to achieve a scientific precision appropriate to his own. But in his age there was little of that certainty which supported the confident articulation of the past.

> To be articulate is a duty, but if the thing itself does not admit complete articulation, we must not attempt it, but be satisfied with so much definiteness as the object yields.

His prose is gray with this knowledge and this regret. Oratory demands assertion, and Hale White was aware that in his day honest writing must be disciplined on the side of understatement and reserve.

Though he belonged to no school, he was drawn—almost in spite of himself—into something of the attitude toward art and life which characterized the Pre-Raphaelites and their generation, of whom he was a profound admirer (particularly Turner, Ruskin, Rossetti, Swinburne, Holman Hunt, and Arthur Hughes). Humphrey House has written:

> Because the Romantic tradition said that Nature was somehow the source of important spiritual experience and because the habit of mind of the following generation, with an empirical scientific philosophy, was to dwell so lovingly on factual detail, a suspicion came about that perhaps the cause of the experience lay in the detail.

This encouraged a tendency to impose ''feeling as an afterthought upon literalness,'' and Hale White's practice was precisely in this direction.

In the final passage of the *Deliverance* we can see on the one hand a straining toward oratorical effects and the expression of high emotion, and on the other a loving attention to scientific accuracy and precise fact. The synthesis of these two tensions is a piece of Doric sublimity of rare quality and power. The emotion is not, however, so much ''imposed'' as worked in, brought to the color of autumn leaves by the precision of a naturalist and the passion of an artist. In passages such as these Hale White perfected his art. His success came in fragments, but such fragments are themselves symbolic of the life of this man—of the particulars in which he found his confidence.

> We were beyond the smoke, which rested like a low black cloud over the city in the north-

east, reaching a third of the way up to the zenith. The beech had changed colour, and glowed with reddish-brown fire. We sat down on a floor made of the leaves of last year. At midday the stillness was profound, broken only by the softest of whispers descending from the great trees which spread over us their protecting arms. Every now and then it died down almost to nothing, and then slowly swelled and died again, as if the gods of the place were engaged in divne and harmonious talk. By moving a little towards the external edge of our canopy we beheld the plain all spread out before us, bounded by the heights of Sussex and Hampshire. It was veiled with the most tender blue, and above it was spread a sky which was white on the horizon and deepened by degrees into azure over our heads. The exhilaration of the air satisfied Marie, although she had no playmate, and there was nothing special with which she could amuse herself. She wandered about looking for flowers and ferns, and was content. We were all completely happy.

(pp. 211-14)

> *Wilfred Stone, in his* Religion and Art of William Hale White (''Mark Rutherford''), *Stanford University Press, 1954, 240 p.*

IRVIN STOCK (essay date 1956)

[*Stock is an American playwright and critic. In the following excerpt, he discusses the essential sincerity that informs all of Rutherford's fiction.*]

There is, of course, a sense in which any serious writer is sincere—honesty is a basic condition of his profession and some kind of truth its necessary raw material—but we are rarely impelled, except perhaps in mitigation of the charge of failure, to place that word in the centre of a critical portrait. With [William] Hale White, however, it must in fact go in the centre: it is the chief distinction of his work and the source of his finest effects. What it helps us express in his case is the feeling he gives of an especially intimate relationship between the man and his writing. In order to understand the unique qualities of the writing, we must for this reason start with the man himself.

And the first thing we must note about him is that by the age of fifty, when he began to write, he had experienced so much unhappiness that life had come to mean for him chiefly the endurance of suffering. ''As we get older,'' he wrote to a son, ''we find that endurance is the exact synonym for life.'' This is sometimes uttered as a commonplace: for him it was the most immediate of realities. He had been poor and for nearly twenty years had had to work from the time of rising to the time of sleeping to support his wife and four children. No one has described better than he the anguish—an ignoble anguish—of having to give up one's life to a boring and degrading job while all higher gifts rust unused or become mere sources of pain. Worse than this was the fact that while she was still in her twenties, his wife became ill with disseminated sclerosis, a progressive paralysis that did not kill her for thirty years but that gradually crippled and blinded her. Most of those thirty years she spent in wheel-chairs or in bed. And though amid her sufferings she preserved a courage that could shame her husband, he was never able to forget for an instant the terrible visitation. That he should have been oppressed by it is natural enough, perhaps, but there was a special reason for vulnerability to misfortune. He had a trial that multiplied the difficulties of every other, and that, indeed, required little support from circumstances to steep his life in gloom. From his early manhood he was afflicted with a tendency to what he called ''hypochondria,'' that is depression, which was not the occasional ''bad mood'' we all know but an attack of horror and panic that lasted for long periods at a time and that, when not actually upon him, was being, as it were, consciously held at bay. It is interesting that the state recurs so often in his fiction, sometimes named, sometimes not—and even in his criticism, where it is seen to be involved in the work of favourite writers— that we are reminded of the sexual abnormality in Proust which ends by turning up everywhere. Of course, it was a sickness. He spent much money on doctors (though in vain), and he does not fail to point out the questionable validity of the ideas about life, produced by it, suggesting that they ought not to be regarded as ''mere logical inferences'' but rather as symptoms which must disappear with returning health. Nevertheless, it was impossible not to regard this ''hypochondria'' most often as the opening of a window on a terrible and undeniable reality, on a vision not less true because the usual pleasure and preoccupations of health (that ''divine narcotic'') mercifully conceal it. The terror of it affected nearly everything he said and did, and those who get to know him well can see its influence in the most unlikely places in his work. It made more precious the simplest pleasures of life, and his serious reflections not only derived from it a kind of desperate urgency but were, by it, forever challenged for their true helpfulness to the soul which struggled and suffered.

It is this which accounts for the chief demand he made on the works of the mind—in art, philosophy, even religion: Do they help men to live? Exclusive preoccupation with the separate disciplines themselves tended to make him impatient all his life. ''Poetry, if it is to be good for anything, must help us to live,'' he remarks in his *Pages from a Journal.* ''It is to this we come at last in our criticism, and if it does not help us to live it may as well disappear, no matter what its fine qualities may be.'' As a rule, we are right to reject such a demand that art, or any other intellectual pursuit, be primarily useful, because it is so often made by those with too narrow a notion of what men need or of the manifold ways in which they can be served. But not only was the demand made in his case by one well aware of the peculiar sanctions and seductions of the intellectual life; it was also made by one who sought help for problems of the utmost complexity, for problems, indeed, which are often insoluble. What he sought above all was help to endure uncrushed life's unavoidable pain, and for this it is not things or society that must be changed—the usual notion of those who demand art as ''a weapon''—but only, if possible, oneself, one's ideas. It is the help ideally offered by religion. And in fact his abnormal need intensified all the influences in his education which had made religious thinking natural to him. For it is an important characteristic of religion that, while it deals in ideas which link the individual to mankind and to the universe, these ideas are related directly to the emotional life. They are attempts (whatever else they also are) to help him understand and endure his inevitable sorrows. This is the reason Hale White never lost his reverence for true faith, his nostalgia for a time when his own could have been perfect, and his sense of the special value of those many religious insights that do not depend on the acceptance of systems of dogma but are clearly the insights of men grappling directly with the eternal problems. And this is why the Bible became for him the most

precious of all books, forever read and reread, though he did not get to know it rightly, he tells us, until after he was expelled from his seminary for questioning its unique inspiration.

If religion had been ideally the source of this help, the nineteenth century had, for men like him, destroyed its perfect sufficiency, and such men now sought its consolations also in philosophy and literature. It is significant that the philosopher who meant most to Hale White was Spinoza. Spinoza attempted to reconcile the great helpful ideas of religion—its identification of virtue with inner peace; its lesson of self-forgetfulness, or rather self-discovery, in the higher, the greater, the whole; its lesson of the necessary and healing acceptance of reality (or God's will)—with the demands of the rational intelligence and the facts of nature, and thereby to provide the grounds for ''a joy continuous and supreme to all eternity.'' This was exactly the problem of Hale White, who liked to emphasize that admitted human motive for Spinoza's philosophic quest. And though Spinoza aimed at joy, it was not a joy available to the weak; he led us toward a love of God which does not demand, as the celebrated proposition has it, that God love us in return. One can understand how a man whose life had taught him that inner peace was not in fact going to be made easy by a God of prompt rewards might be struck by such an idea.

In other intellectual fields, too, he sought—religion, one is tempted to say, but, at any rate, this same help to live. In his essays, which range among the works of scientists and at least one polar explorer, as well as of poets and novelists, he is quick to notice the sense of trouble—sometimes, as with Bradley, the eighteenth-century explorer, it takes the form of physical danger—and the medicine used against it: so often, and not only with Bradley, courage. This gives even to his literary criticism, even, indeed, to his most rigorous philosophic reflection, an amazing note of repressed personal feeling. Not that literature as pleasure, using the work in its widest sense, was beneath his notice. On the contrary, like all pleasure it was thrice precious to one whose life so desperately needed sweetening. There is clear personal gratitude in his remarks on Scott, for instance, whose wonderful tales he had read aloud to his wife and children. (So insistent a ''practical'' emphasis may after all engender a doubt as to whether he was aware of what the art of literature is in itself. Let me not move on without at least a hint that he was. To a friend who told him she did not ''understand'' poetry because she was interested in ''what is said,'' not in ''the way it is said,'' he wrote that the distinction was a fallacy.

The noblest office of genius is *realization*, the making *ex*-plicit the world in which we live, and form, therefore, is emphatically reality.... There is a passage in Milton—indeed, there are many in the poems of this miraculous master, in which accent alone is tremendous fact.

> Grasping ten thousand thunders, which he sent
> Before him, such as in their souls infix'd
> Plagues.

He deserts the ordinary rhythm of heroic blank verse in the last eight syllables: they are all slow and their slowness is a great definite creative act.

This statement is one of many which show how his ultimate choices were never made simply by inability to see and feel what ''opposed'' them.)

One thing more must be understood about the man if we are to understand the reason for his special qualities as a writer. It is the abnormal intensity of his longing for a friend with whom he could share what in youth he called his "heartfelt thinkings." "It is not those who have the least, but those who have the most to give who most want sympathy," he said, and he speaks in *The Autobiography*, after explaining that the reserve often charged against him was due to a longing for self-revelation which had generally been rebuffed, of "a dream which I had . . . of a perfect friendship."

> I always felt (he goes on) that talk with whom I would, I left something unsaid which was precisely what I most wished to say. I wanted a friend who would sacrifice himself to me utterly, and to whom I might offer a similar sacrifice. I found companions for whom I cared, and who professed to care for me; but I was thirsting for deeper draughts of love than any which they had to offer; and I said to myself that if I were to die, not one of them would remember me for more than a week. This was not selfishness, for I longed to prove my devotion as well as to receive that of another. How this ideal haunted me! It made me restless and anxious at the sight of every new face, wondering whether at last I had found that for which I searched as if for the kingdom of heaven. It is superfluous to say that a friend of the kind I wanted never appeared.

As it happens, such a friend did finally appear. And though he was old and she was young, mutual recognition was instantaneous and she became his second wife. Her diary of the seven years they had together at Groombridge, Kent, before he died, tells the story of a union of minds as perfect as any in the history of literature—this in spite of painful troubles due to the difference in age and circumstances or to his unfortunate temperament. And to this woman when she came he said a strange thing: "If I had been given you when I was thirty I would never have let the public hear a syllable from me." The inference is clear that when at the age of fifty he sat down, not at first to the comparative frivolity of story-telling, but to share in secret the history of his own inner struggles and the modest "deliverance" he was able to find, he had chosen the anonymous reader for his perfect friend. It is a fact that the voice—the style—we hear in this work is that of a man alone with such a friend and uttering at last what he had never been able to tell a living soul. And when he offers a reason for making public a tale so "commonplace" and so sad, it is something as distinct from the usual motives for a literary career as this:

> I have observed that the mere knowing that other people have been tried as we have been tried is a consolation to us, and that we are relieved by the assurance that our sufferings are not special and peculiar, but common to us with many others. Death has always been a terror to me, and at times, nay generally, religion and philosophy have been altogether unavailing to mitigate the terror in any way. But it has always been a comfort to me to reflect that whatever death may be, it is the inheritance of the whole human race; that I am not singled out, but shall merely have to pass through what the weakest have had to pass through before me. In the worst of maladies, worst at least to me, those which are hypochondriacal, the healing effect which is produced by the visit of a friend who can simply say, 'I have endured all that,' is most marked. So it is not impossible that some few whose experience has been like mine may, by my example, be freed from that sense of solitude which they find so depressing.

We are now in a position to understand that "sincerity" which so many readers have found peculiarly characteristic of his work. It comes from this: that he writes at the impulse of such strong personal feeling, out of so pressing a sense of the gravity of man's condition and the urgency of his need, that all considerations of mere craft seem to become subordinate, or else to disappear. And it is because he was able to divest himself of pride as few men have ever been, and to confess (though in disguise) the existence within him of one who suffered and struggled, and who did so not as a "hero" but as an ordinary man, that he makes so powerful an appeal to that same unheroic self hidden in all of us, exciting responses more intimate and more moved than are common in literature.

This—so to speak—non-literary character of his work accounts for its chief literary qualities. It accounts for the remarkable style, which is a simple communication, undistorted by the slightest striving for effect and absolutely faithful to what has been intensely felt and clearly seen. "If the truth is of serious importance to us we dare not obstruct it by phrasemaking," he wrote. "We are compelled to be as direct as our inherited feebleness will permit. The cannon ball's path is near to a straight line in proportion to its velocity. 'My boy,' my father once said to me, 'if you write anything you consider particularly fine, strike it out.'" The beauty that results is impossible to imitate because one of its main characteristics is an unparalleled purity and naturalness of English: there is no self-assertive twisting of the idiom to take hold of. It comes to seem merely a beauty of personality. But though the naturalness, purity and simplicity of his writing are most often noticed, these alone would be nothing without the emotion which is equally pervasive. One finds in his work many explicit demands for the right to express intensity, lest moderateness of expression tell its own kind of lie. "There is more insincerity," he remarks in *The Revolution*, "in purposely lowering the expression beneath the thought, and denying the thought thereby than in a little exaggeration." The restraint of his style, like his self-discipline in general, is a visible conquest, and sometimes his short definite sentences resemble nothing so much as the speech of a man who must speak coldly between clenched teeth lest he be overmastered by emotion. This could, of course become oppressive, but in his case it has not, because the conquest has been achieved; the man who speaks so is also a man of mind, aware of more than one perspective on his own experience, and capable of irony directed at himself and of humour. When *his* voice vibrates, we are at a point safely beyond sentimentality or a self-pity that is not justified. In fact, while his expressions are always simple and modest, they are clearly meant by an extremely conscious mind in their widest possible signification. This sets up a tension which is one of his chief effects and which can thrill, like understatement.

The art of his novels, too, takes much of its character from this unusual seriousness and intensity. He has described this art himself, unintentionally, in the following remarks to a son:

Art is art in proportion to its distinctness. Noble art is distinguished from base art by the perfect clearness of the conception which it aims to embody. I do not assert that there are not other contrasts, but this is perhpas the most striking. The vehicle may be obscure, but in the writer or painter the intention is definite and vivid. Otherwise what burden lies on him to speak or paint? Only because he sees or thinks with intensity and consequently with a definition superior to that of ordinary mortals does he become great. . . . The sum and substance, to put it in other words, is *realization.* Whatever we have to speak, let it be bounded by a precise limiting line, so that the thing spoken is marked off from the vague, from chaos, from all other things with absolute precision. . . . Perhaps I could have concluded all I had to say in one word. Our actual *experience,* not what we can invent or dream: and no step a hair's breadth beyond what is real and solid for us, proved and again proved. This should be the character of all our speech.

Exactly such clarity of definition—proceeding from just such warmth of response— appears in his characterization, though this can be of the utmost subtlety, in his development out of it of dramatic clash and climax, and in the underlying conception of the meaning of it all which determines the form of a work. Though he writes in the discursive tradition of George Eliot, which permits him to interrupt and comment at will, his

Rutherford in 1908.

novels have the speed and economy of those of Turgeniev, whom, indeed, he admired. His comments, for that matter, tend rather to increase than to dilute intensity, for he hardly ever interrupts unless he must: he seems driven by emotion to utter his larger thought. The reader may have noticed how sometimes, even before one knows what is to be said, the mere fact that a writer is being thus driven to generalize can in itself be moving.

The intimate relation between his writing and his character accounts, finally, for the peculiar unity of his work noticed by Murry [see excerpt dated 1924]. Never the professional fulfilling merely some literary purpose, he brought to every utterance nothing less than his whole self. This is why, as has been suggested, his highest flights of philosophic reflection are charged throughout with the emotion which was their human origin and are often, oddly, as poignant as his accounts of love or pain. And this is why he can pass directly from such heights to the most humbly practical concerns—the pathos of the workman's fleeting Sunday, or how to break the habit of drink—without the slightest air of incongruity. Such concerns, being for him the true basis of all the rest, are seen naturally in a larger perspective that exposes their furthest meaning and unites them with what is highest. As he wrote of a character, "his passion was informed with intellect, and his intellect glowed with passion. There was nothing in him merely animal or merely rational." For those to whom the novels fully reveal themselves, therefore it is likely that the writer will at last be overshadowed by the man. They will be moved again and again to a response that is more than aesthetic, more than intellectual, and, drawn first perhaps by the quiet triumphs of his art, they may find that the slightest essays or notes, the letters, and not least the lovely *Groombridge Diary* of his second wife, so full of his wise and passionate conversation, grow as precious to them as the ripened works themselves.

All that I have so far tried to make clear can be summed up by a passage from one of his late stories. The passage concerns a certain friend of the narrator called Robert, who has chosen to give up the woman he loves in order to be true to a spiritual vocation which must bar her from his life forever. Though we are shown his particular trouble, however, the significant thing for us now is its intensity and its result.

> What made the separation especially terrible, both to Veronica and Robert, it is hard to say. Here are a couple of lines from one of Robert's letters to me which may partly explain: "There is something in this trouble which I cannot put into words. It is the complete unfolding, the making real to myself, all that is hidden in that word *Never.*" Is it possible to express by speech a white handkerchief waved from the window of the railway train, or the deserted platform where ten minutes before a certain woman stood, where her image still lingers? There is something in this which underlies the life of man. One consequence of this experience was the purest sincerity. All insincerity, everything unsound, everything which could not stand the severest test, was by this trial crushed out of him. His words uniformly stood for facts. Perhaps it was his sincerity which gave him a power over me such as no other man ever possessed.

This is the power of Hale White.

Irvin Stock, in his William Hale White (Mark Rutherford): A Critical Study, *Columbia University Press, 1956, 268 p.*

PATRICIA THOMSON   (essay date 1964)

[*In the following excerpt, Thomson analyzes Rutherford's portrayals of marriage.*]

It was in 1880 that Mark Rutherford wrote a short story entitled **"A Dream of Two Dimensions"** which he revised in 1908. It is a significant little allegory upon which Rutherford obviously bestowed much more care than upon his other short stories, although it suffers, as is often the case, from the abrupt, flat ending. It is interesting because it is the first formulation by Rutherford of what was to become, in his novels, the classic situation of a husband and wife incapable of appreciating or sharing the other's emotional life. In this case it is the husband who is impervious to his wife's qualities of affection and self-lessness because he is convinced that he is possessed of an extra dimension—that of intellectual superiority—to which she can never attain. His is the prototype of a personality which becomes increasingly familiar in the books which follow and which Rutherford does not restrict to one sex—that of the intellectual or idealist who finds he has nothing in common with his life-partner. Sometimes the partner is warm-hearted and limited, sometimes ungiving and commonplace; but in either case the husband and wife move on different planes and the marriage appears a travesty of the conception, so dear to Rutherford, of a shared life. (p. 256)

It is an idea to which his protagonists cling desperately in their misery, despite the fact that Rutherford himself clearly felt that marriage was a fearful gamble, which, for the thoughtful man or woman very seldom came off. "While there is nothing which a man does which is of greater consequence than the choice of a woman with whom he is to live, there is nothing he does in which he is more liable to self-deception." (*The Autobiography,* Ch. V). The dice was loaded heavily against an impulsive choice resulting in a satisfactory partnership for life, a choice made when a man was beyond control of reason "led blindfold over a precipice." In *The Autobiography, Deliverance* and *The Revolution in Tanner's Lane* the procession of unhappy marriages—there are at least seven in the three books—has something of the bleak, factual quality of eye-witness reporting and the raw disillusionment of personal experience. Unlike the later novels where his creative power is greater, where the characters have more independent life, there is a tendency for Rutherford at this point to do what George Eliot deplored—to lapse from the picture to the diagram—perhaps because it is a diagram with whose outlines he is painfully familiar. For almost a quarter of a century Hale White had been married to a woman whose qualities of tenderness, courage and affection must have been a constant reproach to him for the dissatisfaction and frustration he must often have felt at her inability to share his intellectual life. And again and again, in his early books, Rutherford preaches the sermon to others that he must have preached to himself—the sermon of acceptance and gratitude and humility. There can be little doubt that Dr. Stock's sensitive reading of Hale White's first marriage is a true one but I cannot believe that it was only the *young* Hale White who rebelled against his lot. Married incompatibility was always a live issue for Rutherford. No one has conveyed better the devastating effect upon an ardent, sensitive soul, in full flight, of the platitudinous remark, the inadequate reaction. These incidents do not give the impression of pain remembered

and resolved, but of the aching, ever-present disparity between two people that no amount of goodwill can bridge. Occasionally the remark is made coldly and deliberately—or so it seems to the victim; as when in *The Autobiography,* Miss Arbour has been quoting Cowper animatedly and her husband turns to the minister's wife and commiserates with her about her cat; or in *The Revolution in Tanner's Lane* Mrs. Coleman "practices the exquisite art of dropping her husband" by asking him, when everyone is moved by a fervent outburst of Zachariah's, whether he will have another cup of tea. But just as painful, and probably nearer to Rutherford's own case, is the comment made in good faith but in leaden-footed incomprehension, as when in *Catharine Furze* Mrs. Cardew, aware that her husband's remarks have caused embarrassment, comes to his rescue and attempts to sum up his arguments with a platitude.

While *Miriam's Schooling* and *Catharine Furze* are marked off from the three earlier books by their more imaginative and complex handling of character and situation, in fact, in every book except *Clara Hopgood*, Rutherford presents not only the same problem in marriage but posits the same solution. The relationship may be dealt with in two or three pages, as in the discussion of Cardinal and his wife in *The Autobiography,* or it may take over the whole of a book, as in the triangle of Mr. and Mrs. Cardew and Catharine Furze but always, Rutherford suggests, the remedy is there for the using. Whether through his own fault, his self-absorption or excessive idealism, or through his partner's limitations, the protagonist is in despair—the narrator in *The Autobiography* or McKay or Cardinal or Zachariah or George Allen or Miss Arbour or Miriam or Mr. Cardew—and it is only Miss Arbour who cuts clean of her marriage-ties. Their sentiments are all very similar and very moving. Rutherford's *alter ego* draws back for a time from marriage to Ellen: "I saw before me the long days of wedded life with no sympathy, and I shuddered when I thought what I should do with such a wife." Zachariah Coleman, who had married his wife for love three months before, wakens to the truth about her, in a passage reminiscent of Dorothea Brooks's reassessment, in Rome, of Mr. Casaubon:

> It was now three months since his wedding-day and the pomp and beauty of the sunrise, gold and scarlet bars with intermediate lakes of softest blue, had been obscured by leaden clouds, which showed no break and let loose a cold, drizzling rain. How was it? He often asked himself that question but could obtain no satisfactory answer. Had anything changed? Was his wife anything which he did not know her to be three months ago? Certainly not. He could not accuse her of passing herself off upon him with false pretences. What she had always represented herself to be she was now.

And later Zachariah sums up bitterly:

> What a revelation!—By this time he had looked often enough into the soul of the woman whom he had chosen—the woman with whom he was to be forever in this world and had discovered that there was nothing, nothing, absolutely nothing which answered anything in himself with a smile of recognition.

(pp. 257-59)

Mr. Cardew is of all the characters the one for whom Rutherford has perhaps least sympathy because he "has fallen in love with himself and married himself'' and his wife, although inarticulate, was ''a saint'' whom he undervalued. But for him, like all the others, there is a two-part solution—acquiescence in necessity and concentration on the other's good qualities. Even a completely hopeless marriage like Cardinal's is shown to become a little more bearable with such treatment—''hatred might pass into pity and pity into a merciful tenderness to her''—and marriages like McKay's and Cardew's, where the husband has till now been unaware of the wife's virtues, revive and blossom. The two stages are necessary for a real solution. One of the mottoes which head **Miriam's Schooling** is taken from Euripides: ''That man amongst mortals who has acquiesced in Necessity is wise and is acquainted with divine things''—and Rutherford stresses that although Miriam has learned to appreciate her husband's dexterity and mathematical bent, she is still not reconciled to her lot. It is not until the last few pages of the book, when she has a meeting with the countryman, Fitchew (yet another of those unhappily married, extra characters whom Rutherford tended to throw in for good measure, as if he had not already sufficiently made his point) that her problem is solved. His version of Euripides, proved on his own pulse, is a piece of homely philosophy that strikes home to Miriam: ''We are as we are, and we must make the best of it.''

In the fiction he wrote before **Clara Hopgood,** while Rutherford is certainly not unusual in treating married incompatibility—George Eliot, Trollope, Meredith, Hardy and James had all been there before him—he is so, in his inability to let the matter drop and in his own distinctive brand of married misery. A brand which, although it may vary in social class and conditions from book to book, is a remarkably constant conception.

It is interesting to see how he uses literary taste to reveal limitations in character. In a short story, **"The Sweetness of a Man's Friend,"** the wife is condemned by her hustand for her inability to pass an opinion on the allegory in *Alastor.* Like Marianne Dashwood (''Nay, Mama, if he is not to be animated by Cowper!'') Miss Arbour finds her husband wanting in his reaction when she quotes in company. Didymus Farrow's inability to share Miriam's tragic pleasure in *Romeo & Juliet*—Didymus who ''never understood suffering unless it was an ache of some kind''—brings home agonisingly to his wife her remoteness from his ''blessed thoughtlessness.'' As for Catharine Furze and Mr. Cardew—''St. Paul and Milton in him saluted St. Paul and Milton in her,'' while his inarticulate well-meaning wife is stumbling through *Paradise Lost,* Book I, with ''no emphasis, no light and shade'' and missing ''altogether the rhythm of the verse'' in a vain effort to please him.

But while literary taste is used by Rutherford in this way, somewhat formidably, as a test, he is careful to keep the results in proper perspective. The loving heart is, after all, the important thing. It would not have mattered for instance, that Mr. Hexton did not respond to Cowper had he been, like the others, warm-hearted and affectionate. It is only in **Clara Hopgood,** that most surprising of all Rutherford's novels and one of the most surprising in Victorian fiction, that we find him using literary feeling as a vital touchstone to character and influence upon action.

Clara Hopgood is by far the most ambitious of Rutherford's novels in its attempt to do justice to the rival claims of self-sacrifice and self realisation as guiding principles in life and in his treatment of Madge, Clara's sister, Rutherford's teaching not only shocked his contemporaries but was in direct opposition to much that he had made explicit in his earlier writings.

It is a novel which has been greatly undervalued and is, in its own way, more ''advanced'' than either *Tess of the D'Urbervilles* or *The Woman Who Did* which had preceded it. Some discussion of the relationship between Madge and her lover, Frank, is necessary to show why Rutherford's attitude constitutes such a *volte-face.*

Like most of the novels it is set half-a-century earlier, in 1844, and Clara and Madge, the two sisters, are very unusual young women to find in a country town like Fenmarket. Their upbringing has been very different from normal; their enlightened father has aimed at giving them the discipline and knowledge of boys' education and they have finished their schooling at Weimar where they ''could see *Egmont* or hear *Fidelio* or talk with friends about the last utterance upon the *Leben Jesu.*'' The stress in the family is on independence and integrity in all relationships. The father loved the mother still, ''because she had the strength to be what she was when he first knew her and she had so fascinated him.'' She was his ''intimate friend'' but he had no desire to assimilate her (a conception of marriage which must have appealed to Lawrence who admired Rutherford's work greatly). Clara is the sister who is usually thoughtful and deliberate, Madge is impulsive and forthright.

In his treatment of Clara which has been well dealt with by critics, Rutherford remains true to the teaching of salvation through renunciation subscribed to in his earlier books. When Clara's chance of happiness in marriage comes, she deliberately renounces it in favour of her sister and, like Catharine Furze, choose death for herself and contentment for others. But for the first half of the book, the focus is on Madge and for the only time in Rutherford's writings, we find him wholeheartedly in favour of an idealistic course of action, however much suffering it brings. The situation is carefully and subtly worked out by Rutherford, who has travelled a long way from the less sophisticated dilemmas of **The Autobiography** and **Deliverance.**

Madge, like her sister, has thought a great deal about religion, politics and literature on which topics she expresses herself forcefully and freely. When she falls in love with Frank Palmer, a ''generous and courageous'' young man . . . ''a fair specimen of thousands of English public-school boys,'' she has some uneasiness about the fact that Frank's opinions always seem to be second-hand and that he is amiably ready to appropriate ''a sentiment or doctrine of which he was not the lawful owner.'' But his passion kindles equal fervour in her and she suppresses her doubts as Frank blunders his way through one of the most literary wooings in fiction. It is clear that his appreciation of literature is nearer Fenmarket than Weimar standards. He starts off, with a lucky break, in recalling, at a strategic moment, a line of Ferdinand's from an amateur production of the night before—''But by Immortal Providence she's mine''—a quotation which gains him credit with Madge for more literary feeling than he possesses. Clara, the dispassionate, is less easily swayed. Frank has defended the juxtaposition of a farce with the scene from *The Tempest* by saying that all tastes had to be catered for.

> There was something in this remark most irritating to Clara: the word ''tastes,'' for example, as if the difference between Miranda and the chambermaid were a matter of ''taste.''

Even Madge in her infatuation, is perturbed when Frank, after presenting her with a copy of her beloved Tennyson, whom he ''greatly admires,'' admits that he is unfamiliar with the poetry but has "read a very good review of him." She excuses him, however, by recalling his good qualities. (pp. 259-63)

Ironically, it is in an attempt to overcome her intellectual reaction to him that she yields to their mutual physical passion. Frank, knowing that Wordsworth is one of her "divinities" has got by heart the entire *Ode on the Intimations of Immortality* and recites it to her when they are out walking. Madge deflates him by saying that she likes it least of Wordsworth's poems and gives a crushing commentary on the *Ode* which is much admired by certain religiously disposed people to whom thinking is distasteful or impossible." She then repents of her ungracious rejection of what has been, after all, a labour of love, however mistaken, on his part and when they shelter from the thunderstorm the "seduction scene" takes place, which contemporary critics found "singularly unpleasant" but which in fact is referred to only obliquely by the symbolism of lightning striking an elm.

After Madge has given herself to Frank, she realises that she has been right to doubt her feelings for him, that she does not really love him and that "to marry to avoid disgrace would be a crime." Despite all Frank's entreaties, even when she knows she is pregnant, she remains adamant and accepts the help only of her mother and sister. She knows what the world thinks, she is aware that she is bringing sorrow to her family—"the sense of cruel injustice to those who loved her remained with Madge perpetually"—and she is conscious that she is penalising the future of her unborn child. But throughout all the worldly, persuasive arguments of those who love her she holds firm to her principles.

The usual critical approach to *Clara Hopgood* is to differentiate between the sisters by describing Madge as trusting to her instincts and Clara to her principles. That seems to me not only to underestimate the complexity of their characters, the blend in each of instinct and theory, but to ignore what is surely a purposeful piece of literary symbolism early in the book. When Madge recites at a concert, her first choice is *The Destruction of Sennacherib*—obviously finding a temperamental affinity in the passion and fire of Byron. But her encore is a very different poem, Wootton's *Happy Life*—a poem of thoughtful reflection upon integrity and independence of judgement and the need to be impervious to public opinions. It is this second side of Madge, the result of her upbringing—which now comes into play—just as Clara, the deliberate, is, in her turn, to allow her life to be changed by a flashing impulse towards self-sacrifice, as instinctive as any ever experienced by her sister. In holding on stubbornly to her vision of what a marriage should be—and even more what it should not be—Madge is as idealistic and high-principled as Clarissa or (possibly a more potent recent influence upon Rutherford) as *The Woman Who Did*. Grant Allen's credo of marriage has clearly something in common with Madge's: "The moment you feel you love me no more don't pollute your own body by yielding it up to a man you have ceased to desire. . . . Be mine as much as you will, as long as you will, to such an extent as you will; but before all things be your own." Madge is equally vehement. "I know what is the crime to the world: but it would have been a crime, perhaps a worse crime, *if a ceremony had been performed before-hand by a priest,* and the worst of crimes would be that ceremony now" [italics are the critic's].

The revolutionary Lawrentian nature of this assertion of Madge's has not, I think, had full justice done to it in critical discussion. She is not only refusing to legitimise her child by marrying its father for whom she has a great deal of affection. That was a shocking enough decision for most Victorian readers, and one which Rutherford had to defend hotly. She is, at the same time, expressing her conviction that physical love-making between husband and wife is a crime, when either is aware that real love is lacking. It is substantially the same position as Grant Allen had taken up the year before, in the book which he had written "solely to satisfy my own taste and my own conscience" and there is an almost doctrinaire ring about it, which does not square with an interpretation of Madge as solely a creature of instinct. Certainly both attitudes are in complete opposition to Rutherford's explicit statements about marriage in his earlier books. The arguments of Mrs. Caffyn, Frank and Clara are very familiar to those already acquainted with Rutherford's doctrines of the need to acquiesce in necessity, to recognise good qualities in others and to eschew the unattainable.

Mrs. Caffyn sensibly disposes of Madge's argument that she will wrong Frank by accepting him.

> My dear, you take my word for it, he isn't so particklar as a woman. He goes about his work and has all sorts of things in his head, and if a woman makes him comfortable when he comes home, he's all right. I won't say as one woman is much the same as another to a man—least ways to all men—but still they are *not* particklar.

Frank tells her that she *ought* to marry him, if only for the sake of their child, with the love she still has for him which is "greater than the love which thousands feel for one another"—so that Madge is forced to ask herself whether she "ought to expect a refinement of relationship to which I have no right?"

And Clara, while sympathetic to Madge's principles, is realistic about the situation.

> I have sometimes wondered whether you have not demanded a little too much of yourself and Frank. It is always a question of how much. There is no human truth which is altogether true, no love which is altogether perfect. You may possibly have neglected virtue or devotion such as you could not find elsewhere, overlooking it because some failing or the lack of sympathy on some unimportant point may at the moment have been prominent. Frank loved you, Madge.

But although all these arguments are cogent and Madge feels their force, Rutherford leaves us in no doubt that these well meaning people are, in this case, acting as Devil's Advocates. "Clara, Clara! You know not what you do!"—the scriptural ring of Madge's tortured cry, in response to Clara's persuasion, puts her sister momentarily in the rôle of anti-Christ. For Rutherford, Madge, as she defends her faith, is a divine soul. "Precious and rare are those divine souls for whom a pale vision possesses an authority they are forced unconditionally to obey."

The "pale vision" is that of an ideal relationship, of two people so "closely akin that they find their meaning in each other," and it is a marriage, to which Madge finally attains, by the self-sacrifice of her sister. But on her journey, she runs through all the dangerous attitudes against which Rutherford has uttered so many heartfelt warnings. She sets her gaze upon the unattainable; she "indulges in singular behaviour" and does not "bind herself by the common laws of humanity," she guides herself by abstract principles; she brings suffering upon others and runs the risk of inflicting very much more upon her illegitimate child; she does not "discern the duty of thankfully receiving any scrap of love offered . . . however imperfect it might be" nor does she consider that an affectionate heart will be enough compensation for what her marriage will lack. And, finally, she refuses to acquiesce in what most people would have accepted as necessity. When Frank finds comfort in the remark "to what is inevitable we must submit," Rutherford is scathing.

> This new phrase struck Frank very much, and it seemed very philosophic to him, a maxim for guidance through life. It did not strike him that it was generally either a platitude or an excuse for weakness, and that a nobler duty is to find out what is inevitable and what is not.

In short, in his treatment of Madge Hopgood, Rutherford runs counter to all his earlier teaching on marriage although not, perhaps, to the underlying spirit of much of his writing. His sympathies had always been instinctively with the idealists, but until *Clara Hopgood* he had invariably recommended coming to terms with the situation, allowing compassion and humility to blur the vision of the unattainable. Now, in his last novel, he allows one of his characters, not only to impose her own terms upon life, but to find that ideal relationship for which all his other protagonists had yearned in vain—and which he himself, it is pleasing to remember, was also able to reach before it was too late. (pp. 263-67)

> Patricia Thomson, "The Novels of Mark Rutherford," in Essays in Criticism, Vol. XIV, No. 3, July, 1964, pp. 256-67.

STEPHEN MERTON   (essay date 1967)

[*Merton is an American critic. In the following excerpt, he examines the social background of Rutherford's writings.*]

There is a strain of quiet but enterprising sensibility in the nineteenth century that is common to authors as varied as Matthew Arnold, Gerard Manley Hopkins, Francis Kilvert, Emily Dickinson, and Henry David Thoreau. Not "Victorian" in the vulgar sense, their work is marked by the kind of poignant awareness that distinguishes both the poetic and the religious experience, as well as by a tact that shuns effusiveness or sentimentality. To this group of authors belongs William Hale White.

Better known under his pseudonym "Mark Rutherford," Hale White reflects from many angles the interests and tastes of the Victorian man of sensibility. His curious mind touched upon most of the nineteenth-century compromises, in politics and philosophy, in science and religion, and in fiction and literary criticism. And it touched upon them always with a certain fervor, discriminating and intense. His novels, too, are marked by this quality. They remain indeed the single clear echo of an extremely powerful and rather small segment of English culture—the Calvinistic minority that reached back to Oliver Cromwell and to John Bunyan and that had, one suspects, a determining influence on the Victorian milieu. (p. 21).

A sense of seriousness, compounded of a Calvinistic search for salvation and a Victorian search for truth, underlies all Hale White's work. It determines the distinctive tone of his masterpieces, *The Autobiography of Mark Rutherford* and *The Rev-*

olution in Tanner's Lane. Hale White never descends to the trivial. The search was always going on within him. To Miss Dorothy Vernon Smith, whom he married at the age of eighty, he remarked, "You are the only person who does not mind my being serious. I can't *help* being serious."

The search started in his youth, after his awakening under the influence of the *Lyrical Ballads.* "Of more importance, too," he notes of this influence, "than the decay of systems was the birth of a habit of inner reference and a dislike to occupy myself with anything which did not in some way or other touch the soul, or was not the illustration or embodiment of some spiritual law." From this time onward he felt that there was some destiny he had to fulfill. "I have a strange fancy—that there is one word which I was sent into the world to say. At times I can dimly make it out but I cannot speak it. Nevertheless it seems to make all other speech beside the mark and futile." But he had not a hint of self-importance. He realized the tendency to self-deception in all human nature, especially his own. "It is curious that I always have such a sense of insincerity when I try to speak on solemn subjects, even when I do my best to say what I mean and no more than what I mean."

He pounced on superficiality at once. A book for him, if it was anything at all, was the essence of a life—to be cultivated as part of a spacious domain. For this reason he arose habitually between five and six every morning to read and write. This was the only portion of a heavily chartered day he could afford for his central vocation. (Even during his last years, after he retired, his wife reports of him, "when I woke it was generally to find him with a volume of Shakespeare or Spenser or a book from the London library in his hand.") Superficiality in people repelled him in the same way. "Never try to say anything remarkable," he advises. "It is sure to be wrong." He approached his friends as devoutly as he did his books. "For what do my friends stand? Not for the clever things they say: I do not remember them half an hour after they are spoken. It is always the unspoken, the unconscious which is their reality to me." (pp. 22-3)

In an age of three-decker novels, the slim volumes of Hale White, critical, searching, and unadorned, stand apart. An anonymous reviewer of *The Autobiography of Mark Rutherford* said just after its publication, "It is remarkable. It is short and that in itself is a merit in these days of weary three volumes." Hale White's first two novels crossed the Atlantic and were reviewed by William Dean Howells in *Harper's New Monthly Magazine;* he immediately recognized their distinction [see excerpt dated 1886].

The locale of these novels, when it is not London, is typically a small English market town like Hale White's native Bedford on the meadow flats of the eastern midlands. In the opening chapter of *Catharine Furze,* which of all his novels recaptures most lovingly the country of his boyhood, the scene is given in a single encompassing sentence:

> The malthouses and their cowls, the wharves and the gaily painted sailing barges alongside, the fringe of slanting willows turning the silver-gray sides of their foliage towards the breeze, the island in the middle of the river with bigger willows, the large expanse of sky, the soft clouds distinct in form almost to the far distant horizon, and, looking eastwards, the illimitable distance towards the fens and the sea—all of this made up a landscape, more suitable perhaps to

some persons than rock or waterfall, although
no picture had ever been painted of it and nobody had ever come to see it.

Actually, this is the charming countryside we are shown in
John Constable's paintings. This land of meadow and wood
and river, of farm and mill and wharf had been the scene of
Constable's own Suffolk childhood in the valley of the river
Stour, which separates that county on the south from Essex.
These counties occupy those very fenlands stretching eastward
from Bedford and Cambridge to the sea. These "scenes of his
boyhood," Constable had been fond of saying, "made him a
painter." He had celebrated them on his canvases during the
first four decades of the century, decades which included Hale
White's own boyhood. In Constable's pictures we are given
the landscape of Hale White's "Cowfolds." Hale White pays
his tribute to those "fields by the banks of the Stour." "It is
Constable's country," he says in his *Early Life,* "and in its
way not to be matched in England. Although there is nothing
striking in it, its influence, at least upon me, is greater than
that of celebrated mountains and waterfalls."

All Hale White's characters are taken from his own life in a
sense more literal than is true for most novelists. "He never
created a character in his life," his wife records, "never sat
down to write without having somebody before his mind's
eye." These novels, written in his fifties and sixties, in the
London of the 1880's and 1890's, re-create the rural countryside of the early decades of the century—a world that has all
but disappeared: the River Ouse with its bridges and barges,
the spicy talk of the farmers drinking whiskey in back parlors,
the bustle and anger of politics—Chartism, Reform—against
the still vivid memory of the French Revolution.

Hale White's world is one that has not altogether found a place
in the great novels. It is not quite the circle of *Adam Bede,*
nor at all that of *Barchester Towers,* nor of *The Way of All
Flesh.* Thackeray was not aware of it, and Dickens merely
caricatured it. It is the world which Hale White himself came
from and which he knew best. "I seem to have come from an
honest set," he writes to his future wife, "but socially nothing
much above farmers who may have been and indeed very likely
were officers in Oliver's army." Their forebears were the Saxons, who having in the fourteenth century been driven to the
towns by the Black Death, had become merchants and developed a vigorously independent style of life. Their religion was
simple, with none of the ornateness that flourished among the
Norman feudal lords and that was later to develop into "Anglicanism." From this Saxon tradition of the fenlands came—
together with Bunyan and Cromwell's soldiers—the shopkeepers, ironmongers, brewers, printers, and booksellers of Hale
White's novels, a working class homely of speech, of manner,
and of religion, independent, and, when occasion demanded,
rebellious of thought and temper. To this world Hale White
restricts himself in his novels, and by so doing becomes its
principal spokesman. "He is by his own right," William Learoyd Sperry delimits it finely, "the spokesman for mid-Victorian Independency, a world which without his witness would
have been mute and perhaps ultimately forgotten. He has done
for the humble nonconformity of his own midland counties
what Trollope did for the Establishment in sleepy Cathedral
towns, what George Eliot did for Methodism through the countryside, and what Jane Austen and Miss Mitford did for in-
nocuous gentility at large. 'Cowfold' is the 'Barchester' of
Dissent" [see Additional Bibliography].

Hale White's milieu is as far removed from Barchester as
Barchester is from London. His "Cowfolds" are, as he puts
it in the *Autobiography,* "a sort of condensation of the agricultural country round." Like Gray's *Elegy,* Hale White's novels celebrate the romance that lies implicit, and that can at
times achieve a glory of its own, in the annals of the poor.
But these annals for him are not short nor simple. In them lie
entangled the very complexities of motive and deed that dominate the courts and capitals of the world. (pp. 33-5)

It was this "uncovering of the 'commonplace,'" as she phrased
it, which first drew Dorothy Vernon Smith, later his second
wife, to his books. Hale White himself intimates in one sentence of *Catharine Furze* the meaning of his novels: "When
we grow old we find that what is commonplace is true. . . ."
With the Romantic bias which was sharpened under the influence of Wordsworth, his purpose is to present the ordinary in
an unusual way. "In Wordsworth the miraculous inherent in
the commonplace, but obscured by 'the film of familiarity,' is
restored to it," he has observed. The discoveries that he embodies in his stories are however his own. The facts which
unsettle and propel him are peculiarly urban. His are among
the first of the "proletarian" novels. "What are the facts?"
he asks in one of his detached notes. "Not those in Homer,
Shakespeare or even the Bible. The facts for most of us are a
dark street, crowds, hurry commonplaceness, loneliness, and,
worse than all, a terrible doubt which can hardly be named as
to the meaning and purpose of the world." Nor is it the peasant
mentality to which his Romantic inheritance draws him. It is
in "second-rate sensitive minds" exposed to the rootlessness
of modern life that he is interested.

The protagonists of Hale White's novels are essentially pro-
jections of his own youthful temperament. "I wish not to judge
others," he says in the *Autobiography* "but the persons who
to me have proved themselves most attractive, have been those
who have passed through such a process as that through which
I myself passed; those who have had in some form or other an
enthusiastic stage in their history, when the story of Genesis
and the Gospels has been rewritten, when God has visibly
walked in the garden, and the Son of God has drawn men away
from their daily occupations to the divinest of dreams."

Hale White combines in a remarkable way strands from the
seventeenth century and from the nineteenth. The latter appear
in the intellectual conflict of his characters; the former are
implicit in their stern, Puritan idealism, which intesifies that
conflict. The story of Genesis and the Gospels has been rewritten by his heroes. Hale White's special achievement is to
restore to the Christian terminology its original meaning in
existential terms. "Nearly every doctrine in the college creed
had once had a natural origin in the necessities of human nature,
and might therefore be so interpreted as to become a necessity
again," says Mark Rutherford in the *Autobiography* during his
short career as a theological student. Ironically, he learned that
it was just such interpretation, leading back to the origins of
creed, that the authorities feared and misunderstood: "To reach
through to that original necessity; to explain the atonement as
I believed it appeared to Paul, and the sinfulness of man as it
appeared to the prophets, was my object. But it was precisely
this reaching after a meaning which constituted heresy."

Hale White's theology . . . was to develop quickly in the direction of a symbolism which read the old creed in terms of
an ever new existence. His novels embody these views and
their growth. What must one do to be saved? The answer to
this question is the persistent theme of his fiction. In the earlier

autobiographical novels—whose protagonist, Mark Rutherford, is Hale White himself "under a semi-transparent disguise"—the metaphysical problem of the age, echoed in poets like Clough and Arnold and Tennyson, is expressed by Hale White in the very specific context of the Calvinistic creed. Mark is torn by the loss of the old belief and relives the words of the twenty-second Psalm, "My God, my God, why hast thou forsaken me?" His need is not for the rationalized deity of the schools but for a personal union. In these earlier novels Hale White has undertaken to show us the disintegration of a religion. Part of his aim is to contrast a fading Puritanism with the fiery ardor of the earlier sect. This ardor is relit in a few isolated souls, like Mark Rutherford and Zachariah Coleman, incarnations of pristine nonconformity in the nineteenth-century muddle. The fading is a symptom of prosperity and middle-class attitudes. Calvinism has climbed almost to the respectability of Anglicanism. It is this climb which evokes the dominant note of irony in the novels.

Hale White's early male protagonists are Job-like heroes of endurance; his later, female protagonists tend to be, like Ibsen's Nora, more rebellious. Hale White's special subject is the predicament of ardent, Christ-like spirits in a prosperous, alien world; his special contribution to English fiction is the rendition, unsentimental and acute, of their endurance. No one equals him in projecting into fiction the stoical lesson which was impressed upon him by Carlyle and which he expresses as follows: "Carlyle feels the contradictions of the universe as keenly as any man can feel them. He knows how easy it is to appear profound by putting anew riddles which nobody can answer; he knows how strong is the temptation toward the insoluable. But upon these subjects he also knows how to hold his tongue; he does not shriek in the streets, but he bows his head.

Gradually, in the later novels, the exigencies of living apply their balm to the pain of youthful frustration. Solutions begin to appear: absorption in work (*Mark Rutherford's Deliverance*), and politics and love (*The Revolution in Tanner's Lane*). The problem is blunted but the ache is still there. It persists through all the later novels under the guise of new circumstance. The most radical alteration in these later novels is, as their titles indicate, that their protagonists are women, and that the change of sex is accompanied by a change in the phrasing of the question. The search for a God becomes a search for a human relationship. It is as though women, with their sense of the practical, can confer another perspective, can view the problem of salvation naturalistically. In these novels the "new woman" of the later nineteenth century (modeled for Hale White in many features by George Eliot) emerges.

For all their concern with the problem of love, these later novels are however not "love stories." They are quite as concentrated as were the earlier novels on the issues of struggle and salvation. This is what distinguishes them, the sense they establish of the dependence of the immediate on the ultimate. They convey a Spinozistic view of the human situation *sub specie aeternitatis*. If they are not love stories, neither are they "religious novels" in any pious sense; they are so only if we interpret religion broadly enough to include a secular non-supernatural humanism. Then they are truly so. They are ever questioning both the dogma and the skepticism of the nineteenth century. Apropos of the "entertainment" provided at the monthly Sunday evening meetings of his congregation during his term as minister, Mark Rutherford comments on the pious books used for the public readings: "I was reduced to that class of literature which of all others I most abominated, and which always seemed to me the most profane,—religious and sectarian gossip, religious novels designed to make religion attractive, and other slip-slop of this kind." Hale White's own approach is quiet and direct. His seriousness is rarely without its touch of irony. His editorial asides, which are frequent, are woven into the fabric of his stories without noticeable shift of tone, and they do not offend. Even the professional sermons of his ministers are convincing, and keep within the narrow bounds of a fiction reader's patience. Thomas Seccombe has observed of these: "He interpolates several sermons into his novels and these are the only sermons we have read for many years.

The personalities of Hale White's protagonists are derived especially from the idols of his youth. Their qualities of sincerity, skepticism, sensitivity, aloofness, and fearlessness are those Hale White inherited from his own father and discovered anew in one or two older friends and in such literary favorites as Carlyle and Byron. Upon Hale White's heroines the influence of George Eliot (who for him was very much a friend before she was an author) is noticeable. His heroes, men like the Reverend Bradshaw in the *Revolution*, are modeled in part upon the old breed of minister that was passing from the scene in Hale White's childhood. One such, the Reverend Samuel Hilliard, had occupied the pulpit of Bunyan Meeting, the chapel at Bedford, in Hale White's childhood. For half a century he had fearlessly maintained the connection between Dissent and political reform that dated back to Cromwell. He was succeeded by the Reverend John Jukes, neo-orthodox and careful in his politics, the type of the sanctimonious, pussyfooting minister, representative of a decadent, mammonized Dissent, who was to be satirized in the Reverend John Broad of the *Revolution*. When Hale White was eighteen, he came under the influence of an eloquent Welsh preacher, Caleb Morris, who more than any other person except his father influenced his life. Recalling one of Morris' sermons he has written: "I can feel even now the force which streamed from him that night, and swept me with it, as if I were a leaf on a river in a flood. . . . I never beheld a man in whom Christianity, or rather Christ, was so vitally inherent."

Such intensities of realization flash out in the protagonists of Hale White's novels. Caleb Morris represented for him the heroic culmination of qualities in his father and in his father's favorite authors, to which as a boy he had learned to respond. Matthew Arnold has described religion as "the power not ourselves that makes for righteousness." Religion, divested of its theology, was for Hale White too essentially a moral power. As such it came to be articulated for him by great literary spokesmen like Carlyle. Carlyle indeed had been the particular idol of his father, whose religion was colored by the fervor and skepticism of the Scotch author much as Hale's was to be colored by the pantheism of Wordsworth. Fervor and skepticism became the distinguishing traits of Hale White's great male characters, Mark Rutherford and Zachariah Coleman. Byron, too, with his scorn for the petty and the vulgar, his flair for the grand possibilities in life, vanquished with his rhetoric both father and son. Standing at his composing desk, the Puritan printer would declaim from memory long passages from Byron to the enthralled young Hale. The father loved poetry of a sublime cast, especially Milton, and Hale White could in his old age remember his reciting passages from "Comus," his special favorite. Pervasively do Hale White's various interests—in religion and politics, in philosophy and science—

inform his novels, but from his literary admirations these novels catch their special note.

The kinship among the protagonists of his novels, the literary and personal heroes of his youth, and Hale White himself, has its origins deep within the Victorian conscience and the Victorian temper. Carlyle, Byron, George Eliot, Caleb Morris, William White, Sr., were all products of the religious awakening that marked the opening decades of the century—an awakening that is evident also in Newman, Arnold, and Ruskin, all temperamentally akin to Hale White and all emergent from similar severe Protestant backgrounds. All of them modified the dogma of the old creed but retained its impassioned moral dedication. Protestant in the sense that the early Reformation leaders were, each forged from his own experience, which frequently involved a painful "soul crisis," a religion of his own. Hale White's novels record the agonizing and liberating progress of his own personal religion. In so doing they give us an insight into the Victorian moral ferment as it worked its way from the great spokesmen of the age and was filtered through the sensibility of an intensely individual author. (pp. 36-40)

Stephen Merton, in his Mark Rutherford (William Hale White), *Twayne Publishers, Inc., 1967, 189 p.*

SIR WILLIAM HALEY (essay date 1971)

[*In the following excerpt, Haley argues the need for a reassessment of Rutherford's works.*]

Mark Rutherford, of all people, needed no excuse for writing a book about John Bunyan. But he felt he did. "The properties of light" he wrote "are revealed by the object which reflects or absorbs it. We are struck with the peculiar dryness of the criticism of Shakespeare in the eighteenth century. It was dry, not because the eighteenth century was deficient in intellect, but because there was so much in Shakespeare to which it could not respond. It did not ask the questions we ask, or demand what we demand." So, too, he thought, it was with Bunyan. So, too, it is with himself.

William Hale White, to give Mark Rutherford his real name—and there are times when it is necessary to distinguish between the two—has never had a wide general appeal. Yet he finds readers in each generation. The mysteries which agitated him, not only in the semi-confessional, semi-fictional period of his early life depicted in *The Autobiography of Mark Rutherford* and *Mark Rutherford's Deliverance* but in some degree throughout his 81 years, have little relevance to the great majority of people today. Yet, sometimes at the heart of them, sometimes on their periphery, there are other mysteries which have a greater force now than they had when he wrote over three-quarters of a century ago. Three major works about him have been published since the end of the last war. Also there has been Professor Basil Willey's luminous and moving essay in *More Nineteenth Century Studies* [see Additional Bibliography].

All these have depicted, analysed, and sought to explain Mark Rutherford as the deeply religious man he never ceased to be. Indeed the slow clarification of his religion was what mattered most to Hale White at all times. He set little store by his books. At his life's end he could remember only one of them, *Miriam's Schooling,* a tale perhaps significant in one regard, but that not central to his beliefs.

What he could and could not believe over-rode all else. Nonetheless I am not going to add yet another set of footprints over that ground. For one thing, I am not qualified to do so. I have read Mark Rutherford for close on 50 years in spite of his religious obsessions, not because of them. For another, I think Mark Rutherford's future will depend on his holding his place as a story-teller who wrote fine prose. And I believe that long after the realities of Dissent, Broad Church, Independents, Arminianism, Predestination, Election, and Reprobation have been forgotten, that future will still be secure.

There is perhaps one requirement. It is a re-ordering of the estimation in which Mark Rutherford's individual books are held, and particularly an abandonment of the supposed pre-eminence of *The Revolution in Tanner's Lane.* Too often it is cited as his masterpiece. It is not. It is a broken-backed work; really two novels in one. Both are powerful and vividly written. The fortuitous overlap of some characters does not make the two parts one whole.

Many years ago I elaborated on the idea that in each generation there is vital importance in the order in which a famous author's works are read. Often the most praised books are best left to the last. If the initiation of the next generation of readers is to depend on *The Revolution in Tanner's Lane,* or even more on *The Autobiography of Mark Rutherford* and *Mark Rutherford's Deliverance,* then in all too many cases these will fall on stony ground. Better would be the three volumes of his *Journal* (which contain many short tales); better still would be *Catharine Furze;* best of all, *Clara Hopgood.*

It is in *Clara Hopgood* and *Catharine Furze* and, to a lesser extent, *Miriam's Schooling,* that Hale White's gifts as a novelist are at their best. The first of these gifts is his ability to tell a story that holds the reader. Much present day fiction gives little weight to this. Its importance to ordinary readers, as distinct from literary critics, is still great. Even when we least care about Mark Rutherford's doubts and mental discomforts we are still anxious to know whom he will marry, how he will manage to support himself, and what will become of his friend, Mardon, and Mardon's daughter, Mary. When Miss Arbour passionately reveals to Rutherford the secret of her own married life in order to persuade him not to make a mistake himself, it does not seem—as some interpolated short stories in famous novels do—a digression to be skipped or at least got through as quickly as possible. For ten pages we become as absorbed in her fortunes as we have been in Rutherford's own. Very occasionally the tale Hale White has to tell, or an episode in it, may seem melodramatic. The coincidence of the two savings from drowning in "**Michael Trevanion**" make it a contrived religious anecdote. Hale White himself must have felt the sudden conversion and confession of Orkid Jim (also after being saved from drowning) was likely not to win belief, for he appeals to "John Bunyan's account of the strange behaviour of Mr. Tod" at Hertford Assizes to show that his story is not impossible. Be that as it may, his ability to hold the reader's interest survives.

The reason we care what happens to Hale White's characters (he denied he had ever created one; they were all, he said, the fruits of observation) is that we see them so clearly from the outset. Hale White had Tolstoy's gift of introducing each person in his tale simply and directly, in a few matter-of-fact strokes. The man or woman's character is quickly set. Thereafter he or she acts according to it. One of the fascinations of *Clara Hopgood* is the way one becomes aware, despite apparent surprises, of Hale White's consistency in this novel also.

It must be said that Hale White's range of characters is limited. The world he peoples is a relatively narrow one. He is no

Balzac or Tolstoy, and while he has been compared to George Eliot, in some respects appropriately, not in the sum total of all his works does he encompass the range of *Middlemarch*.

Considering wherein his strength as a novelist lay and his purpose—for Hale White was always a writer with a purpose—the fact he limited his scene to his experience was not a disadvantage. He depicts it minutely and accurately. His picture of the delicately separated social strata of a provincial town in early Victorian England is exact, and amusing. He gives it a quiet, ironical humour. Whether the daughters of an auctioneer, a bank clerk, a druggist, a bootmaker could or could not be taken as pupils by the Misses Pratt depended on hairlines of social distinction. Mrs. Furze, as the daughter of a Cambridge draper, had been a cut above what she became as the wife of an Eastthorpe ironmonger. Bank managers, merchants, shopkeepers, clergymen, farmers, all had stations into which Providence had called them and out of which those above and below them were watchful they should not stray. The caste system embraced locality as well as occupation. Mrs. Furze was clear that only if she could bully or bamboozle her poor, ineffectual mouse of a husband into moving the family's home away from the shop into The Terrace would it be even remotely possible for Mrs. Colston, the brewer's wife, to condescend to call on her. (When Mrs. Colston does call, the chapter of accidents that turns what should have been a triumph into a disaster shows Hale White's gift for comedy. So does the chat of the three farmers in the parlour behind Mr. Furze's shop on market day.) Mrs. Furze was also sure that if the move from the High Street to The Terrace was to be socially successful, there must at the same time be a transfer of attendance from the chapel to the church. Here, too, she was disappointed. Instead of bringing them respectability it was one cause of their ruin.

The social comedy of the Victorian middle-class in the provinces was no more Hale White's aim in *Catharine Furze* and *Clara Hopgood* than the depiction of London squalor was in *Mark Rutherford's Deliverance* and *Miriam's Schooling*. Every one of Hale White's novels has at its core the problem of a personal relationship. That relationship is often affected by the relationship of one or both participants to God, but this is not always decisive.

Catharine Furze is the story of two such relationships: the girl Catharine's controlled love for the clergyman, Mr. Cardew and, growing directly out of it, Mr. Cardew's late-flowering love for his wife. Of the two the latter is the more moving. Hale White had a tender insight into certain kinds of marriage. Because of the beautiful love between himself and Dorothy Vernon that gave a radiance to his last years—*The Groombridge Diary* is the record of it—and because little is so generally known about his first wife, this at first surprises. The fictional Mark Rutherford—and it must always be remembered that in his factual *Early Life* Hale White said that *The Autobiography of Mark Rutherford* and *Mark Rutherford's Deliverance* had contained much that was entirely fictitious—stays in the mind as an essentially lonely and isolated man coming into a matrimonial refuge only towards his life's end. Professor Basil Willey has provided the key to what might seem a mystery by pointing out that early in Hale White's first marriage his wife became a victim of disseminated sclerosis. "Both he and she" Professor Willey quotes their eldest son, Sir William Hale-White, as saying, "bore this 30 year long tragedy without wincing, devoted in their affection for one another."

The disparity between Mr. Cardew and his wife is not between health and sickness, however. He is an eager talker; she can never find words at all. There is a touching scene in which Mrs. Cardew tries to take lessons from Catharine in being articulate, using *Paradise Lost* as a "set book." The trouble between M'Kay and his wife in *Mark Rutherford's Deliverance* is that her uncritical admiration of him makes her not a companion but a maddening echo of all he says. In *Miriam's Schooling,* her husband, Didymus is too prosaic. Where Hale White is distinctive as a novelist is that in all these cases there is an abundance of love. It is communication that is lacking. Eventually the Cardews are brought to understand each other through Catharine's death. Miriam has an altogether new awareness of her husband when he constructs an orrery for Mr. Armstrong, the vicar of a neighbouring village, and Didymus educates her in the movements of the planets.

The relationships in *Clara Hopgood* are numerous. There is more crisscrossing than in any other of his novels. *Clara Hopgood* is a relatively short book. (Hale White had an ability to pace and proportion his tales; each is given what it needs, without padding or compression.) In some 50,000 words we have the relations of Clara with her sister, Madge; Madge's with Frank Palmer, who seduces her; Clara's renunciation of Baruch Cohen; Baruch's bitter awakening to his son Benjamin's feelings about him (involving another escape from drowning); Baruch's marriage to Madge; Clara's enchantment by Mazzini; and Mrs. Caffyn's motherly care of almost everyone. With all this Hale White still leaves himself room to fix his characters firmly in their settings.

Madge and Clara Hopgood are, I think, Hale White's diploma pieces as a novelist. The amount of Hale White himself in Mark Rutherford disqualifies that character. At first it seems as if the contrast between the two sisters is to be one of lightness and strength. Then Madge surprises us by her steadfastness in refusing to marry Frank who, weak though he is, does, albeit with diminishing determination, try to make the mother of his child his wife. Clara's strength is of a different kind, leading her finally to death in Italy as one of Mazzini's martyrs. The shape the novel takes in our memory justifies Clara's monopoly of its title.

Mention of seduction and sea rescues must not be allowed to give a false impression. Violence plays little part in Hale White's stories. Often it is the slight pressure of a hand, a word left unspoken, a look, that decides a lifetime's future. The most powerful and ubiquitous of all Hale White's characters is what, in *The Autobiography of Mark Rutherford,* he calls the silent monitor. This force "gentle and incomprehensible, but nevertheless unmistakable . . . none the less the peremptory, although its voice was so soft and low that it might easily have been overlooked" is felt by many of his characters. It restrains Mark from declaring his love to Theresa. It forbids Clara to allow Baruch to propose to her. It impels Catharine to dismiss Mr. Cardew. It can be positive as well as negative. By those with conscience and sensibility it is never to be denied. Much has been written about Hale White's "black moments," those occasions when he found himself looking into the abyss. Undoubtedly they were real. They were comparatively rare. They came and went. "The silent monitor" was always at his side.

It gives him his abiding relevance. Mark Rutherford tells M'Kay that "with the departure of a belief in the supernatural departs once and for ever the chance of regenerating the race except by the school and by science." In a footnote Hale White asks his readers to bear in mind the difference between the early Victorian days he is depicting and the time he is writing (1884) "when socialism, nationalism of the land, and other projects have renewed in men the hope of regeneration by political processes.'' That hope—or delusion—is still with us. So is the still, small voice. Because of it Mark Rutherford's observation that ''As we get older we find that all life is given to us on conditions of uncertainty, and yet we walk courageously on'' is still true. It is seen in this light that Hale White's writings meet the demands of today. (pp. 39-42)

Sir William Haley, ''William Hale White: Alias Mark Rutherford,'' in Contemporary Review, *Vol. 218, No. 1260, January, 1971, pp. 38-42*

GERRY H. BROOKES   (essay date 1986)

[*In the following excerpt, Brookes contends that* The Autobiography of Mark Rutherford *and* Mark Rutherford's Deliverance *can be best understood when viewed as fiction rather than as autobiography.*]

For Victorian scholars William Hale White's *Autobiography of Mark Rutherford* and *Mark Rutherford's Deliverance* raise the question of how literary criticism should deal with works that seem a mix of fictional and autobiographical materials. They may be treated as mixed works, but doing so avoids a leading question in genre theory, whether there is an informing principle, fictional or autobiographical, to which the various elements may be subordinated.

[In] the *Autobiography* the fictional and any autobiographical elements are subordinated to the dramatic representation of an egotistical character in a particular predicament that is worked out according to the principles of plot. Although *Deliverance* takes up again the narrative of the life of the same character, White shifts his focus onto communal principles of adaptation to modern life, which he exemplifies in various lives, giving his work an exemplary shape, that of an apologue. Both works have forms that approximate those of narrative fiction, and they should be judged accordingly.

Although some critics have been content to consider the works amorphous fictionalized autobiography, interpretation from the start has been dominated by the hypothesis that the works have the coherence and power of autobiography, that is, that their effect depends on their representing experience that is prior to the text, which is what I seek to deny. In reviewing both books, William Dean Howells remarked, ''When you have read the books you feel that you have witnessed the career of a man as you might have witnessed it in the world and not in a book. We could not give too strong an impression of this incomparable sincerity'' [see excerpt dated 1886]. White himself encouraged the tendency to read the works as autobiographical. Referring to the *Autobiography* and *Deliverance* in *The Early Life of Mark Rutherford (W. Hale White)*—a title that indicates his public identification with his protagonist—White remarked, ''I have been asked at 78 years old to set down what I remember of my early life. A good deal of it has been told before under a semi-transparent disguise, with much added which is entirely fictitious.'' While his remarks encourage viewing the works as at least mixed in genre, they do not provide an indication of the principles according to which he uses both fictional and autobiographical materials. His claim that much of the narrative is fictional has not been sufficient to discourage critics from viewing it as essentially self-expressive, in part because no fictional form seems evident to them. On the other hand, the works are clearly not pure autobiography. Originally, in responding to Howells, even White himself seemed momentarily convinced that he had not invented any of the narrative but

had simply recorded it. He wrote Howells that he ''never should have dreamed of publishing anything if it had not struck me when I was fifty that perhaps some of my experiences were worth recording for the sake of those who were brought up as I was.'' This justification for publishing is, of course, very close to that claimed by his protagonist in the opening pages of the *Autobiography*. White apparently could not bring himself to admit that the impression of sincerity could be a creation of his art and was not simply implicit in a bare account of his own life. White seems to have been willing to risk confusion about the extent to which the works were records of verifiable experiences. The autobiographical impression that the works created, a strain of expressive criticism ready to embrace such an impression, and White's cooperation in allowing himself and his protagonist to be confused have all made it difficult to escape seeing the works as autobiography. James Anthony Froude, whose *The Nemesis of Faith* suffered from similar confusion in readers' minds, added a note to his text insisting that his protagonist's experience was not his own. . . . White never wrote such a note.

This view, that White wrote only autobiography, rests on much that cannot be verified, often on an apparent intuition that some higher truth about the author is being told, rather than any literal one. An obvious reason for thinking that no literal truth is being told is that Rutherford's and White's lives do not conform in many details. Important influences on White, such as his father and Caleb Morris, for example, are not present, and the significant episode in *Deliverance* of opening a room for the working poor of Drury Lane has no analogue in White's life. Any intrusion of White's father, for example, who recited Byron from memory and was drawn away from the meeting house by Carlyle's early works, would have forced White to change significantly the course of Mark Rutherford's life. Catherine Macdonald Maclean has even suggested that the life story actually presented resembles those of two of White's friends, William Chignell and William Macall, more closely than his own. . . . The discrepancies between White's life and his protagonist's seem to suggest that he is turning his materials away from whatever meaning might be inherent in the story of his own life and toward something else. Yet these fictionalized details commonly drive the critics back into a more ineffable realm of essential truths, unknown facts, and psychological mysteries. Wilfred Stone, for example, who knows White's life more intimately than anyone, insists that all explanations of the details in the works must be biographical: the Drury Lane episode, for example, cannot be imaginary but must be based on some experience that White had but we cannot document. . . . Obviously, any work in some measure arises from its author's experience. The real question is what is the form that ''formulates'' his experience. (pp. 247-49)

If Rutherford's life is significantly different from White's, he clearly uses autobiographical materials and presents ideas and observations of his own, which appear elsewhere in his journals and other works. But the fictional and autobiographical materials are shaped within forms that make them intelligible, satisfying, and important, apart from the complex, extra-literary context of White's life. Both the *Autobiography* and *Deliverance* can be understood without a sense that some external truths or facts about the author are at issue or have the power to confirm or deny the substance of the narratives, as is certainly the case with overt autobiographies like Newman's *Apologia* or Mill's *Autobiography*. Rather than telling his own story, White fuses fictional and autobiographical materials into a dramatic account of the life of a hypothetical person in the *Au-*

tobiography and then, in *Deliverance,* into a set of hypothetical examples of how some people adapt to the disabling conditions of modern life. Stone remarks that whenever White used personal experience in the *Autobiography,* he distorted it in order to make Rutherford's situation worse than his own had been. . . . Indeed, some of his former schoolmates objected to his apparent unfairness to the president of the college he attended, a version of whom oppresses Rutherford. . . . These distortions are necessary to the consistent effect White wishes to create. Ultimately the books are powerful evidence of the nature of White's view of the world, but they are only indirect evidence of his personal experience.

A number of framing devices, like the use of a fictional author and editor, point to the hypothetical nature of the narratives, inclining one to think that the experiences described are not necessarily true or are at least intended to seem more hypothetical than actual. The devices certainly work to forestall the reader's inclination to test the narratives against other accounts of the same life. The reader asks whether the text presents a plausible and internally consistent life story, not whether it presents a plausible version of the life of an actual person who may be inquired after. Yet a much more powerful indication of the nature of the narratives resides in the familiar informing shapes of fiction, in the principles governing the forms of the works. One need not be surprised to discover from external sources that, as in much fiction, some episodes are versions of real events, but their power resides fully in the context of these works, where it lies in their probability, not in their verifiability or their accuracy as records of William Hale White's experience. Tacitly, one perceives that a whole, actual life could not arrange itself so neatly to fit the demands of the implicit forms, and it is hard to conceive of any reader, with vision unclouded by biography or romantic bias, becoming persuaded that these books are true and accurate accounts of the life of a real man. (pp. 250-51)

> *Gerry H. Brookes, "Fictional Forms in William Hale White's 'Autobiography of Mark Rutherford' and 'Mark Rutherford's Deliverance',' " in Biography, Vol. 9, No. 3, Summer, 1986, pp. 247-68.*

ADDITIONAL BIBLIOGRAPHY

Allen, Walter. "The Novel from 1881 to 1914." In his *The English Novel: A Short Critical History,* pp. 305-409. New York: E. P. Dutton, 1954.
    Briefly discusses Rutherford's work, concluding that he was "not more than a minor novelist," although his novels are important because of their unprecedented treatment of English Dissenters.

Baker, Ernest A. "Mark Rutherford and Others." In his *The History of the English Novel: The Day Before Yesterday,* pp. 97-121. London: H. F. and G. Witherby, 1938.
    Discusses Rutherford's principal works.

Buchmann, Ursula. *William Hale White (Mark Rutherford) and the Problem of Self-Adjustment in a World of Changing Values.* Zurich: Juris-Verlag, 1950, 143 p.
    Traces the evolution of Rutherford's theological stance through an analysis of moral conclusions in his novels.

Cunningham, Valentine. "Was There a Revolution in Tanner's Lane?" In his *Everywhere Spoken Against,* pp. 249-277. Oxford: Clarendon Press, 1975.
    Explores the relationship of Rutherford's religious background to his work.

Daiches, David. Chapter Three. In his *Some Late Victorian Attitudes,* pp. 87-123. New York: W. W. Norton and Co., 1969.
    Considers *The Autobiography of Mark Rutherford* as the quintessential expression of Victorian loss of faith.

Harwood, H. C. "Mark Rutherford." *The London Mercury* III, No. 16 (February 1921): 388-97.
    Analyzes the stoic moral philosophy which underlies all Rutherford's work, maintaining that "Rutherford is a great writer only in so far as he is a moral writer."

Hughes, Linda K. "Madge and Clara Hopgood: William Hale White's Spinozan Sisters." *Victorian Studies* XVIII, No. 1 (September 1974): 57-75.
    Considers the actions of the protagonists of the novel *Clara Hopgood* as an explanation of Spinoza's concept of the relation between passion and intellect.

Low, Frances. "Mark Rutherford: An Appreciation." *Fortnightly Review* 90 (1 September 1908): 458-73.
    Positive assessment of style and content in Rutherford's fiction.

Lucas, John. "William Hale White and the Problems of Deliverance." In his *The Literature of Change: Studies in the Nineteenth-Century Provincial Novel,* pp. 57-118. Sussex: Harvester Press, 1977.
    Discussion of political and religious themes in Rutherford's work, focusing in particular on *The Revolution in Tanner's Lane.*

MacLean, Catherine MacDonald. *Mark Rutherford: A Biography of William Hale White.* London: MacDonald, 1955, 416 p.
    Comprehensive, noncritical biography.

"Recent Novels." *The Nation* 45, No. 1151 (21 July 1887): 56-58.
    Review of *The Revolution in Tanner's Lane* concluding: "with all the discursive talk, the multiplicity of incidents and character, and the general diffuseness that make a reader's final feeling . . . one of disappointment, there is at the same time a breadth of view which is uncommon and praiseworthy."

Nicoll, W. Robertson. *Memories of Mark Rutherford.* London: Unwin, 1924, 127 p.
    Memoir written by a close friend.

Noble, James Ashcroft. Review of *Catharine Furze,* by Mark Rutherford. *The Academy* 45, No. 1140 (10 March 1894): 206-07.
    Finds *Catharine Furze* "worth reading because it is an unconventional story which does not cheapen its unconventionality by italicising and advertising it."

Rayson, R. J. "Is *The Revolution in Tanner's Lane* Broken-Backed?" *Essays in Criticism* XX, No. 1 (January 1970): 71-80.
    Argues that the two seemingly unrelated halves of *The Revolution in Tanner's Lane* represent a conscious effort on Rutherford's part to explore both "the historical and perennial" implications of Dissent.

Salgado, Gamini. "The Rhetoric of Sincerity: *The Autobiography of Mark Rutherford* as Fiction." In *Renaissance and Modern Essays,* edited by G. R. Hibbard, pp. 159-68. London: Routledge and Kegan Paul, 1966.
    Contends that *The Autobiography of Mark Rutherford* can only be properly interpreted when viewed as pure fiction.

Sperry, Willard Learoyd. "Mark Rutherford." *Harvard Theological Review* VII, No. 2 (April 1914): 166-92.
    Lengthy biographical and critical essay.

Swann, Charles. "The Author of 'Mark Rutherford'; or, Who Wrote *Miriam's Schooling?*" *The Yearbook of English Studies* 9 (1979): 270-78.
    Argues that in creating the personas of Mark Rutherford and Reuben Shapcott, White was not simply attempting to preserve his anonymity, but was experimenting with a new approach to literature: fictional works created by a fictional character.

Taylor, A. E. "The Novels of Mark Rutherford." In *Essays and Studies by Members of the English Association,* vol. 5, edited by Oliver Elton, pp. 51-74. Oxford: Clarendon Press, 1914.

Discusses major themes in Rutherford's fiction.

Tempest, E. Vincent. "Optimism in Mark Rutherford." *Westminster Review* 180, No. 2 (August 1913): 174-84.
    Discusses the influence of Wordsworth and Spinoza on Rutherford's moral philosophy.

Trilling, Lionel. Foreword to *William Hale White (Mark Rutherford)*, by Irvin Stock, pp. v-x. New York: Columbia University Press, 1956.
    Discusses Rutherford's art and philosophy.

White, Dorothy V. *Groombridge Diary*. London: Oxford University Press, 1924, 503 p.
    Memoirs and correspondence from Rutherford's final years compiled by his second wife.

Willey, Basil. "Mark Rutherford." In his *More Nineteenth Century Studies: A Group of Honest Doubters*, pp. 186-247. New York: Columbia University Press, 1956.
    Considers the Victorian element of loss of religious faith as the central feature of Rutherford's work.

Amalie (Bertha) Skram

1847-1905

Norwegian novelist, dramatist, and short story writer.

Skram is among the most important Scandinavian authors to follow the principles of late nineteenth-century literary Naturalism. Most notably, she produced the four-volume peasant family saga *Hellemyrsfolket*, which is considered a classic of Naturalist fiction in Norwegian literature. Focusing on social issues and employing a direct narrative style, Skram's fiction emphasizes a few central themes, including the despair of a loveless marriage, the degrading poverty of the lower classes, and the victimization of the insane, subjects which shocked her contemporaries. Commentators regard her fiction as forceful but essentially bleak; according to H. G. Topsöe-Jensen "Skram is the North's most consistent exponent of Naturalism, and she is the most complete pessimist among the writers of that period."

Born into a middle-class family in Bergen on the west coast of Norway, Skram was the second child of a merchant couple who owned a farm supply store. She received a superior education at an exclusive girls' school in Bergen, but when she was seventeen her father deserted the family after a business venture left him bankrupt, and it is thought that Skram became engaged soon after in an effort to bring financial security to her family. Her marriage to a sea captain elevated her family socially and enabled Skram to travel widely and to gain experiences later incorporated into her fiction. However, neither this marriage nor a second marriage were successful. Biographers have noted that Skram's unhappy marriages profoundly affected her, and it has been suggested that her fiction reflects the emotional traumas of her own life. Works such as *Forrådt* and *Fru Inés* portray the differences between men and women as virtually irreconcilable; thus marriage is seen to provide only nominal assurance of mutual concern, support, and faithfulness.

In 1878 Skram and her first husband were separated and two years later, divorced. After a brief stay in a psychiatric hospital (due to the strain of the collapse of her marriage), Skram entered the society of liberal artists and intellectuals in Christiania (now Oslo), and there she was influenced by fiction writers who emulated the Naturalist works of Emile Zola. Adopting the Naturalist's belief that all life is controlled by natural laws, Skram perceived human existence to be actuated by a "race impulse" that determines behavior through biological urges, making men and women slaves to a natural instinct of propagation. Skram commented: "If passion did not exist, love would be eternal—What difference would it make if mankind ceased to propagate its kind? It seems to me that many enough have lived already." Occasionally called "Zola's pupil from Bergen," Skram subsequently wrote fiction in which the common life of the proletariat, precise description of social milieu, and a preoccupation with sexuality are the principal characteristics.

Skram married a Danish writer named Erik Skram in 1884 and moved to Copenhagen, where she produced her first novel, *Constance Ring*. Published in 1885, the book was immediately condemned as immoral and scandalous by conservative critics

because Skram, a socially prominent woman from a respectable family, had frankly portrayed a woman's sexual life in a novel that appeared to be autobiographical. Throughout her career, Skram depicted events apparently based on her personal crises; for instance, the play *Agnete* examines the economic and romantic struggles of a beautiful young divorcée. Biographers suggest that Skram's second divorce, finalized in 1900, led her to commit herself once again to a psychiatric hospital, an experience that formed the basis of *Professor Hieronimus* (*Professor Hieronimus*) and *På St. Jørgen*. These novels, which describe her treatment for nervous disorders, were used by Skram to criticize the care of the insane and drew international attention to this problem. Because she believed Danish readers favored her artistry more than Norwegian readers, Skram remained in Copenhagen for the rest of her life, and was eventually awarded a small pension from the Danish government. Upon her death in 1905 her tombstone was inscribed with the epitaph "Danish citizen, Danish subject and Danish author."

Skram was called a "modern documentor" during her lifetime, in reference to the Naturalist writer's role as scientific recorder of social and psychological forces that debase human life. Skram's tetralogy *Hellemyrsfolket,* for instance, portrays the corrupting effects of poverty, illness, and alcoholism, and the series has been described as intensely and sordidly Naturalist.

Nevertheless, critics have also found a romantic vision in her novels. This vision is most conspicuously displayed in a central conflict that recurs throughout Skram's fiction: the struggle of a woman whose love is frustrated by an inconsiderate and unfaithful man. Brian Downs has described Skram's novels as "matrimonial tragedies" involving "the imperative demands of all-transcending love and the lethal obstacles in the way of following its call." In *Fru Inés,* for example, a woman commits suicide because she inspires love but is unable to return it. For such storylines, Skram has been called a disappointed romantic whose fiction combines a Naturalist narrative style with romantic emotionalism. This emotionalism, as well as the autobiographical elements in Skram's work, have led some critics to emphasize the ways in which her work departs from the Naturalism practiced by Zola and his followers. Downs, for example, contends that Skram's fiction was more innovative in its portrayal of eroticism than in its Naturalism. Generally, however, Skram's work has been appreciated as an important expression of Naturalism in Scandinavian literature, and her manner of conveying empathy for her character's struggles and defeats has been seen as an enduring quality of her fiction. As Harold Beyer has commented: "The profound humanity which fills her best works, the passion that burns beneath the surface, and the intense psychological analysis, and her incomparable pictures of the life of her times—all of these contribute to the unmistakable effect of reality and genuineness which keeps [Amalie Skram's] books alive."

PRINCIPAL WORKS

Constance Ring (novel) 1885
**Sjur Gabriel* (novel) 1887
**To Venner* (novel) 1887
Lucie (novel) 1888
**S. G. Myre* (novel) 1890
Forrådt (novel) 1891
Fru Inés (novel) 1891
Agnete (drama) [first publication] 1893
På St. Jørgen (novel) 1895
Professor Hieronimus (novel) 1895
  [*Professor Hieronimus,* 1899]
**Afkom* (novel) 1898
Sommer (short stories) 1899
Julehelg (novel) 1900

*These volumes comprise the series *Hellemyrsfolket.*

LAURA MARHOLM HANSSON   (essay date 1896)

[*Hansson was a German critic of Norwegian descent. Hermione Ramsden has said of Hansson's perspective: "In all her writings, Laura Marholm looks at life through the spectacles of a happy marriage; she believes that matured thought and widened views can—in a woman's case—be only the direct result of marriage, and consequently she considers marriage to be absolutely indispensable to every woman, and that without it she is both mentally and morally undeveloped." Regarding the women she discusses in Das Buch der Frauen (Modern Women), including Eleonora Duse, Amalie Skram, and Marie Bashkirtseff, Hansson has commented: "They were out of harmony with themselves, suffering from a conflict which made its first appearance in the world when the 'woman question' came to the fore, causing an unnatural breach between the needs of the intellect and the requirements of their womanly nature. Most of them succumbed in the struggle."*

In the following excerpt, Hansson praises Skram for the breadth of experience depicted in her novels, attributing her development as a writer to the travel and contacts her marriages afforded her.]

When the woman's rights movement made its appearance in Norway, authoresses sprang up as numerous as mushrooms after the rain. Women claimed the right to study, to plead, and to legislate in the local body and the state; they claimed the suffrage, the right of property, and the right to earn their own living; but there was one very simple right to which they laid no claim, and that was the woman's right to love. To a great extent this right had been thrust aside by the modern social order, yet there were plenty of Scandinavian authors who claimed it, it was only amongst the lady writers that it was ignored. They did not want to risk anything in the company of man, they did not want any love on the fourth storey with self-cooked meals, they preferred to criticise man and all connected with him, and they wrote books about the hard-working woman and the more or less contemptible man. The two sexes were a vanquished standpoint. These were completed by the addition of beings who were neither men nor women, and, in consequence of the law of adaptability, they continued to improve with time, and woman became a thinking, working, neutral organism.

Good heavens! When women think!

Among the group of celebrated women-thinkers: Leffler, Ahlgren, Agrell, &c., who criticised love as though it were a product of the intelligence, followed by a crowd of maidenly amazons, there suddenly appeared an author named Amalie Skram, whom one really could not accuse of being too thoughtful. It is true that in her first book there was the intellectual woman and the sensual man, and a seduced servant girl, grouped upon the chess-board of moral discussion with a measured proportion of light and shade—that was the usual method of treating the deepest and most complicated moments of human life. But this book contained something else, which no Scandinavian authoress had ever produced before; her characters came and went, each in his own way, every one spoke his own language and had his own thoughts, there was no need for inky fingers to point the way, life lived itself, and the horizon was wide with plenty of fresh air and blue sky—there was nothing cramped about it like the wretched little extract of life to which the other ladies confined themselves. There was a wealth of minute observation about this book, brought to life by careful painting and critical descriptions, a trustworthy memory and an untroubled honesty; one recognised true naturalism below the hard surface of a problem novel, and one felt that if her talent grew upon the sunny side, the North would gain its first woman naturalist who did not write about life in a critical, moralising, and polemical manner, but in whom life would reveal itself as bad and as stupid, as full of unnecessary anxiety and unconscious cruelty, as easy-going, as much frittered away and led by the senses as it actually is.

Two years passed by and **Constance Ring,** the story of a woman who was misunderstood, was followed by **Sjur Gabriel,** the story of a starving west coast fisherman. There is not a single false note in the book, and not one awkward description or superfluous word. It resembles one of those sharp-cut bronze medallions of the Renaissance, wherein the intention of the artist is executed with a perfected technical power in the use of the material. This perfection was the result of an intimate knowledge of the material, and that was Fru Skram's secret. Her soul was sufficiently uncultured, and her sense of harmony spontaneous enough to enable her to reproduce the simplest cause in the heart's fibre. She describes human beings as they are to be found alone with nature, with a raw, niggardly, unreliable, Northern nature; she tells of their never-ending, unfruitful toil, whether field labour or child-bearing, the stimulating effect of brandy, the enervating influence of their fear of a harsh God—the God of a severe climate—the shy, unspoken love of the father, and the overworked woman who grows to resemble an animal more and more. Such are the contents of this simplest of all books, which is so intense in its absolute straightforwardness. The story is told in the severest style, in few words without reflections, but with a real honesty which looks facts straight in the face with unterrified gaze, and is filled with a knowledge of life and of people combined with a breadth of experience, which is generally the property of men, and not many men. We are forced to ask ourselves where a woman can have obtained such knowledge, and we wonder how this unconventional mode of thinking can have found its way into the tight-laced body and soul of a woman?

A second book appeared the same year called *Two Friends*. It is the story of a sailing vessel of the same name, which travels backwards and forwards between Bergen and Jamaica, and Sjur Gabriel's grandson is the cabin boy on board. This book offers such a truthful representation of the life, tone of conversation, and work on board a Norwegian sailing vessel, that it would do credit to an old sea captain. The tone is true, the characters are life-like, and the humour which pervades the whole is thoroughly seamanlike. The description of how the entire crew, including the captain, land at Kingston one hot summer night to sacrifice to the Black Venus, and the description of the storm and the shipwreck of the *Two Friends* on the Atlantic Ocean, the gradual destruction of the ship, the state of mind of the crew, and the captain's suddenly awakened piety;—it is all so perfectly life-like, so characteristically true of the sailor class, and so full of local Norwegian colouring, that we ask ourselves how a woman ever came to write it,—not only to experience it, but to describe it at all, describe it as she does with such masterly confidence and such plain expressions, without any affectation, prudery, or conceit, and without any trace of that dilettantism of style and subject, which has hitherto been regarded as inseparable from the writings of Scandinavian women.

Whence comes this sudden change from the dilettante book, *Constance Ring,* with its Björnson-like reflections, to the matured style of *Sjur Gabriel* and *Two Friends*?

I could not understand it all at first, but the day came when I understood. Amalie Skram as a woman and an author had come on to the sunny side.

I have often wondered why it is that so few people come on to the sunny side. I have studied life until I became the avowed enemy of all superficial pessimism and superficial naturalism. I have discovered a secret attraction between happiness and individualism, an attraction deeper than Zola is able to apprehend; it is the complete human beings who, with wide-opened tentacles, are able to appropriate to their own use every thing that their inmost being has need of, but whether a person is or is not a complete human being, that fate decides for them before they are born.

Fru Amalie Skram was, in her way, one of these complete women. She passed unscathed through a girl's education, was perhaps scarcely influenced by it, and with sparkling eyes and glowing cheeks she gazed upon the world and society with the look of a barbaric Northern woman, who retains the full use of her instinct. When quite young she married the captain of a ship, by whom she had two sons. She went with him on a long sea voyage round the world, she saw the Black Sea, the Sea of Azof, and the shores of the Pacific and Atlantic oceans. She saw life on board ship, and life on land—man's life. Her mind was like a photographic plate that preserves the impressions received until they are needed, and when she reproduced them, they were as fresh and complete as at the moment when they were first taken. These impressions were not the smallware of a lady's drawing-room, they represented the wide horizon, the rough ocean of life with its many dangers. It was the kind of life that brings with it freedom from all prejudice, the kind of life which is no longer found on board a modern steamer going to and fro between certain places at certain intervals.

But it was not to be expected that the monotony of the life could satisfy her. She separated herself from her husband, and remained on shore, where she became interested in various social problems, and wrote *Constance Ring*.

It was then that she made the acquaintance of Erik Skram.

The man with the head of Gustavus-Adolphus is Denmark's most Danish critic. His name is little known elsewhere, and he cannot be said to have a very great reputation, but this may be partly accounted for by the fact that he has no ambition, and partly because he has one of those profound natures that are rendered passive by the depth of their intellect. He is a man of one book, a novel called *Gertrude Colbjörnson,* and he is never likely to write another. But he contributes to newspapers and periodicals, where his spontaneous talent is accompanied by that quiet, delicate, easy-going style, which is one of the forms of expression peculiar to the Danish sceptics.

Fru Amalie Müller became Fru Amalie Skram, and the bold Bergen woman, who was likewise the dissatisfied lady reformer of Christiania, became the wife of a born critic, and went to live at Copenhagen. She was an excitable little *brunette,* he a fair, phlegmatic man, and together they entered upon the struggle for the mastery, which marriage always is.

In this struggle Fru Amalie Skram was beaten; every year she became more of an artist, more natural, more simple, more herself, and more of all that a woman never can become when she is left to herself. Her husband's superior culture liberated her fresh, wild, primitive nature from the parasites of social problems; the experienced critic saw that her strength lay in her keen observation, her happy incapacity for reasoning and moralising, her infallible memory for the impressions of the senses and emotions, and her good spirits, which are nothing more than the result of physical health. He cautiously pushed her into the direction to which she is best suited, to the naturalism which is natural to her. Her books were no longer drawn out, neither were they as poor in substance as books by women generally are, even the best of them; they grew to be more laconic than the majority of men's books, but clear and vivid—there was nothing in them to betray the woman. And after he had done this much for her, the experienced man did yet one thing more—he gave her the courage of her recollections.

Amalie Skram's talent culminated in *Lucie.* In this book we see her going about in an untidy, dirty, ill-fitting morning gown, and she is perfectly at home. It would scandalise any lady. Authoresses who struggle fearlessly after honest realism—like Frau von Ebner-Eschenbach and George Eliot—might perhaps have touched upon it, but with very little real knowledge of the subject. Amalie Skram, on the other hand, is perfectly at home in this dangerous borderland. She is much better informed than Heinz Tovote, for instance, and he is a poet who sings of women who are not to be met with in drawing-rooms. She describes the pretty ballet girl with genuine enjoyment and true sympathy; but the book falls into two halves, one of which has succeeded and the other failed. Everything that concerns Lucie is a success, including the part about the fine, rather weak-kneed gentleman who supports her, and ends by marrying her, although his love is not of the kind that can be called "ennobling." All that does not concern Lucie and her natural surroundings is a failure, especially the fine gentleman's social circle, into which Lucie enters after her marriage, and where she seems to be as little at home as Amalie Skram herself. Many an author and epicurean would have hesitated before writing such a book as *Lucie.* But Amalie Skram's naturalism is of such an honest and happy nature, that any secondary considerations would not be likely to enter her mind, and in the last chapter the brutal naturalism of the story reaches its highest pitch. In the whole of Europe there are only two genuine and honest naturalists, and they are Emile Zola and Amalie Skram.

Her later books—take, for instance, her great Bergen novel, *S. G. Myre, Love in North and South, Betrayed,* &c.—are not to be compared with the three that we have mentioned. They are naturalistic, of course, their naturalism is of the best kind, they are still *un coin de la nature* ["a corner of nature"], but they are no longer entirely *vu à travers un tempérament* ["seen through a temperament"]. They are no longer quite Amalie Skram.

Norwegian naturalism—we might almost say Teutonic naturalism—culminated in Amalie Skram, this off-shoot of the Gallic race. Compared with her, Fru Leffler and Fru Ahlgren are good little girls, in their best Sunday pinafores; Frau von Ebner is a maiden aunt, and George Eliot a moralising old maid. All these women came of what is called "good family," and had been trained from their earliest infancy to live as became their position. All the other women whom I have sketched in this book belonged to the upper classes, and like all women of their class, they only saw one little side of life, and therefore their contribution to literature is worthless as long as it tries to be objective. Naturalism is the form of artistic expression best suited to the lower classes, and to persons of primitive culture, who do not feel strong enough to eliminate the outside world, but reflect it as water reflects an image. They feel themselves in sympathy with their surroundings, but they have not the refined instincts and awakened antipathies which belong to isolation. Where the character differs from the individual consciousness, they do not think of sacrificing their soul as a highway for the multitude, any more than their body—*à la* Lucie—to the *commune bonum.* (pp. 132-41)

> Laura Marholm Hansson, "The Woman Naturalist: Amalie Skram," in her Modern Women, *translated by Hermione Ramsden, John Lane/The Bodley Head, 1896, pp. 127-41.*

THE BOOKMAN, LONDON   (essay date 1899)

[*In the following excerpt, the critic reviews the English translation of* Professor Hieronimus *and praises the novel for its characterization.*]

The translators of *Professor Hieronimus* have revealed to us a very powerful Danish writer. Amalie Skram's other work is unknown to us, but this book, at least, is courageous, vital, and startlingly vivid. The story lays itself open to argument

and contradiction, without doubt, since it paints a state of things that most readers will deny the existence of, and perhaps rightly. That a nervous patient, who was willing to pay for privacy and exceptional care, whose chief symptom was sleeplessness, should be confined in the asylum, to which she voluntarily goes for rest and advice, in a room opening on a ward full of lunatics and imbeciles, and immediately above the place where dangerous maniacs bellow and fight; that she should be subjected to every kind of suspicion, indignity, and brutality, though she is patently sane, seems to us incredible. And yet to read the story is inevitably to feel that such a condition of things does exist somewhere, since it is described with a graphic simplicity that it would be impossible to surpass. Besides—and Amalie Skram is a declared naturalist—the writer spent some time voluntarily in such an institution, and her story has been treated in Denmark as a *roman à clef.* But even if the circumstances she depicts be exaggerated, there is one thing in her book absolutely true to life—the personality of Professor Hieronimus. We only get the briefest glimpses of him. There is hardly any description. He comes in to see his patients, barely speaks, and vanishes quickly; yet we know him perfectly and dread him as much. He is the fanatic, the instinctive tyrant, given absolute authority. His kingdom is a kingdom of the irresponsible, the insane, the weak-willed and the weak-nerved. His assistants are no curb; he is the man of special knowledge; he has the power of favour or ruin. They learn that the first condition of a tolerable life is cringing. That performed, there are legends of his benevolence. Professor Hieronimus does not rule over lunatic asylums alone. Indeed, he may be, in these humanitarian days, an impossibility there. But he lives still, an evil blighting force, under a solemn respectable guise; and Amalie Skram has doubtless strengthened a few arms to deal the wholesome blows that will liberate some helpless creatures from his grasp.

> A review of "Professor Hieronimus," in The Bookman, *London, Vol. 16, No. 92, May, 1899, p. 56.*

THE ATHENAEUM   (essay date 1899)

[*In the following review of* Professor Hieronimus, *the critic finds this novel less powerful than the novel series* Hellemyrsfolket, *while praising its realistic depiction of a private asylum.*]

Fru Skram is one of the hardiest representatives of the naturalistic school in the North; indeed, there are some of her admirers who boast that she could give points to Zola himself if required. This, so far as we are aware, is the first time that she has appeared in an English dress, and although *Prof. Hieronimus* is nothing like so powerful as *Hellemyrsfolket,* and other of her stories which we forbear to mention, it is none the less convincing because it is perfectly decent. It also possesses a strong personal interest. It is supposed to relate the author's own experiences in a private lunatic asylum controlled by an eminent psychiatrical expert, whose altogether extraordinary influence over every one who comes within his ken will be quite inexplicable to the readers of the story. The chief impression we carry away of the omnipotent Hieronimus is that of a mean and crafty tyrant, who deliberately irritates and ill-uses those of his patients who do not cringe to him. Of anything like power or striking individuality—qualities which one might naturally expect to find in a man in such a unique position of trust—there is no trace. Either Fru Skram's characterization is here for once at fault, or she is intentionally satirizing a person she detests. On the other hand, the horrors of the private asylum described in these pages are real enough, and if only a tithe of the abuses and irregularities described be true, it is high time the Folkthing amended the existing lunacy laws in Denmark which make such outrages possible. The whole narrative seems to bear the impress of truth, so vividly realistic is it in every detail.

A review of "Professor Hieronimus," in The Athenaeum, Vol. 114, No. 3749, September 2, 1899, p. 318.

WILLIAM MORTON PAYNE   (essay date 1899)

[*The long-time literary editor for several Chicago publications, Payne reviewed books for twenty three years at the* Dial, *one of America's most influential journals of literature and opinion in the early twentieth century. In the following excerpt, Payne refutes the critical praise received by* Professor Hieronimus.]

Fru Amalie Skram, a Norwegian woman who is the wife of a well-known Danish scholar, has elected to write fiction under the banner of "naturalism," and has been seriously likened to M. Zola. Her work is now first introduced to the English public by a well-made translation of *Professor Hieronimus*. Herr Björnson, who is a warm admirer of the writer, has characterized the book in these terms: "It is the first time that a great author in full possession of her mental powers has had the opportunity of making such a study. Seeking quiet and treatment for a nervous affection, Fru Skram of her own free will became an inmate of a lunatic asylum. Thus she had a chance of studying one of those specialists in mental disease who are too apt to mistake rebelliousness for a sign of mental derangement. Of this doctor, of the patients, the nurses, her whole environment, she gives a picture so vivid, of such absorbing interest, that it can vie with the most thrilling romance." This praise seems to us overdrawn, and, assuming the writer's purpose to be that of establishing abuses in the treatment of the insane, she is only half-convincing. It is indeed a chamber of horrors into which she leads us, but, barring a few minor instances of heedlessness, the asylum seems to be conducted upon humane and scientific principles. As far as Hieronymus is concerned, we cannot make out what the writer is driving at. He is certainly an unsympathetic figure, but certainly not the monster she would have us think him. We should warn prospective readers that the book has no plot whatsoever; it is the bare journal, day by day, of the asylum experiences of the heroine, and does not even end with her release. This suggests possibilities of more volumes of the same sort, which may Heaven avert.

William Morton Payne, in The Dial, Vol. 27, No. 318, September 16, 1899, p. 177.

H. G. TOPSÖE-JENSEN   (essay date 1929)

[*In the following excerpt, Topsöe-Jensen surveys Skram's major works.*]

[Amalie Skram] is the North's most consistent exponent of Naturalism, and she is the most complete pessimist among the writers of the period. (p. 90)

Amalie Skram's aim was to reproduce reality unabridged and in its most merciless form, to lay bare the hopeless woe and misery of life. Her very first work, the sketch *Mrs. Höier's Tenants,* dealing with a miserably poor family which is thrown out on the street, is coal-black in its pessimism. Her first novel, *Constance Ring* . . . , with its attack on marriage and especially on the unfaithfulness of the husband and his lack of consideration, was her contribution to the great controversy on sex morality. In it she sketches in sharp, glaring outlines a type which recurs in several of her books—the woman who cannot love and who therefore wearies of life. We meet her again in the heroine of *Fru Inez* . . . , who always inspires love but is unable to reciprocate it, and who finally, disgusted with life, kills herself. We meet her also in the important novel, *Betrayed* . . . , which goes far deeper in its delineation of men and women than does the rather tiresome *Constance Ring*. The chief character, Mrs. Ory, reminds one somewhat of Hedda Gabler; the idea of the book is the impassable abyss, the racial difference between man and woman.

Upon this lack of any possibility of understanding between the sexes is based the interesting play, *Agnete*. . . . Quiet and intimate in style are the short story, **"Summer"** . . . , which bears the impress of her marital shipwreck, and the novel *Christmas Holiday* . . . , whose chief male character is created after the memory of her fine and noble brother, Johan Ludvig.

Amalie Skram's greatest achievement, however, is the series of novels bearing the general title *The People of Hellemyr* and consisting of *Siur Gabriel* . . . , *Two Friends* . . . , *S. G. Myre* . . . and *Offspring*. . . . It is a family history as Naturalism loves to tell it, as we find it in Zola, for example, a demonstration of that school's theory of heredity in its most pessimistic form. The action takes place in Bergen, and the series, in so far, forms a companion piece to the Stavanger novels of Kielland. Not the least part of their interest lies in the shifting pictures of the enterprising commercial city through half a century. But the keynote here, as in all the works of Amalie Skram, is gloomy and sad.

The first little book, *Siur Gabriel,* forms an introduction to the work; it gives us a foundation for the understanding of its plot. It tells of a poor Stril family (the Strils are the fisher-folk in the vicinity of Bergen) and its hopeless struggle for an existence which has nothing to offer but adversity, want, and sorrow. The wife is a drunkard. The husband, the industrious and serious-minded Siur Gabriel, finally yields to the same temptation after the death of his youngest son, Little Gabriel, who had been the only bright spot in his somber existence. We are told that "from that day both the husband and the wife at Hellemyr drank."

The chief character in the other three novels of this series is Siur Gabriel's grandson, Sivert Jensen. In the excellent sea tale, *Two Friends,* which in its descriptions of sea folk and seamanship approaches considerably nearer to reality than Jonas Lie, we meet him as a brisk, clever boy with a firm determination to rise in the world. But his racial heritage makes itself known in an ominous manner; he is guilty of petty thievery, is given to lying, and is not to be depended upon.

The events narrated in *S. G. Myre* take place about 1860 and picture Sivert's efforts to raise himself to the middle class from the working class to which he belongs by birth. The description of the death and burial of the grandfather, Siur Gabriel, is brutal and repulsive. After many tribulations Sivert is presently successful in reaching his goal; he becomes the merchant S. G. Myre, but it is only by marrying the mistress of the Consul and establishing himself with the latter's money.

In *Offspring,* Amalie Skram's chief work, Sivert's home is pictured. His son, Severin, is a refined edition of his father. He is a promising young man, but he, too, lies and steals, and in the end he commits suicide. The daughter, Fia, is seduced by a rather decent lieutenant and marries a worthless and brutal man. Sivert's wife is cold as ice by nature, evil and hard-hearted, embittered toward life—which has not fulfilled her ambitious expectations. Sivert himself sinks lower and lower, forges a check, and dies in prison. As a contrast to the sinister home of the Myres with all its brutality, the author has painted in bright colors the home of Severin's friend, Henrik Smith; and Henrik's aunt, the fine and animated Milla Munthe, who is Amalie Skram's ideal woman, impresses one as a positive figure in the otherwise negative pessimism. The book contains a throng of persons clearly and sharply drawn; it is the most vivid and the most humanly sympathetic of her novels.

Amalie Skram is surely one of the most important woman writers of the North, but her talent has something morbid about it. She is bolder in her choice of subjects and in her descriptions than most of her contemporaries, but her imagination is attracted chiefly by the hideous and ugly aspects of life; she exaggerates because of her pessimism. Her art is utterly lacking in humor. This pessimism has its deepest foundation in an unsatisfied need to love; the experiences of her own life, which held little happiness, have determined her entire outlook on existence, particularly her views of the relations between men and women. Her strength is her forthright honesty. Her observations always bear the stamp of experience and of having been seen with her own eyes. For this reason her style is more vividly effective than that of Kielland, for example. The interplay between her remorseless realism and her deep need for tenderness in the midst of her despair gives her otherwise masculine writing the true womanly note that is always found in it. (pp. 91-5)

> *H. G. Topsöe-Jensen, "Naturalism," in his* Scandinavian Literature from Brandes to Our Day, *translated by Isaac Anderson, The American-Scandinavian Foundation—W. W. Norton & Company, Inc., 1929, pp. 65-122.*

THEODORE JORGENSON (essay date 1933)

[*Jorgenson is an educator, author, and critic specializing in Norwegian culture and literature. In the following excerpt, he describes the quality of intensity he finds in Skram's fiction and relates it to her theory of naturalism.*]

The inner intensity which raises expression to significant art was in [Arne] Garborg due to the disparity existing between life as it ought to be from the point of view of the rational intellect and as it is when experienced intuitively day by day or as it is when moving within the framework of social institutions. (pp. 346-47)

In the case of Amalie Skram the intensity is attained through a fiery indignation.... Her indignation is a violent denunciation of life itself, the cry of an outraged soul who spits in the face of the torturer.... [She] knew the meaning of religious mysticism. But she found no deep joy in this knowledge. She had been betrayed. Life had betrayed her; human beings had betrayed her. The beauty and the spirituality of the soul and the world of ideals was entirely undermined by the passions of the animal world. A curse rested upon the existence she knew and that curse she thought ingrained in the very constitutional law of man's being. No Norwegian writer possesses a temperament so natively in harmony with the precepts of naturalism as Amalie Skram. (p. 347)

Amalie Skram began her artistic activity as a theoretical naturalist. The subject matter was mankind's subjection to the

tyranny of natural laws, and her style was gray and heavy in conformity with the scientific emphasis which discouraged imagination and color. The portion of her production which raised her to immortality is, however, far more personal than any dogma of art. As Garborg did in the religious books beginning with *The Lost Father,* as Kielland attempted in the Lövdahl trilogy, and as many others have tried to create a monumental work, so Amalie Skram set forth what life had meant to her in the great tetralogy, *The People of Hellemyr.* In this effort she created the classic product of Norwegian naturalism.

The first volume, *Sjur Gabriel,* tells about life among the Stril fishermen. It is indescribably sordid but at the same time grippingly intense. *Two Friends* is a sea story based largely on her own experiences. It is at the other extreme from Jonas Lie's *The Pilot and His Wife.* Nordahl Grieg's *The Ship Sails On* comes in the naturalistic classification, though there is in Grieg a romantic note which gives relief. Such is foreign to Amalie Skram. *S. G. Myre* is the story of ambition; of how people by hook or crook try to gain wealth and distinction. Here too the natural law works. Sivert cannot sever his contacts with the past. The burden of heredity is upon him. In *Generation* the topic of heredity is made central. Not only is the present world contaminated by brute passion. Heredity makes the curse self-perpetuating. Truly, from this point of view, the logical deed for all mankind is suicide. (p. 352)

> *Theodore Jorgenson, "Naturalism," in his* History of Norwegian Literature, *The Macmillan Company, 1933, pp. 311-82.*

HARALD BEYER (essay date 1956)

[*In the following excerpt, Beyer examines prominent characteristics of Skram's works.*]

[The] opposition that held Amalie Skram back was due to her being altogether too modern, too crass for the taste of her public. Many people were particularly offended that a woman would write like this. Camilla Collett had idealized female love and maintained a woman's right to make her own decisions. Amalie Skram tried to give an unadorned picture of the inner life of women, and particularly of women who are unable to love. Camilla Collett had stirred up discussion, but Amalie Skram caused consternation.

The keynote of her writing was pessimistic. Her favorite Bible passages must surely have been "the wages of sin is death" and "the misdeeds of the fathers are visited upon the children." Throughout her books runs a feeling that life is a hopeless struggle for sensitive individuals and a bottomless morass for most human beings. Nevertheless the best of her writing is not depressing because it is infused with a sympathy that elevates the spirit and gives a deeper understanding.

Some of her novels, particularly those that grew out of her personal experiences, are direct attacks on individuals and institutions. But when she herself was not so directly involved she tended rather to explain than to condemn. As a pure naturalist she was content to document, and did not wish to be understood as a writer with a purpose. When the last volume of her main work, the four-volume *People of Hellemyr,* appeared, she was bitterly attacked on the grounds that her novel was an accusation. Then she answered, "I have never portrayed evil, for I have never met it on my path. That which superficial and doctrinaire persons call evil is to me a necessity, a result.

If I have had any purpose whatever in my writing, it has been to make one or another understand, and to moderate their judgments." She was convinced that heredity, education, and environment were what caused people to stagnate and made them vicious and petty. Above all she attributed it to poverty and the joylessness of life. Very few of her characters avoid this fate, and happiness is rare in their lives once they have reached adulthood. (p. 239)

[*Constance Ring*] was praised by Arne Garborg and the radicals, but branded as immoral by the conservatives. A more direct contribution to the sexual discussion of the times was *Lucie*. . . . A third novel, *Mrs Inés* (*Fru Inés* . . .), showed an artistic advance. Her mastery in this field came with the sea story *Betrayed* (*Forraadt* . . .). Here, the relationship between the very young girl and her older, "experienced" husband is not seen exclusively from the girl's point of view. Ory drives her husband to insanity. Bjørnson wrote about this tragic tale that it "leaves an impression as if you were out at sea and look down into the water and there you see a pair of eyes, large, large eyes in a head that cannot be discerned, but the eyes keep opening and closing, opening and closing, cold as the sea itself."

But it would be a reduction of Amalie Skram's talent to speak only of her depiction of feminine psychology. She is also a student of the child. No Norwegian writer has had a deeper understanding of the defenselessness of the child's position in an adult world, whether in childhood, adolescence, or the transition to adulthood—its religious difficulties, its relationship to parents and the other children in the family. No one has understood better the influence of social circumstances on the child's mind. In her portraits of childhood we often find a brighter atmosphere than otherwise in her writing. When children and young people are allowed to be together without thinking of the grownups or their homes, or when brother and sister share their deepest intimacies, the atmosphere can be lighthearted and free. (p. 240)

Amalie Skram was not a fastidious stylist or a great artist. But the profound humanity which fills her best works, the passion that burns beneath the surface, the intense psychological analysis, and her incomparable pictures of the life of her times— all of these contribute to the unmistakable effect of reality and genuineness which keeps these books alive. (p. 241)

> *Harald Beyer, "Novelists of Realism," in his A History of Norwegian Literature, edited and translated by Einar Haugen, New York University Press, 1956, pp. 228-50.*

BRIAN W. DOWNS (essay date 1966)

[*Downs was an English educator, author, and critic whose works include a study of Norwegian literature. In the following excerpt, he emphasizes the autobiographical nature of Skram's works, using her drama* Agnete *as a representative portrayal of themes Skram developed more fully in her novels.*]

Not until 1882, her thirty-seventh year, did [Amalie Skram] publish a piece of imaginative writing; not till 1885 her first novel. For fifteen years after that she continued fairly prolific, with tales, novels and two plays.

Amalie Skram's second play *Agnete* . . . [is] amenable to the same critical standards as her fiction. It deals with an idle, youngish *divorcée* who has been resorting to petty thefts, false pretenses and untruthful hard-luck stories to finance the easy life to which she has been accustomed when she falls deeply in love with an upright law don, long an admirer of hers. He tells her straight out that her reputation forbids his marrying her; she refuses a clandestine *liaison* (as she does a loveless marriage offered by another) and finally goes off to earn an honest livelihood as a housekeeper far away. For once, Amalie Skram has presented two lovers who seem pretty well "made for one another," but the theme of the play—to recur over and over again in her writings—is the formidable difficulty, arising from temperament as well as convention, of adjusting passion and marriage in the social conditions of her time. This theme it is, not unskilfully varied in sub-plots and sustained by plausible characters and dialogue, which holds *Agnete* together, rather than any elaborate plot or even the vicissitudes of the heroine. By the standards of the day it was a thoroughly untidy play about untidy people—the Bohemian *milieu* and scrappy construction resemble Strindberg's recent *Comrades*—and, as one of the earliest of that kind, it met with scant applause at first. But on audiences that knew Chekhov it was to leave a deep impression.

Half of Amalie Skram's novels are built on themes akin to that of *Agnete*. *Constance Ring* . . . , which makes the start, tells of a middle-class young woman's ill-starred marriages. The first is to a considerably older, insensitive man whom she has never loved and whose embraces revolt her, terminated, before the divorce she is contemplating, by his being accidentally drowned. The second union, with a younger, considerate and cultivated husband, is a more promising and more complicated affair. Constance comes to love him and is happy for a while, but the discovery of a former mistress—whom he still sees, but hardly does more than see—kills her love and her happiness stone dead; and a second discovery, that the seemingly inoffensive lover to whom she gives herself is likewise "entangled," drives her, frantic with disgust at him and herself, to suicide.

Regarded as a novel, *Constance Ring* is an amateurish performance and, in varying degrees, this is true of all the author's work. For all her experiences and distresses, the heroine raises no interest and sympathy in herself; often enough the reader cannot make out what she and the story are "at"; the tragic end is huddled up; and the style lacks all distinction. But its publication caused a great scandal, even in the years when marital and extra-marital relations were under constant debate (*A Doll's House, Ghosts, A Gauntlet,* Kielland's *Poison*). The chief conservative newspaper of Norway stigmatized it as more indecent than [Emile Zola's] *Nana*. The outcry was chiefly provoked by the exhibition of a "respectable" lady constantly preoccupied, decently veiled though they might be, with the carnal concomitants of marriage and "love," and also by the suspicion that the well-known Fru Skram had given the public bits from her autobiography.

Hazardous though it may be to refer everything that an author presents to an actual experience in the flesh, it can scarcely be doubted that in *Constance Ring* and other stories Amalie Skram was fighting—and trying to fight out—her own battle. The short novel *Betrayed* (*Forraadt* . . .) throws a clearer light on this than *Constance Ring*. Aurora Ingstad at 17½ marries the considerably older sea-captain Riber and at once accompanies him on his ship. She is horrified by all associations with the marriage-bed and still more horrified at her husband's previous fornications, which she morbidly forces him to recount in detail. In return she "gives him hell." Riber, passionate, but also understanding, is so broken down by the sense of guilt and hopelessness which her recriminations and frigidity have engendered that he throws himself overboard. Something like the first half of this, one is constrained to believe, must have happened when, at about the same age as Aurora, the authoress married her first husband and sailed the seas with him.

It has been argued from **Constance Ring, Betrayed** and **Madame Inès** (**Fru Inès** . . .)—the story of a seemingly hot-blooded Spaniard who obtains no satisfaction when flirtation gives way to something more serious—that wherever the sexual element predominates in Amalie Skram's compositions they are "tragedies of women who cannot love." This cannot be upheld. Constance Ring, Agnete and Petra Fridmann (to whom we shall shortly come), at least, are perfectly *capable* of love. What shatters them is the proximity of the highest erotic ecstasy to the "swinishness" with which they brand all sexual relations falling short of this ecstasy, the fatal ease with which this proximity can be betrayed and the material difficulties of entering upon and preserving the "marriage of true minds" which would sanctify the marriage of the body. Amalie Skram may not be the first clinician of female frigidity, but she did, to use Ibsen's phrase, "move the frontier-posts" by putting into the forefront of a literary work the bewilderment, fear, desperate disillusionments and tragic heart-searchings of women who, imperfectly mated, are racked in mind and body from their failure to attain the "miracle of miracles" (Nora Helmer's *vidunderligste*). Her revered predecessor Camilla Collett, in her pioneer novel of "the woe of women," had stopped short at the altar. But, it may be noted, the twin focal points round which her junior's matrimonial tragedies revolve are the same as those of *The Sheriff's Daughters*—the imperative demands of all-transcending love and the lethal obstacles in the way of following its call.

The first of these points is, in any interpretation of the word, romantic. But the author who clung so desperately to this romantic principle is most commonly celebrated for something on the face of it quite alien—as the founder of Norwegian naturalistic fiction. Unless (as was done, for instance, in condemnations of Ibsen's *Ghosts* and Kielland's *Else*) naturalism is summarily identified with indecency and indecency with any allusion to sexual relations, that claim is principally based on some works of hers not yet mentioned. Both in order of time and for the completeness with which it conforms to the naturalistic programme, the short story **"Ma Høier's Lodgers"** (**"Madam Høiers Leiefolk,"**) stands at their head. With unbroken objectivity and as much material detail as the limited compass allows, it presents the wife of a drunken, one-legged labourer, who is evicted from Mrs Høier's slum tenement, and, by giving her new-born twins spirits in order to lull them to sleep, brings a sentence of three years' imprisonment for infanticide upon herself—a sentence she accepts with gratitude, since it means at least a roof over her head.

Of greater substance are five novels: [**Sjur Gabriel, The "Two Friends"** (**To Venner**), **S. G. Myre, Offspring** (**Afkom**) and **Lucie**] . . . , the last-named Amalie Skram's tepid contribution to the literature of prostitution then proliferating in Norway. The remaining four were designed as a series, under the collective title **The Hellemyr Folk** (**Hellemyrsfolket**). They make up the family saga of a wretchedly poor fisherman-crofter from Hellemyr, Sjur Gabriel, his wife and their descendants through three generations, who make their livings as seamen or as dock-labourers and ships' chandlers in the lower quarters of Bergen. Nothing spectacular or exciting comes within their ken. Respectability is the limit of their ambition; none of them attains

to or even dreams of *grandeurs*. But there is abundance of *misères*, almost unalloyed; their surroundings are sordid when they are not squalid; the practices of a lifeless pietism alternate with the workaday struggle for existence, beset by accidents, debt, horrible smells, death and disease; small wonder if some of them—but only *some*—give way to drunkenness, incontinence and crime. Amalie Skram said of herself that she "wept her way through her books"; no fiction outdoes **The Hellemyr Folk** in calling up and sustaining an atmosphere of sheer grim misery.

"Zola's pupil from Bergen," it is facile to conclude. An unflinching realist Amalie Skram may truly be called, but she was a *naturaliste* with a difference. She was never anyone's disciple. As a girl she was carried away by Byron (Byron!—but chiefly because in *Cain* he had said "We, who know the truth, must speak it"). She venerated Camilla Collett, she came to venerate Tolstoy, but her art was that of an autodidact: her consistently flat style and total neglect of "construction" show it. As for Zola, we may believe her when she said at the time of **"Ma Høier's Lodgers"** that she had read very little of him, and at no time did she come nearer to him than there. She resembles him in the prominence she gives to accurately described *milieu* and its formative influence, in the inclusion of the proletariat within her purview and in her obsession with sexuality. In at least one very important respect, however—apart from temperament—the difference between them was radical. Any intention she may have had of making **The Hellemyr Folk** a quasi-biological object-lesson in heredity and degeneracy, like [Zola's] *Les Rougon-Macquart*, soon evaporated. **Sjur Gabriel** is about two irredeemable drunkards; but their descendants are not conspicuously a family of alcoholics. More than that, the last of the line to be introduced seem the soundest: young Severin in **Offspring,** a sturdy lad, and his sister Fie, who may have gone off the rails temporarily with an army officer, but settles down as the respectable wife of a skin-and-hide dealer. Sympathy was always there; there is a glint of hope at the end. The pessimistic, impassible, "scientific" determinism of the Naturalistic school is in abeyance.

A wretched microcosm, the world Amalie Skram knew as a girl, is faithfully presented in the saga of the Hellemyr Folk. A greater interest, however, even here lies in the purely personal realm, in the life-histories of Sivert, Sjur Gabriel's grandson, and his wife Petra. As he is the most fully portrayed of his family, so he may be designated the worst: he is the undetected murderer of his grandmother, he is a dishonest shopkeeper, defrauds his benefactor and dies in gaol on a charge of forgery; but his fallings away from honest resolution genuinely puzzle him; he thinks himself, on the whole, a decent fellow, and Amalie Skram's conscientious, compassionate record almost makes us come to think so too. With his wife we are back at the kind of problem broached in **Constance Ring.** An able, respectable working-class girl, Petra Fridmann is introduced as housekeeper to Consul Smith, whose wife is a bed-ridden invalid. Petra becomes his mistress. Her intercourse with him breeds passionate love in her, but it is unreciprocated. When Fru Smith dies, the consul takes a second wife from his own social circle and promotes the marriage between his ex-mistress and his sometime house-boy, Sivert. Petra's heart dies within her. She becomes an ugly, venomous shrew; the hell which her lovelessness makes of her home is shown as a much greater power for evil than indigence or hereditary alcoholism.

The figure of Petra Fridmann, if nothing else, demonstrates that no hard and fast line can be drawn between the author's social novels, on the one hand, and the psychological, erotic on the other. The naturalist Amalie Skram and the romantic Amalie Skram were one. That gives her work its singular and stimulating, if artistically unattractive, character. With her primarily erotic delineations she was more truly the pioneer, but it was the others which, on the whole, have won her the greater fame. Several, with less success, tried to follow in her footsteps; but only Arne Garborg can, as far as Norway is concerned, dispute the naturalist laurel with her. (pp. 93-8)

Brian W. Downs, "Kielland and Amalie Skram," in his Modern Norwegian Literature: 1860-1918, *Cambridge at the University Press, 1966, pp. 80-98.*

ADDITIONAL BIBLIOGRAPHY

Grondahl, Illit, and Raknes, Ola. "Some Writers of the Present." In their *Chapters in Norwegian Literature,* pp. 268-97. Copenhagen: Gyldendal, 1923.

Sketches the changing critical perspectives on Skram's work.

The Spectator 82, No. 3691 (25 March 1899): 419.

Unfavorable review of *Professor Hieronimus.* The critic comments: "Amateurs of the gruesome, or those persons, if any such exist, who may need some artificial means of abating the exuberance of their animal spirits, may safely embark on Skram's recital of the sufferings of the tortured wife and the diabolical cruelty of the unscrupulous 'alienist.' But we cannot honestly recommend the volume to normally constituted readers, least of all to those recovering from influenza."

Pauline (Urmson) Smith

1882-1959

(Also wrote under pseudonyms Janet Tamson and Janet Urmson) South African novelist, short story writer, dramatist, and poet.

Smith is best known for her penetrating and compassionate portraits of Afrikaners, the South African Dutch settlers who are also known as Boers. Her fiction is based on Afrikaner life in the Little Karoo region in the southernmost tip of Africa, where she spent the first twelve years of her life, and focuses on a few central concerns, including the inflexible nature of Afrikaner traditions and values and the relationships in Afrikaner culture between man and woman, master and servant, and individual and community. While she is to a certain extent considered a regionalist, Smith has also been praised for revealing universal aspects of human nature: critics have noted that, in the process of depicting the unique character of the Afrikaner and the Little Karoo, Smith's fiction encompasses such important human experiences as love, suffering, aging, isolation, oppression, and death.

The daughter of a Scottish nurse and London physician, Smith was born in a town centered in the Little Karoo region of the Cape Province called Oudtshoorn, also known as Platkops. Described as patriarchal, slow, and pastoral, Oudtshoorn was a pre-industrial community whose residents led an agrarian life, growing tobacco, grains, and vines and raising ostriches where the land was fertile enough to support them. Smith's father, who had moved his family from England to improve his health, was the first properly qualified doctor to settle in Oudtshoorn. He sometimes took his daughter along when visiting patients in the region, and in this way Smith was introduced to the descendants of the first European colonizers of South Africa, the Afrikaners, who had settled the Cape Province some seventy-five years before and would later fight the English in the Anglo-Boer War (1899-1902). These excursions through both farm country and desert plains made a lasting impression on Smith, and later she often wrote of the simple dignity of the impoverished bywoners, or tenant farmers, of the region.

Smith was taught by governesses until she was twelve, when her father sent her to school in Aberdeen, Scotland, to receive a formal education; she never again lived in South Africa. Four years later, her father died. In an essay tracing her development as an author, Smith explained that she began writing after her father's death because it provided her with an opportunity "to set down for my own comfort the memories of . . . happier days." Smith's first stories, later collected in *Platkops Children,* recall her early years and have been admired for their ability to convey the natural beauty of South Africa with the intensity and wonder of a child's point of view. Smith soon left school because of ill health, traveling with her mother in England and Scotland, and it was in the Aberdeen newspapers the *Evening Gazette* and the *Weekly Free Press* that her first published story, "A Tenantry Dinner," appeared in 1902. Smith's progress as a writer was furthered by her meeting in 1909 with the English novelist Arnold Bennett, who encouraged her efforts and advised her to write about the Little Karoo, suggesting she create a more definite sense of local color in her descriptions of this region to "exploit the quality of rareness

and remoteness" in her material. Guided by Bennett's suggestions, Smith thereafter wrote stories almost exclusively about the Little Karoo, publishing one of the earliest of these, "The Sisters," in the *New Statesman* in 1915. Smith received her first notable success as a writer when John Middleton Murry, on Bennett's recommendation, accepted Smith's short story "The Pain" for publication in the *Adelphi;* many of her subsequent stories were also published in that journal. Collected in 1925 in *The Little Karoo,* these stories received favorable reviews, with "The Pain" being singled out for particular praise. Smith was in her forties when she began work on *The Beadle,* her first sustained attempt at writing a novel. Published in 1926, the novel was for the most part well received and was compared to Thomas Hardy's *Tess of the d'Urbervilles* and Nathaniel Hawthorne's *The Scarlet Letter* for its treatment of the theme of the social outcast in a closed society. Despite these successes, Smith produced few other works, for she struggled throughout her life with intermittent illness that made writing increasingly difficult for her. Arnold Bennett's death in 1931 deprived her of the advice that had served her, at least in part, as impetus to write between periods of illness. In the remaining twenty-eight years of her life Smith wrote very little. She died in England in 1959.

The most important and distinctive feature of Smith's stories in *The Little Karoo* and her novel *The Beadle* is her characterization of Afrikaners and Afrikaner life. In describing *The Little Karoo,* Alan Paton has stated: "Though not herself an Afrikaner, [Smith] produced one of the most remarkable collections of Afrikaner stories ever written. She never avoided the harsh and ugly, nor the fiercest of passions, nor the strange compound of religiousness and lovelessness, nor the despair and melancholy of these lonely Afrikaners who asked for nothing and got it." Through her characterizations, Smith portrayed men and women isolated from one another by their own intense preoccupations: husbands whose suffering and solitude leads them to reject their wives' comforts, as in "The Sinner" and "The Miller"; fathers whose fierce ambition drives them to jeopardize their children's happiness, as in "The Sisters" and "The Father"; and churchwomen whose righteous faith causes them to act mercilessly, as in *The Beadle.* Pared down to dominant traits which, taken to an extreme, become self-destructive flaws, such characterizations express a sense of tragedy that has led critics to liken Smith's works to Greek drama. Smith's primary method of characterization was through dialogue: by employing translated Afrikaans in place of formal English, she maintained the flavor of the Afrikaners' language, thus conveying a sense of their cultural identity. Critics have noted that as a result of inverted word order, un-English phraseology, and an occasional insertion of an untranslated Afrikaans phrase, Smith was able to evoke the biblical cadences of the Afrikaans language with authenticity and immediacy. However, some critics contend that Smith's translated Afrikaans contributes to a romantic sentimentality in her fiction. South African novelist and translator J. M. Coetzee further alleges that Smith "validates" and thereby "perpetuates" the romanticized myth of the Afrikaner as Israelite—a myth, he notes, that has historically supported a belief in racial supe-

375

riority. Defending Smith against the charge of being reactionary and sentimental, Geoffrey Haresnape argues that readers must learn to read Smith's fiction on its own terms, recognizing that it represents a continuation of the Victorian sensibilities of the nineteenth century. Nevertheless, Haresnape also asserts that "Pauline Smith can on occasion undercut the dogmatic foundations on which the conservative, Puritan-oriented society of her fiction is erected."

While characterization and stylistic techniques in Smith's fiction reflect her pervasive interest in Afrikaner society and values, Smith's desire to address South African social issues, particularly racial inequality, is a subject of debate. Because white South Africans were not receptive to criticism of the racial inequities caused by apartheid, recent critics have proposed that Smith substituted a general "theme of oppression" for specific references to racial oppression in her work. Smith's rendering of relationships between husband and wife and between master and servant has led Dorothy Driver to suggest "the possibility that Smith had an Afrikaans audience in mind as well as an English one, that she was referring to inequalities *within* the Afrikaner community (landowner, poor white, Christian, Jew) because she felt that was the simplest way to reveal to the Afrikaner other inequalities, at least as serious but, at the same time, less open to his sympathy." One "theme of oppression" that Driver detects in Smith's fiction involves the treatment of women, and Driver called "The Sisters"—a story in which a woman is married off to secure water rights for her father—Smith's "feminist statement." Although Smith did not regard herself as a feminist, her fiction has been interpreted from a feminist perspective because it typically portrays women's role in society as limited by social and economic necessity. However, whether such a portrayal can serve as a symbol for the condition of black South Africans remains in question. In Smith's entire career only the story "Ludovitje" treats the relationship between the Afrikaners and the native African, yet this story is regarded as Smith's most ambiguous work because it apparently offers a purely mystical solution to the racial division caused by apartheid. Even though the racial tensions that exist in such a social system are not discussed openly in Smith's fiction, her private writings suggest that she was not indifferent to the racial problems of her age. As Smith wrote in her journal: "All Dutchmen and many English colonials as well, would, I think, go back to slaves with a relish." Elsewhere in her journal Smith expressed her indignation at the English imperialist assumption of superiority over the Afrikaner, at the upper-class Afrikaner's self-serving beneficence toward the working class, and at the attitude of both English and Afrikaner toward black South Africans.

During the 1920s and 1930s Smith's fiction was widely acclaimed by English and American critics. Thereafter it was all but forgotten until the 1960s, when she began to receive increased attention from South African critics. This revival culminated in various events celebrating the centenary of her birth, including new editions of her major fiction, a special edition of previously uncollected work, a museum exhibit, and public lectures. Summarizing Smith's literary achievement, Michael Gardiner has observed: "Pauline Smith is a highly deliberate and remarkably intelligent writer despite the modesty of her personal statements."

PRINCIPAL WORKS

The Little Karoo (short stories) 1925
The Beadle (novel) 1926
The Last Voyage (drama) 1929; published in *Eleven One Act Plays*
A. B. '. . . a Minor Marginal Note' (memoir) 1933
Platkops Children (short stories and poetry) 1935
Miscellaneous Writings (short stories and diaries) 1983
South African Journal, 1913-14 (journal) 1983

THE CAPE TIMES (essay date 1925)

[*In the following excerpt from a review first published in the* Cape Times, *21 March 1925, a South African critic praises the insights and intensity of description in Smith's first book,* The Little Karoo *but notes the paucity of description of the lighter moments in Afrikaner life.*]

An unpretentious little volume [*The Little Karoo*] holds the eight stories in which Miss Pauline Smith sets before her readers the life of some twenty years ago in the remoter parts of the Little Karoo, in the tiny dorps, the distant farms. She shows them in the days before the railway ran through Oudtshoorn, before the farmers had Ford cars—those barer, simpler, humbler days when there was much loneliness on outlying farms, stern poverty unquestioningly accepted for struggling bijwoners and their families, an almost unrelieved monotony, a hard routine of toil from youth to old age, a widespread illiteracy and lack of culture. Happiness depended on loving, dutiful faith in God and loving, dutiful service in the home. The best of these sturdy folk breathed the pure and strengthening air of Heaven; the worst at times went down into a very hard and cruel hell, made up of bodily and mental suffering, of weak despair, of hysterical hatreds and obsessions.

Miss Smith has seen it all, felt it, absorbed it. She has possessed it and it has possessed her, till she is able to make it known to all the world, to as many as care to read her tales.

Many will read them. They are worthy of being read more than once, both for the sound stuff that is in them and for the beauty of the telling. They are no trivial commonplace, conventional productions, turned out to sell. They throb with vital force; they stir the reader as life stirs him.

Their writer looks very steadily at her world, and as yet she is most conscious of its pain, and therefore of our imperative need of mutual tender pity. An ancestral streak of Aberdeenshire granite is very noticeable in the strong substance of pity as Miss Smith understands it. There is no softness in these tales, no weak relenting, but a clear spiritual beauty and unswerving courage.

The longest of the little collection is **"The Pain,"** which attracted considerable attention when it appeared in Mr. Middleton Murry's monthly review, *The Adelphi*. No lovelier tale of old age has ever been written, and it reveals at once the chief secret of the writer's power. She has a rare gift of insight. She passes unerringly from the fact which can be observed to the interpretation which lies beyond. Her honest directness of vision is indissolubly linked with a deep intuitive sympathy, a true creative element.

How understanding she is! How reverent of the simple, homely, foundation virtues! An old man, an old woman, bijwoners, poor and childless, dull and ignorant, the woman gripped by a slow and torturing disease. It is so small and so everyday in its pitiable facts, but it is transfigured into lasting beauty by its profound tenderness. That is the writer's characteristic genius. Like a good portrait painter she sees and renders the inner soul.

The defect of the tales as a series of sketches depicting life in the more primitive parts of the Cape is their neglect of its lighter social side. Afrikaners are not usually gay, but they are gregarious and cheerful and much given to homely entertainments. The only entertainments noticed in this volume are the annual thanksgiving, which is fully and charmingly described, and a children's picnic, which is just mentioned in passing, being a necessary introduction to a ghastly scene of sudden madness. As detached stories the sketches are beautiful and true. As a collection they do not escape monotony of subject, and they do not make a full picture of that pleasant region with its endearing name of Little Karoo. They all sound a tragic note, except **"The Sinner,"** an errant husband, who, as we take our leave of him, has painfully realised that the way of the transgressor is very hard indeed, and is putting his poor bundle of oddments together, preparatory to going back thankfully and hopefully to the home where love is waiting to welcome him. When one considers that this is the cheeriest tale in the book, it is obvious that Miss Smith is not a frivolous writer.

The tales treat of old age, intermittent homicidal fury, an obsession of morbid hatred, the prodigal husband, a peculiarly heartless scoundrel, an old maid's love story, a child mystic and missionary suffering from mortal disease, a bad and mad old man. Not one of them but has beauty and truth fast woven in its fabric, yet the total result is too sombre as a representation of the country life of sunny South Africa. It must be admitted that we are not a people of sprightly and polished wit, but we do exude a humour, albeit of the obvious kind, which plays most readily about the family hearth and the local market.

High praise must be given to Miss Smith's manner of writing. There is in it the true Karoo note with echoes of her Scottish antecedents. She wisely avoids any ugly hotch-potch of English and Dutch. The stories are essentially Dutch in their content, and she tells them with a spontaneous directness and intimate simplicity which brings us very near to the homely, heartfelt charm of Afrikaans. In the conversational passages, the constructions, though good English, are often unwonted English; moreover, the tense emotional quality differs from that of English, and in a very illuminating way. Take, for instance, Andries Lombard in **"The Miller,"** one of the finest tales in the book:

> Andries . . . was a stupid kindly man whom illness had turned into a morose and bitter one. . . . Round his neck he wore an eelskin which his wife Mintje had tramped sixteen miles down the Aangenaam valley to borrow from old Tan' Betje Ferreira of Vetkuil. The eelskin had cured many coughs in Tan' Betje's family, but God knows how it was, though Andries wore it day and night it did not cure him of spitting blood. And in the month of September, when, in the Aangenaam valley, other men planted their lands with sweet potatoes and pumpkins and mealies, the miller said to his wife: "I will not plant my lands. If I plant me now my lands surely by the time it comes for me to dig my potatoes and gather me my mealies I shall be dead of this cough that I have from the dust in the mill. And so surely as I

am dead, the day that I am buried they will drive you out of this house in the rocks and to the man that comes after me they will give my potatoes and mealies."

(pp. 85-6)

This present volume of short stories, fine though they are, conveys no definite assurance that the writer has the large and sustained power needful for a novel of genius, but it affords ample proof that she has a great work to accomplish in the interpretation, to South Africa and to the bigger world outside, of a people, strange to cities, and but now slowly emerging from their long isolation, with all its profoundly interesting influences on a virile and pious race. (p. 87)

> *"'A New South African Writer': Review of 'The Little Karoo',"* in Pauline Smith, *edited by Dorothy Driver, McGraw-Hill Book Company, 1983, pp. 85-7.*

BROOKS SHEPARD   (essay date 1925)

[*In the following excerpt, Shepard reviews* The Little Karoo, *praising Smith's portrayal of Afrikaners and her treatment of universal themes.*]

It is a very startling thing to blunder all unwarned into so fine a book as [*The Little Karoo*]. Who ever heard of Pauline Smith? Who, for that matter, ever heard of the Little Karoo? Who, learning that it is a great plateau in Cape Colony, cares to read a mean-looking little book of short stories about it—even though Arnold Bennett may have prefaced it? . . .

It is difficult to say whether Pauline Smith has sought to capture and preserve the feeling of this remote district and its patient humble people, or whether in writing of these folk she has all mankind at heart. Probably the first. Her childhood was passed in the Little Karoo, and her mind was packed, during the impressionable years, with the sound and smell and color and feel of it. One doubts that she has said to herself, Lo, I will be a Universalist. She is utterly un-self-conscious, and she withdraws herself almost uncannily from the action of her stories. And she has succeeded overwhelmingly in breathing life into the Karoo, with its remote farms and hamlets, its laborious journeyings in a rumbling ox cart, its stern, sober, simple, shrewd men and women, its utter detachment from the world and civilization—especially this detachment, the Karoo's completeness in itself, economic and ethical; but she has succeeded also in picturing the man and woman in each of us, so that the people and the country of which she writes with strange brooding pity seem only incidental to her brooding upon mankind, and the Karoo is only her name for the world, conveniently isolated for sympathetic study.

Arnold Bennett speaks of her "strange, austere, and ruthless talent." Austere in that Pauline Smith stands always aside, watching life as it goes by, interpretor and not participant. Tender, yes; infinitely tender and sympathetic and comprehending, toward men and women alike. Ruthless? Not for an instant. She is like Hardy; a brooding pity breathes from every page. Bennett writes: "I . . . had to answer many times the question: 'Who is Pauline Smith?' I would reply: 'She is a novelist.' 'What are her novels?' came the inquiry. 'She hasn't written any yet,' I would say, 'but she will'."

This may be. But it is no small feat to compress into a few small pages the material of a novel, and still convey a sense of time and space and growth and significance; and this is what

Pauline Smith has done. Novelist or no, she is a great short story writer.

Brooks Shepard, ''A Fine Talent,'' in The Saturday Review of Literature, *Vol. 1, No. 39, April 25, 1925, p. 703.*

PERCY A. HUTCHISON   (essay date 1927)

[*In the following excerpt, Hutchison compares* The Beadle *with Nathaniel Hawthorne's* The Scarlet Letter *(1850).*]

Pauline Smith, who wrote a single short story of Africa which attracted attention—*The Little Karoo*—has now returned to the veldt for a novel. She appears to have found good hunting, as one might say, for in *The Beadle* she has produced a tale of singularly delicate beauty.

It cannot be said that the plot of *The Beadle* (if plot it may be called) is strictly new. In fact, the captious critic may be somewhat distressed at a superficial resemblance between this story of the veldt and a certain masterpiece of about a century ago. This is not to accuse the author of plagiarism, or even of imitation; old songs, as once noted by a well-known poet, have a tendency to turn up again; and if an author can lend to them freshness and a kind of novelty—set the old words to new music, as it were—the result can be a genuinely original product. Having noted, then, that there is a superficial resemblance between *The Beadle* and *The Scarlet Letter*, the matter may be dismissed.

And Miss Smith's story does not go over the same ground as Hawthorne's. The author of *The Beadle* has begun where the biographer of Hester Prynne and Arthur Dimmesdale left off. What of little, wayward, beautiful Pearl, with her heritage of beauty and passion? Hawthorne, intent upon a study of adult romance flowering out of the dank, rocky soil of Puritanism, left the question unanswered. Either he was not interested, or it was a problem with which he did not feel himself able to cope. Indeed, it is possible that it was a problem beyond his age; that before the twentieth century revaluation of the feminine the question could not be answered. Nor does Pauline Smith, in her study of the little Boer girl Andrina, attempt to lay down any general proposition or draw any universal conclusions. She has posed one particular case, concentrated on it and left the others to reason therefrom as they may. This is the function of the storyteller and she does not exceed her prerogatives. The story of *The Beadle* could not have been laid anywhere else than in Dutch Africa, unless, perhaps, in one of those portions of North America inhabited by strictly practicing Puritanic sects. In their dour religious life—if we are to believe Pauline Smith—the Boers of the African veldt approximate closely the social conditions surrounding Hester and Pastor Dimmesdale. But in all other respects the two civilizations would seem to be wide apart. The Boers, it would appear, although they work hard and take life sternly, are not unresponsive to such natural beauty as they find about them—green prairies, molded hills, brightly colored flowers. Hence Miss Smith finds more light to mingle with the sombre background of *The Beadle* than Hawthorne could justly employ, and the result is a story of much softer outlines.

It is a dangerous theme which the author of *The Beadle* has attempted to handle; or, rather, it would be dangerous for one of less skill. She has to render two characters convincing, the Beadle and Andrina; and she must leave the reader with the feeling that the man who, under a rough classification, could only be called the villain of the piece, was not more of a villain than nature had made him. And it is just in this last that she is least successful. One winces a little, even when it is fiction, at what can only be characterized as willful seduction. In the case of the present story the author would have done better to have made her roving Englishman in search of health and adventure an out-and-out rascal rather than the purely helpless puppet of passion which her character is. But it is clearly throughout her purpose never to heighten the note, as any such change would undoubtedly have done. And as her single goal is the ultimate regeneration of the Beadle through his acknowledgement of his paternity, to which he is led by the spectacle of Andrina's martyrdom to love, she may, perhaps, be forgiven some lapse in conceiving and drawing a character which is merely instrumental to the aim of the book. Nevertheless, the truly great novelist does not err even in a minor personage. In *The Beadle*, although a tragic story, there is curiously lacking the impression of tragedy. And this can be due only to a faltering of the author's hand in delineating the character which is productive of the tragedy.

On the other hand, all criticism ceases when one turns to the picture of the little Dutch child—for in the beginning Andrina is a child—to follow her wistful story, with all its delicacy of beauty, through to the end. And this character, Andrina, is truly a creation; moreover, it is a creation which is an addition to English letters, for there exists no one else quite like her in a long line of novels resplendent with enduring women. There is a certain magic touch in the way Pauline Smith has drawn this intensely human, yet always somewhat eerie, girl. Toward the close of the book there is a passage which, one is almost convinced, must have been almost the first thing the author wrote.

> What was it she [Andrina] felt? She did not know. Amazement, terror, joy and sadness— her heart held them all. Shame she did not feel. The child she bore within her was not for her the sign and seal of her sin, but the sign and seal of her love. What was it Christ had said to His disciples? ''I will not leave you comfortless.'' What made her think of this now? She did not know. Christ as the Son of God meant nothing to her, yet suddenly His tenderness meant everything and her own troubled heart answered to it with a tenderness which embraced even the Englishwoman for whose sake her child must forever be fatherless. The burden of her jealousy was lifted from her.

Herein is the key to the book; the note which the author sounded for her guidance at the outset. It was no light task to keep throughout on such a note. Over against the stern, moralistic theology of the Dutch Puritans of whose stock Andrina is sprung and among whom she is reared, the girl must convince as the vital expression of a more humane interpretation of religion than she finds surrounding her. And it is just this which the author accomplishes. The sanctimonious old Beadle, not so dramatically as Arthur Dimmesdale, but with equal contriteness of spirit, acknowledges his sin toward Andrina's mother and takes to himself Andrina and her child.

It was a dangerous theme, then, which was undertaken by Pauline Smith when she projected *The Beadle*. The pitfalls were innumerable; and almost every one of them could be fatal. The book lacks the dramatic power of *The Scarlet Letter;* but in place of this it has a subdued but glowing intensity which in a measure at least makes up. Andrina is not Hester Prynne's daughter, little Pearl. Whatever might have been Pearl's fate it could not have been the fate of Andrina. But the Dutch girl is the descendant of Pearl, with the latter's own inheritance.

Whether Miss Smith's Dutch-Puritan setting is not too nearly identical with Hawthorne's Puritan New England to permit a working out of the theme in quite the fashion she has selected is a nice question. It is possible she has imported into Dutch Africa something a little too English or too American, something too much of a twentieth century which has not yet spread to the veldt. Of this each reader will judge for himself. But in any case *The Beadle* must stand as a noteworthy accomplishment.

Percy A. Hutchison, "New England Vintage in South African Bottles," in The New York Times Book Review, *March 20, 1927, p. 5.*

HERMAN CHARLES BOSMAN   (essay date 1945)

[*Bosman was a South African poet, novelist, and short story writer. An Afrikaner who wrote in English, Bosman has been praised for achieving in his fiction what one critic has described as a "singularly vivid, objective portrait of a remote Afrikaner community." In the following excerpt from an essay that originally appeared in the journal* South African Opinion *in 1945, Bosman comments on Smith's use of language in her fiction.*]

Pauline Smith knows what she is writing about. She understands the Afrikaner and the veld. Not with the detached understanding of the intellect, which is a brittle thing and betrays you the very moment you start relying on it, but with the warm comprehension of the heart. Pauline Smith's knowledge of her subject is profound and penetrative and strong, passionately so, and her approach is essentially feminine. Her stories are pure with light and very tenderly told and brave. One requires nothing more than this from a woman story-teller. But, also, one demands nothing less.

The result is that there is a wider, more all-embracing truth about life and about the veld that Pauline Smith does not deal with at all. But I want to make clear that for the sake of her art it is right that she cannot see the autumn as melodrama, and that her warm understanding of the spirit of the Afrikaner does not rise to the height of that other love and that further knowing, in which stark tragedy has also got its tinsel side and sorrow is the mask for a carnival.

The wider form of literary creation belongs with the ultimates of art. And it is well that Pauline Smith does not essay this furthest flight of all. She would lay waste her heart if she were to emerge from the high purpose of her inwardness and attempt to depict life in the colours of more starry truth, where a knowledge of humanity comes near to, and therefore is not, mockery.

The strange thing about Pauline Smith's language is that it is more like Afrikaans than English. By this I don't mean that she uses an affected style, or that she overloads her prose with the adventitious introduction of Afrikaans words and phrases, twisting her sentences round to conform to the Afrikaans idiom. It is easy to get a specious sort of local colour this way. For intance, if you want to write a novel about the Middle Ages and you don't know too much about medieval spirit you can achieve a fair degree of success with the judicious use of words like "quotha," "scurvy," "beshrew," "knave," and whatnot. But you have got to be an artist to do it successfully. Lots

of people, writing about the backveld, have employed this same trick, in order to get atmosphere. The result is that their stories read like Robert Louis Stevenson's *Black Arrow*.

Pauline Smith's stories are written in an English of a purity to which not even Fowler could object. But there is more than that to her style. Take the last sentence of **"The Sinner"**: "With stupid, fumbling fingers, and eyes made redder than ever with tears, he tied his bundles together and took the road to Platkops dorp." As for me, more than once, reading her stories—particularly **"The Sisters"**—I was brought to realise, with something almost like a start, that the page in front of me was printed, not in Afrikaans, but in English.

Pauline Smith's stories are already for ever a part of South African literature. They depict South African life with a truth and a beauty which no writer has so far achieved in the short story form written in Afrikaans. (pp. 99-100)

Herman Charles Bosman, "The Truth of the Veld: 'The Little Karoo' by Pauline Smith," in Pauline Smith, *edited by Dorothy Driver, McGraw-Hill Book Company, 1983, pp. 98-100.*

WILLIAM PLOMER   (essay date 1949)

[*Plomer is a South African fiction writer and critic. In the following excerpt, he surveys themes in the short stories collected in* The Little Karoo.]

Pauline Smith's stories are about people belonging to the ethnic group variously known as the South African Dutch (or just "the Dutch"), the Boers, or the Afrikaners. Her characters may be presumed to be living in the first decade or two of the present century. They live on the land without such mechanical aids as motor-cars, radios, or telephones. They do not travel far from home, and they do not seem to read newspapers, talk politics, or bother at all about the rest of the world: this storyteller's concern, it is true, is chiefly with what goes on in their hearts. (pp. 13-14)

It is indeed a great advantage to a fictionist to be able to write about an isolated community with, as Bennett put it, "the most rigid standards of conduct—from which standards the human nature in them is continually falling away." The homogeneity of such a group of people at once imposed one kind of unity on any writing about them; every falling away from those rigid standards is of itself dramatic; and the concentration of family life leads to strains and crises which are the more significant and the more deeply felt since there is so little to distract attention from them. Relationships that go wrong are haunted by the ghost of the purpose—deflected, maimed, perverted, or extinguished—that they were to go right; life, though it may be lived at a slow pace, is lived with the whole being; nothing is cheapened; and under that huge clean sky it is, or was, easier to be wicked than vulgar. These stories are a reminder that a life "narrow in its setting, harsh in its poverty" may allow, as it did to Dientje Mostert, dignity and grace: "narrow" is the important word—one would not over-hopefully look for those qualities nowadays in an overcrowded urban proletariat.

The intelligent reader can dismiss any suspicion that the somewhat biblical simplicity of [the stories in *The Little Karoo*] suggests them to be the work of a writer who sees life in terms too plain and elemental. There is no lack of subtlety in Pauline Smith's understanding of human nature. She shows us **"The Pastor's Daughter,"** conscious that love can be "beautiful and cruel and selfish and bitter, and who can tell where the one begins and the other ends?'' She does not, like some facile idealists, dodge the fact that pugnacity is an attribute of the human male—of Piet Pienaar, for example, for whom ''battle was the natural means of intercourse with his fellow-men.'' She can face the truth, even when it takes the form of a paranoiac miser; and she can thrust deeply into the truth, as in that appalling glimpse of the father who ''sought fiercely to wound, and so to reach and possess, the mind of his son.'' Or she can show how much, in these narrow settings in the wide veld, small, choice possessions may mean to their owners; Deltje's shell-covered box goes with her like a talisman, and upon Koba Nooi's shell-framed looking-glass has come to depend her very technique of seduction.

The nearer Pauline Smith comes to the themes of death or disaster—as in **''The Pain''** or **''Desolation''**—the nearer to poetry is her presentation of human nature in the face of these things. When Anna Coetzee is discovered feverishly turning the handle of that broken musical box, the symbolism of this situation may be a trifle emphatic, but it is none the less poetically true and whatever we are meant, in **''Ludovitje,''** to read into the revelation that only Maqwasi the Kaffir can dig the graves of white Piet and his wife, it has great force, like something in an epic legend. It is to be noted that when, in this same story, this author has occasion to touch most nearly upon South Africa's most open sore—the poisoned rift between white citizens and black—she pours upon it, like a healing oil, the magic unction of evangelical mysticism, so that the child and the servant are brought into communion and rapt away into the supra-mundane sphere for which their innocence and the reasonless fervour kindled by a few bizarre old phrases have fitted them. (pp. 15-17)

> *William Plomer, in a preface to* The Little Karoo *by Pauline Smith, The Vanguard Press, Inc., 1952, pp. 13-18.*

PAULINE SMITH   (essay date 1959?)

[*In the following essay, Smith reveals the influences that contributed to her development as a writer. Since this essay was published posthumously and its date of composition cannot be fixed, the editors have placed it in the year of Smith's death.*]

To neither the ''Why'' nor the ''How'' is there any very definite or romantic answer, but I seem to have set about it, at a very early age, with prayer. The first of my prayers, however, was not for a pen but for ''a beard like my father and a tail like my dog Tycho.'' The beard and the tail were never granted me. Yet it was with the same hopeful importunity that, a little later, I prayed: ''Give me an orphanage and make me an author.'' The orphanage has never been achieved, and if at last I am an author it is author of so very little that the title now embarrasses me much as, in earlier days, the beard and the tail might have done.

Though I made my wishes known thus early and clearly to heaven I can remember no remarkable or precocious plunge into authorship in childhood. It was in fact only slowly, through years of ill-health, that I came to write at all, and though ill-health may have made me a little more sensitive and impressionable than other robuster children it did not make me an imaginative genius. It did not even make me, so far as I can remember, particularly bookish, for books in quantity played no great part in the out-of-door life we led as children in our small Dutch village in the Little Karoo. But for that very reason, perhaps, such books as we did read made a tremendous

impression upon me. Among these were *Rab and His Friends,* the tales of Mrs. Ewing, *Robinson Crusoe,* and the amazing and terrifying *Fairchild Family.* But the three which influenced me most deeply, though I was then too young to realize their beauty as literature, were the Old Testament, *The Ancient Mariner,* and *The Vicar of Wakefield.* To these three books and to my father's insistence always that our use of the English language, both written and spoken, should be simple and direct, the ''author'' in me owes much.

Much too, I owe, to the unconscious storing up in my memory, through those impressionable years, of all that was dear and familiar to me, as well as that which was mysterious and strange, in the small world—set in a wide sun-parched plain, bounded north, south, east and west by mountain ranges—which made my universe. In those unhustled days, when a visit to the nearest neighbouring village meant a day's journey by cart or a several days' journey by ox-wagon ''over the mountains,'' the Dutch farmers among whom my father's work as a doctor lay, still lived in a primitive simplicity close to their God. Among these people we had many friends and all their way of life, and their slow and brooding talk which fell so naturally in translation into the English of the Old Testament, was full of interest to us. Often my father took us with him when he visited their farms, and these journeys with him across the wide empty veld: the long low white-washed homesteads we came to—some bare and treeless and poor as they were bare, some set in green lands in narrow fertile valleys among the mountain foot-hills; the mountains themselves, varying always in colour, over which, once a year, we travelled to the sea: the long quiet village its streets lined with giant eucalyptus trees, poplars and willows, to which we returned from all our wanderings with such deep content—all these things were beautiful to me as a child. And when, at school in England, after my father's death, I did at last begin to write, it was to set down for my own comfort the memories of these happier days.

These sketches of a South African childhood were followed later by others of Scottish village life, but all I wrote (and it was little) was written slowly through years of ill-health. Authorship as a career, in spite of my earlier prayers, was something that I felt to be for ever beyond me. I knew no literary people, and had no guidance in my work whatever. My only asset, if asset it can be called, was patience. And with patience I began at last to write a novel.

I had written about a third of my novel when, in Switzerland, I met my first literary critic. With the severity of a schoolmaster this famous man asked to see my work, and with timidity of a school-girl I gave it to him. A few days later I was asked to tea. And after tea I was told that anybody could have written my Scottish sketches (which had found publication in a north-country newspaper): that not everybody could have written the South African sketches (which had never been published): and that the novel was no good and that the ''artist'' in me, having achieved the South African children sketches, must know as well as he did just how bad it was.

This ''damning'' of my novel brought me an astonishing sense of relief, and established my faith in the critic's judgment as no praise would have done. I knew nothing about the undeveloped ''artist'' within me but I did know that this adverse criticism of my novel was just and that in damning it the critic had done for me what I had not had the courage to do for myself. I destroyed those opening chapters and never afterwards regretted it. And I began to work, with a clearer purpose, for this self-appointed master.

Yet, as always, everything I did was done slowly and painfully, with many long breaks. A second novel, begun in France, was ended by illness in Italy, and all the little I had written despairingly destroyed. Still the "master" insisted that I must write—and after a year spent among our old friends in the Little Karoo I turned again to the writing of South African sketches, dealing now not with children but with their elders.

From the first these short stories, written at long intervals, won the critic's praise, but their gloom and austerity, he declared, would make it almost impossible to place them with any ordinary English magazine, and they remained in my desk. There came at last, however, a moment when even he rebelled against the austerity of these Little Karoo tales, and the "bare bones" of my next short story, he insisted, must be "clothed." This story had lain for long in my mind, and I set to work upon it now in the way he indicated. But the result filled me with so despairing a sense of failure that I sent him my manuscript only half-finished asking if what I was doing was really worth while. Three days later we met, and with the air of a triumphant fellow-schoolboy-conspirator he returned my half-finished manuscript crying: "Now you've done it! Now you've done it! And *I've* shown you *how* to do it!" Then he added sharply, the school-boy no longer but the school-master: "And now you'll go home and finish it!"

I did finish it. And again the sense of failure oppressed me. Again, it seemed to me I failed to do justice to these people as I saw them—so fine in their simplicity and humility, so courageous in their poverty. But I satisfied my critic. "God knows whom I'll get to publish this," he said, after three words of praise, "but it has got to be published."

It was published—by Middleton Murry in the *Adelphi*, and it was called **"The Pain."**

And that is how and why, so far as I can judge, I became an author. (pp. 150-53)

> Pauline Smith, "Why and How I Became an Author," in English Studies in Africa, *Vol. 6, No. 2, September, 1963, pp. 150-53.*

ALAN PATON (essay date 1959)

[*Paton is a South African novelist whose fiction exposes the results of the racist policies of his country's elite ruling class, revealing not only the consequences for the exploited but also for South Africa as a whole. In addition to his writing, he has devoted much of his life to social and political reform in South Africa. In the following excerpt, Paton praises Smith for her characterizations of Afrikaners in* The Little Karoo.]

Of all our South African writers, none was ever more generally accepted and admired, and excited less controversy and opposition, than Pauline Smith. That was partly because the body of her work was so slight, partly because of her own gentle and unassertive nature; but also because of the purity, strength and tenderness of her work, which excited admiration rather than envy, and spared her from the deathly kisses of fellow-writers....

In *The Little Karoo,* Pauline Smith, though not herself an Afrikaner, produced one of the most remarkable collections of Afrikaner stories ever written. She never avoided the harsh and the ugly, nor the fiercest of passions, nor the strange compound of religiousness and lovelessness, nor the despair and melancholy of these lonely Afrikaners who asked nothing and got it. When she writes of love and fortitude and self-sacrifice and

mercy, she does not do it to compensate us for the harshness and bitterness of life, but because she sees them, too. She weaves them altogether into a tragic and beautiful cloth of life; one feels that for her, life is something that can be led only with fortitude.

Her stories remind me of that great collection of pictures, "The Family of Man," portraying the humble majesty of humankind, sometimes joyful, sometimes desperate, but never mean. Pauline Smith could not write meanly about life and man, because she loved them; she certainly wrote lovingly about the loving and the gentle and the courageous, and one might well suppose she had a prejudice in favor of them, but she wrote lovingly about the others, too. She wrote about cruelty, but never cruelly, she wrote about sex, but never sexily. Mankind emerged from her creative hands, battered, lined, old, bent, but beautiful. It is a rare genius that is able to look upon life, to know it and to suffer it, to find it beautiful, and to make it so for others.

Such a one was Pauline Smith.

> Alan Paton, "A Classic of South Africa," in New York Herald Tribune Book Review, *Vol. 36, No. 11, October 18, 1959, p. 8.*

CHARLES EGLINGTON (essay date 1960)

[*Eglington is a South African poet, short story writer, and critic. In the following excerpt, he examines the "quaintness" that many readers observe in Smith's prose style.*]

[In the process of investigating the relative popularity of the stories in *The Little Karoo* over the novel *The Beadle,* I discovered that among readers of these works] nearly all of them had been struck by something "quaint" in Pauline Smith's style.

What was quaint about it? The answers amounted almost invariably to this: "Her English is a bit unusual." Or, "She seems to have tried to reproduce the flavour of Afrikaans in her English." Or, "Her style is very old-fashioned and Biblical." So far as I could gather the "quaintness" was generally less apparent to Afrikaans-speaking readers than to English-speaking readers; although readers in both groups discerned "something Afrikaans" in Pauline Smith's writing.

I soon became reasonably sure of where they considered this "quaintness" to be. But to determine more specifically, I asked a number of them to study four excerpts from the stories and the novel, and to put their fingers on what they thought was quaint. These were the four excerpts:

> (A) Through the long, hot days, still, moonlit nights that followed, the loneliness of the old people, and for Juriaan the sense of a God withdrawn, steadily increased. The ways of the hospital, the order and routine necessary for the running of it, remained to the end incomprehensible to them both. For fifty years on their mountain-side in the Aangenaam Valley life had been for them as simple as were their daily needs, as humble as were their hearts. In this new and bewildering world the kindness of the English doctor, of the matron, and of the nurse reached them only as the kindness of human beings reaches the suffering of dumb animals. On neither side was there, nor could there be

complete understanding. The doctor and the matron might know all that was to be known about the pain in Deltje's side. About the pain in her heart and in Juriaan's they knew nothing. And from the inquisitiveness of the other patients in the ward the little old woman shrank with a gentle timidity that increased her isolation.

(B) It was in the kitchen that on this particular day Andrina's services were needed at the homestead. The kitchen was a big sunny room with a fire place resembling a low raised platform taking up one entire side of it. At one end of this platform was the door of the great brick oven, built out into the yard. At the other was a small modern stove. The stove was seldom used and most of the cooking was done in three-legged pots and pans over an open fire in the centre of the platform. The fire was lighted always between two large stones set at some distance apart, and across which, to support a big black kettle, rested the flattened-out iron rims of two old wagon wheels. In a corner, close to the oven door, stood a long wooden oven-shovel.

(C) "I will not plant my lands. If I plant me now my lands surely by the time it comes for me to dig my potatoes and gather me my mealies I shall be dead of this cough that I have from the dust in the mill. And so surely as I am dead, the day that I am buried they will drive you out of this house in the rocks and to the man that comes after me they will give my potatoes and mealies. So I will not plant my lands. God help you, Mintje, when I am dead and they drive our children and you out in the veld the day that I am buried, but I will not plant my lands for the man that comes after me."

(D) "Jan Beyers," she said, plunging at once, with cheerful decision into the young man's affairs: "Look now! It was a mistake that I made when I gave you the name of Andrina du Toit for your wife. It is Betje Ferreira that you must marry. Give me your letter and I will now change the name from Andrina to Betje."

"No, what, Juffrouw," said the young man miserably, producing his letter but not giving it up, "Andrina's and not Betje's is the name that I will keep for my letter. That is how it is with me now!"

"Jan Beyers," cried Tan' Linda in alarm, "what mean you?"

"No, what, Juffrouw! Did not you yourself first choose Andrina for me? Why now must I marry Betje?"

"Jan Beyers, when first I chose Andrina for you you would not hear her name! Why now will you hear no other?"

"No, what," confided the young man in his misery. "See how it is! So soon as Andrina said that she would not take my letter, then I knew it was she and not Betje Ferreira or Toontje van Niekerk that I wished to marry. And three whole hours has it been so with me now. It was for this that I came to you. To ask you to speak with Andrina for me."

None of the persons asked could point to anything really "quaint" in passage (A); and they admitted that passage (B) was good, effective prose. But in both passages (C) and (D) they found the English "quaint," because in them Pauline Smith had "translated Afrikaans literally into English." None of them thought it worthwhile to mention in what important respects the four passages differed one from the other. Yet the differences are fairly obvious.

From an examination of the passages one can learn a good deal about Pauline Smith's prose style and the devices she uses in her dialogue. It is on the basis of these excerpts that I would like to make some observations about these two aspects of her writing.

*　　*　　*

Excerpt (A) is from her celebrated short story, **"The Pain,"** in which the author is conveying to the reader something about the feelings and state of mind of two simple, primitive old people from the Aangenaam Valley: a sick woman and her husband, who has taken her for treatment to a hospital in a Karoo town.

Excerpt (B) is a straightforward description of the kitchen in a homestead in the Aangenaam Valley, and is from **The Beadle**.

Excerpt (C) is from a story in **The Little Karoo** called **"The Miller"**: the miller, Andries Lombard, is complaining bitterly to his wife.

Passage (D), from **The Beadle,** is part of a conversation between Tan' Linda, the meddlesome Aangenaam Valley matchmaker, and Jan Beyers, who has suddenly decided that he would rather marry Andrina, the novel's tragic heroine, than any of the other girls previously recommended to him by Tan' Linda.

There is, of course, nothing quaint to be found in the first two passages for a very obvious reason: they are passages of narrative and descriptive prose. It is only a curious illusion in many readers that there is something quaint about Pauline Smith's prose style. The diction of the last two passages *is* un-English, however, and has an Afrikaans tone; this is quite deliberate on the part of the author, who wishes the reader to know that the characters in both cases are Afrikaners, speaking their own language in their own particular way.

The probable reason why the readers I questioned did not notice the difference between the four passages, even to the extent of distinguishing between dialogue and ordinary prose, is that Pauline Smith's Afrikaans-into-English dialogue leaves an echo in the mind—an echo which tends to condition the memory of readers and leave them with the impression that the diction in the dialogue is to some extent characteristic of her prose in general. This erroneous impression may be attributed to inattention, lack of a selective memory, or a poor inner ear, in the reader; but I am inclined to believe that the illusion, curious as it may seem, is both more complex and significant than that. I think it is attributable not so much to any lack in the reader, as to qualities in Pauline Smith's writing which are entirely to her credit.

The diction used in her dialogue, where Afrikaans characters are involved, performs a specific function; her prose style has not only one, but several, attributes. The best way to define the function of the dialogue, and the various attributes of her prose style, is to particularize the important differences in the four excerpts quoted.

*   *   *

In passage (A) the author is trying to induce the reader to identify himself as closely as possible with the condition and state of mind of the characters: a bewildered old couple, in utterly alien, incomprehensible surroundings, faced by an exigency all the more distressing because they do not understand it. The writing in this passage is subjective; it contains a number of latent suggestions intended to work on the imagination of the reader. The prose moves at a slow, almost stumbling, pace; its simplicity is the simplicity of the old people themselves, numb and almost stupid with too many new, bewildering experiences.

Similar examples could be found in Pauline Smith's work to show that her so-called Biblical simplicity is not paucity of feeling or expression; that it is not a false, affected or inept simplicity. The pace, pitch and tone of her subjective writing varies according to the nature of the latent suggestions it carries.

Quite different in pace, pitch and tone is passsage (B). Here the author is making no attempt to condition the reader's response. She aims simply at describing a certain kitchen: she keeps the scene steadily before her mind's eye and sets it down before the reader in clear, careful language. She evokes a picture which she keeps as plain and as sharply-focused as possible, so that the reader will remember it. Later this particular description will fall into place beside other equally objective descriptions, to form a complex of images constituting the setting against which the story is told.

Again, other examples could be chosen to show how sensitively and carefully Pauline Smith's prose is composed, in accordance with the demands of the purpose to be achieved.

She is not a remarkable prose stylist, in the sense that her style is a conspicuous expression of her personality. As narrator and commentator, she keeps her personality as much out of the picture as possible. Indeed, her austere suppression of her own personality often imparts to her prose a certain drabness. But, in general, her curious distinction as a writer lies in her not obtruding much on the reader's attention; in her interposing nothing between the reader and her writing. Even her subjectivity is subdued; when she is not describing objectively, the suggestions latent in her prose are made to work on the reader's attention, more by means of emotive diction, than by a calculated selection of images and metaphors. Thus her emotive writing very often does reflect the salient characteristics of the people or the events she is concerned with. This may have a good deal to do with the illusion of "quaintness" which some readers have about her writing. But that illusion is created principally by her Afrikaans-into-English dialogue.

*   *   *

In passage (C) Pauline Smith is bringing the reader as close as she knows how to the feelings, mental process and power of expression of a simple, bitter, stubborn and defiant man. This monologue gives a necessary clue to the characterization of the miller, and to the tragic predicament in which he finds himself. All this is implicit in the diction, in the pace and cadence of the prose; and in the disrupted syntax. Could formal

English have been so effective? This is a matter to which I shall have to return a little later.

In passage (D) the object to be achieved is altogether different; and, accordingly, the use of Afrikaans-into-English is quite different. This is a comic scene, about which there is nothing gratuitous. Its purpose is manifold. Two characters are depicted: Tan' Linda, the matchmaker, is important to the story; Jan Beyers is relatively unimportant. But in this amusing scene both Tan' Linda and Beyers are sharply and firmly fixed in their relation to Andrina, the heroine of the novel. Beyers is trying, with Tan' Linda's help, to win the hand of Andrina in marriage, because he has been told that she will bring him a dowry of cattle. His motives are entirely selfish and, through them, he becomes an agent of the bitter Aalst Volkman, the beadle, whose twisted mind and tortured emotions are such powerful influences on Andrina's fate. Tan' Linda, however, has other plans for Andrina: she is busy furthering the affair between Andrina and the stranger to the Aangenaam Valley, the Englishman: an affair which turns out so fatally.

Here the Afrikaans-into-English dialogue is given a comic lightness—light in an appropriately bucolic way. The reader will remember this absurd scene because, later, the comedy will turn out to have had tragic undertones. Tan' Linda's gabby meddlesomeness, although kindly intended, and Jan Beyers's oafish designs—so well depicted in their speech—play a considerable part in the development of the story, both directly and indirectly. This particular conversation is, in fact, a good example not only of how Pauline Smith uses dialogue to delineate character and, with great economy, to carry the narrative along; but also of how subtly she can invest seemingly insignificant dialogue with an import that gradually becomes apparent.

A comparison of these two passages (and any number of other passages could be compared as effectively) shows that Pauline Smith's Afrikaans-into-English device is not simply a formula to provide "local colour," or to indicate that the people she is writing about are strange primitives. She does not resort to the shallow expedient of literal, or quasi-literal, translation: an expedient which, at best, becomes mechanical and incapable of conveying a rich range of differences between one character and another, and, at worst, degenerates into the kind of caricature language one sometimes comes across in bad books, or encounters in jokes or burlesques. Occasionally she does translate a phrase or expression literally—e.g. "Look, now," "No, what"; and these are quite effective in an unimportant way. But almost invariably her Afrikaans-into-English dialogue is done with poetic precison and sensitivity; in her hands the device does not become monotonous or mechanical; her characters—although, as it were, all speaking in the same literary lingo—do not *sound* alike. Although a comparison between several passages of dialogue, spoken by different characters, will often show that the words and expressions used are very much alike, and the syntactical peculiarities almost identical, the various speakers do not become confused with each other in the reader's mind. (pp. 49-55)

The question whether a novelist should try to indicate in his English dialogue that the characters are really talking another language, has been vexed by a good many irrelevant considerations. It must in the long run remain a matter of individual opinion. Some readers are genuinely irritated by foreign-sounding dialogue and feel that it is seldom, if ever, justified. All that can be said is that, if such dialogue is clumsily handled by a writer whose ear is not true, it is dreadful, and certainly has nothing to recommend it.

Is Pauline Smith's Afrikaans-into-English dialogue justified? Could she have achieved the same object if she had written it in ordinary English?

My own feeling is that her device is entirely justified; not only because her dialogue is consistently written with tact, sensitivity and profoundly poetic precison; but because in it she has created a language which fits the characters as naturally as their own skins. I do not think that she could have made ordinary English do as well, she needed to create for her characters a language that could convey clearly the singularity of their lives, of their outlook on life, and of their time and place. She created such a language, not by a formal statement of their thoughts, feelings and beliefs, but by means of a diction which remained imaginatively close to their manner of expression. Formal English could not have conveyed so accurately or so poetically the individuality of the people of the Aangenaam Valley. (p. 56)

> Charles Eglington, "'Quaintness' in Pauline Smith: Observations on Her Style and Dialogue," in English Studies in Africa, Vol. 3, No. 1, March, 1960, pp. 48-56.

ARTHUR RAVENSCROFT (essay date 1963)

[*Ravenscroft is a South African critic and educator. He has stated that his most urgent concern is "trying to understand the savagery at the center of European (indeed North Atlantic) civilization when it has unleashed itself on the Third World, trying to understand why any human beings can imagine themselves dignified by their humiliation of their fellows. . . . Such wondering about a civilization that has produced both Beethoven and Buchenwald has arisen out of my South African origins, the intimate relationship between apartheid and Auschwitz, and, in the last twenty years, my reading of Third World literature." In the following excerpt, Ravenscroft examines themes and narrative techniques in Smith's fiction.*]

[What] fired Pauline Smith's imagination as she pondered over her memories of the isolated Afrikaner people of the Little Karoo was not a condescending interest in rural quaintness, but a rich, warm comprehension of the grey tones in which life and the will of God were revealed to them. That she, of English origin, should have been able to grasp this is in itself remarkable, but the lasting value of her artistry lies not in the sure, concrete details with which she presents their daily lives, but in the realization, through these details, of an organic community, with a way of life, identity, and consciousness of its own. The sympathetic intimacy with which she presents an insulated, entirely pre-industrial culture and the sensitivity and emotional logic with which she senses where stresses within individuals and between individuals and the community are likely to occur, rank her work, despite its small extent, with that of the George Eliot of *Silas Marner*. She has little of George Eliot's massiveness of intellect, but her austere art, superficially so simple, but in reality wise and imaginative in the fullest sense, explores the mentally claustrophobic limits of the Little Karoo people with fine precision and an accurate penetration to the common humanity that lies beneath their regional and racial peculiarities.

These peculiarities are there, convincingly and throughout; they are encompassed within her understanding of an elemental human condition, yet their rendering is one of the means not the end of her art. This is no mere regionalism, though there is

evidence that some of her admirers have found her "charm" as a writer to extend no further. And it is all too easy to be captivated by the exoticism to the non-South African reader of the setting of the stories, and by what a *New York Times* reviewer refers to as Pauline Smith's "almost Biblical eloquence." This is chiefly the level on which they have been praised. But "biblical" is not a useful critical term.

There are echoes sometimes for specific purposes (as in the story **"Ludovitje"**), of biblical cadences and phraseology, but on the whole they occur in order to show how life in the Little Karoo resembles for its people that of Israel in the Old Testament. To this extent the dialogue of Pauline Smith's stories is "biblical," but she is clearly less interested in echoing the Bible than the accents of the leisurely, metaphor-laden language actually used by her people. To do this in English for Afrikaans speech, she tries to give their dialogue a distinctly un-English flavour by such means as literal renderings of Afrikaans exclamations and endearments ("No, what!," "Now look now," "My little springbok," "My little heart-thief"), by the use of Afrikaans sentence patterns which invert normal English word order ("Say for me now. . .", "After you will I send. . ."), and occasionally by the insertion of an untranslated Afrikaans expression, such as "a-le-wereld." The biblicality is only part of this transliteration of colloquial Afrikaans speech, which contributes so largely to the authenticity and immediacy of her characters.

The faithful recording of actual speech is at the centre of her artistic method and has its counterparts on other levels too. Real geographical names are interchanged or but slightly altered, many of the surnames of her characters are well known in the Oudtshoorn district, and the description of Platkops village and its hospital in **"The Pain"** is still recognizably that of Oudtshoorn, even after fifty years of change. Yet the art is not flat representationalism. With locality and mode of life firmly rooted in her actual experience of it, Pauline Smith goes on to probe the emotional lives of individuals whose desires, whether selfish or generous, are delineated with profound imaginative insight. The "simple" setting of a homogeneous community primitively close to a reluctant soil enables her to concentrate fully on an order of human experience shorn of incidental elaborations. Her narrative techniques are shaped by this environmental severity. What gives the language of **The Little Karoo** and **The Beadle** their real eloquence is a rigorous critical faculty which forbids excrescence, irrelevance or slackness. The description, for instance, in **"Desolation"** of the terrain over which Old Alie and her grandson travel to Hermansdorp:

> Throughout the first day it was in the Verlatenheid, with frequent outspans, that they journeyed. And here, from sun-up to sun-down they met no human being and saw in the distance only one white-washed and deserted farmhouse, bare and treeless in the drought-stricken veld. Every *kuil* or water-hole they passed was dry, and near every *kuil* were the skeletons of donkeys and sheep which had come there but to perish of their thirst. Of living things they saw only, now and then, a couple of *koorhan* rising suddenly in flight, or a lizard basking lazily in the sun. And once, bright as a jewel in that desert of sand and stone, they came upon a small green bush poisonous to sheep and cattle alike.

Turned off the land, old Alie alone stands between the child and destitution. She makes for the village where 50 years before she worked happily as a mattress-maker and now hopes to resume her trade. But the village too is blighted by drought and where she expected to find the pleasant cottage of her youth there now stands an impersonal orphanage. The passage conveys the grim ironic pathos of the story: the signs of calamitous drought are listed with remorseless exactness, culminating in the final irony that the only green bush in the desolate immensity is poisonous.

Within the narrow compass, the range and depth of human emotions explored is impressive. The theme of **"The Pain"** is the tender old-age love of Juriaan and Deltje which through their fifty hard, childless years together has been the one sure sensuous fact of their existence, threatened only once—by the foreign efficiency of the Platkops hospital. When Deltje finds that their enforced lying apart brings pain to their hearts more unendurable even than her physical pain, they steal away at night and return home with a deep content to await her death. This is the most tender of all the stories, though human capacity for selfless devotion occurs as a theme also in **"Desolation"** and **"The Pastor's Daughter,"** and supremely in the nature of Andrina's love of the easy-going Englishman in *The Beadle*.

Pauline Smith handles the relationship between Andrina and the Englishman with fearlessness and a stress upon the sanctity of sex that cannot fail to remind one of D. H. Lawrence. Whether Andrina is in narrowly realistic terms a successful creation is perhaps beside the point. She is treated as completely innocent and childlike, and the very sparseness of her physical and mental environment makes genuine and moving the touching into life of her emotional and spiritual potentialities, even by an irresponsible Englishman from across the mountains. Her naïve trust is emphasized in order to show the unspoiled generosity of her nature, contrasted with her aunt Johanna's bitter righteousness and inability to forgive an old wrong, and with the beadle's tortured moroseness that conceals his unexpiated sin. The flowering of Andrina's love coincides with her admission to church membership and she interprets the joy her love brings her as a sign of God's mercy and bounty. In her poverty she can give the Enlishman only her body and this she does unselfconsciously with the same sacramental intensity that accompanies her other means of ministering to him. (pp. 61-4)

Though the Englishman is identified with an arrogant world "which sent out judges and administrators to its colonies," he is not merely callous. He cossets himself with semi-imaginary invalidism and makes that the moral excuse for his actions, but without being a villainous seducer. Incapable of fathoming Andrina's fatalistic acceptance of God's will (whether it brings pain or joy) he misreads it as an admirable "emancipated" courage. He needs to justify his actions before his own conscience, and Pauline Smith sets forth his morally self-deluding arguments with an ironic sympathy that shows a grasp almost as sure of this kind of sophisticated mind as of the "simpler" minds of the Little Karoo people.

> He had taken nothing from Andrina which she had not been willing to give. He had given her nothing which she had not been eager to have. He had done her no harm. Again and again, as if in argument with an opponent, he insisted upon this—he had done her no harm.

Despite his desertion and her desolation, she joyously looks forward to the birth of the child that will be her comforter.

Their relationship and the exploration of its enriching effect upon Andrina do not constitute the whole core of the novel. This again lies in the setting of the Aangenaam valley and the nature of the forces that work upon its inhabitants. The bitter feud between Johanna Steenkamp and the beadle, Mijnheer van der Merwe's stern patriarchy, his wife's beneficence, the comic, well-intentioned matrimonial manipulation of Tan' Linda of the post office, and the canny motives behind Jan Beyers's wife-seeking—all these form a skilfully integrated pattern both for the characterization of a people and for the working out of Andrina's fate.

One of Pauline Smith's creative strengths is her ability to present the warping, through a variety of pressures, of human feeling into perverse self-torture and cruelty to others. A father in anguish over dangers to his child but unable to prevent them because he is too proud to acknowledge that she is, illegitimately, his. An outcast finding peace and love but destroying both in the same kind of fit of demented rage that had driven him thousands of miles from home. In *The Beadle* one sees it particularly in the beadle's treatment of Jacoba Steenkamp, whose forgiveness of his ancient infidelity twists his conscience-stricken mind into uttering the cruel words that hasten her death. A tubercular miller dies without being able to articulate the tender words that will wipe out the effect of his self-pitying outbursts of rage against a timid wife whom he had loved dearly before his illness. One of the most powerful of the stories is **"The Father,"** which unfolds the process by which Piet Pienaar acquires, and tries to push a holding of farmland to the river bank by scrimping and piecemeal purchase. This passion is frustrated by Mijnheer van Reenen, a shrewd landowner with a reputation for "evil-living." Pienaar gradually becomes so unhinged that he convinces himself of the illegitimacy of his only son, "whose birth had closed Aantje's womb to those other sons for whose creating he had married her." His delusion leads to an attempt upon his son's life so that he may triumph over the combined mockery of himself by God, Mijnheer and Aantje.

Pauline Smith has nothing to say about black-white racial tensions in South Africa. **"Ludovitje,"** the least successful of her stories, is the only one which, on a mystical-religious plane, deals specifically with relations between Afrikaner and African. But her grasp of the situation is summed up with caustic economy in this passage from *The Beadle:*

> When the last of the dishes was cleared away, the great Bible was placed before Mijnheer. From a drawer in the sideboard Andrina brought the psalm-books—one for each person round the table and one for the Englishman among the rest. From the kitchen quarters came the native servants, crowding in the doorway without entering the room and squatting down there upon the floor. The chapter was read. The psalm was sung. Jantje, slipping from his chair, walked up to his grandfather's knee and repeated his evening prayer. From the doorway came the indentured children and they too, at their master's knee, repeated a prayer. "Make me to be obedient to my mistress, oh Lord," prayed Spaasie in her rough, hoarse voice. "Make me to run quickly when my master calls," prayed Klaas.

Her art deals uncompromisingly with the passions of an obscure community. It is never likely to be "popular," but its influence is to be found in the work of subsequent South African writers, both in English and in Afrikaans, among them Alan Paton. Ten months before Pauline Smith died at Broadstone in Dorset, on 29 January 1959, a group of South African writers acknowledged their indebtedness by presenting her with an illuminated scroll as "a tribute of our admiration." More widely, her stories form a small but living contribution to the specifically English literary tradition inspired by the best qualities of English puritan fidelity. (pp. 65-7)

Arthur Ravenscroft, "Pauline Smith," in A Review of English Literature, *Vol. 4, No. 2, April, 1963, pp. 55-67.*

NADINE GORDIMER   (essay date 1963)

[*Gordimer is a South African fiction writer and critic who has achieved international recognition for examining the effects of the South African system of apartheid on both the ruling whites and the oppressed blacks. Showing the victimization of the whites as well as blacks by the apartheid system, Gordimer's novel* A World of Strangers *(1958) depicts the alienation of classes and races in a stratified society, and* The Late Bourgeois World *(1966) focuses on the isolation of the white middle class. In the following excerpt from an essay that originally appeared in the* New York Times Book Review *in June 1963, Gordimer compares the ethos of present-day Afrikaners and Afrikaners as portrayed in* The Beadle.]

It is irresistible to compare with South Africa today the South Africa of Pauline Smith's novel [*The Beadle*], which deals not with the period, 37 years ago, in which it was originally published, but with that of the latter half of the nineteenth century. To readers who are accustomed to the facile shock-a-day picture of the country that emerges from newspaper reports, or even the depth and complexity of the picture given by the country's contemporary creative writing, the author's picture will be, at first glance, unrecognizable. But if they look again at the lonely life of the isolated Boer community of Harmonie, in the Little Karoo, they may find a rare opportunity to learn something of what the Afrikaners were like nearly a hundred years ago, before gold and diamonds had been discovered to make the country rich and bring about an industrial revolution, and before the word apartheid had been coined.

For myself, I am puzzled and uneasy as I trace the origins, admirable if narrow, of some of the uglier manifestations of the present-day Afrikaner ethos. Is it possible that patient submission to the will of God can become the licence of those who feel themselves God-ordained to dispose of the lives of others? Can simplicity of heart swell up into self-righteousness? Is it power, then, that lies like a distorting glass across these people now, magnifying grotesquely into the modern world what were once, in a small, humble context, such wonderfully human qualities?

These questions and the possibility of finding answers are not the real reasons for reading this book. Conversely, people who are bored with Africa should not allow themselves to miss it. Like the author's famous *The Little Karoo* stories, this little-known novel has the beauty and authority of insight that reaches out beyond a historical view of life. Even stylistically it transcends the period in which it was written, the period about which it was written and this decade in which it has now been republished. It is a nineteenth-century narrative without the sermonizing; a modern novel with the classic economy but not the "absurd" philosophy of an Albert Camus; the exploration of guilt but not the Catholic refuge of a Graham Greene.

The guilt of Aalst Vlokman, the beadle, toward Jacoba and Johanna Steenkamp and their dead sister's child, Andrina du Toit, is like a train of gunpowder he tracks helplessly, on the soles of his shoes, through the book. It is acknowledged in the silence of hard Johanna, the stunted personality of gentle Jacoba, and the ignorance and innocence of the young woman, Andrina, of the destiny to which her mother's passionate nature and her father's failure to accept responsibility for her inevitably lead her. When the girl falls in love, one watches, fascinated, while she unknowingly repeats in her life the pattern of her own parents. She loves the young Englishman who has come to the Karoo to play at learning to farm and plays at loving, too. She comes to grief as she came to be born: through a human being who does not accept the responsibilities of human involvement.

Theme and story move along with a most remarkable unity and skill. Without ever resorting to interior monologue, with scarcely any dialogue, Pauline Smith makes the lives of these people surge up through the quiet narrative. When there is an exchange of words between them—sometimes only a bare sentence—a whole situation or turn of events bursts devastatingly upon one's consciousness. This is one of the great novels that should never be allowed to go out of print. It will always be rediscovered with astonishment and admiration. (pp. 101-02)

Nadine Gordimer, "'For Andrina Destiny Was Bitter': Review of 'The Beadle'," in Pauline Smith, *edited by Dorothy Driver, McGraw-Hill Book Company, 1983, pp. 101-02.*

GEOFFREY HARESNAPE   (essay date 1969)

[*Haresnape is a South African poet, fiction writer, biographer, and critic. In the following excerpt from his book-length study of Smith's life and work, he discusses symbolism in Smith's fiction, paying particular attention to* The Beadle.]

It is apparent that Pauline Smith wishes her reader to be moved in a special way by places like the Aangenaam Valley, the Credo Mountains and the farm Harmonie. He is expected to feel through them her intuition of a remote and perfect region. They are, as has been made clear, suggestions of Eden. This talent of hers to invest ordinary objects and situations with poetic strength gives power to her work.

The high land where the van Royens live above the Aangenaam Valley is a place to be close to spiritual reality. The cold, square hospital on the banks of the river in Platkops dorp, standing in its open yard, is symbolic of the brashness and lack of compassion in the practical medicine which it subserves. Many other descriptions and situations point to specific meanings which are suggested by but lie beyond themselves. These save the stories from becoming colonial sketches of interest primarily for their local colour.

Even the cycle of the seasons is invested with a certain poetical meaningfulness in stories like "**The Miller**" and "**The Schoolmaster,**" and especially in *The Beadle*. Its symbolism seems to state that when a man accepts and conforms to the seasons he has interior peace. Sin and bitter self-righteousness throw him out of gear with the round of nature. This is true of Andries Lombard who refuses to plant his lands in spring and digs a grave when his neighbours are bringing in the harvest. Only at the moment of his death does he become one with the year, by bringing his repentance as "fruit" to the thank-offering service.

The Beadle's strong seasonal pattern gives the book shape and plays an important part in the development of the characters of Aalst Vlokman and Andrina. The book is divided into four parts. The first of these plays itself out in early spring. When Henry Nind comes into the Aangenaam Valley he sees that "the corn was already up and the fresh young green of mealies was showing through the dark grey soil. The little orchards were pink with peach blossom and the veld too, grey and bare for so many months of each year, was gay with spring flowers."

With the spring there is a general stirring in the Harmonie community. Harry feels lawless and exultant. It is a special year for Andrina who, ever the child of nature, is growing into womanhood with the awakening season. At this time her aunts set about making her sacrament dress, suggestive of her womanhood, and Jacoba gives her a mirror, one of the tokens of self-awareness which occur frequently in Pauline Smith's work. This spring also makes demands on Aalst Vlokman. But, like Andries Lombard, his bitterness and past sin make him go against it. He hates to think that Andrina is growing up, and is lonely and sullen.

The second part covers only a short period of time, the weeks of "high spring." Action is centered mainly in Mevrouw van der Merwe's garden. At this time, when blood is hot, Henry Nind and Andrina are attracted strongly to each other. The sacrament dress is completed, and the church service ratifies that she has now reached womanhood by admitting her to the adult congregation. In this part Aalst Vlokman receives his greatest blows. His offer to the Lord of two plough-oxen to save Andrina is rejected. Johanna gains the mastery of him and his whole attempt at guarding his illegitimate daughter seems to be in ruins. For him it is a period of bitterness and disillusion.

In part three "the clear spring days grew warmer with the approaching heat of summer." It is in early summer that Andrina and Harry become lovers—the heated blood and rising emotions of the spring have reached their fruition. Throughout the summer Andrina has "a life of dear and secret intimacy with the Englishman." All this while Aalst Vlokman is dazed and unhappy. Life is empty and dark for him. He is in complete opposition to the summer. Autumn and the fall of the year come on with the end of this section. Harry, who in his own opinion has philandered long enough, decides to go away. Andrina, always in harmony with her surroundings, experiences sorrow and emptiness after his departure at the same time as the onset of winter.

The fourth part has for its time span autumn and winter, concluding with the re-arrival of spring. Thus it brings the book round full circle in a pleasing and appropriate manner. In autumn Aalst Vlokman slowly begins to show the fruits of regeneration. By early winter, the time of the thanksgiving service, his repentance and resignation are ripe. Down at the church, in front of all the congregation, he confesses that he is Andrina's father and takes the responsibility for Jacoba's death upon his own shoulders. Although he does not realise it, he is now conforming to the spirit of the thanksgiving service. He has to leave Harmonie and all which is dear to him, once more plunging into isolation. But this time he has a purpose—to find out where his daughter is and to offer to work for her. His personal winter is now in harmony with the season. It is a healthy state, the period of sapless wood which must precede the new bud.

During this winter Andrina is compelled to leave her home. She is assailed by desolation and despair after Harry has left and is tempted to be jealous of Lettice Featherstone. With the knowledge that she is bearing a child, she leaves Uitkijk and throws herself upon the protection of old Hans Rademeyer, who takes her to the toll-house in the Cortes district where his sister lives. Both father and daughter have to leave their old ways of life and journey in uncertainty and solitude before they can meet with new love and understanding in the next spring. Aalst Vlokman is no longer bitter and against the seasons; he accepts the re-awakening year with a certain simple wonder and happiness. When Andrina is lying in the toll-house room waiting for her father to enter, she thinks: "At Harmonie now, in the orchard there, the peach trees were surely in blossom." But this spring there is a new child, "the little grandson . . . with his round bald head." Aalst Vlokman who was filled with bitterness and resentment as his child became a woman, can now accept the infant and ask if he may work for it.

As Mr. William Plomer suggests in his preface to *The Little Karoo* [see excerpt dated 1949] the symbolic situation of Anna Coetzee cranking at the handle of her broken musical box may be a trifle emphatic. However, other situations and objects have a poetic strength which is both luminous and intriguing. Their more compelling hold derives, perhaps, from the fact that their meanings are not as obvious.

One of the more important of these symbolic objects is a mirror in a frame of shells. It is mentioned three times in *The Little Karoo* and *The Beadle*. First it is part of a small box and one of Deltje van Royen's treasured possessions in **"The Pain."** As she travels across the wide, desolate veld in her husband's trek-cart, racked with pain and afraid on her momentous journey to the Platkops dorp hospital, she keeps it close to her, almost—as Mr. Plomer suggests—like a talisman. What can this small seemingly worthless object mean to her? Is it some consolation, a reminder of a happier past? Or does it represent self-awareness?

It takes another short story, **"The Sinner,"** to give the mirror a more definite symbolic meaning. Here it is owned by Jacoba Nooi, the silly woman with a tongue like a running sluice, who persuades Niklaas Dampers to abandon his wife, life, and family to rush madly into the Kombuis. The mirror was such as "had never before been seen by any bijwoner's wife or daughter in the Platkops district." It represents a new dimension in self-awareness and is a potential temptation to pride and vanity. Niklaas's wife and neighbours realise this, but he has been so wrapped up in himself that Jacoba catches him unawares. When he sits with her on the river bank and she suddenly brings her mirror into play, "Niklaas saw before him part of his own wild and sorrowful face, and part of Koba Nooi's plump, round, childish one pressing against it."

Apart from the old cracked glass at which he had glanced when dressing for church, the *bywoner* had never used a mirror before. Now he was seeing his own image, languorously and with intense self-awareness, for the first time. He sees the outward manifestations of his inner state and finds himself imperfect and disordered. At once he gives himself up in a frenzied despair and tries to forget everything in making love with Jacoba Nooi. Although the mirror itself always remains the same, its effect differs, depending on the kind of person who looks into it. For Deltje van Royen the looking-glass could never be dangerous. She can see herself without getting unbalanced from pride or fear. It is only people who are not one with themselves who are put off their stroke by the mirror.

The looking-glass with its frame of shells appears a third time in *The Beadle*. And here it has both of these effects. Jacoba Steenkamp, the humble, innocent sister of the self-righteous Johanna, buys the mirror for Andrina. The aunt is happy on account of the young woman's beauty and no doubt wants her niece to see herself and keep herself in trim. There is no pride here, harmless vanity at the most. Wonder and mystery are the greatest meanings the mirror has for her. In the scene where Jacoba hands it over to Andrina these qualities are stressed. They are near some graves—mysterious, unchanging death beside them—and the time is dusk.

> Together, with beating hearts, they peered at themselves in the little square of glass through the fading light. . . . Andrina asked for no explanation of this miraculous gift, and Jacoba offered none.

Aalst Vlokman, like Niklaas Dampers, is filled with harsh self-righteousness. He sees the mirror only as dangerous pride. When he thinks bitterly how his daughter may be seduced by Henry Nind, his mind moves to the mirror: "Jacoba, poor fool, might God forgive her! had given the child a mirror in which to learn her beauty." But Andrina is simple and unself-conscious enough to escape this pitfall.

> Of her gifts Andrina herself remained as unaware as she was of any God but Jehovah. In the little mirror rimmed with shells she had seen no beauty that was worthy of the Englishman's regard.

Aalst Vlokman has no doubt been afraid of what the mirror will do to Andrina, because he cannot face his own image. Upright and fiercely competitive, Johanna realises this immediately after she has challenged the beadle to declare what his right to Andrina is. On an impulse she brings the mirror into the room.

> "Look now, Aalst Vlokman," she said, propping it up against a dish on the table before him, "look well now into Jacoba's present, for there you will see the face of the man that took Klaartje to Platkops dorp and yet thinks he can say what Andrina shall wear and whom she shall marry!"

Like Niklaas Dampers, Aalst Vlokman sees in his own image the outward sign of his restless and inconsistent spirit. Proud and striving for perfection, he cannot face up to what he sees—"a man abandoned by his God"—and rises hurriedly to leave the room. As he goes, the mirror slips from the table and breaks at the leg of his stool. This scene suggests that he cannot face himself or others in his present state. Willy-nilly, he must break and change before he can escape from his own remorse and misery.

Another striking symbol in *The Beadle* is Andrina's sacrament dress. It has been shown how the girl's acceptance into the church was a sign of her achieved womanhood. The dress which the two aunts make for her indicates to all the world that she is a child no longer. It is made from a print material which "had a pale grey ground, closely sprinkled with pin-prick black dots over which were scattered small pink roses and little blue forget-me-nots." Tan' Jacoba, we are told, was thrilled with the flowers. For her they suggested the beauty, delicacy, and fruitfulness of life and of Andrina's growing up. Tan' Johanna took a grim comfort from the frequency of the little black dots. Andrina's maturity will bring austerity and disappointment as well as joy. In this way the dress becomes a symbol for the whole of Andrina's new life.

At first Aalst Vlokman is antagonistic both to this new, attractive young woman and to her dress. With bitter pangs of fear and inward protest he sees her in her new glory at the church service. The dress becomes associated in his mind with her sexual maturity and her chance of being seduced by Henry Nind. He reproaches the Steenkamp sisters bitterly for dressing her up like a doll for the Englishman to play with. Yet it is the same dress which helps him to find Andrina at the end of the novel. Alone and without obsessions, after confessing his sin at Harmonie, the beadle is walking along the Cortes-dorp-Losberg road. Suddenly he sees Andrina's sacrament dress hanging out on a bush to dry. For the first time he can see the dress in its beauty:

> Those little pink roses—those little blue flowers on their background of grey, closely sprinkled with pin-prick black dots—anywhere on earth would the beadle have known them.

The way in which he goes up to the bush and touches the dress reminds us of Tan' Jacoba's simple wonder at the colour of the material. As a symbol, the dress has remained the same. It still speaks of Andrina's new maturity. But Aalst Vlokman has changed. His acceptance has made him one with the seasons and put him in harmony with his whole world. Consequently the sacrament dress, which once had driven him nearly to distraction, has become an ally, showing him the way back to his daughter. It is "a sign from the Lord."

The two plough-oxen which Aalst Vlokman offers to Jan Beyers if he will marry Andrina have symbolic significance in giving a picture of the beadle's spiritual state at that time. By sacrificing the beasts, he is trying to make a bargain with God. This is the Old Testament conception of justice: I give you this and you give me that—an eye for an eye and a tooth for a tooth. Appropriately, the oxen are typical sacrifice animals. Pauline Smith shows that this desire to bargain with God and human nature is inadequate and ridiculous. Her method of doing this is through a comic episode in which Jan Beyers tries to press his suit to Andrina. Whenever Andrina moved away from him, it seemed to Jan Beyers as if "the two plough-oxen were retreating with her." It is not until the beadle's pride is broken that he understands the inadequacy of this type of justice and reaches the understanding of Mevrouw Alida van der Merwe that "sin would pass, sorrow would pass, but the compassion which had sent the Redeemer into the world to forgive and heal—this would never pass."

He confesses his past and trudges away from the Harmonie community, a wanderer with no possessions save the bag upon his back. In this he ceases to be the Old Testament man, offering his goods as the pledge of a bargain with God. His new role is reminiscent of the disciples whom Christ sent by twos to announce the arrival of the new Kingdom.

Many other parts of Pauline Smith's writing are rich in poetic suggestion. The grave which Maqwasi digs for Ludovitje in the clay-stone *koppie,* the trees, the furrows, and the jailhouse which old Alie van Staden thinks of before she sets out on her long and desolate trek, are amongst them. Even the Southeaster in that rather thin one-act play, *The Last Voyage,* is effectively symbolic when we come to realise that it represents the attrition of old age against which John Tunstall has fought so long. This poetry behind the facts is one of the most important characteristics of Pauline Smith's writing. Its effectiveness and prevalence form one of her strongest claims to excellence. (pp. 131-38)

Geoffrey Haresnape, in his Pauline Smith, *Twayne Publishers, Inc., 1969, 198 p.*

SHEILA SCHOLTEN   (essay date 1977)

[*In the following excerpt from an essay that originally appeared in* New South African Writing *(1977), Scholten surveys the stories and poems collected in* Platkops Children.]

Pauline Smith's collection of children's sketches and poems entitled **Platkops Children** was published by Jonathan Cape in only one edition, that of 1935. . . . Although this book comprises her very earliest stories, it was the last of her works to be published; her reputation as an author had already been established by the **Little Karoo** collection of 1925 and by her only novel, **The Beadle,** first published in 1926. Her only other book to find publication was her moving and revealing tribute to Arnold Bennett entitled **A. B. '. . . a Minor Marginal Note'** which appeared a while after his death.

It was Bennett who first recognised what he later described in an introduction to the first edition of **The Little Karoo** as her "strange, austere, tender, and ruthless talent," and it was in the Platkops stories (although they are little more than sketches) that he first recognised that talent. What was it in these Karoo sketches which drew Bennett's discerning attention? At first glance today they would appear to have little if any literary value. Although originally written for children about children, they would not appeal to the average modern child. They are written in the language and spelling of her childhood, a language which today seems strangely naive. For example, in the introductory sketch:

> An' Nickum says we can write what we like in our book but we're not on no account to menshun his hair, which is red. So in course we're not goin' to. Which is a great pity you know, because the chiefest part of Nickum is his hair, which is red.
>
> (pp. 138-39)

A second and closer look at the stories can be very rewarding, especially when it is realised that they are all autobiographical. Pauline Smith, born in 1882 in Oudtshoorn, was the elder of the two daughters born to Dr. Herbert Urmson Smith and his wife Jessie. They had come to South Africa in the late 1870s, and were highly-respected and much-loved members of a predominantly Dutch community. The "dokter" often took "Polly" (as she was known) with him in his white-hooded buggy on his rounds of the district, and in this way she came to know and love the people of the Little Karoo. In particular she loved to visit the farm Vlakteplatz and the Schoeman family. She describes the approach to the farm in the sketch entitled **"Oupa Carel's"** thus:

> An' oh, but it is beautiful! With tremenjous great red rocks goin' high up in to the sky, an' wild white geese flyin' about among them, an' the river far away down below. But instead of bein' one great river like it is when the floods come an' nobody, not even the Pos'-cart, can get through it for days, it was three little rivers

all by theirselves with great wide bits of sand in between.

> (p. 139)

This farm lies in the lower foothills of the Swartberg towards Uniondale, and the early memory of it was to feature in her short story **"The Schoolmaster,"** included in the **Little Karoo** collection. It was not so much the settings, however, but the characterizations in the early sketches which drew Bennett's attention. Even though she had been thousands of miles away at a cold boarding school in Scotland she was able to evoke the personalities of the people of that warm and happy childhood which she had left at the age of twelve. Her father had been her adored parent, friend and companion; a wise and just man, who had guided her in all things—not least her reading, which at first had been the Bible, *The Vicar of Wakefield,* and "The Ancient Mariner." It is mainly to this background that the sincerity and poignancy of the stories is due for she started to write them in her grief when he died so soon after settling the girls at school.

Regarding her early reading, it is interesting to note that the style in **Platkops Children** shows a marked influence of the Bible as in the following passage from **"The B'loon Man"**:

> An' by'm-bye the B'loon man came out hisself, an' the people cheered, an' he made a very perlite bow an' said how pleased he was to see everybody. An' then he came an' talked to Red Nose, an' then he went back to the b'loon again.
>
> An' Red Nose came up to the fig-trees an' hel' up his ole cap an' said Would we kindly pay our two shillin'ses?
>
> An' Nickum said What for?
>
> An' he said Seein' the b'loon go up.
>
> An' Six said, We hadn' seen no b'loon go up. . . .

Years later, in a pamphlet entitled **"Why and How I Became an Author"** [see excerpt dated 1959] she refers to the "slow and brooding talk [of the Dutch farmers] which fell so naturally in translation into the English of the Old Testament." (pp. 139-40)

In spite of the childish spelling and grammar, the characters are drawn faithfully and economically—this economy of description would be seen in her short stories of the Little Karoo years later. For example, a wealth of meaning is implicit in **"Concits an' thin's"** in her description of the clown of the circus whose friend had died through ill-treatment:

> An' all of a sudden out of the dressin' tent came the funnies' man you ever saw, in a white dress with red spots on it, an' frills roun' his neck an' his legs, an' white hair an' a white tall cap, an' a white face with red spots on his cheecks an' his nose an' his chin.
>
> An' he looked at us an' we looked at him, none of us sayin' anythin', we were so serprised.
>
> An' he said Don't you know me?
>
> An' Paoli fell out of the fig-trees, an' ran up to him, sayin' Oh Joey!
>
> An' Joey said, Why Paoli! What's the matter?
>
> But the Paoli one didn' know. So she couldn' tell him. She jes' stood there holdin' his han' an' sayin' nothin'.

One is thus aware of tragedy simply through a picture which has been drawn for us of a funny-faced clown whose misery conveys itself, despite his make-up, to the sensitive little girl.

Many of the tales are really very funny indeed, and again it is her economy of style which gives point to a situation, as in the story of Perceval Gordon-Gordon, the **"Perlite English Boy"** who falls into the dam in his "welwet" suit when he goes sailing in a tub with Nickum D. She writes:

> So Nickum brought the tub to the edge of the dam an' the English boy got in. But the English boy was much heavier than Nickum, an' the tub, it tipped, an' there they were both in the dam together. An' although it didn' matter much to Nickum whose clo'es were all under the quince hedge it did to Arthur Perceval Gordon-Gordon who had his on. An'. . . .
>
> (pp. 141-42)

A few stories are very sad, especially the one called simply **"Jackie"**—about the baby brother (one of the twins) who died when he was barely a year old. It is the understatement which underlines the poignancy—as when the governess Miss Cherry takes the little girls with her to lie down in her bedroom and gently breaks the news that their little brother has died. She starts off by telling them how Jesus loves little children, and teaches them the text "Suffer little children."

> An' it took us a long time to learn. . . .
>
> An' she said That was why he sometimes sent for little babies to go up to heaven before they grew up, an' that when he did so we mus' always remember it was only Jesus takin' them up in his arms an' carryin' them home to God.
>
> An' we said Yes. An' the room was very dark an' still an' there was a pain in the Paoli one's throat that she couldn' swallow.
>
> (p. 142)

At an early age Smith was very much aware of hardship and tragedy in the lives of others; her sensitive response to sadness is shown in several stories, such as when by chance the children come across Ou-pa Carel's coffin under a bed during a game of hide and seek. (It was of course the custom to have the coffin ordered and ready long before time in those days.)

Apart from the twelve sketches or short stories which make up *Platkops*, there are seven poems. These are written in ballad form and although not literary they are delightfully evocative of the Little Karoo. They could well be set to music. It is possible that not all the poems were written at the same time as the sketches, but whatever the case, they complement them charmingly. A few stanzas from **"Katisje's Patchwork Dress"** will illustrate (Katisje was their coloured nanny):

> When Sunday came and Old Katis',
> In patchwork dress and kapje,
> Stood on the stoep to show herself
> What ayah was more happy?
>
> Of many a print the dress was made
> (All sizes were the pieces),
> And starched so stiff she'd not sit down
> For fear of making creases.

> And so she'd stand, our old Katis',
> With make-pretence of myst'ry,
> And whisper low at our request
> Of every patch the hist'ry.
>
> "Dis from de Predikant's wife came,
> It was her dochter's baby's;
> And dis de Jedge's cook give me,
> It was de Jedge's lady's. . . .
>
> An' dis? Yo' Pa give me dis flag
> To show how I be loyal
> At Jooblee time—look, here's de Queen,
> An' all her Fam'ly Royal. . . ."
>
> And as she went we'd hear her croon
> "Oh bless de Lord? I'm happy
> In dis here petchwork dress of mine
> An' dis here white-starched kapje!"

In the poems as well as the stories of *Platkops* (which was of course Oudtshoorn) Smith has achieved an authentic picture of life in a small Karoo town at the turn of the century. The pages are redolent of the veld; such words as "mielie-lans," "quince hedges," "pig lilies," etc., fill one with nostalgia for the small dorp of one's childhood. This great love of the Little Karoo never left her throughout her long life, although she lived in England. She did, however, pay several return visits to South Africa and stayed with old friends in Oudtshoorn and the surrounding district and these visits provided her with material for her later work. (pp. 142-43)

> *Sheila Scholten, "'Platkops Children'—The Child-hood Sketches of Pauline Smith: A Commentary," in* Pauline Smith, *edited by Dorothy Driver, Mc-Graw-Hill Book Company, 1983, pp. 138-43.*

GEORGE DALE (essay date 1979)

> [*Dale is a South African critic. In the following excerpt, he examines structure, style, and symbolism in* The Beadle.]

The Beadle is close-knit and excellently shaped; its form and structure weld the story into a satisfying and living unity.

The opening chapter sets out the essentials of the environment and the people whom fate and circumstance have brought together, and it also indicates the cause of the conflict: that act of tremendous consequence which Johanna performs in a spirit of righteous indignation. In other words the chapter prepares the design and points the theme. As the tale progresses we become aware of certain elements which recur like a theme in a musical composition so that we are led on and yet recall what has gone before. The sacrament dress, symbol of the unremitting conflict between Johanna and Aalst Vlokman, is just such an element. It is the beginning and the end; a symbol of love, antagonism and tortured conscience; a constant reminder of Aalst Vlokman, of his past sin and present suffering; and finally it is the sign of his redemption and his release from his burden of guilt. That dress which initially aroused his fears and indignation finally draws him to peace and reconciliation.

Another instance of the use of patterning is the repeated taunt which the self-righteous and terrible Johanna utters like the pronouncement of some Old Testament prophet: "And who then is Aalst Vlokman that he should say to us what Klaartje's child should wear?" The cruel accusation of these words and the irony of the reference to Klaartje's child is like a leit-motif associated with Aalst Vlokman, sounding its most devastating note when he turns the phrase against the boundless forgiveness of Jacoba. "Keep your letter to yourself as Johanna kept hers. What is Klaartje's child to me?"

There is also a subtle echo of the phrase in Oom Hans's words: "And if I let none that have sinned travel in my wagon who then would travel in it, Andrintje?" It is through the phrase and its echoes that we see Christian love and charity in sharp contrast to the righteous indignation of Johanna and the tortured denial of guilt that falls from Aalst Vlokman's lips. Such echoes reinforce and bind the elements of the story.

The isolation of individuals from their fellows, and of the community from the wider world, is another recurring element, emphasized by the repeated references to the taciturn and secretive behaviour of the beadle, especially when his behaviour is set against the sociability of the Boers at those times when they do come together for the regular occasions of the church calendar. It is at these times that we are most conscious of the way the beadle has cut himself off from his fellows, and recall the comment in the first chapter—"there was no man who called him friend, no child who called him Oom." His isolation is most harshly underlined at the time of the Thanksgiving Service, when he responds to the greeting of Tan Betje who has "come to Harmonie for her last sacrament." But this brief conversation brings him no joy or comfort since he learns from Tan Betje that he has failed to bribe Jan Beyers into marrying Andrina. His desolation is total for he is sure that his fears for Andrina will be realised and that his God has abandoned him. So it is that he is driven to make his public confession and as an outcast leave the community to seek "the child of his sin who is now also an outcast," for he believes that "God who had refused all his sacrifices with his sin unconfessed would surely now, for the sake of His son, the Redeemer of the world, take pity on him and grant him this."

The events of Andrina's life and those associated with her, follow the cycle of the seasons and their rhythms. The nagmaal at which she is received into the church is in September, the spring of the year, and the growth of her love for Nind and the sadness which flows from it, are parallelled by the seasons. The birth of her child and her discovery of her real father come at the end of the winter like a sign, just as the birth of the Saviour was, that salvation and true happiness have come to Andrina and the father, who has at last found her.

As in so many of the best novels the conclusion seems inevitable and fitting. In *The Beadle* one has a sense of the working of a divine providence that shapes the destiny of Aalst Vlokman and Andrina, and those whose lives are interwoven with theirs. It is not blind chance but the design of a loving Creator that brings sinners to true repentance and redemption.

There is, then a clearly marked design to the book which gives the reader a satisfying feeling of organic development and completeness.

But the shaping of the book would not of itself give it life and artistic worth. For this we must have a perceptive and sympathetic picture of real people, and this Pauline Smith gives us. She recreates in vivid and telling terms the physical environment, the Aangenaam Valley "closed to the North by the Zwartkops Range, which, like a jagged bar of steel, cut Platkops off from the Great Karroo," and brings to life the people of this isolated community. She does this in language which subtly evokes the cadences and flavour of their speech; she wins our sympathy for and appreciation of the Boers of the Valley without resorting to special pleading or propaganda;

and most important of all she tells a tale as a moving as Hardy's *Tess* or Conrad's *Chance* and tells it with honest frankness.

And what of the growth of Andrina's love for Henry Nind, a love that is true and unselfish, artless and naive? Can one accept that a young girl could be as ignorant of the facts of reproduction as she was? In 1978 it is hard for anyone unfamiliar with the twenties to appreciate how cut off a farming community could be, how remote from city life, newspapers, and books, with no radio and only the horse-cart or ox-wagon for transport. Furthermore Andrina grew up in a household where there was no normal family life—no parents, no births, no brothers or sisters; a life without formal schooling and the infective curiosity of other children. She was a child of nature, responding shyly yet warmly to those around her, accepting quite humbly her role of helper to Mevrou and nursemaid to Jantje, all her actions unselfconsciously informed by her simple faith in the beneficence of God. The writer's account of Andrina's religious belief and her conception of God and the Saviour is all the more convincing for being couched in terms that so aptly reflect her thinking and her responses. (pp. 19-21)

Her humility and her expectation of some divine adventure are both her downfall and her shield, making her susceptible to the irresponsible approaches of Henry Nind, yet giving her the capacity to accept what befalls her. It is her tenderness and her simple faith in Nind's love that draws us to her and touches our sympathy. There is a nobility about the way she accepts Nind's going as right and inevitable, cruelly though she herself feels it. Her last words are both a farewell and a courageous concealment of the desolation in her heart: "If Mijnheer will but let me," she said, "I will now pack for him."

The love which has irradiated her being gives her the strength to withstand even the cruel uncharitableness of Mevrou Cornelius. There can be very few parallels to Mevrou's bitter taunt: "Is your child then the Son of God that his father cannot be named?" Rejected and denied her wish to return to the warmth of her Aunt Jacoba's love and the security of Harmonie, bewildered but still able to believe in the goodness of people, she goes in trust and hope to Oom Hans's wagon. In him she finds one as compassionate and understanding as Mevrou Cornelius is cruel and unchristian. How simply and movingly he responds to Andrina's expression of her own unworthiness. "And if I let none that have sinned travel in my wagon who then will travel in it, Andrintje? Our Father!"

The language which Pauline Smith employs catches the cadences and the idiom of the Afrikaans of these people, and does so in an unobtrusive way. She uses very few borrowings from Afrikaans, relying chiefly on word order and differences in usage. The conversation between Jantje and Andrina on their walk to the mill is a delightful example of this accurate reflection, not only of their speech but also of the artless chatter of Andrina's young charge and companion. (pp. 21-2)

Pauline Smith said of the speech and thought of men like Mijnheer van der Merwe: It was "the slow and brooding talk which fell so naturally in translation into the English of the Old Testament." She not only uses the English of the Old Testament where appropriate, but also brings in allusions to Biblical persons and events so that the story of these patriarchal people is given added colour by the parallels with the life of the people of the Old Testament. We smile at Jafta, the postcart driver whose bugle "was to him like a voice in the wilderness," and see Mijnheer van der Merwe all the more clearly because of the Biblical terms in which his faith is described. "[He] was conscious always of the presence of his God. His God was not, as he was for his wife Alida, a God of love drawing his people towards Him like little children. He was Jehovah—the God of justice and of righteousness: the God to whom vengeance belongeth: the God who, showing mercy unto thousands of them that keep his commandments, would in His own time, bring His chosen people into their full inheritance." (p. 22)

Another example of the authenticity of the dialogue and language is to be found in the account of Jan Beyers's visit to that indefatigable match-maker, Tan Linda. Not only is the idiom typical but her advice to Jan Beyers in his dilemma is shrewd and humorously expressed, exposing the weakness in her make-up and the acquisitive motive behind Jan Beyers's quest for a wife.

A particularly striking feature of the book is the sympathy with which she writes of these people without becoming sentimental or trying to build a special case for them. Her account of the origins of the Boers and of their way of life is nicely judged and as unemotively expressed as any I have come across. Again, though the novel has a South African setting, it ranks a high place in any company, for its theme is universally valid and the characterization convincing. An American reading the book might miss the full effect of the language and the setting, since he would have no local knowledge to supplement the art of the writer, but he would have no difficulty in appreciating the sensitivity of the writing and the moving tale Pauline Smith has to tell. The Calvinist faith of these people is quite comprehensible and not simply the expression of a belief peculiar to a small and isolated community. These people, preoccupied with sin and often more concerned about justice than mercy, cherish also a proper Christian concept of salvation for the repentant and of the grace which a truly Christian outlook brings. Aalst Vlokman's story would not touch one so deeply were it not for the sincerity of his convictions, and of his strong views on sin and the weaknesses of the flesh. While some may find his public confession melodramatic and improbable, I find it completely in character—the logical response of a tortured conscience which can find no other way to reconciliation with God and man. One may well see his journey to the tollhouse and his single-minded determination to accept in humility and love his duty and his right to care for his daughter, as a re-birth in the Christian sense. "Except ye be converted and become as little children, ye shall not enter the kingdom of heaven."

Pauline Smith uses symbolism to great effect, evoking images and thoughts which radiate in many directions, giving richness to what might at first seem straightforward and plain. In the opening chapter of Part II the description of Mevrou's garden is not only realistically evocative (as so many of the descriptions are) but also suggests much about its place in Jantje's world for whom it will always be an enchanted spot. Tan Linda's character is reflected in her determined collection of unnamed cuttings and her random planting with her long steel knife, which she uses in the garden, much in the way that she imposes her solutions on the affairs of others. We sense too that this wilderness full of strange and beautiful and unexpected things watered by the stream from the mill in a sense represents the lives of the Aangenaam people fed by the water of life.

The Beadle is a moral book in the best sense. The reader is required to evaluate the behaviour of the characters but not simply to classify them into sheep and goats. Some are obviously admirable and virtuous (Mevrou van der Merwe and

Jacoba for instance) or like Henry Nind selfish, shallow, and without principle, but what of Tan Linda whose besetting sin is to interfere and attempt to regulate the lives of others, or Johanna whose righteousness is both arrogant and vindictive? It is true that Pauline Smith passes judgment on her characters but she expresses her evaluation subtly and in a manner quite free from sententiousness. She exposes their faults and weaknesses and leaves us to judge them by their actions and their influence upon the lives of others. The tension of the narrative is maintained by the constant expectation of the consequences of the actions of the beadle, the Englishman, Andrina, Johanna and the others, and by our certainty that sin must be expiated and salvation earned; but a structural factor comes into play as well. Note how most chapters conclude with a short decisive statement which carries one forward and stimulates the curiosity. A perfect example is the final line of the first chapter, but there are many others. Particularly striking are the endings of the chapters in Part I.

The writer is adept at crystallising a scene or evoking an emotion in vivid but simple language. I am reminded of the suggestive power of the old ballads which stir the imagination by what is left unsaid. The concluding sentence of the book is a superb instance of such economy. Andrina's invitation to the beadle embraces the entire story, epitomising as it does the plot, reminding one of the course events have taken, and showing obliquely that the beadle has expiated his sins and found peace and fulfilment: the design is complete. The man whom no one called friend and whom no child caled Oom is now Oupa. His suffering and his burden of guilt are lifted from him by the birth of Andrina's child. "Come in then, Oupa," she said. "Come in, and see the little grandson that you have, with his round, bald head." (pp. 22-3, 28)

George Dale, "Art or Artifice? Some Thoughts on 'The Beadle'," in Crux, *Vol. 13, No. 1, February, 1979, pp. 19-23, 28.*

GUY BUTLER (essay date 1981)

[*Butler is a South African poet, dramatist, and critic. Concerning the background to his poetic works, he has written: "Much of my poetry—but by no means all—is generated by the European-African encounter as experienced by someone of European descent, who feels himself to belong to Africa. I am, I think, a product of the old, almost forgotten Eastern Cape Frontier tradition, with its strong liberal and missionary admixture." In the following essay, Butler, who grew up in the Karoo region, argues that too much emphasis has been placed on Smith's regionalism.*]

The title [*The Little Karoo*] invites us to see the work as regional: and regional it is in evocation of heat and space, of niggardly grey plains alternating with valleys in whose groins shine small homesteads, green fields and orchards, with an occasional water mill, or a focal white-washed church.

But since the mid-twenties that space has been defeated by the railway bus and the motor car, and the inner *lebensraum* of its people invaded by the vulgarities of chain stores, consumerism, Springbok Radio and S.A.T.V. By 1940 the class from which most of her characters are drawn—the Poor Whites—had all but ceased to exist in the countryside. A book such as Yvonne Burgess's *A Life to Live* (Johannesburg 1971) gives some idea of what their migration into the cities could entail, and makes the important observation that rural poverty is seldom as squalid as urban.

But it would be a mistake, having discovered an arcadian archetype behind these stories, to rest in it. Nowhere does our author invite us to think in idyllic terms. On the contrary, she creates with a striking insistence, beneath the lucidly sketched landscape of every story, the shimmer of a biblical desert that can blossom as the rose. How could it be otherwise? That is what her characters saw.

It was not any obsession with the Karoo landscape that impelled her to write: it was devotion to the people who inhabited it:

> I always felt that what had been written about them did not do them full justice, and I made up my mind to write about them as I had known them.

Again, after writing her masterpiece, **"The Pain,"**

> . . . A sense of failure oppressed me. Again it seemed to me that I failed to do justice to these people as I saw them—so fine in their simplicity, so courageous in their poverty. . . . [To] do justice to these people. Who were they?

She tells us that "the Dutch farmers among whom my father's work as a doctor lay, still lived in primitive simplicity close to God. Among these people we had many friends, and all their way of life, and their slow and brooding talk which fell so naturally into the English of the Old Testament, was full of interest to us."

It is true that there is a greater similarity between the English of the King James Version of the Old Testament and Afrikaans than there is between the English of the 19th century novel and Afrikaans; and there are indeed phrases and idioms in the sometimes quaint English of these stories which are self-conscious Afrikanerisms. To stop here, however, is to be satisfied with an explanation of certain incidentals of her style, not its essentials.

There is far more to the English of the Old Testament, or indeed any translation of the Old Testament, than this; and more attention should be given to the narrative style of that great book, which exerts such a formative force on the lives and speech of her characters, and on the entire style of *The Little Karoo*. What, for instance, distinguishes it from much of the meticulously accurate description in some South African writing of the social realist school?

I suspect it is her subtle integration of the temporal circumstances of her characters with their ultimate destiny. Whatever we may think, they think their souls are immortal; and their belief in an eternal background suffuses the foreground with a significance not found in merely graphic description. Her method of characterisation is by ontological predicament, rather than by class dynamics or psychological determinism.

Her stories have closer affinities with compact forms like the old ballad and drama than with the discursive novel. Her imagination seizes upon extreme situations in the approaches to death. Indeed, a bare outline of these stories might suggest that she had a morbid addiction to the more lurid and melodramatic happenings of the community. But, as in good tragedies and ballads, the violent incident is merely the generator of the agonies and triumphs of souls put to the final test by some terrible crisis.

Her preoccupation with the tragic had to be endured, no matter what the short term consequences for her writing. "I wrote with little hope of publication for we (Arnold Bennett & herself)

both believed that no editor . . . would accept stories so uniformly tragic as those of *The Little Karoo*—and I knew I could write no others until my mind was relieved of the burden of these."

She wrote them slowly, painfully, and, above all, with truth to a vision which was compassionate without being sentimental. The patience which her long illnesses had taught her entered into her art. She would refuse to force a story because her understanding of human experience forbade its reduction to sequences of interesting incidents fabricated to make moral or social points.

"I could not *make* situations to suit the needs of a story as a story—all I could do was to describe, often after long waiting, the slow development in the lives of my characters which lay outside my will."

Her prime consideration, then, was to do justice to her characters' experience; and those characters saw themselves as fallen creatures living under a God whose justice was harsh and whose mercy was mysterious. Her own determination to do justice to them is bound up with their own concern with justice; and her compassionate stance is related to the mercy which demands that we should forgive as we need be forgiven:

> "God forgive me, Niklaas, if I should judge you, for there is not one of us who has not sinned." . . . and then it was as if in pity and forgiveness God Himself had spoken. **"The Sinner."**

Character after character grows, and is pruned, or hacked, into that unique shape which bears the tragic fruit: ripeness is all.

Some do not, of course, bear such fruit—like Alie's son in **"Desolation"**—"a weak and obstinate man who saw in his God a power actively engaged in direct opposition to himself, and at each blow dealt to him by his God, he lifted up his voice and cried aloud in his injury." Or the tuberculotic Miller, who refuses the ancient benisons of contrition and humility offered by the Pastor:

> Is it by gifts alone that a man shall be judged? Surely not, my children . . . The sacrifices to God are a broken spirit: a broken and contrite heart He will not despise.

He dies dumbly fumbling a belated gesture of love towards his wife, in whose arms he is allowed to die. Similarly, the most sadistic and insane of these sufferers, whose obsession with God's injustice drives him to attempt the murder of his own son, dies in the arms of the young woman who has stopped him.

> The stricken man looked up at the son . . . who had thus, to the last, eluded him—but speech was beyond him. So, too, perhaps, was hatred. So too, perhaps, were bitterness and unjust suspicion . . . All that was known and could afterwards be told was that, with his last conscious movement, it was towards Dientje and away from his son that he turned—and under her compassionate gaze that he closed his eyes upon the world. **"The Father."**

It is no accident that Pauline Smith chose to end the volume with this cautious yet unequivocal suggestion of the redeeming power of compassion.

We return, then, to what many critics regard as the great achievement of this book: the creation of the landscape of an entire region. No one will question Pauline Smith's powers of description. It is the weight given to this aspect of her work which needs adjustment. As Ridley Beeton has observed, the book received its regional character almost by accident.

> Bennett realised, quite suddenly, that one of the defects of her work was that it had, in the assumption of its truthfulness, concerned itself too little with conveying a sense of locality to those who did not know the Karoo. He advised her to try to produce not a greater authenticity (for this was always there), but the better communication of a setting. Her short story, **"The Pain,"** one of her undoubted masterpieces, was the result. . . .

It would be interesting to know what, if any, any additions of detail she made to the settings of the already written stories once *The Adelphi*'s acceptance of **"The Pain"** had broken the publisher's ice.

On one thing one may be sure: no addition would have been made which falsified that "landscape of the mind" which her characters inhabited: Karoo in the foreground, biblical in its symbolical depths; a landscape so simplified and intensified that the profound moral mathematics of their beings, and of ours, becomes ruthlessly, mercifully, clearer. (pp. vii-xi)

> *Guy Butler, in a foreword to* The Little Karoo *by Pauline Smith, revised edition, A. A Balkema, 1981, pp. vii-xi.*

MICHAEL GARDINER (essay date 1983)

[*In the following excerpt, Gardiner discusses* The Beadle *as an illustration of his contention that Smith's artistry is more subtle and complex than critics have generally assumed.*]

Two decades of published criticism on Pauline Smith's fiction have done little more than reinforce the view that her work is and will remain an unobtrusive monument in South African prose without sufficient intrinsic interest to merit full critical attention. Many of the articles commenting on her work after the publication of the only book-length study have been occasional; and her work is perceived as so irrevocably minor in quality that even in those articles prompted by a disinterested desire to share insights which the writing itself has generated, there is a critical holding back, a general lightness of touch. Critical discussion of Pauline Smith's fiction has accepted and emphasised consistently the consolatory, pietistic and resigned elements in the writing because critics have regarded Pauline Smith as more of a medium, a transmitter of the restricted lives of an Afrikaner community than as a deliberate artist: as a passive rather than an active intelligence. (p. 1)

It is important to insist that the experience of reading Pauline Smith's writing as fiction points decidedly away from the adequacy of regarding her method as fundamentally descriptive. Critical assumptions about Pauline Smith's relationship as author to her characters, their community and its circumstances govern what commentators are prepared to admit can take place in her prose. I would like to draw an example from *The Beadle*.

In their chapter on this novel, the authors of *Perspectives on South African Fiction* make this observation:

> The good angel of Harmonie is Mevrouw, who is characterised by her unfailing devotion to the command "my little children, love one another." . . . By an internal logic, Mevrouw's goodness is complemented by that of the pastor. . . . The loving faith of Mevrouw converges with that of the pastor at the great dramatic climax where Aalst Vlokman makes his confession [see Christie entry in Additional Bibliography].

The entire passage (of which I have quoted only three sentences) is a representative example of the orthodox critical attitude which is inimical to Pauline Smith's art.

The most obvious limitation of this account of the "loving faith" of Mevrouw and the pastor is to be seen in the repeated word "good" which not only suggests an uncritically bland view of the situation but implies that the authors are oblivious of the treatment which that word receives in the text of the novel:

> The talk drifted to those who had already arrived for the coming Sacrament and camped out in the church-land. Old Tan' Betje Ferreira was mentioned. Many, many months, the pastor explained to the Englishman, had Tan' Betje lain helpless on her bed, and now, in answer to prayer, her pain had been so much eased that it had been possible for her son Hans to bring her to Harmonie for the Sacrament on a swinging bed-frame in a borrowed wagon. Hans was a good son and in young Betje he had a good daughter as old Betje had a good grandchild. Poor they were, as so many Aangenaam people were, but rich in their affection for one another. Young Betje would make a good wife, and he, the pastor, hoped there was truth in the report that Jan Beyers wished to marry her. Jan Beyers was an upright and well-doing young man, and Betje, for her kindness to her grandmother, deserved a good husband. "But others also deserve good husbands," cried Tan' Linda, smiling archly across the table to Andrina. "Others also!" . . .

The comfortably undiscriminating and complacent level of conversation invites a near-satirical response to the pastor. The account of his near-sighted view of the members of his flock, while he dines with the "aristocracy" of Harmonie, stops short of satire because the pastor is speaking in a language unusual to him. Even so, he manages to be condescending both about the poor and to the Englishman. We have here in miniature, as well, an example of how self-justifying myths about a people are propagated. It is important to remember at this point that the "upright and well-doing young man" Jan Beyers has had difficulty in choosing between Toontje with her three sheep, and Betje who has a sewing machine. It is the pastor's failure to perceive the role of necessity in the lives of people that also highlights the level of personal convenience in his attitudes.

Curiously enough, on a different occasion, Geoffrey Hutchings, when commenting on the related attitudes of the pastor and the beadle towards Andrina, says the following:

> What is most significant about the contrasting reactions of the two men is that they are based, not upon knowledge of Andrina, but upon their

own characters and experience: the pastor's simple piety, the beadle's guilt.

Here lies a neglected clue to discovering Pauline Smith's authorial stance towards her fictional characters, characters whose qualities cause critics to suspend normally alert judgement and thereby to fall into an orthodoxy of attitude which fails to see what is so clearly suggested. Mevrouw's attitude to members of the Harmonie community as "little children," with the best will in the world, cannot cope adequately with the full range of human experience. Mevrouw's reaction to the letter from her son Cornelius, in which he gives a self-justifying account of his wife's expulsion of the pregnant Andrina, is critically placed by its own evident limitations:

> All this did Mevrouw read sitting quietly in the window with tears trickling down her cheeks. Sorrow for her was not anguish, and sin brought her no horror. In both sin and sorrow she saw but the passing ills of those little children whose duty it was to love one another, and who, in sin or in sorrow, were safe in the keeping of a compassionate Father. Sin would pass, sorrow would pass, but the compassion which had sent the Redeemer into the world to forgive and to heal—this would never pass.
>
> So were her thoughts moving slowly to the slow, unnoticed tears of her serene and gentle old age when Classina October burst into the room.
>
> "Mevrouw, Mevrouw!" she cried. "Down by the Steenkamp house they cry that Juffrouw Jacoba lies dead."

Particular care should be taken not to grant uncritical credence to views which happen to be religious. Terence Edgecombe's remarks are useful here:

> The authoress's total grasp of her subject . . . allows the reader to participate completely in a dimension of experience normally very difficult of imaginative access. This is because her interest in the religious life of her characters is not doctrinal but directed towards an illumination of the human aspirations of which it is an expression and the human hungers which it satisfies.

Mevrouw's religious attitudes are consonant with her position as the dominant woman in the Harmonie society, her selfish attitude towards Andrina (a view which Jean Marquard corroborates) and are among the factors which make the Harmonie society a closed one. The connexion between Mevrouw and the grandmother in **"The Schoolmaster"** is evident in a number of ways.

The basis for much inappropriate and inaccurate opinion about Pauline Smith and her writing is not to be found in the apparently small range of her fictional interests nor in what might be seen as the restricted aspirations and circumstances of her characters. Current opinion has been shaped, I believe, by the assumptions that have been made consistently by critics about her religious convictions, her ethical concerns and, most particularly, about the relationship between characters and author. Evidence from Pauline Smith's fiction points strongly to her acute awareness of the relative nature of human beliefs, convictions and commitments. The skill with which she represents

and understands the values and aspirations of her characters within their communities should not be mistaken for her vision as a writer of fiction. The following account of the history of the people from whom the Harmonie community derives will serve to make the point:

> In that strange new land of their adoption it was to the Bible that they turned for help, guidance and comfort in all the crises of a life which, in its simplicity and in the physical conditions of the country in which it was led, closely resembled that of the Patriarchs of the Old Testament. . . . Together they were, like Israel of old, a people chosen of God for the redeeming of this portion of the earth. . . .

Why assume that a passage like this (and the whole reinforces the point) carries full authorial approval when its rhythms are so evidently those of the religious and political spokesman, and when the context makes it plain that this sense of nationhood is both a simplification and a self-perception in which discomforting historical events (like the freeing of the slaves) are labelled as "injustices" to themselves and mere confirmation of the conveniently self-generated myth?

> The freeing of the slaves by the English was for him, and remains for many of his descendants, an incomprehensible act of injustice towards himself and of indifference to the warnings of the prophets. And with each succeeding act of injustice towards himself the Dutchman has been driven to a deeper, fiercer belief in his race as a persecuted but chosen people whose pilgrimage is not yet over. . . .

John Coetzee's remark [see Additional Bibliography] that "the historical consequences of this myth . . . have been serious" is obvious enough. But to imply that Pauline Smith actively collaborates in the perpetuation of that myth is to blame her for the critical misinterpretations of her fiction and to deny the validity of her novel. Is it just and valid to ignore the ferocious egotism suggested in that account of racial history?—we should notice the repeated "him." Does Pauline Smith share that belief in "the warnings of the prophets?" I don't believe that she does: instead, it is this element in Pauline Smith which links her to Herman Charles Bosman. How can the reader of **The Beadle** reconcile the steady analyses in the novel of customary, communal, emotional, circumstantial and religious oppression and its effects with the critical assertion that Pauline Smith propagates such myths?

A more transparent example of Pauline Smith's flexibility of authorial stance is reflected in Andrina's notion of God:

> Andrina's God was a serene and beneficent being who bore a perfectly natural resemblance to Mevrouw van der Merwe. . . .

Only the most literal-minded of readers will refuse to see the irony and wry humour beneath the startling directness of Andrina's innocent complacency. We ordinarily expect, and comment quite easily upon, the subtleties of the relationship between author and fiction in the writing of American and English authors. The refusal of critics to perceive irony and humour in Pauline Smith's fiction suggests that they regard her writing as dealing only in reverential solemnity.

One reason for the limitations imposed by critics upon the fiction is a preoccupation with the author as a reflector and not as an artist. The writing is not read as fiction but as many other things, such as the revelation of the humanity of an Afrikaner community, as the exemplification of the author's personal values, as Pauline Smith's wish to "assert certain myths about the Afrikaner." These attitudes towards the author are accompanied by a general agreement among critical commentators about her "objectivity" and her detachment, coupled with the belief that Pauline Smith never judges her characters. The consequence of these attitudes has been the acceptance of the fiction's concerns at a comfortable face-value with the inevitable inability to link insights of detail (many of which are very perceptive and suggestive) into anything like a coherent point of view. As Lukács has pointed out, "the premature closing of the circle" causes the "form to disintegrate into disparate, heterogeneous parts."

By positing both authorial objectivity and immediacy, criticism has made decisions about the writing which inhibits its full fictional impact. Criticism has sought to account for qualities sensed in the writing by linking details, events and episodes to Pauline Smith's biographical data and journal entries. Comparisons with other writers have been mildly attempted; schemes of relationships, diagrams and image-chasing have represented sporadic attempts to account for what can be only adequately perceived within the fiction once critics are prepared to recognise that in this case, as in others, the artistic intentions that underpin the fiction determine the ethical and compositional structure of the whole.

If one looks at the precise points at which references are made in *The Beadle* to coffee (to take an example of significant detail), most occur, expectedly, as part of hospitality in the tradition which the Harmonie homestead exemplifies. However, coffee is sold at a "coffee-house" in Platkops dorp, three days and nights inland, to which Klaartje, Andrina's mother, fled when she made the break from the Harmonie community. Klaartje embodied a spirit which sought expression other than that possible in the Aangenaam valley: her spirit represents a challenge to the attempts by the community leaders (like the Van der Merwe family) to prevent change by retarding the effects of time and history. The coffee-house in Platkops dorp is part of a movement from an enclosed rural community to an urban society with very different social relationships. That movement suggests a development from the closed, circular view of landscape and of time (in which the recurrent gives the impression of the eternal), towards a linear conception of time and history, which ends in this novel with the birth of Andrina's son in the toll-house on the Cortes-Losberg road. Immediately afterwards, the nucleus of a community is established when the bond between father and daughter is acknowledged, irrevocably outside the circle of the Harmonie community.

The suggested shifts in societal development and the tensions between individuals and the community are elements which contribute to a controlling and signifying context for the attitudes and beliefs of Andrina, as without it they would be merely idiosyncratic. Initially, Andrina seems entirely part of the Harmonie community, but as the novel develops she expresses in her private experiences of love and religion values that the community endorses in the abstract but which it denies in practice. Andrina represents an affirmation of the ideals of her community—in her selfless desire to serve, her incarnation of the godhead, her trust in life and in her sense of the miraculous immanent in the everyday—but she transgresses its laws in her expression of religion and love.

As assistant-cum-servant to Mevrouw van der Merwe, and not "one of the family," as Mevrouw conveniently rationalises her use of Andrina because of the distinctions between bywoner and farm owner, Andrina is seen at work in kitchen, pantry and dining room, frequently dispensing coffee. The intimacy associated with this beverage in early-morning bedrooms and with the family around the dining-room table eventually develops to the point where the serving of coffee to the Englishman is a prelude to Andrina's making love with him and suggests most powerfully the fusion of the erotic and spiritual in Andrina's natural experience:

> Up at the homestead, Andrina, left alone in the yard, went slowly back into the house to make fresh coffee for the Englishman. She was troubled and happy, happy and troubled. The native servants had gone to their huts, as was their custom, and silence hung about the quiet, half-darkened rooms like a drapery. She went into the larder to get the little red cakes which the Englishman loved. They were kept in a deep, brown canister which she had to unlock. She spent some time in choosing the lightest, the crispest of these. To do so gave her a strange, almost physical pleasure. It gave her the same pleasure to wash again the spotless cup and saucer which he would use for his coffee. He would never know with what care she had chosen his cakes, with what care she had polished his cup and saucer, yet this service brought her so exquisite a joy that her heart cried out in thankfulness to heaven for it. There was so little she could do for her dear love, and not anything that she would not do! Alone in that quiet, darkened house her heart cried out for service to him as it had never cried before, her body trembled at the thought of his caresses, her soul sang its innocent magnificat of humility and desire. . . .

Of course it is not coffee nor the serving of coffee which indicates a major cultural shift in the historical evolution of a people, or which can express adequately Andrina's erotic spirituality. Although the tracing of references to the deliberately repeated motif can lead to a perception of Pauline Smith's technique of exploring an aspect of the domestic fabric of a community to depict the social and personal significance of the habitual and traditional, that significance is only discernible in the full context of the novel provided that the underlying forces at work in the novel are acknowledged.

Despite her intimate association with it, Andrina is as tenuously connected to the Harmonie community as her father, Aalst Vlokman is. Having violated its laws, he attempts vainly to gain re-admission. The inability to acknowledge his fatherhood of Andrina cannot be seen in this context merely as his refusal to admit the truth to that community. The religious and social laws which govern the community in practice make no provision for such truth. Vlokman's bitterness, loneliness and grotesque anxieties are as much part of his own incapacity to admit a dimension of life that is within him as they are manifestations of the ethos of that community. His eventual confession to the congregation quite logically leads to his leaving that community altogether.

This partial reading of *The Beadle* points, I suggest, to Pauline Smith's intentions in this novel. For the purposes of my argument it is not agreement with this reading that I seek as much as a willingness to recognise that Pauline Smith's fiction gives rise to, and is capable of sustaining, critical discussion of this kind. (pp. 4-10)

> *Michael Gardiner, "Critical Responses and the Fiction of Pauline Smith," in* Theoria, *Pietermaritzburg, Vol. LX, May, 1983, pp. 1-12.*

DOROTHY DRIVER   (essay date 1984)

[*In the following excerpt, Driver defines thematic concerns in Smith's fiction as they relate to personal concerns expressed in her journal about the various forms of oppression and inequalities she observed in South Africa.*]

Smith remains relatively unknown in the English-speaking world beyond that of her birth. To repair something of this gap I should like now to explore her social concerns, first in a general sense, as they relate to class, exploitation, and imperialism and then in a specifically feminist sense, in an attempt both to rescue Smith from the easy cliches and benevolent patronization that have skewed some of the local critical judgements of her, as well as to present her as a writer worthy of even closer scrutiny than this necessarily introductory analysis can give. Other women writers in southern Africa have had far more attention—one thinks of Olive Schreiner, Nadine Gordimer, Doris Lessing, and, to a lesser degree, Sarah Gertrude Millin—perhaps because they deal with black-white relations to a greater extent and their social concerns are more explicitly expressed. Yet Smith is not merely to be dismissed as a local colorist, a sensitive regional voice, or a depicter of pastoral types; apart from the seriousness of her other social concerns, she makes a profound effort to deal with women and female sexuality that has not yet been aired in critical debate.

From Smith's nonfiction writings, her social concerns are apparent. In her memoir of Bennett she wrote of his *Imperial Palace,* which is set in a luxury hotel and packed with trivial detail about its fittings and furnishings, "Here was a world which I had no desire to share and of whose worth and importance . . . I remained still sociologically and artistically doubtful." . . . For her fictional world she turned elsewhere: "in my own work my most deeply-felt interest lay with the poor and the narrowing circumstances of their lives." . . . Her 1913-1914 journal, written twenty years earlier [during a holiday in South Africa], shows her to be antiimperialist, anticapitalist, and, in a gentler way, anticlerical, anti-Calvinist and even in a sense at odds with Christianity: a worldly woman with a tolerant attitude and a sense of humor that does not conform to the public self she presented, which seems to have left friends and critics with an image of overriding timidity and diffidence. (pp. 47-8)

Her sympathies were consistently with the working class. She was appalled at the attitudes of the colonists to the 1914 railway strikers (8 January 1914):

> I was told again and again how well paid they are. Free coal, free schools, cheap groceries, etc. The fact that they were fighting against what to them seemed unjust retrenchment was a fact to the middle classes of no importance whatever. . . . The *Cape Times* so hopelessly prejudiced, no possibility of getting at the truth from that at all. . . . The patriotism—red cross nurses, girl and boy scouts,—all a bit sickening when it was justice one wanted to get hold of.

The attitudes of the white farmers to their black workers often dismayed her, and she remarked on "the old trouble about labour, the old meanness about wages. All Dutchmen, and many English colonials as well, would, I think, go back to slaves with relish" (22 January 1914). One comment, though it shows a blinkered view of the land problem that existed at the time, reveals at least some awareness of the rights of the indigenous people of South Africa (23 April 1914): "Here [the land] was not owned, that is farmed and possessed, till the colonists came, though even the colonists stole what grazing rights existed from the tribes who owned cattle."

Her journal was kept specifically for the purposes of what Smith called "copy" (1 March 1914). The trip gave her back her childhood world, the Little Karoo, just south of Olive Schreiner's Great Karoo and marginally less vast and barren, in the days before it became rich through the fashion in ostrich feathers. Apart from the indigenous people (with whom Smith is not directly concerned in her fiction), it was populated by small Afrikaans farming communities, patriarchal and Calvinist, who viewed with suspicion the outside world, and particularly the world of British rule from which they had trekked some seventy-five years before, and by which some of them had recently been imprisoned during the Anglo-Boer War (1899-1902). With the exception of **"Desolation,"** which is set in the "grey and desolate region" of the Great Karoo, the stories in *The Little Karoo* are set in one or another farming community in this area, with occasional excursions to the town of Platkops (Oudtshoorn). Whereas in *The Beadle* the predominant sense of security provided by what are virtually feudal relations offsets the harshness of the countryside, the atmosphere of the short stories is pervaded by poverty and deprivation; the set of master-servant relations, which form a backdrop to most of the stories, introduces the theme of oppression in its most basic manifestation. In **"Desolation,"** to cite just one instance, a farmer "made harsher by a drought which had brought him closer to ruin" throws off his farm the old mother of his hired hand and her grandson, thereby depriving them of their home and sole means of livelihood in an economically depressed time and place. While the short stories focus on the relations between white farmer and white *bywoner*, the landless tenant laborer or sharecropper, the novel casts its net over a wider variety of master-servant relations, dealing also with the relations between the English and the Afrikaans, as colonizer and colonized, and, to take the implications of the concept even further, the relation of fictional character to God. Moreover, both generic forms explore the relations between men and women, which are closely bound to or dependent on the other sets of relations. While in neither are black-white relations more than briefly dealt with, they are given an allusive force in *The Beadle,* acting as a reminder of the potentialities of inequality and oppression, much as Christian-Jew relations are used in both *The Beadle* and **"The Miller."** (pp. 49-50)

Smith's fiction generally concerns itself with the establishment or reinforcement of community and familial bonds, a theme reinforced by the use of folktale motifs—the movement in and out of the community for regenerative purposes and the deployment of "a stranger to the district" (*Little Karoo* . . .) for instance. The especial horror of what may well be her best story **"Desolation"** is that the institutionalized care of Alie's grandson strips Alie of her last familial bond. (p. 52)

That the social order is founded upon deprivation and suffering the author periodically reminds us: the homestead with its enormous shuttered windows, its wide stone hearth, its brass-bound chests, its furniture of stinkwood or teak was "achieved so many years ago for the van der Merwe family by the labour of slaves" (**Beadle** . . .); the bell of the church land "had once been the slave-bell." . . . The social atmosphere is tinged with the memories of personal and national suffering that give to the beadle "a strange bitterness of spirit which drove men from him" . . . and to the Afrikaner as a group a nationalist intensity that feeds on resentment towards the English and "bitter contempt" towards the "heathen" from whom he had taken the land. . . . The religious atmosphere is warped by a Calvinist obscssion with the Jchovah of vengeance and righteousness that keeps alive, for the Russian-Jewish refugee, the threat of persecution. *The Beadle* is very much concerned with suffering at the hands of Christians—"one of those inspirations to cruelty which in some natures are the strange and bitter fruit of righteousness." . . . (p. 52)

Although Smith's identification of what she takes to be an "inspiration to cruelty" provides a major impetus to her corrective social vision, it is important to understand the precise nature of her attitude towards the Afrikaners as a group, as a cultural force: her precarious sympathy both for them and for the patriarchal system softens the corrective tones. The clearest way in which one can see this sympathy is in the comparisons she makes, both in her fiction and her journal, between the Afrikaner and the English, against whom the Afrikaner felt so many grudges. (pp. 52-3)

[In *The Beadle*, the Englishman's] seduction of Andrina is put in terms to take it a metaphor for the essentially irresponsible treatment of the colony by the British: he justifies it by reflecting that he "had taken nothing from Andrina which she had not been willing to give. He had given her nothing which she had not been eager to have" . . . and is nagged only by a feeling "which wavered curiously between a tender regret for the child whom he must hurt and something which came perilously near to the resentment felt by the oppressor towards the oppressed." . . . That the Afrikaner felt persecuted by the English is made quite clear in *The Beadle*: it was the Afrikaner who was the "rightful owner of a country which he, and not the Englishman, had taken from the heathen" . . . ; it was the Afrikaner who suffered from the abolition of slavery by the English, an act which "was for him, and remains for many of his descendents, an incomprehensible act of injustice." . . . These reasons are not without a sharp ironic edge; nevertheless, it is clear where Smith's sympathies lay: she abhorred what she called on one occasion the "cocky and pleased" attitude of some visiting English and even referred to herself as "a 'pro-Boer' at heart" (Journal, 18 November 1913).

Certainly what Smith responded to very warmly in the Little Karoo that she drew on was the relation of the Dutch Reformed Church church to the people. (pp. 53-4)

Indeed, it is in Smith's attitude to the conversion to Christianity of the indigenous population—there is no reference to black churchgoers—that is manifest the precarious sympathy of her authorial attitude towards the Afrikaner. In *The Beadle* she presents an incident that was initially recounted in her journal and has to do with the blatant humiliations suffered by the indentured black children at a farm she stayed at (29 November 1913):

> Alie, now sitting at the head of the table, and
> quite regardless of their feelings, ordering Betje

to sing, and *cry,* for our pleasure, and listening to the prayers of Easach and Yacob who stumped in with crossed hands and closed eyes to perform the evening devotion in public!

But the tale is given in *The Beadle* in rather more idyllic terms . . . :

> The chapter was read. The psalm was sung. Jantje, slipping from his chair, walked up to his grandfather's knee and repeated his evening prayer. From the doorway came the indentured children and they too, at their master's knee, repeated a prayer, "Make me to be obedient to my mistress, oh Lord," prayed Spaasie in her rough, hoarse voice. "Make me to run quickly when my master calls," prayed Klaas.

The attitude in the journal is overtly disapproving, while in the novel there seems simply to be a covert qualification to the atmosphere of harmonious patriarchy. In a novel that deals with such a variety of master-servant relationships, particularly with the beadle's self-righteous and self-destructive service to God, and Andrina's combination of domestic service, sacramental service, and connubial service, the prayers for obedience certainly provide a subtle ironic counterpoint. Smith is, after all, in various other ways that will emerge later, treating the nature of the patriarchal community as problematic. One can perhaps account for her occasional sentimentalization of the Afrikaner—for example, in **"The Pain,"** with its emphasis on the "simple hearts" of Juriaan and Deltje van Royen—by noting her effort to translate one culture for another, to redress the contemporary view of the Afrikaner, a people who, according to a confidante of hers, the "trivial novelists, busy with externals, very often misunderstand and traduce . . . , a lapse which has far-reaching Imperial consequences." Indeed, Smith was, much later, to write in a letter to her publisher that "in the present bitterness of racial and political differences any link of sympathy & understanding between Dutch and English is of value" (21 November 1948).

If the benevolent eye that Smith casts on the rural Afrikaner becomes more benevolent when the Afrikaner is seen in relation to the English oppressor, it becomes less benevolent when the Afrikaner is examined in isolation. There is even the possibility that Smith had an Afrikaans audience in mind as well as an English one, that she was referring to inequalities *within* the Afrikaner community (landowner, poor white, Christian, Jew) because she felt that that was the simplest way to reveal to the Afrikaner other inequalities, at least as serious but, at the same time, less open to his sympathy. An entry in her journal reads: "I cannot imagine the Dutch fighting to raise the standing of their own poor whites, I *can* imagine them fighting to reintroduce slavery" (25 April 1914). Her authorial stance is such that she clearly and continually creates situations in which the excesses of patriarchy and Calvinism show up the weaknesses of the system. The solution that she suggests is one offered by women.

Smith may well have had much the same aloofness from the hurly, burly of feminist politics as had Virginia Woolf (they were, incidentally, born in the same year); what she does reveal very clearly in her journal is distaste for the self-importance and preciousness of some of the upper-class suffragettes (9 March 1914):

> They did a deal of congratulating one another on the marvellous marvellous uplifting among

women. The *pride* in the sex and I don't know what more, and the harping back in gentle dignity to pre-natal conditions . . . , a sort of "not nice" subject to be approached only by a woman of her dignity and superiority. Oh dear me I *did* enjoy myself and was awful sorry to leave for no one noticed me in the least.

Yet, from a conversation that she reports in which a new acquaintance asks her if she is a suffragette, it seems that she regards herself as at least a passive supporter (19 August 1913):

I said I was not political at all. "Oh well, it is wicked, wicked for women to be suffragettes. I don't know how any thinking woman can *be* a suffragette. The Bible is so clearly against it. And the harm they do!!" P. "Oh, well, it's the wild unthinking ones who do the harm." Miss B. "But they're *all* unthinking and all wicked. No thinking woman *can* be a suffragette. The Bible says it's wrong." So I got off the subject.

While Smith was by no means the polemicist that Woolf was, there is no doubt that her fiction is very much concerned with the status and role of women in a traditional community, and was seen as such at the time by at least one reviewer, who noted: "The women in Pauline Smith's chapters are often slaves of the farm; unpaid, unthanked day labourers, whose children are yoked with them by an autocratic father's will" (*British Weekly,* 14 January 1932). In an introductory essay, it is simply not possible to do full justice to Smith as a woman writing about the experience of women. One hopes, of course, that feminist critics will begin to take note of her work; what is being offered here are simply some signals of her stature, not only as a woman writer who can be seen in terms of so many of the stereotypes of her time, both biographically and creatively, but also as a woman writer who attended to some of the literary questions posed by the female literary tradition. (pp. 54-7)

Broadly speaking, Smith's writing style combines the Austen-Eliot lines in a manifestation of a quietly ironic I that qualifies the acquiescent accent, combined with a robust sense of comedy and social life. In at least two respects she makes a significant contribution to the literature of the female tradition: in her imagery of sexual awakening and in her evaluation of female sensibility.

Like so many women writers before her, Smith employs an imagery of enclosure and entrapment—the pantry in *The Beadle,* the walled garden, the "little black box" of **"Anna's Marriage"**—and even presents what Ellen Moers, in a piece of fascinating critical speculation on the use of metaphor and imagery in women's literature, has identified as a "female landscape," a topography of the female genital parts. (pp. 57-8)

While there is not a great amount of sensory detail in Smith's work, she is clearly alert to sensory stimuli. Like the beadle, she responds, though more warmly, to "All this small world—the sights, the sounds, the very smell of it." . . . If her presentation of sensuality is not much more than an indication that the repressions of the Victorian era were coming to an end, she is markedly more direct in her presentation of women's emotions regarding sex and women's sensuality than other women writers of the time generally were. Indeed, she takes authorial delight in physical contact between women as well as between men and women. In **"The Sisters"** the narrator says of her

sister Marta: "And she drew me down on to the pillow beside her, and took me into her arms, and I cried there until far into the night." . . . (p. 58)

In her presentation of women Smith also makes an interesting statement though she may not, strictly speaking, be breaking new ground in this respect any more than she is in her use of sensory and sexual imagery. In virtually all her fiction she adopts the stereotypical image of the woman as angel or redeemer. The traditional means through which redemption is achieved is love; Smith defines that love by means of the notion of service, which she presents in cautionary tones. Traditionally, the object of redemption is a male character; Smith . . . incorporates the community. (p. 60)

In her presentation of women Smith, though by no means openly rebellious, is part of the "revisionary and revolutionary" trend revealed even by women writers whom "we usually think of as models of angelic resignation" [Sandra M. Gilbert and Susan Gubar, *The Madwoman in the Attic*], Ann Brontë, for instance. While her women characters, too, seem resigned simply to accepting their fate with as much grace as they can muster, they in fact have, psychologically, an active role in the community. The men, on the other hand, as incapable as the women of improving their socioeconomic status as "poor whites," become bitter and cruel, an interesting subversion of the traditional differentiation in literature between active men and inactive women. While Smith employs traditional literary stereotypes—the angel-redeemer, the lady bountiful, the matchmaking postmistress, the flirt with "a tongue like a running sluice" (**"The Sinner"** . . .), to name the most obvious—these are to varying degrees treated problematically. Moreover, Smith's sensitivity to the social situation of women comes through not only in her depiction of women as servants (**"The Father"**) or as financially at the mercy of their husbands (**"The Sisters"**) but also in her conflation of self-expression and the expression of love. For women, creativity becomes the creation of love. They must seize what self-expression they can: Niccoline Joanna in **"The Pastor's Daughter"** must transform her unused wedding dress into a dress for the child of the man she should have married, but couldn't; Engela in **"The Schoolmaster"** can caress Jan Boetje and speak her words of love to him only when he is dead (a situation that takes one into the tradition of Jane Eyre and her crippled, blinded Rochester).

In a world in which "life, for most, was the bearing of unbearable things" (*Beadle* . . .), it is the women who consistently manage to create whatever kind of love is possible. In the words of Engela's Grandmother Delport, "love comes at the last to be but what one makes it" . . .—or, as Cherry Wilhelm amends, "God, like love, is what you make of Him." . . . Smith's female characters are the active bearers of love and tenderness, pity, and forgiveness; expressing love, they express God. They are, in fact, like God. (pp. 63-4)

Dorothy Driver, "Pauline Smith: 'A Gentler Music of Her Own'," in Research in African Literatures, *Vol. 15, No. 1, Spring, 1984, pp. 45-71.*

SHEILA ROBERTS (essay date 1984)

[*An educator, fiction writer, and critic, Roberts was born in South Africa, but emigrated to the United States in 1977. Concerning her work, she has stated: "The political situation in South Africa has strongly influenced my writing, as well as the experience of the 'underdogs'—blacks, women, children, failures." In the fol-*

lowing excerpt, Roberts expresses reservations about The Beadle
as a realistic portrayal of Afrikaner culture.]

For me, and arguably for other modern South African readers, there are a number of obstacles to entering and remaining comfortably within the world of *The Beadle*. One is Pauline Smith's rendering of a conceivably imagined Afrikaans into English; the second is the way her works contribute towards upholding certain myths about the Afrikaner—myths that have had and are still having important political implications; and the third is the temperamental narrowness of her characters, their tendency towards single, consuming obsessions.

Clearly Pauline Smith's choice to render Afrikaans into English was not made for the superficial purpose of displaying local manners and setting but, being closely linked to her writing intentions, was consistent with the essence of her vision of the Afrikaner. In other words, language and style form an integral part of structure, a structure formed on a simple but major repetition and supporting the minor repetitions or cycles of a hard pastoral and religious life in an isolated and immutable landscape. The implied author, the anonymous narrating observer, is part of this life. Events related by the narrator alone, that is, events not conveyed in the free indirect speech or dialogue of the characters, are frequently couched in the manner of the Little Karoo speech, and most images and details are confined to this very world. For some readers today, even while they must acknowledge the tightness of Pauline Smith's craftsmanship, the rhythmic yet cumbrous style can prove unremittingly intrusive. I know it did for me. For example, the following conversation takes place between Jan Beyers, a young man in search of a wife, and Tan' Linda, who has agreed to write his love letters for him:

> "Surely I will write for you, Jan Beyers," cried Tan' Linda, her eyes alight with interest, "but you yourself must first say to me if it is Betje Ferreira or Toontje van Niekerk that you would marry."
>
> "Juffrouw, I cannot say," confessed the young man miserably. "See how it is with me! When I call by Toontje's house, then I think it is Betje. But as soon as I go by Betje's house, then I think it is Toontje."
>
> "Jan Beyers," said Tan' Linda wisely, "for a man to marry one woman and think all his days of another is sorrow and madness. And you cannot now have two wives. Neither Betje Ferreira nor Toontje van Niekerk should you marry if that is how it is with you."
>
> "But, Juffrouw, think now! If I marry Toontje, three sheep will she bring to my kraal, and if I marry Betje, there will be in our house the sewing-machine. . . ."

Each person in the Harmonie village in the Aangenaam valley exists and functions in a clearly defined position in an unchallenged social hierarchy. Mijnheer van der Merwe, the builder of the church at Harmonie, is the richest man in the district and its leader. Under him the small farmers, the *bijwoners*, and the hired hands (all white) take their assigned places. Mijnheer van der Merwe, and not the pastor, has the power to reward Aalst Vlokman for services rendered by appointing him beadle of the church. Alida van der Merwe, his wife, can call at will for help in her kitchen from the Steenkamp women, the

postmistress, Tan' Linda and any of the other wives beneath her in status.

Within the unchanging arrangement of personal place in the Aangenaam valley, the Steenkamp women, Johanna, Jacoba and young Andrina, seem to have to live forever in the shadow of Klaartje's disgrace. That is their lot. Esther Shokolowsky, the storekeeper, remains eternally nothing but the "Jew-woman," Henry Nind is always only the "Englishman," Aalst Vlokman continues to make his routinely silent way from the fields to the church, and the few faceless, generally nameless black servants working for the van der Merwes gather each night without deviation beyond the sitting-room door to hear the prayers and the reading:

> To the smell of coffee, of lamp oil, of rich food . . . was added the human odour of the two small native children, indentured in service to Mevrouw and Mijnheer, who, alert and eager as monkeys, watched the proceedings from behind their master's and mistress's chairs . . . and they too, at their master's knee, repeated a prayer. "Make me to be obedient to my mistress, oh Lord," prayed Spaasie in her rough, hoarse voice. "Make me to run quickly when my master calls," prayed Klaas.
>
> (pp. 232-34)

Apart from little Spaasie, Klaas, and Classina the maid, no other black people are ever mentioned in the book. It must strike any South African reader as odd that in a farming community such as the Aangenaam valley there were no black labourers, that there was no "location" nearby nor black people living in huts on the peripheries of the farmlands. It is inconceivable that the white farmers did all the work without black assistance. Yet Pauline Smith excludes black people from her book along with any intimation of the nature of the relationship between the blacks and the whites, an exclusion that makes this assertion on her part inadequate:

> I always felt that what had been written about them [the Afrikaners] did not do them full justice and I made up my mind that I would try to write about them as I had known them.

But, to return to the matter of the social hierarchy in the Aangenaam valley: in such a structured society, where each person adheres to his place as solidly as the heavy red rocks in the landscape, change is impossible. The only variability the book provides is a passing reference to women's print dresses coming into fashion and the daring wearing of hats by the richer farmers' wives. Two people try leaving the Aangenaam valley: Klaartje, who dies giving birth to Andrina, and Andrina, who merely gets as far as the tollhouse and is, we can assume, brought back by Aalst Vlokman.

One interesting example of the inability of the inhabitants of Aangenaam to move freely out of their pre-ordained social positions is Andrina's way of addressing the Englishman. Even after they have become lovers, and in spite of his insistence on her use of his nickname "Harry," she persists with a kind of automatism in addressing him as "Mijnheer." Mentally she will call him Harry, but not to his face.

At certain erotic moments in the book, this form of address could border on the comical were it not for the reader's irritation at her unquestioning subservience and pity for the thoroughness of her conditioning. I doubt whether Pauline Smith intended such reader response and see it therefore as part of the problem of reading her work today. In effect, Andrina's place in life is that of a servant, and she has been so well trained in it that she cannot disregard it even in the arms of the man she loves.

An important facet of the pre-ordained social hierarchy of the Aangenaam community is a person's position within the family. When the time is right for Jan Beyers to marry, it is not *whom* he will marry that is of deepest concern to him but simply that he marry a woman with some possessions, in this case, sheep or oxen or even a sewing machine. And Pauline Smith does not attribute the impersonality of Jan Beyers's choice to him alone: the postmistress meddles among the candidates and Aalst Vlokman goes so far as to offer Andrina to him, throwing in two plough oxen as inducement. Once he is married, Jan Beyers can claim equality with, if not superiority over, an older man like Aalst Vlokman who has remained a bachelor. As spinsters, Johanna and Jacoba assume humble positions on the social scale. Some of the humour of the book arises from the postmistress' ignorance of the Englishman's indifference to the gradations of status among the Aangenaam people (which is not to say that he is indifferent to these gradations among his own). Hoping to get the Englishman to marry Andrina, she confides in him, not quite accurately it seems, that the girl descends from a famous Steenkamp, a pastor and school-teacher. She is mystified when he refers to pastors and school-masters as "Johnnies" and "Ninnies," and remains unimpressed by Andrina's antecedents.

The Aangenaam valley, in which rests the village of Harmonie, is cut off to the north by both the Aangenaam hills and the Swartkops range, which Smith describes as "a jagged bar of steel." To the south lie the Teniquota mountains. Into this confined world various strangers have come: first Esther Shokolowsky and her grandson, who never become fully integrated members of the community; then the baby Andrina, the so-called orphan child of the runaway Klaartje; and finally the Englishman, who is seen as a guest and as someone not to be taken too seriously. Aalst Vlokman remains something of an outsider to the Aangenaam folk, in spite of his position as beadle, because of his close reticence. If the reader asks what these four outsiders have in common, the answer soon makes itself apparent: in some way or another they are all outside of the religious life of the community. Esther is Jewish; the Englishman is at the very least a freethinker; Andrina cannot reconcile Christ's sacrifice with his divinity; and Aalst Vlokman feels himself rejected by the God of his people because of the subterfuge surrounding his life. As the reader discovers that all of the Aangenaam community's rituals, deriving from the seasons or otherwise, occur in or around the church, he must acknowledge the fitness of the book's social outsiders being heretical. That probably three out of the four would be hard put to articulate the nature of their heresy is not important. They do not live close to the centre of the sustaining hub of the group and thus cannot or will not look to the centre for comfort or guidance.

This brings me to the matter of Pauline Smith's validation of Afrikaner myths. One of these myths is of the Afrikaner as Israelite, as the Chosen of God, journeying across a Promised Land, preserving the Covenant and (less urgently) converting the heathen. Pauline Smith's competent fleshing-out of this myth provides us with a novel of almost classical sombreness and power, one in which cause and effect dominate grimly. Yet, even while we are moved by this power and solemnity, we are alienated by the depiction of the Afrikaner, and the Afrikaner alone, as the inheritor of the Southern African earth. And the believability of her depiction of these generally gentle and pious "Israelites" is hugely challenged by a comparison with Olive Schreiner's depiction of them in *A Story of an African Farm,* or Sol Plaatje's portrayal in *Mhudi.*

As I have mentioned, life in the Aangenaam valley revolves around religious observance: the daily prayers, the Bible class, the yearly sacrament, and the Thanksgiving. Apart from the four outsiders referred to, the other characters in the book respond religiously to their world and to other people in one of two not necessarily mutually exclusive ways. One impulse, felt by Jacoba Steenkamp and Alida van der Merwe, for example, is to perceive God as a loving father, compassionate and forgiving towards his children (Andrina's tendency is, of course, to carry this impulse further: she can only encompass intellectually and emotionally the humanity of God). The contrary, or perhaps complementary response, is to view God as Jehovah—just, righteous, and vengeful—as do Stephan van der Merwe, Aalst Vlokman, and Johanna Steenkamp. Because these two religious responses, one probably deriving from the New Testament and the other from the Old, can be maintained without real tension within an established dogma and in a single community, Pauline Smith creates a world devoid of villains, and this is arguably one of her strengths. She is able to portray sympathetically characters as diverse as Johanna and Jacoba, Aalst Vlokman and Hans Rademeyer. The reader suffers with and pities the self-induced misery arising from inflexibility in such as Johanna and Aalst, and admires the generosity of spirit in such as Jacoba and Alida. To assess where Pauline Smith's own preference lay, one could perhaps turn to the walk-on, walk-off character Hans Rademeyer, who godlike, gentle and fatherly, comes into the book at the end and takes the pregnant and destitute Andrina to his sister at the tollhouse where she can give birth to her son in relative comfort among kindly people. Yet for all Pauline Smith's conviction of the necessity for mercy in men and women's dealings with each other, it is noticeable that the most materially successful characters in the book, Alida and Stephan van der Merwe, present these two religious impulses in harmonious conjunction, his tending towards judgement and hers towards mercy. Their household and farm are well run, their children are hardworking and useful, and husband and wife combine exactitude and charity in their leadership of the community.

In devising the plot of *The Beadle,* Pauline Smith sets herself certain problems which are, in my opinion, not totally successfully worked out. Aalst Vlokman has to redeem himself from his earlier sin if he is to achieve a reunited family and be accepted, according to his own lights, into the full religious life of the community. His sin was to contrive at the escape from Harmonie of his fiancee's sister, Klaartje. When Klaartje would not accept his advances thereafter, he raped her and later failed to acknowledge his responsibility as father of her child. Pauline Smith patterns a repetition of events to provide the beadle with a second chance. Andrina resembles her mother Klaartje very closely; like Klaartje she has no sense of sin (although unlike Klaartje's vivacious seductiveness, Andrina's sensuality is depicted as entirely innocent). Like Klaartje Andrina leaves the Aangenaam valley and gives birth to a child. By going after Andrina, having publicly admitted his paternity, Aalst Vlokman not only gains absolution of his previous ill-doing, but is also endowed with strong familial status. The last words of the novel come from Andrina calling out to him, "Come in then, Ou-pa . . . Come in then and see the little grandson that you have. . . ."

To avoid an exact repetition of Klaartje's life in Andrina, Pauline Smith places in the humble, self-effacing Andrina's path a sophisticated, leisurely and, because of his Englishness, not easily understandable young man. Henry Nind is presented as no rapist. In fact, he thinks that he has made it clear to Andrina that he wants nothing from her that is not freely given. Because he has no apprehension of the extent of her love, he does not realize or is perhaps too shallow to realize that what she offers him is not some sensation on loan but her utter devotion. Andrina makes the reverse mistake: she overestimates the Englishman's love and gives herself to him with a lack of restraint that even he finds at times curious.

It is in the scenes of seduction that Smith's problem of repetition-with-variation is not entirely solved. To begin with, the reader is not convinced of Henry Nind's attractiveness—he remains too thinly drawn, too superficial, too snide. The reader has an even harder time believing that a farm girl like Andrina would not have had a more direct awareness of the ordinary physicality of sex and its consequences, or even, at her age, some distaste for or fear of intimacy. Even though her religious beliefs deviate from those of her people, it seems unlikely that she would not have imbibed some sexual inhibition and some moral conditioning from the church's teaching. She is, after all, no rebel like her mother and is thoroughly conditioned in every other social aspect. Pauline Smith wanted to exact the reader's sympathy for Andrina while holding her character aloft beyond any possible taint of criticism or guilt. Because Henry Nind must not be a rapist, Andrina has to be a pure child of nature. Had she been an ordinarily sensual woman, the reader in Pauline Smith's day, and perhaps even in ours, might have responded with, "You got what you deserved, my girl." Then Smith would have had to kill her off, like Klaartje, and Aalst Vlokman would not have had his second chance. But such are the problems of authors.

A further question which the unrelenting realist might ask is why Aalst Vlokman lives in the same house with the Steenkamp sisters. We know that he wishes to remain near his unacknowledged child Andrina, but how, we wonder, can he bear to live with one sister who hates him and with another who annoyingly persists in forgiving him for his unrepentent desertion of her? This household arrangement is clearly a contrivance of the author's to keep before the eyes of Aalst Vlokman the product of his sin, and we are forced to accept the necessity of such contrivance, when the author restricts himself to characters nursing single obsessions. She may not distract their attention by a world of variety and possibility.

Certainly Pauline Smith has importance as a regional writer. She paints the topography of the Little Karoo, the farms, the houses and everything that is in them, with fine detail, and she even offers two full pages of historical background to the Afrikaner community of that region. It is because of this richness and the bold simplicity of her stories that both *The Beadle* and *The Little Karoo* are enjoying a current popularity and are generating a good deal of critical writing. But I cannot resist putting in my pennyworth of caution: I don't believe that her work is "informative about the social . . . character of the Little Karoo," nor do I accept that while she relaxed on Arnold Bennett's yacht in the Mediterranean writing, as the gossip goes, she intended to give her readership a set of "universals." For me the Aangenaam community is a nostalgic, wish-fulfilling one and if its inhabitants are (because such a community never existed as Smith portrays it) allegorical of "human nature," then I would like to know *whose* "human nature"? (pp. 234-38)

Sheila Roberts, "A Confined World: A Rereading of Pauline Smith," in World Literature Written in English, *Vol. 24, No. 2, Autumn, 1984, pp. 232-38.*

CHARLES PONNUTHURAI SARVAN   (essay date 1984)

[*In the following excerpt, Sarvan analyzes Smith's treatment of Christianity in* The Beadle.]

William Plomer in his preface to the 1950 edition of Pauline Smith's collection of short stories, *The Little Karoo . . .* , describes them as "the best collection . . . yet written in English on South African themes." Arnold Bennett, having read the manuscript of her novel, *The Beadle,* exclaimed "I wish to God . . . I had thought . . . of this myself!" Yet, for several reasons, Pauline Smith is now not often remembered. The increasing stridency of the "colour conflict" in South Africa, the concern of modern criticism with ideology, and the very slim amount of work Pauline Smith was able to produce go towards an explanation. But it would be a loss if what she did not write about made us neglect what she has produced. I shall here confine myself to her only novel, *The Beadle.* (p. 244)

Aalst Vlokman, the beadle from whom this novel takes its title, lives in the home of two middle-aged sisters, Johanna and Jacoba Steenkamp, and their niece, Andrina du Toit. Andrina is seventeen and is being prepared spiritually and theologically for admission to the church and to receive the holy sacrament for the first time. The past lives and inter-relations of these three adults are fully clarified only near the end of the story, but from the beginning it is evident that there is much bitterness, pain and brooding in Johanna and the beadle. There is reference too to the death of Andrina's mother Klaartje in "sin" and shame, and as events lead Andrina in her turn to "sin" and pain, we are conscious of an earlier tragedy. The beadle and Jacoba had once been in love but the vivacious Klaartje had persuaded Aalst Vlokman to help her escape from her strict and austere father. She hides in Vlokman's wagon and he drives her away. On the journey, the unpremeditated happens, and Klaartje conceives. She marries Herman du Toit, who abandons her when he discovers she is pregnant. However, Andrina's paternity is not suspected and she is known as Andrina du Toit. Into Andrina's life there now comes Henry Nind, an Englishman sent to Platkops for his health. Andrina's love for the foreigner is deep, but for Henry the relationship is an enjoyable dalliance. The tragedy arises not only because one individual is self-indulgent and dishonest, and the other innocent and trusting, but because they represent two worlds with different values. That Henry is always referred to as "the Englishman" emphasizes this difference:

> She came of a race for whom time moved as slowly as did their wagons across the wide open spaces of the veld, and for whom thought moved as slowly as did time . . . That craving for mental excitement and change of environment which fashioned the Englishman's outlook on life and which, when gratified, lapsed so quickly into boredom, played no part in theirs. Their slow habit of mind was . . . to accept both adventure and weariness with equal philosophy. . . .

The beadle perceives Andrina's love for the Englishman and fears its outcome, but because he has not confessed his claim to concern, he has forfeited his right to intervene and protect. Eventually the Englishman and Andrina are left alone and their relationship is consummated.

Wagons, so much associated with early Boer history, are linked to the fate of individuals in this society. Klaartje's escape was in Vlokman's wagon; seventeen years later, Vlokman, now the beadle, worrying about Andrina, does not see the wagon, "strange vehicle of Andrina's fate," take Mevrouw van der Merwe away, leaving Andrina alone with the Englishman. A few months later, pregnant, Andrina escapes by hiding in the wagon of kind old Hans Rademeyer: "The movement soothed her . . . For generations her people had found security in their wagons, and for generations had the women of her race, homeless but for their wagons, borne their children kneeling on the ground behind them." . . . Wagons, associated with the protection of the womb but also with transience and fragility, are a miniature of life.

The Englishman receives a letter from a woman who had once rejected him and immediately returns to England to marry her, leaving Andrina to experience the meaning of Aunt Jacoba's words "Death is but one end to love. There are others that are harder." The beadle, learning that Andrina, alone and distraught, has gone in search of the man she thinks is her father, confesses his sin at the church door and goes in search of her. Guided and influenced by Hans Rademeyer, daughter and father come together: "Come in then, Ou-pa . . . and see the little grandson that you have, with his round bald head." The similarity with *The Scarlet Letter* is not only in Smith's description of a secluded, intensely religious community or her story of "sin" and public confession in one closely associated with the church, but also in her interest in sin, judgement, oppression and suffering and in the strange psychology of human individuals. Andrina could well have repeated the Reverend Roger Chillingworth's words and claimed (with greater truth) that she had never violated the sanctity of the human heart.

Though the novel takes its title from him, there is little analysis of or comment on the beadle. But this makes his silently burning, self-consuming presence all the more pervasive. He is taciturn, fierce and isolated. Andrina and her Aunt Jacoba are similar and in the former there was "no saving sense of sin" but only that "dangerous charity which made her Aunt Jacoba so tolerant towards sinners, so pitiful towards saints." . . . The two aunts form a sharp contrast: Jacoba's pity turns life's shadows to consoling shade . . . and her gentle presence somehow robs even shameful things of their shame . . . ; Johanna is harsh and unrelenting in her righteousness. Pauline Smith probes the harshly virtuous: behind Johanna's righteousness is a craving for moral domination, that is, for power and Jacoba is her immediate victim. Carrying into the twentieth century that iconoclasm which was a feature of the end of the Victorian age, Smith states that righteousness can prove "a terrible weapon for evil," and boldly posits the paradox that had Johanna sinned, she would have been a better woman.

The Englishman, more than a foreigner merely serving as catalyst, is analysed with clarity and quiet vehemence. Henry Nind's amiability and good humour are weapons "against the world and a shield against his own conscience." . . . What appears to be a punctilious honesty restrains him from ever using the word "love" to Andrina, but this proves to be a "deliberate determination to safeguard himself against possible complications in the future." . . . "Untutored" Andrina—it is ironic that Henry Nind is appointed her tutor—responds to what she believes is Henry's honesty, unaware that selfishness can turn even honesty to its own purpose. At the end, Henry feels only that impatience and resentment of the oppressor for those whom he oppresses. . . . (The author does not deal with the political implication of this psychological reaction.) Henry's selfishness is "strengthened by the selfishness of semi-invalidism behind which it was so easy to seek moral shelter." . . . (Her own state of health must have warned Pauline Smith of this temptation to self-indulgence.)

In the two previous paragraphs, I have tried to convey something of the clarity of Pauline Smith's analysis of character and action, and of the boldness of her moral position. In her treatment of Christianity, in her rejection of the conventional, and in the sceptical questioning of orthodox religious positions, Pauline Smith was individualistic and iconoclastic. She was a rebel but gentle; beset by ill-health, extraordinarily shy and retiring but courageous and earnest in her ethical and religious questioning.

In keeping with the simple and intense faith of the small Boer community, *The Beadle* is told and developed with implicit reference to Christianity. As the novel commences, Andrina is about to join the church, though with "no religious convictions whatever. But because she was joining it her heart was filled with a vague gentle expectancy of some divine adventure outside her daily life." . . . This vague but intense receptiveness is fulfilled by the sudden arrival of the Englishman. The taking of the sacrament implies a new birth and with Henry's coming and what she believes is his love for her, a new Andrina comes into being. . . . More to challenge and infuriate the beadle than to please Andrina, Johanna with Jacoba's trembling help makes a sacrament dress for Andrina. It will be Andrina's first new dress, and the pale grey material is sprinkled with black dots, small pink roses and little blue forget-me-nots. The pie Mevrouw van der Merwe bakes for the Englishman and which Andrina takes out of the oven is decorated with rose leaves, and we see Andrina as an offering not to God but to the Englishman. The little garden in which the Englishman and Andrina meet is an Eden, a wilderness full of roses and strange, beautiful and unexpected things, watered by a little stream known as the "Water of Life." As the pastor dwells on the love of God, Andrina thinks of her greater love for the Englishman, and when asked if she is grateful to God, Andrina can answer with sincerity in the affirmative because of her "dear and secret joy." On the evening of her final examination before the elders of the church, the Englishman kisses Andrina for the first time, and she goes into the "House of God" still feeling his lips on hers. The mystery of the sacrament is matched by her "mysteriously developing body" and Andrina thanks God for His love and care, evidenced by His sending of the Englishman. The coffee Andrina shyly shares with the Englishman just prior to her seduction is to her a holy and joyful sacrament; the "new sweet joy" of which she had been assured when she joined the church is now hers and "her soul sang its innocent magnificat of humility and desire." . . . The Christian references are used to celebrate innocence and human love. The Englishman is proud, for godlike he has called a "new Andrina into being"; his is "the triumph of a creator." The last evening meal of which the Englishman partakes is a sombre one, with everyone present subdued, though for different reasons. A sense of sadness brought by the knowledge of coming abandonment and pain makes this meal Andrina's Last Supper. Finally, as the shepherds were brought to the place of the virgin birth by a star, so the beadle, searching for his daughter and grandson, is at last arrested by seeing Andrina's sacrament dress hung out on a line to dry—the garment she presumably was wearing when she gave birth to her illegitimate son.

A recurrent term and concept in the novel is fatherhood, God's and man's. Andrina is "a child of sin" and therefore believed to be fatherless; Aalst Vlokman, because he did not confess his "sin," was unable to exercise his fatherhood and protect Andrina; the pastor repeatedly talks of the fatherhood of God; when the Englishman leaves, Andrina cries out to "Our Father" and, pregnant, sets out to find the man she thinks is her earthly father. Against the love, care and protection implied by the term fatherhood, there is the Englishman's insistence on the individual's complete freedom of action. . . . Through this and other oppositions, using the Christian frame of reference, Pauline Smith expresses her secular and ethical perceptions and concerns.

The novelist insists that no experience could deprive Andrina of her innocence, that innocence is not a condition of the body but of the soul and mind. When Andrina realizes that she is pregnant, she feels amazement, terror, joy and sadness, but "Shame she did not feel. The child she bore within her was not for her the sign and the seal of her sin, but . . . of her love." . . . What is to be feared is not mistaken notions of sin, but pain and sorrow. . . . Smith was reaching out to a new definition of morality; sin is that which causes pain and sorrow. In this sense, superficially Christian, respectable middle-class attitudes could be seen as sin. The van der Merwes' married daughter, with whom Andrina is staying when her pregnancy is discovered, is puzzled and outraged. To Antoinette, "comfortably" married, sure of the affection of her husband and children, there is no greater sin than that from which, "as a wife and mother, she felt herself to be secure." Yet in Andrina, "with this evil of evils went a natural goodness of heart that . . . became, in some way which she could not properly define, a threat to her own moral security." . . . It is Antoinette who, telling Andrina that she is a sinner causing scandal and shame, brings her out of a natural and innocent Eden into the unkind social reality.

Fleeing from Antoinette and the world as revealed to her, Andrina is assisted by Hans Rademeyer. Adapting Christ's words, Oom Hans asks "if I let none that have sinned travel in my wagon, who then would travel in it?" The compassion and generosity of this old man, Andrina feels, is "the tenderness of Christ made real." Later she thinks that Oom Hans, with his kind eyes and smile, is Christ, "Christ grown old, grown old. . . ." Thus it is man who draws man to God; indeed, God is but the word for that sublime compassion, love, generosity and nobility which we sometimes encounter in life. The criticism of social values and attitudes is telling, though quietly made.

Through Andrina, Pauline Smith questions the nature and existence of God. "While the Englishman prided himself upon being a free agent Andrina knew herself to be entirely in the hands of her God" . . .—and her God does not protect her. Rather, God's peace is calm and indifferent, like the peace of the Great Karoo, and absorbs man and his labours as things of naught. . . . Like Euripides, the novelist asks: if no man escapes the will of God . . . , what is the nature of Him who permits, if not wills, painful and tragic happenings? Perhaps there is no good and "the crowning tragedy of the Jewish teacher's life" was that his followers had thrust a godhead upon him. Christ died, but knowing that he would rise again and go to heaven. "Out of all eternity where lay the sacrifices, in time, of a life on earth of thirty years?" . . . "If Christ had been but the son of Joseph, not of God, if He had died not to rise again, but to lie forever in his grave, then . . . she could have understood and loved Him. . . ."

Even more quietly, Pauline Smith draws attention to the education and upbringing of girls. Andrina is trained to be undemanding, unobstrusive and ever of service to adults, especially to men. The chief obligation of men, on the other hand, is to make the most of any experience that comes their way. . . . Andrina's seduction is partly attributable to a wish to obey and to minister to a man's needs and requests. Pauline Smith writes of women having a sexuality of their own, equal and similar to that of men. To women too, love can be "a passionate adventure of the body or the soul" . . . and Andrina's body has a "hunger" for Henry's.

Pauline Smith questioned many beliefs and practices, and with respect to the injustice done to black Africans she was either unperceiving or silent. Esther Shokolowsky, the old "Jew-woman" to whom terrible things had happened in her own country in eastern Europe "at the hands of Christians," is treated sympathetically. But the black Africans to whom terrible things were also happening in their own country escape her attention and therefore her sympathy. She does point briefly, by way of comment, to the Boers' reaction to the freeing of the slaves by the English—"an incomprehensible act of injustice." She makes a similar passing, ironic observation about the treatment and upbringing of indentured children: Spaasie prays, "Make me to be obedient" and Klaas prays, "Make me run quickly when my master calls."

Sin brings bitterness and isolation to the beadle and Johanna, but Jacoba and Andrina transcend sin through compassion, forgiveness and love. From sin comes sorrow but through sorrow one can attain peace. . . . The Great Karoo helps Andrina—though she still loves and longs for her Englishman—to attain a measure of acceptance.

> If she were indeed as insignificant as at some moments in this space and stillness she felt herself to be, of what account were her joys and her sorrows, her hopes and her fears? Of what account was time . . . Of what account were love and anguish? . . .

Rather early in life, Andrina du Toit learns that life is the bearing of unbearable things. . . .

The Beadle is a short novel, not without humour and like Greek tragedy, perceptive, moving and ennobling. (pp. 244-49)

> *Charles Ponnuthurai Sarvan, "Pauline Smith: A Gentle Rebel," in* World Literature Written in English, *Vol. 24, No. 2, Autumn, 1984, pp. 244-50.*

ADDITIONAL BIBLIOGRAPHY

Bennett, Arnold. Introduction to *The Little Karoo*, by Pauline Smith, pp. 7-11. 1925. Reprint. New York: The Vanguard Press, 1952.
    Biographical sketch describing the geographical and cultural background of *The Little Karoo*.

Christie, Sarah; Hutchings, Geoffrey; and Maclennan, Don. "Pauline Smith: *The Beadle*." In their *Perspectives On South African Fiction*, pp. 57-69. Johannesburg: Donker, 1980.
    General discussion intended for African university students.

Coetzee, John M. "Pauline Smith and the Afrikaans Language." *English in Africa* 8, No. 1 (March 1981): 25-32.
    Assesses Smith's rendering of the Afrikaans language into English, which Coetzee calls "transfer" rather than translation, because Smith "transfers" into English linguistic traits of the

original language. Coetzee concludes: "Smith wishes to assert certain myths about the Afrikaner, or rather to validate pre-existent myths with what will look like evidence: the trace of a characteristic Afrikaner consciousness inscribed in his language, or in his language as thrown into relief through the medium of transfer. In particular, Smith's text asserts, and the practice of transfer is meant to validate, the myth (a myth received with sympathy if with condescension in liberal circles in England before, during and for a while after the South African war) in terms of which the Afrikaner has his type in the Israelite, tender of flocks, member of an elect race (*volk*) set apart from the tribes of the idolatrous, living by simple and not-to-be-questioned divine commandments, afflicted with trials by an inscrutable Jehovah but destined for great things."

Driver, Dorothy, ed. *Pauline Smith*. Johannesburg: McGraw-Hill Book Co., 1983, 235 p.

Collection of seminal reviews and essays on Smith, including studies by William Plomer, Arthur Ravenscroft, Alan Paton, Cherry Clayton, Kay McCormick, Geoffrey Haresnape, and J. M. Coetzee, with a detailed chronology of Smith's life by the editor. Several essays in this collection are excerpted above.

Haresnape, Geoffrey. "Barriers of Race and Language: Pauline Smith's Critique of a Rural Society." *English in Africa* 4, No. 1: 40-6.

Places Smith's depiction of black South Africans in a historical context. Haresnape explains: "The way in which [Smith] portrays blacks and their relationships with whites forms a small but important part of her critique of the rural society. One needs immediately to be reminded that she was dealing with a pre-1925 situation (and almost certainly harking back even further) in a region where racial confrontation was not particularly stressful or widespread. Here, as elsewhere, her critical method is characteristically oblique. For these reasons she did not have much to say overtly about the racial theme."

Muir, Edwin. Review of *The Beadle*. *The Nation and Athenaeum* XL, No. 2 (16 October 1926): 88-9.

Mixed review. Muir comments that *The Beadle* "is neither quite enough a story, nor quite enough a picture of manners. But the quiet grace of the writing, the serenity and decision of the delineation, set it securely above mediocrity. . . . Miss Smith's picture of the life of the Boer peasants is charming, but it is obvious that she takes them too much at their own valuation, and this gives the book a faint trace of sentimentality. But allowing for this *The Beadle* is a genre picture of great charm and occasionally of moving beauty."

Scheub, Harold. "Pauline Smith and the Oral Tradition: The Koenraad Tales." *English in Africa* 8, No. 1 (March 1981): 1-11.

Examines Smith's use of the folkloric archetype of the trickster in "Horse Thieves" and "The Cart." Drawing on evidence from Smith's journal, in which she records the origin of the stories in Afrikaner oral tradition, Scheub also comments on the alterations found in Smith's fictional versions.

Sumeli-Weinberg, Grazia. "Naturalism in Pauline Smith." *Quarry* (1980-1982): 91-102.

Examines naturalism in Smith's narrative technique and compares her approach to that of Italian author Giovanni Verga.

Voss, Tony. "Die Perels van Pauline; or, The History of Smith." *English in Africa* 11, No. 1 (May 1984): 107-17.

Reviews the criticism of Pauline Smith's fiction.

Wilhelm, Cherry. "The Style of Poverty: The Language of Pauline Smith's Little Karoo." *English Studies in Africa* 20, No. 2 (September 1977): 65-77.

Compares Smith's prose style in her fiction with the prose style she employed in her memoir of Arnold Bennett.

Oswald Spengler

1880-1936

German philosopher and essayist.

Spengler is the author of *Der Untergang des Abendlandes* (*The Decline of the West*), a treatise in the philosophy of history that is considered one of the most important and influential books of the twentieth century. In this work Spengler rejected the theories of historians who explained history, principally that of Western Europe, as an unbroken sequence of events which has been developing from antiquity to modern times and which may be seen as either progressive or degenerative in accord with varying criteria of cultural value. As an alternative to this model of a continuous history, Spengler proposed one in which civilizations and historical periods previously regarded as being significantly related—such as those of the Roman Empire and medieval Europe—are instead viewed as belonging to separate cultures, each having a unique identity yet each undergoing the same process of birth, growth, decay, and death. It is this process that is the keystone of Spengler's thesis in *The Decline of the West,* upholding a comparative science of history that would enable historians to fix the specific juncture at which a culture has arrived through analogies with past cultures. Thus derives the title of the work in which Spengler proclaimed that the West is nearing its final phase of existence.

Spengler was born at Blankenburg, a small town in the Harz mountains of central Germany. His father worked in the local mining industry, but after the mines failed the family moved to Halle. There Spengler received his secondary and university education, later pursuing advanced studies at the universities of Munich and Berlin. While his university curriculum focused on natural science and mathematics, he also acquired a wide knowledge of literature, history, and philosophy, writing his doctoral dissertation on the Greek philosopher Heraclitis. Spengler taught at secondary schools in several German cities until 1911, when he moved to Munich and there lived on a small legacy he had received as well as the negligible income he earned as a book reviewer. With the advent of the First World War, Spengler's financial situation worsened considerably, and it was during these years that he wrote *The Decline of the West.*

After being rejected by every German publisher to which it was submitted, *The Decline of the West* was finally published in Austria in 1918. A second revised edition, which appeared in 1923, gained international renown and made Spengler an intellectual celebrity whose opinions were eagerly solicited. However, his subsequent work, which consists largely of essays on historical and political topics, does not compete with the power and vision displayed in *The Decline of the West.* Beyond its intrinsic qualities, the popularity of *The Decline of the West* is often attributed to the philosophical ambiance of the time, a climate of desperation that made readers receptive to prophecies of a disintegrating world. As Donald O. White has explained: "Spengler, the man of the perpetual scowl, became a whole generation's symbol for the futility of human endeavor." Embracing the demise of Western culture, Spengler wrote that "we have no right to expect anything good in the face of facts. . . . Only dreamers believe there is a way out. Optimism is cowardice. We are born into this time and must

bravely follow the path to the destined end." This "destined end" predicted by Spengler was to be a period typified by great wars and the conquests of a new Caesar. Spengler's forecast was especially attractive to a rising Nazi party, but the appeal was not mutual: he remained conspicuously aloof from the ruthless proceedings of National Socialism, disdained its anti-Semitism, and ultimately fell into disfavor with the fanatics of a revitalized Germany. In his later years Spengler was restricted in his activities by the Nazi regime. He died in 1936.

In *The Decline of the West,* the cross-cultural continuum that earlier historians construed from the multifarious data of world history is replaced by a "comparative morphology" of cultures. Spengler maintained that seven cultures have appeared in the course of human civilization, including those of Egypt, China, classical Greece and Rome, and the present culture of the West. Each of these cultures possesses a distinct spirit which is reflected in every aspect of its life and which may be represented by symbols relating to the perception members of a given society have of the space in which they live. For example, Spengler found that people of classical antiquity are characterized by their strict orientation to the finite world and that the spatial confines of the Doric column and nude sculpture serve as symbols of this highly localized perspective. By contrast, the Western world expresses a sense of the infinite in the reaching spires of Gothic cathedrals and the deep perspectives of European painting, which symbolize the Faustian ambition of the West. Spengler observes that, given this diversity in the essence and expression of individual cultures, there can be no genuine understanding among them. Nevertheless, comparisons among these different cultures reveal analogies which Spengler employs to argue for the uniformity of their structure and course of evolution. Considering parallels between ancient Greece and Europe, Spengler states: "We might have found the *alter ego* of our own actuality in establishing the correspondence, item by item, from the Trojan War and the Crusades, Homer and the Nibelungenlied, through Doric and Gothic, Dionysian movement and Renaissance, Polycletus and Johann Sebastian Bach, Athens and Paris, Aristotle and Kant, Alexander and Napoleon, to the world-city and the imperialism common to both cultures."

Fundamental to Spengler's vision of history in *The Decline of the West* is the analogy between a culture and a living organism, both of which are born at a random moment, grow to maturity, decline in vitality, and then perish. Whereas previous historians speculated on the progress or purpose of history beyond the life-span of defunct cultures, Spengler viewed even geographically and temporally proximate cultures as having no collective future or shared influences: each proceeded through its organic cycle in isolation. However, Spengler did posit a type of influence, termed "pseudomorphosis," in which a new culture arising in proximity to an established one is forced to develop in ways antithetical to its natural spirit. An example of such malformation is the Russian culture, which was significantly altered when European influences were imposed upon it by Peter the Great in the eighteenth century and by the Bolsheviks in the twentieth century. Illustrating the natural phases of a culture's existence, Spengler employed the analogy of the four seasons. In Western culture, spring took place during the Middle Ages, a heroic era when society was dominated by the aristocracy and the church, wars and strong spiritual feelings flourished, peasants sustained the ties of humanity to the land and to nature, and the arts were practiced anonymously as a means of collective rather than personal expression. Summer in the West arrived with the Renaissance, a time when city-states became the focus of power and activity, a shift from agrarian to urban life had begun, and great individuals such as Shakespeare and Michelangelo became prominent in the arts. Autumn occurred in the eighteenth century, bringing Western culture to fruition and initiating its exhaustion as cities and commerce dramatically expanded, power converged in a few monarchies, the creative spirit achieved full maturity in the work of Wolfgang Amadeus Mozart, Johann Wolfgang von Goethe, and Immanuel Kant, and seemingly eternal social and religious traditions came under the inquiry of enlightenment thinkers. With the appearance of winter, Spengler makes a distinction between a culture in the true sense—that is, a community having a unique spiritual character—and a "civilization," which Spengler characterizes as a soulless aggregate of people whose achievements are primarily those of technology, political administration, and military aggression, with artistic life now either exhausted or a parasitic derivation of the past. Indications of the approaching winter of Western culture are the rise of dictatorships, a science devoted mainly to industrial and militaristic ends, and colossal cities that mirror one another in their formless expansion. Furthermore, if Napoleon's career in the eighteenth century parallels that of Alexander the Great in the classical world, then, according to Spengler, the West can expect to witness a modern counterpart to Caesar—a conqueror who will inaugurate the closing epoch of the Western world.

Although *The Decline of the West* enjoyed considerable popularity when it was first published and continues to be regarded as a modern classic, Spengler's study has always been subject to severe criticism. The most serious objections have been concerned with three central issues: first, the validity of Spengler's assertion that cultures are isolated and discontinuous phenomena, a doctrine that is crucial to the method of comparative morphology; second, the accuracy of Spengler's scholarship and the manner in which he deploys historical facts to support his arguments; and third, the moral soundness of Spengler's deterministic view of history, which has been censured as pessimistic, fatalistic, and defeatist. A key argument against the conclusions of *The Decline of the West* is articulated by William Harlan Hale, who observes that Spengler's philosophy "often repeats the assertion that separate cultures leave no heritage, that their meaning is unattainable by an alien observer, that therefore history can never reveal their soul. But Spengler's whole structure is reared upon his conviction that he precisely understands the soul and meaning of cultures removed from him by vast distances of time and area." Summarizing many of the criticisms of comparative morphology, R. G. Collingwood has stated that "Spengler's so-called philosophy of history . . . is lacking in orientation, because it reduces history to a plurality of cultures between whose fundamental ideas there is no relation whatever; it is unsound on fundamentals, because its purpose—that of 'predetermining the future'—is impossible in itself and in any case unrealizable by his methods; it is ill thought-out, because he shows no signs of having seen the fatal objections to it; and it is committed to the methodical falsification of facts because it distorts every fact falling—or alleged to fall—within a given culture, into an abstract and one-sided idea which is fancied to represent the essence of that culture." In a 1974 reexamination of *The Decline of the West,* Northrop Frye has found that critical rebukes such as those of Hale and Collingwood "arise from the fact that the reader's point of view differs from that of the writer, and he is apt to project these differences into the book as inconsistencies within it." Illustrating these differences in viewpoint at their most extreme are the judgments on *The Decline of the West* offered by Lewis Mumford and Thomas Mann, who regard Spengler's thought entirely from a moral perspective. "Through its emotional impact," Mumford writes, "Spengler's work as a whole constitutes a morbid saga of Barbarism. It began as a poem of defeat; it finally became an epic justification of the fascist attack on the very humanity of man." Similarly, Mann condemns Spengler as a "defeatist of humanity" and his philosophy as one of "fatalism." By contrast, Adda B. Bozeman's recent reappraisal of Spengler's work explains that "contrary to numerous respected theorists and historians in the Occident, who accentuate the themes of evolution in their work and who are programmatically 'upbeat' in conjecturing the future in terms of progress, Spengler was convinced that the full measure of life can be discovered only when decline and decay are perceived and assessed as clearly as beginnning and becoming. It is this dual focus that seems to have irritated many of his detractors, causing them to charge Spengler with the social sin of pessimism."

Whatever pronouncements have been made concerning the value of *The Decline of the West* as a work of scholarship or prophecy, critics have acknowledged the rhetorical force of its prose, often recognizing its claim to be considered the work of a visionary, as well as being, in the words of Northrop Frye, "one of the world's great Romantic poems." Regarding *The Decline of the West* not as an objective document of historical theory but as the expression of a personal vision, George Santayana praised Spengler's work as "subjective, moral, lyrical," and Kenneth Burke concluded that "however much one may snipe at Spengler's book, it remains a stupendous piece of work, formidable, lugubrious, and passionate." While its prestige as a treatise in the philosophy of history has always been unstable, and its intellectual influence greatly diminished after the Second World War, *The Decline of the West* has retained its stature as a seminal expression of the spiritual infirmities of the modern era.

PRINCIPAL WORKS

Heraklit (dissertation) 1904
Der Untergang des Abendlandes. 2 vols.   (philosophy)
    1918-22
    [*The Decline of the West,* 1926-28]
Preussentum und Sozialismus (essay) 1919
    ["Prussianism and Socialism" published in *Selected
    Essays,* 1967]
Politische Pflichten der deutschen Jugend (lecture) 1924
Der Mensch und die Technik (philosophy) 1931
    [*Man and Technics,* 1932]
Politische Schriften (essays) 1932
Jahre der Entscheidung (philosophy) 1933
    [*The Hour of Decision,* 1934]
Reden und Aufsätze (lectures and essays) 1937
Gedanken (aphorisms) 1941
    [*Aphorisms,* 1967]
Briefe, 1913-1936 (letters) 1963
    [*Letters, 1913-1936,* 1966]
Selected Essays (essays) 1967

THOMAS MANN (essay date 1922)

[*Mann was a German novelist, short story writer, essayist, and critic who singlehandedly raised the German novel to an international stature which it had not enjoyed since the time of the Romantics. Like his contemporaries James Joyce and Marcel Proust, Mann keenly reflected the intellectual currents of his age, particularly the belief that European realism was no longer viable for the inhabitants of a sophisticated and complex century. Yet, while Joyce and Proust expressed this predicament through the form of their writing, Mann maintained the outward convention of realistic fiction, emphasizing an ironic vision of life and a deep, often humorous, sympathy for humanity. In the following excerpt from an essay originally published in Mann's* Rede und Antwort *in 1922, Mann condemns* The Decline of the West *for its advocacy of defeatism and denial of spiritual values.*]

Spengler denies that he is a pessimist. Still less, I suppose, would he call himself an optimist. He is a fatalist. But his fatalism, summed up in the sentence, "We must will the inevitable or nothing," is far from having the tragic, the heroic, the dionysiac character possessed by Nietzsche's resolution of the contradiction between optimism and pessimism. Rather it is a malicious demonstration of hostility to the future, in the disguise of scientific ruthlessness. It is not *amor fati*—indeed with *amor* of any kind it has little to do; that is the repellent thing about it. Neither pessimism nor optimism is in question. Though we may envisage but darkly the fate of mankind, thinking it doomed to suffer through endless ages; though we may shroud ourselves in the profoundest scepticism and refuse to believe in any hypothetic future happiness; yet we shall not

thereby relish the more, by a single grain, the schoolmasterish insensibility of the Spenglerian brand of pessimism. Pessimism is not lovelessness. It does not necessarily mean a cold-blooded, "scientific" mastery over the forces of evolution and a contemptuous disregard of such imponderabilia as are manifested by the spirit and the will of man, since these perhaps add to the process an element of irrationality not accessible to scientific calculation. But such presumption, and such disregard of the human element, are what Spengler represents. He might be as cynical as the devil himself—but no, he is only fatalist. And it is ill done of him to speak of Goethe, Nietzsche and Schopenhauer as the forerunners of his own hyenalike gift of prophecy. For they were human beings, while he is a defeatist of humanity.

I assume that my readers have read the **Decline of the West:** I can do so confidently, for it has achieved world-wide reputation, due to certain great characteristics; nobody would dispute its possession of these. Its theory, in a nutshell, is this: what we call history is the life-course of certain vegetative and structurally similar organisms, each possessing its own span of life and its own individual characteristics. Each of these is a "culture." So far there have been eight of them: the Egyptian, Indian, Babylonian, Chinese, "classical," Arabic, Occidental (our own) and the Mayan (Central American). But though alike in their general structure and their common fate, these cultures are strictly self-contained forms of life; each inevitably committed to its own laws of style, in all its thinking, seeing, feeling, living—and each quite shut off from all understanding of the others. Herr Spengler, and he alone, understands all of them; he knows what to say about one and all in a way that is a joy to hear. Otherwise, as I have said, there reigns a profound lack of mutual understanding. Sheer absurdity to speak of a continuity of life, of ultimate spiritual unity, of that humanity which, according to Novalis, is the higher meaning of our planet, the star that links us with the upper world, the eye it lifts to heaven. Vain to remind oneself that a single work of love—like Mahler's "Song of the Earth," which takes an old-Chinese lyric and fuses it into an organic human unity with the most developed tonal art of the West—knocks into a cocked hat this whole conception of the essential unrelatedness between civilisations! Since there is no humanity, there is, according to Spengler, likewise no mathematics, no art of painting, no physics; there are only as many mathematics, physics and arts of painting as there are cultures; and these are essentially disparate things. There reigns a Babylonian confusion of tongues; but Herr Spengler again, endowed with the gift of intuition, can understand them all. Each culture, he says, has a span of life like a human being. Born of its parent landscape, each blossoms, ripens, fades and dies. Dies, after it has manifested its characteristics, exhausted all the possibilities of picturesque expression with which it was endowed—such as nationalities, religions, literatures, arts, sciences, forms of government. And the grey old age of each, its transition into nothingness and the rigor mortis of no-history, that is what we know as civilisation. But since any stage of a given culture can be deduced from all the others, we have in the first place a new and diverting conception of contemporaneity, and in the second—for people in the know—an astronomical certainty of what is going to happen. Take, for instance, our own culture, the occidental—which at the beginning of the nineteenth century entered the old-age phase of "civilisation," and whose immediate future will be "contemporaneous" with the century of the Roman soldier-emperors—its course is quite fixed. Astronomically, biologically, morphologically fixed. Appallingly fixed. And if there is anything more appalling than fate, it is the human being who bears it without lifting a finger.

This to do is what the adamantine scholar admonishes us. We must, he says, will the inevitable or nothing; heedless that that is no alternative; that man, by willing only that which inexorable science says must be, simply ceases to will—which is after all not precisely human. And this inevitable—what is it? It is the decline of the west. That is the writing on the wall: a decline not precisely in so many words, not in the material sense, though much material decline will be bound up with it; but the decline of the occident as a culture. China still exists, and many millions of Chinese, but the Chinese culture is dead. So it is with Egypt: since Roman times it is no longer occupied by an indigenous cultural population but by fellaheen. And the fellaheen state is, so Spengler says, the final condition of all folk life. When its culture has lived itself out a people passes into the fellaheen stage; it reverts to its primitive, unhistoried condition. But the intellectual, political and economical instrument of this result is civilisation. It is the spirit of the city: it brings on the conception of the fourth estate, the masses; and these masses, the nomads of the big city, are no longer the people, they are formlessness, the end, nothingness. For the west, as for every culture, the rise of formless, traditional forces (Napoleon) coincides with the beginning of civilisation. But Napoleonism passes into Caesarism, the parliamentary democracy into the dictatorship of single individuals of power and race, unscrupulous economic conquistadors of the type of Cecil Rhodes. The Caesarist stage is a feature of all declining cultures and lasts all of two centuries. In China it is called "the time of the fighting states." This is our own stage. At the beginning of the twentieth century private power as a political force succeeded the power of parliamentary parties, these being always conditioned by abstract ideals. The personal power, the single great man, rules over nerveless multitudes of fellaheen, which he treats like cattle. Another Caesar can always rise—another Goethe never; and it is sheer flabby sentimentality to spend any time to-day on cultural affairs—art, poetry, education. Such things are not for fellaheen. The literary life of to-day has no significance whatever save as a futile struggle between the intellectualised art of the cities and the backward, idyllic art of the soil. He who grasps the forces of destiny will pay no heed to such trifles; he will cling to those things which are all the future has and is: to the machine, technique, economics, and perhaps still politics. Laughter is the portion of those who believe in goodwill and flatter themselves that goodness, spirit and will belong to a worthier order of mankind, that they too might have some influence over the course of our world. What is to come is fixed: wars on the vastest scale for power and plunder; rivers of blood; for the fellaheen populations, silence and submission. Man, relapsed into the cosmic, zoologic, post-historied, will live as a peasant bound to the soil, or dully grubbing among the ruins of cities. To lull his suffering soul he will produce the so-called "second state of religion," a substitute for his earlier cultural and creative kind, with just effectiveness enough to help him bear his sufferings with resignation.

The man who possesses this refreshing outlook on life is a peculiarly puzzling phenomenon. His theory is cold, scientific, emotionless, lifted above all human prejudice; relentlessly deterministic; it seems to be pure knowledge. Yet through it is manifest a will, a conception of the world, sympathies and antipathies; it is then at bottom *not* emotionless, it is secretly conservative. For one does not set up a creed of this kind, does not so marshal his facts, so identify history and culture, so

sharply emphasise the antithesis between form and spirit, unless he is a conservative, unless in his heart he accepts form and culture and shudders at the decay of civilisation. The complexity and the perversity of the Spengler position consists— or seems to consist—in that despite this second, secret conservatism he does not affirm culture, does not like a preacher threaten death and decay in order to ward them off, but, on the contrary, affirms "civilisation," wilfully accepts it with a kind of fatalistic fury, and with ruthless scorn takes its side against culture, because forsooth the future belongs to it, and all that is cultural is doomed to death. To such cruel self-conquest and self-denial the stern heroic thinker goads himself on. Secretly conservative, a man of culture, he seems to be affirming civilisation only in a contrary spirit; but no, that is only the seeming of a seeming, a double delusion; for he is genuinely affirming it—not only with his words, against which his being revolts, but with his being as well!

That which he denies, even while he prophesies, he portrays, he *is*, himself: civilisation. All that belongs to it, all that it consists in: intellectualism, rationalism, relativism, cult of causality, of the "natural law"—with all that his theory is saturated; and against that leaden historical materialism the materialism of a Marx is sheer blue-sky idealism. It is all pure nineteenth century, utterly *vieux jeu*, bourgeois through and through. It writes "civilisation" on the wall, as a revelation of what is to come; but all the while itself is but civilisation's swan-song and dying echo.

The author has borrowed from Goethe the conception of morphology, but in his hands the idea developed—just as did in Darwin's the idea of evolution, likewise Goethe's. From Nietzsche he learned how to write, how to invest his words with the accents of fate. But his false and loveless austerity learned not a whit from him whose message was as unspeakably new as his spirit was sternly loving. He is a foe to spirit—not in the sense of culture but in that of the materialistic civilisation whose kingdom is of yesterday and not to-morrow. He is its true son, its latest master; inexorably and pessimistically prophesying its coming, while at the same time showing himself a secret conservative and a member of the party of culture.

In a word, he is a snob; and shows himself such in his attachment to nature, the natural law, and his contempt for spirit. "Might not the unchangeable laws of nature be a deception, and highly unnatural?" Novalis asks. "Everything acts according to law, and nothing acts according to law. Laws are simple, easily seen relations; we seek them for the sake of convenience." Yes, forsooth, for the sake of scientific convenience, and in sheer dictatorial lovelessness. And out of a self-complacency that lusts to betray its kind, that sides with nature against spirit and man, in nature's name arrogantly lays down the law to spirit and thinks itself monstrously elevated and irreproachable the while. But the problem of aristocracy, comprised of course in the conflict between nature and spirit, is not to be resolved by any such renegade attitude as this; and he who seeks, as does Spengler, to represent nature against spirit, must belong to the aristocracy of nature—like Goethe, who stood for it against Schiller's aristocracy of the spirit. Otherwise he is simply that which I just called the talented author of the **Decline:** namely, a snob, and a member of the very large class of modern personalities who uncomfortably indoctrinate views which they are unsuited to hold. (pp. 219-27)

Thomas Mann, "On the Theory of Spengler," in his Past Masters and Other Papers, *translated by H. T. Lowe-Porter, Alfred A. Knopf, 1933, pp. 217-27.*

WALDO FRANK (essay date 1926)

[*Frank was an American novelist and critic who was best known as an interpreter of contemporary civilization, particularly that of Latin America. A socialist and supporter of various radical groups in the United States, he was a founding editor of* The Seven Arts *(1916-1917), a leftist,* avant-garde *magazine of literature and opinion. One of Frank's most significant works of criticism,* Our America *(1919), derides the "genteel tradition" in American letters and is considered an influential work in its support of realism in the nation's literature. In the following excerpt, Frank takes issue with the philosophical theses propounded in* The Decline of the West, *though he praises the poetic force of the work.*]

Oswald Spengler's *The Decline of the West,* from 1918 to 1926, sold in Germany almost a hundred thousand copies. It would be inspiriting to believe that a profound historical and philosophical work could have so large a sale in any modern land. But the originality of Spengler does not reside in his erudition; it is poetic. The book's metaphysics is eclectic rather than sound; its historical research is vast rather than uniformly deep. *Der Untergang des Abendlandes* is an epos, a myth. So, if Germany has not bought a hundred thousand copies of a great philosophic work, it has at least welcomed a personal mythos of deep interest: one whose elements are philosophy, history, esthetics: one whose comprehension requires of the reader a great familiarity with comparative history and comparative religion.

I think at once of *The Outline of History* of H. G. Wells, which had an analogous popular appeal in America and England. Wells, like Spengler, under the guise of writing history, offered a thesis and a myth. Here the analogy stops. The story in Wells is a vulgar, obvious narrative of "events": his thesis is the most illiterate notion of "human progress" and his myth is a mere flatulent, optimistic dream. Spengler's work is formally beautiful. He builds, not by storytelling, but by the presentation and analysis of analogies. And he concludes on a note as darkly glamorous as it is pessimistic. The Winter is upon us, he declares in doom words that are closer to the note of the prophets than he would care to admit. Our salvation is to perform, nobly and perfectly, the work of Winter: to understand ourselves, to set down as the Seal of our glorious dying life a ruthless scrutiny of what we were.

I shall criticize Spengler harshly enough. Let it be, however, always clear that Spengler has written a work of heroic poetic power. The land that dared to welcome such a volume still possesses culture.

The book's main thesis seems to be disguised in the title. *The Decline of the West*—is it not a misnomer? Has not Spengler really written a history and a morphology of Cultures? But no. Though the title may mislead—may, indeed, have misled its author and its readers, it is a true self-confession of the poet's veritable purpose. Spengler has composed this erudite, overpoweringly brilliant thesis on the anatomy and physiology of cultures, in order to prove that *his* Culture (the Culture of the West) is dying. This is where his heart lies. He has written a swan song. And since he is a citizen of the world whose most valid mythic material is no longer the personal legend, the hero, the war, the romance; is, on the other hand, metaphysics, history, epistemology and science, Spengler has employed these elements to make his tragic tale.

And the value of the book lies not in its thesis and its proof. This decline of the West is obvious enough. Spengler shares his conviction of it with a great measure of good Europeans. (pp. 188-89)

Spengler's value (and it is very real) lies in his attitude toward this decline of the West and in the method whereby he establishes it. His attitude is poetic. He despises the Superman construction whereby Nietzsche cheated his despair of tomorrow: he is closer to the marvelous poet Rimbaud who accepted the complete negation of all values, without hope of heavens or nirvanas, and who, yet, made of his acceptance a last song. Spengler is in love with winter. So bitter-passionate is his embrace of the death he feels in his own soul that he has written a vast book to prove the inevitability of his love. The romantic "proves" the perfection of his lady by showing how the birds and the trees and the winds sing her praises. Thus has Spengler bent the art and mathematics of the Greeks, the religion of the Jews and Arabs, the cultures of Egypt, India and China to his one loved purpose: he has made them over into ineluctable signs of the winter upon Europe.

Before such thorough passion one must be respectful. This is a song—a death song the Prussian is singing. The work of art is a matter of focus. Here a man with the whole world's learning in his hand has *focused* it to make refrain for a great downgoing. He has seen mankind whole, in order to make that whole the accomplice of his own particular end. He has warped history, maimed philosophy, chain-ganged science, perverted art. But he is an artist himself. He has written a book which is poor history, worse anthropology, perhaps. So was Dante's *Divina Commedia.*

Spengler, I have said, is a poet, his metaphysics eclectic rather than sound, his historical research vast rather than uniformly deep. Spengler's masters, as regards the material with which he works out his conception, are almost legion, nor has he always done them justice. The notion of a culture-organism, independent, impenetrable, yet somehow mirroring the universe within its autonomous self, and moved only by God in the mysterious shape of Destiny, is very close to Leibnitz with his Monads. Spengler, indeed, is an instance, with Whitehead and Bertrand Russell, of the revival of Leibnitz, whose realistic, pluralistic universe was for a time submerged under the idealistic waves of Kant and Hegel. To this Leibnitzian base, Spengler adds a good measure of Hegel. His treatment of mathematics, science, history, all the attributes of culture from geometry to esthetics, as expressions of Spirit and as subjective, is Hegelian or Kantian idealism. On the other hand, his radical differentiation of mathematical time (which is reversible) from the irreversible Time which he calls Destiny brings to mind Bergson who opposed creative Time, the signature of Life, to the false, spatial, materialistic time which he condemns as a constructed figment of the intellect. Spengler's anti-intellectualism, whereas it is as logical as Hegel, springs from Bergson, as does, likewise, his hostility to the geneticisms of Darwin and of Marx. His treatment, however, of the art-phenomena of any age as physiognomic traits of its people is a brilliant evolution of what Taine and Renan themselves derived from Hegel.

Spengler avows Goethe as his master. He is forever quoting Goethe, appealing to him as the scientific and philosophic source of his conception. And he is right, in so far as both these men are poets. Spengler is very far from the ideas of Goethe; but in his use of ideas toward an absolute, mythmaking end, he is allied to the creator of Faust.

Goethe's philosophic master was Spinoza. This manifest fact would be inadmissible to Spengler who regards Goethe as the last master of the Faustian soul and Spinoza as an anomalous survival, out of time and out of place, from the alien Magian or Arabian culture. Spengler's thesis of intact, autonomous culture-organisms does not allow that a master from one culture can do more than impede the evolution of another. Spinoza, he declares, shows his strangeness from Western (Faustian) Culture in that he lacks the *force-element* which is that culture's primary trait. Faust denotes force tending toward the infinite. But why cannot the same be said of the personal nature of any of the Hebrew prophets or of Prometheus? In Spinoza, it is true that this trait of personal force is assimilated—or, rather, it is equated—in that balance of individual wills whose sum is God. The point is that whereas Goethe as artist depicted personal force in Faust, he transcended it as a philosopher precisely in his acceptance of the Spinozistic synthesis of forces. Goethe, maturing as a thinker, transcended the concept of personal will as ultimate. Spengler has taken Goethe's esthetic creation of the individual, *willing* Faust, and made of it a philosophic symbol for an entire culture.

Let us take Spengler for a while, as he demands to be taken, critically. My notes of specific disagreements with the Spenglerian presentation of facts and of conclusions would cover many pages. This is no place to print them. Yet I cannot avoid some minimum of analytical discussion.

The major thesis is the critical issue. Spengler considers the culture as an organism. He discerns in history a number of such cultures. He examines the Chinese, the Egyptian, the Indian (Hindu), the Classical (Greek and Roman), the Magian (Jewish-Persion—early Christian-Arab), and the Western or Faustian (roughly Western Europe since 900 C.E.). He discovers in each of these cultures a regular life span of four seasons: spring, summer, autumn, winter. They sum to about one thousand years. The form and length of this course never varies. Each culture has a *soul*: this it expresses through a chief spiritual attitude, through an individual vision of life and through a specific symbol. The mathematics, science, art, religion, political, financial and economic forms of every culture express its soul, its vision—are symbols of its attitude toward life. These expressions go, with the culture itself, through the seasons to decrepitude from youth. Each epoch in any culture is strictly homogeneous with the "contemporary" epoch of any other culture. In the spring, that is, of Classical culture, you will find manifestations in every activity of man which are analogous to those of the spring of Western or of Chinese culture. Each culture lives out its own destiny, dies its own death. No other culture can do more than impede it, even as one tree may impede another's sunlight. There is no interpenetration. There is no mutual understanding. It is an illusion on the part of the Western soul to believe it understands the Chinese, the Arabian, the Greek. The inherent growth of each culture is a matter not of geneticisms and material evolutions, but of Destiny. There is no cause and effect; there are monadlike cultural units, mapped through irreversible Time from birth to death.

Now, the trouble with these organisms is that they are placed *in vacuo*. They are described as evolving their destiny sheerly out of themselves, without relational struggle, drama, reaction, interference. And yet they are also described as having the nature of biologic organisms: i.e., they have youth, maturity, old age; they have a specific lifespan. But no organisms known to man exist in this utter isolation. One and all, they arise from other organisms like them, they live in a continuum of interaction with other organisms like them, they give birth before

death or in death to other organisms like them. The culture-organisms of Spengler do not seem to be really alive: they are mere synthetic constructions of the author. In order to prove them alive, Spengler has been forced to a progressive and virtuosic deforming of the facts.

When I say that the Spenglerian culture-organism, absolute, monadlike, impenetrable, does not exist, I do not mean that there is no valid view of cultures as organic within their rise and fall. Before I can come to this, I must examine in at least one detail the Spenglerian proof.

Each culture, Spengler undertakes to show, has a soul unique and radically different from that of any other culture. (If this is so, why is there such strict analogy in the forms, seasons and lifespan of all cultures?) This soul's Weltanschauung is its own. And its prime symbol is its idea of space or of extension. From this symbol each culture-soul constructs its mathematics, its sciences, its religion, its architecture, etc. They are all expressions of the prime symbol. Therefore every mathematics, science system, religion, etc., differs radically from every other. Moreover, there is no one mathematics, no one system of physics, etc. There are as many as there are cultures. Each is true, and true uniquely for *its* culture.

To prove his thesis of the individual prime symbol of each culture, Spengler bravely ventures to establish that Greek "number" and "space" and "mathematics" differ radically from the Western. The Classical prime symbol is the finite unit, the entity, the *here and now*. It denies infinitude, past, future. It considers space as the mere emptiness between objects. Therefore it looks on number (Pythagoras) as the essence of all things: and by all things it means literally things perceptible to the senses. From this prime symbol has come the Classical esthetic unit—the human body: the Greek tragedy of episode and exterior fate: the political unit, a small city (polis): the coin, etc. But the Western (Faustian) soul has infinity as its prime symbol. Space for it is infinite and comes prior to the objects which have their being *within* it. Western mathematics is, therefore, one of function, analysis, relation. Its geometry is non-Euclidean. Its State is a cosmic empire. Its money is credit, not the coin. Its signal art is not sculpture but atmospheric painting and contrapuntal music. Its architecture is not the interiorless Greek temple, but the infinitely soaring Gothic church.

To make his thesis absolute instead of merely suggestive, Spengler is forced to explain away the Dionysian (anti-Apollonian) element in Greek culture and the Renaissance in Western Europe: to ignore the mystical in Pythagoras and Plato, together with the Aristotelian elements of medieval thought and modern science. The idea of the infinite and of aspiration toward it existed, indeed, in Greece. It came over, organically, from Egypt. Classic Greece did not lose it, but formed it, rather; and transformed it. Moreover, the modern mathematics is different from the classic and the Newtonian only in so far as it is a growth. Infinity was a problem evaded by the classical geometers: admitted as insoluble by the Cartesians: and *eliminated as solved* by the non-Euclidean mathematicians of the nineteenth century. The Classical attitude toward ultimate problems was a status of childhood. It admitted only the object and the material. So it evolved materialistic systems like those of Thales, Democritus, Heraclitus; or turned the abstractions of ideas into quasi materials called essences, as in Plato. The Faustian attitude was one of adolescence. It stressed the unsolved and aspirational: the concept of infinite space, the autonomy of the personal will. Faust is a growth from Œdipus;

even as the Cathedral is a growth from the Temple. To differentiate the prime symbols of cultures which so obviously were interpenetrated, not alone one by the other, but each by still other cultures (such as the Egyptian and the Hebrew), is to do them violence. It is an unnecessary abstraction. Why Spengler wanted to make this abstraction we shall see in the sequel.

Here is a book packed with intricate allusions. To criticize it in detail would take almost page for page. I must confine myself to one more example. One of the cultures discussed by Spengler is the Arabian—the culture of the Magian soul. Its prime space-symbol is the *world-cave*. It lacks the force element of the Faustian, and the unit-object notion of the Greek. The individual, here, is a mere passive emanation within God, as within an aloof yet immanent and defining Cave. The Arab arch, the mosque-dome, the mosaic painting, are alike expressions of this symbol. As are also algebra (the arithmetic of indefinite number), the arguments of Talmudry, the fatalism of the Moslem. The Magian culture-soul was born about the first year of our era. Precultural to it was the whole pre-Christian history of Judea, Persia, Arabia. Now, as "springtime scruptures," come the Gospels, come the philosophies of Origen, Philo, Plotinus, Iamblichus, Mani. With Augustine and the Nestorians we are at the summer. Mohammed marks the decline into the autumnal dryness whose strawlike flowers are the Arab and Judaic thinkers of Babylon and Spain.

Perhaps this amazing violence done to such various spirits as ancient Hebrew prophet, Berber mystic, Alexandrian pseudepigraphist, Arab Moslem and Granadan Moor, in the attempt to enclose them all within one organic cultural conception, born at the birth of Christ, reaching summer about 400, drooping in 800 and dead with the *rigor mortis* of "civilization" at the year 1,000, will most briefly prove the dangers of the Spenglerian method.

Of course, there are analogies between St. Augustine and Ibn Gabirol. Are there, then, none between Faust and Job? between the writers of the Upanishads and Whitman? between the sculptors of Egypt and the painters of Spain? If Maimonides is a "Magian Winter man," why is Aquinas a "Faustian Spring man"? If kinship of "prime symbol" bring Philo, Plotinus, Mohammed, Rabbi Akiba and Jehuda Halevi together as seasonal expressions of a single culture, why not prove for the entire world one spiritual Body, one organic culture—with its systoles and diastoles, of course, its tides, its shifts, and yet as well with its deep unity of purpose, its continuity of form and of method of creation?

Death is a breaking up; a lapse from unity into multiplicity. When a human being dies, only his unity is gone. Disease means *dis-wholeness*. Spengler breaks up the world into these absolute cultures which are really fragments, because there is the tendency toward death—toward disunity—in his own high Prussian soul. *He* is breaking and so is his particular portion of the world. Let him, therefore, make conscription of all the wisdom of his world to prove that his experience is the Law.

Nowhere is the man's will to see crooked plainer than in his virtual ignoring of the Jews. The whole Scriptural era before the Gospels is set aside as "inorganic"—not cultural at all. Now, Spengler's thesis is that the pure mystical religious ethos is the trait of the birth of a culture. Legalism, materialism, socialism, communism, the various systems of utiliarianism, mark that culture's end and herald the "state of suspended death" which he calls civilization and which, with all its wintry

signs, he declares now to be upon the European and American worlds. But if, hypothetically, he had deigned to consider the Hebrews and Jews as a culture, what would he have found? Mosaism (read: materialism, legalism, utilitarianism) came first! "Civilization" or death came before culture or birth. And from this winter a gradual unfolding toward the spring of the prophets. He would have found matter even more disquieting than that. For this "organism" of the Jews is hopelessly irregular: its seasons and states recur and are intermingled. Nor does Spengler's millennial limit for the entire story tell one-half of its creative tale. He would have found, moreover, that this hypothetic culture interpenetrated with others: revived and created others, was revived by others.

And, looking from the Jews back to his Greeks and Faustians, he would have found a similar intricate story. He would have found, in other words, hope in lieu of his dear despair. Wherefore he looked elsewhere, reasoned otherwise.

The culture-organism is a notion abstracted from human life. It *is* an abstraction. And abstractions are needed for intellectual work. They are right when they are fruitful. To regard the life of Greece as a strict cultural whole is wrong: yet pragmatically it may be correct to do so, since it enables us to get the results which observation in isolated status alone brings. The danger rises when we forget that abstractions are of use qua abstractions. Take them for real and they turn monsters.

Indeed, the idea of the periodic rise and fall of man is probably a similar abstraction. Yet it is justified so long as we employ it either to criticize the past or to envisage a greater future. Both of these acts require the analytic method: and analysis *is* abstraction. And now we are at the root of what ails Spengler. His "cultures" are counters of the analyst. And these he has turned into a poet's bodies. This is why his book, although its impulse is poetic, cannot rank as great poetic art. He tells us a good deal about the cultures which have filled the world. And much of what he says is true and is profound. Nowhere, for instance, have I encountered better comment on German music, on the deep significances of Classic and Gothic architecture. Yet the cultures themselves, whereof he speaks as breathing entities, do not become plastically real. We learn much in detail about their traits. *They* neither breathe for us nor move. They cannot. For they are not persons of a drama: they are tools of an argument.

Human spirit takes forms, of course, and all forms die. But the *constant* is the human spirit. And it is poor philosophy to take its forms as really abstracted from each other. Even the painter of a group of persons must relate them, one and all, upon his canvas if he aims to achieve esthetic truth.

Among the forms of human spirit are the arts which rise and fall; are social entites like state and city, which are builded and broken. But the Spenglerian assumption that the human spirit has no other life than in the splendor of great buildings, great realms, great arts, is a profanation. To prove that the abstraction called Rome was "decadent" in the year 400 is not to prove that Man, then, was less great than in the days when Caesar strutted. It may require a peculiar conjunction of poetic genius and social readiness to produce a Vergil. But there are other ways to the light. And some of them are always open.

Spengler feels death in his own soul. Wherefore he marshals a whole retrospect of life to funeral him in true Prussian glory. But human history is subtler. Man is a variable constant. He can achieve greatness with the ruins of a world as his sole instruments, as well as with the aid of outward fortune. Here, too, the evidence of the Jew might have saved Spengler—from the writing of his book! Variant circumstance has infinitely varied the expressions of this people. They have been warlike and humble; unphilosophical and later, abstruse beyond the Greeks and Hindus. They have had no drama and flooded the stage: no worldly arts at all, and later supplied such arts for all the world. They have been pastoral, and adverse from the soil. They have been creators, politically, of Greek polis, of Oriental empires, and of invisible, Platonic Zions.

Only in so far as Man remained alive among the Jews was Jewish culture a constant. And this is true of any culture. The undying kernel is humanity: this is the locus of organic growth and of organic permanence which Spengler should have studied. For cultures are never isolate. Cut them off from their immerision in other cultures—in Life, they will die uprooted. They move upon and within each other: they fall to rise, fade to be transfigured.

Above all, the human spirit, in any cultural body, is capable of *unprecedented transformation,* provided an unprecedented new element of life comes fertilely upon it. This is the destiny of evolution. And evolution is true, however discarded the mechanistic form of it may be which Darwin degraded from Lamarck. And this crucial fact—that the culture, if to be regarded as an organism at all, must be taken as a transforming organism; an organism related to the genus, not to the individual, to the possibly infinite genus, not to the sharply delimited and mortal person—is entirely ignored by Spengler.

Look on cultures, not as biologic bodies with their youth and age, but as indefinite series like those in mathematics, and you have a fertile abstraction in lieu of a dead one. These series have, each, their inner laws, perhaps, but they are intertwined and any figure belonging in one place to one series may differently occupy other series. Paul, then, who in the Spenglerian sense was a "winter man" for the Jews, could be a "spring man" for Western Europe. And Jesus, his strict contemporary in time and race, could have in him all seasons.

Or take America. Spengler would rightly say that America was born of the dying of European culture. So he condemns us to the *rigor mortis* of civilization; to a noisier Egyptian fellahdom. But why of the new mythmakers, the springtime men, those creatures of pure ethos—Whitman, Lincoln, Melville, Thoreau? In an organic body, shut by Destiny, they have no place, and Spengler doubtless would deny them. In a life series, self-contained yet indefinitely progressing, they are in place. For with such a series each integer is at once the conclusion of what came before and the outset of an infinity beyond. . . . (pp. 190-201)

> Waldo Frank, "Reflections on Spengler," in his *In the American Jungle* [1925-1936], *Farrar & Rinehart, Incorporated, 1937, pp. 188-201.*

KENNETH BURKE (essay date 1926)

[*In the following excerpt which originally appeared in the* Dial *in 1926, Burke summarizes the system of cultural analysis put forth in* The Decline of the West *and debates the validity of Spengler's conclusions.*]

Over against the H. G. Wells concept of history as a straight line progressing from savagery to modernity, Spengler [in *The Decline of the West*] opposes the concept of numberless cultural systems, each of which has followed through a cycle of its own, growing, flourishing, and decaying in a fixed order or "periodicity." These cultural cycles, by Spengler's doctrine, evolve in an irreversible sequence through "spring, summer, autumn, and winter" aspects, any "season" of one culture being comparable with the corresponding season of any other culture. These analogous stages of different cultural systems are called "contemporaneous"; and by aligning the stages of our own cultural cycle (that of Europe and European America, which Spengler dates from about 1000 A.D.) with the contemporaneous stages of other cultural cycles, Spengler claims to produce a series of co-ordinates for determining which of the cultural seasons is now upon us.

Homer, in the Graeco-Roman cycle, would be contemporaneous with the northern sagas in our own, this era always being "rural and intuitive," and marked by the "birth of a myth of the grand style, expressing a new God-feeling." This spring gradually metamorphoses into summer, a period of "ripening consciousness" and of the "earliest urban and critical stirrings"—the pre-Socratics of the sixth and fifth centuries being analogous to Galileo, Bacon, and Descartes. In autumn the city assumes a leading position in the life of the culture. This is the age of "enlightenment" (Socrates and Rousseau) in which the traditional code is now subjected to a rigorous questioning, although it is still powerful as a religious and creative force. The mathematics characteristic of the culture is now definitely formulated, and the "great conclusive" metaphysical systems are constructed (Plato and Aristotle having their contemporaneous parallel in Goethe and Kant).

But each culture, while exemplifying the laws of growth and decay common to all cultures, is a self-contained unit, talking in a language addressed to itself alone. When it has passed, it leaves us its monuments and its scripts, but the experience which these works symbolized has vanished, so that subsequent cultures inherit a body of rigid symbols to which they are psychically alien—much the way one of Jung's typical extraverts would be alien to a typical introvert. In this sense, ancient Greek is as undecipherable a language as Etruscan, since there is no word in the Greek vocabulary which corresponds, in its cultural background, to the word which we select as its equivalent in any one of our modern languages. Consider, for instance, the difference in content between "man" as one of a race who stole the fire from heaven and "man" as a link in the evolutionary chain. It is not hard to imagine how a work of art arising out of the one attitude could be "alien" to a reader in whom the other attitude was ingrained.

Spengler lays great emphasis upon this cultural subjectivism, and even insists upon the subjective element in natural science. For even though science deals with empirically provable facts, a specific kind of mentality is required to meditate upon these facts rather than others. The possible modes of natural investigation are dependent upon the interests of the investigators. Spengler characterizes the science of any given culture as the conversion of its religion into an irreligious field—such concepts as "force" and "energy," for instance, merely being an altered aspect of the omnipotent and omnipresent God conceived at an earlier stage in the same culture.

The growth of science is also the evidence of a radical change in a culture's evolution. At this stage, the intellectualistic, critical, and irreligious elements of the culture gradually rise to the ascendancy. The emotional certainty of the earlier epochs, when religious, metaphysical, and aesthetic systems were built up spontaneously, is now past. The culture becomes a civilization. "In the one period life *reveals* itself, the other has life as its *object*.'' In place of the city we have the metropolis, and the ''ethical-practical tendencies of an irreligious and unmetaphysical cosmopolitanism.'' Winter, thereby, is upon us. Hellenistic-Roman Stoicism after 200—returning to our concept of the contemporaneous—is paralleled by ethical socialism after 1900. The theatricality of Pergamene art is matched by Liszt, Berlioz, and Wagner—and Hellenistic painting finds its equivalent in impressionism. The American skyscraper, instead of being looked upon as the evidence of a new ''dawn,'' is interpreted by Spengler as the symptom of decay corresponding to the ''architectural display in the cities of the Diadochi.''

Spengler thus finds that the high point of our culture has been passed, while we go deeper into the closing period, the era of civilization. With intellectualistic elements predominant, we are no longer fitted for the production of great works of art, but for technical exploits, for economic, commercial, political, and imperialistic activities. We are, like Rome, which was the civilization of Greek culture, ordained to be superior as road-builders and inferior as artists. And by his doctrine of cultural subjectivism, even those great works of art which our culture in its more youthful and vigorous stages produced as the symbolization of Western-European experience will become alien as this experience itself recedes before the rise of other cultures having other modes of experience to symbolize. In conclusion, then: (a) Even the greatest works of art are couched, not in the language of ''mankind,'' but in the language of a specific cultural tradition, and the loss of the tradition is like the loss of the dictionary; and (b) since art is inevitably inferior in an era of civilization, we are invited to abandon all hope of further artisic excellence in our cultural cycle.

Let us consider first Spengler's subjectivist argument. In discussing each cultural cycle, he finds some dominant trait which characterizes the entire mode of experience peculiar to the culture. Arabic culture, for instance, is ''magian,'' our own is ''Faustian,'' and the Graeco-Roman is ''Apollinian.'' He then shows how these dominant traits manifest themselves in all the various aspects of a culture's ''behaviour.'' The Apollinian trait can be expanded as a sense of the ''pure present,'' a concrete ''thisness and hereness,'' which is to be found equally in the repose of the Greek temple, the ''corporeality'' of Greek mathematics, and the Greek indifference to time (the Greeks had no system of chronological reckoning comparable to our method of dating from the birth of Christ). This same attitude naturally resulted in the develoment of sculpture into a major art. In contrast to this, the Faustian culture has a pronounced historic sense, a mathematics of function and time, an ''aspiring'' architecture; and it has developed music into a major art. In painting, the ''corporeal'' mentality of the Greeks led to the exclusion of sky-blue as a colour, and the disinterest in perspective; while the Faustian culture, with its feeling for distance, showed a marked preference for this very blue, and developed perspective exhaustively. Spengler considers this as evidence of totally different subjective states; yet could it not, as well, be used to indicate a very fundamental kind of similarity? If blue and perspective are employed by the Faustian for the same reason that they are rejected by the Apollinian, does not this argue a common basis of choice? It is to grant, categorically, that blue and perspective symbolize for both cultures a sense of distance. A genuinely subjective difference between cultures would be undetectable, for it would involve a situation in which the symbols could be employed with directly opposite content. Blue and perspective would then, for the Greek, mean pure present; and we could have formed the Greek temple, rather than the Gothic cathedral, as our symbol of aspiration. The aesthetic symbols of an alien culture could give us no clue as to the mode of experience behind them.

Furthermore, it seems arbitrary that Spengler should stop at cultural subjectivism. Why not epochal subjectivism? If a difference in the traits of a culture involves a difference in the content of its expressionistic symbols, does not his division of a culture into seasons indicate that each season symbolizes a mode of experience peculiar to itself? If a culture speaks a language of its own, then each season has its own dialect of that language.

Why, then, does Spengler not go on to this further stage? What ''vested interests'' could be endangered for this savant who would so willingly sacrifice an entire culture? The fact is that epochal subjectivism would interfere with his two major conclusions: cultural subjectivism and aesthetic defeatism.

Spengler's division into spring, summer, autumn, and winter is at bottom the formulation of four subjective types, four typical modes of experience which recur in each cultural cycle. Thus, subjectivity is seen to produce its alliances as well as its estrangements. And contemporaneous epochs of different cultural cycles might even be considered to have more in common than different epochs of the same culture—our ''irreligious and cosmopolitan'' winter, for instance, being nearer to the same mode of experience in the Graeco-Roman cycle than to its own ''rural and intuitive'' spring. At least, there is more of Apuleius than of Beowulf in the modern *Weltanschauung*. Epochal subjectivity, looked upon in this way, would tend to counteract the estrangements of cultural subjectivity. Cultural subjectivity would not be an *absolute* condition, but an *approximate* one—and the modes of experience in different eras of the world's history would be capable of an approach towards identity. Epochal subjectivity, furthermore, would constitute a sanction of the modern artist. It would force us to recognize that winter, purely by being a different mode of experience from spring, summer, or autumn, is categorically entitled to symbolize this mode of experience in art.

In any case, how can Spengler call modern art inferior? By what subtlety does this absolute judgement manage to creep into a relativistic theory? There is no criterion of excellence inherent in the analysis of a genetic process. His logical machinery provides for no step beyond the observation that in spring we must have the symbolizations of spring and in winter the symbolizations of winter. To emerge with a judgement in such a case would be like concluding, after an explanation of the earth's seasons as being caused by the planet's revolution about the sun, ''therefore autumn is better than winter.''

The pessimistic connotation which he puts upon the civilization aspect of the culture-civilization dichotomy is purely arbitrary. We might, with as much authority, use a different analogy from that of the seasons, perhaps considering all the earlier stages of a cultural cycle as periods of upbuilding, of pioneering, of grim, hard-working zealotry. Culture, we could say, struggles and wrestles with its environment to amass an inheritance which civilization, coming after it, has the leisure to enjoy. For when a culture is in full swing, it is not only politically and religiously intolerant, but aesthetically intolerant as well. And in any case, the people of Bach's time did not have Beethoven, and those of Beethoven's time did not have Wagner—while in the course of a New York winter we have them all.

Yet, however much one may snipe at Spengler's book, it remains a stupendous piece of work, formidable, lugubrious, and passionate. His historical perspectives are often brilliant and fertile; his methodology unquestionably has a future. And European culture does seem to be undergoing some weakening of the pure cultural strain: whatever interpretation we may put upon the fact, we must recognize that our culture is no longer thorough-bred. We now question, where we once asserted— and even art is trammelled by considerations which prey upon it much the way epistemology has preyed upon metaphysics. Such phenomena are given an elaborate orientation in Spengler's system. (pp. 289-94)

> Kenneth Burke, "A 'Logic' of History," in A Dial Miscellany, *edited by William Wasserstrom, Syracuse University Press, 1963, pp. 289-95.*

R. G. COLLINGWOOD (essay date 1927)

[*Collingwood was a highly-respected English archaeologist and philosopher whose writings often center on the relationship between philosophy and history. In the following excerpt, he criticizes* The Decline of the West *as unsound in its scholarship, logic, methodology, and fundamental philosophy.*]

Spengler's view of history presents it as a succession of cultures, each having a peculiar physiognomy of its own which it maintains and works out down to the smallest details, and each following a definite course of development through a sequence of phases that is identical for all. Every culture has its spring, its dawning phase, economically based on rural life and spiritually recognizable by a rich mythological imagination expressing in epic and legend the whole world-view which, later, is to be developed in philosophical and scientific form. Then follows its summer, at once a revolt against the mythology and scholasticism of the spring and their continuation; a period in which a young and vigorous urban intelligence pushes religion into the background and brings to the fore a strictly scientific form of consciousness. The autumn of the culture pushes this consciousness to its limit, while at the same time it sees the decay of religion and the impoverishment of inward life; rationalism, enlightenment, are its obvious marks. Last comes winter, the decay of culture and the reign of civilization, the materialistic life of the great cities, the cult of science only so far as science is useful, the withering of artistic and intellectual creativeness, the rise of academic and professional philosophy, the death of religion, and the drying-up of all the springs of spiritual life. The four-fold distinction of phases is not a necessity; at times it is convenient to distinguish more or fewer than four; but however many are distinguished in one culture the same number is necessarily distinguishable in all others. (pp. 311-12)

This conception is set forth at enormous length in a formless and chaotic volume, heavy with erudition and illuminated by a brilliant play of analogical insight, and a still more brilliant power of discrimination. The unforgettable things in the book are the passages in which the author characterizes such fundamental differences as those between classical things and their modern analogues: in which he illustrates the thesis that "Classical culture possessed no memory, no organ of history in the highest sense," or that the ancients thought of space as the non-existent—this he proves not simply by quoting philosophers but by analysing sculpture and architecture—whereas western man regards infinite space as his true home and proper environment; which again is proved not from Kant but from a

study of Gothic and oil-painting. For the philosopher only makes explicit in his own peculiar way an idea which has necessarily been the common heritage of his entire culture; and nothing is more admirable than the way in which Spengler sees and expounds this important truth.

The strange thing is that he seems to think his ideas altogether new. Learned as he is, he is either very ignorant or very reticent concerning the history of his own science. He asserts over and over again that the morphology of historical cultures is a wholly new thing. He seems ready to admit, in a single cautious sentence, that with regard to political history the idea is old; but he denies that anyone has applied it to "*all* branches of a culture." That may be; all is a large word; but if he really knew of the cyclical doctrines of Plato, Polybius, Machiavelli, and above all Vico, which last both anticipates his own in all essentials and goes far beyond it in historical profundity; if he even knew of Professor Petrie's recent and fascinating exposition of the same doctrine, he cannot be acquitted of *suppressio veri*. He cannot claim to have omitted them for lack of space; his book consists largely of repetitions, and of its 250,000 words it would have been easy to devote 250 to naming his predecessors in the field. The fact that he has not done so, makes it incumbent on a critic like the present writer to confess that not only has the main thesis of Spengler's book been familiar to him all his life, but that the reading of it has not given him a single genuinely new idea; for all the applications of the thesis are mechanical exercises which, so far as the present writer is acquainted with the ground, he has long ago carried out for himself. This one may say without claiming to possess a quarter of Spengler's erudition.

This erudition, gigantic as it is, shows one gap. Spengler is at his worst in discussion philosophy. He shows what must be called a complete misunderstanding of Plato when he mistakes a deliberately "mythical" literary form for a "mystical" type of thought (what philosopher was ever less "mystical" than Plato?); he consistently attributes to the Stoics the fundamental conception of the Epicureans, and incidentally misunderstands its meaning; and he commits the appalling blunder of asserting that for Descartes the soul is in space—a statement which falsifies the whole modern conception of the relation between space and thought and goes far to explain his long rambling polemics against what he takes to be the philosophy of Kant.

This is not a matter of mere ignorance concerning one department of human history. He is not only ill-informed on the history of philosophy, he is ill at ease in philosophy itself; and this means that whenever he tries to handle a fundamental problem he does so clumsily and without firmness or penetration. Brilliant on the surface, glittering in its details with a specious cleverness and apparent profundity, his "philosophy of history" is at bottom lacking in orientation, unsound on fundamentals, ill thought-out, and in consequence committed to a method which falsifies even its detail when a crucial case arises. These are serious charges; they are only made because Spengler's is a serious book which deserves to be taken seriously; and the first step towards proving them must be to quote falsified details. They are numerous; here are a few.

"The Greek and Roman alike sacrificed to the gods of the place in which he happened to stay or reside; all other deities were outside his range of vision." This *must* be true, because it follows from the fundamentally spaceless and timeless character of the classical mind, its insistence on the here-and-now as the only reality. But it is *not* true. Even Odysseus prays to his own Athene as he struggles for life in the stormy sea; and the Roman carries to the ends of the empire the Juppiter Optimus Maximus of the Capitol. The first half of Spengler's sentence is true; the second is false. This means that he has represented as the whole of the classical mind what was in reality only a part. The tendency to worship the gods of the land was very real; but it was only one tendency, and it was constantly balanced and checked by a counter-tendency to carry with one the cult of one's own place. *Caelum non animum mutant, qui trans mare currunt.*

Similarly, he asserts more than once that the classical mind was essentially polytheistic, and opposes to it "Magian monotheism," that is, alleges that monotheism is characteristic of the Arabian culture that filled the first millennium of our era. But this is, once more, inaccurate. All the Greek philosophers, until the decadence, were monotheists; and Spengler knows that philosophy is only a reasoned statement of ideas common to the culture. The monotheism of the philosophers can only indicate a profound strain of monotheism in the whole Graeco-Roman world. And indeed Spengler himself would recognize that strain (for its existence is notorious enough) did not his faulty logic compel him to ignore it in the interests of his morphology. (pp. 313-15)

These are not superficial flaws. They are not minor errors or inconsistencies such as much exist in any great work. They are sacrifices of truth to method; they are symptoms of a logical fallacy which underlies the whole book and has actually been erected into a principle. The fallacy lies in the attempt to characterize a culture by means of a single idea or tendency or feature, to deduce everything from this one central idea without recognizing that a single idea, asserted in this way, calls up its own opposite in order to have something to assert itself against, and henceforth proceeds, not by merely repeating itself, but by playing a game of statement and counter-statement with this opposite. Everything in the classical mind is by Spengler deduced from the here-and-now of the immediate, sense-given, bodily present. But to assert the present is to deny the absent; therefore the absent must be present to the classical mind as *that which it is denying,* and it is impossible to concentrate one's mind on denying anything unless one vividly feels the need of denying it; feels that it is *there* to be denied, that someone, or some obscure force within oneself, is asserting it. Further, when one has denied it, and denied it effectively and overwhelmingly, it reasserts itself in a new form; and one has to begin over again, in order to meet this new peril. So the attempt to frame a whole life—political, artistic, religious, scientific, and so forth—by working out the implications of a single fundamental idea is foredoomed to failure; the idea can only live in conflict with its own opposite, and unless that opposite is present as an effective force there is no conflict and no life.

This conception of the mind's life as a conflict between opposing ideas or tendencies is, nowadays, one would have thought, a commonplace. Indeed, Spengler himself says it is. It is the more curious that he should not himself possess the conception; or rather, that he should base his entire system of historical cycles on denying it. For this is what, in effect, he does. It is true that classical art or thought tends to be easily intelligible, while modern or western tends to be obscure to the many and intelligible only to the few; therefore, says Spengler, this is the whole truth; "everything that is classical is comprehensible in *one* glance"; instead of obscure philosophers, for instance, the classical world has philosophers who can be understood by the man in the street; and in this context he actually mentions

Heraclitus, without adding that he was nicknamed "the Obscure." Magian monotheism is dualistic, therefore Jewish religion, being Magian, opposes to Jahweh (whom? you would never guess)—Beelzebub! The classical culture only cared for the present, therefore the Hellenes, unlike the Vikings, did not bury their dead in great barrows; and what of the tombs on the Via Appia? . . . These are merely examples of the way in which, to bring them into the scheme, facts are constantly impoverished, robbed of one element merely because it is recessive, in order that the other, dominant as it is, may be erected into a false absolute. No one, probably, will deny that the elements which Spengler identifies as characteristic of this or that culture really are characteristic of it; where he fails is in thinking out what he means by "characteristic." He thinks that the characteristic is a fundamental something whose logical consequences flow smoothly and unopposedly into all its manifestations; whereas it is really the dominant partner in a pair of opposites, asserting itself only so far as it can keep its opposite in check and therefore always coloured by the hidden presence and underground activity of this opposite. To see the dominant characteristic and miss the recessive is to see history with the eye of the superficial student.

The same fault comes out in a different way in his view of the relation of cultures to one another. Vico, whose work he so curiously ignores, pointed out that the feudal barbarism of the Middle Ages differed from the Homeric feudal barbarism because it contained in itself Christianity, which summarizes and transcends ancient thought. And even Spengler, when it comes to mathematics, notices that Euclidean geometry is still retained today as elementary or school geometry, so that modern mathematics contains and transcends Greek mathematics. But though he sees this fact, he does not understand it; for him, every culture is just radically different from every other, based on its own idea and not on the idea of any but itself. Each culture is wholly self-enclosed; within its limits, it proceeds on a type-pattern exactly like that of the rest, but this similarity of structure is its *only* relation to the rest. For him, therefore, it is a misfortune that our elementary geometry is still Euclidean; it gets us into bad mathematical habits and sets an unnecessary obstacle in the way of our understanding modern non-Euclidean geometry. Thus the whole idea of "classical education" is, we infer, a gigantic blunder. Similarly, it was a misfortune, he thinks, that the "Magian" culture grew up under the tutelage of decaying classical civilization, whose petrified relics prevented the new culture from rising spontaneously, because unopposed, in the Roman Imperial age. But surely it is not very hard to see that non-Euclidean geometry is based on Euclidean even while it transcends and opposes it; and that the "Magian" culture, far from being stifled by the Roman Empire, used it as a scaffolding for its own building, a trellis for its own climbing flowers. The reason why Spengler denies these obvious facts is because he cannot grasp the true dynamic relation between opposites; his philosophical error leads him into the purely historical blunder of thinking that one culture, instead of stimulating another by its very opposition, can only crush it or be crushed by it. He thinks of cultures atomistically, each as a self-contained or closed system, precisely as Epicurus thought of the "worlds" whose plurality he asserted; and just as Epicurus could do nothing better with the spaces between his worlds than to hand them over to the gods as a dwelling, surrendering all attempt to make sense of the relation between world and world, so Spengler plugs the gap between one culture and the next with a crude, cultureless human life which insulates each culture from its neighbours and makes it impossible to envisage an historical whole of which every culture is a part. He actually claims that the abandonment of the historical whole, and the atomistic view of cultures, is a grand merit of his system; and so it is, for it cuts out the real problem of history, the problem of *interrelating* the various cultures, which is the problem that requires profound and penetrating thought, and leaves only the problem of *comparing* them, a far easier task for those shallow minds that can accept it. And if, as Spengler says, this is the age of shallow and decadent thought, of unphilosophical philosophy and unscientific science, his philosophy of history is, as he says it is, precisely what our age needs.

The fact is that Spengler, with all his erudition and historical learning, lacks the true historical mind. Learning does not make the historian; there is a *sense* of history which is not acquired through erudition, and for this historical sense we look to Spengler in vain. History deals with the individual in all its individuality; the historian is concerned to discover the facts, the whole facts and nothing but the facts. Now comparative anatomy is not history but science; and Spengler's morphology is simply the comparative anatomy of historical periods. The historical morphologist is concerned not to discover what happened, but, assuming that he knows what happened, to generalize about its structure as compared with the structure of other happenings. His business is not to *work at* history, but to *talk about* it, on the assumption that someone else has already done the work—the work, that is, of finding out what the facts are, the historian's work. In this sense, Spengler nowhere shows the slightest desire to do a piece of historical work, or the slightest sign of having done one. His history consists of readymade facts which he has found in books; and what he wants to do is to arrange these in patterns. When the man with historical sense reads a statement in a history book, he at once asks, is that really so? What evidence is there? How can I check the statement? and he sets to work doing over again, for himself, the work of determining the fact. This is because the historical sense means the feeling for historical thought as living thought, a thought that goes on within one's own mind, not a dead thought that can be treated as a finished product, cut adrift from its roots in the mind that thinks it, and played with like a pebble. Now the extraordinary thing about Spengler is that, after giving us a penetrating and vivid description of the difference between history and nature, and setting up the demand that we shall envisage "the world as history"—an admirable demand admirably stated—he goes on to consider the world not as history but precisely as nature, to study it, that is to say, through scientific and not historical spectacles, and to substitute for a truly genetic narrative, which would be history, a self-confessed morphology, which is science. And he is forced into doing this by his own philosophical errors, his errors, that is to say, concerning the structure of his own thought. He prepares us for all this, it is true, by his open scorn of logic and his statement that Goethe and Nietzsche are his only two masters; for neither Goethe nor Nietzsche, with all their poetic gifts and fine intelligence, had any grasp on the distinction between nature and history. And Spengler himself praises Goethe for confusing the two, for treating Nature as history and a culture as an organism.

The touchstone of the historical sense is the future. Science determines the future, foretells an eclipse or the like, just because the object of science is Nature and "Nature has no history." The laws of Nature are timeless truths. For history, time is the great reality; and the future is the infinite well-spring of those events which, when they happen, become present, and whose traces left upon the present enable us to reconstruct them

when they are past. We cannot know the future, just because the future has not happened and therefore cannot leave its traces in the present. The historian who tries to forecast the future is like a tracker anxiously peering at a muddy road in order to descry the footsteps of the next person who is going to pass that way. All this, the historian knows instinctively. Ask him to forecast a single instant of the future, and he will laugh in your face. If anyone offers to foretell events, he speaks not as an historian but as a scientist or a clairvoyant. And if he offers to foretell events by means of historical thinking, he is either hoaxing his audience or saying historical when he means scientific. Spengler again and again claims that his morphology enables him to foretell the future. He even says that therein lies its chief merit and novelty; in which context, as usual, he refrains from mentioning his predecessors, the crowd of sociological writers, led by Marx, who have made just that claim.

But his claim to foretell the future is absolutely baseless. Just as his morphology does not work at history but only talks about it, does not *determine* the past but, assuming it as already determined, attaches labels to it, so this same method does not determine the future, but only provides a set of labels—the same old set—for a future that is undetermined. For instance, Spengler tells us that between A.D. 2000 and 2200 someone will arise corresponding to Julius Caesar. Well, we ask, what will he do? Where will he live? What will he look like? Whom will he conquer? All Spengler can say is, he will correspond to Julius Caesar; he will do the kind of things that a person would do, who corresponded to Julius Caesar; he will live in a place corresponding to Julius Caesar's Rome; he will look like a person corresponding to Julius Caesar, and so forth. But, we must reply, this is not predetermining history. . . . Spengler's claim to foretell the future is on a par with saying that the possession of a clock will enable its possessor to foretell the future because he can say that twelve will happen an hour after eleven. No doubt; but what will be going on at twelve?

There is another reason why the claim is wholly futile. On his own showing, the decay of classical culture in Rome synchronized with the rise of Magian culture in the very same culture-area. Thus cultures may overlap both in space and in time. In Hadrian's reign, then, a Spengler might have diagnosed a general petrifaction and decay of everything classical, and said that the Roman world was a dying world. And when someone pointed to the Pantheon, and said, "is that a symptom of decay?" the answer would be, "that is an example of imperial display by means of material and mass," . . . "and therefore it is meaningless, barren, vulgar civilization-architecture." But a counter-Spengler would retort, "not at all; the Pantheon is *the first Mosque* . . . and therefore belongs to the exuberant springtime of a nascent culture." Now it follows from the atomistic view of cultures that a new culture may begin anywhere, at any moment, irrespective of any circumstances whatever; and there is no possible proof that one is not beginning now. But if so, what becomes of "predetermining the future"?

It is all the more hopeless because there is no possible way, according to Spengler, of discovering what will be the fundamental idea of any hitherto undeveloped or unexamined culture. This, of course, follows from the atomistic conception; but its results are very serious. If any two cultures happened to have the same fundamental idea, they would be indistinguishable; the person corresponding to Julius Caesar would be Julius Caesar himself, repeated identically, name and all, at another date. That this possibility follows logically from Spengler's conception shows how profoundly anti-historical that conception is; that he has not observed it to follow, shows how ill he has thought out his own position. But on the other hand, if the fundamental idea of one culture differs from that of another, how can the one understand the other? Spengler unhesitatingly answers, it cannot. We do not understand the classical world; what we see in it is our own image in an opaque mirror. Very well, but how does he know this to be merely our image? How does he know that we are not understanding the past as it really was? There is no answer, and can be no answer; for the fact is, unless we understand the ancients well enough to know that we do not understand them completely, we can never have reason to suspect that our errors about them are erroneous. Spengler, by denying the possibility of understanding other cultures than our own, has denied the possibility of history itself. Here again, bad philosophy—a crude half-baked subjective idealism—brings its own punishment. If history is possible, if we can understand other cultures, we can do so only by re-thinking for ourselves their thoughts, cherishing within us the fundamental idea which framed their lives; and in that case their culture lives on within ours, as Euclidean geometry lives on within modern geometry and Herodotean history within the mind of the modern historian. But this is to destroy the idea of atomic cultures, and to assert not a mere plurality of cultures but a unity of that plurality, a unity which is the present culture, the heir of all its past. Against that conception Spengler struggles, because, having no historical sense, he does not *feel* it, and, being a bad philosopher, cannot understand it; yet that conception is presupposed on every page of his work. "The unities of place, time and action" I read, opening it at random, "are . . . an indication of what classical man felt about life." And how does Spengler know what classical man felt? Only by putting himself into the position of classical man and feeling it too. Unless he has done that, he is deliberately deceiving us; no man knows what another feels if he is incapable of feeling it himself.

Spengler's so-called philosophy of history is therefore, we may repeat, lacking in orientation, because it reduces history to a plurality of cultures between whose fundamental ideas there is no relation whatever; it is unsound on fundamentals, because its purpose—that of "predetermining the future"—is impossible in itself and in any case unrealizable by his methods; it is ill thought-out, because he shows no signs of having seen the fatal objections to it; and it is committed to the methodical falsification of facts because it distorts every fact falling—or alleged to fall—within a given culture, into an example of an abstract and one-sided idea which is fancied to represent the essence of that culture. In all four respects, it is an unworthy child of the historical studies of the last two hundred years. In each respect it violates elementary dictates of the historical consciousness; in each respect it is far surpassed by the cyclical doctrines of Hegel, a hundred, and Vico, two hundred years ago. (pp. 315-22)

> *R. G. Collingwood, "Oswald Spengler and the Theory of Historical Cycles," in* Antiquity, *Vol. I, September, 1927, pp. 311-25.*

GEORGE SANTAYANA (essay date 1929)

[*Santayana was a Spanish-born philosopher, poet, novelist, and literary critic who was for the most part educated in the United States, taking his undergraduate and graduate degrees at Harvard where he later taught philosophy. His earliest published works were the poems of* Sonnets, and Other Verses *(1894). Although Santayana is regarded as no more than a fair poet, his facility*

with language is one of the distinguishing features of his later philosophical works. Written in an elegant, non-technical prose, Santayana's major philosophical work of his early career is the five-volume Life of Reason *(1905-06). These volumes reflect their author's materialist viewpoint applied to such areas as society, religion, art, and science, and along with* Scepticism and Animal Faith *(1923) and the four-volume* Realms of Being *(1927-40) put forth the view that while reason undermines belief in anything whatever, an irrational animal faith suggests the existence of a "realm of essences" which leads to the human search for knowledge. Late in his life Santayana stated that "reason and ideals arise in doing something that at bottom there is no reason for doing." "Chaos," he wrote earlier, "is perhaps at the bottom of everything." In the following excerpt from an essay originally published in the* New Adelphi, *March 1929, Santayana argues that the value of* The Decline of the West *lies in the work's poetic vision rather than in the accuracy of Spengler's historical and philosophical analysis.*]

[Spengler's two thick volumes of **The Decline of the West**] are swollen with a bewildering variety of alleged facts, insubstantial enough in themselves; for we know nowadays better than a hundred years ago, at the dawn of romantic philosophy and history, how fast the most authoritative academic views change on every subject, how often they contradict one another, and on what slender evidence they are apt to rest. Even if Spengler were a leading professor in each of the branches of learning which he deflowers so sweepingly, we might suspect that there was more fancy than fact in his science. For what is his thesis? That there is a certain order of phases which recur and must recur in the rise and fall of every great society. Spengler does not follow, like Hegel, a thread of true history, interpreting it dialectically and giving it out as alone central or significant: he surveys instead the whole panorama, and creates a sort of botany of events; and this in two stages, one obvious and Linnaean, another more Pythagorean and occult. On the surface, he picks out the brighter flowers from the weedy garden of history, counts their petals, notes their colors, and considers their manner of growth and of going to seed. We are pelted with multitudinous assertions which, poor wights, we have no means of testing; and we are filled, in any case, with that emotion of *Reichtum* and *Fülle* ["richness" and "fullness"] so dear to the German heart. But, attempting to go deeper, Spengler offers us an occult botany as well; for where the form, color, and growth of his flowers are by no means identical, as in Egypt compared with China, or in the Greek world compared with the modern, he nevertheless persuades himself that they exactly correspond, and are *really* forms of the same species. Here is a revival, in respect to history, of that theory of fixed species and eternal *genres* which once found favor in biology and in the arts. As a tragedy, in whatever age or language composed, was required to have five acts and three unities, at the risk of not being a tragedy according to Aristotle, so now every civilization is required to pass through a classical, a magian, a Faust-like, and an imperial phase, at the risk of not being a civilization according to Spengler. Naturally, these necessary phases appear in so many disguises that it is hard to say what, precisely, they may be; but if we compare Spengler with Hegel and with Houston Stewart Chamberlain, who seem to be his next-of-kin, we may observe that his philosophy of history is more impartial. Spengler has more respect for the exotic, and more knowledge of it; he is not content to describe the principal ingredients of a single tradition, Hebraic, Hellenic, Germanic, as if nothing else counted in his snug universe, made to declare the glory of one chosen people or of one chosen idea; he sees in his own times neither the culmination of the world nor its collapse, but a phase in its mutation, such as has often occurred before and may often occur again. Germany and the present age are thus put where they belong in the midst of a flux of events in which they have no pre-eminence. The dogma of progress disappears and, for that very reason, instances of actual and finite progress in specific directions can be honestly traced, when we have taken for the moment the point of view of some living interest. The botanist recognizes his struggling flowers, however widely dispersed and curiously modified; the logician, taking a bird's-eye view of history, thinks he can discern the same patterns endlessly repeated in every part.

Thus the superstition of historical idealism is abandoned, but the illusion of it is retained; and the consequent advantage is not unmixed. The views of Hegel and Chamberlain represent a last revision of Hebraic prophecy: they express the vitality, the faith, the arrogance of a stubborn people struggling against infinite odds: if intellectually preposterous, they are morally powerful or even sublime. In them romanticism at least bravely takes its life in its hands, and rushes to a passionate suicide. In Spengler all this narrow zeal and party-spirit are absent; the idealism which in the others was a war-cry, in him is only a hobby; and we may ask ourselves why, having reformed his national philosophy so far, he could not reform it altogether. I am perhaps no philosopher myself; but I can hardly understand what pleasure anyone can find in wanton extravagance. If various plants or institutions can be traced back materially to a common source, this fact is interesting; and if affinities appear between various forms, even when different in origin, this circumstance is interesting too; but in both cases the divergencies are no less real than the similarities, and all the profit of tracing either the one or the other lies in clarifying and elaborating the picture of each particular thing in its own ideal individuality. A cultivated mind clings as to its natural friends to the salient moments of history, when men were noble and arts perfect; but these moments are rare and traversed inwardly by the most disquieting infections and rumblings of decay. On the other hand, minor beauties, incipient arts, and joyful accidents are scattered broadcast even in the darkest ages and in the most savage lives; the desert has its palms and the moor its heather; the bleakest down breaks here and there into a copse, or slopes into a dale, a rivulet, or a meadow. Why deprive these odd nooks and high stony places of their beautiful singularity? Why say that there are only nine kinds of possible nooks, or only one form of true mountain? The metaphysical pretensions of Spengler's idealism, in seeking to impose a pet pattern on the flux of existence, not only do violence to the incorrigible variety of Nature, but in the effort to conceal their falseness they compromise the purity of the intuitions which they express abusively. Such pretensions may make a system; they may even make a reputation; but are they worthy of a philosophic mind?

The whole force of Spengler's perceptions—and they have sometimes a remarkable force—seems to me to lie in another quarter. It is subjective, moral, lyrical. Like the epic and tragic poets of Greece, we may transport our own passions into the irrevocable past, and give them a nobler expression in that distant setting. We may vivify a slender tradition with a fresh wonder and a new moral; the vivid fiction will have an interest for us quite apart from its historical truth, because poetry, as Aristotle says, is truer than history; that is, it is nearer to the roots of action and estimation in ourselves. Now Spengler's political botany, the tragic pattern which he discovers repeated everywhere, is a help to intuition: it dramatizes the past for our imaginative pleasure. Analogies are the wings of memory;

they are seven-league boots by which we may traverse formidable distances, and sweep aside irrelevant details or contrary facts which would only oppress the mind if it could retain them. Intuition, far from penetrating by a miraculous feminine gift to the truth of things distant, falsifies even things present: it substitutes a luminous essence for their obscure diffusion; and dramatic intuition in particular synthesizes elements never themselves co-existent. A man's view of history is necessarily personal: it exhibits his politics, and his politics, if genuine, exhibit his heart. As Plato's *Republic* was avowedly a means of writing large the economy of the civilized Greek soul, so any intuitive philosophy of history will be a means of writing large the sympathies and capacities of the philosopher's mind. In Spengler's case, for instance, we can easily see that his private studies and his nationality are responsible for the part assigned to mathematics in his Only Possible Idea of Culture, as well as for the appearance there of a special Faust-like or musical phase. These personal notes would offend, if we could seriously regard such a philosophy as a study of forces actually governing events; but the same peculiarities become innocent and even amiable, when we take them for private vistas, tragic insights of a mind deeply engaged in the very flux which it thus attempts to dominate poetically; that is, always with a profound reference to its own loves and its own fate. The romantic poet crying in the wilderness of history is then like a Homeric hero telling us how manfully he vanquished the god Scamander when caught and almost carried away in that rushing stream. (pp. 88-93)

George Santayana, "Spengler," in his The Idler and His Works and Other Essays, *edited by Daniel Cory, George Braziller, Inc., 1957, pp. 87-96.*

JOHN DEWEY (essay date 1932)

[*Dewey was one of the most celebrated American philosophers of the twentieth century and the leading philosopher of pragmatism after the death of William James. Like James's pragmatism, Dewey's philosophy, which he named "instrumentalism," was an action-oriented form of speculation which judged ideas by their practical results, especially in furthering human adaptation to the changing circumstances of existence. Dewey criticized the detached pursuit of truth for its own sake and advocated a philosophy with the specific aim of seeking improvements in human life. Much of Dewey's influence has been felt in the fields of education and political theory. In the following excerpt, he reviews* Man and Technics.]

The preoccupation of so much of contemporary thought with the machine and its technology finds its place in the problem of the relation of past and future history. It also gives striking evidence that the force of nineteenth century thought is still with us; that we are still far removed from any universally shared apprehension of the machine in terms of what we can do with it. The more vocal contemporary part of thought still thinks of the machine as something outside of human purpose, as a force proceeding from the past and bound to sweep on and carry us whither it will. As yet, the most obvious sign of change from the nineteenth century temper is the transformation of paeans into lamentations. Instead of jubilation because the machine is sure to usher us automatically into a promised land, we now have the jeremiad that it is sure to land us in waste lands.

But even with respect to the machine, to technology, and the industrial operations which have accompanied the machine, there are signs of a change of attitude. There are an increasing number who remind us that after all the machine was invented and constructed by man, that it is used by man, and that man will be its creature instead of its creator only just as long as he chooses that role for himself. There was no trait of our late prosperity and the "new economic era" more amusing, except that it was alarming, than the assumption so loudly trumpeted by those accepted as leaders that at last we had attained a constantly expanding régime of production equated to consumption which was automatically guaranteed to continue by some inherent process. The tragic collapse of the fact has reacted somewhat—though not as much as one would expect—against the theory. But one may fairly say that at least the problem is now raised. Must man helplessly abdicate before his own production? Can human beings check the tendencies of industrialization which have swept us along for a generation? Can we arrest machine industry at the point of reasonable subordination to other interests, and then turn it to account as a servant of other values? Or are we enslaved by some necessary inescapable cosmic force?

Spengler's little book, **Man and Technics,** both belongs and does not belong to the class of books in which is raised this fundamental issue. He has a vivid sense of the importance of "technics"; he has a much clearer grasp on their nature than most writers. He heartily accepts the idea of mutation; everything decisive in world history has happened suddenly, without warning. He is temperamentally against evolution by gradual cumulative changes; they are too tame and domesticated for him; he demands something dramatic in the way of change. He also sees how fully the issue of our present culture is bound up with what happens to our machine technology. But his analysis and his prophecy are couched wholly in terms of something called destiny. He sees life and history as an inspired oracle of old might have conceived a Greek tragedy of fate, if the oracle had also been gifted with the potentially vast audience of that modern oracle, the publicity agent. For Spengler fairly press-agents Doom, and in the end his technic becomes a mere puppet playing the part assigned to it in the tragedy of destiny.

The volume was originally conceived as an account of prehistoric times; as a story of origins told after the method and manner of **The Decline of the West.** The canvas has been reduced in order to be accommodated to the vision of the reader who is unfitted to grasp the whole scene in the total grandiose pictorial form in which it appears in the **Decline.** Reference to early epochs coming before the age of "High Cultures" remains, but it is now set forth as the first act of the drama which fate is playing with mankind.

A few ideas, strikingly stated, dominate the volume. Technics is not to be identified with the machine or even with the implement and tool. It covers all the ways in which a fighting animal contends with its environment striving to get the better of it as an adversary. It is exemplified equally when the word is used as a weapon (as by the diplomat) and when stalking is employed by the lion. In every technique, things are subordinated to purposive activity, to an idea. Machines are no part of mere economics because they are simply means in the universal conflict of man with nature. The importance of technics in culture was totally overlooked until the nineteenth century. Culture has been supposed in the entire literary and philosophic tradition to be something elevated far above the machine; this tradition measured culture in terms of books, pictures by idealists and ideologues.

The utilitarian, materialistic, socialist movement of the nineteenth century corrected this error but only to fall into a more shallow one. It thought of the machine as the means by which the ease and comfort of humanity were surely to be achieved; its ideal was a devastating state of tranquility which Spengler describes in terms which remind one of William James's account of the tedium of the eternal tea-party with which the millennium has been identified. Man being a beast of prey, his technics, including the machine, is the armory from which are drawn the weapons with which man fights nature. Since every work of man is artificial, the machine is unnatural, an act of rebellion, of intentional matricide. The higher a culture, the greater is the rift between man and nature, and the more must man become the bitter enemy of nature. Since nature is the stronger, every culture is a defeat: the destiny of tragic doom is within it.

The machine is simply the most powerful of the weapons of man in his combat with nature. But it has created a whole series of tensions in the life of man; tensions between the few leaders and the mass which is led; between the processes of work and its results; between the industrialized nations and the rest of the world; between life and organization, since vital things are dying in the grip of mechanical organization. The machine is failing even from the standpoint or economy of production. In consequence, man is in revolt against the machine which has enslaved him. The knell of this machine culture is sounded, and with its doom there is enacted another act in the tragic destiny of mankind. But to this doom we were born. It is as cowardly as it is futile to strive to resist it and to divert the course of history. What we can do is to perish heroically; or, as a correspondent of mine has put it, we can "wade in chin high" to meet the destroying flood.

I am quite aware that a summary like the one which I have just given may appear like a parody, although it is as faithful an epitome as space permits. But this book indicates what many readers of Spengler's earlier book must have suspected, that the real significance of his work does not lie at all where he himself conceives it to lie but somewhere else. In other words, Mr. Spengler's vast generalizations have a fustian quality. They are rhetorical rather than eloquent; they are tags pasted on, rather than convictions growing directly from the material dealt with. Mr. Spengler has real strength. But it lies in swift, penetrating, incidental remarks. There are a dozen insights in this little volume which are rare and precious. But they have almost nothing to do with the march of any argument; they do not support his final conclusions; they can be converted to many another intellectual use than that which their author makes of them.

It is a pity that Spengler's passion for sparks and glitter is so great. He raises a real problem; he says many things which will have to be taken into account in its solution. But it is extremely doubtful whether many readers will carry from the book the intellectual provocation which a less partisan book might have given. He is committed in advance to write history as a high tragedy, moving from catastrophe to catastrophe on an ever vaster scale. He is committed to looking at all attempts to plan for the future so as to divert forces now operating into more humane channels, with contemptuous indifference. He is a learned German Mencken, but with an obsession that he was born to write high tragedy instead of to be amused at the spectacle of human folly and stupidity. Hence it is that he belongs and does not belong among the thinkers who realize that the most important problem of the present is what we are to do with the new techniques which have come with the advent of the machine. He perceives that the present age is what it is because of the new technology, but his discussion is completely controlled by his concern with destiny and doom. It is, of course, conceivable that the present culture is to collapse; in its present economic form it surely will in time—and probably with only a few to mourn it. But the total destruction because of machine technology of all factors in civilization will occur only if all the rest of us—from levity and routine rather than from a sense of tragedy—agree with Spengler that human desire and thought are impotent. It does not help to say that we are completely in the grip of an overwhelming cosmic force, when in reality we are faced with the problem of what we are to do with a tool we have ourselves created. (pp. 581-82)

> John Dewey, "Self-Saver or Frankenstein?" in The Saturday Review of Literature, Vol. VIII, No. 34, March 12, 1932, pp. 581-82.

WILLIAM HARLAN HALE   (essay date 1932)

[*Hale was an American journalist, biographer, historian, and novelist. In the following excerpt from his* Challenge to Defeat: Modern Man in Goethe's World and Spengler's Century, *Hale examines Spengler's denial of reason and humanism in* The Decline of the West.]

Here is the first puzzle of Spenglerism: The philosophy scorns all mechanism and materialism, and sees each culture as the product of one thing only: of the soul of man awakening from the surrounding chaos. But this vaunted all-productive soul actually produces nothing, since . . . it becomes completely extinguished after every short period. The cultures and their souls disappear, but the world goes on, a mechanical process, a wholly material thing. Soul culminates in soullessness.

Here is the second puzzle: The philosophy categorically denies the absoluteness of any idea or truth, and insists that the world is purely one of flow and change. Yet the whole philosophy rests upon one assumption: the undoubted absoluteness of the idea, the truth which Spengler has first recognized: the law of "morphology." This is the very opposite of flow and change.

Here is the third puzzle: The philosophy often repeats the assertion that the separate cultures leave no heritage, that their meaning is unattainable by an alien observer, that therefore history can never reveal their soul. But Spengler's whole structure is reared upon his conviction that he precisely understands the soul and meaning of cultures removed from him by vast distances of time or area. He insists that we are utterly unable to penetrate into the Classical, or Indian, or Magian mind; but without that penetration, there could be no Spengler.

Here is the fourth puzzle: The philosophy is built on an elaborate structure of historical analogies and comparisons, of which the following—fractionally quoted for the reader who has not had contact with the *Decline*—are examples:

> Who . . . realizes that between the Differential Calculus and the dynastic principle of politics in the age of Louis XIV, between the Classical city-state and the Euclidean geometry, between the space-perspective of Western oil-painting and the conquest of space by railroad, telephone, and long-range weapon, between contrapuntal music and credit economics, there are deep uniformities?

We might have found the *alter ego* of our own actuality in establishing the correspondence, item by item, from the "Trojan War" and the Crusades, Homer and the Nibelungenlied, through Doric and Gothic, Dionysian movement and Renaissance, Polycletus and John Sebastian Bach, Athens and Paris, Aristotle and Kant, Alexander and Napoleon, to the world-city and the imperialism common to both Cultures.

It is impossible to escape the force and suggestion of these comparisons; the facts seem mutually to illuminate each other. But suppose some one should object, for example, to Spengler's preposterous dismissal of the Renaissance as merely a minor eddy in the history of western culture—"minor" only because it obviously lacks any analogous phenomenon in any culture of the past? Spengler has armored himself against such criticism. He has denied the value of all rationality and scientific examination; one must proceed, he says, by intuition, feeling, soul. He has "felt" the Renaissance thus; we bring historical proofs to the contrary; but of course we do not register. Causality, judgment, examination are to play no part in his theory. He is not to be tested by the standards of men. He stands above us, he claims a superior validity. His work is messianic, not scholarly. So, while Spengler can criticize all other historians, no one can effectively criticize him.

And yet, is not his theory too built up on books, on relics, on studied evidences and scholarly fragments of the archaeologist's past?

To conclude the specific criticisms of Spengler's method, before questioning his philosophy in general: the whole use of selected historical data to prove a universal thesis is a dangerous business; it may act as a boomerang. Its force lies in the first impression: one is surprised, intoxicated, carried away by the revelation of hitherto unsuspected relationships. And the comparison or juxtaposition of facts always carries apparent clarity and strength. But when one begins to go from the facts he has mentioned to those he has not, then the joyousness may pass. How is it, for instance, that the man who undertakes to deliver a complete analysis and prophecy of his own age, does not know, or refuses to recognize, the cultural facts of that age? He proves our entire artistic destiny today by the evidences of the ancient past; he does not deem the present manifestations worthy of examination, for he has already come to his conclusion. He says: "There has been no architecture for these one hundred years." Why not? Because his theory does not allow it to exist. Apparently he is ignorant of the challenging and unprecedented new movements in building and design which have revolutionized the art beginning from Austria (Hoffmann, Behrens, Paul), passing through Germany (Gropius, Mendelssohn, Taut, Loos), Holland (Oud, Dudok), France (Le Corbusier) and reaching profoundly over to America (Sullivan, Wright, etc.). To have dismissed as nonexistent the only actually new style of architecture since the Baroque, to have ignored the surpassing vitality of all our modern conceptions of building and our philosophy of the art, casts heavy shadows on Spengler's method of historical "proof."

One might go further into his apparent fear of recognizing any modern artistic facts, and examine the strange statement that "the modern artist is a workman, not a creator"; one might presume to question the remnant enthusiasm which he withdraws from the modern French school and gives over to "Marées, Spitzweg, Diez, Leibl"; or in such a remark as "Rembrandt's mighty landscapes lie essentially in the universe, Manet's near a railway station''—one might detect that scolding prejudice against all modern reality which is so typical of the cloistered scholar.

But it is not our function here to go into a precise criticism of the details of the work. Hundreds of German professors have delivered their specialized objections to Spengler's dealings with advanced or obscure subjects; usually the professors have completely missed or avoided the challenge of the whole. Here we begin only by noticing several of the puzzles, inconsistencies, and omissions of the vast *Decline*. What interests us more is the validity of the general principles that underlie it.

Is it possible to construct any philosophy, or to deliver any prophecy meaningful for thinking modern man, while absolutely denying and excluding the factor of reason? What sort of a strange doctrine was it—nourished through an entire century—that believed that we could learn the absolute reality of things by merely living, feeling, and relying on intuition? Few things in the history of thought seem to have been more disrupting than the separation of experience from idea, imagination from reason. For how can the mere consciousness recognize the entire reality or plan of an environment? Are not observation, examination, intelligence, factors that fundamentally lead us toward that? A man may unconsciously feel the relation that lies between some objects and experiences; but he cannot intuit the entirety of the world. Mere experience is a havoc of sensations; our reactions and impressions can be clarified and made intelligible only as another power acts upon them—the reasoned, the reflective.

All this seems obvious and close to schoolmasterly; but it is not obvious at all. The whole Spenglerian point of view rests on the denial of it. It rests on the denial, that is, of the unifying conceptions which appear through the aid of rational method; and it enthrones those conceptions which rest only on suggestion, a ''deep mysteriousness'' of intuition, and kindred beautiful but vague approaches. It is inevitable therefore that Spengler should lack any true realization of unity or law or principle; but it is not at all inevitable that we must accept these sweeping negations.

It is all very well to talk about the Decline of the West; but it is manifest inconsistency for a man who worships soul and life-feeling to herald the utter extinction of that soul and life. From the rational point of view, it is equally unsatisfactory: for if we logically consider history (which Spengler does) as similar to the biological process of a life, we cannot end with its utter disappearance and total lack of influence. The facts of elementary chemistry convince us of the conservation of matter and energy, and biology always demonstrates that the individual, after his death and decay, essentially contributes to the production and nourishment of the individuals that follow. The whole Decline-theory is based on the belief in complete discontinuity; and yet neither its spiritual basis nor its biological basis can for one moment countenance such a belief.

If Spenglerism loses its force by a blunt disregard of the fundamental needs of reason, it loses almost as much by a complete disregard of the fundamental truths of humanity. This separation of theory and thought from society is a thing we have reviewed too often to warrant further consideration; but here it approaches its limit. Spengler is not merely a determinist, a fatalist, he is a conscious and deliberate opponent of human principles; he represents something ultimately Mephistophelian; or, to put it in slightly different words, he seems to lie in that tradition of ''Satanism'' which was so brilliantly for-

mulated in poetry by Baudelaire. In Spenglerian theory the deeds of man are creative—yes indeed; the soul is the genesis of all things. But the whole movement of creation is toward decay: each deed, instead of being the fulfillment of a possibility, is the elimination of one. That is, since the cycle of culture is predestined and automatic, each work of art, each discovery of science, each summary of philosophy, is merely an automatic step further away from the primitive soul to the decaying intellect. The essence of life, according to Spengler, is ''Direction.'' But whereto? Why, direction turned on itself. Each progressive fact of life in a culture is negative in that it leads inevitably and irreversibly toward the quick death of that culture and the unredeemable extinction of its soul. Each great creative act is a step into creative death: a culture asserts itself chiefly to destroy itself.

There is no deeper irony than this, there is no more tragic, anti-human conception possible; it is the summit (and it is the conclusion) of the European nihilism that Nietzsche foresaw.

Think back a moment to the figure who is Spengler's sworn master, and consider his attitude to the same world of deed. Goethe in his lasting belief in the supreme reality of outward, concrete activity could say: Deed is always a creation of order, an organizing, a forming *(Gestalten);* and he could sum up with the memorable sentence, *Die Wirkung jedes Getanen reicht ins Unendliche*—the effect of every deed reaches into the infinite.

But now, the effect of every deed reaches toward death: the act of advance or progress is the move into decay. The more deeds there are—the more there is written and thought and painted and played—the faster will come the complete collapse. As Robinson Jeffers said . . . : ''You making haste haste on decay.'' The more you do, the quicker you become undone. What then? The only rational answer would be, Do Nothing.

The Spenglerian is of course basically a Goethian: [that can be seen] as the deep foundation for Spengler's thought. What are the essential concepts of Goethe? We might best present them as *Das Schaffende*—the creating; *Das Bildende*—the developing; *Das Ewig-Weibliche, das uns hinan zieht*—the power of love, that eternally draws us upward and on. Without the knowledge of these ideas of growth and power unending, Goethe's life and work become meaningless.

And now the consummate follower of Goethe, rounding out his historical picture and at last arriving at the point where he delivers an ethical doctrine to the world, resolutely and completely denies the entire Goethian mind that was his master. We now find that growth and power are anything but unending; that in fact today growth and power have come to a full stop. Western man—whose deepest essence, according to Spengler, is typified by the striving and straining of Faust—suddenly must deny his entire soul, go back on his whole development, and surrender all the spirit which he held most cherished.

This is his last word. The master philosophical mind, the historical wizard who would offer us a ''creative'' understanding of our position and our fate, started out with Goethe; and when he comes to counsel us, he ends by utterly denying any remote Goethian possibility, and by plunging us into a confusion far greater than any from which he may have lifted us. We must renounce—not our too proud emotions, but our entire will to do and to create. We must submit—not to the laws of man and order and society, but to the blind unaccountable cycle of mechanical nature. We must die—not in the attempt to fulfill our great and tragic ambitions, but in the blank necessity of decay.

The philosophy of doom avoids the rational, then, and it avoids the human. It denies the continuity of deed, matter, and law. It casts out the enduring fact of human will, energy, man's onward thrust. All that it holds as true is the isolation of moments, and the cessation of activity. Starting from the biological plan of individual life, it ends by refusing any biology of the life beyond mere individuals. Beginning with the enthronement of the soul, it concludes with the overthrow of the soul's endurance.

And now we see in full relief the insufficiencies to which a century of Separation led. We realize how little strength can lie in an ultimate philosophy that ignores two basic sides of what we call existence. The world-denial which Spengler formulates is merely his own denial of reason and humanism. When we re-introduce these great elements into the philosophic picture, the theories of denial and decline lose their force.

Already Spenglerism and the mood of downfall begin to appear as matters of the past, conclusions to tendencies that in these moods and theories reached their last possible extremity. Already we become vividly conscious of the bankruptcy of the thought of decadence and dissolution. Our innate life senses the overdoing of apartness, division, of arts and theories built on single and exclusive points of view; we are reacting, we are unconsciously, inevitably desiring a fuller participation of our unified faculties in this spiritual world. We are beginning to doubt the whole religion of discontinuous events, scattered particles, and meaningless wholes. If indeed we are to be convinced that our entire civilization is doomed to a quick collapse, we mean once more before we surrender to seek the opposite religion, the belief which should give us strength and fertility.

Still, the prophet of doom will reply, how is it that today the soul of western man seems for the first time to be weary, exhausted, and wishful for death? But, one replies, is that the soul of western man, or is it the soul of a century—the soul of the vast and tragic century that has now come to its conclusion? And indeed, it is no special weariness of the present hour, this longing of western soul to escape the "overlong daylight" and to flee homeward to the dark mother of mystic night and death. (pp. 153-64)

And how can Spengler reconcile his view of the unprecedented world-weariness of present-day man with the deep funereal and morbid literature of the seventeenth century (that is, in English writing—a tradition that he sees fit to ignore)? How are his pictures of the glorious Baroque and the conquering Descartian world to be joined to the world of a Donne—"Whoever comes to shroud me"—or that of a Sir Thomas Browne—"For the world, I count it not an inn, but an hospital; and a place not to live in, but to die in"? And even in that splendid early eighteenth century, with its colonies and navies and vast states growing, we hear one of the grandest of all voices—Swift's—dissolving the world into mad ruin; we get the resignation and death-longing of the older Bach; we get the utter weariness and expiration of the Rococo. And only then, on all this accumulation, comes the birth of romanticism and symbolism, and the final beauty of death's abyss.

It is hard to believe that, as Spengler says, a sudden world-weariness has spread over a culture that never, except during the early Gothic, had known it before. There is a deeper continuity underlying the surface changes which Spengler so brilliantly detects. Always there is with us the passionate love for

death. And always that love exists by the very side of the passionate love for life. Faust would never have reached for the poison, if he had not reached for the whole world. And when he had touched the bottle to his lips, he reached for that world again; his human spirit was not so easily conquered. Below the manifestations of a day such as ours—one that is marked by doubt and loneliness and exhaustion and despair—there are the manifestations of lasting humanity. Western man seems no nearer his death-agony now than each man has been sometime in the middle of his striving life. He has gone through an era which was the break-up of society, the denial of humanity, the revolt against reason, and the final grand fall of reality. In Spenglerism he too lifted the poison to his lips. But the last vision, through the clouds of chaos, of an abiding, producing, vital outside world, turns him back to life; and the irrevocable essence of his nature calls him to rebuild the structure he so proudly overthrew. Western man is changing; and more deeply, he stays the same. (pp. 165-67)

> *William Harlan Hale, "The World Again," in his* Challenge to Defeat: Modern Man in Goethe's World and Spengler's Century, *Harcourt Brace Jovanovich, 1932, pp. 151-202.*

WILLIAM MacDONALD (essay date 1934)

[*MacDonald is an American educator and critic. In the following excerpt, he reviews* The Hour of Decision.]

[*The Hour of Decision*], Spengler tells us, grew out of a lecture on **"Germany in Danger,"** which he delivered in Hamburg in 1932 "without meeting with much comprehension." The larger part of the first half of the book was finished a year ago, and that part is now published without alteration, "for I write," he declares, "not for a few months ahead or for next year, but for the future. What is true cannot be made null by an event." "I offer no wish-picture of the future," he announces elsewhere in his introduction.

> still less a program for its realization—as is the fashion amongst us Germans—but a clear picture of the facts as they are and will be. I see further than others. I see not only great possibilities but also great dangers, their origin and perhaps the way to avoid them. And if no one else has the courage to see and to tell what it is he sees, I mean to do so. I have a *right* to criticism, since by means of it I have repeatedly demonstrated that which *must* happen because it will *happen*.

The passage just quoted is Spengler's own testimony to the supreme self-confidence with which he has gone at his task. No one who has read *The Decline of the West* is likely to think him lacking in assurance, but for the present purpose he is more assured than ever of the soundness of his position, of the complete accuracy of the historical analysis upon which it rests, and of what Germany and the rest of the world ought to think about it. The eloquent passages which dot the pages of *The Decline of the West* are conspicuous by their absence: the language is rather that of an indictment, punctuated, to be sure, with keen or scornful criticism strikingly phrased, but with no concession to opposing opinions and no sympathy for such as will not follow.

Nominally, the subject is Germany, its present state and pressing duty. Since Germany, however, "more than any other country,'' is ''bound up with the fate of all the others,'' what has happened to Germany and what Germany needs if it is to survive have world interest and application. Woven into the exposition are the fundamental ideas which Spengler's other writings have made familiar: The rise and growth of cultures and their decay when culture becomes civilization, the dependence of the present upon the past, and the inescapable destiny which orders events. The historical illustrations, wide as usual in their range, are drawn most often from classical times, and particularly from those of Rome. The problems of contemporary Germany, however, are not those of a single or isolated nation, for Germany ''is not an island,'' but the weaknesses from which it suffers and the difficulties which it faces are typical of those with which other nations of the present time must deal.

What, in Spengler's view, is the trouble with Germany? ''If a stable foundation,'' Spengler declares, ''is to be laid for a great future, one on which coming generations may build, ancient traditions must continue effective.'' Germany, however, unlike other nations, has had ''no educative past.'' ''It has had 700 years of the petty provincial régime of small States, with never a breath of greatness, an idea, an aim.'' From the time of the Hohenstaufen and the Hansa ''the German has shut himself up in inumerable little fatherlands and petty local interests,'' ''dreaming hungrily and miserably of a kingdom in the clouds'' and calling it ''German idealism.'' He shares the ''universal dread of reality'' which is the ''spiritual weakness'' of men of the higher civilizations who live in cities, cut off from the soil and ''the natural experiencing of destiny, time and death.'' A general view of world politics and economics has become impossible, and true statesmen are ''rarer and rarer.'' A prevailing rationalism provides the mind with catchwords, romanticism seeks to reform the world with ''noble talk of poetic theories'' and the ''everlasting 'youths' '' are with us, ''Immature, destitute of the slightest experience or even real desire for experience, but writing and talking away about politics, fired by uniforms and badges and clinging fantastically to some theory or other.''

The ''domination of the rootless urban intellect'' Spengler sees drawing to a close and in its place emerges skepticism as ''a final way of understanding things as they are.'' The international situation of the moment, however, we are all in danger of misreading. The long period of peace from 1870 to 1914 ''rendered all white men self-satisfied, covetous, void of understanding and incapable of bearing misfortune.'' The age in which we live is ''the greatest that the Western civilization has ever known or will know,'' but ''all the more diminutive are the people in it.'' To those who shout against war while desiring class war, Spengler insists that ''man is a beast of prey'' and conflict ''the original fact of life.''

> The dreary train of world-improvers has now come to an end of its amble through these centuries, leaving behind it, as sole monument of its existence, mountains of printed paper. The Caesars will now take its place.

Spengler, accordingly, not only sees world wars continuing for the present century and perhaps the next, but he interprets them as indicating the transition from a world of States to some kind of world empire. Who won the last world war was easier to say in 1918 than it is now. What has come about is ''a new form of world'' as ''the precondition for future crises which must one day set in with crushing force.'' Russia, Spengler declares, has been ''reconquered morally by Asia''; ''it is

doubtful if the British Empire any longer has its centre of gravity in Europe''; Germany is again becoming a frontier against Asia, Italy will be powerful as long as Mussolini lives and may lay the foundation of world power in the Mediterranean, and France, ''who once more considers herself lord of Europe,'' is the heart of a system to which the League of Nations and some of the States of Southeastern Europe belong.

Victor or vanquished, however, the end of a State is chaos if it follows the road of democracy and representative government. ''A modern republic is nothing but the ruin of a monarchy that has given itself up.'' No State can govern itself in any proper connotation of that phrase; it must be governed just as an army must be led, ''and as long as it possesses healthy instincts it likes to be governed.'' Parties are subversive because, unlike monarchs and statesmen, they are wholly irresponsible, and the place of economics is in subordination to politics. Thanks to the development which traces through the Manchester free trade school and reaches its theoretical culmination in the Communist manifesto, we have ''the dethronement of politics by economics, of the State by the counting-house, of the diplomatist by the trade-union leader. . . . *This whole crushing depression* [the italics are Spengler's] *is purely and simply the result of the decline of State power.*''

Until 1914 the decline of State authority, as Spengler sees it, had stopped short at the standing armies; but where, until then, the army had been a conservative force and its officers aloof from politics, the conscript army of today, thanks to the inroads of party and propaganda, has become a very different influence. Since the end of the eighteenth century, moreover, the nations have gone in for economic war; witness the ''economic offensive'' of the Russian Five-Year Plan, the raids on the pound, currency inflation, trade quotas and restrictions and the Dawes and Young plans. ''What it really amounts to is that the life of one's own nation has to be gained at the cost of destroying that of others. It is the struggle on the keel of the overturned boat.''

Out of the chaos, Spengler predicts, new world powers will develop, but ''none of the world powers of today,'' he reminds us, ''stands so firmly that one can say with certainty that it will still be a power in a hundred or in fifty years, or even exist at all.'' Russia consists of ''a ruling horde, called the Communist party, with its chieftains and almighty Khan, and a downtrodden, defenseless mass of people some hundred times as large.'' It can conduct foreign wars only by propaganda, and it must reckon with Japan. The United States is ''neither a real nation nor a real State,'' its life is ''organized exclusively from the economic side and consequently lacks depth,'' it has a social dictatorship which affects everything—''flirtation and church-going, shoes and lipsticks, dances and novels *a la mode*, thought, food and recreation''—and its underworld and its unemployed are a menace. England has lost heavily of its best blood through wars and migration, it ''lacks the racial foundation of a tough peasantry,'' its ''thirst for adventure is dying,'' it can no longer keep its navy superior to all others, and the dominions are becoming independent.'' As for the Latin countries, including France, they ''have no more than a provincial significance.''

Still other influences and conditions, not confined to State lines, retard the coming of the new world power. The dictatorship of the proletariat is to Spengler ''an accomplished fact.'' The cities, draining their massed population from the land, hold a genuine mob of the restless, incompetent, criminal, vengeful and pathetic from which ''the heroes of the moment

Spengler's apartment in Munich.

of all popular movements and radical parties arise." "High culture is inseparably bound up with luxury and wealth," and wealth, concentrated in the hands of a few and in ruling classes, is one of the foundations for "the training of generations of leading minds," but a proletarian society hates wealth and class distinctions and will have leaders only of its own kind. Bolshevism, commonly thought of as a Russian product, originated in fact in the proletarian and liberal circles of Western Europe and has Christian theology as its "grandmother." Hence the mischievouus predominance of the "worker," with rights but no obligations, and of the labor union, the cult of class warfare, and attacks upon property and capital. The world economic crisis which we are undergoing, and which will continue, is "in all essentials . . . the product of the deliberate work of the leaders of the proletariat. . . . The labor leader won the war."

Yet the victory, such as it was, is apparently to be short-lived. Spengler sees, looming larger and nearer, a vast labor struggle between the white and the colored peoples. The danger was great even by 1900, for the structure of the white economic system, with its specialized and large-scale industry and agriculture, was "already undermined." The World War brought to the white world economic collapse. Labor was paid for the war in shorter working hours and the maintenance of high wages, but the thirty millions of unemployed are not found among the colored races of India or Africa or in Asiatic Russia. What would happen, Spengler asks, "if, one day, class war

and race war joined forces to make an end of the white world?" "Would the white leaders of the class war ever hesitate if colored outbreaks opened up a way for them? They have never been fastidious in the means they use."

Such is the situation. Where, if anywhere, in this chaos of world revolution, is the way out? For Germany, the battlefield of the ages and the source from which new world power must spring, the path is through what Spengler characterizes as "Prussianism." The elements of the new Prussianism are the disciplining of economic life "by a powerful State," this being "the precondition of free initiative in private enterprise"; "the aristocratic ordering of life according to the grade of achievement"; "the undisputed precedence of foreign policy . . . over internal policy," and "a character which disciplines itself." With Prussianism, but with Prussianism alone, there will be "the starting point for the ultimate overcoming of the world revolution."

Spengler is at pains to make clear, on the other hand, that his Prussianism is not exclusively German. "Not every one is a Prussian who is born in Prussia; the type is possible anywhere in the white world and actually occurs, though rarely." It is the idea which stands opposed to "finance-liberalism as well as to labor-socialism," regards as suspect "everything that is 'Left,'" and resists "any weakening of the State" and "any desecrating misuse of it for economic interests." It is conservative and "grows out of whatever fundamental life-forces still exist in Nordic peoples: instinct for power and possessions; for possessions as power; for inheritance, fecundity and family, which three belong together; for distinctions of rank and social gradation." It is, in short, "a preliminary step toward Caesarism," and "the riper the age, the more prospects does this road open up."

Criticism of this latest chapter of Spengler's social philosophy must, of course, take account of the doctrine of inevitableness which inheres in his conception of history. To Spengler, what has happened must have happened, and the future in this respect will be as the past. One quickly begins to question, however, in reading his outspoken and dogmatic arraignment of things as they are, whether he has not laid aside the role of interpreter and assumed that of preacher and prophet. There runs through his forcible criticism of democracy, party government, proletarian dominance and all the rest a note of personal irritation that such things should be, and a pretty clear suggestion of a belief that it is within the power of peoples, certainly of the German people, to make them different; yet if nothing has happened except what could not have been avoided there can be, apparently, no recourse save to accept bolshevism, labor unions and self-seeking politicians as the inevitable marks of a decaying culture, and await, as calmly as may be, the hour of social collapse.

The actual novelty of the book lies chiefly in the striking way in which its criticisms and contentions are put. It is not news that inefficiency in government, internal disorder and external danger have produced, in many quarters, a conservative reaction and that Caesarism is on the way, or that liberalism has often turned out to be only a valley of indecision and reform a short-lived exercise of the self-constituted elect, or that high wages, shorter hours and unemployment are found together in every industrial State, or that physical vigor and fecundity tend to decline with the flocking of population to cities, or that property, family and inheritance are conserving forces. We knew already, even if we did not keenly realize, that the British Empire appears to be slowly disintegrating, that Mussolini is a masterful ruler and France a State on the defensive, that Russia is autocratically governed, and that the American underworld is a menace and the unemployed a peril. It is not from Spengler that we learn for the first time of the fundamental antagonism between white and colored peoples, or of the threat to Western civilization that lies in the long hours, low wages, historic resentments and sheer weight of numbers in Africa, India and Asia.

What Spengler holds out as a way of escape for a demoralized and distracted Western world is the conception of a State whose watchwords are discipline, class distinctions and authority. The idea is not much elaborated, and "Prussianism" is chosen as the distinctive characterization, one suspects, only because Spengler is writing first of all for Germans. To the German people, distracted as they have been by the World War and its aftermath, yet with traditions of submission to authority which have not been wholly forgotten, the idea may well carry inspiration, and the more because of the crucial position in Europe and the world which Spengler sees Germany occupying and the vision of world dominion which he describes. It is the old theory of an enlightened despotism, but furbished with new plausibilities because much within and without is chaotic; the conception of a nation wisely governed by its best minds, achieving "individual initiative" through discipline imposed from above, and directing its foreign policy to the attainment of a place in the sun.

Wide as will be the dissent from the analysis and the program, there will be no denial of the importance of the situation which Spengler has exposed. It is well to be shown, with the brutal audacity which is here his manner, the road we have been traveling and the evils through which it has led. If it be true, as Spengler insists, that no people can govern itself, that authority is on the march, and that world power is to lie with the disciplined State whose people are physically the strongest and most prolific, the time cannot be far distant when the doctrine will be put to the test. For the moment, however, ***The Hour of Decision*** is neither a philosophy nor a guide; it is an indictment and a challenge. (pp. 1, 18)

William MacDonald "Spengler's New Challenge," in The New York Times Book Review, *February 11, 1934, pp. 1, 18.*

LEWIS MUMFORD (essay date 1939-44)

[*Mumford is an American sociologist, historian, philosopher, and author whose primary interest is the relationship between the modern individual and his or her environment. Influenced by the works of Patrick Geddes, a Scottish sociologist and pioneer in the field of city planning, Mumford has worked extensively in the area of city and regional planning, and has contributed several important studies of cities, including* The Culture of Cities *(1938),* City Development *(1945), and* The City in History *(1961). All of these works examine the interrelationship between cities and civilization over the centuries. Also indicative of much of his work is Mumford's concern with firm moral values to assure the growth of civilization. Writing in the* Saturday Evening Post, *Mumford noted that "the test of maturity, for nations as well as for individuals, is not the increase of power, but the increase of self-understanding, self-control, self-direction, and self-transcendence. For in a mature society, man himself, not his machines or his organizations, is the chief work of art." In the following excerpt from an essay written over a five year period and so dated by Mumford, he decries* The Decline of the West *as an apology for barbarism, discussing Spengler's theories as rationalization for German militarism before World War I and for the development of European fascism after the war.*]

Barbarism had many prophets during the last century, from Houston Stewart Chamberlain to Georges Sorel, from Nietzsche to Pareto; but the man whose work most fully displays the sinister lure of barbarism was Oswald Spengler, the author of **"The Downfall of the Western World,"** timidly translated into English as ***The Decline of the West***. Spengler had a free mind and a servile emotional attitude; he presented a formidable upright figure, with a domed bald head and a keen eye, but in the presence of authority, particularly military authority, his backbone crumpled. Representing the intellect he yet abased the function of intellect before the power of "blood"; elaborating the concept of the organic in history he used it to justify the acceptance of the machine.

Conceived before the First World War, published first in Vienna in 1918, before the war had ended, Spengler's treatise was something more than a philosophy of history. To begin with it was, from the German standpoint, a work of consolation. It was written to rationalize the state in which the new German found himself: he had acquired great wealth and high physical organization by repressing most of his vital impulses except those that directly or deviously served his will-to-power. But in his heart, he was not at home in this new environment. Measured by humane standards, the relatively feeble, industrially backward, politically divided country of the Enlightenment had been a better place for the spirit: Kant in Koenigsberg, Goethe and Schiller in Weimar, Mozart and Beethoven in Vienna had put the Germans on a higher cultural level than centralized Berlin had achieved.

If Germany was defeated in her attempt to gain military and economic control of Europe, all was lost; but if Germany won, how much was gained? Nothing was left except to go on with the empty conquests of the past forty years, building railroads to Baghdad, throwing steamship lines across new trade routes, manufacturing genuine Scotch marmalade in Hamburg, and above all, giving larger scope to Junker arrogance and prowess: the too easy sack of Peking had but whetted army appetites. Thought itself had become technicized, indeed partly militarized: it tended toward adding-machine accuracy, but the values algebraically represented in this process came to so many zeros. Those who still felt a sentimental pull toward the older and deeper German culture were appalled by the battlefront bleakness of the intellectual landscape. Spengler himself was appalled: in this he was more keenly alive than that army of American scholars who had imitated German methods with clever facility without realizing how little they had gained or how much they were to lose.

Drawing upon world history for consoling comparisons and precedents, Spengler found them in his theory of historic development. According to him, there are two kinds of peoples in the world: those who merely live and those who enact history. The first, if they exist before the cultural cycle begins, are mere vegetables: their life is directionless: they endure on a timeless level of pure being. If they come at the end of the cycle they also tumble into a Spenglerian limbo: they are "fellaheen," without ambition, without creative capacity, different from the true peasant because they clothe themselves in the tattered garments of an old civilization, containing its forms even though they progressively lose all its meanings.

Opposed to this dull village chorus are the actors, the creators: the latter experience "Destiny"; they are drawn by a dominating idea from a state of culture, in which life is bound up with a common soil and a deep intuitive sense of the importance of blood and race and caste, to a state of civilization, in which their waking consciousness progressively transcends their more instinctive earlier life, and in which the external conquest of nature takes the place of the harmonious cultivation of life. In this second state, they cease to be fettered to a particular region and become, instead, cosmopolitan, highly urbanized, increasingly indifferent to all the vital processes that meant so much to both townsman and peasant during the earlier period, deeply hostile to those unconscious or unformulated forces that cannot be glibly translated into word-symbols or money-symbols. Rationalism and humanitarianism devitalize their will-to-power. Pacificism gives rise to passivism. Optimistic and cowardly to the end, the denizens of this civilization are ripe for butchery.

In the phase of culture, life germinates and flourishes; in the state of civilization, the sap sinks to the roots, the stem and leaves become brittle, and the whole structure of the organism becomes incapable of further growth. The promise of culture's springtime ends in the dormant period of civlization's winter. From the organic to the inorganic, from the living to the mechanical, from the subjectively conditioned to the objectively conditioned—this, said Spengler, is the line of development for all societies.

By making the rise and fall of cultures an immanent, automatic process, Spengler got caught in the net of his organic metaphor: he was thus forced to treat each culture as a unified body,

dominated by a specific idea, which in turn would be symbolized by its architecture, its mathematics, its painting, its statecraft, its technics. Not merely is a culture incapable of receiving the ideas or contributions of other cultures; it cannot even understand them. All intercourse with outside cultures is impossible: all carryovers from the past are for Spengler an illusion. The processes of self-repair, self-renewal, self-transcendence, which are as observable in cultures as in persons, were completely overlooked by Spengler. His many vital perceptions of the historic process served only one purpose which he kept steadfastly in view: as apology for barbarism.

Applying his theory to "Faustian" culture, that of the last thousand years, Spengler pointed out that the Western European was about to enter the frigid state of winter. Poetry, art, philosophy were no longer open possibilities; civilization meant the deliberate abdication of the organic and vital elements: the unqualified reign of the mechanical, the desiccated, the devitalized. The region was shriveling to a point: the world city or Megalopolis. (The original Megalopolis in fourth century Greece had emptied out a whole countryside in order to create a single large center.) The earth itself was now being plated with stone and steel and asphalt: man dreamed of growing crops in tanks, taking food in capsules, transplanting foetuses to protoplasmic incubators, conquering the air in stratoliners by means of oxygen tanks, and burrowing into underground cities in order to have security against his wonderful conquest of the more rarefied medium. In that process, the individual shrank once more into a mechanical atom in a formless mass of humanity: the sourest satire of Aldous Huxley's *Brave New World* or Zamiatin's *We* scarcely did justice to the regimentation that was actually under way. To succeed in terms of such a civilization, one must be hard. What remained of life, if one could call it life, belonged to the engineer, the business man, the soldier; in short, to pure technicians, devoid of any concern for life or the values of life, except in so far as they served the machine. Was there no way for life, then, to reassert itself? Spengler answered Yes: by brutality, by brutality and conquest. The sole outlet open to the victims of civilization was to replenish their barbarism and consummate their will-to-destruction. In politics the hour of Caesarism was at hand.

This invocation to barbarism fascinated many of Spengler's more literate contemporaries. Hence it is important to realize, not so much the illegitimacy of the poetic figure Spengler used, as the even deeper unsoundness of the grand division Spengler made between culture and civilization, by putting them at opposite ends of a cycle. These two terms represent the spiritual and the material aspects of every society; and the fact is that one is never found without the other. The overdevelopment of fortifications and castles in the fourteenth century, for example, was as much a mechanical fact, an example of sheer externalization, as the overdevelopment of subways in the modern megalopolis, though the first belonged to a vernal feudalism of blood and caste, while the other belongs to finance capitalism. So, again, the building of new towns on rectangular plans was as much a characteristic of the springtide of Faustian culture as it was of the autumnal period of the nineteenth century. Spengler's theory of cultural isolationism—unfortunately a typical example of Germanic egoism—prevented him from correctly interpreting the organic inter-relations his theory pretends to demonstrate. At every point his organicism gives place to dualism: for without that dualism he could not sanction barbarism.

To follow the real drift of the **"Downfall"** one must read the pamphlets which were all that Spengler published in the following years: here the hidden aim was unveiled. In *Man and Technics,* and in *The Hour of Decision,* Spengler divested himself completely of the forms of scholarly judgment: he beat a frenzied tattoo on the tribal drum, attempting to summon together the forces of reaction. For Spengler was no Aristotle: he was the revived Fichte of the barbarian revolution whose name was fascism in Italy, Nazism in Germany, and totalitarianism everywhere. In its very characteristics as a work of art, a poem of devilish hate and darkening fate, Spengler's **"Downfall"** was an image of the fascist states that were to be erected during the next two decades: their irrationalities, their phobias, their humorless limitations, their colossal brutalities, their perverse animus against all life, except at the blindest levels of the id, were prophetically mirrored in his work. He who understood the significance of Spengler's act of prophecy had little to learn from the further course of Europe's history. (pp. 218-21)

For all his breadth of vision, Spengler succeeded only in reading back into world history the limitations of his own country, his own generation. In his scheme of living he had no place for the very class he represented: the priest, the artist, the intellectual, the scientist, the maker and conserver of ideas and ideal patterns were not operative agents: he not merely asserted that no fact has ever altered a faith, but he even said that no idea had ever modified an act. If that were true, he need not have spent so much time attempting to shout down the ideas of those who opposed the acts he favored.

Every society consists of organizers, energizers, creators, and followers: in each group and association within society a similar social division of labor can be detected; and all social action is the result of their combined efforts. For Spengler, the organizers, the men of blood and will, were supreme. The work of the creators, strange to say, he associated with death: the fixed, the immobilized, the no-saying seemed to him their only attributes; and he hated the activities of the men of religion and the men of thought because it curbed the raw outbreaks of animal passion and physical prowess that his drill sergeant's mind gloried in.

The truth is that Spengler feared the deep humanness of humanity, as he feared those domestic sentiments, truly native to man, that work against the rule of his mythical "carnivore." Spengler recoiled from the fact, so obvious in history, that dehumanized power in the long run is as pitifully weak, as impotent and sterile, as a merely wishful humanitarianism. He hated the independent power of the mind, creating values, erecting standards, subduing ferine passions, laying the basis for a more universal society, precisely because he knew in his heart of hearts, for all his loud contempt, that this *was* a power: a power men obeyed, a power even the humblest could feel within himself, at least in milliamperes, as in a radio receiving set, recording the same feelings, the same hopes and dreams, that had left the original transmitting station at full strength.

What makes Spengler so significant was that he expressed in so many words the premises upon which Western society as a whole acted: the man of fact, who despised values, was the product of the New World idolum, native to that habitat, flourishing there almost without competitors like the jack-rabbit in Australia. With the rest of Western society in decay, the antivital tendencies of the mechanical ideology now could exercise themselves unrestrained. Nothing that Spengler advocated for the coming dictatorships was outside current practice: the gangsterism he preached on a large scale had already been achieved in the one-man rule of the American political boss, petty but sometimes not so petty: his contempt for the poet and

the painter, his devaluation of all ideal activity, were but the working principles of the successful philistine in every land: his glorification of technique at the expense of rational content was the very principle by which men currently advanced themselves in medicine or in education, in law or business: did not advertising condition the masses to this philosophy?

Unlike his liberal and democratic opponents, Oswald Spengler drew the inevitable conclusion from this situation. If values are unreal and if humane purposes are chimerical, then even scientific technique must ultimately become subservient to brute force: the need for rational restraint and self-discipline of any kind disappears. Thus technicism leads directly to irrationality—and the cult of barbarian power salvages the technician's otherwise growing sense of frustration and futility. (pp. 222-23)

Spengler ignored all the creative tendencies in modern life, except those associated with the machine: little though he relished the thought, his essential creed favored Russia and the United States even more than it did the fascist countries. Spengler accepted as "real" only those elements which emphasized modern man's automatism, his deflation of values, his subservience to mechanical organization, and the savage irrationality which takes the place of reason in other parts of the personality. And because these forces cannot be confined within their original frontiers, Spengler predicted, far more accurately than hopeful philosophers, the disastrous downward course that modern civilization is still following, at a steadily accelerating pace. Through its emotional impact, Spengler's work as a whole constitutes a morbid Saga of Barbarism. It began as a poem of defeat; it finally became an epic justification of the fascist attack on the very humanity of man. . . . (pp. 223-24)

> *Lewis Mumford, "Spengler: Dithyramb to Doom,"*
> *in his* Interpretations and Forecasts, 1922-1972: Studies in Literature, History, Biography, Technics, and Contemporary Society, *Harcourt Brace Jovanovich, Inc., 1973, pp. 218-24.*

H. STUART HUGHES   (essay date 1952)

[*An American historian, Hughes is the author of the biographical and critical study* Oswald Spengler. *In the following excerpt from that work, he evaluates the structure and style of* The Decline of the West.]

In its final version . . . *The Decline of the West* is annoyingly long and repetitious. It never seems to have occurred to Spengler that his theories might gain in clarity and impact if presented in somewhat tighter form. But long, wretchedly organized books have been the tradition in Germany, and we may wonder whether a shorter, more lucid volume would have achieved the same reputation for profundity. In Germany, a book that is not hard to read is scarcely considered worth reading. As finally constituted, the German edition of the *Decline* runs to nearly twelve hundred pages and is full of repetitions of ideas, phrases, and, in one case, even of an entire paragraph. The sequence of thought is frequently difficult to grasp. Part of this difficulty is doubtless due to Spengler's highly personal method of writing. He composed his ideas originally in the form of aphorisms, which he kept in a portable trunk and left with friends whenever he went off on a journey. Many of his books—more particularly his later political works—started simply as collections of aphorisms.

Hence the lapidary, pictorial character of Spengler's writing. It is, as he himself noted in the preface to his revised first volume, "intuitive and deceptive through and through, written in a language which seeks to present objects and relations illustratively instead of offering an army of ranked concepts, It addresses itself solely to readers who are capable of living themselves into the word-sounds and pictures as they read." To others, trained in a smoother and more continuous style of exposition, the *Decline* may look like a disconnected series of massive, boldly-hewn segments of undifferentiated thought and deeply-colored imagery.

More closely regarded, however, Spengler's writing reveals its own characteristic logic. Its very repetitions and constant returns to familiar guiding principles begin to conform to a special sort of design. This pattern, Spengler subsequently complained, eluded nearly all his readers. They failed to grasp that thoughts like his could be conveyed only through examples, and that to fasten too literal-mindedly on any one of them meant to lose sight of its relation to the others. "For here everything hangs together so tightly that to take one particular point out of its context is already to fall into error."

Hence even the back-trackings and repetitions play their part, indeed are nearly indispensable, in the tightly woven, all-interrelated effect that the author seeks to convey. Actually the *Decline* can hardly be said to start and end at any particular point. It is not to be read as a logical sequence. It is rather—to use the language of music to which Spengler was so deeply attracted—a theme and variations, a complex contrapuntal arrangement, in which no one idea necessarily follows another, but in which a group of ideas, whose mutual relationship is symbolically experienced rather than specifically understood, summon, answer, and balance one another in the sort of lofty cosmic harmony that Goethe's angels had proclaimed in the prologue and concluding stanzas of *Faust*. (pp. 66-7)

H. Stuart Hughes, in his Oswald Spengler: A Critical Estimate, *Charles Scribner's Sons, 1952, 176 p.*

BRUCE MAZLISH   (essay date 1966)

[*An American historian, Mazlish is best known as the author of works in "psychohistory," a controversial discipline whose practitioners psychoanalyze historical figures through the examination of secondary sources in an attempt to achieve a better understanding of their subjects' personalities and function in history. Mazlish, who notes that psychohistory is the "fusion of psychoanalysis and history (not a mere application of one to the other)," has utilized this method in studies of Richard Nixon, Jimmy Carter, and Henry Kissinger. In the following discussion of* The Decline of the West, *Mazlish examines Spengler's political views, postulates upon the metaphysical basis of his theory of history, and presents theoretical aspects of his historical analysis.*]

The political affects Spengler's work [*The Decline of the West*] in two ways (1) it is an integral part of his philosophy of history, being part of any culture which he treats; and (2) it is an external element which anachronistically colors his approach to all the cultures which he studies. Let us look more closely at both these points.

In any culture, according to Spengler, the political elements must be completely in tune with the general "spirit" of the whole organism. . . . [We] can perceive here that Spengler is merely restating the "holistic" position. For example, his vision of an integral connection between the dynastic principle of Louis XIV and the differential calculus, or the Greek polis and Euclidean geometry, is really comparable to Marx's view of the connection of the windmill and the feudal lord. The spring or unifying element behind the two conceptions is dif-

ferent, in one case, spiritual . . . , in the other, economic, but the basic principle is the same.

It follows from this view that the political element in a culture is neither accidental nor transmittible as a tool is to some other time or place. Within all political arrangements, however, there is one constant for Spengler: law and political rule are always "class" devices. In this surprising affirmation of Marx, Spengler asserts that "every historical world-picture contains a political-economic *tendency* dependent, not upon what this man or that thinks, but upon what is practically intended by the class which in fact commands the power and, with it, the legislation." While Spengler defines class, somewhat differently from Marx—Spengler's class is more political than economic—he, too, insists on a class struggle taking place, even if ony in constitutional guise. At one point, undoubtedly with Montesquieu in mind, Spengler makes the significant comment that "the spirit of laws is always a party spirit."

The aim of all politics, internal and external, is survival. Man, as Spengler remarks in one of his works (*Man and Technics*), is a "beast of prey." In addition to such Darwin-like metaphors, Spengler also talks of the will of the strongest, and repeats with Hegel that "World-history is the world-court," adding that "it has ever decided in favor of the stronger, fuller, and more self-assured life—decreed to it, namely, the right to exist, regardless of whether its right would hold before a tribunal of waking-consciousness."

For Spengler, the internal and external arrangements of a political body are always related, but the the external must dominate; that is, foreign policy takes precedence over domestic, and the class conflict of the latter must be subordinated to the national struggles of the former. Reversing Clausewitz's dictum, Spengler insists that policy is only war by other means. Spengler's approval of war as a natural and commendable act of creativity takes concrete affirmation in his proud affirmation of the "uprising of 1914," which, he tells us, was "Prussian through and through" and "transformed souls in one moment." In the light of his declared view about politics as survival and the will of the strongest, Spengler's protests about the harshness of the Treaty of Versailles sound a bit incongruous; however, his exhortations to his people to prepare for another war looked forward to a reversal of that decision.

Espousing external war, Spengler also embraces many of the cliché positions of early nineteenth-century conservatism. Glorifying both the nobility and the peasantry, he constantly denigrates the middle classes and the urban "mob." He contrasts virtuous "Blood" with filthy "Money." At one point in his rather naïve and mixed-up passages on economics, he characterizes trade and the middleman as "parasitism, completely unproductive and, therefore, land-alien." In a vague way, Spengler is even on the side of entail.

Along with such social-economic views, Spengler has the usual assortment of conservative or reactionary political notions. He is opposed to parliamentarianism, and sees (alas, in 1918, perhaps correctly) elections degenerating into farces. As against political parties, which essentially, he feels, can only be bourgeois in nature, Spengler favors the struggle of factions, which he views as in some way "organic." Freedom of the press and such-like "liberal" notions are only illusions, for they mean simply the freedom of Money to corrupt and control the people in the bourgeoisie's own narrow interest. While Spengler identifies all of the elements listed above, economic and political, as existing at a certain stage—the decline—in all cultures, it is obvious that on the eve of 1918 and the Weimar Republic they take on a rather special contemporary importance.

On the positive side, Spengler favors what he calls "Prussianism." This catchall term embraces not only Socialism, but Imperialism and Nationalism. By Socialism, Spengler does not mean Marx's theory "but Frederick William I's Prussian practice which long preceded Marx and will yet displace him—the socialism, inwardly akin to the system of Old Egypt, that comprehends and cares for permanent economic relations, trains the individual in his duty to the whole, and glorifies hard work as an affirmation of Time and Future." In Spengler's scheme of economics, work is not a commodity but a duty, and the individual seeks not his own selfish betterment but the service of the state. To effect this, the whole national productive force is to be brought under the state's control, while leaving a certain amount of scope for personal enterprise. As one commentator sums it up, "For a society conceived in these terms, corporatism is the logical form of government." This corporate state, however, from which political parties will be absent, is to be under the rule of a hereditary monarch, like Frederick William I, and graced and by a nobility which, to use Spengler's sporting term, is "in form."

Now, it is this last element which . . . perhaps most distinguished Spengler's politics from the Nazi movement. While his stress on the nation, its aggressive foreign policy, and its "socialist" economy lent itself readily to an identification with National Socialism, the tone and meaning of Spengler's formulation was quite different. "The traditions of an old monarchy," he prophesied, "of an old aristocracy, of an old polite society, in so much as they are still healthy enough to keep clear of professional or professorial politics, in so far as they possess honor, abnegation, discipline, the geniune sense of a great mission (*race-quality,* that is, and training), sense of duty and sacrifice—can become a centre which holds together the being-stream of an entire people and enables it to outlast this time and make its landfall in the future." Alas, the charismatic upstart, Hitler, was neither polite nor possessed of a sense of honor, and Spengler was true enough to his ideal to hold himself aloof, and even to oppose, the Nazi movement which had enough in common with his own political beliefs to betray them effectively.

Spengler believed that it was Germany's mission to try to make the "landfall" sketched above. But his historical sense told him that Western culture was in its decline, and that "Caesarism" was more likely than a traditional monarchy to succeed the present reign of Money. Nevertheless, he seems not to have recognized Hitler as one of the "great fact-men" who seize the role of Caesar. Rather, Spengler imagined the modern Caesar as a successor to the Cecil Rhodes type of leader. In any case, whereas Burckhardt (with his *terribles simplificateurs*) and Nietzsche (with his commanders of the herd who, pretending to follow, will lead with an iron will) had merely foreseen the coming Caesarism, Spengler identified and described his coming as a predetermined point on a fated cyclical movement.

In the *Decline,* the elements of what I have called Spengler's "conservatism" are omnipresent. And this brings us to the second point with which I started: that the political is not only an integral part of any culture which Spengler studies, but that his own political convictions anachronistically color his studies of all cultures. Only if we recognize this fact—one which, admittedly, can only be tested as we go into his theory—can we deal effectively with Spengler's philosophy of history, making allowance for his and our political bias, and concentrating on his critical and speculative theories about history. Spengler himself claimed that his treatment would "employ no distorting modulus of personal ideals, set no personal origin of co-ordinates, be influenced by none of the personal hopes and fears and other inward impulses which count for so much in practical life; and such a detachment will—to use the words of Nietzsche . . .—enable one to view the whole fact of Man from an immense distance, to regard the individual Cultures, one's own included, as one regards the range of mountain peaks along a horizon." While it must be flatly stated that Spengler fell far short of his own ideal, we ought to follow his injunction in our own approach to him as one of the "mountain peaks" in the field of philosophy of history.

Spengler gave to his political-cum-philosophy of history work the title *Der Untergang des Abendlandes.* We are also told that he approved the use of *Decline of the West* as an English rendering of his title. Now, the word "Untergang" in German has an astronomical significance, as in the idea of the "declining" or "setting" of the sun. Thus, the thought arises that Spengler intended by his title to implant in his reader's imagination the idea, not of a decline of a society owing to naturalistic or historical reasons, but of a decline which is inevitable because it is "in our stars." Basically, I believe, Spengler was what I shall call an astrological historian. He is really talking about his own work when he says, "Astrology, in the form in which from Gothic to Baroque the Western soul knew it—was dominated by it even in denying it—was the attempt to master one's *whole* future life-course; the Faustian horoscope, of which the best-known example is perhaps that drawn out for Wallenstein by Kepler, *presupposes* a steady and purposeful direction in the existence that has yet to be accomplished."

My suspicion that Spengler saw himself as the modern historical Kepler, drawing up the Faustian horoscope, is made greater by a number of rather occult references to the influence over our destiny exercised by the heavenly bodies. Thus, talking of certain critical points in history, Spengler comments that they are "yet another hint that the Cosmic flowings in the form of human lives upon the surface of a minor star are not self-contained and independent, but stand in deep harmony with the unending movedness of the universe." Elsewhere, he talks of "the belief in his star which every born man of action possesses," and defines race, or the feeling for a common destiny, as "*something cosmic and psychic,* periodic in some obscure way, and in its inner nature partly conditioned by major astronomical relations."

Spengler's astrological view of history is, I believe, of the greatest importance in his work. It allows him to see a cyclical movement in history—an eternal recurrence—one which results from the astronomical theory of the revolution of the heavenly bodies. Further, it permits Spengler to claim powers of divination and prediction, whereby he can perceive human destiny. At the same time, it provides him with a periodization scheme which allows him to say at what point on the cycle our destiny stands at a given moment. Moreover, causation, for Spengler, resolves itself into cosmic destiny, and is therefore no longer a problem for the historian. In general, too, astronomic images, such as rise and fall, or dawn and decline, permit a historian like Spengler to embrace the notion that culture or society is an entity which moves *as a whole* in cyclic fashion. Thus, he need not entertain the disturbing idea that one part of the culture, for example, the political, may be progressing while another, possibly the social, may be suffering a reverse.

Nevertheless, while in my judgment the "astrological" is the major motif in Spengler's philosophy of history, its note is rarely sounded aloud. It serves only as the great cosmic backdrop for Spengler's more microscopic drama of life. Thus, for the bulk of his work, Spengler uses other, "biological" images. Perhaps he realized that his astrological approach was too unacceptable, suggesting charlatanism, or that, once stated, it could not readily be applied in the fine detail of actual cultural history. In any case, the inspiration of Kepler gave way in practice to that of Goethe.

The prime question Spengler set for himself was: "Is there a logic of history?" His answer was "yes," but it is an *"organic logic."* This logic, Spengler tells us, is "an instinctive, dream-sure logic of all existence as opposed to the *logic of the inorganic,* the logic of understanding and of things understood— a logic of direction as against a logic of extension—and no systematist, no Aristotle or Kant, has known how to deal with it." What this new organic logic tells us, and Spengler overlooks the tautological aspect of his remark, is that there is a world-as-history in contrast to a world-as-nature. The world-as-history relates to becoming; the world-as-nature, to the system of all things become. According to Spengler, the first man before him to divine this distinction was the immortal Goethe. "That which Goethe called *Living Nature,*" Spengler proclaims, "is exactly that which we are calling here world-history, world-as-history."

Thus, following Goethe, Spengler makes a fundamental distinction between the historical and the natural worlds. As a result, for Spengler, the unity of the positive, scientific universe is broken. Over the world-as-history lies what Spengler calls the "Destiny Idea," while the "Causality Principle" reigns over the world-as-nature. Again and again, Spengler stresses this basic dualism in the **Decline,** working it out in an involved and involuted fashion wherein each member of the pair reappears in a new garb. I list only some of the ingenious masquerades worn by the dualism: world-as-history versus world-as-nature; Destiny versus Causality (which are related as Time and Space); Form (*Gestalt*) versus Law (*Gesetz*); Physiognomic versus Systematic; Will versus Thought; Cosmic versus Microcosmic; periodity versus polarity; feel (*Fühlen*) versus feeling (*Empfinden*); Being (*Dasein*) versus waking-being (*Wachsein*); plant-like beings versus animal-beings; reason (*Vernunft*) versus understanding (*Verstand*); Race versus Language; Totem versus Taboo; Politics versus Religion; Castle versus Cathedral; and Female versus Male. Spengler's brilliance, undoubtedly somewhat perverted here, is demonstrated by the skill with which he spins out this seemingly endless dance of the two partners.

Erratic, despite its ingenuity, as Spengler's *development* of the dualism may appear, the idea itself is a fundamental position in modern philosophy of history. Simply stated, it holds that history is *not* subsumed under the generalizing sciences. Nor are its methods the same as those of the natural sciences. What the historian needs, according to Spengler, is an *eye,* "The power of seeing and not that of calculating, depth and not intellect." Speaking of Goethe, Spengler remarks: "Sympathy, observation, comparison, immediate and inward certainly, intellectual *flair*—these were the means whereby he was enabled to approach the secrets of the phenomenal world in motion. *Now these are the means of historical research*—precisely these and no others." *Par excellence,* Spengler informs us, the method of history is "intuitive perception." Contemplation and vision (*Anschauen*) are the desired experiences, for, as a

becoming, history can only be experienced, lived through (*erleben*), and not cognized in the form of mechanical laws.

History, then, is the study of unique "becomings," which can only be contemplated intuitively. This, let us note, is a basic historicist position. At one point, Spengler tries to sum it up with a quotation from Goethe, who, writing to his friend Eckermann, remarks, "The Godhead is effective in the living and not in the dead, in the becoming and the changing, not in the become and the set-fast; and therefore, similarly, the reason (*Vernunft*) is concerned only to strive towards the divine through the becoming and the living, and the understanding (*Verstand*) only to make use of the become and the set-fast." Obviously, we have already encountered these words in our treatment of the *Decline,* and Spengler himself confessed about the quotation above, "This sentence comprises my entire philosophy."

Enjoined by Spengler to look at the world-as-history intuitively and with an organic logic, we discover that all "history is founded upon general biographic archetypes," organic beings, which, like everything organic, go through the phases of birth, youth, age, and death. More specifically, these organic beings are *cultures.* In Spengler's words, "*Cultures are organisms,* and world-history is their collective biography." Thus, Spengler clearly identifies for us the subject and object of history: instead of Hegel's "nation" or Marx's "class," it is "culture" which acts in history and which is also the object of our historical study.

Spengler's view of cultures as "biographic archetypes" or as organisms also allows him to add a refinement to his general historical method. Now, to intuition the historian can join a more scientific approach: comparative morphology. Again it is Goethe who supplies the hint with his distinction in biology between the term *homology,* signifying morphological or structural equivalence, and the term *analogy,* relating to functional equivalence. Thus, the lungs of terrestrial and the swim bladders of aquatic animals are homologous, while lungs and gills are analogous. Extended to history, this method allows us to go beyond shallow analogies and comparisons, such as that of Napoleon and Caesar, and to perceive, for example, that the homologous form to Napoleon is Alexander the Great: both stand in the same phase of a declining culture, while Caesar comes later. Hence, for Spengler, Napoleon and Alexander are "contemporaries," while Caesar's contemporary is yet to appear in the Western culture.

With his new morphological method, Spengler can run through all of past history, correctly estimating relationships, or so he claims, which were previously misconceived. Thus, for Spengler, the Classical Dionysiac movement is homologous with the Renaissance and only analogous with the Reformation. He also claims that he can fill in gaps, for example, from known elements in art to corresponding unknown elements in the political forms, or, as in Chinese Culture, to "predict" (by comparison with the Western Gothic phase) the existence of a mystical period *even though* no data relating to it has survived. Shocking and strained as some of Spengler's morphological relationships appear at first sight, they at least suggest a new approach to the ancient and frequently jejune practice of superficial historical analogy.

How did Spengler come upon these discoveries? By seeing with the eyes of Goethe. "The deep, and scarcely appreciated, idea of Goethe, which he discovered in his 'living nature' and always made the basis of his morphological researches," Spengler tells us, "we shall here apply—in its most precise sense—to all the formations of man's history." Thus, when studying natural phenomena, Goethe lived into (*erfühlen*) instead of dissecting them. As a result, Spengler informs us, referring to the great poet's strange, interesting, and debatable scientific achievements, "To the spiritual eye of Goethe the idea of the prime plant was clearly visible in the form of every individual plant that happened to come up, or even that could possibly come up. In his investigation of the 'os intermaxillare' his starting-point was the *prime phenomenon of the vertebrate type;* and in other fields it was geological stratification, or the leaf as the prime form of the plant-organism, or the metamorphosis of the plants as the prime form of all organic becoming."

I cannot discuss Goethe's scientific work here—his real contribution to the study of plant life and of anatomy, or his odd battle against Newton's theory of color—but only underline the fact that Spengler derived from him the notion of an intuitively perceived culture as the prime, organic historical phenomenon. Goethe's great enemy, in the eyes of Spengler, was Darwin. Thus, in spite of the fact that Spengler, sometimes unknowingly, fills his pages with Darwinistic images of struggle and survival, he has nothing but scorn for the English naturalist. It was Darwin, Spengler charges, who had sacrificed Goethe's Nature-Theory to the nineteenth-century cult of the useful and the material. As a result, "the organic logic of the facts of life was supplanted by a mechanics in physiological garb. Heredity, adaptation, natural selection, are utility-causes of purely mechanical connotation." The consequence for history is that "the historical *dispensations* were superseded by a naturalistic *movement* 'in space' . . . the word 'process' eliminated Destiny and unveiled the secret of becoming, and lo! there was no longer a tragic but only an exact mathematical structure of world-happening. And thereupon the 'exact' historian enunciated the proposition that in the history-picture we had before us a sequence of 'states' of mechanical type which were amenable to rational analysis like a physical experiment or a chemical reaction, and that therefore causes, means, methods and objects were capable of being grouped together as a comprehensible system on the visible surface. It all becomes astonishingly simple." In sum along with Darwin, an indictment against Condorcet, Comte, Marx, and their ilk is strongly implied.

Abandoning, too, the idea of linear progress held by both the positivist historians and, supposedly, by Darwin, Spengler effects what he calls his "Copernican discovery." Instead of the Ptolemaic system of history, whereby modern Western man saw all world-happenings as circling around him and his development, Spengler substitutes a new perspective: the Copernican, wherein eight mighty cultures—Indian, Babylonian, Chinese, Egyptian, Arabic, Mexican, as well as the Classical and Western—flourish independently and go through their fated cycles of birth and death as separate worlds of self-contained values. As such, each must develop its own possibilities of self-expression.

One result of Spengler's new vision is the destruction of the old periodization scheme. What he calls the "jejune" subdivision of history into "Ancient," "Medieval," and "Modern" is entirely shattered. . . . In its place are merely the separate cultures, passing through their organic life cycles. Another result, already foreshadowed in Spengler's recommended method of intuition, is the elimination of the possibility of "history-in-itself." There are only various *perspectives* on history, enjoyed by each culture. Moreover, historical consciousness itself

differs for each culture; thus, to jump ahead a bit, according to Spengler the Greeks were ahistorical in comparison to Western man who views history as an infinite development.

A new perspective and a new periodization scheme (or absence of one), these are the concomitants of Spengler's organic logic of history. To them Spengler adds a suggestion as to the language in which history is written and, therefore, how it is to be read. His task, Spengler tells us, is comparable to Galileo's, who perceived that the book of the world-as-nature was written in mathematical language. Spengler's great discovery is that historical phenomena are not merely events or objects (for the understanding) but *symbols*—expressions of the spiritual. Thus, facts are not important in themselves (history-in-itself?) but only because they form the symbol language of history. Interpreting this language with marvelous ingenuity and acuteness, Spengler presents us with a dazzling analysis of the symbolic meaning attaching to such diverse phenomena as the colors and brushstrokes used by artists of different cultures and different time periods; the clothes worn by different people; the different sorts of mathematics, drama, and funeral customs; the different ways of fighting wars and arranging political matters; and so on and on.

Obviously, what Spengler is seeking is the "spirit" of a culture or a period. This, for him, is the substance of history, for he has already disposed of the search for the "causes" of happenings in the world-as-history. Naturally, each spirit will be *sui generis* for each culture, and will pervade all aspects of the culture. Because it pervades and animates all aspects, every fact and happening in the culture serves, in turn, as we have seen, as a symbol of that culture and spirit.

Basic to every culture-spirit is a people's conception of time and space. These are the great categories which impose their forms on every perception. But Spengler's vision is not Kantian. Time and space are *not* the same for everyone, eternal verities which thereby allow for universal truths. They are specific and different ways of seeing, enjoyed by each culture, and differentiating it from every other. Opposed to universal mankind, a common humanity, Spengler poses culture-man, unique and cut off from men of another culture. Thus, for classical man, time and space are bounded and nonextended—for example, a Euclidean geometry of magnitudes and a drama of the "blind Causal of the moment" were all he could perceive—whereas, for Western man, time and space are unlimited and infinite, and his mathematics typically a differential calculus of functions and his drama "an *inexorable* logic of becoming." In short, time and space in Spengler are relative to a given culture.

Indeed, it is this apparently overwhelming "relativism" of Spengler which most impressed many of his original readers. Spengler made no bones about his relativism. Concerning philosophy, he announced that "there are no eternal truths. Every philosophy is the expression of its own and only its own time." Similarly, "There is no timeless and solely-true way of art, but only a history of art." Ethics, of course, are in the same situation.

Now, bold as Spengler thought his declarations, they were really only the commonplace dictums of the day. Certainly, Nietzsche had sounded forth the relativity of philosophy—merely the "confession of the philosopher," as he called it—and of ethics in no uncertain terms. And Spengler's views on art were the small change of reaction to Winckelmann and his ideal of timeless art drawn from his Greek studies, a reaction in effect ever since the early nineteenth century, joined now by Spengler with borrowings, often unacknowledged, from the debates of the German art historians of his time, men like Riegl, Semper, Worringer, and others. What Spengler added to the existing relativism, however, was a persistence in demonstrating this relativity in *all* fields, including, significantly, modern science, and, further, a treatment of this relativism in terms of *culture as a whole.*

Spengler realized, indeed, that the most fundamental challenge to his relativism came from the field of mathematics. Surely, here was a field in which knowledge was cumulative, carrying over from one culture to another, *regardless* of their different conceptions of time, space, and destiny? No, says Spengler, mathematics is a *part* of philosophy, and we have already seen that every philosophy is merely the expression of its own time. *"There is no mathematic but only mathematics,"* Spengler announces. "What we call 'the history of mathematics'—implying merely the progressive actualizing of a single invariable ideal—is in fact, below the deceptive surface of history, a complex of self-contained and independent developments, an ever-repeated process of bringing to birth new form-worlds amd appropriating, transforming and sloughing alien form-worlds, a purely organic story of blossoming, ripening, wilting and dying within the set period." Thus, the Western appropriation of classical geometry is merely an outward possession of a thing learnt, and not an inward development of the Western soul.

Similarly, Spengler undercuts the claim of natural science to cumulative objectivity by attaching science to religion. Thus, against the prevailing rationalist view of a conflict of science and religion, Spengler views the two as related attempts to do away with fear by setting up laws of causality. "Always," he informs us, "science has grown up on a religion and under all the spiritual prepossessions of that religion, and always it signifies nothing more or less than an abstract melioration of these doctrines, considered as false because less abstract." Thus, for example, the Renaissance notion of God approximates the idea of pure endless space. Religion and its companion, science, therefore, are only intellectual form-worlds which are true for the particular culture in which they take shape, flourish, and then die.

What are we to say of Spengler's seemingly total relativism? The first thing to remark is that he supports his position by an informed and perceptive knowledge of such matters as mathematics—which he had concentrated on in school—art, literature, and music. Of all the philosophers of history with whom we have dealt, Spengler is probably the most gifted in these areas (though undoubtedly surpassed by Condorcet and Comte as a pure mathematician). Thus, his pursuit of relativism in these subjects, even if ultimately we judge it incorrect, is a *tour de force.* We gain constantly from his brilliant *aperçus.*

The second thing to note is that Spengler's work joins, on one side, to the investigations undertaken by ethnologists, anthropologists, and psychologists concerning the different conceptions of time and space (which, of course, underlie all mathematics) held by primitive, mythical-minded peoples. On the other side, it relates to the speculations and researches of the sociologists of knowledge. Without going into details, I suggest the validity and value of a comparison of Spengler with, say, Mircea Eliade on myth, or Karl Mannheim on the epistemological basis of knowledge.

Finally, we must study the connection of Spengler's relativism with skepticism, and the significance of this connection for Spengler's own work in philosophy of history. The only possible philosophy, Spengler tells us, for modern Western man is that which corresponds to Classical Skepticism. In a rather tricky passage, Spengler defines the difference between the two skepticisms. "The Classical skepticism is ahistoric, it doubts by denying outright. But that of the West . . . is obliged to be historical through and through. Its solutions are got by treating everything as relative, as a historical phenomenon, and its procedure is psychological. Whereas the Skeptic philosophy arose within Hellenism as the negation of philosophy—declaring philosophy to be purposeless—we, on the contrary, regard the *history of philosophy* as, in the last resort, philosophy's gravest theme. This *is* 'skepsis,' in the true sense." Thus, Spengler's skepticism concerns *absolute* knowing, it does not deny *relative,* i.e., historical, knowledge. From a given perspective we can gain knowledge which is correct, relative to that perspective, by definition. Hence, all knowledge is *historical*—situated in time and space—i.e., it is becoming.

The problem we are left with, however, is to reconcile Spengler's historical knowledge, even though relative in the sense above, with his earlier view that cultures are, in essence, unknowable one to another. One or two quotations from the **Decline** will set up the problem. "Truths are truths only in relation to a particular mankind." Thus, Spengler admits, "my own philosophy is able to express and reflect only the Western (as distinct from the Classical, Indian, or other) soul, and that soul *only* in its present civilized phase by which its conception of the world, its practical range and its sphere of effect are specified." Or, talking of the world of the Bible, he remarks "how alien to us all the inner life of Jesus is," and concludes that "Such sensations are unapproachably remote from men who live in and with a dynamical world-picture."

How, then, does Western man come to feel—for surely Spengler has already disdained mere understanding (*Verstand*)—the soul-forms of other cultures? Ah, says Spengler, we must learn to *see* with different eyes, "not from this or that 'standpoint,' but in a high, time-free perspective embracing whole millenniums of historical world-forms." We must duplicate Copernicus' act in the world-as-nature with a similar act in the world-as-history. By so doing, we emancipate ourselves from "the evident present in the name of infinity." Only if we can put "our Western feeling" out of action shall we be able to penetrate, for example, "into the essence of the world-image that underlay the Classical attitude."

Fortunately, before Spengler's eyes "there seems to emerge, as a vision, a hitherto unimagined mode of superlative historical research that is truly Western . . . a morphology of becoming for *all* humanity . . . a duty of penetrating the world-feeling not only of our proper soul but of all souls whatsoever that have contained grand possibilities and have expressed them in the field of actuality as grand Cultures." This research "presupposes the eye of an artist, and of an artist who can feel the whole sensible and apprehensible environment dissolve into a deep infinity of mysterious relationships." This artist, it would seem, by his vision is able to rise above the relative knowledge which Spengler previously claimed was all that was permitted to mortal man. Spengler hails this artist's coming with the glad cry that "Now, at last, it is possible to take the decisive step of sketching an image of history that is independent of the accident of standpoint, of the period in which this or that observer lives—independent too of the personality of the observer himself, who as an interested member of his own Culture is tempted, by its religious, intellectual, political and social tendencies, to order the material of history according to a perspective that is limited as to both space and time.''

Then, having transcended space and time, Spengler adds that it is the historian's business not to praise or blame the ''material'' of history, i.e., the symbols of a culture, but solely to consider them morphologically. Admittedly, the reader is shaken after this declaration about historical impartiality by Spengler's vehement ''I prefer one Roman aqueduct to all Roman temples and statues'' and numerous other such apparently ''partial'' statements, but Spengler's casual defense is simply that items such as the temples and statues were not ''in harmony with the tendency of the age.''

According to Spengler, the reason we know what is the tendency of the age is because we are the first culture to have escaped our own perspective—in fact, this is *our* spiritual tendency—and therefore are able to view from on high the *necessary* course of every culture. Hence, intimately tied to Spengler's transcendence of his own ''relative history'' is his unwavering conviction that the history of every culture is predetermined. Its destiny is inevitable, and indeed it is the triumph of *our* culture that we alone ''can foresee the way that destiny has chosen for it.''

Now, by determinism and inevitability, Spengler emphatically does not mean that history is under the necessity of causal laws. Causality . . . can be applied only to the world-as-nature. For Spengler, ''Real history is heavy with fate but free of laws.'' As such, we can *divine* the future but not reckon or calculate it. This divinable fate, however, does not take away our freedom; it is, instead, our necessary freedom. Obedience to the ''laws'' (in Spengler's terms, the destiny) of history is what makes us free. ''We have not the freedom to reach to this or to that,'' Spengler tells us on the last page of the *Decline*, ''but the freedom to do the necessary or to do nothing. And a task that history necessarily has set *will* be accomplished with the individual or against him.'' (pp. 314-34)

Bruce Mazlish, ''Spengler,'' in his The Riddle of
History: The Great Speculators from Vico to Freud,
Harper & Row, Publishers, 1966, pp. 307-50.

NORTHROP FRYE   (essay date 1974)

[*Frye has exerted a tremendous influence in the field of twentieth-century literary scholarship, mainly through his study* Anatomy of Criticism *(1957). In this seminal work, Frye makes controversial claims for literature and literary critics, arguing that judgments are not inherent in the critical process and asserting that literary criticism can be ''scientific'' in its methods and its results without borrowing concepts from other fields of study. Literary criticism, in Frye's view, should be autonomous in the manner that physics, biology, and chemistry are autonomous disciplines. For Frye, literature is schematic because it is wholly structured by myth and symbol. The critic becomes a near-scientist, determining how symbols and myth are ordered and function in a given work. The critic need not, in Frye's view, make judgments of value about the work; a critical study is structured by the fact that the components of literature, like those of nature, are unchanging and predictable. Frye believes that literature occupies a position of extreme importance within any culture. Literature, as he sees it, is ''the place where our imaginations find the ideal that they try to pass on to belief and action, where they find the vision which is the source of both the dignity and the joy of life.'' The literary critic serves society by studying and ''translating'' the structures in which that vision is encoded. In the following excerpt from an essay originally published in* Daedalus, Winter

1974, Frye evaluates thematic, analytic, and methodological aspects of The Decline of the West.]

The philosophical framework of Spengler's argument [in *The Decline of the West*] is a Romantic one, derived ultimately from Fichte's adaptation of Kant. The objective world, the world that we know and perceive, the phenomenal world, is essentially a spatial world: it is the domain of Nature explored by science and mathematics, and so far as it is so explored, it is a mechanical world, for when living things are seen objectively they are seen as mechanisms. Over against this is the world of time, organism, life and history. The essential reality of this world eludes the reasoner and experimenter: it is to be attained rather by feeling, intuition, imaginative insight, and, above all, by symbolism. The time in which this reality exists is a quite different time from the mechanical or clock time of science, which is really a dimension of space. It follows that methods adequate for the study of nature are not adequate for the study of history. The true method of studying living forms, Spengler says, is by analogy, and his whole procedure is explicitly and avowedly analogical. The problem is to determine what analogies in history are purely accidental, and which ones point to the real shape of history itself. Thanks to such works as Bernard Lonergan's *Insight* (1957), we know rather more about the positive role of analogy in constructive thought than was generally known in 1918, and it is no longer possible to dismiss Spengler contemptuously as ''mythical'' or ''irrational'' merely because his method is analogical. He may be, but for other reasons. (p. 180)

[The] morphological view of history, which sees history as a plurality of cultural developments, is, Spengler claims, an immense improvement on the ordinary ''linear'' one which divides history into ancient, medieval, and modern periods. Here Spengler seems to me to be on very solid ground, at least to the extent that linear history is really, at bottom, a vulgar and complacent assumption that we represent the inner purpose of all human history. The Hebrews gave us our religion, the Greeks our philosophy, the Romans our law, and these contributions to our welfare descended from the Middle Ages to us. The Chinese and Indians had little to do with producing us; they only produced more Chinese and Indians, so they don't really belong to history. ''Better fifty years of Europe than a cycle of Cathay,'' as the man says in Tennyson. Hegel has been often and most unfairly ridiculed for advocating a view of history which made the Prussian state of his day its supreme achievement. But whenever we adopt this linear view, especially in its progressive form, which asserts that the later we come in time the better we are, we do far worse than Hegel. The linear view of history is intellectually dead, and Spengler has had a by no means ignoble role in assisting at its demise.

Spengler's view of history includes, however, a rather similar distinction between human life with history and human life without it. If we study the history of one of the great cultures, we find that institutions evolve, classes rise, and conquests expand in what seems a logical, but is really an organic, way. But if we try to write a history of Patagonians or Zulus or Mongols, we can produce only a series of events or incidents. These people live and die and reproduce; they trade and think and fight as we do; they make poems and pots and buildings. But their stories are chronicles or annals, not coherent histories. Lapland in the eighteenth century is much like Lapland in the thirteenth: we do not feel, as we feel when we compare eighteenth-century with thirteenth-century England, that it is five centuries *older*. Similarly, after a culture has completely exhausted itself, it passes out of "history." There are, therefore, two forms of human life: a primitive existence with the maximum of continuity and the minimum of change, and life within a growing or declining culture, which is history properly speaking.

A parallel distinction reappears within the cultural developments themselves. People have constantly been fascinated by the degree of accident in history, by the fact that, as Pascal says, history would have been quite different if Cleopatra's nose had been longer. Spengler distinguishes what he calls destiny from incident. The incidents of a man's life will depend on the job he takes, the woman he marries, the town he decides to life in, and these are often determined by sheer accident. But nothing will alter the fact that it will be his life. Cultures, too, have their real lives as well as the incidents those lives bring to the surface. Spengler does not mention Cleopatra's nose, but he does say that if Mark Antony had won the battle of Actium the shape of Magian culture would have been much easier to recognize. The incidents of Western history would have been quite different if Harold had won at Hastings or Napoleon at the Nile, but the same kind of history would have appeared in other forms. A modern reader would doubtless prefer some other word to "destiny," but the distinction itself is valid, granted Spengler's premises. In what a culture produces, whether it is art, philosophy, military strategy, or political and economic developments, there are no accidents: everything a culture produces is equally a symbol of that culture.

Certain stock responses to Spengler may be set aside at once. In the first place, his view of history is not a cyclical view, even if he does use the names of the four seasons to describe its main phases. A cyclical theory would see a mechanical principle, like the one symbolized by Yeats's double gyre, as controlling the life of organisms, and for Spengler the organism is supreme: there is no superorganic mechanism. Brooks Adams's *The Law of Civilization and Decay* (1895), which appears to have wrought such disaster in the impresssionable mind of Ezra Pound, does give us a rather crude cyclical theory of history as an alternating series of movements of aggressiveness and usury, with apparently some preference for the former. Yeats's *Vision,* as just implied, is also cyclical, because it is astrological, and therefore sees history as following the mechanical rhythms of nature rather than the organic ones. It seems to me that Spengler's distinction between primitive and historical existence is the real basis of Yeats's distinction between "primary" cultures and the "antithetical" ones that rise out of them, but the spirits who supplied Yeats with his vision did not know much history.

In a way Spengler does give an illusion of a cyclical view: he knows very little about Chinese and Indian civilizations, and relegates the possibility of other such developments in Babylonia or pre-Columbian America to bare mentions. Fair enough: nobody expects omniscience. But this leaves us with a series of five that do run in sequence: the Egyptian, the Classical, the Magian, the Western, and the Russian. This sequence may have its importance, as I shall suggest later, but for Spengler himself cultures grow up irregularly, like dandelions. There was no inevitability that a new Russian culture would appear in the decline of a Western one, nor is there any carryover of contrasting characteristics from one to the other (except in the negative and distorting form of "pseudomorphosis"), such as a genuinely cyclical theory would postulate.

Spengler's analogical method of course rests, not only on the analogies among the cultures themselves, but on a further analogy between a culture and an organism. It is no good saying that a culture is not an organism, and that therefore we can throw out his whole argument. The question whether a culture "is" an organism or not belongs to what I call the fallacy of the unnecessary essence. It is an insoluble problem, and insoluble problems are insoluble because they have been wrongly formulated. The question is not whether a culture is an organism, but whether it behaves enough like one to be studied on an organic model. "Let the words youth, growth, maturity, decay . . . be taken at last as objective descriptions of organic states," Spengler says. Spengler's massed evidence for these characteristicss in a variety of cultures seems to me impressive enough to take seriously. It is no good either denouncing him on the ground that his attitude is "fatalistic" or "pessimistic," and that one ought not to be those things. It is not fatalism to say that one grows older every year; it is not pessimism to say that whatever is alive will eventually die. Or if it is, it doesn't matter.

Again, I am not much worried about the "contradictions" or "ambiguities," which can probably be found by job-lots in Spengler's work. Anybody can find contradictions in any long and complex argument. Most of them are verbal only, and disappear with a little application to the real structure of the argument itself. Most of the rest arise from the fact that the reader's point of view differs from that of the writer, and he is apt to project these differences into the book as inconsistencies within it. There may remain a number of genuine contradictions which really do erode the author's own case, and I think there are some in Spengler. But for a book of the kind he wrote the general principle holds that if one is in broad sympathy with what he is trying to do, no errors or contradictions or exaggerations seem fatal to the general aim; if one is not in sympathy with it, everything, however correct in itself, dissolves into chaos.

Spengler's book is not a work of history; it is a work of historical popularization. It outlines one of the mythical shapes in which history reaches everybody except professional historians. Spengler would not care for the term popularization: he is proud of the length and difficulty of his work, speaks with contempt of the popular; and of his efforts to popularize his own thesis, such as **"Prussianism and Socialism"** . . . or *Man and Technics* . . . , the less said the better. Nevertheless, his book is addressed to the world at large, and historians are the last people who should be influenced by it. What Spengler has produced is a vision of history which is very close to being a work of literature—close enough, at least, for me to feel some appropriateness in examining it as a literary critic. If *The Decline of the West* were nothing else, it would still be one of the world's great Romantic poems. There are limits to this, of course: Spengler had no intention of producing a work of *pure* imagination, nor did he do so. A work of literature, as such, cannot be argued about or refuted, and Spengler's book has been constantly and utterly refuted ever since it appeared. But it won't go away, because in sixty years there has been no alternative vision of the data it contemplates.

What seems to me most impressive about Spengler is the fact that everybody does accept his main thesis in practice, whatever they think or say they accept. Everybody thinks in terms of a "Western" culture to which Europeans and Americans belong; everybody thinks of that culture as old, not young; everybody realizes that its most striking parallels are with the Roman period of Classical culture; everybody realizes that some crucial change in our way of life took place around Napoleon's time.

At that I am not counting the people who have a sentimental admiration for medieval culture because it represents our own lost youth, or the people who cannot listen with pleasure to any music later than Mozart or Beethoven, or the people who regard the nineteenth century as a degenerate horror, or the Marxists who talk about the decadence of bourgeois culture, or the alarmists who talk about a return to a new Dark Ages, or the Hellenists who regard Latin literature as a second-hand imitation of Greek literature. All these have a more or less muddled version of Spengler's vision as their basis. The decline, or aging, of the West is as much a part of our mental outlook today as the electron or the dinosaur, and in that sense we are all Spenglerians. (pp. 183-88)

For students of English literature, at least, the most famous attack on Spengler occurs in Wyndham Lewis's *Time and Western Man* [see Additional Bibliography], as part of his general onslaught on the "time philosophy." And a most instructive attack it is. In the first place, we notice that Lewis has no alternative philosophy. He makes vague remarks about attaching more importance to space and painting and less to time and music, and says such things as "I am for the physical world." But his book is actually a quite lucid, often brilliant, example of the very procedure he proposes to attack. He shows how twentieth-century philosophy, literature, politics, popular entertainment, music and ballet, and half a dozen other social phenomena all form a single interwoven texture of "time philosophy," and are all interchangeable symbols of it. We are thus not surprised to find that Lewis's targets of attack are formative influences on his other work, as Joyce influenced his fiction and Bergson his theory of satire. And as *Time and Western Man* is really a Spenglerian book, doing essentially the kind of thing Spengler would do, including taking a hostile and polemical tone toward most contemporary culture, we are not surprised either to find that Lewis seldom comes to grips with Spengler's actual arguments. He does make some effective points, such as showing how a *Zeitgeist* patter can rationalize irresponsible political leadership by explaining that history says it's "time" for another war. But this would apply to a lot of people besides Spengler. What Lewis mainly attacks and ridicules are Spengler's sound effects.

It is true that Spengler's sound effects are sometimes hard to take, and the reason for their existence brings us to a problem that the literary critic is constantly having to face. I have elsewhere tried to show that it is intellectually dishonest to call a man's work reactionary, whatever his personal attitudes may have been, because it is the use made of it by others that will determine whether it will be reactionary or not. The pseudo-critic is constantly looking for some feature of a writer's attitude, inside or outside his books, that will enable him to plaster some ready-made label on his author. Genuine criticism is a much more difficult and delicate operation, especially in literature, where a man may be a great poet and still be little better than an idiot in many of his personal attitudes.

In a large number, at least, of important writers we find an imagination which makes them important, and something else, call it an ego, which represents the personality trying to *say* something, to assert and argue and impress. A great deal of criticism revolves around the problem of trying to separate these two elements. We have Eliot the poet and Eliot the snob; Pound the poet and Pound the crank; Yeats the poet and Yeats the poseur; Lawrence the poet and Lawrence the hysteric. Further back, Milton, Pope, Blake, Shelley, Whitman, all present aspects of personality so distasteful to some critics that they cannot really deal critically with their poetry at all. For somebody on the periphery of literature, like Spengler, the task of separation is still more difficult, and requires even more patience. It does a writer no service to pretend that the things which obstruct his imagination are not there, or, if there, can be rationalized or explained away. In my opinion Spengler has a permanent place in twentieth-century thought, but so far as his reputation is concerned, he was often his own worst enemy, and a stupid and confused Spengler is continually getting in the way of the genuine prophet and visionary.

We may suspect, perhaps, some illegitimate motivation in Spengler's writing, some desire to win the war on the intellectual front after being left out of the army. It would be easy to make too much of this, but he does say in the preface to the revised edition that he has produced what he is "proud to call *a German philosophy*" (italics original), although the real thesis of his book is that there are no German philosophies, only Western ones. In any case, he belonged all his life to the far right of the German political spectrum, and carried a load of the dismal *Völkisch* ["racial"] imbecilities that played so important a part in bringing Hitler to power. Hitler in fact represents something of a nemesis for Spengler the prophet, even though Spengler died in 1936, before Hitler had got really started on his lemming march. Unless he has unusual sources of information, a prophet is well advised to stick to analyzing the present instead of foretelling the future. Spengler wanted and expected a German leader in the Bismarckian and Prussian military tradition, and he doubted whether this screaming *lumpen-Künstler* ["trumpery artist"] was it. He greeted the Nazis in a book called in English *The Hour of Decision* . . ., which the Nazis, when they got around to reading it, banned from circulation. But his general political attitude was sufficiently close to Nazism to enable him to die in his bed.

These personal attitudes account for many of the more unattractive elements in his rhetoric, which has all the faults of a prophetic style: harsh, dogmatic, prejudiced, certain that history will do exactly what he says, determined to rub his reader's nose into all the toughness and grimness of his outlook. He has little humor, though plenty of savage and sardonic wit, and a fine gift for gloomy eloquence. He is fond of murky biological language, like calling man a "splendid beast of prey," and much of his imagery is Halloween imagery, full of woo-woo noises and shivery Wagnerian whinnies about the "dark" goings-on of nature and destiny. Thus:

> With the formed state, high history also lays itself down weary to sleep. Man becomes a plant again, adhering to the soil, dumb and enduring. The timeless village and the "eternal" peasant reappear, begetting children and burying seed in Mother Earth. . . . There, in the souls, world-peace, the peace of God, the bliss of grey-haired monks and hermits, is become actual—and there alone. It has awakened that depth in the endurance of suffering which the historical man in the thousand years of his development has never known. Only with the end of grand History does holy, still Being reappear. It is a drama noble in its aimlessness, noble and aimless as the course of the stars, the rotation of the earth, and alternance of land and sea, of ice and virgin forest upon its face. We may marvel at it or we may lament it—but it is there.

It may not be everybody's poetry, but it is genuine enough of its kind. But occasionally we come across elements connected with this kind of rhetoric that are more objectionable. For example, Spengler knows that his argument really has nothing to do with the conception of "race," and in *The Hour of Decision* he makes it clear—well, fairly clear—that he regards the Nazi attitude to race as suicidal frenzy. But he *cannot* give up the notion that Jews are a separate entity: if he did, one of the most dearly cherished *Völkisch* prejudices would go down the drain:

> Spinoza, a Jew and therefore, spiritually, a member of the Magian Culture, could not absorb the Faustian force-concept at all, and it has no place in his system. And it is an astounding proof of the secret power of root-ideas that Heinrich Hertz, the only Jew amongst the great physicists of the recent past, was also the only one of them who tried to resolve the dilemma of mechanics by eliminating the idea of force.

According to Spengler's own thesis, a man who spends his life in seventeenth-century Holland belongs to the Western Baroque, whatever his religious or racial affinities. Most of Spinoza's contemporaries called themselves Christians, which is equally a "Magian" religion according to Spengler. But of course one never knows when such a prejudice will come in handy. "It is something fundamental in the essence of the Magian soul that leads the Jew, as entrepreneur and engineer, to stand aside from the creation proper of machines and devote himself to the business side of their production." This remark follows closely on a critique of Marx. As the Nazis said, capitalism and communism are both Jewish inventions. The biological function of women is also a fruitful topic for dark symbolization.

> Endless Becoming is comprehended in the idea of Motherhood. Woman as Mother *is* Time and *is* Destiny. Just as the mysterious act of depth-experience fashions, out of sensation, extension and world, so through motherhood the bodily man is made an individual member of this world, in which thereupon he *has* a Destiny. All symbols of Time and Distance are also symbols of maternity. *Care* is the root-feeling of future, and all care is motherly.

It is little surprise to learn that Ibsen's Nora "is the very type of the provincial derailed by reading." That is, if Nora had really responded to the *Zeitgeist,* and understood that she *was* Time and Destiny, she would have done nothing so unfeminine as read books, but would have remained illiterate, pregnant, and absorbed in her doll-house.

There is also the unnecessary value judgment implied in the word "decline" itself. Strictly speaking, according to Spengler Western art is not getting any better or worse as it changes from medieval to Renaissance to Baroque conventions; it is simply growing older. But Spengler wants it to decline and exhaust its possibilities, because he wants his contemporaries, at least the German ones, to devote themselves to the things required by their cultural age, which for him are technological, national socialist, and military:

> I would sooner have the fine mind-begotten forms of a fast steamer, a steel structure, a precision-lathe, the subtlety and elegance of

many chemical and optical processes, than all the pickings and stealings of present-day "arts and crafts," architecture and painting included. I prefer one Roman aqueduct to all Roman temples and statues. . . .

The Romans who built aqueducts and carried out huge massacres and purges also produced Lucretius, Virgil, Ovid, Horace and Catullus. Not one of these names appears in Spengler's indexes (except Horace by courtesy of the translator). He would say, with the Hellenists mentioned above, that Latin poetry was an inorganic repetition of Greek poetry, but it wasn't. But, of course, for him as for others the word "decline" is an easy way of dismissing anything in the contemporary arts that one finds puzzling or disturbing. When Spengler's book was published, the fashionable myth was the myth of progress, and Spengler's evidence that technological advance could just as easily be seen as a hardening of the cultural arteries was useful as a counterweight. But its usefulness, like so many other things in history, has exhausted its possibilities now that this aspect of technology is obvious to everybody.

After all this has been said, and a great deal more that could be said taken for granted, it is still true that very few books, in my experience, have anything like Spengler's power to expand and exhilarate the mind. The boldness of his leaping imagination, the kaleidoscopic patterns that facts make when he throws them together, the sense of the whole of human thought and culture spread out in front of one, the feeling that the blinkers of time and space have been removed from one's inward eyes when Greek sculptors are treated as the "contemporaries" of Western composers, all make up an experience not easily duplicated. I first encountered him as an undergraduate, and I think this is the best time to read him, because his perspective is long range and presbyopic, and his specific judgments all too often wrong headed. Some of his comparative passages, such as his juxtaposing of colors in Western painting with tonal effects in Western music, read almost like free association. Any number of critics could call these comparisons absurd or mystical balderdash. But Spengler has the power to challenge the reader's imagination, as critics of that type usually have not, and he will probably survive them all even if all of them are right.

The best-known philosophy of history after Spengler, at least in English, is that of Arnold Toynbee, whose *Study of History* began appearing while Spengler was still alive. Toynbee has twenty-one cultures to Spengler's seven or eight, and twenty of them follow, more or less, Spengler's organic scheme of youth, maturity, decline (accompanied by a "time of troubles") and dissolution. But the twenty-first is Toynbee's own Western culture, and that one has just got to be different: to assume that it will go the way of the others would be "fatalism," which is what he professes to object to in Spengler. So he develops a "challenge and response" theory which enables him to use a mechanical metaphor instead of an organic one at the stage corresponding to "decline," and talk of "breakdown" instead. But the sequence of genesis, growth, breakdown and disintegration in Toynbee seems more jumbled than Spengler's consistently organic model. He begins his discussion of the causes of "breakdown," at the beginning of Volume Four, with a critique of Spengler which has all the air of a dodged issue. He says that it is too early to say whether Western culture has come to its "time of troubles" yet, which is quite a statement to make in 1939; he says Spengler is a "fatalist," which as we have seen is irrelevant, and he says that Spengler treats a metaphor as though it were a fact. But every historical overview of this kind, including Toynbee's, is and has to be metaphorical. When we look at Toynbee's own table of contents we find "nemesis of creativity," "schism and palingenesis," "withdrawal and return," and if those are not metaphors I don't know the meaning of the word. He also seems to feel that ignoring Spengler's distinction between destiny and incident will give more sense of freedom to man by putting more emphasis on the accidental factors of history. There is of course a great deal that is of value and interest in Toynbee's books, but as a Spenglerian revisionist he seems to me to be something of a bust. Except for one thing.

That one thing is his account of the passing of Classical into Western culture. He says that when a culture dies it forms an internal and an external proletariat. The late Roman Empire had its internal proletariat in the bread-and-circus mobs of Rome and the other big cities, and its external proletariat in the Goths and Vandals breaking through the periphery of the Empire. Out of these two forms of proletariat there emerged a "universal Church," which acted as the tomb of the old culture and the womb of the new one. Spengler also speaks of a "second religiousness" which enters a culture in its final stages: it seems to be one of his most useful and suggestive ideas. But he thinks of Toynbee's internal proletariat simply as a rabble: "The mass is the end, the radical nullity," he says. He overlooks both the connection of primitive Christianity with the proletariat and its extraordinary power of organization. It seems to me that Toynbee gives a more rational explanation of the historical role of Christianity in this period than Spengler gives. Toynbee ignores Spengler's "Magian" intermediate culture, but his own view does not necessarily do away with it: it merely points to something else that was also happening, to different aspects of what was happening, and to a process which would also account for the "cavern" imagery that Spengler associates with Byzantine culture. It also provides a means of explaining something very important that Spengler leaves out.

This is the curious fascination of Western culture with the idea of making itself into a reborn Classical culture. In its "spring" period its poets devoted great energies to recreating the visions of Virgil and Ovid; in its political life, it revolved around the conception of a reborn Augustus, a Christianized Roman Emperor. Why is the central mythical figure of English literature King Arthur, who has so vague and hazy a historical existence? At best he was merely a local British leader making a temporary rally against the Saxons, who of course won in the end. Why not make more of, say, Alfred, who really was a great man, and whose historical existence is not open to doubt? When we read in Geoffrey of Monmouth that Arthur conquered the armies of Rome, and remember that his colleague in romance was Charlemagne, we get a clue: he is a prototype of the reborn Christian Caesar, the Holy Roman Emperor. This symbolism of recreating Classical culture reaches its climax with the Renaissance, a word which means the "rebirth" of Classicism. It is highly significant that Spengler is rather silly about the Renaissance, which he treats as an un-German interruption of the development of German Gothic into German Baroque. He also seems unaware of the extent to which the same idea dominated, to or past the verge of obsession, a long series of German writers, from Winckelmann through Hölderlin to Nietzsche and George, the last two of whom Spengler certainly knew well. Of course Toynbee's death and rebirth pattern does introduce a more cyclical element into history than Spengler admits. Vico is often regarded as a precursor of Spengler,

though I see no evidence that Spengler had read him, but Toynbee brings us much closer to what Vico means by the *ricorso* than anything in Spengler.

If one culture can recreate another one in this way, we have to abandon what seems to me in any case a profoundly unacceptable element in Spengler's argument: his insistence that every culture is a windowless monad, and cannot be genuinely influenced by another culture. "To the true Russian the basic proposition of Darwinism is as devoid of meaning as that of Copernicus is to a true Arab." This remark may be a curious anticipation of the Lysenko business in Stalinist Russia, but on the whole such observations are clearly nonsense: there are a lot of Arabs who know that the earth goes round the sun, and they are not bogus ones. In fact science, in general, is the great obstacle to Spengler's cultural solipsism. Granted that different cultures will construct different scientific world-pictures, there is an obviously translatable quality in science, which makes its principles quite as comprehensible to Chinese or Indians as to Germans or Americans. Such science might even develop a world view on a supercultural scale. We notice that Spengler casts some uneasy glances at what he calls "the ruthlessly cynical hypothesis of the Relativity theory." He tries to see it, of course, as "exhausting the possibilities" of Western science, but he seems to be not quite sure that its view of time will be content to confine itself to the world of measurement and stay out of his dark existential territory.

Apart from this, however, perhaps the fact that Western culture has spread over the world means something more than simply

A letter from Spengler to his sister Adele.

the capacity for expansion which Spengler assigns to the Faustian spirit. If science is a universal structure of knowledge, it can help mankind to break out of culture-group barriers. Spengler of course thinks this is a pipe dream, and insists that the people of Asia and Africa have no interest in Western science or technology except as a means of destroying the West. But Marx is a far more effective prophet in the world today than Spengler, and the reason is that he emphasizes something uniform and global in the human situation. The factors which are the same throughout the world, such as the exploitation of labor, have always been, if not less important, at any rates less powerful in history than conflicts of civilizations. Now they are more important, and growing in power. The industrial revolution brings a new factor into the situation which cannot be wholly absorbed into a dialectic of separate "cultures," important as those have been. The question whether Western civilization will survive, decline or break down is out of date, for the world is trying to outgrow the conception of "a" civilization, and reach a different kind of perspective.

If the death-to-rebirth transition from Classical to Western culture happened once, something similar could happen again in our day, though the transition would be to something bigger than another culture. This would imply three major periods of human existence: the period of primitive societies, the period of the organic cultures, and a third period now beginning. Spengler, we saw, attacks and ridicules the three-period view of ancient, medieval and modern ages with, we said, a good deal of justification. But he also remarks that the notion of three ages has had a profound appeal to the Faustian consciousness, from Joachim of Floris in the thirteenth century onward. It is possible that what is now beginning to take shape is the real "Third Reich," of which the Nazis produced so hideous a parody.

The detail of Spengler's vision is all around us, in the restless wandering of great masses of people, in the violence and overcrowding of our almost unmanageable cities, in the strong ethical sense in some social areas, which Spengler compares with Buddhism in India and Stoicism in Rome, neutralized by dictatorships and police states in others, in the "second religiousness" of Oriental cults and the like, in the brutality and vacuousness of our standard forms of entertainment, in the physical self-indulgence paralleling the Roman cult of the bath, in the rapid series of vogues and fashions in the arts which distract us from their inner emptiness. It would be disastrous to pretend that these are not features of cultural aging. It would be still more disastrous to underestimate the powerful inertia in society that wants to "decline" still further, give up the freedom that demands responsibility, and drop out of history. What Spengler said would happen is happening, to a very considerable degree. But while Spengler is one of our genuine prophets, he is not our definitive prophet: other things are also happening, in areas that still invite our energies and loyalties and are not marked off with the words "too late." (pp. 189-98)

Northrop Frye, "Spengler Revisited," in his Spiritus Mundi: Essays on Literature, Myth, and Society, *Indiana University Press, 1976, pp. 179-98.*

ADDA B. BOZEMAN (essay date 1983)

[*Bozeman is a Latvian-born American writer on law and international relations. Her works include* Politics and Culture in International History *(1960) and* The Future of Law in a Multicultural World *(1971). In the following excerpt, she discusses Spengler's cultural analysis in* The Decline of the West *and applies Spengler's ideas to situations in present-day global relations.*]

Reflections on Spengler allow for the thought that his own biography is an eloquent metaphor for one of the most pervasive themes in his work, that, namely, which centers upon the place of the creative individual in culture, society, and time. Spengler held with Goethe that humanity is an abstraction, and that there have always been only men. Only the individual—*der Einzelne*—thinks and has ideas. Humanity, or mankind, he notes, has no goal, no plan, and no ideas; it is an empty, zoological term. These were not fashionable thoughts in an age marked by crass materialism and totalitarian systems of rule, but Spengler never wavered in his commitment to acknowledge the primacy of ideas and the distinctiveness of men who bring them forth.

In praising the wondrous life of ideas, however, Spengler never forgot that all life is change, that concepts undergo transformation and that becoming and declining are two aspects of one and the same organic process. Contrary to numerous respected theorists and historians in the Occident, who accentuate the themes of evolution in their work and who are programmatically "upbeat" in conjecturing the future in terms of progress, Spengler was convinced that the full measure of life can be discovered only when decline and decay are perceived and assessed as clearly as beginning and becoming. It is this dual focus that seems to have irritated many of his detractors, causing them to charge Spengler with the social sin of pessimism.

Spengler was quite conscious of this clash of orientations in the West. He knew that men are generally disdainful of experience and that, driven by limitless and uncontrolled hope, they like to conceptualize the future in terms of what they consider the desirable rather than the likely course of events. In counterpoint to these, in his view, irrational trends, he remarked that optimism is naïve and in some respects even vulgar, and that it surely stands for cowardice when one is afraid to face the fact that life is fleeting and transient in all its aspects.

These thoughts touch a major motif in Spengler's philosophy which critics tend to ignore, namely the recognition of the place of tragedy in the Occidental cultural world. Tragic modes of experiencing life can only evolve there, where the individual human being is presumed autonomous in his feelings, thoughts, and actions, and where he is therefore vulnerable to the agony of having to make choices between conflicting interests and commitments. They are thus absent in the high cultures of the Orient, where human beings are generally subsumed in the superior concept of the consensus or in the social roles assigned them. In fact, they have been fully developed only in the cultures of the West, and in this context, again, Spengler suggests that they have been more enduring in continental Europe than in England, where they atrophied under the weight of utilitarianism and pragmatism, and in the United States, where "the longing for the happy ending" came to set the tone for life.

Spengler's pessimism, then, is strictly qualified. And the same holds for his determinism. He notes that there is nothing absolutely inevitable about the passage from one phase in the history of a culture, a nation, or a state to the other, and that none of these three organisms is bound to wither away. Decline will set in only when living human beings choose to play light with their society's moral and legal ground rules and when they voluntarily indulge in the mechanization of their intellectual and sentimental lives. Indices of decline are man-made, after all—hence Spengler's distinction between possible and actual culture. Indeed, there is a strong suggestion in his work that biography is, in the final analysis, dominant over the flux of time. Just as he himself had the courage to fathom the idea of decline without ever suspending efforts to arrest this process, so does he seem to have believed that intelligent men must always be ready to size up the epoch and the milieu in which they find themselves so that they may take constructive action in response to the demands of the hour. Statesmanship in particular, he tells us, is just not conceivable without this dimension of thought.

Spengler announces his unifying scheme in Volume I of *Der Untergang des Abendlandes*. . . . It is the *Dasselbe* ["that which remains the same"] in the rush of life and the flow of time which Spengler was determined to uncover and identify. What he looked for in his attempts to understand a folk, a nation, or a culture was the human unit's integral sustaining essence. He concluded that this essence which radiates "inner certainty" to successive generations and which therefore stands for the group's destiny (*Schicksal*) is not a function either of race or of language. Just look at the Romans, he counsels the reader: they were neither Etruscan nor Latin but specifically Roman. Or consider the Persians: once they were Indian heroes riding West, later they were Parthians or Mongolians who incorporated the sentiment of Persian nationalism and accepted Persian speech forms. The vital question in each case is rather, Spengler insists, what does it *mean* to be a Roman or a Persian? And the answer can be found and formulated only after one has come to terms with the given group's "unity of experience."

Since a culture—and it usually encompasses different but fundamentally like-minded peoples or nations—is such a field of unified human experience, the fact must be accepted that there are as many cultures as there are distinct modes of experiencing unity in thought and life styles. Spengler elucidates this point on page after page, as, for example, when he takes certain 19th- and 20th-century European thinkers to task (Nietzsche and Ibsen in particular) for their blithe assumption that abstract truths argued from the records of Europe's history are valid for man everywhere. Other peoples, other truths, Spengler concludes; and for the thinking man all truths are relevant or none is.

This proposition is the core of Spengler's philosophy of culture and history. We are thus reminded forcefully that mankind could not have rallied to *one* number system, because there *are* several modes of mathematical thought, several *Zahlenwelten,* and hence several cultures. Moreover, each distinct mathematical language is linked to other culturally discrete languages and symbols, among them those implicit in music and architecture. The Gothic dome and the Islamic mosque tell at a glance of radically different human strivings and spatial orientations. Further, and quite contrary to long dominant persuasions in the Western European world, few other realms subscribe to the principle of progression in time, and even fewer rely on history as the major repository of a society's "unity of experience" in time. And in this connection Spengler notes explicitly what is generally being overlooked today, namely, that all dispositions to space and time, including those bearing on the organization and maintenance of society, are inextricably linked to a given group's relationship to writing.

Spengler begins with the recognition that whereas speech relates to what is present, near, and actual, writing is the great symbol of distance, continuity, the future, and the yearning for eternity. History as distinguished from mere consciousness of the past thus presupposes writing; the state and law are preconditioned by it, and "world history," which is predicated on recorded relationships between states, cannot be fathomed without it. Spengler's main conclusion, presented in eloquent, often poetic prose, is, in effect, that the real meaning of any *one* category or order of thought can be experienced only *within* the particular culture that has brought it forth.

These insights or reminders help explain why societies which rose and matured in conditions of nonliterary, as, for example, those in sub-Saharan Africa, simply cannot take to Western models of the state and law, and why it is difficult for us to understand societies for which history or secular law is not normatively significant.

Cultures rise, change, and decline. Spengler does not pretend to solve the mystery of a culture's birth. But he points out that there are moments when the character of a culture becomes established, and when, therefore, a new reading of the universe becomes socially operative. These culture traits do not take form simultaneously in all fields of life. Rather, they appear in specific contexts which then become what he calls centers of force, shaping first an elite and thereafter the culture's structure in general.

Comparisons of eight high cultural histories (Egyptian, Sumero-Babylonian, Greco-Roman, Indian, Chinese, Maya-Aztec, Levantine, and West European) convinced Spengler that a moment arose in each of these great life courses when the critical-intellectual faculties of man gained ascendancy over the lyric-instinctual. A brief period of enlightened creativity then unfolded, but it always ended in exhaustion, sterility, mechanical repetition, and ultimately in confusion and dissolution. Spengler's frame of reference here was deeply influenced by Goethe who had outlined a sequence of four stages as normal to all culture cycles and who associated the last phase with the following characteristics:

> And so, the force of every mystery is undone, the people's religion itself profaned; distinctions that formerly grew from each other in natural development now work against each other as contradictory elements, and thus we have the Tohuwa-Bohu chaos again; but not the first, gravid, fruitful one; rather, a dying one running to decay, from which not even the spirit of God could create for itself a worthy world.

These are the major symptoms of decline also perceived by Spengler. Surveying his own West European culture, he thus took early note of the mechanization of intellectual activities, the meaninglessness of all forms of political life, the rise of cosmopolitan world cities and rootless masses, and the advent of a second, rather primitive religiosity.

Spengler's diagnoses of the ills of culture are so far-reaching, vivid, and explicit that they are apt to induce depression. It is therefore helpful to remember that his time frame is not that of our "now" generations. In Spengler's conception, decline is a most protracted process, in no way comparable, metaphorically speaking, to the sinking of an ocean liner. He thus notes that it took approximately one thousand years for creativity to spend itself in China (the nuclear creative epoch here is the period of "The Warring States"), and that the cultures of India and the Levant had also been fulfilled in all essentials when the decline set in hundreds of years before overt notice was taken of their exhaustion. In short, each of these cultures was burnt-out; in Spengler's language it had become *Fellahin.*

Western Europe's Faustian culture, which began to unfold itself in the 10th century A.D., reached its autumn period in the 18th century and began its wintering phase during the 19th century, i.e. nine hundred years after its inception.

Spengler's thesis, that cultures follow essentially parallel courses, but that each culture transforms itself in accordance with its own guiding and sustaining ideas, holds for all stages of evolution, including those marked by decline. In combination with his conviction that one must distinguish between possible or potential culture and actual culture, it has the effect of correcting the impression left by a casual reading of his works, namely that *everything* is predetermined. Determinism is strictly qualified also by yet another distinctly Spenglerian and, in my opinion, politically and theoretically revolutionary complex of ideas. It is the one that addresses the problem of intercultural relations.

Spengler starts with the proposition that cultures are mutually incomprehensible in the sense that the denizens of one cannot fully understand the ideas and values guiding men in another culture. Misunderstandings thus ensue as a matter of course, even when deliberate efforts are made to approximate, even merge, culturally separate peoples by transposing concepts and institutions from one to the other.

The transplantation of Buddhism from India to China in the first millennium A.D. is a case in point. In Spengler's view there had not been such a movement of "Buddhism" but rather an acceptance of part of the Indian Buddhists' store of images by Chinese of a certain spiritual tendency. They then fashioned a *new* mode of religious expression having meaning for Chinese, and only Chinese, Buddhists. Other particularly interesting variations on the theme of cultural borrowing relate to interactions between the cultures of the Near East and Western Europe. Spengler thus observed that the Magian realm (which encompasses Judaism, early Christianity, and Islam) is the midmost of the group of higher cultures because it has been in touch with practically all others, and that in respect of both space and time. Yet nothing in any of these records persuaded him that a culturally unified world society can be created by a fiat of will. After all, Greeks and Persians had long coexisted in geographically close quarters, but Alexander's intricate strategic design to fuse these two peoples turned out to be a failure. And the same holds for his methodical endeavors to merge these two societies with Bactria (Afghanistan today) and northwest India.

The relevance of these and analogous historical records for the present is obvious. Had scholars and statesmen in the United States followed some of Spengler's leads and come to an understanding of the cultural structures underlying modern Islamic society, they might well have tempered their trust in the principle of "economic determinism," according to which all 20th-century peoples would gladly forsake their values and worn-out traditions—which consigned them to poverty—so as to "develop" into economically advanced nation-states on models enacted by the modern West. Political decision-makers in our nation might also have learnt how to distinguish meaningfully between different strains in the Magian, notably the Islamic, world. Knowledge of pre-Islamic Iran's heritage would surely have led them to the awareness that the 20th-century Pahlavi monarchs were in fact determined to build a Western-type secular nation, not by relying on borrowed Western blueprints, but by resuscitating some of their own Achaemenid traditions of statecraft in counterpoint to those espoused by the Shiite religious establishment. The full meaning of Ayatollah Khomeini's declaratory injunction (1979) that Iranians must choose between the *Book of Kings* and the Koran would have been instantly understood by Spengler in its full significance. American scholars, journalists, and diplomats, by contrast, failed to assess the relevance of this remark.

Some of the episodes in the dialogue between Europe and the Levant—perhaps including the one just mentioned—are aspects of a phenomenon which Spengler calls "historical pseudo-morphosis." This concept, viewed by some commentators as the most daring construction in *The Decline of the West,* relates to situations in which an older alien culture lies so massively over a land that a young indigenuous culture cannot develop its own self-consciousness. No authentic positive or constructive feelings and ideas can arise in such conditions. What grows and festers instead is hatred for "the alien." Spengler thus points out that an important segment of the Magian realm had developed in just this way under Greek and Roman pressures until it suddenly, with Mohammed, broke free, allowing Islam to evolve its own culture. And he makes the same case for northern Europe's culture which began its evolution under the heavy cover of both classical Greco-Roman and Levantine Biblical influences and which came into its own only after the original Magian forms of Christianity had been recast so as to bring them into an organic relationship to Europe's indigenuous (non-Magian) character.

Spengler illustrates the poignancy of the ongoing dialogue between the West and the East by calling attention to the fact that Magian man is mainly an integral part of the consensus which, emerging from God, excludes error and the very possibility of a self-asserting ego. Truth here is thus something other than in the Occident, where the human being thinks of himself in terms of an essentially self-determining ego. Such a norm is explicitly denied in Magian thought, and Western epistemological methods must be dismissed as madness and infatuation in the Levant because they rest upon individual judgment.

Spengler had a keen understanding for yet another aspect of cultural borrowing that has not received the attention it deserves from modern Western scholars and diplomats. This relates to the psychological "backlash" that has been ensuing regularly when borrowed Western ideas, whether pertaining to science, economics, law, or government, do not produce desired or expected results in non-Western societies. With special regard to the phenomenon of pseudo-morphosis in the Middle East, Spengler thus knew what we seem to have been discovering only lately, namely that this kind of failure does not induce self-criticism on the part of the receiving people. Rather, and as he observes succinctly, it vents itself routinely in indictments of the Occident, which is pronounced guilty of the crime of corrupting Islam or, in the jargon of the post-Spengler era, of committing "cultural aggression," a concept launched by the Chinese communists.

Another case of pseudo-morphosis singled out by Spengler is the Russia that was shaped by Peter the Great and his successors in near total deference to Western European norms, styles, and institutions. Here as elsewhere the process bypassed the folk of the countryside—the carriers of the Russian soul, in Spengler's terms. It affected mainly city elites, but even in these strata Westernization did not penetrate to great depths, Spengler found. What he perceived and watched was the rise, under the surface of imparted forms, of a "near-apocalyptic hatred" for the Occident.

''Pseudo-Morphosis'' may be an awkward term, but the concepts and processes it conveys are certainly alive and well today as non-Western societies in Africa and the Orient shake off the Western norms that had made for self-determination and national independence in order to return to roots. The chief casualties in this revolutionary process of transformation are the Occidental idea of the sovereign state, secular constitutional law including individuated civil rights, and the entire apparatus of parliamentary institutions. Spengler had foreseen precisely these developments at a time when his contemporaries in academe and politics were confident about the world-wide applicability of all of these Occidental designs. Not being one to succumb to dreams of sameness, brotherhood, and peace for which supporting evidence was altogether lacking, he had become persuaded that other peoples bring forth other politically effective forms, just as they create other art styles, religions, and musical modes. It would therefore not have occurred to him to apply the term ''state'' to a tribe, a village, or a church. For one thing, the state presupposes writing in his frame of reference. For another, it is associated with ''a nation,'' and a nation—in Spengler's view—is always identified with a major idea. Further, he holds that only those peoples are ''nations'' who are conscious of history and whose existence makes for world history.

Still, not all nations can accommodate the idea of the territorially-defined state as this had evolved in the classical and Christian West. After the passing of ancient Persia, the concept thus proved meaningless or irrelevant in the Magian Near East, where the region's essentially Semitic culture developed in terms not of ''nation states'' but of communities of believers or freely floating sects unconfined by spatial bounds. In fact, the near total refutation of ''the state'' which set in after the eclipse of the Persian and Byzantine states is in Spengler's view the main reason for the stubborn incidence throughout the centuries of that ''magic type of formless violence'' which has been finding continuous expression in one and the same kind of insurrection. (pp. 183-93)

Next, the Occidental state is traditionally defined in terms of law, and it is therefore not surprising that imported norms of constitutional or other public law have also been ejected by non-Western societies. Being keenly aware of law as a symbol of a nation's culture and therefore as a suitable measure for comparisons of Occidental and Oriental legal orders, Spengler notes that whereas the classical Western law was made by burghers on the basis of practical experience, the Arabian and the Jewish came from God. In the first case a man regards law as an expression of another human being's will. In the latter, law is an element of divine dispensation. Western jurists are thus culturally conditioned to seek the truth by pondering the records of human experience compiled by other men in similar circumstances, whereas Levantine jurists are concerned with discovering the general conviction of their associates in regard to the mind of God. (p. 193)

In short, Spengler did not think of the state as a natural political organism. Although he identified its existence in several nations and cultures, he shows in each case that the concept of ''the state'' is as fragile and as subject to transformation and decomposition as all other great forms and ideas. Closely related themes which also absorbed Spengler throughout his life related, first, to parallelisms among classical Rome, ancient China, and modern Europe, chief among them the role of state-sustaining elites and the conceptualization of foreign policy, and second, to the association of ''the state'' with ''world history.''

Spengler's classical state in the Apollinian culture realm is the ''absolute'' polis as represented, specifically, by Rome. ''Absolute'' here refers to the condition which comes about when the nobility—which Spengler considers cognate with the state ''down to the roots''—has put itself wholly at the state's service. At that point in evolution Spengler finds that the nation is ''in condition'' in the sense that it is unified by a common and voluntary acceptance of moral and legal precepts, standards of manners, diplomatic and strategic codes, and canons of taste in art, thought, and expression. The difficulties arise when this classical state expands. Conquests thus produce a juxtaposition of the polis and the subjugated border regions which encircle it—a state of affairs illustrated in the Hellenistic-Roman world first by Carthage, which was destined to degenerate into a mere core city after it had acquired a Mediterranean empire, and, after Caesar had fashioned his Gallic empire, by Rome itself. These developments—which Spengler likens to the advent of Napoleonism in the later European Faustian culture—herald the transition from ''culture'' to ''civilization.'' ''With this,'' Spengler writes, ''which is the preface to unredeemed historical formlessness, dawns the real day of the great individual.''

Rome is, in Spengler's view, ''a perfectly unique and marvelous phenomenon in world history'' because it managed to remain in form in circumstances that have doomed all other states. This accomplishment, he writes, is not due to the Roman people but to the class which had brought Rome into ''condition'' in the first place—a class that has no counterparts elsewhere. The human element here in play is identified by him as an eminently talented elite which had no constitutionally established status but ''found its constitutional engine in the Senate,'' which knew how to keep social revolutions within constitutional limits and when to incorporate the upper strata of such other classes as the plebs, and which succeeded, gradually, in drawing the rest of the Mediterranean societies into Rome's ''bed'' of sustaining values and ideas.

The particular qualities that made this elite so ''popular and yet historically successful'' are, in Spengler's analysis, functions of its continuous commitment to government as a public service, an avocation, and an art. These men were no ideologues, Spengler notes approvingly. Well read and highly educated, they yet disdained to perceive facts through the prism of abstractions. Here were no theories and no critical literature such as had been the ruin of Athens; what we have instead is only ''a praxis in the grand style.'' Thus there came into being a government such as no megalopolis in any other culture has possessed and a tradition to which it would be impossible to find parallels, save perhaps in the Venice and the Papal Curia of the Baroque. Rome's decline set in only when freedom was granted to a vast slave population which came from Mediterranean border lands and could not be integrated because it had no roots in Rome. It was the growth of these people's influence during the Gracchi period that ruined what Spengler assesses to have been a marvel in the annals of statehood.

The second important model of the state in Spengler's design is the princely state in Ancient China which began evolving in the ''Spring and Autumn Period'' just before the onset of the epoch of the ''Contending States'' (Spengler's dates here are 480-230 B.C.). The latter—which marks the transition from Napoleonism to Caesarism in China—ends with the victory of what Spengler calls the ''Roman'' state of Tsin (Ch'in) over all other warring states and the establishment, in 221 B.C., of a unified empire.

Spengler begins by drawing attention to the numerous parallels between the period of China's Warring States and the 19th-century European "age of gigantic conflicts." Next, he makes a compelling case for correspondence between the "chain of statemen and generals centered on Tsin (Ch'in) and the sequence of classical Roman figures leading from the Scipios, the Catos, and the Gracchi to Marius, Sulla, Pompey, Caesar, and Augustus. All leading Chinese statesmen of the time, Spengler writes,

> were finished orators and all from time to time wrote on philosophy . . . but they did so not as professional philosophers, but because *otium cum dignitate* was the habit of cultivated gentlemen. In business hours they were masters of fact, whether on battle fields or in high politics, and precisely the same is true of the Chancellors Chang-I and Su-tsin; the dreaded diplomatist Fan-Sui (Fan-Chu) who overthrew Pe-Ki (Po-chi'i), the general; Wei-Yang the legislator of Tsin; . . . and others.

And most of them, Spengler adds, were deeply influenced by the war theorist Sun Tzu and by Kuei-Ku-Tzu, whose knowledge of men, deep sense of the historically possible, and command of the diplomatic technique of the age known as "art of the vertical and the horizontal"—i.e., the art of manipulating the North/South and West/East alliance systems—was unsurpassed.

This learned elite of state-serving Legalists or Realists was renowned for its efficient ruthlessness in domestic administration, diplomacy, and warfare. But, as Spengler rightly observes, it coexisted—usually in bitter contention—with rival schools of thinkers, prominent among them the Confucians and the Taoists. The German scholar thus takes note of "the China of Lao Tse," likening it to the Athens of the Sophists and the Europe of Montesquieu on the ground that all three exemplify the inordinate influence of books and abstract systems upon the art of government. In his perspective it is therefore no accident that the "Roman state of Tsin" rose in the unphilosophical North-West, whereas the focus of the opposition was in the kingdom of Ch'u in the Taoist South. Here, he writes, we have in fact the opposition of Rome and the Hellenistic East: on the one side, hard, clear will-to-power; on the other, the tendency to dreaming and world-improvement.

Both Rome and Ch'in forfeited statehood as they expanded into empires. But there is a difference between them in this transformation which Spengler identifies in its full poignancy. Chinese myths and legends—contrary to those of Roman susceptibilities—make a powerful case for the superiority of the imperial principle over that of the state, and the victorious king of Ch'in could thus assume the legendary title of emperor which invited claims to universal rule. Further, imperial Chinese administrations could rely in this context upon the richly suggstive concept of "the Middle Kingdom"—a notion entirely alien to the classical European world and to India—which allowed for a system of conducting foreign relations that is unique to China. As one of China's sages put it: "For the ruler of the Middle there is no foreign land."

Spengler's reading of modern European history, in particular of what we customarily call the modern European states-system, differs considerably from conventionally established wisdom. The period of "the absolute state" in the Faustian world thus covers scarcely a century and a half in his perspective,

from 1660, when Bourbon triumphs over Hapsburg and the Stuarts return to England, to the Coalition Wars against the French Revolution. Spengler's exemplar of the state here is Prussia as fashioned by Frederick II (the Great). Identified by Spengler as the last great Occidental nation, it was in his judgment a masterwork in political organization because Frederick II conceived of it as a "service state" and succeeded in associating it with an ethic of duty in accordance with which the monarch had to think of himself as "the first servant of the State."

The counterplayer to Frederick II is Napoleon, who represents the principle of unlimited individualized power. For in the degree in which nations cease to be politically "in condition," Spengler argues, possibilities open up for the energetic private person who *means* to be politically creative and who will have power at any price. Such a "fact-man" then becomes "the destiny" of an entire people or culture, and in that situation events become unpredictable, a development which Spengler views as the preface to unredeemed formlessness.

The social substratum of the state has been totally transformed by this time, for the first estate which had supplied a state-conscious elite is now replaced by the urban bourgeoisie which experiences the state as a burden, being mainly concerned with its own well-being. It is in this context too that intellectuals become a new political force, wholly different from the educated state-serving elites in classical Rome, ancient China, Venice, or Prussia in the sense that they wish the state to actualize "justice" or "the rights of man" rather than the force of historical facts, and to defend freedom of criticism rather than respect for nationally accepted moral and religious norms. In short, the new times herald the emergence of "abstract concepts" as guides for rule.

Spengler tells us that government in 19th- and 20th-century Europe reflects the culture's general decline into civilization. Quite contrary to most Western political scientists and historians, who view the rise of modern democracy as the Occident's most solid and admirable achievement and as a decidely progressive force in world affairs, Spengler is dubious on this score. He is thus persuaded that parliamentarism in France and England has actually been in full decay throughout this period of transition to Caesarism and that democratic institutions of government merely mask the real political power of finance capital and of its major agent, the press. This estimate is qualified in the case of England, for Spengler notes with admiration that the aristocratic elite of *Tatsachen-Menschen* ["fact men"] was able, at least temporarily, to rule indirectly under the cover of the "unwritten constitution." But he did not believe that either of the uniquely British norms and arrangements was exportable. It was thus a "catastrophic" notion in his opinion to attempt a transfer of English institutions to Germany—a finding analogous to his conclusion that the earlier massive borrowing of Roman law by the Germans had interfered negatively with that nation's fortunes.

Spengler was, of course, deeply concerned with the past, present, and future of the German nation. The norms for its optimal development had in his judgment been set by Prussia, but attempts to approximate this ideal were consistently thwarted by other, mainly geopolitical factors. In a set of deeply probing reflections that illumine such later developments in East/West relations as the Yalta agreement, the settlement of the Oder/Neisse line, and the recent Helsinki accord which confirmed the actual war-induced boundaries of Germany and the Soviet Union's Eastern European satellite states, he thus notes in *Jahre der Entscheidung* that Germany could not become an organically sound state because it functioned throughout history as the battlefield for "real" states. And in the same but extended context he points to the indisputable fact that the German realm emerges from Eurasian history as *die Mitte* ["the middle"] between Occident and Orient. In that capacity, Spengler continues, it has served as the rampart of the West, for the oriental limits of Occidental culture have always coincided with the advance lines reached by German colonization.

The Eurasian plain beyond this fluctuating frontier has been traditionally feared by continental Europeans because it has regularly unleashed hordes of barbarian invaders bent on ravaging the West's countryside and culture. But thus vast Eastern realm has also long been the home of the Russians, and they occupy a somewhat enigmatic place in Spengler's comparative culture history. Spengler does not include them in the concert of Western or Faustian nations. Nor does he acknowledge Russia as a state. In his scheme it is definitely part of the Byzantine Magian realm and should therefore never have been pressed into the European order of things. Further, and as noted earlier, Spengler views the tsardom of Peter the Great as a pseudomorphosis and the entire era of the Romanovs as a mere episode in a history that is yet to unfold itself, possibly in alignment with the kind of Magian religiosity represented by Dostoevsky.

Nor does Spengler acknowledge Bolshevik Russia as a "state." In developing the motif of Caesarism he points to Lenin as a "Private Power Man" of the type also represented by Cecil Rhodes, and to Trotzky as one in the line of Russia's "alien executioners" (another being Genghis Khan). All of these, he writes, are "very little different from most of the pretenders of the Latin-American republics, whose private struggles have long since put an end to the form-rich age of the Spanish Baroque." Indeed, under Stalin as previously under the Mongols, Russia was just a country that had fallen prey to the rule of a barbarian horde, this time in the form of the Communist Party.

These and related aspects of Russian history persuaded Spengler to assign Russia to the ranks of "the colored nations," those which are attracted to Western culture and its miracle of "economic development" but prove incapable of making it yield its boons to them. None of these peoples should be supplied with our cultural and technical armor, he holds, for all of them are in the final analysis Western culture's enemies. Yet, and somewhat in counterpoint to these devaluations of Russia, Spengler projects the possibility that something entirely new may well arise in the eastern vastness between the Weichsel (Vistula) and the Amur after the decline of the West has become a *fait accompli*. It is poignant to recall in light of recent developments in this area that the Weichsel had been a German river feeding Danzig, an old German trading town, until Germany was defeated in two world wars.

The United States occupies a similarly enigmatic position in Spengler's universe. It is identified mainly as a region or "a country," not as a solid state. Not unlike the Soviet Union, it is territorially so vast, Spengler finds, that its citizenry cannot experience the kind of national danger that makes for consciousness of a common destiny. In fact, the essential elements of nationhood may be lacking here since America is a country of immigrants whose spiritual roots and legacies are elsewhere in the world and who tend to fashion the challenges of life in essentially materialistic terms. In short, Spengler finds that the United States lacks depth as a state and as a nation, never more so than in the 20th century which marked its entry into the arena of world politics. Furthermore, he finds that the American cause is poorly served by a form of government which insists, following Montesquieu, that the executive and the legislative must have parallel powers—an arrangement ill-suited for political emergencies when it is apt to make way for "formless powers" of the kind with which Mexico and South America have long been associated.

The modern state, then, is critically embattled in its function as the outer normative form of national life. In Spengler's judgment this crisis stems mainly from the ills afflicting the state's inner life—a diagnosis which he extends to the United States. Spengler thus points out that the mechanistic economic world view, which has peaked 200 years after Puritanism, had been nurtured assiduously by English commitments to ideals of "utilitarianism" and of "the greatest happiness of the greatest number of people" before it became the "real" religion of our times. Faustian man, whose passion for the inventive intellectual life is in Spengler's view unequaled in other cultures, was thus destined to become the slave of this, his own and latest creation; for in calling forth a spectacular technological environment, he lost his bearings in his culture. His proud inventions tire him now, and he is possessed by longings for a return to the simple pastoral life. The non-Europeans (i.e., the colored peoples including Russia), meanwhile, whom Faustian men regarded as major beneficiaries of all new Western breakthroughs, fail conspicuously to appreciate the intrinsic meanings and promises of all these Western achievements. True, they are eager to appropriate the Euro/American "secret," but only because they value Faustian techniques as weapons in their struggle against this inventive civilization. In Spengler's prognosis, then, there is no future for the West's *Technik*: it will end with Faustian man—forgotten and destroyed.

World realities today confirm the substance of these predictions and premonitions. As the West's power wanes in Africa and Asia, the West's machinery, so recently installed in many provinces of these continents for the furtherance of health, education, and economic development, has also been grinding to a halt, in some places as a result of simple carelessness and neglect, in others by virtue of ruling policies and ideologies which insist that these imported tools are the satanic devices of an evil enemy.

Spengler identifies the triumph and the tragedy of the European state in this era with the prominence of the third estate. He praises the urban bourgeoisie for its creativity, love of freedom, and determination to uphold the cause of Occidental culture. He also notes, though, that this social class was at no time wholly master of its actions and that its individualist and antisymbolic attitude toward life clearly presaged the transition from "culture" to "civilization." The analysis thus notes that the third estate never had a *positive* inner unity. Refuting all differentiation in rank and function that cannot be justified by reason and utility, it stands instead for *negative* unity only—a unity that expresses itself more or less exclusively in moments of opposition to something. "To be free from something—that, all wanted," Spengler notes.

The state-related functions of this "non-estate" as Spengler calls it are today, as in historically parallel periods, fatally compromised and undercut by the rise of the masses—the fourth estate—in the great cities which alone now speak the decisive words. This conglomeration of rootless fragments of populations stands outside all established social relationships.

Elements drawn from all classes and conditions belong to it instinctively—uprooted peasantry, literates, ruined businessmen, and above all (as the age of Catiline shows with terrifying clarity) derailed nobles. Their power is far in excess of their numbers, for they are always on the spot, always on hand at the big decisions, ready for anything. . . .

This city mob feels no attachment to a vocational class; indeed, it is not even prepared to identify itself as "the real working class." Refuting the very idea of culture and antagonistic to all political form as well as to ordered property and ordered knowledge, these populations do not or cannot acknowledge their past and do not have a future as a group. The fourth estate thus represents "the new nomadism" of the cosmopolis, which marks the transition from history to non-history. *Die Masse ist das Ende, das radikale Nichts* ["the masses are the end, the radical nothingness."]

The bourgeoisie looks at these masses with real uneasiness, seeking to separate itself from them, Spengler observes. But in the presence of overpowering realities, the separating frontier cannot be drawn; "wherever the bourgeoisie throws into the scale against the older orders its feeble weight of aggressiveness, this mass has forced itself into their ranks, pushed to the front, imparted most of the drive that wins the victory, and very often managed to secure the conquered position for itself—not seldom with the continued idealistic support of the educated who are intellectually captivated, or the material backing of the money powers. . . ." At this point of time, then, when "civilization" is developing into full bloom, there stands the miracle of the Cosmopolis which Spengler portrays in the following way:

> . . . the great petrifact, a symbol of the formless—vast, splendid, spreading in insolence. It draws within itself the being-streams of the now impotent countryside, human masses that are wafted as dunes from one to another or flow like loose sand into the chinks of the stone. Here money and intellect celebrate their greatest and their last triumphs. It is the most artificial, the cleverest phenomenon manifested in the light-world of human eyes—uncanny, "too good to be true," standing already almost beyond the possibilities of cosmic formation.

No evocation of the big modern city—be it Berlin in the 20's and 30's, or London, Tokyo, Rome, and New York today—has in my judgment captured the construction, inner life, and atmosphere of "radical chic" more vividly and accurately than Spengler's. And few modern evaluations of the relevance of this complex urban phenomenon for the fortunes of the state in foreign relations come to mind as convincing as his. One of Spengler's main motifs in this context . . . is the malaise that urban reason experiences in its relationship to the state. For this "non-estate" the state is definitely a burden, and the same holds for its disposition to the idea of the nation. The very thought that the whole people should be "in form" or simply disciplined in its commitment to the well-being of the whole does not arise, Spengler reasons, because the individual himself is inwardly no longer disciplined or "in form." And this holds not only for morals, the arts, and in modes of thinking, but also and most importantly, for politics. The result is, Spengler concludes, that the bourgeoisie is not inclined to think in terms of foreign policy and world history. Whether the state

is able to hold its own at all amongst other states, is a question no one asks. All that matters is whether it secures men's "rights."

This is so, Spengler explains, because bourgeois urbans equate their own "class" ideals with historical actuality. Led and tutored by the era's bookmen (*Büchermenschen*) who disdain nationalism as they propagate abstract truths for men everywhere, these city people willingly subscribe to such catchwords as liberty and equality for all, nowhere more so than in the United States, where the Declaration of Independence proclaims the universality of typically European values and standards. To think in terms of the primacy of a "world society" and "world citizenry" rather than in those of the nation's survival, and to aim at international understanding and world reconciliation rather than at unity and harmony within the state, thus become the policy objectives for which priority is claimed. In all these ways history is being canceled today as it also was in the age of imperial Rome when humankind ceased to live as nations and when actualities were distorted by the blithe propagation of such slogans as humanity, happiness, economic development, enlightenment, the freedom of the peoples, the subjection of nature, or world peace—all understood as absolute measures of the records of millennia.

Real or genuine history has never taken notice of abstract propositions such as these, which lose themselves in the moving crush of facts. It just is not apolitical cultural history as understood by philosophers that counts. Rather, Spengler holds, it is the history of war, of diplomacy, and of states. And in the world of facts with which history deals, the choice is not between peace and war but between victory and defeat. Taking a cue from Heraclitus, Spengler thus warns us (see *Preussentum und Sozialismus*) that the superiority of a nation or an ideology is in the final analysis determined by its capacity to win in war. True, "world peace" has often been said to exist, but what precisely are the connotations of this condition? Spengler describes them tersely as follows:

> world peace . . . involves the private renunciation of war on the part of the immense majority, but along with this it involves an unavowed readiness to submit to being the booty of others who do *not* renounce it. It begins with the State-destroying wish for universal reconciliation, and it ends in nobody's moving a finger so long as misfortune only touches his neighbor.

The state of being "in form" then passes from nations to bands and retinues of adventurers, self-styled Caesars, seceding generals, barbarian kings, and what not—in whose eyes the population becomes in the end merely a part of the landscape.

"World peace" is phony even as a catchword in our times, when we watch the annihilation of nation after nation while hearing boastful announcements that "we are at peace." Spengler could not have pondered the guerrilla wars, civil wars, and surrogate wars that brought ruin to nation after nation in Africa, Asia, and Latin America, yet he seems to have known the basic score and scenario of these exercises in violence better than most of our statesmen and academicians. "The wars of the age of world-peace are private wars, more fearful than any State wars because they are formless," he concludes after telling us first that there are only private histories, private destinies, private ambitions, from top to bottom, from the miserable troubles of the fellaheen to the dreary feuds of Caesars for the private possession of the world. Spengler's last published words addressed precisely this set of issues. In response to the question "what are the possibilities of world peace?" which reached him from America in early 1936, he telegraphed back: "Pacifism will remain an ideal, and war a fact, and if the white peoples are resolved to wage war no more, the colored will do so and will be the rulers of the earth."

Reflections on the future of states and nations in the Occident led Spengler to conclude that it falls to us to live in the most trying times known to the history of a great culture and that this challenge must be met by mustering the will to endure as an authentic thought world. The main task before us is to shape up and live by daring to act, and the example here is Achilles—not the moody anxious intellectuals, *die Menschen der ewigen Angst* ["the people of external fear"], who initiate the decline of cultures with their sermons on moral self-disarmament. (pp. 194-207)

> *Adda B. Bozeman, "Decline of the West? Spengler Reconsidered," in* The Virginia Quarterly Review, *Vol. 59, No. 2, Spring, 1983, pp. 181-207.*

ADDITIONAL BIBLIOGRAPHY

T. W. Adorno. "Spengler after the Decline." In his *Prisms*, pp. 51-72. London: Neville Spearman, 1967.

> Maintains that "the course of world history vindicated [Spengler's] immediate prognoses to an extent that would astonish if they were still remembered. Forgotten, Spengler takes his revenge by threatening to be right."

Beard, Charles A. "Cheers for Caesar." *New York Herald Tribune Books* 5, No. 9 (18 November 1928): 1, 6.

> Reviews the English translation of Volume II of *The Decline of the West*, maintaining that "even if most of [Spengler's] analogies are indefensible and his conclusions wrong, still his *Decline* is a great work—one of the few mighty books of our time—mighty in its challenge, in its psychological analysis, in its efforts to grasp at the hem of Destiny."

Bentley, Eric Russell. "Oswald Spengler and German Historiography." In his *A Century of Hero-Worship*, pp. 205-13. Philadelphia: J. B. Lippincott, 1944.

> Summarizes the principal ideas put forth in *The Decline of the West*. Bentley disputes the argument that the book is primarily a presentation of Spengler's cyclical theory of history and is therefore inaptly named, stating that the work "was a polemic against the plutocratic democracy which, *he hoped,* was on the decline; the book is a philippic against England and France and an elegy on the Kaiser's Germany. The apparatus of historical analogy is a persuasive strategy."

Callan, Edward. "W. B. Yeats's Learned Theban: Oswald Spengler." *Journal of Modern Literature* 4, No. 3 (February 1975): 593-609.

> Analyzes the influence of *The Decline of the West* on Yeats's poetry.

Chesterton, G. K. "On the Contiguous Past." In his *All I Survey*, pp. 162-67. Reprint. 1933. Freeport, N.Y.: Books for Libraries Press, 1967.

> Dismisses as invalid Spengler's theory of discrete and mutually incomprehensible historical periods but speculates upon the "horrible possibility that what he says falsely about our past may be said truly about our future," warning against the modern tendency to forget the past.

Dahlström, Carl E. W. L. "Spengler's Views of Art." *PMLA* XLIX, No. 4 (December 1934): 1182-98.

Summarizes the historical theses presented in *The Decline of the West* and discusses Spengler's views of art as an outgrowth of his general theory of civilizations.

Fennelly, John F. *Twilight of the Evening Lands: Oswald Spengler—A Half Century Later*. New York: The Brookdale Press, 1972, 181 p.

> Presents Spengler's theories and examines their relevance to the contemporary world.

Friedman, George. "Spengler." In his *The Political Philosophy of the Frankfurt School*, pp. 79-86. Ithaca, N.Y.: Cornell University Press, 1981.

> Examines the influence of Spengler's works on the Frankfurt School of philosophy.

Goddard, E. H., and Gibbons, P. A. *Civilisation or Civilisations: An Essay on the Spenglerian Philosophy of History*. New York: Boni & Liveright, 1926, 245 p.

> A popularization of Spengler's ideas.

Gottfried, Paul. "Oswald Spengler and the Inspiration of the Classical Age." *Modern Age* 26, No. 1 (Winter 1982): 68-75.

> Examines Spengler's treatment of classical civilization in *The Decline of the West,* focusing upon his adoption of aspects of classical Greek thought and his glorification of Roman society as a model for the future of Western civilization.

Hausheer, Herman. "Plato's Conception of the Future as Opposed to Spengler's." *The Monist* XXXIX, No. 2 (April 1929): 204-24.

> Attempts "to determine if Spengler's dogmatic assertion that the Greeks had no sense of the future is valid in so far as the evidence of Plato's dialogues is concerned." Hausheer concludes that Spengler's assertion is indefensible and that his own sense of time as evidenced in his writings is based to a large extent on classical Greek conceptions of time.

Heller, Erich. "Oswald Spengler and the Predicament of the Historical Imagination." In his *The Disinherited Mind: Essays in Modern German Literature and Thought*, pp. 181-98. New York: Farrar, Straus and Cudahy, 1952.

> Dismisses *The Decline of the West* as a product of "a crude and wicked mind."

Lattimore, Owen. "Spengler and Toynbee." *The Atlantic Monthly* CLXXXI, No. 4 (April 1948): 104-05.

> Appraises Spengler's and Arnold Toynbee's philosophies of history.

Lewis, Wyndham. "The 'Chronological' Philosophy of Spengler." In his *Time and Western Man*, pp. 260-97. New York: Harcourt, Brace, 1928.

> Analyzes the function of time in Spengler's philosophy of history.

Muir, Edwin. "Oswald Spengler." In his *Essays on Western Literature and Society*, pp. 125-33. Cambridge, Mass.: Harvard University Press, 1967.

> Contends that "Spengler was an excellent pamphleteer with an astonishing gift for facile generalization; he was not, as a thinker, of any importance."

Mumford, Lewis. "The Hour of Disintegration." *The New Republic* LXXVIII, No. 1003 (21 February 1934): 51-2.

> Scathing review of *The Hour of Decision*. Mumford maintains that "as a contribution to thought, *The Hour of Decision* is trash. As as stimulus to action it will encourage only those who, like Spengler himself, apparently, are already beyond the point where rational thinking can sharpen their blunt and defective sense of reality."

Slochower, Harry. "Faustian Fascism: Oswald Spengler." In his *No Voice Is Wholly Lost: Writers and Thinkers in War and Peace*, pp. 201-04. New York: Creative Age Press, 1945.

> Asserts that "Spengler openly calls for the reactionary program which Nazism carries out under the veil of revolutionary phraseology."

Sorokin, Pitrim A. "Oswald Spengler." In his *Social Philosophies in an Age of Crisis,* pp. 72-112. Boston: The Beacon Press, 1950.
    Outlines the principal arguments put forth in *The Decline of the West*.

Toynbee, Arnold J. "My View of History." In his *Civilization on Trial,* pp. 3-15. New York: Oxford University Press, 1948.
    Mentions *The Decline of the West* in a discussion of the development of Toynbee's own thought. Toynbee calls Spengler's views on the genesis of civilizations "unilluminatingly dogmatic and deterministic" and "disappointingly unworthy of Spengler's brilliant genius."

Untermeyer, Louis. "Oswald Spengler." In his *Makers of the Modern World,* pp. 553-58. New York: Simon and Schuster, 1955.
    Brief biographical and critical essay.

Ivan Vazov

1850-1921

(Also transliterated as Vasoff and Vazoff) Bulgarian poet, novelist, short story writer, dramatist, and essayist.

Regarded as Bulgaria's most important modern author, Vazov was a fervent patriot whose numerous writings forcefully proclaim their creator's nationalist sentiments. His most renowned works, the novel *Pod igoto (Under the Yoke)* and the poetic cycle *Epopeya na zabravenite,* are sympathetic accounts of the Bulgarian struggle for independence from the Ottoman Empire during the final decades of the nineteenth century; many of his other writings celebrate the pastoral beauty of his homeland. Vazov consciously sought to supply his nascent country with a native modern literature by creating works in all genres, and in so doing he set the standards by which all subsequent Bulgarian literature was evaluated. In addition, with the translation of *Under the Yoke* into all of the major Western languages, Vazov succeeded in bringing Bulgarian literature international attention.

Vazov was born in the village of Sopot, now known as Vazovgrad, where his father was a successful and moderately wealthy merchant. From an early age, Vazov displayed an interest in literature and he studied the French and Russian classics during his secondary education, despite his father's wish that he prepare himself for a place in the family business. In 1870 Vazov was sent to Rumania, where he was to be trained for a career in international commerce, but he soon became involved with the emigré leaders of the Bulgarian independence movement and abruptly abandoned his career plans to join their cause. During the next decade Vazov participated in the struggle to overthrow the Turks, promulgating the cause of freedom both as a soldier and as a journalist. He also recorded many events of the revolution in poetry, most notably in the epic *Epopeya na zabravenite*. After the successful revolution of 1878, Vazov was able to devote much more of his time to writing, and he began to produce work in all genres.

In 1886, as a result of political conflicts within the Bulgarian government, Vazov was temporarily exiled to Russia, and it was in Odessa that he began work on *Under the Yoke*. The publication of *Under the Yoke* and its subsequent translation into several European languages brought Vazov worldwide recognition and markedly increased his fame within his native country. Upon his return from exile, he was urged to participate in the newly formed Bulgarian government, and he eventually became minister of education. After 1899, Vazov retired from public life and devoted himself entirely to writing. In honor of his literary accomplishments, the occasion of his seventieth birthday was marked by an enormous state celebration. He died of heart failure one year later.

Critic Charles Moser has stated that "patriotism is the backbone of all Vazov's writing, both in prose and in verse." In Vazov's early works, his patriotism usually took the form of incitements to rebel against the Turkish oppressors. Yet Moser has also pointed out that Vazov was not as ardently militaristic as many other Bulgarian revolutionaries, and even among his earliest patriotic poems there are pastoral lyric pieces which quietly but lavishly praise the beauty of the Bulgarian countryside.

(Poems of this type fill several collections which bear such titles as "Fields and Forests" and "A May Bouquet.") Later, when the revolution had succeeded, Vazov felt compelled to commemorate the heroic deeds of the Bulgarian revolutionists so that their sacrifices would not be forgotten or undervalued by succeeding generations, and it was this impulse which led to the creation of *Epopeya na zabravenite* and *Under the Yoke*. In *Epopeya na zabravenite,* literally "Epic of the Forgotten," Vazov related the actions of the revolution's most outstanding heroes while denouncing the barbarism of their Turkish opponents. Similarly, in *Under the Yoke,* Vazov's fictional characters take part in historically accurate events and thus represent the many Bulgarians whose names are not recorded in accounts of the revolution but who nevertheless made enormous sacrifices to obtain Bulgarian freedom. Vazov's extensive documentation of historical events in this novel has led to comparisons with Leo Tolstoy's *War and Peace* and with Victor Hugo's *Les miserables,* two of his strongest literary influences, although critics note that in his attempts to chronicle a major and extremely complex political situation, Vazov was unable to match the narrative coherence of those writers.

Vazov's work represents a major accomplishment in the development of Bulgarian literature, and the period between 1890 and 1920 is known as "the Age of Vazov" in that country.

Although many of his more topical writings have not survived into the second half of the twentieth century, his historical and elegiac works are still widely read, as evidenced by the continuing republication of his more popular stories and novels. In addition, his example has been followed by younger Bulgarian writers and has led to the establishment of a large and respected body of native Bulgarian literature.

PRINCIPAL WORKS

Pryaporets i gusla (poetry) 1876
Tagite na Bulgaria (poetry) 1877
Izbavlenie (poetry) 1878
*Gusla (poetry) 1881
Mitrofam i Dormidolski (novel) 1882
Ruska (drama) [first publication] 1883
*Polya i gori (poetry) 1884
Chichovtsi (novel) 1885
Slivnitsa (poetry) 1886
Razkazi (short stories) 1891
Pod igoto (novel) 1893
   [*Under the Yoke*, 1894]
Draski i sharki. 2 vols. (short stories) 1893-95
Zvukove (poetry) 1893
Nova zemya (novel) 1896
Pod nashete nebe (poetry) 1900
Kazalarskata tsaritsa (novel) 1903
Velika Rilska pustina (travel essays) 1904
   [*The Great Rila Wilderness*, 1969]
Svetoslav terter (novel) 1907
Borislav (drama) [first publication] 1910
Legendi pri Tsarevets (poetry) 1910
Pod grama na pobedite (poetry) 1914
Pesni za Makedonia (poetry) 1916
Novi ekove (poetry) 1917
Lyulyaka mi zamirisa (poetry) 1919
Ne shte zagine (poetry) 1919
Sabranie sachineniya (poetry, short stories, novellas,
    novels, dramas, and essays) 1955-57
Ivan Vazov: Selected Stories (short stories) 1967

*These collections include the two parts of Vazov's epic cycle, *Epopeya na zabravenite*.

EDMUND GOSSE (essay date 1894)

[*Gosse's importance as a critic is due primarily to his introduction of Henrik Ibsen's "new drama" to an English audience. He was among the chief English translators and critics of Scandinavian literature and was decorated by the Norwegian, Swedish, and Danish governments for his efforts. Among his other works are studies of John Donne, Thomas Gray, Sir Thomas Browne, and important early articles on French authors of the late nineteenth century. Although Gosse's works are varied and voluminous, he was largely a popularizer, with the consequence that his commentary lacks depth and is not considered in the first rank of modern critical thought. However, his broad interests and knowledge of foreign literatures lend his works much more than a documentary value. In the following essay, which appeared as the introduction to the 1894 publication of* Under the Yoke, *Gosse discusses Vazov's works.*]

If there is a certain gratification in presenting to the English public the first specimen of the literature of a new people, that gratification is lifted above triviality, and grounded upon a serious critical basis, when the book so presented is in itself a masterpiece. I do not think that it will be questioned that *Under the Yoke* is a romance of modern history of a very high class indeed. That it should be the earliest representation of Bulgarian *belles-lettres* translated into a Western tongue may be curious and interesting, but the book rests its claim upon English readers on no such accidental quality. In any language, however hackneyed, the extreme beauty of this heroic novel, so simply and yet so artfully constructed, so full of ideal charm, permeated with so pure and fiery a passion, so human and tender, so modern and yet so direct and primitive, must have been assured among all imaginative readers.

The story is one of false dawn before the sunrise. The action proceeds, as may gradually be discovered, in the years 1875 and 1876, and the scene is laid in that corner of Bulgaria which is not even yet completely freed from Turkish rule—the northwest part of Thrace—overshadowed by the Balkan on the north, and now forming part of the anomalous suzerainty of Eastern Roumelia. *Pod Igoto* is the title of the book, and I am instructed that in Bulgarian the three words *Pod Igo-to* mean, literally translated, **Under the Yoke**. The whole story is the chronicle of one of those abortive attempts which were made throughout Bulgaria and Roumelia a generation ago, under the hope of help from Russia, to throw off the intolerable Turkish yoke of tyranny. The tale ends tragically, with the failure of the particular and partial insurrection described, and the martyrdom of the leading patriots who took a part in it; but the reader is preserved from finding this failure depressing by the consciousness that relief was at hand, and that an end was soon afterwards to be put to all the horrors of bondage, to the incessant zaptié at the door, to the hateful Turkish rapine, to the misery of Christian servitude under a horde of Oriental officials. (pp. v-vi)

Ivan Vazoff, by far the most distinguished writer of modern Bulgaria, was born in August 1850, at Sopot, a large Bulgarian village in what is now Eastern Roumelia, at the foot of the Balkan, and about forty miles to the north of Philippopolis. I have not been able to find Sopot marked in a very good map of the peninsula, but the locality indicated is identical with the centre of the district obviously described in **Under the Yoke,** and I should not be surprised to learn that Bela Cherkva, the little town so lovingly and so picturesquely pictured by M. Vazoff as the centre of his novel, was Sopot under a disguise.

The other scenes of action—Klissoura, Karlovo, Koprivshtitsa, and the rest—appear in the course of this romance under their real names, and are the towns of a lovely pastoral district. The story passes in the heart of the famous Valley of Roses, where the attar is made; and over these billowy meadows, heavy with the redundant rose, over the hurrying water-courses, the groves of walnut and pear trees, the white cupolas ringed about with poplars, the little sparkling cities—over all this foreground of rich fertility there rises the huge bulwark of the inaccessible Balkan, snow-clad all through the tropic summer, and feeding the flowery plain with the wealth of its cascades and torrents.

M. Ivan Vazoff was educated at the school of his native village. From Sopot his father, a small trader, sent him to Kalofer and then to Philippopolis. At that time . . . Bulgarian literature consisted of nothing but a few school-books and political pamphlets, possessed of no literary pretensions. Like all other Bulgarians who have made their mark in new Bulgaria, M. Vazoff was driven to seek his facts and his ideas from foreign sources. None but works written in alien languages were worthy to be read. He set himself to study Russian and then French, taking advantage of the school libraries existing in the chief centres of population. When the budding spirit of Bulgaria put forth that first tender leaf, *The Periodic Review,* published at Braila, over the frontiers of friendly Roumania, he was one of the first to contribute poems to it.

From 1870 to 1872 M. Vazoff resided, like so many educated Bulgarians of that time, in Roumania. But in the latter year he went back to Sopot, hesitating between the only two employments open to such men as he, teaching and trade. He chose the latter, and entered his father's business. He was not very successful, attending to it, we may believe, not much more closely than his hero, Ognianoff, does to school-work. No doubt, not a little of M. Vazoff's personal history is here mingled with his fiction, for we find that he grew more and more an object of suspicion to the Turkish authorities, until in 1876, the year of smouldering and futile insurrection, he had to fly north across the Balkan for his life. He reached Roumania in safety, and at Bucharest joined the Bulgarian Revolutionary Committee. The three stormy years that followed saw the final development of his genius, and the publication of three famous volumes of his patriotic lyrical poetry, ***The Banner and the Guzla, The Sorrows of Bulgaria, The Deliverance,*** in which the progressive story of Bulgarian emancipation may be read in admirable verse.

He returned in 1878 to find Sopot destroyed, and his father murdered by the Bashi-bozouks. The impression made upon his imagination by the horrors of his bleeding country may be clearly marked in the later chapters of ***Under the Yoke.*** M. Vazoff accepted from the Russians, who were then in occupation of Bulgaria, a judicial appointment. In 1879 he was elected a member of the Permanent Committee of the Provincial Assembly in the new and anomalous country of Eastern Roumelia. He settled in the new capital, Philippopolis, and here he published his earliest prose works, his stories of ***Not Long Ago, Mitrofan, Hadji Akhil,*** and ***The Outcast,*** his comedy of ***Mikhalaki,*** and issued, besides, two new collections of poetry, entitled ***Fields and Woods*** and ***Italy*** respectively. The last-mentioned was published in 1884, after the author had been travelling in the country it celebrated.

During the Serbo-Bulgarian war of 1885, M. Vazoff visited the battle-fields of Slivnitza, Tsaribrod and Pirot, sang the valour of his countrymen in dithyrambic strains, and inveighed—in a volume entitled ***Slivnitza***—against the fratricidal madness of King Milan. Dissatisfied with the turn taken by affairs in the peninsula after the abdication of Prince Alexander of Battenberg, M. Vazoff in 1886 left for Russia. It was while residing in Odessa that he wrote the romance of ***Pod Igoto*** (***Under the Yoke***), which is generally admitted to be his masterpiece. In 1889 he returned to Bulgaria, and settled in Sofia, where he had inherited some property from an uncle. ***Pod Igoto*** first appeared, in serial form, in the excellent *Sbornik* (or Miscellany) published by the Bulgarian Ministry of Public Instruction. The same review issued in 1892 a book by M. Vazoff entitled ***The Great Rila Wilderness,*** and another this year, called ***In the Heart of the Rhodope.*** In 1891-92 our author undertook the editorial management of the monthly periodical *Dennitsa* (''The Morning Star''). He is now, without a rival, the leading writer of Bulgaria, and actively engaged in the production of prose and verse.

The poems of Vazoff enjoy a great popularity in his own country, and selections from them have been translated into Russian, Czech, Slovenian, and Servian. The Bohemians may read him in a version by Voracek, published at Prague in 1891, which is recommended to me as particularly admirable. But alas! Bohemia is itself remote, and a poet to whom a translation into Czech appears to be an introduction to the Western world seems to us inaccessible indeed. Professor Gueshoff considers that Vazoff will hold in the history of Bulgarian literature a place analogous to that of Chaucer in our own. Having no Bulgarian models to follow, and no native traditions of poetical style, Vazoff has had to invent the very forms of versification that he uses. His success has already led to the creation of a school of young Bulgarian poets, but, though many have imitated Vazoff with talent, not one approaches him in the melody of his metrical effects or in his magical command of the resources of the Bulgarian language.

Written during an epoch of intense national excitement, in a language quite unused before, Vazoff's poems are described to me as reflecting with extraordinary directness and simple passion the woes and burdens, the hopes and the pleasures, of a pastoral people, long held in servitude but at length released. Most of the figures celebrated in his ballads and his odes are the heroes of contemporary patriotism—men, unknown till yesterday, who rose into momentary fame by fighting and dying for their country. They live crystallised in this beautiful verse, already classical, already the food and inspiration of Bulgarian youth—verse written by a son of the new country, one who suffered and struggled with her through her worst years of hope deferred. How tantalising it is that we cannot read such poetry, with the dew of the morning of a nation upon it! It is almost enough to tempt the busiest of us to turn aside to the study of Bulgarian.

We may regret our wider loss the less, since it is now practicable to read in English what all Bulgarians seem to admit is the leading prose product of their nation. In ***Pod Igoto*** (***Under the Yoke***) Vazoff is understood to have concentrated in riper form than elsewhere the peculiar gifts of his mind and style. The first quality which strikes the critic in reading this very remarkable book is its freshness. It is not difficult to realise that, in its original form, this must be the earliest work of genius written in an unexhausted language. Nor, if Vazoff should live eighty years, and should write with unabated zeal and volume, is it very likely that he will ever recapture this first fine careless rapture. ***Under the Yoke*** is a historical romance, not constructed by an antiquary or imagined by a poet out of vague and insufficient materials accidentally saved from a distant past, but recorded by one who lived and fought and suffered through the scenes that he sets himself to chronicle. It is like seeing *Old Mortality* written by Morton, or finding the autobiography of Ivanhoe. It is history seen through a powerful telescope, with mediaeval figures crossing and recrossing the seventies of our own discoloured nineteenth century.

When the passion which animates it is taken into consideration, the moderate and artistic tone of ***Under the Yoke*** is worthy of great praise. In an episode out of the epic of an intoxicated nation, great extravagance, great violence might have been expected and excused. But this tale of forlorn Bulgarian patriotism is constructed with delicate consideration, and passes nowhere into bombast. The author writes out of his heart things which he has seen and felt, but the moment of frenzy has gone by, and his pulse as an observer has recovered its precision. The passion is there still, the intense conviction of intolerable wrongs, scarcely to be wiped out with blood. He reverts to the immediate past—

Seeing how with covered face and plumeless wings,
    With unreverted head
    Veiled, as who mourns his dead,
Lay Freedom, couched between the thrones of kings,
    A wearied lion without lair,
And bleeding from base wounds, and vexed with alien air—

but already the image is settled, and has taken the monumental and marmoreal aspect of past history.

The strenuous political fervour of this romance is relieved by a multitude of delicate, touching, and humorous episodes. The scene in the theatre, where, in the presence of the indulgent and indolent Turkish Bey, songs of Bulgarian insurrection are boldly introduced into a sentimental farce, a spurious running translation being supplied to the unsuspecting governor; the thrilling slaughter of the bandits at the Mill; the construction of the hollow cherry-tree cannon, which bursts so ignominiously at the moment of trial; the beautiful and heroic love-scenes between Ognianoff and Rada, cunningly devised and prepared as the very food of patriotism for youthful native readers; the copious and recurrent, but never needless or wire-drawn, descriptions of the scenery of the Balkan valleys; the vignettes of life in Bulgarian farmsteads, and cafés, and mon-asteries, and water-mills—all these are but the embroidery of a noble piece of imaginative texture, unquestionably one of the finest romances that Eastern Europe has sent into the West. (pp. vi-xii)

> *Edmund Gosse, in an introduction to* Under the Yoke:
> A Novel *by Ivan Vazoff, William Heinemann, 1894,*
> *pp. v-xii.*

THE BOOKMAN, LONDON   (essay date 1894)

[*In the following essay, the critic considers some flaws and merits of* Under the Yoke.]

The first book translated from the Bulgarian into English is bound to have an interest of its own. That it contains, too, a story of stirring times still fresh in the memories of those that are not the most venerable among us, is a matter of additional interest. It is a story that enlists our keen sympathies for the hopes, the foiled efforts, the heroism, and the suffering of which it tells. Let **Under the Yoke** present itself with these recommendations, and it will find readers. To label it a mas-terpiece, as Mr. Gosse does [see excerpt dated 1894], is to do it wrong. It is not even a good novel, but it is a book full of sincerity and enthusiasm, with many scattered passages of real power—the book of a genius, if you will—and M. Vazoff is a writer for a young country to be justly proud of. The story, a formless one, is of a futile insurrection to throw off the Turkish yoke just before the Russo-Turkish war. The central character is an escaped political prisoner from the fortress of Diarbekir, who, in the guise of a district schoolmaster, carries on a revolutionary propaganda. When the troubles begin he flies to the hills and woods, where he lives protected by his own brave heart, and the kindliness of the Bulgarians, who will not betray him. Leader of the insurrection that ends so lamentably, he escapes the slaughter only to fall into the hands of the Turkish gendarmes, and dies fighting to the last, his sweetheart and his friend sharing his fate. M. Vazoff makes us understand the workings of Bulgarian hearts and minds, but he hardly makes us feel the living presence of Bulgarians. He

is better at drawing plans than pictures. In the story of the oppression there is no exaggeration. A humane spirit seems to flow from the writer's pen; we feel in him a man of many sides, many sympathies. He presents no over-gloomy impres-sion, in spite of the tragedy of the end. Indeed, his observation of life leads him to say this, "With all its hardships, bondage has yet this one advantage: it makes a nation merry. Where the arena of political and scientific activity is closely barred, where the desire of rapid enrichment finds no stimulant, and far-reaching ambition has no scope for its development, the community squanders its energy on the trivial and personal cares of its daily life, and seeks relief and recreation in simple and easily obtainable material enjoyment. . . . When a man is irretrievably ruined he often puts a bullet through his head, or ends his life in some equally rapid and decisive manner. But a nation, however hopeless its bondage, never ends its own existence; it eats, drinks, begets children. It enjoys itself." Interesting! Is it true? There is much humour and human nature in the book. The unsuspecting boy listening to the revolutionary songs in the theatre is a delightful scene, and so is that where Marko, the staid father of a family, yet pledged to the insur-rection by his conscience against his interest, says, of his chil-dren:

"Thank goodness, they're out of it at least. God bless 'em. I'm in for it, that's quite enough." But a bitter thought occurred to him, he added sadly, "What, haven't the rascals got blood in their veins? Have I brought them up to be traders? But no— no—let 'em keep aloof, one in a house is enough." Going home he finds a large cupboard secretly turned into a regular arsenal, and the old grandmother says the boys have done it, "they're in and out of it all day up to something." Marko became confused. "The devil take the young brigands," he cried, scratching his head. . . . Mad—mad! God bless 'em!"

The translator has had a difficult task, which she has done very creditably. It is not her fault that the story drags so often. Only when the writer is at a white heat of enthusiasm does he com-mand all our attention.

> *A review of "Under the Yoke," in* The Bookman,
> London, *Vol. V, No. 29, February, 1894, p. 160.*

RADOSLAV A. TSANOFF   (essay date 1908)

[*In the following excerpt, Tsanoff praises Vazov's prose and po-etry.*]

Pod Igoto is "one of the best pieces of literature that the East has sent to the West." During the baker's dozen years since its publication in the miniature fatherland, the novel has put on the garb of wellnigh every European language, from the Swedish of the ice-clad fjords to the Italian of the sun-basked South. . . . Literary circles received the Balkan visitor with a hundred welcomes; the critics pronounced the romance "the best novel published in English during 1893"; and to say that **Pod Igoto** made a sensation would hardly be an exaggeration. From a folklorist's standpoint it is a veritable mine of romantic tradition—it is a living monument of the epoch immediately preceding the revolt of '76. Yet the value of Vazoff's work is of a far more permanent and intrinsic nature. The character portrayal is masterly. The hero, Boitcho Ognianoff, a figure conceived on a vast scale, proves none the less genuine under the scrutiny of the most minute analysis. In the complexity of his nature, primitively chivalrous, yet toughened by long, weary years of Diarbekir exile—one witnesses all the savage grandeur of a Zagloba and a good share of Insaroff's tragic heroism.

There is a womanly nobility about Rada, a quiet intensity of emotion, which reminds one of the heroine of *On the Eve*. The "schoolma'am" of Bela Tcherkva,—Vazoff's romance name for his native Sopot,—with her vain endeavors to dominate and pacify her fervid patriotism by a calm exterior, is in full contrast with the headstrong Geena, a woman of naïve effusiveness and happy go lucky abandon, who flings her frank "prokliatia" under the very nose of the Moslem authorities and cares not an iota about the loyalty reputation of her family. Geena's character is one full of surprises for the reader; yet beneath the apparently jocular exterior of her moral makeup one discerns at times a will-bravery of veritable steel. When Rada herself is on the brink of despair Geena stands unperturbed. Among the old-styled *tchorbadjis* and family patriarchs of the day, outwardly bewailing the restless hubbub and rebellious disregard of authority rampant among the rising generation, one meets not infrequently a Marko who would occasionally perjure himself and steal a revolutionary letter to save Boitcho Ognianoff; or perchance find himself in the midst of a dozen old-fashioned *tchitchovtzy* (uncles), reading the future liberation of the country in the occult significance of the number-values of old Slavonic letters. To counteract as it were the quasi-learned modernity of Kandoff, with his university Russisms and his heterodox ideas, Vazoff has pictured for our benefit scores of delightfully primitive figures—peasant lads and lassies, moving in a region untouched by Western civilization with its frippery and its pretense of pseudo-refinement and culture—men and women of genuine simplicity and intrinsic worth. And, adding a touch of romantic pathos to the whole, the rebels are shadowed by the imbecile Muntcho, whose good intentions almost cost the life of Boitcho Ognianoff. Side by side with this Balkan Quasimodo towers the Cyclopean frame of Ivan Kill-the-Bear, a combination belfry-tower and canyon bugle of Bela Tcherkva, whose bag-pipe lungs thunder to all the valley the consoling accents of: "Listen, every one of you yonder! We shall just try the cherry-tree cannon this afternoon! Don't get scared!" A touch of cynicism is apparent at times—for had not the irony of fate played fast and loose with the god-forsaken Balkaneers? Right after the sewing party of Altinovo, with all its frolic and gaiety, the blood of revenge is shed and the Revolution bursts in all its fury.

The story has been penned with Vazoff's own heart's blood. The volcanic panorama that we face from the smoky Balkan heights, with the Valley of Roses a maelstrom of blood and fire, is permeated with a gloomy melancholy of dashed hopes and everlasting despair, of an intensity approaching "L'Epoppee dans la Rue St. Denis." Had Vazoff written nothing else, his claim to reserved space in a library of the World's Best Literature would have still been secure.

Heinrich Heine sought respite and balm for his love-shattered yearnings in the nature-soul of the Harz. Ivan Vazoff found peace and forgetfulness in the desert ravines of the Balkans. [*The Great Rila Wilderness*] and *In the Heart of the Rhodope* would do honor to the author of a Harzreise. In both of these poems in prose Vazoff sings the beauty of the miniature Fatherland. The story of the poet's love affairs would make melancholy reading, and we shall spare the reader a painful chapter. But to one love Vazoff has remained ever constant; he has never ceased being in close communion with the native *vylla* of the Balkan chasms. That muse of the Balkan canyons speaks to Vazoff with a language that he alone understands. Listen to this passage from his sketch.

> Musallah: "I have seen this Switzerland. I have climbed those Alps, with their blue lakes and everlasting glaciers. But while all these wonders have astounded me, they have left me cold, unmoved. They have not whispered to my heart the strange names of their strange horizons, in the strange language that sounds there. That scenery is alien to me, and I am alien to it. I have admired it, but never loved it. But Bulgaria, Balkandom? All is akin to me here, all is close to my very heart and soul. Every grove and glen, every peak and precipice speak to me in a language that I understand. I feel that they are all mine, ours, Bulgarian, that I belong to them and they to me, that I am almost part of them, flesh of their flesh. One air and one sun have nourished and raised us both. All her charms are precious to me, all her grandeurs grander still to my proud heart. And it seems to me that no other land is quite as beautiful,—which is perhaps the reason for my national egotism. Who says that Bulgaria is not beautiful, divinely beautiful and fair? Who is that Thomas? Come, come and see!"

While he is loyal forever to the beauties of the Balkan *vylla*, Vazoff is nevertheless not insensible to the charms of alien Alpland. He writes love ballads to the Jungfrau, and the balmy air of the land of Dante and Petrarch soothes his ever-restless heart. The statue of the creator of the *Divine Comedy* fills him with reverence and awe:

> Alighieri! whither dost thou stare?
> Of thy torrential thought what is the goal?
> Thy world, what dreamy sprites are living there?
> Does Beatrice's face enchant thy soul,
> Or art thou brooding over Satan's lair,
> Or breathing the divinely vibrant air,
> Where the grand hymns of the Eternal roll? . . .

Son of the bouldery Balkans though he is, Vazoff has a decided penchant for the sea. The elemental grandeur of the deep has a hypnotic fascination for him, though it may fill his soul with melancholy.

> Waves, where are you pulsing—days, where do you glide?
> —From Eternity's ebb to Eternity's tide.
>
> Clouds, lazily floating o'er the canopy blue,
> Who is your pilot? We are wanderers, too.
>
> Yon eagle, why hover'st thou up in the sky?
> —Of the desert o'erhead the proud sheikh am I.
>
> Love, love, what is thy goal? Back, back whence I came.
> Thou! Hope of my heart? I know not yet my name!
>
> And thou, grief eternal, thou hell's sharpest dart,
> Why stay'st *thou* forever, tormenting my heart?
> —O wretch, I am wingless: I cannot depart.

Life has been so scant in joy and happiness, so merciless at times, to everything dear to the poet, that one is tempted to mistake the occasional wave of pessimism for the steady tide. Vazoff, in the last analysis, is confessedly an optimist. He has admitted it again and again. He feels that somehow, in some as yet unseen way the great life of the world is moving on to progress. Yet he is at a loss to grasp the why and wherefore of it all. Life is at times a perfectly enigmatic tangle:

> The soul and the sky and the sea—
> Three words—three dark secrets for me;
> The sea and the soul and the sky—
> Three worlds where all mysteries lie.

His intellectual makeup seems quite tinged with doubt, which fact may be accounted for by Vazoff's close communion with the French thinkers of the Revolutionary period. France, the mother of everything free, the inspiration goddess of all liberty lovers, dominates the religious nature of the poet. Apotheoses of Voltaire are not infrequent in his poems; together with him he hates all Popery—social, political, religious. Yet an orthodox strain sounds its old-time chords now and then amidst the modern liberalism of his song. **"Lines to an Old-Fashioned Icon"** is one example. (pp. 105-08)

Since 1890 the story of Vazoff's life has been a series of literary successes. Poems, stories, and dramas, sketches, novels, and romances—all have followed in quick succession. Vazoff is a prolific writer; a complete list of his works would call forth in the mind of the reader the names of Maurus Jokai or Dumas. A good share of his work is admittedly but phosphates for the literary pasture of Balkandom. Some of the output, however, has upon it the stamp of undying life. It is as yet too early to attempt any final analysis of Vazoff's ultimate rank as a writer; but to every clear-sighted critic there is not much doubt as to the permanent worth of *Pod Igoto* and *The Epic of the Forgotten Ones*. The student of Vazoff should not forget his *Poems*, a collection containing the entire *Epic* as well as that gorgeous fantasia steeped in rich folklore, *In Fairyland;* the drama *Hushove*, the sketch-books *Things Seen and Heard* and *Pustur Svet* (*All Sorts of Folks*); the verse collections, *A Wanderer's Songs,* and *Under Our Sky,* and lastly the poet's latest novel [*The Czarina of Kazalar*], an attempt to deal on a large scale with Balkan life of to-day, permeated in certain aspects as it is with Western culture,—yes, and Western vice. (p. 109)

> *Radoslav A. Tsanoff, "Ivan Vazoff: Balkan Poet and Novelist," in* Poet Lore, *Vol. XIX, No. 1, Spring, 1908, pp. 98-110.*

THE BOOKMAN, LONDON (essay date 1913)

[*In the following essay, the critic praises* Under the Yoke.]

A wholly exceptional interest attaches to a novel describing a nation's struggle for freedom, when written by one of the active participators in that struggle. Be it never so badly written it bears the stamp of actuality; it lives; it is a fact, not a mere tissue woven of the imagination. But [*Under the Yoke*] is not badly written. It is the work of a great artist as well as a great patriot. Dumas himself could not have strung together a series of more thrilling and breathless incidents. Victor Hugo's *Les Misérables* hardly excites more of our sympathy with the suffering magnanimous hero. Like Jean Valjean he develops, grows to the stature of a perfect man. At first a mere hunted fugitive, then, what is not much more exalted, a mere wreaker of primitive punishment of lust and cruelty in the great scene in the mill, and the perpetrator of an act of thoughtlessness which entails much suffering afterwards, he rises and grows into the kindly, great souled patriot. This development of his personality proceeds through and by means of a succession of glowing scenes of Bulgarian life and labour. Truth to tell the brilliancy of these different pictures, the detailed portraiture of numbers of dramatis personae rather difficult to remember by their Bulgarian names that give no clue to sex, rather stays and hampers the main action. It is *Romola* over again, but with this great difference that it is *Romola* written by a Florentine of the Medici age. So we do not by any means grudge the time and attention expended on these full-blooded, many-coloured pictures: Marko supping with his joyous family under the ivied

wall; the nunnery a perfect *School for Scandal;* the monastery, with its imbecile, its glutton, and its Robin Hood for a prior; the wedding dinner at the usurers; the gay and sparkling sewing party—in everyone there is a rush of vivacity, an abundance of life such as is all too seldom found in English novels. In short, we welcome *con amore* this, the first-fruits of Bulgarian genius.

> *A review of "Under the Yoke," in* The Bookman, *London, Vol. XLIII, No. 256, January, 1913, p. 237.*

CLARENCE A. MANNING AND ROMAN SMAL-STOCKI (essay date 1960)

[*In the following excerpt, Manning and Smal-Stocki discuss Vazov's major works.*]

Ivan Vazov rose slowly to prominence and maintained an almost undisputed leadership as Bulgaria's foremost literary figure for the half century after the liberation. Critics in the early twentieth century might regard him as old-fashioned and limited, but he went on his way serenely, secure of his audience, the Bulgarian people. He also became the first Bulgarian author to have his works translated and thus made known abroad. (p. 80)

It is very hard to classify Vazov's work or to identify him with any school of writing, for he painted the virtues and the vices of the Bulgarian people without resorting to panegyrics or whitewashing their vices and at the same time without overstressing the negative elements as did many writers of the naturalistic school. He equally avoided the extremes of the Symbolists of the next generation. He simply wrote of his country as he knew and loved her, and the people, in return, read his works, even though some of the younger critics tried to deride his influence and ideas and regarded him as hopelessly outmoded. Today the Bulgarian Communists either condemn him for his failure to maintain the revolutionary fervor of his younger days and his attempts to give Bulgaria a conservative and solid government or they treat only those works which can be made to serve their purposes. So far as they can, they ignore some of his best works, the writings of his mature years, which conflict with their ideas. (pp. 85-6)

His early collections of poems, such as *The May Garland,* still show some of the naïveté and the irresponsible nature of much of his early poetry; but with the suppression of the revolt of 1876, he wrote such poems as **"The Complaints of the Mother,"** which reveal the terrible conditions under which the Bulgarians were compelled to live, the **"Ode to Alexander II"** and the **"Buried Soldiers,"** which reflect the joy of the people in their final liberation.

Vazov in all of his poetical works reflects the moods of the people and their varying emotions. He does not directly and forcibly express his own feelings of the moment and his own experiences in those troubled times. Here he differs entirely from [Khristo] Botev in whom life and poetry were inextricably mixed. Botev's life was his poetry and his poetry was his life. Vazov, in a sense, is outside the events which he describes. Despite this detachment, he so perfectly reflects the emotions and the thoughts of his people that he gives a more vivid picture of the times than he perhaps could have done if his own personality were at the center of his work.

In the early period after the liberation he reached what may be the high point of his poetic genius when he celebrated the heroic figures of the revival in his *Epic of the Forgotten*. Here, in separate poems, he pays homage to Father Paisi, to Rakovski, the Brothers Miladinov, the actual fighters such as Levski and the volunteers who fought side by side with the Russians at Shipka. In a somewhat different vein, in the *Legends of Tsarevets,* the old palace hill in Tirnovo, he describes in ballad form all those historical events that were connected with the Second Bulgarian Empire from its beginning to its tragic close at the hands of the Turks. Yet, even while he is glorifying the Bulgarian past, he cannot forget the tragedy of the individual that must accompany every successful victory, and in **"The News"** he shows how the same dispatch must carry the message of triumph and of death.

He carries this almost dualistic attitude into his poems in other fields. He shows himself thoroughly aware of the great progress that the Bulgarians made after they secured their independence, but he cannot overlook their many faults. Recognizing their patriotism and service to their people, he still saw and condemned in relatively strong language the hypocritical politicians who contrived under the cloak of idealism to serve their own interests and the interest of foreign powers. He also censured the liberated people, who all too often acted as if they were still the helpless and oppressed slaves of the days before the liberation. He condemned the quasi-intellectuals who hid their own inadequacy behind progressive slogans, as in **"The Progressive."** In his philosophy he showed himself optimistic concerning the future, but at the same time in **"To a Child"** he painted a bleak picture of life as it is really lived. Death is a reality and it can put an end to the higher hopes of a man, but it can be disregarded for something higher. The good will ultimately prevail but only after a hard struggle, and man must not become discouraged if, for the moment, evil seems to be in the saddle. It is remarkable, too, that Vazov, who began his work with frivolous love poems, should pay so little attention to the theme of personal love in his lyric poems. Perhaps this omission was a result of his personal experience. In fact satire plays a far larger role as a weapon with which he can lash his people's defects.

He wrote a number of longer poems on romantic themes, largely unhappy, in which he pointed out the unfortunate results of arranged marriages. One of his longer, romantic works is *Zikhra,* a poem about a girl confined in a harem by the sultan lest she meet someone to love her. Here we can see clearly the romantic devices of Byron and Pushkin, although the fact that Vazov was living in a country which only a few years before knew these themes as a reality added to the poignancy of his works.

Vazov wrote many travel sketches summarizing his journeys throughout Bulgaria and to Italy. In these ecstatic sketches he gives really fresh pictures of the beauty of the Bulgarian landscape, which he felt deeply and included in many of his poems. At the same time his ability to see the humor of many situations that would have annoyed the ordinary traveller provided him with the objectivity needed to carry out his purpose of showing the Bulgarian land and people as they really were.

He uses the same methods in his many stories. Some of these, such as *The Chichovtsi,* are frankly satirical, and we cannot help laughing at the pretensions and claims of the rival village leaders as they compete for the position of overseer of the local school while their ardent admirers quarrel about Greek influence and the influence of Voltaire, subjects that they are entirely unprepared to discuss intelligently. He shows the appeal to the superstitions of the village, the elaborate system of tabus and meaningless prohibitions which have been applied to life. However, he does it all with good humor and leaves the reader

with a sense not of complete despair but a consciousness that man by his own efforts can in freedom adjust these grotesque traditions and rise worthily to human dignity. He does this too in **"Tsoncho's Revenge"** in which a village half-wit, the butt of the entire community and especially the pretty girls, saves one of these girls from a rockfall in a cave at the cost of his own life, a sacrifice that is made voluntarily without a moment's hesitation.

He uses the same tactics in describing new Bulgaria when he scourges the self-important intellectuals for their half-baked theories. Though he was himself the son of a *chorbadji,* he could impress upon his people the dignity of honest labor on the land. In his prose as in his poetry Vazov pictured Bulgaria both as it was and as he hoped it would become.

Undoubtedly the greatest single work of Vazov was *Under the Yoke,* which he published in 1889. This describes the situation in Bulgaria in 1876 before and after the insurrection of that year. It pictures all facets of life and classes of Bulgarians of the day. It is done in the typical Vazov manner on the basis of the approved historical novel of the time, although it refers to events that took place but a few years before. Still, those years cover the period between an enslaved and an independent Bulgaria, a period which might have been decades or centuries long, so great was the difference in the state of mind that rapidly evolved even in the same individual.

The scene is the small Bulgarian city of Bela Cherkva. There appears in it a revolutionist known as Boycho Ognyanov, whose real name is Ivan Kralich. He has escaped from a Turkish prison and has chosen Bela Cherkva as the seat of his next operations because of his father's friend, the *chorbadji* Marko. After various adventures, Marko gives him false papers and makes it possible for him to stay and become the village teacher. Here, too, he wins the youth and also the love of a village teacher, Rada Gospojina, but he infuriates the leading Turkophile *chorbadji* and finally has to flee to escape arrest.

He returns on the eve of the revolution and identifies himself to his friends, Rada and Dr. Sokolov, and promises to marry Rada. Then the revolution breaks out in Klisora on April 2, 1876. Ognyanov is appointed to lead the fight and goes to Klisora. Rada also follows with a student who worships her. The peasants are aroused, but at the approach of Turkish punitive forces, they lose heart. Ognyanov escapes to Wallachia and Rada who has tried to commit suicide by blowing up the supply of gunpowder is saved and taken back to Bela Cherkva.

A little later Ognyanov, too, arrives in Bela Cherkva on the false assumption that the revolution has spread to that city. He hides in a mill and is there joined by Rada and Dr. Sokolov, but the Turks break in and kill the three.

In this novel Vazov gives a romantic picture of the tragic events of the April Uprising, showing the reaction of all classes of the population. There is the monk, the Hegumen Natanail, who is ready to use his monastery as an arsenal, and there are other priests who do not want to sacrifice themselves for the cause of the people. There are the Turkophile *chorbadji* who care only for their own safety and property. There are peasants who are willing to die for the cause but have no sense of organization or knowledge of military tactics and are easily demoralized. Vazov even brings in the famous cannon made out of a cherry log which the peasants made and tried to use without success. Rada is a typically novelistic heroine of the nineteenth century. The reader, whether he be Bulgarian or not, can learn from the volume how the Bulgarians as a whole and individually reacted in the crisis, but Vazov very emphatically did not try to probe deeply into the psychology of even his main characters. That was not his way, for his aim was to picture events and not to explain why they occurred. Yet his method makes **Under the Yoke** good reading, and we can see why it was the first Bulgarian story to be translated into nearly all the languages of western Europe as well as Russian.

Later Vazov in a way continued the novel in another work, **The New Land.** The hero, Nayden Stremski, is the son of the *chorbadji* Marko, who was killed by the Turks. During the boy's attempt to escape he saves the life of Nevena Shamura, the daughter of an enemy of his father. He secures a post in the Russian revolutionary government in Ruse and later meets Nevena again, falls in love with her, and marries her. Stremski becomes a deputy in the Rumelian parliament and then travels in Switzerland and France. On his return to Plovdiv, the union of the two regions has taken place and on the outbreak of the Bulgarian-Serbian War, he immediately volunteers.

The novel did not win as great popularity as **Under the Yoke,** for the events which it described were the mundane ones surrounding the forming of a new and efficient government. The story lacks the appeal and the adventure of the futile revolt and the struggle for independence. The scene is basically the same but a few years later, and some of the characters who have survived reappear. It does show Vazov's personal experiences during the troublous times when the young leaders of the Bulgarian people were trying to make their new form of government function. However, it is constructed again on the principle of all of Vazov's art, and, like most continuations, it lacks the freshness of the first work.

In a third novel, [**The Czarina of Kazalar**], written late in the nineties, Vazov again pays his respects with considerable irony to the populist intelligentsia and contrasts with them the limited and self-satisfied teacher Chakalov and his wife, both of whom have no intellectual interests but desire to build up a model economy and become rich at all costs. The novel shows Vazov's own conservative principles. It expresses his efforts to put the intellectual life and especially the teaching profession on a sound basis which could offer the means for constructive work for the people; and it makes plain that he prefers conservatism to the stormy advocacy of doubtful doctrines.

Vazov also did for the Bulgarian theatre what he did for lyric poetry and artistic prose. When he was in Plovdiv in the eighties, there was a call for plays for the local theatre, and of course he supplied the need. He dramatized some of his more romantic stories and wrote other plays. He dramatized, too, some of his comic sketches and produced a long series of comedies, poking fun at the foibles of the Bulgarian people, but almost always with that kindly attitude that was his forte. Still later he turned to the historical drama, and in such works as **Borislav** and **Ivaylo** he drew upon the life of the Second Bulgarian Empire to present a picture of the Bulgarians in the past, showing in his dramas that same facility that he exhibited in other branches of literature.

All this assures Vazov of a unique place in Bulgarian literature. He was a true artist, a conscientious and hard-working creator of a new literature, which he launched on a high plane on the world stage. No one before him had applied himself so diligently to the field of literature. No one since has had the wide knowledge of the Bulgarian people, the wide grasp of Bulgarian life in the past and in the present, and no one has been able to speak with his authority and experience. There have been men of perhaps greater and deeper talent, but there has been no one who more correctly and carefully interpreted the thoughts and ideas of the great masses of the Bulgarian people and expressed them in such beautiful, fluent and poetic language. It is small wonder that Vazov on the fiftieth anniversary of his literary career should have been greeted by all classes of the population and the literary world, even by those critics who had previously been his warmest opponents. (pp. 87-92)

> *Clarence A. Manning and Roman Smal-Stocki, "Ivan Vazov," in their* The History of Modern Bulgarian Literature, *Bookman Associates, 1960, pp. 80-93.*

CHARLES A. MOSER　(essay date 1972)

[*Moser is an American critic who specializes in the study of Slavic literatures. In the following excerpt, he considers the prominent features of Vazov's work.*]

Patriotism is the backbone of all Vazov's writing, both in prose and in verse. The existence of **Pod igoto** alone is sufficient witness to this. In verse Vazov published not only certain collections with patriotic titles in the final years of the 1870s, but also the **Epopeja na zabravenite.** Beyond that his patriotism is exhibited in a multitude of specific details. It appears in its crudest form—verging on the chauvinism which he displayed during the First World War—in a poem like **"Belgarskijat vojnik"** (**"The Bulgarian Soldier"**), a paean to Bulgaria's military exploits during the war with Serbia of 1885. Though at first contemptuous of the Bulgarian fighting man, according to Vazov, the enemy quickly learns to retreat at first sight of his righteously wrathful opponent. Vazov's patriotism was not blind, though, for in an earlier poem of 1876, **"Južnoslavjanska solidarnost"** (**"South Slavic Solidarity"**), he had spoken eloquently of the necessity for cooperation between Serbs and Bulgarians; he had discovered no reason to alter this viewpoint after the passage of another decade. That this is so may be discerned from a poem written after 1885, the overdone **"V okopa"** (**"In the Trenches"**). Here the poet pictures a Bulgarian and a Serbian soldier who have just wounded each other mortally and who realize before they die that ten years previously they had fought side by side in the war of 1876 between Serbia and Turkey, when Bulgarian volunteers came to the aid of their neighbors. The thought of strife between the two Orthodox South Slavic nations grieves Vazov, although of course if he must choose between them he will unhesitatingly support his own country. His implacable wrath—to the extent that he was capable of such an emotion, for unlike Botev he was very mild-mannered (compare the stanza from **"Ne sem borec"** [1888-1889]: "I am no fighter, no hero glorious, / but I have never crawled humbly on the ground, / I have never begged for mercy in unequal conflict / and I have not trampled a fallen enemy")—was reserved for the Catholics, those natural enemies of Eastern Orthodoxy, and for the English. Vazov rarely mentions the Turks specifically as the enemy in his poetry, but he brands the English perfidious traitors because of their role in partially undoing the Bulgarian liberation. As for the Catholic church, after visiting the Vatican during his Italian journey of 1884 the poet wrote a not entirely original poem attacking it for having sought to suppress men like Galileo, Hus, Gutenberg and Voltaire. Once anathematized by Catholicism as "devils," they are now revered by the whole world, Vazov exults.

Vazov greatly admired the Russians. The strong pro-Russian strain in his work is clear in the poem **"Rusija"** (**"Russia,"**

1876), where the writer recalls that when he was a small child his mother would show him a portrait of Nicholas I and tell him that he was the "Czar of Bulgaria." Doubtless many Russians of Nicholas' time would have been dumbfounded to learn of the esteem in which he was held by the Bulgarians, but for Vazov the might of the Russian people was embodied in the monarch.

Vazov's interest in history and geography blended well with his desire to define and foster the national spirit. This aim was served most plainly in his travel impressions, composed in prose and in verse, for his best work in this genre was inspired by visits to historic sites associated with stirring events or notable people of the national past. Thus once when he passed near Mt. Athos he wrote a sonnet, included in the **"Makedonski soneti"** (**"Macedonian Sonnets"**), evoking the shade of Paisij Xilendarski, who had lived and worked there. Vazov reverently avoided naming Paisij outright in the text, instead referring to him as "he" and elucidating the reference for his less informed readers in a footnote. Again, while visiting the spot where Botev fell mortally wounded, the poet entered a trancelike state and reconstructed the entire scene in his mind. Viewing historic sites powerfully stimulated Vazov's poetic imagination.

Finally, Vazov also used the Bulgarian language to sharpen the national consciousness, as Paisij had done more than a century before him. In **"Belgarskijat ezik"** (**"The Bulgarian Language"**) he lauds the "beauty and power" of his native tongue, castigates those who maintain that elevated thoughts cannot be expressed in Bulgarian, and declares that he will seek poetic inspiration in his language's "black shame." And Vazov did contribute to the creation of a standard modern Bulgarian literary language despite the contamination of his own style by Russian forms and words. Through the quantity and quality of his writing he raised his native tongue to a level of subtlety it had not known theretofore. (pp. 99-101)

Like many others, Vazov anticipated a moral regeneration of the Bulgarian people after the liberation. . . . (p. 101)

[In *Epopeja na zabravenite*] the theme of the liberation received its most superlative expression. . . . The poems on Levski, Benkovski, Kočo, the Žekovi, and Kableškov appeared in the collection *Gusla* of 1881, the remaining seven poems in *Polja i gori* of 1884. These pieces are written in a tone of almost religious awe at their subjects' feats. Such an attitude is prominent in a passage near the end of **"Levski"** describing the revolutionary's martyrdom: "He was hanged. Oh glorious gallows! / In shame and grandeur equal to the cross!" The anti-Turkish revolutionaries sacrificed themselves so that their people might be resurrected and they themselves might live on in the nation's heart; the gallows was the instrument of their sanctification. Most of the poems in *Epopeja na zabravenite* are dedicated to individuals, but they are always depicted against the background of the Bulgarian nation. And the last poem of the sequence, **"Opelčencite na Šipka"** (**"Volunteers at Šipka"**), which Vazov later considered the work's high point and one of his greatest poetic achievements in general, is a poem with a collective hero: the group of Bulgarian volunteers who fought furiously at the battle of the Šipka Pass to expunge with blood the shame of their nation's slavery. Individuals like Levski and Benkovski concentrated in themselves that which was finest in the spirit of the Bulgarian nation as a whole.

What *Epopeja na zabravenite* was in poetry, *Pod igoto* was in prose. Although the novel suffers from centrifugal, kaleidoscopic tendencies inevitable in any attempt to paint a broad

picture of the national movement of 1876, it is held together by the figure of the revolutionary Bojčo Ognjanov, who arrives in a town after escaping from a Turkish prison. The book recounts his tender and oversentimentalized love affair with a local schoolteacher (Rada Gospožina), his difficulties with Turkish occupiers and Bulgarian traitors and cowards, the burst of national pride in the hearts of the Bulgarian population which longs to be rid of its tormentors, the outbreak and quick suppression of the April uprising, and Ognjanov's hopeless last stand against the Turks, when he and Rada perish together and his severed head is exhibited as a trophy by the victors.

In *Pod igoto* Vazov was at his best when he described, not revolutionaries, but the old patriarchal milieu presided over by the wealthy *čorbadžii* and simple but good persons of the type pictured in *Čičovci*. Vazov takes the revolutionary movement as his chief subject, but he is unable to delineate it with the sympathetic familiarity with which he draws the ordinary society of the sleepy pre-liberation town. Moreover, Vazov had no sympathy with notions of internal social conflict, and so firmly rejected the doctrines of men like Botev, for whom a social revolution within the Bulgarian population was fully as important as the political one needed to drive out the Turks. Indeed Vazov is so understanding that he cannot pronounce an unreserved condemnation of outright traitors to the patriotic cause, much less the rich Bulgarians who at least did not oppose the revolution. He is at pains to emphasize the national unity in speaking of the popular ardor for the fight:

> When they were told: "Be ready, you must die!" the church gave its priest, the school its master, the field its ploughman, the mother her son. The idea spread everywhere with irresistible force, it laid hold of everything. . . . Even the *čorbadžii*, the branded class, the obstacle in the way of the people's progress, were fascinated by the idea which had fired the minds of the people about them. It is true that their share in the patriotic movement was relatively small, but they did nothing to hinder it, for they did not betray it.

Vazov writes favorably of the church . . . : even though the local monastery is a hotbed of malicious gossip, even though a young deacon tries to break and run at a critical moment, in the end the deacon dies a hero's death and an elderly priest willingly donates his life's savings to the cause. The author further emphasizes the nation's unity of purpose by having Ognjanov and others polemicize with a radical named Kandov, who mouths socialist doctrine and advocates social revolution. "The ideas you express," Ognjanov tells him at one point,

> merely prove how widely read you are, but they are a deucedly eloquent sign of your ignorance of the Bulgarian question. Under such a banner you'd find yourself alone. . . . As to the principles of socialism to which you've treated us, they are not for our stomachs, Bulgarian common sense rejects them, nor can they now or ever find favorable soil in Bulgaria. . . . We can depend on none but the people, and among the people we find both the *čorbadžii* and the clergy: they are a power, and we shall make use of them.

Of course Vazov would not dream of reading a Kandov out of the national movement either: his aim was to treat all elements of society equitably.

Vazov's novel has numerous shortcomings, among which are the overuse of coincidence, the employment of the mechanical device of alternating peaceful tableaux with scenes of excitement and danger (a scheme which the critic Malčo Nikolov has attributed to Victor Hugo's pernicious influence), nature descriptions given for their own sake and not integrated into the novel's fabric, the flat characterization of many of the heroes, and a patriotic naiveté which sits badly with foreign readers. Despite these defects, *Pod igoto* displays a power in its evocation of the national arousal and a simplicity in the portrayal of its characters which make it possible for the reader to form an affection for them even when they are not wholly credible, and a love for the Bulgarian nation which ensure that it will endure as the classic work of Bulgarian literature. Upon first reading it a foreigner may be at a loss to comprehend the novel's reputation, but further acquaintance with Bulgarian culture and another perusal or two will usually lead to a much better appreciation of it.

Vazov's second novel, *Nova zemja,* ends with the Union of 1885, an event which he thought nearly as important as the Russo-Turkish war. An autobiographical strain is obvious in *Nova zemja:* its main hero, Stremski, like Vazov, starts out in Bjala Čerkva and later moves to Plovdiv, the center of the unification movement. Several characters from *Pod igoto* reappear in *Nova zemja* in less epic settings, for a principal theme of the book is disillusion with the realities of independent national life. The main plot line describes Stremski's political and love affairs, but around it are clustered a number of subplots and independent vignettes. Intended to give the reader a feel for the social fabric of the era, they instead frequently cause him to lose his way in a welter of detail. For all this, and even though *Nova zemja* enjoys a reputation distinctly inferior to that of *Pod igoto,* it sustains the reader's interest to the end, and not solely through the sensationalism which was a significant factor in the book's success.

In *Nova zemja* Vazov continued his polemic against the Bulgarian socialists, who by the mid-1890s had gained much influence in Bulgarian intellectual life. He gently caricatures one wild-eyed young socialist and has Stremski argue that socialist ideas derive too purely from western European conditions to find any application in Bulgaria. Further, in his description of the Union of 1885, interpreted as a bloodless revolution, the author emphasizes that it was precisely the population's unswerving desire for union which brought that event to pass so effortlessly. He maintains that the nation is an organic whole and thus opposes the advocates of internal social upheaval. (pp. 101-06)

Vazov attained his greatest fame as a novelist on the strength of his first novel, *Pod igoto,* and each new novel he published afterwards was inferior to its predecessor. After painting a broad portrait of Bulgarian society from the liberation through the Union of 1885 in *Nova zemja,* he brought the story down to the 1890s in the third book of what may be considered a historical trilogy, *Kazalarskata carica (The Czarina of Kazalar).* In this work the author hangs his story upon a slight plot involving the amatory affairs of two young ladies, though in fact he was trying to describe society of the 1890s as a whole, not concoct an intricate plot. Dr. Krestev proclaimed the novel beneath critical contempt, but it sold well when first published. Time has confirmed the critic's judgment, however, and it is now little read. Even less read than *Kazalarskata carica* were Vazov's later short novels, set in the distant historical past: *Ivan Aleksander* and *Svetoslav Terter* (both 1907). These works

deal with events at the end of the thirteenth and the middle of the fourteenth centuries respectively.

Vazov was much concerned with the history of medieval Bulgaria, especially during the first ten years of this century. His travel sketches have a way of becoming meditations on Bulgaria's past historical glories. He had a gift for nature description, and his travel sketches set standards for this genre in Bulgarian literature. But Vazov did not write nature descriptions merely to quiet his lyrical urge. It was patriotism which led him to praise the natural beauties of his homeland and utilize historic sites as stimuli for ruminations upon Bulgaria's past glories. Unhappily, destruction and years of neglect had done their work so well that little more than pedestals and pieces of walls remained of the medieval structures in such cities as Pliska and Ternovo, but Vazov's imagination fed upon even this scanty fare. For example, in a piece written in 1900 about Ternovo, Vazov contemplates the remnants of the city's medieval fortress and recalls with pride how once upon a time Bulgarian power had extended from that spot over an area almost double that granted Bulgaria by the Treaty of San Stefano. "This grandeur has vanished without trace today," Vazov writes. "And a quiet pain embraces the soul, which is filled to overflowing with grandiose and mysterious visions but which stands before the ugly reality of desolation and death. But nevertheless I cast insatiable glances at the bare summit, for I expect that there will appear to me there the shade of some Czar with his golden helmet." Vazov also remarks upon how appropriate it would have been to return to this "improbable, impossible city" (Ternovo hangs precariously on rugged steeps above a river) its pride of place, to make it the capitol of liberated Bulgaria. It was precisely this capacity for never losing sight of his country's historical aspirations and heritage which helped make Vazov the national poet he is today. (pp. 163-64)

> *Charles A. Moser, "The Post Liberation Epoch (1878-1896)" and "The Age of Modernism and Individualism (1896-1919)," in his* A History of Bulgarian Literature: 865-1944, *Mouton, 1972, pp. 91-119, 120-80.*

MARCO MINCOFF (essay date 1976)

[*In the following excerpt, Mincoff assesses the importance of* Under the Yoke *in the development of both Bulgarian and world literatures.*]

Vazov is . . . the classic of Bulgarian literature, and his novel **Under the Yoke** is a part of the literary inheritance, of the cultural background, of every Bulgarian man and woman. To a foreigner, skimming over the pages of the book, this may at first seem strange: its weakness lies patent on the surface—a certain helplessness as regards the mechanics of writing, repetitions and clichés, a simplicity and monotony of sentence structure that may strike one as a mannerism, but whose roots lie deeper than that, a banality in the not infrequent comments that the author makes on characters and situations, a tawdriness whenever the grandiose is attempted. For the Bulgarian such points are somewhat masked by the quaint, old-fashioned air that the language and style give out, for though it is well under a century since **Under the Yoke** was first published, the language has developed with extraordinary rapidity since then. To reproduce this quaintness in a translation is however scarcely possible, the effect would not be the same, and it would merely seem like affectation if one were to try and dress it in the language of Pepys or Deloney. When Vazov began to write, scarcely any Bulgarian literature existed—no novels, no tales worthy the name, and verse that, with the exception—and it is a great exception—of a marvellous wealth of folk-songs, both lyrical and epic, is the merest doggerel. It was Vazov and the men of his generation, like Botev and Karavelov, that moulded the language into a vehicle of literary expression, who took the speech of the market-place, the café, of the small-town gossips, and made it capable of expressing the high thoughts and aspirations and emotions that for the ordinary man would remain vague and undefinable, because unexpressed. And it was Vazov, if only through the greater volume of his work, who probably contributed more than anyone to the elevation of the language. Seen in this light it is not Vazov's weakness that should surprise us, but rather the miracle he did achieve.

For if Vazov was merely one of the chief formers of the Bulgarian literary language, any interest he aroused would be historical and local. But *Under the Yoke* has already won for itself a certain niche in the literature of the world. It has been translated, and not without success, into most of the chief languages of Europe. It is an exciting tale, vividly told. But it is more than that—it may remind one of a romance by Walter Scott, but it is not an imaginative reconstruction of past events, it is told by a contemporary and to some extent even an eye-witness of the events and circumstances it describes. The defence of Klissoura, the cherry-tree cannon, the revolutionary committees, are all historical facts, and the background out of which they grow is the background of Vazov's own youth. Byala Cherkva is merely a transparent disguise for his native Sopot, and the men and women he describes are the men and women he grew up with. His heroes, Boicho and Rada, and his villain, Stefchov, may have much of the conventional figures of romance about them, nevertheless it is convention moulded in a local, definite form, and often enough taking on real life, as with Rada pirouetting before the mirror and sticking out her tongue at herself because she looks so pretty; and the so-called minor characters, Bai Marko, old Chorbadji Diamandiev, Bai Micho, Borimechka, Aunt Ghinka, Hadji Rovoahma and the rest, have been seen and set down with real mastery by one who knew and had caught their every gesture and inflection. And, as with Scott or Dickens, it is the minor characters that give their life to the novel. As a picture of life in Bulgaria on the eve of the Liberation, it is beyond praise. (pp. 10-12)

> *Marco Mincoff, in an introduction to* Under the Yoke *by Ivan Vazov, edited by Marco Mincoff, translated by Marguerite Alexieva and Theodora Atanassova, Sofia Press, 1976, pp. 9-17.*

CHARLES A. MOSER (essay date 1979)

[*In the following excerpt, Moser examines the disparity between Vazov's supreme importance in the literature of his own country and his relatively low international reputation.*]

The extent to which a great writer in a small (or little known) culture may be recognized internationally is a special case of the general problem of reputation, or, more precisely, reputation for excellence. The connection between actual achievement in any particular field—including literature and art, scholarship, or statecraft—and national or international reputation for excellence poses thorny sociological questions and resists neat analysis. This becomes more evident as we consider the "market" in reputation, for an individual of renown may lapse into total obscurity after his death while one of little prominence

may years later be considered among the most talented individuals of his time and place. An elucidation of the entire problem of reputation would require at least a large book, but perhaps a shorter study may promote clarification by observing a writer considered great by nearly all those who know his work in detail, but whose international reputation (by which we mean primarily his reputation in Western Europe and America) is relatively limited: the modern Bulgarian writer Ivan Vazov.

Ivan Vazov . . . published poetry, prose, travel sketches, essays, and plays, and indeed the 1880s saw his output as nearly co-extensive with Bulgarian literature of that time. Scholars and critics both within Bulgaria and without agree that Vazov most fully embodied the national spirit of his day and that, moreover, he is his country's greatest writer. Though other writers may surpass him in particular genres or areas, it is plain that Vazov's oeuvre overshadows that of any other Bulgarian author. In his brief *Panorama* of modern Bulgarian literature, written in 1936, Georges Hateau devoted an entire chapter to Vazov; the Italian scholar Lavinia Borriero Picchio, in her 1961 survey of Bulgarian literature, also allocated a number of pages to him, and explicitly termed him "the greatest Bulgarian writer"; the division of space in Clarence Manning and Roman Smal-Stocki's *History of Modern Bulgarian Literature* [see excerpt dated 1960] clearly indicates that they agree with this evaluation. Other such examples could easily be cited.

One difficulty a national writer faces in achieving an international reputation is that the more closely bound he is to a particular time and people, the less likely in the long term he is to appeal to an international audience which knows little of his native culture. Vazov sought to be the conscience of his country, and to delineate its unique character. Hateau remarks that his poetic lyricism is most frequently stimulated by "love of his country and appreciation of nature" . . . , and that nature is largely Bulgarian. Much of his writing consists of historical fiction or drama, poems on national topics, and travelogues of an historical and cultural bent.

Vazov exhibited a quite limited international perspective, rarely writing on foreign themes. One of the few such poetic cycles he ever produced was *Italija* . . . , a collection of poems he wrote during a journey to Italy where he hoped to recover from an unhappy love affair. These works demonstrate his appreciation of the natural and man-made beauties of an ancient land: in the lyric **"Italija,"** for instance, he extends Bulgaria's greeting to this "land of ringing song, / of genius, of beauty." While sailing past Greece en route to Italy, he paid poetic tribute to Lord Byron's sacrifice in the struggle for Greek independence; he dedicated individual poems to paintings viewed in Italian galleries, or to the galleries themselves. Vazov was certainly no Baj Ganju (Aleko Konstantinov's philistine tourist) but he always remembers who he is: in the poem **"Slavjanskijat zvuk"** (**"Slavic Sounds"**) he rejoices upon overhearing a young Russian woman speaking Russian on board ship; in **"Kapuanska dolina"** (**"The Valley of Capua"**) he writes of a beautiful Italian valley which evokes memories of the even more lovely Valley of Roses in his native country. . . . Though the *Italy* poems may be internally balanced between nationalism and internationalism, the cycle as a whole is an anomaly in the corpus of Vazov's work, since otherwise he was little interested in the achievements of foreign cultures. He was too busy creating a national literature and culture for his own land.

To be sure, Vazov's concern with Bulgarian history and culture also helped him to gain an international reputation. That very concern impelled him to compose the poetic *Epopeja na za-bravenite* (*Epic of the Forgotten* . . .), in which he celebrated the heroes of Bulgaria's Renascence and Liberation; and especially the prose work *Pod igoto* (*Under the Yoke* . . .), a historical novel describing the abortive April Uprising of 1876 which preceded the Liberation of 1878. His most powerful work, *Under the Yoke,* came to the attention of influential individuals in the West; in a short time, in 1894, it was rendered into English and published in England. Georges Hateau observes that such a novel as *Under the Yoke* may attract foreign readers by its "documentary interest" . . . and perhaps this is so, for the foreign reader can learn much about Bulgarian society of a century ago from its pages. And yet, in his introduction to the 1894 edition, the eminent British critic Edmund Gosse stressed not the book's documentary value, but rather its universal aesthetic appeal:

> In any language, however hackneyed, the extreme beauty of this heroic novel, so simple and yet so artfully constructed, so full of ideal charm, permeated with so pure and fiery a passion, so human and tender, so modern and yet so direct and primitive, must have been assured among all imaginative readers. . . . The first quality which strikes the critic in reading this very remarkable book is its freshness. It is not difficult to realise that, in its original form, this must be the earliest work of genius written in an unexhausted language.

That which Gosse perceived in the novel attracted others as well. By 1959 it had appeared in thirty-one Bulgarian editions and had been translated into twenty-eight foreign languages, with three English editions and five French editions (although it should be noted that a portion of these translations were done in Sofia). The Germans were slow to translate it, and when they did, the author of the brief introduction to the first German translation of 1917 or 1918 felt obliged to apologize for the delay. By now Vazov has become the most frequently translated Bulgarian author, and *Under the Yoke* the Bulgarian novel most often published in foreign languages. . . . There can be no question, then, that *Under the Yoke* is known to a degree in Western Europe, and it certainly remains the work upon which Vazov's international reputation rests.

The extent of that reputation is another matter. Among the general Western European reading public—or among the intelligentsia which might be expected to take an interest in such things without any specialized knowledge of Bulgarian literature—Vazov's reputation seems to be limited. In 1951 the Bulgarian critic Nikolaj Dončev published an article summarizing the commemoration in other countries of the hundredth anniversary of Vazov's birth. Most of the articles appearing abroad in the popular press at that time came out in the Soviet Union, or in other Eastern European countries, where cultural anniversaries are force-fed to readers. Some pieces published in Austria (then still under Soviet occupation) emphasized the links between Vazov's work and Russian literature, but those printed in France, Italy, or Belgium were done by Bulgarian contributors, with Dončev himself producing several of them. This would seem to indicate that Western European interest in Bulgaria's greatest writer is rather mild.

An article of 1955 on Vazov published by Charles Hyart in the Belgian journal *Synthèses* corroborates this surmise. Hyart comments that in Vazov's case the saying that a prophet is not without honor save in his own country must be reversed: Vazov enjoys full recognition within Bulgaria, but he too has been unable to breach the barricade of unfamiliarity which separates the West from such great writers as Puškin, Lermontov, Ostrovskij, Mickiewicz, and Słowacki. Hyart then summarizes Vazov's career, paying special attention to *Under the Yoke,* and concludes that since Vazov's writing unquestionably contains "valuable human messages across space and time," it is regrettable that his work is not better known at the opposite end of Europe. (pp. 87-9)

We must conclude, then, that Ivan Vazov, despite his reputation within Bulgaria and among foreign specialists as an author worthy of comparison with well-known Western writers, enjoys at best a very limited reputation in intellectual circles of Western Europe and America. Moreover, no other Bulgarian writer boasts an international reputation even approaching Vazov's. There are several reasons for this situation.

First any writer in a small culture is more likely to win recognition abroad if he publishes prose rather than poetry, since poetry is so intimately bound up with language. This helps to explain why even Puškin's reputation outside Russia is so insubstantial, and why Vazov's foreign reputation rests primarily upon one novel. Second, a writer who hopes to achieve an international reputation must depend upon that much maligned individual, the translator, to faithfully render his work into a major European language, thus accessible to a wider reading public. *Under the Yoke* has been fortunate in this respect, having been published many times in major European languages. Even Russian literature was little appreciated in the West until Constance Garnett published her monumental translations of the Russian classics. Translators are a necessity for any writer from a small country who wishes to be known internationally.

Likewise important for the development of a writer's reputation are critics, writing for a general intellectual audience and preferably foreign, who appreciate his work and promote it consistently. Vazov did arouse the approbation of a critic like Edmund Gosse, but it was not sustained. Of course he did receive continuing support from Alfred Jensen and some other foreign historians of Bulgarian literature. Specialists, however, are often thought to suffer from a certain *parti pris,* and moreover they write for limited audiences. Vazov's writing never found an independent, general, foreign critic who liked it sufficiently to promote it over several years. And that is probably the chief reason for his relative lack of international renown.

An ancillary contributing factor here is the character of Vazov's writing, which is so deeply bound up with the culture of a small country. One may conjecture that a writer who catches a national spirit too adeptly and too consistently has little chance of becoming well known outside his native land. To this extent Krestev was correct in arguing that a man of international culture like Penčo Slavejkov had a better chance of acquiring international standing than Vazov. The flaw in Krestev's reasoning was that Slavejkov as a poet was made, not born: he lacked any great innate poetic talent.

Thus it develops that a writer in a small culture, no matter how remarkable his talent, must depend much more heavily for his international reputation upon others than a great author in a major culture. If he never attracts the translators and critics he requires, he will remain unknown to the outside world. If he attracts them only to a degree—as did Vazov—he may become only the best-known representative of an obscure culture, which is little enough in absolute terms. (pp. 91-2)

Charles A. Moser, "National Renown and International Reputation: The Case of Ivan Vazov," in Slavic and East-European Journal, *n.s. Vol. 23, No. 1, Spring, 1979, pp. 87-93.*

ADDITIONAL BIBLIOGRAPHY

Cunliffe, John W., and Thorndike, Ashley H. "Ivan Vazoff." In their *The World's Best Literature*, pp. 263-65. New York: Warner Library, 1917.
    Brief discussion of Vazov's literary influences and translations of three short poems.

Matejic, Mateja; Dimitrova, Elena; Lekov, Docho; and Sarandev, Ivan. "Ivan Vazov." In *A Biobibliographical Handbook of Bulgarian Authors*, pp. 141-49. Edited by Karen L. Black. Translated by Predrag Matejic. Columbus, Ohio: Slavica Publishers, 1981.
    Biographical and critical sketch, with a bibliography of primary and secondary sources in Bulgarian and English.

Werner, Alfred. "Ivan Vazov." *Books Abroad* 24, No. 3 (Summer 1950): 242-44.
    Discusses Vazov's reputation in Bulgaria.

Appendix

The following is a listing of all sources used in Volume 25 of *Twentieth-Century Literary Criticism*. Included in this list are all copyright and reprint rights and acknowledgments for those essays for which permission was obtained. Every effort has been made to trace copyright, but if omissions have been made, please let us know.

THE EXCERPTS IN TCLC, VOLUME 25, WERE REPRINTED FROM THE FOLLOWING PERIODICALS:

The Academy, n.s. v. XVI, October 4, 1879; v. CVI, February 4, 1899.

African Studies, v. 2, 1943.

American Mercury, v. XXVIII, January, 1933 for "The Genesis of Spoon River" by Edgar Lee Masters. Copyright 1933, renewed 1960, by American Mercury Magazine, Inc. Reprinted by permission of the Literary Estate of Edgar Lee Masters.

Antiquity, v. I, September, 1927.

The Athenaeum, n. 2791, April 23, 1881; n. 3590, August 15, 1896; n. 3749, September 2, 1899; n. 3891, May 24, 1902; n. 3976, January 9, 1904.

The Atlantic Monthly, v. XXI, January, 1868; v. XXXIV, December, 1874; v. LI, May, 1883.

The Australian Quarterly, v. VII, June, 1935; v. IX, September, 1937.

Biography, v. 9, Summer, 1986. © 1986 by the Biographical Research Center. All rights reserved. Reprinted by permission of the publisher.

The Book News Monthly, v. 27, April, 1909.

The Bookman, London, v. V, February, 1894; v. 16, May, 1899; v. XLIII, January, 1913.

The Bookman, New York, v. XXIX, April, 1909; v. XXXIII, April, 1911; v. XXXVI, November, 1912; v. XLVII, April, 1918; v. LVIII, September, 1923; v. LXXIII, April, 1931.

Bulletin, 1903.

Canadian Literature, n. 5, Summer, 1960 for "Venture on the Verge" by George Woodcock; n. 90, Autumn, 1981 for "Drummond—The Legend & the Legacy" by Gerald Noonan. Both reprinted by permission of the respective authors.

THE EXCERPTS IN TCLC, VOLUME 25, WERE REPRINTED FROM THE FOLLOWING BOOKS:

Anderson, Frederick. From a preface to *"Ah Sin": A Dramatic Work*. By Mark Twain and Bret Harte, edited by Frederick Anderson. The Book Club of California, 1961. Copyright 1961 by The Mark Twain Company and The Bret Harte Company. Reprinted by permission of the Literary Estates of Mark Twain and Bret Harte.

Argyle, Barry. From *An Introduction to the Australian Novel: 1830-1930*. Oxford at the Clarendon Press, Oxford, 1972. © Oxford University Press 1972. Reprinted by permission of Oxford University Press.

Atkinson, Brooks. From an introduction to *Sixteen Famous American Plays*. Edited by Bennett Cerf and Van H. Cartmell. The Modern Library, 1941. Copyright 1941, renewed 1968, by Random House, Inc. Reprinted by permission of Random House, Inc.

Barnes, John. From *Joseph Furphy*. Edited by John Barnes. Portable Australian Authors. University of Queensland Press, 1981. © University of Queensland Press 1981. Reprinted by permission of the publisher.

Bassan, Maurice. From *Hawthorne's Son: The Life and Literary Career of Julian Hawthorne*. Ohio State University Press, 1970. Copyright © 1970 by the Ohio State University Press. All rights reserved. Reprinted by permission of the publisher.

Bennett, Arnold. From *The Journal of Arnold Bennett: 1896-1928*. Viking Press, 1933. Copyright 1932, 1933, renewed 1959, 1960 by The Viking Press, Inc. Reprinted by permission of A. P. Watt Ltd. on behalf of Madame V. Eldin.

Bergonzi, Bernard. From *Heroes' Twilight: A Study of the Literature of the Great War*. Second edition. The Macmillan Press Ltd., 1980. © Bernard Bergonzi, 1965, 1980. All rights reserved. Reprinted by permission of A. D. Peters & Co. Ltd.

Beyer, Harald. From *A History of Norwegian Literature*. Edited and translated by Einar Haugen. New York University Press, 1956.

Blunden, Edmund. From an introduction to *Her Privates We*. By Frederic Manning. Peter Davies, 1964. Reprinted by permission of A. D. Peters & Co. Ltd.

Brooks, Cleanth, John Thibaut Purser, and Robert Penn Warren. From *An Approach to Literature*. Third edition. Appleton-Century-Crofts, 1952. Copyright, 1952, by Appleton-Century-Crofts, Inc. Renewed 1980 by Cleanth Brooks, John Thibaut Purser, and Robert Penn Warren. Excerpted by permission of Prentice-Hall, Inc., Englewood Cliffs, NJ.

Brooks, Cleanth and Robert Penn Warren. From *Understanding Fiction*. Edited by Cleanth Brooks and Robert Penn Warren. Appleton-Century-Crofts, Inc., 1943. Copyright 1943 by F. S. Crofts & Co., Inc. Renewed 1970 by Cleanth Brooks and Robert Penn Warren. Excerpted by permission of Prentice-Hall, Inc., Englewood Cliffs, NJ.

Brown, E. K. From *On Canadian Poetry*. Revised edition. The Ryerson Press, 1944.

Butler, Guy. From a foreword to *The Little Karoo*. By Pauline Smith. Revised edition. A. A. Balkema, 1981. Reprinted by permission of the publisher.

Canby, Henry Seidel. From *The Short Story in English*. Henry Holt and Company, 1909.

Conrad, Joseph. From *Nostromo: A Tale of the Seaboard*. J. M. Dent & Sons, 1918.

Cox, C. B. From *Joseph Conrad: The Modern Imagination*. J. M. Dent & Sons, Ltd., 1974. © C. B. Cox, 1974. All rights reserved. Reprinted by permission of the publisher.

Curle, Richard. From *Joseph Conrad: A Study*. Doubleday, Page & Company, 1914.

Dathorne, O. R. From *The Black Mind: A History of African Literature*. University of Minnesota Press, 1974. © Copyright 1974 by the University of Minnesota. All rights reserved. Reprinted by permission of the publisher.

Dawson, W. J. From *The Makers of English Fiction*. Fleming H. Revell Company, 1905.

Douglas, Drake. From *Horror!* The Macmillan Company, 1966. Copyright © 1966 by Drake Douglas. All rights reserved. Permission granted by Bertha Klausner International Literary Agency, Inc.

Downs, Brian W. From *Modern Norwegian Literature: 1860-1918*. Cambridge at the University Press, 1966. © Cambridge University Press 1966. Reprinted by permission of the publisher.

Drake, William A. From *Contemporary European Writers*. The John Day Company, 1928.

Duckett, Margaret. From *Mark Twain and Bret Harte*. University of Oklahoma Press, 1964. Copyright 1964 by the University of Oklahoma Press, Publishing Division of the University. Reprinted by permission of the publisher.

Efros, Israel. From an introduction to *Selected Poems of Hayyim Nahman Bialik*. By Hayyim Nahman Bialik, edited by Israel Efros. Revised edition. Bloch Publishing Company, 1965. Reprinted by permission of the publisher.

Ewers, John K. From *Creative Writing in Australia: A Selective Survey*. Revised edition. Georgian House, 1956.

Fleishman, Avrom. From *Conrad's Politics: Community and Anarchy in the Fiction of Joseph Conrad*. The Johns Hopkins Press, 1967. Copyright © 1967 by The Johns Hopkins Press. All rights reserved. Reprinted by permission of the publisher.

France, Anatole. From *On Life & Letters, third series*. Translated by D. B. Stewart. John Lane/The Bodley Head Ltd., 1922.

Frank, Waldo. From *In the American Jungle* [*1925-1936*]. Farrar & Rinehart, Incorporated, 1937.

Franklin, Miles. From *Laughter, Not for a Cage*. Angus & Robertson, 1956.

Gérard, Albert S. From *Four African Literatures: Xhosa, Sotho, Zulu, Amharic*. University of California Press, 1971. Copyright © 1971 by The Regents of the University of California. Reprinted by permission of the publisher.

Goldstein, Israel. From *Toward a Solution*. G. P. Putnam's Sons, 1940.

Gosse, Edmund. From an introduction to *Under the Yoke: A Novel*. By Ivan Vazoff. William Heinemann, 1894.

Green, H. M. From *A History of Australian Literature: Pure and Applied, 1789-1923, Vol. I*. Angus & Robertson, 1961. © Dorothy Green 1962, 1984. Reprinted by permission of Angus & Robertson Publishers.

Guerard, Albert J. From *Conrad the Novelist*. Cambridge, Mass.: Harvard University Press, 1958. Copyright © 1958 by The President and Fellows of Harvard College. Renewed 1986 by Albert J. Guerard. Reprinted by permission of the author.

Haining, Peter. From *The Gaston Leroux Bedside Companion*. Edited by Peter Haining. Victor Gollancz Ltd., 1980. © Seventh Zenith Ltd. 1980. Reprinted by permission of the publisher.

Hale, William Harlan. From *Challenge to Defeat: Modern Man in Goethe's World and Spengler's Century*. Harcourt Brace Jovanovich, 1932. Copyright 1932, 1960, by William Harlan Hale. Reprinted by permission of Harcourt Brace Jovanovich, Inc.

Hansson, Laura Marholm. From *Modern Women*. Translated by Hermione Ramsden. John Lane/The Bodley Head, 1896.

Haresnape, Geoffrey. From *Pauline Smith*. Twayne, 1969. Copyright 1969 by Twayne Publishers. All rights reserved. Reprinted with the permission of Twayne Publishers, a division of G. K. Hall & Co., Boston.

Hawthorne, Julian. From *Confessions and Criticisms*. Ticknor and Company, 1887.

Haycraft, Howard. From *Murder for Pleasure: The Life and Times of the Detective Story*. Appleton-Century Company, 1941. A Hawthorne Book. Copyright 1941 by D. Appleton-Century Co., Inc. Renewed 1968 by Howard Haycraft. All rights reserved. Reprinted by permission of E. P. Dutton, a division of NAL Penguin Inc.

Henry, Stuart. From *French Essays and Profiles*. Dutton, 1921. Copyright, 1921, by E. P. Dutton & Company. Renewed 1948 by Stuart Henry. All rights reserved. Reprinted by permission of the publisher, E. P. Dutton, a division of NAL Penguin Inc.

Heredia, José de. From a preface to *A Romance of Youth*. By François Coppée. Maison Mazarin, 1905.

Hicks, Granville. From *The Great Tradition: An Interpretation of American Literature Since the Civil War*. Revised edition. Macmillan Publishing Company, 1935.

Hughes, H. Stuart. From *Oswald Spengler: A Critical Estimate*. Charles Scribner's Sons, 1952. Copyright, 1952, by Charles Scribner's Sons. Renewed 1980 by H. Stuart Hughes. All rights reserved. Reprinted with the permission of Charles Scribner's Sons, a division of Macmillan, Inc.

Hyman, Stanley Edgar. From *The Critic's Credentials: Essays & Reviews*. Edited by Phoebe Pettingell. Atheneum, 1978. Copyright © 1978 by Phoebe Pettingell. All rights reserved. Reprinted with the permission of Atheneum Publishers, a division of Macmillan, Inc.

Jorgenson, Theodore. From *History of Norwegian Literature*. The Macmillan Company, 1933.

Wagenknecht, Edward. From *Cavalcade of the American Novel: From the Birth of the Nation to the Middle of the Twentieth Century*. Holt, Rinehart and Winston, 1952. Copyright 1952 by Henry Holt and Company, Inc. Renewed 1980 by Edward Wagenknecht. Reprinted by permission of the author.

Ward, A. C. From *The Nineteen-Twenties: Literature and Ideas in the Post-War Decade*. Methuen & Co. Ltd., 1930.

Warren, Robert Penn. From " 'The Great Mirage': Conrad and 'Nostromo'," in *Selected Essays*. Random House, 1958. Copyright 1951, renewed 1979, by Random House, Inc. Reprinted by permission of the publisher.

Wells, Carolyn. From *The Technique of the Mystery Story*. Edited by J. Berg Esenwein. Revised edition. The Home Correspondence School, 1929.

Wilde, Oscar. From *Essays, Criticisms and Reviews*. N.p., 1901.

Work, James C. From "The Moral in Austin's 'The Land of Little Rain'," in *Women and Western American Literature*. Edited by Helen Winter Stauffer and Susan J. Rosowski. The Whitston Publishing Company, 1982. Copyright 1982 Helen Winter Stauffer & Susan J. Rosowski. Reprinted by permission of the author.

Wrenn, John H. and Margaret M. Wrenn. From *Edgar Lee Masters*. Twayne, 1983. Copyright © 1983 by Twayne Publishers. All rights reserved. Reprinted with the permission of Twayne Publishers, a division of G. K. Hall & Co., Boston.

Wright, Walter F. From *Romance and Tragedy in Joseph Conrad*. University of Nebraska Press, 1949. Copyright 1949 by University of Nebraska Press. Renewed 1976 by Walter F. Wright. Reprinted by permission of the publisher.

Yates, Norris W. From *The American Humorist: Conscience of the Twentieth Century*. Iowa State University Press, 1964. © 1964 by the Iowa State University Press, Ames, Iowa 50010. All rights reserved. Reprinted by permission of the publisher.

Yudkin, Leon I. From *Escape into Siege: A Survey of Israeli Literature Today*. Routledge & Kegan Paul, 1974. © Leon I. Yudkin 1974. Reprinted by permission of Routledge & Kegan Paul PLC.

Appendix

Literary Criticism Series
Cumulative Author Index

This index lists all author entries in the Gale Literary Criticism Series and includes cross-references to other Gale sources. For the convenience of the reader, references to the *Yearbook* in the *Contemporary Literary Criticism* series include the page number (in parentheses) after the volume number. References in the index are identified as follows:

AITN: *Authors in the News*, Volumes 1-2

CAAS: *Contemporary Authors Autobiography Series*, Volumes 1-5

CA: *Contemporary Authors* (original series), Volumes 1-120

CABS: *Contemporary Authors Bibliographical Series*, Volumes 1-2

CANR: *Contemporary Authors New Revision Series*, Volumes 1-20

CAP: *Contemporary Authors Permanent Series*, Volumes 1-2

CA-R: *Contemporary Authors* (revised editions), Volumes 1-44

CDALB: *Concise Dictionary of American Literary Biography*

CLC: *Contemporary Literary Criticism*, Volumes 1-45

CLR: *Children's Literature Review*, Volumes 1-13

DLB: *Dictionary of Literary Biography*, Volumes 1-58

DLB-DS: *Dictionary of Literary Biography Documentary Series*, Volumes 1-4

DLB-Y: *Dictionary of Literary Biography Yearbook*, Volumes 1980-1986

LC: *Literature Criticism from 1400 to 1800*, Volumes 1-6

NCLC: *Nineteenth-Century Literature Criticism*, Volumes 1-16

SAAS: *Something about the Author Autobiography Series*, Volumes 1-3

SATA: *Something about the Author*, Volumes 1-48

TCLC: *Twentieth-Century Literary Criticism*, Volumes 1-25

YABC: *Yesterday's Authors of Books for Children*, Volumes 1-2

Author Index

Anderson, Maxwell 1888-1959 .... TCLC **2**
See also CA 105
See also DLB 7

Anderson, Poul (William)
1926-..........................CLC **15**
See also CAAS 2
See also CANR 2, 15
See also CA 1-4R
See also SATA 39
See also DLB 8

Anderson, Robert (Woodruff)
1917-..........................CLC **23**
See also CA 21-24R
See also DLB 7
See also AITN 1

Anderson, Roberta Joan 1943-
See Mitchell, Joni

Anderson, Sherwood
1876-1941............TCLC **1, 10, 24**
See also CAAS 3
See also CA 104
See also DLB 4, 9
See also DLB-DS 1

Andrade, Carlos Drummond de
1902-..........................CLC **18**

Andrewes, Lancelot 1555-1626 ...... LC **5**

Andrews, Cicily Fairfield 1892-1983
See West, Rebecca

Andreyev, Leonid (Nikolaevich)
1871-1919..................TCLC **3**
See also CA 104

Andrézel, Pierre 1885-1962
See Dinesen, Isak
See also Blixen, Karen (Christentze Dinesen)

Andrić, Ivo 1892-1975 ....CLC **8**
See also CA 81-84
See also obituary CA 57-60

Angelique, Pierre 1897-1962
See Bataille, Georges

Angell, Roger 1920-................CLC **26**
See also CANR 13
See also CA 57-60

Angelou, Maya 1928- .... CLC **12, 35**
See also CANR 19
See also CA 65-68
See also DLB 38

Annensky, Innokenty
1856-1909..................TCLC **14**
See also CA 110

Anouilh, Jean (Marie Lucien Pierre)
1910-............ CLC **1, 3, 8, 13, 40**
See also CA 17-20R

Anthony, Florence 1947-
See Ai

Anthony (Jacob), Piers 1934-.......CLC **35**
See also Jacob, Piers A(nthony)
D(illingham)
See also DLB 8

Antoninus, Brother 1912-
See Everson, William (Oliver)

Antonioni, Michelangelo 1912- .....CLC **20**
See also CA 73-76

Antschel, Paul 1920-1970
See Celan, Paul
See also CA 85-88

Anwar, Chairil 1922-1949 .... TCLC **22**

Apollinaire, Guillaume
1880-1918.................TCLC **3, 8**
See also Kostrowitzki, Wilhelm Apollinaris de

Appelfeld, Aharon 1932- ....CLC **23**
See also CA 112

Apple, Max (Isaac) 1941-....... CLC **9, 33**
See also CANR 19
See also CA 81-84

Aquin, Hubert 1929-1977.........CLC **15**
See also CA 105
See also DLB 53

Aragon, Louis 1897-1982....... CLC **3, 22**
See also CA 69-72
See also obituary CA 108

Arbuthnot, John 1667-1735..........LC **1**

Archer, Jeffrey (Howard)
1940-.........................CLC **28**
See also CA 77-80

Archer, Jules 1915-..............CLC **12**
See also CANR 6
See also CA 9-12R
See also SATA 4

Arden, John 1930-.......... CLC **6, 13, 15**
See also CAAS 4
See also CA 13-16R
See also DLB 13

Arenas, Reinaldo 1943-............CLC **41**

Arguedas, José María
1911-1969................ CLC **10, 18**
See also CA 89-92

Argueta, Manlio 1936- ....CLC **31**

Ariosto, Ludovico 1474-1533........ LC **6**

Armah, Ayi Kwei 1939- .... CLC **5, 33**
See also CA 61-64

Armatrading, Joan 1950-...........CLC **17**
See also CA 114

Arnim, Achim von (Ludwig Joachim von Arnim) 1781-1831........... NCLC **5**

Arnold, Matthew 1822-1888 ...... NCLC **6**
See also DLB 32, 57

Arnow, Harriette (Louisa Simpson)
1908-1986.............. CLC **2, 7, 18**
See also CANR 14
See also CA 9-12R
See also obituary CA 118
See also DLB 6
See also SATA 42

Arp, Jean 1887-1966..............CLC **5**
See also CA 81-84
See also obituary CA 25-28R

Arquette, Lois S(teinmetz)
See Duncan (Steinmetz Arquette), Lois
See also SATA 1

Arrabal, Fernando 1932- ..... CLC **2, 9, 18**
See also CANR 15
See also CA 9-12R

Arrick, Fran 19??-................CLC **30**

Artaud, Antonin 1896-1948 .... TCLC **3**
See also CA 104

Arthur, Ruth M(abel)
1905-1979....................CLC **12**
See also CANR 4
See also CA 9-12R
See also obituary CA 85-88
See also SATA 7
See also obituary SATA 26

Arundel, Honor (Morfydd)
1919-1973....................CLC **17**
See also CAP 2
See also CA 21-22
See also obituary CA 41-44R
See also SATA 4
See also obituary SATA 24

Asch, Sholem 1880-1957......... TCLC **3**
See also CA 105

Ashbery, John (Lawrence)
1927-.....CLC **2, 3, 4, 6, 9, 13, 15, 25, 41**
See also CANR 9
See also CA 5-8R
See also DLB 5
See also DLB-Y 81

Ashton-Warner, Sylvia (Constance)
1908-1984....................CLC **19**
See also CA 69-72
See also obituary CA 112

Asimov, Isaac
1920-............. CLC **1, 3, 9, 19, 26**
See also CLR 12
See also CANR 2, 19
See also CA 1-4R
See also SATA 1, 26
See also DLB 8

Astley, Thea (Beatrice May)
1925-.........................CLC **41**
See also CANR 11
See also CA 65-68

Aston, James 1906-1964
See White, T(erence) H(anbury)

Asturias, Miguel Ángel
1899-1974...............CLC **3, 8, 13**
See also CAP 2
See also CA 25-28
See also obituary CA 49-52

Atheling, William, Jr. 1921-1975
See Blish, James (Benjamin)

Atherton, Gertrude (Franklin Horn)
1857-1948................... TCLC **2**
See also CA 104
See also DLB 9

Atwood, Margaret (Eleanor)
1939-....... CLC **2, 3, 4, 8, 13, 15, 25, 44 (145)**
See also CANR 3
See also CA 49-52
See also DLB 53

Auchincloss, Louis (Stanton)
1917-............. CLC **4, 6, 9, 18, 45**
See also CANR 6
See also CA 1-4R
See also DLB 2
See also DLB-Y 80

Auden, W(ystan) H(ugh)
1907-1973..... CLC **1, 2, 3, 4, 6, 9, 11, 14, 43**
See also CANR 5
See also CA 9-12R
See also obituary CA 45-48
See also DLB 10, 20

Audiberti, Jacques 1899-1965 . . . . . .CLC 38
See also obituary CA 25-28R

Auel, Jean M(arie) 1936- . . . . .CLC 31
See also CA 103

Austen, Jane 1775-1817 . . . . . . .NCLC 1, 13

Austin, Mary (Hunter)
1868-1934 . . . . TCLC 25

Avison, Margaret 1918- . . . . CLC 2, 4
See also CA 17-20R
See also DLB 53

Ayckbourn, Alan
1939- . . . . .CLC 5, 8, 18, 33
See also CA 21-24R
See also DLB 13

Aymé, Marcel (Andre)
1902-1967 . . . . .CLC 11
See also CA 89-92

Ayrton, Michael 1921-1975 . . . . .CLC 7
See also CANR 9
See also CA 5-8R
See also obituary CA 61-64

Azorín 1874-1967 . . . . .CLC 11
See also Martínez Ruiz, José

Azuela, Mariano 1873-1952 . . . . . . TCLC 3
See also CA 104

"Bab" 1836-1911
See Gilbert, (Sir) W(illiam) S(chwenck)

Babel, Isaak (Emmanuilovich)
1894-1941 . . . . .TCLC 2, 13
See also CA 104

Babits, Mihály 1883-1941 . . . . TCLC 14
See also CA 114

Bacchelli, Riccardo 1891-1985 . . . . . .CLC 19
See also obituary CA 117
See also CA 29-32R

Bach, Richard (David) 1936- . . . . . . .CLC 14
See also CANR 18
See also CA 9-12R
See also SATA 13
See also AITN 1

Bachman, Richard 1947-
See King, Stephen (Edwin)

Bacovia, George 1881-1957 . . . . . . TCLC 24

Bagehot, Walter 1826-1877 . . . . . . NCLC 10

Bagnold, Enid 1889-1981 . . . . .CLC 25
See also CANR 5
See also CA 5-8R
See also obituary CA 103
See also SATA 1, 25
See also DLB 13

Bagryana, Elisaveta 1893- . . . . CLC 10

Bailey, Paul 1937- . . . . .CLC 45
See also CANR 16
See also CA 21-24R
See also DLB 14

Baillie, Joanna 1762-1851 . . . . NCLC 2

Bainbridge, Beryl
1933- . . . . . . .CLC 4, 5, 8, 10, 14, 18, 22
See also CA 21-24R
See also DLB 14

Baker, Elliott 1922- . . . . .CLC 8
See also CANR 2
See also CA 45-48

Baker, Russell (Wayne) 1925- . . . . . .CLC 31
See also CANR 11
See also CA 57-60

Bakshi, Ralph 1938- . . . . .CLC 26
See also CA 112

Baldwin, James (Arthur)
1924- . . . . . .CLC 1, 2, 3, 4, 5, 8, 13, 15,
                                                    17, 42
See also CANR 3
See also CA 1-4R
See also CABS 1
See also SATA 9
See also DLB 2, 7, 33
See also CDALB 1941-1968

Ballard, J(ames) G(raham)
1930- . . . . .CLC 3, 6, 14, 36
See also CANR 15
See also CA 5-8R
See also DLB 14

Balmont, Konstantin Dmitriyevich
1867-1943 . . . . .TCLC 11
See also CA 109

Balzac, Honoré de 1799-1850 . . . . . NCLC 5

Bambara, Toni Cade 1939- . . . . .CLC 19
See also CA 29-32R
See also DLB 38

Banim, John 1798-1842
See Banim, John and Banim, Michael

Banim, John 1798-1842 and **Banim,
Michael** 1796-1874 . . . . NCLC 13

Banim, Michael 1796-1874
See Banim, John and Banim, Michael

Banim, Michael 1796-1874 and **Banim,
John** 1798-1842
See Banim, John and Banim, Michael

Banks, Iain 1954- . . . . CLC 34 (29)

Banks, Lynne Reid 1929- . . . . .CLC 23
See also Reid Banks, Lynne

Banks, Russell 1940- . . . . .CLC 37
See also CA 65-68
See also CANR 19

Banville, Théodore (Faullain) de
1832-1891 . . . . .NCLC 9

Baraka, Amiri
1934- . . . . . .CLC 1, 2, 3, 5, 10, 14, 33
See also Baraka, Imamu Amiri
See also Jones, (Everett) LeRoi
See also DLB 5, 7, 16, 38

Baraka, Imamu Amiri
1934- . . . . . . .CLC 1, 2, 3, 5, 10, 14, 33
See also Baraka, Amiri
See also Jones, (Everett) LeRoi
See also DLB 5, 7, 16, 38
See also CDALB 1941-1968

Barbellion, W. N. P.
1889-1919 . . . . TCLC 24

Barbera, Jack 1945- . . . . CLC 44 (431)

Barbey d'Aurevilly, Jules Amédée
1808-1889 . . . . .NCLC 1

Barbusse, Henri 1873-1935 . . . . TCLC 5
See also CA 105

Barea, Arturo 1897-1957 . . . . TCLC 14
See also CA 111

Barfoot, Joan 1946- . . . . .CLC 18
See also CA 105

Baring, Maurice 1874-1945 . . . . TCLC 8
See also CA 105
See also DLB 34

Barker, George (Granville)
1913- . . . . .CLC 8
See also CANR 7
See also CA 9-12R
See also DLB 20

Barker, Howard 1946- . . . . .CLC 37
See also CA 102
See also DLB 13

Barker, Pat 1943- . . . . .CLC 32
See also CA 117

Barnes, Djuna
1892-1982 . . . . CLC 3, 4, 8, 11, 29
See also CANR 16
See also CA 9-12R
See also obituary CA 107
See also DLB 4, 9, 45

Barnes, Julian 1946- . . . . .CLC 42
See also CANR 19
See also CA 102

Barnes, Peter 1931- . . . . .CLC 5
See also CA 65-68
See also DLB 13

Baroja (y Nessi), Pío
1872-1956 . . . . TCLC 8
See also CA 104

Barondess, Sue K(aufman) 1926-1977
See Kaufman, Sue
See also CANR 1
See also CA 1-4R
See also obituary CA 69-72

Barrett, (Roger) Syd 1946-
See Pink Floyd

Barrett, William (Christopher)
1913- . . . . .CLC 27
See also CANR 11
See also CA 13-16R

Barrie, (Sir) J(ames) M(atthew)
1860-1937 . . . . TCLC 2
See also CA 104
See also YABC 1
See also DLB 10

Barrol, Grady 1953-
See Bograd, Larry

Barry, Philip (James Quinn)
1896-1949 . . . . TCLC 11
See also CA 109
See also DLB 7

Barth, John (Simmons)
1930- . . . . . .CLC 1, 2, 3, 5, 7, 9, 10, 14,
                                                       27
See also CANR 5
See also CA 1-4R
See also CABS 1
See also DLB 2
See also AITN 1, 2

Barthelme, Donald
1931- . . . . . .CLC 1, 2, 3, 5, 6, 8, 13, 23
See also CANR 20
See also CA 21-24R
See also SATA 7
See also DLB 2
See also DLB-Y 80

Barthelme, Frederick 1943- . . . . .CLC 36
See also CA 114
See also DLB-Y 85

Author Index

Caldwell, (Janet Miriam) Taylor (Holland)
1900-1985........CLC 2, 28, 39 (301)
See also CANR 5
See also CA 5-8R
See also obituary CA 116

Calhoun, John Caldwell
1782-1850................. NCLC 15
See also DLB 3

Calisher, Hortense
1911-................CLC 2, 4, 8, 38
See also CANR 1
See also CA 1-4R
See also DLB 2

Callaghan, Morley (Edward)
1903-................. CLC 3, 14, 41
See also CA 9-12R

Calvino, Italo
1923-1985.......CLC 5, 8, 11, 22, 33,
39 (305)
See also CA 85-88
See also obituary CA 116

Cameron, Peter 1959-........ CLC 44 (33)

Campana, Dino 1885-1932...... TCLC 20
See also CA 117

Campbell, John W(ood), Jr.
1910-1971..................,....CLC 32
See also CAP 2
See also CA 21-22
See also obituary CA 29-32R
See also DLB 8

Campbell, (John) Ramsey
1946-.......................CLC 42
See also CANR 7
See also CA 57-60

Campbell, (Ignatius) Roy (Dunnachie)
1901-1957.................. TCLC 5
See also CA 104
See also DLB 20

Campbell, (William) Wilfred
1861-1918................... TCLC 9
See also CA 106

Camus, Albert
1913-1960...... CLC 1, 2, 4, 9, 11, 14,
32
See also CA 89-92

Canby, Vincent 1924-.............CLC 13
See also CA 81-84

Canetti, Elias 1905-......... CLC 3, 14, 25
See also CA 21-24R

Cape, Judith 1916-
See Page, P(atricia) K(athleen)

Čapek, Karel 1890-1938......... TCLC 6
See also CA 104

Capote, Truman
1924-1984........CLC 1, 3, 8, 13, 19,
34 (320), 38
See also CANR 18
See also CA 5-8R
See also obituary CA 113
See also DLB 2
See also DLB-Y 80, 84
See also CDALB 1941-1968

Capra, Frank 1897-..............CLC 16
See also CA 61-64

Caputo, Philip 1941-.............CLC 32
See also CA 73-76

Card, Orson Scott 1951-..... CLC 44 (163)

Cardenal, Ernesto 1925-...........CLC 31
See also CANR 2
See also CA 49-52

Carey, Ernestine Gilbreth 1908-
See Gilbreth, Frank B(unker), Jr. and
Carey, Ernestine Gilbreth
See also CA 5-8R
See also SATA 2

Carey, Peter 1943-................CLC 40

Carleton, William 1794-1869...... NCLC 3

Carlisle, Henry (Coffin) 1926-......CLC 33
See also CANR 15
See also CA 13-16R

Carman, (William) Bliss
1861-1929.................. TCLC 7
See also CA 104

Carpenter, Don(ald Richard)
1931-....................CLC 41
See also CANR 1
See also CA 45-48

Carpentier (y Valmont), Alejo
1904-1980.............. CLC 8, 11, 38
See also CANR 11
See also CA 65-68
See also obituary CA 97-100

Carr, John Dickson 1906-1977 ......CLC 3
See also CANR 3
See also CA 49-52
See also obituary CA 69-72

Carr, Virginia Spencer
1929-................. CLC 34 (419)
See also CA 61-64

Carrier, Roch 1937- ....CLC 13
See also DLB 53

Carroll, James (P.) 1943-..........CLC 38
See also CA 81-84

Carroll, Jim 1951-...............CLC 35
See also CA 45-48

Carroll, Lewis 1832-1898........ NCLC 2
See also Dodgson, Charles Lutwidge
See also CLR 2
See also DLB 18

Carroll, Paul Vincent
1900-1968....................CLC 10
See also CA 9-12R
See also obituary CA 25-28R
See also DLB 10

Carruth, Hayden
1921-................CLC 4, 7, 10, 18
See also CANR 4
See also CA 9-12R
See also DLB 5

Carter, Angela (Olive)
1940-................. CLC 5, 41
See also CANR 12
See also CA 53-56
See also DLB 14

Carver, Raymond 1938-....... CLC 22, 36
See also CANR 17
See also CA 33-36R
See also DLB-Y 84

Cary, (Arthur) Joyce
1888-1957.................. TCLC 1
See also CA 104
See also DLB 15

Casares, Adolfo Bioy 1914-
See Bioy Casares, Adolfo

Casely-Hayford, J(oseph) E(phraim)
1866-1930.................. TCLC 24

Casey, John 1880-1964
See O'Casey, Sean

Casey, Michael 1947- ....CLC 2
See also CA 65-68
See also DLB 5

Casey, Warren 1935-
See Jacobs, Jim and Casey, Warren
See also CA 101

Cassavetes, John 1929-............CLC 20
See also CA 85-88

Cassill, R(onald) V(erlin)
1919-.................... CLC 4, 23
See also CAAS 1
See also CANR 7
See also CA 9-12R
See also DLB 6

Cassity, (Allen) Turner
1929-.................... CLC 6, 42
See also CANR 11
See also CA 17-20R

Castaneda, Carlos 1935?-..........CLC 12
See also CA 25-28R

Castro, Rosalía de 1837-1885 ..... NCLC 3

Cather, Willa (Sibert)
1873-1947................ TCLC 1, 11
See also CA 104
See also SATA 30
See also DLB 9, 54
See also DLB-DS 1

Catton, (Charles) Bruce
1899-1978..................CLC 35
See also CANR 7
See also CA 5-8R
See also obituary CA 81-84
See also SATA 2
See also obituary SATA 24
See also DLB 17
See also AITN 1

Caunitz, William 1935-....... CLC 34 (35)

Causley, Charles (Stanley)
1917-.......................CLC 7
See also CANR 5
See also CA 9-12R
See also SATA 3
See also DLB 27

Caute, (John) David 1936-.........CLC 29
See also CAAS 4
See also CANR 1
See also CA 1-4R
See also DLB 14

Cavafy, C(onstantine) P(eter)
1863-1933................. TCLC 2, 7
See also CA 104

Cavanna, Betty 1909-.............CLC 12
See also CANR 6
See also CA 9-12R
See also SATA 1, 30

Cayrol, Jean 1911- ....CLC 11
See also CA 89-92

Cela, Camilo José 1916-........ CLC 4, 13
See also CA 21-24R

Celan, Paul 1920-1970 .... CLC 10, 19
See also Antschel, Paul

Author Index

Didion, Joan 1934- .... CLC 1, 3, 8, 14, 32
See also CANR 14
See also CA 5-8R
See also DLB 2
See also DLB-Y 81, 86
See also AITN 1

Dillard, Annie 1945- ....CLC 9
See also CANR 3
See also CA 49-52
See also SATA 10
See also DLB-Y 80

Dillard, R(ichard) H(enry) W(ilde)
1937- ....CLC 5
See also CANR 10
See also CA 21-24R
See also DLB 5

Dillon, Eilís 1920- ....CLC 17
See also CAAS 3
See also CANR 4
See also CA 9-12R
See also SATA 2

Dinesen, Isak 1885-1962....... CLC 10, 29
See also Blixen, Karen (Christentze
Dinesen)

Disch, Thomas M(ichael)
1940- .... CLC 7, 36
See also CAAS 4
See also CANR 17
See also CA 21-24R
See also DLB 8

Disraeli, Benjamin 1804-1881 ..... NCLC 2
See also DLB 21

Dixon, Paige 1911-
See Corcoran, Barbara

Döblin, Alfred 1878-1957........ TCLC 13
See also Doeblin, Alfred

Dobrolyubov, Nikolai Alexandrovich
1836-1861.................. NCLC 5

Dobyns, Stephen 1941- ....CLC 37
See also CANR 2, 18
See also CA 45-48

Doctorow, E(dgar) L(aurence)
1931- ....CLC 6, 11, 15, 18, 37,
44 (166)
See also CANR 2
See also CA 45-48
See also DLB 2, 28
See also DLB-Y 80
See also AITN 2

Dodgson, Charles Lutwidge 1832-1898
See Carroll, Lewis
See also YABC 2

Doeblin, Alfred 1878-1957...... TCLC 13
See also CA 110

Doerr, Harriet 1910-........ CLC 34 (151)
See also CA 117

Donleavy, J(ames) P(atrick)
1926-......... CLC 1, 4, 6, 10, 45
See also CA 9-12R
See also DLB 6
See also AITN 2

Donnadieu, Marguerite 1914-
See Duras, Marguerite

Donnell, David 1939?-....... CLC 34 (155)

Donoso, José 1924- ....CLC 4, 8, 11, 32
See also CA 81-84

Donovan, John 1928- ....CLC 35
See also CLR 3
See also CA 97-100
See also SATA 29

Doolittle, Hilda 1886-1961
See H(ilda) D(oolittle)
See also CA 97-100
See also DLB 4, 45

Dorn, Ed(ward Merton)
1929-.................... CLC 10, 18
See also CA 93-96
See also DLB 5

Dos Passos, John (Roderigo)
1896-1970..... CLC 1, 4, 8, 11, 15, 25,
34 (419)
See also CANR 3
See also CA 1-4R
See also obituary CA 29-32R
See also DLB 4, 9
See also DLB-DS 1

Dostoevski, Fedor Mikhailovich
1821-1881.................NCLC 2, 7

Douglass, Frederick
1817-1895................... NCLC 7
See also SATA 29
See also DLB 1, 43, 50

Dourado, (Waldomiro Freitas) Autran
1926-.......................CLC 23
See also CA 25-28R

Dowson, Ernest (Christopher)
1867-1900.................... TCLC 4
See also CA 105
See also DLB 19

Doyle, (Sir) Arthur Conan
1859-1930.................. TCLC 7
See also CA 104
See also SATA 24
See also DLB 18

Dr. A 1933-
See Silverstein, Alvin and Virginia
B(arbara Opshelor) Silverstein

Drabble, Margaret
1939-........... CLC 2, 3, 5, 8, 10, 22
See also CANR 18
See also CA 13-16R
See also DLB 14

Dreiser, Theodore (Herman Albert)
1871-1945............... TCLC 10, 18
See also SATA 48
See also CA 106
See also DLB 9, 12
See also DLB-DS 1

Drexler, Rosalyn 1926-.......... CLC 2, 6
See also CA 81-84

Dreyer, Carl Theodor
1889-1968....................CLC 16
See also obituary CA 116

Drieu La Rochelle, Pierre
1893-1945................ TCLC 21
See also CA 117

Droste-Hülshoff, Annette Freiin von
1797-1848.................. NCLC 3

Drummond, William Henry
1854-1907................ TCLC 25

Drummond de Andrade, Carlos 1902-
See Andrade, Carlos Drummond de

Drury, Allen (Stuart) 1918-........CLC 37
See also CANR 18
See also CA 57-60

Dryden, John 1631-1700 .... LC 3

Duberman, Martin 1930-..........CLC 8
See also CANR 2
See also CA 1-4R

Dubie, Norman (Evans, Jr.)
1945-...................... CLC 36
See also CANR 12
See also CA 69-72

Du Bois, W(illiam) E(dward) B(urghardt)
1868-1963........... CLC 1, 2, 13
See also CA 85-88
See also SATA 42
See also DLB 47, 50

Dubus, André 1936- .... CLC 13, 36
See also CANR 17
See also CA 21-24R

Ducasse, Isidore Lucien 1846-1870
See Lautréamont, Comte de

Duclos, Charles Pinot 1704-1772 ..... LC 1

Dudek, Louis 1918-........... CLC 11, 19
See also CANR 1
See also CA 45-48

Dudevant, Amandine Aurore Lucile Dupin
1804-1876
See Sand, George

Duerrenmatt, Friedrich 1921-
See also CA 17-20R

Duffy, Maureen 1933-.............CLC 37
See also CA 25-28R
See also DLB 14

Dugan, Alan 1923-............. CLC 2, 6
See also CA 81-84
See also DLB 5

Duhamel, Georges 1884-1966 ....CLC 8
See also CA 81-84
See also obituary CA 25-28R

Dujardin, Édouard (Émile Louis)
1861-1949.................. TCLC 13
See also CA 109

Duke, Raoul 1939-
See Thompson, Hunter S(tockton)

Dumas, Alexandre (Davy de la Pailleterie)
(*père*) 1802-1870 .... NCLC 11
See also SATA 18

Dumas, Alexandre (*fils*)
1824-1895................ NCLC 9

Dumas, Henry (L.) 1934-1968.......CLC 6
See also CA 85-88
See also DLB 41

Du Maurier, Daphne 1907- ..... CLC 6, 11
See also CANR 6
See also CA 5-8R
See also SATA 27

Dunbar, Paul Laurence
1872-1906................ TCLC 2, 12
See also CA 104
See also SATA 34
See also DLB 50, 54

Duncan (Steinmetz Arquette), Lois
1934-......................CLC 26
See also Arquette, Lois S(teinmetz)
See also CANR 2
See also CA 1-4R
See also SAAS 2
See also SATA 1, 36

Duncan, Robert (Edward)
    1919- . . . . CLC 1, 2, 4, 7, 15, 41
    See also CA 9-12R
    See also DLB 5, 16

Dunlap, William 1766-1839 . . . . NCLC 2
    See also DLB 30, 37

Dunn, Douglas (Eaglesham)
    1942- . . . . CLC 6, 40
    See also CANR 2
    See also CA 45-48
    See also DLB 40

Dunn, Elsie 1893-1963
    See Scott, Evelyn

Dunn, Stephen 1939- . . . . .CLC 36
    See also CANR 12
    See also CA 33-36R

Dunne, John Gregory 1932- . . . . . . .CLC 28
    See also CANR 14
    See also CA 25-28R
    See also DLB-Y 80

**Dunsany, Lord (Edward John Moreton Drax
    Plunkett)** 1878-1957 . . . . TCLC 2
    See also CA 104
    See also DLB 10

Durang, Christopher (Ferdinand)
    1949- . . . . CLC 27, 38
    See also CA 105

Duras, Marguerite
    1914- . . . . . . CLC 3, 6, 11, 20, 34 (161),
                                                        40
    See also CA 25-28R

Durban, Pam 1947- . . . . CLC 39 (44)

Durcan, Paul 1944- . . . . .CLC 43

Durrell, Lawrence (George)
    1912- . . . . .CLC 1, 4, 6, 8, 13, 27, 41
    See also CA 9-12R
    See also DLB 15, 27

Dürrenmatt, Friedrich
    1921- . . . . .CLC 1, 4, 8, 11, 15, 43
    See also Duerrenmatt, Friedrich

Dwight, Timothy 1752-1817 . . . . . . NCLC 13
    See also DLB 37

Dworkin, Andrea 1946- . . . . .CLC 43
    See also CANR 16
    See also CA 77-80

Dylan, Bob 1941- . . . . .CLC 3, 4, 6, 12
    See also CA 41-44R
    See also DLB 16

East, Michael 1916-
    See West, Morris L.

Eastlake, William (Derry) 1917- . . . . .CLC 8
    See also CAAS 1
    See also CANR 5
    See also CA 5-8R
    See also DLB 6

Eberhart, Richard 1904- . . . . CLC 3, 11, 19
    See also CANR 2
    See also CA 1-4R
    See also DLB 48
    See also CDALB 1941-1968

Eberstadt, Fernanda
    1960- . . . . CLC 39 (48)

**Echegaray (y Eizaguirre), José (María
    Waldo)** 1832-1916 . . . . TCLC 4
    See also CA 104

Eckert, Allan W. 1931- . . . . .CLC 17
    See also CANR 14
    See also CA 13-16R
    See also SATA 27, 29

Eco, Umberto 1932- . . . . .CLC 28
    See also CANR 12
    See also CA 77-80

Eddison, E(ric) R(ucker)
    1882-1945 . . . . TCLC 15
    See also CA 109

Edel, Leon (Joseph)
    1907- . . . . CLC 29, 34 (534)
    See also CANR 1
    See also CA 1-4R

Eden, Emily 1797-1869 . . . . NCLC 10

Edgar, David 1948- . . . . .CLC 42
    See also CANR 12
    See also CA 57-60
    See also DLB 13

Edgerton, Clyde 1944- . . . . CLC 39 (52)
    See also CA 118

Edgeworth, Maria 1767-1849 . . . . . NCLC 1
    See also SATA 21

Edmonds, Helen (Woods) 1904-1968
    See Kavan, Anna
    See also CA 5-8R
    See also obituary CA 25-28R

Edmonds, Walter D(umaux)
    1903- . . . . .CLC 35
    See also CANR 2
    See also CA 5-8R
    See also SATA 1, 27
    See also DLB 9

Edson, Russell 1905- . . . . .CLC 13
    See also CA 33-36R

Edwards, G(erald) B(asil)
    1899-1976 . . . . .CLC 25
    See also obituary CA 110

Edwards, Gus 1939- . . . . .CLC 43
    See also CA 108

Ehle, John (Marsden, Jr.)
    1925- . . . . .CLC 27
    See also CA 9-12R

Ehrenbourg, Ilya (Grigoryevich) 1891-1967
    See Ehrenburg, Ilya (Grigoryevich)

Ehrenburg, Ilya (Grigoryevich)
    1891-1967 . . . . CLC 18, 34 (433)
    See also CA 102
    See also obituary CA 25-28R

Eich, Guenter 1907-1971
    See also CA 111
    See also obituary CA 93-96

Eich, Günter 1907-1971 . . . . .CLC 15
    See also Eich, Guenter

Eichendorff, Joseph Freiherr von
    1788-1857 . . . . NCLC 8

Eigner, Larry 1927- . . . . .CLC 9
    See also Eigner, Laurence (Joel)
    See also DLB 5

Eigner, Laurence (Joel) 1927-
    See Eigner, Larry
    See also CANR 6
    See also CA 9-12R

Eiseley, Loren (Corey)
    1907-1977 . . . . .CLC 7
    See also CANR 6
    See also CA 1-4R
    See also obituary CA 73-76

Ekeloef, Gunnar (Bengt) 1907-1968
    See Ekelöf, Gunnar (Bengt)
    See also obituary CA 25-28R

Ekelöf, Gunnar (Bengt)
    1907-1968 . . . . .CLC 27
    See also Ekeloef, Gunnar (Bengt)

Ekwensi, Cyprian (Odiatu Duaka)
    1921- . . . . .CLC 4
    See also CANR 18
    See also CA 29-32R

Eliade, Mircea 1907- . . . . .CLC 19
    See also CA 65-68
    See also obituary CA 119

Eliot, George 1819-1880 . . . . . . NCLC 4, 13
    See also DLB 21, 35

Eliot, John 1604-1690 . . . . .LC 5
    See also DLB 24

Eliot, T(homas) S(tearns)
    1888-1965 . . . . CLC 1, 2, 3, 6, 9, 10,
                        13, 15, 24, 34 (387; 523), 41
    See also CA 5-8R
    See also obituary CA 25-28R
    See also DLB 7, 10, 45

Elkin, Stanley (Lawrence)
    1930- . . . . CLC 4, 6, 9, 14, 27
    See also CANR 8
    See also CA 9-12R
    See also DLB 2, 28
    See also DLB-Y 80

Elledge, Scott 19??- . . . . CLC 34 (425)

Elliott, George P(aul)
    1918-1980 . . . . .CLC 2
    See also CANR 2
    See also CA 1-4R
    See also obituary CA 97-100

Elliott, Sumner Locke 1917- . . . . . . .CLC 38
    See also CANR 2
    See also CA 5-8R

Ellis, A. E. 19??- . . . . .CLC 7

Ellis, Alice Thomas 19??- . . . . .CLC 40

Ellis, Bret Easton 1964- . . . . . . CLC 39 (55)
    See also CA 118

Ellis, (Henry) Havelock
    1859-1939 . . . . TCLC 14
    See also CA 109

Ellison, Harlan (Jay)
    1934- . . . . .CLC 1, 13, 42
    See also CANR 5
    See also CA 5-8R
    See also DLB 8

Ellison, Ralph (Waldo)
    1914- . . . . CLC 1, 3, 11
    See also CA 9-12R
    See also DLB 2
    See also CDALB 1941-1968

Elman, Richard 1934- . . . . .CLC 19
    See also CAAS 3
    See also CA 17-20R

Éluard, Paul 1895-1952 . . . . TCLC 7
    See also Grindel, Eugene

Elvin, Anne Katharine Stevenson 1933-
  See Stevenson, Anne (Katharine)
  See also CA 17-20R

Elytis, Odysseus 1911- ....**CLC 15**
  See also CA 102

Emecheta, (Florence Onye) Buchi
  1944-........................**CLC 14**
  See also CA 81-84

Emerson, Ralph Waldo
  1803-1882...................**NCLC 1**
  See also DLB 1

Empson, William
  1906-1984..........**CLC 3, 8, 19, 33,**
             34 (335; 538)
  See also CA 17-20R
  See also obituary CA 112
  See also DLB 20

Enchi, Fumiko 1905-..............**CLC 31**

Ende, Michael 1930- ....**CLC 31**
  See also CA 118
  See also SATA 42

Endo, Shusaku 1923- ....**CLC 7, 14, 19**
  See also CA 29-32R

Engel, Marian 1933-1985.........**CLC 36**
  See also CANR 12
  See also CA 25-28R
  See also DLB 53

Engelhardt, Frederick 1911-1986
  See Hubbard, L(afayette) Ron(ald)

Enright, D(ennis) J(oseph)
  1920-...................**CLC 4, 8, 31**
  See also CANR 1
  See also CA 1-4R
  See also SATA 25
  See also DLB 27

Enzensberger, Hans Magnus
  1929-.......................**CLC 43**
  See also CA 116, 119

Ephron, Nora 1941- ....**CLC 17, 31**
  See also CANR 12
  See also CA 65-68
  See also AITN 2

Epstein, Daniel Mark 1948-........**CLC 7**
  See also CANR 2
  See also CA 49-52

Epstein, Jacob 1956-..............**CLC 19**
  See also CA 114

Epstein, Joseph 1937-.......**CLC 39 (463)**
  See also CA 112, 119

Epstein, Leslie 1938-..............**CLC 27**
  See also CA 73-76

Erdman, Paul E(mil) 1932- ....**CLC 25**
  See also CANR 13
  See also CA 61-64
  See also AITN 1

Erdrich, Louise 1954-.......**CLC 39 (128)**
  See also CA 114

Erenburg, Ilya (Grigoryevich) 1891-1967
  See Ehrenburg, Ilya (Grigoryevich)

Eseki, Bruno 1919-
  See Mphahlele, Ezekiel

Esenin, Sergei (Aleksandrovich)
  1895-1925..................**TCLC 4**
  See also CA 104

Eshleman, Clayton 1935-...........**CLC 7**
  See also CA 33-36R
  See also DLB 5

Espriu, Salvador 1913-1985........**CLC 9**
  See also obituary CA 115

Evans, Marian 1819-1880
  See Eliot, George

Evans, Mary Ann 1819-1880
  See Eliot, George

Evarts, Esther 1900-1972
  See Benson, Sally

Everson, Ronald G(ilmour)
  1903-.......................**CLC 27**
  See also CA 17-20R

Everson, William (Oliver)
  1912-................**CLC 1, 5, 14**
  See also CANR 20
  See also CA 9-12R
  See also DLB 5, 16

Evtushenko, Evgenii (Aleksandrovich) 1933-
  See Yevtushenko, Yevgeny

Ewart, Gavin (Buchanan)
  1916-.......................**CLC 13**
  See also CANR 17
  See also CA 89-92
  See also DLB 40

Ewers, Hanns Heinz
  1871-1943.................**TCLC 12**
  See also CA 109

Ewing, Frederick R. 1918-
  See Sturgeon, Theodore (Hamilton)

Exley, Frederick (Earl)
  1929-....................**CLC 6, 11**
  See also CA 81-84
  See also DLB-Y 81
  See also AITN 2

Ezekiel, Tish O'Dowd
  1943-..................**CLC 34 (46)**

Fagen, Donald 1948-
  See Becker, Walter and Fagen, Donald

Fagen, Donald 1948- and
    Becker, Walter 1950-
  See Becker, Walter and Fagen, Donald

Fair, Ronald L. 1932-.............**CLC 18**
  See also CA 69-72
  See also DLB 33

Fairbairns, Zoë (Ann) 1948- ....**CLC 32**
  See also CA 103

Fairfield, Cicily Isabel 1892-1983
  See West, Rebecca

Fallaci, Oriana 1930- ....**CLC 11**
  See also CANR 15
  See also CA 77-80

Faludy, George 1913- ....**CLC 42**
  See also CA 21-24R

Fargue, Léon-Paul 1876-1947 ....**TCLC 11**
  See also CA 109

Farigoule, Louis 1885-1972
  See Romains, Jules

Fariña, Richard 1937?-1966 ....**CLC 9**
  See also CA 81-84
  See also obituary CA 25-28R

Farley, Walter 1920-..............**CLC 17**
  See also CANR 8
  See also CA 17-20R
  See also SATA 2, 43
  See also DLB 22

Farmer, Philip José 1918- ......**CLC 1, 19**
  See also CANR 4
  See also CA 1-4R
  See also DLB 8

Farrell, J(ames) G(ordon)
  1935-1979....................**CLC 6**
  See also CA 73-76
  See also obituary CA 89-92
  See also DLB 14

Farrell, James T(homas)
  1904-1979............**CLC 1, 4, 8, 11**
  See also CANR 9
  See also CA 5-8R
  See also obituary CA 89-92
  See also DLB 4, 9
  See also DLB-DS 2

Farrell, M. J. 1904-
  See Keane, Molly

Fassbinder, Rainer Werner
  1946-1982....................**CLC 20**
  See also CA 93-96
  See also obituary CA 106

Fast, Howard (Melvin) 1914-.......**CLC 23**
  See also CANR 1
  See also CA 1-4R
  See also SATA 7
  See also DLB 9

Faulkner, William (Cuthbert)
  1897-1962....... **CLC 1, 3, 6, 8, 9, 11,**
           14, 18, 28
  See also CA 81-84
  See also DLB 9, 11, 44
  See also DLB-Y 86
  See also DLB-DS 2
  See also AITN 1

Fauset, Jessie Redmon
  1884?-1961...................**CLC 19**
  See also CA 109

Faust, Irvin 1924- ....**CLC 8**
  See also CA 33-36R
  See also DLB 2, 28
  See also DLB-Y 80

Federman, Raymond 1928- ....**CLC 6**
  See also CANR 10
  See also CA 17-20R
  See also DLB-Y 80

Federspiel, J(ürg) F. 1931-........**CLC 42**

Feiffer, Jules 1929- ....**CLC 2, 8**
  See also CA 17-20R
  See also SATA 8
  See also DLB 7, 44

Feinstein, Elaine 1930- ....**CLC 36**
  See also CA 69-72
  See also CAAS 1
  See also DLB 14, 40

Feldman, Irving (Mordecai)
  1928-.......................**CLC 7**
  See also CANR 1
  See also CA 1-4R

Fellini, Federico 1920- ....**CLC 16**
  See also CA 65-68

Felsen, Gregor 1916-
  See Felsen, Henry Gregor

Author Index

Jacob, (Cyprien) Max
    1876-1944................... TCLC 6
    See also CA 104

Jacob, Piers A(nthony) D(illingham) 1934-
    See Anthony (Jacob), Piers
    See also CA 21-24R

Jacobs, Jim 1942-
    See Jacobs, Jim and Casey, Warren
    See also CA 97-100

Jacobs, Jim 1942- and
    Casey, Warren 1935-.........CLC 12

Jacobs, W(illiam) W(ymark)
    1863-1943................. TCLC 22

Jacobson, Dan 1929-........... CLC 4, 14
    See also CANR 2
    See also CA 1-4R
    See also DLB 14

Jagger, Mick 1944-
    See Jagger, Mick and Richard, Keith

Jagger, Mick 1944- and
    Richard, Keith 1943-.........CLC 17

Jakes, John (William) 1932- ....CLC 29
    See also CANR 10
    See also CA 57-60
    See also DLB-Y 83

James, C(yril) L(ionel) R(obert)
    1901-........................CLC 33
    See also CA 117

James, Daniel 1911-
    See Santiago, Danny

James, Henry (Jr.)
    1843-1916.............TCLC 2, 11, 24
    See also CA 104
    See also DLB 12

James, M(ontague) R(hodes)
    1862-1936.................. TCLC 6
    See also CA 104

James, P(hyllis) D(orothy)
    1920-........................CLC 18
    See also CA 21-24R

James, William 1842-1910...... TCLC 15
    See also CA 109

Jandl, Ernst 1925-......... CLC 34 (194)

Janowitz, Tama 1957-.............CLC 43
    See also CA 106

Jarrell, Randall
    1914-1965......... CLC 1, 2, 6, 9, 13
    See also CLR 6
    See also CANR 6
    See also CA 5-8R
    See also obituary CA 25-28R
    See also CABS 2
    See also SATA 7
    See also DLB 48, 52
    See also CDALB 1941-1968

Jarry, Alfred 1873-1907....... TCLC 2, 14
    See also CA 104

Jean Paul 1763-1825............. NCLC 7

Jeffers, (John) Robinson
    1887-1962............CLC 2, 3, 11, 15
    See also CA 85-88
    See also DLB 45

Jefferson, Thomas 1743-1826 .... NCLC 11
    See also DLB 31

Jellicoe, (Patricia) Ann 1927-.......CLC 27
    See also CA 85-88
    See also DLB 13

Jennings, Elizabeth (Joan)
    1926-..................... CLC 5, 14
    See also CAAS 5
    See also CANR 8
    See also CA 61-64
    See also DLB 27

Jennings, Waylon 1937-...........CLC 21

Jensen, Laura (Linnea) 1948- ......CLC 37
    See also CA 103

Jerrold, Douglas William
    1803-1857................... NCLC 2

Jerome, Jerome K.
    1859-1927.................. TCLC 23
    See also CA 119
    See also DLB 10, 34

Jewett, (Theodora) Sarah Orne
    1849-1909................. TCLC 1, 22
    See also CA 108
    See also SATA 15
    See also DLB 12

Jhabvala, Ruth Prawer
    1927-................... CLC 4, 8, 29
    See also CANR 2
    See also CA 1-4R

Jiles, Paulette 1943-..............CLC 13
    See also CA 101

Jiménez (Mantecón), Juan Ramón
    1881-1958................... TCLC 4
    See also CA 104

Joel, Billy 1949-..................CLC 26
    See also Joel, William Martin

Joel, William Martin 1949-
    See Joel, Billy
    See also CA 108

Johnson, B(ryan) S(tanley William)
    1933-1973.................. CLC 6, 9
    See also CANR 9
    See also CA 9-12R
    See also obituary CA 53-56
    See also DLB 14, 40

Johnson, Charles 1948-.............CLC 7
    See also CA 116
    See also DLB 33

Johnson, Diane 1934- .... CLC 5, 13
    See also CANR 17
    See also CA 41-44R
    See also DLB-Y 80

Johnson, Eyvind (Olof Verner)
    1900-1976...................CLC 14
    See also CA 73-76
    See also obituary CA 69-72

Johnson, James Weldon
    1871-1938............... TCLC 3, 19
    See also Johnson, James William
    See also CA 104

Johnson, James William 1871-1938
    See Johnson, James Weldon
    See also SATA 31

Johnson, Lionel (Pigot)
    1867-1902.................. TCLC 19
    See also CA 117
    See also DLB 19

Johnson, Marguerita 1928-
    See Angelou, Maya

Johnson, Pamela Hansford
    1912-1981............... CLC 1, 7, 27
    See also CANR 2
    See also CA 1-4R
    See also obituary CA 104
    See also DLB 15

Johnson, Uwe
    1934-1984..........CLC 5, 10, 15, 40
    See also CANR 1
    See also CA 1-4R
    See also obituary CA 112

Johnston, Jennifer 1930- ....CLC 7
    See also CA 85-88
    See also DLB 14

Jones, D(ouglas) G(ordon)
    1929-.......................CLC 10
    See also CANR 13
    See also CA 29-32R
    See also CA 113
    See also DLB 53

Jones, David
    1895-1974......... CLC 2, 4, 7, 13, 42
    See also CA 9-12R
    See also obituary CA 53-56
    See also DLB 20

Jones, David Robert 1947-
    See Bowie, David
    See also CA 103

Jones, Diana Wynne 1934-........CLC 26
    See also CANR 4
    See also CA 49-52
    See also SATA 9

Jones, Gayl 1949- .... CLC 6, 9
    See also CA 77-80
    See also DLB 33

Jones, James
    1921-1977...... CLC 1, 3, 10, 39 (404)
    See also CANR 6
    See also CA 1-4R
    See also obituary CA 69-72
    See also DLB 2
    See also AITN 1, 2

Jones, (Everett) LeRoi
    1934-....CLC 1, 2, 3, 5, 10, 14, 33
    See also Baraka, Amiri
    See also Baraka, Imamu Amiri
    See also CA 21-24R

Jones, Madison (Percy, Jr.)
    1925-........................CLC 4
    See also CANR 7
    See also CA 13-16R

Jones, Mervyn 1922-..............CLC 10
    See also CAAS 5
    See also CANR 1
    See also CA 45-48

Jones, Mick 1956?-
    See The Clash

Jones, Nettie 19??-........... CLC 34 (67)

Jones, Preston 1936-1979..........CLC 10
    See also CA 73-76
    See also obituary CA 89-92
    See also DLB 7

Jones, Robert F(rancis) 1934- ....CLC 7
    See also CANR 2
    See also CA 49-52

Jones, Terry 1942?-
    See Monty Python
    See also CA 112, 116

Macaulay, (Dame Emile) Rose
1881-1958 . . . . TCLC 7
See also CA 104
See also DLB 36

MacBeth, George (Mann)
1932- . . . . CLC 2, 5, 9
See also CA 25-28R
See also SATA 4
See also DLB 40

MacCaig, Norman (Alexander)
1910- . . . . CLC 36
See also CANR 3
See also CA 9-12R
See also DLB 27

MacDermot, Thomas H.
1870-1933 . . . . See Redcam, Tom

MacDiarmid, Hugh
1892-1978 . . . . CLC 2, 4, 11, 19
See also Grieve, C(hristopher) M(urray)
See also DLB 20

Macdonald, Cynthia 1928- . . . . . CLC 13, 19
See also CANR 4
See also CA 49-52

MacDonald, George
1824-1905 . . . . TCLC 9
See also CA 106
See also SATA 33
See also DLB 18

MacDonald, John D(ann)
1916-1986 . . . . CLC 3, 27, 44 (406)
See also CANR 1, 19
See also CA 1-4R
See also DLB 8
See also DLB-Y 86

Macdonald, (John) Ross
1915-1983 . . . . CLC 1, 2, 3, 14,
34 (416), 41
See also Millar, Kenneth

MacEwen, Gwendolyn 1941- . . . . CLC 13
See also CANR 7
See also CA 9-12R
See also DLB 53

Machado (y Ruiz), Antonio
1875-1939 . . . . TCLC 3
See also CA 104

Machado de Assis, (Joaquim Maria)
1839-1908 . . . . TCLC 10
See also CA 107

Machen, Arthur (Llewellyn Jones)
1863-1947 . . . . TCLC 4
See also CA 104
See also DLB 36

MacInnes, Colin 1914-1976 . . . . . CLC 4, 23
See also CA 69-72
See also obituary CA 65-68
See also DLB 14

MacInnes, Helen (Clark)
1907-1985 . . . . CLC 27, 39 (349)
See also CANR 1
See also CA 1-4R
See also obituary CA 65-68
See also SATA 22, 44

Macintosh, Elizabeth 1897-1952
See Tey, Josephine
See also CA 110

Mackenzie, (Edward Montague) Compton
1883-1972 . . . . CLC 18
See also CAP 2
See also CA 21-22
See also obituary CA 37-40R
See also DLB 34

Mac Laverty, Bernard 1942- . . . . CLC 31
See also CA 116, 118

MacLean, Alistair (Stuart)
1922- . . . . CLC 3, 13
See also CA 57-60
See also SATA 23

MacLeish, Archibald
1892-1982 . . . . CLC 3, 8, 14
See also CA 9-12R
See also obituary CA 106
See also DLB 4, 7, 45
See also DLB-Y 82

MacLennan, (John) Hugh
1907- . . . . CLC 2, 14
See also CA 5-8R

MacNeice, (Frederick) Louis
1907-1963 . . . . CLC 1, 4, 10
See also CA 85-88
See also DLB 10, 20

Macpherson, (Jean) Jay 1931- . . . . . . CLC 14
See also CA 5-8R
See also DLB 53

MacShane, Frank 1927- . . . . . CLC 39 (404)
See also CANR 3
See also CA 11-12R

Macumber, Mari 1896-1966
See Sandoz, Mari (Susette)

Madden, (Jerry) David
1933- . . . . CLC 5, 15
See also CAAS 3
See also CANR 4
See also CA 1-4R
See also DLB 6

Madhubuti, Haki R. 1942- . . . . CLC 6
See also Lee, Don L.
See also DLB 5, 41

Maeterlinck, Maurice
1862-1949 . . . . TCLC 3
See also CA 104

Maginn, William 1794-1842 . . . . NCLC 8

Mahapatra, Jayanta 1928- . . . . CLC 33
See also CANR 15
See also CA 73-76

Mahon, Derek 1941- . . . . CLC 27
See also CA 113
See also DLB 40

Mailer, Norman
1923- . . . . . . CLC 1, 2, 3, 4, 5, 8, 11, 14,
28, 39 (416)
See also CA 9-12R
See also CABS 1
See also DLB 2, 16, 28
See also DLB-Y 80, 83
See also DLB-DS 3
See also AITN 2

Mais, Roger 1905-1955 . . . . TCLC 8
See also CA 105

Major, Clarence 1936- . . . . CLC 3, 19
See also CANR 13
See also CA 21-24R
See also DLB 33

Major, Kevin 1949- . . . . CLC 26
See also CLR 11
See also CA 97-100
See also SATA 32

Malamud, Bernard
1914-1986 . . . . . CLC 1, 2, 3, 5, 8, 9, 11,
18, 27, 44 (411)
See also CA 5-8R
See also obituary CA 118
See also CABS 1
See also DLB 2, 28
See also DLB-Y 80, 86
See also CDALB 1941-1968

Malherbe, François de 1555-1628 . . . . . LC 5

Mallarmé, Stéphane
1842-1898 . . . . NCLC 4

Mallet-Joris, Françoise 1930- . . . . CLC 11
See also CANR 17
See also CA 65-68

Maloff, Saul 1922- . . . . CLC 5
See also CA 33-36R

Malone, Michael (Christopher)
1942- . . . . CLC 43
See also CANR 14
See also CA 77-80

Malouf, David 1934- . . . . CLC 28

Malraux, (Georges-) André
1901-1976 . . . . CLC 1, 4, 9, 13, 15
See also CAP 2
See also CA 21-24R
See also obituary CA 69-72

Malzberg, Barry N. 1939- . . . . CLC 7
See also CAAS 4
See also CANR 16
See also CA 61-64
See also DLB 8

Mamet, David
1947- . . . . CLC 9, 15, 34 (217)
See also CANR 15
See also CA 81-84
See also DLB 7

Mamoulian, Rouben 1898- . . . . CLC 16
See also CA 25-28R

Mandelstam, Osip (Emilievich)
1891?-1938? . . . . TCLC 2, 6
See also CA 104

Mandiargues, André Pieyre de
1909- . . . . CLC 41
See also CA 103

Manley, (Mary) Delariviere
1672?-1724 . . . . LC 1
See also DLB 39

Mann, (Luiz) Heinrich
1871-1950 . . . . TCLC 9
See also CA 106

Mann, Thomas
1875-1955 . . . . TCLC 2, 8, 14, 21
See also CA 104

Manning, Frederic
1882-1935 . . . . TCLC 25

Manning, Olivia 1915-1980 . . . . . CLC 5, 19
See also CA 5-8R
See also obituary CA 101

Mano, D. Keith 1942- . . . . CLC 2, 10
See also CA 25-28R
See also DLB 6

McCarthy, Mary (Therese)
1912-.....CLC 1, 3, 5, 14, 24, 39 (484)
See also CANR 16
See also CA 5-8R
See also DLB 2
See also DLB-Y 81

McCartney, (James) Paul
1942-....................CLC 35
See also Lennon, John (Ono) and
McCartney, Paul

McClure, Michael 1932-........ CLC 6, 10
See also CANR 17
See also CA 21-24R
See also DLB 16

McCourt, James 1941-.............CLC 5
See also CA 57-60

McCrae, John 1872-1918....... TCLC 12
See also CA 109

McCullers, (Lula) Carson
1917-1967............CLC 1, 4, 10, 12
See also CANR 18
See also CA 5-8R
See also obituary CA 25-28R
See also CABS 1
See also SATA 27
See also DLB 2, 7
See also CDALB 1941-1968

McCullough, Colleen 1938?-.......CLC 27
See also CANR 17
See also CA 81-84

McElroy, Joseph 1930-.............CLC 5
See also CA 17-20R

McEwan, Ian 1948-................CLC 13
See also CA 61-64
See also DLB 14

McGahern, John 1935-.......... CLC 5, 9
See also CA 17-20R
See also DLB 14

McGinley, Patrick 1937-..........CLC 41
See also CA 120

McGinley, Phyllis 1905-1978.......CLC 14
See also CA 9-12R
See also obituary CA 77-80
See also SATA 2, 44
See also obituary SATA 24
See also DLB 11, 48

McGinniss, Joe 1942-.............CLC 32
See also CA 25-28R
See also AITN 2

McGivern, Maureen Daly 1921-
See Daly, Maureen
See also CA 9-12R

McGrath, Thomas 1916- ....CLC 28
See also CANR 6
See also CA 9-12R
See also SATA 41

McGuane, Thomas (Francis III)
1939-...................CLC 3, 7, 18
See also CANR 5
See also CA 49-52
See also DLB 2
See also DLB-Y 80
See also AITN 2

McHale, Tom 1941-1982 .... CLC 3, 5
See also CA 77-80
See also obituary CA 106
See also AITN 1

McIlvanney, William 1936-........CLC 42
See also CA 25-28R
See also DLB 14

McIlwraith, Maureen Mollie Hunter 1922-
See Hunter, Mollie
See also CA 29-32R
See also SATA 2

McInerney, Jay 1955-........ CLC 34 (81)
See also CA 116

McIntyre, Vonda N(eel) 1948-......CLC 18
See also CANR 17
See also CA 81-84

McKay, Claude 1890-1948....... TCLC 7
See also CA 104
See also DLB 4, 45

McKuen, Rod 1933- .... CLC 1, 3
See also CA 41-44R
See also AITN 1

McLuhan, (Herbert) Marshall
1911-1980...................CLC 37
See also CANR 12
See also CA 9-12R
See also obituary CA 102

McManus, Declan Patrick 1955-
See Costello, Elvis

McMurtry, Larry (Jeff)
1936-.....CLC 2, 3, 7, 11, 27, 44 (253)
See also CANR 19
See also CA 5-8R
See also DLB 2
See also DLB-Y 80
See also AITN 2

McNally, Terrence 1939- ..... CLC 4, 7, 41
See also CANR 2
See also CA 45-48
See also DLB 7

McPhee, John 1931- ....CLC 36
See also CA 65-68

McPherson, James Alan 1943- .....CLC 19
See also CA 25-28R
See also DLB 38

McPherson, William
1939-................... CLC 34 (85)
See also CA 57-60

McSweeney, Kerry 19??- .... CLC 34 (579)

Mead, Margaret 1901-1978........CLC 37
See also CANR 4
See also CA 1-4R
See also obituary CA 81-84
See also SATA 20
See also AITN 1

Meaker, M. J. 1927-
See Kerr, M. E.
See Meaker, Marijane

Meaker, Marijane 1927-
See Kerr, M. E.
See also CA 107
See also SATA 20

Medoff, Mark (Howard)
1940-..................... CLC 6, 23
See also CANR 5
See also CA 53-56
See also DLB 7
See also AITN 1

Megged, Aharon 1920-.............CLC 9
See also CANR 1
See also CA 49-52

Mehta, Ved (Parkash) 1934- ....CLC 37
See also CANR 2
See also CA 1-4R

Mellor, John 1953?-
See The Clash

Meltzer, Milton 1915-.............CLC 26
See also CA 13-16R
See also SAAS 1
See also SATA 1

Melville, Herman
1819-1891................NCLC 3, 12
See also DLB 3

Mencken, H(enry) L(ouis)
1880-1956.................. TCLC 13
See also CA 105
See also DLB 11, 29

Mercer, David 1928-1980..........CLC 5
See also CA 9-12R
See also obituary CA 102
See also DLB 13

Meredith, George 1828-1909..... TCLC 17
See also CA 117
See also DLB 18, 35, 57

Meredith, William (Morris)
1919-.................. CLC 4, 13, 22
See also CANR 6
See also CA 9-12R
See also DLB 5

Mérimée, Prosper 1803-1870...... NCLC 6

Merkin, Daphne 1954- .... CLC 44 (62)

Merrill, James (Ingram)
1926-.......... CLC 2, 3, 6, 8, 13, 18,
                                    34 (225)
See also CANR 10
See also CA 13-16R
See also DLB 5
See also DLB-Y 85

Merton, Thomas (James)
1915-1968...... CLC 1, 3, 11, 34 (460)
See also CA 5-8R
See also obituary CA 25-28R
See also DLB 48
See also DLB-Y 81

Merwin, W(illiam) S(tanley)
1927-..... CLC 1, 2, 3, 5, 8, 13, 18, 45
See also CANR 15
See also CA 13-16R
See also DLB 5

Metcalf, John 1938-...............CLC 37
See also CA 113

Mew, Charlotte (Mary)
1870-1928.................. TCLC 8
See also CA 105
See also DLB 19

Mewshaw, Michael 1943-...........CLC 9
See also CANR 7
See also CA 53-56
See also DLB-Y 80

Meyer-Meyrink, Gustav 1868-1932
See Meyrink, Gustav
See also CA 117

Meyrink, Gustav 1868-1932...... TCLC 21
See also Meyer-Meyrink, Gustav

Meyers, Jeffrey 1939-........ CLC 39 (427)
See also CA 73-76

Meynell, Alice (Christiana Gertrude
    Thompson) 1847-1922 .... **TCLC 6**
  See also CA 104
  See also DLB 19

Michaels, Leonard 1933- .... **CLC 6, 25**
  See also CA 61-64

Michaux, Henri 1899-1984...... **CLC 8, 19**
  See also CA 85-88
  See also obituary CA 114

Michener, James A(lbert)
    1907-...............**CLC 1, 5, 11, 29**
  See also CA 5-8R
  See also DLB 6
  See also AITN 1

Mickiewicz, Adam 1798-1855 ..... **NCLC 3**

Middleton, Christopher 1926- ......**CLC 13**
  See also CA 13-16R
  See also DLB 40

Middleton, Stanley 1919- .... **CLC 7, 38**
  See also CA 25-28R
  See also DLB 14

Miguéis, José Rodrigues 1901- .....**CLC 10**

Miles, Josephine (Louise)
    1911-1985......**CLC 1, 2, 14, 34 (243),**
                    39 (352)
  See also CANR 2
  See also CA 1-4R
  See also obituary CA 116
  See also DLB 48

Mill, John Stuart 1806-1873 ..... **NCLC 11**

Millar, Kenneth 1915-1983
  See Macdonald, Ross
  See also CANR 16
  See also CA 9-12R
  See also obituary CA 110
  See also DLB 2
  See also DLB-Y 83

Millay, Edna St. Vincent
    1892-1950................... **TCLC 4**
  See also CA 104
  See also DLB 45

Miller, Arthur
    1915-.......... **CLC 1, 2, 6, 10, 15, 26**
  See also CANR 2
  See also CA 1-4R
  See also DLB 7
  See also CDALB 1941-1968
  See also AITN 1

Miller, Henry (Valentine)
    1891-1980....... **CLC 1, 2, 4, 9, 14, 43**
  See also CA 9-12R
  See also obituary CA 97-100
  See also DLB 4, 9
  See also DLB-Y 80

Miller, Jason 1939?- ....**CLC 2**
  See also CA 73-76
  See also DLB 7
  See also AITN 1

Miller, Sue 19??- .... **CLC 44 (67)**

Miller, Walter M(ichael), Jr.
    1923-.................... **CLC 4, 30**
  See also CA 85-88
  See also DLB 8

Millhauser, Steven 1943- ....**CLC 21**
  See also CA 108, 110, 111
  See also DLB 2

Milne, A(lan) A(lexander)
    1882-1956................... **TCLC 6**
  See also CLR 1
  See also CA 104
  See also YABC 1
  See also DLB 10

Miłosz, Czesław
    1911-...............**CLC 5, 11, 22, 31**
  See also CA 81-84

Miner, Valerie (Jane) 1947-........**CLC 40**
  See also CA 97-100

Minot, Susan 1956- .... **CLC 44 (77)**

Minus, Ed 1938- .... **CLC 39 (79)**

Miró (Ferrer), Gabriel (Francisco Víctor)
    1879-1930................... **TCLC 5**
  See also CA 104

Mishima, Yukio
    1925-1970......... **CLC 2, 4, 6, 9, 27**
  See also Hiraoka, Kimitake

Mistral, Gabriela 1889-1957 ...... **TCLC 2**
  See also CA 104

Mitchell, James Leslie 1901-1935
  See Gibbon, Lewis Grassic
  See also CA 104
  See also DLB 15

Mitchell, Joni 1943-..............**CLC 12**
  See also CA 112

Mitchell (Marsh), Margaret (Munnerlyn)
    1900-1949................... **TCLC 11**
  See also CA 109
  See also DLB 9

Mitchell, W(illiam) O(rmond)
    1914-........................**CLC 25**
  See also CANR 15
  See also CA 77-80

Mitford, Mary Russell
    1787-1855................... **NCLC 4**

Mitford, Nancy
    1904-1973.............. **CLC 44 (482)**

Modiano, Patrick (Jean) 1945- .....**CLC 18**
  See also CANR 17
  See also CA 85-88

Modarressi, Taghi 1931-...... **CLC 44 (82)**

Mofolo, Thomas (Mokopu)
    1876-1948................. **TCLC 22**

Mohr, Nicholasa 1935- ....**CLC 12**
  See also CANR 1
  See also CA 49-52
  See also SATA 8

Mojtabai, A(nn) G(race)
    1938-...............**CLC 5, 9, 15, 29**
  See also CA 85-88

Molnár, Ferenc 1878-1952...... **TCLC 20**
  See also CA 109

Momaday, N(avarre) Scott
    1934- .... **CLC 2, 19**
  See also CANR 14
  See also CA 25-28R
  See also SATA 30, 48

Monroe, Harriet 1860-1936...... **TCLC 12**
  See also CA 109
  See also DLB 54

Montagu, Elizabeth 1720-1800 .... **NCLC 7**

Montague, John (Patrick)
    1929-........................**CLC 13**
  See also CANR 9
  See also CA 9-12R
  See also DLB 40

Montale, Eugenio
    1896-1981............... **CLC 7, 9, 18**
  See also CA 17-20R
  See also obituary CA 104

Montgomery, Marion (H., Jr.)
    1925-........................**CLC 7**
  See also CANR 3
  See also CA 1-4R
  See also DLB 6
  See also AITN 1

Montgomery, Robert Bruce 1921-1978
  See Crispin, Edmund
  See also CA 104

Montherlant, Henri (Milon) de
    1896-1972................. **CLC 8, 19**
  See also CA 85-88
  See also obituary CA 37-40R

Monty Python......................**CLC 21**
  See also Cleese, John

Moodie, Susanna (Strickland)
    1803-1885................. **NCLC 14**

Mooney, Ted 1951- ....**CLC 25**

Moorcock, Michael (John)
    1939-..................... **CLC 5, 27**
  See also CAAS 5
  See also CANR 2, 17
  See also CA 45-48
  See also DLB 14

Moore, Brian
    1921-.........**CLC 1, 3, 5, 7, 8, 19, 32**
  See also CANR 1
  See also CA 1-4R

Moore, George (Augustus)
    1852-1933................... **TCLC 7**
  See also CA 104
  See also DLB 10, 18, 57

Moore, Lorrie 1957- ...... **CLC 39 (82), 45**
  See also Moore, Marie Lorena

Moore, Marianne (Craig)
    1887-1972...... **CLC 1, 2, 4, 8, 10, 13,**
                      19
  See also CANR 3
  See also CA 1-4R
  See also obituary CA 33-36R
  See also DLB 45
  See also SATA 20

Moore, Marie Lorena 1957-
  See Moore, Lorrie
  See also CA 116

Moore, Thomas 1779-1852....... **NCLC 6**

Morand, Paul 1888-1976 ....**CLC 41**
  See also obituary CA 69-72

Morante, Elsa 1918-1985...........**CLC 8**
  See also CA 85-88
  See also obituary CA 117

Moravia, Alberto
    1907-........... **CLC 2, 7, 11, 18, 27**
  See also Pincherle, Alberto

Moréas, Jean 1856-1910........ **TCLC 18**

Morgan, Berry 1919- ....**CLC 6**
  See also CA 49-52
  See also DLB 6

Morgan, Edwin (George)
1920-.........................CLC 31
See also CANR 3
See also CA 7-8R
See also DLB 27

Morgan, Frederick 1922-..........CLC 23
See also CA 17-20R

Morgan, Janet 1945-........ CLC 39 (436)
See also CA 65-68

Morgan, Robin 1941-..............CLC 2
See also CA 69-72

Morgenstern, Christian (Otto Josef Wolfgang)
1871-1914...................TCLC 8
See also CA 105

Mori Ōgai 1862-1922 .... TCLC 14
See also Mori Rintaro

Mori Rintaro 1862-1922
See Mori Ōgai
See also CA 110

Mörike, Eduard (Friedrich)
1804-1875.................. NCLC 10

Moritz, Karl Philipp 1756-1793 ...... LC 2

Morris, Julian 1916-
See West, Morris L.

Morris, Steveland Judkins 1950-
See Wonder, Stevie
See also CA 111

Morris, William 1834-1896 .... NCLC 4
See also DLB 18, 35, 57

Morris, Wright (Marion)
1910-............ CLC 1, 3, 7, 18, 37
See also CA 9-12R
See also DLB 2
See also DLB-Y 81

Morrison, James Douglas 1943-1971
See Morrison, Jim
See also CA 73-76

Morrison, Jim 1943-1971..........CLC 17
See also Morrison, James Douglas

Morrison, Toni 1931- .... CLC 4, 10, 22
See also CA 29-32R
See also DLB 6, 33
See also DLB-Y 81

Morrison, Van 1945-..............CLC 21
See also CA 116

Mortimer, John (Clifford)
1923-............... CLC 28, 43
See also CA 13-16R
See also DLB 13

Mortimer, Penelope (Ruth)
1918-.........................CLC 5
See also CA 57-60

Mosley, Nicholas 1923-............CLC 43
See also CA 69-72
See also DLB 14

Moss, Howard 1922-........ CLC 7, 14, 45
See also CANR 1
See also CA 1-4R
See also DLB 5

Motley, Willard (Francis)
1912-1965...................CLC 18
See also obituary CA 106
See also CA 117

Mott, Michael (Charles Alston)
1930-.............. CLC 15, 34 (460)
See also CANR 7
See also CA 5-8R

Mowat, Farley (McGill) 1921-......CLC 26
See also CANR 4
See also CA 1-4R
See also SATA 3

Mphahlele, Es'kia 1919-
See Mphahlele, Ezekiel

Mphahlele, Ezekiel 1919-..........CLC 25
See also CA 81-84

Mqhayi, S(amuel) E(dward) K(rune Loliwe)
1875-1945.................. TCLC 25

Mrożek, Sławomir 1930- .... CLC 3, 13
See also CA 13-16R

Mueller, Lisel 1924- ....CLC 13
See also CA 93-96

Muir, Edwin 1887-1959 .... TCLC 2
See also CA 104
See also DLB 20

Mujica Láinez, Manuel
1910-1984...................CLC 31
See also CA 81-84
See also obituary CA 112

Muldoon, Paul 1951-..............CLC 32
See also CA 113
See also DLB 40

Mulisch, Harry (Kurt Victor)
1927-.......................CLC 42
See also CANR 6
See also CA 9-12R

Mull, Martin 1943- ....CLC 17
See also CA 105

Munford, Robert 1637?-1784 .... LC 5
See also DLB 31

Munro, Alice 1931-......... CLC 6, 10, 19
See also CA 33-36R
See also SATA 29
See also DLB 53
See also AITN 2

Munro, H(ector) H(ugh) 1870-1916
See Saki
See also CA 104
See also DLB 34

Murdoch, (Jean) Iris
1919-......CLC 1, 2, 3, 4, 6, 8, 11, 15,
22, 31
See also CANR 8
See also CA 13-16R
See also DLB 14

Murphy, Richard 1927-..........CLC 41
See also CA 29-32R
See also DLB 40

Murphy, Sylvia 19??- .... CLC 34 (91)

Murray, Les(lie) A(llan) 1938-......CLC 40
See also CANR 11
See also CA 21-24R

Murry, John Middleton
1889-1957.................. TCLC 16
See also CA 118

Musgrave, Susan 1951-............CLC 13
See also CA 69-72

Musil, Robert (Edler von)
1880-1942.................. TCLC 12
See also CA 109

Musset, (Louis Charles) Alfred de
1810-1857.................. NCLC 7

Myers, Walter Dean 1937-.........CLC 35
See also CLR 4
See also CANR 20
See also CA 33-36R
See also SAAS 2
See also SATA 27, 41
See also DLB 33

Nabokov, Vladimir (Vladimirovich)
1899-1977....... CLC 1, 2, 3, 6, 8, 11,
15, 23, 44 (463)
See also CANR 20
See also CA 5-8R
See also obituary CA 69-72
See also DLB 2
See also DLB-Y 80
See also DLB-DS 3
See also CDALB 1941-1968

Nagy, László 1925-1978 ....CLC 7
See also obituary CA 112

Naipaul, Shiva(dhar Srinivasa)
1945-1985........... CLC 32, 39 (355)
See also CA 110, 112
See also obituary CA 116
See also DLB-Y 85

Naipaul, V(idiadhar) S(urajprasad)
1932-.......... CLC 4, 7, 9, 13, 18, 37
See also CANR 1
See also CA 1-4R
See also DLB-Y 85

Nakos, Ioulia 1899?-
See Nakos, Lilika

Nakos, Lilika 1899?-..............CLC 29

Nakou, Lilika 1899?-
See Nakos, Lilika

Narayan, R(asipuram) K(rishnaswami)
1906-............... CLC 7, 28
See also CA 81-84

Nash, (Frediric) Ogden
1902-1971...................CLC 23
See also CAP 1
See also CA 13-14
See also obituary CA 29-32R
See also SATA 2, 46
See also DLB 11

Nathan, George Jean
1882-1958.................. TCLC 18
See also CA 114

Natsume, Kinnosuke 1867-1916
See Natsume, Sōseki
See also CA 104

Natsume, Sōseki
1867-1916............... TCLC 2, 10
See also Natsume, Kinnosuke

Natti, (Mary) Lee 1919-
See Kingman, (Mary) Lee
See also CANR 2

Naylor, Gloria 1950-..............CLC 28
See also CA 107

Neihardt, John G(neisenau)
1881-1973...................CLC 32
See also CAP 1
See also CA 13-14
See also DLB 9

Nekrasov, Nikolai Alekseevich
1821-1878.................. NCLC 11

Nelligan, Émile 1879-1941 .... TCLC 14
See also CA 114

Author Index

Nelson, Willie 1933- ....CLC 17
  See also CA 107

Nemerov, Howard
    1920-................CLC 2, 6, 9, 36
  See also CANR 1
  See also CA 1-4R
  See also CABS 2
  See also DLB 5, 6
  See also DLB-Y 83

Neruda, Pablo
    1904-1973.......CLC 1, 2, 5, 7, 9, 28
  See also CAP 2
  See also CA 19-20
  See also obituary CA 45-48

Nerval, Gérard de 1808-1855 ..... NCLC 1

Nervo, (José) Amado (Ruiz de)
    1870-1919................. TCLC 11
  See also CA 109

Neufeld, John (Arthur) 1938- ......CLC 17
  See also CANR 11
  See also CA 25-28R
  See also SAAS 3
  See also SATA 6

Neville, Emily Cheney 1919- ....CLC 12
  See also CANR 3
  See also CA 5-8R
  See also SAAS 2
  See also SATA 1

Newbound, Bernard Slade 1930-
  See Slade, Bernard
  See also CA 81-84

Newby, P(ercy) H(oward)
    1918-................. CLC 2, 13
  See also CA 5-8R
  See also DLB 15

Newlove, Donald 1928-.............CLC 6
  See also CA 29-32R

Newlove, John (Herbert) 1938- .....CLC 14
  See also CANR 9
  See also CA 21-24R

Newman, Charles 1938- ....CLC 2, 8
  See also CA 21-24R

Newman, Edwin (Harold)
    1919-.....................CLC 14
  See also CANR 5
  See also CA 69-72
  See also AITN 1

Newton, Suzanne 1936-............CLC 35
  See also CANR 14
  See also CA 41-44R
  See also SATA 5

Ngugi, James (Thiong'o)
    1938-................CLC 3, 7, 13, 36
  See also Ngugi wa Thiong'o
  See also Wa Thiong'o, Ngugi
  See also CA 81-84

Ngugi wa Thiong'o
    1938-................CLC 3, 7, 13, 36
  See also Ngugi, James (Thiong'o)
  See also Wa Thiong'o, Ngugi

Nichol, B(arrie) P(hillip) 1944- .....CLC 18
  See also CA 53-56
  See also DLB 53

Nichols, John (Treadwell)
    1940-.....................CLC 38
  See also CAAS 2
  See also CANR 6
  See also CA 9-12R
  See also DLB-Y 82

Nichols, Peter (Richard)
    1927-.................... CLC 5, 36
  See also CA 104
  See also DLB 13

Nicolas, F.R.E. 1927-
  See Freeling, Nicolas

Niedecker, Lorine
    1903-1970................ CLC 10, 42
  See also CAP 2
  See also CA 25-28
  See also DLB 48

Nietzsche, Friedrich (Wilhelm)
    1844-1900.............. TCLC 10, 18
  See also CA 107

Nightingale, Anne Redmon 1943-
  See Redmon (Nightingale), Anne
  See also CA 103

Nin, Anaïs
    1903-1977........ CLC 1, 4, 8, 11, 14
  See also CA 13-16R
  See also obituary CA 69-72
  See also DLB 2, 4
  See also AITN 2

Nissenson, Hugh 1933-.......... CLC 4, 9
  See also CA 17-20R
  See also DLB 28

Niven, Larry 1938- ....CLC 8
  See also Niven, Laurence Van Cott
  See also DLB 8

Niven, Laurence Van Cott 1938-
  See Niven, Larry
  See also CANR 14
  See also CA 21-24R

Nixon, Agnes Eckhardt 1927- ......CLC 21
  See also CA 110

Nkosi, Lewis 1936- ....CLC 45
  See also CA 65-68

Nordhoff, Charles 1887-1947..... TCLC 23
  See also CA 108
  See also SATA 23
  See also DLB 9

Norman, Marsha 1947-............CLC 28
  See also CA 105
  See also DLB-Y 84

Norris, (Benjamin) Frank(lin)
    1870-1902.................. TCLC 24
  See also CA 110
  See also DLB 12

Norris, Leslie 1921-...............CLC 14
  See also CANR 14
  See also CAP 1
  See also CA 11-12
  See also DLB 27

North, Andrew 1912-
  See Norton, Andre

North, Christopher 1785-1854
  See Wilson, John

Norton, Alice Mary 1912-
  See Norton, Andre
  See also CANR 2
  See also CA 1-4R
  See also SATA 1, 43

Norton, Andre 1912-.............CLC 12
  See also Norton, Mary Alice
  See also DLB 8

Norway, Nevil Shute 1899-1960
  See Shute (Norway), Nevil
  See also CA 102
  See also obituary CA 93-96

Nossack, Hans Erich 1901-1978 .....CLC 6
  See also CA 93-96
  See also obituary CA 85-88

Nova, Craig 1945-.............. CLC 7, 31
  See also CANR 2
  See also CA 45-48

Novalis 1772-1801 .... NCLC 13

Nowlan, Alden (Albert) 1933- ......CLC 15
  See also CANR 5
  See also CA 9-12R
  See also DLB 53

Noyes, Alfred 1880-1958 .... TCLC 7
  See also CA 104
  See also DLB 20

Nunn, Kem 19??-............ CLC 34 (94)

Nye, Robert 1939-............ CLC 13, 42
  See also CA 33-36R
  See also SATA 6
  See also DLB 14

Nyro, Laura 1947-.................CLC 17

Oates, Joyce Carol
    1938-......CLC 1, 2, 3, 6, 9, 11, 15, 19,
                                                33
  See also CA 5-8R
  See also DLB 2, 5
  See also DLB-Y 81
  See also AITN 1

O'Brien, Darcy 1939-.............CLC 11
  See also CANR 8
  See also CA 21-24R

O'Brien, Edna
    1932-............. CLC 3, 5, 8, 13, 36
  See also CANR 6
  See also CA 1-4R
  See also DLB 14

O'Brien, Flann
    1911-1966.......... CLC 1, 4, 5, 7, 10
  See also O Nuallain, Brian

O'Brien, Richard 19??-............CLC 17

O'Brien, (William) Tim(othy)
    1946-.................. CLC 7, 19, 40
  See also CA 85-88
  See also DLB-Y 80

Obstfelder, Sigbjørn
    1866-1900.................. TCLC 23

O'Casey, Sean
    1880-1964......... CLC 1, 5, 9, 11, 15
  See also CA 89-92
  See also DLB 10

Ochs, Phil 1940-1976 ....CLC 17
  See also obituary CA 65-68

O'Connor, Edwin (Greene)
    1918-1968...................CLC 14
  See also CA 93-96
  See also obituary CA 25-28R

O'Connor, (Mary) Flannery
    1925-1964...... CLC 1, 2, 3, 6, 10, 13,
                                            15, 21
  See also CANR 3
  See also CA 1-4R
  See also DLB 2
  See also DLB-Y 80
  See also CDALB 1941-1968

O'Connor, Frank
 1903-1966................ **CLC 14, 23**
 See also O'Donovan, Michael (John)

O'Dell, Scott 1903- ....**CLC 30**
 See also CLR 1
 See also CANR 12
 See also CA 61-64
 See also SATA 12
 See also DLB 52

Odets, Clifford 1906-1963 ...... **CLC 2, 28**
 See also CA 85-88
 See also DLB 7, 26

O'Donovan, Michael (John) 1903-1966
 See O'Connor, Frank
 See also CA 93-96

Ōe, Kenzaburō 1935- .... **CLC 10, 36**
 See also CA 97-100

O'Faolain, Julia 1932- .... **CLC 6, 19**
 See also CAAS 2
 See also CANR 12
 See also CA 81-84
 See also DLB 14

O'Faoláin, Seán
 1900-................**CLC 1, 7, 14, 32**
 See also CANR 12
 See also CA 61-64
 See also DLB 15

O'Flaherty, Liam
 1896-1984........... **CLC 5, 34** (355)
 See also CA 101
 See also obituary CA 113
 See also DLB 36
 See also DLB-Y 84

O'Grady, Standish (James)
 1846-1928................... **TCLC 5**
 See also CA 104

O'Hara Family
 See Banim, John and Banim, Michael

O'Hara, Frank
 1926-1966.............. **CLC 2, 5, 13**
 See also CA 9-12R
 See also obituary CA 25-28R
 See also DLB 5, 16

O'Hara, John (Henry)
 1905-1970...... **CLC 1, 2, 3, 6, 11, 42**
 See also CA 5-8R
 See also obituary CA 25-28R
 See also DLB 9
 See also DLB-DS 2

O'Hehir, Diana 1922-..............**CLC 41**
 See also CA 93-96

Okigbo, Christopher (Ifenayichukwu)
 1932-1967....................**CLC 25**
 See also CA 77-80

Olds, Sharon 1942- ...... **CLC 32, 39** (186)
 See also CANR 18
 See also CA 101

Olesha, Yuri (Karlovich)
 1899-1960....................**CLC 8**
 See also CA 85-88

Oliphant, Margaret (Oliphant Wilson)
 1828-1897.................. **NCLC 11**
 See also DLB 18

Oliver, Mary 1935- ...... **CLC 19, 34** (246)
 See also CANR 9
 See also CA 21-24R
 See also DLB 5

Olivier, (Baron) Laurence (Kerr)
 1907-.....................**CLC 20**
 See also CA 111

Olsen, Tillie 1913-............. **CLC 4, 13**
 See also CANR 1
 See also CA 1-4R
 See also DLB 28
 See also DLB-Y 80

Olson, Charles (John)
 1910-1970...... **CLC 1, 2, 5, 6, 9, 11, 29**
 See also CAP 1
 See also CA 15-16
 See also obituary CA 25-28R
 See also CABS 2
 See also DLB 5, 16

Olson, Theodore 1937-
 See Olson, Toby

Olson, Toby 1937-................**CLC 28**
 See also CANR 9
 See also CA 65-68

Ondaatje, (Philip) Michael
 1943-................... **CLC 14, 29**
 See also CA 77-80

Oneal, Elizabeth 1934-
 See Oneal, Zibby
 See also CA 106
 See also SATA 30

Oneal, Zibby 1934-................**CLC 30**
 See also Oneal, Elizabeth

O'Neill, Eugene (Gladstone)
 1888-1953................. **TCLC 1, 6**
 See also CA 110
 See also AITN 1
 See also DLB 7

Onetti, Juan Carlos 1909- ...... **CLC 7, 10**
 See also CA 85-88

O'Nolan, Brian 1911-1966
 See O'Brien, Flann

O Nuallain, Brian 1911-1966
 See O'Brien, Flann
 See also CAP 2
 See also CA 21-22
 See also obituary CA 25-28R

Oppen, George
 1908-1984.........**CLC 7, 13, 34** (358)
 See also CANR 8
 See also CA 13-16R
 See also obituary CA 113
 See also DLB 5

Orlovitz, Gil 1918-1973 ....**CLC 22**
 See also CA 77-80
 See also obituary CA 45-48
 See also DLB 2, 5

Ortega y Gasset, José
 1883-1955................... **TCLC 9**
 See also CA 106

Ortiz, Simon J. 1941-.............**CLC 45**

Orton, Joe 1933?-1967 ...... **CLC 4, 13, 43**
 See also Orton, John Kingsley
 See also DLB 13

Orton, John Kingsley 1933?-1967
 See Orton, Joe
 See also CA 85-88

Orwell, George
 1903-1950.............**TCLC 2, 6, 15**
 See also Blair, Eric Arthur
 See also DLB 15

Osborne, John (James)
 1929-............. **CLC 1, 2, 5, 11, 45**
 See also CA 13-16R
 See also DLB 13

Osceola 1885-1962
 See Dinesen, Isak
 See also Blixen, Karen (Christentze Dinesen)

Oshima, Nagisa 1932-.............**CLC 20**
 See also CA 116

Ossoli, Sarah Margaret (Fuller marchesa d')
 1810-1850
 See Fuller, (Sarah) Margaret
 See also SATA 25

Otero, Blas de 1916-..............**CLC 11**
 See also CA 89-92

Owen, Wilfred (Edward Salter)
 1893-1918................... **TCLC 5**
 See also CA 104
 See also DLB 20

Owens, Rochelle 1936-.............**CLC 8**
 See also CAAS 2
 See also CA 17-20R

Owl, Sebastian 1939-
 See Thompson, Hunter S(tockton)

Oz, Amos 1939-...... **CLC 5, 8, 11, 27, 33**
 See also CA 53-56

Ozick, Cynthia 1928- .... **CLC 3, 7, 28**
 See also CA 17-20R
 See also DLB 28
 See also DLB-Y 82

Ozu, Yasujiro 1903-1963 ....**CLC 16**
 See also CA 112

Pa Chin 1904-....................**CLC 18**
 See also Li Fei-kan

Pack, Robert 1929-...............**CLC 13**
 See also CANR 3
 See also CA 1-4R
 See also DLB 5

Padgett, Lewis 1915-1958
 See Kuttner, Henry

Padilla, Heberto 1932-............**CLC 38**
 See also AITN 1

Page, Jimmy 1944-
 See Page, Jimmy and Plant, Robert

Page, Jimmy 1944- and
 Plant, Robert 1948- ....**CLC 12**

Page, Louise 1955-................**CLC 40**

Page, P(atricia) K(athleen)
 1916-................... **CLC 7, 18**
 See also CANR 4
 See also CA 53-56

Paget, Violet 1856-1935
 See Lee, Vernon
 See also CA 104

Palamas, Kostes 1859-1943 .... **TCLC 5**
 See also CA 105

Palazzeschi, Aldo 1885-1974 ....**CLC 11**
 See also CA 89-92
 See also obituary CA 53-56

Paley, Grace 1922- .... **CLC 4, 6, 37**
 See also CANR 13
 See also CA 25-28R
 See also DLB 28
 See also AITN 1

Author Index

Prokosch, Frederic 1908- . . . . .CLC 4
  See also CA 73-76
  See also DLB 48

Prose, Francine 1947- . . . . .CLC 45
  See also CA 109, 112

Proust, Marcel 1871-1922 . . . . . TCLC 7, 13
  See also CA 104

Pryor, Richard 1940- . . . . .CLC 26

P'u Sung-ling 1640-1715 . . . . LC 3

Puig, Manuel 1932- . . . . . . .CLC 3, 5, 10, 28
  See also CANR 2
  See also CA 45-48

Purdy, A(lfred) W(ellington)
  1918- . . . . CLC 3, 6, 14
  See also CA 81-84

Purdy, James (Amos)
  1923- . . . . .CLC 2, 4, 10, 28
  See also CAAS 1
  See also CANR 19
  See also CA 33-36R
  See also DLB 2

Pushkin, Alexander (Sergeyevich)
  1799-1837 . . . . NCLC 3

Puzo, Mario 1920- . . . . .CLC 1, 2, 6, 36
  See also CANR 4
  See also CA 65-68
  See also DLB 6

Pym, Barbara (Mary Crampton)
  1913-1980 . . . . .CLC 13, 19, 37
  See also CANR 13
  See also CAP 1
  See also CA 13-14
  See also obituary CA 97-100
  See also DLB 14

Pynchon, Thomas (Ruggles, Jr.)
  1937- . . . . . . .CLC 2, 3, 6, 9, 11, 18, 33
  See also CA 17-20R
  See also DLB 2

Quasimodo, Salvatore
  1901-1968 . . . . .CLC 10
  See also CAP 1
  See also CA 15-16
  See also obituary CA 25-28R

Queen, Ellery 1905-1982 . . . . CLC 3, 11
  See also Dannay, Frederic
  See also Lee, Manfred B(ennington)

Queneau, Raymond
  1903-1976 . . . . .CLC 2, 5, 10, 42
  See also CA 77-80
  See also obituary CA 69-72

Quin, Ann (Marie) 1936-1973 . . . . . . .CLC 6
  See also CA 9-12R
  See also obituary CA 45-48
  See also DLB 14

Quinn, Simon 1942-
  See Smith, Martin Cruz

Quiroga, Horacio (Sylvestre)
  1878-1937 . . . . TCLC 20
  See also CA 117

Quoirez, Françoise 1935-
  See Sagan, Françoise
  See also CANR 6
  See also CA 49-52

Rabelais, François 1494?-1553 . . . . LC 5

Rabe, David (William)
  1940- . . . . CLC 4, 8, 33
  See also CA 85-88
  See also DLB 7

Rabinovitch, Sholem 1859-1916
  See Aleichem, Sholom
  See also CA 104

Rachen, Kurt von 1911-1986
  See Hubbard, L(afayette) Ron(ald)

Radcliffe, Ann (Ward)
  1764-1823 . . . . NCLC 6
  See also DLB 39

Radnóti, Miklós 1909-1944 . . . . . . TCLC 16
  See also CA 118

Rado, James 1939-
  See Ragni, Gerome and
    Rado, James
  See also CA 105

Radomski, James 1932-
  See Rado, James

Radvanyi, Netty Reiling 1900-1983
  See Seghers, Anna
  See also CA 85-88
  See also obituary CA 110

Raeburn, John 1941- . . . . CLC 34 (477)
  See also CA 57-60

Ragni, Gerome 1942-
  See Ragni, Gerome and Rado, James
  See also CA 105

Ragni, Gerome 1942- and
    Rado, James 1939- . . . . .CLC 17

Rahv, Philip 1908-1973 . . . . .CLC 24
  See also Greenberg, Ivan

Raine, Craig 1944- . . . . .CLC 32
  See also CA 108
  See also DLB 40

Raine, Kathleen (Jessie)
  1908- . . . . CLC 7, 45
  See also CA 85-88
  See also DLB 20

Rampersad, Arnold
  19??- . . . . CLC 44 (506)

Rand, Ayn
  1905-1982 . . . . .CLC 3, 30, 44 (447)
  See also CA 13-16R
  See also obituary CA 105

Randall, Dudley (Felker) 1914- . . . . . .CLC 1
  See also CA 25-28R
  See also DLB 41

Ransom, John Crowe
  1888-1974 . . . . CLC 2, 4, 5, 11, 24
  See also CANR 6
  See also CA 5-8R
  See also obituary CA 49-52
  See also DLB 45

Rao, Raja 1909- . . . . .CLC 25
  See also CA 73-76

Raphael, Frederic (Michael)
  1931- . . . . CLC 2, 14
  See also CANR 1
  See also CA 1-4R
  See also DLB 14

Rathbone, Julian 1935- . . . . .CLC 41
  See also CA 101

Rattigan, Terence (Mervyn)
  1911-1977 . . . . .CLC 7
  See also CA 85-88
  See also obituary CA 73-76
  See also DLB 13

Raven, Simon (Arthur Noel)
  1927- . . . . .CLC 14
  See also CA 81-84

Rawlings, Marjorie Kinnan
  1896-1953 . . . . TCLC 4
  See also CA 104
  See also YABC 1
  See also DLB 9, 22

Ray, Satyajit 1921- . . . . .CLC 16
  See also CA 114

Read, Herbert (Edward)
  1893-1968 . . . . .CLC 4
  See also CA 85-88
  See also obituary CA 25-28R
  See also DLB 20

Read, Piers Paul 1941- . . . . . . CLC 4, 10, 25
  See also CA 21-24R
  See also SATA 21
  See also DLB 14

Reade, Charles 1814-1884 . . . . NCLC 2
  See also DLB 21

Reade, Hamish 1936-
  See Gray, Simon (James Holliday)

Reaney, James 1926- . . . . .CLC 13
  See also CA 41-44R
  See also SATA 43

Rechy, John (Francisco)
  1934- . . . . .CLC 1, 7, 14, 18
  See also CAAS 4
  See also CANR 6
  See also CA 5-8R
  See also DLB-Y 82

Redcam, Tom 1870-1933 . . . . TCLC 25

Redgrove, Peter (William)
  1932- . . . . CLC 6, 41
  See also CANR 3
  See also CA 1-4R
  See also DLB 40

Redmon (Nightingale), Anne
  1943- . . . . .CLC 22
  See also Nightingale, Anne Redmon
  See also DLB-Y 86

Reed, Ishmael
  1938- . . . . .CLC 2, 3, 5, 6, 13, 32
  See also CA 21-24R
  See also DLB 2, 5, 33

Reed, John (Silas) 1887-1920 . . . . . . TCLC 9
  See also CA 106

Reed, Lou 1944- . . . . .CLC 21

Reid, Christopher 1949- . . . . .CLC 33
  See also DLB 40

Reid Banks, Lynne 1929-
  See Banks, Lynne Reid
  See also CANR 6
  See also CA 1-4R
  See also SATA 22

Reiner, Max 1900-
  See Caldwell, (Janet Miriam) Taylor
    (Holland)

Remark, Erich Paul 1898-1970
  See Remarque, Erich Maria

Rohmer, Eric 1920-...............CLC 16
    See also Scherer, Jean-Marie Maurice

Roiphe, Anne (Richardson)
    1935-........................ CLC 3, 9
    See also CA 89-92
    See also DLB-Y 80

Rolfe, Frederick (William Serafino Austin
    Lewis Mary) 1860-1913..... TCLC 12
    See also CA 107
    See also DLB 34

Rolland, Romain 1866-1944...... TCLC 23
    See also CA 118

Rölvaag, O(le) E(dvart)
    1876-1931................. TCLC 17
    See also DLB 9

Romains, Jules 1885-1972 ....CLC 7
    See also CA 85-88

Romero, José Rubén
    1890-1952................. TCLC 14
    See also CA 114

Ronsard, Pierre de 1524-1585........ LC 6

Rooke, Leon 1934-....... CLC 25, 34 (250)
    See also CA 25-28R

Rosa, João Guimarães
    1908-1967....................CLC 23
    See also obituary CA 89-92

Rosen, Richard (Dean)
    1949-.................. CLC 39 (194)
    See also CA 77-80

Rosenberg, Isaac 1890-1918...... TCLC 12
    See also CA 107
    See also DLB 20

Rosenblatt, Joe 1933- ....CLC 15
    See also Rosenblatt, Joseph
    See also AITN 2

Rosenblatt, Joseph 1933-
    See Rosenblatt, Joe
    See also CA 89-92

Rosenthal, M(acha) L(ouis)
    1917-........................CLC 28
    See also CANR 4
    See also CA 1-4R
    See also DLB 5

Ross, (James) Sinclair 1908- ....CLC 13
    See also CA 73-76

Rossetti, Christina Georgina
    1830-1894................... NCLC 2
    See also SATA 20
    See also DLB 35

Rossetti, Dante Gabriel
    1828-1882................... NCLC 4
    See also DLB 35

Rossetti, Gabriel Charles Dante 1828-1882
    See Rossetti, Dante Gabriel

Rossner, Judith (Perelman)
    1935-............. CLC 6, 9, 29
    See also CANR 18
    See also CA 17-20R
    See also DLB 6
    See also AITN 2

Rostand, Edmond (Eugène Alexis)
    1868-1918................. TCLC 6
    See also CA 104

Roth, Henry 1906-...........CLC 2, 6, 11
    See also CAP 1
    See also CA 11-12
    See also DLB 28

Roth, Philip (Milton)
    1933-......CLC 1, 2, 3, 4, 6, 9, 15, 22,
                                             31
    See also CANR 1
    See also CA 1-4R
    See also DLB 2, 28
    See also DLB-Y 82

Rothenberg, Jerome 1931-..........CLC 6
    See also CANR 1
    See also CA 45-48
    See also DLB 5

Roumain, Jacques 1907-1944 .... TCLC 19
    See also CA 117

Rourke, Constance (Mayfield)
    1885-1941.................. TCLC 12
    See also CA 107
    See also YABC 1

Roussel, Raymond 1877-1933 .... TCLC 20
    See also CA 117

Rovit, Earl (Herbert) 1927-.........CLC 7
    See also CA 5-8R
    See also CANR 12

Rowson, Susanna Haswell
    1762-1824................... NCLC 5
    See also DLB 37

Roy, Gabrielle 1909-1983...... CLC 10, 14
    See also CANR 5
    See also CA 53-56
    See also obituary CA 110

Różewicz, Tadeusz 1921- .... CLC 9, 23
    See also CA 108

Ruark, Gibbons 1941-.............CLC 3
    See also CANR 14
    See also CA 33-36R

Rubens, Bernice 192?- .... CLC 19, 31
    See also CA 25-28R
    See also DLB 14

Rudkin, (James) David 1936- ......CLC 14
    See also CA 89-92
    See also DLB 13

Rudnik, Raphael 1933-.............CLC 7
    See also CA 29-32R

Ruiz, José Martínez 1874-1967
    See Azorín

Rukeyser, Muriel
    1913-1980..........CLC 6, 10, 15, 27
    See also CA 5-8R
    See also obituary CA 93-96
    See also obituary SATA 22
    See also DLB 48

Rule, Jane (Vance) 1931-..........CLC 27
    See also CANR 12
    See also CA 25-28R

Rulfo, Juan 1918-1986 ....CLC 8
    See also CA 85-88
    See also obituary CA 118

Runyon, (Alfred) Damon
    1880-1946.................. TCLC 10
    See also CA 107
    See also DLB 11

Rush, Norman 1933-........ CLC 44 (91)

Rushdie, (Ahmed) Salman
    1947-................... CLC 23, 31
    See also CA 108, 111

Rushforth, Peter (Scott) 1945-......CLC 19
    See also CA 101

Ruskin, John 1819-1900........ TCLC 20
    See also CA 114
    See also SATA 24

Russ, Joanna 1937-...............CLC 15
    See also CANR 11
    See also CA 25-28R
    See also DLB 8

Russell, George William 1867-1935
    See A. E.
    See also CA 104

Russell, (Henry) Ken(neth Alfred)
    1927-........................CLC 16
    See also CA 105

Rutherford, Mark 1831-1913 .... TCLC 25
    See also DLB 18

Ruyslinck, Ward 1929-............CLC 14

Ryan, Cornelius (John)
    1920-1974....................CLC 7
    See also CA 69-72
    See also obituary CA 53-56

Rybakov, Anatoli 1911?- ....CLC 23

Ryder, Jonathan 1927-
    See Ludlum, Robert

Ryga, George 1932-...............CLC 14
    See also CA 101

Sabato, Ernesto 1911-......... CLC 10, 23
    See also CA 97-100

Sachs, Marilyn (Stickle) 1927-......CLC 35
    See also CLR 2
    See also CANR 13
    See also CA 17-20R
    See also SAAS 2
    See also SATA 3

Sachs, Nelly 1891-1970............CLC 14
    See also CAP 2
    See also CA 17-18
    See also obituary CA 25-28R

Sackler, Howard (Oliver)
    1929-1982....................CLC 14
    See also CA 61-64
    See also obituary CA 108
    See also DLB 7

Sade, Donatien Alphonse François, Comte de
    1740-1814................... NCLC 3

Sadoff, Ira 1945-..................CLC 9
    See also CANR 5
    See also CA 53-56

Safire, William 1929- ....CLC 10
    See also CA 17-20R

Sagan, Carl (Edward) 1934- ....CLC 30
    See also CANR 11
    See also CA 25-28R

Sagan, Françoise
    1935-............. CLC 3, 6, 9, 17, 36
    See also Quoirez, Françoise

Sahgal, Nayantara (Pandit)
    1927-........................CLC 41
    See also CANR 11
    See also CA 9-12R

Sainte-Beuve, Charles Augustin
    1804-1869................... NCLC 5

Sainte-Marie, Beverly 1941-
    See Sainte-Marie, Buffy
    See also CA 107

Sainte-Marie, Buffy 1941- ....CLC 17
    See also Sainte-Marie, Beverly

Author Index

Škvorecký, Josef (Václav)
    1924-.............. CLC 15, 39 (220)
    See also CAAS 1
    See also CANR 10
    See also CA 61-64

Slade, Bernard 1930- ....CLC 11
    See also Newbound, Bernard Slade
    See also DLB 53

Slaughter, Frank G(ill) 1908- ......CLC 29
    See also CANR 5
    See also CA 5-8R
    See also AITN 2

Slavitt, David (R.) 1935-........ CLC 5, 14
    See also CAAS 3
    See also CA 21-24R
    See also DLB 5, 6

Slesinger, Tess 1905-1945........ TCLC 10
    See also CA 107

Slessor, Kenneth 1901-1971.......CLC 14
    See also CA 102
    See also obituary CA 89-92

Słowacki, Juliusz 1809-1849 ..... NCLC 15

Smart, Christopher 1722-1771 .... LC 3

Smith, A(rthur) J(ames) M(arshall)
    1902-1980...................CLC 15
    See also CANR 4
    See also CA 1-4R
    See also obituary CA 102

Smith, Betty (Wehner)
    1896-1972...................CLC 19
    See also CA 5-8R
    See also obituary CA 33-36R
    See also SATA 6
    See also DLB-Y 82

Smith, Cecil Lewis Troughton 1899-1966
    See Forester, C(ecil) S(cott)

Smith, Clark Ashton
    1893-1961...................CLC 43

Smith, Dave 1942-......... CLC 22, 42
    See also Smith, David (Jeddie)
    See also DLB 5

Smith, David (Jeddie) 1942-
    See Smith, Dave
    See also CANR 1
    See also CA 49-52

Smith, Florence Margaret 1902-1971
    See Smith, Stevie
    See also CAP 2
    See also CA 17-18
    See also obituary CA 29-32R

Smith, Lee 1944-................CLC 25
    See also CA 114, 119
    See also DLB-Y 83

Smith, Martin Cruz 1942-.........CLC 25
    See also CANR 6
    See also CA 85-88

Smith, Martin William 1942-
    See Smith, Martin Cruz

Smith, Mary-Ann Tirone
    1944-.................. CLC 39 (97)
    See also CA 118

Smith, Patti 1946-................CLC 12
    See also CA 93-96

Smith, Pauline (Urmson)
    1882-1959................. TCLC 25
    See also CA 29-32R
    See also SATA 27

Smith, Sara Mahala Redway 1900-1972
    See Benson, Sally

Smith, Stevie
    1902-1971...... CLC 3, 8, 25, 44 (431)
    See also Smith, Florence Margaret
    See also DLB 20

Smith, Wilbur (Addison) 1933-.....CLC 33
    See also CANR 7
    See also CA 13-16R

Smith, William Jay 1918-..........CLC 6
    See also CA 5-8R
    See also SATA 2
    See also DLB 5

Smollett, Tobias (George)
    1721-1771..................... LC 2
    See also DLB 39

Snodgrass, W(illiam) D(e Witt)
    1926-.................CLC 2, 6, 10, 18
    See also CANR 6
    See also CA 1-4R
    See also DLB 5

Snow, C(harles) P(ercy)
    1905-1980....... CLC 1, 4, 6, 9, 13, 19
    See also CA 5-8R
    See also obituary CA 101
    See also DLB 15

Snyder, Gary (Sherman)
    1930-............. CLC 1, 2, 5, 9, 32
    See also CA 17-20R
    See also DLB 5, 16

Snyder, Zilpha Keatley 1927- ......CLC 17
    See also CA 9-12R
    See also SAAS 2
    See also SATA 1, 28

Sokolov, Raymond 1941- ....CLC 7
    See also CA 85-88

Sologub, Fyodor 1863-1927 .... TCLC 9
    See also Teternikov, Fyodor Kuzmich

Solomos, Dionysios
    1798-1857.................. NCLC 15

Solwoska, Mara 1929-
    See French, Marilyn

Solzhenitsyn, Aleksandr I(sayevich)
    1918-.....CLC 1, 2, 4, 7, 9, 10, 18, 26,
                                     34 (480)
    See also CA 69-72
    See also AITN 1

Somers, Jane 1919-
    See Lessing, Doris (May)

Sommer, Scott 1951-..............CLC 25
    See also CA 106

Sondheim, Stephen (Joshua)
    1930-............. CLC 30, 39 (172)
    See also CA 103

Sontag, Susan
    1933-........... CLC 1, 2, 10, 13, 31
    See also CA 17-20R
    See also DLB 2

Sorrentino, Gilbert
    1929-........... CLC 3, 7, 14, 22, 40
    See also CANR 14
    See also CA 77-80
    See also DLB 5
    See also DLB-Y 80

Soto, Gary 1952-.................CLC 32
    See also CA 119

Souster, (Holmes) Raymond
    1921-.................... CLC 5, 14
    See also CANR 13
    See also CA 13-16R

Southern, Terry 1926- ....CLC 7
    See also CANR 1
    See also CA 1-4R
    See also DLB 2

Southey, Robert 1774-1843 .... NCLC 8

Soyinka, Akinwande Oluwole 1934-
    See Soyinka, Wole

Soyinka, Wole
    1934-....... CLC 3, 5, 14, 36, 44 (276)
    See also CA 13-16R
    See also DLB-Y 1986

Spacks, Barry 1931- ....CLC 14
    See also CA 29-32R

Spanidou, Irini 1946- ... CLC 44 (104)

Spark, Muriel (Sarah)
    1918-........CLC 2, 3, 5, 8, 13, 18, 40
    See also CANR 12
    See also CA 5-8R
    See also DLB 15

Spencer, Elizabeth 1921- ....CLC 22
    See also CA 13-16R
    See also SATA 14
    See also DLB 6

Spencer, Scott 1945- ....CLC 30
    See also CA 113
    See also DLB-Y 86

Spender, Stephen (Harold)
    1909-............. CLC 1, 2, 5, 10, 41
    See also CA 9-12R
    See also DLB 20

Spengler, Oswald 1880-1936 ..... TCLC 25
    See also CA 118

Spenser, Edmund 1552?-1599........ LC 5

Spicer, Jack 1925-1965......... CLC 8, 18
    See also CA 85-88
    See also DLB 5, 16

Spielberg, Peter 1929-.............CLC 6
    See also CANR 4
    See also CA 5-8R
    See also DLB-Y 81

Spielberg, Steven 1947-............CLC 20
    See also CA 77-80
    See also SATA 32

Spillane, Frank Morrison 1918-
    See Spillane, Mickey
    See also CA 25-28R

Spillane, Mickey 1918-......... CLC 3, 13
    See also Spillane, Frank Morrison

Spitteler, Carl (Friedrich Georg)
    1845-1924.................. TCLC 12
    See also CA 109

Spivack, Kathleen (Romola Drucker)
    1938-........................CLC 6
    See also CA 49-52

Spoto, Donald 1941- .... CLC 39 (444)
    See also CANR 11
    See also CA 65-68

Springsteen, Bruce 1949-..........CLC 17
    See also CA 111

Spurling, Hilary 1940- ...... CLC 34 (494)
    See also CA 104

Author Index

Author Index

Author Index

Author Index

Cumulative Index to Nationalities

NEPALI
Devkota, Laxmiprasad   23

NEW ZEALAND
Mansfield, Katherine   2, 8

NICARAGUAN
Darío, Rubén   4

NORWEGIAN
Bjørnson, Bjørnstjerne   7
Grieg, Nordhal   10
Hamsun, Knut   2, 14
Ibsen, Henrik   2, 8, 16
Kielland, Alexander   5
Lie, Jonas   5
Obstfelder, Sigbjørn   23
Skram, Amalie   25
Undset, Sigrid   3

PERUVIAN
Vallejo, César   3

POLISH
Borowski, Tadeusz   9
Reymont, Wladyslaw
Stanislaw   5
Schulz, Bruno   5
Sienkiewitz, Henryk   3
Witkiewicz, Stanislaw
Ignacy   8

PUERTO RICAN
Hostos, Eugenio María de   24

RUMANIAN
Bacovia, George   24

RUSSIAN
Aldanov, Mark   23
Andreyev, Leonid   3
Annensky, Innokenty   14
Babel, Isaak   2, 13
Balmont, Konstantin
Dmitriyevich   11
Bely, Andrey   7
Blok, Aleksandr   5
Bryusov, Valery   10
Bulgakov, Mikhail   2, 16
Bunin, Ivan   6
Chekhov, Anton   3, 10
Esenin, Sergei   4
Gorky, Maxim   8
Hippius, Zinaida   9
Ilf, Ilya   21
Khlebnikov, Velimir   20
Khodasevich, Vladislav   15
Korolenko, Vladimir   22
Kuprin, Aleksandr   5
Mandelstam, Osip   2, 6
Mayakovsky, Vladimir   4, 18
Petrov, Evgeny   21
Pilnyak, Boris   23
Platonov, Andrei   14
Sologub, Fyodor   9
Tolstoy, Alexey
Nikolayevich   18
Tolstoy, Leo   4, 11, 17
Trotsky, Leon   22
Tsvetaeva, Marina   7

Zamyatin, Yevgeny
Ivanovich   8
Zhdanov, Andrei   18
Zoshchenko, Mikhail   15

SCOTTISH
Barrie, J. M.   2
Bridie, James   3
Davidson, John   24
Gibbon, Lewis Grassic   4
Graham, R. B.
Cunninghame   19
Lang, Andrew   16
MacDonald, George   9
Muir, Edwin   2
Tey, Josephine   14

SOUTH AFRICAN
Campbell, Roy   5
Mqhayi, S.E.K.   25
Schreiner, Olive   9
Smith, Pauline   25

SPANISH
Barea, Arturo   14
Baroja, Pío   8
Benavente, Jacinto   3
Blasco Ibáñez, Vicente   12
Echegaray, José   4
García Lorca, Federico   1, 7
Jiménez, Juan Ramón   4
Machado, Antonio   3
Martínez Sierra, Gregorio   6
Miró, Gabriel   5
Ortega y Gasset, José   9

Pereda, José María de   16
Salinas, Pedro   17
Unamuno, Miguel de   2, 9
Valera, Juan   10
Valle-Inclán, Ramón del   5

SWEDISH
Dagerman, Stig   17
Heidenstam, Verner von   5
Lagerlöf, Selma   4
Strindberg, August   1, 8, 21

SWISS
Spitteler, Carl   12
Walser, Robert   18

TURKISH
Sait Faik   23

UKRAINIAN
Bialik, Chaim Nachman   25

URUGUAYAN
Quiroga, Horacio   20

WELSH
Davies, W. H.   5
Lewis, Alun   3
Machen, Arthur   4
Thomas, Dylan   1, 8

YIDDISH
Aleichem, Sholom   1
Asch, Sholem   3
Peretz, Isaac Leib   16

Nationality Index

TCLC Cumulative Title Index

Title Index

Title Index

Title Index

Title Index

Title Index

Title Index

"Fair Day" **22**:147
*The Fair Haven: A Work in Defence of the
   Miraculous Element in Our Lord's
   Ministry upon Earth, Both as against
   Rationalistic Impugners and Certain
   Orthodox Defenders* **1**:134
"The Fair Lady" **5**:94
The Fair Lavinia, and Others **9**:73
Fair Margaret **10**:146, 151, 155
The Fair Prosperina
   See *Sundarī Projerpinā*
"The Fairer Hope, a Brighter Morn"
   14:260
The Fairground Booth **5**:99, 100
Fairy and Folk Tales of the Irish Peasantry
   11:537, 539
The Fairy Chessman **10**:265, 269, 274,
   276
The Fairy Child
   See *Das Feenkind*
"The Fairy Curate" **3**:212-13
"The Fairy Foster-Mother" **3**:504
"A Fairy Funeral" **6**:387
"Fairy Godmothers" **22**:191
"The Fairy Goldsmith" **8**:521-22
"Fairy Land" **17**:241
"A Fairy Tale" **8**:235
Fairy-Tales (Čapek) **6**:85
Fairy Tales (Sologub) **9**:447-49
The Fairy's Dilemma **3**:209
"Faith" (Graham) **19**:112, 119, 131
"Faith" (Rutherford) **25**:341
"The Faith Cure Man" **12**:120
The Faith of Men **9**:262
The Faithful Wife (Tagore)
   See *Satī*
The Faithful Wife (Undset)
   See *Den trofaste hustru*
*Falcons of France: A Tale of Youth and the
   Air* **23**:58, 65, 67
"Falk" **13**:102
"The Fall" **2**:486
Der Fall Deruga (The Deruga Trial)
   13:243, 252
Der Fall Maurizius (The Maurizius Case)
   6:511, 517-19
"The Fall of Babbulkund" **2**:136
"The Fall of the House of Usher" **1**:84
"Der Fall Wagner: Ern Muskikanten-
   Problem" (The Case of Wagner) **10**:391,
   393
The Fallen Angel **22**:253
"A Fallen Yew" **4**:440
En fallit (The Bankrupt) **7**:104, 107, 111,
   113
Der falsche Nero **3**:187
"The False Coupon" **11**:464
"False Dawn" **3**:559; **9**:550
"The False Heart" **18**:41
"False Prophet" **8**:536
The False Sound of the Lute
   See *Koto no sorane*
"The Falsehood of Truth" **14**:88
"Fame" **8**:294, 298
Die Familie Grossglück **3**:66
Familjen paa Gilje (The Family at Gilje)
   5:323-24, 330
"Une famille d'arbes" **17**:302
"The Family" **3**:340
The Family
   See *Ie*
The Family at Gilje
   See *Familjen paa Gilje*

"A Family Feud" **2**:131; **12**:106-07
Family Happiness
   See *Semeinoe schaste*
"Family Life in America" **1**:81
A Family without a Name **6**:495-96, 501
Famira kifared (Thamiras Cytharede;
   Thamyras the Cythara Player) **14**:17-18,
   21-3, 28
Famous Imposters **8**:394
Le fanal bleu (The Blue Lantern) **1**:192;
   5:169-70; **16**:118, 131
"The Fanatics" **12**:112
The Fanatics **2**:129, 132; **12**:107, 111-13,
   118-19, 123
Fancies versus Fads **6**:109
"Fanny" **20**:213
Fanny and the Servant Problem **23**:88
Fanny Essler **4**:142, 144
Fanny's First Play **21**:324
"Fantasi" **23**:177
"Fantasia" (Scott) **6**:387
"Fantasia" (Zangwill) **16**:461
"Fantasia of the Unconscious" **2**:346-48;
   9:215-16; **16**:284, 293-94, 306
"Fantasie printaniere" **24**:447
"Fantasies" **14**:371
Fantastic Dialogues
   See *Diálogos fantásticos*
Fantastic Fables **1**:87-8, 94; **7**:89
A Fantastic Tale **18**:378, 382
Fantastics, and Other Fancies **9**:125-26,
   134-37
Les fantoches **19**:331-32, 338, 340-43,
   345
Le fantôme **17**:138, 153, 155
La fantôme de l'opéra (The Phantom of the
   Opera) **25**:256, 258, 260
"Un fantôme de nuées" **3**:33
Fantôme d'Orient **11**:356
Far and Near Ones
   See *Dalekie i bliskie*
"The Far and the Near" **4**:519
The Far-Away Bride
   See *Tobit Transplanted*
"Far Away, Far Away"
   See "Messze . . . Messze"
"Far Away the Rachel-Jane" **17**:227
Far End **11**:411, 419
Far from the Madding Crowd **4**:147-49,
   153, 155-56, 158, 160, 168, 175, 177;
   10:217, 226, 229; **18**:87, 92, 111
Far Future Calling **22**:327, 333
"Far in a Western Brookland" **10**:247,
   252
"Far Known to Sea and Shore" **10**:247
Far Off Things **4**:278, 280, 285
"Le fard des Argonautes" **22**:64
"Farda" (To-Morrow) **21**:75
"Farewell, Go with God" **9**:523
Farewell, My Friend
   See *Śesher kavitā*
Farewell My Heart **20**:164
Farewell, My Lovely **1**:172, 175-76;
   7:167-68, 172-75, 179
"The Farewell of Paracelsus to Aprile"
   7:208
"The Farewell of the Sun"
   See "Auringon hyvästijättö"
Farewell to Autumn
   See *Pożegnanie jesieni*
"Farewell to Florida" **12**:367
Farewell to Mary
   See *Pożegnanie z Maria*

Farewell to Poesy, and Other Poems
   5:199-200
Farewell to the Theatre **2**:195-96
Farfetched Fables **3**:397; **9**:425
A farkas (The Wolf) **20**:159-60, 166, 169
The Farm **11**:77-8, 85-9
"Farmer" (Hamsun)
   See "Bonde"
"Farmer" (Shimazaki)
   See "Nōfu"
"Farmer Finch" **22**:146
"The Farmer's Bride" **8**:294, 296-300
The Farmer's Bride (Saturday Market)
   8:294-99
A Farmer's Year **11**:241, 245
Farn mabul (Three Cities: A Trilogy) **3**:67-9
"Faro en la noche" (Nocturnal Beacon)
   5:446
Farsa de la enamorada del rey **5**:483
Farsang (Carnival) **20**:166, 170
The Fascinating Mr. Vanderveldt **6**:420-21
Fascist Socialism **21**:35-7
Fashions for Men
   See *Úri divat*
"The Fat Man" **20**:329
"Fata morgana" **11**:36
"The Fatal Cipher" **19**:96
The Fatal Eggs
   See *Rokovye iaitsa*
The Fatal Force **7**:208
Fatal Interview **4**:311, 313, 315
A Fatal Wedding
   See *Bodas de sangre*
Fatalitas! **25**:260
"Fate" **23**:116
Fate
   See *Unmei*
"Fate o' Women"
   See "Frauenschicksal"
"The Fate of Humphrey Snell" **24**:226
"The Fate of King Feargus" **3**:503
*The Fate of the Jury: An Epilogue to
   Domesday Book* **2**:471; **25**:299, 303,
   315-16
The Fateful Game of Love **6**:84
Fateful Journey
   See *Schicksalreise*
"The Fates" **5**:374
"The Father" (Bjørnson) **7**:112
"The Father" (Smith) **25**:385, 393, 399
The Father
   See *Fadren*
"Father against Mother"
   See "Pai contra mãe"
"Father and Son"
   See "Baba oğul"
"Father Archangel of Scotland" **19**:101
Father Archangel of Scotland **19**:101
"Father Garasse" **8**:439
Father Sergius
   See *Otetz Sergii*
"Father, Son" **13**:151, 153-54
"Fatherlands" **5**:383
Fatherlands **5**:379
"Father's Last Escape"
   See "Ostatnia ucieczka ojca"
Fattige skjaebner (Poor Fortunes) **3**:522
"Les faulx visaiger" **20**:323
"The Faun" (Sterling) **20**:372, 374
"The Faun" (Tolstoy) **18**:377
"Fauns at Noon" **11**:426
"Faustina, ein Gespräch über die Liebe"
   6:514

Title Index

Title Index

Title Index

Title Index

Title Index

Title Index

Title Index

"The March"
  See "Pokhod"
The March of Literature from Confucius'
  Day to Our Own **15**:87, 93
"The March of Progress" **5**:140
March to Quebec: Journals of the Members
  of Arnold's Expedition **23**:236, 239
Marcha triufal **4**:56, 59
"La marchande des journaux" **25**:120
La marchanta **3**:76
Das Märchen **4**:388
Das Märchen der 672. Nacht, und andere
  Erzahlungen **11**:302-03
"Marching" **12**:288, 297, 302
Marching Men **1**:35, 38, 40, 44, 48, 55-7;
  10:32-3, 36-7, 42, 44, 50; **24**:30
"The Marching Morons" **8**:219-21
The Marching Morons **8**:221
"Marching Song"
  See "Marschlied"
"Marching to Zion" **5**:175
The Marchioness Rosalinda
  See *La marquesa Rosalinda*
Marco Millions **1**:385; **6**:329, 331-32
"Marcus Curtius" **15**:101
Mare nostrum **12**:31-2, 35, 38, 43, 50
"Mare Ships" **4**:115-16
Marevo (Mirage) **11**:38
"Margaret Fuller Black" **25**:314
Margaret Ogilvy **2**:47
"Margery" **11**:407
"Margery of the Fens" **11**:426
Margherita Spoletina **8**:119
Margret Howth: A Story of To-Day **6**:147,
  150-53, 155
"I mari del sud" (The South Seas) **3**:339,
  341
Maria (Mary) (Asch) **3**:68-70, 72
Maria (Babel)
  See *Mariia*
"Maria Cora" **10**:296
María Luisa **3**:75, 77
"Maria Moroni" **8**:114
Maria Stuart (Mary, the Queen of Scots)
  17:429, 442, 457
Maria Stuart i Skotland (Mary Stuart in
  Scotland) **7**:100, 103, 109, 111, 113-14,
  116
"Maria Vetsera"
  See "Mariya Vechora"
"Maria Who Made Faces and a Deplorable
  Marriage" **18**:39
Le mariage de Barillon **22**:89
Le mariage de Loti (Rarahu; or, The
  Marriage of Loti) **11**:351, 353-54, 356,
  359-61, 365-67
"Marian Drury" **7**:135, 139, 146
"Mariana" **10**:291, 296
Mariana **4**:96, 98, 101, 103
Mariana Pineda **1**:320; **7**:291-93, 296, 300
Marianna Sirca **23**:36-7, 39
"Marie" **3**:37, 39
Marie **11**:243, 246, 255
Marie Antoinette **7**:39
Marie-Magdeleine (Mary Magdalene)
  3:323, 331
"Marie Vaux of the Painted Lips" **15**:412
"An Mariechen" **15**:209
Marietta: A Maid of Venice **10**:148, 151
Mariia (Maria) **2**:23-4; **13**:30-1
"Un marino" **16**:380
Marino Faliero **8**:432-33

Mario and the Magician
  See *Mario und der Zauberer*
Mario und der Zauberer (Mario and the
  Magician) **2**:439; **8**:264; **14**:332, 358
"Marion" **8**:113, 119, 121
Marion Darche **10**:143-44, 146, 150
The Marionette **2**:486
"Mariposa" **4**:315
Mariquita y Antonio **10**:506, 508
Il marito amante della moglie (The Husband
  in Love with His Wife) **7**:307, 309, 313
Il marito di Elena (Helen's Husband) **3**:548
"Mariya Vechora" (Maria Vetsera) **20**:130,
  139
"Marizibill" **3**:36
"Marjatan poika" (Mary's Son) **24**:371
The Mark on the Wall **1**:527
Mark Only **9**:360-62, 365, 369, 375-76
Mark Rutherford's Deliverance **25**:335,
  340, 342-43, 345, 350-51, 355-56,
  360-64
Mark Twain's Autobiography **6**:460;
  12:437-38; **19**:385
Markens grøde (Growth of the Soil) **2**:202,
  204-08; **14**:221-22, 224-26, 228-31, 235,
  237, 240-41, 243, 248
"The Market"
  See "A vásár"
"Market Day" **24**:472
Markiza dezes (Marquise Desaix) **20**:136
"Marklake Witches" **17**:207
Marlowe **7**:175
"The Marmozet" **18**:39
The Marne **3**:572
La marquesa Rosalinda **5**:472-73, 486
El Marquésda Lumbrí **9**:511, 515
The Marquis of Keith
  See *Der Marquis von Keith*
The Marquis of Lossie **9**:292, 308
Der Marquis von Keith (The Marquis of
  Keith) **7**:580, 582, 585, 590
Marquise Desaix
  See *Markiza dezes*
Die Marquise von Arcis (The Mask of
  Virtue) **8**:368, 373, 378
"Marrakech" **6**:345
"Marriage" **25**:146
Marriage (Döblin)
  See *Die Ehe*
Marriage (Strindberg)
  See *Giftas*
Marriage (Wells) **6**:525-26, 529, 531,
  539; **12**:495-96, 508
"Marriage à la mode" **8**:282-85
"Marriage for One" **10**:181
Marriage Is No Joke **3**:131
"Marriage Made Easy" **14**:312
"The Marriage of Phaedra" **11**:100
Married
  See *Giftas*
Married Life
  See *Et samliv*
The Married Lover
  See *Duo*
"A Married Man's Story" **2**:451;
  8:281-82, 292
"The Marring of Malyn" **7**:135
The Marrow of Tradition **5**:133-34,
  138-40
"The Marry Month of May" **19**:180
The Marrying of Ann Leete **2**:193-97
Mars Child **8**:216
"Marschlied" (Marching Song) **10**:480, 490

The Marsden Case **15**:88, 93
"Marsh Fire" **4**:142
A Marsh Island **1**:359, 367, 369; **22**:135,
  138
"Marsh Rosemary" **22**:125, 129, 133,
  146
"The Marshland" **16**:27
Marshlands
  See *Paludes*
"Marstube" **8**:215
"Marsyas" (Carman) **7**:149
"Marsyas" (Masters) **25**:289
"Marsyas" (Roberts) **8**:320
Marsyas; or, On the Margin of Literature
  6:85
Marthe **7**:404, 407, 410
Marthe and the Madman
  See *Marthe et l'enragé*
Marthe et l'enragé (Marthe and the
  Madman) **19**:59, 61, 63-6
"Martin Chuzzlewit" **2**:262
Martin Eden **9**:255, 257, 260, 263, 265,
  268-70, 273, 275-77; **15**:255-56, 260-61,
  271-72, 277
Martin Luther **7**:486-87
"Martin Luther on Celibacy and Marriage"
  10:61
Martin Paz **6**:490
"Martinique Sketches" **9**:133
"Martin's Close" **6**:206, 212-13
"The Martyr"
  See "Hōkyōnin no shi"
"The Martyr of Alabama" **14**:260, 263
The Martyr of Alabama, and Other Poems
  14:263
Le martyre de Saint Sébastien **6**:136-37
"Maruja" **25**:213, 223
The Marvelous Land of Oz **7**:14, 20-3, 25,
  27
"Marx" **16**:341
"Marxism Is a Weapon, a Method of
  Firearm Quality—So Use This Method
  Knowledgeably!" **18**:269
Mary
  See *Maria*
"Mary and Gabriel" **7**:122
"Mary and Martha" **22**:147
"Mary and Veronica" **11**:20
"Mary at the Feet of Christ" **14**:260
Mary Baker Eddy **17**:442
Mary Baker Eddy; oder, Wunder in
  Amerika (Mary Baker Eddy) **10**:483
"The 'Mary Gloster'" **8**:191
Mary Magdalen **8**:343, 346, 348-49, 352
Mary Magdalene
  See *Marie-Magdeleine*
Mary, Mary
  See *The Charwoman's Daughter*
Mary of Magdala **8**:118-19
Mary of Scotland **2**:4-6, 8
Mary Oliver **3**:434-35, 437-38, 440-42;
  11:411, 413-17, 419-20, 422
"Mary Postgate" **8**:195; **17**:213
Mary Rose **2**:43-4, 49
"Mary Shepherdess" **21**:243, 245, 250
"Mary Smith" **9**:467
Mary Stuart **8**:432-33
Mary Stuart in Scotland
  See *Maria Stuart i Skotland*
Mary, the Queen of Scots
  See *Maria Stuart*
Mary the Third **19**:75, 77, 80-1, 84
"Mary Tired" **21**:245, 250

Title Index

Title Index

Title Index

Title Index

Title Index

Title Index

Title Index

Title Index

Title Index